The HUTCHINSON
FACTFINDER

FACTS • FIGURES
DATES • EVENTS

The HUTCHINSON FACTFINDER

FACTS • FIGURES
DATES • EVENTS

Helicon

This edition published 1999
by BCA by arrangement with Helicon Publishing Group plc

Copyright © Helicon Publishing Ltd 1999

CN 7877

Printed and bound in Slovenia by
DELO-Tiskarna, d,d.,
by arrangement with Korotan-Ljubljana

Editorial Director
Hilary McGlynn

Managing Editor
Roger Tritton

Project Editor
Catherine Thompson

Technical Projects Editor
Tracey Auden

Text Editors
Sara Jenkins-Jones
Karen Young

Production
Tony Ballsdon

Art and Design Manager
Terence Caven

Typesetting and Page Make-up
TechType

Contents

ASTRONOMY

—————————— ✳ ——————————

Astronomy is the science of the celestial bodies: the Sun, the Moon, and the planets; the stars and galaxies; and all other objects in the universe. It is concerned with their positions, motions, distances, and physical conditions and with their origins and evolution. It is divided into fields such as astrophysics, celestial mechanics, and cosmology.

Astronomy is perhaps the oldest recorded science; there are observational records from ancient Babylonia, China, Egypt, and Mexico. The first true astronomers were the Greeks, who deduced the Earth to be a sphere and attempted to measure its size. A summary of Greek astronomy is provided in Ptolemy of Alexandria's *Almagest*. The Arabs developed the astrolabe and produced good star catalogues. In 1543 the Polish astronomer Copernicus demonstrated that the Sun, not the Earth, is the centre of our planetary system. The Italian scientist Galileo was the first to use a telescope for astronomical study, in 1609–10. In the 17th and 18th centuries astronomy was mostly concerned with positional measurements. The British astronomer William Herschel's suggestions on the shape of our galaxy were verified in 1923 by the US astronomer Edwin Hubble's telescope at the Mount Wilson Observatory, California. The most remarkable recent extension of the powers of astronomy to explore the universe is in the use of rockets, satellites, space stations, and space probes, while the launching of the Hubble Space Telescope into permanent orbit in 1990 has enabled the detection of celestial phenomena seven times more distant than any Earth-based telescope.

THE SOLAR SYSTEM

The Solar System consists of the Sun, a central star which contains 99.86% of the of the Solar System's mass, and all the bodies orbiting it: the nine planets (Mercury, Venus, Earth, Mars, Jupiter, Saturn, Uranus, Neptune, and Pluto), their moons, the asteroids, and the comets. Thought to have formed by condensation from a cloud of gas and dust in space about 4.6 billion years ago, the Solar System gives every indication of being a strongly unified system having a common origin and development. It is isolated in space; all the planets go round the Sun in orbits that are nearly circular and coplanar, and in the same direction as the Sun itself rotates; moreover this same pattern is continued in the regular system of satellites that accompany Jupiter, Saturn, and Uranus.

Apollo asteroid member of a group of asteroids whose orbits cross that of the Earth. They are named after the first of their kind, Apollo, discovered in 1932 and then lost until 1973. Apollo asteroids are so small and faint that they are difficult to see except when close to Earth (Apollo is about 2 km/1.2 mi across).

asteroid or **minor planet,** any of many thousands of small bodies, composed of rock and iron, that orbit the Sun. Most lie in a belt between the orbits of Mars and Jupiter, and are thought to be fragments left over from the formation of the Solar System. About 100,000 may exist, but their total mass is only a few hundredths the mass of the Moon.

They include Ceres (the largest asteroid, 940 km/584 mi in diameter), Vesta (which has a light-coloured surface, and is the brightest as seen from Earth), Eros, and Icarus. Some asteroids are in orbits that bring them close to Earth, and some, such as the Apollo asteroids, even cross Earth's orbit; at least some of these may be remnants of former comets. One group, the Trojans, moves along the same orbit as Jupiter,

60° ahead and behind the planet. One unusual asteroid, Chiron, orbits beyond Saturn.

aurora coloured light in the night sky near the Earth's magnetic poles, called **aurora borealis** ('northern lights') in the northern hemisphere and **aurora australis** in the southern hemisphere. Although aurorae are usually restricted to the polar skies, fluctuations in the solar wind occasionally cause them to be visible at lower latitudes. An aurora is usually in the form of a luminous arch with its apex towards the magnetic pole followed by arcs, bands, rays, curtains, and coronas, usually green but often showing shades of blue and red, and sometimes yellow or white. Aurorae are caused at heights of over 100 km/60 mi by a fast stream of charged particles from solar flares and low-density 'holes' in the Sun's corona.

Baily's beads bright spots of sunlight seen around the edge of the Moon for a few seconds immediately before and after a total eclipse of the Sun, caused by sunlight shining between mountains at the Moon's edge. Sometimes one bead is much

The Largest Asteroids

Name	Diameter		Average distance from Sun	Orbital period (years)
	km	mi	(Earth = 1)	
Ceres	940	584	2.77	4.6
Pallas	588	365	2.77	4.6
Vesta	576	358	2.36	3.6
Hygeia	430	267	3.13	5.5
Interamnia	338	210	3.06	5.4
Davida	324	201	3.18	5.7

Some Major Comets

(– = not known.)

Name	First recorded sighting	Orbital period (yrs)	Interesting facts
Halley's comet	240 BC	76	parent of Eta Aquarid and Orionid meteor showers
Comet Tempel-Tuttle	AD 1366	33	parent of Leonid meteors
Biela's comet	1772	6.6	broke in half in 1846; not seen since 1852
Encke's comet	1786	3.3	parent of Taurid meteors
Comet Swift-Tuttle	1862	130	parent of Perseid meteors; reappeared 1992
Comet Ikeya-Seki	1965	880	so-called 'Sun-grazing' comet, passed 500,000 km/ 300,000 mi above surface of the Sun on 21 October 1965
Comet Kohoutek	1973	–	observed from space by *Skylab* astronauts
Comet West	1975	500,000	nucleus broke into four parts
Comet Bowell	1980	–	ejected from Solar System after close encounter with Jupiter
Comet IRAS-Araki Alcock	1983	–	passed only 4.5 million km/2.8 million mi from the Earth on 11 May 1983
Comet Austin	1989	–	passed 32 million km/20 million mi from the Earth in 1990
Comet Shoemaker-Levy 9	1993	–	made up of 21 fragments; crashed into Jupiter in July 1994
Comet Hale-Bopp	1995	1,000	spitting out of gas and debris produced a coma, a surrounding hazy cloud of gas and dust, of greater volume than the Sun; the bright coma is due to an outgassing of carbon monoxide; clearly visible with the naked eye in March 1997
Comet Hyakutake	1996	–	passed 15 million km/9,300,000 mi from the Earth

brighter than the others, producing the so-called **diamond ring** effect. The effect was described in 1836 by the English astronomer Francis Baily (1774–1844).

Callisto second-largest moon of Jupiter, 4,800 km/3,000 mi in diameter, orbiting every 16.7 days at a distance of 1.9 million km/1.2 million mi from the planet. Its surface is covered with large craters.

Ceres the largest asteroid, 940 km/584 mi in diameter, and the first to be discovered (by Italian astronomer Giuseppe Piazzi 1801). Ceres orbits the Sun every 4.6 years at an average distance of 414 million km/257 million mi. Its mass is about one-seventieth of that of the Moon.

Chiron unusual Solar-System object orbiting between Saturn and Uranus, discovered 1977 by US astronomer Charles T Kowal (1940–). Initially classified as an asteroid, it is now believed to be a giant cometary nucleus about 200 km/120 mi across, composed of ice with a dark crust of carbon dust. It has a 51-year orbit and a coma (cloud of gas and dust) caused by evaporation from its surface, resembling that of a comet. It is classified as a centaur.

chromosphere layer of mostly hydrogen gas about 10,000 km/6,000 mi deep above the visible surface of the Sun (the photosphere). It appears pinkish red during eclipses of the Sun.

comet small, icy body orbiting the Sun, usually on a highly elliptical path. A comet consists of a central nucleus a few kilometres across, and has been likened to a dirty snowball because it consists mostly of ice mixed with dust. As a comet approaches the Sun its nucleus heats up, releasing gas and dust which form a tenuous coma, up to 100,000 km/60,000 mi wide, around the nucleus. Gas and dust stream away from the coma to form one or more tails, which may extend for millions of kilometres. There are two distinct types of comet: one rich in methanol

Comets

Comet Hale-Bopp

(C/1995 01) Large and exceptionally active comet, which in March 1997 made its closest flyby to Earth since 2000 BC, coming within 190 million km/118 million mi. It has a diameter of approximately 40 km/25 mi and an extensive gas coma (when close to the Sun Hale-Bopp released 10 tonnes of gas every second). Unusually, Hale-Bopp has three tails: one consisting of dust particles, one of charged particles, and a third of sodium particles.

Comet Hale-Bopp was discovered independently in July 1995 by two amateur US astronomers, Alan Hale and Thomas Bopp.

Comet Shoemaker-Levy 9

A comet that crashed into Jupiter in July 1994. The fragments crashed into Jupiter at 60 kps/37 mps over the period 16–22 July 1994. The impacts occurred on the far side of Jupiter, but the impact sites came into view of Earth about 25 minutes later. Analysis of the impacts shows that most of the pieces were solid bodies about 1 km /0.6 mi in diameter, but that at least three of them were clusters of smaller objects.

When first sighted in 24 March 1993 by US astronomers Carolyn and Eugene Shoemaker and David Levy, it was found to consist of at least 21 fragments in an unstable orbit around Jupiter. It is believed to have been captured by Jupiter in about 1930 and fragmented by tidal forces on passing within 21,000 km/ 13,050 mi of the planet in July 1992.

Encke's comet

Comet with the shortest known orbital period, 3.3 years. It is named after German mathematician and astronomer Johann Franz Encke (1791–1865), who calculated its orbit in 1819 from earlier sightings.

Encke's comet was first seen in 1786 by the French astronomer Pierre Méchain (1744–1804). It is the parent body of the Taurid meteor shower and a fragment of it may have hit the Earth in the Tunguska Event in 1908.

In 1913, it became the first comet to be observed throughout its entire orbit when it was photographed near aphelion (the point in its orbit furthest from the Sun) by astronomers at Mount Wilson Observatory in California, USA.

Halley's comet

Comet that orbits the Sun about every 76 years, named after Edmond Halley who calculated its orbit. It is the brightest and most conspicuous of the periodic comets. Recorded sightings go back over 2,000 years. It travels around the Sun in the opposite direction to the planets. Its orbit is inclined at almost 20° to the main plane of the Solar System and ranges between the orbits of Venus and Neptune. It will next reappear 2061.

The comet was studied by space probes at its last appearance in 1986. The European probe *Giotto* showed that the nucleus of Halley's comet is a tiny and irregularly shaped chunk of ice, measuring some 15 km/10 m long by 8 km/5 m wide, coated by a layer of very dark material, thought to be composed of carbon-rich compounds. This surface coating has a very low albedo, reflecting just 4% of the light it receives from the Sun. Although the comet is one of the darkest objects known, it has a glowing head and tail produced by jets of gas from fissures in the outer dust layer. These vents cover 10% of the total surface area and become active only when exposed to the Sun. The force of these jets affects the speed of the comet's travel in its orbit.

---

and one low in methanol. Evidence for this comes in part from observations of the spectrum of Comet Hyakutake in 1996.

Comets are believed to have been formed at the birth of the Solar System. Billions of them may reside in a halo (the **Oort cloud**) beyond Pluto. The gravitational effect of passing stars pushes some towards the Sun, when they eventually become visible from Earth. Most comets swing around the Sun and return to distant space, never to be seen again for thousands or millions of years, although some, called **periodic comets,** have their orbits altered by the gravitational pull of the planets so that they reappear every 200 years or less. Periodic comets are thought to come from the Kuiper belt, a zone just beyond Neptune. Of the 800 or so comets whose orbits have been calculated, about 160 are periodic. The one with the shortest known period is Encke's comet, which orbits the Sun every 3.3 years.

corona faint halo of hot (about 2,000,000°C/ 3,600,000°F) and tenuous gas around the Sun, which boils from the surface. It is visible at solar eclipses or through a **coronagraph,** an instrument that blocks light from the Sun's brilliant disc. Gas flows away from the corona to form the solar wind.

crater bowl-shaped depression in the ground, usually round and with steep sides. Craters are formed by explosive events such as the eruption of a volcano or the impact of a meteorite. The Moon has more than 300,000 craters over 1 km/0.6 mi in diameter, formed by meteorite bombardment; similar craters on Earth have mostly been worn away by erosion. Craters are found on many other bodies in the Solar System.

Deimos one of the two moons of Mars. It is irregularly shaped, 15 × 12 × 11 km/9 × 7.5 × 7 mi, orbits at a height of 24,000 km/15,000 mi every 1.26 days, and is not as heavily cratered as the other moon, Phobos. Deimos was discovered in 1877 by US astronomer Asaph Hall (1829–1907), and is thought to be an asteroid captured by Mars's gravity.

Earth third planet from the Sun. More information on the Earth is given in the chapter *Physical World*.

eclipse passage of an astronomical body through the shadow of another.

The term is usually employed for solar and lunar eclipses, which may be either partial or total, but also, for example, for eclipses by Jupiter of its satellites. An eclipse of a star by a body in the Solar System is called an occultation.

A **solar eclipse** occurs when the Moon passes in front of the Sun as seen from Earth, and can happen only at new Moon. During a total eclipse the Sun's corona can be seen. A total solar eclipse can last up to 7.5 minutes. When the Moon is at its farthest from Earth it does not completely cover the face of the Sun, leaving a ring of sunlight visible. This is an **annular eclipse** (from the Latin word *annulus* 'ring'). Between two and five solar eclipses occur each year.

A **lunar eclipse** occurs when the Moon passes into the shadow of the Earth, becoming dim until emerging from the shadow. Lunar eclipses may be partial or total, and they can happen only at full Moon. Total lunar eclipses last for up to 100 minutes; the maximum number each year is three.

Eros asteroid, discovered in 1898, that can pass 22 million km/14 million mi from the Earth, as observed in 1975. Eros was the first asteroid to be discovered that has an orbit coming within that of Mars. It is elongated, measures about 36 × 12 km/22 × 7 mi, rotates around its shortest axis every 5.3 hours, and orbits the Sun every 1.8 years. The Near Earth Asteroid Rendezvous (NEAR) launched February 1996 is estimated to take three years to reach Eros. It will spend a year

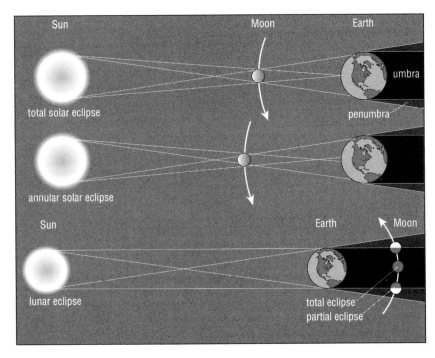

eclipse The two types of eclipse: lunar and solar. A lunar eclipse occurs when the Moon passes through the shadow of the Earth. A solar eclipse occurs when the Moon passes between the Sun and the Earth, blocking out the Sun's light. During a total solar eclipse, when the Moon completely covers the Sun, the Moon's shadow sweeps across the Earth's surface from west to east at a speed of 3,200kph/2,000mph.

circling the asteroid in an attempt to determine what it is made of.

Europa fourth-largest moon of the planet Jupiter, diameter 3,140 km/1,950 mi, orbiting 671,000 km/417,000 mi from the planet every 3.55 days. It is covered by ice and criss-crossed by thousands of thin cracks, each some 50,000 km/30,000 mi long.

NASA's robot probe, *Galileo*, began circling Europa in February 1997 and is expected to send back around 800 images from 50 different sites by 1999. One of the first discoveries was that what were thought to be cracks covering the surface of the moon are in fact low ridges. NASA announced plans to launch *Europa Observer* in 2003. Its aim will be to search for water beneath Europa's icy surface.

flare, solar brilliant eruption on the Sun above a sunspot, thought to be caused by release of magnetic energy. Flares reach maximum brightness within a few minutes, then fade away over about an hour. They eject a burst of atomic particles into space at up to 1,000 kps/600 mps. When these particles reach Earth they can cause radio blackouts, disruptions of the Earth's magnetic field, and aurorae.

Ganymede largest moon of the planet Jupiter, and the largest moon in the Solar System, 5,260 km/3,270 mi in diameter (larger than the planet Mercury). It orbits Jupiter every 7.2 days at a distance of 1.1 million km/700,000 mi. Its surface is a mixture of cratered and grooved terrain. Molecular oxygen was identified on Ganymede's surface in 1994.

The space probe *Galileo* detected a magnetic field around Ganymede in 1996; this suggests it may have a molten core. *Galileo* photographed Ganymede at a distance of 7,448 km/4,628 mi. The resulting images were 17 times clearer than those taken by *Voyager 2* in 1979, and show the surface to be extensively cratered and ridged, probably as a result of forces similar to those that create mountains on Earth. *Galileo* also detected molecules containing both carbon and nitrogen on the surface March 1997. Their presence may indicate that Ganymede harboured life at some time.

Jupiter

Jupiter is the fifth planet from the Sun, and the largest in the Solar System, with a mass equal to 70% of all the other planets combined, 318 times that of Earth's. It is largely composed of hydrogen and helium, liquefied by pressure in its interior, and probably with a rocky core larger than Earth. Its main feature is the Great Red Spot, a cloud of rising gases, 14,000 km/8,500 mi wide and 30,000 km/20,000 mi long, revolving anticlockwise.
mean distance from the Sun 778 million km/484 million mi
equatorial diameter 142,800 km/88,700 mi
rotation period 9 hr 51 min
year (complete orbit) 11.86 Earth years
atmosphere consists of clouds of white ammonia crystals, drawn out into belts by the planet's high speed of rotation (the fastest of any planet). Darker orange and brown clouds at lower levels may contain

sulphur, as well as simple organic compounds. Further down still, temperatures are warm, a result of heat left over from Jupiter's formation, and it is this heat that drives the turbulent weather patterns of the planet.
surface although largely composed of hydrogen and helium, Jupiter probably has a rocky core larger than Earth.

In 1995, the *Galileo* probe revealed Jupiter's atmosphere to consist of 0.2% water, less than previously estimated.
satellites Jupiter has 16 moons. The four largest moons, Io, Europa (which is the size of our Moon), Ganymede, and Callisto, are the **Galilean satellites,** discovered in 1610 by Galileo (Ganymede, which is about the size of Mercury, is the largest moon in the Solar System). Three small moons were discovered 1979 by the Voyager space probes, as was a faint ring of dust around

Jupiter's equator 55,000 km/34,000 mi above the cloud tops.

The Great Red Spot was first observed in 1664. Its top is higher than the surrounding clouds; its colour is thought to be due to red phosphorus. Jupiter's strong magnetic field gives rise to a large surrounding magnetic 'shell', or magnetosphere, from which bursts of radio waves are detected. The Southern Equatorial Belt in which the Great Red Spot occurs is subject to unexplained fluctuation. In 1989 it sustained a dramatic and sudden fading.

Comet Shoemaker-Levy 9 crashed into Jupiter in July 1994. Impact zones were visible but are not likely to remain.

Jupiter's faint rings are made up of dust from its moons, particularly the four inner moons. The discovery was made in 1998 from images taken by *Galileo*.

heliosphere region of space through which the solar wind flows outwards from the Sun. The **heliopause** is the boundary of this region, believed to lie about 100 astronomical units from the Sun, where the flow of the solar wind merges with the interstellar gas.

Icarus Apollo asteroid 1.5 km/1 mi in diameter, discovered 1949. It orbits the Sun every 409 days at a distance of 28–300 million km/18–186 million mi (0.19–2.0 astronomical units). It was the first asteroid known to approach the Sun closer than does the planet Mercury. In 1968 it passed 6 million km/4 million mi from the Earth.

interplanetary matter gas and dust thinly spread through the Solar System. The gas flows outwards from the Sun as the solar wind.

Fine dust lies in the plane of the Solar System, scattering sunlight to cause the zodiacal light. Swarms of dust shed by comets enter the Earth's atmosphere to cause meteor showers.

Io third-largest moon of the planet Jupiter, 3,630 km/2,260 mi in diameter, orbiting in 1.77 days at a distance of 422,000 km/262,000 mi. It is the most volcanically active body in the Solar System, covered by hundreds of vents that erupt not lava but sulphur, giving Io an orange-coloured surface.

Kuiper belt ring of small, icy bodies orbiting the Sun beyond the outermost planet. The Kuiper belt, named after US astronomer Gerard Kuiper who proposed its existence in 1951, is thought to be the source of comets that orbit the Sun with periods of less than 200 years. The first member

of the Kuiper belt was seen in 1992. In 1995 the first comet-sized objects were discovered; previously the only objects found had diameters of at least 100 km/63 mi (comets generally have diameters of less than 10 km/6.3 mi).

mare plural **maria**, dark lowland plain on the Moon. The name comes from Latin 'sea', because these areas were once wrongly thought to be water.

Mercury

Mercury the closest planet to the Sun. Its mass is 0.056 that of Earth. On its sunward side the surface temperature reaches over 400°C/752°F, but on the 'night' side it falls to −170°C/−274°F.
mean distance from the Sun 58 million km/36 million mi
equatorial diameter 4,880 km/3,030 mi
rotation period 59 Earth days
year 88 Earth days
atmosphere Mercury has an atmosphere with minute traces of argon and helium
surface composed of silicate rock often in the form of lava flows. In 1974 the US space probe *Mariner 10* showed that Mercury's surface is cratered by meteorite impacts
satellites none

meteor flash of light in the sky, popularly known as a **shooting** or **falling star,** caused by a particle of dust, a **meteoroid,** entering the atmosphere at speeds up to 70 kps/45 mps and burning up by friction at a height of around 100 km/60 mi. On

Mars

Mars is the fourth planet from the Sun. It is much smaller than Venus or Earth, with a mass 0.11 that of Earth. Mars is slightly pear-shaped, with a low, level northern hemisphere, which is comparatively uncratered and geologically 'young', and a heavily cratered 'ancient' southern hemisphere.
mean distance from the Sun 227.9 million km/141.6 million mi
equatorial diameter 6,780 km/4,210 mi
rotation period 24 hr 37 min
year 687 Earth days

atmosphere 95% carbon dioxide, 3% nitrogen, 1.5% argon, and 0.15% oxygen. Red atmospheric dust from the surface whipped up by winds of up to 450 kph/280 mph accounts for the light pink sky. The surface pressure is less than 1% of the Earth's atmospheric pressure at sea level
surface the landscape is a dusty, red, eroded lava plain. Mars has white polar caps (water ice and frozen carbon dioxide) that advance and retreat with the seasons
satellites two small satellites:

Phobos and Deimos
There are four enormous volcanoes near the equator, of which the largest is Olympus Mons 24 km/15 mi high, with a base 600 km/375 mi across, and a crater 65 km/40 mi wide. To the east of the four volcanoes lies a high plateau cut by a system of valleys, Valles Marineris, some 4,000 km/2,500 mi long, up to 200 km/120 mi wide and 6 km/4 mi deep; these features are apparently caused by faulting and wind erosion. Recorded temperatures vary from −100°C/−148°F to 0°C/32°F.

any clear night, several **sporadic meteors** can be seen each hour.

Several times each year the Earth encounters swarms of dust shed by comets, which give rise to a **meteor shower.** This appears to radiate from one particular point in the sky, after which the shower is named; the **Perseid** meteor shower in August appears in the constellation Perseus. The **Leonids** shoot out from the constellation Leo and are caused by dust from Comet Tempel-Tuttle, which orbits the Sun every 33 years. The Leonid shower reaches its peak when the comet is closest to the Sun.

When is a bomb a meteorite?

■ An explosion in Northern Ireland in December 1997 was blamed on terrorists, but was later discovered to be caused by a meteorite. It left a 1.2-m/4-ft wide crater.

---

meteorite piece of rock or metal from space that reaches the surface of the Earth, Moon, or other body. Most meteorites are thought to be fragments from asteroids, although some may be pieces from the heads of comets. Most are stony, although some are made of iron and a few have a mixed rock-iron composition.

Stony meteorites can be divided into two kinds: **chondrites** and **achondrites.** Chondrites contain chondrules, small spheres of the silicate minerals olivine and orthopyroxene, and comprise 85% of meteorites. Achondrites do not contain chondrules. Meteorites provide evidence for the nature of the Solar System and may be similar to the Earth's core and mantle, neither of which can be observed directly.

moon any natural satellite that orbits a planet. Mercury and Venus are the only planets in the Solar System that do not have moons.

Oort cloud spherical cloud of comets beyond Pluto, extending out to about 100,000 astronomical units (1.5 light years) from the Sun. The gravitational effect of passing stars and the rest of our Galaxy disturbs comets from the cloud so that they fall in towards the Sun on highly elongated orbits, becoming visible from Earth. As many as 10 trillion comets may reside in the Oort cloud, named after Dutch astronomer Jan Oort who postulated its existence in 1950.

Phobos one of the two moons of Mars, discovered 1877 by the US astronomer Asaph Hall (1829–1907). It is an irregularly shaped lump of

Heaviest Meteorites

(N/A = not available.)

Name and location	Weight (tonnes)	Year found	Dimensions	Composition
Hoba West, Grootfontein, Namibia	60	1920	2.7 × 2.7 × 1.1 m/9 × 9 × 3.5 ft	nickel-rich iron
Ahnighito, Greenland	30	–	–	–
Bacuberito, Mexico	27	1863	3.6 m/12 ft long	iron
Mbosi, Tanzania	26	1930	4.1 × 1.2 × 1.3 m/13.5 × 4 × 4 ft	iron
Agpalik, Greenland	20	–	–	–
Armanty, Mongolia	20	1935 (known in 1917)	–	iron
Chupaderos, Mexico	14	known for centuries; first mentioned in 1852	2 masses	iron
Willamette (OR), USA	14	1902	–	iron
Campo del Cielo, Argentina	13	–	–	–
Mundrabilla, Western Australia	12	–	–	–
Morito, Mexico	11	known in 1600	–	iron

Moon

The Moon is the natural satellite of Earth, 3,476 km/2,160 mi in diameter, with a mass 0.012 (approximately one-eightieth) that of Earth.

Its surface gravity is only 0.16 (one-sixth) that of Earth. Its average distance from Earth is 384,400 km/238,855 mi, and it orbits in a west-to-east direction every 27.32 days (the **sidereal month**). It spins on its axis with one side permanently turned towards Earth. The Moon has no atmosphere and was thought to have no water till ice was discovered on its surface in 1998.

phases The Moon is illuminated by sunlight, and goes through a cycle of phases of shadow, waxing from **new** (dark) via **first quarter** (half Moon) to **full**, and waning back again to new every 29.53 days (the **synodic month** or **lunation**). On its sunlit side, temperatures reach 110°C/230°F, but during the two-week lunar night the surface temperature drops to –170°C/–274°F.

origins The origin of the Moon is still open to debate. Scientists suggest the following theories: that it split from the Earth; that it was a separate body captured by Earth's gravity; that it formed in orbit around Earth; or that it was formed from debris thrown off when a body the size of Mars struck Earth.

research The far side of the Moon was first photographed from the Soviet *Lunik 3* in October 1959. Much of our information about the Moon has been derived from this and other photographs and measurements taken by US and Soviet Moon probes, from geological samples brought back by US Apollo astronauts and by Soviet Luna probes, and from experiments set up by the US astronauts in 1969–72. The US probe, *Lunar Prospector,* launched January 1998, examined the composition of the lunar crust, recorded gamma rays, and mapped the lunar magnetic field.

composition The Moon's composition is rocky, with a surface heavily scarred by meteorite impacts that have formed craters up to 240 km/150 mi across. Seismic observations indicate that the Moon's surface extends downwards for tens of kilometres; below this crust is a solid mantle about 1,100 km/688 mi thick, and below that a silicate core, part of which may be molten. Rocks brought back by astronauts show the Moon is 4.6 billion years old, the same age as Earth. It is made up of the same chemical elements as Earth, but in different proportions, and differs from Earth in that most of the Moon's surface features were formed within the first billion years of its history when it was hit repeatedly by meteorites. The youngest craters are surrounded by bright rays of ejected rock. The largest scars have been filled by dark lava to produce the lowland plains called seas, or **maria** (plural of mare). These dark patches form the so-called 'man-in-the-Moon' pattern. Inside some craters that are permanently in shadow is 300 million–300 billion tonnes of ice existing as a thin layer of crystals.

rock, cratered by meteorite impacts. Phobos is 27 x 22 x 19 km/17 x 13 x 12 mi across, and orbits Mars every 0.32 days at a distance of 9,400 km/5,840 mi from the planet's centre. It is thought to be an asteroid captured by Mars' gravity.

Neptune

Neptune is the eighth planet in average distance from the Sun. It is a gas giant (hydrogen, helium, methane) planet, with a mass 17.2 times that of Earth. It has the highest winds in the Solar System.

mean distance from the Sun 4.4 billion km/2.794 billion mi

equatorial diameter 48,600 km/30,200 mi

rotation period 16 hr 7 min

year 164.8 Earth years

atmosphere methane in its atmosphere absorbs red light and gives the planet a blue colouring. Consists primarily of hydrogen (85%) with helium (13%) and methane (1–2%)

surface hydrogen, helium and methane. Its interior is believed to have a central rocky core covered by a layer of ice

satellites of Neptune's eight moons, two (Triton and Nereid) are visible from Earth. Six were discovered by the *Voyager 2* probe in 1989, of which Proteus (diameter 415 km/260 mi) is larger than Nereid (300 km/200 mi)

rings there are four faint rings: Galle, Le Verrier, Arago, and Adams (in order from Neptune). Galle is the widest at 1,700 km/1,060 mi. Leverrier and Arago are divided by a wide diffuse particle band called the plateau

research Neptune was located 1846 by German astronomers Johan Galle and Heinrich d'Arrest (1822–1875) after calculations by English astronomer John Couch Adams and French mathematician Urbain Leverrier had predicted its existence from disturbances in the movement of Uranus. *Voyager 2,* which passed Neptune in August 1989, revealed various cloud features, notably an Earth-sized oval storm cloud, the Great Dark Spot, similar to the Great Red Spot on Jupiter, but images taken by the Hubble Space Telescope in 1994 show that the Great Dark Spot has disappeared. A smaller dark spot DS2 has also gone.

Neptune's Satellites

Satellite	Year of discovery	Diameter		Mean distance from Neptune	
		km	mi	km	mi
Triton	1846	2,700	1,678	355,000	221,000
Nereid	1949	340	211	5,513,000	3,426,000
Despina	1989	180	112	53,000	33,000
Galatea	1989	150	93	62,000	39,000
Larissa	1989	190	118	74,000	46,000
Naiad	1989	50	31	48,000	30,000
Proteus	1989	400	249	118,000	73,000
Thalassa	1989	80	50	50,000	31,000

photosphere visible surface of the Sun, which emits light and heat. About 300 km/200 mi deep, it consists of incandescent gas at a temperature of 5,800K (5,530°C/9,980°F). Rising cells of hot gas produce a mottling of the photosphere known as **granulation,** each granule being about 1,000 km/620 mi in diameter. The photosphere is often marked by large, dark patches called sunspots.

planet large celestial body in orbit around a star, composed of rock, metal, or gas. There are nine planets in the Solar System: Mercury, Venus, Earth, Mars, Jupiter, Saturn, Neptune, Uranus, and Pluto. The inner four, called the **terrestrial planets,** are small and rocky, and include the planet Earth. The outer planets, with the exception of Pluto, are called the **major planets,** and consist of large balls of rock, liquid, and gas; the largest is Jupiter, which contains a mass equivalent to 70% of all the other planets combined. Planets do not produce light, but reflect the light of their parent star.

As seen from the Earth, all the historic planets are conspicuous naked-eye objects moving in looped paths against the stellar background. The size of these loops, which are caused by the Earth's own motion round the Sun, are inversely proportional to the planet's distance from the Earth.

prominence bright cloud of gas projecting from the Sun into space 100,000 km/60,000 mi or more. **Quiescent prominences** last for months, and are held in place by magnetic fields in the

The Planets

(– = not applicable.)

Planet	Main constituents	Atmosphere	Average distance from the Sun		Orbital period	Diameter		Average density
			km (millions)	mi (millions)	(Earth yrs)	km (thousands)	mi (thousands)	(water = 1 unit)
Mercury	rock, ferrous	–	58	36	0.241	4.88	3.03	5.4
Venus	rock, ferrous	carbon dioxide	108	67	0.615	12.10	7.51	5.2
Earth	rock, ferrous	nitrogen, oxygen	150	93	1.00	12.76	7.92	5.5
Mars	rock	carbon dioxide	228	141	1.88	6.78	4.21	3.9
Jupiter	liquid hydrogen, helium	–	778	484	11.86	142.80	88.73	1.3
Saturn	hydrogen, helium	–	1,427	886	29.46	120.00	74.56	0.7
Uranus	ice, hydrogen, helium	hydrogen, helium	2,870	1,783	84.00	50.80	31.56	1.3
Neptune	ice, hydrogen, helium	hydrogen, helium	4,497	2,794	164.80	48.60	30.20	1.8
Pluto	ice, rock	methane	5,900	3,666	248.50	2.30	1.40	~2

Pluto

Pluto is the smallest and, usually, outermost planet of the Solar System. The existence of Pluto was predicted by calculation by Percival Lowell and the planet was located by Clyde Tombaugh in 1930. Its highly elliptical orbit occasionally takes it within the orbit of Neptune, as in 1979–99. Pluto has a mass about 0.002 of that of Earth.
mean distance from the Sun 5.9 billion km/3.6 billion mi
equatorial diameter 2,300 km/1,438 mi
rotation period 6.39 Earth days
year 248.5 Earth years
atmosphere thin atmosphere with small amounts of methane gas
surface low density, composed of rock and ice, primarily frozen methane; there is an ice cap at Pluto's north pole
satellites one moon, Charon

Sun's corona. **Surge prominences** shoot gas into space at speeds of 1,000 kps/600 mps. **Loop prominences** are gases falling back to the Sun's surface after a solar flare.

solar wind stream of atomic particles, mostly protons and electrons, from the Sun's corona, flowing outwards at speeds of between 300 kps/200 mps and 1,000 kps/600 mps. The fastest streams come from 'holes' in the Sun's corona that lie over areas where no surface activity occurs. The solar wind pushes the gas of comets' tails away from the Sun, and 'gusts' in the solar wind cause geomagnetic disturbances and aurorae on Earth.

solstice either of the days on which the Sun is farthest north or south of the celestial equator each year. The **summer solstice,** when the Sun is farthest north, occurs around 21 June; the **winter solstice** around 22 December.

Sun
- The further out from the Sun, the hotter it is: the Sun's corona is 1,994,000°C/3,589,000°F hotter than the Sun itself.

Sun the star at the centre of the Solar System. Its diameter is 1,392,000 km/865,000 mi; its temperature at the surface is about 5,800K (5,500°C/9,900°F), and at the centre 15,000,000K (about 15,000,000°C/27,000,000°F). It is composed of about 70% hydrogen and 30% helium, with other elements making up less than 1%. The Sun's energy is generated by nuclear fusion reactions that turn hydrogen into helium at its centre. The gas core is far denser than mercury or lead on Earth. The Sun is about 4.7 billion years old, with a predicted lifetime of 10 billion years.

sunspot dark patch on the surface of the Sun, actually an area of cooler gas, thought to be caused by strong magnetic fields that block the outward flow of heat to the Sun's surface. Sunspots consist of a dark central **umbra,** about 4,000K (3,700°C/6,700°F), and a lighter surrounding **penumbra,** about 5,500K (5,200°C/9,400°F). They last from

Saturn

Saturn is the second-largest planet in the Solar System, sixth from the Sun, and encircled by bright and easily visible equatorial rings. Viewed through a telescope it is ochre. Its polar diameter is 12,000 km/7,450 mi smaller than its equatorial diameter, a result of its fast rotation and low density, the lowest of any planet. Its mass is 95 times that of Earth, and its magnetic field 1,000 times stronger.
mean distance from the Sun 1.427 billion km/0.886 billion mi
equatorial diameter 120,000 km/75,000 mi
rotational period 10 hr 14 min at equator, 10 hr 40 min at higher latitudes
year 29.46 Earth years
atmosphere visible surface consists of swirling clouds, probably made of frozen ammonia at a temperature of −170°C/−274°F, although the markings in the clouds are not as prominent as Jupiter's. The space probes *Voyager 1* and *2* found winds reaching 1,800 kph/1,100 mph
surface Saturn is believed to have a small core of rock and iron, encased in ice and topped by a deep layer of liquid hydrogen
satellites 18 known moons, more than for any other planet. The largest moon, Titan, has a dense atmosphere. Other satellites include Epimetheus, Janus, Pandor, and Prometheus. The rings visible from Earth begin about 14,000 km/9,000 mi from the planet's cloudtops and extend out to about 76,000 km/47,000 mi. Made of small chunks of ice and rock (averaging 1 m/3 ft across), they are 275,000 km/170,000 mi rim to rim, but only 100 m/300 ft thick. The Voyager probes showed that the rings actually consist of thousands of closely spaced ringlets, looking like the grooves in a gramophone record.

Selected Satellites of Saturn

Satellite	Year of discovery	Diameter		Mean distance from Saturn	
		km	mi	km	mi
Titan	1655	5,150	3,200	1,222,000	759,000
Iapetus	1671	1,460	910	3,561,000	2,213,000
Rhea	1672	1,530	950	527,000	327,000
Dione	1684	1,120	700	377,000	234,000
Tethys	1684	1,050	650	295,000	183,000
Enceladus	1789	500	310	238,000	148,000
Mimas	1789	390	245	186,000	116,000
Hyperion	1848	shape irregular 410 × 260 × 220	shape irregular 255 × 160 × 135	1,481,000	920,000
Phoebe	1898	220	135	12,950,000	8,047,000

several days to over a month, ranging in size from 2,000 km/1,250 mi to groups stretching for over 100,000 km/62,000 mi.

Sunspots are more common during active periods in the Sun's magnetic cycle, when they are sometimes accompanied by nearby flares. The number of sunspots visible at a given time varies from none to over 100, in a cycle averaging 11 years. There was a lull in sunspot activity, known as the Maunder minimum, 1645–1715, that coincided with a cold spell in Europe.

superior planet planet that is farther away from the Sun than the Earth is: that is, Mars, Jupiter, Saturn, Uranus, Neptune, and Pluto.

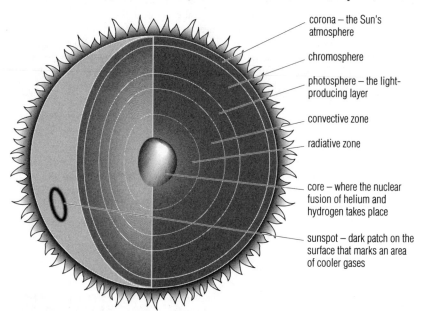

corona – the Sun's atmosphere

chromosphere

photosphere – the light-producing layer

convective zone

radiative zone

core – where the nuclear fusion of helium and hydrogen takes place

sunspot – dark patch on the surface that marks an area of cooler gases

Sun The structure of the Sun. Nuclear reactions at the core releases vast amounts of energy in the form of light and heat that radiate out to the photosphere and corona. Surges of glowing gas rise as prominences from the surface of the Sun and cooler areas, known as sunspots, appear as dark patches on the giant stars surface.

Uranus

Uranus is the seventh planet from the Sun, discovered by William Herschel in 1781. It is twice as far out as the sixth planet, Saturn. Uranus has a mass 14.5 times that of Earth. The spin axis of Uranus is tilted at 98°, so that one pole points towards the Sun, giving extreme seasons.

mean distance from the Sun 2.9 billion km/1.8 billion mi

equatorial diameter 50,800 km/31,600 mi

rotation period 17.2 hr

year 84 Earth years

atmosphere deep atmosphere composed mainly of hydrogen and helium

surface composed primarily of hydrogen and helium but may also contain heavier elements, which might account for Uranus's mean density being higher than Saturn's

satellites 17 moons (two discovered in 1997); 11 thin rings around the planet's equator were discovered in 1977.

Uranus has a peculiar magnetic field, whose axis is tilted at 60° to its axis of spin, and is displaced about a third of the way from the planet's centre to its surface. Uranus spins from east to west, the opposite of the other planets, with the exception of Venus and possibly Pluto. The rotation rate of the atmosphere varies with latitude, from about 16 hours in mid-southern latitudes to longer than 17 hours at the equator.

Uranus's equatorial ring system comprises 11 rings. The ring furthest from the planet centre (51,000 km/31,800 mi), Epsilon, is 100 km/62 mi at its widest point. In 1995, US astronomers determined the ring particles contained long-chain hydrocarbons. Looking at the brightest region of Epsilon, they were also able to calculate the precession of Uranus as 264 days, the fastest known precession in the Solar System.

tektite small, rounded glassy stone, found in certain regions of the Earth, such as Australasia. Tektites are probably the scattered drops of molten rock thrown out by the impact of a large meteorite.

Uranus
- All Uranus' moons are named after characters from Shakespeare, including Miranda, Ariel, Oberon, and Titania.

Venus

Venus is the second planet from the Sun. It can approach Earth to within 38 million km/24 million mi, closer than any other planet. Its mass is 0.82 that of Earth. Venus rotates on its axis more slowly than any other planet, from east to west, the opposite direction to the other planets (except Uranus and possibly Pluto).

mean distance from the Sun 108.2 million km/67.2 million mi

equatorial diameter 12,100 km/7,500 mi

rotation period 243 Earth days

year 225 Earth days

atmosphere Venus is shrouded by clouds of sulphuric acid droplets that sweep across the planet from east to west every four days. The atmosphere is almost entirely carbon dioxide, which traps the Sun's heat by the greenhouse effect and raises the planet's surface temperature to 480°C/900°F, with an atmospheric pressure of 90 times that at the surface of the Earth.

surface consists mainly of silicate rock and may have an interior structure similar to that of Earth: an iron–nickel core, a mantle composed of more mafic rocks (rocks made of one or more ferromagnesian, dark-coloured minerals), and a thin siliceous outer crust. The surface is dotted with deep impact craters. Some of Venus's volcanoes may still be active

satellites no moons

The first artificial object to hit another planet was the Soviet probe *Venera 3*, which crashed on Venus on 1 March 1966. Later Venera probes parachuted down through the atmosphere and landed successfully on its surface, analysing surface material and sending back information and pictures. In December 1978 a US Pioneer Venus probe went into orbit around the planet and mapped most of its surface by radar, which penetrates clouds. In 1992 the US space probe *Magellan* mapped 99% of the planet's surface to a resolution of 100 m/ 330 ft.

The largest highland area is Aphrodite Terra near the equator, half the size of Africa. The highest mountains are on the northern highland region of Ishtar Terra, where the massif of Maxwell Montes rises to 10,600 m/35,000 ft above the average surface level. The highland areas on Venus were formed by volcanoes.

Venus has an ion-packed tail 45 million km/28 million mi in length that stretches away from the Sun and is caused by the bombardment of the ions in Venus's upper atmosphere by the solar wind. It was first discovered in the late 1970s but it was not until 1997 that the Solar Heliospheric Observatory (SOHO) revealed its immense length.

Van Allen radiation belts two zones of charged particles around the Earth's magnetosphere, discovered in 1958 by US physicist James Van Allen. The atomic particles come from the Earth's upper atmosphere and the solar wind, and are trapped by the Earth's magnetic field. The inner belt lies 1,000–5,000 km/620–3,100 mi above the Equator, and contains protons and electrons. The outer belt lies 15,000–25,000 km/9,300–15,500 mi above the Equator, but is lower around the magnetic poles. It contains mostly electrons from the solar wind.

zodiac zone of the heavens containing the paths of the Sun, Moon, and planets. When this was devised by the ancient Greeks, only five planets were known, making the zodiac about 16° wide. In astrology, the zodiac is divided into 12 signs, each 30° in extent: Aries, Taurus, Gemini, Cancer, Leo, Virgo, Libra, Scorpio, Sagittarius, Capricorn, Aquarius, and Pisces. These do not cover the same areas of sky as the astronomical constellations.

The 12 astronomical constellations are uneven in size and do not between them cover the whole zodiac, or even the line of the ecliptic, much of which lies in the constellation of Ophiuchus.

Prime meridian
English astronomer John Flamsteed. After petitioning Charles II for a national observatory, he was made the first Astronomer Royal 1675 and founded the Royal Observatory at Greenwich, London. He determined the latitude of Greenwich, which from then on has been used as 0°, the prime meridian. Flamsteed also computed the positions of 3,000 stars in his catalogue *Historia Coelestis Britannica* (1725). *Private collection*

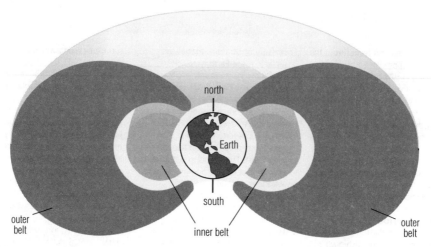

Van Allen radiation belts The Van Allen belts of trapped charged particles are a hazard to spacecraft, affecting on-board electronics and computer systems. Similar belts have been discovered around the planets Mercury, Jupiter, Saturn, Uranus, and Neptune.

STARS, GALAXIES, AND THE UNIVERSE

The Universe is thought to have formed 10 to 20 billion years ago with the Big Bang. The largest features of our Universe are galaxies, congregations of millions or billions of stars, held together by gravity. Galaxies are classified as spiral, elliptical, or irregular. They vary in size, structure, and luminosity, and, like stars, are found alone, in pairs, or in clusters. Most galaxies occur in clusters, containing anything from a few to thousands of members.

Our own galaxy, the Milky Way, is a spiral galaxy about 100,000 light years in diameter, and contains at least 100 billion stars. The Sun lies in one of its spiral arms, about 25,000 light years from the centre of the galaxy. The Milky Way is a member of a small irregular cluster, referred to as the Local Group.

Galaxies are composed of stars, luminous globes of gas, mainly hydrogen and helium, which produce their own heat and light by nuclear reactions. Although stars shine for a very long time – many billions of years – they are not eternal, and have been found to change in appearance at different stages in their lives. A **main-sequence** star, like our Sun, is formed from interstellar matter that contracts under the influence of gravity. At about 10 million°C/18 million°F, a temperature hot enough for a nuclear reaction to begin, contraction stops and the star begins to shine. A star with the mass of the Sun takes a few million years to reach the main sequence, and then remains on it for about 10 billion years. The Sun is expected to remain at this stage for another 5 billion years.

As the main-sequence star ages, all the hydrogen at the core is converted into helium, at which time the star swells to become a **red giant**. Depending on its mass, the red giant star either will collapse in on itself eventually to form a small and very dense body called a **white dwarf**, or further nuclear transformations will take place until the star explodes into a brilliant **supernova**. Part of the core remaining after the explosion may collapse to form a small superdense star, called a **neutron star**. But if the collapsing core of the supernova has a mass more than twice that of the Sun, it does not form a neutron star; instead it forms a **black hole**, a region so dense that its gravity not only draws in all nearby matter but also all radiation, including its own light.

Algol or **Beta Persei,** eclipsing binary, a pair of orbiting stars in the constellation Perseus, one of which eclipses the other every 69 hours, causing its brightness to drop by two-thirds.

Alpha Centauri or **Rigil Kent,** brightest star in the constellation Centaurus and the third-brightest star in the sky. It is actually a triple star; the two brighter stars orbit each other every 80 years, and the third, Proxima Centauri, is the closest star to the Sun, 4.2 light years away, 0.1 light years closer than the other two.

Brightest star
- The brightest known star is the Pistol Star, discovered near the centre of the Milky Way in 1997 by the Hubble Space Telescope. It emits as much energy in seconds as the Sun does in one year, making it 10 million times brighter and 100 times larger.

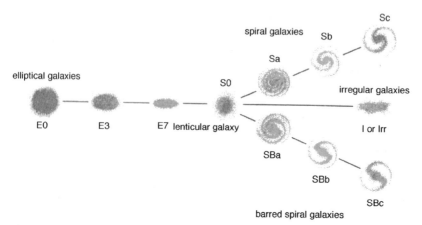

Sc

spiral galaxies   Sb

Sa

elliptical galaxies

S0

irregular galaxies

E0   E3   E7   lenticular galaxy   I or Irr

SBa

SBb

SBc

barred spiral galaxies

galaxy Galaxies were classified by US astronomer Edwin Hubble in 1925. He placed the galaxies in a 'tuning-fork' pattern, in which the two prongs correspond to the barred and non-barred spiral galaxies. A third prong was added later for irregular galaxies.

Andromeda galaxy galaxy 2.2 million light years away from Earth in the constellation Andromeda, and the most distant object visible to the naked eye. It is the largest member of the Local Group of galaxies. Like the Milky Way, it is a spiral orbited by several companion galaxies but contains about twice as many stars. It is about 200,000 light years across.

Barnard's star second-closest star to the Sun, six light years away in the constellation Ophiuchus. It is a faint red dwarf of 10th magnitude, visible only through a telescope. It is named after the US astronomer Edward E Barnard (1857–1923), who discovered in 1916 that it has the fastest proper motion of any star, crossing 1 degree of sky every 350 years.

Big Bang hypothetical 'explosive' event that marked the origin of the universe as we know it. At the time of the Big Bang, the entire universe was squeezed into a hot, superdense state. The Big Bang explosion threw this compact material outwards, producing the expanding universe. The cause of the Big Bang is unknown; observations of the current rate of expansion of the universe suggest that it took place about 10–20 billion years ago. The Big Bang theory began modern cosmology.

According to a modified version of the Big Bang, called the **inflationary theory,** the universe underwent a rapid period of expansion shortly after the Big Bang, which accounts for its current large size and uniform nature. The inflationary theory is supported by the most recent observations of the cosmic background radiation.

Scientists have calculated that one 10^{-36} second (equivalent to one million-million-million-million-million-millionth of a second) after the Big Bang, the universe was the size of a pea, and the temperature was 10 billion million million million°C (18 billion million million million°F). One second after the Big Bang, the temperature was about 10 billion°C (18 billion°F).

binary star pair of stars moving in orbit around their common centre of mass. Observations show that most stars are binary, or even multiple – for example, the nearest star system to the Sun, Alpha Centauri.

One of the stars in the binary system Epsilon Aurigae may be the largest star known. Its diameter is 2,800 times that of the Sun. If it were in the position of the Sun, it would engulf Mercury, Venus, Earth, Mars, Jupiter, and Saturn. A spectroscopic binary is a binary in which two stars are so close together that they cannot be seen separately, but their separate light spectra can be distinguished by a spectroscope.

black hole object in space whose gravity is so great that nothing can escape from it, not even light. Thought to form when massive stars shrink at the end of their lives, a black hole sucks in more matter, including other stars, from the space around it. Matter that falls into a black hole is squeezed to infinite density at the centre of the hole. Black holes can be detected because gas falling towards them becomes so hot that it emits X-rays.

Black holes containing the mass of millions of stars are thought to lie at the centres of quasars. Satellites have detected X-rays from a number of objects that may be black holes, but only four likely black holes in our Galaxy had been identified by 1994.

brown dwarf object less massive than a star, but heavier than a planet. Brown dwarfs do not have enough mass to ignite nuclear reactions at their centres, but shine by heat released during their contraction from a gas cloud. Some astronomers believe that vast numbers of brown dwarfs exist throughout the Galaxy. Because of the difficulty of detection, none were spotted until 1995, when US astronomers discovered a brown dwarf, GI229B, in the constellation Lepus. It is about 20–40 times as massive as Jupiter but emits only 1% of the radiation of the smallest known star. In 1996 UK astronomers discovered four possible brown dwarfs within 150 light years of the Sun.

Cepheid variable yellow supergiant star that varies regularly in brightness every few days or weeks as a result of pulsations. The time that a Cepheid variable takes to pulsate is directly related to its average brightness; the longer the pulsation period, the brighter the star. This relationship, the **period luminosity law** (discovered by US astronomer Henrietta Leavitt), allows astronomers to use Cepheid variables as 'standard candles' to measure distances in our Galaxy and to nearby galaxies. They are named after their prototype, Delta Cephei, whose light variations were observed 1784 by English astronomer John Goodricke (1764–1786).

constellation one of the 88 areas into which the sky is divided for the purposes of identifying and naming celestial objects. The first constellations were simple, arbitrary patterns of stars in which early civilizations visualized gods, sacred beasts, and mythical heroes.

The constellations in use today are derived from a list of 48 known to the ancient Greeks, who inherited some from the Babylonians. The current list of 88 constellations was adopted by the International Astronomical Union, astronomy's governing body, in 1930.

cosmic background radiation or **3° radiation,** electromagnetic radiation left over from the original formation of the universe in the Big Bang around 15 billion years ago. It corresponds to an overall background temperature of 3K (−270°C/−454°F), or 3°C above absolute zero. In 1992 the Cosmic Background Explorer satellite, COBE, detected slight 'ripples' in the strength of the background radiation that are believed to mark the first stage in the formation of galaxies.

Cosmic background radiation was first detected in 1965 by US physicists Arno Penzias (1933–   ) and Robert Wilson (1936–   ), who in 1978 shared the Nobel Prize for Physics for their discovery.

dark matter matter that, according to current theories of cosmology, makes up 90–99% of the mass of the universe but so far remains undetected. Dark matter, if shown to exist, would explain many currently unexplained gravitational effects in the movement of galaxies.

Theories of the composition of dark matter include unknown atomic particles (cold dark matter) or fast-moving neutrinos (hot dark matter) or a combination of both.

Part of the dark matter may be in the form of stray planets and brown dwarfs, and possibly, stars that have failed to light up. These objects are known as MACHOs (massive astrophysical compact halo objects) and may make up approximately half of the dark matter in the Milky Way's halo.

double star two stars that appear close together. Many stars that appear single to the naked eye appear double when viewed through a telescope. Some double stars attract each other due to gravity, and orbit each other, forming a genuine binary star, but other double stars are at different distances from Earth, and lie in the same line of sight only by chance. Through a telescope both types look the same.

Double stars of the second kind, which are of little astronomical interest, are referred to as 'optical pairs'; those of the first as 'physical pairs' or, more usually, 'visual binaries'. They are the principal source from which is derived our knowledge of stellar masses.

eclipsing binary binary (double) star in which the two stars periodically pass in front of each other as seen from Earth.

When one star crosses in front of the other the total light received on Earth from the two stars declines. The first eclipsing binary to be noticed was Algol.

Constellations

A constellation is one of the 88 areas into which the sky is divided for the purposes of identifying and naming celestial objects. The first constellations were simple, arbitrary patterns of stars in which early civilizations visualized gods, sacred beasts, and mythical heroes. (– = not applicable.)

Constellation	Abbreviation	Popular name	Constellation	Abbreviation	Popular name
Andromeda	And	–	Lacerta	Lac	Lizard
Antlia	Ant	Airpump	Leo	Leo	Lion
Apus	Aps	Bird of Paradise	Leo Minor	LMi	Little Lion
Aquarius	Aqr	Water-bearer	Lepus	Lep	Hare
Aquila	Aqi	Eagle	Libra	Lib	Balance
Ara	Ara	Altar	Lupus	Lup	Wolf
Aries	Ari	Ram	Lynx	Lyn	–
Auriga	Aur	Charioteer	Lyra	Lyr	Lyre
Boötes	Boo	Herdsman	Mensa	Men	Table
Caelum	Cae	Chisel	Microscopium	Mic	Microscope
Camelopardalis	Cam	Giraffe	Monoceros	Mon	Unicorn
Cancer	Cnc	Crab	Musca	Mus	Southern Fly
Canes Venatici	CVn	Hunting Dogs	Norma	Nor	Rule
Canis Major	CMa	Great Dog	Octans	Oct	Octant
Canis Minor	CMi	Little Dog	Ophiuchus	Oph	Serpent-bearer
Capricornus	Cap	Sea-goat	Orion	Ori	–
Carina	Car	Keel	Pavo	Pav	Peacock
Cassiopeia	Cas	–	Pegasus	Peg	Flying Horse
Centaurus	Cen	Centaur	Perseus	Per	–
Cepheus	Cep	–	Phoenix	Phe	Phoenix
Cetus	Cet	Whale	Pictor	Pic	Painter
Chamaeleon	Cha	Chameleon	Pisces	Psc	Fishes
Circinus	Cir	Compasses	Piscis Austrinus	PsA	Southern Fish
Columba	Col	Dove	Puppis	Pup	Poop
Coma Berenices	Com	Berenice's Hair	Pyxis	Pyx	Compass
Corona Australis	CrA	Southern Crown	Reticulum	Ret	Net
Corona Borealis	CrB	Northern Crown	Sagitta	Sge	Arrow
Corvus	Crv	Crow	Sagittarius	Sgr	Archer
Crater	Crt	Cup	Scorpius	Sco	Scorpion
Crux	Cru	Southern Cross	Sculptor	Scl	–
Cygnus	Cyn	Swan	Scutum	Sct	Shield
Delphinus	Del	Dolphin	Serpens	Ser	Serpent
Dorado	Dor	Goldfish	Sextans	Sex	Sextant
Draco	Dra	Dragon	Taurus	Tau	Bull
Equuleus	Equ	Foal	Telescopium	Tel	Telescope
Eridanus	Eri	River	Triangulum	Tri	Triangle
Fornax	For	Furnace	Triangulum Australe	TrA	Southern Triangle
Gemini	Gem	Twins	Tucana	Tuc	Toucan
Grus	Gru	Crane	Ursa Major	UMa	Great Bear
Hercules	Her	–	Ursa Minor	UMi	Little Bear
Horologium	Hor	Clock	Vela	Vel	Sails
Hydra	Hya	Watersnake	Virgo	Vir	Virgin
Hydrus	Hyi	Little Snake	Volans	Vol	Flying Fish
Indus	Ind	Indian	Vulpecula	Vul	Fox

globular cluster spherical or near-spherical star cluster containing from approximately 10,000 to millions of stars. More than a hundred globular clusters are distributed in a spherical halo around our Galaxy. They consist of old stars, formed early in the Galaxy's history. Globular clusters are also found around other galaxies.

Local Group cluster of about 30 galaxies that includes our own, the Milky Way. Like other groups of galaxies, the Local Group is held together by the gravitational attraction among its members, and does not expand with the expanding universe. Its two largest galaxies are the Milky Way and the Andromeda galaxy; most of the others are small and faint.

Magellanic Clouds two galaxies nearest to our own galaxy. They are irregularly shaped, and appear as detached parts of the Milky Way, in the southern constellations Dorado, Tucana, and Mensa.

The Large Magellanic Cloud spreads over the constellations of Dorado and Mensa. The Small Magellanic Cloud is in Tucana. The Large Magellanic Cloud is 169,000 light years from Earth, and about a third the diameter of our Galaxy; the Small Magellanic Cloud, 180,000 light years away, is about a fifth the diameter of our Galaxy. They are named after the navigator Ferdinand Magellan, who first described them.

magnitude measure of the brightness of a star or other celestial object. The larger the number denoting the magnitude, the fainter the object. Zero or first magnitude indicates some of the brightest stars. Still brighter are those of negative magnitude, such as Sirius, whose magnitude is –1.46. **Apparent magnitude** is the brightness of an object as seen from Earth; **absolute magnitude** is the brightness at a standard distance of 10 parsecs (32.6 light years).

Each magnitude step is equal to a brightness difference of 2.512 times. Thus a star of magnitude 1 is $(2.512)^5$ or 100 times brighter than a sixth-magnitude star just visible to the naked eye. The apparent magnitude of the Sun is –26.8, its absolute magnitude +4.8.

Milky Way faint band of light crossing the night sky, consisting of stars in the plane of our Galaxy. The name Milky Way is often used for the Galaxy itself. It is a spiral galaxy, 100,000 light years in diameter and 2,000 light years thick, containing at least 100 billion stars. The Sun is in one of its spiral arms, about 25,000 light years from the centre, not far from its central plane.

The densest parts of the Milky Way, towards the Galaxy's centre, lie in the constellation Sagittarius. In places, the Milky Way is interrupted by lanes of dark dust that obscure light from the stars beyond, such as the Coalsack nebula in Crux (the Southern Cross). It is because of these that the Milky Way is irregular in width and appears to be divided into two between Centaurus and Cygnus.

Mira or **Omicron Ceti,** brightest long-period pulsating variable star, located in the constellation Cetus. Mira was the first star discovered to vary periodically in brightness.

nebula cloud of gas and dust in space. Nebulae are the birthplaces of stars, but some nebulae are produced by gas thrown off from dying stars. Nebulae are classified depending on whether they emit, reflect, or absorb light. An **emission nebula,** such as the Orion nebula, glows brightly because its gas is energized by stars that have formed within it. In a **reflection nebula,** starlight reflects off grains of dust in the nebula, such as surround the stars of the Pleiades cluster. A **dark nebula** is a dense cloud, composed of molecular hydrogen, which partially or completely absorbs light behind it. Examples include the Coalsack nebula in Crux and the Horsehead nebula in Orion.

neutron star very small, 'superdense' star composed mostly of neutrons. They are thought to form when massive stars explode as supernovae, during which the protons and electrons of the star's atoms merge, owing to intense gravitational collapse, to make neutrons. A neutron star may have the mass of up to three Suns, compressed into a globe only 20 km/12 mi in diameter.

Heaviest star

■ Neutron stars are so condensed that a fragment the size of a sugar cube would weigh as much as all the people on Earth put together.

nova faint star that suddenly erupts in brightness by 10,000 times or more, remains bright for a few days, and then fades away and is not seen again for very many years, if at all. Novae are believed to occur in close binary star systems, where gas from one star flows to a companion white dwarf. The gas ignites and is thrown off in an explosion at speeds of 1,500 kps/930 mps or more. Unlike a supernova, the star is not completely disrupted by the outburst. After a few weeks or months it subsides to its previous state; it may erupt many more times.

oscillating universe theory that states that the gravitational attraction of the mass within the universe will eventually slow down and stop the expansion of the universe. The outward motions of the galaxies will then be reversed, eventually resulting in a 'Big Crunch' where all the matter in the universe would be contracted into a small volume of high density. This could undergo a further Big Bang, thereby creating another expansion phase. The theory suggests that the universe would alternately expand and collapse through alternate Big Bangs and Big Crunches.

planetary nebula shell of gas thrown off by a star at the end of its life. Planetary nebulae have nothing to do with planets. They were named by William Herschel, who thought their rounded shape resembled the disc of a planet. After a star such as the Sun has expanded to become a red giant, its outer layers are ejected into space to form a planetary nebula, leaving the core as a white dwarf at the centre.

Plaskett's star most massive binary star known, consisting of two supergiants of about 40 and 50 solar masses, orbiting each other every 14.4 days. Plaskett's star lies in the constellation Monoceros and is named after Canadian astronomer John S Plaskett (1865–1941), who identified it as a binary star and discovered its massive nature in 1922.

Polaris or **Pole Star** or **North Star**, bright star closest to the north celestial pole, and the brightest star in the constellation Ursa Minor. Its position is indicated by the 'pointers' in Ursa Major. Polaris is a yellow supergiant about 500 light years away. It currently lies within 1° of the north celestial pole; precession (Earth's axial wobble) will bring Polaris closest to the celestial pole (less than 0.5° away) in about year 2100. Then its distance will start to increase, reaching 1° in 2205 and 47° in 2800.

Pole Star another name for Polaris, the northern pole star.

Proxima Centauri closest star to the Sun, 4.2 light years away. It is a faint red dwarf, visible only with a telescope, and is a member of the Alpha Centauri triple-star system. It is called Proxima because it is about 0.1 light years closer to us than its two partners.

pulsar celestial source that emits pulses of energy at regular intervals, ranging from a few seconds to a few thousandths of a second. Pulsars are thought to be rapidly rotating neutron stars, which flash at radio and other wavelengths as they spin. They were discovered in 1967 by Jocelyn Bell Burnell and Antony Hewish at the Mullard Radio Astronomy Observatory, Cambridge, England. Over 500 radio pulsars are now known in our Galaxy, although a million or so may exist.

quasar from **qua**si-stellar object (*QSO*) one of the most distant extragalactic objects known, discovered in 1963. Quasars appear starlike, but each emits more energy than 100 giant galaxies. They are thought to be at the centre of galaxies, their brilliance emanating from the stars and gas falling towards an immense black hole at their nucleus. Most quasars are found in elliptical galaxies. Quasar light shows a large red shift, indicating that they are very distant. Some quasars emit radio waves, which is how they were first identified, but most are radio-quiet. The furthest are over 10 billion light years away.

radio galaxy galaxy that is a strong source of electromagnetic waves of radio wavelengths. All galaxies, including our own, emit some radio waves, but radio galaxies are up to a million times more powerful. In many cases the strongest radio emission comes not from the visible galaxy but from two clouds, invisible through an optical telescope, that can extend for millions of light years either side of the galaxy. This double structure at radio wavelengths is also shown by some quasars, suggesting a close relationship between the two types

Star: Nearest Stars

Star	Distance (light years)	Star	Distance (light years)
Proxima Centauri	4.2	UV Ceti A	8.4
Alpha Centauri A	4.3	UV Ceti B	8.4
Alpha Centauri B	4.3	Sirius A	8.6
Barnard's Star	6.0	Sirius B	8.6
Wolf 359	7.7	Ross 154	9.4
Lalande 21185	8.2	Ross 249	10.4

of object. In both cases, the source of energy is thought to be a massive black hole at the centre. Some radio galaxies are thought to result from two galaxies in collision or recently merged.

red dwarf any star that is cool, faint, and small (about one-tenth the mass and diameter of the Sun). Red dwarfs burn slowly, and have estimated lifetimes of 100 billion years. They may be the most abundant type of star, but are difficult to see because they are so faint. Two of the closest stars to the Sun, Proxima Centauri and Barnard's Star, are red dwarfs.

red giant any large bright star with a cool surface. It is thought to represent a late stage in the evolution of a star like the Sun, as it runs out of hydrogen fuel at its centre and begins to burn heavier elements, such as helium, carbon, and silicon. Because of more complex nuclear reactions that then occur in the red giant's interior, it eventually becomes gravitationally unstable and begins to collapse and heat up. The result is either explosion of the star as a supernova, leaving behind a neutron star, or loss of mass by more gradual means to produce a white dwarf. Red giants have diameters between 10 and 100 times that of the Sun. They are very bright because they are so large, although their surface temperature is lower than that of the Sun, about 2,000–3,000K (1,700–2,700°C/3,000–5,000°F).

Seyfert galaxy galaxy whose small, bright centre is caused by hot gas moving at high speed around a massive central object, possibly a black hole. Almost all Seyferts are spiral galaxies. They seem to be closely related to quasars, but are about 100 times fainter. They are named after their discoverer Carl Seyfert (1911–1960).

steady-state theory rival theory to that of the Big Bang, which claims that the universe has no origin but is expanding because new matter is being created continuously throughout the universe. The theory was proposed in 1948 by Hermann Bondi, Thomas Gold (1920–), and Fred Hoyle, but was dealt a severe blow in 1965 by the discovery of cosmic background radiation (radiation left over from the formation of the universe) and is now largely rejected.

supernova the explosive death of a star, which temporarily attains a brightness of 100 million Suns or more, so that it can shine as brilliantly as a small galaxy for a few days or weeks. Very approximately, it is thought that a supernova explodes in a large galaxy about once every 100 years. Many supernovae – astronomers estimate some 50% – remain undetected because of obscuring by interstellar dust.

variable star star whose brightness changes, either regularly or irregularly, over a period ranging from a few hours to months or years. The Cepheid variables regularly expand and contract in size every few days or weeks.

Stars that change in size and brightness at less precise intervals include **long-period variables,** such as the red giant Mira in the constellation Cetus (period about 330 days), and **irregular variables,** such as some red supergiants. **Eruptive variables** emit sudden outbursts of light. Some suffer flares on their surfaces, while others, such as a nova, result from transfer of gas between a close pair of stars. A supernova is the explosive death of a star. In an **eclipsing binary,** the variation is due not to any change in the star itself, but to the periodic eclipse of a star by a close companion. The

Our Expanding Universe

The universe is all of space and its contents, the study of which is called cosmology. The universe is thought to be between 10 billion and 20 billion years old, and is mostly empty space, dotted with galaxies for as far as telescopes can see. The most distant detected galaxies and quasars lie 10 billion light years or more from Earth, and are moving farther apart as the universe expands. Several theories attempt to explain how the universe came into being and

evolved; for example, the Big Bang theory of an expanding universe originating in a single explosive event, and the contradictory steady-state theory.

Apart from those galaxies within the Local Group, all the galaxies we see display red shifts in their spectra, indicating that they are moving away from us. The farther we look into space, the greater are the observed red shifts, which implies that the more distant galaxies are receding

at ever greater speeds.

This observation led to the theory of an expanding universe, first proposed by Edwin Hubble in 1929, and to Hubble's law, which states that the speed with which one galaxy moves away from another is proportional to its distance from it. Current data suggest that the galaxies are moving apart at a rate of 50–100 kps/30–60 mps for every million parsecs of distance.

different types of variability are closely related to different stages of stellar evolution.

white dwarf small, hot star, the last stage in the life of a star such as the Sun. White dwarfs make up 10% of the stars in the Galaxy; most have a mass 60% of that of the Sun, but only 1% of the Sun's diameter, similar in size to the Earth. Most have surface temperatures of 8,000°C/14,400°F or more, hotter than the Sun. Yet, being so small, their overall luminosities may be less than 1% of that of the Sun. The Milky Way contains an estimated 50 billion white dwarfs.

SPACE EXPLORATION

Apollo project US space project to land a person on the Moon, achieved 20 July 1969, when Neil Armstrong was the first to set foot there. He was accompanied on the Moon's surface by 'Buzz' Aldrin; Michael Collins remained in the orbiting command module.

The programme was announced in 1961 by President Kennedy. The world's most powerful rocket, *Saturn V,* was built to launch the Apollo spacecraft, which carried the three astronauts. When the spacecraft was in orbit around the Moon, two astronauts would descend to the surface in a lunar module to take samples of rock and set up experiments that would send data back to Earth. After three other preparatory flights, *Apollo 11* made the first lunar landing. Five more crewed landings followed, the last in 1972. The total cost of the programme was over \$24 billion.

Apollo–Soyuz test project joint US–Soviet space mission in which an Apollo and a Soyuz craft docked while in orbit around the Earth on 17 July 1975. The craft remained attached for two days and crew members were able to move from one craft to the other through an airlock attached to the nose of the Apollo. The mission was designed to test rescue procedures as well as having political significance.

Ariane launch vehicle built in a series by the European Space Agency (first flight in 1979). The launch site is at Kourou in French Guiana. *Ariane* is a three-stage rocket using liquid fuels. Small solid-fuel and liquid-fuel boosters can be attached to its first stage to increase carrying power. Since 1984 it has been operated commercially by Arianespace, a private company financed by European banks and aerospace industries. A more powerful version, *Ariane 5,* was launched on 4 June 1996, and was intended to carry astronauts aboard the Hermes spaceplane. However, it disintegrated during a test flight owing to a fault in the software controlling the takeoff trajectory. A successful test flight for *Ariane 5* was completed in 1998.

Ariel series of six UK satellites launched by the USA 1962–79, the most significant of which was *Ariel 5* in 1974, which made a pioneering survey of the sky at X-ray wavelengths.

astronaut person making flights into space; the term **cosmonaut** is used in the West for any astronaut from the former Soviet Union.

Atlas rocket US rocket, originally designed and built as an intercontinental missile, but subsequently adapted for space use. Atlas rockets launched astronauts in the Mercury series into orbit, as well as numerous other satellites and space probes.

Cape Canaveral promontory on the Atlantic coast of Florida, USA, 367 km/228 mi north of Miami, used as a rocket launch site by NASA.

Cassini joint space probe of the US agency NASA and the European Space Agency to the planet Saturn. *Cassini* was launched in October 1997, to go into orbit around Saturn 2004, dropping off a sub-probe, *Huygens,* to land on Saturn's largest moon, Titan.

Challenger orbiter used in the US space shuttle programme which on 28 January 1986 exploded on takeoff, killing all seven crew members.

Delta rocket US rocket used to launch many scientific and communications satellites since 1960, based on the Thor ballistic missile. Several increasingly powerful versions produced as satellites became larger and heavier. Solid-fuel boosters were attached to the first stage to increase lifting power.

Energiya most powerful Soviet space rocket, first launched 15 May 1987. Used to launch the Soviet space shuttle, the *Energiya* booster is capable, with the use of strap-on boosters, of launching payloads of up to 190 tonnes into Earth orbit.

escape velocity minimum velocity with which an object must be projected for it to escape from the gravitational pull of a planetary body. In the case of the Earth, the escape velocity is 11.2 kps/6.9 mps; the Moon, 2.4 kps/1.5 mps; Mars, 5 kps/3.1 mps; and Jupiter, 59.6 kps/37 mps.

European Space Agency (*ESA*), organization of European countries (Austria, Belgium, Denmark, Finland, France, Germany, Ireland, Italy, the Netherlands, Norway, Spain, Sweden, Switzerland, and the UK) that engages in space research and technology. It was founded in 1975, with headquarters in Paris.

ESA has developed various scientific and communications satellites, the *Giotto* space probe, and the *Ariane* rockets. ESA built *Spacelab,* and plans to build its own space station, *Columbus,* for attachment to a US space station.

Explorer series of US scientific satellites. *Explorer 1*, launched January 1958, was the first US satellite in orbit and discovered the Van Allen radiation belts around the Earth.

Galileo spacecraft launched from the space shuttle *Atlantis* October 1989, on a six-year journey to Jupiter. *Galileo's* probe entered the atmosphere of Jupiter December 1995. It radioed information back to the orbiter for 57 minutes before it was destroyed by atmospheric pressure.

Gemini project US space programme (1965–66) in which astronauts practised rendezvous and docking of spacecraft, and working outside their spacecraft, in preparation for the Apollo Moon landings.

Gemini spacecraft carried two astronauts and were launched by Titan rockets.

Giotto space probe built by the European Space Agency to study Halley's comet. Launched by an Ariane rocket in July 1985, *Giotto* passed within 600 km/375 mi of the comet's nucleus on 13 March 1986. On 2 July 1990, it flew 23,000 km/14,000 mi from Earth, which diverted its path to encounter another comet, Grigg-Skjellerup, on 10 July 1992.

Goddard Space Flight Center NASA installation at Greenbelt, Maryland, USA, responsible for the operation of NASA's unmanned scientific satellites, including the Hubble Space Telescope. It is also home of the National Space Science Data centre, a repository of data collected by satellites.

Hipparcos acronym for **high precision parallax collecting satellite,** satellite launched by the European Space Agency in 1989. Named after the Greek astronomer Hipparchus, it is the world's first astrometry satellite and is providing precise positions, distances, colours, brightnesses, and apparent motions for over 100,000 stars.

Infrared Space Observatory ISO, orbiting telescope with a 60-cm/24-in diameter mirror. It was launched in November 1995 by the European Space Agency and spent 18 months in an elongated orbit giving it a range from the Earth of 1,000–70,500 km/620–43,800 mi and keeping it as much as possible outside the radiation belts that would swamp its detectors.

Intelsat acronym for **International Telecommunications Satellite Organization,** organization established in 1964 to operate a worldwide system of communications satellites. In 1994 it had 134 member nations and 22 satellites in orbit. Its headquarters are in Washington, DC. Intelsat satellites are stationed in geostationary orbit (maintaining their positions relative to the Earth) over the Atlantic, Pacific, and Indian Oceans. The first Intelsat satellite was *Early Bird*, launched in 1965.

IRAS acronym for **Infrared Astronomy Satellite,** joint US–UK–Dutch satellite launched in 1983 to survey the sky at infrared wavelengths, studying areas of star formation, distant galaxies, possible embryo planetary systems around other stars, and discovering five new comets in our own Solar System. It operated for 10 months.

Johnson Space Center NASA installation at Houston, Texas, home of mission control for crewed

Galileo The *Galileo* spacecraft about to be detached from the Earth-orbiting space shuttle *Atlantis* at the beginning of its six-year journey to Jupiter. *National Aeronautical Space Agency*

space missions. It is the main centre for the selection and training of astronauts.

Kennedy Space Center NASA launch site on Merritt Island, near Cape Canaveral, Florida, used for Apollo and space-shuttle launches. The first flight to land on the Moon (1969) and *Skylab,* the first orbiting laboratory (1973), were launched here.

Mars Global Surveyor US spacecraft that went into orbit around Mars on 12 September 1997 to conduct a detailed photographic survey of the planet commencing March 1998. The spacecraft used a previously untried technique called **aerobraking** to turn its initially highly elongated orbit into a 400 km/249 mi circular orbit by dipping into the outer atmosphere of the planet.

Marshall Space Flight Center NASA installation at Huntsville, Alabama, where the series of Saturn rockets and the space-shuttle engines were developed. It also manages various payloads for the space shuttle, including the Spacelab space station.

Mars Observer NASA space probe launched in 1992 to orbit Mars and survey the planet, its atmosphere, and the polar caps over two years. The probe was also scheduled to communicate information from the robot vehicles delivered by Russia's Mars 94 mission. The $1 billion project miscarried, however, when the probe unaccountably stopped transmitting in August 1993, three days before it was due to drop into orbit.

Mars Pathfinder US spacecraft that landed in the Ares Vallis region of Mars on 4 July 1997. It carried a small six-wheeled roving vehicle called **Sojourner** which examined rock and soil samples around the landing site. *Mars Pathfinder* was the first to use air bags instead of retro-rockets to cushion the landing

Mercury project US project to put a human in space in the one-seat Mercury spacecraft 1961–63.

The first two Mercury flights, on Redstone rockets, were short flights to the edge of space and back. The orbital flights, beginning with the third in the series (made by John Glenn), were launched by Atlas rockets.

Mir Soviet space station, the core of which was launched on 20 February 1986. It is intended to be a permanently occupied space station.

NASA acronym for **National Aeronautics and Space Administration,** US government agency for spaceflight and aeronautical research, founded in 1958 by the National Aeronautics and Space Act. Its headquarters are in Washington, DC, and its main installation is at the Kennedy Space Center in Florida. NASA's early planetary and lunar programmes included Pioneer spacecraft from 1958, which gathered data for the later crewed missions, the most famous of which took the first people to the Moon in *Apollo 11* on 16–24 July 1969.

In the early 1990s, NASA moved towards lower-budget 'Discovery missions', which should not exceed a budget of $150 million (excluding launch costs), nor a development period of three years.

Pioneer probe any of a series of US space probes 1958–78. The probes *Pioneer 4–9* went into solar orbit to monitor the Sun's activity during the 1960s and early 1970s. *Pioneer 5,* launched in 1960, was the first of a series to study the solar wind between the planets. *Pioneer 10,* launched March in 1972, was the first probe to reach Jupiter (December 1973) and to leave the Solar System in 1983. *Pioneer 11,* launched April 1973, passed Jupiter December 1974, and was the first probe to reach Saturn (September 1979), before also leaving the Solar System. NASA ceased to operate *Pioneer 10* in April 1997. The probe had functioned for 25 years and reached a distance of 10 billion km from the Sun. *Pioneer 11* ceased to function in 1995.

Pioneer 10 and *11* carry plaques containing messages from Earth in case they are found by other civilizations among the stars. Pioneer Venus probes were launched May and August 1978. One orbited Venus, and the other dropped three probes onto the surface. The orbiter finally burned up in the atmosphere of Venus 1992. In 1992 *Pioneer 10* was more than 8 billion km/4.4 billion mi from the Sun. Both it and *Pioneer 11* were still returning data measurements of starlight intensity to Earth.

Pioneer 1, 2, and *3,* launched in 1958, were intended Moon probes, but *Pioneer 2's* launch failed, and *1* and *3* failed to reach their target, although they did measure the Van Allen radiation belts. *Pioneer 4* began to orbit the Sun after passing the Moon.

Proton rocket Soviet space rocket introduced in 1965, used to launch heavy satellites, space probes, and the *Salyut* and *Mir* space stations. Proton consists of up to four stages as necessary. It has never been used to launch humans into space.

Redstone rocket short-range US military missile, modified for use as a space launcher. Redstone rockets launched the first two flights of the Mercury project. A modified Redstone, *Juno 1*, launched the first US satellite, *Explorer 1*, in 1958.

Rosetta project of the European Space Agency, due for launch in 2003, to send a spacecraft to Comet Wirtanen. *Rosetta* is expected to go into orbit around the comet in 2011 and land two probes on the nucleus a year later. The spacecraft will stay with the comet as it makes its closest approach to the Sun in October 2013.

What is a rocket?

A rocket is a projectile driven by the reaction of gases produced by a fast-burning fuel. Unlike jet engines, which are also reaction engines, modern rockets carry their own oxygen supply to burn their fuel and do not require any surrounding atmosphere. For warfare, rocket heads carry an explosive device.

Rockets have been valued as fireworks over the last seven centuries, but their intensive development as a means of propulsion to high altitudes, carrying payloads, started only in the interwar years with the state-supported work in Germany (primarily by Wernher von Braun) and of Robert Hutchings Goddard (1882–1945) in the USA. Being the only form of propulsion available that can function in a vacuum, rockets are essential to exploration in outer space. Multistage rockets have to be used, consisting of a number of rockets joined together.

Two main kinds of rocket are used: one burns liquid propellants, the other solid propellants. The fireworks rocket uses gunpowder as a solid propellant. The US space shuttle's solid rocket boosters use a mixture of powdered aluminium in a synthetic rubber binder. Most rockets, however, have liquid propellants, which are more powerful and easier to control. Liquid hydrogen and kerosene are common fuels, while liquid oxygen is the most common oxygen provider, or oxidizer.

One of the biggest rockets ever built, the *Saturn V* Moon rocket, was a three-stage design, standing 111 m/ 365 ft high. It weighed more than 2,700 tonnes/3,000 tons on the launch pad, developed a takeoff thrust of some 3.4 million kg/7.5 million lb, and could place almost 140 tonnes/150 tons into low Earth orbit. In the early 1990s, the most powerful rocket system was the Soviet Energiya, capable of placing 100 tonnes/110 tons into low Earth orbit. The US space shuttle can put only 24 tonnes/ 26 tons into orbit.

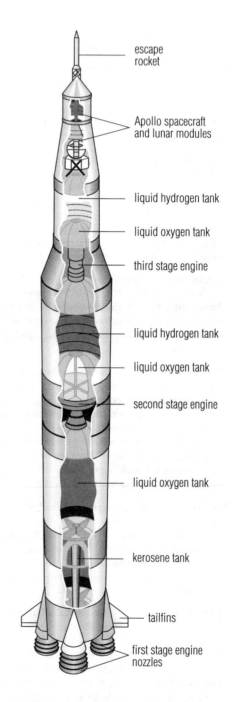

escape rocket

Apollo spacecraft and lunar modules

liquid hydrogen tank

liquid oxygen tank

third stage engine

liquid hydrogen tank

liquid oxygen tank

second stage engine

liquid oxygen tank

kerosene tank

tailfins

first stage engine nozzles

rocket The three-stage *Saturn V* rocket used in the Apollo moonshots of the 1960s and 1970s. It stood 111 m/365 ft high, as tall as a 30-storey skyscraper, weighed 2,700 tonnes/3,000 tons when loaded with fuel, and developed a power equivalent to 50 Boeing 747 jumbo jets.

Crewed Space Flight: Chronology

1903 Russian scientist Konstantin Tsiolkovsky published the first practical paper on astronautics.

1926 US engineer Robert Goddard launched the first liquid-fuel rocket.

1937–45 In Germany, Wernher von Braun developed the *V2* rocket.

1957 4 Oct: The first space satellite, *Sputnik 1* (USSR, Russian 'fellow-traveller'), orbited the Earth at a height of 229–898 km/142–558 mi in 96.2 min. 3 Nov: *Sputnik 2* was launched carrying a dog, 'Laika'; it died on board seven days later.

1961 12 April: the first crewed spaceship, *Vostok 1* (USSR), with Yuri Gagarin on board, was recovered after a single orbit of 89.1 min at a height of 142–175 km/88–109 mi.

1962 20 Feb: John Glenn in *Friendship 7* (USA) became the first American to orbit the Earth. *Telstar* (USA), a communications satellite, sent the first live television transmission between the USA and Europe.

1963 16–19 June: Valentina Tereshkova in *Vostok 1* (USSR) became the first woman in space.

1967 27 Jan: US astronauts Virgil Grissom, Edward White, and Roger Chaffee were killed during a simulated countdown when a flash fire swept through the cabin of *Apollo 1*. 24 April: Vladimir Komarov was the first person to be killed on a mission, when his ship, *Soyuz 1*

(USSR), crash-landed on the Earth.

1969 20 July: Neil Armstrong of *Apollo 11* (USA) was the first person to walk on the Moon.

1970 10 Nov: *Luna 17* (USSR) was launched; its space probe, *Lunokhod*, took photographs and made soil analyses of the Moon's surface.

1971 19 April: *Salyut 1* (USSR), the first orbital space station, was established; it was later visited by the *Soyuz 11* crewed spacecraft.

1973 *Skylab 2*, the first US orbital space station, was established.

1975 15–24 July: *Apollo 18* (USA) and *Soyuz 19* (USSR) made a joint flight and linked up in space.

1979 The European Space Agency's satellite launcher, *Ariane 1*, was launched.

1981 12 April: The first reusable crewed spacecraft, the space shuttle *Columbia* (USA), was launched.

1986 Space shuttle *Challenger* (USA) exploded shortly after take-off, killing all seven crew members.

1988 US shuttle programme resumed with launch of *Discovery*. Soviet shuttle *Buran* was launched from the rocket *Energiya*. Soviet cosmonauts Musa Manarov and Vladimir Titov in space station *Mir* spent a record 365 days 59 min in space.

1991 5 April: The Gamma Ray Observatory was launched from the space shuttle *Atlantis*

to survey the sky at gamma-ray wavelengths. 18 May: Astronaut Helen Sharman, the first Briton in space, was launched with Anatoli Artsebarsky and Sergei Krikalev to *Mir* space station, returning to Earth 26 May in *Soyuz TM-11* with Viktor Afanasyev and Musa Manarov. Manarov set a record for the longest time spent in space, 541 days, having also spent a year aboard *Mir* 1988.

1992 16 May: Space shuttle *Endeavour* returned to Earth after its first voyage. During its mission, it circled the Earth 141 times and travelled 4 million km/2.5 million mi. 23 Oct: *LAGEOS II* (Laser Geodynamics Satellite) was released from the space shuttle *Columbia* into an orbit so stable that it will still be circling the Earth in billions of years. Dec: Space shuttle *Endeavour* successfully carried out mission to replace the Hubble Space Telescope's solar panels and repair its mirror.

1994 4 Feb: Japan's heavy-lifting *H-2* rocket was launched successfully, carrying an uncrewed shuttle craft.

1995 June: the US space shuttle *Atlantis* docked with *Mir*, exchanging crew members.

1996 4 June: the *Ariane 5* rocket disintegrated almost immediately after takeoff, destroying the four Cluster satellites.

1997 July: *Mir* underwent increasing difficulties, following a collision with a cargo ship in June that depressurized one of its modules, *Spektr*.

Salyut series of seven space stations launched by the USSR 1971–82. Salyut was cylindrical in shape, 15 m/50 ft long, and weighed 19 tonnes/21 tons. It housed two or three cosmonauts at a time, for missions lasting up to eight months.

Salyut 1 was launched 19 April 1971. It was occupied for 23 days in June 1971 by a crew of three, who died during their return to Earth when their Soyuz ferry craft depressurized. In 1973 *Salyut 2* broke up in orbit before occupation. The first fully successful Salyut mission was a 14-day visit to *Salyut 3* July 1974. In 1984–85 a team of three cosmonauts endured a record 237-day flight in *Salyut 7*. In 1986 the Salyut series was superseded by *Mir*, an improved design capable of being enlarged by additional modules sent up from Earth.

Saturn rocket family of large US rockets, developed by Wernher von Braun (1912–1977) for the Apollo project. The two-stage *Saturn IB* was used for launching Apollo spacecraft into orbit around the Earth. The three-stage *Saturn V* sent Apollo spacecraft to the Moon, and launched the *Skylab* space station. The liftoff thrust of a *Saturn V* was 3,500 tonnes. After Apollo and *Skylab,* the Saturn rockets were retired in favour of the space shuttle.

Skylab US space station, launched 14 May 1973, made from the adapted upper stage of a *Saturn V* rocket. At 75 tonnes/82.5 tons, it was the heaviest object ever put into space, and was 25.6 m/84 ft long. *Skylab* contained a workshop for carrying out experiments in weightlessness, an observatory for monitoring the Sun, and cameras for photographing the Earth's surface.

Damaged during launch, it had to be repaired by the first crew of astronauts. Three crews, each of three astronauts, occupied *Skylab* for periods of up to 84 days, at that time a record duration for human spaceflight. *Skylab* finally fell to Earth on 11 July 1979, dropping debris on Western Australia.

SOHO acronym for **Solar and Heliospheric Observatory,** space probe launched in 1995 by the European Space Agency to study the solar wind of atomic particles streaming towards the Earth from the Sun. It also observes the Sun in ultraviolet and visible light, and measures slight oscillations on the Sun's surface that can reveal details of the structure of the Sun's interior. It is positioned 1.5 million km/938,000 mi from Earth towards the Sun. SOHO is operated jointly with NASA and costs $1.2 billion.

SOHO's hydrazine fuel froze in June 1998 causing contact with it to be lost. Ground control at Goddard Space Flight Center finally regained command of SOHO in September 1998, when SOHO was turned so that its solar power arrays faced the Sun. Some data and instruments may have been permanently damaged by exposure to extreme temperatures.

SOHO carries equipment for 11 separate experiments, including the study of the Sun's corona, measurement of its magnetic field, and of solar winds. The **Coronal Diagnostic Spectrometer** (CDS) detects radiation at extreme ultraviolet wavelengths and allows the study of the Sun's atmosphere. The **Michelson Doppler Imager** (MDI) measures Doppler shifts in light wavelengths and can detect winds caused by convention beneath the Sun's surface. The **Extreme-Ultraviolet Imaging Telescope** (EIT) investigates the mechanisms that heat the Sun's corona. The **Large-Angle Spectroscopic Coronagraph** (LASCO) images the corona by detecting sunlight scattered by the coronal gases.

Solar Maximum Mission satellite launched by the US agency NASA in 1980 to study solar activity, which discovered that the Sun's luminosity increases slightly when sunspots are most numerous. It was repaired in orbit by astronauts from the space shuttle in 1984 and burned up in the Earth's atmosphere in 1989.

Soyuz Soviet series of spacecraft, capable of carrying up to three cosmonauts. Soyuz spacecraft consist of three parts: a rear section containing engines; the central crew compartment; and a forward compartment that gives additional room for working and living space. They are now used for ferrying crews up to space stations, though they were originally used for independent space flight.

Spacelab small space station built by the European Space Agency, carried in the cargo bay of the US space shuttle, in which it remains throughout each flight, returning to Earth with the shuttle. *Spacelab* consists of a pressurized module in which astronauts can work, and a series of pallets, open to the vacuum of space, on which equipment is mounted. It is used for astronomy, Earth observation, and experiments utilizing the conditions of weightlessness and vacuum in orbit. The first *Spacelab* mission, consisting of a pressurized module and pallets, lasted ten days November–December 1983.

Space Probe: Chronology

1959 13 Sept: *Luna 2* (USSR) hit the Moon, the first craft to do so. 10 Oct: *Luna 3* photo-graphed the far side of the Moon.

1962 14 Dec: *Mariner 2* (USA) flew past Venus; launch date 26 Aug 1962.

1964 31 July: *Ranger 7* (USA) hit the Moon, having sent back 4,316 pictures before impact.

1965 14 July: *Mariner 4* flew past Mars; launch date 28 Nov 1964.

1966 3 Feb: *Luna 9* achieved the first soft landing on the Moon, having transmitted 27 close up panoramic photographs; launch date 31 Jan 1966. 2 June: *Surveyor 1* (USA) landed softly on the Moon and returned 11,150 pictures; launch date 30 May 1965.

1971 13 Nov: *Mariner 9* entered orbit of Mars; launch date 30 May 1971.

1973 3 Dec: *Pioneer 10* (USA) flew past Jupiter; launch date 3 March 1972.

1974 29 March: *Mariner 10* flew past Mercury; launch date 3 Nov 1973.

1975 22 Oct: *Venera 9* (USSR) landed softly on Venus and returned its first pictures; launch date 8 June 1975.

1976 20 July: *Viking 1* (USA) first landed on Mars; launch date 20 Aug 1975. 3 Sept: *Viking 2* transmitted data from the surface of Mars.

1977 20 Aug: *Voyager 2* (USA) launched. 5 Sept: *Voyager 1* launched.

1978 4 Dec: *Pioneer-Venus 1* (USA) orbited Venus; launch date 20 May 1978.

1979 5 March and 9 July: *Voyager 1* and *Voyager 2* encountered Jupiter, respectively.

1980 12 Nov: *Voyager 1* reached Saturn.

1981 25 Aug: *Voyager 2* flew past Saturn.

1982 1 March: *Venera 13* transmitted its first colour pictures of the surface of Venus; launch date 30 Oct 1981.

1983 10 Oct: *Venera 15* mapped the surface of Venus from orbit; launch date 2 June 1983.

1985 2 July: *Giotto* (European Space Agency) launched to Halley's comet.

1986 24 Jan: *Voyager 2* encountered Uranus. 13–14 March: *Giotto* met Halley's comet, closest approach 596 km/370 mi, at a speed 50 times faster than that of a bullet.

1989 4 May: *Magellan* (USA) launched from space shuttle *Atlantis* on a 15-month cruise to Venus across 15 million km/ 9 million mi of space. 25 Aug: *Voyager 2* reached Neptune (4,400 million km/2,700 million mi from Earth), approaching it to within 4,850 km/3,010 mi. 18 Oct: *Galileo* (USA) launched from space shuttle *Atlantis* for six-year journey to Jupiter.

1990 10 Aug: *Magellan* arrived at Venus and transmitted its first pictures 16 Aug 1990. 6 Oct: *Ulysses* (European Space Agency) launched from space shuttle *Discovery*, to study the Sun.

1991 29 Oct: *Galileo* made the closest-ever approach to an asteroid, Gaspra, flying within 1,600 km/990 mi.

1992 8 Feb: *Ulysses* flew past Jupiter at a distance of 380,000 km/236,000 mi from the surface, just inside the orbit of Io and closer than 11 of Jupiter's 16 moons. 10 July: *Giotto* (USA) flew at a speed of 14 kms/8.5 mps to within 200 km/124 mi of comet Grigg-Skellerup, 12 light years (240 million km/150 mi) away from Earth. 25 Sept: *Mars Observer* (USA) launched from Cape Canaveral, the first US mission to Mars for 17 years. 10 Oct: *Pioneer-Venus 1* burned up in the atmosphere of Venus.

1993 21 Aug: *Mars Observer* disappeared three days before it was due to drop into orbit around Mars. 28 Aug: *Galileo* flew past the asteroid Ida.

1995 Dec: *Galileo*'s probe entered the atmosphere of Jupiter. It radioed information back to the orbiter for 57 minutes before it was destroyed by atmospheric pressure.

1996 NASA's Near Earth Asteroid Rendezvous (NEAR) was launched to study Eros.

1997 The US spacecraft *Mars Pathfinder* landed on Mars. Two days later the probe's rover *Sojourner*, a six-wheeled vehicle controlled by an Earth-based operator, began to explore the area around the spacecraft. The US space probe *Galileo* began orbiting Jupiter's moons.

(continued)

Space Probe: Chronology (continued)

It took photographs of Europa for a potential future landing site, and detected molecules containing carbon and nitrogen on Callisto, suggesting that life once existed there. The US *Near Earth Asteroid Rendezvous* (NEAR) spacecraft flew within 1,200 km/746 mi of the asteroid Mathilde, taking high-resolution photographs and revealing a 25-km/15.5-mi crater covering the 53-km/

33-mi asteroid. The US spacecraft *Mars Global Surveyor* went into orbit around Mars to conduct a detailed photographic survey of the planet, commencing in March 1998, and reported the discovery of bacteria on Mars.

1998 The US probe *Lunar Prospector* was launched to go into low orbits around the Moon and transmit data on the composition of its crust,

record gamma rays, and map its magnetic field. The satellite detected 11 million tonnes of water on the Moon in the form of ice. Analysis of high resolution images from the *Galileo* spacecraft suggested that the icy crust of Europa, Jupiter's fourth-largest moon, may hide a vast ocean warm enough to support life. 4 July: Japan's Planet-B was launched to study Mars.

space shuttle reusable crewed spacecraft. The first was launched 12 April 1981 by the USA. It was developed by NASA to reduce the cost of using space for commercial, scientific, and military purposes. After leaving its payload in space, the space-shuttle orbiter can be flown back to Earth to land on a runway, and is then available for reuse.

Four orbiters were built: *Columbia, Challenger, Discovery,* and *Atlantis. Challenger* was destroyed in a midair explosion just over a minute after its tenth launch 28 January 1986, killing all seven crew members, the result of a failure in one of the solid rocket boosters. Flights resumed with redesigned boosters in September 1988. A replacement orbiter, *Endeavour,* was built, which had its first flight in May 1992. At the end of the 1980s, an average of $375 million had been spent on each space-shuttle mission.

The USSR produced a shuttle of similar size and appearance to the US one. The first Soviet shuttle, *Buran,* was launched without a crew by the *Energiya* rocket 15 November 1988.

space sickness or **space adaptation syndrome,** feeling of nausea, sometimes accompanied by vomiting, experienced by about 40% of all astronauts during their first few days in space. It is akin to travel sickness, and is thought to be caused by confusion of the body's balancing mechanism, located in the inner ear, by weightlessness. The sensation passes after a few days as the body adapts.

space station any large structure designed for human occupation in space for extended periods of time. Space stations are used for carrying out

astronomical observations and surveys of Earth, as well as for biological studies and the processing of materials in weightlessness. The first space station was *Salyut 1,* and the USA has launched *Skylab.*

space suit protective suit worn in space. It provides an insulated, air-conditioned cocoon in which people can live and work for hours at a time while outside the spacecraft. Inside the suit is a cooling garment that keeps the body at a comfortable temperature even during vigorous work. The suit provides air to breathe, and removes exhaled carbon dioxide and moisture. The suit's outer layers insulate the occupant from the extremes of hot and cold in space (−150°C/ −240°F in the shade to +180°C/+350°F in sunlight), and from the impact of small meteorites. Some space suits have a jet-propelled backpack, which the wearer can use to move about.

Sputnik series of ten Soviet Earth-orbiting satellites. *Sputnik 1* was the first artificial satellite, launched 4 October 1957. It weighed 84 kg/185 lb, with a 58 cm/23 in diameter, and carried only a simple radio transmitter which allowed scientists to track it as it orbited Earth. It burned up in the atmosphere 92 days later. Sputniks were superseded in the early 1960s by the Cosmos series.

Stardust US project to obtain a sample of dust and gas from the head of a comet. Due for launch in February 1999, the *Stardust* space probe will fly through the head Comet Wild 2 in January 2004, passing within 100 km/62 mi of the 4 km/2.5 mi nucleus. It will return to Earth with its samples in January 2006.

Tanegashima Space Centre Japanese rocket-launching site on a small island off southern Kyushu. Tanegashima is run by the National Space Development Agency (NASDA), responsible for the practical applications of Japan's space programme (research falls under a separate organization based at Kagoshima Space Centre). NASDA, founded in 1969, has headquarters in Tokyo; a tracking and testing station, the Tsukuba Space Centre, in eastern central Honshu; and an Earth observation centre near Tsukuba.

Telstar US communications satellite, launched on 10 July 1962, which relayed the first live television transmissions between the USA and Europe. *Telstar* orbited the Earth in 158 minutes, and so had to be tracked by ground stations, unlike the geostationary satellites of today.

Titan rocket family of US space rockets, developed from the Titan intercontinental missile. Two-stage Titan rockets launched the Gemini crewed missions. More powerful Titans, with additional stages and strap-on boosters, were used to launch spy satellites and space probes, including the Viking and Voyager probes and *Mars Observer*.

transfer orbit elliptical path followed by a spacecraft moving from one orbit to another, designed to save fuel although at the expense of a longer journey time.

Space probes travel to the planets on transfer orbits. A probe aimed at Venus has to be 'slowed down' relative to the Earth, so that it enters an elliptical transfer orbit with its perigee (point of closest approach to the Sun) at the same distance as the orbit of Venus; towards Mars, the vehicle has to be 'speeded up' relative to the Earth, so that it reaches its apogee (furthest point from the Sun) at the same distance as the orbit of Mars. **Geostationary transfer orbit** is the highly elliptical path followed by satellites to be placed in geostationary orbit around the Earth (an orbit coincident with Earth's rotation). A small rocket is fired at the transfer orbit's apogee to place the satellite in geostationary orbit.

Ulysses space probe to study the Sun's poles, launched in 1990 by a US space shuttle. It is a joint project by NASA and the European Space Agency. In February 1992, the gravity of Jupiter swung *Ulysses* on to a path that looped it first under the Sun's south pole in 1994 and then over its north pole in 1995 to study the Sun and solar wind at latitudes not observable from the Earth.

Voskhod (Russian 'ascent') Soviet spacecraft used in the mid-1960s; it was modified from the single-seat Vostok, and was the first spacecraft capable of carrying two or three cosmonauts. During *Voskhod 2's* flight in 1965, Aleksi Leonov made the first space walk.

Vostok (Russian 'east') first Soviet spacecraft, used 1961–63. *Vostok* was a metal sphere 2.3 m/7.5 ft in diameter, capable of carrying one cosmonaut. It made flights lasting up to five days. *Vostok 1* carried the first person into space, Yuri Gagarin.

Voyager probes two US space probes. *Voyager 1,* launched on 5 September 1977, passed Jupiter in March 1979, and reached Saturn in November 1980. *Voyager 2* was launched earlier, on 20 August 1977, on a slower trajectory that took it past Jupiter in July 1979, Saturn in August 1981, Uranus in January 1986, and Neptune in August 1989. Like the Pioneer probes, the *Voyagers* are on their way out of the Solar System; at the start of 1995, *Voyager 1* was 8.8 billion km/5.5 billion mi from Earth, and *Voyager 2* was 6.8 billion km/ 4.3 billion mi from Earth. Their tasks now include helping scientists to locate the position of the heliopause, the boundary at which the influence of the Sun gives way to the forces exerted by other stars.

Both *Voyagers* carry specially coded long-playing records called *Sounds of Earth* for the enlightenment of any other civilizations that might find them.

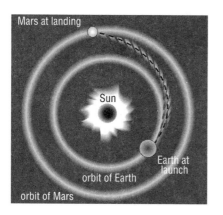

Transfer orbit The transfer orbit used by spacecraft when travelling from Earth to Mars. The orbit is chosen to minimize the fuel needed by the spacecraft; the craft is in free fall for most of the journey.

Useful Terms

Major Ground-Based Telescopes and Observatories

Observatory/ Telescope	Location	Description	Year opened	Run by
Algonquin Radio Observatory	Ontario, Canada	radio telescope, 46 m/150 ft in diameter	1966	National Research Council (NRC) of Canada
Arecibo Observatory	Puerto Rico	home of the largest radar-radio telescope in the world; a 305-m/1,000-ft diameter spherical reflector with a surface made up of nearly 40,000 perforated aluminium panels. Each panel can be adjusted to maintain a precise spherical shape that varies less than 3 mm/0.12 in over the whole 20 acre surface.	inaugurated in 1963; upgraded in 1974, and again in the mid-1990s	National Astronomy and Ionosphere Center, which is operated by Cornell University and the National Science Foundation
Australia Telescope National Facility	New South Wales, Australia	giant radio telescope consisting of six 22-m/72-ft antennae at Culgoora, a similar antenna at Siding Spring Mountain, and the 64-m/210-ft Parkes radio telescope; together they simulate a dish 300 km/186 mi across	1993	Commonwealth Scientific and Industrial Research Organization (CSIRO)
Cerro Tololo Inter-American Observatory	Cerro Tololo mountain in the Chilean Andes	main instrument is a 4-m/158-in reflector, a twin of that at Kitt Peak, Arizona, USA	1974	Association of Universities for Research into Astronomy (AURA)
David Dunlap Observatory	Richmond Hill, Ontario, Canada	1.88-m/74-in reflector, the largest optical telescope in Canada	1935	University of Toronto
Dominion Radio Astrophysical Observatory	Penticton, British Columbia, Canada	26-m/84-ft radio dish and an aperture synthesis radio telescope	1996	NRC of Canada through its Herzberg Institute of Astrophysics
Effelsberg Radio Telescope	near Bonn, Germany	the world's largest fully steerable radio telescope; 100-m/328-ft radio dish	1971	Max Planck Institute for Radio Astronomy
European Southern Observatory	La Silla, Chile	telescopes include: 3.6-m/142-in reflector 3.58-m/141-in New Technology Telescope	1976 1990	operated jointly by Belgium, Denmark, France, Germany, Italy, the Netherlands, Sweden, and Switzerland
Gemini 8-Meter Telescopes Project	Mauna Kea (HI), USA; Cerro Pachon, Chile	Very Large Telescope (VLT), consisting of four 8-m/315-in reflectors mounted independently but capable of working in combination	1999	international partnership of USA, UK, Canada, Chile, Argentina, and Brazil
		two 8-m/26-ft Aperture Optical/Infrared Telescopes	1999; 2001	
Jodrell Bank	Cheshire, UK	Lovell Telescope, a 76-m/250-ft radio dish	1957, modified 1970	Nuffield Radio Astronomy Laboratories of the University of Manchester
		elliptical radio dish 38 m × 25 m/125 ft × 82 ft capable of working at shorter wavelengths	1964	
Keck I	Mauna Kea (HI), USA	world's largest optical telescope, with a primary mirror 10- m/33-ft in diameter, with 36 hexagonal sections, each controlled by a computer to generate single images of the objects observed	first images 1990	jointly owned by the California Institute of Technology and the University of California/Lick Observatory

Major Ground-Based Telescopes and Observatories (continued)

Observatory/ Telescope	Location	Description	Year opened	Run by
Keck II	Mauna Kea (HI), USA	identical to Keck I: primary mirror 10 m/33 ft in diameter, with 36 hexagonal sections, each controlled by a computer	1996	jointly owned by the California Institute of Technology and the University of California/Lick Observatory
Kitt Peak National Observatory	Quinlan Mountains near Tucson (AZ), USA	numerous telescopes including the 4-m/ 158-in Mayall reflector	1973	AURA in agreement with the National Science Foundation of the USA
		McMath-Pierce Solar Telescope, the world's largest of its type	1960	National Solar Observatory (NSO)
		3.5-m/138-in reflecting telescope	1994	WIYN consortium (University of Wisconsin, Indiana University, Yale University, and National Optical Astronomy Observatories (NOAO))
La Palma Observatory or the Observatorio del Roque de los Muchachos	La Palma, Canary Islands	Isaac Newton Group of telescopes, including the 4.2- m/165-in William Herschel Telescope	1987	Royal Greenwich Observatories (RGO)
Las Campanas Observatory	Chile	2.5-m/100-in Irénée du Pont telescope	1977	Carnegie Institution of Washington
Lick Observatory or the University of California/Lick Observatory	Mount Hamilton (CA), USA	several instruments including: 3.04-m/120-in Shane reflector	1959	University of California and Mount Hamilton
		91-cm/36-in refractor, the second-largest refractor in the world	1888	
Lowell Observatory	Flagstaff (AZ), USA	8 telescopes, including the 61- cm/24-in Alvan Clark refractor	1894	Lowell Observatory staff
	Anderson Mesa	several telescopes, including the 1.83-m/72-in Perkins reflector		Ohio State and Ohio Wesleyan universities
McDonald Observatory	Davis Mountains (TX), USA	2.72-m/107-in reflector	1969	University of Texas
		2.08-m/82-in reflector	1939	
		9.2-m/30-ft Hobby-Eberly telescope (HET) for spectral analysis	1997	Penn State University, Stanford University, and the Ludwig-Maximilians Universität
Magellan	Las Campanas, Chile	6.5-m/21.3-ft honeycomb-back optical mirror	1997	Carnegie Institution of Washington, University of Arizona, and Harvard College Observatory

(continued)

Major Ground-Based Telescopes and Observatories (continued)

Observatory/ Telescope	Location	Description	Year opened	Run by
Mauna Kea	Mauna Kea (HI), USA	telescopes include: the 2.24-m/88-in University of Hawaii reflector	1970	University of Hawaii
		3.8-m/150-in United Kingdom Infrared Telescope (UKIRT) (also used for optical observations)	1978	Royal Observatory, Edinburgh
		3-m/120-in NASA Infrared Telescope Facility (IRTF)	1979	NASA
		3.6-m/142-in Canada-France–Hawaii Telescope (CFHT), designed for optical and infrared work	1979	NRC of Canada, University of Hawaii, and Centre National de la Recherche Scientifique of France
		15-m/50-ft diameter UK/Netherlands James Clerk Maxwell Telescope (JCMT), the world's largest telescope specifically designed to observe millimetre wave radiation from nebulae, stars, and galaxies	1987	Joint Astronomy Centre in Hilo (HI) for the NRC of Canada, Particle Physics and Astronomy Research Council (PPARC) of the UK, and Netherlands Organization for Scientific Research (NOSR)
		Keck I and Keck II telescopes *see under* Keck		
Mount Palomar	80 km/50 mi northeast of San Diego (CA), USA	5-m/200-in diameter reflector called the Hale; 1.2-m/48-in Schmidt telescope; it was the world's premier observatory during the 1950s	1948	California Institute of Technology and the University of California/Lick Observatory
Mount Wilson Observatory	San Gabriel Mountains, near Los Angeles (CA), USA	several telescopes including: 2.5-m/100-in Hooker telescope, with which Edwin Hubble discovered the expansion of the universe	1917	Mount Wilson Institute
		solar telescopes in towers 18.3 m/60 ft and 45.7 m/150 ft tall	1912	operated presently by University of California (UCLA)
Mullard Radio Astronomy Observatory	Cambridge, UK	Ryle Telescope, eight dishes 12.8 m/42 ft wide in a line 5 km/3 mi long	1972	University of Cambridge, UK
Multiple Mirror Telescope	Mt Hopkins (AZ), USA	6.5-m/21.3-ft honeycomb-back optical telescope conversion	1979	University of Arizona and the Smithsonian Institute
		6 mirrors of 1.8-m/72-in aperture, which perform as a single 4.5 m/176 in mirror	1996	
New Technology Telescope	La Silla, Chile	optical telescope that forms part of the European Southern Observatory; it has a thin, lightweight mirror, 3.38 m/141 in across with active optics, which is kept in shape by computer-adjustable supports	1991	operated jointly by Belgium, Denmark, France, Germany, Italy, the Netherlands, Sweden, and Switzerland with headquarters near Munich

Major Ground-Based Telescopes and Observatories (continued)

Observatory/ Telescope	Location	Description	Year opened	Run by
Royal Greenwich Observatory (RGO)	Cambridge, UK	operates Isaac Newton Group of telescopes, including:	founded 1675 (moved to Cambridge in 1990)	RGO
	La Palma, Canary Islands	4.2-m/165-in William Herschel Telescope	1987	Anglo-Australian Observatory
Siding Spring Mountain	400 km/250 mi northwest of Sydney, Australia	1.2-m/48-in UK Schmidt Telescope	1973	
		3.9-m/154-in Anglo-Australian Telescope	1975	
South African Astronomical Observatory	Sutherland, South Africa	main telescope is a 1.88-m/74-in reflector	founded 1973	Council for Scientific and Industrial Research of South Africa
Subaru ('Pleiades')	Mauna Kea (HI), USA	8-m/26.4-ft optical-infrared telescope	1999	National Astronomical Observatory (NAO) of the University of Tokyo
United Kingdom Infrared Telescope (UKIRT)	Mauna Kea (HI), USA	3.8-m/150-in reflecting telescope for observing at infrared wavelengths	1979	Royal Observatory, Edinburgh
US Naval Observatory	Washington DC, USA	several telescopes including: 66-cm/26-in refracting telescope	1873	US Naval Observatory
	Flagstaff (AZ), USA	1.55-m/61-in reflector for measuring positions of celestial objects	1964	
Very Large Array (VLA)	Plains of San Augustine (NM), USA	largest and most complex single-site radio telescope in the world, comprising 27 dish antennae, each 25 m/82 ft in diameter, forming a Y-shaped array	1981	NRAO
Very Large Telescope (VLT)	Cerro Paranal, Chile	4 × 8 m/5 × 26 ft optical array	1999	European Southern Observatory consisting of eight European countries
Very Long Baseline Array (VLBA)	St Croix (VI); Hancock (NH); North Liberty (IA); Fort davis (TX); Los Alamos (NM); Pie Town (NM); Kitt Peak (AZ); Owens Valley (CA); Brewster (WA); Mauna Kea (HI), USA	system of 10 radio telescopes, each a 25-m/82-ft diameter dish antenna, controlled remotely from the Array Operations Center in Socorro, New Mexico, that work together as the world's largest dedicated, full-time astronomical instrument		NRAO
Yerkes Observatory	Wisconsin, USA	houses the world's largest refracting optical telescope, with a lens of diameter 102 cm/40 in	observatory founded 1897	University of Chicago Department of Astronomy and Astrophysics
Zelenchukskaya	Caucasus Mountains of Russia	site of the world's largest single mirror optical telescope, with a mirror of 6 m/236 in diameter	1976	Special Astrophysical Observatory of the Russian Academy of Sciences (RAS) in St Petersburg
		Radio Astronomy Telescope of the Russian Academy of Sciences (RATAN) 600 radio telescope, consisting of radio reflectors in a circle 600 m/2,000 ft in diameter		

aberration of starlight apparent displacement of a star from its true position, due to the combined effects of the speed of light and the speed of the Earth in orbit around the Sun (about 30 km per second/18.5 mi per second).

Aberration, discovered in 1728 by English astronomer James Bradley (1693–1762), was the first observational proof that the Earth orbits the Sun.

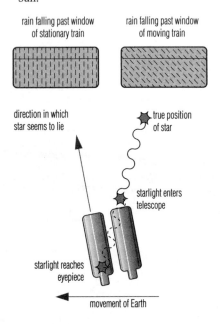

rain falling past window of stationary train

rain falling past window of moving train

direction in which star seems to lie

true position of star

starlight enters telescope

starlight reaches eyepiece

movement of Earth

aberration of starlight The aberration of starlight is an optical illusion caused by the motion of the Earth. Rain falling appears vertical when seen from the window of a stationary train; when seen from the window of a moving train, the rain appears to follow a sloping path. In the same way, light from a star 'falling' down a telescope seems to follow a sloping path because the Earth is moving. This causes an apparent displacement, or aberration, in the position of the star.

albedo the fraction of the incoming light reflected by a body such as a planet. A body with a high albedo, near 1, is very bright, while a body with a low albedo, near 0, is dark. The Moon has an average albedo of 0.12, Venus 0.76, Earth 0.37.

aphelion the point at which an object, travelling in an elliptical orbit around the Sun, is at its furthest from the Sun. The Earth is at its aphelion on 5 July.

apogee the point at which an object, travelling in an elliptical orbit around the Earth, is at its furthest from the Earth.

arc minute, arc second units for measuring small angles, used in geometry, surveying, map-making, and astronomy. An arc minute (symbol ´) is one-sixtieth of a degree, and an arc second (symbol ´´) is one-sixtieth of an arc minute. Small distances in the sky, as between two close stars or the apparent width of a planet's disc, are expressed in minutes and seconds of arc.

astrometry measurement of the precise positions of stars, planets, and other bodies in space. Such information is needed for practical purposes including accurate timekeeping, surveying and navigation, and calculating orbits and measuring distances in space. Astrometry is not concerned with the surface features or the physical nature of the body under study.

Before telescopes, astronomical observations were simple astrometry. Precise astrometry has shown that stars are not fixed in position, but have a proper motion caused as they and the Sun orbit the Milky Way Galaxy. The nearest stars also show parallax (apparent change in position), from which their distances can be calculated. Above the distorting effects of the atmosphere, satellites such as *Hipparcos* can make even more precise measurements than ground telescopes, so refining the distance scale of space.

astronomical unit (AU) unit equal to the mean distance of the Earth from the Sun: 149,597,870 km/92,955,800 mi. It is used to describe planetary distances. Light travels this distance in approximately 8.3 minutes.

Cassegrain telescope or **Cassegrain reflector** type of reflecting telescope in which light collected by a concave primary mirror is reflected on to a convex secondary mirror, which in turn directs it back through a hole in the primary mirror to a focus behind it. As a result, the telescope tube can be kept short, allowing equipment for analyzing and recording starlight to be mounted behind the main mirror. All modern large astronomical telescopes are of the Cassegrain type. It is named after the 17th century French astronomer, Cassegrain who first devised it as an improvement to the simpler Newtonian telescope.

celestial mechanics the branch of astronomy that deals with the calculation of the orbits of celestial bodies, their gravitational attractions (such as those that produce the Earth's tides), and also the orbits of artificial satellites and space probes. It is

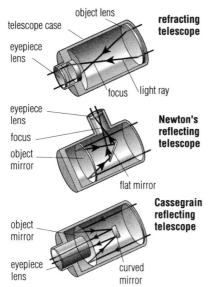

object lens

telescope case

eyepiece
lens

focus   light ray

**refracting
telescope**

eyepiece
lens

focus

object
mirror

**Newton's
reflecting
telescope**

flat mirror

object
mirror

eyepiece
lens   curved
mirror

**Cassegrain
reflecting
telescope**

telescope Three kinds of telescope. The refracting telescope uses a large objective lens to gather light and form an image which the smaller eyepiece lens magnifies. A reflecting telescope uses a mirror to gather light. The Cassegrain telescope uses a corrective lens to achieve a wide field of view. It is one of the most widely used tools of astronomy.

based on the laws of motion and gravity laid down by Isaac Newton.

celestial sphere imaginary sphere surrounding the Earth, on which the celestial bodies seem to lie. The positions of bodies such as stars, planets, and galaxies are specified by their coordinates on the celestial sphere. The equivalents of latitude and longitude on the celestial sphere are called declination and right ascension (which is measured in hours from 0 to 24). The **celestial poles** lie directly above the Earth's poles, and the **celestial equator** lies over the Earth's Equator. The celestial sphere appears to rotate once

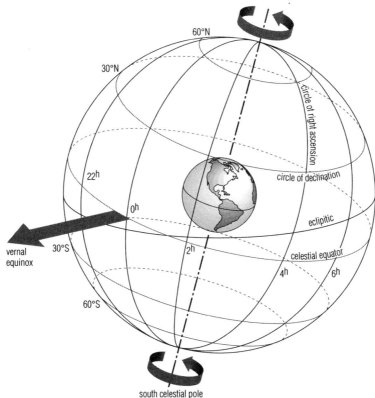

60°N

30°N

circle of right ascension

22h

0h

2h

circle of declination

ecliptic

celestial equator

4h   6h

vernal
equinox

30°S

60°S

south celestial pole

celestial sphere The main features of the celestial sphere. The equivalents of latitude and longitude on the celestial sphere are declination and right ascension. Declination runs from 0° at the celestial equator to 90° at the celestial poles. Right ascension is measured in hours eastwards from the vernal equinox, one hour corresponding to 15° of longitude.

around the Earth each day, actually a result of the rotation of the Earth on its axis.

conjunction the alignment of two celestial bodies as seen from Earth. A superior planet (or other object) is in conjunction when it lies behind the Sun. An inferior planet (or other object) comes to **inferior conjunction** when it passes between the Earth and the Sun; it is at **superior conjunction** when it passes behind the Sun.

  Planetary conjunction takes place when a planet is closely aligned with another celestial object, such as the Moon, a star, or another planet.

cosmology branch of astronomy that deals with the structure and evolution of the universe as an ordered whole. Its method is to construct 'model universes' mathematically and compare their large-scale properties with those of the observed universe.

  Modern cosmology began in the 1920s with the discovery that the universe is expanding, which suggested that it began in an explosion, the Big Bang. An alternative – now discarded – view, the steady-state theory, claimed that the universe has no origin, but is expanding because new matter is being continually created.

declination coordinate on the celestial sphere (imaginary sphere surrounding the Earth) that corresponds to latitude on the Earth's surface. Declination runs from 0° at the celestial equator to 90° at the north and south celestial poles.

ecliptic path, against the background of stars, that the Sun appears to follow each year as it is orbited by the Earth. It can be thought of as the plane of the Earth's orbit projected on to the celestial sphere (imaginary sphere around the Earth).

  The ecliptic is tilted at about 23.5° with respect to the celestial equator, a result of the tilt of the Earth's axis relative to the plane of its orbit around the Sun.

elongation angular distance between the Sun and a planet or other Solar System object. This angle is 0° at conjunction, 90° at quadrature, and 180° at opposition.

equinox the points in spring and autumn at which the Sun's path, the ecliptic, crosses the celestial equator, so that the day and night are of approximately equal length. The **vernal equinox** occurs about 21 March and the **autumnal equinox,** 23 September.

geostationary orbit circular path 35,900 km/22,300 mi above the Earth's Equator on which a satellite takes 24 hours, moving from west to east, to complete an orbit, thus appearing to hang stationary over one place on the Earth's surface. Geostationary orbits are used particularly for communications satellites and weather satellites. They were first thought of by the author Arthur C Clarke. A **geosynchronous orbit** lies at the same distance from Earth but is inclined to the Equator.

gravitational lensing bending of light by a gravitational field, predicted by Einstein's general theory of relativity. The effect was first detected in 1917 when the light from stars was found to be bent as it passed the totally eclipsed Sun. More remarkable is the splitting of light from distant quasars into two or more images by intervening galaxies. In 1979 the first double image of a quasar produced by gravitational lensing was discovered and a quadruple image of another quasar was later found.

Hertzsprung–Russell diagram graph on which the surface temperatures of stars are plotted against their luminosities. Most stars, including the Sun, fall into a narrow band called the **main sequence.** When a star grows old it moves from the main sequence to the upper right part of the graph, into the area of the giants and supergiants. At the end of its life, as the star shrinks to become a white dwarf, it moves again, to the bottom left area. It is named after the Dane Ejnar Hertzsprung (1873–1967) and the American Henry Norris Russell (1877–1957), who independently devised it in the years 1911–13.

Hubble constant measure of the rate at which the universe is expanding, named after Edwin Hubble. Observations suggest that galaxies are moving apart at a rate of 50–100 kps/30–60 mps for every million parsecs of distance. This means that the universe, which began at one point according to the Big Bang theory, is between 10 billion and 20 billion years old (probably closer to 20). Observations by the Hubble Space Telescope in 1996 produced a revised constant of 73 kps/45 mps.

Hubble's law the law that relates a galaxy's distance from us to its speed of recession as the universe expands, announced in 1929 by Edwin Hubble. He found that galaxies are moving apart

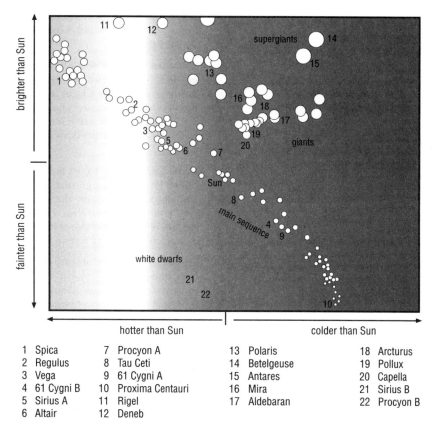

1	Spica	7	Procyon A	13	Polaris	18	Arcturus
2	Regulus	8	Tau Ceti	14	Betelgeuse	19	Pollux
3	Vega	9	61 Cygni A	15	Antares	20	Capella
4	61 Cygni B	10	Proxima Centauri	16	Mira	21	Sirius B
5	Sirius A	11	Rigel	17	Aldebaran	22	Procyon B
6	Altair	12	Deneb				

Hertzsprung–Russell diagram The Hertzsprung–Russell diagram relates the brightness (or luminosity) of a star to its temperature. Most stars fall within a narrow diagonal band called the main sequence. A star moves off the main sequence when it grows old. The Hertzsprung–Russell diagram is one of the most important diagrams in astrophysics.

at speeds that increase in direct proportion to their distance apart. The rate of expansion is known as Hubble's constant.

inclination angle between the ecliptic and the plane of the orbit of a planet, asteroid, or comet. In the case of satellites orbiting a planet, it is the angle between the plane of orbit of the satellite and the equator of the planet.

Kepler's laws three laws of planetary motion formulated in 1609 and 1619 by the German mathematician and astronomer Johannes Kepler: (1) the orbit of each planet is an ellipse with the Sun at one of the foci; (2) the radius vector of each planet sweeps out equal areas in equal times; (3) the squares of the periods of the planets are proportional to the cubes of their mean distances from the Sun.

Kepler derived the laws after exhaustive analysis of numerous observations of the planets, especially Mars, made by Tycho Brahe without telescopic aid. Isaac Newton later showed that Kepler's Laws were a consequence of the theory of universal gravitation. *See illustration on page 40.*

Lagrangian points five locations in space where the centrifugal and gravitational forces of two bodies neutralize each other; a third, less massive body located at any one of these points will be held in equilibrium with respect to the other two. Three of the points, L1–L3, lie on a line joining the two large bodies. The other two points, L4 and L5, which are the most stable, lie on either side of this line. Their existence was predicted in 1772 by French mathematician Joseph Louis Lagrange.

light year the distance travelled by a beam of light in a vacuum in one year, approximately

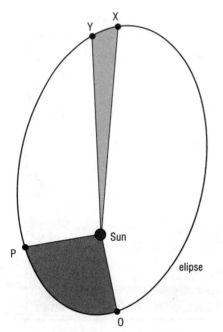

Kepler's laws Kepler's second law states that the light-shaded area equals the dark-shaded area if the planet moves from P to O in the same time that it moves from X to Y. The law says, in effect, that a planet moves fastest when it is closest to the Sun.

9.46 trillion (million million) km/5.88 trillion miles.

luminosity or **brightness** amount of light emitted by a star, measured in magnitudes. The apparent brightness of an object decreases in proportion to the square of its distance from the observer. The luminosity of a star or other body can be expressed in relation to that of the Sun.

magnetosphere volume of space, surrounding a planet, controlled by the planet's magnetic field, and acting as a magnetic 'shell'. The Earth's magnetosphere extends 64,000 km/40,000 mi towards the Sun, but many times this distance on the side away from the Sun.

The extension away from the Sun is called the **magnetotail.** The outer edge of the magnetosphere is the **magnetopause.** Beyond this is a turbulent region, the **magnetosheath,** where the solar wind is deflected around the magnetosphere. Inside the magnetosphere, atomic particles follow the Earth's lines of magnetic force. The magnetosphere contains the Van Allen radiation belts. Other planets have magnetospheres, notably Jupiter.

nadir the point on the celestial sphere vertically below the observer and hence diametrically opposite the **zenith.**

Newtonian telescope simple reflecting telescope in which light collected by a parabolic primary mirror is directed to a focus at the side of the tube by a flat secondary mirror placed at 45 degrees to the optical axis. It is named after Isaac Newton, who constructed such a telescope in 1668.

nutation slight 'nodding' of the Earth in space, caused by the varying gravitational pulls of the Sun and Moon. Nutation changes the angle of the Earth's axial tilt (average 23.5°) by about 9 seconds of arc to either side of its mean position, a complete cycle taking just over 18.5 years.

occultation temporary obscuring of a star by a body in the Solar System. Occultations are used to provide information about changes in an orbit, and the structure of objects in space, such as radio sources, for example, the rings of Uranus were discovered when that planet occulted a star in 1977.

Olbers' paradox question put forward 1826 by Heinrich Olbers, who asked: If the universe is infinite in extent and filled with stars, why is the sky dark at night? The answer is that the stars do not live infinitely long, so there is not enough starlight to fill the universe. A wrong answer, fre-

Astronomical Constants

Constant	Value
Astronomical unit (AU)	149,597,870 km
Speed of light in a vacuum (c)	299,792.458 km/sec
Solar parallax	8.794148 arc seconds
Mass of the Sun	1.9891×10^{30} kg
Mass of the Earth	5.9742×10^{24} kg
Mass of the Moon	7.3483×10^{22} kg
Light year (ly)	9.4605×10^{12} km (or 0.30660 pc)
Parsec (pc)	30.857×10^{12} km (or 3.26161 ly)
Obliquity of the elliptic (2000)	23° 26′ 21.448′
General precession (2000)	50.290966 arc seconds/year
Constant of nutation (2000)	9.2025 arc seconds
Constant of aberration (2000)	20.49552 arc seconds

quently given, is that the expansion of the universe weakens the starlight.

opposition moment at which a body in the Solar System lies opposite the Sun in the sky as seen from the Earth and crosses the meridian at about midnight.

orbit path of one body in space around another, such as the orbit of Earth around the Sun, or the Moon around Earth. When the two bodies are similar in mass, as in a binary star, both bodies move around their common centre of mass. The movement of objects in orbit follows Johann Kepler's laws, which apply to artificial satellites as well as to natural bodies. As stated by the laws, the orbit of one body around another is an ellipse. The ellipse can be highly elongated, as are comet orbits around the Sun, or it may be almost circular, as are those of some planets. The closest point of a planet's orbit to the Sun is called **perihelion**; the most distant point is **aphelion**. (For a body orbiting the Earth, the closest and furthest points of the orbit are called **perigee** and **apogee**.)

parallax change in the apparent position of an object against its background when viewed from two different positions. Nearby stars show a shift owing to parallax when viewed from different positions on the Earth's orbit around the Sun. A star's parallax is used to deduce its distance from the Earth. Nearer bodies such as the Moon, Sun, and planets also show a parallax caused by the motion of the Earth. **Diurnal parallax** is caused by the Earth's rotation.

parsec (symbol pc) unit used for distances to stars and galaxies. One parsec is equal to 3.2616 light years, 2.063×10^5 astronomical units, and 3.086×10^{13} km. It is the distance at which a star would have a parallax (apparent shift in position) of one second of arc when viewed from two points the same distance apart as the Earth's distance from the Sun; or the distance at which one astronomical unit subtends an angle of one second of arc.

perigee the point at which an object, travelling in an elliptical orbit around the Earth, is at its closest to the Earth. The point at which it is furthest from the Earth is the apogee.

perihelion the point at which an object, travelling in an elliptical orbit around the Sun, is at its closest to the Sun. The point at which it is furthest from the Sun is the aphelion.

precession slow wobble of the Earth on its axis, like that of a spinning top. The gravitational pulls of the Sun and Moon on the Earth's equatorial bulge cause the Earth's axis to trace out a circle on the sky every 25,800 years. The position of the celestial poles is constantly changing owing to precession, as are the positions of the equinoxes (the points at which the celestial equator intersects the Sun's path around the sky). The **precession of the equinoxes** means that there is a gradual westward drift in the ecliptic – the path that the Sun appears to follow – and in the coordinates of objects on the celestial sphere.

This is why the dates of the astrological signs of the zodiac no longer correspond to the times of year when the Sun actually passes through the constellations. For example, the Sun passes through Leo from mid-August to mid-September, but the astrological dates for Leo are between about 23 July and 22 August.

Precession also occurs in other planets. Uranus has the Solar System's fastest known precession (264 days) determined in 1995.

proper motion gradual change in the position of a star that results from its motion in orbit around our Galaxy, the Milky Way. Proper motions are slight and undetectable to the naked eye, but can be accurately measured on telescopic photographs taken many years apart. Barnard's Star is the star with the largest proper motion, 10.3 arc seconds per year.

radio astronomy study of radio waves emitted naturally by objects in space, by means of a radio telescope. Radio emission comes from hot gases (**thermal radiation**); electrons spiralling in magnetic fields (**synchrotron radiation**); and specific wavelengths (**lines**) emitted by atoms and molecules in space, such as the 21-cm/8-in line emitted by hydrogen gas.

Radio astronomy began in 1932 when US astronomer Karl Jansky detected radio waves from the centre of our Galaxy, but the subject did not develop until after World War II. Radio astronomy has greatly improved our understanding of the evolution of stars, the structure of galaxies, and the origin of the universe. Astronomers have mapped the spiral structure of the Milky Way from the radio waves given out by interstellar gas, and they have detected many individual radio sources within our Galaxy and beyond.

Among radio sources in our Galaxy are the remains of supernova explosions, such as the

Crab nebula and pulsars. Short-wavelength radio waves have been detected from complex molecules in dense clouds of gas where stars are forming. Searches have been undertaken for signals from other civilizations in the Galaxy, so far without success. Strong sources of radio waves beyond our Galaxy include radio galaxies and quasars. Their existence far off in the universe demonstrates how the universe has evolved with time. Radio astronomers have also detected weak **background radiation** thought to be from the Big Bang explosion that marked the birth of the universe.

radio telescope instrument for detecting radio waves from the universe in radio astronomy. Radio telescopes usually consist of a metal bowl that collects and focuses radio waves the way a concave mirror collects and focuses light waves. Radio telescopes are much larger than optical telescopes, because the wavelengths they are detecting are much longer than the wavelength of light. The largest single dish is 305 m/1,000 ft across, at Arecibo, Puerto Rico. **Interferometry** is a technique in which the output from two dishes is combined to give better resolution of detail than with a single dish. **Very long baseline interferometry** (VBLI) uses radio telescopes spread across the world to resolve minute details of radio sources.

red shift lengthening of the wavelengths of light from an object as a result of the object's motion away from us. It is an example of the Doppler effect. The red shift in light from galaxies is evidence that the universe is expanding.

Lengthening of wavelengths causes the light to move or shift towards the red end of the spectrum, hence the name. The amount of red shift can be measured by the displacement of lines in an object's spectrum. By measuring the amount of red shift in light from stars and galaxies, astronomers can tell how quickly these objects are moving away from us. A strong gravitational field can also produce a red shift in light; this is termed **gravitational red shift.**

satellite any small body that orbits a larger one, either natural or artificial. Natural satellites that orbit planets are called moons. The first **artificial satellite**, Sputnik 1, was launched into orbit around the Earth by the USSR in 1957. Artificial satellites are used for scientific purposes, communications, weather forecasting, and military applications. The brightest artificial satellites can be seen by the naked eye.

sidereal period orbital period of a planet around the Sun, or a moon around a planet, with reference to a background star. The sidereal period of a planet is in effect a 'year'. A synodic period is a full circle as seen from Earth.

singularity point in space-time at which the known laws of physics break down. Singularity is predicted to exist at the centre of a black hole, where infinite gravitational forces compress the infalling mass of a collapsing star to infinite den-

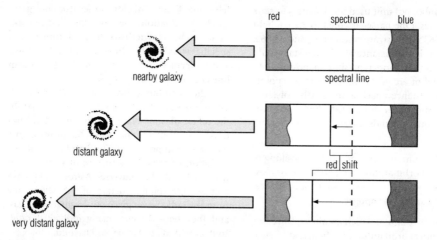

red shift The red shift causes lines in the spectra of galaxies to be shifted towards the red end of the spectrum. More distant galaxies have greater red shifts than closer galaxies. The red shift indicates that distant galaxies are moving apart rapidly, as the universe expands.

Largest Natural Planetary Satellites

Planet	Satellite	Diameter		Mean distance from centre of primary planet		Orbital period (Earth days)	Reciprocal mass (planet = 1)
		km	mi	km	mi		
Jupiter	Ganymede	5,262	3,300	1,070,000	664,898	7.16	12,800
Saturn	Titan	5,150	3,200	1,221,800	759,226	15.95	4,200
Jupiter	Callisto	4,800	3,000	1,883,000	1,170,096	16.69	17,700
Jupiter	Io	3,630	2,240	421,600	261,982	1.77	21,400
Earth	Moon	3,476	2,160	384,400	238,866	27.32	81.3
Jupiter	Europa	3,138	1,900	670,900	416,897	3.55	39,700
Neptune	Triton	2,700	1,690	354,300	220,162	5.88	770

sity. It is also thought, according to the Big Bang model of the origin of the universe, to be the point from which the expansion of the universe began.

speckle interferometry technique whereby large telescopes can achieve high resolution of astronomical objects despite the adverse effects of the atmosphere through which light from the object under study must pass. It involves the taking of large numbers of images, each under high magnification and with short exposure times. The pictures are then combined to form the final picture. The technique was introduced by the French astronomer Antoine Labeyrie in 1970.

synodic period the time taken for a planet or moon to return to the same position in its orbit as seen from the Earth; that is, from one opposition to the next. It differs from the sidereal period because the Earth is moving in orbit around the Sun.

transit passage of a smaller object across the visible disc of a larger one. Transits of the inferior

Telescopes

Telescopes are optical instruments that magnify images of faint and distant objects, or more broadly, any device for collecting and focusing light and other forms of electromagnetic radiation. A telescope with a large aperture, or opening, can distinguish finer detail and fainter objects than one with a small aperture. The **refracting telescope** uses lenses, and the **reflecting telescope** uses mirrors. A third type, the **catadioptric telescope**, is a combination of lenses and mirrors.

Refractor
In a refractor, light is collected by a lens called the **object glass** or **objective**, which focuses light down a tube, forming an image magnified by an **eyepiece**. Invention of the refractor is attributed to a Dutch optician, Hans Lippershey, in 1608. Hearing of the invention in 1609,

Galileo quickly constructed one for himself and went on to produce a succession of such instruments which he used from 1610 onwards for astronomical observations. The largest refracting telescope in the world, at Yerkes Observatory, Wisconsin, USA, has an aperture of 102 cm/40 in.

Reflector
In a reflector, light is collected and focused by a concave mirror. The first reflector was built about 1670 by Isaac Newton. Large mirrors are cheaper to make and easier to mount than large lenses, so all the largest telescopes are reflectors. The largest reflector with a single mirror, 6 m/236 in, is at Zelenchukskaya, Russia. Telescopes with larger apertures composed of numerous smaller segments have been built, such as the Keck Telescope on Mauna Kea, Hawaii. A **multiple-mirror telescope**

was installed on Mount Hopkins, Arizona, USA, in 1979. It consists of six mirrors of 1.8-m/72-in aperture, which perform like a single 4.5-m/176-in mirror. **Schmidt telescopes** are used for taking wide-field photographs of the sky. They have a main mirror plus a thin lens at the front of the tube to increase the field of view.

Telescopes in space
Large telescopes can now be placed in orbit above the distorting effects of the Earth's atmosphere. Telescopes in space have been used to study infrared, ultraviolet, and X-ray radiation that does not penetrate the atmosphere but carries much information about the births, lives, and deaths of stars and galaxies. The 2.4-m/94-in Hubble Space Telescope, launched in 1990, can see the sky more clearly than can any telescope on Earth.

planets occur when they pass directly between the Earth and the Sun, and are seen as tiny dark spots against the Sun's disc.

Other forms of transit include the passage of a satellite or its shadow across the disc of Jupiter and the passage of planetary surface features across the central meridian of that planet as seen from Earth. The passage of an object in the sky across the observer's meridian is also known as a transit.

universal time (UT) another name for Greenwich Mean Time. It is based on the rotation of the Earth, which is not quite constant. Since 1972, UT has been replaced by **coordinated universal time** (UTC), which is based on uniform atomic time.

X-ray astronomy detection of X-rays from intensely hot gas in the universe. Such X-rays are prevented from reaching the Earth's surface by the atmosphere, so detectors must be placed in rockets and satellites. The first celestial X-ray source, Scorpius X-1, was discovered by a rocket flight in 1962.

Since 1970, special satellites have been put into orbit to study X-rays from the Sun, stars, and galaxies. Many X-ray sources are believed to be gas falling on to neutron stars and black holes.

zenith uppermost point of the celestial horizon, immediately above the observer; the nadir is below, diametrically opposite.

Noteworthy Astronomers

Aristarchus of Samos (*c.* 320–*c.* 250 BC) Greek astronomer who was the first to argue that the Earth orbits the Sun

Bessel Friedrich Wilhelm (1784–1846) German astronomer and mathematician who was the first person to calculate the distance of a star other than the Sun

Boksenberg Alexander (1936–) English astronomer and physicist who developed a light-detecting system for telescopes, thereby greatly enhancing their optical power

Bradley James (1693–1762) English astronomer who calculated the speed of light in 1728

Brahe Tycho (1546–1601) Danish astronomer whose accurate calculation of the motion of the Sun led to the reform of the calendar in 1582, with the adoption of the Gregorian Calendar; he discovered and reported a supernova explosion in 1572

Cannon Annie Jump (1863–1941) US astronomer who first classified stars by their spectra

Celsius Anders (1701–1744) Swedish astronomer, physicist, and mathematician who introduced the Celsius scale of temperature in 1742

Copernicus Nicolaus (Latinized form of **Mikołaj Kopernik**) (1473–1543) Polish astronomer who argued that the Sun is the centre of the Solar System

Flamsteed John (1646–1719) English astronomer who became the first Astronomer Royal at Greenwich and pioneered work on the cataloguing of stars

Fowler William Alfred (1911–1995) US astrophysicist who worked on the life cycle of stars and the origin of chemical elements

Galileo (properly **Galileo Galilei**) (1564–1642) Italian mathematician, astronomer, and physicist who developed the astronomical telescope and confirmed that planets orbit the Sun

Gill David (1843–1914) Scottish astronomer who pioneered the use of photographic techniques in the cataloguing of stars

Greenstein Jesse Leonard (1909–) US astronomer who helped discover the interstellar magnetic field and quasars

Halley Edmond (or **Edmund**) (1656–1742) English astronomer who, in 1705, identified the comet now named after him; he also compiled a catalogue of stars and researched stellar motion

Heraklides of Pontus (388–315 BC) Greek astronomer and philosopher who was one of the first to recognize the 24 hour rotation of the Earth from west to east on its axis

Herschel (Frederick) William (1738–1822) German-born English astronomer who discovered the planet Uranus in 1781 and outlined the basic form of the Milky Way

Herschel John Frederick William (1792–1871) English astronomer who carried out a survey of the stars in the southern hemisphere and measured the brightness of stars

Hertzsprung Ejnar (1873–1967) Danish astronomer and physicist who introduced the concept of the absolute magnitude (brightness) of a star

Hipparchus (c. 190–c. 120 BC) Greek astronomer and mathematician who calculated the lengths of the solar year and lunar month

Hubble Edwin (1889–1953) US astronomer who discovered the existence of other galaxies and found evidence for the expansion of the universe

Huygens Christiaan (1629–1695) Dutch mathematical physicist and astronomer who observed Saturn's rings; he was also famous for his work in the field of optics

Jeans James Hopwood (1877–1946) English scientist and astronomer who did much to popularize astronomy through books and television broadcasts

Kepler Johannes (1571–1630) German mathematician and astronomer who described how planets orbit the Sun; he is particularly remembered for what are now termed Kepler's laws of motion

Laplace Pierre Simon (1749–1827) French astronomer and mathematician who formulated the nebular hypothesis of the origin of the solar system and developed the field of celestial mechanics

Lemaître Georges Edouard (1894–1966) Belgian cosmologist who proposed the Big Bang theory of the origin of the universe

Lowell Percival (1855–1916) US astronomer who predicted the existence of Pluto

Messier Charles (1730–1817) French astronomer who produced a catalogue of the locations of nebulae and star clusters

Minkowski Rudolph Leo (1895–1976) German-born US astrophysicist who compiled the National Geographic Society Palomar Observatory Sky Survey and was a pioneer in the field of radio-astronomy

Moore Patrick Alfred Calderwell (1923–) English astronomer, author, and broadcaster who has promoted the public understanding of astronomy through his popular television series *The Sky at Night* and more than 60 books

Newcomb Simon (1835–1909) Canadian-born US mathematician and astronomer who standardized the system of astronomical constants

Newton Isaac (1642–1727) English physicist, mathematician, and astronomer whose work is fundamental to the development of science; his theories on the nature of space and the action of force at a distance contributed greatly to the modern understanding of the universe

Ptolemy (Claudius Ptolemaeus) (c. 100–c. 170) Egyptian astronomer and geographer who developed the geocentric view of the Solar System

Schiaparelli Giovanni Virginio (1835–1910) Italian astronomer who drew attention to 'canals', or linear markings, on Mars

Shapley Harlow (1885–1972) US astronomer who established that our galaxy is much larger than was previously thought

Van Allen James Alfred (1914–) US physicist who discovered two zones of intense radiation around the Earth

Astronomy: Chronology

2300 BC Chinese astronomers made their earliest observations.

2000 Babylonian priests made their first observational records.

1900 Stonehenge was constructed: first phase.

434 Anaxagoras claims the Sun is made up of hot rock.

365 The Chinese observed the satellites of Jupiter with the naked eye.

3rd century Aristarchus argued that the Sun is the centre of the

Solar System.

2nd century AD Ptolemy's complicated Earth-centred system was promulgated, which dominated the astronomy of the Middle Ages.

1543 Copernicus revived the

(*continued*)

Astronomy: Chronology (continued)

ideas of Aristarchus in *De Revolutionibus*.

1608 Hans Lippershey invented the telescope, which was first used by Galileo in 1609.

1609 Johannes Kepler's first two laws of planetary motion were published (the third appeared in 1619).

1632 The world's first official observatory was established in Leiden in the Netherlands.

1633 Galileo's theories were condemned by the Inquisition.

1675 The Royal Greenwich Observatory was founded in England.

1687 Isaac Newton's *Principia* was published, including his 'law of universal gravitation'.

1705 Edmond Halley correctly predicted that the comet that had passed the Earth in 1682 would return in 1758; the comet was later to be known by his name.

1781 William Herschel discovered Uranus and recognized stellar systems beyond our Galaxy.

1796 Pierre Laplace elaborated his theory of the origin of the solar system.

1801 Giuseppe Piazzi discovered the first asteroid, Ceres.

1814 Joseph von Fraunhofer first studied absorption lines in the solar spectrum.

1846 Neptune was identified by Johann Galle, following predictions by John Adams and Urbain Leverrier.

1859 Gustav Kirchhoff explained dark lines in the Sun's spectrum.

1887 The earliest photographic star charts were produced.

1889 Edward Barnard took the first photographs of the Milky Way.

1908 Fragment of comet fell at Tunguska, Siberia.

1920 Arthur Eddington began the study of interstellar matter.

1923 Edwin Hubble proved that the galaxies are systems independent of the Milky Way, and by 1930 had confirmed the concept of an expanding universe.

1930 The planet Pluto was discovered by Clyde Tombaugh at the Lowell Observatory, Arizona, USA.

1931 Karl Jansky founded radio astronomy.

1945 Radar contact with the Moon was established by Z Bay of Hungary and the US Army Signal Corps Laboratory.

1948 The 5-m/200-in Hale reflector telescope was installed at Mount Palomar, California, USA.

1957 The Jodrell Bank telescope dish in England was completed.

1957 The first Sputnik satellite (USSR) opened the age of space observation.

1962 The first X-ray source was discovered in Scorpius.

1963 The first quasar was discovered.

1967 The first pulsar was discovered by Jocelyn Bell and Antony Hewish.

1969 The first crewed Moon landing was made by US astronauts.

1976 A 6-m/240-in reflector telescope was installed at Mount Semirodniki, USSR.

1977 Uranus was discovered to have rings.

1977 The spacecraft *Voyager* 1 and 2 were launched, passing Jupiter and Saturn 1979–1981.

1978 The spacecraft *Pioneer Venus* 1 and 2 reached Venus.

1978 A satellite of Pluto, Charon, was discovered by James Christy of the US Naval Observatory.

1986 Halley's comet returned. *Voyager 2* flew past Uranus and discovered six new moons.

1987 Supernova SN1987A flared up, becoming the first supernova to be visible to the naked eye since 1604. The 4.2-m/165-in William Herschel Telescope on La Palma, Canary Islands, and the James Clerk Maxwell Telescope on Mauna Kea, Hawaii, began operation.

1988 The most distant individual star was recorded – a supernova, 5 billion light years away, in the AC118 cluster of galaxies.

1989 *Voyager 2* flew by Neptune and discovered eight moons and three rings.

1990 Hubble Space Telescope was launched into orbit by the US space shuttle.

1991 The space probe *Galileo* flew past the asteroid Gaspra, approaching it to within 26,000 km/16,200 mi.

1992 COBE satellite detected ripples from the Big Bang that mark the first stage in the formation of galaxies.

(continued)

Astronomy: Chronology (continued)

1994 Fragments of comet Shoemaker–Levy struck Jupiter.

1996 US astronomers discovered the most distant galaxy so far detected. It is in the constellation Virgo and is 14 billion light years from Earth.

1997 Data from the satellite *Hipparicos* improved estimates of the age of the universe, and the distances to many nearby stars. Two new moons were discovered circling Uranus, bringing its total number of moons up to 17.

1998 NASA announced the discovery of up to 300 million tonnes of ice on the surface of the Moon. The ice exists as a thin layer of crystals inside some craters that are permanently in shadow.

THE PHYSICAL WORLD

---　✳　---

The scientific study of the planet Earth as a whole is referred to as earth science. The mining and extraction of minerals and gems, the prediction of weather and earthquakes, the pollution of the atmosphere, and the forces that shape the physical world all fall within its scope of study. The emergence of the discipline reflects scientists' concern that an understanding of the global aspects of the Earth's structure and its past will hold the key to how humans affect its future, ensuring that its resources are used in a sustainable way. It is a synthesis of several traditional subjects such as geology, meteorology, oceanography, geophysics, geochemistry, and palaeontology.

EARTH'S INTERIOR

The Earth's interior is thought to be composed of a number of concentric layers: an inner core of solid iron and nickel; an outer core of molten iron and nickel; and a mantle of mostly solid rock, separated by the Mohorovic discontinuity from the Earth's crust.

Evidence for the layered structure has been gathered by scientists surveying the paths taken by seismic waves (earthquake waves), which travel at different speeds through different materials. The crust and the topmost layer of the mantle (the lithosphere) form about 12 large moving plates, some of which carry the continents.

anticline rock layers or beds folded to form a convex arch (seldom preserved intact) in which older rocks comprise the core. Where relative ages of the rock layers, or stratigraphic ages, are not known, convex upward folded rocks are referred to as **antiforms.** The fold of an anticline may be undulating or steeply curved. A steplike bend in otherwise gently dipping or horizontal beds is a **monocline.** The opposite of an anticline is a syncline.

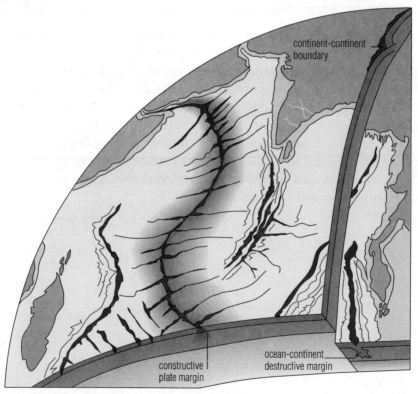

lithosphere The surface of the Earth is made up of plates with different kinds of margins. In mid-ocean, there are constructive plate margins, where magma wells up from the Earth's interior, forming new crust. On continent–continent margins, mountain ranges are flung up by the collision of two continents. At an ocean–continent destructive margin, ocean crust is forced under the denser continental crust, forming an area of volcanic instability.

The Earth

Earth is the third planet from the Sun. It is almost spherical, flattened slightly at the poles, and is composed of three concentric layers: the core, the mantle, and the crust. About 70% of the surface (including the north and south polar icecaps) is covered with water. The Earth is surrounded by a life-supporting atmosphere and is the only planet on which life is known to exist.

mean distance from the Sun 149,500,000 km/92,860,000 mi

equatorial diameter 12,756 km/ 7,923 mi

circumference 40,070 km/24,900 mi

rotation period 23 hr 56 min 4.1 sec

year (complete orbit, or sidereal period) 365 days 5 hr 48 min 46 sec. Earth's average speed around the Sun is 30 kps/18.5 mps; the plane of its orbit is inclined to its equatorial plane at an angle of 23.5°, the reason for the changing seasons

atmosphere nitrogen 78.09%; oxygen 20.95%; argon 0.93%; carbon dioxide 0.03%; and less than 0.0001% neon, helium, krypton, hydrogen, xenon, ozone, radon

surface land surface 150,000,000 sq km/57,500,000 sq mi (greatest height above sea level 8,872 m/29,118 ft Mount Everest); water surface 361,000,000 sq km/ 139,400,000 sq mi (greatest depth 11,034 m/36,201 ft Mariana Trench in the Pacific). The interior is thought to be an inner core about 2,600 km/1,600 mi in diameter, of solid iron and nickel; an outer core about 2,250 km/1,400 mi thick, of molten iron and nickel; and a mantle of mostly solid rock about 2,900 km/1,800 mi thick, separated from the Earth's crust by the Mohorovičić discontinuity. The crust and the topmost layer of the mantle form about twelve major moving plates, some of which carry the continents. The plates are in constant, slow motion

satellite the Moon

age 4.6 billion years. The Earth was formed with the rest of the Solar System by consolidation of interstellar dust. Life began 3.5–4 billion years ago

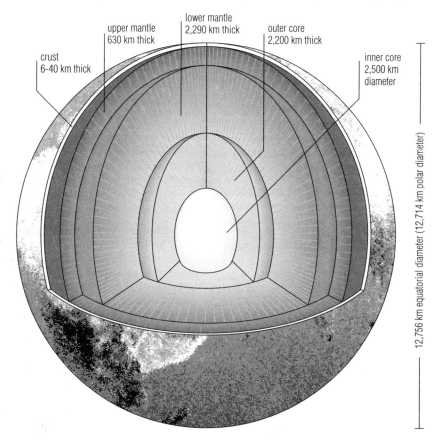

upper mantle 630 km thick

lower mantle 2,290 km thick

outer core 2,200 km thick

crust 6-40 km thick

inner core 2,500 km diameter

12,756 km equatorial diameter (12,714 km polar diameter)

Earth The surface of the Earth is a thin crust about 6 km/4 mi thick under the sea and 40 km/25 mi thick under the continents. Under the crust lies the mantle about 2,900 km/1,800 mi thick and with a temperature of 1,500–3,000°C/2,700–5,400°F. The outer core is about 2,250 km/ 1,400 mi thick, of molten iron and nickel. The inner core is probably solid iron and nickel at about 5,000°C/9,000°F.

asthenosphere a layer within Earth's mantle lying beneath the lithosphere, typically beginning at a depth of approximately 100 km/63 mi and extending to depths of approximately 260 km/160 mi. Sometimes referred to as the 'weak sphere', it is characterized by being weaker and more elastic than the surrounding mantle.

The asthenosphere's elastic behaviour and low viscosity allow the overlying, more rigid plates of lithosphere to move laterally in a process known as plate tectonics. Its elasticity and viscosity also allow overlying crust and mantle to move vertically in response to gravity to achieve **isostatic equilibrium.**

core innermost part of Earth. It is divided into an outer core, which begins at a depth of 2,898 km/1,800 mi, and an inner core, which begins at a depth of 4,982 km/3,095 mi. Both parts are thought to consist of iron-nickel alloy. The outer core is liquid and the inner core is solid.

The fact that seismic shear waves disappear at the mantle–outer core boundary indicates that the outer core is molten, since shear waves cannot travel through fluid. Scientists infer the iron-nickel-rich composition of the core from Earth's density and its moment of inertia. The temperature of the core, as estimated from the melting point of iron at high pressure, is thought to be at least 4,000°C/7,232°F, but remains controversial. Earth's magnetic field is believed to be the result of the motions involving the inner and outer cores.

craton or **shield** core of a continent, a vast tract of highly deformed metamorphic rock around which the continent has been built. Intense mountain-building periods shook these shield areas in Precambrian times before stable conditions set in.

Cratons exist in the hearts of all the continents, a typical example being the Canadian Shield.

crust the outermost part of the structure of Earth, consisting of two distinct parts, the oceanic crust and the continental crust. The **oceanic** crust is on average about 10 km/6.2 mi thick and consists mostly of basaltic types of rock. By contrast, the **continental** crust is largely made of granite and is more complex in its structure. Because of the movements of plate tectonics, the oceanic crust is in no place older than about 200 million years. However, parts of the continental crust are over 3 billion years old.

Beneath a layer of surface sediment, the oceanic crust is made up of a layer of basalt, followed by a layer of gabbro. The composition of the oceanic crust overall shows a high proportion of *si*licon and *ma*gnesium oxides, hence named **sima** by geologists. The continental crust varies in thickness from about 40 km/25 mi to 70 km/45 mi, being deeper beneath mountain ranges. The surface layer consists of many kinds of sedimentary and igneous rocks. Beneath lies a zone of metamorphic rocks built on a thick layer of granodiorite. *Si*licon and *al*uminium oxides dominate the composition and the name **sial** is given to continental crustal material.

dating science of determining the age of geological structures, rocks, and fossils, and placing them in the context of geological time. The techniques are of two types: relative dating and absolute dating. **Relative dating** can be carried out by identifying fossils of creatures that lived only at certain times (marker fossils), and by looking at the physical relationships of rocks to other rocks of a known age. **Absolute dating** is achieved by measuring how much of a rock's radioactive elements have changed since the rock was formed, using the process of radiometric dating.

epicentre the point on the Earth's surface immediately above the seismic focus of an earthquake. Most damage usually takes place at an earthquake's epicentre. The term sometimes refers to a point directly above or below a nuclear explosion ('at ground zero').

fault fracture in the Earth either side of which rocks have moved past one another. Faults involve displacements, or offsets, ranging from the microscopic scale to hundreds of kilometres. Large offsets along a fault are the result of the accumulation of smaller movements (metres or less) over long periods of time. Large motions cause detectable earthquakes.

Faults are planar features. Fault orientation is described by the inclination of the fault plane with respect to horizontal (see dip) and its direction in the horizontal plane. Faults at high angle with respect to horizontal (in which the fault plane is steep) are classified as either **normal faults,** where one block has apparently moved downhill along the inclined fault plane, or **reverse faults,** where one block appears to have moved uphill along the fault plane. Normal

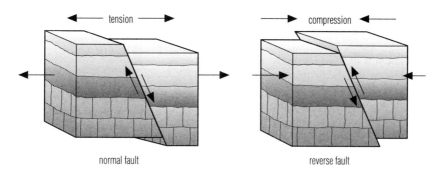

fault Faults are caused by the movement of rock layers, producing such features as mountains and rift valleys. A normal fault is caused by a tension or stretching force acting in the rock layers. A reverse fault is caused by compression forces. Faults can continue to move for thousands or millions of years.

faults occur where rocks on either side have moved apart. Reverse faults occur where rocks on either side have been forced together. A reverse fault that forms a low angle with the horizontal plane is called a **thrust fault.**

fold bend in beds or layers of rock. If the bend is arched up in the middle it is called an **anticline**; if it sags downwards in the middle it is called a **syncline.** The line along which a bed of rock folds is called its axis. The axial plane is the plane joining the axes of successive beds.

fossil a cast, impression, or the actual remains of an animal or plant preserved in rock. Fossils were created during periods of rock formation, caused by the gradual accumulation of sediment over millions of years at the bottom of the sea bed or an inland lake. Fossils may include footprints, an internal cast, or external impression. A few fossils are preserved intact, as with mammoths fossilized in Siberian ice, or insects trapped in tree resin (amber). The study of fossils is called palaeontology. Palaeontologists are able to

deduce much of the geological history of a region from fossil remains.

geological time scale see geological time feature.

igneous rock rock formed from cooling magma or lava, and solidifying from a molten state. Igneous rocks are largely composed of silica (SiO_2) and they are classified according to their crystal size, texture, method of formation, or chemical composition, for example by the proportions of light and dark minerals.

intrusion mass of igneous rock that has formed by 'injection' of molten rock, or magma, into existing cracks beneath the surface of the Earth, as distinct from a volcanic rock mass which has erupted from the surface. Intrusion features include vertical cylindrical structures such as stocks, pipes, and necks; sheet structures such as dykes that cut across the strata and sills that push between them; laccoliths, which are blisters that push up the overlying rock; and batholiths, which represent chambers of solidified magma and contain vast volumes of rock.

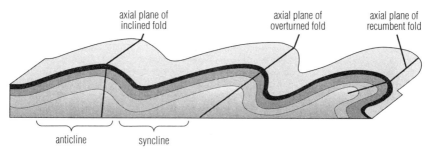

fold The folding of rock strata occurs where compression causes them to buckle. Over time, folding can assume highly complicated forms, as can sometimes be seen in the rock layers of cliff faces or deep cuttings in the rock. Folding contributes to the formation of great mountain chains such as the Himalayas.

lava molten rock (usually 800–1,100°C/1,500–2,000°F) that erupts from a volcano and cools to form extrusive igneous rock. It differs from magma in that it is molten rock on the surface; **magma** is molten rock below the surface. Lava that is viscous and sticky does not flow far; it forms a steep-sided conical composite volcano. Less viscous lava can flow for long distances and forms a broad flat shield volcano.

The viscosity of lava, and thus the form of volcano they form, depends on silica content, temperature, and degree of solidification upon extrusion. It is often said that viscosity increases with silica content because silica polymerizes, but this rule can be misleading. Lavas having the composition of basalt, which is low in silica content, tend to flow easily and form broad flat volcanoes as in the Hawaiian Islands. But some very silica-rich lavas of rhyolite composition can also flow readily. Lavas that are especially viscous are often of andesite composition and intermediate in silica content. Andesite lavas can therefore give rise to explosive volcanoes like the island of Montserrat, West Indies.

lithosphere topmost layer of the Earth's structure, forming the jigsaw of plates that take part in the movements of plate tectonics. The lithosphere comprises the crust and a portion of the upper mantle. It is regarded as being rigid and moves about on the more elastic and less rigid asthenosphere. The lithosphere is about 100 km/63 mi thick.

magma molten rock material beneath the Earth's (or any of the terrestrial planets) surface from which igneous rocks are formed. Lava is magma that has extruded on to the surface.

mantle see Earth's mantle feature below.

metamorphic rock rock altered in structure and composition by pressure, heat, or chemically active fluids after original formation. (If heat is sufficient to melt the original rock, technically it becomes an igneous rock upon cooling.) The term was coined in 1833 by Scottish geologist Charles Lyell (1797–1875).

metamorphism geological term referring to the changes in rocks of the Earth's crust caused by increasing pressure and temperature. The resulting rocks are metamorphic rocks. All metamorphic changes take place in solid rocks. If the rocks melt and then harden, they become igneous rocks.

Mohorovičić discontinuity also **Moho** or **M-discontinuity** boundary that separates the Earth's crust and mantle, marked by a rapid increase in the speed of earthquake waves. It follows the variations in the thickness of the crust and is found approximately 32 km/20 mi below the continents and about 10 km/6 mi below the oceans. It is named after the Yugoslav geophysicist Andrija Mohorovičić (1857–1936), who suspected its presence after analysing seismic waves from the Kulpa Valley earthquake in 1909.

permeable rock rock that allows water to pass through it. Rocks are permeable if they have cracks or joints running through them or if they are porous, containing many interconnected pores. Examples of permeable rocks include limestone (which is heavily jointed) and chalk (porous).

The Earth's mantle

The mantle is the intermediate zone of the Earth between the crust and the core, accounting for 82% of Earth's volume. The boundary between the mantle and the crust above is the Mohorovičić discontinuity, located at an average depth of 32 km/20 mi. The lower boundary with the core is the Gutenburg discontinuity at an average depth of 2,900 km/1,813 mi.

The mantle is subdivided into **upper mantle, transition zone,** and **lower mantle,** based upon the different velocities with which seismic waves travel through these regions.

The upper mantle includes a zone characterized by low velocities of seismic waves, called the **low velocity zone,** at 72 km/45 mi to 250 km/155 mi depth. This zone corresponds to the asthenosphere upon which Earth's tectonic plates of lithosphere glide. Seismic velocities in the upper mantle are overall less than those in the transition zone and those of the transition zone are in turn less than those of the lower mantle. Faster propagation of seismic waves in the lower mantle implies that the lower mantle is more dense than the upper mantle.

The mantle is composed primarily of magnesium, silicon, and oxygen in the form of silicate minerals. In the upper mantle, the silicon in silicate minerals, such as olivine, is surrounded by four oxygen atoms. Deeper in the transition zone greater pressures promote denser packing of oxygen such that some silicon is surrounded by six oxygen atoms, resulting in magnesium silicates with garnet and pyroxene structures. Deeper still, all silicon is surrounded by six oxygen atoms so that the new mineral $MgSiO_3$-perovskite predominates.

Metamorphic Rocks

typical depth and temperature	primary material (before metamorphism)		
	shale with several minerals	sandstone with only quartz	limestone with only calcite
50,000 ft/570°F	slate	quartzite	marble
65,000 ft/750°F	schist		
82,000 ft/930°F	gneiss		
98,500 ft/1,100°F	hornfels	quartzite	marble

Geological Time

Time scale embracing the history of the Earth from its physical origin to the present day. Geological time is traditionally divided into eons (Archaean or Archaeozoic, Proterozoic and Phanerozoic in ascending chronological order), which in turn are subdivided into eras, periods, epochs, ages, and finally chrons.

The terms eon, era, period, epoch, age and chron are **geochronological units** representing intervals of geological time. Rocks representing an interval of geological time comprise a **chronostratigraphic unit.** Each of the hierarchical geochronological terms has a chronostratigraphic equivalent. Thus, rocks formed during an eon (a geochronological unit) are members of an eonothem (the chronostratigraphic unit equivalent of eon). Rocks of an era belong to an erathem. The chronostratigraphic equivalents of period, epoch, age, and chron are system, series, stage, and chronozone, repectively.

Archaean (or **Archaeozoic**) widely used term for the earliest era of geological time; the first part of the Precambrian **Eon,** spanning the interval from the formation of Earth to about 2,500 million years ago.

Cambrian period of geological time 570–510 million years ago; the first period of the Palaeozoic era. All invertebrate animal life appeared, and marine algae were widespread. The **Cambrian Explosion** 530–520 million years ago saw the first appearance in the fossil record of all modern animal phyla; the earliest fossils with hard shells, such as trilobites, date from this period.

The name comes from Cambria, the medieval Latin name for Wales, where Cambrian rocks are typically exposed and were first described.

Carboniferous period of geological time 362.5–290 million years ago, the fifth period of the Palaeozoic era. In the USA it is divided into two periods: the Mississippian (lower) and the Pennsylvanian (upper).

Typical of the lower-Carboniferous rocks are shallow-water limestones, while upper-Carboniferous rocks have delta deposits with coal (hence the name). Amphibians were abundant, and reptiles evolved during this period.

Cretaceous period of geological time approximately 144.2–65 million years ago. It is the last period of the Mesozoic era, during which angiosperm (seed-bearing) plants evolved, and dinosaurs reached a peak before their extinction at the end of the period. The north European chalk, which forms the white cliffs of Dover, was deposited during the latter half of the Cretaceous.

Devonian period of geological time 408–360 million years ago, the fourth period of the Palaeozoic era. Many desert sandstones from North America and Europe date from this time. The first land plants flourished in the Devonian period, corals were abundant in the seas, amphibians evolved from air-breathing fish, and insects developed on land.

The name comes from the county of Devon in southwest England, where Devonian rocks were first studied.

Eocene second epoch of the Tertiary period of geological time, 56.5–35.5 million years ago. Originally considered the earliest division of the Tertiary, the name means 'early recent', referring to the early forms of mammals evolving at the time, following the extinction of the dinosaurs.

Gondwanaland southern landmass formed 200 million years ago by the splitting of the single world continent Pangaea. (The northern landmass was Laurasia.) It later fragmented into the continents of South America, Africa, Australia, and Antarctica, which have since moved slowly to their present positions. The baobab tree found in both Africa and Australia is a relic of this ancient land mass.

A database of the entire geology of Gondwanaland has been constructed by geologists in South Africa. The database, known as Gondwana Geoscientific Indexing Database (GO-GEOID), displays information as a map of Gondwana 155 million years ago, before the continents broke apart.

Holocene epoch of geological time that began 10,000 years ago, the second and current epoch of the Quaternary period. During this epoch the glaciers retreated, the climate became warmer, and humans developed significantly.

Geological Time (continued)

Iapetus Ocean (or **Proto-Atlantic**) sea that existed in early Palaeozoic times between the continent that was to become Europe and that which was to become North America. The continents moved together in the late Palaeozoic, obliterating the ocean. When they moved apart once more, they formed the Atlantic.

ice age any period of glaciation occurring in the Earth's history, but particularly that in the Pleistocene epoch, immediately preceding historic times. On the North American continent, glaciers reached as far south as the Great Lakes, and an ice sheet spread over northern Europe, leaving its remains as far south as Switzerland.

There were several glacial advances separated by interglacial stages during which the ice melted and temperatures were higher than today. There is a possibility that the Pleistocene ice age is not yet over. It may reach another maximum in another 60,000 years.

Formerly there were thought to have been only three or four glacial advances, but recent research has shown about 20 major incidences. For example, ocean-bed cores record the absence or presence in their various layers of such cold-loving small marine animals as radiolaria, which indicate a fall in ocean temperature at regular intervals. Other ice ages have occurred throughout geological time: there were four in the Precambrian era, one in the Ordovician, and one at

the end of the Carboniferous and beginning of the Permian. The occurrence of an ice age is governed by a combination of factors (the **Milankovitch hypothesis**): (1) the Earth's change of attitude in relation to the Sun, that is, the way it tilts in a 41,000-year cycle; (2) the precession of equinoxes, that is, the way Earth wobbles on its axis in a 22,000-year cycle, making the time of its closest approach to the Sun come at different seasons; and (3) the 92,000-year cycle of eccentricity in its orbit round the Sun, changing it from an elliptical to a near circular orbit, the severest period of an ice age coinciding with the approach to circularity.

The theory of ice ages was first proposed in the 19th century by, among others, Swiss civil engineer Ignace Venetz 1821 and Swiss naturalist Louis Agassiz 1837. (Before, most geologists had believed that the rocks and sediment they left behind were caused by the biblical flood.) The term 'ice age' was first used by botanist Karl Schimper in 1837.

K-T boundary geologists' shorthand for the boundary between the rocks of the Cretaceous and the Tertiary periods 65 million years ago. It coincides with the end of the extinction of the dinosaurs and in many places is marked by a layer of clay or rock enriched in the element iridium. Extinction of the dinosaurs at the K-T boundary and deposition of the iridium layer are thought to be the result of either impact of a meteorite (or comet) that crashed into the Yucatán Peninsula (forming the **Chicxulub crater**) or the result of intense volcanism on the continent of India.

Mesozoic era of geological time 245–65 million years ago, consisting of the Triassic, Jurassic, and Cretaceous periods. At the beginning of the era, the continents were joined together as Pangaea; dinosaurs and other giant reptiles dominated the sea and air; and ferns, horsetails, and cycads thrived in a warm climate worldwide. By the end of the Mesozoic era, the continents had

begun to assume their present positions, flowering plants were dominant, and many of the large reptiles and marine fauna were becoming extinct.

Miocene fourth epoch of the Tertiary period of geological time, 23.5–5.2 million years ago. At this time grasslands spread over the interior of continents, and hoofed mammals rapidly evolved.

Oligocene third epoch of the Tertiary period of geological time, 35.5–3.25 million years ago. The name, from Greek, means 'a little recent', referring to the presence of the remains of some modern types of animals existing at that time.

Ordovician period of geological time 510–439 million years ago; the second period of the Palaeozoic era. Animal life was confined to the sea: reef-building algae and the first jawless fish are characteristic.

The period is named after the Ordovices, an ancient Welsh people, because the system of rocks formed in the Ordovician period was first studied in Wales.

Palaeozoic era of geological time 570–245 million years ago. It comprises the Cambrian, Ordovician, Silurian, Devonian, Carboniferous, and Permian periods. The Cambrian, Ordovician, and Silurian constitute the Lower or Early Palaeozoic; the Devonian, Carboniferous, and Permian make up the Upper or Late Palaeozoic. The era is that of the evolution of hard-shelled multicellular life forms in the sea; the invasion of land by plants and animals; and the evolution of fish, amphibians, and early reptiles. The earliest identifiable fossils date from this era.

The climate at this time was mostly warm with short ice ages. The continents were very different from the present ones but, towards the end of the era, all were joined together as a single world continent called Pangaea.

Paleocene first epoch of the Tertiary period of geological time, 65–55 million years ago. Many types of mammals spread rapidly after the

Major Ice Ages

Name	Date (years ago)
Pleistocene	1.64 million–10,000
Permo-Carboniferous	330–250 million
Ordovician	440–430 million
Verangian	615–570 million
Sturtian	820–770 million
Gnejso	940–880 million
Huronian	2,700–1,800 million

Geological Time (continued)

disappearance of the great reptiles of the Mesozoic.

At the end of the Palaeocene there was a mass extinction that caused more than half of all bottom-dwelling organisms to disappear worldwide, over a period of around one thousand years. Surface-dwelling organisms remained unaffected, as did those on land. The cause of this extinction remains unknown, though US palaeontologists have found evidence (released 1998) that it may have been caused by the Earth releasing tonnes of methane into the oceans causing increased water temperatures.

Pangaea or **Pangea** single land mass, made up of all the present continents, believed to have existed between 300 and 200 million years ago; the rest of the Earth was covered by the Panthalassa ocean. Pangaea split into two land masses – Laurasia in the north and Gondwanaland in the south – which subsequently broke up into several continents. These then drifted slowly to their present position.

The existence of a single 'supercontinent' was proposed by German meteorologist Alfred Wegener in 1912.

Permian period of geological time 290–245 million years ago, the last period of the Palaeozoic era. Its end was marked by a significant change in marine life, including the extinction of many corals and trilobites. Deserts were widespread, terrestrial amphibians and mammal-like reptiles flourished, and cone-bearing plants

(gymnosperms) came to prominence. In the oceans, 49% of families and 72% of genera vanished in the late Permian. On land, 78% of reptile families and 67% of amphibian families disappeared.

Phanerozoic eon in Earth history, consisting of the most recent 570 million years. It comprises the Palaeozoic, Mesozoic, and Cenozoic eras. The vast majority of fossils come from this eon, owing to the evolution of hard shells and internal skeletons. The name means 'interval of well-displayed life'.

Precambrian time from the formation of Earth (4.6 billion years ago) up to 570 million years ago. Its boundary with the succeeding Cambrian period marks the time when animals first developed hard outer parts (exoskeletons) and so left abundant fossil remains. It comprises about 85% of geological time and is divided into two periods: the Archaean, in which no life existed, and the Proterozoic, in which there was life in some form.

Proterozoic eon of geological time, 3.5 billion to 570 million years ago, the second division of the Precambrian. It is defined as the time of simple life, since many rocks dating from this eon show traces of biological activity, and some contain the fossils of bacteria and algae.

Quaternary period of geological time that began 1.64 million years ago and is still in process. It is divided

into the Pleistocene and Holocene epochs.

Silurian period of geological time 439–409 million years ago, the third period of the Palaeozoic era. Silurian sediments are mostly marine and consist of shales and limestone. Luxuriant reefs were built by coral-like organisms. The first land plants began to evolve during this period, and there were many ostracoderms (armoured jawless fishes). The first jawed fishes (called acanthodians) also appeared.

Tertiary period of geological time 65–1.64 million years ago, divided into five epochs: Palaeocene, Eocene, Oligocene, Miocene, and Pliocene. During the Tertiary period, mammals took over all the ecological niches left vacant by the extinction of the dinosaurs, and became the prevalent land animals. The continents took on their present positions, and climatic and vegetation zones as we know them became established. Within the geological time column the Tertiary follows the Cretaceous period and is succeeded by the Quaternary period.

Triassic period of geological time 245–208 million years ago, the first period of the Mesozoic era. The continents were fused together to form the world continent Pangaea. Triassic sediments contain remains of early dinosaurs and other reptiles now extinct. By late Triassic times, the first mammals had evolved.

The climate was generally dry; desert sandstones are typical Triassic rocks.

EARTH'S SURFACE

alluvial deposit layer of broken rocky matter, or sediment, formed from material that has been carried in suspension by a river or stream and dropped as the velocity of the current decreases. River plains and deltas are made entirely of alluvial deposits, but smaller pockets can be found in the beds of upland torrents.

Alluvial deposits can consist of a whole range of particle sizes, from boulders down through cobbles, pebbles, gravel, sand, silt, and clay. The raw materials are the rocks and soils of upland areas that are loosened by erosion and washed away by mountain streams. Much of the world's richest farmland lies on alluvial deposits. These deposits can also provide an economic source of minerals. River currents produce a sorting action, with particles of heavy material deposited first while lighter materials are washed downstream.

Antarctic Circle imaginary line that encircles the South Pole at latitude 66° 32′ S. The line encompasses the continent of Antarctica and the Antarctic Ocean. The region south of this line experiences at least one night in the southern summer during which the Sun never sets, and at least one day in the southern winter during which the Sun never rises.

> **Antarctica**
> ■ The ice that covers Antarctica is 4,776 m/ 15,669 ft deep at its thickest point.

aquifer a body of rock through which appreciable amounts of water can flow. The rock of an aquifer must be porous and permeable (full of interconnected holes) so that it can conduct water. Aquifers are an important source of fresh water, for example, for drinking and irrigation, in many arid areas of the world, and are exploited by the use of artesian wells.

An aquifer may be underlain, overlain, or sandwiched between less permeable layers, called aquicludes or **aquitards,** which impede water

> **Astonishing aquifer**
> ■ The Ogallala aquifer in the USA contains 4 trillion tonnes of water – more than Lake Huron, the second-largest of the North American Great Lakes.

movement. Sandstones and porous limestones make the best aquifers.

archipelago group of islands, or an area of sea containing a group of islands. The islands of an archipelago are usually volcanic in origin, and they sometimes represent the tops of peaks in areas around continental margins flooded by the sea. Volcanic islands are formed either when a hot spot within the Earth's mantle produces a chain of volcanoes on the surface, such as the Hawaiian Archipelago or at a destructive plate margin where the subduction of one plate beneath another produces an arc-shaped island group called an 'island arc', such as the Aleutian Archipelago. Novaya Zemlya in the Arctic Ocean, the northern extension of the Ural Mountains, resulted from continental flooding.

Arctic Circle imaginary line that encircles the North Pole at latitude 66° 33′ north. Within this line there is at least one day in the summer during which the Sun never sets, and at least one day in the winter during which the Sun never rises.

atoll continuous or broken circle of coral reef and low coral islands surrounding a lagoon.

avalanche fall or flow of a mass of snow and ice down a steep slope under the force of gravity. Avalanches occur because of the unstable nature of snow masses in mountain areas.

Changes of temperature, sudden sound, or earth-borne vibrations may trigger an avalanche, particularly on slopes of more than 35°. The snow compacts into ice as it moves, and rocks may be carried along, adding to the damage caused.

Avalanches leave slide tracks, long gouges down the mountainside that can be up to 1 km/ 0.6 mi long and 100 m/330 ft wide. These slides have a similar beneficial effect on biodiversity as do forest fires, clearing the land of snow and mature mountain forest, enabling plants and shrubs that cannot grow in shade to recolonize and creating wildlife corridors.

badlands barren landscape cut by erosion into a maze of ravines, pinnacles, gullies and sharp-edged ridges. Areas in South Dakota and Nebraska, USA, are examples.

barrier reef coral reef that lies offshore, separated from the mainland by a shallow lagoon.

butte Chimney Rock near Shiprock, New Mexico, USA – a notable example of this geological formation. *K G Preston-Mafham/ Premaphotos Wildlife*

butte steep-sided, flat-topped hill, formed in horizontally layered sedimentary rocks, largely in arid areas. A large butte with a pronounced tablelike profile is a mesa.

Buttes and mesas are characteristic of semi-arid areas where remnants of resistant rock layers protect softer rock underneath, as in the plateau regions of Colorado, Utah, and Arizona, USA.

caldera very large basin-shaped crater. Calderas are found at the tops of volcanoes, where the original peak has collapsed into an empty chamber beneath. The basin, many times larger than the original volcanic vent, may be flooded, producing a crater lake, or the flat floor may contain a number of small volcanic cones, produced by volcanic activity after the collapse. Typical calderas are Kilauea, Hawaii; Crater Lake, Oregon, USA; and Ngorongoro, Tanzania.

cave roofed-over cavity in the Earth's crust usually produced by the action of underground water or by waves on a seacoast. Caves of the former type commonly occur in areas underlain by limestone, such as Kentucky and many Balkan regions, where the rocks are soluble in water. A **pothole** is a vertical hole in rock caused by water descending a crack; it is thus open to the sky.

limestone caves Most inland caves are found in karst regions, because limestone is soluble when exposed to ground water. As the water makes its way along the main joints, fissures, and bedding planes, they are constantly enlarged into potential cave passages, which ultimately join to form a complex network. Stalactites and stalagmites and columns form due to water rich in calcium carbonate dripping from the roof of the cave. The collapse of the roof of a cave produces features such as **natural arches** and **steep-sided gorges.** Limestone caves are usually found just below the water-table, wherever limestone outcrops on the surface. The biggest cave in the world is over 70 km/32 mi long, at Holloch, Switzerland.

sea caves Coastal caves are formed where relatively soft rock or rock containing definite lines of weakness, like basalt at tide level, is exposed to severe wave action. The gouging process (corrasion) and dissolution (corrosion) of weaker, more soluble rock layers is exacerbated by subsidence, and the hollow in the cliff face grows still larger because of air compression in the chamber. Where the roof of a cave has fallen in, the vent up to the land surface is called a **blow-hole.** If this grows, finally destroying the cave form, the outlying truncated 'portals' of the cave are known as stacks or columns. The Old Man of Hoy (137 m/85 mi high), in the Orkney Islands, is an example of a stack.

coastal erosion the erosion of the land by the constant battering of the sea's waves, primarily by the processes of hydraulic action, corrasion, attrition and corrosion. Hydraulic action occurs when the force of the waves compresses air pockets in coastal rocks and cliffs. The air expands explosively, breaking the rocks apart. Rocks and pebbles flung by waves against the cliff face wear it away by the process of corrasion. Chalk and limestone coasts are often broken down by solution (also called corrosion). **Attrition** is the process by which the eroded rock particles themselves are worn down, becoming smaller and more rounded.

Frost shattering (or freeze-thaw), caused by the expansion of frozen sea water in cavities, and biological weathering, caused by the burrowing of rock-boring molluscs, also result in the breakdown of the coastal rock.

Where resistant rocks form headlands, the sea erodes the coast in successive stages. First it exploits weaknesses, such as faults and cracks, in cave openings and then gradually wears away the interior of the caves until their roofs are pierced through to form blowholes. In time, caves at either side of a headland may unite to form a natural arch. When the roof of the arch collapses, a stack is formed. This may be worn down further to produce a stump and a wave-cut platform.

Beach erosion occurs when more sand is eroded and carried away from the beach than is deposited by longshore drift. Beach erosion can occur due to the construction of artificial barriers, such as groynes, or due to the natural periodicity of the **beach cycle,** whereby high tides and the high waves of winter storms tend to carry sand away from the beach and deposit it offshore in the form of bars. During the calmer summer season some of this sand is redeposited on the beach.

continental drift theory that, about 250–200 million years ago, the Earth consisted of a single large continent (Pangaea), which subsequently broke apart to form the continents known today. The theory was proposed 1912 by German meteorologist Alfred Wegener, but such vast continental movements could not be satisfactorily explained until the study of plate tectonics in the 1960s.

The term 'continental drift' is not strictly correct, since land masses do not drift through the oceans. The continents form part of a plate, and the amount of crust created at divergent plate margins must equal the amount of crust destroyed at subduction zones.

delta tract of land at a river's mouth, composed of silt deposited as the water slows on entering the sea. Familiar examples of large deltas are those of the Mississippi, Ganges, and Nile.

desert arid area with sparse vegetation (or, in rare cases, almost no vegetation) and irregular rainfall of less than 250 mm/19.75 in per year. Soils are poor, and many deserts include areas of shifting sands. Deserts can be either hot or cold. Tropical deserts have a big diurnal temperature range and

Upper Carboniferous period

Eocene

Lower Quaternary

continental drift The continents are slowly shifting their positions, driven by convection in the mantle beneath the Earth's lithosphere. Over 200 million years ago, there was a single large continent called Pangaea. By 200 million years ago, the continents had started to move apart. By 50 million years ago, the continents were approaching their present positions.

very high daytime temperatures (58°C/136.4°F has been recorded at Azizia in Libya), whereas mid-latitude deserts have a wide annual range and much lower winter temperatures (in the Mongolian desert the mean temperature is below

What is a continent?

A continent is any one of the seven large land masses of the Earth, as distinct from the oceans. They are Asia, Africa, North America, South America, Europe, Australia, and Antarctica. Continents are constantly moving and evolving. A continent does not end at the coastline; its boundary is the edge of the shallow continental shelf, which may extend several hundred kilometres out to sea.

At the centre of each continental mass lies a shield or craton, a deformed mass of old metamorphic rocks dating from Precambrian times. The shield is thick, compact, and solid (the Canadian Shield is an example), having undergone all the mountain-building activity it is ever likely to, and is usually worn flat. Around the shield is a concentric pattern of mountains comprised of folded rock, with older ranges, such as the Rockies, closest to the shield, and younger ranges, such as the coastal ranges of North America, farther away. This general concentric

pattern is modified when two continental masses have moved together and they become welded with a great mountain range along the join, the way Europe and northern Asia are joined along the Urals. If a continent is torn apart, the new continental edges have no mountains formed by wrinkling and folding of the crust; for instance, the western coast of Africa, which rifted apart from South America 200 million years ago.

freezing point for half the year). Almost 33% of the Earth's land surface is desert, and this proportion is increasing.

The **tropical desert** belts of latitudes from 5° to 30° are caused by the descent of air that is heated over the warm land and therefore has lost its moisture. Other natural desert types are the **continental deserts,** such as the Gobi, that are too far from the sea to receive any moisture; **rain-shadow deserts,** such as California's Death Valley, that lie in the lee of mountain ranges, where the ascending air drops its rain only on the windward slopes; and **coastal deserts,** such as the Namib, where cold ocean currents cause local dry air masses to descend. Desert surfaces are usually rocky or gravelly, with only a small proportion being covered with sand. Deserts can be created by changes in climate, or by the human-aided process of desertification.

desert An open forest of small eucalyptus trees covered this barren landscape in Western Australia only a few years previously. Once the land was cleared for agriculture, the unstable soils in this very dry zone were rapidly blown away by the winds, leaving a total desert. This process is called desertification. *Food and Agriculture Organization*

dune mound or ridge of wind-drifted sand common on coasts and in deserts. Loose sand is blown and bounced along by the wind, up the windward side of a dune. The sand particles then fall to rest on the lee side, while more are blown up from the windward side. In this way a dune moves gradually downwind.

earthquake abrupt motion that propagates through the Earth and along its surfaces. Earthquakes are caused by the sudden release in rocks of strain accumulated over time as a result of tectonics. The study of earthquakes is called

Largest Deserts in the World

Desert	Location	Area[1]	
		sq km	sq mi
Sahara	northern Africa	9,065,000	3,500,000
Gobi	Mongolia/northeastern China	1,295,000	500,000
Patagonian	Argentina	673,000	260,000
Rub al-Khali	southern Arabian peninsula	647,500	250,000
Chihuahuan	Mexico/southwestern USA	362,600	140,000
Taklimakan	northern China	362,600	140,000
Great Sandy	northwestern Australia	338,500	130,000
Great Victoria	southwestern Australia	338,500	130,000
Kalahari	southwestern Africa	260,000	100,000
Kyzyl Kum	Uzbekistan	259,000	100,000
Thar	India/Pakistan	259,000	100,000
Sonoran	Mexico/southwestern USA	181,300	70,000
Simpson	Australia	103,600	40,000
Mojave	southwestern USA	51,800	20,000

[1] Desert areas are very approximate because clear physical boundaries may not occur.

seismology. Most earthquakes occur along faults (fractures or breaks) and Benioff zones. Plate tectonic movements generate the major proportion: as two plates move past each other they can become jammed. When sufficient strain has accumulated, the rock breaks, releasing a series of elastic waves (seismic waves) as the plates spring free. The force of earthquakes (magnitude) is measured on the Richter scale, and their effect (intensity) on the Mercalli scale. The point at which an earthquake originates is the **seismic focus** or **hypocentre**; the point on the Earth's surface directly above this is the **epicentre**. See 20th-century earthquakes table on page 62.

Equator or **terrestrial equator** the great circle whose plane is perpendicular to the Earth's axis (the line joining the poles). Its length is 40,092 km/24,901.8 mi, divided into 360 degrees of longitude. The Equator encircles the broadest part of the Earth, and represents 0° latitude. It divides the Earth into two halves, called the northern and the southern hemispheres. The **celestial equator** is the circle in which the plane of the Earth's Equator intersects the celestial sphere.

Some 20th-Century Earthquakes

(N/A = not available.)

Date	Location	Magnitude (Richter scale)	Estimated number of deaths
18–19 April 1906	San Francisco (CA), USA	7.7-7.9	503
16 August 1906	Valparaiso, Chile	8.6	20,000
28 December 1908	Messina, Italy	7.5	83,000
16 December 1920	Gansu Province, China	8.6	200,000
1 September 1923	Yokohama, Japan	8.3	143,000
22 May 1927	Nan-Shan, China	8.3	200,000
26 December 1932	Gansu, China	7.6	70,000
31 May 1935	Quetta, India	7.5	60,000
24 January 1939	Chillan, Chile	7.8	30,000
26 December 1939	Erzincan, Turkey	7.9	23,000
21 December 1946	Honshu, Japan	8.4	2,000
28 June 1948	Fukui, Japan	7.3	5,130
6 October 1948	Iran/USSR	7.3	100,000
5 August 1949	Pelileo, Ecuador	6.8	6,000
15 August 1950	Assam, India	8.7	1,530
10–17 June 1956	northern Afghanistan	7.7	2,000
29 February 1960	Agadir, Morocco	5.7	12,000
1 September 1962	northwestern Iran	7.1	12,000
27 March 1964	Anchorage (AL), USA	9.2	131
31 August 1968	northeastern Iran	7.4	11,600
5 January 1970	Yunan Province, China	7.7	10,000
31 May 1970	Chimbote, Peru	7.8	67,000
10 April 1972	southern Iran	7.1	5,000
23 December 1972	Managua, Nicaragua	6.2	5,000
28 December 1974	Kashmir, Pakistan	6.3	5,200
4 February 1976	Guatemala City, Guatemala	7.5	22,778
28 July 1976	Tangshan, China	8.0	255,000[1]
4 March 1977	Romania	7.5	1,541
16 September 1978	northeastern Iran	7.7	25,000
12 December 1979	Colombia/Ecuador	7.9	800
10 October 1980	northern Algeria	7.7	3,000
23 November 1980	southern Italy	7.2	4,800
19, 21 September 1985	Mexico City, Mexico	8.1	5,000[2]
7 December 1988	Armenia, USSR	6.8	25,000
17 October 1989	San Francisco (CA), USA	7.1	62
20–21 June 1990	northwestern Iran	7.7	37,000
13, 15 March 1992	Erzincan, Turkey	6.7	2,000
12 December 1992	Flores Island, Indonesia	7.5	2,500
29 September 1993	Maharashtra, India	6.3	9,800
16 January 1995	Kobe, Japan	7.2	5,500
14 June 1995	Sakhalin Island, Russia	7.6	2,000
4 February 1998	Takhar province, Afghanistan	6.1	>3,800

[1] Early estimates put the death toll as high as 750,000; the figure shown is the official one.
[2] Some estimates put the death toll as high as 20,000.

erosion wearing away of the Earth's surface, caused by the breakdown and transportation of particles of rock or soil (by contrast, weathering does not involve transportation). Agents of erosion include the sea, rivers, glaciers, and wind.

estuary river mouth widening into the sea, where fresh water mixes with salt water and tidal effects are felt.

fjord or **fiord** narrow sea inlet enclosed by high cliffs. Fjords are found in Norway, New Zealand, and western parts of Scotland. They are formed when an overdeepened U-shaped glacial valley is drowned by a rise in sea-level. At the mouth of the fjord there is a characteristic lip causing a shallowing of the water. This is due to reduced glacial erosion and the deposition of moraine at this point.

flood plain area of periodic flooding along the course of river valleys. When river discharge exceeds the capacity of the channel, water rises over the channel banks and floods the adjacent low-lying lands. As water spills out of the channel some alluvium (silty material) will be deposited on the banks to form levees (raised river banks). This water will slowly seep into the flood plain, depositing a new layer of rich fertile alluvium as it does so.

geyser natural spring that intermittently discharges an explosive column of steam and hot water into the air due to the build-up of steam in underground chambers. One of the most remarkable geysers is Old Faithful, in Yellowstone National Park, Wyoming, USA. Geysers also occur in New Zealand and Iceland.

What is a glacier?

A glacier is a tongue of ice, originating in mountains in snowfields above the snowline, which moves slowly downhill and is constantly replenished from its source. The geographic features produced by the erosive action of glaciers (glacial erosion) are characteristic and include glacial troughs (U-shaped valleys), corries, and arêtes. In lowlands, the laying down of rocky debris carried by glaciers (glacial deposition) produces a variety of landscape features, such as moraines, eskers, and drumlins.

Glaciers form where annual snowfall exceeds annual melting and drainage. The area at the top of the glacier is called the zone of **accumulation**. The lower area of the glacier is called the **ablation zone**. In the zone of accumulation, the snow compacts to ice under the weight of the layers above and moves downhill under the force of gravity. The ice moves plastically under pressure, changing its shape and crystalline structure permanently. Partial melting of ice at the sole of the glacier also produces a sliding component of glacial movement, as the ice travels over the bedrock. In

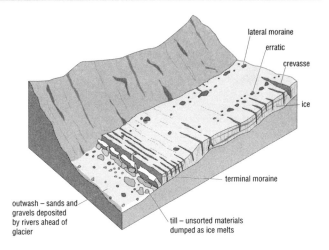

glacial deposition A glacier picks up large boulders and rock debris from the valley and deposits them at the snout of the glacier when the ice melts. Some deposited material is carried great distances by the ice to form erratics.

the ablation zone, melting occurs and glacial till is deposited.

When a glacier moves over an uneven surface, deep **crevasses** are formed in rigid upper layers of the ice mass; if it reaches the sea or a lake, it breaks up to form **icebergs**. A glacier that is formed by one or several valley glaciers at the base of a mountain is called a **piedmont** glacier. A body of ice that covers a large land surface or continent, for example Greenland or Antarctica, and flows outward in all directions is called an **ice sheet**.

geyser Echinus geyser in Yellowstone National Park, Wyoming, USA. *Jean Preston-Mafham/Premaphotos Wildlife*

groundwater water collected underground in porous rock strata and soils; it emerges at the surface as springs and streams. The groundwater's upper level is called the **water table.** Sandy or other kinds of beds that are filled with groundwater are called **aquifers.** Recent estimates are that usable ground water amounts to more than 90% of all the fresh water on Earth; however, keeping such supplies free of pollutants entering the recharge areas is a critical environmental concern.

International Date Line (IDL) imaginary line that approximately follows the 180° line of longitude. The date is put forward a day when crossing the line going west, and back a day when going east. The IDL was chosen at the International Meridian Conference 1884.

island area of land surrounded entirely by water. Australia is classed as a continent rather than an

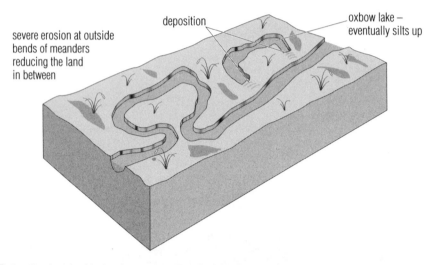

severe erosion at outside
bends of meanders
reducing the land
in between

deposition

oxbow lake –
eventually silts up

lake The formation of an oxbow lake. As a river meanders across a flood plain, the outer bends are gradually eroded and the water channel deepens; as the loops widen, the neck of the loop narrows and finally gives way, allowing the water to flow in a more direct route, isolating the old water channel and forming an oxbow lake.

island, because of its size. Islands can be formed in many ways. **Continental islands** were once part of the mainland, but became isolated (by tectonic movement, erosion, or a rise in sea level, for example). **Volcanic islands,** such as Japan, were formed by the explosion of underwater volcanoes. **Coral islands** consist mainly of coral, built up over many years. An **atoll** is a circular coral reef surrounding a lagoon; atolls were formed when a coral reef grew up around a volcanic island that subsequently sank or was submerged by a rise in sea level. **Barrier islands** are found by the shore in shallow water, and are

formed by the deposition of sediment eroded from the shoreline.

lake body of still water lying in depressed ground without direct communication with the sea. Lakes are common in formerly glaciated regions, along the courses of slow rivers, and in low land near the sea. The main classifications are by origin: **glacial lakes,** formed by glacial scouring; **barrier lakes,** formed by landslides and glacial moraines; **crater lakes,** found in volcanoes; and **tectonic lakes,** occurring in natural fissures.

Crater lakes form in the calderas of extinct

Largest Lakes in the World

Lake	Location	Area sq km	Area sq mi	Lake	Location	Area sq km	Area sq mi
Caspian Sea	Azerbaijan/Russia/Kazakhstan/ Turkmenistan/Iran	370,990	143,239	Malawi	Malawi/Tanzania/ Mozambique	28,867	11,146
Superior	USA/Canada	82,071	31,688	Great Slave	Canada	28,560	11,027
Victoria	Tanzania/Kenya/Uganda	69,463	26,820	Erie	USA/Canada	25,657	9,906
Aral Sea	Kazakhstan/Uzbekistan	64,500	24,903	Winnipeg	Canada	25,380	9,799
Huron	USA/Canada	59,547	22,991	Ontario	USA/Canada	19,010	7,340
Michigan	USA	57,735	22,291	Balkhash	Kazakhstan	18,421	7,112
Tanganyika	Tanzania/Democratic Republic of Congo/Zambia/Burundi	32,880	12,695	Ladoga	Russia	17,695	6,832
Baikal	Russia	31,499	12,162	Chad	Chad/Cameroon/Nigeria	16,310	6,297
Great Bear	Canada	31,316	12,091	Maracaibo	Venezuela	13,507	5,215

volcanoes, for example Crater Lake, Oregon. Subsidence of the roofs of limestone caves in karst landscape exposes the subterranean stream network and provides a cavity in which a lake can develop. Tectonic lakes form during tectonic movement, as when a rift valley is formed. Lake Tanganyika was created in conjunction with the East African Great Rift Valley. Glaciers produce several distinct types of lake, such as the lochs of Scotland and the Great Lakes of North America.

Lakes are mainly freshwater, but salt and bitter lakes are found in areas of low annual rainfall and little surface runoff, so that the rate of evaporation exceeds the rate of inflow, allowing mineral salts to accumulate. The Dead Sea has a salinity of about 250 parts per 1,000 and the Great Salt Lake, Utah, about 220 parts per 1,000. Salinity can also be caused by volcanic gases or fluids, for example Lake Natron, Tanzania.

landslide sudden downward movement of a mass of soil or rocks from a cliff or steep slope. Landslides happen when a slope becomes unstable, usually because the base has been undercut or because materials within the mass have become wet and slippery.

A **mudflow** happens when soil or loose material is soaked so that it no longer adheres to the slope; it forms a tongue of mud that reaches downhill from a semicircular hollow. A **slump** occurs when the material stays together as a large mass, or several smaller masses, and these may form a tilted steplike structure as they slide. A **landslip** is formed when beds of rock dipping towards a cliff slide along a lower bed. Earthquakes may precipitate landslides.

latitude and longitude imaginary lines used to locate position on the globe. Lines of latitude are drawn parallel to the Equator, with 0° at the Equator and 90° at the north and south poles. Lines of longitude are drawn at right angles to these, with 0° (the Prime Meridian) passing through Greenwich, England.

marsh low-lying wetland. Freshwater marshes are common wherever groundwater, surface springs, streams, or run-off cause frequent flooding or more or less permanent shallow water. A marsh is alkaline whereas a bog is acid. Marshes develop on inorganic silt or clay soils. Rushes are typical marsh plants. Large marshes dominated by papyrus, cattail, and reeds, with standing water throughout the year, are commonly called swamps. Near the sea, salt marshes may form.

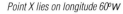
Point X lies on longitude 60°W

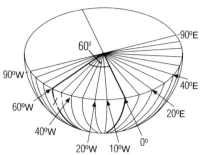

Point X lies on latitude 20°S

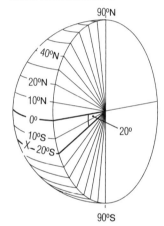

latitude and longitude Locating a point on a globe using latitude and longitude. Longitude is the angle between the terrestrial meridian through a place and the standard meridian 0° passing through Greenwich, England. Latitude is the angular distance of a place from the equator.

meander loop-shaped curve in a mature river flowing sinuously across flat country. As a river flows, any curve in its course is accentuated by the current. On the outside of the curve the velocity, and therefore the erosion, of the current is greatest. Here the river cuts into the outside bank, producing a **cutbank** or **river cliff** and the river's deepest point, or **thalweg**. On the curve's inside the current is slow and deposits any transported material, building up a gentle slip-off slope. As each meander migrates in the direction of its cutbank, the river gradually changes its course across the flood plain. A loop in a river's flow may become so accentuated that it becomes cut off from the normal course and forms an oxbow lake.

Mercalli Scale

The Mercalli scale shown here is the Modified Mercalli Intensity Scale, developed in 1931 by US seismologists Harry Wood and Frank Neumann.

Intensity value	Description
I	not felt except by a very few under especially favourable conditions
II	felt only by a few persons at rest, especially on upper floors of buildings
III	felt quite noticeably by persons indoors, especially on upper floors of buildings; many people do not recognize it as an earthquake; standing motor cars may rock slightly; vibrations similar to the passing of a truck; duration estimated
IV	felt indoors by many, outdoors by few during the day; at night, some awakened; dishes, windows, doors disturbed; walls make cracking sound; sensation like heavy truck striking building; standing motor cars rock noticeably
V	felt by nearly everyone; many awakened; some dishes, windows broken; unstable objects overturned; pendulum clocks may stop
VI	felt by all, many frightened; some heavy furniture moved; a few instances of fallen plaster; damage slight
VII	damage negligible in buildings of good design and construction; slight to moderate in well-built ordinary structures; considerable damage in poorly-built or badly-designed structures; some chimneys broken
VIII	damage slight in specially-designed structures; considerable damage in ordinary substantial buildings with partial collapse; damage great in poorly-built structures; fall of chimneys, factory stacks, columns, monuments, walls; heavy furniture overturned
IX	damage considerable in specially-designed structures; well-designed frame structures thrown out of plumb; damage great in substantial buildings, with partial collapse; buildings shifted off foundations
X	some well-built wooden structures destroyed; most masonry and frame structures with foundations destroyed; rails bent
XI	few, if any (masonry) structures remain standing; bridges destroyed; rails bent greatly
XII	damage total; lines of sight and level are distorted; objects thrown into the air

Mercalli scale scale used to measure the intensity of an earthquake. It differs from the Richter scale, which measures **magnitude.** It is named after the Italian seismologist Giuseppe Mercalli (1850–1914). Intensity is a subjective value, based on observed phenomena, and varies from place to place with the same earthquake.

meridian half a great circle drawn on the Earth's surface passing through both poles and thus through all places with the same longitude. Terrestrial longitudes are usually measured from the Greenwich Meridian.

An astronomical meridian is a great circle passing through the celestial pole and the zenith (the point immediately overhead).

moraine rocky debris or till carried along and deposited by a glacier. Material eroded from the side of a glaciated valley and carried along the glacier's edge is called a **lateral moraine;** that worn from the valley floor and carried along the base of the glacier is called a **ground moraine.** Rubble dropped at the snout of a melting glacier is called a **terminal moraine.**

When two glaciers converge their lateral moraines unite to form a **medial moraine.** Debris that has fallen down crevasses and becomes embedded in the ice is termed an **englacial moraine;** when this is exposed at the surface due to partial melting it becomes ablation moraine.

mountain natural upward projection of the Earth's surface, higher and steeper than a hill. Mountains are at least 330 m/1000 ft above the surrounding topography. The process of mountain building (orogeny) consists of volcanism, plutonism, folding, faulting, and thrusting, resulting from the collision of two tectonic plates (see plate tectonics) at a **convergent margin.** The existing rock is also subjected to high temperatures and pressures causing metamorphism.

peat fibrous organic substance found in bogs and formed by the incomplete decomposition of plants such as sphagnum moss. Northern Asia, Canada, Finland, Ireland, and other places have

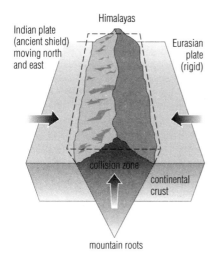

Indian plate (ancient shield) moving north and east

Himalayas

Eurasian plate (rigid)

collision zone

continental crust

mountain roots

mountain Mountains are created when two continental plates collide and no subduction takes place, resulting in the land at the collision zone being squeezed together and thrust upwards.

large deposits, which have been dried and used as fuel from ancient times. Peat can also be used as a soil additive.

Peat bogs began to be formed when glaciers retreated, about 9,000 years ago. They grow at the rate of only a millimetre a year, and large-scale digging can result in destruction both of the bog and of specialized plants growing there.

permafrost condition in which a deep layer of soil does not thaw out during the summer.

Permafrost occurs under periglacial conditions. It is claimed that 26% of the world's land surface is permafrost. Permafrost gives rise to a poorly drained form of grassland typical of northern Canada, Siberia, and Alaska known as tundra.

plateau elevated area of fairly flat land, or a mountainous region in which the peaks are at the same height. An **intermontane plateau** is one surrounded by mountains. A **piedmont plateau** is one that lies between the mountains and low-lying land. A **continental plateau** rises abruptly from low-lying lands or the sea. Examples are the Tibetan Plateau and the Massif Central in France.

polder area of flat reclaimed land that used to be covered by a river, lake, or the sea. Polders have been artificially drained and protected from flooding by building dykes. They are common in the Netherlands.

pole either of the geographic north and south points of the axis about which the Earth rotates. The geographic poles differ from the magnetic poles, which are the points towards which a freely suspended magnetic needle will point.

rainforest dense forest usually found on or near the Equator where the climate is hot and wet. Moist air brought by the converging tradewinds rises because of the heat producing heavy rainfall. Over half the tropical rainforests are in Central and South America, primarily the lower Amazon and the coasts of Ecuador and

What is plate tectonics?

Plate tectonics is the theory formulated in the 1960s to explain the phenomena of continental drift and seafloor spreading, and the formation of the major physical features of the Earth's surface. The Earth's outermost layer, the lithosphere, is regarded as a jigsaw puzzle of rigid major and minor plates that move relative to each other, probably under the influence of convection currents in the mantle beneath. At the margins of the plates, where they collide or move apart, major landforms such as mountains, volcanoes, ocean trenches, and ocean ridges are created. The rate of plate movement is at most 15 cm/6 in per year.

The concept of plate tectonics brings together under one unifying theory many previously unrelated phenomena observed in the Earth's crust. The size of the plates is variable, as they are constantly changing, but six or seven large plates now cover much of the Earth's surface, the remainder being occupied by a number of smaller plates. Each large plate may include both continental and ocean crust. As a result of seismic studies it is known that the lithosphere is a rigid layer extending to depths of 50–100 km/30–60 mi, overlying the upper part of the mantle (the asthenosphere), which is composed of rocks very close to melting point, with a low shear strength. This zone of mechanical weakness allows the movement of the overlying plates. The margins of the plates are defined by major earthquake zones and belts of volcanic and tectonic activity, which have been well known for many years. Almost all earthquake, volcanic, and tectonic activity is confined to the margins of plates, and shows that the plates are in constant motion. *See illustration on* *page 68.*

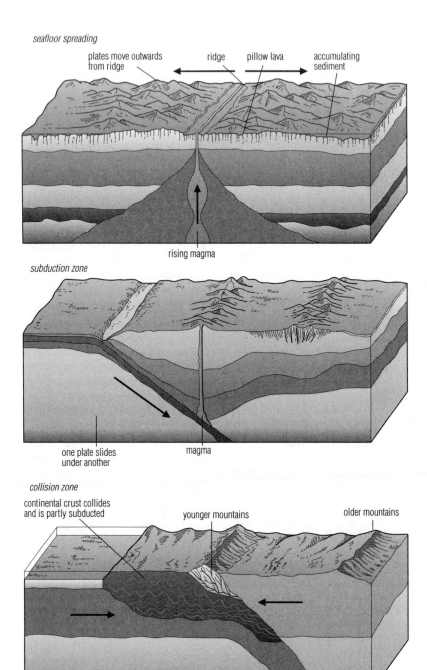

seafloor spreading

plates move outwards from ridge   ridge   pillow lava   accumulating sediment

rising magma

subduction zone

one plate slides under another   magma

collision zone

continental crust collides and is partly subducted   younger mountains   older mountains

plate tectonics The three main types of action in plate tectonics. (top) **Seafloor spreading** The upwelling of magma forces apart the plates, producing new crust at the joint. Rapid extrusion of magma produces a domed ridge; more gentle spreading produces a central valley. (middle) **Subduction** The drawing downwards of a plate with oceanic crust beneath a plate with more bouyant continental crust produces a range of volcanic mountains parallel to the plate edge. (bottom) **Collision** Collision of continental plates produces immense mountains, such as the Himalayas.

The plates of the Earth's lithosphere are always changing in size and shape as material is added at constructive margins and removed at destructive margins.

Richter Scale

Magnitude	Relative amount of energy released	Examples	Year
1	1		
2	31		
3	960		
4	30,000	Carlisle, England (4.7)	1979
5	920,000	Wrexham, Wales (5.1)	1990
6	29,000,000	San Fernando (CA) (6.5)	1971
		northern Armenia (6.8)	1988
7	890,000,000	Loma Prieta (CA) (7.1)	1989
		Kobe, Japan (7.2)	1995
		Rasht, Iran (7.7)	1990
		San Francisco (CA) (7.7–7.9)[1]	1906
8	28,000,000,000	Tangshan, China (8.0)	1976
		Gansu, China (8.6)	1920
		Lisbon, Portugal (8.7)	1755
9	850,000,000,000	Prince William Sound (AK) (9.2)	1964

[1] Richter's original estimate of a magnitude of 8.3 has been revised by two recent studies carried out by the California Institute of Technology and the US Geological Survey.

Columbia. The rest are in Southeast Asia (Malaysia, Indonesia, and New Guinea) and in West Africa and the Congo.

Tropical rainforest once covered 14% of the Earth's land surface, but are now being destroyed at an increasing rate as their valuable timber is harvested and the land cleared for agriculture, causing problems of deforestation. Although by 1991 over 50% of the world's rainforest had been removed, they still comprise about 50% of all growing wood on the planet, and harbour at least 40% of the Earth's species (plants and animals).

Richter scale scale based on measurement of seismic waves, used to determine the magnitude of an earthquake at its epicentre. The magnitude of an earthquake differs from its intensity, measured by the Mercalli scale, which is subjective and varies from place to place for the same earthquake. The scale is named after US seismologist Charles Richter. An earthquake's magnitude is a function of the total amount of energy released, and each point on the Richter scale represents a thirtyfold increase in energy over the previous point. The greatest earthquake ever recorded, in 1920 in Gansu, China, measured 8.6 on the Richter scale.

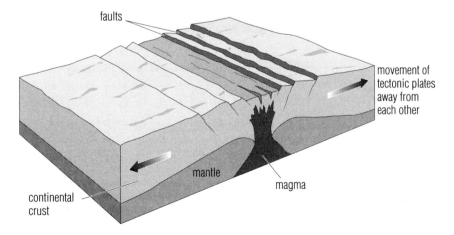

faults

movement of tectonic plates away from each other

mantle

magma

continental crust

rift valley The subsidence of rock resulting from two or more parallel rocks moving apart is known as a graben. When this happens on a large scale, with tectonic plates moving apart, a rift valley is created.

rift valley valley formed by the subsidence of a block of the Earth's crust between two or more parallel faults. Rift valleys are steep-sided and form where the crust is being pulled apart, as at ocean ridges, or in the Great Rift Valley of East Africa. *See illustration on page 69.*

river large body of water that flows down a slope along a channel restricted by adjacent banks and levées. A river originates at a point called its **source,** and enters a sea or lake at its **mouth.** Along its length it may be joined by smaller rivers called **tributaries**; a river and its tributaries are contained within a drainage basin. The point at which two rivers join is called the confluence.

Rivers are formed and moulded over time chiefly by the processes of erosion, and by the **transport** and **deposition** of sediment. Rivers are able to work on the landscape because the energy stored in the water, or potential energy, is converted as it flows downhill into the kinetic energy used for erosion, transport, and deposition. The amount of potential energy available to a river is proportional to its initial height above sea level. A river follows the path of least resistance downhill, and deepens, widens and lengthens its channel by erosion.

One way of classifying rivers is by their stage of development. A youthful stream is typified by a narrow V-shaped valley with numerous waterfalls, lakes, and rapids. Because of the steep gradient of the topography and the river's height above sea level, the rate of erosion is greater than the rate of deposition and downcutting occurs by **vertical corrasion.** These characteristics may also be said to typify a river's **upper course.**

In a mature river, the topography has been

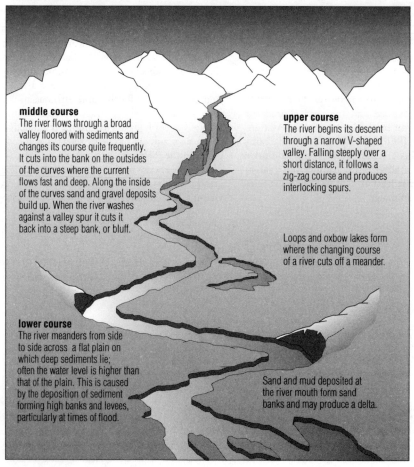

river The course of a river from its source of a spring or melting glacier, through to maturity where it flows into the sea.

middle course
The river flows through a broad valley floored with sediments and changes its course quite frequently. It cuts into the bank on the outsides of the curves where the current flows fast and deep. Along the inside of the curves sand and gravel deposits build up. When the river washes against a valley spur it cuts it back into a steep bank, or bluff.

upper course
The river begins its descent through a narrow V-shaped valley. Falling steeply over a short distance, it follows a zig-zag course and produces interlocking spurs.

Loops and oxbow lakes form where the changing course of a river cuts off a meander.

lower course
The river meanders from side to side across a flat plain on which deep sediments lie; often the water level is higher than that of the plain. This is caused by the deposition of sediment forming high banks and levees, particularly at times of flood.

Sand and mud deposited at the river mouth form sand banks and may produce a delta.

Longest Rivers in the World

River	Location	Approximate length		River	Location	Approximate length	
		km	mi			km	mi
Nile	Africa	6,695	4,160	Yenisei	Russia	4,100	2,548
Amazon	South America	6,570	4,083	Parana	Brazil	3,943	2,450
Chang Jiang (Yangtze)	China	6,300	3,915	Mississippi	USA	3,779	2,348
Mississippi–Missouri–Red Rock	USA	6,020	3,741	Murray–Darling	Australia	3,751	2,331
				Missouri	USA	3,726	2,315
Huang He (Yellow River)	China	5,464	3,395	Volga	Russia	3,685	2,290
Ob–Irtysh	China/Kazakhstan/Russia	5,410	3,362	Madeira	Brazil	3,241	2,014
				Purus	Brazil	3,211	1,995
Amur–Shilka	Asia	4,416	2,744	São Francisco	Brazil	3,199	1,988
Lena	Russia	4,400	2,734	Yukon	USA/Canada	3,185	1,979
Congo–Zaire	Africa	4,374	2,718	Rio Grande	USA/Mexico	3,058	1,900
Mackenzie–Peace–Finlay	Canada	4,241	2,635	Indus	Tibet/Pakistan	2,897	1,800
Mekong	Asia	4,180	2,597	Danube	eastern Europe	2,858	1,776
Niger	Africa	4,100	2,548				

eroded down over time and the river's course has a shallow gradient. This mature river is said to be graded. Erosion and deposition are delicately balanced as the river meanders (gently curves back and forth) across the extensive flood plain (sometimes called an inner delta). **Horizontal corrasion** is the dominant erosive process. The flood plain is an area of periodic flooding along the course of river valleys made up of fine silty material called alluvium deposited by the flood water. Features of a the mature river (or the **lower course** of a river) include extensive meanders, ox-bow lakes, and braiding.

scarp and dip two slopes formed when a sedimentary bed outcrops as a landscape feature. The scarp is the slope that cuts across the bedding plane; the dip is the opposite slope which follows the bedding plane. The scarp is usually steep, while the dip is a gentle slope.

sedimentary rock rock formed by the accumulation and cementation of deposits that have been laid down by water, wind, ice, or gravity. Sedimentary rocks cover more than two-thirds of the Earth's surface and comprise three major categories: clastic, chemically precipitated, and organic (or biogenic). Clastic sediments are the largest group and are composed of fragments of pre-existing rocks; they include clays, sands, and gravels.

Chemical precipitates include some limestones and evaporated deposits such as gypsum and halite (rock salt). Coal, oil shale, and limestone made of fossil material are examples of organic sedimentary rocks.

soil loose covering of broken rocky material and decaying organic matter overlying the bedrock of the Earth's surface. It is comprised of minerals, organic matter (called humus) derived from decomposed plants and organisms, living organisms, air, and water. Soils differ according to climate, parent material, rainfall, relief of the bedrock, and the proportion of organic material. The study of soils is **pedology.**

Living soil
■ A handful of soil contains up to 5,000 species of bacteria.

soil erosion the wearing away and redistribution of the Earth's soil layer. It is caused by the action of water, wind, and ice, and also by improper methods of agriculture. If unchecked, soil erosion results in the formation of deserts (desertification). It has been estimated that 20% of the world's cultivated topsoil was lost between 1950 and 1990. If the rate of erosion exceeds the rate of soil formation (from rock and decomposing organic matter), then the land will become infertile. The removal of forests (deforestation) or other vegetation often leads to serious soil erosion, because plant roots bind soil, and without them the soil is free to wash or blow away, as in the American dust bowl. The effect is worse on hillsides, and there has been devastating loss of soil where forests have been cleared from mountainsides, as in Madagascar.

stalactite and stalagmite cave structures formed by the deposition of calcite dissolved in ground water. **Stalactites** grow downwards from the roofs or walls and **Stalagmites** grow upwards from the cave floor. Growing stalactites and stalagmites may meet to form a continuous column from floor to ceiling.

syncline fold in the rocks of the Earth's crust in which the layers or beds dip inwards, thus forming a trough-like structure with a sag in the middle. The opposite structure, with the beds arching upwards, is an anticline.

taiga or **boreal forest** Russian name for the forest zone south of the tundra, found across the northern hemisphere. Here, dense forests of conifers (spruces and hemlocks), birches, and poplars occupy glaciated regions punctuated with cold lakes, streams, bogs, and marshes. Winters are prolonged and very cold, but the summer is warm enough to promote dense growth. The varied fauna and flora are in delicate balance because the conditions of life are so precarious. This ecology is threatened by mining, forestry, and pipeline construction.

tectonics study of the movements of rocks on the Earth's surface. On a small scale tectonics involves the formation of folds and faults, but on a large scale plate tectonics deals with the movement of the Earth's surface as a whole.

topography the surface shape and composition of the landscape, comprising both natural and artificial features, and its study. Topographical features include the relief and contours of the land; the distribution of mountains, valleys, and human settlements; and the patterns of rivers, roads, and railways.

tropics the area between the tropics of Cancer and Capricorn, defined by the parallels of latitude approximately 23° 30' north and south of the Equator. They are the limits of the area of Earth's surface in which the Sun can be directly overhead. The mean monthly temperature is over 20°C/68°F.

Climates within the tropics lie in parallel bands. Along the Equator is the intertropical convergence zone, characterized by high temperatures and year-round heavy rainfall. Tropical rainforests are found here. Along the tropics themselves lie the tropical high-pressure zones, characterized by descending dry air and desert conditions. Between these, the conditions vary seasonally between wet and dry, producing the tropical grasslands.

Crime sometimes pays
- Mt Pelée volcano in Martinique erupted in 1902. All but one of the port of Saint-Pierre's 30,000 inhabitants were killed by the force of the eruption; the survivor was protected by the thick walls of his jail cell.

---

waterfall cascade of water in a river or stream. It occurs when a river flows over a bed of rock that resists erosion; weaker rocks downstream are worn away, creating a steep, vertical drop and a plunge pool into which the water falls. Over time, continuing erosion causes the waterfall to retreat upstream forming a deep valley, or gorge.

water table the upper level of ground water (water collected underground in porous rocks). Water that is above the water table will drain downwards; a spring forms where the water table cuts the surface of the ground. The water table rises and falls in response to rainfall and the rate at which water is extracted, for example, for irrigation and industry.

Highest Waterfalls in the World

Waterfall	Location	Total drop		Waterfall	Location	Total drop	
		m	ft			m	ft
Angel Falls	Venezuela	979	3,212	Great Karamang River Falls	Guyana	488	1,600
Yosemite Falls	USA	739	2,425	Mardalsfossen–North	Norway	468	1,535
Mardalsfossen–South	Norway	655	2,149	Della Falls	Canada	440	1,443
Tugela Falls	South Africa	614	2,014	Gavarnie Falls	France	422	1,385
Cuquenan	Venezuela	610	2,000	Skjeggedal	Norway	420	1,378
Sutherland	New Zealand	580	1,903	Glass Falls	Brazil	404	1,325
Ribbon Fall, Yosemite	USA	491	1,612				

Volcano

A volcano is a crack in the Earth's crust through which hot magma (molten rock) and gases well up. The magma is termed lava when it reaches the surface. A volcanic mountain, usually cone shaped with a crater on top, is formed around the opening, or vent, by the build-up of solidified lava and ash (rock fragments). Most volcanoes arise on plate margins, where the movements of plates generate magma or allow it to rise from the mantle beneath. However, a number are found far from plate-margin activity, on 'hot spots' where the Earth's crust is thin.

There are two main types of volcano: **Composite volcanoes**, such as Stromboli and Vesuvius in Italy, are found at destructive plate margins (areas where plates are being pushed together), usually in association with island arcs and coastal mountain chains. The magma is mostly derived from plate material and is rich in silica. This makes a very stiff lava such as andesite, which solidifies rapidly to form a high, steep-sided volcanic mountain. The magma often clogs the volcanic vent, causing violent eruptions as the blockage is blasted free, as in the eruption of Mount St Helens, USA, in 1980. The crater may collapse to form a caldera.

Shield volcanoes, such as Mauna Loa in Hawaii, are found along the rift valleys and ocean ridges of constructive plate margins (areas where plates are moving apart), and also over hot spots. The magma is derived from the Earth's mantle and is quite free-flowing. The lava formed from this magma – usually basalt – flows for some distance over the surface before it sets and so forms broad low volcanoes. The lava of a shield volcano is not ejected violently but simply flows over the crater rim.

composite volcano

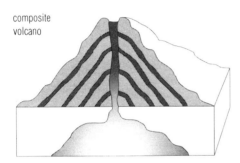

cinder cone

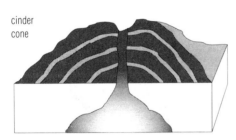

shield volcano

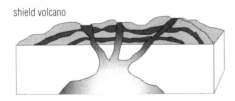

volcano There are two types of volcano, but three distinctive cone shapes. Composite volcanoes emit a stiff, rapidly solidifying lava which forms high, steep-sided cones. Volcanoes that regularly throw out ash build up flatter domes known as cider cones: The lava from a shield volcano is not ejected violently, flowing over the crater rim forming a broad low profile.

Major Volcanic Eruptions in the 20th Century

Volcano	Location	Year	Estimated number of deaths
Santa María	Guatemala	1902	1,000
Pelée	Martinique	1902	28,000
Taal	Philippines	1911	1,400
Kelut	Java, Indonesia	1919	5,500
Vulcan	Papua New Guinea	1937	500
Lamington	Papua New Guinea	1951	3,000
St Helens	USA	1980	57
El Chichon	Mexico	1982	1,880
Nevado del Ruiz	Colombia	1985	23,000
Lake Nyos	Cameroon	1986	1,700
Pinatubo	Luzon, Philippines	1991	639
Unzen	Japan	1991	39
Mayon	Philippines	1993	70
Loki[1]	Iceland	1996	0
Soufriere	Montserrat	1997	23
Merapi	Java, Indonesia	1998	38

[1] The eruption caused severe flooding, and melted enough ice to create a huge sub-glacial lake.

ATMOSPHERE AND OCEANS

abyssal zone dark ocean region 2,000–6,000 m/ 6,500–19,500 ft deep; temperature 4°C/39°F. Three-quarters of the area of the deep-ocean floor lies in the abyssal zone, which is too far from the surface for photosynthesis to take place. Some fish and crustaceans living there are blind or have their own light sources. The region above is the bathyal zone; the region below, the hadal zone.

atmosphere mixture of gases surrounding a planet. Planetary atmospheres are prevented from escaping by the pull of gravity. On Earth, atmospheric pressure decreases with altitude. In its lowest layer, the atmosphere consists of nitrogen (78%) and oxygen (21%), both in molecular form (two atoms bonded together) and 1% argon. Small quantities of other gases are important to the chemistry and physics of the Earth's atmosphere, including water and carbon dioxide. The atmosphere plays a major part in the various cycles of nature (the water cycle, the carbon cycle, and the nitrogen cycle).

barometer instrument that measures atmospheric pressure as an indication of weather. Most often used are the **mercury barometer** and the **aneroid barometer.**

Atmosphere: Composition

Gas	Symbol	Volume (%)	Role
nitrogen	N_2	78.08	cycled through human activities and through the action of microorganisms on animal and plant waste
oxygen	O_2	20.94	cycled mainly through the respiration of animals and plants and through the action of photosynthesis
carbon dioxide	CO_2	0.03	cycled through respiration and photosynthesis in exchange reactions with oxygen. It is also a product of burning fossil fuels
argon	Ar	0.093	chemically inert and with only a few industrial uses
neon	Ne	0.0018	as argon
helium	He	0.0005	as argon
krypton	Kr	trace	as argon
xenon	Xe	trace	as argon
ozone	O_3	0.00006	a product of oxygen molecules split into single atoms by the Sun's radiation and unaltered oxygen molecules
hydrogen	H_2	0.00005	unimportant

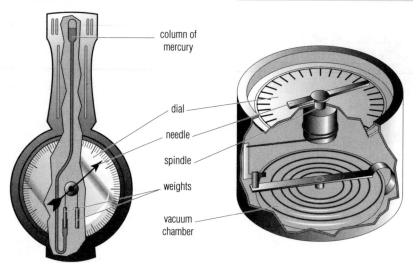

column of mercury

dial

needle

spindle

weights

vacuum chamber

mercury barometer

aneroid barometer

barometer The mercury barometer (left) and the aneroid barometer (right). In the mercury barometer, the weight of the column of mercury is balanced by the pressure of the atmosphere on the lower end. A change in height of the column indicates a change in atmospheric pressure. In the aneroid barometer, any change of atmospheric pressure causes the metal box which contains the vacuum to be squeezed or to expand slightly. The movements of the box sides are transferred to a pointer and scale via a chain of levers.

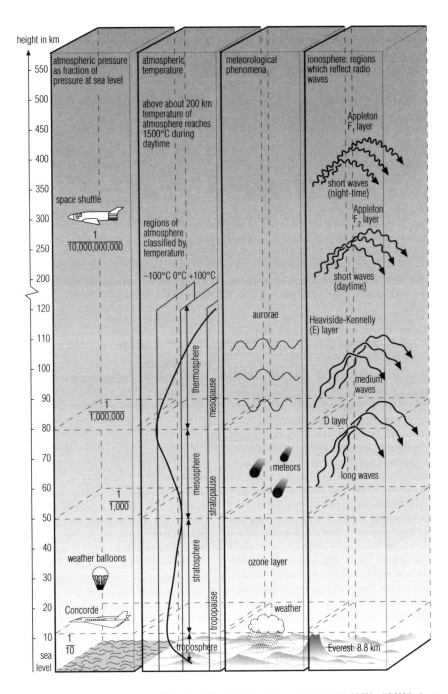

atmosphere All but 1% of the Earth's atmosphere lies in a layer 30 km/19 mi above the ground. At a height of 5,500 m/18,000 ft, air pressure is half that at sea level. The temperature of the atmosphere varies greatly with height; this produces a series of layers, called the troposphere, stratosphere, mesosphere, and thermosphere.

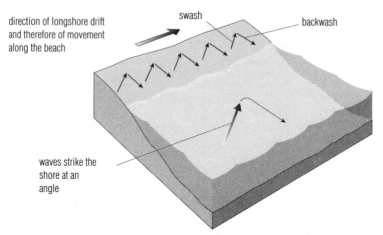

direction of longshore drift
and therefore of movement
along the beach

swash

backwash

waves strike the
shore at an
angle

beach Waves sometimes hit the beach at an angle. The incoming waves (swash) carry sand and shingle up onto the shore and the outgoing wave takes some material away with it. Gradually material is carried down the shoreline in the same direction as the longshore current. This is known as longshore drift.

bathyal zone upper part of the ocean, which lies on the continental shelf at a depth of between 200 m/650 ft and 2,000 m/6,500 ft.

beach strip of land bordering the sea, normally consisting of boulders and pebbles on exposed coasts or sand on sheltered coasts. It is usually defined by the high- and low-water marks. A berm, a ridge of sand and pebbles, may be found at the farthest point that the water reaches.

The unconsolidated material of the beach consists of a rocky debris eroded from exposed rocks and headlands by the processes of coastal erosion, or material carried in by rivers. The material is transported to the beach, and along the beach, by longshore drift. Incoming waves (swash) hit the beach at an angle and carry sand onto the beach. Outgoing waves (backwash) draw back at right angles to the beach carrying sand with them. This zigzag pattern results in a net movement of the material in one particular direction along the coast.

When the energy of the waves decreases due to interaction with currents or changes in the coastline, more sand is deposited than is transported, building up to create depositional features such as spits, bars, and **tombolos.**

Attempts often are made to artificially halt longshore drift and increase deposition on a beach by erecting barriers (groynes) at right angles to the beach. These barriers cause sand to build up on their upstream side but deplete the beach on the downstream side, causing beach erosion. The finer sand can be moved about by the wind, forming sand dunes.

Beaufort scale system of recording wind velocity (speed), devised by Francis Beaufort in 1806. It is a numerical scale ranging from 0 to 17, calm being indicated by 0 and a hurricane by 12; 13–17 indicate degrees of hurricane force. In 1874 the scale received international recognition; it was modified in 1926. Measurements are made at 10 m/33 ft above ground level.

climate see **climate** feature.

cloud water vapour condensed into minute water particles that float in masses in the atmosphere. Clouds, like fogs or mists, which occur at lower levels, are formed by the cooling of air containing water vapour, which generally condenses around tiny dust particles.

Coriolis effect the effect of the Earth's rotation on the atmosphere and on all objects on the Earth's surface. In the northern hemisphere it causes moving objects and currents to be deflected to the right; in the southern hemisphere it causes deflection to the left. The effect is named after its discoverer, French mathematician Gaspard de Coriolis (1792–1843).

current flow of a body of water or air, or of heat, moving in a definite direction. Ocean currents are fast-flowing currents of sea water generated by the wind or by variations in water density between two areas. They are partly responsible for transferring heat from the Equator to the poles and thereby evening out the global heat imbalance.

Beaufort Scale

The Beaufort scale is a system of recording wind velocity (speed).

Number and description	Features	Air speed	
		kph	mph
0 calm	smoke rises vertically; water smooth	0–2	0–1
1 light air	smoke shows wind direction; water ruffled	2–5	1–3
2 light breeze	leaves rustle; wind felt on face	6–11	4–7
3 gentle breeze	loose paper blows around	12–19	8–12
4 moderate breeze	branches sway	20–29	13–18
5 fresh breeze	small trees sway, leaves blown off	30–39	19–24
6 strong breeze	whistling in telephone wires; sea spray from waves	40–50	25–31
7 near gale	large trees sway	51–61	32–38
8 gale	twigs break from trees	62–74	39–46
9 strong gale	branches break from trees	75–87	47–54
10 storm	trees uprooted; weak buildings collapse	88–101	55–63
11 violent storm	widespread damage	102–117	64–73
12 hurricane	widespread structural damage	above 118	above 74

There are three basic types of ocean current: **drift currents** are broad and slow-moving; **stream currents,** such as the Gulf Stream, are narrow and swift-moving; and **upwelling currents,** such as the Peru (Humboldt) current, bring cold, nutrient-rich water from the ocean bottom.

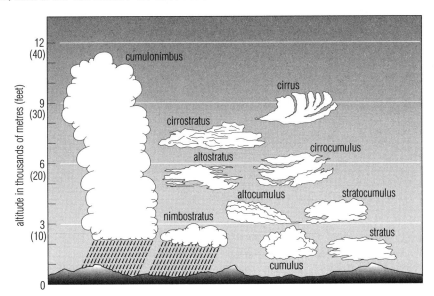

cloud Standard types of cloud. The height and nature of a cloud can be deduced from its name. Cirrus clouds are at high levels and have a wispy appearance. Stratus clouds form at low level and are layered. Middle-level clouds have names beginning with 'alto'. Cumulus clouds, ball or cottonwool clouds, occur over a range of height.

What is climate?

Climate is combination of weather conditions at a particular place over a period of time – usually a minimum of 30 years. A classification of climate encompasses the averages, extremes, and frequencies of all meteorological elements such as temperature, atmospheric pressure, precipitation, wind, humidity, and sunshine, together with the factors that influence them. The primary factors involved are: the Earth's rotation and latitudinal effects; ocean currents; large-scale movements of wind belts and air masses over the Earth's surface; temperature differences between land and sea surfaces; and topography.

climatology The scientific study of climate, includes the construction of computer-generated models, and considers not only present-day climates, their effects and their classification, but also long-term climate changes, covering both past climates (palaeoclimates) and future predictions. Climatologists are especially concerned with the influence of human activity on climate change, among the most important of which, at both a local and global level, are those currently linked with ozone depleters and the greenhouse effect.

climate classification The word climate comes from the Greek *klima*, meaning an inclination or slope (referring to the angle of the Sun's rays, and thus latitude) and the earliest known classification of climate was that of the ancient Greeks, who based their system on latitudes. In recent times, many different systems of classifying climate have been devised, most of which follow that formulated by the German climatologist Wladimir Köppen (1846–1940) in 1900. These systems use vegetation-based classifications such as desert, tundra, and rainforest. Classification by air mass is used in conjunction with this method. This idea was first introduced in 1928 by the Norwegian meteorologist Tor Bergeron, and links the climate of an area with the movement of the air masses it experiences.

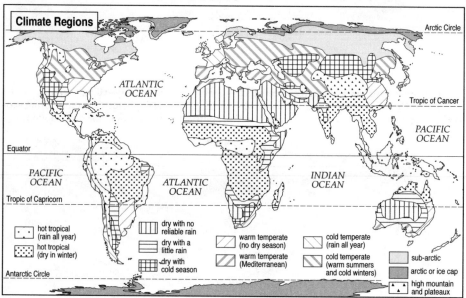

climate The world's climatic zones. There are many systems of classifying climate. One system, that of Wladimir Köppen, was based on temperature and plant type. Other systems take into account the distribution of global winds.

cyclone alternative name for a depression, an area of low atmospheric pressure. A severe cyclone that forms in the tropics is called a tropical cyclone or hurricane.

depression or **cyclone** or **low** region of low atmospheric pressure. In mid latitudes a depres-

sion forms as warm, moist air from the tropics mixes with cold, dry polar air, producing warm and cold boundaries (fronts) and unstable weather – low cloud and drizzle, showers, or fierce storms. The warm air, being less dense, rises above the cold air to produce the area of low pressure on the ground. Air spirals in towards the centre of the depression in an anticlockwise direction in the northern hemisphere, clockwise in the southern hemisphere, generating winds up to gale force. Depressions tend to travel eastwards and can remain active for several days.

doldrums area of low atmospheric pressure along the Equator, in the intertropical convergence zone where the northeast and southeast trade winds converge. The doldrums are characterized by calm or very light winds, during which there may be sudden squalls and stormy weather. For this reason the areas are avoided as far as possible by sailing ships.

exosphere the uppermost layer of the atmosphere. It is an ill-defined zone above the thermosphere, beginning at about 700 km/435 mi and fading off into the vacuum of space. The gases are extremely thin, with hydrogen as the main constituent.

fog cloud that collects at the surface of the Earth, composed of water vapour that has condensed on particles of dust in the atmosphere. Cloud and fog are both caused by the air temperature falling below dew point. The thickness of fog depends on the number of water particles it contains. Officially, fog refers to a condition when visibility is reduced to 1 km/0.6 mi or less, and mist or haze to that giving a visibility of 1–2 km or about 1 mi.

There are two types of fog. An **advection fog** is formed by the meeting of two currents of air, one cooler than the other, or by warm air flowing over a cold surface. Sea fogs commonly occur where warm and cold currents meet and the air above them mixes. A **radiation fog** forms on clear, calm nights when the land surface loses

heat rapidly (by radiation); the air above is cooled to below its dew point and condensation takes place. A **mist** is produced by condensed water particles, and a haze by smoke or dust.

In drought areas, for example, Baja California, Canary Islands, Cape Verde Islands, Namib Desert, Peru, and Chile, coastal fogs enable plant and animal life to survive without rain and are a potential source of water for human use (by means of water collectors exploiting the effect of condensation).

front the boundary between two air masses of different temperature or humidity. A **cold front** marks the line of advance of a cold air mass from below, as it displaces a warm air mass; a **warm front** marks the advance of a warm air mass as it rises up over a cold one. Frontal systems define the weather of the mid-latitudes, where warm tropical air is constantly meeting cold air from the poles.

Warm air, being lighter, tends to rise above the cold; its moisture is carried upwards and usually falls as rain or snow, hence the changeable weather conditions at fronts. Fronts are rarely stable and move with the air mass. An **occluded front** is a composite form, where a cold front catches up with a warm front and merges with it.

frost condition of the weather that occurs when the air temperature is below freezing, 0°C/32°F. Water in the atmosphere is deposited as ice crystals on the ground or exposed objects. As cold air is heavier than warm, ground frost is more common than hoar frost, which is formed by the condensation of water particles in the same way that dew collects.

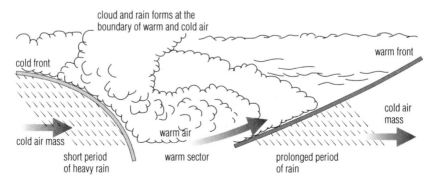

front The boundaries between two air masses of different temperature and humidity. A warm front is when warm air displaces cold air, if cold air replaces warm air, it is a cold front.

greenhouse effect phenomenon of the Earth's atmosphere by which solar radiation, trapped by the Earth and re-emitted from the surface as infrared radiation, is prevented from escaping by various gases in the air. Greenhouse gases trap heat because they readily absorb infrared radiation. The result is a rise in the Earth's temperature (global warming). The main greenhouse gases are carbon dioxide, methane, and chlorofluorocarbons (CFCs) as well as water vapour. Fossil-fuel consumption and forest fires are the principal causes of carbon dioxide build-up; methane is a by-product of agriculture (rice, cattle, sheep).

The United Nations Environment Programme estimates that by 2025, average world temperatures will have risen by 1.5°C/2.7°F with a consequent rise of 20 cm/7.9 in in sea level. Low-lying areas and entire countries would be threatened by flooding and crops would be affected by the change in climate. However, predictions about global warming and its possible climatic effects are tentative and often conflict with each other.

gyre circular surface rotation of ocean water in each major sea (a type of current). Gyres are large and permanent, and occupy the northern and southern halves of the three major oceans. Their movements are dictated by the prevailing winds and the Coriolis effect. Gyres move clockwise in the northern hemisphere and anticlockwise in the southern hemisphere.

hail precipitation in the form of pellets of ice (hailstones). It is caused by the circulation of moisture in strong convection currents, usually within cumulonimbus clouds. Water droplets freeze as they are carried upwards. As the circulation continues, layers of ice are deposited around the droplets until they become too heavy to be supported by the currents and they fall as a hailstorm.

> **Hailstones can kill**
> ■ In the Gopalganji region of Bangladesh in 1988, 92 people died after being hit by huge hailstones weighing up to 1 kg/2.2 lb.

hurricane or **tropical cyclone** or **typhoon** severe depression (region of very low atmospheric pressure) in tropical regions, called **typhoon** in the North Pacific. It is a revolving storm originating at latitudes between 5° and 20° N or S of the Equator, when the surface temperature of the ocean is above 27°C/80°F. A central calm area,

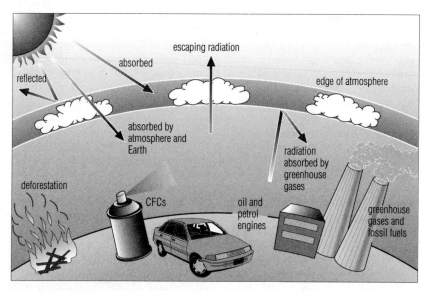

greenhouse effect The warming effect of the Earth's atmosphere is called the greenhouse effect. Radiation from the Sun enters the atmosphere but is prevented from escaping back into space by gases such as carbon dioxide (produced for example, by the burning of fossil fuels), nitrogen oxides (from car exhausts), and CFCs (from aerosols and refrigerators). As these gases build up in the atmosphere, the Earth's average temperature is expected to rise.

Hurricanes: Worst of the 20th Century

Year	Date	Location	Deaths
1900	Aug–Sept	Galveston, Texas	6,000
1926	20 Oct	Cuba	600
1928	6–20 Sept	Southern Florida	1,836
1930	3 Sept	Dominican Republic	2,000
1938	21 Sept	Long Island, New York, New England	600
1942	15–16 Oct	Bengal, India	40,000
1963	4–8 Oct	(Flora) Caribbean	6,000
1974	19–20 Sept	(Fifi) Honduras	2,000
1979	30 Aug–7 Sept	(David) Caribbean, eastern USA	1,100
1989	16–22 Sept	(Hugo) Caribbean	504

called the eye, is surrounded by inwardly spiralling winds (anticlockwise in the northern hemisphere) of up to 320 kph/200 mph. A hurricane is accompanied by lightning and torrential rain, and can cause extensive damage. In meteorology, a hurricane is a wind of force 12 or more on the Beaufort scale.

hydrological cycle alternative name for the water cycle, by which water is circulated between the Earth's surface and its atmosphere. It is a complex system involving a number of physical processes (such as evaporation, precipitation, and throughflow) and stores (such as rivers, oceans, and soil).

isobar line drawn on maps and weather charts linking all places with the same atmospheric pressure (usually measured in millibars). When used in weather forecasting, the distance between the isobars is an indication of the barometric gradient (the rate of change in pressure). Where the isobars are close together, cyclonic weather is indicated, bringing strong winds and a depression, and where far apart anticyclonic, bringing calmer, settled conditions.

jet stream narrow band of very fast wind (velocities of over 150 kph/95 mph) found at altitudes of 10–16 km/6–10 mi in the upper troposphere or lower stratosphere. Jet streams usually occur about the latitudes of the Westerlies (35°–60°).

lagoon coastal body of shallow salt water, usually with limited access to the sea. The term is normally used to describe the shallow sea area cut off by a coral reef or barrier islands.

lightning high-voltage electrical discharge between two charged rainclouds or between a

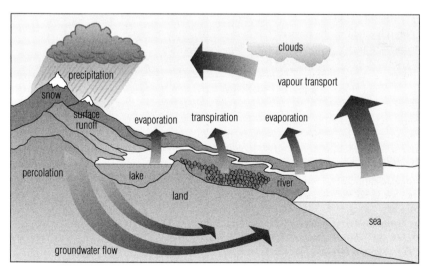

hydrological cycle About one-third of the solar energy reaching the Earth is used in evaporating water. About 380,000 cubic km/95,000 cubic mi is evaporated each year. The entire contents of the oceans would take about one million years to pass through the water cycle.

cloud and the Earth, caused by the build-up of electrical charges. Air in the path of lightning ionizes (becomes conducting), and expands; the accompanying noise is heard as thunder. Currents of 20,000 amperes and temperatures of 30,000°C/54,000°F are common. Lightning causes nitrogen oxides to form in the atmosphere and approximately 25% of the atmospheric nitrogen oxides are formed in this way.

magnetic storm sudden disturbance affecting the Earth's magnetic field, causing anomalies in radio transmissions and magnetic compasses. It is probably caused by sunspot activity.

Mariana Trench lowest region on the Earth's surface; the deepest part of the sea floor. The trench is 2,400 km/1,500 mi long and is situated 300 km/200 mi east of the Mariana Islands, in the northwestern Pacific Ocean. Its deepest part is the gorge known as the Challenger Deep, which extends 11,034 m/36,201 ft below sea level.

Under pressure in the Mariana Trench
■ A column of 10,000 tonnes of sea water presses down on every square metre of the ocean floor in the Mariana Trench.

Mediterranean climate climate characterized by hot dry summers and warm wet winters. Mediterranean zones are situated in either hemisphere on the western side of continents, between latitudes of 30° and 60°. During the winter rain is brought by the Westerlies; in summer Mediterranean zones are under the influence of the trade winds. The regions bordering the Mediterranean Sea, California, central Chile, the Cape of Good Hope, and parts of southern Australia have such climates.

mesosphere layer in the Earth's atmosphere above the stratosphere and below the thermosphere. It lies between about 50 km/31 mi and 80 km/50 mi above the ground.

meteorology scientific observation and study of the atmosphere, so that weather can be accurately forecast.

Data from meteorological stations and weather satellites are collated by computer at central agencies, and forecast and weather maps based on current readings are issued at regular intervals. Modern analysis, employing some of the most powerful computers, can give useful

---

Bolts from the blue
■ There are an estimated 8 million bolts of lightning worldwide every day.

---

forecasts for up to six days ahead.

At meteorological stations readings are taken of the factors determining weather conditions: atmospheric pressure, temperature, humidity, wind (using the Beaufort scale), cloud cover (measuring both type of cloud and coverage), and precipitation such as rain, snow, and hail (measured at 12-hour intervals). Satellites are used either to relay information transmitted from the Earth-based stations, or to send pictures of cloud development, indicating wind patterns, and snow and ice cover.

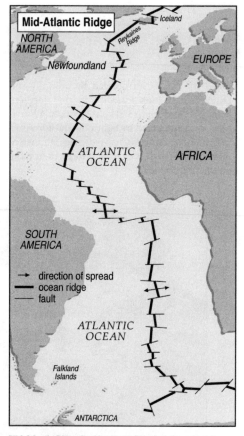

Mid-Atlantic Ridge The Mid-Atlantic Ridge is the boundary between the crustal plates that form America, and Europe and Africa. An oceanic ridge cannot be curved since the material welling up to form the ridge flows at a right angle to the ridge. The ridge takes the shape of small straight sections offset by fractures transverse to the main ridge.

Mid-Atlantic Ridge ocean ridge, formed by the movement of plates described by plate tectonics, that runs along the centre of the Atlantic Ocean, parallel to its edges, for some 14,000 km/8,800 mi – almost from the Arctic to the Antarctic.

The Mid-Atlantic Ridge is central because the ocean crust beneath the Atlantic Ocean has continually grown outwards from the ridge at a steady rate during the past 200 million years. Iceland straddles the ridge and was formed by volcanic outpourings.

monsoon wind pattern that brings seasonally heavy rain to South Asia; it blows towards the sea in winter and towards the land in summer. The monsoon may cause destructive flooding all over India and Southeast Asia from April to September, leaving thousands of people homeless each year.

The monsoon cycle is believed to have started about 12 million years ago with the uplift of the Himalayas.

ocean great mass of salt water. Strictly speaking three oceans exist – the Atlantic, Indian, and Pacific – to which the Arctic is often added. They cover approximately 70% or 363,000,000 sq km/ 140,000,000 sq mi of the total surface area of the Earth. Water levels recorded in the world's oceans have shown an increase of 10–15 cm/4–6 in over the past 100 years.

depth (average) 3,660 m/12,000 ft, but shallow ledges (continental shelves) 180 m/600 ft run out from the continents, beyond which the continental slope reaches down to the abyssal zone, the largest area, ranging from 2,000–6,000 m/ 6,500–19,500 ft. Only the deep-sea trenches go deeper, the deepest recorded being 11,034 m/ 36,201 ft (by the *Vityaz*, USSR) in the Mariana Trench of the western Pacific in 1957

features deep trenches (off eastern and southeast Asia, and western South America), volcanic belts (in the western Pacific and eastern Indian Ocean), and ocean ridges (in the mid-Atlantic, eastern Pacific, and Indian Ocean)

temperature varies on the surface with latitude (–2°C to +29°C); decreases rapidly to 370 m/ 1,200 ft, then more slowly to 2,200 m/7,200 ft; and hardly at all beyond that

water contents salinity averages about 3%; minerals commercially extracted include bromine, magnesium, potassium, salt; those potentially recoverable include aluminium, calcium, copper, gold, manganese, silver.

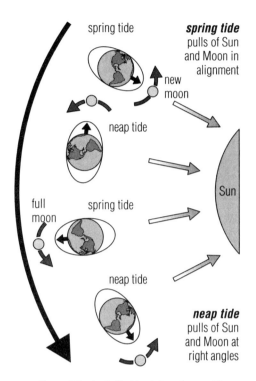

ocean The gravitational pull of the Moon is the main cause of the tides. Water on the side of the Earth nearest the Moon feels the Moon's pull and accumulates directly under the Moon. When the Sun and the Moon are in line, at new and full moon, the gravitational pull of Sun and Moon are in line and produce a high spring tide. When the Sun and Moon are at right angles, lower neap tides occur.

ocean current fast-flowing current of seawater generated by the wind or by variations in water density between two areas. Ocean currents are partly responsible for transferring heat from the Equator to the poles and thereby evening out the global heat imbalance.

ocean ridge mountain range on the seabed indicating the presence of a constructive plate margin (where tectonic plates are moving apart and magma rises to the surface;). Ocean ridges, such as the Mid-Atlantic Ridge, consist of many segments offset along transform faults, and can rise thousands of metres above the surrounding seabed.

Ocean ridges usually have a rift valley along their crests, indicating where the flanks are being pulled apart by the growth of the plates of the lithosphere beneath. The crests are generally free of sediment; increasing depths of sediment are found with increasing distance down the flanks.

Major Oceans and Seas in the World

Ocean/sea	Area[1]		Average depth	
	sq km	sq mi	m	ft
Pacific Ocean	166,242,000	64,186,000	3,939	12,925
Atlantic Ocean	86,557,000	33,420,000	3,575	11,730
Indian Ocean	73,429,000	28,351,000	3,840	12,598
Arctic Ocean	13,224,000	5,106,000	1,038	3,407
South China Sea	2,975,000	1,149,000	1,464	4,802
Caribbean Sea	2,754,000	1,063,000	2,575	8,448
Mediterranean Sea	2,510,000	969,000	1,501	4,926
Bering Sea	2,261,000	873,000	1,491	4,893
Sea of Okhotsk	1,580,000	610,000	973	3,192
Gulf of Mexico	1,544,000	596,000	1,614	5,297
Sea of Japan	1,013,000	391,000	1,667	5,468
Hudson Bay	730,000	282,000	93	305
East China Sea	665,000	257,000	189	620
Andaman Sea	565,000	218,000	1,118	3,667
Black Sea	461,000	178,000	1,190	3,906
Red Sea	453,000	175,000	538	1,764
North Sea	427,000	165,000	94	308
Baltic Sea	422,000	163,000	55	180
Yellow Sea	294,000	114,000	37	121
Persian Gulf	230,000	89,000	100	328
Gulf of California	153,000	59,000	724	2,375
English Channel	90,000	35,000	54	177
Irish Sea	89,000	34,000	60	197

[1] All figures are approximate, as boundaries of oceans and seas cannot be exactly determined.

ocean trench deep trench in the seabed indicating the presence of a destructive margin (produced by the movements of plate tectonics). The subduction or dragging downwards of one plate of the lithosphere beneath another means that the ocean floor is pulled down. Ocean trenches are found around the edge of the Pacific Ocean and the northeastern Indian Ocean; minor ones occur in the Caribbean and near the Falkland Islands.

Ocean trenches represent the deepest parts of the ocean floor, the deepest being the Mariana Trench which has a depth of 11,034 m/36,201 ft. At depths of below 6 km/3.6 mi there is no light and very high pressure; ocean trenches are inhabited by crustaceans, coelenterates (for example, sea anemones), polychaetes (a type of worm), molluscs, and echinoderms.

rain form of precipitation in which separate drops of water fall to the Earth's surface from clouds. The drops are formed by the accumulation of fine droplets that condense from water vapour in the air. The condensation is usually brought about by rising and subsequent cooling of air.

Rain can form in three main ways – frontal (or cyclonic) rainfall, orographic (or relief) rainfall, and convectional rainfall. **Frontal rainfall** takes place at the boundary, or front, between a mass of warm air from the tropics and a mass of cold air from the poles. The water vapour in the warm air is chilled and condenses to form clouds and rain.

Orographic rainfall occurs when an airstream is forced to rise over a mountain range. The air becomes cooled and precipitation takes place. **Convectional rainfall,** associated with hot climates, is brought about by rising and abrupt cooling of air that has been warmed by the extreme heat of the ground surface. The water vapour carried by the air condenses and so rain falls heavily. Convectional rainfall is usually accompanied by a thunderstorm, and it can be intensified over urban areas due to higher temperatures.

seafloor spreading growth of the ocean crust outwards (sideways) from ocean ridges. The concept of seafloor spreading has been combined with that of continental drift and incorporated into plate tectonics.

Seafloor spreading was proposed 1960 by US geologist Harry Hess (1906–1969), based on his observations of ocean ridges and the relative youth of all ocean beds. In 1963, British geophysicists Fred Vine and Drummond Matthews observed that the floor of the Atlantic Ocean was made up of rocks that could be arranged in strips, each strip being magnetized either normally or reversely (due to changes in the Earth's polarity when the North Pole becomes the South Pole and vice versa, termed polar reversal). These strips were parallel and formed identical patterns on both sides of the ocean ridge. The implication was that each strip was formed at some stage in geological time when the magnetic field was polarized in a certain way. The seafloor magnetic-reversal patterns could be matched to dated magnetic reversals found in terrestrial rock. It could be shown that new rock forms continuously and spreads away from the ocean ridges, with the oldest rock located

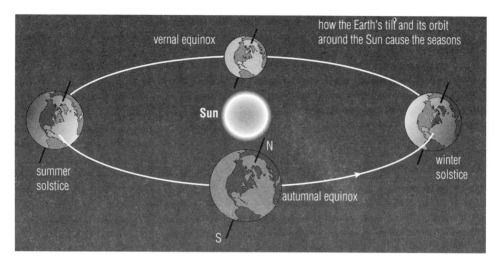

how the Earth's tilt and its orbit around the Sun cause the seasons

vernal equinox

Sun

N

summer solstice

winter solstice

autumnal equinox

S

season The cause of the seasons. As the Earth orbits the Sun, its axis of rotation always points in the same direction. This means that, during the northern hemisphere summer solstice (21 June), the Sun is overhead in the northern hemisphere. At the northern hemisphere winter solstice (22 December), the Sun is overhead in the southern hemisphere.

farthest away from the midline. The observation was made independently 1963 by Canadian geologist Lawrence Morley, studying an ocean ridge in the Pacific near Vancouver Island.

season period of the year having a characteristic climate.

snow precipitation in the form of soft, white, crystalline flakes caused by the condensation in air of excess water vapour below freezing point. Light reflecting in the crystals, which have a basic hexagonal (six-sided) geometry, gives snow its white appearance.

thunderstorm severe storm of very heavy rain, thunder, and lightning. Thunderstorms are usually caused by the intense heating of the ground surface during summer. The warm air rises rapidly to form tall cumulonimbus clouds with a characteristic anvil-shaped top. Electrical charges accumulate in the clouds and are discharged to the ground as flashes of lightning. Air in the path of lightning becomes heated and

expands rapidly, creating shock waves that are heard as a crash or rumble of thunder.

The rough distance between an observer and a lightning flash can be calculated by timing the number of seconds between the flash and the thunder. A gap of three seconds represents about a kilometre; five seconds represents about a mile.

tornado extremely violent revolving storm with swirling, funnel-shaped clouds, caused by a rising column of warm air propelled by strong wind. A tornado can rise to a great height, but with a diameter of only a few hundred metres or less. Tornadoes move with wind speeds of 160–480 kph/100–300 mph, destroying everything in their path. They are common in central USA and Australia.

tsunami ocean wave generated by vertical movements of the sea floor resulting from earthquakes or volcanic activity. Unlike waves generated by surface winds, the entire depth of water is involved in the wave motion. In the open ocean the tsunami takes the form of several successive waves, rarely in excess of 1 m/3 ft in height but travelling at speeds of 650–800 kph/400–500 mph. In the coastal shallows tsunamis slow down and build up producing huge swells over 15 m/45 ft high in some

---

Thunderstorms worldwide

■ There are an estimated 44,000 thunderstorms worldwide every day.

Major Floods and Tsunamis of the 20th Century

Year	Location	Number of deaths
1918	Kuril Islands/Russia/Japan/Hawaii	23
1923	Kamchatka/Hawaii	3
1944	Japan	998
1946	Japan	1,997
	Aleutian Islands/Hawaii/California	159
1952	Kamchatka/Kuril Islands/Hawaii	many
1960	Chile/Hawaii/Japan	5,000
1964	Alaska/Aleutian Islands/California	122
1976	Philippines	5,000
1979	Indonesia	539
1983	Japan/South Korea	107
1990	Bangladesh	370

cases and over 30 m/90 ft in rare instances. The waves sweep inland causing great loss of life and property.

weather day-to-day variation of atmospheric and climatic conditions at any one place over a short period of time. Such conditions include humidity, precipitation, temperature, cloud cover, visibility, and wind, together with extreme phenomena such as storms and blizzards. Weather differs from climate in that the latter is a composite of the average weather conditions of a locality or region over a long period of time (at least 30 years). Meteorology is the study of short-term weather patterns and data within a circumscribed area; climatology is the study of weather over longer timescales on a zonal or global basis.

weathering process by which exposed rocks are broken down on the spot by the action of rain, frost, wind, and other elements of the weather. It differs from erosion in that no movement or transportation of the broken-down material takes place. Two types of weathering are recognized: physical (or mechanical) and chemical. They usually occur together.

wind the lateral movement of the Earth's atmosphere from high-pressure areas (anticyclones) to low-pressure areas (depression). Its speed is measured using an anemometer or by studying its effects on, for example, trees by using the Beaufort scale. Although modified by features such as land and water, there is a basic worldwide system of trade winds, westerlies, and polar easterlies.

A belt of low pressure (the doldrums) lies along the Equator. The trade winds blow towards this from the horse latitudes (areas of high pressure at about 30° N and 30° S of the Equator), blowing from the northeast in the northern hemisphere, and from the southeast in the southern. The Westerlies (also from the horse latitudes) blow north of the Equator from the southwest and south of the Equator from the northwest.

Cold winds blow outwards from high-pressure areas at the poles. More local effects result from landmasses heating and cooling faster than the adjacent sea, producing onshore winds in the daytime and offshore winds at night.

The monsoon is a seasonal wind of southern Asia, blowing from the southwest in summer and bringing the rain on which crops depend. It blows from the northeast in winter.

Famous or notorious warm winds include the **chinook** of the eastern Rocky Mountains, North America; the **föhn** of Europe's Alpine valleys; the **sirocco** (Italy)/**khamsin** (Egypt)/

Weathering

physical weathering

temperature changes	weakening rocks by expansion and contraction
frost	wedging rocks apart by the expansion of water on freezing
unloading	the loosening of rock layers by release of pressure after the erosion and removal of those layers above

chemical weathering

carbonation	the breakdown of calcite by reaction with carbonic acid in rainwater
hydrolysis	the breakdown of feldspar into china clay by reaction with carbonic acid in rainwater
oxidation	the breakdown of iron-rich minerals due to rusting
hydration	the expansion of certain minerals due to the uptake of water

sharav (Israel), spring winds that bring warm air from the Sahara and Arabian deserts across the Mediterranean; and the **Santa Ana,** a periodic warm wind from the inland deserts that strikes the California coast. The dry northerly **bise** (Switzerland) and the **mistral,** which strikes the Mediterranean area of France, are unpleasantly cold winds.

Rocks and Minerals

agate cryptocrystalline (with crystals too small to be seen with an optical microscope) silica, SiO_2, composed of cloudy and banded chalcedony, sometimes mixed with opal, that forms in rock cavities.

amethyst variety of quartz, SiO_2, coloured violet by the presence of small quantities of impurities such as manganese or iron; used as a semiprecious stone. Amethysts are found chiefly in the Ural Mountains, India, the USA, Uruguay, and Brazil.

anthracite hard, dense, shiny variety of coal, containing over 90% carbon and a low percentage of ash and impurities, which causes it to burn without flame, smoke, or smell. Because of its purity, anthracite gives off relatively little sulphur dioxide when burnt. Anthracite gives intense heat, but is slow-burning and slow to light; it is therefore unsuitable for use in open fires. Its characteristic composition is thought to be due to the action of bacteria in disintegrating the coal-forming material when it was laid down during the Carboniferous period. Among the chief sources of anthracite coal are Pennsylvania in the USA; South Wales, UK; the Donbas, Ukraine and Russia; and Shanxi province, China.

apatite common calcium phosphate mineral, $Ca_5(PO_4)_3(F,OH,Cl)$. Apatite has a hexagonal structure and occurs widely in igneous rocks, such as pegmatite, and in contact metamorphic rocks, such as marbles. It is used in the manufacture of fertilizer and as a source of phosphorus.

Carbonate hydroxylapatite, $Ca_5(PO_4,CO_3)_3$ $(OH)_2$, is the chief constituent of tooth enamel and, together with other related phosphate minerals, is the inorganic constituent of bone.

aquamarine blue variety of the mineral beryl. A semiprecious gemstone, it is used in jewellery.

basalt see **Basalt throughout the Solar System** feature.

bauxite principal ore of aluminium, consisting of a mixture of hydrated aluminium oxides and hydroxides, generally contaminated with compounds of iron, which give it a red colour. It is formed by the chemical weathering of rocks in tropical climates. Chief producers of bauxite are Australia, Guinea, Jamaica, Russia, Kazakhstan, Suriname, and Brazil.

bitumen impure mixture of hydrocarbons, including such deposits as petroleum, asphalt, and natural gas, although sometimes the term is restricted to a soft kind of pitch resembling asphalt.

Solid bitumen may have arisen as a residue from the evaporation of petroleum. If evaporation took place from a pool or lake of petroleum, the residue might form a pitch or asphalt lake, such as Pitch Lake in Trinidad.

chalcedony form of the mineral quartz, SiO_2, in which the crystals are so fine-grained that they are impossible to distinguish with a microscope (cryptocrystalline). Agate, onyx, and carnelian are gem varieties of chalcedony.

chalk soft, fine-grained, whitish sedimentary rock composed of calcium carbonate, $CaCO_3$,

Basalt throughout the Solar System

Basalt is the commonest volcanic igneous rock in the Solar System. Much of the surfaces of the terrestrial planets Mercury, Venus, Earth, and Mars, as well as the Moon, are composed of basalt. Earth's ocean floor is virtually entirely made of basalt. Basalt is mafic, that is, it contains relatively little silica: about 50% by weight. It is usually dark grey but can also be green, brown, or black. Its essential constituent minerals are calcium-rich feldspar and calcium- and magnesium-rich pyroxene.

The groundmass may be glassy or finely crystalline, sometimes with large crystals embedded. Basaltic lava tends to be runny and flows for great distances before solidifying. Successive eruptions of basalt have formed the great plateaus of Colorado and the Deccan plateau region of southwest India. In some places, such as Fingal's Cave in the Inner Hebrides of Scotland and the Giant's Causeway in Antrim, Northern Ireland, shrinkage during the solidification of the molten lava caused the formation of hexagonal columns.

The dark-coloured lowland mare regions of the Moon are underlain by basalt. Lunar mare basalts have higher concentrations of titanium and zirconium and lower concentrations of volatile elements like potassium and sodium relative to terrestrial basalts. Martian basalts are characterized by low ratios of iron to manganese relative to terrestrial basalts, as judged from some martian meteorites (shergottites, a class of the **SNC** meteorites) and spacecraft analyses of rocks and soils on the Martian surface.

extensively quarried for use in cement, lime, and mortar, and in the manufacture of cosmetics and toothpaste. **Blackboard chalk** in fact consists of gypsum (calcium sulphate, $CaSO_4.2H_2O$). It is composed chiefly of coccolithophores, unicellular lime-secreting algae, and hence primarily of plant origin. It is formed from deposits of deep-sea sediments called oozes.

cinnabar mercuric sulphide mineral, HgS, the only commercially useful ore of mercury. It is deposited in veins and impregnations near recent volcanic rocks and hot springs. The mineral itself is used as a red pigment, commonly known as **vermilion.** Cinnabar is found in the USA (California), Spain (Almadén), Peru, Italy, and Slovenia.

clay very fine-grained sedimentary deposit that has undergone a greater or lesser degree of consolidation. When moistened it is plastic, and it hardens on heating, which renders it impermeable. It may be white, grey, red, yellow, blue, or black, depending on its composition. Clay minerals consist largely of hydrous silicates of aluminium and magnesium together with iron, potassium, sodium, and organic substances. The crystals of clay minerals have a layered structure, capable of holding water, and are responsible for its plastic properties. According to international classification, in mechanical analysis of soil, clay has a grain size of less than 0.002 mm/0.00008 in.

diagenesis physical and chemical changes by which a sediment becomes a sedimentary rock. The main processes involved include compaction of the grains, and the cementing of the grains together by the growth of new minerals deposited by percolating groundwater.

diamond generally colourless, transparent mineral, an allotrope of carbon. It is regarded as a precious gemstone, and is the hardest substance known. Present sources are Australia and Southern Africa. Diamonds may be found as alluvial diamonds on or close to the Earth's surface in riverbeds or dried watercourses; on the sea bottom (off southwest Africa); or, more commonly, in diamond-bearing volcanic pipes composed of 'blue ground', kimberlite or lamproite, where the original matrix has penetrated the Earth's crust from great depths. They are sorted from the residue of crushed ground by X-ray and other recovery methods.

dolomite white mineral with a rhombohedral structure, calcium magnesium carbonate $(CaMg (CO_3)_2)$. Dolomites are common in geological successions of all ages and are often formed when limestone is changed by the replacement of the mineral calcite with the mineral dolomite.

emerald a clear, green gemstone variety of the mineral beryl. It occurs naturally in Colombia, the Ural Mountains in Russia, Zimbabwe, and Australia. The green colour is caused by the presence of the element chromium in the beryl.

flint compact, hard, brittle mineral (a variety of chert), brown, black, or grey in colour, found as nodules in limestone or shale deposits. It consists of cryptocrystalline (grains too small to be visible even under a light microscope) silica, SiO_2, principally in the crystalline form of quartz. Implements fashioned from flint were widely used in prehistory.

gabbro mafic (consisting primarily of dark-coloured crystals) igneous rock formed deep in the Earth's crust. It contains pyroxene and calcium-rich feldspar, and may contain small amounts of olivine and amphibole. Its coarse crystals of dull minerals give it a speckled appearance. Gabbro is the plutonic version of basalt (that is, derived from magma that has solidified below the Earth's surface), and forms in large, slow-cooling intrusions.

garnet group of silicate minerals with the formula $X_3Y_3(SiO_4)_3$, where X is calcium, magnesium, iron, or manganese, and Y is usually aluminium or sometimes iron or chromium. Garnets are used as semiprecious gems (usually pink to deep red) and as abrasives. They occur in metamorphic rocks such as gneiss and schist.

gem mineral valuable by virtue of its durability (hardness), rarity, and beauty, cut and polished for ornamental use, or engraved. Of 120 minerals known to have been used as gemstones, only about 25 are in common use in jewellery today; of these, the diamond, emerald, ruby, and sapphire are classified as precious, and all the others semiprecious; for example, the topaz, amethyst, opal, and aquamarine.

granite coarse-grained intrusive igneous rock, typically consisting of the minerals quartz, feldspar, and biotite mica. It may be pink or grey, depending on the composition of the

granite The smooth granite domes near Ambalavo, Madagascar, that are typical of this area. *K G Preston-Mafham/Premaphotos Wildlife*

feldspar. Granites are chiefly used as building materials.

Granites often form large intrusions in the core of mountain ranges, and they are usually surrounded by zones of metamorphic rock (rock that has been altered by heat or pressure). Granite areas have characteristic moorland scenery. In exposed areas the bedrock may be weathered along joints and cracks to produce a tor, consisting of rounded blocks that appear to have been stacked upon one another.

graphite blackish-grey, laminar, crystalline form of carbon. It is used as a lubricant and as the active component of pencil lead. Graphite, like diamond and fullerene, is an allotrope of carbon. The carbon atoms are strongly bonded together in sheets, but the bonds between the sheets are weak, allowing other atoms to enter regions between the layers causing them to slide over one another. Graphite has a very high melting point (3,500°C/6,332°F), and is a good conductor of heat and electricity. It absorbs neutrons and is therefore used to moderate the chain reaction in nuclear reactors.

hematite principal ore of iron, consisting mainly of iron(III) oxide, Fe_2O_3. It occurs as **specular hematite** (dark, metallic lustre), **kidney ore** (reddish radiating fibres terminating in smooth, rounded surfaces), and a red earthy deposit.

impermeable rock rock that does not allow water to pass through it – for example, clay, shale, and slate. Unlike permeable rocks, which absorb water, impermeable rocks can support rivers. They therefore experience considerable erosion (unless, like slate, they are very hard) and commonly form lowland areas.

kaolinite white or greyish clay mineral, hydrated aluminium silicate, $Al_2Si_2O_5(OH)_4$, formed

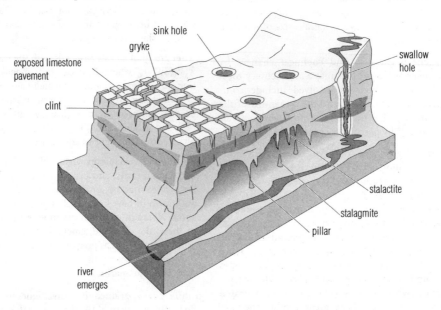

limestone The physical weathering and erosion of a limestone landscape. The freezing and thawing of rain and its mild acidic properties cause cracks and joints to enlarge, forming limestone pavements, potholes, caves and caverns.

mainly by the decomposition of feldspar in granite. It is made up of platelike crystals, the atoms of which are bonded together in two-dimensional sheets, between which the bonds are weak, so that they are able to slip over one another, a process made more easy by a layer of water. China clay (kaolin) is derived from it. It is mined in France, the UK, Germany, China, and the USA.

lapis lazuli rock containing the blue mineral lazurite in a matrix of white calcite with small amounts of other minerals. It occurs in silica-poor igneous rocks and metamorphic limestones found in Afghanistan, Siberia, Iran, and Chile. Lapis lazuli was a valuable pigment of the Middle Ages, also used as a gemstone and in inlaying and ornamental work.

limestone sedimentary rock composed chiefly of calcium carbonate $CaCO_3$, either derived from the shells of marine organisms or precipitated from solution, mostly in the ocean. Various types of limestone are used as building stone. Marble is metamorphosed limestone. Certain so-called marbles are not in fact marbles but fine-grained fossiliferous limestones that take an attractive polish. Caves commonly occur in limestone. Karst is a type of limestone landscape.

Mohs scale scale of hardness for minerals (in ascending order): 1 talc; 2 gypsum; 3 calcite; 4 fluorite; 5 apatite; 6 orthoclase; 7 quartz; 8 topaz; 9 corundum; 10 diamond.

The scale is useful in mineral identification because any mineral will scratch any other mineral lower on the scale than itself, and similarly it will be scratched by any other mineral higher on the scale.

obsidian black or dark-coloured glassy volcanic rock, chemically similar to granite, but formed by cooling rapidly on the Earth's surface at low pressure. The glassy texture is the result of rapid cooling, which inhibits the growth of crystals. Obsidian was valued by the early civilizations of Mexico for making sharp-edged tools and ceremonial sculptures.

onyx semiprecious variety of chalcedonic silica (SiO_2) in which the crystals are too fine to be detected under a microscope, a state known as cryptocrystalline. It has straight parallel bands of different colours: milk-white, black, and red. **Sardonyx**, an onyx variety, has layers of brown or red carnelian alternating with lighter layers of onyx. It can be carved into cameos.

ooze sediment of fine texture consisting mainly of organic matter found on the ocean floor at depths greater than 2,000 m/6,600 ft. Several kinds of ooze exist, each named after its constituents. **Siliceous ooze** is composed of the silica shells of tiny marine plants (diatoms) and animals (radiolarians). **Calcareous ooze** is formed from the calcite shells of microscopic animals (foraminifera) and floating algae (coccoliths).

opal form of hydrous silica $(SiO_2.nH_2O)$, often occurring as stalactites and found in many types

Mohs Scale

Number	Defining mineral	Other substances compared
1	talc	
2	gypsum	fingernail $2\frac{1}{2}$
3	calcite	copper coin $3\frac{1}{2}$
4	fluorite	
5	apatite	steel blade $5\frac{1}{2}$
6	orthoclase	glass $5\frac{3}{4}$
7	quartz	steel file 7
8	topaz	
9	corundum	
10	diamond	

note that the scale is not regular; diamond, at number 10 the hardest natural substance, is 90 times harder in absolute terms than corundum, number 9

opal Formed by silica-rich waters, opals can occur in the cavities of many rocks, and are often close to the surface. Here at the White Cliffs opal mines in Australia, the 'mines' are shallow craters. *Australian High Commission*

of rock. The common opal is translucent, milk-white, yellow, red, blue, or green, and lustrous. Precious opal is opalescent, the characteristic play of colours being caused by close-packed silica spheres diffracting light rays within the stone.

Opal is cryptocrystalline, that is, the crystals are too fine to be detected under an optical microscope. Opals are found in Hungary; New South Wales, Australia (black opals were first discovered there in 1905); and Mexico (red fire opals).

petrology branch of geology that deals with the study of rocks, their mineral compositions, and their origins.

rock constituent of the Earth's crust composed of minerals or materials of organic origin that have consolidated into hard masses as igneous, sedimentary, or metamorphic rocks. Rocks are formed from a combination (or aggregate) of minerals, and the property of a rock will depend on its components. Where deposits of economically valuable minerals occur they are termed ores. As a result of weathering, rock breaks down into very small particles that combine with organic materials from plants and animals to form soil. In geology the term 'rock' can also include unconsolidated materials such as sand, mud, clay, and peat.

---

rock

■ The oldest known rocks are found near the Great Slave and Great Bear lakes in Canada. The rocks, which include granite, are 4.03 billion years old.

---

ruby the red transparent gem variety of the mineral corundum Al_2O_3, aluminium oxide. Small amounts of chromium oxide, Cr_2O_3, substituting for aluminium oxide, give ruby its colour. Natural rubies are found mainly in Myanmar (Burma).

sand loose grains of rock, sized 0.0625–2.00 mm/0.0025–0.08 in in diameter, consisting most commonly of quartz, but owing their varying colour to mixtures of other minerals. Sand is used in cement-making, as an abrasive, in glass-making, and for other purposes. Sands are classified into marine, freshwater, glacial, and terrestrial. Some 'light' soils contain up to 50% sand. Sands may eventually consolidate into sandstone.

sandstone sedimentary rocks formed from the consolidation of sand, with sand-sized grains (0.0625–2 mm/0.0025–0.08 in) in a matrix or cement. Their principal component is quartz. Sandstones are commonly permeable and porous, and may form freshwater aquifers. They are mainly used as building materials.

Sandstones are classified according to the matrix or cement material (whether derived from clay or silt; for example, as calcareous sandstone, ferruginous sandstone, siliceous sandstone).

sapphire deep-blue, transparent gem variety of the mineral corundum Al_2O_3, aluminium oxide. Small amounts of iron and titanium give it its colour. A corundum gem of any colour except red (which is a ruby) can be called a sapphire; for example, yellow sapphire.

sediment any loose material that has 'settled' – deposited from suspension in water, ice, or air, generally as the water current or wind speed decreases. Typical sediments are, in order of increasing coarseness, clay, mud, silt, sand, gravel, pebbles, cobbles, and boulders.

silica silicon dioxide, SiO_2, the composition of the most common mineral group, of which the most familiar form is quartz. Other silica forms are chalcedony, chert, opal, tridymite, and cristobalite. Common sand consists largely of silica in the form of quartz.

Noteworthy Earth Scientists

Agassiz (Jean) Louis (Rodolphe) (1807–1873) Swiss-born US palaeontologist and geologist who developed the idea of the ice age

Beaufort Francis (1774–1857) British naval officer and hydrographer who devised the Beaufort scale of wind force

Bjerknes Vilhelm Firman Koren (1862–1951) Norwegian scientist who was a pioneer in weather forecasting

Bowen Norman Levi (1887–1956) Canadian-born US geologist who pioneered the study of petrology, particularly silicates and igneous rocks

Brongniart Alexandre (1770–1847) French naturalist and geologist who first used fossils to date the strata of rock

Crutzen Paul (1933–) Dutch meteorologist who helped explain the formation and decomposition of ozone

Cuvier Georges Léopold Chrétien Frédéric Dagobert (1769–1832) French comparative anatomist who was the founder of palaeontology

Davis William Morris (1850–1934) US geomorphologist who studied the role of rain in the process of erosion; he also studied the development of rivers

Edinger Tilly (Johanna Gabrielle Ottilie) (1897–1967) German-born US palaeontologist who pioneered research in vertebrate palaeontology

Elsasser Walter Maurice (1904–1991) German-born US geophysicist who pioneered analysis of the Earth's magnetic fields

Ewing (William) Morris (1906–1974) US marine geologist who studied mid-ocean ridges and the theory of plate tectonics

Hall James (1761–1832) Scottish geologist who was one of the founders of experimental geology

Hess Harry Hammond (1906–1969) US geologist who proposed the theory of seafloor spreading

Holmes Arthur (1890–1965) English geologist who pioneered geochronology and dating techniques; he also studied the mechanism of continental plate movement

Humboldt (Friedrich Wilhelm Heinrich) Alexander (1769–1859) German geophysicist, botanist, and geologist who is considered a founder of ecology

Hutton James (1726–1797) Scottish geologist who was the founder of geology as an academic discipline

Lyell Charles (1797–1875) Scottish geologist who contributed . to the acceptance of Charles Darwin's views on evolution

Maury Matthew Fontaine (1806–1873) US hydrographer and naval officer who was the founder of the US Naval Oceanographic Office

Mercator Gerardus (Latinized form of Gerhard Kremer) (1512–1594) Flemish map-maker who devised the first modern atlas

Murchison Roderick Impey (1792–1873) Scottish geologist who named the Silurian period and worked with Sedgwick on the identification of the Devonian system in southwest England

Powell John Wesley (1834–1902) US geologist who pioneered work on erosion and mountain formation

Richter Charles Francis (1900–1985) US seismologist who devised the Richter scale to measure earthquakes

Sedgwick Adam (1785–1873) English geologist who studied the stratigraphy of the British Isles and identified the Devonian system in southwest England

Smith William (1769–1839) English geologist who was the founder of stratigraphical geology

Vine Frederick J(ohn) (1939–1988) English geophysicist who worked on the hypothesis of seafloor spreading

Wegener Alfred Lothar (1880–1930) German meteorologist who originally proposed the theory of continental drift

Werner Abraham Gottlob (1749–1817) German geologist who was the first to develop a classification of rocks and worked on a theory of deposition

Wilson John Tuzo (1908–1993) Canadian geologist and geophysicist who developed the concept of plate tectonics

Earth Science: Chronology

1735 English lawyer George Hadley described the circulation of the atmosphere as large-scale convection currents centred on the equator.

1743 Christopher Packe produced the first geological map, of southern England.

1744 The first map produced on modern surveying principles was produced by César-François Cassini in France.

1745 In Russia, Mikhail Vasilievich Lomonosov published a catalogue of over 3,000 minerals.

1746 A French expedition to Lapland proved the Earth to be flattened at the poles.

1760 Mikhail Vasilievich Lomonosov explained the formation of icebergs. John Mitchell proposed that earthquakes are produced when one layer of rock rubs against another.

1766 The fossilized bones of a huge animal (later called *Mosasaurus*) were found in a quarry near the River Meuse, the Netherlands.

1776 James Keir suggested that some rocks, such as those making up the Giant's Causeway in Ireland, may have formed as molten material that cooled and then crystallized.

1779 French naturalist Comte George de Buffon speculated that the Earth may be much older than the 6,000 years suggested by the Bible.

1785 Scottish geologist James Hutton proposed the theory of uniformitarianism: all geological features are the result of processes that are at work today, acting over long periods of time.

1786 German–Swiss Johann von Carpentier described the European ice age.

1793 Jean Baptiste Lamarck argued that fossils are the remains of once-living animals and plants.

1794 William Smith produced the first large-scale geological maps of England.

1795 In France, Georges Cuvier identified the fossil bones discovered in the Netherlands in 1766 as being those of a reptile, now extinct.

1804 French physicists Jean Biot and Joseph Gay-Lussac studied the atmosphere from a hot-air balloon.

1809 The first geological survey of the eastern USA was produced by William Maclure.

1815 In England, William Smith showed how rock strata (layers) can be identified on the basis of the fossils found in them.

1822 Mary Ann Mantell discovered on the English coast the first fossil to be recognized as that of a dinosaur (an iguanodon). In Germany, Friedrich Mohs introduced a scale for specifying mineral hardness.

1825 Cuvier proposed his theory of catastrophes as the cause of the extinction of large groups of animals.

1830 Scottish geologist Charles Lyell published the first volume of *The Principles of Geology*, which described the Earth as being several hundred million years old.

1839 In the USA, Louis Agassiz described the motion and laying down of glaciers, confirming the reality of the ice ages.

1842 English palaeontologist Richard Owen coined the name 'dinosaur' for the reptiles, now extinct, that lived about 175 million years ago.

1846 Irish physicist William Thomson (Lord Kelvin) estimated, using the temperature of the Earth, that the Earth is 100 million years old.

1850 US naval officer Matthew Fontaine Maury mapped the Atlantic Ocean, noting that it is deeper near its edges than at the centre.

1852 Edward Sabine in Ireland showed a link between sunspot activity and changes in the Earth's magnetic field.

1853 James Coffin described the three major wind bands that girdle each hemisphere.

1854 English astronomer George Airy calculated the mass of the Earth by measuring gravity at the top and bottom of a coal mine.

1859 Edwin Drake drilled the world's first oil well at Titusville, Pennsylvania, USA.

1872 The beginning of the world's first major oceanographic expedition, the four-year voyage of the *Challenger*.

1882 Scottish physicist Balfour Stewart postulated the existence of the ionosphere (the ionized

Earth Science: Chronology (continued)

layer of the outer atmosphere) to account for differences in the Earth's magnetic field.

1884 German meteorologist Vladimir Köppen introduced a classification of the world's temperature zones.

1895 In the USA, Jeanette Picard launched the first balloon to be used for stratospheric research.

1896 Swedish chemist Svante Arrhenius discovered a link between the amount of carbon dioxide in the atmosphere and the global temperature.

1897 Norwegian-US meteorologist Jacob Bjerknes and his father Vilhelm developed the mathematical theory of weather forecasting.

1902 British physicist Oliver Heaviside and US engineer Arthur Edwin Kennelly predicted the existence of an electrified layer in the atmosphere that reflects radio waves. In France, Léon Teisserenc discovered layers of different temperatures in the atmosphere, which he called the troposphere and stratosphere.

1906 Richard Dixon Oldham proved the Earth to have a molten core by studying seismic waves.

1909 Yugoslav physicist Andrija Mohorovičić discovered a discontinuity in the Earth's crust, about 30 km/18 mi below the surface, that forms the boundary between the crust and the mantle.

1912 In Germany, Alfred Wegener proposed the theory of continental drift and the existence of a supercontinent, Pangaea, in the distant past.

1913 French physicist Charles Fabry discovered the ozone layer in the upper atmosphere.

1914 German-US geologist Beno Gutenberg discovered the discontinuity that marks the boundary between the Earth's mantle and the outer core.

1922 British meteorologist Lewis Fry Richardson developed a method of numerical weather forecasting.

1925 A German expedition discovered the Mid-Atlantic Ridge by means of sonar. Edward Appleton discovered a layer of the atmosphere that reflects radio waves; it was later named after him.

1929 By studying the magnetism of rocks, Japanese geologist Motonori Matuyama showed that the Earth's magnetic field reverses direction from time to time.

1935 US seismologist Charles Francis Richter established a scale for measuring the magnitude of earthquakes.

1936 Danish seismologist Inge Lehmann postulated the existence of a solid inner core of the Earth from the study of seismic waves.

1939 In Germany, Walter Maurice Elsasser proposed that eddy currents in the molten iron core cause the Earth's magnetism.

1950 Hungarian-US mathematician John Von Neumann made the first 24-hour weather forecast by computer.

1956 US geologists Bruce Charles Heezen and Maurice Ewing discovered a global network of oceanic ridges and rifts that divide the Earth's surface into plates.

1958 Using rockets, US physicist James Van Allen discovered a belt of radiation (later named after him) around the Earth.

1960 The world's first weather satellite, *TIROS 1*, was launched. US geologist Harry Hammond Hess showed that the sea floor spreads out from ocean ridges and descends back into the mantle at deep-sea trenches.

1963 British geophysicists Fred Vine and Drummond Matthews analyzed the magnetism of rocks in the Atlantic Ocean floor and found conclusive proof of seafloor spreading.

1985 A British expedition to the Antarctic discovered a hole in the ozone layer above the South Pole.

1991 A borehole in the Kola Peninsula in Arctic Russia, begun in the 1970s, reached a depth of 12,261 m/40,240 ft (where the temperature was found to be 210°C/410°F).

1996 US geophysicists detected a difference between the spinning time of the core and that of the rest of the Earth.

1998 The wind patterns of El Niño were shown to have slowed the Earth's rotation by 0.4 milliseconds to each day.

LIFE ON EARTH

————————✳————————

Life on Earth may have begun about 4 billion years ago when a chemical reaction produced the first organic substance. Over time, life has evolved from primitive single-celled organisms to complex multicellular ones. Almost all living organisms share certain basic characteristics, which include reproduction, growth, metabolism, movement, responsiveness, and adaptation.

Living things are greatly dependent on their physical surroundings and are also interdependent on other life forms. At the same time, each organism is adapted to its own particular environment which must provide the right conditions for it to survive. For example, all living things require water and a range of other chemical substances, and life as we know it can exist only within a limited range of temperatures. There are now some 1.4 million different species of plants and animals living on the Earth.

EVOLUTION AND GENETICS

Evolution is the slow, gradual process by which life has developed by stages from single-celled organisms into the multiplicity of animal and plant life, extinct and existing, that inhabit the Earth. The current theory of evolution, neo-Darwinism, combines Charles Darwin's theory of natural selection with the theories of Austrian biologist Gregor Mendel on genetics. Natural selection occurs because those individuals better adapted to their particular environments reproduce more effectively, thus contributing their characteristics (in the form of genes) to future generations. Heritable changes arise from genetic mutations which occur spontaneously in all organisms.

Genetics, the branch of biology concerned with the study of heredity and variation, attempts to explain how characteristics of living organisms are passed on from one generation to the next. Genes, the basic units of heredity, are present in the cells of all organisms, from bacteria and viruses to higher plants and animals, including humans. The study of the molecular basis of life, including the biochemistry of molecules such as DNA, RNA, and proteins, is becoming increasingly important to understanding the mechanisms of evolution.

There are several lines of evidence for evolution: the fossil record, the existence of similarities or homologies between different groups of organisms, embryology, and geographical distribution. It is now also clear that evolutionary change does not always occur at a constant rate, but that the process can have long periods of relative stability interspersed with periods of rapid change. Of the 1.4 million identifiable species existing on Earth at the present time, every one is the result of a long line of extinct species. Bacteria are among the earliest known species of life on Earth and still survive today.

living fossil

The coelacanth is a large dark brown to blue-grey fish with bony, overlapping scales, and muscular lobe (limblike) fins. Coelacanth fossils exist dating back over 400 million years and coelacanths were believed to be extinct until one was caught in 1938 off the coast of South Africa

Coelacanths live in the deep waters (200 m/650 ft) of the western Indian Ocean around the Comoros Islands and also off Sulawesi, Indonesia. They can grow to about 2 m/6 ft in length, and weigh up to 73 kg/160 lb. They feed on other fish, and give birth to live young rather than shedding eggs as most fish do.

Coelacanths are now threatened, and have been listed as endangered by CITES since 1991, although the discovery in 1998 of a coelacanth caught off Sulawesi, Indonesia means that the Comoros population (estimated at 500) is not the only population, as had previously been thought.

coelacanth The coelacanth is the sole survivor of an ancient group of fishes.

adaptation All cacti are xerophytes adapted to life in very dry conditions. This is a *Copiapoa* cactus in Pan De Azucar national park, Chile. *K G Preston-Mafham/Premaphotos Wildlife*

Biodiversity: Number of Species Worldwide

	Number identified	% of estimated total number of species
microorganisms	5,800	3–27%
invertebrates	1,021,000	3–27%
plants	322,500	67–100%
fish	19,100	83–100%
birds	9,100	94–100%
reptiles and amphibians	12,000	90–95%
mammals	4,000	90–95%
total	1,393,500	

	Number of species	% identified
low estimate of all species	4.4 million	31
high estimate of all species	80 million	2

adaptation any change in the structure or function of an organism that allows it to survive and reproduce more effectively in its environment. In evolution, adaptation is thought to occur as a result of random variation in the genetic make-up of organisms coupled with natural selection. Species become extinct when they are no longer adapted to their environment – for instance, if the climate suddenly becomes colder.

adaptive radiation formation of several species, with adaptations to different ways of life, from a single ancestral type. Adaptive radiation is likely to occur whenever members of a species migrate to a new habitat with unoccupied ecological niches. It is thought that the lack of competition in such niches allows sections of the migrant population to develop new adaptations, and eventually to become new species.

The colonization of newly formed volcanic islands has led to the development of many unique species. The 13 species of Darwin's finch on the Galápagos Islands, for example, are probably descended from a single species from the South American mainland. The parent stock evolved into different species that now occupy a range of diverse niches.

allele one of two or more alternative forms of a gene at a given position (locus) on a chromosome, caused by a difference in the DNA. Blue and brown eyes in humans are determined by different alleles of the gene for eye colour.

artificial selection selective breeding of individuals that exhibit the particular characteristics that a plant or animal breeder wishes to develop. In plants, desirable features might include resistance to disease, high yield (in crop plants), or attractive appearance. In animal breeding, selection has led to the development of particular breeds of cattle for improved meat production (such as the Aberdeen Angus) or milk production (such as Jerseys).

balance of nature the idea that there is an inherent equilibrium in most ecosystems, with plants and animals interacting so as to produce a stable, continuing system of life on Earth. The activities of human beings can, and frequently do, disrupt the balance of nature.

base pair linkage of two base (purine or pyrimidine) molecules in DNA. They are found in nucleotides, and form the basis of the genetic code.

cell see **What is a cell?** feature on pages 106–07.

clone an exact replica. In genetics, any one of a group of genetically identical cells or organisms. An identical twin is a clone; so, too, are bacteria living in the same colony.

codon a triplet of bases in a molecule of DNA or RNA that directs the placement of a particular amino acid during the process of protein (polypeptide) synthesis. There are 64 codons in the genetic code.

coevolution evolution of those structures and behaviours within a species that can best be understood in relation to another species. For example, insects and flowering plants have evolved together: insects have produced mouthparts suitable for collecting pollen or drinking nectar, and plants have developed chemicals and flowers that will attract insects to them.

competition interaction between two or more organisms, or groups of organisms (for example, species), that use a common resource which is in short supply. Competition invariably results in a reduction in the numbers of one or both competitors, and in evolution contributes both to the decline of certain species and to the evolution of adaptations.

continuous variation the slight difference of an individual character, such as height, across a sample of the population. Although there are very tall and very short humans, there are also many people with an intermediate height. The same applies to weight. Continuous variation can result from the genetic make-up of a population, or from environmental influences, or from a combination of the two.

convergent evolution independent evolution of similar structures in species (or other taxonomic groups) that are not closely related, as a result of living in a similar way. Thus, birds and bats have wings, not because they are descended from a common winged ancestor, but because their respective ancestors independently evolved flight.

chromosome see **What is a chromosome?** feature.

deoxyribonucleic acid full name of DNA.

diploid having paired chromosomes in each cell. In sexually reproducing species, one set is derived from each parent, the gametes, or sex cells, of each parent being haploid (having only one set of chromosomes) due to meiosis (reduction cell division).

DNA abbreviation for **deoxyribonucleic acid,** complex giant molecule that contains, in chemically coded form, the information needed for a cell to make proteins. DNA is a ladderlike double-stranded nucleic acid which forms the

What is a chromosome?

A chromosome is a structure in a cell nucleus that carries the genes. Each chromosome consists of one very long strand of DNA, coiled and folded to produce a compact body. The point on a chromosome where a particular gene occurs is known as its locus. Most higher organisms have two copies of each chromosome, together known as a **homologous pair** (they are diploid) but some have only one (they are haploid). There are 46 chromosomes in a normal human cell.

Variable shrews
- The number of chromosomes in the cells of common shrews varies from 20–25 in females and 21–27 in males. They are the only mammals not to have a constant number of chromosomes.

chromosome The 23 pairs of chromosomes of a normal human male.

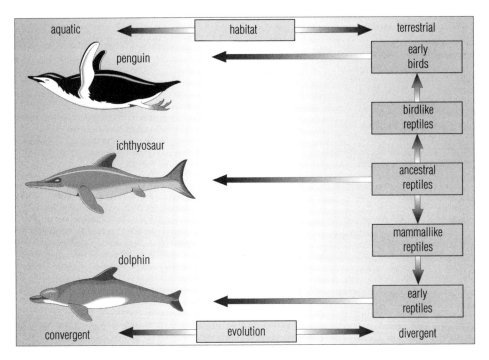

aquatic — habitat — terrestrial

penguin

early birds

birdlike reptiles

ichthyosaur

ancestral reptiles

mammallike reptiles

dolphin

early reptiles

convergent — evolution — divergent

convergent evolution Convergent evolution produced the superficially similar streamlined bodies of the dolphin and penguin. Despite their very different evolutionary paths – one as a mammal, the other as a bird – both have evolved and adapted to the aquatic environment they now inhabit.

basis of genetic inheritance in all organisms, except for a few viruses that have only RNA. DNA is organized into chromosomes and, in organisms other than bacteria, it is found only in the cell nucleus.

Genes by the thousand
■ Human DNA contains more than 80,000 genes.

enzyme biological catalyst produced in cells, and capable of speeding up the chemical reactions necessary for life. They are large, complex proteins, and are highly specific, each chemical reaction requiring its own particular enzyme. The enzyme's specificity arises from its **active site,** an area with a shape corresponding to part of the molecule with which it reacts (the substrate). The enzyme and the substrate slot together forming an enzyme–substrate complex that allows the reaction to take place, after which the enzyme falls away unaltered.

evolution see **What is evolution?** feature on page 102.

evolutionary stable strategy (ESS), in sociobiology, an assemblage of behavioural or physical characters (collectively termed a 'strategy') of a population that is resistant to replacement by any forms bearing new traits, because the new traits will not be capable of successful reproduction.

extinction complete disappearance of a species or higher taxon. Extinctions occur when an animal becomes unfit for survival in its natural habitat usually to be replaced by another, better-suited animal. An organism becomes ill-suited for survival because its environment is changed or because its relationship to other organisms is altered. For example, a predator's fitness for survival depends upon the availability of its prey.

gene unit of inherited material, encoded by a strand of DNA and transcribed by RNA. In higher organisms, genes are located on the chromosomes. A gene consistently affects a particular character in an individual – for example, the gene for eye

What is evolution?

Evolution is the the slow, gradual process of change from one form to another during the development of life on Earth, from single-celled organisms into the multiplicity of animal and plant life, extinct and existing, that inhabit the Earth. The English naturalist Charles Darwin attributed the main role in evolutionary change to natural selection acting on randomly occurring variations. These variations in species are now known to be adaptations produced by mutations in the genetic material of organisms. There are several lines of evidence for evolution: the fossil record, the existence of similarities or homologies (for example, similarities in limb structures in animals with similar lifestyles that are unrelated to each other) between different groups of organisms, embryology, and geographical distribution.

Evolutionary changes have not taken place in a linear manner, but as a branching process of descent from a common ancestor; this is often portrayed as an evolutionary tree, with humans at the top of the tree. Of the 1.4 million identifiable species existing on Earth at the present time, every one is the result of a long line of extinct species. Bacteria are among the earliest known species of life on Earth and still survive today. The human body contains ten times more bacteria cells than it does human cells.

mechanisms of evolution

Although the broad outlines of the evolutionary sequence are known, much research is still necessary to fill in the details and to discover the mechanisms of evolutionary change. Evolution depends on the presence of heritable variations in a population which confers a selective advantage on the individuals displaying them. The phrase 'survival of the fittest' is misleading since it implies the death of the 'unfit' individuals. From an evolutionary point of view, fertility is much more important than survival since if one type regularly leaves more offspring than another, the frequency of the more fertile type in the population is bound to increase. Fertility depends on many things including general vigour, the length of the reproductive period, and the ability to mate successfully.

Heritable changes arise from genetic mutations which occur spontaneously in all organisms. Many investigations that are currently being made into the genetic structures of living plant and animal populations show the relative importance of mutations and isolation in the origin of new species.

It is believed that the processes now occurring on a very small scale are the same as those which have caused the evolution of the major groups over a vast period of geological time. These studies should therefore throw light on the mechanism of evolution.

natural selection, sexual selection, and chance The idea of continuous evolution can be traced as far back as Roman philosopher Lucretius in the 1st century BC, but it did not gain wide acceptance until the 19th century following the work of Scottish geologist Charles Lyell, French naturalist Jean Baptiste Lamarck, Charles Darwin together with Alfred Russel Wallace, and English biologist T H Huxley. Natural selection occurs because those individuals better adapted to their particular environments reproduce more effectively, thus contributing their characteristics (in the form of genes) to future generations. The current theory of evolution, neo-Darwinism, combines Darwin's theory of natural selection with the theories of Austrian biologist Gregor Mendel on genetics.

colour. Also termed a Mendelian gene, after Austrian biologist Gregor Mendel, it occurs at a particular point, or locus, on a particular chromosome and may have several variants, or alleles, each specifying a particular form of that character – for example, the alleles for blue or brown eyes. Some alleles show dominance. These mask the effect of other alleles, known as recessive.

gene amplification technique by which selected DNA from a single cell can be duplicated indefinitely until there is a sufficient amount to analyse by conventional genetic techniques.

genetic code the way in which instructions for building proteins, the basic structural molecules of living matter, are 'written' in the genetic material DNA. This relationship between the sequence of bases (the subunits in a DNA molecule) and the sequence of amino acids (the subunits of a protein molecule) is the basis of heredity. The code employs codons of three bases each; it is the same in almost all organisms, except for a few minor differences recently discovered in some protozoa.

genome the full complement of genes carried by a single (haploid) set of chromosomes. The term may be applied to the genetic information carried by an individual or to the range of genes found in a given species. The human genome is made up of 75,000 genes.

genotype the particular set of alleles (variants of genes) possessed by a given organism. The term is usually used in conjunction with phenotype, which is the product of the genotype and all environmental effects.

haploid having a single set of chromosomes in each cell. Most higher organisms are diploid – that is, they have two sets – but their gametes (sex cells) are haploid. Some plants, such as mosses, liverworts, and many seaweeds, are haploid, and male honey bees are haploid because they develop from eggs that have not been fertilized.

heterozygous having two different alleles for a given trait. In homozygous organisms, by contrast, both chromosomes carry the same allele. In an outbreeding population an individual organism will generally be heterozygous for some genes but homozygous for others.

homozygous having two identical alleles for a given trait. Individuals homozygous for a trait always breed true; that is, they produce offspring that resemble them in appearance when bred with a genetically similar individual; inbred varieties or species are homozygous for almost all traits.

Recessive alleles are only expressed in the homozygous condition.

human species, origins of evolution of humans from ancestral primates. The African apes (gorilla and chimpanzee) are shown by anatomical and molecular comparisons to be the closest living relatives of humans. The oldest known **hominids** (of the human group), the australopithecines, found in Africa, date from 3.5–4.4 million years ago. The first to use tools came 2 million years later, and the first humanoids to use fire and move out of Africa appeared 1.7 million years ago. Neanderthals were not direct ancestors of the human species. Modern humans are all believed to descend from one African female of 200,000 years ago, although there is a rival theory that humans evolved in different parts of the world simultaneously.

karyotype set of chromosomes characteristic of a given species. It is described as the number, shape, and size of the chromosomes in a single cell of an organism. In humans for example, the karyotype consists of 46 chromosomes, in mice 40, crayfish 200, and in fruit flies 8.

Mendelism theory of inheritance originally outlined by Austrian biologist Gregor Mendel. He suggested that, in sexually reproducing species, all characteristics are inherited through indivisible 'factors' (now identified with genes) contributed by each parent to its offspring.

mutation change in the genes produced by a change in the DNA that makes up the hereditary material of all living organisms. Mutations, the raw material of evolution, result from mistakes during replication (copying) of DNA molecules. Only a few improve the organism's performance and are therefore favoured by natural selection. Mutation rates are increased by certain chemicals and by radiation.

natural selection the process whereby gene frequencies in a population change through certain individuals producing more descendants than others because they are better able to survive and reproduce in their environment.

The accumulated effect of natural selection is to produce adaptations such as the insulating coat of a polar bear or the spadelike forelimbs of a mole. The process is slow, relying firstly on random variation in the genes of an organism being produced by mutation and secondly on the genetic recombination of sexual reproduction. It was recognized by Charles Darwin and English

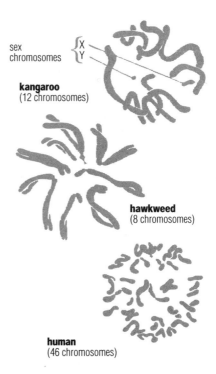

sex chromosomes {X Y

kangaroo
(12 chromosomes)

hawkweed
(8 chromosomes)

human
(46 chromosomes)

karyotype The characteristics, or karyotype, of the chromosomes vary according to species. The kangaroo has 12 chromosomes, the hawkweed has 8, and a human being has 46.

naturalist Alfred Russel Wallace as the main process driving evolution.

nature–nurture controversy or **environment–heredity controversy** long-standing dispute among philosophers and psychologists over the relative importance of environment, that is, upbringing, experience, and learning ('nurture'), and heredity, that is, genetic inheritance ('nature'), in determining the make-up of an organism, as related to human personality and intelligence.

neo-Darwinism the modern theory of evolution, built up since the 1930s by integrating the 19th-century English scientist Charles Darwin's theory of evolution through natural selection with the theory of genetic inheritance founded on the work of the Austrian biologist Gregor Mendel.

nucleotide organic compound consisting of a purine (adenine or guanine) or a pyrimidine (thymine, uracil, or cytosine) base linked to a sugar (deoxyribose or ribose) and a phosphate group. DNA and RNA are made up of long chains of nucleotides.

operon group of genes that are found next to each other on a chromosome, and are turned on and off as an integrated unit. They usually produce enzymes that control different steps in the same biochemical pathway. Operons were discovered in 1961 (by the French biochemists François Jacob and Jacques Monod) in bacteria.

phenotype visible traits, those actually displayed by an organism. The phenotype is not a direct reflection of the genotype because some alleles are masked by the presence of other, dominant alleles. The phenotype is further modified by the effects of the environment (for example, poor nutrition stunts growth).

phylogeny historical sequence of changes that occurs in a given species during the course of its evolution. It was once erroneously associated with ontogeny (the process of development of a living organism).

polymorphism the coexistence of several distinctly different types in a population (groups of animals of one species). Examples include the different blood groups in humans, different colour forms in some butterflies, and snail shell size, length, shape, colour, and stripiness.

polymorphism Polymorphism in whelks. There are a variety of shell colours and patterns in any whelk population. *Dr Rod Preston-Mafham/ Premaphotos Wildlife*

preadaptation fortuitous possession of a character that allows an organism to exploit a new situation. In many cases, the character evolves to solve a particular problem that a species encounters in its preferred habitat, but once evolved may allow the organism to exploit an entirely different situation. The ability to extract oxygen directly from the air evolved in some early fishes, probably in response to life in stagnant, deoxygenated pools; this later made it possible for their descendants to spend time on land, so giving rise eventually to the air-breathing amphibians.

prehistoric life the diverse organisms that inhabited Earth from the origin of life about 3.5 billion years ago to the time when humans began to keep written records, about 3500 BC. During the course of evolution, new forms of life developed and many other forms, such as the dinosaurs, became extinct. Prehistoric life evolved over this vast timespan from simple bacteria-like cells in the oceans to algae and protozoans and complex multicellular forms such as worms, molluscs, crustaceans, fishes, insects, land plants, amphibians, reptiles, birds, and mammals. On a geological timescale human beings evolved relatively recently, about 4 million years ago, although the exact dating is a matter of some debate.

punctuated equilibrium model evolutionary theory developed by Niles Eldredge and US palaeontologist Stephen Jay Gould in 1972 to explain discontinuities in the fossil record. It claims that periods of rapid change alternate with periods of relative stability (stasis), and that the appearance of new lineages is a separate process from the gradual evolution of adaptive changes within a species.

replication production of copies of the genetic material DNA; it occurs during cell division (mitosis and meiosis). Most mutations are caused by mistakes during replication.

ribosome protein-making machinery of the cell. Ribosomes are located on the endoplasmic reticulum (ER) of eukaryotic cells, and are made of proteins and a special type of RNA, ribosomal RNA. They receive messenger RNA (copied from the DNA) and amino acids, and 'translate' the messenger RNA by using its chemically coded instructions to link amino acids in a specific order, to make a strand of a particular protein.

RNA abbreviation for **ribonucleic acid,** nucleic acid involved in the process of translating the genetic material DNA into proteins. It is usually single-stranded, unlike the double-stranded DNA, and consists of a large number of nucleotides strung together, each of which comprises the sugar ribose, a phosphate group, and one of four bases (uracil, cytosine, adenine, or guanine). RNA is copied from DNA by the formation of base pairs, with uracil taking the place of thymine.

saltation idea that an abrupt genetic change can occur in an individual, which then gives rise to a new species. The idea has now been largely discredited, although the appearance of polyploid individuals can be considered an example.

sex determination process by which the sex of an organism is determined. In many species, the sex of an individual is dictated by the two sex chromosomes (X and Y) it receives from its parents. In mammals, some plants, and a few insects, males are XY, and females XX; in birds, reptiles, some amphibians, and butterflies the reverse is the case. In bees and wasps, males are produced from unfertilized eggs, females from fertilized eggs.

sexual selection process similar to natural selection but relating exclusively to success in finding a mate for the purpose of sexual reproduction and producing offspring. Sexual selection occurs when one sex (usually but not always the female) invests more effort in producing young than the other. Members of the other sex compete for access to this limited resource (usually males competing for the chance to mate with females).

species distinguishable group of organisms that resemble each other or consist of a few distinctive types (as in polymorphism), and that can all interbreed to produce fertile offspring. Species are the lowest level in the system of biological classification.

transcription process by which the information for the synthesis of a protein is transferred from the DNA strand on which it is carried to the messenger RNA strand involved in the actual synthesis.

translation process by which proteins are synthesized. During translation, the information coded as a sequence of nucleotides in messenger RNA is transformed into a sequence of amino acids in a peptide chain. The process involves the 'translation' of the genetic code.

X chromosome larger of the two sex chromosomes, the smaller being the Y chromosome. These two chromosomes are involved in sex determination. Females have two X chromosomes, males have an X and a Y. Genes carried on the X chromosome produce the phenomenon of sex linkage.

Y chromosome smaller of the two sex chromosomes. In male mammals it occurs paired with the other type of sex chromosome (X), which carries far more genes. The Y chromosome is the smallest of all the mammalian chromosomes and is considered to be largely inert (that is, without direct effect on the physical body). There are only 20 genes discovered so far on the human Y chromosome, much fewer than on all other human chromosomes.

What is a cell?

A cell is the basic structural unit of life. It is the smallest unit capable of independent existence which can reproduce itself exactly. All living organisms – with the exception of viruses – are composed of one or more cells. Single cell organisms such as bacteria, protozoa, and other microorganisms are termed **unicellular,** while plants and animals which contain many cells are termed **multicellular** organisms. Highly complex organisms such as human beings consist of billions of cells, all of which are adapted to carry out specific functions – for instance, groups of these specialized cells are organized into tissues and organs. Although these cells may differ widely in size, appearance, and function, their essential features are similar.

Cells divide by mitosis, or by meiosis when gametes are being formed.

The cytoplasm of all cells contains ribosomes, which carry out protein synthesis, and DNA, the coded instructions for the behaviour and reproduction of the cell and the chemical machinery for the translation of these instructions into the manufacture of proteins. Viruses lack this translation machinery and so have to parasitize cells in order to reproduce themselves.

eukaryote cells In eukaryote cells, found in protozoa, fungi, and higher animals and plants, DNA is organized into chromosomes and is contained within a nucleus. Each eukaryote has a surrounding membrane, which is a thin layer of protein and fat that restricts the flow of substances in and out of the cell and encloses the cytoplasm, a jellylike material containing the nucleus and other structures (organelles) such as mitochondria. The nuclei of some cells contain a dense spherical structure called the nucleolus, which contains ribonucleic acid (RNA) for the synthesis of ribosomes. The only cells of the human body which have no nucleus are the red blood cells.

In general, plant cells differ from animal cells in that the membrane is surrounded by a cell wall made of cellulose. They also have larger vacuoles (fluid-filled pouches), and contain chloroplasts that convert light energy to chemical energy for the synthesis of glucose.

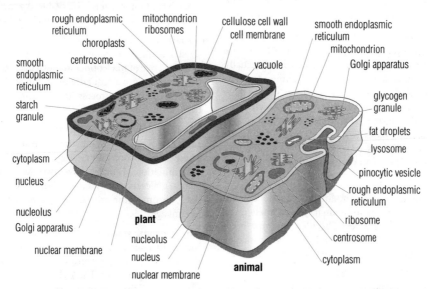

cell structure Typical plant and animal cell. Plant and animal cells share many structures, such as ribosomes, mitochondria, and chromosomes, but they also have notable differences: plant cells have chloroplasts, a large vacuole, and a cellulose cell wall. Animal cells do not have a rigid cell wall but have an outside cell membrane only.

What is a cell? (continued)

prokaryote cells

In prokaryote cells, found in bacteria and cyanobacteria, the DNA forms a simple loop and there is no nucleus. The prokaryotic cell also lacks organelles such as mitochondria, chloroplasts, endoplasmic reticulum, Golgi apparatus, and centrioles, which perform specialized tasks in eukaryotic cells.

cell composition

Primarily, cells are composed of the elements that make up the majority of organic compounds – namely, oxygen, hydrogen, carbon, and nitrogen – and the complete contents of a cell are called the protoplasm. The composition of the protoplasm varies, but the products of its breakdown when the cell dies are mostly proteins. It also contains carbohydrates, fats, and the lipoids, lecithin and cholesterin, besides inorganic salts such as the phosphates and chlorides of potash, soda, and lime. Water, which provides a favourable environment for biochemical reactions, makes up 60 to 65% of a cell. Its distribution through the cell membrane is controlled by osmosis. Most cells contain vacuoles, which are spaces within cells surrounded by membrane and containing a solution. Plant cells have large vacuoles containing a solution of sugars and other substances called cell sap; animal cells have smaller vacuoles which may contain either food or water. Some cells have flexible, hairlike attachments called cilia and flagellum; these are found on protozoa as well as in human oviducts and respiratory tracts and are used for locomotion, capturing food, and removing particles of foreign material.

cell function

The cell wall in most animal cells is not a substantial membrane, and the shape of the cell is maintained by surface tension or chemical action. All cells are dynamic at some stage of their life cycle, in the sense that they use energy to perform a variety of cell functions: movement, growth, maintenance and repair of cell structure, reproduction of the cell, and manufacture of specialized cell products such as enzymes and hormones. These functions are also the result of interactions of organic molecules. The endoplasmic reticulum (ER), which is found in all cells, is a system of membranes running throughout the cytoplasm and is the site for the production of fats and proteins. Connected to this is the Golgi apparatus, a collection of vesicles and folded membranes, which stores and later transports the proteins manufactured by the ER. Mitochondria are also found in all cells. These are sometimes called the 'powerhouses' of the cell as they contain the enzymes involved in the cell's metabolic activities that enable the release of energy from food by combining it with oxygen. Chloroplasts are only found in plant cells. They contain chlorophyll which absorbs sunlight and converts this to energy through the process of photosynthesis.

cell reproduction

New cells are produced from existing cells. They reproduce by division (mitosis), with each cell dividing to produce two new cells, both of which contain a copy of the genetic programme. Simple cell division, or asexual reproduction, normally results in the production of two identical daughter cells, each containing a set of chromosomes identical with those of the parent cell. In sexual reproduction, the DNA of two different organisms of the same species combines to produce a cell with a new combination of genes. When this occurs between single-celled organisms, it is called conjugation. In multicellular organisms, sexual reproduction requires the production of male and female germ cells (sperm and eggs) by a process called meiosis. During this process a cell divides twice, but its chromosomes are duplicated only once. Thus, four germ cells are produced, each containing half the normal number of chromosomes. In the male organism the germ cells develop into sperm; in the female they develop into eggs. A sperm and an egg then unite (fertilization) to form a new cell, called a zygote, which has a complete set of chromosomes, and which has received half its genetic information from each parent, thus producing a new individual. Cell differentiation is the process by which a daughter cell becomes different from its parent in appearance or function, or both, even though both parent and daughter cell contain identical genetic information.

cell death

Like all living things, cells die. Within the human body, about 3 billion cells die every minute; at the same time, these are replaced by about the same number of new cells. External cells, such as skin cells, flake off, while the dead cells from internal organs are passed out of the body with waste products. The life span of cells varies – for example, white blood cells live for about 13 days, red blood cells live about 120 days, and liver cells live about 18 months. Nerve cells can live for as long as 100 years.

ELEMENTS THAT SUSTAIN LIFE

An ecosysem is an integrated unit consisting of a community of living organisms – bacteria, animals, and plants – and the physical environment – air, soil, water, and climate – that they inhabit. Individual organisms interact with each other and with their environment, or habitat, in a series of relationships that depends on the flow of energy and nutrients through the system. These relationships are usually complex and finely balanced, and in theory natural ecosystems are self-sustaining. However, major changes to an ecosystem, such as climate change, overpopulation, or the removal of a species, may threaten the system's sustainability and result in its eventual destruction. For instance, the removal of a major carnivore predator can result in the destruction of an ecosystem through overgrazing by herbivores.

One of the main features of an ecosystem is its biodiversity. Members are usually classified as producers (those that can synthesize the organic materials they need from inorganic compounds in the environment) or consumers (those that are unable to manufacture their own food directly from these sources and depend upon producers to meet their needs). Thus plants, as producers, capture energy originating from the sun through a process of photosynthesis and absorb nutrients from the soil and water; these stores of energy and nutrients then become available to the consumers – for example, they are passed via the herbivores that eat the plants, to the carnivores that feed on the herbivores. The sequence in which energy and nutrients pass through the system is known as a food chain, and the energy levels within a food chain are termed trophic levels. At each stage of assimilation, energy is lost by consumer functioning, and so there are always far fewer consumers at the end of the chain.

abiotic factor a nonorganic variable within the ecosystem, affecting the life of organisms. Examples include temperature, light, and soil structure. Abiotic factors can be harmful to the environment, as when sulphur dioxide emissions from power stations produce acid rain.

acclimation *or* **acclimatization,** the physiological changes induced in an organism by exposure to new environmental conditions. When humans move to higher altitudes, for example, the number of red blood cells rises to increase the oxygen-carrying capacity of the blood in order to compensate for the lower levels of oxygen in the air.

aerobic term used to describe those organisms that require oxygen (usually dissolved in water) for the efficient release of energy contained in food molecules, such as glucose. They include almost all organisms (plants as well as animals)

> **Sharks never stop**
> ■ Sharks have to keep swimming to survive. The great white shark must swim constantly at about 3.5 kph/2.2 mph to ensure enough oxygen reaches its bloodstream. An immobile shark (or one dragged backwards) drowns.

with the exception of certain bacteria, yeasts, and internal parasites.

anaerobic (of living organisms) not requiring oxygen for the release of energy from food molecules such as glucose. Anaerobic organisms include many bacteria, yeasts, and internal parasites.

autotroph any living organism that synthesizes organic substances from inorganic molecules by using light or chemical energy. Autotrophs are the **primary producers** in all food chains since the materials they synthesize and store are the energy sources of all other organisms. All green plants and many planktonic organisms are autotrophs, using sunlight to convert carbon dioxide and water into sugars by photosynthesis.

basal metabolic rate (BMR), minimum amount of energy needed by the body to maintain life. It is measured when the subject is awake but resting, and includes the energy required to keep the heart beating, sustain breathing, repair tissues, and keep the brain and nerves functioning. Measuring the subject's consumption of oxygen gives an accurate value for BMR, because oxygen is needed to release energy from food.

biodiversity contraction of **biological diversity** measure of the variety of the Earth's animal, plant, and microbial species; of genetic differences within species; and of the ecosystems that support those species. Its maintenance is important for ecological stability and as a resource for research into, for example, new drugs and crops. In the 20th century, the destruction of habitats is believed to have resulted in the most severe and rapid loss of biodiversity in the history of the planet.

biomass the total mass of living organisms present in a given area. It may be specified for a particular species (such as earthworm biomass) or for a general category (such as herbivore biomass). Estimates also exist for the entire global plant biomass. Measurements of biomass can be used to study interactions between organisms, the stability of those interactions, and variations in population numbers. Where dry biomass is measured, the material is dried to remove all water before weighing.

biosphere the narrow zone that supports life on our planet. It is limited to the waters of the Earth, a fraction of its crust, and the lower regions of the atmosphere. The biosphere is made up of all the Earth's ecosystems. It is affected by external forces such as the Sun's rays, which provide energy, the gravitational effects of the Sun and Moon, and cosmic radiations.

biosynthesis synthesis of organic chemicals from simple inorganic ones by living cells – for example, the conversion of carbon dioxide and water to glucose by plants during photosynthesis. Other biosynthetic reactions produce cell constituents including proteins and fats.

camouflage colours or structures that allow an animal to blend with its surroundings to avoid detection by other animals. Camouflage can take the form of matching the background colour, of countershading (darker on top, lighter below, to counteract natural shadows), or of irregular patterns that break up the outline of the animal's body. More elaborate camouflage involves closely resembling a feature of the natural environment, as with the stick insect; this is closely akin to mimicry.

carnivore mammal of the order Carnivora. Although its name describes the flesh-eating

carnivore A cheetah family *Acinonyx jubatus* feeding on the carcass of an impala that they have killed in a game park in Kenya. A female cheetah may have up to four cubs, though it is relatively unusual for all to survive. The family will remain together until the cubs are fully matured and sometimes longer, though cheetahs are otherwise fairly solitary animals. *Ken Preston/Mafham Premaphotos Wildlife*

carnivore Some plants are sometimes described as carnivorous (or more accurately insectivorous). The insect traps of North American pitcher plants are modified leaves. Insects are lured into the pitchers by sweet secretions and then tumble into the fluid at the base, where they drown and are slowly digested. Insectivorous plants grown in nitrogen-poor soil.

ancestry of the order, it includes pandas, which are herbivorous, and civet cats, which eat fruit.

carrying capacity maximum number of animals of a given species that a particular area can support. When the carrying capacity is exceeded, there is insufficient food (or other resources) for the members of the population. The population may then be reduced by emigration, reproductive failure, or death through starvation.

chemosynthesis method of making protoplasm (contents of a cell) using the energy from chemical reactions, in contrast to the use of light energy employed for the same purpose in photosynthesis. The process is used by certain bacteria, which can synthesize organic compounds from carbon dioxide and water using the energy from special methods of respiration.

chemotropism movement by part of a plant in response to a chemical stimulus. The response by the plant is termed 'positive' if the growth is towards the stimulus or 'negative' if the growth is away from the stimulus.

commensalism relationship between two species whereby one (the commensal) benefits from the association, whereas the other neither benefits nor suffers. For example, certain species of millipede and silverfish inhabit the nests of army ants

and live by scavenging on the refuse of their hosts, but without affecting the ants.

decomposer any organism that breaks down dead matter. Decomposers play a vital role in the ecosystem by freeing important chemical substances, such as nitrogen compounds, locked up in dead organisms or excrement. They feed on some of the released organic matter, but leave the rest to filter back into the soil as dissolved nutrients, or pass in gas form into the atmosphere, for example as nitrogen and carbon dioxide.

The principal decomposers are bacteria and fungi, but earthworms and many other invertebrates are often included in this group. The nitrogen cycle relies on the actions of decomposers.

decomposition process whereby a chemical compound is reduced to its component substances. In biology, it is the destruction of dead organisms either by chemical reduction or by the action of decomposers, such as bacteria and fungi.

ectoparasite parasite that lives on the outer surface of its host.

endoparasite parasite that lives inside the body of its host.

food chain sequence showing the feeding relationships between organisms in a particular ecosystem. Each organism depends on the next lowest member of the chain for its food. A pyramid of numbers can be used to show the reduction in food energy at each step up the food chain. In reality food chains are an oversimplification as they are actually interlinked as **food webs**.

herbivore animal that feeds on green plants (or photosynthetic single-celled organisms) or their products, including seeds, fruit, and nectar. The most numerous type of herbivore is thought to be the zooplankton, tiny invertebrates in the surface waters of the oceans that feed on small photosynthetic algae. Herbivores are more numerous than

Herbivorous hippos
■ During a nightly grazing session, a hippo can eat up to 40 kg/88 lb of grass and dead leaves. This is the equivalent of about 12 full sacks of food.

Ants and fungus farming

■ Leaf-cutter ants feed their larvae on a fungus that they cultivate themselves in underground gardens. The ants depend on the fungus for food, and the fungus cannot reproduce without the ants. When a new queen takes flight to establish another colony, she takes some of the fungus with her in a special mouth pouch.

other animals because their food is the most abundant. They form a vital link in the food chain between plants and carnivores.

heterotroph any living organism that obtains its energy from organic substances produced by other organisms. All animals and fungi are heterotrophs, and they include herbivores, carnivores, and saprotrophs (those that feed on dead animal and plant material).

migration the movement, either seasonal or as part of a single life cycle, of certain animals, chiefly birds and fish, to distant breeding or feeding grounds.

nitrogen cycle the process of nitrogen passing through the ecosystem. Nitrogen, in the form of inorganic compounds (such as nitrates) in the soil, is absorbed by plants and turned into organic compounds (such as proteins) in plant tissue. A proportion of this nitrogen is eaten by herbivores, with some of this in turn being passed on to the carnivores, which feed on the

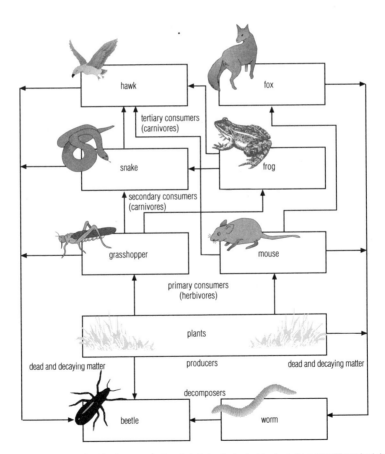

food chain The complex interrelationships between animals and plants in a food web. A food web shows how different food chains are linked in an ecosystem. Note that the arrows indicate movement of energy through the web. For example, an arrow shows that energy moves from plants to the grasshopper, which eats the plants.

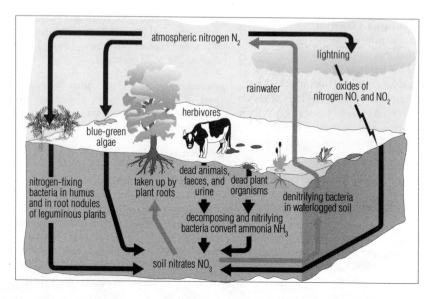

atmospheric nitrogen N_2

lightning

rainwater

oxides of nitrogen NO, and NO_2

herbivores

blue-green algae

nitrogen-fixing bacteria in humus and in root nodules of leguminous plants

taken up by plant roots

dead animals, faeces, and urine

dead plant organisms

denitrifying bacteria in waterlogged soil

decomposing and nitrifying bacteria convert ammonia NH_3

soil nitrates NO_3

nitrogen cycle The nitrogen cycle is one of a number of cycles during which the chemicals necessary for life are recycled. The carbon, sulphur, and phosphorus cycles are others. Since there is only a limited amount of these chemicals in the Earth and its atmosphere, the chemicals must be continuously recycled if life is to go on.

herbivores. The nitrogen is ultimately returned to the soil as excrement and when organisms die and are converted back to inorganic form by decomposers.

nitrogen fixation the process by which nitrogen in the atmosphere is converted into nitrogenous compounds by the action of microorganisms, such as cyanobacteria and bacteria, in conjunction with certain legumes.

omnivore animal that feeds on both plant and animal material. Omnivores have digestive adaptations intermediate between those of herbivores and carnivores, with relatively unspecialized digestive systems and gut microorganisms that can digest a variety of foodstuffs. Omnivores include humans, chimpanzees, cockroaches, and ants.

parasite organism that lives on or in another organism (called the host) and depends on it for nutri-

tion, often at the expense of the host's welfare. Parasites that live inside the host, such as liver flukes and tapeworms, are called **endoparasites;** those that live on the exterior, such as fleas and lice, are called **ectoparasites.**

photosynthesis process by which green plants trap light energy from the Sun. This energy is used to drive a series of chemical reactions which lead to the formation of carbohydrates. The carbohydrates occur in the form of simple sugar, or glucose, which provides the basic food for both plants and animals. For photosynthesis to occur, the plant must possess chlorophyll and must have a supply of carbon dioxide and water. Photosynthesis takes place inside chloroplasts which are found mainly in the leaf cells of plants.

The by-product of photosynthesis, oxygen, is of great importance to all living organisms, and virtually all atmospheric oxygen has originated by photosynthesis.

respiration metabolic process in organisms in which food molecules are broken down to release energy. The cells of all living organisms need a continuous supply of energy, and in most plants and animals this is obtained by **aerobic** respiration. In this process, oxygen is used to break down the glucose molecules in food. This

---

Lousy birds

■ Birds support a vast variety of parasites. A curlew may carry over 1,000 feather lice, and a single grouse can harbour 10,000 nematode worms within its intestines.

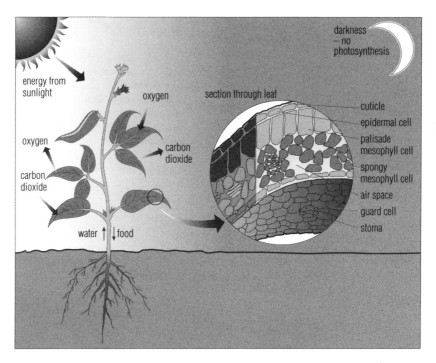

photosynthesis Process by which green plants and some bacteria manufacture carbohydrates from water and atmospheric carbon dioxide, using the energy of sunlight. Photosynthesis depends on the ability of chlorophyll molecules within plant cells to trap the energy of light to split water molecules, giving off oxygen as a by-product. The hydrogen of the water molecules is then used to reduce carbon dioxide to simple carbohydrates.

releases energy in the form of energy-carrying molecules (ATP), and produces carbon dioxide and water as by-products. Respiration sometimes occurs without oxygen, and this is called **anaerobic** respiration. In this case, the end products are energy and either lactose acid or ethanol (alcohol) and carbon dioxide; this process is termed fermentation.

sensitivity in biology, the ability of an organism, or part of an organism, to detect changes in the environment. All living things are capable of some sensitivity, and any change detected by an organism is called a stimulus. Plant response to stimuli (for example, light, heat, moisture) is by directional growth (tropism). In animals, the body cells that detect the stimuli are called receptors, and these are often contained within a sense organ. For example, the eye is a sense organ, within which the retina contains rod and cone cells which are receptors. The part of the body that responds to a stimulus, such as a muscle, is called an effector, and the communication of stimuli from receptors to effectors is termed 'coordination'; messages are passed from receptors to effectors either via the nerves or by means of chemicals called hormones. Rapid communication and response to stimuli, such as light, sound, and scent, can be essential to an animal's well-being and survival, and evolution has led to the development of highly complex mechanisms for this purpose.

transpiration the loss of water from a plant by evaporation. Most water is lost from the leaves through pores known as stomata, whose primary function is to allow gas exchange between the plant's internal tissues and the atmosphere. Transpiration from the leaf surfaces causes a

Sweet feet
■ The sensors on the feet of a red admiral butterfly are 200 times more sensitive to sugar than the human tongue.

continuous upward flow of water from the roots via the xylem, which is known as the transpiration stream.

tropism or **tropic movement,** the directional growth of a plant, or part of a plant, in response to an external stimulus such as gravity or light. If the movement is directed towards the stimulus it is described as positive; if away from it, it is negative. **Geotropism** for example, the response of plants to gravity, causes the root (positively geotropic) to grow downwards, and the stem (negatively geotropic) to grow upwards.

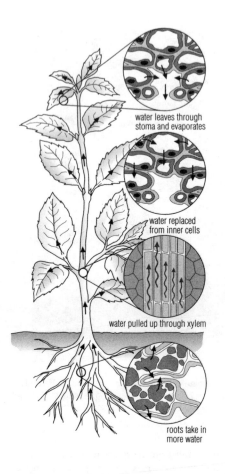

water leaves through
stoma and evaporates

water replaced
from inner cells

water pulled up through xylem

roots take in
more water

transpiration The loss of water from a plant by evaporation is known as transpiration. Most of the water is lost through the surface openings, or stomata, on the leaves. The evaporation produces what is known as the transpiration stream, a tension that draws water up from the roots through the xylem, water-carrying vessels in the stem.

THE LIFE CYCLE

A life cycle is the sequence of developmental stages through which members of a given species pass. Most vertebrates have a simple life cycle consisting of fertilization of sex cells or gametes, a period of development as an embryo, a period of juvenile growth after hatching or birth, an adulthood including sexual reproduction, and finally death. Invertebrate life cycles are generally more complex and may involve major reconstitution of the individual's appearance (metamorphosis) and completely different styles of life. Plants have a special type of life cycle with two distinct phases, known as alternation of generations. Many insects such as cicadas, dragonflies, and mayflies have a long larvae or pupae phase and a short adult phase. Dragonflies live an aquatic life as larvae and an aerial life during the adult phase. In many invertebrates and protozoa there is a sequence of stages in the life cycle, and in parasites different stages often occur in different host organisms.

Reproduction, the process by which a living organism produces other organisms more or less similar to itself, is a major part of the life cycle. The ability to reproduce is considered one of the fundamental attributes of living things. The ways in which species reproduce differ, but the two main methods are by asexual reproduction and sexual reproduction.

aestivation state of inactivity and reduced metabolic activity, similar to hibernation, that occurs during the dry season in species such as lungfish and snails. In botany, the term is used to describe the way in which flower petals and sepals are folded in the buds. It is an important feature in plant classification.

> **As rare as an old frog ...**
> ■ Common frogs can live for about six years but only about 1 in 10,000 will successfully evade predators and disease to live to this ripe old age.

ageing in common usage, the period of deterioration of the physical condition of a living organism that leads to death; in biological terms, the entire life process.

> **... or as common as an old mussel**
> ■ The European freshwater mussel *Margaritifera margaritifera* lives for at least 90 years.

alternation of generations see **Alternation of generations** feature on page 116.

asexual reproduction reproduction that does not involve the manufacture and fusion of sex cells, nor the necessity for two parents. The process carries a clear advantage in that there is no need to search for a mate nor to develop complex pollinating mechanisms; every asexual organism can reproduce on its own. Asexual reproduction can therefore lead to a rapid population build-up. *See illustration on page 116.*

binary fission form of asexual reproduction, whereby a single-celled organism, such as the amoeba, divides into two smaller 'daughter' cells. It can also occur in a few simple multicellular organisms, such as sea anemones, producing two smaller sea anemones of equal size.

birth act of producing live young from within the body of female animals. Both viviparous and ovoviviparous animals give birth to young. In viviparous animals, embryos obtain nourishment from the mother via a placenta or other means. In ovoviviparous animals, fertilized eggs develop and

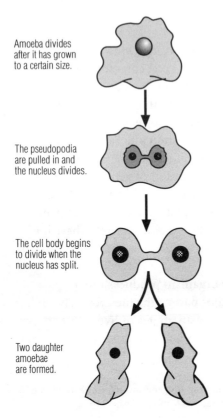

Amoeba divides after it has grown to a certain size.

The pseudopodia are pulled in and the nucleus divides.

The cell body begins to divide when the nucleus has split.

Two daughter amoebae are formed.

asexual reproduction Asexual reproduction is the simplest form of reproduction, occurring in many simple plants and animals. Binary fission, shown here occurring in an amoeba, is one of a number of asexual reproduction processes

hatch in the oviduct of the mother and gain little or no nourishment from maternal tissues.

budding type of asexual reproduction in which an outgrowth develops from a cell to form a new individual. Most yeasts reproduce in this way.

death cessation of all life functions, so that the molecules and structures associated with living

Grieving hippos

■ When a hippopotamus dies, other hippos surround the corpse and lick it. They may remain like this for a whole day, driving away any hungry crocodiles. They only abandon the corpse when the crocodiles become too numerous to deter.

Alternation of generations

This is the typical life cycle of terrestrial plants and some seaweeds, in which there are two distinct forms occurring alternately: **diploid** (having two sets of chromosomes) and **haploid** (one set of chromosomes). The diploid generation produces haploid spores by meiosis, and is called the sporophyte, while the haploid generation produces gametes (sex cells), and is called the gametophyte. The gametes fuse to form a diploid zygote which develops into a new sporophyte; thus the sporophyte and gametophyte alternate.

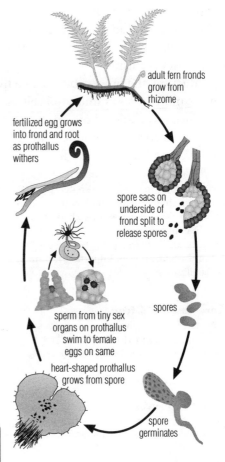

adult fern fronds grow from rhizome

fertilized egg grows into frond and root as prothallus withers

spore sacs on underside of frond split to release spores

spores

sperm from tiny sex organs on prothallus swim to female eggs on same

heart-shaped prothallus grows from spore

spore germinates

alternation of generations The life cycle of a fern. Ferns have two distinct forms that alternate during their life cycle. For the main part of its life, a fern consists of a short stem (or rhizome) from which roots and leaves grow. The other part of its life is spent as a small heart-shaped plant called a prothallus.

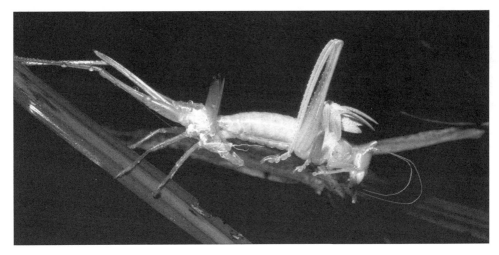

ecdysis A bush cricket or katydid (family Tettigoniidae) sheds its skin at night in a rainforest in Costa Rica. The insect is very vulnerable to attack at this time, so it is an advantage for ecdysis to take place during the hours of darkness. *K G Preston-Matham/Premaphotos Wildlife*

things become disorganized and indistinguishable from similar molecules found in nonliving things. In medicine, a person is pronounced dead when the brain ceases to control the vital functions, even if breathing and heartbeat are maintained artificially.

ecdysis periodic shedding of the exoskelton to allow for growth.

egg in animals, the ovum, or female gamete (reproductive cell). After fertilization by a sperm cell, it begins to divide to form an embryo. Eggs may be deposited by the female (ovipary) or they may develop within her body (vivipary and ovovivipary). In the oviparous reptiles and birds, the egg is protected by a shell, and well supplied with nutrients in the form of yolk.

embryo early developmental stage of an animal or a plant following fertilization of an ovum (egg cell), or activation of an ovum by parthenogenesis. In humans, the term embryo describes the fertilized egg during its first seven weeks of existence; from the eighth week onwards it is referred to as a fetus. *See illustration on page 118.*

fertilization union of two gametes (sex cells, often called egg and sperm) to produce a zygote, which combines the genetic material contributed by each parent. In self-fertilization the male and female gametes come from the same plant; in cross-fertilization they come

Section through a fertilized egg

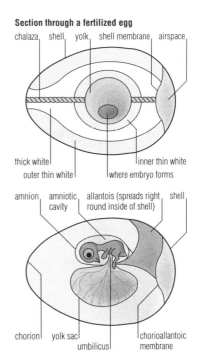

egg Section through a fertilized bird egg. Inside a bird's egg is a complex structure of liquids and membranes designed to meet the needs of the growing embryo. The yolk, which is rich in fat, is gradually absorbed by the embryo. The white of the egg provides protein and water. The chalaza is a twisted band of protein which holds the yolk in place and acts as a shock absorber. The airspace allows gases to be exchanged through the shell. The allantois contains many blood vessels which carry gases between the embryo and the outside.

egg Sea slug eggs (pink fronds) on the Great Barrier Reef, Australia.
Chris McTernan

from different plants. Self-fertilization rarely occurs in animals; usually even hermaphrodite animals cross-fertilize each other.

fetus or **foetus** stage in mammalian embryo development. The human embryo is usually termed a fetus after the eighth week of development, when the limbs and external features of the head are recognizable.

gamete cell that functions in sexual reproduction by merging with another gamete to form a zygote. Examples of gametes include sperm and egg cells. In most organisms, the gametes are haploid (they contain half the number of chromosomes of the parent), owing to reduction division or meiosis.

germination initial stages of growth in a seed, spore, or pollen grain. Seeds germinate when they are exposed to favourable external conditions of moisture, light, and temperature, and when any factors causing dormancy have been removed.

gestation in all mammals except the monotremes (platypus and spiny anteaters), the period from the time of implantation of the embryo in the uterus to birth. This period varies among species; in humans it is about 266 days, in elephants 18–22 months, in cats about 60 days, and in some species of marsupial (such as opossum) as short as 12 days.

hermaphrodite organism that has both male and female sex organs. Hermaphroditism is the norm in such species as earthworms and snails, and is common in flowering plants. Cross-fertilization is the rule among hermaphrodites, with the parents functioning as male and female simultaneously, or as one or the other sex at different stages in their development. Human hermaphrodites are extremely rare.

hibernation state of dormancy in which certain animals spend the winter. It is associated with a

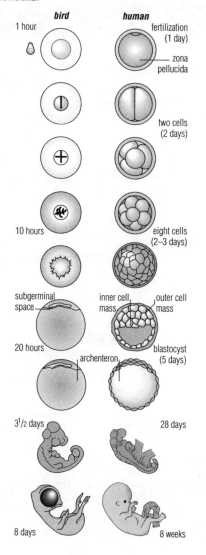

embryo The development of a bird and a human embryo. In the human, division of the fertilized egg, or ovum, begins within hours of conception. Within a week, a hollow, fluid-containing ball – a blastocyte – with a mass of cells at one end has developed. After the third week, the embryo has changed from a mass of cells into a recognizable shape. At four weeks, the embryo is 3 mm/0.1 in long, with a large bulge for the heart and small pits for the ears. At six weeks, the embryo is 1.5 cm/0.6 in long with a pulsating heart and ear flaps. By the eighth week, the embryo (now technically a fetus) is 2.5 cm/1 in long and recognizably human, with eyelids and small fingers and toes.

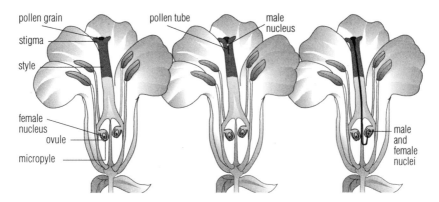

fertilization In a flowering plant pollen grains land on the surface of the stigma, and if conditions are acceptable the pollen grain germinates, forming a pollen tube, through which the male gametes pass, entering the ovule via the micropyle in order to reach the female egg.

dramatic reduction in all metabolic processes, including body temperature, breathing, and heart rate. It is a fallacy that animals sleep throughout the winter.

larva stage between hatching and adulthood in those species in which the young have a different appearance and way of life from the adults. Examples include tadpoles (frogs) and caterpillars (butterflies and moths). Larvae are typical of the invertebrates, some of which (for example,

Legless fleas

■ The wormlike larvae of fleas are eyeless and legless. They do not suck blood, but feed on digested blood excreted by the adult flea.

hibernation Ladybirds hibernating on a pine tree. Many animals hibernate during the winter months, when food is scarce, in order to conserve energy. *K G Preston-Mafham/Premaphotos Wildlife*

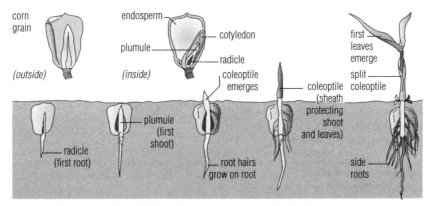

germination The germination of a corn grain. The plumule and radicle emerge from the seed coat and begin to grow into a new plant. The coleoptile protects the emerging bud and the first leaves.

Gestation Periods

Animal	Gestation (days)	Average longevity/ maximum longevity (years)	Animal	Gestation (days)	Average longevity/ maximum longevity (years)
ass	365	12/35.8	lion	100	15/25
baboon	187	20/35.5	monkey (rhesus)	164	15/–
bear (black)	219	18/36.8	moose	240	12/–
bear (grizzly)	225	25/–	mouse (meadow)	21	3/–
bear (polar)	60	20/34.7	mouse (dom. white)	19	3/3.5
beaver	122	5/20.5	opossum (American)	14–17	1/–
buffalo (American)	278	15/–	pig (domestic)	112	10/27
camel, bactrian	406	12/29.5	puma	90	12/19
cat (domestic)	63	12/28	rabbit (domestic)	31	5/13
chimpanzee	231	20/44.5	rhinoceros (black)	450	15/–
chipmunk	31	6/8	rhinoceros (white)	480	20/–
cow	284	15/30	sea lion (California)	350	12/28
deer (white-tailed)	201	8/17.5	sheep (domestic)	154	12/20
dog (domestic)	61	12/20	squirrel (grey)	44	10/–
elephant (African)	675	35/60	tiger	105	16/26.3
elephant (Asian)	645	40/70	wolf (maned)	63	5/–
elk	250	15/26.5	zebra (Grant's)	365	15/–
fox (red)	52	7/14			
giraffe	425	10/33.5			
goat (domestic)	151	8/18	**Incubation time (days)**		
gorilla	257	20/39.3			
guinea pig	68	4/7.5	chicken	21	
hippopotamus	238	25/–	duck	30	
horse	330	20/46	goose	30	
kangaroo	42	7/–	pigeon	18	
leopard	98	12/19.3	turkey	26	

longevity figures refer to animals in captivity; an animal's potential life span is rarely attained in nature

shrimps) have two or more distinct larval stages. Among vertebrates, it is only the amphibians and some fishes that have a larval stage.

meiosis process of cell division in which the number of chromosomes in the cell is halved. It only occurs in eukaryotic cells, and is part of a life cycle that involves sexual reproduction because it allows the genes of two parents to be combined without the total number of chromosomes increasing.

menopause in women, the cessation of reproductive ability, characterized by menstruation (see menstrual cycle) becoming irregular and eventu-

ally ceasing. The onset is at about the age of 50, but varies greatly. Menopause is usually uneventful, but some women suffer from complications such as flushing, excessive bleeding, and nervous disorders. Since the 1950s, hormone-replacement therapy (HRT), using oestrogen alone or with progestogen, a synthetic form of progesterone, has been developed to counteract such effects.

menstrual cycle cycle that occurs in female mammals of reproductive age, in which the body is prepared for pregnancy. At the beginning of the cycle, a Graafian (egg) follicle develops in the ovary, and the inner wall of the uterus forms a soft spongy lining. The egg is released from the ovary, and the uterus lining (endometrium) becomes vascularized (filled with blood vessels). If fertilization does not occur, the corpus luteum (remains of the Graafian follicle) degenerates, and the uterine lining breaks down, and is shed. This is what causes

---

Menopausal mammals

■ All female mammals undergo the menopause, not just humans.

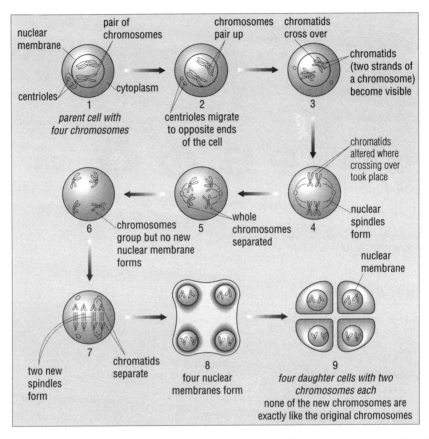

1
parent cell with
four chromosomes

nuclear membrane
pair of chromosomes
centrioles
cytoplasm

2
centrioles migrate
to opposite ends
of the cell

chromosomes pair up

3
chromatids cross over
chromatids (two strands of a chromosome) become visible

4
chromatids altered where crossing over took place
nuclear spindles form

5
whole chromosomes separated

6
chromosomes group but no new nuclear membrane forms

7
two new spindles form
chromatids separate

8
four nuclear membranes form

9
four daughter cells with two chromosomes each
none of the new chromosomes are exactly like the original chromosomes
nuclear membrane

meiosis Meiosis is a type of cell division that produces gametes (sex cells, sperm and egg). This sequence shows an animal cell but only four chromosomes are present in the parent cell (1). There are two stages in the division process. In the first stage (2–6), the chromosomes come together in pairs and exchange genetic material. This is called crossing over. In the second stage (7–9), the cell divides to produce four gamete cells, each with only one copy of each chromosome from the parent cell.

the loss of blood that marks menstruation. The cycle then begins again. Human menstruation takes place from puberty to menopause, except during pregnancy, occurring about every 28 days. *See illustration on page 122.*

fish, during which the individual's body changes from one form to another through a major reconstitution of its tissues. For example, adult frogs are produced by metamorphosis from tadpoles, and butterflies are produced from caterpillars following metamorphosis within a pupa.

Synchronized fertility
■ The menstrual cycles of women living in close proximity to each other become synchronized. This could be due to pheromones released in the sweat and may have evolved as means of thwarting male infidelity.

No time for tadpoles
■ Certain frogs do not spend time as tadpoles. The female of a species of tiny Brazilian frog lays a single egg which hatches as a single froglet, rather than going through a tadpole phase first.

metamorphosis period during the life cycle of many invertebrates, most amphibians, and some

mitosis process of cell division by which identical daughter cells are produced. During mitosis the

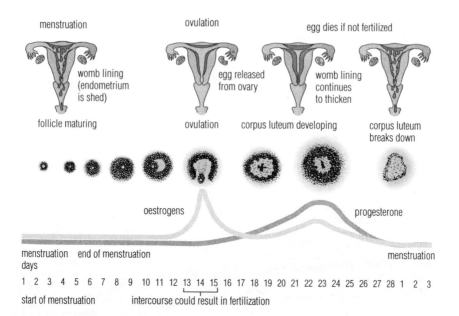

menstrual cycle From puberty to the menopause, most women produce a regular rhythm of hormones that stimulate the various stages of the menstrual cycle. The change in hormone levels may cause premenstrual tension. This diagram shows an average menstrual cycle. The dates of each stage vary from woman to woman.

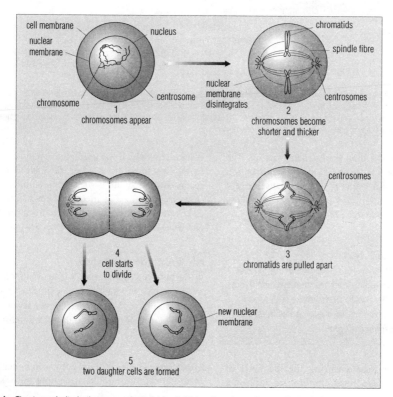

mitosis The stages of mitosis, the process of cell division that takes place when a plant or animal cell divides for growth or repair. The two daughter cells each receive the same number of chromosomes as were in the original cell.

DNA is duplicated and the chromosome number doubled, so new cells contain the same amount of DNA as the original cell.

The genetic material of eukaryotic cells is carried on a number of chromosomes. To control movements of chromosomes during cell division so that both new cells get the correct number, a system of protein tubules, known as the spindle, organizes the chromosomes into position in the middle of the cell before they replicate. The spindle then controls the movement of chromosomes as the cell goes through the stages of division: **interphase, prophase, metaphase, anaphase,** and **telophase**. See also meiosis.

ovum plural **ova** female gamete (sex cell) before fertilization. In animals it is called an egg, and is produced in the ovaries. In plants, where it is also known as an egg cell or oosphere, the ovum is produced in an ovule. The ovum is non-motile. It must be fertilized by a male gamete before it can develop further, except in cases of parthenogenesis.

parthenogenesis development of an ovum (egg) without any genetic contribution from a male. Parthenogenesis is the normal means of reproduction in a few plants (for example, dandelions) and animals (for example, certain fish). Some sexually reproducing species, such as aphids, show parthenogenesis at some stage in their life cycle to accelerate reproduction to take advantage of good conditions.

pollen the grains of seed plants that contain the male gametes. In angiosperms (flowering plants) pollen is produced within anthers; in most gymnosperms (cone-bearing plants) it is produced in male cones. A pollen grain is typically yellow and, when mature, has a hard outer wall. Pollen of insect-pollinated plants is often sticky and spiny and larger than the smooth, light grains produced by wind-pollinated species.

pollination process by which pollen is transferred from one plant to another. The male gametes are contained in pollen grains, which must be transferred from the anther to the stigma in angiosperms (flowering plants), and from the male cone to the female cone in gymnosperms (cone-bearing plants). Fertilization

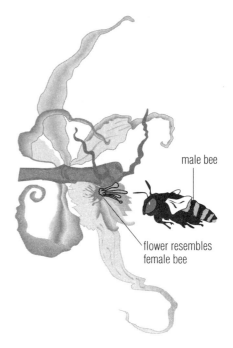

male bee

flower resembles female bee

pollination The male bee, attracted to the orchid because of its resemblance to a female bee, attempts to mate with the flower. The bee's efforts cover its body with pollen, which is carried to the next flower it visits. This method of pollination is known as pseudocopulation.

(not the same as pollination) occurs after the growth of the pollen tube to the ovary. Self-pollination occurs when pollen is transferred to a stigma of the same flower, or to another flower on the same plant; cross-pollination occurs when pollen is transferred to another plant. This involves external pollen-carrying agents, such as wind (anemophily), water (hydrophily), insects, birds (ornithophily), bats, and other small mammals.

pregnancy in humans, the period during which an embryo grows within the womb. It begins at conception and ends at birth, and the normal length is 40 weeks. Menstruation usually stops on conception. About one in five pregnancies fails, but most of these failures occur very early on, so the woman may notice only that her period is late. After the second month, the breasts become tense and tender, and the areas round the nipples become darker. Enlargement of the uterus can be felt at about the end of the third month, and thereafter the abdomen enlarges progressively. Fetal movement can be felt at about 18 weeks; a heart-beat may be heard during the sixth month.

puberty stage in human development when the individual becomes sexually mature. It may occur from the age of ten upwards. The sexual organs take on their adult form and pubic hair grows. In girls, menstruation begins, and the breasts develop; in boys, the voice breaks and becomes deeper, and facial hair develops.

pupa nonfeeding, largely immobile stage of some insect life cycles, in which larval tissues are broken down, and adult tissues and structures are formed.

seed the reproductive structure of higher plants (angiosperms and gymnosperms). It develops from a fertilized ovule and consists of an embryo and a food store, surrounded and protected by an outer seed coat, called the testa. The food store is contained either in a specialized nutritive tissue, the endosperm, or in the cotyledons of the embryo itself. In angiosperms the seed is enclosed within a fruit, whereas in gymnosperms it is usually naked and unprotected, once shed from the female cone. Following germination the seed develops into a new plant.

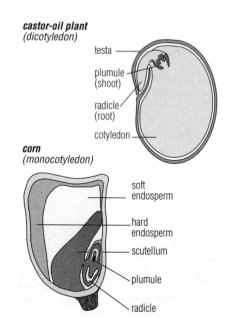

castor-oil plant
(dicotyledon)

testa
plumule (shoot)
radicle (root)
cotyledon

corn
(monocotyledon)

soft endosperm
hard endosperm
scutellum
plumule
radicle

seed The structure of seeds. The castor is a dicotyledon, a plant in which the developing plant has two leaves, developed from the cotyledon. In maize, a monocotyledon, there is a single leaf developed from the scutellum.

sexual reproduction reproductive process in organisms that requires the union, or fertilization, of gametes (such as eggs and sperm).

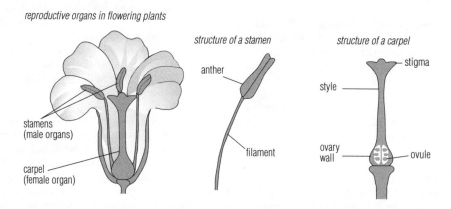

reproductive organs in flowering plants

stamens (male organs)
carpel (female organ)

structure of a stamen

anther
filament

structure of a carpel

stigma
style
ovary wall
ovule

sexual reproduction Reproductive organs in flowering plants. The stamens are the male parts of the plant. Each consists of a stalklike filament topped by an anther. The anther contains four pollen sacs which burst to release tiny grains of pollen, the male sex cells. The carpels are the female reproductive parts. Each carpel has a stigma which catches the pollen grain. The style connects the stigma to the ovary. The ovary contains one or more ovules, the female sex cells. Buttercups have many ovaries; the lupin has only one.

female reproductive system

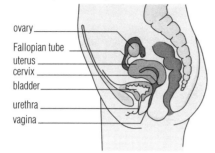

- ovary
- Fallopian tube
- uterus
- cervix
- bladder
- urethra
- vagina

male reproductive system

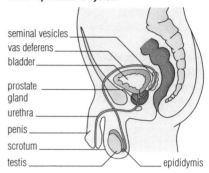

- seminal vesicles
- vas deferens
- bladder
- prostate gland
- urethra
- penis
- scrotum
- testis
- epididymis

sexual reproduction The human reproductive organs. In the female, gametes called ova are released regularly in the ovaries after puberty. The Fallopian tubes carry the ova to the uterus or womb, in which the baby will develop. In the male, sperm is produced inside the testes after puberty; about 10 million sperm cells are produced each day, enough to populate the world in six months. The sperm duct or vas deferens, a continuation of the epididymis, carries sperm to the urethra during ejaculation.

These are usually produced by two different individuals, although self-fertilization occurs in a few hermaphrodites such as tapeworms. Most organisms other than bacteria and cyanobacteria (blue-green algae) show some sort of sexual process. Except in some lower organisms, the gametes are of two distinct types

Pregnant males

- In sea horses it is the male that carries the babies. The female deposits her eggs into his brood pouch, where he fertilizes them. They remain there for up to six weeks while he nourishes them till they reach independence.

sperm Female bush cricket *Eupholidoptera chabrieri* with a spermatophore. The male produces the spermatophore containing his sperm and deposits it in the female's cloaca during their courtship ritual. Internal fertilization can then take place. *R A Preston-Mafham/Premaphotos Wildlife*

Giant sperm

■ The fruit fly *Drosophila bifurca* (1.5 cm/0.6 in long) has sperm cells that are 6 cm/2.4 in long (1,200 times longer than human sperm). Its testes take up 50% of its abdominal cavity and *D. bifurca* produces fewer than 20 sperm cells at a time (human males produce millions).

spore Fruiting bodies of the slime mould *Comatricha nigra*. The fruiting bodies release spores that will form the single-celled slime moulds that are the first stage in the life cycle of cellular slime moulds. *K G Preston-Mafham/Premaphotos Wildlife*

called eggs and sperm. The organisms producing the eggs are called females, and those producing the sperm, males. The fusion of a male and female gamete produces a **zygote,** from which a new individual develops.

sperm or **spermatozoon** male gamete of animals. Each sperm cell has a head capsule containing a nucleus, a middle portion containing mitochondria (which provide energy), and a long tail (flagellum).

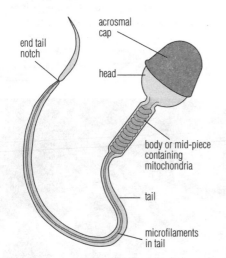

sperm Only a single sperm is needed to fertilize an egg, or ovum. Yet up to 500 million may start the journey towards the egg. Once a sperm has fertilized an egg, the egg's wall cannot be penetrated by other sperm. The unsuccessful sperm die after about three days.

spore small reproductive or resting body, usually consisting of just one cell. Unlike a gamete, it does not need to fuse with another cell in order to develop into a new organism. Spores are produced by the lower plants, most fungi, some bacteria, and certain protozoa. They are generally light and easily dispersed by wind movements.

Plant spores are haploid and are produced by the sporophyte, following meiosis.

succession in ecology, a series of changes that

succession These seedlings are a pioneer species, quickly colonizing this steep muddy river bank along the Bohorok River, Sumatra, Indonesia, following a landslide which had removed all existing vegetation. *Ken Preston-Mafham/Premaphotos Wildlife*

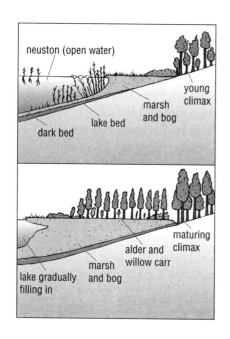

occur in the structure and composition of the vegetation in a given area from the time it is first colonized by plants (**primary succession**), or after it has been disturbed by fire, flood, or clearing (**secondary succession**).

zygote ovum (egg) after fertilization but before it undergoes cleavage to begin embryonic development.

succession The succession of plant types along a lake. As the lake gradually fills in, a mature climax community of trees forms inland from the shore. Extending out from the shore, a series of plant communities can be discerned with small, rapidly growing species closest to the shore.

PLANT LIFE

Plants are organisms that carry out photosynthesis, have cellulose cell walls and complex cells, and are immobile. A few parasitic plants have lost the ability to photosynthesize but are still considered to be plants. Plants are autotrophs, that is, they make carbohydrates from water and carbon dioxide, and are the primary producers in all food chains, so that all animal life is dependent on them. They play a vital part in the carbon cycle, removing carbon dioxide from the atmosphere and generating oxygen. The study of plants is known as botany.

Many of the lower plants (the algae and bryophytes) consist of a simple body, or thallus, on which the organs of reproduction are borne. Simplest of all are the threadlike algae, for example *Spirogyra*, which consist of a chain of cells.

The seaweeds (algae) and mosses and liverworts (bryophytes) represent a further development, with simple, multicellular bodies that have specially modified areas in which the reproductive organs are carried. Higher in the morphological scale are the ferns, club mosses, and horsetails (pteridophytes).

The pteridophytes have special supportive water-conducting tissues, which identify them as vascular plants, a group which includes all seed plants, that is the gymnosperms (conifers, yews, cycads, and ginkgos), and the flowering plants, which are called angiosperms. The seed plants are the largest group, and structurally the most complex. They are usually divided into three parts: root, stem, and leaves. Stems grow above or below ground. Their cellular structure is designed to carry water and salts from the roots to the leaves in the xylem, and sugars from the leaves to the roots in the phloem. The leaves manufacture the food of the plant by means of photosynthesis, which occurs in the chloroplasts they contain. Flowers and cones are modified leaves arranged in groups, enclosing the reproductive organs from which the fruits and seeds result.

Plant communication

■ Plants can communicate with each other. A wounded plant may release a gaseous hormone that warns its neighbours to prepare their defences for insect attack, thus limiting potential damage.

---

algae singular **alga** highly varied group of plants, ranging from single-celled forms to large and complex seaweeds. They live in both fresh and salt water, and in damp soil. Algae do not have true roots, stems, or leaves.

Marine algae help combat global warming by removing carbon dioxide from the atmosphere during photosynthesis.

angiosperm flowering plant in which the seeds are enclosed within an ovary, which ripens into a fruit. Angiosperms are divided into monocotyledons (single seed leaf in the embryo) and dicotyledons (two seed leaves in the embryo). They include the majority of flowers, herbs, grasses, and trees except conifers.

bryophyte member of the Bryophyta, a division of the plant kingdom containing three classes: the Hepaticae (liverwort), Musci (moss), and Anthocerotae (hornwort). Bryophytes are generally small, low-growing, terrestrial plants with no vascular (water-conducting) system as in higher plants. Their life cycle shows a marked alternation of generations. Bryophytes chiefly occur in damp habitats and require water for

chloroplast structure (organelle) within a plant cell containing the green pigment chlorophyll. Chloroplasts occur in most cells of the green plant that are exposed to light, often in large numbers. Typically, they are flattened and disclike, with a double membrane enclosing the stroma, a gel-like matrix. Within the stroma are stacks of fluid-containing cavities, or vesicles, where photosynthesis occurs.

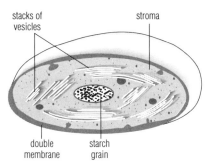

chloroplast Green chlorophyll molecules on the membranes of the vesicle stacks capture light energy to produce food by photosynthesis.

bryophyte Liverworts belong to a group of plants, called the Bryophyta, that also includes the mosses. Neither mosses nor liverworts possess true roots and both require water to enable the male gametes to swim to the female sex organs to fertilize the eggs. Unlike mosses most liverworts have no, or only very frail, leaves.

the dispersal of the male gametes (antherozoids).

cactus plural **cacti** strictly, any plant of the family Cactaceae, although the word is commonly used to describe many different succulent and prickly plants. True cacti have a woody axis (central core) surrounded by a large fleshy stem, which takes various forms and is usually covered with spines (actually reduced leaves). They are all specially adapted to growing in dry areas.

chlorophyll green pigment present in most plants; it is responsible for the absorption of light energy during photosynthesis.

The pigment absorbs the red and blue-violet parts of sunlight but reflects the green, thus giving plants their characteristic colour.

Fishy chlorophyll
- The deepsea fish *Malecosteus niger* has chlorophyll in the retina of its eye. This is the only known instance of chlorophyll being found in an organism that is not plant or bacteria.

fern any of a group of plants related to horsetails and clubmosses. Ferns are spore-bearing, not flowering, plants and most are perennial, spreading by slow-growing roots. The leaves, known as fronds, vary widely in size and shape. Some taller types, such as tree ferns, grow in the tropics. There are over 7,000 species. (Order Filicales.)

Common old bracken
- Bracken is one of the world's six most common plants and also one of the six oldest, being at least 90 million years old.

fungus plural **fungi** any of a unique group of organisms that includes moulds, yeasts, rusts, smuts, mildews, mushrooms, and toadstools. There are around 70,000 species of fungi known to science, though there may be as many as

Fungi everywhere
- Fungi have twice the total biomass of all the Earth's animals.

Major Divisions in the Plant Kingdom

Phylum	Examples	Phylum	Examples
Bryophyta	mosses, liverworts, hornworts	Cycadophyta	cycads
Psilophyta	whisk ferns	Ginkgophyta	ginkgo
Sphenophyta	horsetails	Coniferophyta	cedar, cypress, juniper, pine, redwood
Filicinophyta	ferns	Anthophyta	flowering plants

Classes of flowering plants

Dicotyledons	magnolia, laurel, water lily, buttercup, poppy, pitcher plant, nettle, walnut, cacti, peonies, violet, begonia, willow, primrose, rose, maple, holly, grape, honeysuckle, African violet, daisy
Monocotyledons	flowering rush, eel grass, lily, iris, banana, orchid, sedge, pineapple, grasses, palms, cat tail

1.5 million actually in existence. They are not considered to be plants for three main reasons: they have no leaves or roots; they contain no chlorophyll (green colouring) and are therefore unable to make their own food by photosynthesis; and they reproduce by spores. Some fungi are edible but many are highly poisonous; they often cause damage and sometimes disease to the organic matter they live and feed on, but some fungi are exploited in the production of food and drink (for example, yeasts in baking and brewing) and in medicine (for example, penicillin).

What is a flower?

A flower is the reproductive unit of an angiosperm or flowering plant, typically consisting of four whorls of modified leaves: sepals, petals, stamens, and carpels. These are borne on a central axis or receptacle. The many variations in size, colour, number, and arrangement of parts are closely related to the method of pollination. Flowers adapted for wind pollination typically have reduced or absent petals and sepals and long, feathery stigmas that hang outside the flower to trap airborne pollen. In contrast, the petals of insect-pollinated flowers are usually conspicuous and brightly coloured.

grass any of a very large family of plants, many of which are economically important because they provide grazing for animals and food for humans

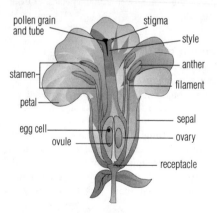

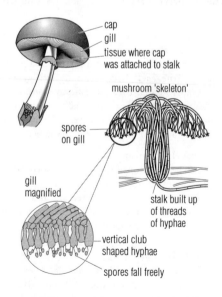

flower Cross section of a typical flower showing its basic components: sepals, petals, stamens (anthers and filaments), and carpel (ovary and stigma). Flowers vary greatly in the size, shape, colour, and arrangement of these components.

fungus Fungi grow from spores as fine threads, or hyphae. These have no distinct cellular structure. Mushrooms and toadstools are the fruiting bodies formed by the hyphae. Gills beneath the caps of these aerial structures produce masses of spores.

gymnosperm (Greek 'naked seed') any plant whose seeds are exposed, as opposed to the structurally more advanced angiosperms, where they are inside an ovary. The group includes conifers and related plants such as cycads and ginkgos, whose seeds develop in cones. Fossil gymnosperms have been found in rocks about 350 million years old.

hydrophyte plant adapted to live in water, or in waterlogged soil.

insectivorous plant plant that can capture and digest live prey (normally insects), to obtain nitrogen compounds that are lacking in its usual marshy habitat. Some are passive traps, for example, the pitcher plants *Nepenthes* and *Sarracenia*. One pitcher-plant species has container-traps holding 1.6 l/3.5 pt of the liquid that 'digests' its food, mostly insects but occasionally even rodents. Others, for example, sundews *Drosera*, butterworts *Pinguicula*, and Venus flytraps *Dionaea muscipula*, have an active trapping mechanism. Insectivorous plants have adapted to grow in poor soil conditions where the number of microorganisms recycling nitrogen compounds is very much reduced. In these circumstances other plants cannot gain enough nitrates to grow.

leaf lateral outgrowth on the stem of a plant, and in most species the primary organ of

sorghum Sorghum is a type of grass that was originally cultivated in Africa to provide grain for animal fodder and to make flour for bread or porridge. There are other kinds of sorghums which have been used to provide hay, molasses or syrup, and even brushes and brooms.

in the form of cereals. There are about 9,000 species distributed worldwide except in the Arctic regions. Most are perennial, with long, narrow leaves and jointed, hollow stems; flowers with both male and female reproductive organs are borne on spikelets; the fruits are grainlike. Included in the family are bluegrass, wheat, rye, maize, sugarcane, and bamboo.

Classification of Carnivorous Plants

Plants that obtain at least some of their nutrition by capturing and digesting prey are called carnivorous plants. Such plants have adaptations that allow them to attract, catch, and break down or digest prey once it is caught. Estimates of the number of species of carnivorous plants number from 450 to more than 600. Generally, these plants are classified into genera based upon the mechanism they have for trapping and capturing their prey. The major genera of these plants are listed in the table.

Common name	Genus	Scientific name	Trapping mechanism
bladderwort	*Utricularia*	*Utricularia vulgaris*	active trap; shows rapid motion during capture
butterwort	*Pinguicula*	*Pinguicula vulgaris*	semi-active trap; two-stage trap in which prey is initially caught in sticky fluid
calf's head pitcher plant	*Darlingtonia*	*Darlingtonia californica*	passive trap; attracts prey with nectar and then drowns prey in fluid contained within plant
flypaper plant	*Byblis*	*Byblis liniflora*	passive trap; attracts prey with nectar and then drowns prey in fluid contained within plant
sundew	*Drosera*	*Drosera linearis*	semi-active trap; two-stage trap in which prey is initially caught in sticky fluid
Venus flytrap	*Dionaea*	*Dionaea muscipula*	active trap; shows rapid motion during capture

leaf margins

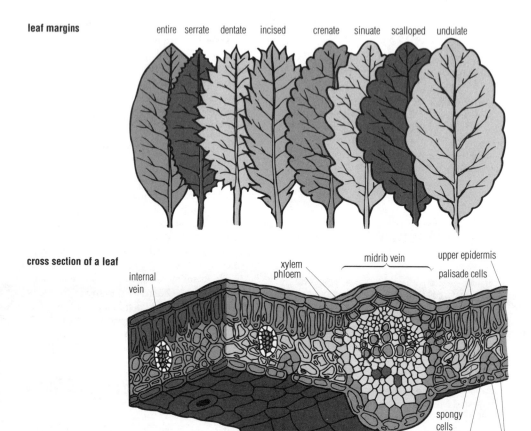

entire serrate dentate incised crenate sinuate scalloped undulate

cross section of a leaf

internal vein

xylem phloem

midrib vein

upper epidermis

palisade cells

spongy cells

air space

guard cells of stoma

lower epidermis

leaf Leaf shapes and arrangements on the stem are many and varied; in cross section, a leaf is a complex arrangement of cells surrounded by the epidermis. This is pierced by the stomata through which gases enter and leave.

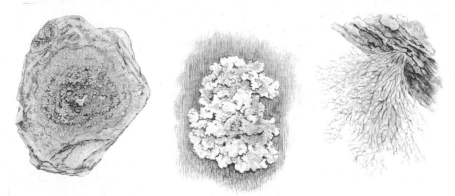

lichen A lichen is a symbiotic association between an alga and a fungus – in other words, each lichen is not one organism but two. Lichens grow very slowly, usually as encrustations on rocks, walls, or wood. They are found throughout the world but are unable to survive where the atmosphere is polluted, so they are good indicators of clean air.

photosynthesis. The chief leaf types are cotyledons (seed leaves), scale leaves (on underground stems), foliage leaves, and bracts (in the axil of which a flower is produced).

lichen any organism of a unique group that consists of a specific fungus and a specific algae living together in a mutually beneficient relationship. Found on trees, rocks, and other surfaces, lichens flourish in harsh conditions..

moss small nonflowering plant of the class Musci (10,000 species), forming with the liverworts and the hornworts the order Bryophyta. The stem of each plant bears rhizoids that anchor it; there are no true roots. Leaves spirally arranged on its lower portion have sexual organs at their tips. Most mosses flourish best in damp conditions where other vegetation is thin.

mould furlike growth caused by any of a group of fungi living on foodstuffs and other organic matter; a few are parasitic on plants, animals, or each other. Many moulds are of medical or industrial importance; for example, the antibiotic penicillin comes from a type of mould.

mould The mould *Dactylium dendroides* engulfing *Pholiota squarrosa* toadstools. Fungi are decomposers, breaking down dead matter; decomposers, themselves, will eventually be broken down by other decomposers. *K G Preston-Mafham/Premaphotos Wildlife*

phylum plural **phyla** major grouping in biological classification. In classifying plants (where the term 'division' often takes the place of 'phylum'), there are between four and nine phyla depending on the criteria used; all flowering plants belong to a single phylum, Angiospermata, and all conifers to another, Gymnospermata. Related phyla are grouped together in a kingdom; phyla are subdivided into classes.

pteridophyte simple type of vascular plant. The pteridophytes comprise four classes: the Psilosida, including the most primitive vascular plants, found mainly in the tropics; the Lycopsida, including the club mosses; the Sphenopsida, including the horsetails; and the Pteropsida, including the ferns. They do not produce seeds.

rhizome or **rootstock** horizontal underground plant stem. It is a perennating organ in some species, where it is generally thick and fleshy, while in other species it is mainly a means of vegetative reproduction, and is therefore long and slender, with buds all along it that send up new plants. The potato is a rhizome that has two distinct parts, the tuber being the swollen end of a long, cordlike rhizome.

stem main supporting axis of a plant that bears the leaves, buds, and reproductive structures; it may be simple or branched. The plant stem usually grows above ground, although some grow underground, including rhizomes, corms, rootstocks, and tubers. Stems contain a continuous vascular system that conducts water and food to and from all parts of the plant.

stoma plural **stomata** a pore in the epidermis of a plant. Each stoma is surrounded by a pair of guard cells that are crescent-shaped when the stoma is open but can collapse to an oval shape, thus closing off the opening between them. Stomata allow the exchange of carbon dioxide and oxygen (needed for photosynthesis and respiration) between the internal tissues of the plant and the outside atmosphere. They are also the main route by which water is lost from the plant, and they can be closed to conserve water, the movements being controlled by changes in turgidity of the guard cells.

succulent plant thick, fleshy plant that stores water in its tissues; for example, cacti and

Varieties of roots

The root is the part of a plant that is usually underground, and whose primary functions are anchorage and the absorption of water and dissolved mineral salts. Roots usually grow downwards and towards water (that is, they are positively geotropic and hydrotropic. Plants such as epiphytic orchids, which grow above ground, produce aerial roots that absorb moisture from the atmosphere. Others, such as ivy, have climbing roots arising from the stems, which serve to attach the plant to trees and walls.

root nodule Root nodules containing nitrogen-fixing bacteria, on the roots of the lupin. *Ken Preston-Mafham/Premaphotos Wildlife*

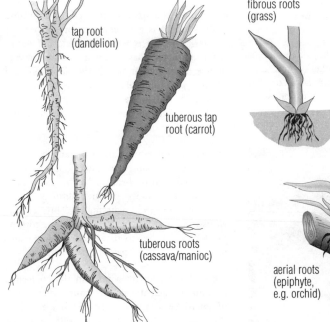

root Types of root. Many flowers (dandelion) and vegetables (carrot) have swollen tap roots with smaller lateral roots. The tuberous roots of the cassava are swollen parts of an underground stem modified to store food. The fibrous roots of the grasses are all of equal size. Prop roots grow out from the stem and then grow down into the ground to support a heavy plant. Aerial roots grow from stems but do not grow into the ground; many absorb moisture from the air.

stonecrops *Sedum*. Succulents live either in areas where water is very scarce, such as deserts, or in places where it is not easily obtainable because of the high concentrations of salts in the soil, as in salt marshes. Many desert plants are xerophytes.

Succulent stench
- The flowers of the stapeliads of Africa and southern Asia look very like dung or decaying meat. This is because they rely on carrion-feeding beetles to pollinate them. So convincing are the flowers that they are often covered with maggots that have hatched from eggs mistakenly laid on them.

Giant Trees of the USA

Source: Courtesy of American Forests

The measurements listed represent the largest known specimen of that species.

Tree type	Girth at 4.5 ft		Height		Crown spread		Location
	mm	in	m	ft	m	ft	
Douglas fir	11,125	438	100.28	329	18.29	60	Coos Country (OR)
American elm	7,950	313	26.52	87	23.16	76	Louisville (KY)
sugar maple	5,918	233	26.52	87	30.48	100	Kingston (NH)
white oak	9,500	374	24.08	79	31.09	102	Wye Mills State Park (MD)
loblolly pine	4,775	188	45.11	148	25.30	83	Warren (AR)
pinyon pine	5,410	213	21.03	69	15.85	52	Cuba (NM)
sugar pine	11,227	442	70.71	232	8.84	29	Dorrington (CA)
coast redwood	21,463	845	95.40	313	30.78	101	Prairie Creek (CA)
giant sequoia	25,349	998	83.82	275	32.61	107	Sequoia National Park (CA)
black willow	10,160	400	23.16	76	28.04	92	Grand Traverse (MI)

taxonomy another name for the classification of living organisms.

Tallest tree

■ The tallest tree ever measured was an Australian eucalyptus (*Eucalyptus regnans*), reported in 1872. It was 132 m/435 ft tall.

tree perennial plant with a woody stem, usually a single stem (trunk), made up of wood and protected by an outer layer of bark. It absorbs water through a root system. There is no clear dividing line between shrubs and trees, but sometimes a minimum achievable height of 6 m/20 ft is used to define a tree.

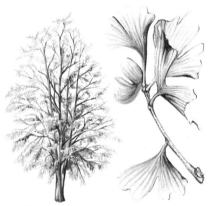

tree The ginkgo tree has existed virtually unchanged for at least 160 million years. The bright green leaves resemble those of the maidenhair fern and give the ginkgo its common name, the maidenhair tree.

Longest-Lived Trees in the USA

Common name	Scientific name	Life span/expectancy (years)
bristlecone pine	*Pinus longaeva*	3,000–4,700
giant sequoia	*Sequoiadendron giganteum*	2,500
redwood	*Sequoia sempervirens*	1,000–3,500
Douglas fir, Oregon	*Pseudotsuga menziesii*	750
bald cypress	*Taxodium distichum*	600

ANIMAL LIFE

alimentary canal in animals, the tube through which food passes; it extends from the mouth to the anus. It is a complex organ, adapted for digestion. In human adults, it is about 9 m/30 ft long, consisting of the mouth cavity, pharynx, oesophagus, stomach, and the small and large intestines.

amoeba see **microscopic life** feature on pages 152–153.

amphibian (Greek 'double life') member of the vertebrate class Amphibia, which generally spend

their larval (tadpole) stage in fresh water, transferring to land at maturity (after metamorphosis) and generally returning to water to breed. Like fish and reptiles, they continue to grow throughout life, and cannot maintain a temperature greatly differing from that of their environment. The class contains 4,553 known species, 4,000 of which are

What is an animal?

An animal is a member of the kingdom Animalia, one of the major categories of living things, the science of which is **zoology.** Animals are all heterotrophs (they obtain their energy from organic substances produced by other organisms); they have eukaryotic cells (the genetic material is contained within a distinct nucleus) bounded by a thin cell membrane rather than the thick cell wall of plants. Most animals are capable of moving around for at least part of their life cycle.

In the past, it was common to include the single-celled protozoa with the animals, but these are now classified as protists, together with single-celled plants. Thus all animals are multicellular. The oldest land animals known date back 440 million years.

feeding types Animals can be divided into three feeding types: **herbivores** eat plants and plant products, **carnivores** eat other animals, and **omnivores** eat both. Since few animals can digest cellulose, herbivores have either symbiotic cellulose-digesting bacteria or protozoa in their guts, or grinding mechanisms, such as the large flattened teeth of elephants, to release the plant protoplasm from its cellulose-walled cells. Carnivores are adapted for hunting and eating flesh, with well-developed sense

organs and fast reflexes, and weapons such as sharp fangs, claws, and stings. Omnivores eat whatever they can find, and often scavenge among the remains of carnivores' prey; because of the diversity of their diet, they have more versatile teeth and guts than herbivores or carnivores. Many animals are adapted for a parasitic way of life, living on other animals or plants, and feeding solely by absorbing fluids from their hosts. Some animals absorb food directly into their body cells; others have a digestive system in which food is prepared for absorption by body tissues.

movement The mechanisms by which living organisms move vary from the flowing protoplasm of an amoeba to the complex muscle-and-bone movements of a bird's wing in flight. Wriggling, crawling, swimming, and the internal flow of fluids are often assisted by minute cellular organelles, *cilia*, which beat in a rhythmic pattern. Most animals have contractile tissue to assist with movement; the increased complexity of muscle systems in higher animals, coupled with a stiff skeleton, allows greater flexibility of movement.

circulation In order to contract, muscles must have energy, which is obtained by breaking down sugars produced by the digestion of food, usually by combining them with

oxygen. In simple animals, the sugars and oxygen diffuse through the body to the contractile tissue; in higher animals they are carried by a blood circulatory system, which is pumped by the heart, to the muscles. In insects, the oxygen is carried through tiny branching air-filled tubes, called **trachea.**

excretion The circulatory system also carries waste products away from the cells. These are separated from the blood (in the kidneys of higher animals), and are excreted together with undigested food. The excretory systems of aquatic animals are also responsible for maintaining a correct fluid balance within the animals. This is particularly important in freshwater creatures, which tend to absorb water by osmosis.

nervous system The movement and behaviour of animals are controlled by the nervous system. Impulses pass from centres of control – often grouped to form a brain – to the various muscles and glands. As animals become more advanced, their brains become more complex, and their nervous control more complete. Behaviour varies from the simplest reflex action to the highly complex learned and intelligent behaviour of the higher primates. In many animals special behaviour patterns form an integral part of courtship.

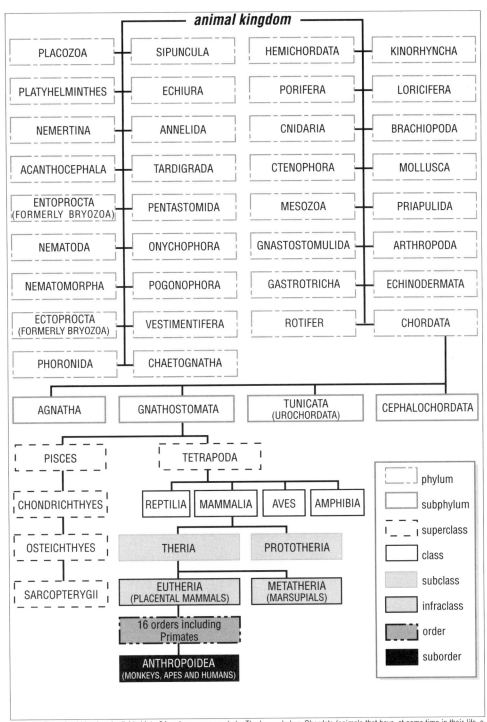

animal The animal kingdom is divided into 34 major groups or phyla. The large phylum Chordata (animals that have, at some time in their life, a notochord, or stiff rod of cells running along the length of their body) is subdivided into four subphyla, of which two, the Agnatha and the Gnathostomata, are vertebrates (animals with backbones). The subphyla are divided into classes and subclasses.

annelid any segmented worm of the phylum Annelida. Annelids include earthworms, leeches, and marine worms such as lugworms.

arachnid or **arachnoid** type of arthropod of the class Arachnida, including spiders, scorpions,

annelid Annelids are worms with segmented bodies. The ragworm, lugworm, and peacock worm shown here are all marine species. Ragworms commonly live in mucous-lined burrows on muddy shores or under stones, and lugworms occupy U-shaped burrows. The peacock worm, however, builds a smooth, round tube from fine particles of mud.

arachnid The pink-toed tarantula *Avicularia avicularia* (family Theraphosidae) has few enemies. Its venom is not particularly potent but it has a covering of irritant hairs that act as a strong deterrent to predators. Tarantulas, like all spiders, are arachnids. *Mark Preston-Mafham/Premaphotos Wildlife*

frogs and toads, 390 salamanders, and 163 caecilians (wormlike in appearance).

section through a long bone (the femur)

spongy bone

periosteum

epiphysis

periosteum

blood vessel

concentric lamellae

marrow cavity

diaphysis

blood vessel

Haversian canal

epiphysis

trabeculae

articular cartilage

bone Bone is a network of fibrous material impregnated with mineral salts and as strong as reinforced concrete. The upper end of the thighbone or femur is made up of spongy bone, which has a fine lacework structure designed to transmit the weight of the body. The shaft of the femur consists of hard compact bone designed to resist bending. Fine channels carrying blood vessels, nerves, and lymphatics interweave even the densest bone.

ticks, and mites. They differ from insects in possessing only two main body regions, the cephalothorax and the abdomen, and in having eight legs.

arthropod member of the phylum Arthropoda; an invertebrate animal with jointed legs and a segmented body with a horny or chitinous casing (exoskeleton), which is shed periodically and replaced as the animal grows. Included are arachnids such as spiders and mites, as well as crustaceans, millipedes, centipedes, and insects.

bacteria see **microscopic life** feature on pages 152–153.

bird backboned animal of the class Aves, the biggest group of land vertebrates, characterized by warm blood, feathers, wings, breathing through lungs, and egg-laying by the female. Birds are bipedal; feet are usually adapted for perching and never have more than four toes. Hearing and eyesight are well developed, but the sense of smell is usually poor. No existing species of bird possesses teeth.

Most birds fly, but some groups (such as ostriches) are flightless, and others include flightless members. Many communicate by sounds (nearly half of all known species are

---

The naming of birds
■ Rifleman, short-tailed pygmy tyrant, frilled coquette, bobwhite, tawny frogmouth, trembler, wattle-eye, fuscous honeyeater, dickcissel, common grackle, and forktailed drongo are all common names for species of bird.

---

songbirds) or by visual displays, in connection with which many species are brightly coloured, usually the males. Birds have highly developed patterns of instinctive behaviour. There are nearly 8,500 species of birds.

blue-green algae see **microscopic life** feature on pages 152–153.

bone hard connective tissue comprising the skeleton of most vertebrate animals. Bone is composed of a network of collagen fibres impregnated with mineral salts (largely calcium phosphate and calcium carbonate), a combination that gives it great density and strength, comparable in some cases with that of reinforced concrete. Enclosed within this solid matrix are bone cells, blood vessels, and nerves. The interior of the long bones of the limbs

---

Classification of Major Bird Groups

Order	Examples	Order	Examples
Tinamiformes	tinamou	Charadriiformes	wader, gull, auk, oyster-catcher, plover, puffin, tern
Rheiformes	rhea		
Struthioniformes	ostrich	Gaviiformes	diver
Casuariiformes	cassowary, emu	Columbiformes	dove, pigeon, sandgrouse
Apterygiformes	kiwi	Psittaciformes	parrot, macaw, parakeet
Podicipediformes	grebe	Cuculiformes	cuckoo, roadrunner
Procellariiformes	albatross, petrel, shearwater, storm petrel	Strigiformes	owl
		Caprimulgiformes	nightjar, oilbird
Sphenisciformes	penguin	Apodiformes	swift, hummingbird
Pelecaniformes	pelican, booby, gannet, frigate bird	Coliiformes	mousebird
Anseriformes	duck, goose, swan	Trogoniformes	trogon
Phoenicopteriformes	flamingo	Coraciiformes	kingfisher, hoopoe
Ciconiiformes	heron, ibis, stork, spoonbill	Piciformes	woodpecker, toucan, puffbird
Falconiformes	falcon, hawk, eagle, buzzard, vulture	Passeriformes	finch, crow, warbler, sparrow, weaver, jay, lark, blackbird, swallow, mockingbird, wren, thrush
Galliformes	grouse, partridge, pheasant, turkey		
Gruiformes	crane, rail, bustard, coot		

consists of a spongy matrix filled with a soft marrow that produces blood cells.

brain in higher animals, a mass of interconnected nerve cells forming the anterior part of the central nervous system, whose activities it coordinates and controls. In vertebrates, the brain is contained by the skull. At the base of the brainstem, the **medulla oblongata** contains centres for the control of respiration, heartbeat rate and strength, and blood pressure. Overlying this is the **cerebellum,** which is concerned with coordinating complex muscular processes such as maintaining posture and moving limbs.

The cerebral hemispheres (**cerebrum**) are paired outgrowths of the front end of the forebrain, in early vertebrates mainly concerned with the senses, but in higher vertebrates greatly developed and involved in the integration of all sensory input and motor output, and in thought, emotions, memory, and behaviour.

Bryozoan, moss animals or **sea-mats** plant-like animal in the phylum Bryozoa which form colonies arising from the continual budding of the cells. There are 4,300 known species. The majority are marine, but many occur in fresh water. Colonies exhibit a wide variation in form and habit, occurring as crusts on rocks, masses, broad fronds, or branched growths.

Chordata phylum of animals, members of which are called chordates.

chordate animal belonging to the phylum Chordata, which includes vertebrates, sea squirts, amphioxi, and others. All these animals, at some stage of their lives, have a supporting rod of tissue (notochord or backbone) running down their bodies.

circulatory system system of vessels in an animal's body that transports essential substances (blood or other circulatory fluid) to and from the different parts of the body. It was first discovered and described by English physician, William Harvey. All mammals except for the simplest kinds – such as sponges, jellyfish, sea anemones, and corals – have some type of circulatory system. Some invertebrates (animals without a backbone), such as insects, spiders, and most shellfish, have an 'open' circulatory system which consists of a simple network of tubes and hollow spaces. Other invertebrates have pumplike structures that send blood through a system of blood vessels. All vertebrates (animals with a backbone), including human beings, have a 'closed' circulatory system which principally consists of a pumping organ – the heart – and a network of blood vessels.

class in biological classification, a group of related orders. For example, all mammals belong to the class Mammalia and all birds to the class Aves. Among plants, all class names end in 'idae' (such as Asteridae) and among fungi in 'mycetes'; there are no equivalent conventions among animals. Related classes are grouped together in a phylum.

classification arrangement of organisms into a hierarchy of groups on the basis of their similarities in biochemical, anatomical, or physiological characters. The basic grouping is a species, several of which may constitute a genus, which in turn are grouped into families, and so on up through orders, classes, phyla (in plants, sometimes called divisions), to kingdoms.

Coral Reef Biological Diversity

location	coral species	fish species
Philippines	400	1,500
Great Barrier Reef (Australia)	350	1,500
New Caledonia	300	1,000
French Polynesia	168	800
Aqaba	150	400
Toliara (Madagascar)	147	552
Society Islands	120	633

location	coral species	fish species
St Gilles (Réunion)	120	258
Tadjoura (Djibouti)	65	180
Baie Possession (Réunion)	54	109
Tutia Reef (Tanzania)	52	192
Hermitage (Réunion)	30	81
Kuwait	23	85

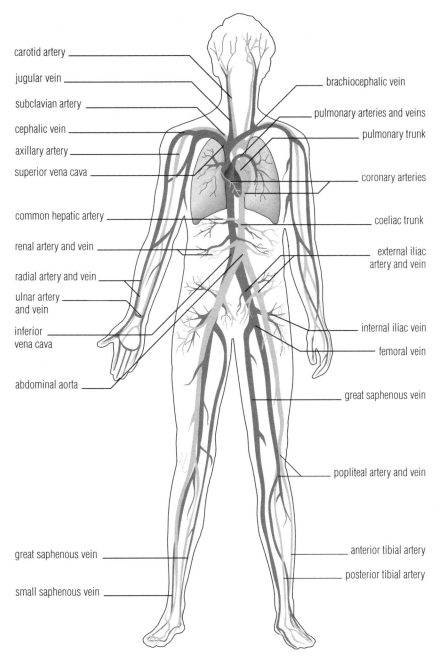

carotid artery

jugular vein

subclavian artery

cephalic vein

axillary artery

superior vena cava

common hepatic artery

renal artery and vein

radial artery and vein

ulnar artery
and vein

inferior
vena cava

abdominal aorta

great saphenous vein

small saphenous vein

brachiocephalic vein

pulmonary arteries and veins

pulmonary trunk

coronary arteries

coeliac trunk

external iliac
artery and vein

internal iliac vein

femoral vein

great saphenous vein

popliteal artery and vein

anterior tibial artery

posterior tibial artery

circulatory system Blood flows through 96,500 km/60,000 mi of arteries and veins, supplying oxygen and nutrients to organs and limbs. Oxygen-poor blood (dark grey) circulates from the heart to the lungs where oxygen is absorbed. Oxygen-rich blood (light grey) flows back to the heart and is then pumped round the body through the aorta, the largest artery, to smaller arteries and capillaries. Here oxygen and nutrients are exchanged with carbon dioxide and waste products and the blood returns to the heart via the veins. Waste products are filtered by the liver, spleen, and kidneys, and nutrients are absorbed from the stomach and small intestine.

coral Brain coral in the Red Sea at Eilat, Israel. So-called because of it's resemblance to a brain, the structure is made up of the hard lime skeletons of a colony of millions of coral polyps. The structure grows slowly as the coral polyps grow and reproduce. *Chris McTernan*

coral marine invertebrate of the class Anthozoa in the phylum Cnidaria, which also includes sea anemones and jellyfish. It has a skeleton of lime (calcium carbonate) extracted from the surrounding water. Corals exist in warm seas, at moderate depths with sufficient light. Some coral is valued for decoration or jewellery, for example, Mediterranean red coral *Corallum rubrum. See table on page 140.*

crustacean one of the class of arthropods that includes crabs, lobsters, shrimps, woodlice, and barnacles. The external skeleton is made of protein and chitin hardened with lime. Each segment bears a pair of appendages that may be modified as sensory feelers (antennae), as mouthparts, or as swimming, walking, or grasping structures.

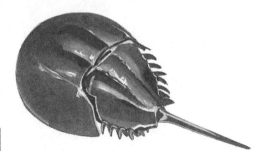

crustacean The king crab is an ancient life form, almost identical to fossils from the Triassic period about 225 million years ago. It is caught for food in large numbers off the eastern coast of N America from Florida to Nova Scotia, and off the eastern coast of Asia.

Lobsters queue for efficiency
■ When spiny lobsters migrate, they do so by walking in queues of up to 65 along the sea-bed, each clinging with its claws to the rear of the one in front. Scientific experiments with dead lobsters, weights and pulleys have shown that such an arrangement reduces drag and allows a 25% improvement in speed through the water.

diatom see **microscopic life** feature on pages 152–153.

digestive system all the organs and tissues involved in the digestion of food. In animals, these consist of the mouth, stomach, intestines, and their associated glands. The process of digestion breaks down the food by physical and chemical means into the different elements that are needed by the body for energy and tissue building and repair. Digestion begins in the mouth and is completed in the stomach; from there most nutrients are absorbed into the small intestine from where they pass through the intestinal wall into the bloodstream; what remains is stored and concentrated into faeces in the large intestine. Birds have two additional digestive organs – the crop and gizzard. In smaller, simpler animals such as jellyfish, the digestive system is simply a cavity (coelenteron or enteric cavity) with a 'mouth' into which food is taken; the digestible portion is dissolved and absorbed in this cavity, and the remains are ejected back through the mouth.

echinoderm marine invertebrate of the phylum Echinodermata ('spiny-skinned'), characterized by a five-radial symmetry. Echinoderms have a water-vascular system which transports substances around the body. They include starfishes (or sea stars), brittle-stars, sea lilies, sea urchins, and sea cucumbers. The skeleton is external, made of a series of limy plates. Echinoderms generally move by using tube-feet, small water-filled sacs that can be protruded or pulled back to the body.

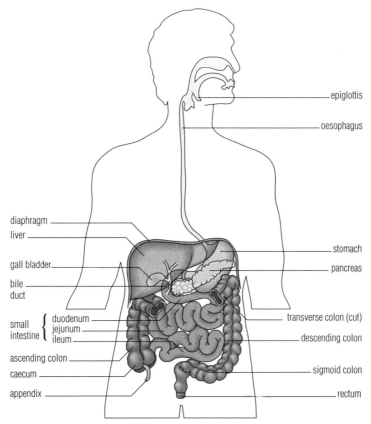

epiglottis
oesophagus
diaphragm
liver
gall bladder
bile duct
small intestine { duodenum jejunum ileum
ascending colon
caecum
appendix
stomach
pancreas
transverse colon (cut)
descending colon
sigmoid colon
rectum

digestive system The human digestive system. When food is swallowed, it is moved down the oesophagus by the action of muscles (peristalsis) into the stomach. Digestion starts in the stomach as the food is mixed with enzymes and strong acid. After several hours, the food passes to the small intestine. Here more enzymes are added and digestion is completed. After all nutrients have been absorbed, the indigestible parts pass into the large intestine and thence to the rectum. The liver has many functions, such as storing minerals and vitamins and making bile, which is stored in the gall bladder until needed for the digestion of fats. The pancreas supplies enzymes. The appendix appears to have no function in human beings.

Endangered Species

Species	Observation
plants	a quarter of the world's plants are threatened with extinction by the year 2010
amphibians	worldwide decline in numbers; half of New Zealand's frog species are now extinct; 25% of species threatened with extinction and 38% of US amphibians were endangered in the late 1990s
birds	three-quarters of all bird species are declining; 11% are threatened with extinction
carnivores	almost all species of cats and bears are declining in numbers
fish	one-third of North American freshwater fish are rare or endangered; half the fish species in Lake Victoria, Africa's largest lake, are close to extinction due to predation by the introduced Nile perch; 33% of species are threatened with extinction
invertebrates	about 100 species are lost each day due to deforestation; half the freshwater snails in the southeastern USA are now extinct or threatened; 50% of crayfish and 56% of mussel species are endangered in the USA; a quarter of German invertebrates are threatened
mammals	half of Australia's mammals are threatened; 40% of mammals in France, the Netherlands, Germany, and Portugal are threatened; 25% of species are threatened with extinction
primates	two-thirds of primate species are threatened
reptiles	over 40% of reptile species are threatened; 20% with extinction

The naming of fish

- Spurdog, alewife, twaite shad, jollytail, tadpole madtom, bummalow, walleye pollock, wrestling halfbeak, mummichog, jolthead porgy, sweetlip emperor, and slippery dick are all common names for species of fish.

fish aquatic vertebrate that uses gills to obtain oxygen from fresh or sea water. There are three main groups: the bony fishes or Osteichthyes (goldfish, cod, tuna); the cartilaginous fishes or Chondrichthyes (sharks, rays); and the jawless fishes or Agnatha (hagfishes, lampreys).

Fishes of some form are found in virtually every body of water in the world except for the very salty water of the Dead Sea and some of the

Fish that can climb trees

- The mudskipper spends three-quarters of its time out of water. Malaysian mudskippers live in mangrove swamps, where they climb among the tangled stems and roots, and sometimes into the branches.

hot larval springs. Of the 30,000 fish species, approximately 2,500 are freshwater.

flatworm invertebrate of the phylum Platyhelminthes. Some are free-living, but many are parasitic (for example, tapeworms and flukes). The body is simple and bilaterally symmetrical, with one opening to the intestine. Many are hermaphroditic (with both male and female sex organs) and practise self-fertilization.

Fighting, flirting flatworms

- In many hermaphrodite flatworm species, the sperm is not received into a genital opening, instead the penis pierces the skin to inject sperm straight into the body. As this causes some damage to the flatworm, in each sexual encounter both flatworms attempt to take the male role. Consequently flatworms will vie with each other for an hour or more with each attempting to stab the other with its penis, whilst avoiding being stabbed itself.

foraminifera any marine protozoan of the order Foraminiferida, with shells of calcium carbonate. Their shells have pores through which filaments project. Some form part of the plankton, others live on the sea bottom.

Classification of Fish

Order	Number of species	Examples
Class Agnatha (jawless fishes)		
Subclass Cyclostomota (scaleless fish with round mouths)		
Petromyzoniformes	30	lamprey
Myxiniformes	15	hagfish
Superclass Pisces (jawed fishes)		
Class Chondrichthyes (cartilaginous fishes)		
Subclass Elasmobranchii (sharks and rays)		
Hexanchiformes	6	frilled shark, comb-toothed shark
Heterodontiformes	10	Port Jackson shark
Lamniformes	200	'typical' shark
Rajiformes	300	skate, ray
Subclass Holocephali (rabbitfishes)		
Chimaeriformes	20	chimaera, rabbitfish
Class Osteichthyes (bony fishes)		
Subclass Sarcopterygii (lobe-finned fishes)		
Coelacanthiformes	1	coelacanth
Ceratodiformes	1	Australian lungfish
Lepidosireniformes	4	South American and African lungfish
Subclass Actinopterygii (ray-finned fishes)		
Polypteriformes	11	bichir, reedfish
Acipensiformes	25	paddlefish, sturgeon
Amiiformes	8	bowfin, garpike
Superorder Teleostei		
Elopiformes	12	tarpon, tenpounder
Anguilliformes	300	eel
Notacanthiformes	20	spiny eel
Clupeiformes	350	herring, anchovy
Osteoglossiformes	16	arapaima, African butterfly fish
Mormyriformes	150	elephant-trunk fish, featherback
Salmoniformes	500	salmon, trout, smelt, pike
Gonorhynchiformes	15	milkfish
Cypriniformes	350	carp, barb, characin, loache
Siluriformes	200	catfish
Myctophiformes	300	deep-sea lantern fish, Bombay duck
Percopsiformes	10	pirate perch, cave-dwelling amblyopsid
Batrachoidiformes	10	toadfish
Gobiesociformes	100	clingfish, dragonets
Lophiiformes	150	anglerfish
Gadiformes	450	cod, pollack, pearlfish, eelpout
Atheriniformes	600	flying fish, toothcarp, halfbeak
Lampridiformes	50	opah, ribbonfish
Beryciformes	150	squirrelfish
Zeiformes	60	John Dory, boarfish
Gasterosteiformes	150	stickleback, pipefish, seahorse
Channiformes	5	snakeshead
Synbranchiformes	7	cuchia
Scorpaeniformes	700	gurnard, miller's thumb, stonefish
Dactylopteriformes	6	flying gurnard
Pegasiformes	4	sea-moth
Pleuronectiformes	500	flatfish
Tetraodontiformes	250	puffer fish, triggerfish, sunfish
Perciformes	6,500	perch, cichlid, damsel fish, gobie, wrass, parrotfish, gourami, marlin, mackerel, tuna, swordfish, spiny eel, mullet, barracuda, sea bream, croaker, ice fish, butterfish

genus plural **genera** group of species with many characteristics in common.

Thus all doglike species (including dogs, wolves, and jackals) belong to the genus *Canis* (Latin 'dog').

Species of the same genus are thought to be descended from a common ancestor species. Related genera are grouped into families.

heart muscular organ that rhythmically contracts to force blood around the body of an animal with a circulatory system. Annelid worms and some other invertebrates have simple hearts consisting of thickened sections of main blood vessels that pulse regularly. An earthworm has ten such hearts. Vertebrates have one heart. A fish heart has two chambers – the thin-walled **atrium** (once called the auricle) that expands to receive blood, and the thick-walled **ventricle** that pumps it out. Amphibians and most reptiles have two atria and one ventricle; birds and mammals have two atria and two ventricles. The beating of the

Classification of Insects

(N/A = not available.)

Order	Number of species	Examples
Class insecta		
Subclass Apterygota (wingless insects)		
Thysanura	350	three-pronged bristletails, silverfish
Diplura	400	two-pronged bristletails, campodeids, japygids
Protura	50	minute insects living in soil
Collembola[1]	1,500	springtails

Subclass Pterygota (winged insects or forms secondary wingless)

Superorder Exopterygota (young resemble adults but have externally-developing wings)

Order	Number of species	Examples
Ephemeroptera	1,000	mayflies
Odonata	5,000	dragonflies, damselflies
Plecoptera	3,000	stoneflies
Grylloblattodea	12	wingless soil-living insects of North America
Orthoptera	20,000	crickets, grasshoppers, locusts, mantids, roaches
Phasmida	2,000	stick insects, leaf insects
Dermaptera	1,000	earwigs
Embioptera	150	web-spinners
Dictyoptera	5,000	cockroaches, praying mantises
Isoptera	2,000	termites
Zoraptera	16	tiny insects living in decaying plants

Order	Number of species	Examples
Psocoptera	1,600	booklice, barklice, psocids
Mallophaga	2,500	biting lice, mainly parasitic on birds
Anoplura	250	sucking lice, mainly parasitic on mammals
Hemiptera	55,000	true bugs, including shield- and bedbugs, froghoppers, pond skaters, water boatmen
Homoptera	N/A	aphids, cicadas
Thysanoptera	5,000	thrips

Superorder Endopterygota (young, unlike adults, undergo sudden metamorphosis)

Order	Number of species	Examples
Neuroptera	4,500	lacewings, alder flies, snake flies, ant lions
Mecoptera	300	scorpion flies
Lepidoptera	165,000	butterflies, moths
Trichoptera	3,000	caddis flies
Diptera	80,000	true flies, including bluebottles, mosquitoes, leatherjackets, midges
Siphonaptera	1,400	fleas
Hymenoptera	100,000	bees, wasps, ants, sawflies, chalcids
Coleoptera	350,000	beetles, including weevils, ladybirds, glow-worms, woodworms, chafers

[1] Some zoologists recognize the Collembola taxon as a class rather than an order.

---

heart is controlled by the autonomic nervous system and an internal control centre or pacemaker, the **sinoatrial node.**

insect any of a vast group of small invertebrate animals with hard, segmented bodies, three pairs of jointed legs, and, usually, two pairs of wings; they belong among the arthropods and are distributed throughout the world. An insect's body is divided into three segments:

> **Accelerating fleas**
> ■ As a flea jumps, its rate of acceleration is 20 times that of the space shuttle during launching. It reaches a speed of 100 m per sec within the first 500th of a second.

> **Tiny insect**
> ■ The world's smallest winged insect is smaller than the eye of a house fly. It is the Tanzanian parasitic wasp, which has a wingspan of 0.2 mm/0.008 in.

head, thorax, and abdomen. On the head is a pair of feelers, or antennae. The legs and wings are attached to the thorax, or middle segment of the body. The abdomen, or end segment of the body, is where food is digested and excreted and where the reproductive organs are located.

Insects vary in size from 0.2 mm/0.008 in to 35 mm/13.5 in in length. The world's smallest insect is believed to be a 'fairy fly' wasp in

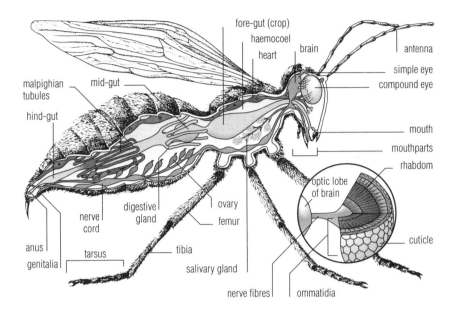

insect Body plan of an insect. The general features of the insect body include a segmented body divided into head, thorax, and abdomen, jointed legs, feelers or antennae, and usually two pairs of wings. Insects often have compound eyes with a large field of vision.

the family Mymaridae, with a wingspan of 0.2 mm/0.008 in. (Class Insecta.)

invertebrate animal without a backbone. The invertebrates comprise over 95% of the million or so existing animal species and include sponges, coelenterates, flatworms, nematodes, annelid worms, arthropods, molluscs, echinoderms, and primitive aquatic chordates, such as sea squirts and lancelets.

Top speeds of animals

Animal	Speed		Animal	Speed	
	kph	mph		kph	mph
			Reindeer	51	32
Cheetah	103	64	Giraffe	51	32
Wildebeest	98	61	White-tailed deer	48	30
Lion	81	50	Wart hog	48	30
Quarterhorse	76	47.5	Grizzly bear	48	30
Elk	72	45	Cat (domestic)	48	30
Cape hunting dog	72	45	Human	45	28
Coyote	69	43	Elephant	40	25
Grey fox	68	42	Black mamba snake	32	20
Hyena	64	40	Squirrel	19	12
Zebra	64	40	Pig (domestic)	18	11
Greyhound	63	39	Chicken	14	9
Whippet	57	35.5	Giant tortoise	0.27	0.17
Rabbit (domestic)	56	35	Three-toed sloth	0.24	0.15
Jackal	56	35	Garden snail	0.05	0.03

Major Invertebrate and Vertebrate Groups

Invertebrates

Taxon[1] Name		Examples
P	Porifera	all sponges
P	Cnidaria	corals, sea anemones, *Hydra*, jellyfishes
P	Ctenophora	sea gooseberries, comb jellies
P	Platyhelminthes	flatworms, flukes, tapeworms
P	Nemertina	nemertine worms, ribbon worms
P	Nematoda	roundworms
P	Mollusca	clams, oysters, snails, slugs, octopuses, squids, cuttlefish
P	Annelida	ringed worms, including lugworms, earthworms, and leeches
P	Arthropoda	(subdivided into classes below)
C	Arachnida	spiders, ticks, scorpions, mites
C	Branchiopoda	water fleas
C	Cirripedia	barnacles
C	Malacostraca	crabs, lobsters, shrimp, woodlice
C	Diplopoda	millipedes
C	Chilopoda	centipedes
C	Insecta	silverfish, dragonflies, mayflies, stoneflies, cockroaches, earwigs, web spinners, termites, booklice, lice, grasshoppers, thrips, lace-wings, scorpion flies, caddis-flies, moths, butterflies, beetles, house flies, fleas, stylopids, ants, bees
P	Echinodermata	sea stars, brittle stars, sea urchins, sand dollars, sea cucumbers
P	Hemichordata	acorn worms, pterobranchs, graptolites

Vertebrates

Taxon[1] Name		Examples
C	Agnatha	(jawless fishes) lampreys, hagfishes
C	Chondricthyes	(cartilaginous fishes) dogfish, sharks, rays, skates
C	Osteichthyes	(bony fishes) salmon, catfishes, perches, flatfishes including flounder and halibut
C	Amphibia	frogs, toads, newts, salamanders, caecilians
C	Reptilia	tuatara, tortoises, turtles, lizards, snakes
C	Aves	rheas, ostriches, moa, penguins, ducks, pheasants, gulls, swifts, kingfishers, sparrows, woodpeckers, pelicans, flamingoes, herons, falcons, cranes, divers, pigeons, parrots, cuckoos, owls
C	Mammalia	duck-billed platypuses, echidnas, kangaroos, opossums, shrews, bats, dogs, seals, whales, dolphins, rats, rabbits, pigs, camels, deer, horses, tapirs, elephants, hyraxes, anteaters, manatees, pangolins, lemurs, monkeys, humans

[1] P represents phylum; C represents class.

Classification of Mammals

Order	Number of species	Examples
Leading class: Mammalia		
Subclass: Prototheria (egg-laying mammals)		
Monotremata	3	echidna, platypus
Subclass: Theria		
Infraclass: Metatheria (pouched mammals)		
Marsupiala	266	kangaroo, koala, opossum
Infraclass: Eutheria (placental mammals)		
Rodentia	1,700	rat, mouse, squirrel, porcupine
Chiroptera	970	all bats
Insectivora	378	shrew, hedgehog, mole
Carnivora	230	cat, dog, weasel, bear
Primates	180	lemur, monkey, ape, human
Artiodactyla	145	pig, deer, cattle, camel, giraffe
Cetacea	79	whale, dolphin
Lagomorpha	58	rabbit, hare, pika
Pinnipedia	33	seal, walrus
Edentata	29	anteater, armadillo, sloth
Perissodactyla	16	horse, rhinoceros, tapir
Hyracoidea	11	hyrax
Pholidota	7	pangolin
Sirenia	4	dugong, manatee
Dermoptera	2	flying lemur
Proboscidea	2	elephant
Tubulidentata	1	aardvark

What is a mammal?

A mammal (Class Mammalia) is any of a large group of warm-blooded vertebrate animals characterized by having mammary glands in the female; these are used for suckling the young. Other features of mammals are hair (very reduced in some species, such as whales); a middle ear formed of three small bones (ossicles); a lower jaw consisting of two bones only; seven vertebrae in the neck; and no nucleus in the red blood cells.

Mammals are divided into three groups:

placental mammals, where the young develop inside the mother's body, in the uterus, receiving nourishment from the blood of the mother via the placenta;

marsupials, where the young are born at an early stage of development and develop further in a pouch on the mother's body where they are attached to and fed from a nipple; and

monotremes, where the young hatch from an egg outside the mother's body and are then nourished with milk.

The monotremes are the least evolved and have been largely displaced by more sophisticated marsupials and placentals, so that there are only a few types surviving (platypus and echidna). Placentals have spread to all parts of the globe, and where placentals have competed with marsupials, the placentals have in general displaced marsupial types. However, marsupials occupy many specialized niches in South America and, especially, Australasia.

According to the Red List of endangered species published by the World Conservation Union (IUCN) for 1996, 25% of mammal species are threatened with extinction.

mammal Yellow meerkats *Cynictis penicillata* on sentry duty just outside their burrow. The open savannah where they live and the large number of their predators, including snakes, jackals, and birds of prey, requires constant vigilance. *K G Preston-Mafham/Premaphotos Wildlife*

mammal The bottlenosed dolphin lives in groups of up to 15 individuals. There is extensive communication and cooperation between individuals. They can produce a range of clicks of various frequencies which they use for echolocation.

---

jellyfish marine invertebrate, belonging among the coelenterates, with an umbrella-shaped body made of a semitransparent jellylike substance, often tinted with blue, red, or orange colours, and stinging tentacles that trail in the water. Most adult jellyfish move freely, but during parts of their life cycle many are polyplike and attached to rocks, the seabed, or another underwater surface. They feed on small animals that are paralysed by stinging cells in the jellyfish tentacles. (Phylum Coelenterata, subphylum Cnidaria.)

microorganism see **microscopic life** feature on pages 152–153.

mollusc any of a group of invertebrate animals, most of which have a body divided into three parts: a head, a central mass containing the main organs, and a foot for movement; the more sophisticated octopuses and related molluscs have arms to capture their prey. The majority of molluscs are marine animals, but some live in fresh water, and a few live on dry land. They

Molluscs: Classification

phylum mollusca

class *Monoplacophora* primitive marine forms, including Neopilina (2 species)	class *Scaphopoda* tusk shells, marine burrowers (350 species)
	class *Bivalvia* molluscs with a double (two-valved) shell (15,000 species): mussels, oysters, clams, cockles, scallops, tellins, razor shells, shipworms
class *Amphineura* wormlike marine forms 1 *Aplacophora* chitons, coat-of-mail 2 *Polyplacophora* shells (1,150 species)	
class *Gastropoda* snail-like molluscs, with single or no shell (9,000 species) 1 *Prosobranchia* limpets, winkles, whelks 2 *Opisthobranchia* seaslugs, land and sea snails 3 *Pulmonata* freshwater snails, slugs	class *Cephalopoda* molluscs with shell generally reduced, arms to capture prey, and beaklike mouth; body bilaterally symmetrical and nervous system well developed (750 species): squids, cuttlefish, octopuses, pearly nautilus, argonaut

include clams, mussels, and oysters (bivalves), snails and slugs (gastropods), and cuttlefish, squids, and octopuses (cephalopods). The body is soft, without limbs (except for the cephalopods), and cold-blooded. There is no internal skeleton, but many species have a hard shell covering the body. (Phylum Mollusca.)

muscle contractile animal tissue that produces locomotion and power, and maintains the movement of body substances. Muscle is made of long cells that can contract to between one-half and one-third of their relaxed length.

nematode any of a group of unsegmented worms that are pointed at both ends, with a tough, smooth outer skin. They include many free-living species found in soil and water, including the sea, but a large number are parasites, such as the roundworms and pinworms that live in

The intelligent molluscs
Common octopus *Octopus vulgaris* in the Farne Islands, off Northumberland, England. Octopuses have highly sophisticated nervous systems and are more intelligent than any other invertebrates. They are able to distinguish between objects using tactile and visual information, and retain the memory of reward signals for several weeks. *Chris McTernan*

humans, or the eelworms that attack plant roots. They differ from flatworms in that they have two openings to the gut (a mouth and an anus). (Phylum Nematoda.)

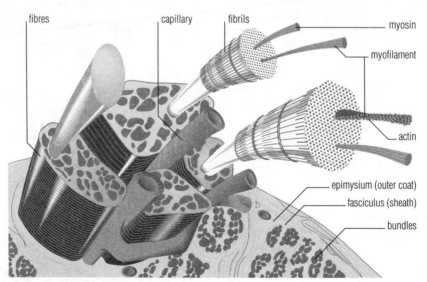

fibres   capillary   fibrils   myosin   myofilament   actin   epimysium (outer coat)   fasciculus (sheath)   bundles

muscle The movements of the arm depend on two muscles, the biceps and the triceps. To lift the arm, the biceps shortens and the triceps lengthens. To lower the arm, the opposite occurs: the biceps lengthens and the triceps shortens.

nervous system the system of interconnected nerve cells of most invertebrates and all vertebrates. It is composed of the central and autonomic nervous systems. It may be as simple as the nerve net of coelenterates (for example, jellyfishes) or as complex as the mammalian nervous system, with a central nervous system comprising brain and spinal cord and a peripheral nervous system connecting up with sensory organs, muscles, and glands.

Platyhelminthes invertebrate phylum consisting of the flatworms.

prokaryote see **microscopic life** feature on pages 152–153.

protozoa see **microscopic life** feature on pages 152–153.

skeleton the rigid or semirigid framework that supports and gives form to an animal's body, protects its internal organs, and provides anchorage points for its muscles. The skeleton may be composed of bone and cartilage (vertebrates), chitin (arthropods), calcium carbonate (molluscs and other invertebrates), or silica (many protists). The human skeleton is composed of 206 bones, with the vertebral column (spine) forming the central supporting structure.

skin the covering of the body of a vertebrate. In mammals, the outer layer (epidermis) is dead

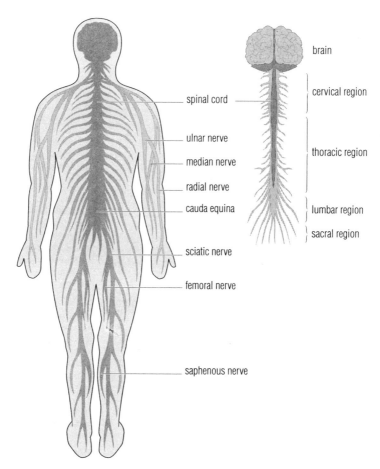

central nervous system The central nervous system (CNS) with its associated nerves. The CNS controls and integrates body functions. In humans and other vertebrates it consists of a brain and a spinal cord, which are linked to the body's muscles and organs by means of the peripheral nervous system.

Microscopic Life

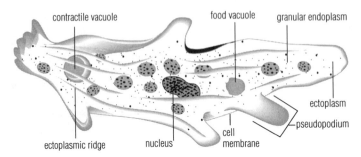

amoeba The amoebae are among the simplest living organisms, consisting of a single cell. Within the cell, there is a nucleus, which controls cell activity, and many other microscopic bodies and vacuoles (fluid-filled spaces surrounded by a membrane) with specialized functions. Amoebae eat by flowing around food particles, engulfing the particle, a process called phagocytosis.

A **microorganism** is a living organism invisible to the naked eye but visible under a microscope. Microorganisms include viruses and single-celled organisms such as bacteria, protozoa, yeasts, and some algae. The term has no taxonomic significance in biology. The study of microorganisms is known as microbiology.

amoeba
one of the simplest living animals, consisting of a single cell and belonging to the protozoa group. The body consists of colourless protoplasm. Its activities are controlled by the nucleus, and it feeds by flowing round and engulfing organic debris. It reproduces by binary fission. Some species of amoeba are harmful parasites.

bacillus
member of a group of rodlike bacteria that occur everywhere in the soil and air. Some are responsible for diseases such as anthrax or for causing food spoilage.

bacteria
microscopic single-celled organisms lacking a nucleus. Bacteria are widespread, present in soil, air, and water, and as parasites on and in

Simplest organism
■ The simplest known free-living organism is the bacterium *Mycoplasma genitalium,* which has 468 genes.

other living things. Some parasitic bacteria cause disease by producing toxins, but others are harmless and may even benefit their hosts. Bacteria usually reproduce by binary fission (dividing into two equal parts), and this may occur approximately every 20 minutes. Only 4,000 species of bacteria are known; bacteriologists believe that around 3 million species may actually exist.

Radioactive resistant bacteria
■ The bacterium *Deinococcus radiourans* can survive at gamma radiation levels of up to 50,000 grays – thousands of times greater than that needed to kill a human.

blue-green algae
single-celled, primitive organisms that resemble bacteria in their internal cell organization, sometimes joined together in colonies or filaments. Blue-green algae are among the oldest known living organisms and, with bacteria, belong to the kingdom Monera; remains have been found in rocks up to 3.5 billion years old. They are widely distributed in aquatic habitats, on the damp surfaces of rocks and trees, and in the soil.

coccus
member of a group of globular bacteria, some of which are harmful to humans. The cocci contain the subgroups **streptococci,** where the bacteria associate in straight chains, and **staphylococci,** where the bacteria associate in branched chains.

diatom
microscopic alga (Division Bacillariophyta.) found in all parts of the world in either fresh or marine waters. Diatoms consist of single cells that secrete a hard cell wall made of silica.
    The cell wall of a diatom is made up of two overlapping valves known as **frustules,** which are impregnated

Microscopic Life (continued)

with silica, and which fit together like the lid and body of a pillbox. Diatomaceous earths (diatomite) are made up of the valves of fossil diatoms, and are used in the manufacture of dynamite and in the rubber and plastics industries.

methanogenic bacteria
one of a group of primitive microorganisms, the Archaea. They give off methane gas as a by-product of their metabolism, and are common in sewage treatment plants and hot springs, where the temperature is high and oxygen is absent. Archaeons were originally classified as bacteria, but were found to be unique in 1996 following the gene sequencing of the deep-sea vent organism *Methanococcus jannaschii*.

plankton
small, often microscopic, forms of plant and animal life that live in the upper layers of fresh and salt water, and are an important source of food for larger animals. Marine plankton are concentrated in areas where rising currents bring mineral salts to the surface.

Pfiesteria piscicida is the only predatory phytoplankton. It stuns its prey by producing a powerful toxin that also causes the deaths of nearby fish and may be harmful to humans exposed to it.

prokaryote
organism whose cells lack organelles (specialized segregated structures such as nuclei, mitochondria, and chloroplasts). Prokaryote DNA is not arranged in chromosomes but forms a coiled structure called a **nucleoid**. The prokaryotes comprise only the **bacteria** and **cyanobacteria**; all other organisms are eukaryotes.

protist
single-celled organism which has a eukaryotic cell, but which is not a

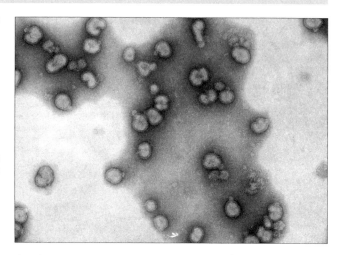

virus An electron micrograph of the influenza virus magnified 100,000 times. The influenza virus can form new strains rapidly, with major epidemics appearing in cycles. Most strains are comparatively mild, but some can kill. *Lesley Calder National Institute for Medical Research*

member of the plant, fungal, or animal kingdoms. The main protists are protozoa.

Single-celled photosynthetic organisms, such as diatoms and dinoflagellates, are classified as protists or algae. Recently the term has also been used for members of the kingdom Protista, which features in certain five-kingdom classifications of the living world. This kingdom may include slime moulds, all algae (seaweeds as well as unicellular forms), and protozoa.

protozoa
group of single-celled organisms without rigid cell walls. Some, such as amoeba, ingest other cells, but most are *saprotrophs* or parasites. The group is polyphyletic (containing organisms which have different evolutionary origins).

virus
infectious particle consisting of a core of nucleic acid (DNA or RNA) enclosed in a protein shell. Viruses are acellular and able to function and reproduce only if they can invade a living cell to use the cell's system to replicate themselves. In the process they may disrupt or alter the host cell's own DNA. The healthy human body reacts by producing an antiviral protein, interferon, which prevents the infection spreading to adjacent cells.

There are around 5,000 species of virus known to science, though there may be as many as 0.5 million actually in existence.

yeast
one of various single-celled fungi that form masses of tiny round or oval cells by budding. When placed in a sugar solution the cells multiply and convert the sugar into alcohol and carbon dioxide. Yeasts are used as fermenting agents in baking, brewing, and the making of wine and spirits. Brewer's yeast (*Saccharomyces cerevisiae*) is a rich source of vitamin B.

What are reptiles?

A reptile is any member of a class (Reptilia) of vertebrates. Unlike amphibians, reptiles have hard-shelled, yolk-filled eggs that are laid on land and from which fully formed young are born. Some snakes and lizards retain their eggs and give birth to live young. Reptiles are cold-blooded, and their skin is usually covered with scales. The metabolism is slow, and in some cases (certain large snakes) intervals between meals may be months. Reptiles date back over 300 million years.

reptile A diamondback rattlesnake *Crotalus atrox* in Arizona, USA. The diamond markings camouflage it against its dusty habitat. Rattlesnakes give birth to live young, usually numbering about 8–12. *Dr Rod Preston-Mafham/Premaphotos Wildlife*

reptile The estuarine or saltwater crocodile, of India, SE Asia, and Australasia, is one of the largest and most dangerous of its family. It has been known to develop a taste for human flesh. Hunted near to extinction for its leather, it is now protected by restrictions and the trade in skins is controlled.

and its cells are constantly being rubbed away and replaced from below; it helps to protect the body from infection and to prevent dehydration. The lower layer (dermis) contains blood vessels, nerves, hair roots, and sweat and sebaceous glands, and is supported by a network of fibrous and elastic cells.

vertebrate any animal with a backbone. The 41,000 species of vertebrates include mammals, birds, reptiles, amphibians, and fishes. They include most of the larger animals, but in terms of numbers of species are only a tiny proportion of the world's animals. The zoological taxonomic group Vertebrata is a subgroup of the phylum Chordata.

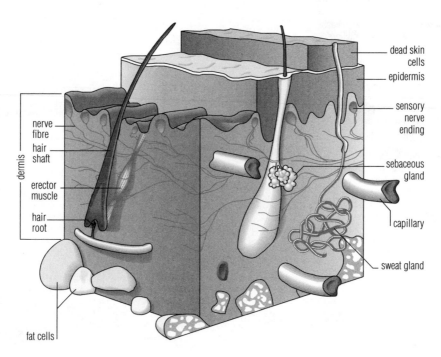

dead skin cells
epidermis
sensory nerve ending
sebaceous gland
capillary
sweat gland

nerve fibre
hair shaft
dermis
erector muscle
hair root

fat cells

skin The skin of an adult man covers about 1.9 sq m/20 sq ft; a woman's skin covers about 1.6 sq m/17 sq ft. During our lifetime, we shed about 18 kg/40 lb of skin.

Noteworthy Biologists

Avery Oswald Theodore (1877–1955) Canadian-born US bacteriologist who established that DNA is responsible for the transmission of heritable characteristics

Bateson William (1861–1926) English geneticist who introduced the term 'genetics' and translated the work of Gregor Mendel into English

Beadle George Wells (1903–1989) US biologist who formed the 'one gene–one enzyme' hypothesis (that a single gene codes for a single kind of enzyme)

Berg Paul (1926–) US molecular biologist who pioneered research on recombinant DNA

Bishop (John) Michael (1936–) US virologist and molecular biologist who helped discover cancer-causing genes known as oncogenes

Brenner Sidney (1927–) South African biologist who was one of the pioneers of genetic engineering and discovered messenger RNA

Brown Michael Stuart (1941–) US geneticist who helped discover how the human body metabolizes cholesterol

Brown Robert (1773–1858) Scottish botanist who investigated the impregnation of plants and noted that living cells contain a nucleus

Carson Rachel Louise (1907–1964) US biologist who inspired the modern environmental movement

Chargaff Erwin (1905–) Czech-born US biochemist who pioneered research on the base composition of DNA

Cohn Ferdinand Julius (1828–1898) German botanist and bacteriologist who developed a classification system for bacteria

Crick Francis Harry Compton (1916–) English biochemist and physicist who pioneered research on DNA

Darwin Charles Robert (1809–1882) English naturalist who developed the modern theory of evolution

Delbrück Max (1906–1981) German-born US biologist who pioneered techniques in molecular biology, studying genetic changes occurring when viruses invade bacteria

De Vries Hugo Marie (1848–1935) Dutch botanist who was a pioneer in the study of plant evolution

Dobzhansky Theodosius (originally **Feodosy Grigorevich Dobrzhansky**) (1900–1975) Ukrainian-born US geneticist who established evolutionary genetics as an independent discipline

Funk Casimir (1884–1967) Polish-born US biochemist who worked on vitamins and a cure for the disease beriberi

Galton Francis (1822–1911) English scientist who studied evolution and eugenics; he is credited with devising the system of fingerprint identification

Gilbert Walter (1932–) US molecular biologist who identified the lac repressor molecule in gene control

Goldstein Joseph Leonard (1940–) US geneticist who helped discover the gene involved in the removal of cholesterol

Golgi Camillo (1843–1926) Italian cell biologist who produced the first detailed knowledge of the fine structure of the nervous system

Gould Stephen Jay (1941–) US palaeontologist who proposed the evolutionary theory of punctuated equilibrium

Haeckel Ernst Heinrich Philipp August (1834–1919) German zoologist and philosopher who supported Charles Darwin's theory of evolution

Haldane J(ohn) B(urdon) S(anderson) (1892–1964) British physiologist, geneticist, and author of popular science books

Hershey Alfred Day (1908–1997) US biologist who pioneered research on DNA

Hill Archibald Vivian (1886–1977) English physiologist who investigated the physiology of muscle and nerve tissue

Hill Robert (1899–1991) British biochemist who demonstrated that during photosynthesis oxygen is produced from water

Holly Robert William (1922–) US biochemist who established the existence of transfer RNA

Hooke Robert (1635–1703) British scientist who pioneered the early use of the microscope

Hooker Joseph Dalton (1817–1911) English botanist who developed the classification of plants and began the compilation of *Index Kewensis*, still the standard reference work today

Hopkins Frederick Gowland (1861–1947) English biochemist who pioneered research on vitamins

Huxley Thomas Henry (1825–1895) English biologist who supported Darwin's theory of evolution vehemently, most notably in the 1860 debate with Bishop Samuel Wilberforce

Jeffreys Alec John (1950–) British geneticist who discovered the DNA probes necessary for genetic fingerprinting

Johanssen Wilhelm Ludwig (1857–1927) Danish botanist and geneticist who introduced the term 'gene' as a unit of heredity

Kendrew John Cowdray (1917–1997) English molecular biologist who determined the crystallographic structure of the muscle protein myoglobin using X-rays

Lamarck Jean Baptiste Pierre Antoine de Monet, Chevalier de (1744–1829) French naturalist who coined the word 'biology' and proposed a theory of evolution

Lederberg Joshua (1925–) US geneticist who showed that bacteria can reproduce sexually, combining genetic material so that offspring possess characteristics of both parent organisms

Leeuwenhoek Anton van (1632–1723) Dutch pioneer of microscopic research

Linnaeus Carolus (Latinized form of Carl von Linné) (1707–1778) Swedish naturalist and physician who developed the modern system of naming and classifying plants and animals

Lorenz Konrad Zacharias (1903–1989) Austrian ethologist who studied the relationship between instinct and behaviour, particularly in birds, and described the phenomenon of imprinting

Maynard Smith John (1920–) British geneticist and evolutionary biologist who applied game theory to animal behaviour

McCollum Elmer Verner (1879–1967) US biochemist who pioneered research into vitamins and discovered that vitamin D could be used in the prevention of rickets

Mendel Gregor Johann (1822–1884) Austrian biologist who pioneered the study of modern genetics

Monod Jacques (1910–1976) French biochemist who won the Nobel Prize, together with François Jacob, for work on genetic control mechanisms

Montagnier Luc (1932–) French molecular biologist who first identified the HIV virus and AIDS in 1983

Morgan Thomas Hunt (1866–1945) US geneticist who developed the chromosome theory of inheritance

Muller Hermann Joseph (1890–1967) US geneticist who was awarded a Nobel prize in 1946 for his work on the use of X-rays to cause genetic mutations

Perutz Max Ferdinand (1914–) Austrian-born biochemist who determined the structure of haemoglobin and myoglobin

Ray John (1627–1705) English naturalist who developed the basic principles of the classification of plants and animals

Sanger Frederick (1918–) English biochemist who determined the structure of insulin

Sharp Phillip Allen (1944–) US molecular biologist who discovered that genes are split into several sections, separated by stretches of DNA known as 'introns'

Schleiden Matthias Jacob (1804–1881) German botanist who developed cell theory by explaining the role of the nucleus in cell formation

Schwann Theodor (1810–1882) German physiologist who is credited with formulating cell theory

Sherrington Charles Scott (1857–1952) English physiologist who worked on the structure and function of the nervous system and introduced the term 'synapse'

Spallanzani Lazzaro (1729–1799) Italian biologist who disproved the theory that microbes spontaneously generate out of rotten food

Sturtevant Alfred Henry (1891–1970) US geneticist who first mapped the position of genes on a chromosome

Tatum Edward Lawrie (1909–1975) US microbiologist who pioneered work in molecular genetics

Waksman Selman Abraham (1888–1973) Ukrainian-born US biochemist who coined the word 'antibiotic' and won a Nobel prize for his work on antibiotics

Wallace Alfred Russel (1823–1913) Welsh naturalist who collected animal and plant specimens in South America and Southeast Asia, and independently arrived at a theory of evolution by natural selection similar to that proposed by Charles Darwin

Watson James Dewey (1928–) US biologist who pioneered research on DNA

Weismann August Friedrich Leopold (1834–1914) German biologist who was one of the founders of genetics

Whipple George Hoyt (1878–1976) US pathologist who helped explain the formation of haemoglobin in the blood

Noteworthy Zoologists

Andrews Roy Chapman (1884–1960) US zoologist who was the first to find fossilized dinosaur eggs

Audubon John James (1785–1851) US ornithologist and bird artist best known for his publication *Birds of America*

Carter Herbert James (1858–1940) English-born Australian entomologist who described over 1,000 new species of beetle

Dawkins (Clinton) Richard (1941–) British scientist and zoologist who popularized the theories of sociobiology and evolution

De Beer Gavin Rylands (1899–1972) British zoologist who disproved the germ-layer theory and developed the concept of paedomorphism

Ehrenberg Christian Gottfried (1795–1876) German naturalist who was the first scientist to study the fossils of microorganisms

Eisner Thomas (1929–) German-born US entomologist and conservation activist who is an authority on the role of chemicals in insect behaviour

Fabre Jean Henri Casimir (1823–1915) French entomologist whose studies of wasps, bees, and other insects have become classics

Fabricus Johann Christian (1745–1808) Danish entomologist who developed a classification system for insects based on the mouth structure; he named and described over 10,000 insects

Fossey Dian (1938–1985) US zoologist who did pioneer studies on mountain gorillas

Frisch Karl von (1886–1982) Austrian zoologist who co-founded ethology with Niko Tinbergen and Konrad Lorenz

Geoffroy Saint-Hilaire Etienne (1772–1844) French zoologist who developed a classification system for the study of apes

Goodall Jane (1934–) English primatologist and conservationist who is a world authority on wild chimpanzees

Gosse Philip Henry (1810–1888) English naturalist who built the first aquarium ever used to house marine animals long-term and wrote influential works on marine zoology

Gray James (1891–1975) British zoologist who helped establish cytology (cell structure) as a distinct branch of zoology

Griffin Donald Redfield (1915–) US zoologist who discovered that bats use echolocation to navigate when flying

Hertwig Oscar Wilhelm August (1849–1922) German zoologist who discovered that fertilization involves the fusion of the nuclei of an egg and one sperm

Hyman Libbie Henrietta (1888–1969) US zoologist whose six-volume *The Invertebrates* provided an encyclopedic account of most invertebrate phyla

Kinsey Alfred Charles (1894–1956) US zoologist and pioneering sexologist who founded the Institute of Sex Research in 1942

Lankester Edwin Ray (1847–1929) English zoologist who demonstrated clear morphological distinctions between the different orders of invertebrates

Leuckart Karl Georg Friedrich Rudolf (1822–1898) German zoologist who developed the taxonomic divisions of jellyfish; he was a pioneer of parasitology

Lorenz Konrad Zacharias (1903–1989) Austrian zoologist who co-founded the study of ethology with Karl von Frisch and Niko Tinbergen

Manton Sidnie Milana (married name Harding) (1902–1979) English embryologist who specialized in the arthropods

Mayr Ernst Walter (1904–   ) German-born US zoologist who was influential in the development of modern evolutionary theories

Mechnikov Ilia Ilich (1845–1916) Russian-born French zoologist who discovered the function of white blood cells and phagocytes

Morgan Ann Haven (1882–1966) US zoologist who promoted the study of ecology and conservation

Morris Desmond John (1928–   ) British zoologist who popularized research on animal and human behaviour

Pennycuick Colin James (1933–   ) British zoologist who pioneered research on bird migration

Schaudinn Fritz Richard (1871–1906) German zoologist who determined the life cycle of the coccidiae (scale insects)

Schultze Max Johann Sigismund (1825–1874) German zoologist who adopted the term protoplasm in reference to the contents of cells

Sutton-Pringle John William (1912–   ) British zoologist who established much of our knowledge of the anatomical mechanisms involved in insect flight

Swammerdam Jan (1637–1680) Dutch naturalist who is considered a founder of both comparative anatomy and entomology

Tinbergen Niko(laas) (1907–1988) Dutch-born British zoologist who co-founded the study of ethology with Konrad Lorenz and Karl von Frisch

Wilson Edmund Beecher (1856–1939) US zoologist who was one of the founders of modern genetics

Wilson E(dward) O(sborne) (1929–   ) US zoologist who helped develop the fields of biogeography and sociobiology; he is a world authority on ants

Wynne-Edwards Vero Copner (1906–1997) English zoologist who argued that animal behaviour is often altruistic, and that animals will behave for the good of the group, even if this entails individual sacrifice

Young J(ohn) Z(achary) (1907–1997) British zoologist who discovered the giant nerve fibres in squid

Zuckerman Solly (1904–1993) South African-born British zoologist who did pioneer research on primates

Biology: Chronology

c. **500 BC** First studies of the structure and behaviour of animals, by the Greek Alcmaeon of Croton.

c. **450** Hippocrates of Kos undertook the first detailed studies of human anatomy.

c. **350** Aristotle laid down the basic philosophy of the biological sciences and outlined a theory of evolution.

c. **300** Theophrastus carried out the first detailed studies of plants.

c. **AD 175** Galen established the basic principles of anatomy and physiology.

c. **1500** Leonardo da Vinci studied human anatomy to improve his drawing ability and produced detailed anatomical drawings.

1628 William Harvey described the circulation of the blood and the function of the heart as a pump.

1665 Robert Hooke used a microscope to describe the cellular structure of plants.

Biology: Chronology (continued)

1672 Marcelle Malphigi undertook the first studies in embryology by describing the development of a chicken egg.

1677 Anton van Leeuwenhoek greatly improved the microscope and used it to describe spermatozoa as well as many microorganisms.

1736 Linnaeus published his systematic classification of plants, so establishing taxonomy.

1768–79 James Cook's voyages of discovery in the Pacific revealed an undreamed-of diversity of living species, prompting the development of theories to explain their origin.

1796 Edward Jenner established the practice of vaccination against smallpox, laying the foundations for theories of antibodies and immune reactions.

1809 Jean-Baptiste Lamarck advocated a theory of evolution through inheritance of acquired characteristics.

1839 Theodor Schwann proposed that all living matter is made up of cells.

1857 Louis Pasteur established that microorganisms are responsible for fermentation, creating the discipline of microbiology.

1859 Charles Darwin published *On the Origin of Species,* expounding his theory of the evolution of species by natural selection.

1865 Gregor Mendel pioneered the study of inheritance with his experiments on peas, but achieved little recognition.

1883 August Weismann proposed

his theory of the continuity of the germ plasm.

1900 Mendel's work was rediscovered and the science of genetics founded.

1935 Konrad Lorenz published the first of many major studies of animal behaviour, which founded the discipline of ethology.

1953 James Watson and Francis Crick described the molecular structure of the genetic material, DNA.

1964 William Hamilton recognized the importance of inclusive fitness, so paving the way for the development of sociobiology.

1975 Discovery of endogenous opiates (the brain's own painkillers) opened up a new phase in the study of brain chemistry.

1976 Har Gobind Khorana and his colleagues constructed the first artificial gene to function naturally when inserted into a bacterial cell, a major step in genetic engineering.

1982 Gene databases were established at Heidelberg, Germany, for the European Molecular Biology Laboratory, and at Los Alamos, USA, for the US National Laboratories.

1985 The first human cancer gene, retinoblastoma, was isolated by researchers at the Massachusetts Eye and Ear Infirmary and the Whitehead Institute, Massachusetts.

1988 The Human Genome Organization (HUGO) was established in Washington DC with the aim of mapping the complete sequence of DNA.

1991 Biosphere 2, an experiment

that attempts to reproduce the world's biosphere in miniature within a sealed glass dome, was launched in Arizona, USA.

1992 Researchers at the University of California, USA, stimulated the multiplication of isolated brain cells of mice, overturning the axiom that mammalian brains cannot produce replacement cells once birth has taken place. The world's largest organism, a honey fungus with underground hyphae (filaments) spreading across 600 hectares/ 1,480 acres, was discovered in Washington State, USA.

1994 Scientists from Pakistan and the USA unearthed a 50-million-year-old fossil whale with hind legs that would have enabled it to walk on land.

1995 New phylum identified and named Cycliophora. It contains a single known species, *Symbion pandora,* a parasite of the lobster.

1996 The sequencing of the genome of brewer's yeast *Saccharomyces cerevisiae* is completed, the first time this has been achieved for an organism more complex than a bacterium. The 12 million base pairs took 300 scientists six years to map. A new muscle was discovered by two US dentists. It is 3 cm/1 in long, and runs from the jaw to behind the eye socket.

1997 The first mammal to be cloned from a non-reproductive cell was born. The lamb had been cloned from an udder cell from a six-year-old ewe.

1998 The first international ban on human cloning was signed by 19 European countries.

PHYSICAL SCIENCES

— ✳ —

Physics is the branch of science concerned with the laws that govern the structure of the universe, and the properties of matter and energy and their interactions. For convenience, physics is often divided into branches such as atomic physics, nuclear physics, particle physics, solid-state physics, molecular physics, electricity and magnetism, optics, acoustics, heat, thermodynamics, quantum theory, and relativity.

Chemistry is the area of science concerned with the study of the structure and composition of the different kinds of matter, the changes which matter may undergo, and the phenomena which occur in the course of these changes. It is commonly divided into **organic chemistry** which deals with carbon compounds; **inorganic chemistry** which deals with the description, properties, reactions, and preparation of all the elements and their compounds, with the exception of carbon compounds; **physical chemistry** is concerned with the quantitative explanation of chemical phenomena and reactions, and the measurement of data required for such explanations; **biochemistry** is concerned with the chemistry of living organisms: the structure and reactions of proteins (such as enzymes), nucleic acids, carbohydrates, and lipids.

PHYSICS

Before the 20th century, physics was known as **natural philosophy**. Newtonian physics is based on the concepts of the English scientist Isaac Newton, before the formulation of quantum theory or Einstein's theory of relativity. Nuclear physics is the study of the properties of the nucleus of the atom, including the structure of nuclei; nuclear forces; the interactions between particles and nuclei; and the study of radioactive decay. The study of elementary particles is particle physics.

absolute zero lowest temperature theoretically possible according to kinetic theory, zero kelvin (0 K), equivalent to −273.15°C/−459.67°F, at which molecules are in their lowest energy state.

acceleration rate of change of the velocity of a moving body. It is usually measured in metres per second per second (m s^{-2}) or feet per second per second (ft s^{-2}). Because velocity is a vector quantity (possessing both magnitude and direction) a body travelling at constant speed may be said to be accelerating if its direction of motion changes. According to Newton's second law of motion, a body will accelerate only if it is acted upon by an unbalanced, or resultant, force.

Acceleration due to gravity is the acceleration of a body falling freely under the influence of the Earth's gravitational field; it varies slightly at different latitudes and altitudes. The value adopted internationally for gravitational acceleration is 9.806 m s^{-2}/32.174 ft s^{-2}.

acoustics in general, the experimental and theoretical science of sound and its transmission; in particular, that branch of the science that has to do with the phenomena of sound in a particular space such as a room or theatre.

alpha particle positively charged, high-energy particle emitted from the nucleus of a radioactive atom. It is one of the products of the spontaneous disintegration of radioactive elements such as radium and thorium, and is identical with the nucleus of a helium atom – that is, it consists of two protons and two neutrons. The process of emission, **alpha decay**, transforms one element into another, decreasing the atomic (or proton) number by two and the atomic mass (or nucleon number) by four.

antimatter form of matter in which most of the attributes (such as electrical charge, magnetic moment, and spin) of elementary particles are reversed. Such particles (antiparticles) can be created in particle accelerators, such as those at

What is an accelerator?

An accelerator is a device to bring charged particles (such as protons and electrons) up to high speeds and energies, at which they can be of use in industry, medicine, and pure physics. At low energies, accelerated particles can be used to produce the image on a television screen and generate X-rays (by means of a cathode-ray tube), destroy tumour cells, or kill bacteria. When high-energy particles collide with other particles, the fragments formed reveal the nature of the fundamental forces.

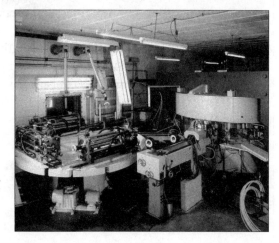

accelerator A cyclotron accelerator that employs a rotating, water-cooled target to produce isotopes. These include gallium-67 (half-life 78 hours) and indium-111 (half-life 67 hours). Sodium-22, cobalt-57, and cadmium-109 (all with half-lives in excess of 150 hours) are made in irradiations extending for up to 150 hours. *AEA Technology*

The structure of the atom

The atom is the smallest unit of matter that can take part in a chemical reaction, and which cannot be broken down chemically into anything simpler. An atom is made up of protons and neutrons in a central nucleus surrounded by electrons. The atoms of the various elements differ in atomic number, relative atomic mass, and chemical behaviour.

Atoms are much too small to be seen by even the most powerful optical microscope (the largest, caesium, has a diameter of 0.0000005 mm/0.00000002 in), and they are in constant motion. However, modern electron microscopes, such as the scanning tunnelling microscope (STM) and the atomic force microscope (AFM), can produce images of individual atoms and molecules.

The arrangement of electrons around the nucleus of an atom are arranged in distinct energy levels, also called orbitals or shells. These shells can be regarded as a series of concentric spheres, each of which can contain a certain maximum number of electrons; the noble gases have an arrangement in which every shell contains this number. The energy levels are usually numbered beginning with the shell nearest to the nucleus. The outermost shell is known as the valency shell as it contains the valence electrons.

Bohr Danish physicist Niels Bohr, one of the major figures of atomic research. Successfully combining Rutherford's classical model of the atom with Planck's quantum theory, he developed a model of the atom that revolutionized atomic theory. *AEA Technology*

CERN in Geneva, Switzerland, and at Fermilab in the USA.

antiparticle particle corresponding in mass and properties to a given elementary particle but with the opposite electrical charge, magnetic properties, or coupling to other fundamental forces. For example, an electron carries a negative charge whereas its antiparticle, the positron, carries a positive one. When a particle and its antiparticle collide, they destroy each other, in the process called 'annihilation', their total energy being converted to lighter particles and/or photons. A substance consisting entirely of antiparticles is known as antimatter.

atom see **structure of the atom** feature.

beta particle electron ejected with great velocity from a radioactive atom that is undergoing spontaneous disintegration. Beta particles do not exist in the nucleus but are created on disintegration, **beta decay**, when a neutron converts to a proton to emit an electron.

Boyle's law law stating that the volume of a given mass of gas at a constant temperature is inversely proportional to its pressure. For example, if the pressure of a gas doubles, its volume will be reduced by a half, and vice versa. The law was discovered in 1662 by Irish physicist and chemist Robert Boyle.

centre of mass point in or near an object at which the whole mass of the object may be considered to be concentrated. A symmetrical homogeneous object such as a sphere or cube has its centre of mass at its geometrical centre; a hollow object (such as a cup) may have its centre of mass in space inside the hollow.

chain reaction fission reaction that is maintained because neutrons released by the splitting of some atomic nuclei themselves go on to split others, releasing even more neutrons. Such a reaction can be controlled (as in a nuclear reactor) by using moderators to absorb excess neutrons. Uncontrolled, a chain reaction produces a nuclear explosion (as in an atom bomb).

change of state change in the physical state (solid, liquid, or gas) of a material. For instance, melting, boiling, evaporation, and their opposites, solidification and condensation, are changes of state. The former set of changes are brought about by heating or decreased pressure; the latter by cooling or increased pressure. *See illustration on page 166.*

Uncontainable boron

■ Boron becomes liquid at 2,100°C/ 3812°F and is so corrosive that it cannot be contained at all.

circuit arrangement of electrical components through which a current can flow. There are two basic circuits, series and parallel. In a series circuit, the components are connected end to end so that the current flows through all components one after the other. In a parallel circuit, compo-

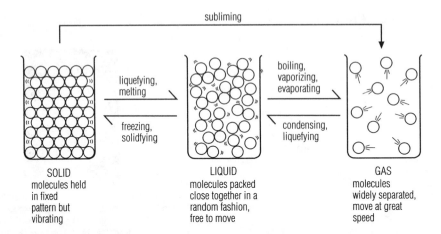

change of state The state (solid, liquid, or gas) of any substance is not fixed but varies with changes in temperature and pressure.

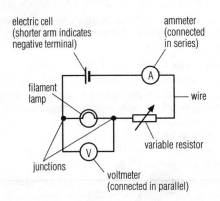

circuit diagram A circuit diagram shows in graphical form how the components of an electric circuit are connected together. Each component is represented by an internationally recognized symbol, and the connecting wires are shown by straight lines. A dot indicates where wires join.

nents are connected side by side so that part of the current passes through each component. A circuit diagram shows in graphical form how components are connected together, using standard symbols for the components.

critical mass minimum mass of fissile material that can undergo a continuous chain reaction. Below this mass, too many neutrons escape from the surface for a chain reaction to carry on; above the critical mass, the reaction may accelerate into a nuclear explosion.

cryogenics science of very low temperatures (approaching absolute zero), including the production of very low temperatures and the exploitation of special properties associated with them, such as the disappearance of electrical resistance (superconductivity).

density measure of the compactness of a substance; it is equal to its mass per unit volume and is measured in kg per cubic metre/lb per cubic foot. Density is a scalar quantity. The average density D of a mass m occupying a volume V is given by the formula:

$$D = m/V$$

Relative density is the ratio of the density of a substance to that of water at 4°C/32.2°F.

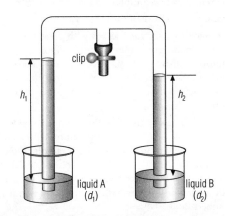

density Hare's apparatus is used to compare the density of two liquids. When air is removed from the top of the apparatus, the liquids rise in the tubes to heights which are inversely proportional to their densities.

Densities of Some Common Substances

Substance Density in kg m^{-3}

Solids		Liquids	
balsa wood	200	milk	1,030
oak	700	sea water	1,030
butter	900	glycerine	1,260
ice	920	Dead Sea brine	1,800
ebony	120		
sand (dry)	1,600	**Gases** (at standard temperature and pressure of 0°C and 1 atm)	
concrete	2,400		
aluminium	2,700		
steel	7,800	air	1.30
copper	8,900	hydrogen	0.09
lead	11,300	helium	0.18
uranium	19,000	methane	0.72
		nitrogen	1.25
Liquids		oxygen	1.43
water	1,000	carbon dioxide	1.98
petrol, paraffin	800	propane	2.02
olive oil	900	butane (iso)	2.60

diffraction the spreading out of waves when they pass through a small gap or around a small object, resulting in some change in the direction of the waves. In order for this effect to be observed the size of the object or gap must be comparable to or smaller than the wavelength of the waves. Diffraction occurs with all forms of progressive waves – electromagnetic, sound, and water waves – and explains such phenomena as why long-wave radio waves can bend round hills better than short-wave radio waves.

dispersion particular property of refraction in which the angle and velocity of waves passing through a dispersive medium depends upon their frequency. In the case of visible light the frequency corresponds to colour. The splitting of white light into a spectrum when it passes through a prism occurs because each component frequency of light moves through at a slightly different angle and speed. A rainbow is formed when sunlight is dispersed by raindrops.

efficiency general term indicating the degree to which a process or device can convert energy from one form to another without loss. It is normally expressed as a fraction or percentage, where 100% indicates conversion with no loss. The efficiency of a machine, for example, is the ratio of the work done by the machine to the energy put into the machine; in practice it is always less than 100% because of frictional heat losses. Certain electrical machines with no moving parts, such as transformers, can approach 100% efficiency.

elasticity ability of a solid to recover its shape once deforming forces (stresses modifying its dimensions or shape) are removed. An elastic material obeys Hooke's law, which states that its deformation is proportional to the applied stress up to a certain point, called the **elastic limit**, beyond which additional stress will deform it permanently. Elastic materials include metals and rubber; however, all materials have some degree of elasticity.

electric charge property of some bodies that causes them to exert forces on each other. Two bodies both with positive or both with negative charges repel, each other, whereas bodies with opposite or 'unlike' charges attract each other, since each is in the electric field of the other. In atoms, electrons possess a negative charge, and protons an equal positive charge. The SI unit of electric charge is the coulomb (symbol C).

electric current the flow of electrically charged particles through a conducting circuit due to the presence of a potential difference. The current at any point in a circuit is the amount of charge flowing per second; its SI unit is the ampere (coulomb per second).

electricity all phenomena caused by electric charge, whether static or in motion. Electric

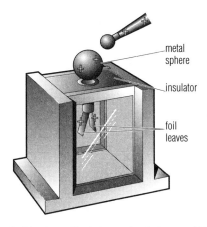

electric charge The electroscope is a simple means of detecting electric charge. The metal foil leaves diverge when a charge is applied to the metal sphere.

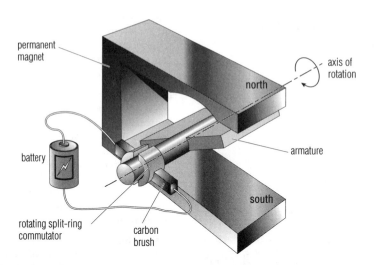

permanent magnet

axis of rotation

north

battery

armature

rotating split-ring commutator

carbon brush

south

electric motor In an electric motor, magnetic fields generated by electric currents push against each other, causing a shaft (the armature) to rotate.

charge is caused by an excess or deficit of electrons in the charged substance, and an electric current is the movement of charge through a material. Substances may be electrical conductors, such as metals, that allow the passage of electricity through them readily, or insulators, such as rubber, that are extremely poor conductors. Substances with relatively poor conductivities that can be improved by the addition of heat or light are known as semiconductors.

electrodynamics branch of physics dealing with electric charges, electric currents and associated forces. Quantum electrodynamics (QED) studies the interaction between charged particles and their emission and absorption of electromagnetic radiation. This field combines quantum theory and relativity theory, making accurate predictions about subatomic processes involving charged particles such as electrons and protons.

electromagnetic waves oscillating electric and magnetic fields travelling together through space at a speed of nearly 300,000 km/186,000 mi per second. The (limitless) range of possible wavelengths and frequencies of electromagnetic waves, which can be thought of as making up the **electromagnetic spectrum**, includes radio waves, infrared radiation, visible light, ultraviolet radiation, X-rays, and gamma rays.

electron stable, negatively charged elementary particle; it is a constituent of all atoms, and a member of the class of particles known as leptons. The electrons in each atom surround the nucleus in groupings called shells; in a neutral atom the number of electrons is equal to the number of protons in the nucleus. This electron structure is responsible for the chemical properties of the atom.

energy capacity for doing work. Energy can exist in many different forms. For example, potential energy (PE) is energy deriving from position; thus a stretched spring has elastic PE, and an object raised to a height above the Earth's surface, or the water in an elevated reservoir, has gravitational PE. Moving bodies possess kinetic energy (KE). Energy can be converted from one form to another, but the total quantity in a system stays the same (in accordance with the conservation of energy principle). Energy cannot be created or destroyed. For example, as an apple falls it loses gravitational PE but gains KE.

Although energy is never lost, after a number of conversions it tends to finish up as the kinetic energy of random motion of molecules (of the air, for example) at relatively low temperatures. This is 'degraded' energy that is difficult to convert back to other forms.

engine device for converting stored energy into useful work or movement. Most engines use a

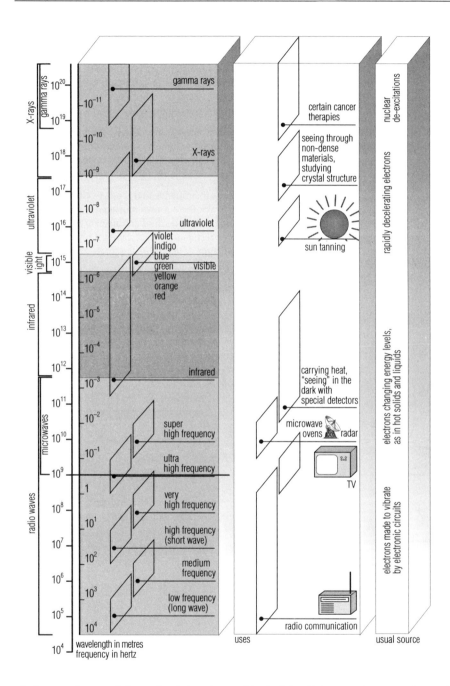

electromagnetic waves Radio waves have the lowest frequency. Infrared radiation, visible light, ultraviolet radiation, X-rays, and gamma rays have progressively higher frequencies.

fuel as their energy store. The fuel is burnt to produce heat energy – hence the name 'heat engine' – which is then converted into move-ment. Heat engines can be classified according to the fuel they use (petrol engine or diesel engine), or according to whether the fuel is burnt inside (internal combustion engine) or outside (steam engine) the engine, or according to whether they produce a reciprocating or rotary motion (turbine or Wankel engine).

entropy in thermodynamics, a parameter representing the state of disorder of a system at the atomic, ionic, or molecular level; the greater the disorder, the higher the entropy. Thus the fast-moving disordered molecules of water vapour have higher entropy than those of more ordered liquid water, which in turn have more entropy than the molecules in solid crystalline ice.

equilibrium unchanging condition in which an undisturbed system can remain indefinitely in a state of balance. In a **static equilibrium**, such as an object resting on the floor, there is no motion. In a **dynamic equilibrium**, in contrast, a steady state is maintained by constant, though opposing, changes. For example, in a sealed bottle half-full of water, the constancy of the water level is a result of molecules evaporating from the surface and condensing on to it at the same rate.

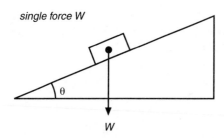

single force W

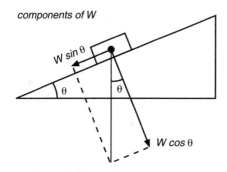

components of W

resolution of forces In mechanics, the resolution of forces is the division of a single force into two parts that act at right angles to each other. In the diagram, the weight W of an object on a slope, tilted at an angle θ, can be resolved into two parts or components: one acting at a right angle to the slope, equal to Wcosθ, and one acting parallel to and down the slope, equal to Wsinθ.

field region of space in which an object exerts a force on another separate object because of certain properties they both possess. For example, there is a force of attraction between any two objects that have mass when one is in the gravitational field of the other.

fission splitting of a heavy atomic nucleus into two or more major fragments. It is accompanied by the emission of two or three neutrons and the release of large amounts of nuclear energy.

force any influence that tends to change the state of rest or the uniform motion in a straight line of a body. The action of an unbalanced or resultant force results in the acceleration of a body in the direction of action of the force, or it may, if the

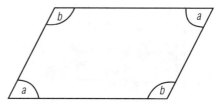

(i) opposite sides and angles are equal

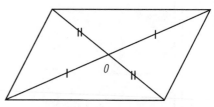

(ii) diagonals bisect each other at 0

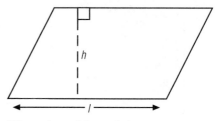

(iii) area of a parallelogram l x h

forces The diagram shows how the parallelogram of forces can be used to calculate the resultant (combined effect) of two different forces acting together on an object. The two forces are represented by two lines drawn at an angle to each other. By completing the parallelogram (of which the two lines are sides), a diagonal may be drawn from the original angle to the opposite corner to represent the resultant force vector.

body is unable to move freely, result in its deformation. Force is a vector quantity, possessing both magnitude and direction; its SI unit is the newton.

forces, fundamental four fundamental interactions believed to be at work in the physical universe. There are two long-range forces: **gravity**, which keeps the planets in orbit around the Sun, and acts between all particles that have mass; and the **electromagnetic force**, which stops solids from falling apart, and acts between all particles with electric charge. There are two very short-range forces which operate only inside the atomic nucleus: the **weak nuclear force**, responsible for the reactions that fuel the Sun and for the emission of beta particles from certain nuclei; and the **strong nuclear force**, which binds together the protons and neutrons in the nuclei of atoms. The relative strengths of the four forces are: strong, 1; electromagnetic, 10^{-2}; weak, 10^{-6}; gravitational, 10^{-40}.

frequency number of periodic oscillations, vibrations, or waves occurring per unit of time. The SI unit of frequency is the hertz (Hz), one hertz being equivalent to one cycle per second. Frequency is related to wavelength and velocity by the relationship:

$$f = \frac{v}{\lambda}$$

where f is frequency, v is velocity and λ is wavelength.

Frequency is the reciprocal of the period T:

$$f = \frac{1}{T}$$

friction force that opposes the relative motion of two bodies in contact. The **coefficient of friction** is the ratio of the force required to achieve this relative motion to the force pressing the two bodies together.

fundamental constant physical quantity that is constant in all circumstances throughout the whole universe. Examples are the electric charge of an electron, the speed of light, Planck's constant, and the gravitational constant.

grand unified theory sought-for theory that would combine the theory of the strong nuclear force (called quantum chromodynamics) with the theory of the weak nuclear and electromagnetic forces. The search for the grand unified theory is part of a larger programme seeking a unified field theory, which would combine all the forces of nature (including gravity) within one framework.

gravity force of attraction that arises between objects by virtue of their masses. On Earth, gravity is the force of attraction between any object in the Earth's gravitational field and the Earth itself. It is regarded as one of the four fundamental forces of nature, the other three being the electromagnetic force, the strong nuclear force, and the weak nuclear force. The gravitational force is the weakest of the four forces, but it acts over great distances. The particle that is postulated as the carrier of the gravitational force is the graviton.

Fast rain

■ The maximum speed with which a falling raindrop can hit you is about 29 kmph/ 18 mph. In a vacuum, the further an object falls, the more speed it gains, but in the real world, air resistance eventually balances out the accelerating effect of gravity.

---

half-life during radioactive decay, the time in which the strength of a radioactive source decays to half its original value. In theory, the decay process is never complete and there is always some residual radioactivity. For this reason, the half-life of a radioactive isotope is measured, rather than the total decay time. It may vary from millionths of a second to billions of years.

Half-life

Isotope	Half-life
(least stable)	
lithium-5	4.4×10^{-22} sec
polonium-213	4.2×10^{-6} sec
lead-211	36 min
lead-209	3.3 hours
uranium-238	4.551×10^9 years
thorium-232	1.39×10^{10} years
tellurium-128	1.5×10^{24} years
(most stable)	

Physical Constants

Physical constants, or fundamental constants, are standardized values whose parameters do not change.

Constant	Symbol	Value in SI units
acceleration of free fall	g	9.80665 m s^{-2}
Avogadro's constant	N_A	$6.0221367 \times 10^{23} \text{ mol}^{-1}$
Boltzmann's constant	k	$1.380658 \times 10^{-23} \text{ J K}^{-1}$
elementary charge	e	$1.60217733 \times 10^{-19} \text{ C}$
electronic rest mass	m_e	$9.1093897 \times 10^{-31} \text{ kg}$
Faraday's constant	F	$9.6485309 \times 10^4 \text{ C mol}^{-1}$
gas constant	R	$8.314510 \text{ J K}^{-1} \text{ mol}^{-1}$
gravitational constant	G	$6.672 \times 10^{-11} \text{ N m}^2 \text{ kg}^{-2}$
Loschmidt's number	N_L	$2.686763 \times 10^{25} \text{ m}^{-3}$
neutron rest mass	m_n	$1.6749286 \times 10^{-27} \text{ kg}$
Planck's constant	h	$6.6260755 \times 10^{-34} \text{ J s}$
proton rest mass	m_p	$1.6726231 \times 10^{-27} \text{ kg}$
speed of light in a vacuum	c	$2.99792458 \times 10^8 \text{ m s}^{-1}$
standard atmosphere	atm	$1.01325 \times 10^5 \text{ Pa}$
Stefan–Boltzmann constant	θ	$5.67051 \times 10^{-8} \text{ W m}^{-2} \text{ K}^{-4}$

heat form of energy possessed by a substance by virtue of the vibrating movement (kinetic energy) of its molecules or atoms. Heat energy is transferred by conduction, convection, and radiation. It always flows from a region of higher temperature (heat intensity) to one of lower temperature. Its effect on a substance may be simply to raise its temperature, or to cause it to expand, melt (if a solid), vaporize (if a liquid), or increase its pressure (if a confined gas).

Hooke's law law stating that the deformation of a body is proportional to the magnitude of the deforming force, provided that the body's elastic limit is not exceeded. If the elastic limit is not reached, the body will return to its original size once the force is removed. The law was discovered by Robert Hooke 1676.

hydrodynamics branch of physics dealing with fluids (liquids and gases) in motion.

hydrostatics branch of statics dealing with fluids in equilibrium – that is, in a static condition. Practical applications include shipbuilding and dam design.

inertia tendency of an object to remain in a state of rest or uniform motion until an external force is applied, as described by Isaac Newton's first law of motion.

interference phenomenon of two or more wave motions interacting and combining to produce a resultant wave of larger or smaller amplitude (depending on whether the combining waves are in or out of phase with each other).

isotope one of two or more atoms that have the same atomic number (same number of protons), but which contain a different number of neutrons, thus differing in their atomic mass. They may be stable or radioactive, naturally occurring or synthesized. For example, hydrogen has the isotopes ^2H (deuterium) and ^3H (tritium). The term was coined by English chemist Frederick Soddy, pioneer researcher in atomic disintegration.

kinetic theory theory describing the physical properties of matter in terms of the behaviour – principally movement – of its component atoms or molecules. The temperature of a substance is dependent on the velocity of movement of its constituent particles, increased temperature being accompanied by increased movement. A gas consists of rapidly moving atoms or molecules and, according to kinetic theory, it is their continual impact on the walls of the containing vessel that accounts for the pressure of the gas. The slowing of molecular motion as temperature falls, according to kinetic theory, accounts for the physical properties of liquids and solids, culminating in the concept of no molecular motion at absolute zero (0K/–273°C).

laser (acronym for **light amplification by stimulated emission of radiation**) device for producing a narrow beam of light, capable of travelling over vast distances without dispersion, and of being focused to give enormous power densities (10^8 watts per cm^2 for high-energy lasers). The laser operates on a principle similar to that of the maser (a high-frequency microwave amplifier or oscillator). The uses of lasers include communications (a laser beam can carry much more information than can radio waves), cutting, drilling, welding, satellite tracking, medical and biological research, and surgery. Sound wave vibrations from the window glass of a room can be picked up by a reflected laser beam. Lasers are also used as entertainment in theatres, concerts, and light shows.

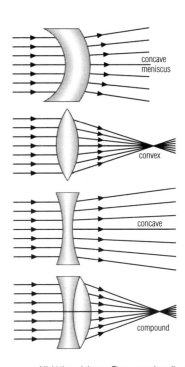

lens The passage of light through lenses. The concave lens diverges a beam of light from a distant source. The convex and compound lenses focus light from a distant source to a point. The distance between the focus and the lens is called the focal length. The shorter the focus, the more powerful the lens.

Platinum into gold

■ The Petawatt, the world's most powerful laser, generates 1,200 times as much power as the entire electrical grid of the USA. When focused on platinum, it turns it into gold.

---

lens in optics, a piece of a transparent material, such as glass, with two polished surfaces – one concave or convex, and the other plane, concave, or convex – that modifies rays of light. A convex lens brings rays of light together; a concave lens makes the rays diverge. Lenses are essential to spectacles, microscopes, telescopes, cameras, and almost all optical instruments.

lever simple machine consisting of a rigid rod pivoted at a fixed point called the fulcrum, used for shifting or raising a heavy load or applying force. Levers are classified into orders according to where the effort is applied, and the

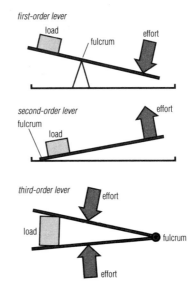

lever Types of lever. Practical applications of the first-order lever include the crowbar, seesaw, and scissors. The wheelbarrow is a second-order lever; tweezers or tongs are third-order levers.

load-moving force developed, in relation to the position of the fulcrum.

light electromagnetic waves in the visible range, having a wavelength from about 400 nanometres in the extreme violet to about 770 nanometres in the extreme red. Light is considered to exhibit particle and wave properties, and the fundamental particle, or quantum, of light is called the photon. The speed of light (and of all electromagnetic radiation) in a vacuum is approximately 300,000 km/186,000 mi per second, and is a universal constant denoted by c.

luminescence emission of light from a body when its atoms are excited by means other than raising its temperature. Short-lived luminescence is called fluorescence; longer-lived luminescence is called phosphorescence.

magnetism phenomena associated with magnetic fields. Magnetic fields are produced by moving charged particles: in electromagnets, electrons flow through a coil of wire connected to a battery; in permanent magnets, spinning electrons within the atoms generate the field.

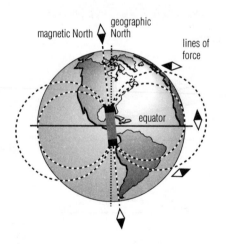

magnetism The Earth's magnetic field is similar to that of a bar magnet with poles near, but not exactly at, the geographic poles. Compass needles align themselves with the magnetic field, which is horizontal near the equator and vertical at the magnetic poles.

mass quantity of matter in a body as measured by its inertia. Mass determines the acceleration produced in a body by a given force acting on it, the acceleration being inversely proportional to the mass of the body. The mass also determines the

force exerted on a body by gravity on Earth, although this attraction varies slightly from place to place. In the SI system, the base unit of mass is the kilogram.

matter anything that has mass. All matter is made up of atoms, which in turn are made up of elementary particles; it ordinarily exists in one of three physical states: solid, liquid, or gas.

mechanics branch of physics dealing with the motions of bodies and the forces causing these motions, and also with the forces acting on bodies in equilibrium. It is usually divided into dynamics and statics.

momentum the product of the mass of a body and its velocity. If the mass of a body is m kilograms and its velocity is v m s^{-1}, then its momentum is given by:

$$momentum = mv$$

Its unit is the kilogram metre-per-second (kg m s^{-1}) or the newton second.

The momentum of a body does not change unless a resultant or unbalanced force acts on that body.

Newton's laws of motion three laws that form the basis of Newtonian mechanics. (1) Unless acted upon by an unbalanced force, a body at rest stays at rest, and a moving body continues moving at the same speed in the same straight line. (2) An unbalanced force applied to a body gives it an acceleration proportional to the force (and in the direction of the force) and inversely proportional to the mass of the body. (3) When a body A exerts a force on a body B, B exerts an equal and opposite force on A; that is, to every action there is an equal and opposite reaction.

nuclear fusion process whereby two atomic nuclei are fused, with the release of a large amount of energy. Very high temperatures and pressures are thought to be required in order for the process to happen. Under these conditions the atoms involved are stripped of all their electrons so that the remaining particles, which together make up a **plasma**, can come close together at very high speeds and overcome the mutual repulsion of the positive charges on the atomic nuclei. At very close range the strong nuclear force will come into play, fusing the particles together to form a larger nucleus. As fusion is accompanied by the release of large amounts of energy, the process might one day be harnessed to form the basis of commercial energy production. Methods of achieving controlled fusion are therefore the subject of research around the world.

particle physics see feature on page 174.

optics branch of physics that deals with the study of light and vision – for example, shadows and mirror images, lenses, microscopes, telescopes, and cameras. For all practical purposes light rays travel in straight lines, although Albert Einstein demonstrated that they may be 'bent' by a gravitational field. On striking a surface they are reflected or refracted with some absorption of energy, and the study of this is known as geometrical optics.

potential, electric relative electrical state of an object. The potential at a point is equal to the energy required to bring a unit electric charge from infinity to the point. The SI unit of potential is the volt (V). Positive electric charges will flow 'downhill' from a region of high potential to a region of low potential.

power rate of doing work or consuming energy. It is measured in watts (joules per second) or other units of work per unit time.

pressure in a fluid, the force that would act normally (at right angles) per unit surface area of a body immersed in the fluid. The SI unit of pressure is the pascal (Pa), equal to a pressure of one newton per square metre. In the atmosphere, the pressure declines with height from about 100 kPa at sea level to zero where the atmosphere fades into space. Pressure is commonly measured with a barometer, manometer, or Bourdon gauge. Other common units of pressure are the bar and the torr.

proton positively charged subatomic particle, a constituent of the nucleus of all atoms. It belongs to the baryon subclass of the hadrons. A proton is extremely long-lived, with a lifespan of at least 10^{32} years. It carries a unit positive charge equal to the negative charge of an electron. Its mass is almost 1,836 times that of an electron, or 1.67×10^{-27} kg. Protons are composed of two up quarks and one down quark held together by gluons. The number of protons in the atom of an element is equal to the atomic number of that element.

quantum theory or **quantum mechanics** theory that energy does not have a continuous range of values, but is, instead, absorbed or radiated discontinuously, in multiples of definite, indivisible units called quanta. Just as earlier theory showed how light, generally seen as a wave motion, could also in some ways be seen as composed of discrete particles (photons), quantum theory shows how atomic particles such as electrons may also be seen as having wavelike properties. Quantum theory is the basis of particle physics, modern theoretical chemistry, and the solid-state physics that describes the behaviour of the silicon chips used in computers.

radioactive decay process of disintegration undergone by the nuclei of radioactive elements, such as radium and various isotopes of uranium and the transuranic elements. This changes the element's atomic number, thus transmuting one element into another, and is accompanied by the emission of radiation. Alpha and beta decay are the most common forms.

radiation emission of radiant energy as particles or waves – for example, heat, light, alpha particles, and beta particles.

radioisotope contraction of **radioactive isotope** naturally occurring or synthetic radioactive form of an element. Most radioisotopes are made by bombarding a stable element with neutrons in the core of a nuclear reactor. The radiations given off by radioisotopes are easy to detect (hence their use as tracers), can in some instances penetrate substantial thicknesses of materials, and have profound effects (such as genetic mutation) on living matter.

reflection the throwing back or deflection of waves, such as light or sound waves, when they hit a surface. The **law of reflection** states that the angle of incidence (the angle between the ray and

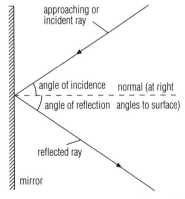

reflection The law of reflection: the angle of incidence of a light beam equals the angle of reflection of the beam.

What is particle physics?

Particle physics is the study of the particles that make up all atoms, and of their interactions. More than 300 subatomic particles have now been identified by physicists, categorized into several classes according to their mass, electric charge, spin, magnetic moment, and interaction. Subatomic particles include the elementary particles (quarks, leptons, and gauge bosons), which are believed to be indivisible and so may be considered the fundamental units of matter; and the hadrons (baryons, such as the proton and neutron, and mesons), which are composite particles, made up of two or three quarks. The proton, electron, and neutrino are the only stable particles (the neutron being stable only when in the atomic nucleus). The unstable particles decay rapidly into other particles, and are known from experiments with particle accelerators and cosmic radiation.

Pioneering research took place at the Cavendish laboratory, Cambridge, England. In 1897 English physicist J J Thomson discovered that all atoms contain identical, negatively charged particles (electrons), which can easily be freed. By 1911 New Zealand physicist Ernest Rutherford had shown that the electrons surround a very small, positively-charged nucleus. In the case of hydrogen, this was found to consist of a single positively charged particle, a proton. The nuclei of other elements are made up of protons and uncharged particles called neutrons.

1932 saw the discovery of a particle (whose existence had been predicted by British theoretical physicist Paul Dirac in 1928) with the mass of an electron, but an equal and opposite charge – the positron. This was the first example of

antimatter; it is now believed that all particles have corresponding antiparticles. In 1934 Italian-born US physicist Enrico Fermi argued that a hitherto unsuspected particle, the neutrino, must accompany electrons in beta-emission.

particles and fundamental forces By the mid-1930s, four types of fundamental force interacting between particles had been identified. The electromagnetic force acts between all particles with electric charge, and is thought to be related to the exchange between these particles of gauge bosons called photons, packets of electromagnetic radiation.

In 1935 Japanese physicist Hideki Yukawa suggested that the strong nuclear force (binding protons and neutrons together in the nucleus) was transmitted by the exchange of particles with a mass about one-tenth of that of a proton; these particles, called pions (originally pi mesons), were found by British physicist Cecil Powell in 1946. Yukawa's theory was largely superseded from 1973 by the theory of quantum chromodynamics, which postulates that the strong nuclear force is transmitted by the exchange of gauge bosons called gluons between the quarks and antiquarks making up protons and neutrons. Theoretical work on the weak nuclear force began with Enrico Fermi in the 1930s. The existence of the gauge bosons was confirmed in 1983 at CERN, the European nuclear research organization.

Gauge bosons carry forces between other particles. There are four types: gluon, photon, weakon, and graviton. The gluon carries the strong nuclear force, the photon the electromagnetic force, the weakons the weak nuclear force, and the

graviton the force of gravity, which is experienced by all matter.

leptons The electron, muon, tau, and their neutrinos comprise the leptons – light particles with half-integral spin that 'feel' the weak nuclear and electromagnetic force but not the strong force. There are 12 types: the electron, muon, tau; their neutrinos, the electron neutrino, muon neutrino, and tau neutrino; and the antiparticles of each. These particles are influenced by the weak nuclear force.

mesons and baryons The hadrons (particles that 'feel' the strong nuclear force) were found in the 1950s and 1960s. They are classified into mesons, with whole-number or zero spins, and baryons (which include protons and neutrons), with half-integral spins. It was shown in the early 1960s that if hadrons of the same spin are represented as points on suitable charts, simple patterns are formed. This symmetry enabled a hitherto unknown baryon, the omega-minus, to be predicted from a gap in one of the patterns; it duly turned up in experiments.

quarks In 1964, US physicists Murray Gell-Mann and George Zweig suggested that all hadrons were built from three 'flavours' of a new particle with half-integral spin and a charge of magnitude either $\frac{1}{3}$ or $\frac{2}{3}$ that of an electron; Gell-Mann named the particle the **quark**. There are 12 types of quark (up, down, charm, strange, top, and bottom, plus the antiparticles of each). Mesons are quark–antiquark pairs (spins either add to one or cancel to zero), and baryons are quark triplets. To account for new mesons such as the psi (J) particle the number of quark flavours had risen to six by 1985.

Principal Subatomic Particles

	Group	Particle	Symbol	Charge	Mass (MeV)	Spin	Lifetime (sec)
elementary particle	quark	up	u	$\frac{2}{3}$	336	$\frac{1}{2}$	?
		down	d	$-\frac{1}{3}$	336	$\frac{1}{2}$	?
		(top)	t	$(\frac{2}{3})$	(<600,000)	$(\frac{1}{2})$	?
		bottom	b	$-\frac{1}{3}$	4,700	$\frac{1}{2}$	?
		strange	s	$-\frac{1}{3}$	540	$\frac{1}{2}$	?
		charm	c	$\frac{2}{3}$	1,500	$\frac{1}{2}$	?
	lepton	electron	e^-	−1	0.511	$\frac{1}{2}$	stable
		electron neutrino	ν_e	0	(0)	$\frac{1}{2}$	stable
		muon	μ^-	−1	105.66	$\frac{1}{2}$	2.2×10^{-6}
		muon neutrino	ν_μ	0	(0)	$\frac{1}{2}$	stable
		tau	τ^-	−1	1,784	$\frac{1}{2}$	3.4×10^{-13}
		tau neutrino	ν_τ	0	(0)	$\frac{1}{2}$	?
	gauge boson	photon	γ	0	0	1	stable
		graviton	g	0	(0)	2	stable
		gluon	g	0	0	1	?
		weakon	$W^\pm$	±1	81,000	1	?
			Z	0	94,000	1	?
hadron	meson	pion	Π^+	1	139.57	0	2.6×10^{-8}
			Π^0	0	134.96	0	8.3×10^{-17}
		kaon	K^+	1	493.67	0	1.2×10^{-8}
			K^{0S}	0	497.67	0	8.9×10^{-11}
			K^{0L}	0	497.67	0	5.18×10^{-8}
		psi	ψ	0	3,100	1	6.3×10^{-2}
		upsilon	Υ	0	9,460	1	$\sim 1 \times 10^{-20}$
	baryon	nucleon:					
		proton	p	1	938.28	$\frac{1}{2}$	stable
		neutron	n	0	939.57	$\frac{1}{2}$	920
		hyperon:					
		lambda	Λ	0	1,115.6	$\frac{1}{2}$	2.63×10^{-10}
		sigma	Σ^+	1	1,189.4	$\frac{1}{2}$	8.0×10^{-11}
			Σ^-	−1	1,197.3	$\frac{1}{2}$	1.5×10^{-10}
			Σ^0	0	1,192.5	$\frac{1}{2}$	5.8×10^{-20}
		xi	X^-	−1	1,321.3	$\frac{1}{2}$	1.64×10^{-10}
			X^0	0	1,314.9	$\frac{1}{2}$	2.9×10^{-10}
		omega	Ω	−1	1,672.4	$\frac{3}{2}$	8.2×10^{-11}

? indicates that the paricle's lifetime has yet to be determined
( ) indicates that the property has been deduced but not confirmed
MeV = million electron volts

What is relativity?

Relativity is the theory of the relative rather than absolute character of motion and mass, and the interdependence of matter, time, and space, as developed by German-born US physicist Albert Einstein in two phases:

special theory of relativity (1905)
Starting with the premises that (1) the laws of nature are the same for all observers in unaccelerated motion, and (2) the speed of light is independent of the motion of its source, Einstein arrived at some rather unexpected consequences. Intuitively familiar concepts, like mass, length, and time, had to be modified. For example, an object moving rapidly past the observer will appear to be both shorter and heavier than when it is at rest (that is, at rest relative to the observer), and a clock moving rapidly past the observer will appear to be running slower than when it is at rest.

Costly relativity
■ The manuscript for Einstein's special theory of relativity sold for $5 million in 1996.

These predictions of relativity theory seem to be foreign to everyday experience merely because the changes are quite negligible at speeds less than about 1,500 km s^{-1}, and they only become appreciable at speeds approaching the speed of light.

general theory of relativity (1915)
The geometrical properties of space-time were to be conceived as modified locally by the presence of a body with mass. A planet's orbit around the Sun (as observed in three-dimensional space) arises from its natural trajectory in modified space-time; there is no need to invoke, as Isaac Newton did, a force of gravity coming from the Sun and acting on the planet. Einstein's general theory accounts for a peculiarity in the behaviour of the motion of the perihelion of the orbit of the planet Mercury that cannot be explained by Newton's theory. The new theory also said that light rays should bend when they pass by a massive object. The predicted bending of starlight was observed during the eclipse of the Sun in 1919. A third corroboration is found in the shift towards the red in the spectra of the Sun and, in particular, of stars of great density – white

---

Einstein and fridges
■ Einstein collaborated with Hungarian physicist Leo Szilard on a number of designs for a refrigerator. A series of patents was taken out in their names, although nothing was actually developed commercially.

---

dwarfs such as the companion of Sirius.

Who was Einstein?
Albert Einstein was a German-born US physicist whose theories of relativity revolutionized our understanding of matter, space, and time. Einstein established that light may have a particle nature and deduced the **photoelectric law**, for which he was awarded the Nobel Prize for Physics in 1921. Einstein also showed that mass is related to energy by the famous equation $E = mc^2$, which indicates the enormous amount of energy that is stored as mass, some of which is released in radioactivity and nuclear reactions, for example in the Sun.

---

a perpendicular line drawn to the surface) is equal to the angle of reflection (the angle between the reflected ray and a perpendicular to the surface).

refraction the bending of a wave when it passes from one medium into another. It is the effect of the different speeds of wave propagation in two substances that have different densities. The amount of refraction depends on the densities of the media, the angle at which the wave strikes the surface of the second medium, and the amount of bending and change of velocity corresponding to the wave's frequency (dispersion). Refraction occurs with all types of progressive waves – electromagnetic waves, sound waves, and water waves – and differs from reflection, which involves no change in velocity.

relativity see feature.

resistance property of a conductor that restricts the flow of electricity through it, associated with

the conversion of electrical energy to heat; also the magnitude of this property. Resistance depends on many factors, such as the nature of the material, its temperature, dimensions, and thermal properties; degree of impurity; the nature and state of illumination of the surface; and the frequency and magnitude of the current. The SI unit of resistance is the ohm.

$$resistance = \frac{voltage}{current}$$

This is known as Ohm's law.

resonance rapid amplification of a vibration when the vibrating object is subject to a force varying at its natural frequency. In a trombone, for example, the length of the air column in the instrument is adjusted until it resonates with the note being sounded. Resonance effects are also produced by many electrical circuits. Tuning a radio, for example, is done by adjusting the natural frequency of

Decibel Scale

The decibel scale is used primarily to compare sound intensities although it can be used to compare voltages.

Decibels	Typical sound	Decibels	Typical sound
0	threshold of hearing	65–90	train
10	rustle of leaves in gentle breeze	75–80	factory (light/medium work)
10	quiet whisper	90	heavy traffic
20	average whisper	90–100	thunder
20–50	quiet conversation	110–140	jet aircraft at take-off
40–45	hotel; theatre (between performances)	130	threshold of pain
50–65	loud conversation	140–190	space rocket at take-off
65–70	traffic on busy street		

the receiver circuit until it coincides with the frequency of the radio waves falling on the aerial.

semiconductor material with electrical conductivity intermediate between metals and insulators and used in a wide range of electronic devices. Certain crystalline materials, most notably silicon and germanium, have a small number of free electrons that have escaped from the bonds between the atoms. The atoms from which they have escaped possess vacancies, called holes, which are similarly able to move from atom to atom and can be regarded as positive charges. Current can be carried by both electrons (negative carriers) and holes (positive carriers). Such materials are known as **intrinsic semi conductors**.

sound physiological sensation received by the ear, originating in a vibration that communicates itself as a pressure variation in the air and travels in every direction, spreading out as an expanding sphere. All sound waves in air travel with a speed dependent on the temperature; under ordinary conditions, this is about 330 m/1,070 ft per second. The pitch of the sound depends on the number of vibrations imposed on the air per second (frequency), but the speed is unaffected. The loudness of a sound is dependent primarily on the amplitude of the vibration of the air.

spectroscopy study of spectra associated with atoms or molecules in solid, liquid, or gaseous phase. Spectroscopy can be used to identify unknown compounds and is an invaluable tool in science, medicine, and industry (for example, in checking the purity of drugs).

spectrum plural **spectra** arrangement of frequencies or wavelengths when electromagnetic radiations are separated into their constituent parts. Visible light is part of the electromagnetic spectrum and most sources emit waves over a range of wavelengths that can be broken up or 'dispersed'; white light can be separated into red, orange, yellow, green, blue, indigo, and violet. The visible spectrum was first studied by Isaac Newton, who showed in 1672 how white light could be broken up into different colours.

speed of light speed at which light and other electromagnetic waves travel through empty space. Its value is 299,792,458 m/186,281 mi per second. The speed of light is the highest speed possible, according to the theory of relativity, and its value is independent of the motion of its source and of the observer. It is impossible to accelerate any material body to this speed because it would require an infinite amount of energy.

standard model modern theory of elementary particles and their interactions. According to the standard model, elementary particles are classified as leptons (light particles, such as electrons), hadrons (particles, such as neutrons and protons, that are formed from quarks), and gauge bosons. Leptons and hadrons interact by exchanging gauge bosons, each of which is responsible for a different fundamental force: photons mediate the electromagnetic force, which affects all charged particles; gluons mediate the strong nuclear force, which affects quarks; gravitons mediate the force of gravity; and the weakons (intermediate vector bosons) mediate the weak nuclear force.

states of matter forms (solid, liquid, or gas) in which material can exist. Whether a material is solid, liquid, or gaseous depends on its temperature and the pressure on it. The transition between states takes place at definite temperatures, called melting point and boiling point.

statics branch of mechanics concerned with the behaviour of bodies at rest and forces in equilibrium, and distinguished from dynamics.

stress and strain in the science of materials, measures of the deforming force applied to a body (stress) and of the resulting change in its shape (strain). For a perfectly elastic material, stress is proportional to strain (Hooke's law).

subatomic particle particle that is smaller than an atom. Such particles may be indivisible elementary particles, such as the electron and quark, or they may be composites, such as the proton, neutron, and alpha particle.

superstring theory mathematical theory developed in the 1980s to explain the properties of elementary particles and the forces between them (in particular, gravity and the nuclear forces) in a way that combines relativity and quantum theory.

In string theory, the fundamental objects in the universe are not pointlike particles but extremely small stringlike objects. These objects exist in a universe of ten dimensions, although, for reasons not yet understood, only three space dimensions and one dimension of time are discernible.

supersymmetry theory that relates the two classes of elementary particle, the fermions and the bosons. According to supersymmetry, each fermion particle has a boson partner particle, and vice versa. It has not been possible to marry up all the known fermions with the known bosons, and so the theory postulates the existence of other, as yet undiscovered fermions, such as the photinos (partners of the photons), gluinos (partners of the gluons), and gravitinos (partners of the gravitons). Using these ideas, it has become possible to develop a theory of gravity – called **supergravity** – that extends Einstein's work and considers the gravitational, nuclear, and electromagnetic forces to be manifestations of an underlying superforce. Supersymmetry has been incorporated into the superstring theory, and appears to be a crucial ingredient in the 'theory of everything' sought by scientists.

surface tension property that causes the surface of a liquid to behave as if it were covered with a weak elastic skin; this is why a needle can float on water. It is caused by the exposed surface's tendency to contract to the smallest possible area because of cohesive forces between molecules at the surface. Allied phenomena include the formation of droplets, the concave profile of a meniscus, and the capillary action by which water soaks into a sponge.

temperature degree or intensity of heat of an object and the condition that determines whether it will transfer heat to another object or receive heat from it, according to the laws of thermodynamics. The temperature of an object is a measure of the average kinetic energy possessed by the atoms or molecules of which it is composed. The SI unit of temperature is the kelvin (symbol K) used with the Kelvin scale. Other measures of temperature in common use are the Celsius scale and the Fahrenheit scale.

tension stress (force) set up in a stretched material. In a stretched string or wire it exerts a pull that is equal in magnitude but opposite in direction to the stress being applied at the string ends. Tension is measured in newtons.

thermodynamics branch of physics dealing with the transformation of heat into and from other forms of energy. It is the basis of the study of the efficient working of engines, such as the steam and internal combustion engines. The three laws of thermodynamics are: (1) energy can be neither created nor destroyed, heat and mechanical work being mutually convertible; (2) it is impossible for an unaided self-acting machine to convey heat from one body to another at a higher temperature; and (3) it is impossible by any procedure, no matter how idealized, to reduce any system to the absolute zero of temperature (0K/–273°C/–459°F) in a finite number of operations. Put into mathematical form, these laws have widespread applications in physics and chemistry.

ultrasonics branch of physics dealing with the theory and application of ultrasound: sound waves occurring at frequencies too high to be heard by the human ear (that is, above about 20 kHz).

Table of Equivalent Temperatures

Celsius and Fahrenheit temperatures can be interconverted as follows: C = (F − 32) × 100/180; F = (C × 180/100) + 32.

°C	°F	°C	°F	°C	°F	°C	°F
100	212.0	70	158.0	40	104.0	10	50.0
99	210.2	69	156.2	39	102.2	9	48.2
98	208.4	68	154.4	38	100.4	8	46.4
97	206.6	67	152.6	37	98.6	7	44.6
96	204.8	66	150.8	36	96.8	6	42.8
95	203.0	65	149.0	35	95.0	5	41.0
94	201.2	64	147.2	34	93.2	4	39.2
93	199.4	63	145.4	33	91.4	3	37.4
92	197.6	62	143.6	32	89.6	2	35.6
91	195.8	61	141.8	31	87.8	1	33.8
90	194.0	60	140.0	30	86.0	0	32.0
89	192.2	59	138.2	29	84.2	−1	30.2
88	190.4	58	136.4	28	82.4	−2	28.4
87	188.6	57	134.6	27	80.6	−3	26.6
86	186.8	56	132.8	26	78.8	−4	24.8
85	185.0	55	131.0	25	77.0	−5	23.0
84	183.2	54	129.2	24	75.2	−6	21.2
83	181.4	53	127.4	23	73.4	−7	19.4
82	179.6	52	125.6	22	71.6	−8	17.6
81	177.8	51	123.8	21	69.8	−9	15.8
80	176.0	50	122.0	20	68.0	−10	14.0
79	174.2	49	120.2	19	66.2	−11	12.2
78	172.4	48	118.4	18	64.4	−12	10.4
77	170.6	47	116.6	17	62.6	−13	8.6
76	168.8	46	114.8	16	60.8	−14	6.8
75	167.0	45	113.0	15	59.0	−15	5.0
74	165.2	44	111.2	14	57.2	−16	3.2
73	163.4	43	109.4	13	55.4	−17	1.4
72	161.6	42	107.6	12	53.6	−18	−0.4
71	159.8	41	105.8	11	51.8	−19	−2.2

uncertainty principle or **indeterminacy principle** in quantum mechanics, the principle that it is impossible to know with unlimited accuracy the position and momentum of a particle. The principle arises because in order to locate a particle exactly, an observer must bounce light (in the form of a photon) off the particle, which must alter its position in an unpredictable way.

velocity speed of an object in a given direction. Velocity is a vector quantity, since its direction is important as well as its magnitude (or speed).

viscosity resistance of a fluid to flow, caused by its internal friction, which makes it resist flowing past a solid surface or other layers of the fluid. It applies to the motion of an object moving through a fluid as well as the motion of a fluid passing by an object.

wave oscillations that are propagated from a source. Mechanical waves require a medium through which to travel. Electromagnetic waves do not; they can travel through a vacuum. Waves carry energy but they do not transfer matter. There are two types: in a longitudinal wave, such as a sound wave, the disturbance is parallel to the

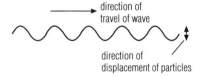

wave The motion of a transverse wave. Light waves are examples of transverse waves: they undulate at right angles to the direction of travel and are characterized by alternating crests and troughs. Simple water waves, such as the ripples produced when a stone is dropped into a pond, are also examples of transverse waves.

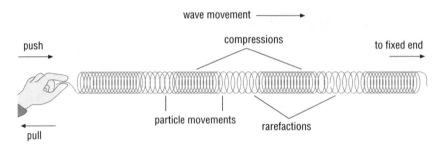

wave The motion of a longitudinal wave. Sound, for example, travels through air in longitudinal waves: the waves vibrate back and forth in the direction of travel. In the compressions the particles are pushed together, and in the rarefactions they are pulled apart.

wave's direction of travel; in a transverse wave, such as an electromagnetic wave, it is perpendicular. The medium (for example the Earth, for seismic waves) is not permanently displaced by the passage of a wave.

weight the force exerted on an object by gravity. The weight of an object depends on its mass – the amount of material in it – and the strength of the Earth's gravitational pull, which decreases with height. Consequently, an object weighs less at the top of a mountain than at sea level. On the surface of the Moon, an object has only one-sixth of its weight on Earth, because the Moon's surface gravity is one-sixth that of the Earth.

work measure of the result of transferring energy from one system to another to cause an object to move. Work should not be confused with energy (the capacity to do work, which is also measured in joules) or with power (the rate of doing work, measured in joules per second).

X-ray band of electromagnetic radiation in the wavelength range 10^{-11} to 10^{-9} m (between gamma rays and ultraviolet radiation). Applications of X-rays make use of their short wavelength (as in X-ray diffraction) or their penetrating power (as in medical X-rays of internal body tissues). X-rays are dangerous and can cause cancer.

Physics: Chronology

c. **400** BC The first 'atomic' theory is put forward by Democritus.

c. **250** BC Archimedes' principle of buoyancy is established.

AD **1600** Magnetism is described by William Gilbert.

1608 Hans Lippershey invents the refracting telescope.

c. **1610** The principle of falling bodies descending to earth at the same speed is established by Galileo.

1642 The principles of hydraulics are put forward by Blaise Pascal.

1643 The mercury barometer is invented by Evangelista Torricelli.

1656 The pendulum clock is invented by Christiaan Huygens.

1662 Boyle's law concerning the behaviour of gases is established by Robert Boyle.

c. **1665** Isaac Newton puts forward the law of gravity,

stating that the Earth exerts a constant force on falling bodies.

1690 The wave theory of light is propounded by Christiaan Huygens.

1704 The corpuscular theory of light is put forward by Isaac Newton.

1714 The mercury thermometer is invented by Daniel Fahrenheit.

1764 Specific and latent heats are described by Joseph Black.

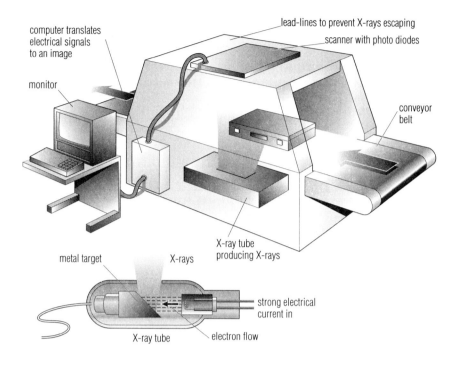

X-ray The X-rays are generated by high-speed electrons impinging on a tungsten target. The rays pass through the specimen and on to a photographic plate or imager.

Physics: Chronology (continued)

1771 The link between nerve action and electricity is discovered by Luigi Galvani.

c. **1787** Charles's law relating the pressure, volume, and temperature of a gas is established by Jacques Charles.

1795 The metric system is adopted in France.

1798 The link between heat and friction is discovered by Benjamin Rumford.

1800 Alessandro Volta invents the Voltaic cell.

1801 Interference of light is discovered by Thomas Young.

1808 The 'modern' atomic theory is propounded by John Dalton.

1811 Avogadro's hypothesis relating volumes and numbers of molecules of gases is proposed by Amedeo Avogadro.

1814 Fraunhofer lines in the solar spectrum are mapped by Joseph von Fraunhofer.

1815 Refraction of light is

explained by Augustin Fresnel.

1820 The discovery of electromagnetism is made by Hans Oersted.

1821 The dynamo principle is described by Michael Faraday; the thermocouple is invented by Thomas Seebeck.

1822 The laws of electrodynamics are established by André Ampère.

1824 Thermodynamics as a branch of physics is proposed by Sadi Carnot.

Physics: Chronology (continued)

1827 Ohm's law of electrical resistance is established by Georg Ohm; Brownian movement resulting from molecular vibrations is observed by Robert Brown.

1829 The law of gaseous diffusion is established by Thomas Graham.

1831 Electromagnetic induction is discovered by Faraday.

1834 Faraday discovers self-induction.

1842 The principle of conservation of energy is observed by Julius von Mayer.

c. **1847** The mechanical equivalent of heat is described by James Joule.

1849 A measurement of speed of light is put forward by French physicist Armand Fizeau (1819–1896).

1851 The rotation of the Earth is demonstrated by Jean Foucault.

1858 The mirror galvanometer, an instrument for measuring small electric currents, is invented by William Thomson (Lord Kelvin).

1859 Spectrographic analysis is made by Robert Bunsen and Gustav Kirchhoff.

1861 Osmosis is discovered.

1873 Light is conceived as electromagnetic radiation by James Maxwell.

1877 A theory of sound as vibrations in an elastic medium is propounded by John Rayleigh.

1880 Piezoelectricity is discovered by Pierre Curie.

1887 The existence of radio waves is predicted by Heinrich Hertz.

1895 X-rays are discovered by Wilhelm Röntgen.

1896 The discovery of radioactivity is made by Antoine Becquerel.

1897 Joseph Thomson discovers the electron.

1899 Ernest Rutherford discovers alpha and beta rays.

1900 Quantum theory is propounded by Max Planck; the discovery of gamma rays is made by French physicist Paul-Ulrich Villard (1860–1934).

1902 Oliver Heaviside discovers the ionosphere.

1904 The theory of radioactivity is put forward by Rutherford and Frederick Soddy.

1905 Albert Einstein propounds his special theory of relativity.

1908 The Geiger counter is invented by Hans Geiger and Rutherford.

1911 The discovery of the atomic nucleus is made by Rutherford.

1913 The orbiting electron atomic theory is propounded by Danish physicist Niels Bohr.

1915 X-ray crystallography is discovered by William and Lawrence Bragg.

1916 Einstein puts forward his general theory of relativity; mass spectrography is discovered by William Aston.

1924 Edward Appleton makes his study of the Heaviside layer.

1926 Wave mechanics is introduced by Erwin Schrödinger.

1927 The uncertainty principle of quantum physics is established by Werner Heisenberg.

1931 The cyclotron is developed by Ernest Lawrence.

1932 The discovery of the neutron is made by James Chadwick; the electron microscope is developed by Vladimir Zworykin.

1933 The positron, the antiparticle of the electron, is discovered by Carl Anderson.

1934 Artificial radioactivity is developed by Frédéric and Irène Joliot-Curie.

1939 The discovery of nuclear fission is made by Otto Hahn and Fritz Strassmann.

1942 The first controlled nuclear chain reaction is achieved by Enrico Fermi.

1956 The neutrino, an elementary particle, is discovered by Clyde Cowan and Fred Reines.

1960 The Mössbauer effect of atom emissions is discovered by Rudolf Mössbauer; the first laser and the first maser are developed by US physicist Theodore Maiman (1927–).

1964 Murray Gell-Mann and George Zweig discover the quark.

1967 Jocelyn Bell (now Bell Burnell) and Antony Hewish

Physics: Chronology (continued)

discover pulsars (rapidly rotating neutron stars that emit pulses of energy).

1971 The theory of superconductivity is announced, where electrical resistance in some metals vanishes above absolute zero.

1979 The discovery of the asymmetry of elementary particles is made by US physicists James W Cronin and Val L Fitch.

1982 The discovery of processes involved in the evolution of stars is made by Subrahmanyan Chandrasekhar and William Fowler.

1983 Evidence of the existence of weakons (W and Z particles) is confirmed at

CERN, validating the link between the weak nuclear force and the electromagnetic force.

1986 The first high-temperature superconductor is discovered, able to conduct electricity without resistance at a temperature of $-238°C/-396°F$.

1989 CERN's Large Electron Positron Collider (LEP), a particle accelerator with a circumference of 27 km/ 16.8 mi, comes into operation.

1991 LEP experiments demonstrate the existence of three generations of elementary particles, each with two quarks and two leptons.

1995 Top quark is discovered at Fermilab, the US particle-physics laboratory, near Chicago. US researchers announce the discovery of a material which is superconducting at the temperature of liquid nitrogen – a much higher temperature than previously achieved.

1996 CERN physicists create the first atoms of antimatter (nine atoms of antihydrogen). The Lawrence Livermore National Laboratory, California, USA, produces a laser of 1.3 petawatts (130 trillion watts).

1998 German physicists discover that as few as 60 atoms will exhibit superfluidity.

Noteworthy Physicists

Alvarez Luis Walter (1911–1988) US physicist who led the research team that discovered the subatomic particle

Ampère André Marie (1775–1836) French physicist who pioneered work in electromagnetism and electrodynamics

Avogadro (Lorenzo Romano) Amedeo Carlo (1776–1856) Italian physicist who was one of the founders of physical chemistry

Bardeen John (1908–1991) US physicist who helped develop the transistor

Becquerel (Antoine) Henri (1852–1908) French physicist who discovered penetrating radiation coming from uranium salts, the first indication of radioactivity

Bohr Niels Henrik David (1885–1962) Danish physicist who developed a new model of atomic structure

Boltzmann Ludwig Eduard (1844–1906) Austrian physicist who studied the kinetic theory of gases

Born Max (1882–1970) German-born British physicist who pioneered quantum theory

Bose Jagadis Chandra (1858–1937) Indian physicist and plant physiologist

Boyle Robert (1627–1691) Irish chemist and physicist who was a pioneer in the use of experiment and scientific method

Bragg William Henry (1862–1942) English physicist who shared with his son Lawrence (1890– 1971) the Nobel Prize for Physics for their research work determining the atomic structure of crystals from their X-ray diffraction patterns

Brewster David (1781–1868) Scottish physicist who made discoveries about the diffraction and polarization of light

Noteworthy Physicists (continued)

Broglie Louis Victor Pierre Raymond de (1892–1987) French theoretical physicist who laid the foundations of wave mechanics

Carnot (Nicolas Léonard) Sadi (1796–1832) French scientist and military engineer who founded the science of thermodynamics

Cavendish Henry (1731–1810) English physicist and chemist who discovered hydrogen

Chadwick James (1891–1974) English physicist who discovered the neutron in the atom

Clausius Rudolf Julius Emanuel (1822–1888) German physicist who was one of the founders of the science of thermodynamics

Cockcroft John Douglas (1897–1967) English physicist who, with Irish physicist Ernest Walton (1903–1995), succeeded in splitting the atom for the first time

Cooper Leon Niels (1930–) US physicist who worked on superconductivity and proposed that at low temperatures electrons would be bound in pairs (since known as Cooper pairs)

Coulomb Charles Augustin de (1736–1806) French physicist who invented the torsion balance for measuring the force of electric and magnetic attraction

Curie Marie (born Maria Skłodowska) (1867–1934) Polish scientist who, with her husband Pierre Curie (1859–1906), discovered two new radioactive elements, polonium and radium

Dirac Paul Adrien Maurice (1902–1984) English physicist who worked out a version of quantum mechanics consistent with special relativity

Doppler Christian Johann (1803–1853) Austrian physicist who enunciated the so-called 'Doppler effect', which explains the frequency variation observed when a vibrating source of waves and the observer approach or recede from one another

Einstein Albert (1879–1955) German-born US physicist who formulated theories of relativity

Fahrenheit Gabriel Daniel (1686–1736) Polish-born Dutch physicist who invented the first accurate thermometer

Faraday Michael (1791–1867) English chemist and physicist who discovered the induction of electric currents and made the first dynamo, the first electric motor, and the first transformer

Fermi Enrico (1901–1954) Italian-born US physicist who proved the existence of new radioactive elements produced by bombardment with neutrons, and discovered nuclear reactions produced by low-energy neutrons

Feynman Richard P(hillips) (1918–1988) US physicist whose work laid the foundations of quantum electrodynamics

Foucault Jean Bernard Léon (1819–1868) French physicist who used a pendulum to demonstrate the rotation of the Earth on its axis, and invented the gyroscope

Franklin Benjamin (1706–1790) US scientist, statesman, and writer who proved that lightning is a form of electricity

Fraunhofer Joseph von (1787–1826) German physicist who studied optics; he developed the prism spectrometer, discovering the dark lines in the Sun's spectrum

Fresnel Augustin Jean (1788–1827) French physicist who refined the theory of polarized light

Gay-Lussac Joseph Luis (1778–1850) French physicist and chemist who investigated the physical properties of gases

Geiger Hans Wilhelm (1882–1945) German physicist who produced the Geiger counter, which is used for detecting radioactive particles

Glashow Sheldon Lee (1932–) US physicist who developed the theory of the electroweak force first postulated by Weinberg and Abdus Salam

Guericke Otto von (1602–1686) German engineer and physicist who developed a primitive version of the vacuum pump

Hahn Otto (1879–1968) German radiochemist who won a Nobel prize for his discovery of nuclear fission

Noteworthy Physicists (continued)

Hawking Stephen William (1942–   ) English physicist whose work has advanced research on a quantum theory of gravity

Heisenberg Werner Karl (1901–1976) German physicist who developed quantum theory

Hertz Heinrich Rudolf (1857–1894) German physicist who studied electromagnetic waves, showing that their behaviour resembles that of light and heat waves

Hooke Robert (1635–1703) English scientist and inventor whose inventions include the telegraph system, marine barometer, and sea gauge; he also pioneered the early use of the microscope

Joule James Prescott (1818–1889) English physicist whose work on the relations between electrical, mechanical, and chemical effects led to the discovery of the first law of thermodynamics

Kelvin William Thomson, 1st Baron Kelvin (1824–1907) Scottish physicist who introduced the Kelvin scale of temperature

Kirchhoff Gustav Robert (1824–1887) German physicist whose work on spectrum analysis led to the discovery of caesium and rubidium; he formulated a law of radiation and a magnetic theory of diffraction

Landau Lev Davidovich (1908–1968) Russian theoretical physicist who was awarded a Nobel prize for his work on condensed matter, particularly helium

Laue Max Theodor Felix von (1879–1960) German physicist who pioneered work on X-ray diffraction in crystals

Lawrence Ernest O(rlando) (1901–1958) US physicist who invented the cyclotron

Lodge Oliver Joseph (1851–1940) British physicist who was a pioneer in the development of radio receivers

Lorentz Hendrik Antoon (1853–1928) Dutch physicist who won a Nobel prize for his work on the Zeeman effect

Mach Ernst (1838–1916) Austrian philosopher and physicist who contributed to the understanding of scientific method; he carried out important experimental work on supersonic projectiles and on the flow of gases

Maxwell James Clerk (1831–1879) Scottish physicist who was a pioneer in research on electromagnetic waves

Meitner Lise (1878–1968) Austrian-born Swedish physicist who worked with German radiochemist Otto Hahn and was the first to realize that they had inadvertently achieved the fission of uranium

Michelson Albert Abraham (1852–1931) German-born US physicist who established the speed of light as a fundamental constant, and who was the first American to be awarded a Nobel prize

Millikan Robert Andrews (1868–1953) US physicist who determined Planck's constant (a fundamental unit of quantum theory)

Newton Isaac (1642–1727) English physicist and mathematician who founded physics as a modern discipline

Oersted Hans Christian (1777–1851) Dutch physicist who founded the science of electromagnetism

Ohm Georg Simon (1789–1854) German physicist and pioneer in the study of electricity

Oppenheimer J(ulius) Robert (1904–1967) US physicist in charge of the Manhattan Project, which developed the first atom bomb

Pauli Wolfgang (1900–1958) Austrian-born Swiss physicist who originated the 'exclusion principle'

Planck Max Karl Ernst (1858–1947) German physicist who developed quantum theory

Röntgen Wilhelm Konrad von (1845–1923) German physicist who discovered X-rays

Rutherford Ernest (1871–1937) New Zealand-born British physicist who was a pioneer of modern atomic science and discovered alpha, beta, and gamma rays

Noteworthy Physicists (continued)

Salam Abdus (1926–1996) Pakistani physicist who proposed a theory linking the electromagnetic and weak interactions of atomic particles

Schrödinger Erwin (1887–1961) Austrian physicist who advanced the study of wave mechanics to describe the behaviour of electrons in atoms

Szilard Leo (1898–1964) Hungarian-born US physicist who was one of the first scientists to realize the importance of nuclear fission

Teller Edward (1908–   ) Hungarian-born US physicist who helped develop the first hydrogen bomb

Tesla Nikola (1856–1943) Croatian-born US physicist and electrical engineer who invented fluorescent lighting and the Tesla induction motor; he also patented the alternating current electrical supply system

Thomson J(oseph) J(ohn) (1856–1940) English physicist who discovered the electron in 1897

Torricelli Evangelista (1608–1647) Italian physicist who established the existence of atmospheric pressure and devised the mercury barometer

Volta Alessandro Giuseppe Antonio Anastasio (1745–1827) Italian physicist who developed the first electric cell

Walton E(rnest) T(homas) S(inton) (1903–1995) Irish physicist who, with Sir John Cockcroft, produced the first disintegration of a nucleus in the first successful use of a particle accelerator

Weinberg Steven (1933–   ) US physicist who developed the theory of the electroweak force first postulated by Weinberg and Abdus Salam

Young Thomas (1773–1829) British physicist who revived the wave theory of light and identified the phenomenon of interferenc

PHYSICAL AND ANALYTICAL CHEMISTRY

This branch of chemistry is concerned with the quantitative explanation of chemical phenomena and reactions, and the measurement of data required for such explanations. It studies in particular the movement of molecules and the effects of temperature and pressure, often with regard to gases and liquids. All matter can exist in three states: gas, liquid, or solid. It is composed of minute particles termed **molecules,** which are constantly moving, and may be further divided into **atoms.** Molecules that contain atoms of one kind only are known as **elements**; those that contain atoms of different kinds are called **compounds.**

acid compound that releases hydrogen ions (H^+ or protons) in the presence of an ionizing solvent (usually water). Acids react with bases to form salts, and they act as solvents. Strong acids are corrosive; dilute acids have a sour or sharp taste, although in some organic acids this may be partially masked by other flavour characteristics. The strength of an acid is measured by its hydrogen-ion concentration, indicated by the pH value. All acids have a pH below 7.0.

activation energy energy required in order to start a chemical reaction. Some elements and compounds will react together merely by bringing them into contact (spontaneous reaction). For others it is necessary to supply energy in order to start the reaction, even if there is ultimately a net output of energy. This initial energy is the activation energy.

affinity force of attraction between atoms that helps to keep them in combination in a molecule. The term is also applied to attraction between molecules, such as those of biochemical significance (for example, between enzymes and substrate molecules).

alkali a base that is soluble in water. Alkalis neutralize acids and are soapy to the touch. The strength of an alkali is measured by its hydrogen-ion concentration, indicated by the pH value. They may be divided into strong and weak alkalis: a strong alkali (for example, potassium hydroxide, KOH) ionizes completely when dissolved in water, wheras a weak alkali (for example, ammonium hydroxide, NH_4OH) exists in a partially ionized state in solution. All alkalis have a pH above 7.0.

anode positive electrode of an electrolytic cell, towards which negative particles (anions), usually in solution, are attracted.

assay determination of the quantity of a given substance present in a sample. Usually it refers to determining the purity of precious metals.

Avogadro's number or **Avogadro's constant,** the number of carbon atoms in 12 g of the carbon-12 isotope (6.022045×10^{23}). The relative atomic mass of any element, expressed in grams, contains this number of atoms. It is named after Amedeo Avogadro.

base substance that accepts protons. Bases can contain negative ions such as the hydroxide ion (OH^-), which is the strongest base, or be molecules such as ammonia (NH_3).

buffer mixture of compounds chosen to maintain a steady pH. The commonest buffers consist of a mixture of a weak organic acid and one of its salts or a mixture of acid salts of phosphoric acid. The addition of either an acid or a base causes a shift in the chemical equilibrium, thus keeping the pH constant.

cathode negative electrode of an electrolytic cell, towards which positive particles (cations), usually in solution, are attracted.

cation ion carrying a positive charge. During electrolysis, cations in the electrolyte move to the cathode (negative electrode).

chain reaction succession of reactions, usually involving free radicals, where the products of one stage are the reactants of the next. A chain reaction is characterized by the continual generation of reactive substances.

What is a chemical equation?

A chemical equation is the method of indicating the reactants and products of a chemical reaction by using chemical symbols and formulae. A chemical equation gives two basic pieces of information: (1) the reactants (on the left-hand side) and products (right-hand side); and (2) the reacting proportions (stoichiometry) – that is, how many units of each reactant and product are involved. The equation must balance; that is, the total number of atoms of a particular element on the left-hand side must be the same as the number of atoms of that element on the right-hand side. For example, the reaction of sodium hydroxide (NaOH) with hydrochloric acid (HCl) to give sodium chloride and water may be represented by:
$NaOH + HCl = NaCl + H_2O$.

colloid substance composed of extremely small particles of one material (the dispersed phase) evenly and stably distributed in another material (the continuous phase). The size of the dispersed particles (1–1,000 nanometres across) is less than that of particles in suspension but greater than that of molecules in true solution. Colloids involving gases include **aerosols** (dispersions of liquid or solid particles in a gas, as in fog or smoke) and **foams** (dispersions of gases in liquids).

compound chemical substance made up of two or more elements bonded together, so that they cannot be separated by physical means. Compounds are held together by ionic or covalent bonds.

conservation of energy principle that states that in a chemical reaction, the total amount of energy in the system remains unchanged.

conservation of mass principle that states that in a chemical reaction the sum of all the masses of the substances involved in the reaction (reactants) is equal to the sum of all of the masses of the substances produced by the reaction (products) – that is, no matter is gained or lost.

cracking reaction in which a large alkane molecule is broken down by heat into a smaller alkane and a small alkene molecule. The reaction is carried out at a high temperature (600°C or higher) and often in the presence of a catalyst. Cracking is a commonly used process in the petrochemical industry.

Collision theory

Collision theory explains how chemical reactions take place and why rates of reaction alter. For a reaction to occur the reactant particles must collide. Only a certain fraction of the total collisions cause chemical change; these are called **fruitful collisions**. The fruitful collisions have sufficient energy (activation energy) at the moment of impact to break the existing bonds and form new bonds, resulting in the products of the reaction. Increasing the concentration of the reactants and raising the temperature bring about more collisions and therefore more fruitful collisions, increasing the rate of reaction.

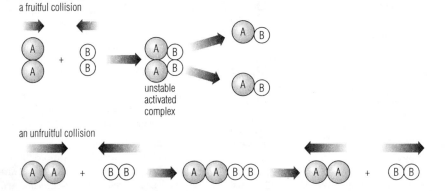

collision theory Collision theory explains how chemical reactions occur and why rates of reaction differ. For a reaction to occur, particles must collide. If the collision causes a chemical change it is referred to as a fruitful collision.

detergent surface-active cleansing agent. The common detergents are made from fats (hydrocarbons) and sulphuric acid, and their long-chain molecules have a type of structure similar to that of soap molecules: a salt group at one end attached to a long hydrocarbon 'tail'. They have the advantage over soap in that they do not produce scum by forming insoluble salts with the calcium and magnesium ions present in hard water.

What is a diffusion?

Diffusion is the spontaneous and random movement of molecules or particles in a fluid (gas or liquid) from a region in which they are at a high concentration to a region of lower concentration, until a uniform concentration is achieved throughout. The difference in concentration between two such regions is called the **concentration gradient**. No mechanical mixing or stirring is involved. For instance, if a drop of ink is added to water, its molecules will diffuse until their colour becomes evenly distributed throughout. Diffusion occurs more rapidly across a higher concentration gradient and at higher temperature.

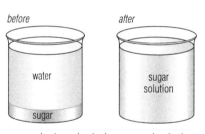

sugar and water molecules become evenly mixed

gas exchange in amoeba

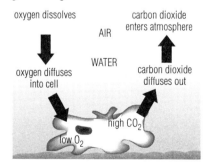

diffusion Diffusion is the movement of molecules from a region of high concentration into a region of lower concentration.

dipole the uneven distribution of magnetic or electrical characteristics within a molecule or substance so that it behaves as though it possesses two equal but opposite poles or charges, a finite distance apart.

dissociation process whereby a single compound splits into two or more smaller products, which may be capable of recombining to form the reactant.

distillation technique used to purify liquids or to separate mixtures of liquids possessing different boiling points. **Simple distillation** is used in the purification of liquids (or the separation of substances in solution from their solvents) – for example, in the production of pure water from a salt solution.

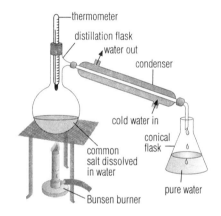

distillation Laboratory apparatus for simple distillation. Other forms of distillation include steam distillation, in which steam is passed into the mixture being distilled, and vacuum distillation, in which air is removed from above the mixture to be distilled.

emulsion a stable dispersion of a liquid in another liquid – for example, oil and water in some cosmetic lotions.

energy of reaction energy released or absorbed during a chemical reaction, also called **enthalpy of reaction** or **heat of reaction**. In a chemical reaction, the energy stored in the reacting molecules is rarely the same as that stored in the product molecules. Depending on which is the greater, energy is either released (an exothermic reaction) or absorbed (an endothermic reaction) from the surroundings. The amount of energy released or absorbed by the quantities of substances represented by the chemical equation is the energy of reaction.

filtration technique by which suspended solid particles in a fluid are removed by passing the mixture through a filter, usually porous paper, plastic, or cloth. The particles are retained by the filter to form a residue and the fluid passes through to make up the filtrate. For example, soot may be filtered from air, and suspended solids from water.

flame test use of a flame to identify metal cations present in a solid.

Flame Test

Element	Colour of flame
sodium	orange-yellow
potassium	lilac
calcium	red or yellow-red
strontium, lithium	crimson
barium, manganese (manganese chloride)	pale green
copper, thallium, boron (boric acid)	bright green
lead, arsenic, antimony	livid blue
copper (copper (II) chloride)	bright blue

formula representation of a molecule, radical, or ion, in which the component chemical elements are represented by their symbols. An **empirical formula** indicates the simplest ratio of the elements in a compound, without indicating how many of them there are or how they are combined. A **molecular formula** gives the number of each type of element present in one molecule. A **structural formula** shows the relative positions of the atoms and the bonds between them. For example, for ethanoic acid, the empirical formula is CH_2O, the molecular formula is $C_2H_4O_2$, and the structural formula is CH_3COOH.

fractionation or **fractional distillation** process used to split complex mixtures (such as petroleum) into their components, usually by repeated heating, boiling, and condensation. In the laboratory it is carried out using a fractionating column.

free radical atom or molecule that has an unpaired electron and is therefore highly reactive. Most free radicals are very short-lived. They are by-products of normal cell chemistry and rapidly oxidize other molecules they encounter. Free radicals are thought to do considerable damage. They are neutralized by protective enzymes.

gas form of matter, such as air, in which the molecules move randomly in otherwise empty space, filling any size or shape of container into which the gas is put.

hydrolysis chemical reaction in which the action of water or its ions breaks down a substance into smaller molecules. Hydrolysis occurs in certain inorganic salts in solution, in nearly all non-metallic chlorides, in esters, and in other organic substances. It is one of the mechanisms for the breakdown of food by the body, as in the conversion of starch to glucose.

immiscible describing liquids that will not mix with each other, such as oil and water. When two immiscible liquids are shaken together, a turbid mixture is produced. This normally forms separate layers on being left to stand.

indicator compound that changes its structure and colour in response to its environment. The commonest chemical indicators detect changes in pH (for example, litmus and universal indicator), or in the oxidation state of a system (redox indicators).

inert gas or **noble gas** any of a group of six elements (helium, neon, argon, krypton, xenon, and radon), so named because they were originally thought not to enter into any chemical reactions. This is now known to be incorrect: in 1962, xenon was made to combine with fluorine, and since then, compounds of argon, krypton, and radon with fluorine and/or oxygen have been described.

Inert Gases: Electronic Structure

Name	Symbol	Atomic number	Electronic arrangement
helium	He	2	2.
neon	Ne	10	2.8.
argon	Ar	18	2.8.8.
krypton	Kr	36	2.8.18.8.
xenon	Xe	54	2.8.18.18.8.
radon	Rn	86	2.8.18.32.18.8.

ion atom, or group of atoms, that is either positively charged (cation) or negatively charged (anion), as a result of the loss or gain of electrons during chemical reactions or exposure to certain forms of radiation. In solution or in the molten state, ionic compounds such as salts, acids, alkalis, and metal oxides conduct electricity. These compounds are known as electrolytes.

ion exchange process whereby an ion in one compound is replaced by a different ion, of the same charge, from another compound. It is the basis of a type of chromatography in which the components of a mixture of ions in solution are separated according to the ease with which they will replace the ions on the polymer matrix through which they flow. The exchange of positively charged ions is called cation exchange; that of negatively charged ions is called anion exchange.

litmus dye obtained from various lichens and used in chemistry as an indicator to test the acidic or alkaline nature of aqueous solutions; it turns red in the presence of acid, and blue in the presence of alkali.

lone pair pair of electrons in the outermost shell of an atom that are not used in bonding. In certain circumstances, they will allow the atom to bond with atoms, ions, or molecules (such as boron trifluoride, BF_3) that are deficient in electrons, forming coordinate covalent (dative) bonds in which they provide both of the bonding electrons.

mass action, law of law stating that at a given temperature the rate at which a chemical reaction takes place is proportional to the product of the active masses of the reactants. The active mass is taken to be the molar concentration of the each reactant.

methylated spirit alcohol that has been rendered undrinkable, and is used for industrial purposes, as a fuel for spirit burners or a solvent.

mixture substance containing two or more compounds that still retain their separate physical and chemical properties. There is no chemical bonding between them and they can be separated from each other by physical means (compare compound).

molecule see **what is a molecule?** feature.

neutralization process occurring when the excess acid (or excess base) in a substance is reacted

What is a molecule?

Molecules are the smallest particles of an element or compound that can exist independently. Hydrogen atoms, at room temperature, do not exist independently. They are bonded in pairs to form hydrogen molecules. A molecule of a compound consists of two or more different atoms bonded together. Molecules vary in size and complexity from the hydrogen molecule (H_2) to the large macromolecules of proteins. They may be held together by ionic bonds, in which the atoms gain or lose electrons to form ions, or by covalent bonds, where electrons from each atom are shared in a new molecular orbital.

Each compound is represented by a chemical symbol, indicating the elements into which it can be broken down and the number of each type of atom present. The symbolic representation of a molecule is known as its formula. For example, one molecule of the compound water, having two atoms of hydrogen and one atom of oxygen, is shown as H_2O.

with added base (or added acid) so that the resulting substance is neither acidic nor basic.

neutron one of the three main subatomic particles, the others being the proton and the electron. The neutron is a composite particle, being made up of three quarks, and therefore belongs to the baryon group of the hadrons. Neutrons have about the same mass as protons but no electric charge, and occur in the nuclei of all atoms except hydrogen. They contribute to the mass of atoms but do not affect their chemistry.

nucleus positively charged central part of an atom, which constitutes almost all its mass. Except for hydrogen nuclei, which have only protons, nuclei are composed of both protons and neutrons. Surrounding the nuclei are electrons, of equal and opposite charge to that of the protons, thus giving the atom a neutral charge.

neutral solution solution of pH7, in which the concentrations of $H^+_{(aq)}$ and $OH^-_{(aq)}$ ions are equal.

oxidation loss of electrons, gain of oxygen, or loss of hydrogen by an atom, ion, or molecule during a chemical reaction.

pH scale from 0 to 14 for measuring acidity or alkalinity. A pH of 7.0 indicates neutrality, below 7 is acid, while above 7 is alkaline. Strong acids, such as those used in car batteries, have a pH of about 2; strong alkalis such as sodium hydroxide are pH 13. *See illustration on page 192.*

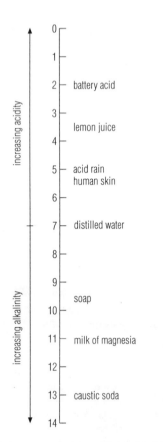

increasing acidity

increasing alkalinity

0	
1	
2	battery acid
3	
4	lemon juice
5	acid rain, human skin
6	
7	distilled water
8	
9	
10	soap
11	milk of magnesia
12	
13	caustic soda
14	

pH The pHs of some common substances. The lower the pH, the more acidic the substance; the higher the pH, the more alkaline the substance.

photolysis chemical reaction that is driven by light or ultraviolet radiation. For example, the light reaction of photosynthesis (the process by which green plants manufacture carbohydrates from carbon dioxide and water) is a photolytic reaction.

precipitation formation of an insoluble solid in a liquid as a result of a reaction within the liquid between two or more soluble substances. If the solid settles, it forms a **precipitate**; if the particles of solid are very small, they will remain in suspension, forming a **colloidal precipitate**.

rate of reaction the speed at which a chemical reaction proceeds. It is usually expressed in terms of the concentration (usually in moles per litre) of a reactant consumed, or product formed, in unit time; so the units would be moles per litre per second ($mol\ l^{-1}\ s^{-1}$). The rate of a reaction may be affected by the concentration of the reactants, the temperature of the reactants (or the amount of light in the case of a photochemical reaction), and the presence of a catalyst. If the reaction is entirely in the gas state, the rate is affected by pressure, and, where one of the reactants is a solid, it is affected by the particle size.

reactivity series chemical series produced by arranging the metals in order of their ease of reaction with reagents such as oxygen, water, and acids. This arrangement aids the understanding of the properties of metals, helps to explain differences between them, and enables predictions to be made about a metal's behaviour, based on a knowledge of its position or properties. It also allows prediction of the relative stability of the compounds formed by an element: the more reactive the metal, the more stable its compounds are likely to be.

redox reaction chemical change where one reactant is reduced and the other reactant oxidized.

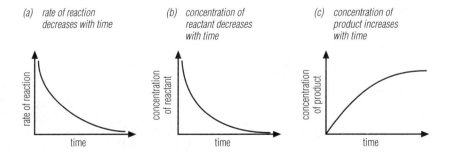

(a) rate of reaction decreases with time

(b) concentration of reactant decreases with time

(c) concentration of product increases with time

rate of reaction The rate of reaction decreases with time whilst the concentration of product increases.

The reaction can only occur if both reactants are present and each changes simultaneously. For example, hydrogen reduces copper(II) oxide to copper while it is itself oxidized to water. The corrosion of iron and the reactions taking place in electric and electrolytic cells are just a few instances of redox reactions.

reduction gain of electrons, loss of oxygen, or gain of hydrogen by an atom, ion, or molecule during a chemical reaction.

relative atomic mass the mass of an atom relative to one-twelfth the mass of an atom of carbon-12. It depends primarily on the number of protons and neutrons in the atom, the electrons having negligible mass. If more than one isotope of the element is present, the relative atomic mass is calculated by taking an average that takes account of the relative proportions of each isotope, resulting in values that are not whole numbers.

salt any compound formed from an acid and a base through the replacement of all or part of the hydrogen in the acid by a metal or electropositive radical. **Common salt** is sodium chloride.

solution two or more substances mixed to form a single, homogenous phase. One of the substances is the **solvent** and the others (**solutes**) are said to be dissolved in it.

solvent substance, usually a liquid, that will dissolve another substance. Although the commonest solvent is water, in popular use the term refers to low-boiling-point organic liquids, which are harmful if used in a confined space. They can give rise to respiratory problems, liver damage, and neurological complaints.

standard temperature and pressure (STP) standard set of conditions for experimental measurements, to enable comparisons to be made between sets of results. Standard temperature is 0°C/32°F (273K) and standard pressure 1 atmosphere (101,325 Pa).

sublimation conversion of a solid to vapour without passing through the liquid phase.

surfactant contraction of **surface-active agent** substance added to a liquid in order to increase its wetting or spreading properties. Detergents are examples.

Common Ions That Form Salts

Positive ions	Negative ions
silver Ag^+	bromide Br^-
aluminium Al^{3+}	chloride Cl^-
barium Ba^{2+}	carbonate CO_3^{2-}
calcium Ca^{2+}	fluoride F^-
copper Cu^{2+}	hydrogencarbonate HCO_3^-
iron(II) Fe^{2+}	hydrogensulphate HSO_4^-
iron(III) Fe^{3+}	iodide I^-
hydrogen H^+	nitrate NO_3^-
potassium K^+	oxide O^{2-}
lithium Li^+	hydroxide OH^-
magnesium Mg^{2+}	sulphide S^{2-}
sodium Na^+	sulphite SO_3^{2-}
ammonium NH_4^+	sulphate SO_4^{2-}
lead Pb^{2+}	
zinc Zn^{2+}	

titration technique to find the concentration of one compound in a solution by determining how much of it will react with a known amount of another compound in solution.

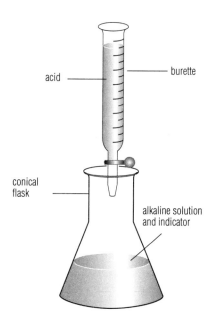

titration Solubility titration is a method used to find the concentration of an acid or an alkali. Typically a burette is filled with an acid of unknown concentration which is slowly (drop by drop) added to an alkali of a known concentration, mixed with an indicator (such as phenolphthalein). The volume of acid needed to neutralize the alkali in the flask can be used to calculate the concentration of the acid.

universal indicator mixture of pH indicators, used to gauge the acidity or alkalinity of a solution. Each component changes colour at a different pH value, and so the indicator is capable of displaying a range of colours, according to the pH of the test solution, from red (at pH 1, strong acid) through green (neutral) to purple (at pH 13, strong alkali).

valency measure of an element's ability to combine with other elements, expressed as the number of atoms of hydrogen (or any other standard univalent element) capable of uniting

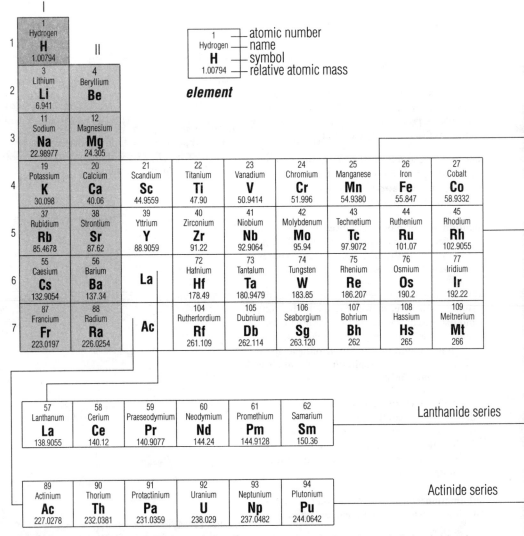

periodic table of the elements The periodic table arranges the elements in horizontal rows (called periods) and vertical columns (called groups) according to their atomic numbers. The elements in a group all have similar properties – for example, all the elements in the far right-hand columns are inert gases.

with (or replacing) its atoms. The number of electrons in the outermost shell of the atom dictates the combining ability of an element.

zwitterion ion that has both a positive and a negative charge, such as an amino acid in neutral solution. For example, glycine contains both a basic amino group (NH_2) and an acidic carboxyl group (COOH); when these are both ionized in aqueous solution, the acid group loses a proton to the amino group, and the molecule is positively charged at one end and negatively charged at the other.

									0
			III	IV	V	VI	VII		2 Helium **He** 4002.60
			5 Boron **B** 10.81	6 Carbon **C** 12.011	7 Nitrogen **N** 14.0067	8 Oxygen **O** 15.9994	9 Fluorine **F** 18.99840		10 Neon **Ne** 20.179
			13 Aluminium **Al** 26.98154	14 Silicon **Si** 28.066	15 Phosphorus **P** 30.9738	16 Sulphur **S** 32.06	17 Chlorine **Cl** 35.453		18 Argon **Ar** 39.948
28 Nickel **Ni** 58.70	29 Copper **Cu** 63.546	30 Zinc **Zn** 65.38	31 Gallium **Ga** 69.72	32 Germanium **Ge** 72.59	33 Arsenic **As** 74.9216	34 Selenium **Se** 78.96	35 Bromine **Br** 79.904		36 Krypton **Kr** 83.80
46 Palladium **Pd** 106.4	47 Silver **Ag** 107.868	48 Cadmium **Cd** 112.40	49 Indium **In** 114.82	50 Tin **Sn** 118.69	51 Antimony **Sb** 121.75	52 Tellurium **Te** 127.75	53 Iodine **I** 126.9045		54 Xenon **Xe** 131.30
78 Platinum **Pt** 195.09	79 Gold **Au** 196.9665	80 Mercury **Hg** 200.59	81 Thallium **Tl** 204.37	82 Lead **Pb** 207.37	83 Bismuth **Bi** 207.2	84 Polonium **Po** 210	85 Astatine **At** 211		86 Radon **Rn** 222.0176
110 Ununnilium **Uun** 269	111 Unununium **Uuu** 272								

63 Europium **Eu** 151.96	64 Gadolinium **Gd** 157.25	65 Terbium **Tb** 158.9254	66 Dysprosium **Dy** 162.50	67 Holmium **Ho** 164.9304	68 Erbium **Er** 167.26	69 Thulium **Tm** 168.9342	70 Ytterbium **Yb** 173.04	71 Lutetium **Lu** 174.97

95 Americium **Am** 243.0614	96 Curium **Cm** 247.0703	97 Berkelium **Bk** 247	98 Californium **Cf** 251.0786	99 Einsteinium **Es** 252.0828	100 Fermium **Fm** 257.0951	101 Mendelevium **Md** 258.0986	102 Nobelium **No** 259.1009	103 Lawrencium **Lr** 260.1054

INORGANIC CHEMISTRY

Inorganic chemistry is the branch of chemistry dealing with the chemical properties of the elements and their compounds, excluding the more complex covalent compounds of carbon, which are considered in organic chemistry.

The origins of inorganic chemistry lay in observing the characteristics and experimenting with the uses of the substances (compounds and elements) that could be extracted from mineral ores. These could be classified according to their chemical properties: elements could be classified as metals or nonmetals; compounds as acids or bases, oxidizing or reducing agents, ionic compounds (such as salts), or covalent compounds (such as gases). The arrangement of elements into groups possessing similar properties led to Mendeleyev's periodic table of the elements, which prompted chemists to predict the properties of undiscovered elements that might occupy gaps in the table. This, in turn, led to the discovery of new elements, including a number of highly radioactive elements that do not occur naturally.

alkali metal any of a group of six metallic elements with similar chemical properties: lithium, sodium, potassium, rubidium, caesium, and francium. They form a linked group (Group One) in the periodic table of the elements. They are univalent (have a valency of one) and of very low density (lithium, sodium, and potassium float on water); in general they are reactive, soft, low-melting-point metals. Because of their reactivity they are only found as compounds in nature.

alkaline-earth metal any of a group of six metallic elements with similar bonding properties: beryllium, magnesium, calcium, strontium, barium, and radium. They form a linked group in the periodic table of the elements. They are strongly basic, bivalent (have a valency of two), and occur in nature only in compounds.

alloy metal blended with some other metallic or nonmetallic substance to give it special qualities, such as resistance to corrosion, greater hardness, or tensile strength. Useful alloys include bronze, brass, cupronickel, duralumin, German silver, gunmetal, pewter, solder, steel, and stainless steel.

aluminium lightweight, silver-white, ductile and malleable, metallic element, symbol Al, atomic number 13, relative atomic mass 26.9815, melting point 658°C. It is the third most abundant element (and the most abundant metal) in the Earth's crust, of which it makes up about 8.1% by mass. It is non-magnetic, an excellent conductor of electricity, and oxidizes easily, the layer of oxide on its surface making it highly resistant to tarnish.

ammonia NH_3 colourless pungent-smelling gas, lighter than air and very soluble in water. It is made on an industrial scale by the Haber (or Haber–Bosch) process, and used mainly to produce nitrogenous fertilizers, nitric acid, and some explosives.

bauxite principal ore of aluminium, consisting of a mixture of hydrated aluminium oxides and hydroxides, generally contaminated with compounds of iron, which give it a red colour. It is formed by the chemical weathering of rocks in tropical climates. Chief producers of bauxite are Australia, Guinea, Jamaica, Russia, Kazakhstan, Suriname, and Brazil.

calcium soft, silvery-white metallic element, symbol Ca, atomic number 20, relative atomic mass 40.08. It is one of the alkaline-earth metals. It is the fifth most abundant element (the third most abundant metal) in the Earth's crust. It is found mainly as its carbonate $CaCO_3$, which occurs in a fairly pure condition as chalk and limestone. Calcium is an essential component of bones, teeth, shells, milk, and leaves, and it forms 1.5% of the human body by mass.

Common Alloys

Name	Approximate composition	Uses
brass	35–10% zinc, 65–90% copper	decorative metalwork, plumbing fittings, industrial tubing
bronze – common	2% zinc, 6% tin, 92% copper	machinery, decorative work
bronze – aluminium	10% aluminium, 90% copper	machinery castings
bronze – coinage	1% zinc, 4% tin, 95% copper	coins
cast iron	2–4% carbon, 96–98% iron	decorative metalwork, engine blocks, industrial machinery
dentist's amalgam	30% copper, 70% mercury	dental fillings
duralumin	0.5 % magnesium, 0.5% manganese, 5% copper, 95% aluminium	framework of aircraft
gold – coinage	10% copper, 90% gold	coins
gold – dental	14–28% silver, 14–28% copper, 58% gold	dental fillings
lead battery plate	6% antimony, 94% lead	car batteries
manganin	1.5% nickel, 16% manganese, 82.5% copper	resistance wire
nichrome	20% chromium, 80% nickel	heating elements
pewter	20% lead, 80% tin	utensils
silver – coinage	10% copper, 90% silver	coins
solder	50% tin, 50% lead	joining iron surfaces
steel – stainless	8–20% nickel, 10–20% chromium, 60–80% iron	kitchen utensils
steel – armour	1–4% nickel, 0.5–2% chromium, 95–98% iron	armour plating
steel – tool	2–4% chromium, 6–7% molybdenum, 90–95% iron	tools

calcium carbonate $CaCO_3$ white solid, found in nature as limestone, marble, and chalk. It is a valuable resource, used in the making of iron, steel, cement, glass, slaked lime, bleaching powder, sodium carbonate and bicarbonate, and many other industrially useful substances.

carbonate CO_3^{2-} ion formed when carbon dioxide dissolves in water; any salt formed by this ion and another chemical element, usually a metal.

element see **What is an element?** feature below.

What is an element?

An element is a substance that cannot be split chemically into simpler substances. The atoms of a particular element all have the same number of protons in their nuclei (their atomic number). Elements are classified in the periodic table of the elements. Of the known elements, 92 are known to occur in nature (those with atomic numbers 1–92). Those elements with atomic numbers above 96 do not occur in nature and are synthesized only, produced in particle accelerators. Of the elements, 81 are stable; all the others, which include atomic numbers 43, 61, and from 84 up, are radioactive.

Elements are classified as metals, nonmetals, or metalloids depending on a combination of their physical and chemical properties; about 75% are metallic.

Metals have lustre and conduct heat and electricity, while **nonmetals** usually lack these properties. **Metalloids** are weakly metallic elements. Some elements occur abundantly (oxygen, aluminium); others occur moderately or rarely (chromium, neon); some, in particular the radioactive ones, are found in minute (neptunium, plutonium) or very minute (technetium) amounts.

The **periodic system**, developed by John Newlands in 1863 and established by Dmitri Mendeleyev in 1869, classified elements according to their relative atomic masses. Those elements that resemble each other in general properties were found to bear a relation to one another by weight, and these were placed in groups or families. Certain anomalies in this system were later removed by classifying the elements according to their atomic numbers. Symbols (devised by Swedish chemist Jöns Berzelius) are used to denote the elements; the symbol is usually the first letter or letters of the English or Latin name (for example, C for carbon, Ca for calcium, Fe for iron, from the Latin ferrum). The symbol represents one atom of the element.

gold heavy, precious, yellow, metallic element; symbol Au, atomic number 79, relative atomic mass 197.0. It is unaffected by temperature changes and is highly resistant to acids. For manufacture, gold is alloyed with another strengthening metal (such as copper or silver), its purity being measured in carats on a scale of 24.

halogen any of a group of five nonmetallic elements with similar chemical bonding properties: fluorine, chlorine, bromine, iodine, and astatine. They form a linked group in the periodic table of the elements, descending from fluorine, the most reactive, to astatine, the least reactive. They combine directly with most metals to form salts, such as common salt (NaCl). Each halogen has seven electrons in its valence shell, which accounts for the chemical similarities displayed by the group.

hydrochloric acid HCl solution of hydrogen chloride (a colourless, acidic gas) in water. The concentrated acid is about 35% hydrogen chloride and is corrosive. The acid is a typical strong, monobasic acid forming only one series of salts, the chlorides. It has many industrial uses, including recovery of zinc from galvanized scrap iron and the production of chlorine. It is also produced in the stomachs of animals for the purposes of digestion.

hydrogen colourless, odourless, gaseous, nonmetallic element, symbol H, atomic number 1, relative atomic mass 1.00797. It is the lightest of all the elements and occurs on Earth chiefly in combination with oxygen as water. Hydrogen is the most abundant element in the universe, where it accounts for 93% of the total number of atoms and 76% of the total mass. Hydrogen's common and industrial uses include the hardening of oils and fats by hydrogenation, the cre-

What is an inorganic compound?

An inorganic compound is a compound found in organisms that are not typically biological.

Water, sodium chloride, and potassium are inorganic compounds because they are widely found outside living cells. The term is also applied to those compounds that do not contain carbon and that are not manufactured by organisms. However, carbon dioxide is considered inorganic, contains carbon, and is manufactured by organisms during respiration.

ation of high-temperature flames for welding, and as rocket fuel.

iron hard, malleable and ductile, silver-grey, metallic element, symbol Fe (from Latin *ferrum*), atomic number 26, relative atomic mass 55.847. It is the fourth most abundant element (the second most abundant metal, after aluminium) in the Earth's crust. Iron occurs in concentrated deposits as the ores hematite (Fe_2O_3), spathic ore ($FeCO_3$), and magnetite (Fe_3O_4). It sometimes occurs as a free metal, occasionally as fragments of iron or iron–nickel meteorites.

metal any of a class of chemical elements with specific physical and chemical characteristics. Metallic elements compose about 75% of the 112 elements in the periodic table of the elements.

Physical properties include a sonorous tone when struck, good conduction of heat and electricity, opacity but good reflection of light, malleability, which enables them to be cold-worked and rolled into sheets, ductility, which permits them to be drawn into thin wires, and the possible emission of electrons when heated (thermionic effect) or when the surface is struck by light (photoelectric effect).

nitrate salt or ester of nitric acid, containing the NO_3^- ion. Nitrates are used in explosives, in the chemical and pharmaceutical industries, in curing meat, and as fertilizers. They are the most water-soluble salts known and play a major part in the nitrogen cycle. Nitrates in the soil, whether naturally occurring or from inorganic or organic fertilizers, can be used by plants to make proteins and nucleic acids. However, runoff from fields can result in nitrate pollution.

nitrite salt or ester of nitrous acid, containing the nitrite ion (NO2–). Nitrites are used as preservatives (for example, to prevent the growth of botulism spores) and as colouring agents in cured meats such as bacon and sausages.

nitric acid or **aqua fortis** HNO3 fuming acid obtained by the oxidation of ammonia or the action of sulphuric acid on potassium nitrate. It is a highly corrosive acid, dissolving most metals, and a strong oxidizing agent. It is used in the nitration and esterification of organic substances, and in the making of sulphuric acid, nitrates, explosives, plastics, and dyes.

nitrogen colourless, odourless, tasteless, gaseous, nonmetallic element, symbol N, atomic number 7, relative atomic mass 14.0067. It forms almost 80% of the Earth's atmosphere by volume and is a constituent of all plant and animal tissues (in proteins and nucleic acids). Nitrogen is obtained for industrial use by the liquefaction and fractional distillation of air. Its compounds are used in the manufacture of foods, drugs, fertilizers, dyes, and explosives.

nonmetal one of a set of elements (around 20 in total) with certain physical and chemical properties opposite to those of metals. Nonmetals accept electrons and are sometimes called electronegative elements.

oxide compound of oxygen and another element, frequently produced by burning the element or a compound of it in air or oxygen.

oxygen colourless, odourless, tasteless, nonmetallic, gaseous element, symbol O, atomic number 8, relative atomic mass 15.9994. It is the most abundant element in the Earth's crust (almost 50% by mass), forms about 21% by volume of the atmosphere, and is present in combined form in water and many other substances. Oxygen is a by-product of photosynthesis and the basis for respiration in plants and animals.

ozone O_3 highly reactive pale-blue gas with a penetrating odour. Ozone is an allotrope of oxygen, made up of three atoms of oxygen. It is formed when the molecule of the stable form of oxygen (O_2) is split by ultraviolet radiation or electrical discharge. It forms the ozone layer in the upper atmosphere, which protects life on Earth from ultraviolet rays, a cause of skin cancer.

phosphate salt or ester of phosphoric acid. Incomplete neutralization of phosphoric acid gives rise to acid phosphates. Phosphates are used as fertilizers, and are required for the development of healthy root systems. They are involved in many biochemical processes, often as part of complex molecules, such as ATP.

plutonium silvery-white, radioactive, metallic element of the actinide series, symbol Pu, atomic number 94, relative atomic mass 239.13. It occurs in nature in minute quantities in pitchblende and other ores, but is produced in quantity only synthetically. It has six allotropic forms and is one of three fissile elements (elements capable of splitting into other elements – the others are thorium and uranium). The element

has awkward physical properties and is the most toxic substance known.

silicon brittle, nonmetallic element, symbol Si, atomic number 14, relative atomic mass 28.086. It is the second-most abundant element (after oxygen) in the Earth's crust and occurs in amorphous and crystalline forms. In nature it is found only in combination with other elements, chiefly with oxygen in silica (silicon dioxide, SiO_2) and the silicates. These form the mineral quartz, which makes up most sands, gravels, and beaches.

silver white, lustrous, extremely malleable and ductile, metallic element, symbol Ag (from Latin *argentum*), atomic number 47, relative atomic mass 107.868. It occurs in nature in ores and as a free metal; the chief ores are sulphides, from which the metal is extracted by smelting with lead. It is one of the best metallic conductors of both heat and electricity; its most useful compounds are the chloride and bromide, which darken on exposure to light and are the basis of photographic emulsions.

sulphate SO_4^{2-} salt or ester derived from sulphuric acid. Most sulphates are water soluble (the exceptions are lead, calcium, strontium, and barium sulphates), and require a very high temperature to decompose them.

sulphide compound of sulphur and another element in which sulphur is the more electronegative element. Sulphides occur in a number of minerals. Some of the more volatile sulphides have extremely unpleasant odours (hydrogen sulphide smells of bad eggs).

sulphite SO_3^{2-} salt or ester derived from sulphurous acid.

sulphur brittle, pale-yellow, nonmetallic element, symbol S, atomic number 16, relative atomic mass 32.064. It occurs in three allotropic forms: two crystalline (called rhombic and monoclinic, following the arrangements of the atoms within the crystals) and one amorphous. It burns in air with a blue flame and a stifling odour. Insoluble in water but soluble in carbon disulphide, it is a good electrical insulator. Sulphur is widely used in the manufacture of sulphuric acid (used to treat phosphate rock to make fertilizers) and in making paper, matches, gunpowder and fireworks, in vulcanizing rubber, and in medicines and insecticides.

The Transuranic Elements

A transuranic element is a chemical element with an atomic number of 93 or more – that is, with a greater number of protons in the nucleus than uranium. All transuranic elements are radioactive. (– = not applicable.)

Atomic number	Name	Symbol	Year discovered	Source of first preparation identified	Isotope	Half-life of first isotope identified
Actinide series						
93	neptunium	Np	1940	irradiation of uranium-238 with neutrons	Np-239	2.35 days
94	plutonium	Pu	1941	bombardment of uranium-238 with deuterons	Pu-238	86.4 years
95	americium	Am	1944	irradiation of plutonium-239 with neutrons	Am-241	458 years
96	curium	Cm	1944	bombardment of plutonium-239 with helium nuclei	Cm-242	162.5 days
97	berkelium	Bk	1949	bombardment of americium-241 with helium nuclei	Bk-243	4.5 h
98	californium	Cf	1950	bombardment of curium-242 with helium nuclei	Cf-245	44 min
99	einsteinium	Es	1952	irradiation of uranium-238 with neutrons in first thermonuclear explosion	Es-253	20 days
100	fermium	Fm	1953	irradiation of uranium-238 with neutrons in first thermonuclear explosion	Fm-235	20 h
101	mendelevium	Md	1955	bombardment of einsteinium-253 with helium nuclei	Md-256	76 min
102	nobelium	No	1958	bombardment of curium-246 with carbon nuclei	No-255	2.3 sec
103	lawrencium	Lr	1961	bombardment of californium-252 with boron nuclei	Lr-257	4.3 sec
Transactinide elements						
104	ruther-fordium	Rf	1969	bombardment of californium-249 with carbon-12 nuclei	Db-257	3.4 sec
105	dubnium	Db	1970	bombardment of californium-249 with nitrogen-15 nuclei	Unp-260	1.6 sec
106	seaborgium	Sg	1974	bombardment of californium-249 with oxygen-18 nuclei	Rf-263	0.9 sec
107	bohrium	Bh	1977	bombardment of bismuth-209 with nuclei of chromium-54	Uns 102	millisec
108	hassium	Hs	1984	bombardment of lead-208 with nuclei of iron-58	Uno-265	1.8 millisec
109	meitnerium	Mt	1982	bombardment of bismuth-209 with nuclei of iron-58	Une	3.4 millisec
110	ununnilium[1]	Uun	1994	bombardment of lead nuclei with nickel nuclei	–	–
111	unununium[1]	Uuu	1994	bombardment of bismuth-209 with nickel nuclei	–	–

[1] Temporary names as proposed by the International Union for Pure and Applied Chemistry.

sulphuric acid or **oil of vitriol** H_2SO_4 a dense, viscous, colourless liquid that is extremely corrosive. It gives out heat when added to water and can cause severe burns. Sulphuric acid is used extensively in the chemical industry, in the refining of petrol, and in the manufacture of fertilizers, detergents, explosives, and dyes. It forms the acid component of car batteries.

transuranic element or **transuranium element** chemical element with an atomic number of 93 or more – that is, with a greater number of protons in the nucleus than has uranium. All transuranic elements are radioactive. Neptunium and plutonium are found in nature; the others are synthesized in nuclear reactions.

uranium hard, lustrous, silver-white, malleable and ductile, radioactive, metallic element of the actinide series, symbol U, atomic number 92, relative atomic mass 238.029. It is the most abundant radioactive element in the Earth's crust, its decay giving rise to essentially all radioactive elements in nature; its final decay product is the stable element lead. Uranium combines readily with most elements to form compounds that are extremely poisonous. The chief ore is pitchblende, in which the element was discovered by German chemist Martin Klaproth in 1789; he named it after the planet Uranus, which had been discovered in 1781.

water chemical compound of hydrogen and oxygen elements, H_2O. It can exist as a solid (ice), liquid (water), or gas (water vapour). Water is the most common element on Earth and vital to all living organisms. It covers 70% of the Earth's surface, and provides a habitat for large

uranium Uranium mining at the Mary Kathleen Uranium Mine, Queensland, Australia. Uranium is found chiefly in pitchblende, a brown ore found in veins and massive crusts. The processes of extraction and refinement are difficult and create large amounts of radioactive waste, but the uranium produced is extremely valuable. *AEA Technology*

numbers of aquatic organisms. It is the largest constituent of all living organisms – the human body consists of about 65% water. Pure water is a colourless, odourless, tasteless liquid which freezes at 0°C/32°F, and boils at 100°C/212°F. Natural water in the environment is never pure and always contains a variety of dissolved substances. Some 97% of the Earth's water is in the oceans; a further 2% is in the form of snow or ice, leaving only 1% available as fresh water for plants and animals. The re-cycling and circulation of water through the biosphere is termed the **water cycle**, or 'hydrological cycle'; regulation of the water balance in organisms is termed osmoregulation.

ORGANIC CHEMISTRY

The branch of chemistry that deals with carbon compounds is called organic chemistry. Organic compounds form the chemical basis of life and are more abundant than inorganic compounds. In a typical organic compound, each carbon atom forms bonds covalently with each of its neighbouring carbon atoms in a chain or ring, and additionally with other atoms, commonly hydrogen, oxygen, nitrogen, or sulphur.

The basis of organic chemistry is the ability of carbon to form long chains of atoms, branching chains, rings, and other complex structures. Compounds containing only carbon and hydrogen are known as **hydrocarbons**. The linking carbon atoms that form the backbone of an organic molecule may be built up from beginning to end without branching, or may throw off branches at one or more points. Sometimes the ropes of carbon atoms curl round and form rings (**cyclic compounds**), usually of five, six, or seven atoms. Open-chain and cyclic compounds may be classified as aliphatic or aromatic depending on the nature of the bonds between their atoms. Compounds containing oxygen, sulphur, or nitrogen within a carbon ring are called **heterocyclic compounds**.

alcohol any member of a group of organic chemical compounds characterized by the presence of one or more aliphatic OH (hydroxyl) groups in the molecule, and which form esters with acids. The main uses of alcohols are as solvents for gums, resins, lacquers, and varnishes; in the making of dyes; for essential oils in perfumery; and for medical substances in pharmacy. The alcohol produced naturally in the fermentation process and consumed as part of alcoholic beverages is called ethanol.

aldehyde any of a group of organic chemical compounds prepared by oxidation of primary alcohols, so that the OH (hydroxyl) group loses its hydrogen to give an oxygen joined by a double bond to a carbon atom (the aldehyde group, with the formula CHO).

aliphatic compound any organic chemical compound in which the carbon atoms are joined in straight chains, as in hexane (C_6H_{14}), or in branched chains, as in 2-methylpentane ($CH_3CH(CH_3)CH_2CH_2CH_3$).

alkane member of a group of hydrocarbons having the general formula $C_nH_{2n\ +\ 2}$,

alkane The lighter alkanes of methane, ethane, propane, and butane, showing the aliphatic chains, where a hydrogen atom bonds to a carbon atom at all available sites.

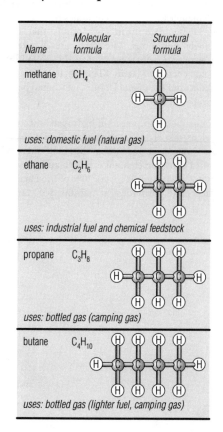

Name	Molecular formula	Structural formula
methane	CH_4	
uses: domestic fuel (natural gas)		
ethane	C_2H_6	
uses: industrial fuel and chemical feedstock		
propane	C_3H_8	
uses: bottled gas (camping gas)		
butane	C_4H_{10}	
uses: bottled gas (lighter fuel, camping gas)		

commonly known as **paraffins**. As they contain only single covalent bonds, alkanes are said to be saturated. Lighter alkanes, such as methane, ethane, propane, and butane, are colourless gases; heavier ones are liquids or solids. In nature they are found in natural gas and petroleum.

alkene member of the group of hydrocarbons having the general formula C_nH_{2n}, formerly known as **olefins**. Alkenes are unsaturated compounds, characterized by one or more double bonds between adjacent carbon atoms. Lighter alkenes, such as ethene and propene, are gases, obtained from the cracking of oil fractions. Alkenes react by addition, and many useful compounds, such as poly(ethene) and bromoethane, are made from them.

alkyne member of the group of hydrocarbons with the general formula C_nH_{2n-2}, formerly known as the **acetylenes**. They are unsaturated compounds, characterized by one or more triple bonds between adjacent carbon atoms. Lighter alkynes, such as ethyne, are gases; heavier ones are liquids or solids.

aromatic compound organic chemical compound in which some of the bonding electrons are delocalized (shared among several atoms within the molecule and not localized in the vicinity of the atoms involved in bonding). The commonest aromatic compounds have ring structures, the atoms comprising the ring being either all carbon or containing one or more different atoms (usually nitrogen, sulphur, or oxygen). Typical examples are benzene (C_6H_6) and pyridine (C_6H_5N).

benzene C_6H_6 clear liquid hydrocarbon of characteristic odour, occurring in coal tar. It is used as a solvent and in the synthesis of many chemicals.

carbon nonmetallic element, symbol C, atomic number 6, relative atomic mass 12.011. It occurs

Formula	Name	Atomic bonding
CH_3	methyl	
CH_2CH_3	ethyl	
CC	double bond	
CHO	aldehyde	
CH_2OH	alcohol	
CO	ketone	
COOH	acid	
CH_2NH_2	amine	
C_6H_6	benzene ring	

carbon Common organic-molecule groupings. Organic chemistry is the study of carbon compounds, which make up over 90% of all chemical compounds. This diversity arises because carbon atoms can combine in many different ways with other atoms, forming a wide variety of loops and chains.

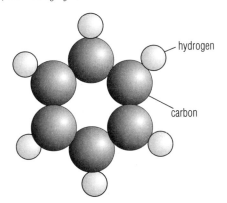

benzene The molecule of benzene consists of six carbon atoms arranged in a ring, with six hydrogen atoms attached. The benzene ring structure is found in many naturally occurring organic compounds.

on its own as diamond, graphite, and as fullerenes (the allotropes), as compounds in carbonaceous rocks such as chalk and limestone, as carbon dioxide in the atmosphere, as hydrocarbons in petroleum, coal, and natural gas, and as a constituent of all organic substances.

carboxyl group –COOH the acidic functional group that determines the properties of fatty acids (carboxylic acids) and amino acids.

ester organic compound formed by the reaction between an alcohol and an acid, with the elimination of water. Unlike salts, esters are covalent compounds.

hydrogen

carbon

oxygen

ester Molecular model of the ester ethyl ethanoate (ethyl acetate) $CH_3CH_2COOCH_3$

ethanoic acid common name **acetic acid** CH_3CO_2H one of the simplest fatty acids (a series of organic acids). In the pure state it is a colourless liquid with an unpleasant pungent odour; it solidifies to an icelike mass of crystals at 16.7°C/62.4°F, and hence is often called glacial ethanoic acid. Vinegar contains 5% or more ethanoic acid, produced by fermentation.

ethanol common name **ethyl alcohol** C_2H_5OH alcohol found in beer, wine, cider, spirits, and other alcoholic drinks. When pure, it is a colourless liquid with a pleasant odour, miscible with water or ether; it burns in air with a pale blue flame. The vapour forms an explosive mixture with air and may be used in high-compression internal combustion engines.

It is produced naturally by the fermentation of carbohydrates by yeast cells. Industrially, it can be made by absorption of ethene and subsequent reaction with water, or by the reduction of ethanal in the presence of a catalyst, and is widely used as a solvent.

ether any of a series of organic chemical compounds having an oxygen atom linking the carbon atoms of two hydrocarbon radical groups (general formula R-O-R'); also the common name for ethoxyethane $C_2H_5OC_2H_5$ (also called diethyl ether).

This is used as an anaesthetic and as an external cleansing agent before surgical operations. It is also used as a solvent, and in the extraction of oils, fats, waxes, resins, and alkaloids.

fatty acid or **carboxylic acid** organic compound consisting of a hydrocarbon chain, up to 24 carbon atoms long, with a carboxyl group (–COOH) at one end. The covalent bonds between the carbon atoms may be single or double; where a double bond occurs the carbon atoms concerned carry one instead of two hydrogen atoms. Chains with only single bonds have all the hydrogen they can carry, so they are said to be **saturated** with hydrogen. Chains with one or more double bonds are said to be **unsaturated**. Fatty acids are produced in the small intestine when fat is digested.

functional group small number of atoms in an arrangement that determines the chemical properties of the group and of the molecule to which it is attached (for example, the carboxyl group COOH, or the amine group NH_2). Organic compounds can be considered as structural skeletons, with a high carbon content, with functional groups attached.

homologous series any of a number of series of organic chemicals with similar chemical properties in which members differ by a constant relative molecular mass.

hydrocarbon any of a class of chemical compounds containing only hydrogen and carbon (for example, the alkanes and alkenes). Hydrocarbons are obtained industrially principally from petroleum and coal tar.

isomer chemical compound having the same molecular composition and mass as another, but with different physical or chemical properties owing to the different structural arrangement of its constituent atoms. For example, the organic compounds butane $(CH_3(CH_2)_2CH_3)$ and methyl propane $(CH_3CH(CH_3)CH_3)$ are isomers, each possessing four carbon atoms and ten hydrogen atoms but differing in the way that these are arranged with respect to each other.

Alkane	Alcohol	Aldehyde	Ketone	Carboxylic acid	Alkene
CH_4 methane	CH_3OH methanol	HCHO methanal	——	HCO_2H methanoic acid	——
CH_3CH_3 ethane	CH_3CH_2OH ethanol	CH_3CHO ethanal	——	CH_3CO_2H ethanoic acid	CH_2CH_2 ethene
$CH_3CH_2CH_3$ propane	$CH_3CH_2CH_2OH$ propanol	CH_3CH_2CHO propanal	CH_3COCH_3 propanone	$CH_3CH_2CO_2H$ propanoic acid	CH_2CHCH_3 propene
methane	methanol	methanal	propanone	methanoic acid	ethene

homologous series and the induced current ionic bond The formation of an ionic bond between a sodium atom and a chlorine atom to form a molecule of sodium chloride. The sodium atom transfers an electron from its outer electron shell (becoming the positive ion Na^+) to the chlorine atom (which becomes the negative chloride ion Cl^-). The opposite charges mean that the ions are strongly attracted to each other. The formation of the bond means that each atom becomes more stable, having a full quota of electrons in its outer shell.

ketone member of the group of organic compounds containing the carbonyl group (C=O) bonded to two atoms of carbon (instead of one carbon and one hydrogen as in aldehydes). Ketones are liquids or low-melting-point solids, slightly soluble in water.

methane CH_4 the simplest hydrocarbon of the paraffin series. Colourless, odourless, and lighter than air, it burns with a bluish flame and explodes when mixed with air or oxygen. It is the chief constituent of natural gas and also occurs in the explosive firedamp of coal mines. Methane emitted by rotting vegetation forms marsh gas, which may ignite by spontaneous combustion to produce the pale flame seen over marshland and known as will-o'-the-wisp.

Fuel from sheep
- The flatulence of a single sheep could power a small lorry for 40 km/25 mi a day. The digestive process produces methane gas, which can be burnt as fuel. According to one New Zealand scientist, the methane from 72 million sheep could supply the entire fuel needs of his country.

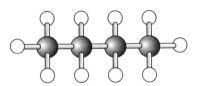

butane $CH_3(CH_2)_2CH_3$

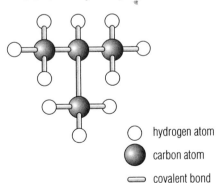

methyl propane $CH_3CH(CH_3)CH_3$

○ hydrogen atom
● carbon atom
⬭ covalent bond

isomer The chemicals butane and methyl propane are isomers. Each has the molecular formula $CH_3CH(CH_3)CH_3$, but with different spatial arrangements of atoms in their molecules.

paraffin common name for alkane, any member of the series of hydrocarbons with the general formula C_nH_{2n+2}. The lower members are gases, such as methane (marsh or natural gas). The middle ones (mainly liquid) form the basis of petrol, kerosene, and lubricating oils, while the higher ones (paraffin waxes) are used in ointment and cosmetic bases.

phenol member of a group of aromatic chemical compounds with weakly acidic properties, which are characterized by a hydroxyl (OH) group attached directly to an aromatic ring. The simplest of the phenols, derived from benzene, is also known as phenol and has the formula C_6H_5OH. It is sometimes called **carbolic acid** and can be extracted from coal tar.

plastic any of the stable synthetic materials that are fluid at some stage in their manufacture, when they can be shaped, and that later set to rigid or semi-rigid solids. Plastics today are chiefly derived from petroleum. Most are polymers, made up of long chains of identical molecules.

polymer compound made up of a large long-chain or branching matrix composed of many repeated simple units (**monomers**) linked together by polymerization. There are many polymers, both natural (cellulose, chitin, lignin) and synthetic (polyethylene and nylon, types of plastic). Synthetic polymers belong to two groups: thermosoftening and thermosetting.

polyunsaturate type of fat or oil containing a high proportion of triglyceride molecules whose

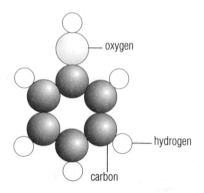

phenol The phenol molecule with its ring of six carbon atoms and a hydroxyl (OH) group attached. Phenol was first extracted from coal tar in 1834. It is used to make phenolic and epoxy resins, explosives, pharmaceuticals, perfumes, and nylon.

fatty acid chains contain several double bonds. By contrast, the fatty-acid chains of the triglycerides in saturated fats (such as lard) contain only single bonds. Medical evidence suggests that polyunsaturated fats, used widely in margarines and cooking fats, are less likely to contribute to cardiovascular disease than saturated fats, but there is also some evidence that they may have adverse effects on health.

propanone CH_3COCH_3 (common name **acetone**) colourless flammable liquid used extensively as a solvent, as in nail-varnish remover. It boils at 56.5°C/133.7°F, mixes with water in all proportions, and has a characteristic odour.

saturated compound organic compound, such as propane, that contains only single covalent

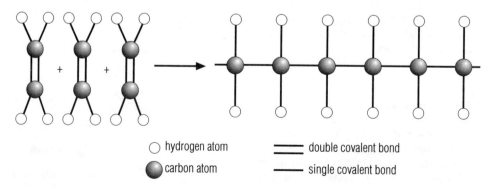

○ hydrogen atom   ═══ double covalent bond
● carbon atom   ─── single covalent bond

polymer In polymerization, small molecules (monomers) join together to make large molecules (polymers). In the polymerization of ethene to polyethene, electrons are transferred from the carbon–carbon double bond of the ethene molecule, allowing the molecules to join together as a long chain of carbon–carbon single bonds.

bonds. Saturated organic compounds can only undergo further reaction by substitution reactions, as in the production of chloropropane from propane.

tetrachloromethane CCl_4 or **carbon tetrachloride** chlorinated organic compound that is a very efficient solvent for fats and greases, and was at one time the main constituent of household dry-cleaning fluids and of fire extinguishers used with electrical and petrol fires. Its use became restricted after it was discovered to be carcinogenic and it has now been largely removed from educational and industrial laboratories.

unsaturated compound chemical compound in which two adjacent atoms are linked by a double or triple covalent bond.

BIOCHEMISTRY

Biochemistry is the science concerned with the chemistry of living organisms: the structure and reactions of proteins (such as enzymes), nucleic acids, carbohydrates, and lipids. Its study has led to an increased understanding of life processes, such as those by which organisms synthesize essential chemicals from food materials, store and generate energy, and pass on their characteristics through their genetic material. A great deal of medical research is concerned with the ways in which these processes are disrupted. Biochemistry also has applications in agriculture and in the food industry (for instance, in the use of enzymes).

ADP abbreviation for **adenosine diphosphate** the chemical product formed in cells when ATP breaks down to release energy.

adrenaline or **epinephrine** hormone secreted by the medulla of the adrenal glands. Adrenaline is synthesized from a closely related substance, noradrenaline, and the two hormones are released into the bloodstream in situations of fear or stress.

ATP abbreviation for **adenosine triphosphate** a nucleotide molecule found in all cells. It can yield large amounts of energy, and is used to drive the thousands of biological processes needed to sustain life, growth, movement, and

What are amino acids?

Amino acids are water-soluble organic molecules, mainly composed of carbon, oxygen, hydrogen, and nitrogen, containing both a basic amino group (NH_2) and an acidic carboxyl (COOH) group. They are small molecules able to pass through membranes. When two or more amino acids are joined together, they are known as peptides; proteins are made up of peptide chains folded or twisted in characteristic shapes.

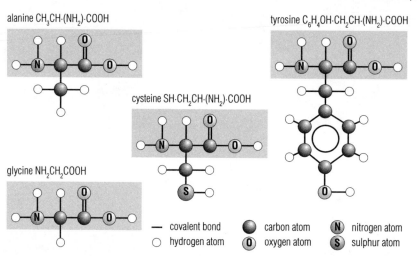

alanine $CH_3CH \cdot (NH_2) \cdot COOH$

tyrosine $C_6H_4OH \cdot CH_2CH \cdot (NH_2) \cdot COOH$

cysteine $SH \cdot CH_2CH \cdot (NH_2) \cdot COOH$

glycine NH_2CH_2COOH

— covalent bond
○ hydrogen atom
● carbon atom
Ⓞ oxygen atom
Ⓝ nitrogen atom
Ⓢ sulphur atom

amino acid Amino acids are natural organic compounds that make up proteins and can thus be considered the basic molecules of life. There are 20 different common amino acids. They consist mainly of carbon, oxygen, hydrogen, and nitrogen. Each amino acid has a common core structure (consisting of two carbon atoms, two oxygen atoms, a nitrogen atom, and four hydrogen atoms) to which is attached a variable group, known as the R group. In glycine, the R group is a single hydrogen atom; in alanine, the R group consists of a carbon and three hydrogen atoms.

Amino Acids

Name	Formula	Name	Formula
glycine	$CH_2(NH_2).COOH$	methionine	$CH_3.S.(CH_2)_2CH.(NH_2).COOH$
alanine	$CH_3CH.(NH_2).COOH$	asparagine	$NH_2CO.CH_2CH.(NH_2).COOH$
phenylalanine	$C_6H_5CH_2CH.(NH_2).COOH$	glutamine	$NH_2CH.(CH_2)_2(CO.NH_2).COOH$
tyrosine	$C_6H_4OH.CH_2CH.(NH_2).COOH$	lysine	$NH_2CH_3CH.(NH_2).COOH$
valine	$(CH_3)_2CH.CH.(NH_2).COOH$	arginine	$NH_2C(NH).NH(CH_2)_3CH.(NH_2).COOH$
leucine	$(CH_3)_2CH.CH_2CH.(NH_2).COOH$	aspartic acid	$COOH.CH_2CH.(NH_2).COOH$
iso-leucine	$(CH_3).CH_2CH(CH_3)CH.(NH_2).COOH$	glutamic acid	$COOH.(CH_2)_2CH.(NH_2).COOH$
serine	$CH_2OH.CH.(NH_2).COOH$	histidine	$C_3H_3N_2.CH_2CH.(NH_2).\ COOH$
threonine	$CH_3CHOH.CH.(NH_2).COOH$	trytophan	$C_4.NH.CH_2CH_2CH.(NH_2).COOH$
cysteine	$SH.CH_2CH.(NH_2).COOH$	proline	$NH.(CH_2)_3CH.COOH$

reproduction. Green plants use light energy to manufacture ATP as part of the process of photosynthesis. In animals, ATP is formed by the breakdown of glucose molecules, usually obtained from the carbohydrate component of a diet, in a series of reactions termed respiration. It is the driving force behind muscle contraction and the synthesis of complex molecules needed by individual cells.

carbohydrate chemical compound composed of carbon, hydrogen, and oxygen, with the basic formula $C_m(H_2O)_n$, and related compounds with the same basic structure but modified functional

What is DNA?

DNA is a complex giant molecule that contains, in chemically coded form, the information needed for a cell to make proteins. DNA is a ladderlike double=stranded nucleic acid which forms the basis of genetic inheritance in all organisms, except for a few viruses that have only RNA. DNA is organized into chromosomes and, in organisms other than bacteria, it is found only in the cell nucleus.

structure DNA is made up of two chains of nucleotide subunits, with each nucleotide containing either a purine (adenine or guanine) or pyrimidine (cytosine or thymine) base.

The bases link up with each other (adenine linking with thymine, and cytosine with guanine) to form base pairs that connect the two strands of the DNA molecule like the rungs of a twisted ladder.

heredity The specific way in which the pairs form means that the base

sequence is preserved from generation to generation. Hereditary information is stored as a specific sequence of bases. A set of three bases – known as a **codon** – acts as a blueprint for the manufacture of a particular amino acid, the subunit of a protein molecule.

codons Geneticists identify the codons by the initial letters of the constituent bases – for example, the base sequence of codon CAG is cytosine–adenine–guanine. The meaning of each of the codons in the genetic code has been worked out by molecular geneticists. There are four different bases, which means that there must be 4 x 4 x 4 = 64 different codons. Proteins are usually made up of only 20 different amino acids, so many amino acids have more than one codon (for example, GGT, GGC, GGA and GGG all code for the same amino acid, glycine).

blueprint for the organism The information encoded by the codons

is transcribed by messenger RNA and is then translated into amino acids in the ribosomes and cytoplasm. The sequence of codons determines the precise order in which amino acids are linked up during manufacture and, therefore, the kind of protein that is to be produced. Because proteins are the chief structural molecules of living matter and, as enzymes, regulate all aspects of metabolism, it may be seen that the genetic code is effectively responsible for building and controlling the whole organism.

Drawn out DNA
■ If the DNA of one human cell was unwound it would be almost 2 m/ 6.6 ft in length. The nucleus that contains the DNA is only 10 micrometres in diameter.

groups. As sugar and starch, carbohydrates are an important part of a balanced human diet, providing energy for life processes including growth and movement. Excess carbohydrate intake can be converted into fat and stored in the body.

disaccharide sugar made up of two monosaccharides or simple sugars. Sucrose, $C_{12}H_{22}O_{11}$, or table sugar, is a disaccharide.

DNA see DNA feature.

enzyme biological catalyst produced in cells, and capable of speeding up the chemical reactions necessary for life. They are large, complex proteins, and are highly specific, each chemical reaction requiring its own particular enzyme. The enzyme's specificity arises from its **active site**, an area with a shape corresponding to part of the molecule with which it reacts (the substrate). The enzyme and the substrate slot together forming an enzyme–substrate complex that allows the reaction to take place, after which the enzyme falls away unaltered.

fat in the broadest sense, a mixture of lipids – chiefly triglycerides (lipids containing three fatty acid molecules linked to a molecule of glycerol). More specifically, the term refers to a lipid mixture that is solid at room temperature (20°C); lipid mixtures that are liquid at room temperature are called **oils**. The higher the proportion of saturated fatty acids in a mixture, the harder the fat.

glucose or **dextrose** or **grape sugar** $C_6H_{12}O_6$ sugar present in the blood and manufactured by green plants during photosynthesis. The respiration reactions inside cells involves the oxidation of glucose to produce ATP, the 'energy molecule' used to drive many of the body's biochemical reactions.

Krebs cycle or **citric acid cycle** or **tricarboxylic acid cycle** final part of the chain of biochemical reactions by which organisms break down food using oxygen to release energy (respiration). It takes place within structures called mitochondria in the body's cells, and breaks down food molecules in a series of small steps, producing energy-rich molecules of ATP.

lipid any of a large number of esters of fatty acids, commonly formed by the reaction of a fatty acid with glycerol. They are soluble in alcohol but not in water. Lipids are the chief constituents of plant and animal waxes, fats, and oils.

metabolism the chemical processes of living organisms enabling them to grow and to function. It involves a constant alternation of building up complex molecules (**anabolism**) and breaking them down (**catabolism**). For example, green plants build up complex organic substances from water, carbon dioxide, and mineral salts (photosynthesis); by digestion animals partially break down complex organic substances, ingested as food, and subsequently resynthesize them for use in their own bodies. Within cells,

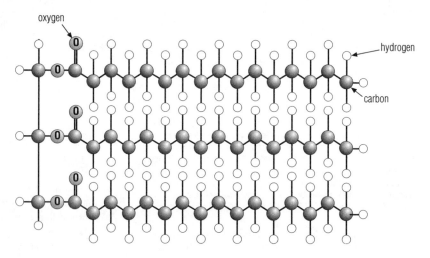

fat The molecular structure of typical fat. The molecule consists of three fatty acid molecules linked to a molecule of glycerol.

polysaccharide A typical polysaccharide molecule, glycogen (animal starch), is formed from linked glucose ($C_6H_{12}O_6$) molecules. A glycogen molecule has 100–1,000 linked glucose units.

complex molecules are broken down by the process of respiration. The waste products of metabolism are removed by excretion.

monosaccharide or **simple sugar** carbohydrate that cannot be hydrolysed (split) into smaller carbohydrate units. Examples are glucose and fructose, both of which have the molecular formula $C_6H_{12}O_6$.

nucleic acid complex organic acid made up of a long chain of nucleotides, present in the nucleus and sometimes the cytoplasm of the living cell. The two types, known as DNA (deoxyribonucleic acid) and RNA (ribonucleic acid), form the basis of heredity. The nucleotides are made up of a sugar (deoxyribose or ribose), a phosphate group, and one of four purine or pyrimidine bases. The order of the bases along the nucleic acid strand contains the genetic code.

nucleotide organic compound consisting of a purine (adenine or guanine) or a pyrimidine (thymine, uracil, or cytosine) base linked to a sugar (deoxyribose or ribose) and a phosphate group. DNA and RNA are made up of long chains of nucleotides.

peptide molecule comprising two or more amino acid molecules (not necessarily different) joined by **peptide bonds**, whereby the acid group of one acid is linked to the amino group of the other (–CO.NH). The number of amino acid molecules in the peptide is indicated by referring to it as a di-, tri-, or polypeptide (two, three, or many amino acids).

polysaccharide long-chain carbohydrate made up of hundreds or thousands of linked simple sugars (monosaccharides) such as glucose and closely related molecules.

amino acids, where R is one of many possible side chains

peptide – this is one made of just three amino acid units. Proteins consist of very large numbers of amino acid units in long chains, folded up in specific ways

protein A protein molecule is a long chain of amino acids linked by peptide bonds. The properties of a protein are determined by the order, or sequence, of amino acids in its molecule, and by the three-dimensional structure of the molecular chain. The chain folds and twists, often forming a spiral shape.

protein complex, biologically important substance composed of amino acids joined by peptide bonds. Proteins are essential to all living organisms. As enzymes they regulate all aspects of metabolism. Structural proteins such as **keratin** and **collagen** make up the skin, claws, bones, tendons, and ligaments; **muscle** proteins produce movement; **haemoglobin** transports oxygen; and **membrane** proteins regulate the movement of substances into and out of cells. For humans, protein is an essential part of the diet, and is found in greatest quantity in soya beans and other grain legumes, meat, eggs, and cheese.

respiration metabolic process in organisms in which food molecules are broken down to release energy. The cells of all living organisms need a continuous supply of energy, and in most plants and animals this is obtained by **aerobic** respiration. In this process, oxygen is used to break down the glucose molecules in food. This releases energy in the form of energy-carrying molecules (ATP), and produces carbon dioxide and water as by-products. Respiration sometimes occurs without oxygen, and this is called **anaerobic** respiration. In this case, the end products are energy and either lactose acid or ethanol (alcohol) and carbon dioxide; this process is termed fermentation.

RNA abbreviation for **ribonucleic acid** nucleic acid involved in the process of translating the genetic material DNA into proteins. It is usually single-stranded, unlike the double-stranded DNA, and consists of a large number of nucleotides strung together, each of which comprises the sugar ribose, a phosphate group, and one of four bases (uracil, cytosine, adenine, or guanine). RNA is copied from DNA by the formation of base pairs, with uracil taking the place of thymine.

saccharide another name for a sugar molecule.

steroid any of a group of cyclic, unsaturated alcohols (lipids without fatty acid components), which, like sterols, have a complex molecular structure consisting of four carbon rings. Steroids include the sex hormones, such as testosterone, the corticosteroid hormones produced by the adrenal gland, bile acids, and cholesterol.

From Biology to Biochemistry

('biology' Greek *bios* 'life', *logos* 'discourse')
Biological research has come a long way towards understanding the nature of life. Increasingly in the 20th century biologists have concentrated on molecular structures: biochemistry, biophysics, and genetics (the study of inheritance and variation).

origins The word 'biology' was first used in 1802 by the German physician Gottfried Reinhold Treviranus (1776–1837), and was popularized by Jean Lamarck. Although medical students such as Hippocrates in the 5th century BC made the first accurate biological observations, describing medicinally useful plants and their properties, attempts at a scientific physiology were bound to fail in the absence of scientific instruments, without a tradition of experiment, or a body of organized knowledge with its own terminology.

developments Only with the Renaissance did free enquiry come into its own. The 16th century saw the production of encyclopedias of natural history, such as that of Konrad Gesner (1516–1565), and the beginnings of modern anatomy, notably at Padua under Vesalius, who was succeeded by Fabricius. William Harvey laid the foundation of modern physiology by his work on the circulation of the blood – the first time any basic function of the body had been scientifically explained. Linnaeus introduced a binomial system of classification.

evolution and genetics During the 19th century, attempts to understand the origins of the great diversity of life forms gave rise to several theories of biological evolution, culminating in Darwin's theory of evolution by natural selection. The ensuing debates over the processes of evolution, together with the elucidation of the structure of DNA by Watson and Crick in 1953, provided the basis for the new science of genetics. The 1970s and 1980s saw the construction of the first artificial gene, the determination of biologically important nucleic-acid-protein complexes, and the discovery of oncogenes, genes carried by viruses that can trigger cancerous growth in normal cells. During the 1990s our knowledge has been further extended as the international Human Genome Project attempts to map the entire genetic code contained in the 23 pairs of human chromosomes.

applying chemical principles
The application of the principles of chemistry to organic substances has led to other developments in biochemistry and molecular biology. An example is the discovery in 1975 of endogenous opiates (the brain's own painkillers), which opened up a new phase of study in brain chemistry. In 1994, G-proteins, a family of proteins that translates messages – in the form of hormones and other chemical signals – into action inside cells, were discovered.

sterol any of a group of solid, cyclic, unsaturated alcohols, with a complex structure that includes four carbon rings; cholesterol is an example. Steroids are derived from sterols.

sucrose or **cane sugar** or **beet sugar** $C_{12}H_{22}O_{11}$ a sugar found in the pith of sugar cane and in sugar beets. It is popularly known as sugar.

urea $CO(NH_2)_2$ waste product formed in the mammalian liver when nitrogen compounds are broken down. It is filtered from the blood by the kidneys, and stored in the bladder as urine prior to release. When purified, it is a white, crystalline solid. In industry it is used to make urea-formaldehyde plastics (or resins), pharmaceuticals, and fertilizers.

Chemistry: Chronology

c. **3000 BC** Egyptians are producing bronze – an alloy of copper and tin.

c. **450 BC** Greek philosopher Empedocles proposes that all substances are made up of a combination of four elements – earth, air, fire, and water – an idea that is developed by Plato and Aristotle and persists for over 2,000 years.

c. **400 BC** Greek philosopher Democritus theorizes that matter consists ultimately of tiny, indivisible particles, *atomos.*

AD 1 Gold, silver, copper, lead, iron, tin, and mercury are known.

200 The techniques of solution, filtration, and distillation are known.

7th–17th centuries Chemistry is dominated by alchemy, the attempt to transform nonprecious metals such as lead and copper into gold. Though misguided, it leads to the discovery of many new chemicals and techniques, such as sublimation and distillation.

12th century Alcohol is first distilled in Europe.

1242 Gunpowder is introduced to Europe from the Far East.

1620 The scientific method of reasoning is expounded by

Francis Bacon in his *Novum Organum.*

1650 Leyden University in the Netherlands sets up the first chemistry laboratory.

1661 Robert Boyle defines an element as any substance that cannot be broken down into still simpler substances and asserts that matter is composed of 'corpuscles' (atoms) of various sorts and sizes, capable of arranging themselves into groups, each of which constitutes a chemical substance.

1662 Boyle describes the inverse relationship between the volume and pressure of a fixed mass of gas (Boyle's law).

1697 Georg Stahl proposes the erroneous theory that substances burn because they are rich in a substance called phlogiston.

1755 Joseph Black discovers carbon dioxide.

1774 Joseph Priestley discovers oxygen, which he calls 'dephlogisticated air'. Antoine Lavoisier demonstrates his law of conservation of mass.

1777 Lavoisier shows air to be made up of a mixture of gases, and shows that one of these – oxygen – is the substance necessary for

combustion (burning) and rusting to take place.

1781 Henry Cavendish shows water to be a compound.

1792 Alessandra Volta demonstrates the electrochemical series.

1807 Humphry Davy passes an electric current through molten compounds (the process of electrolysis) in order to isolate elements, such as potassium, that have never been separated by chemical means. Jöns Berzelius proposes that chemicals produced by living creatures should be termed 'organic'.

1808 John Dalton publishes his atomic theory, which states that every element consists of similar indivisible particles – called atoms – which differ from the atoms of other elements in their mass; he also draws up a list of relative atomic masses. Joseph Gay-Lussac announces that the volumes of gases that combine chemically with one another are in simple ratios.

1811 Amedeo Avogadro's hypothesis on the relation between the volume and number of molecules of a gas, and its temperature and pressure, is published.

Chemistry: Chronology (continued)

1813–14 Berzelius devises the chemical symbols and formulae still used to represent elements and compounds.

1828 Franz Wöhler converts ammonium cyanate into urea – the first synthesis of an organic compound from an inorganic substance.

1832–33 Michael Faraday expounds the laws of electrolysis, and adopts the term 'ion' for the particles believed to be responsible for carrying current.

1846 Thomas Graham expounds his law of diffusion.

1853 Robert Bunsen invents the Bunsen burner.

1858 Stanislao Cannizzaro differentiates between atomic and molecular weights (masses).

1861 Organic chemistry is defined by German chemist Friedrich Kekulé as the chemistry of carbon compounds.

1864 John Newlands devises the first periodic table of the elements.

1869 Dmitri Mendeleyev expounds his periodic table of the elements (based on atomic mass), leaving gaps for elements that have not yet been discovered.

1874 Jacobus van't Hoff suggests that the four bonds of carbon are arranged tetrahedrally, and that carbon compounds can therefore be three-dimensional and asymmetric.

1884 Swedish chemist Svante Arrhenius suggests that

electrolytes (solutions or molten compounds that conduct electricity) dissociate into ions, atoms or groups of atoms that carry a positive or negative charge.

1894 William Ramsey and Lord Rayleigh discover the first inert gases, argon.

1897 The electron is discovered by J J Thomson.

1901 Mikhail Tsvet invents paper chromatography as a means of separating pigments.

1909 Sören Sörensen devises the pH scale of acidity.

1912 Max von Laue shows crystals to be composed of regular, repeating arrays of atoms by studying the patterns in which they diffract X-rays.

1913–14 Henry Moseley equates the atomic number of an element with the positive charge on its nuclei, and draws up the periodic table, based on atomic number, that is used today.

1916 Gilbert Newton Lewis explains covalent bonding between atoms as a sharing of electrons.

1927 Nevil Sidgwick publishes his theory of valency, based on the numbers of electrons in the outer shells of the reacting atoms.

1930 Electrophoresis, which separates particles in suspension in an electric field, is invented by Arne Tiselius.

1932 Deuterium (heavy hydrogen), an isotope of hydrogen, is discovered by Harold Urey.

1940 Edwin McMillan and Philip Abelson show that new elements with a higher atomic number than uranium can be formed by bombarding uranium with neutrons, and synthesize the first transuranic element, neptunium.

1942 Plutonium is first synthesized by Glenn T Seaborg and Edwin McMillan.

1950 Derek Barton deduces that some properties of organic compounds are affected by the orientation of their functional groups (the study of which becomes known as conformational analysis).

1954 Einsteinium and fermium are synthesized.

1955 Ilya Prigogine describes the thermodynamics of irreversible processes (the transformations of energy that take place in, for example, many reactions within living cells).

1962 Neil Bartlett prepares the first compound of an inert gas, xenon hexafluoro-platinate; it was previously believed that inert gases could not take part in a chemical reaction.

1965 Robert B Woodward synthesizes complex organic compounds.

1981 Quantum mechanics is applied to predict the course of chemical reactions by US chemist Roald Hoffmann and Kenichi Fukui of Japan.

1982 Element 109, unnilennium, is synthesized.

1985 Fullerenes, a new class of carbon solids made up of

Chemistry: Chronology (continued)

closed cages of carbon atoms, are discovered by Harold Kroto and David Walton at the University of Sussex, England.

1987 US chemists Donald Cram and Charles Pederson, and Jean-Marie Lehn of France create artificial molecules that mimic the vital chemical reactions of life processes.

1990 Jean-Marie Lehn, Ulrich Koert, and Margaret Harding report the synthesis of a new class of compounds, called nucleohelicates, that mimic the double helical structure of DNA, turned inside out.

1993 US chemists at the University of California and the Scripps Institute synthesize rapamycin, one of a group of complex, naturally occurring antibiotics and immuno-suppressants that are being tested as anticancer agents.

1994 Elements 110 (ununnilium) and 111 (unununium) are discovered at the GSI heavy-ion cyclotron, Darmstadt, Germany.

1995 German chemists build the largest ever wheel molecule, made up of 154 molybdenum atoms surrounded by oxygen atoms. It has a relative

molecular mass of 24,000 and is soluble in water.

1996 Element 112 is discovered at the GSI heavy-ion cyclotron, Darmstadt, Germany.

1997 The International Union of Pure and Applied Chemistry (IUPAC) states that elements 104–109 should be named rutherfordium (104), dubnium (105), seaborgium (106), bohrium (107), hassium (108), and meitnerium (109).

1998 Buckytubes, cylinders of buckminsterfullerene, were proved to be 200 times tougher than any other known fibre.

Noteworthy Chemists

Arrhenius Svante August (1859–1927) Swedish scientist who was one of the founders of physical chemistry

Baekeland Leo Hendrik (1863–1944) Belgian-born US chemist who pioneered the development of plastics and invented Bakelite, the first commercial plastic

Berthollet Claude Lewis (1749–1822) French chemist who determined the composition of ammonia and worked with Lavoisier on a system of nomenclature

Berzelius Jons Jakob (1779–1848) Swedish chemist who devised the system of chemical symbols and formulae

Black Joseph (1728–1799) Scottish chemist who discovered carbon dioxide

Bunsen Robert Wilhelm (1811–1899) German chemist credited with the invention of the Bunsen burner

Butenandt Adolf Friedrich Johann (1903–1995) German biochemist who isolated the first sex hormones

Cannizzaro Stanislaus (1826–1910) Italian organic chemist who established atomic and molecular weights as the basis of chemical calculations

Carothers Wallace Hume (1896–1937) US industrial chemist who developed the synthetic products neoprene and nylon

Chain Ernst Boris (1906–1979) German-born British biochemist who isolated and purified penicillin

Coulson Charles Alfred (1910–1974) English theoretical chemist who developed a molecular orbital theory and studied the concept of partial valency

Curie Marie (born Maria Skłodowska) (1867–1934) Polish scientist, active in France, who, with her husband Pierre Curie (1859–1906) discovered two radioactive elements, polonium and radium

Dalton John (1766–1844) English chemist who first formulated atomic theory

Noteworthy Chemists (continued)

Davy Humphry (1778–1829) English chemist who isolated the elements sodium, potassium, calcium, boron, magnesium, strontium, and barium, and discovered the anaesthetic effect of nitrous oxide (laughing gas)

Faraday Michael (1791–1867) English chemist and physicist who was a pioneer in electromagnetic research

Gay-Lussac Joseph Luis (1778–1850) French chemist and physicist who formulated a law of gas volumes and investigated sodium, potassium, boron, and silicon

Graham Thomas (1805–1869) Scottish chemist who pioneered work on diffusion of gases

Hess Germain Henri (1802–1850) Swiss-born Russian chemist who was a pioneer in thermochemistry and established the law of constant heat summation

Hodgkin Dorothy Mary Crowfoot (1910–1994) English biochemist who analysed the structure of penicillin, insulin, and vitamin B_{12}

Hyatt John Wesley (1837–1920) US inventor who produced the first artificial plastic

Kekulé von Stradonitz Friedrich August (1829–1896) German chemist whose work on the structure of benzene and the tetrahedral carbon atom was fundamental to the development of organic chemistry

Kipping Frederic Stanley (1863–1949) English chemist who pioneered the study of silicon

Kornberg Arthur (1918–) US biochemist whose research led to the discovery of DNA polymerase, the enzyme that synthesizes new DNA

Langmuir Irving (1881–1957) US scientist who won a Nobel prize for his work on surface chemistry

Lavoisier Antoine Laurent (1743–1794) French chemist who described the chemistry of many compounds and who is considered the founder of modern chemistry

Libby Willard Frank (1908–1980) US chemist who developed radiocarbon dating

Liebig Justus von (1803–1873) German organic chemist who introduced the theory of compound radicals

Mendeleyev Dmitri Ivanovich (1834–1907) Russian chemist who framed the periodic law in chemistry

Meyer Julius Lothar von (1830–1895) German chemist who recognized the combination of oxygen with haemoglobin in respiration and discovered the ring structure of benzene

Meyer Viktor (1848–1897) German chemist who invented a method of measuring vapour densities and introduced the term 'stereochemistry'

Mullis Kary Banks (1944–) US molecular biologist who developed the PCR technique in DNA research

Nernst (Walther) Hermann (1864–1941) German physical chemist who formulated the third law of thermodynamics

Newlands John Alexander Reina (1837–1898) English chemist who, in 1865, drew up an early version of the periodic table based on his 'law of octaves'

Nobel Alfred Bernhard (1833–1896) Swedish chemist and engineer who invented dynamite

Ostwald (Friedrich) Wilhelm (1853–1932) Latvian-born German chemist who is regarded as one of the founders of physical chemistry

Pauling Linus Carl (1901–1994) US theoretical chemist and biologist whose ideas on chemical bonding are fundamental to modern theories of molecular structure

Perkin William Henry (1838–1907) English chemist who first extracted the dye mauve, and founded the modern dye industry

Prelog Vladimir (1906–1998) Bosnian-born Swiss organic chemist who developed a comprehensive molecular topology for stereochemistry

Noteworthy Chemists (continued)

Priestley Joseph (1733–1804) English chemist who identified oxygen and several other gases

Ramsay William (1852–1916) Scottish chemist who discovered argon, neon, krypton, and xenon

Regnault Henri Victor (1810–1878) French chemist and physicist who discovered vinyl chloride and refined techniques for determining the specific heats of solids, liquids, and gases

Seaborg Glenn Theodore (1912–   ) US nuclear chemist who helped discover plutonium

Scheele Karl Wilhelm (1742–1786) Swedish chemist and pharmacist who pioneered research on oxygen and respiration

Tiselius Arne Wilhelm Kaurin (1902–1971) Swedish chemist who worked on the analysis of proteins and developed the technique of electrophoresis

Tswett Mikhail Semyonovich (1872–1919) Russian organic chemist who first developed the analytical technique known as chromatography

Willstätter Richard (1872–1942) German organic chemist who researched into alkaloids and their derivations and won a Nobel prize for his work on plant pigments

Windaus Adolf Otto Reinhold (1876–1959) German chemist who identified the structure of cholesterol

Wöler Friedrich (1800–1882) German chemist who prepared specimens of urea and aluminium for the first time

Biochemistry: Chronology

c. **1830** Johannes Müller discovers proteins.

1833 Anselme Payen and J F Persoz first isolate an enzyme.

1862 Haemoglobin is first crystallized.

1869 The genetic material DNA (deoxyribonucleic acid) is discovered by Friedrich Mieschler

1899 Emil Fischer postulates the 'lock-and-key' hypothesis to explain the specificity of enzyme action.

1913 Leonor Michaelis and M L Menten develops a mathematical equation describing the rate of enzyme-catalysed reactions

1915 The hormone thyroxine is first isolated from thyroid gland tissue.

1920 The chromosome theory of heredity is postulated by Thomas H Morgan; growth hormone is discovered by Herbert McLean Evans and J A Long.

1921 Insulin is first isolated from the pancreas by Frederick Banting and Charles Best.

1926 Insulin is obtained in pure crystalline form.

1927 Thyroxine is first synthesized.

1928 Alexander Fleming discovers penicillin.

1931 Paul Karrer deduces the structure of retinol (vitamin A); vitamin D compounds are obtained in crystalline form by Adolf Windaus and Askew, independently of each other.

1932 Charles Glen King isolates ascorbic acid (vitamin C).

1933 Tadeus Reichstein synthesizes ascorbic acid.

1935 Richard Kuhn and Karrer establish the structure of riboflavin (vitamin B_2).

1936 Robert Williams establishes the structure of thiamine (vitamin B_1); biotin is isolated by Kogl and Tonnis.

1937 Niacin is isolated and identified by Conrad Arnold Elvehjem.

1938 Pyridoxine (vitamin B_6) is isolated in pure crystalline form.

1939 The structure of pyridoxine is determined by Kuhn.

1940 Hans Krebs proposes the Krebs (citric acid) cycle;

Biochemistry: Chronology (continued)

Hickman isolates retinol in pure crystalline form; Williams establishes the structure of pantothenic acid; biotin is identified by Albert Szent-Györgyi, Vincent Du Vigneaud, and co-workers.

1941 Penicillin is isolated and characterized by Howard Florey and Ernst Chain.

1943 The role of DNA in genetic inheritance is first demonstrated by Oswald Avery, Colin MacLeod, and Maclyn McCarty.

1950 The basic components of DNA are established by Erwin Chargaff; the alpha-helical structure of proteins is established by Linus Pauling and R B Corey.

1953 James Watson and Francis Crick determine the molecular structure of DNA.

1956 Mahlon Hoagland and Paul Zamecnick discover transfer RNA (ribonucleic acid); mechanisms for the biosynthesis of RNA and DNA are discovered by Arthur Kornberg and Severo Ochoa.

1957 Interferon is discovered by Alick Isaacs and Jean Lindemann.

1958 The structure of RNA is determined.

1960 Messenger RNA is discovered by Sidney Brenner and François Jacob.

1961 Marshall Nirenberg and Ochoa determines the chemical nature of the genetic code.

1965 Insulin is first synthesized.

1966 The immobilization of enzymes is achieved by Chibata.

1968 Brain hormones are discovered by Roger Guillemin and Andrew Schally.

1975 J Hughes and Hans Kosterlitz discover encephalins.

1976 Guillemin discovers endorphins.

1977 J Baxter determines the genetic code for human growth hormone.

1978 Human insulin is first produced by genetic engineering.

1979 The biosynthetic

production of human growth hormone is announced by Howard Goodman and J Baxter of the University of California, and by D V Goeddel and Seeburg of Genentech.

1982 Louis Chedid and Michael Sela develop the first synthesized vaccine.

1983 The first commercially available product of genetic engineering (Humulin) is launched.

1985 Alec Jeffreys devises genetic fingerprinting.

1993 UK researchers introduce a healthy version of the gene for cystic fibrosis into the lungs of mice with induced cystic fibrosis, restoring normal function.

1996 Japanese chemists successfully synthesize cellulose.

1997 US geneticists construct the first artificial human chromosome.

1998 The gene that makes cellulose was identified by Australian biologists.

TRANSPORT

---※---

Significant early transport milestones include the domestication of animals about 8500 BC and the invention of the wheel about 2000 BC. Transport depended on muscle power for thousands of years. During the 12th century, the invention of the stern rudder, together with the developments made in sailing during the Crusades, enabled the use of sails to almost completely supersede that of oars. No new power source was to become available till the first working steam engine in 1712. This paved the way for the development of the railways, and the first internal combustion engine (developed in 1860) eventually lead to horse-drawn carriages being replaced by cars. The first human flight (in a balloon) was made in 1783, but it was not till the early 20th century that a powered heavier-than-air craft was flown.

AIR

aerodynamics branch of fluid physics that studies the forces exerted by air or other gases in motion. Examples include the airflow around bodies moving at speed through the atmosphere (such as land vehicles, bullets, rockets, and aircraft), the behaviour of gas in engines and furnaces, air conditioning of buildings, the deposition of snow, the operation of air-cushion vehicles (hovercraft), wind loads on buildings and bridges, bird and insect flight, musical wind instruments, and meteorology. For maximum efficiency, the aim is usually to design the shape of an object to produce a streamlined flow, with a minimum of turbulence in the moving air. The behaviour of aerosols or the pollution of the atmosphere by foreign particles are other aspects of aerodynamics.

aeronautics science of travel through the Earth's atmosphere, including aerodynamics, aircraft structures, jet and rocket propulsion, and aerial navigation.

aeroplane US **airplane** powered heavier-than-air craft supported in flight by fixed wings. Aeroplanes are propelled by the thrust of a jet engine or airscrew (propeller). They must be designed aerodynamically, since streamlining ensures maximum flight efficiency. The Wright brothers flew the first powered plane (a biplane) in Kitty Hawk, North Carolina, USA in 1903.

afterburning method of increasing the thrust of a gas turbine (jet) aeroplane engine by spraying additional fuel into the hot exhaust duct between the turbojet and the tailpipe where it ignites. Used for short-term increase of power during takeoff, or during combat in military aircraft.

aircraft any aeronautical vehicle capable of flying through the air. It may be lighter than air (supported by buoyancy) or heavier than air (supported by the dynamic action of air on its surfaces). Balloons and airships are lighter-

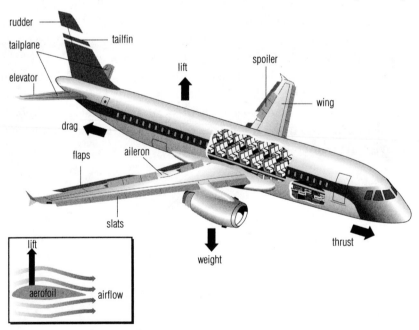

aeroplane In flight, the forces on an aeroplane are lift, weight, drag, and thrust. The lift is generated by the air flow over the wings, which have the shape of an aerofoil. The engine provides the thrust. The drag results from resistance of the air to the aeroplane's passage through it. Various moveable flaps on the wings and tail allow the aeroplane to be controlled. The rudder is moved to turn the aeroplane. The elevators allow the craft to climb or dive. The ailerons are used to bank the aeroplane while turning. The flaps, slats, and spoilers are used to reduce lift and speed during landing.

International Aircraft Registration Prefixes

Source: International Civil Aviation Organization

Most civil aircraft carry one or two letters or a number and a letter to identify their nationality. This nationality mark is painted on both sides of the fuselage or tail. It is also displayed on the underside of the wing. Numbers or letters following the nationality mark on a plane are the registration mark issued to that particular plane in its own country. Each country that belongs to the International Civil Aviation Organization (ICAO) reports its nationality mark to the organization. (As of January 1998.)

Country	ICAO mark	Country	ICAO mark	Country	ICAO mark
Afghanistan	YA	Cyprus	5B	Korea, South	HL
Albania	ZA	Czech Republic	OK	Kuwait	9K
Algeria	7T	Denmark	OY	Kyrgyzstan	EX
Andorra	C3	Djibouti	J2	Laos	RDPL
Angola	D2	Dominica	J7	Latvia	YL
Antigua and Barbuda	V2	Dominican Republic	HI	Lebanon	OD
Argentina	LQ, LV	Ecuador	HC	Lesotho	7P
Armenia	EK	Egypt	SU	Liberia	EL
Australia	VH	El Salvador	YS	Libya	5A
Austria	OE	Equatorial Guinea	3C	Liechtenstein	HB
Azerbaijan	4K	Eritrea	E3	Lithuania	LY
Bahamas	C6	Estonia	ES	Luxembourg	LX
Bahrain	A9C	Ethiopia	ET	Macedonia, Former	
Bangladesh	S2, S3	Fiji Islands	DQ	Yugoslav Republic of	Z3
Barbados	8P	Finland	OH	Madagascar	5R
Belarus	EW	France	F	Malawi	7Q
Belgium	OO	Gabon	TR	Malaysia	9M
Belize	V3	Gambia	C5	Maldives	8Q
Benin	TY	Georgia	4L	Mali	TZ
Bhutan	A5	Germany	D	Malta	9H
Bolivia	CP	Ghana	9G	Marshall Islands	V7
Bosnia-Herzegovina	T9	Greece	SX	Mauritania	5T
Botswana	A2	Grenada	J3	Mauritius	3B
Brazil	PP, PT	Guatemala	TG	Mexico	XA, XB,
Brunei	V8	Guinea	3X		XC
Bulgaria	LZ	Guinea-Bissau	J5	Micronesia	V6
Burkina Faso	XT	Guyana	8R	Moldova	ER
Burundi	9U	Haiti	HH	Monaco	3A
Cambodia	XU	Honduras	HR	Mongolia	BNMAU,
Cameroon	TJ	Hungary	HA		MONGOL,
Canada	C, CF	Iceland	TF		MT
Cape Verde	D4	India	VT	Morocco	CN
Central African Republic	TL	Indonesia	PK	Mozambique	C9
Chad	TT	Iran	EP	Myanmar	XY, XZ
Chile	CC	Iraq	YI	Namibia	V5
China	B	Ireland, Republic of	EI	Nauru	C2
Colombia	HK	Israel	4X	Nepal	9N
Comoros	D6	Italy	I	Netherlands	PH
Congo, Democratic		Jamaica	6Y	New Zealand	ZK, ZL, ZM
Republic of	9Q, 9T	Japan	JA	Nicaragua	YN
Congo, Republic of the	TN	Jordan	JY	Niger	5U
Costa Rica	TI	Kazakhstan	UN	Nigeria	5N
Côte d'Ivoire	TU	Kenya	5Y	Norway	LN
Croatia	9A	Kiribati	T3	Oman	A40
Cuba	CU	Korea, North	P	Pakistan	AP

(continued)

International Aircraft Registration Prefixes (continued)

Country	ICAO mark	Country	ICAO mark	Country	ICAO mark
Panama	HP	Sierra Leone	9L	Tunisia	TS
Papua New Guinea	P2	Singapore	9V	Turkey	TC
Paraguay	ZP	Slovak Republic	OM	Turkmenistan	EZ
Peru	OB	Slovenia	S5	Tuvalu	T2
Philippines	RP	Solomon Islands	H4	Uganda	5X
Poland	SP	Somalia	6O	UK	G
Portugal	CS	South Africa	ZS, ZT, ZU	Ukraine	UR
Qatar	A7	Spain	EC	United Arab Emirates	A6
Romania	YR	Sri Lanka	4R	United Nations	4N
Russia	RA	Sudan	ST	Uruguay	CX
Rwanda	9XR	Suriname	PZ	USA	N
St Kitts and Nevis	V4	Swaziland	3D	Uzbekistan	UK
St Lucia	J6	Sweden	SE	Vanuatu	YJ
St Vincent and the		Switzerland	HB	Vatican City State	HV
Grenadines	J8	Syria	YK	Venezuela	YV
Samoa	5W	Taiwan	B	Vietnam	VN
San Marino	T7	Tajikistan	EY	Yemen	7O
São Tomé and Príncipe	S9	Tanzania	5H	Yugoslavia	YU
Saudi Arabia	HZ	Thailand	HS	Zambia	9J
Senegal	6W	Togo	5V	Zimbabwe	Z
Seychelles	S7	Tonga	A3		

The development of flight

Method of transport in which aircraft carry people and goods through the air. People first took to the air in balloons and began powered flight in 1852 in airships, but the history of flying, both for civilian and military use, is dominated by the aeroplane. The earliest planes were designed for gliding; the advent of the petrol engine saw the first powered flight by the Wright brothers in 1903 in the USA. This inspired the development of aircraft throughout Europe. Biplanes were succeeded by monoplanes in the 1930s. The first jet plane was produced in 1939, and after the end of World War II the development of jetliners brought about a continuous expansion in passenger air travel. In 1969 came the supersonic aircraft Concorde.

history In the 14th century the English philosopher Roger Bacon spoke of constructing an aircraft by means of a hollow globe and liquid fire. He was followed in the 15th century by Albert of Saxony, who also spoke of balloon flight by means of fire in a light sphere. During the 16th and 17th centuries a number of fantastic ideas were put forward; one was that swans' eggs be filled with sulphur or mercury and thereby drawn up to the Sun.

early ideas Francisco de Lana in 1670 proposed that four hollow balls made of very thin brass should be emptied of air. To them should be attached a small boat and sail, and in that way a balloon would be contrived which could carry a person. The idea was not feasible, since the globes, made of brass only 0.1 mm thick, would have collapsed by reason of their own weight. But although de Lana saw this difficulty, he argued that their shape would prevent that.

balloons It was not until the 18th century that the real balloon was invented. The beginning of the development of the balloon was the work of two brothers, Joseph and Etienne Montgolfier, who came to the conclusion that a paper bag filled with a 'substance of a cloud-like nature' would float in the atmosphere. They made a number of experiments which attracted attention and further efforts from others. Progress was made gradually, and the first person-carrying ascent took place in October 1783, when Pilatre de Rozier went up in a Montgolfier captive balloon. The first woman to ascend was Madame Thible, who went up from Lyons in 1784. In 1859 a flight of over 1,600 km/994 mi was made in the USA.

adding power It had long been

recognized that the difficulty with balloons was navigating through the air. Oars were tried, but were not successful. The first attempt to navigate the balloon by means of a small, light engine came in 1852, the experiment being made by Henri Giffard. From 1897 the development of the airship was the special work of Ferdinand Zeppelin. In 1900 he made his first flight with a dirigible balloon carrying five men. It was made of aluminium, supported by gas-bags, and driven by two motors, each of about 12 kW. His first experiment met with some success, a second, more powerful version was wrecked, and a third met with great success. This airship carried 11 passengers and attained a speed of about 55 kph/34 mph, travelling about 400 km/248 mi in 11 hours, but was wrecked by a storm in 1908, caught fire, and was completely destroyed.

powered flight In the late 19th century experiments were being made with soaring machines and hang gliders, chiefly by Otto Lilienthal, who, with an arrangement formed on the plan of birds' wings, attempted to imitate their 'soaring flight'. Following up Lilienthal's ideas, the Wright brothers produced their first powered aeroplane in 1903. Their first successful machine was simply an

than-air craft. Heavier-than-air craft include the aeroplane, glider, autogiro, and helicopter.

airship or **dirigible** any aircraft that is lighter than air and power-driven, consisting of an ellipsoidal balloon that forms the streamlined envelope or hull and has below it the propulsion system (propellers), steering mechanism, and space for crew, passengers, and/or cargo. The balloon section is filled with lighter-than-air gas, either the non-flammable helium or, before helium was industrially available in large enough quantities, the easily ignited and flammable hydrogen. The envelope's form is maintained by internal pressure in the nonrigid (blimp) and semirigid (in which the nose and tail sections have a metal framework connected by a rigid keel) types. The rigid type (zeppelin) maintains its form using an internal metal framework. Airships have been used for luxury travel, polar exploration, warfare, and advertising.

altimeter instrument used in aircraft that measures altitude, or height above sea level. The common type is a form of aneroid barometer, which works by sensing the differences in air pressure at different altitudes. This must continually be recalibrated because of the change in air pressure with changing weather conditions. The radar altimeter measures the height of the aircraft above the ground, measuring the time it takes for radio pulses emitted by the aircraft to be reflected. Radar altimeters are essential features of automatic and blind-landing systems.

autogiro or **autogyro** heavier-than-air craft that supports itself in the air with a rotary wing, or rotor. The Spanish aviator Juan de la Cierva designed the first successful autogiro in 1923. The autogiro's rotor provides only lift and not propulsion; it has been superseded by the helicopter, in which the rotor provides both. The autogiro is propelled by an orthodox propeller.

The development of flight (continued)

aeroplane that flew in a straight line, but this received many modifications; and in 1908 they went to France to carry on experiments, during which Wilbur Wright created a record by remaining in the air for over an hour while carrying a passenger. He also attained a speed of 60 kph/37 mph.

In Europe, at the beginning of the 20th century, France led in aeroplane design and Louis Blériot brought aviation much publicity by crossing the English Channel in 1909, as did the Reims air races of that year. The first powered flight in the UK was made by Samuel Franklin Cody 1908. In 1912 Sopwith and Bristol both built small biplanes. The first big twin-engined aeroplane was the Handley Page bomber 1917. The stimulus of World War I (1914–18) and rapid development of the petrol engine led to increased power, and speeds rose to 320 kph/200 mph. Streamlining the body of planes became imperative: the body, wings, and exposed parts were reshaped to reduce drag. Eventually the biplane was superseded by the internally braced monoplane structure, for example, the Hawker Hurricane and Supermarine Spitfire fighters and Avro Lancaster and Boeing Flying Fortress bombers of World War II (1939–45).

jet aircraft The German Heinkel 178, built in 1939, was the first jet plane; it was driven, not by a propeller as all planes before it, but by a jet of hot gases. The first British jet aircraft, the Gloster E.28/39, flew from Cranwell, Lincolnshire, on 15 May 1941, powered by a jet engine invented by British engineer Frank Whittle. Twin-jet Meteor fighters were in use by the end of WWII. The rapid development of the jet plane led to enormous increases in power and speed until air-compressibility effects were felt near the speed of sound, which at first seemed to be a flight speed limit (the sound barrier). The sound barrier was first broken in the USA in 1947 by a rocket-powered aircraft piloted by Chuck Yeager. To attain supersonic speed, streamlining the aircraft body became insufficient: wings were swept back, engines buried in wings and tail units, and bodies were even eliminated in all-wing delta designs. In the 1950s the first jet airliners, such as the Comet (first introduced in 1949), were introduced into service. Today jet planes dominate both military and civilian aviation, although many light planes still use piston engines and propellers. The late 1960s saw the introduction of the jumbo jet, and in 1976 the Anglo-French Concorde, which makes a transatlantic crossing in under three hours, came into commercial service.

other developments During the 1950s and 1960s research was done on V/STOL (vertical and/or short takeoff and landing) aircraft. The British Harrier jet fighter has been the only VTOL aircraft to achieve commercial success, but STOL technology has fed into subsequent generations of aircraft. The 1960s and 1970s also saw the development of variable geometry ('swing-wing') aircraft, the wings of which can be swept back in flight to achieve higher speeds. In the 1980s much progress was made in 'fly-by-wire' aircraft with computer-aided controls. International partnerships have developed both civilian and military aircraft. The airbus is a wide-bodied airliner built jointly by companies from France, Germany, the UK, the Netherlands, and Spain. The Eurofighter 2000 is a joint project between the UK, Italy, Germany, and Spain. The B-2 bomber, (a stealth bomber) developed by the US Air Force in 1989, is invisible to radar. The altitude record for a solar-powered plane was set in 1997 by Pathfinder, a 30-m/98-ft wingspan aircraft, which reached 20,528 m/67,349 ft above sea level over Hawaii.

automatic pilot control device that keeps an aeroplane flying automatically on a given course at a given height and speed.

aviation term used to describe the science of powered flight.

balloon lighter-than-air craft that consists of a gasbag filled with gas lighter than the surrounding air and an attached basket, or gondola, for carrying passengers and/or instruments. In 1783, the first successful human ascent was in Paris, in a hot-air balloon designed by the Montgolfier brothers Joseph Michel and Jacques Etienne. In 1785, a hydrogen-filled balloon designed by French physicist Jacques Charles travelled across the English Channel.

Bernoulli's principle law stating that the pressure of a fluid varies inversely with speed, an increase in speed producing a decrease in pressure (such as a drop in hydraulic pressure as the fluid speeds up flowing through a constriction in a pipe) and vice versa. The principle also explains the pressure differences on each surface of an aerofoil, which gives lift to the wing of an aircraft. The principle was named after Swiss mathematician and physicist Daniel Bernoulli.

black box popular name for the unit containing an aeroplane's flight and voice recorders. These monitor the plane's behaviour and the crew's conversation, thus providing valuable clues to the cause of a disaster. The box is nearly indestructible and usually painted orange for easy recovery. The name also refers to any compact electronic device that can be quickly connected or disconnected as a unit.

Boeing US military and commercial aircraft manufacturer. Among the models Boeing has produced are the B-17 Flying Fortress, 1935; the B-52 Stratofortress, 1952; the Chinook helicopter, 1961; the first jetliner, the Boeing 707, 1957; the jumbo jet or Boeing 747, 1969; the jetfoil, 1975; and the 777-300 jetliner, 1997.

civil aviation operation of passenger and freight transport by air. With increasing traffic, control of air space is a major problem, and in 1963 Eurocontrol was established by Belgium, France, West Germany, Luxembourg, the Netherlands, and the UK to supervise both military and civil movement in the air space over member countries. There is also a tendency to coordinate services and other facilities between national airlines; for example, the establishment of Air Union in 1963 by France (Air France), West Germany (Lufthansa), Italy (Alitalia), and Belgium (Sabena).

The 10 Worst Aircraft Disasters in Aviation History

Source: National Transportation Safety Board, US Department of Transportation

Fatalities	Date	Airline	Aircraft	Location
582	27 March 1977	Pan American and KLM (Royal Dutch Airlines)	Two Boeing 747s	Tenerife, Canary Islands
520	12 August 1985	Japan Airlines	Boeing 747	Mount Ogura, Japan
349	12 November 1996	Saudi Arabian Air and Kazak Airlines	Boeing 747 and Ilyushin 76TD	Charki Dadri, India
346	3 March 1974	Turkish Air	DC10	northeast of Paris
329	23 June 1985	Air India	Boeing 747	Republic of Ireland coast, Atlantic Ocean
301	19 August 1980	Saudi Arabian Air	Lockheed L-1011	Riyadh, Saudi Arabia
290	3 July 1988	Iran Air	A300 Airbus	Persian Gulf
275	25 May 1979	American Airlines	DC10	Chicago (IL) USA
270	21 December 1988	Pan American	Boeing 747	Lockerbie, Scotland
269	1 September 1983	Korean Airlines	Boeing 747	near Sakhalin Island, Okhokst Sea

Concorde the only supersonic airliner, which cruises at Mach 2, or twice the speed of sound, about 2,170 kph/1,350 mph. Concorde, the result of Anglo-French cooperation, made its first flight in 1969 and entered commercial service seven years later. It is 62 m/202 ft long and has a wing span of nearly 26 m/84 ft. Developing Concorde cost French and British taxpayers £2 billion.

convertiplane vertical takeoff and landing craft (VTOL) with rotors on its wings that spin horizontally for takeoff, but tilt to spin in a vertical plane for forward flight.

delta wing aircraft wing shaped like the Greek letter *delta* Δ. Its design enables an aircraft to pass through the sound barrier with little effect. The supersonic airliner Concorde and the US space shuttle have delta wings.

drag resistance to motion a body experiences when passing through a fluid – gas or liquid. The aerodynamic drag aircraft experience when travelling through the air represents a great waste of power, so they must be carefully shaped, or streamlined, to reduce drag to a minimum. Cars benefit from streamlining, and aerodynamic drag is used to slow down spacecraft returning from space. Boats travelling through water experience hydrodynamic drag on their hulls, and the fastest vessels are hydrofoils, whose hulls lift out of the water while cruising.

flight simulator computer-controlled pilot-training device, consisting of an artificial cockpit mounted on hydraulic legs, that simulates the experience of flying a real aircraft. Inside the cockpit, the trainee pilot views a screen showing a computer-controlled projection of the view from a real aircraft, and makes appropriate adjustments to the controls. The computer monitors these adjustments, changes both the alignment of the cockpit on its hydraulic legs, and the projected view seen by the pilot. In this way a trainee pilot can progress to quite an advanced stage of training without leaving the ground.

G-force force that pilots and astronauts experience when their craft accelerate or decelerate rapidly. One *g* is the ordinary pull of gravity. Early astronauts were subjected to launch and reentry forces of up to six *g* or more; in the space shuttle, more than three *g* is experienced on liftoff. Pilots and astronauts wear *g*-suits that prevent their blood pooling too much under severe *g*-forces, which can lead to unconsciousness.

Harrier the only truly successful vertical takeoff and landing fixed-wing aircraft, often called the **jump jet.** It was built in Britain and made its first flight 1966. It has a single jet engine and a set of swivelling nozzles. These deflect the jet exhaust vertically downwards for takeoff and landing, and to the rear for normal flight. Designed to fly from confined spaces with minimal ground support, it refuels in midair.

helicopter powered aircraft that achieves both lift and propulsion by means of a rotary wing, or rotor, on top of the fuselage. It can take off and land vertically, move in any direction, or remain stationary in the air. It can be powered by piston or jet engine. The autogiro was a precursor.

instrument landing system (ILS) landing aid for aircraft that uses radio beacons on the ground and instruments on the flight deck. One beacon (localizer) sends out a vertical radio beam along the centre line of the runway. Another beacon (glide slope) transmits a beam in the plane at right angles to the localizer beam at the ideal approach-path angle. The pilot can tell from the instruments how to manoeuvre to attain the correct approach path.

jet propulsion method of propulsion in which an object is propelled in one direction by a jet, or stream of gases, moving in the other. This follows from Isaac Newton's third law of motion: 'To every action, there is an equal and opposite reaction.' The most widespread application of the jet principle is in the jet engine, the most common kind of aircraft engine

jumbo jet popular name for a generation of huge wide-bodied airliners including the **Boeing 747,** which is 71 m/232 ft long, has a wingspan of 60 m/196 ft, a maximum takeoff weight of nearly 400 tonnes, and can carry more than 400 passengers.

parachute any canopied fabric device strapped to a person or a package, used to slow down descent from a high altitude, or returning spent missiles or parts to a safe speed for landing, or sometimes to aid (through braking) the landing of a plane or missile. Modern designs enable the parachutist to exercise considerable control of direction, as in skydiving.

propeller screwlike device used to propel some ships and aeroplanes. A propeller has a number

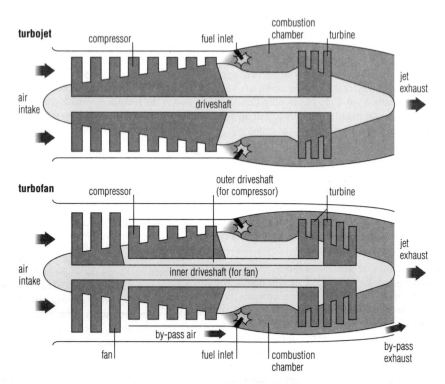

turbojet

compressor | fuel inlet | combustion chamber | turbine

air intake

driveshaft

jet exhaust

turbofan

compressor | outer driveshaft (for compressor) | turbine

air intake

inner driveshaft (for fan)

jet exhaust

by-pass air

fan | fuel inlet | combustion chamber | by-pass exhaust

jet propulsion Two forms of jet engine. In the turbojet, air passing into the air intake is compressed by the compressor and fed into the combustion chamber where fuel burns. The hot gases formed are expelled at high speed from the rear of the engine, driving the engine forwards and turning a turbine which drives the compressor. In the turbofan, some air flows around the combustion chamber and mixes with the exhaust gases. This arrangement is more efficient and quieter than the turbojet.

of curved blades that describe a helical path as they rotate with the hub, and accelerate fluid (liquid or gas) backwards during rotation. Reaction to this backward movement of fluid sets up a propulsive thrust forwards. The marine screw propeller was developed by Francis Pettit Smith in the UK and Swedish-born John Ericson in the USA and was first used in 1839.

seaplane aeroplane capable of taking off from, and landing on, water. There are two major types, floatplanes and flying boats. The floatplane is similar to an ordinary aeroplane but has floats in place of wheels; the flying boat has a broad hull shaped like a boat and may also have floats attached to the wing tips.

sonic boom noise like a thunderclap that occurs when an aircraft passes through the sound barrier, or begins to travel faster than the speed of sound. It happens when the cone-shaped shock wave caused by the plane touches the ground.

swing wing correctly **variable-geometry wing** aircraft wing that can be moved during flight to provide a suitable configuration for either low-speed or high-speed flight. The British engineer Barnes Wallis developed the idea of the swing wing, first used on the US-built Northrop X-4, and since used in several aircraft, including the US F-111, F-114, and the B-1, the European Tornado, and several Soviet-built aircraft. These craft have their wings projecting nearly at right angles for takeoff and landing and low-speed flight, and swung back for high-speed flight.

tilt-rotor aircraft type of vertical takeoff aircraft, also called a convertiplane.

turbojet jet engine that derives its thrust from a jet of hot exhaust gases. Pure turbojets can be very powerful but use a lot of fuel.

turboprop jet engine that derives its thrust partly from a jet of exhaust gases, but mainly from a

swing wing A British Aerospace Tornado F2 swing-wing (variable-geometry) fighter-bomber. It is flying at a relatively low speed and the wings are fully extended. *British Aerospace*

propeller powered by a turbine in the jet exhaust. Turboprops are more economical than turbojets but can be used only at relatively low speeds.

turbulence irregular fluid (gas or liquid) flow, in which vortices and unpredictable fluctuations and motions occur. Streamlining reduces the turbulence of flow around an object, such as an aircraft, and reduces drag.

vertical takeoff and landing craft (VTOL) aircraft that can take off and land vertically. Helicopters, airships, and balloons can do this, as can a few fixed-wing aeroplanes, like the convertiplane.

wind tunnel test tunnel in which air is blown over, for example, a stationary model aircraft, motor vehicle, or locomotive to simulate the effects of movement. Lift, drag, and airflow patterns are observed by the use of special cameras and sensitive instruments. Wind-tunnel testing assesses aerodynamic design, prior to full-scale construction.

Flight: Chronology

1783 First human flight, by Jean F Pilâtre de Rozier and the Marquis d'Arlandes, in Paris, using a hot-air balloon made by Joseph and Etienne Montgolfier; first ascent in a hydrogen-filled balloon by Jacques Charles and M N Robert in Paris.

1785 Jean-Pierre Blanchard and John J Jeffries make the first balloon crossing of the English Channel.

1852 Henri Giffard fly the first steam-powered airship over Paris.

1853 George Cayley flies the first true aeroplane, a model glider 1.5 m/5 ft long.

1891–96 Otto Lilienthal pilots a glider in flight.

1903 First powered and controlled flight of a heavier-than-air craft (aeroplane) by

Orville Wright, at Kitty Hawk, North Carolina, USA.

1908 First powered flight in the UK by Samuel Cody.

1909 Louis Blériot flies across the English Channel in 36 minutes.

1914–18 World War I stimulates improvements in speed and power.

1919 First east–west flight across the Atlantic by Albert C Read, using a flying boat; first nonstop flight across the Atlantic east–west by John William Alcock and Arthur Whitten Brown in 16 hours 27 minutes; first complete flight from Britain to Australia by Ross Smith and Keith Smith.

1923 Juan de la Cieva flies the first autogiro with a rotating wing.

1927 Charles Lindbergh makes the first west–east solo nonstop flight across the Atlantic.

1928 First transpacific flight, from San Francisco to Brisbane, by Charles Kinsford Smith and C T P Ulm.

1930 Frank Whittle patents the jet engine; Amy Johnson becomes the first woman to fly solo from England to Australia.

1937 The first fully pressurized aircraft, the Lockheed XC-35, comes into service.

1939 Erich Warsitz flies the first Heinkel jet plane, in Germany; Igor Sikorsky designs the first helicopter, with a large main rotor and a smaller tail rotor.

1939–45 World War II – developments include the

(continued)

Flight: Chronology (continued)

Hawker Hurricane and Supermarine Spitfire Fighters, and Avro Lancaster and Boeing Flying Fortress bombers.

1947 A rocket-powered plane, the Bell X-1, is the first aircraft to fly faster than the speed of sound.

1949 The de Havilland Comet, the first jet airliner, enters service; James Gallagher makes the first nonstop round-the-world flight, in a Boeing Superfortress.

1953 The first vertical takeoff aircraft, the Rolls-Royce 'Flying Bedstead', is tested.

1968 The world's first supersonic airliner, the Russian TU-144, flies for the first time.

1970 The Boeing 747 jumbo jet enters service, carrying 500 passengers.

1976 Anglo-French Concorde, making a transatlantic crossing in under three hours, comes into commercial service. A Lockheed SR-17A, piloted by Eldon W Joersz and George T Morgan, sets the world air-speed record of 3,529.56 kph/2,193.167 mph over Beale Air Force Base, California, USA.

1978 A US team makes the first transatlantic crossing by

balloon, in the helium-filled *Double Eagle II*.

1979 First crossing of the English Channel by a human-powered aircraft, *Gossamer Albatross*, piloted by Bryan Allen.

1981 The solar-powered *Solar Challenger* flies across the English Channel, from Paris to Kent, taking 5 hours for the 262 km/162.8 mi journey.

1986 Dick Rutan and Jeana Yeager make the first nonstop flight around the world without refuelling, piloting *Voyager*, which completes the flight in 9 days 3 minutes 44 seconds.

1987 Richard Branson and Per Lindstrand make the first transatlantic crossing by hot-air balloon, in *Virgin Atlantic Challenger*.

1988 *Daedelus*, a human-powered craft piloted by Kanellos Kanellopoulos, flies 118 km/74 mi across the Aegean Sea.

1991 Richard Branson and Per Lindstrand cross the Pacific Ocean in the hot-air balloon *Virgin Otsouka Pacific Flyer* from the southern tip of Japan to northwest Canada in 46 hours 15 minutes.

1992 US engineers demonstrate a model radio-controlled ornithopter, the first aircraft to

be successfully propelled and manoeuvred by flapping wings.

1993 The US Federal Aviation Authority makes the use of an automatic on-board collision avoidance system (TCAS-2) mandatory in US airspace.

1994 The US Boeing 777 airliner makes its first flight. A scale model scramjet (supersonic combustion ramjet) is tested and produces speeds of 9,000 kph/5,590 mph (Mach 8.2). The scramjet uses oxygen from the atmosphere to burn its fuel.

1996 Japan tests the first fire-fighting helicopter. It is designed to reach skyscrapers beyond the range of fire-engine ladders.

1998 Swiss balloonist Bertrand Piccard, in the balloon *Breitling Orbiter*, sets a record for the longest nonstop, nonrefuelled flight by an aircraft: 9 days, 17 hours, and 55 minutes.

1998 (August) An unpiloted aircraft crosses the Atlantic. The14-kg/31-lb robot aircraft is designed by Australian and US researchers and it completes the crossing in 26 hours.

RAIL

cable car method of transporting passengers up steep slopes by cable. In the **cable railway,** passenger cars are hauled along rails by a cable wound by a powerful winch. A pair of cars usually operates together on the funicular principle, one going up as the other goes down. The other main type is the **aerial cable car,** where the

passenger car is suspended from a trolley that runs along an aerial cableway.

funicular railway railway with two cars connected by a wire cable wound around a drum at the top of a steep incline. Funicular railways of up to 1.5 km/1 mi exist in Switzerland.

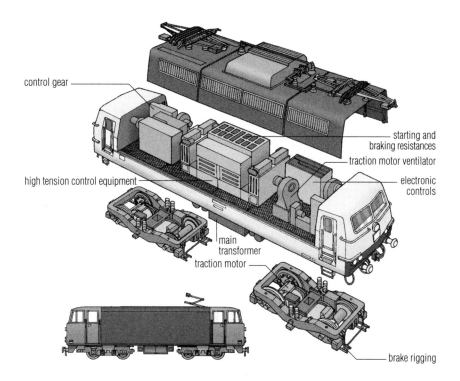

control gear

starting and braking resistances

traction motor ventilator

high tension control equipment

electronic controls

main transformer

traction motor

brake rigging

locomotive The drive of an electric locomotive is provided by powerful electric motors (traction motors) in the bogies beneath the body of the locomotive. The motors are controlled by equipment inside the locomotive. Both AC and DC power supplies are used, although most modern systems use a 2500 V supply.

locomotive engine for hauling railway trains. In 1804 Cornish engineer Richard Trevithick built the first steam engine to run on rails. Locomotive design did not radically improve until British engineer George Stephenson built the *Rocket* in 1829, which featured a multitube boiler and blastpipe, standard in all following **steam locomotives.** Today most locomotives are diesel or electric: **diesel locomotives** have a powerful diesel engine, and **electric locomotives** draw their power from either an overhead cable or a third rail alongside the ordinary track.

London Underground first underground rail line in the world, opened in 1863. At first it was essentially a roofed-in trench. The London Underground is still the world's longest subway, with over 250 mi/400 km of routes.

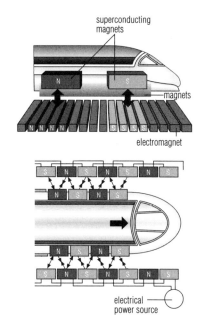

superconducting magnets

magnets

electromagnet

electrical power source

maglev The repulsion of superconducting magnets and electromagnets in the track keeps a maglev train suspended above the track. By varying the strength and polarity of the track electromagnets, the train can be driven forward.

railway The Eurostar, built to run through the Channel Tunnel that connects the UK and France. The train seats 800 passengers and takes 3 hours to travel between London and Paris. *Railtrack plc*

maglev acronym for **magnetic levitation** high-speed surface transport using the repellent force of superconductive magnets to propel and support, for example, a train above a track.

monorail railway that runs on a single rail; the cars can be balanced on it or suspended from it. It was invented in 1882 to carry light loads, and when run by electricity was called a **telpher.**

rack railway railway used in mountainous regions, that uses a toothed pinion running in a

Railway Disasters throughout the World

The worst train disaster ever is considered to be that in Bihar, India, when a train plunged off a bridge over the Bagmati River. The official death toll was given as 268, but as the train was very overcrowded, the number of deaths was probably in excess of 800.

World Railway Disasters Since 1900

Date	Location	Fatalities	Date	Location	Fatalities
8 September 1900	Bolivar (TX)	85	14 November 1960	Pardubice, Czech Republic	110
1 March 1910	Wellington (WA)	96	8 January 1962	Woerden, Netherlands	91
22 May 1915	near Gretna, Scotland	227	3 May 1962	Tokyo, Japan	163
12 December 1917	Modane, France	>540	26 July 1964	Oporto, Portugal	94
9 July 1918	Nashville (TN)	101	4 February 1970	Buenos Aires, Argentina	236
2 November 1918	Brooklyn (NY)	92	16 June 1972	Vierzy, France	107
23 December 1933	Lagny-Polponne, France	230	21 July 1972	Seville, Spain	76
16 July 1937	near Patna, India	107	6 October 1972	Saltillo, Mexico	208
22 December 1939	near Magdeburg, Germany	132	30 August 1974	Zagreb, Yugoslavia	153
	near Friedrichshafen, Germany	99	18 January 1977	Granville, Australia	82
16 January 1944	Leon Province, Spain	>500	6 June 1981	Bihar, India	>800
2 March 1944	near Salerno, Italy	521	27 January 1982	El Asnam, Algeria	130
20 March 1946	Aracaju, Mexico	185	11 July 1982	Tepic, Mexico	120
22 October 1949	near Dwor, Poland	>200	19 February 1983	Empalme, Mexico	100
6 February 1951	Woodbridge (NJ)	84	12 December 1988	London, UK	115
4 March 1952	near Rio de Janeiro, Brazil	119	15 January 1989	Maizdi Khan, Bangladesh	>110
9 July 1952	Rzepin, Poland	160	4 June 1989	Chelyabinsk, former USSR	>600
8 October 1952	Harrow, UK	112	4 January 1990	Sindh Province, Pakistan	>210
3 April 1955	Guadalajara, Mexico	300	14 May 1991	Shigaraki, Japan	42
1 September 1957	Kendal, Jamaica	178	8 March 1994	Durban, South Africa	63
29 September 1957	Montgomery, Pakistan	>250	22 September 1994	Tolunda, Angola	>300
4 December 1957	London, UK	90	20 August 1995	Firozabad, India	>300
8 May 1958	Rio de Janeiro, Brazil	128	3 June 1998	Eschede, Germany	98

Underground: First Underground Railways

city	opened	length (km/mi)	current journeys per year (millions)
London	1863	394/245	775
New York	1867	389/242	1,060
Paris	1900	199/124	1,191

toothed rack to provide traction. The rack usually runs between the rails. Ordinary wheels lose their grip even on quite shallow gradients, but rack railways, like that on Mount Pilatus in Switzerland, can climb slopes as steep as 50% (1 in 2).

railway method of transport in which trains convey passengers and goods along a twin rail track. Following the work of British steam pioneers such as Scottish engineer James Watt, English engineer George Stephenson built the first public steam railway, from Stockton to Darlington, England, in 1825. This heralded extensive railway building in Britain, continental Europe, and North America, providing a fast and economical means of transport and communication. After World War II, steam engines were replaced by electric and diesel engines. At the same time, the growth of road building, air services, and car ownership destroyed the supremacy of the railways.

tramway transport system for use in cities, where wheeled vehicles run along parallel rails. Trams are powered either by electric conductor rails below ground or by conductor arms connected to overhead wires. Greater manoeuvrability is achieved with the trolley bus, similarly powered by conductor arms overhead but without tracks.

Trans-Siberian Railway the world's longest single-service railway, connecting the cities of European Russia with Omsk, Novosibirsk, Irkutsk, and Khabarovsk, and terminating at Nakhodka on the Pacific coast east of Vladivostok. The line was built between 1891 and 1915, and has a total length of 9,289 km/5,772 mi, from Moscow to Vladivostok.

underground US **subway** rail service that runs underground. The first underground line in the world was in London, opened in 1863; it was essentially a roofed-in trench. The London Underground is still the longest, with over 400 km/250 mi of routes. Many large cities throughout the world have similar systems, and Moscow's underground, the Metro, handles up to 6.5 million passengers a day.

Railways: Chronology

1500s Tramways – wooden tracks along which trolleys ran – are in use in mines.

1789 Flanged wheels running on cast-iron rails are first introduced; cars are still horse-drawn.

1804 Richard Trevithick builds the first steam locomotive, and runs it on the track at the Pen-y-darren ironworks in South Wales.

1825 George Stephenson in England builds the first public railway to carry steam trains – the Stockton and Darlington line – using his engine *Locomotion*.

1829 Stephenson designs his locomotive *Rocket*.

1830 Stephenson completes the Liverpool and Manchester Railway, the first steam passenger line. The first US-built locomotive, *Best Friend of Charleston*, goes into service on the South Carolina Railroad.

1835 Germany pioneers steam railways in Europe, using *Der Adler*, a locomotive built by Stephenson.

1863 Robert Fairlie, a Scot, patents a locomotive with pivoting driving bogies, allowing tight curves in the track (this is later applied in the Garratt locomotives). London opens the world's first underground railway, powered by steam.

(*continued*)

Railways: Chronology (continued)

1869 The first US transcontinental railway is completed at Promontory, Utah, when the Union Pacific and the Central Pacific railroads meet. George Westinghouse of the USA invents the compressed-air brake.

1879 Werner von Siemens demonstrates an electric train in Germany. Volk's Electric Railway along the Brighton seafront in England is the world's first public electric railway.

1883 Charles Lartique builds the first monorail, in Ireland.

1885 The trans-Canada continental railway is completed, from Montréal in the east to Port Moody, British Columbia, in the west.

1890 The first electric underground railway opens in London.

1901 The world's longest-established monorail, the Wuppertal Schwebebahn, goes into service in Germany.

1912 The first diesel locomotive takes to the rails in Germany.

1938 The British steam locomotive *Mallard* sets a steam-rail speed record of 203 kph/126 mph.

1941 Swiss Federal Railways introduce a gas-turbine locomotive.

1964 Japan National Railways inaugurates the 515 km/320 mi New Tokaido line between Osaka and Tokyo, on which the 210 kph/130 mph 'bullet' trains run.

1973 British Rail's High Speed Train (HST) sets a diesel-rail speed record of 229 kph/142 mph.

1979 Japan National Railways' maglev test vehicle ML-500 attains a speed of 517 kph/321 mph.

1981 France's Train à Grande Vitesse (TGV) superfast trains begin operation between Paris and Lyons, regularly attaining a peak speed of 270 kph/168 mph.

1987 British Rail sets a new diesel-traction speed record of 238.9 kph/148.5 mph, on a test run between Darlington and York; France and the UK begin work on the Channel Tunnel, a railway link connecting the two countries, running beneath the English Channel.

1988 The West German Intercity Experimental train reaches 405 kph/252 mph on a test run between Würzburg and Fulda.

1990 A new rail-speed record of 515 kph/320 mph is established by a French TGV train, on a stretch of line between Tours and Paris.

1991 The British and French twin tunnels meet 23 km/14 mi out to sea to form the Channel Tunnel.

1993 British Rail privatization plans are announced; government investment is further reduced.

1994 Rail services between England and France start through the Channel Tunnel.

1995 Nerve gas released on Tokyo underground railway by members of a religious cult, caused 12 deaths.

1996 Fifteen people are crushed to death at a railway station in Johannesburg, South Africa, after private security guards use electric cattle prods to control crowds, causing a stampede.

ROAD

aquaplaning phenomenon in which the tyres of a road vehicle cease to make direct contact with the road surface, owing to the presence of a thin film of water. As a result, the vehicle can go out of control (particularly if the steered wheels are involved).

On your bike!
- The world manufacture of bicycles was three times that for cars in 1997; the production rate of bicycles has increased fivefold since the 1960s.

---

bicycle pedal-driven two-wheeled vehicle used in cycling. It consists of a metal frame mounted on two large wire-spoked wheels, with handlebars in front and a seat between the front and back

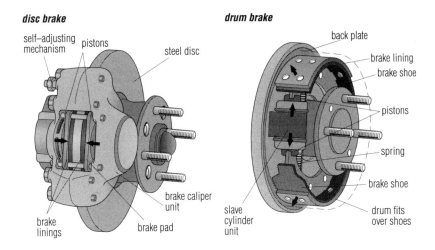

disc brake

self–adjusting mechanism

pistons

steel disc

brake caliper unit

brake linings

brake pad

drum brake

back plate

brake lining

brake shoe

pistons

spring

brake shoe

slave cylinder unit

drum fits over shoes

brake Two common braking systems: the disc brake (left) and the drum brake (right). In the disc brake, increased hydraulic pressure of the brake fluid in the pistons forces the brake pads against the steel disc attached to the wheel. A self-adjusting mechanism balances the force on each pad. In the drum brake, increased pressure of the brake fluid within the slave cylinder forces the brake pad against the brake drum attached to the wheel.

wheels. The bicycle is an energy-efficient, non-polluting form of transport, and it is estimated that 800 million bicycles are in use throughout the world. China, India, Denmark, and the Netherlands are countries with a high use of bicycles. More than 10% of road spending in the Netherlands is on cycleways and bicycle parking.

brake device used to slow down or stop the movement of a moving body or vehicle. The mechanically applied calliper brake used on bicycles uses a scissor action to press hard rubber blocks against the wheel rim. The main braking system of a car works hydraulically: when the driver depresses the brake pedal, liquid pressure forces pistons to apply brakes on each wheel.

cam part of a machine that converts circular motion to linear motion or vice versa. The **edge cam** in a car engine is in the form of a rounded projection on a shaft, the camshaft. When the camshaft turns, the cams press against linkages (plungers or followers) that open the valves in the cylinders.

car small, driver-guided, passenger-carrying motor vehicle; originally the automated version of the horse-drawn carriage, meant to convey people and their goods over streets and roads.

Over 50 million motor cars are produced each year worldwide. The number of cars in the world in 1997 exceeded 500 million. Most are four-wheeled and have water-cooled, piston-type internal-combustion engines fuelled by petrol or diesel. Variations have existed for decades that use ingenious and often nonpolluting power plants, but the motor industry long ago settled on this general formula for the consumer market. Experimental and sports models are streamlined, energy-efficient, and hand-built.

carburation mixing of a gas, such as air, with a volatile hydrocarbon fuel, such as petrol, kerosene, or fuel oil, in order to form an explosive mixture. The process, which ensures that the maximum amount of heat energy is released during combustion, is used in internal-combustion engines. In most petrol engines the liquid fuel is atomized and mixed with air by means of a device called a **carburettor.**

catalytic converter device fitted to the exhaust system of a motor vehicle in order to reduce toxic emissions from the engine. It converts harmful exhaust products to relatively harmless ones by passing the exhaust gases over a mixture of catalysts coated on a metal or ceramic honeycomb (a structure that increases the surface area and therefore the amount of active catalyst with which the exhaust gases will come into contact). **Oxidation catalysts** (small amounts of precious

Motor Vehicle Nationality Abbreviations

Source: United Nations

Many road vehicles display one or more letters to identify their nationality. These letters are in accordance with the 1968 (United Nations) UN Convention on Road Traffic and the 1949 UN Convention on Road Traffic.

Country	Abbreviation	Country	Abbreviation	Country	Abbreviation
Aden	ADN	Greece	GR	Pakistan	PAK
Albania	AL	Grenada	WG	Papua New Guinea	PNG
Alderney	GBA	Guatemala	GCA	Paraguay	PY
Algeria	DZ	Guernsey	GBG	Peru	PE
Andorra	AND	Guyana	GUY	Philippines	RP
Argentina	RA	Haiti	RH	Poland	PL
Australia	AUS	Hong Kong	HK	Portugal	P
Austria	A	Hungary	H	Romania	RO
Bahamas	BS	Iceland	IS	Russia	RUS
Bahrain	BRN	India	IND	Rwanda	RWA
Bangladesh	BD	Indonesia	RI	St Lucia	WL
Barbados	BDS	Iran	IR	St Vincent	WV
Belarus	SU[1]	Ireland, Republic of	IRL	Samoa	WS
Belgium	B	Isle of Man	GBM	San Marino	RSM
Belize	BH	Israel	IL	Senegal	SN
Benin	DY	Italy	I	Seychelles	SY
Bosnia-Herzegovina	BIH	Jamaica	JA	Sierra Leone	WAL
Botswana	RB	Japan	J	Singapore	SGP
Brazil	BR	Jersey	GBJ	Slovak Republic	SK
Brunei	BRU	Jordan	HKJ	Slovenia	SLO
Bulgaria	BG	Kazakhstan	KZ	South Africa	ZA
Cambodia	K	Kenya	EAK	Spain (including	
Canada	CDN	Korea, South	ROK	African localities and	
Central African		Kuwait	KWT	provinces)	E
Republic	RCA	Kyrgyzstan	KS	Sri Lanka	CL
Chile	RCH	Laos	LAO	Suriname	SME
China	RC	Latvia	LV	Swaziland	SD
Congo, Democratic		Lebanon	RL	Sweden	S
Republic of	ZRE	Lesotho	LS	Switzerland	CH
Congo, Republic of the	RCB	Lithuania	LT	Syria	SYR
Costa Rica	CR	Luxembourg	L	Tajikistan	TJ
Côte d'Ivoire	CI	Macedonia, Former		Tanzania	EAT
Croatia	HR	Yugoslav Republic of	MK	Thailand	T
Cyprus	CY	Malawi	MW	Togo	TG
Czech Republic	CZ	Malaysia	MAL	Trinidad and Tobago	TT
Denmark	DK	Mali	RMM	Tunisia	TN
Dominican Republic	DOM	Malta	M	Turkey	TR
Ecuador	EC	Mauritius	MS	Turkmenistan	TM
Egypt	ET	Mexico	MEX	Uganda	EAU
Estonia	EST	Monaco	MC	Ukraine	UA
Faroe Islands	FO	Morocco	MA	Uruguay	ROU
Fiji Islands	FJI	Myanmar	BUR	USA	USA
Finland	FIN	Namibia	NAM	Uzbekistan	UZ
France	F	Netherlands	NL	Vatican City State	V
Gambia	WAG	Netherlands Antilles	NA	Venezuela	YV
Georgia	GE	New Zealand	NZ	Yugoslavia	YU
Germany	D	Nicaragua	NIC	Zambia	RNR
Ghana	GH	Niger	RN	Zanzibar	EAZ
Gibraltar	GBZ	Nigeria	WAN	Zimbabwe	ZW
Great Britain	GB	Norway	N		

[1] Belarus has not yet announced its new distinguishing sign. Therefore the sign 'SU' still appears on this list.

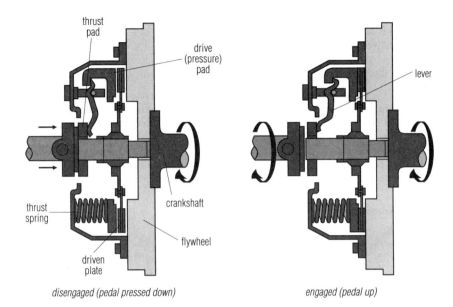

disengaged (pedal pressed down)   *engaged (pedal up)*

clutch The clutch consists of two main plates: a drive plate connected to the engine crankshaft and a driven plate connected to the wheels. When the clutch is disengaged, the drive plate does not press against the driven plate. When the clutch is engaged, the two plates are pressed into contact and the rotation of the crankshaft is transmitted to the wheels.

palladium and platinum metals) convert hydrocarbons (unburnt fuel) and carbon monoxide into carbon dioxide and water, but do not affect nitrogen oxide emissions. **Three-way catalysts** (platinum and rhodium metals) convert nitrogen oxide gases into nitrogen and oxygen.

caterpillar track trade name for an endless flexible belt of metal plates on which certain vehicles such as tanks and bulldozers run, which takes the place of ordinary tyred wheels and improves performance on wet or uneven surfaces.

clutch any device for disconnecting rotating shafts, used especially in a car's transmission system. In a car with a manual gearbox, the driver depresses the clutch when changing gear, thus disconnecting the engine from the gearbox.

diesel engine internal-combustion engine that burns a lightweight fuel oil. The diesel engine operates by compressing air until it becomes sufficiently hot to ignite the fuel. It is a piston-in-cylinder engine, like the petrol engine, but only air (rather than an air-and-fuel mixture) is taken into the cylinder on the first piston stroke (down). The piston moves up and compresses the air until it is at a very high temperature. The

fuel oil is then injected into the hot air, where it burns, driving the piston down on its power stroke. For this reason the engine is called a compression-ignition engine.

differential arrangement of gears in the final drive of a vehicle's transmission system that allows the

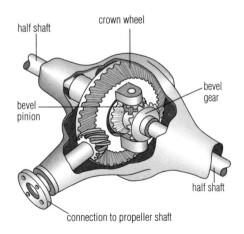

differential The differential lies midway between the driving wheels of a motorcar. When the car is turning, the bevel pinions spin, allowing the outer wheel to turn faster than the inner wheel.

driving wheels to turn at different speeds when cornering. The differential consists of sets of bevel gears and pinions within a cage attached to the crown wheel. When cornering, the bevel pinions rotate to allow the outer wheel to turn faster than the inner.

distributor device in the ignition system of a piston engine that distributes pulses of high-voltage electricity to the spark plugs in the cylinders. The electricity is passed to the plug leads by the tip of a rotor arm, driven by the engine camshaft, and current is fed to the rotor arm from the ignition

coil. The distributor also houses the contact point or breaker, which opens and closes to interrupt the battery current to the coil, thus triggering the high-voltage pulses. With electronic ignition the distributor is absent.

four-stroke cycle the engine-operating cycle of most petrol and diesel engines. The 'stroke' is an upward or downward movement of a piston in a cylinder. In a petrol engine the cycle begins with the induction of a fuel mixture as the piston goes down on its first stroke. On the second stroke (up) the piston compresses the mixture in the

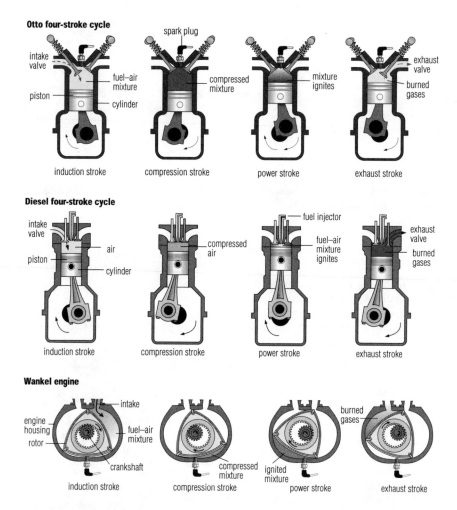

four-stroke cycle Three different types of engine that all function on exactly the same principle of four clearly definable strokes. However, they differ in the way these four stages occur. The Otto engine uses a mixture of fuel and air ignited by a spark; the diesel uses the heat and pressure of compressed air to ignite the fuel sprayed into the piston chamber; and the Wankel uses a fuel-air mixture, but a rotary arm rather than a two-way piston.

top of the cylinder. An electric spark then ignites the mixture, and the gases produced force the piston down on its third, power, stroke. On the fourth stroke (up) the piston expels the burned gases from the cylinder into the exhaust.

fuel injection injecting fuel directly into the cylinders of an internal combustion engine, instead of by way of a carburettor. It is the standard method used in diesel engines, and is now becoming standard for petrol engines. In the diesel engine, oil is injected into the hot compressed air at the top of the second piston stroke and explodes to drive the piston down on its power stroke. In the petrol engine, fuel is injected into the cylinder at the start of the first induction stroke of the four-stroke cycle.

gas engine internal-combustion engine in which a gas (coal gas, producer gas, natural gas, or gas from a blast furnace) is used as the fuel.

The first practical gas engine was built in 1860 by Jean Etienne Lenoir, and the type was subsequently developed by Nikolaus August Otto, who introduced the four-stroke cycle.

gear toothed wheel that transmits the turning movement of one shaft to another shaft. Gear wheels may be used in pairs, or in threes if both shafts are to turn in the same direction. The gear ratio – the ratio of the number of teeth on the two wheels – determines the torque ratio, the turning force on the output shaft compared with the turning force on the input shaft. The ratio of the angular velocities of the shafts is the inverse of the gear ratio.

ignition coil transformer that is an essential part of a petrol engine's ignition system. It consists of two wire coils wound around an iron core. The primary coil, which is connected to the car battery, has only a few turns. The secondary coil, connected via the distributor to the spark plugs, has many turns. The coil takes in a low voltage (usually 12 volts) from the battery and transforms it to a high voltage (about 15,000–20,000 volts) to ignite the engine.

internal-combustion engine heat engine in which fuel is burned inside the engine, contrasting with an external-combustion engine (such as the steam engine) in which fuel is burned in a separate unit. The diesel engine and petrol engine are both internal-combustion engines. Gas turbines and jet and rocket engines are also considered to be internal-combustion engines because they burn their fuel inside their combustion chambers.

linear motor type of electric motor, an induction motor in which the fixed stator and moving armature are straight and parallel to each other (rather than being circular and one inside the other as in an ordinary induction motor). Linear motors are used, for example, to power sliding doors. There is a magnetic force between the stator and armature; this force has been used to support a vehicle, as in the experimental maglev linear motor train.

magneto simple electric generator, often used to provide the electricity for the ignition system of motorcycles and used in early cars. It consists of a rotating magnet that sets up an electric current in a coil, providing the spark.

moped lightweight motorcycle with pedals. Early mopeds (like the autocycle) were like motorized bicycles, using the pedals to start the bike and assist propulsion uphill. The pedals have little function in many mopeds today.

motor anything that produces or imparts motion; a machine that provides mechanical power – for example, an electric motor. Machines that burn fuel (petrol, diesel) are usually called engines, but the internal-combustion engine that propels vehicles has long been called a motor, hence 'motoring' and 'motorcar'. Actually the motor is a part of the car engine.

motorcycle or **motorbike** two-wheeled vehicle propelled by a petrol engine. The first successful motorized bicycle was built in France in 1901, and British and US manufacturers first produced motorbikes 1903.

motorway main road for fast motor traffic, with two or more lanes in each direction, and with special access points (junctions) fed by slip roads. The first motorway (85 km/53 mi) ran from Milan to Varese, Italy, and was completed in 1924; by 1939 some 500 km/300 mi of motorway (*autostrada*) had been built, although these did not attain the standards of later express highways. In Germany some 2,100 km/1,310 mi of *Autobahnen* had been completed by 1942. After World War II motorways were built in a growing number of countries, including the USA, France, and the UK. The most ambitious building

Countries That Drive on the Left

Anguilla	Grenada	Montserrat	South Africa
Antigua	Guyana	Mozambique	Sri Lanka
Australia	Hong Kong	Namibia	Surinam
Bahamas	India	Nepal	Swaziland
Bangladesh	Indonesia	New Zealand	Tanzania
Barbados	Ireland (Republic of)	Norfolk Island	Thailand
Bermuda	Jamaica	Pakistan	Tonga
Bhutan	Japan	Papua New Guinea	Trinidad and Tobago
Botswana	Kenya	St Christopher-Nevis	Tuvalu
Brunei	Kiribati	St Lucia	Uganda
Cook Islands	Lesotho	St Vincent	UK (including Guernsey,
Cyprus	Malaysia	Seychelles	Jersey and the Isle of Man)
Dominica	Malawi	Singapore	Virgin Islands (British)
Falkland Islands	Malta	Solomon Islands	Zambia
Fiji Islands	Mauritius	Somalia	Zimbabwe

programme was in the USA, which by 1974 had 70,800 km/44,000 mi of 'expressway'. Construction of new motorways causes much environmental concern.

petrol engine the most commonly used source of power for motor vehicles, introduced by the German engineers Gottlieb Daimler and Karl Benz in 1885. The petrol engine is a complex piece of machinery made up of about 150 moving parts. It is a reciprocating piston engine, in which a number of pistons move up and down in cylinders. A mixture of petrol and air is introduced to the space above the pistons and ignited. The gases produced force the pistons down, generating power. The engine-operating cycle is repeated every four strokes (upward or downward movement) of the piston, this being known as the four-stroke cycle. The motion of the pistons rotate a crankshaft, at the end of which is a heavy flywheel. From the flywheel the power is transferred to the car's driving wheels via the transmission system of clutch, gearbox, and final drive.

road specially constructed route for wheeled vehicles to travel on.

Reinforced tracks became necessary with the invention of wheeled vehicles in about 3000 BC and most ancient civilizations had some form of road network. The Romans developed engineering techniques that were not equalled for another 1,400 years.

shock absorber any device for absorbing the shock of sudden jarring actions or movements. Shock absorbers are used in conjunction with coil springs in most motor-vehicle suspension systems and are usually of the telescopic type, consisting of a piston in an oil-filled cylinder. The resistance to movement of the piston through the oil creates the absorbing effect.

spark plug plug that produces an electric spark in the cylinder of a petrol engine to ignite the fuel mixture. It consists essentially of two electrodes insulated from one another. High-voltage (18,000 V) electricity is fed to a central electrode via the distributor. At the base of the electrode, inside the cylinder, the electricity jumps to another electrode earthed to the engine body, creating a spark.

speedometer instrument attached to the transmission of a vehicle by a flexible drive shaft, which indicates the speed of the vehicle in miles or kilometres per hour on a dial easily visible to the driver.

stabilizer one of a pair of fins fitted to the sides of a ship, especially one governed automatically by a gyroscope mechanism, designed to reduce side-to-side rolling of the ship in rough weather.

tunnel passageway through a mountain, under a body of water, or underground. Tunnelling is a significant branch of civil engineering in both mining and transport. The difficulties naturally increase with the size, length, and depth of tunnel, but with the mechanical appliances now available no serious limitations are imposed. Granite or other hard rock presents little

The Longest Vehicular Tunnels in the World

Tunnel	Location	Year opened	Length km	mi
Saint Gotthard	Switzerland	1980	16.3	10.1
Arlberg	Austria	1978	14.0	8.7
Fréjus	France–Italy	1980	12.9	8.0
Mont Blanc	France–Italy	1965	11.7	7.3
Gran Sasso	Italy	1976	10.0	6.2
Seelisberg	Switzerland	1979	9.3	5.8
Mount Ena	Japan	1976	8.5	5.3
Rokko 11	Japan	1974	6.9	4.3
San Bernardino	Switzerland	1967	6.6	4.1
Tauren	Austria	1974	6.4	4.0

difficulty to modern power drills. In recent years there have been notable developments in linings (for example, concrete segments and steel liner plates), and in the use of rotary diggers and cutters and explosives.

turbocharger turbine-driven device fitted to engines to force more air into the cylinders, producing extra power. The turbocharger consists of a 'blower', or compressor, driven by a turbine, which in most units is driven by the exhaust gases leaving the engine.

two-stroke cycle operating cycle for internal combustion piston engines. The engine cycle is completed after just two strokes (up or down) of the piston, which distinguishes it from the more common four-stroke cycle. Power mowers and lightweight motorcycles use two-stroke petrol engines, which are cheaper and simpler than four-strokes.

tyre US **tire** inflatable rubber hoop fitted round the rims of bicycle, car, and other road-vehicle wheels. The first pneumatic rubber tyre was patented in 1845 by the Scottish engineer Robert William Thomson (1822–73), but it was Scottish inventor John Boyd Dunlop of Belfast who independently reinvented pneumatic tyres for use with bicycles in 1888–89. The rubber for car tyres is hardened by vulcanization.

Car: Chronology

1769 Nicholas-Joseph Cugnot in France builds a steam tractor.

1801 Richard Trevithick builds a steam coach.

1860 Jean Etienne Lenoir builds a gas-fuelled internal-combustion engine.

1865 The British government passes the Red Flag Act, requiring a person to precede a 'horseless carriage' with a red flag.

1876 Nikolaus August Otto improves the gas engine, making it a practical power source.

1885 Gottlieb Daimler develops a successful lightweight petrol engine and fits it to a bicycle to create the prototype of the present-day motorcycle; Karl Benz fits his lightweight petrol engine to a three-wheeled carriage to pioneer the motorcar.

1886 Gottlieb Daimler fits his engine to a four-wheeled carriage to produce a four-wheeled motorcar.

1891 René Panhard and Emile Levassor establish the present design of cars by putting the engine in front.

1896 Frederick Lanchester introduces epicyclic gearing, which foreshadows automatic transmission.

1899 C Jenatzy breaks the 100-kph barrier in an electric car *La Jamais Contente* at Achères, France, reaching 105.85 kph/65.60 mph.

1901 The first Mercedes takes to the roads; it is the direct ancestor of the present car. Ransome Olds in the USA introduces mass production on an assembly line.

1904 Louis Rigolly breaks the 100 mph barrier, reaching 166.61 kph/103.55 mph in a Gobron-Brillé at Nice, France.

1906 Rolls-Royce introduces the Silver Ghost, which establishes the company's reputation for superlatively engineered cars.

1908 Henry Ford also uses assembly-line production to manufacture his celebrated

(continued)

Car: Chronology (continued)

Model T, nicknamed the Tin Lizzie because it uses light-weight steel sheet for the body.

1911 Cadillac introduces the electric starter and dynamo lighting.

1913 Ford introduces the moving conveyor belt to the assembly line, further accelerating production of the Model T.

1920 Duesenberg begins fitting four-wheel hydraulic brakes.

1922 The Lancia Lambda features unitary (all-in-one) construction and independent front suspension.

1927 Henry Segrave breaks the 200 mph barrier in a Sunbeam, reaching 327.89 kph/203.79 mph.

1928 Cadillac introduces the synchromesh gearbox, greatly facilitating gear changing.

1934 Citroên pioneers front-wheel drive in their 7CV model.

1936 Fiat introduces their baby car, the Topolino, 500 cc.

1938 Germany produces its 'people's car', the Volkswagen Beetle.

1948 Jaguar launches the XK120 sports car; Michelin introduced the radial-ply tyre; Goodrich produces the tubeless tyre.

1950 Dunlop announces the disc brake.

1951 Buick and Chrysler introduce power steering.

1952 Rover's gas-turbine car sets a speed record of 243 kph/152 mph.

1954 Carl Bosch introduces fuel injection for cars.

1955 Citroên produces the advanced DS-19 'shark-front' car with hydropneumatic suspension.

1957 Felix Wankel builds his first rotary petrol engine.

1959 BMC (now Rover) introduces the Issigonis-designed Mini, with front-wheel drive, transverse engine, and independent rubber suspension.

1965 US car manufacturers are forced to add safety features after the publication of Ralph Nader's *Unsafe at Any Speed*.

1966 California introduces legislation regarding air pollution by cars.

1970 American Gary Gabelich drives a rocket-powered car, *Blue Flame*, to a new record speed of 1,001.473 kph/622.287 mph.

1972 Dunlop introduces safety tyres, which seal themselves after a puncture.

1979 American Sam Barrett exceeds the speed of sound in the rocket-engined *Budweiser Rocket*, reaching 1,190.377 kph/ 739.666 mph, a speed not officially recognized as a record because of timing difficulties.

1980 The first mass-produced car with four-wheel drive, the Audi Quattro, is introduced; Japanese car production overtakes that of the USA.

1981 BMW introduces the on-board computer, which monitors engine performance

and indicates to the driver when a service is required.

1983 British driver Richard Noble sets an official speed record in the jet-engined *Thrust 2* of 1,019.4 kph/633.5 mph; Austin Rover introduces the Maestro, the first car with a 'talking dashboard' that alerts the driver to problems.

1987 The solar-powered *Sunraycer* travels 3,000 km/1,864 mi from Darwin to Adelaide, Australia, in six days. Toyota Corona production tops 6 million in 29 years.

1988 California introduces stringent controls on car emissions, aiming for widespread use of zero emission vehicles by 1998.

1989 The first mass-produced car with four-wheel steering, the Mitsubishi Galant, is launched.

1990 Fiat of Italy and Peugeot of France launch electric passenger cars on the market.

1991 Satellite-based car navigation systems are launched in Japan. European Parliament votes to adopt stringent control of car emissions.

1992 Mazda and NEC of Japan develop an image-processing system for cars, which views the road ahead through a video camera, identifies road signs and markings, and helps the driver to avoid obstacles.

1993 A Japanese electric car, the *IZA*, built by the Tokyo Electric Power Company, reaches a speed of 176

Car: Chronology (continued)

kph/109 mph (10 kph/6 mph faster than the previous record for an electric car).
1995 Greenpeace designs its own environmentally friendly car to show the industry how 'it could be done'. It produces a modified Renault Twingo

with 30% less wind resistance, capable of doing 67–78 mi to the gallon (100 km per 3–3.5 litres).

1996 Daimler–Benz unveils the first fuel-cell-powered car. It is virtually pollution-free.

1997 RAF fighter pilot Andy Green breaks the sound barrier in *Thrust SCC*, a car with two Rolls-Royce Spey engines (the same kind used in RAF Phantom jets), setting a speed of 1,149.3 kph/714.1 mph.

WATER

bathyscaph or **bathyscaphe** or **bathyscape** deep-sea diving apparatus used for exploration at great depths in the ocean. In 1960, Jacques Piccard and Don Walsh took the bathyscaph *Trieste* to a depth of 10,917 m/35,820 ft in the Challenger Deep in the Mariana Trench off the island of Guam in the Pacific Ocean.

buoy floating object used to mark channels for shipping or warn of hazards to navigation. Buoys come in different shapes, such as a pole (spar buoy), cylinder (car buoy), and cone (nun buoy). Light buoys carry a small tower surmounted by a flashing lantern, and bell buoys house a bell, which rings as the buoy moves up and down with the waves. Mooring buoys are heavy and have a ring on top to which a ship can be tied.

canal artificial waterway constructed for drainage, irrigation, or navigation. **Irrigation canals** carry

Canals and Waterways

name	country	opened	length (km/mi)
Amsterdam	Netherlands	1876	26.6/16.5
Baltic–Volga	Russian Federation, Belarus, Ukraine	1964	2,430/1,510
Baltic–White Sea	Russian Federation	1933	235/146
Corinth	Greece	1893	6.4/4
Elbe and Trave	Germany	1900	66/41
Erie	USA	1825	580/360
Göta	Sweden	1832	185/115
Grand Canal	China	485 BC–AD 1972	1,050/650
Kiel	Germany	1895	98/61
Manchester	England	1894	57/35.5
Panama	Panama (US zone)	1914	81/50.5
Princess Juliana	Netherlands	1935	32/20
St Lawrence	Canada	1959	3,770/2,342
Sault Ste Marie	USA	1855	2.6/1.6
Sault Ste Marie	Canada	1895	1.8/1.1
Welland	Canada	1929	45/28
Suez	Egypt	1869	166/103

water for irrigation from rivers, reservoirs, or wells, and are designed to maintain an even flow of water over the whole length. **Navigation and ship canals** are constructed at one level between locks, and frequently link with rivers or sea inlets to form a waterway system. The Suez Canal in 1869 and the Panama Canal in 1914 eliminated long trips around continents and dramatically shortened shipping routes.

catamaran (Tamil 'tied log') twin-hulled sailing vessel, based on the native craft of South America and the Indies, made of logs lashed together, with an outrigger. A similar vessel with three hulls is known as a trimaran. Car ferries with a wave-piercing catamaran design are also in use in parts of Europe and North America. They have a pointed main hull and two outriggers and travel at a speed of 35 knots (84.5 kph/52.5 mph).

echo sounder or **sonar device** device that detects objects under water by means of sonar – by using reflected sound waves. Most boats are equipped with echo sounders to measure the water depth beneath them. An echo sounder consists of a transmitter, which emits an ultrasonic pulse, and a receiver, which detects the pulse after reflection from the seabed. The time between transmission and receipt of the reflected signal is a measure of the depth of water. Fishing boats use echo

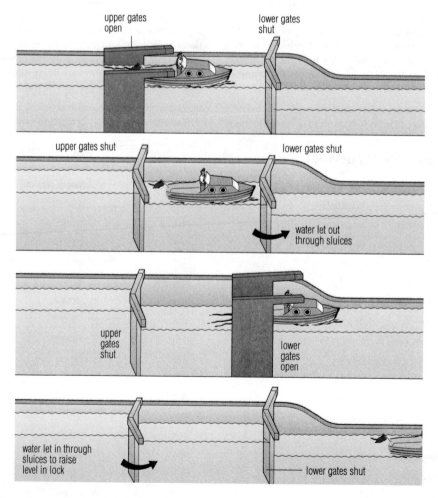

lock Travelling downstream, a boat enters the lock with the lower gates closed. The upper gates are then shut and the water level lowered by draining through sluices. When the water level in the lock reaches the downstream level, the lower gates are opened.

sounders to detect shoals of fish and navies use them to find enemy submarines.

hovercraft vehicle that rides on a cushion of high-pressure air, free from all contact with the surface beneath, invented by British engineer Christopher Cockerell in 1959. Hovercraft need a smooth terrain when operating overland and are best adapted to use on waterways. They are useful in places where harbours have not been established.

hydrofoil wing that develops lift in the water in much the same way that an aeroplane wing develops lift in the air. A hydrofoil boat is one whose hull rises out of the water owing to the lift, and the boat skims along on the hydrofoils. The first hydrofoil was fitted to a boat 1906. The first commercial hydrofoil went into operation 1956. One of the most advanced hydrofoil boats is the Boeing jetfoil. Hydrofoils are now widely used for fast island ferries in calm seas.

jetfoil advanced type of hydrofoil boat built by Boeing, propelled by water jets. It features horizontal, fully submerged hydrofoils fore and aft and has a sophisticated computerized control system to maintain its stability in all waters

locks allow boats or ships to travel from one level to another in waterways . The earliest form, the

flash lock, was first seen in the East in 1st-century-AD China and in the West in 11th-century Holland. By this method barriers temporarily dammed a river and when removed allowed the flash flood to propel the waiting boat through or over any obstacle. This was followed in 12th-century China and 14th-century Holland by the **pound lock.** In this system the lock has gates at each end. Boats enter through one gate when the levels are the same both outside and inside. Water is then allowed in (or out of) the lock until the level rises (or falls) to the new level outside the other gate.

Locks are important to shipping where canals link oceans of differing levels, such as the Panama Canal, or where falls or rapids are replaced by these adjustable water 'steps'.

merchant navy the passenger and cargo ships of a country. Most are owned by private companies. To avoid strict regulations on safety, union rules on crew wages, and so on, many ships are today registered under 'flags of convenience', that is, flags of countries that do not have such rules.

navigation the science and technology of finding the position, course, and distance travelled by a ship, plane, or other craft. Traditional methods include the magnetic compass and sextant. Today the gyrocompass is usually used, together with highly sophisticated electronic methods,

Merchant Fleets of the World

Source: Marine Administration, US Department of Transportation

1997

Country of registry	Total number of ships[1]	Number of combination passenger and cargo ships	Number of general cargo ships	Number of bulk carriers	Number of tankers
Antigua and Barbuda	378	0	264	9	11
Bahamas	954	47	443	142	241
Brazil	188	1	31	53	83
Bulgaria	105	1	44	34	14
China: mainland	1,513	33	791	354	233
Cyprus	1,476	18	610	555	165
Denmark	315	0	163	11	71
Egypt	110	1	69	18	14

(continued)

Merchant Fleets of the World (continued)

Country of registry	Total number of ships[1]	Number of combination passenger and cargo ships	Number of general cargo ships	Number of bulk carriers	Number of tankers
Germany	404	11	172	1	31
Greece	874	19	132	406	286
Honduras	256	3	208	10	28
Hong Kong	223	0	45	124	15
India	305	2	64	140	83
Indonesia	446	9	287	18	118
Iran	123	0	45	47	28
Italy	352	17	503	36	194
Japan	744	15	148	162	299
Korea, South	449	0	151	124	105
Liberia	1,587	38	269	461	642
Malaysia	303	0	121	50	96
Malta	1,113	9	441	337	265
Netherlands	4,454	9	302	8	71
Norway (NIS)	626	14	177	102	285
Panama	3,988	54	1,528	1,086	893
Philippines	534	6	199	232	65
Poland	125	1	47	69	4
Romania	223	0	161	39	12
Russia	1,655	10	1,203	129	271
St Vincent and the Grenadines	683	1	420	121	99
Singapore	753	1	166	126	331
Spain	81	0	29	1	16
Sweden	198	4	88	10	88
Taiwan	202	0	40	55	19
Thailand	288	1	160	35	82
Turkey	516	7	238	177	74
UK	140	20	27	6	60
Ukraine	415	8	326	21	29
USA	495	15	147	15	173
Vanuatu	98	0	48	32	12
World total	26,858	427	11,471	5,694	6,384

[1] This total includes other ships and is not simply a total of all ships accounted for in this table.

employing beacons of radio signals, such as Decca, Loran, and Omega. Satellite navigation uses satellites that broadcast time and position signals.

port point where goods are loaded or unloaded from a water-based to a land-based form of transport. Most ports are coastal, though inland ports on rivers also exist. Ports often have specialized equipment to handle cargo in large quantities (for example, container or roll-on/roll-off facilities).

ship large seagoing vessel. The Greeks, Phoenicians, Romans, and Vikings used ships extensively for trade, exploration, and warfare. The 14th century was the era of European exploration by sailing ship, largely aided by the invention of the compass. In the 15th century Britain's Royal Navy was first formed, but in the 16th–19th centuries Spanish and Dutch fleets dominated the shipping lanes of both the Atlantic and Pacific.

The ultimate sailing ships, the fast US and British tea clippers, were built in the 19th century. Also in the 19th century, iron was first used for some shipbuilding instead of wood. Steam-propelled ships of the late 19th century were followed by compound engine and turbine-propelled vessels from the early 20th century.

sonar acronym for **sound navigation and ranging,** method of locating underwater objects by the reflection of ultrasonic waves. The time taken for an acoustic beam to travel to the object and back to the source enables the distance to be found since the velocity of sound in water is known. Sonar devices, or **echo sounders,** were developed in 1920, and are the commonest means of underwater navigation.

submarine underwater warship. The first underwater boat was constructed in 1620 for James I of England by the Dutch scientist Cornelius van Drebbel (1572–1633). A naval submarine, or submersible torpedo boat, the *Gymnote,* was launched by France in 1888. The conventional submarine of World War I was driven by diesel engine on the surface and by battery-powered electric motors underwater.

The diesel engine also drove a generator that produced electricity to charge the batteries.

submersible vessel designed to operate under water, especially a small submarine used by engineers and research scientists as a ferry craft to support diving operations. The most advanced submersibles are the so-called lock-out type, which have two compartments: one for the pilot, the other to carry divers. The diving compartment is pressurized and provides access to the sea.

triangulation technique used in surveying and navigation to determine distances, using the properties of the triangle. To begin, surveyors measure a certain length exactly to provide a base line. From each end of this line they then measure the angle to a distant point, using a theodolite. They now have a triangle in which they know the length of one side and the two adjacent angles. By simple trigonometry they can work out the lengths of the other two sides.

Notable Shipwrecks and Disappearances

Date	Vessel	Location	Fatalities
Atlantic Ocean and Surrounding Seas			
22 August 1711	eight English transports	wrecked in storm at Egg Island, Labrador	around 2,000
6 September 1776	100 merchant vessels	wrecked by hurricane at Point Bay, Martinique	around 6,000
9 October 1780	seven Dutch ships	wrecked by hurricane at St Eustatius, Lesser Antilles	around 5,000
22 December 1810	*Minotaur,* British frigate	lost off a reef off the coast of the Netherlands	570
12 September 1857	*Central America,* American mail steamship	sank off Florida coast	427
25 March 1865	*General Lyon,* steamship	caught fire off Cape Hatteras, North Carolina	400
5 November 1872	*Marie Celeste,* US half-brig	abandoned in the Atlantic Ocean	unknown
1 April 1873	*Atlantic,* British steamer	wrecked off Nova Scotia, Canada	585
17 March 1891	*Utopia,* liner, and a battleship	collided in the Bay of Gibraltar	576

(*continued*)

Notable Shipwrecks and Disappearances (continued)

Date	Vessel	Location	Fatalities
28 June 1904	*Norge*, Danish steamer	wrecked on Rockall Island, Scotland	651
14–15 April 1912	*Titanic*, British steamer	sank after hitting iceberg in the North Atlantic	1,517
7 May 1915	*Lusitania*, British steamer	torpedoed and sunk by German submarine off Ireland	1,198
9 July 1917	*Vanguard*, British battleship	Scapa Flow, Scotland	804
6 December 1917	*Mont Blanc*, French ammunition ship, and *Imo*, Belgian steamer	collided in Halifax Harbor, Canada	1,600
9 September 1919	*Valbanera*, Spanish steamer	lost off Florida coast	500
16 April 1947	*Grandcamp*, French freighter	exploded in Texas City (TX), USA	510
6 March 1987	*Herald of Free Enterprise*, British ferry	capsized off Zeebrugge, Belgium	188
17 February 1993	*Neptune*, ferry	capsized off Port-au-Prince, Haiti	>500
28 September 1994	*Estonia*, ferry	sank in the Baltic Sea when water entered bow door	1,049

Indian Ocean and Surrounding Seas

Date	Vessel	Location	Fatalities
1 February 1807	*Blenheim*, 74-gun war ship	wrecked by hurricane near the island of Rodriguez	around 600
28 July 1909	*Waratah*, British steamer	vanished in Indian Ocean	300
December 1944	3 US Third Fleet destroyers	sank during typhoon in the Philippine Sea	790
14 December 1991	*Salem Express*, ferry	rammed coral reef off Egyptian coast	462

Mediterranean Sea

Date	Vessel	Location	Fatalities
17 March 1800	*Queen Charlotte*, British frigate	burned off Livorno, Italy	700
17 March 1891	*Utopia*, British steamer, and *Anson*, British ironclad	collided off Gibraltar coast	562
26 February 1916	*Provence*, French cruiser	sank in the Mediterranean sea	3,100
17 January 1919	*Chaonia*, French steamer	lost in the Straits of Messina, Italy	460

Pacific Ocean and Surrounding Seas

Date	Vessel	Location	Fatalities
4 August 1846	*Cataraqui*, immigrant ship	ran aground in a storm in the Bass Strait between Australia and Tasmania	414
4 November 1875	*Pacific*, US steamer	sank after collision off Cape Flattery (WA), USA	236
19 September 1890	*Ertogrul*, Turkish frigate	foundered off Japan	587
28 September 1912	*Kichemaru*, Japanese steamer	sank off Japanese coast	1,000
29 August 1916	*Hsin Yu*, Chinese steamer	sank off Chinese coast	1,000
25 April 1918	*Kiang-Kwan*, Chinese steamer	sank after collision off Hankow, China	500
12 July 1918	*Kawachi*, Japanese battleship	blew up in Tokayama Bay, Japan	500
18 March 1921	*Hong Koh*, steamer	sank near Swatow	1,000
3 December 1948	*Kiangya*, Chinese refugee ship	wrecked in explosion south of Shanghai, China	>1,100
November 1949	Chinese army evacuation ship	exploded and sank off South Manchuria	6,000
26 September 1954	*Toyo Maru*, Japanese ferry	sank in Tsugaru Strait, Japan	2,750
27 January 1981	*Tamponas II*, Indonesian passenger ship	caught fire and sank in the Java Sea	580
20 December 1987	*Dona Paz*, Philippine ferry, and *Victor*, oil tanker	collided in the Tablas Strait, Philippines	3,000

World Waterways and Rivers

Date	Vessel	Location	Fatalities
26–27 April 1865	*Sultana*, US side-wheeled steamer	exploded and burned near Memphis, Tennessee	>1,500
3 September 1878	*Princess Alice*, British steamer	sank after collision in the River Thames, UK	645

Notable Shipwrecks and Disappearances (continued)

Date	Vessel	Location	Fatalities
15 June 1904	*General Slocum*, excursion steamer	burned in Hudson River, New York (NY), USA	1,030
29 May 1914	*Empress of Ireland*, British steamer, and Norwegian collier	collided in St Lawrence River, Canada	1,014
24 July 1915	*Eastland*, excursion steamer	capsized in Chicago River	852
6 August 1988	Indian ferry	capsized on the Ganges River, India	>400
20 August 1989	*Bowbelle*, British barge, and *Marchioness*, British pleasure cruiser	collided on the River Thames, UK	56
21 May 1996	*Bukoba*, ferry	sank in Lake Victoria, Uganda, Kenya, and Tanzania	500

Ships: Chronology

8000–7000 BC Reed boats are developed in Mesopotamia and Egypt; dugout canoes are used in northwest Europe.

4000–3000 The Egyptians use single-masted square-rigged ships on the Nile.

1200 The Phoenicians build keeled boats with hulls of wooden planks.

1st century BC The Chinese invent the rudder.

200–300 The Arabs and Romans develop fore-and-aft rigging that allows boats to sail across the direction of wind.

800–900 Square-rigged Viking longboats cross the North Sea to Britain, the Faroe Islands, and Iceland.

1090 The Chinese invent the magnetic compass.

1400–1500 Three-masted ships are developed in western Europe, stimulating voyages of exploration.

1620 Dutch engineer Cornelius Drebbel invents the submarine.

1777 The first boat with an iron hull is built, in Yorkshire, England.

1783 Frenchman Jouffroy d'Abbans builds the first paddle-driven steamboat.

1802 Scottish engineer William Symington launches the first stern paddle-wheel steamer, the *Charlotte Dundas*.

1807 The first successful steamboat, the *Clermont*, designed by US engineer and inventor Robert Fulton, sails between New York and Albany.

1836 The screw propeller is patented, by Francis Pettit Smith in the UK.

1838 British engineer Isambard Kingdom Brunel's *Great Western*, the first steamship built for crossing the Atlantic, sails from Bristol to New York in 15 days.

1845 The first clipper ship, *Rainbow*, is launched in the USA.

1863 *Plongeur*, the first submarine powered by an air-driven engine, is launched in France.

1866 The British clippers *Taeping* and *Ariel* sail, laden with tea, from China to London in 99 days.

1886 German engineer Gottlieb Daimler builds the first boat powered by an internal-combustion engine.

1897 English engineer Charles Parson fits a steam turbine to *Turbinia*, making it the fastest boat of the time.

1902 The French ship *Petit-Pierre* becomes the first boat to be powered by a diesel engine.

1955 The first nuclear-powered submarine, *Nautilus*, is built in the USA; the hovercraft is patented by British inventor Christopher Cockerell.

1959 The first nuclear-powered surface ship, the Soviet ice-breaker *Lenin*, is commissioned; the US *Savannah* becomes the first nuclear-powered merchant (passenger and cargo) ship.

1980 Launch of the first wind-assisted commercial ship for half a century, the Japanese tanker *Shin-Aitoku-Maru*.

Ships: Chronology (continued)

1983 German engineer Ortwin Fries invents a hinged ship designed to bend into a V-shape in order to scoop up oil spillages in its jaws.

1990 *Hoverspeed Great Britain*, a wave-piercing catamaran, crosses the Atlantic in 3 days, 7 hours, and 52 minutes, setting a record for the fastest crossing by a passenger vessel. The world's largest car and passenger ferry, the *Silja Serenade*, enters service between Stockholm and Helsinki, carrying 2,500 passengers and 450 cars.

1992 Japanese propellerless ship *Yamato* driven by magnetohydrodynamics completes its sea trials. The ship uses magnetic forces to suck in and eject sea water like a jet engine.

1997 The biggest cruise ship ever, the *Carnival Destiny*, is launched. It is as long as three football pitches, taller than the Statue of Liberty, and too wide to pass through the Panama Canal.

COMPUTING

———————— ✳ ————————

A computer is a programmable electronic device that processes data and performs calculations and other symbol manipulation tasks. There are three types: the **digital computer**, which manipulates information coded as binary numbers (the digits 0 and 1, representing two different signals, on and off, with an individual digit being known as a binary digit or bit); the **analogue computer**, which works with continuously varying quantities; and the **hybrid computer**, which has characteristics of both analogue and digital computers.

The first mechanical computer was conceived by Charles Babbage in 1835. He designed a general-purpose mechanical computing device for performing different calculations according to a program input on punched cards. In the 1880s Herman Hollerith devised the first device for high-volume data processing, a mechanical tabulating machine. In 1943 Thomas Flowers built Colossus, the first electronic computer. John Von Neumann's computer, EDVAC, built in 1949, was the first to use binary arithmetic and to store its operating instructions internally. His design still forms the basis of today's computers.

COMPUTER ARCHITECTURE

application program or job designed for the benefit of the end user. Examples of **general purpose** application programs include word processors, desktop publishing programs, databases, spreadsheet packages, and graphics programs (see CAD and CAM). **Application-specific** programs include payroll and stock control systems. Applications may also be **custom designed** to solve a specific problem, not catered for in other types of application.

The term is used to distinguish such programs from those that control the computer (systems programs) or assist the programmer, such as a compiler.

artificial intelligence (AI) branch of science concerned with creating computer programs that can perform actions comparable with those of an intelligent human. Current AI research covers such areas as planning (for robot behaviour), language understanding, pattern recognition, and knowledge representation.

baud unit of electrical signalling speed equal to one pulse per second, measuring the rate at which signals are sent between electronic devices such as telegraphs and computers; 300 baud is about 300 words a minute.

binary number system system of numbers to base two, using combinations of the digits 1 and 0. Codes based on binary numbers are used to represent instructions and data in all modern digital computers, the values of the binary digits (contracted to 'bits') being stored or transmitted as, for example, open/closed switches, magnetized/unmagnetized disks and tapes, and high/low voltages in circuits.

bit contraction of **binary digit** single binary digit, either 0 or 1. A bit is the smallest unit of data stored in a computer; all other data must be coded into a pattern of individual bits. A byte represents sufficient computer memory to store a single character of data, and usually contains eight bits. For example, in the ASCII code system used by most microcomputers the capital letter A would be stored in a single byte of memory as the bit pattern 01000001.

boot or **bootstrap** process of starting up a computer. Most computers have a small, built-in boot program that starts automatically when the computer is switched on – its only task is to load a slightly larger program, usually from a hard disk, which in turn loads the main operating system.

In microcomputers the operating system is often held in the permanent ROM memory and the boot program simply triggers its operation.

Number Systems

Decimal Number System (base 10)

In the decimal number system numbers can be seen as written under columns based on the number 10, for example 2,567 below.

1000s	100s	10s	1s
(10^3)	(10^2)	(10^1)	(10^0)
2	5	6	7

Binary Number System (base 2)

In the binary number system numbers can be seen as written under columns based on the number 2. The binary number 1101 corresponds to the decimal number 13.

8s	4s	2s	1s
(2^3)	(2^2)	(2^1)	(2^0)
1	1	0	1

Octal Number System (base 8)

In the octal number system numbers can be seen as written under columns based on the number 8. The octal number 2,164 corresponds to the decimal number 1,140.

512s	64s	8s	1s
(8^3)	(8^2)	(8^1)	(8^0)
2	1	6	4

Hexadecimal Number System (base 16)

In the hexadecimal number system numbers can be seen as written under columns based on the number 16. Since digits up to a value of decimal 15 are permitted, the letters A to F are used to represent digits corresponding to decimal 10 to 15. The hexadecimal number 23BF corresponds to the decimal number 9,151.

4096s	256s	16s	1s
(16^3)	(16^2)	(16^1)	(16^0)
2	3	B	F

bug error in a program. It can be an error in the logical structure of a program or a syntax error, such as a spelling mistake. Some bugs cause a program to fail immediately; others remain dormant, causing problems only when a particular combination of events occurs. The process of finding and removing errors from a program is called **debugging.**

byte sufficient computer memory to store a single character of data. The character is stored in the byte of memory as a pattern of bits (binary digits), using a code such as ASCII. A byte usually contains eight bits – for example, the capital letter F can be stored as the bit pattern 01000110.

CD-ROM abbreviation for **compact-disc read-only memory** computer storage device developed from the technology of the audio compact disc. It consists of a plastic-coated metal disk, on which binary digital information is etched in the form of microscopic pits. This can then be read optically by passing a laser beam over the disk. CD-ROMs typically hold about 650 megabytes of data, and are used in distributing large amounts of text, graphics, audio, and video, such as encyclopedias, catalogues, technical manuals, and games.

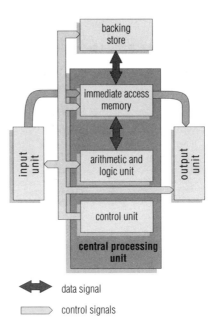

data signal

control signals

central processing unit The relationship between the three main areas of a computer's central processing unit. The arithmetic and logic unit (ALU) does the arithmetic, using the registers to store intermediate results, supervised by the control unit. Input and output circuits connect the ALU to external memory, input, and output devices.

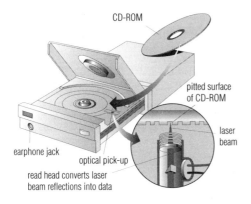

CD-ROM drive Data is obtained by the CD-ROM drive by converting the reflections from a disk's surface into digital form.

central processing unit (CPU) main component of a computer, the part that executes individual program instructions and controls the operation of other parts. It is sometimes called the central processor or, when contained on a single integrated circuit, a microprocessor.

charge-coupled device (CCD) device for forming images electronically, using a layer of silicon that releases electrons when struck by incoming light. The electrons are stored in pixels and read off into a computer at the end of the exposure. CCDs are used in digital cameras, and have now almost entirely replaced photographic film for applications such as astrophotography where extreme sensitivity to light is paramount.

chip or **silicon chip,** another name for an **integrated circuit** a complete electronic circuit on a slice of silicon (or other semiconductor) crystal only a few millimetres square.

client–server architecture system in which the mechanics of looking after data are separated from the programs that use the data. For example, the 'server' might be a central database, typically located on a large computer that is reserved for this purpose. The 'client' would be an ordinary program that requests data from the server as needed.

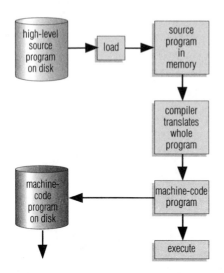

compiler The process of compilation; a program written in a high-level language is translated into a program that can be run without the original source being present.

compiler computer program that translates programs written in a high-level language into machine code (the form in which they can be run by the computer). The compiler translates each high-level instruction into several machine-code instructions – in a process called **compilation** – and produces a complete independent program that can be run by the computer as often as required, without the original source program being present.

CPU abbreviation for central processing unit.

data singular **datum** facts, figures, and symbols, especially as stored in computers. The term is often used to mean raw, unprocessed facts, as distinct from information, to which a meaning or interpretation has been applied.

database structured collection of data, which may be manipulated to select and sort desired items of information. For example, an accounting system might be built around a database containing

What is a computer?

Any programmable electronic device that processes data and performs calculations and other symbol-manipulation tasks can be called a computer. The first mechanical computer was conceived by English mathematician Charles Babbage in 1835. He designed an analytical engine, a general-purpose mechanical computing device for performing different calculations according to a program input on punched cards (an idea borrowed from the Jacquard loom). His device was never built, but it embodied many of the principles on which digital computers are based.

The US inventor Herman Hollerith devised the first device for high-volume data processing, a mechanical tabulating machine. Hollerith's tabulator was widely publicized after being successfully used in the 1890 census. The firm he established, the Tabulating Machine Company, was later one of the founding companies of IBM.

In 1943, more than a century after Babbage's analytical engine, Thomas Flowers (1905–98) built Colossus, the first electronic computer. Working with him at the time was Alan Turing, a mathematician who seven years earlier had published a paper on the

theory of computing machines that had a major impact on subsequent developments. John Von Neumann's computer, EDVAC, built in 1949, was the first to use binary arithmetic and to store its operating instructions internally. This design still forms the basis of today's computers.

types of computer Today, there are three types of computer: the **digital computer,** which manipulates information coded as binary numbers (see binary number system); the **analogue computer,** which works with continuously varying quantities; and the **hybrid computer,** which has characteristics of both analogue and digital computers.

There are four types of digital computer, corresponding roughly to their size and intended use. **Microcomputers** are the smallest and most common, used in small businesses, at home, and in schools. They are usually single-user machines. **Minicomputers** are found in medium-sized businesses and university departments. They may support from around 10 to 200 users at once. **Mainframes,** which can often service several hundred users simultaneously, are found in large

organizations, such as national companies and government departments. **Supercomputers** are mostly used for highly complex scientific tasks, such as analysing the results of nuclear physics experiments and weather forecasting.

Microcomputers now come in a range of sizes, from battery-powered pocket personal computers (PCs) and electronic organizers, notebook and laptop PCs, to floor-standing tower systems that may serve local area networks or work as minicomputers. Most minicomputers are now built using low-cost microprocessors, and large-scale computers built out of multiple microprocessors are starting to challenge traditional mainframe and supercomputer designs.

binary number code Instructions and data in all modern digital computers are represented by a binary number code, a code based on the binary number system. For example, in the ASCII code system used by most microcomputers, the capital letter A is represented by the binary number 01000001. Because binary numbers use only the digits 0 and 1, they can be represented by any device that can exist in two different states.

database table
containing customer details

data format
options

database
containing
customer
details

database An example of the type of information that may be stored on a database. The information may be stored in various formats, enabling it to be sorted and output to other software programs.

What is a computer? (continued)

In a digital computer several different two-state devices are used to store or transmit binary number codes – for example, circuits, which may or may not carry a voltage; disks or tapes, parts of which may or may not be magnetized; and switches, which may be open or closed. Digital computers are designed in this way for two reasons. Firstly, it is much easier and cheaper to construct two-state devices than devices that can exist in more than two states. Secondly, communication between two-state devices is very reliable because only two different signals, 0 or 1 (on or off), need to be recognized.

programming Computers are controlled by the input of instructions in various programming languages. In **procedural programming,** programs are written as lists of instructions for the computer to obey in sequence, and this is by far the most popular form of programming. **Declarative programming,** as used in the programming language PROLOG, does not describe how to solve a problem, but rather describes the logical structure of the problem. Running such a program is more like proving an assertion than following a

procedure. **Functional programming** is a style based largely on the definition of functions. There are very few functional programming languages, HOPE and ML being the most widely used, though many more conventional languages (for example C) make extensive use of functions. **Object-oriented programming,** the most recently developed style, involves viewing a program as a collection of objects that behave in certain ways when they are passed certain 'messages'. For example, an object might be defined to represent a table of figures, which will be displayed on screen when a 'display' message is received.

   Programming languages may be classified as high-level languages or low-level languages. A high-level programming language is designed to suit the requirements of the programmer; it is independent of the internal machine code of any particular computer. High-level languages are used to solve problems – for example, BASIC was designed to be easily learnt by first-time programmers; COBOL is used to write programs solving business problems; and FORTRAN is used for programs solving scientific and

mathematical problems. In contrast, low-level languages, such as assembly languages, closely reflect the machine code of specific computers.

basic components At the heart of a computer is the **central processing unit** (CPU), which executes individual program instructions and controls the operation of other parts. The CPU has three main components: the **arithmetic and logic unit** (ALU), where all calculations and logical operations are carried out; a **control unit,** which decodes, synchronizes, and executes program instructions; and the **immediate access memory,** which stores the data and programs on which the computer is currently working. All these components contain registers, which are memory locations reserved for specific purposes. A main power supply is needed and, for a mainframe or minicomputer, a cooling system. The computer's 'device driver' circuits control the peripheral devices that can be attached. These will normally be keyboards and VDUs (visual display units) for user input and output, disk drive units for mass memory storage, and printers.

details of customers and suppliers. In larger computers, the database makes data available to the various programs that need it, without the need for those programs to be aware of how the data are stored. The term is also sometimes used for simple record-keeping systems, such as mailing lists, in which there are facilities for searching, sorting, and producing records.

data compression techniques for reducing the amount of storage needed for a given amount of data. They include word tokenization (in which frequently used words are stored as shorter codes), variable bit lengths (in which common characters are represented by fewer bits than less common ones), and run-length encoding (in which a repeated value is stored once along with a count).

desktop publishing (DTP) use of microcomputers for small-scale typesetting and page makeup. DTP systems are capable of producing camera-ready pages (pages ready for photographing and printing), made up of text and graphics, with text set in different typefaces and sizes. The page can be previewed on the screen before final printing on a laser printer.

disk drive mechanical device that reads data from, and writes data to, a magnetic disk.

DOS acronym for **disk operating system** computer operating system specifically designed for use with disk storage; also used as an alternative name for a particular operating system, MS-DOS.

DTP abbreviation for **desktop publishing.**

EPROM acronym for **erasable programmable read-only memory** computer memory device in the form of an integrated circuit (chip) that can record data and retain it indefinitely. The data can be erased by exposure to ultraviolet light, and new data recorded. Other kinds of computer memory chips are ROM (read-only memory), PROM (programmable read-only memory), and RAM (random-access memory).

error fault or mistake, either in the software or on the part of the user, that causes a program to stop running (crash) or produce unexpected results. Program errors, or bugs, are largely eliminated in the course of the programmer's initial testing procedure, but some will remain in most programs. All computer operating systems are designed to produce an **error message** (on the display screen, or in an error file or printout) whenever an error is detected, reporting that an error has taken place and, wherever possible, diagnosing its cause.

fifth-generation computer anticipated new type of computer based on emerging microelectronic technologies with high computing speeds and parallel processing. The development of very large-scale integration (VLSI) technology, which can put many more circuits on to an integrated circuit (chip) than is currently possible, and developments in computer hardware and

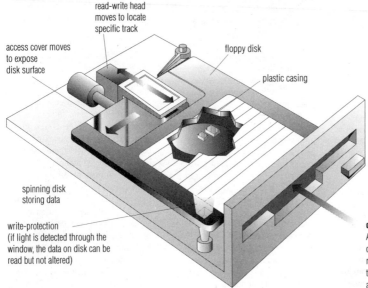

read-write head
moves to locate
specific track

access cover moves
to expose
disk surface

floppy disk

plastic casing

spinning disk
storing data

write-protection
(if light is detected through the
window, the data on disk can be
read but not altered)

disk drive A floppy disk drive. As the disk is inserted into the drive, its surface is exposed to the read-write head, which moves over the spinning disk surface to locate a specific track.

software design may produce computers far more powerful than those in current use.

floppy disk storage device consisting of a light, flexible disk enclosed in a cardboard or plastic jacket. The disk is placed in a disk drive, where it rotates at high speed. Data are recorded magnetically on one or both surfaces.

gigabyte measure of memory capacity, equal to 1,024 megabytes. It is also used, less precisely, to mean 1,000 billion bytes.

Which disk is which?

A **disk** is a common medium for storing large volumes of data (an alternative is magnetic tape). A **magnetic disk** is rotated at high speed in a disk-drive unit as a read/write (playback or record) head passes over its surfaces to record or read the magnetic variations that encode the data. Recently, **optical disks,** such as CD-ROM (compact-disc read-only memory) and WORM (write once, read many times), have been used to store computer data. Data are recorded on the disk surface as etched microscopic pits and are read by a laser-scanning device. Optical disks have an enormous capacity – about 550 megabytes (million bytes) on a compact disc, and thousands of megabytes on a full-size optical disk.

Magnetic disks come in several forms: **fixed hard disks** are built into the disk-drive unit, occasionally stacked on top of one another. A fixed disk cannot be removed: once it is full, data must be deleted in order to free space or a complete new disk drive must be added to the computer system in order to increase storage capacity. Small hard drives typically store 2,000 megabytes or 2 gigabytes (GB) of data, but can store up to 9 GB or more. Arrays of such disks are also used to store minicomputer and mainframe data in RAID storage systems, replacing large fixed disks and removable hard disks.

Removable hard disks are still found in minicomputer and mainframe systems. The disks are contained, individually or as stacks (disk packs), in a protective plastic case, and can be taken out of the drive unit and kept for later use. By swapping such disks around, a single hard-disk drive can be made to provide a potentially infinite storage capacity. However, access speeds and capacities tend to be lower than those associated with large fixed hard disks. A **floppy disk** (or diskette) is the most common form of backing store for microcomputers. It is much smaller in size and capacity than a hard disk, normally holding 0.5–2 megabytes of data. The floppy disk is so called because it is manufactured from thin flexible plastic coated with a magnetic material. The earliest form of floppy disk was packaged in a card case and was easily damaged; more recent versions are contained in a smaller, rigid plastic case and are much more robust. All floppy disks can be removed from the drive unit.

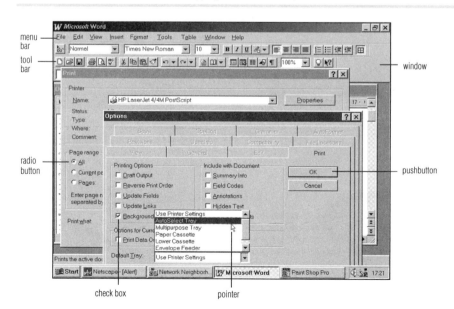

graphical user interface A typical graphical user interface (GUI), where the user moves around the system by clicking on representative buttons or icons using the mouse.

graphical user interface (GUI) type of user interface in which programs and files appear as icons (small pictures), user options are selected from pull-down menus, and data are displayed in windows (rectangular areas), which the operator can manipulate in various ways. The operator uses a pointing device, typically a mouse, to make selections and initiate actions. *See illustration on page 261.*

hard disk storage device usually consisting of a rigid metal disk coated with a magnetic material. Data are read from and written to the disk by means of a disk drive. The hard disk may be permanently fixed into the drive or in the form of a disk pack that can be removed and exchanged with a different pack. Hard disks vary from large units with capacities of more than 3,000 megabytes, intended for use with mainframe computers, to small units with capacities as low as 20 megabytes, intended for use with microcomputers.

Hardware

The term **hardware** refers to a computer's mechanical, electrical, and electronic components, as opposed to its various programs, which constitute software. Hardware associated with a microcomputer might include the power supply and housing of its processor unit, its circuit boards, VDU (screen), disk drive, keyboard, and printer.

hexadecimal number system or **hex,** number system to the base 16, used in computing. In hex the decimal numbers 0–15 are represented by the characters 0, 1, 2, 3, 4, 5, 6, 7, 8, 9, A, B, C, D, E, F.

Hexadecimal numbers are easy to convert to the computer's internal binary code and are more compact than binary numbers.

icon small picture on the computer screen, or VDU, representing an object or function that the user may manipulate or otherwise use. It is a

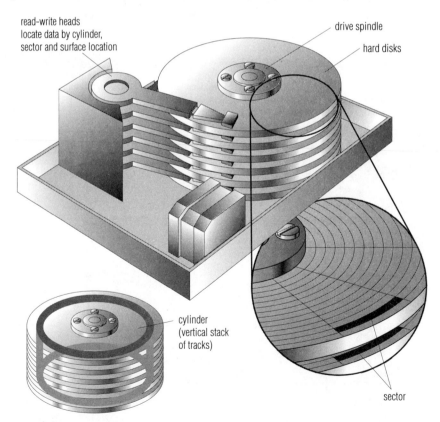

read-write heads
locate data by cylinder,
sector and surface location

drive spindle

hard disks

cylinder
(vertical stack
of tracks)

sector

hard disk On a hard disk data is stored in sectors within cylinders and is read by a head which passes over the spinning surface of each disk.

feature of graphical user interface (GUI) systems. Icons make computers easier to use by allowing the user to point to and click with a mouse on pictures, rather than type commands.

information technology (IT) collective term for the various technologies involved in processing and transmitting information. They include computing, telecommunications, and microelectronics.

input device device for entering information into a computer. Input devices include keyboards, joysticks, mice, light pens, touch-sensitive screens, scanners, graphics tablets, speech-recognition devices, and vision systems. Compare output device.

joystick input device that signals to a computer the direction and extent of displacement of a hand-held lever. It is similar to the joystick used to control the flight of an aircraft.

kilobyte (K or KB) unit of memory equal to 1,024 bytes. It is sometimes used, less precisely, to mean 1,000 bytes.

knowledge-based system (KBS) computer program that uses an encoding of human knowledge to help solve problems. It was discovered during research into artificial intelligence that adding heuristics (rules of thumb) enabled programs to tackle problems that were otherwise difficult to solve by the usual techniques of computer science.

laptop computer portable microcomputer, small enough to be used on the operator's lap. It consists of a single unit, incorporating a keyboard, floppy disk and hard disk drives, and a screen. The screen often forms a lid that folds back in use. It uses a liquid-crystal or gas-plasma display, rather than the bulkier and heavier cathode-ray tubes found in most display terminals. A typical laptop computer measures about 210 x 297 mm/8.3 x 11.7 in (A4), is 5 cm/2 in in depth, and weighs less than 3 kg/6 lb 9 oz. In the 1980s there were several types of laptop computer, but in the 1990s designs converged on systems known as notebook computers.

liquid-crystal display (LCD) display of numbers (for example, in a calculator) or pictures (such as on a pocket television screen) produced by molecules of a substance in a semiliquid state with some crystalline properties, so that clusters of molecules align in parallel formations. The display is a blank until the application of an electric field, which 'twists' the molecules so that they reflect or transmit light falling on them. The two main types of LCD are **passive matrix** and **active matrix.**

Macintosh range of microcomputers originally produced by Apple Computer. The Apple Macintosh, introduced in 1984, was the first popular microcomputer with a graphical user interface. The success of the Macintosh prompted other manufacturers and software companies to create their own graphical user interfaces. Most notable of these are Microsoft Windows, which runs on IBM PC-compatible microcomputers, and OSF/Motif, from the Open Software Foundation, which is used with many UNIX systems.

magnetic tape narrow plastic ribbon coated with an easily magnetizable material on which data can be recorded. It is used in sound recording, audiovisual systems (videotape), and computing. For mass storage on commercial mainframe computers, large reel-to-reel tapes are still used, but cartridges are becoming popular. Various types of cartridge are now standard on minis and PCs, while audio cassettes are sometimes used with home computers.

mainframe large computer used for commercial data processing and other large-scale operations. Because of the general increase in computing power, the differences between the mainframe, supercomputer, minicomputer, and microcomputer (personal computer) are becoming less marked. *See illustration on page 264.*

microcomputer small desktop or portable computer, typically designed to be used by one person at a time, although individual computers can be linked in a network so that users can share data and programs. Its central processing unit is a microprocessor, contained on a single integrated circuit.

microprocessor complete computer central processing unit contained on a single integrated circuit, or chip. The appearance of the first microprocessor in 1971 designed by Intel for a pocket calculator manufacturer heralded the introduction of the microcomputer. The microprocessor has led to a dramatic fall in the size and cost of computers, and dedicated computers can now be found in washing machines, cars, and so

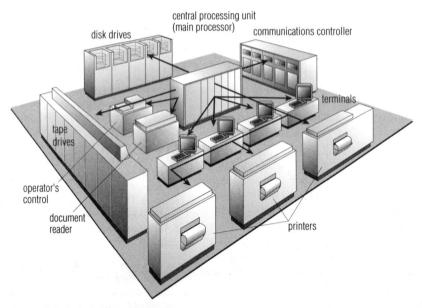

central processing unit
(main processor)

disk drives

communications controller

terminals

tape drives

operator's control

document reader

printers

mainframe A mainframe computer functionally has the same component parts as a microcomputer, but on a much larger scale. The central processing unit is at the hub, and controls all the attached devices.

on. Examples of microprocessors are the Intel Pentium family and the IBM/Motorola PowerPC, used by Apple Computer.

modem contraction of **modulator/demodulator** device for transmitting computer data over tele-

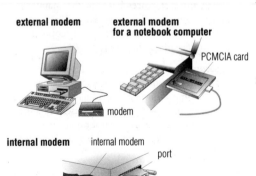

external modem

external modem for a notebook computer

PCMCIA card

modem

internal modem   internal modem

port

expansion slot

modem Modems are available in various forms: microcomputers may use an external device connected through a communications port, or an internal device, which takes the form of an expansion board inside the computer. Notebook computers use an external modem connected via a special interface card.

phone lines. Such a device is necessary because the digital signals produced by computers cannot, at present, be transmitted directly over the telephone network, which uses analogue signals. The modem converts the digital signals to analogue, and back again.

motherboard printed circuit board that contains the main components of a microcomputer. The power, memory capacity, and capability of the microcomputer may be enhanced by adding expansion boards to the motherboard.

mouse input device used to control a pointer on a computer screen. It is a feature of graphical user interface (GUI) systems. The mouse is about the size of a pack of playing cards, is connected to the computer by a wire, and incorporates one or more buttons that can be pressed. Moving the mouse across a flat surface causes a corresponding movement of the pointer. In this way, the operator can manipulate objects on the screen and make menu selections.

MS-DOS abbreviation for **Microsoft Disk Operating System** computer operating system produced by Microsoft Corporation, widely used on microcomputers with Intel x 86 and Pentium family microprocessors. A version called

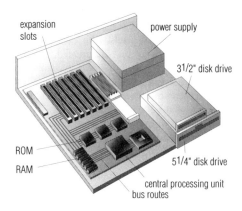

expansion slots

power supply

31/2" disk drive

ROM

RAM

51/4" disk drive

central processing unit
bus routes

motherboard The position of a motherboard within a computer's system unit. The motherboard contains the central processing unit, Random Access Memory (RAM) chips, Read-Only Memory (ROM), and a number of expansion slots.

PC-DOS is sold by IBM specifically for its personal computers. MS-DOS and PC-DOS are usually referred to as DOS. MS-DOS first appeared in 1981, and was similar to an earlier system from Digital Research called CP/M.

multimedia computerized method of presenting information by combining audio and video components using text, sound, and graphics (still, animated, and video sequences). For example, a multimedia database of musical instruments may allow a user not only to search and retrieve text about a particular instrument but also to see pictures of it and hear it play a piece of music. Multimedia applications emphasize interactivity between the computer and the user.

online system originally a system that allows the computer to work interactively with its users, responding to each instruction as it is given and prompting users for information when

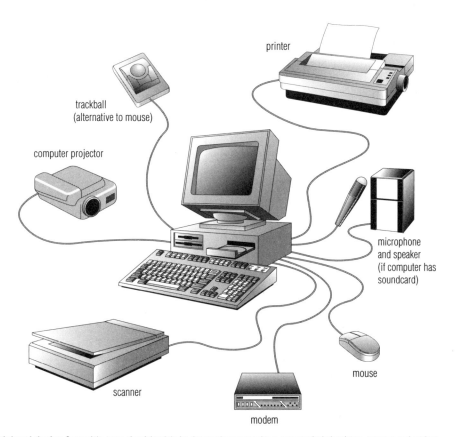

printer

trackball
(alternative to mouse)

computer projector

microphone
and speaker
(if computer has
soundcard)

scanner

modem

mouse

peripheral device Some of the types of peripheral device that may be connected to a computer include printers, scanners, and modems.

necessary. Since almost all the computers used now work this way, 'online system' is now used to refer to large database, electronic mail, and conferencing systems accessed via a dial-up modem. These often have tens or hundreds of users from different places – sometimes from different countries – 'on line' at the same time.

operating system (OS) program that controls the basic operation of a computer. A typical OS controls the peripheral devices such as printers, organizes the filing system, provides a means of communicating with the operator, and runs other programs.

output device any device for displaying, in a form intelligible to the user, the results of processing carried out by a computer.

parallel processing emerging computer technology that allows more than one computation at the same time.

parity of a number, the state of being either even or odd. In computing, the term refers to the number of 1s in the binary codes used to represent data. A binary representation has **even parity** if it contains an even number of 1s and **odd parity** if it contains an odd number of 1s.

peripheral device any item connected to a computer's central processing unit (CPU). Typical peripherals include keyboard, mouse, monitor, and printer. Users who enjoy playing games might add a joystick or a trackball; others might connect a modem, scanner, or integrated services digital network (ISDN) terminal to their machines. *See illustration on page 265.*

pixel derived from **picture element** single dot on a computer screen. All screen images are made up of a collection of pixels, with each pixel being either off (dark) or on (illuminated, possibly in colour). The number of pixels available determines the screen's resolution. Typical resolutions of microcomputer screens vary from 320 x 200 pixels to 800 x 600 pixels, but screens with 1,024 x 768 pixels or more are now common for high-quality graphic (pictorial) displays.

plotter or **graph plotter** device that draws pictures or diagrams under computer control.

Plotters are often used for producing business charts, architectural plans, and engineering drawings. **Flatbed plotters** move a pen up and down across a flat drawing surface, whereas **roller plotters** roll the drawing paper past the pen as it moves from side to side.

printed circuit board (PCB) electrical circuit created by laying (printing) 'tracks' of a conductor such as copper on one or both sides of an insulating board. The PCB was invented in 1936 by Austrian scientist Paul Eisler, and was first used on a large scale in 1948.

printer output device for producing printed copies of text or graphics. Types include the daisywheel printer, which produces good-quality text but no graphics; the dot matrix printer, which produces text and graphics by printing a pattern of small dots; the ink-jet printer, which creates text and graphics by spraying a fine jet of quick-drying ink onto the paper; and the laser printer, which uses electro-

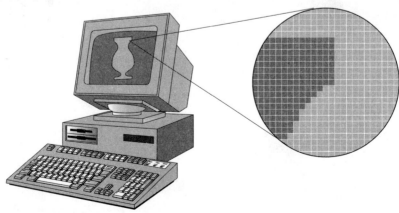

pixel Computer screen images are made of a number of pixels ('dots'). The greater the number of pixels the greater the resolution of the image; most computer screens are set at 640 × 480 pixels, although higher resolutions are available.

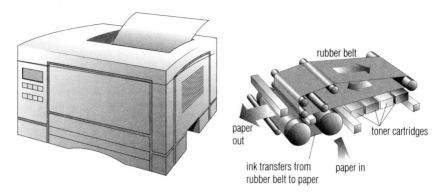

printer A laser printer works by transferring tiny ink particles contained in a toner cartridge to paper via a rubber belt. The image is produced by laser on a light-sensitive drum within the printer.

static technology very similar to that used by a photocopier to produce high-quality text and graphics.

processor another name for the central processing unit or microprocessor of a computer.

PROM acronym for **programmable read-only memory** a memory device in the form of an integrated circuit (chip) that can be programmed after manufacture to hold information permanently. PROM chips are empty of information when manufactured, unlike ROM (read-only memory) chips, which have information built into them. Other memory devices are EPROM (erasable programmable read-only memory) and RAM (random-access memory).

RAM acronym for **random-access memory** memory device in the form of a collection of integrated circuits (chips), frequently used in microcomputers. Unlike ROM (read-only memory) chips, RAM chips can be both read from and written to by the computer, but their contents are lost when the power is switched off.

real-time system program that responds to events in the world as they happen. For example, an automatic-pilot program in an aircraft must respond instantly in order to correct deviations from its course. Process control, robotics, games, and many military applications are examples of real-time systems.

RISC acronym for **reduced instruction-set computer** microprocessor (processor on a single chip) that carries out fewer instructions than other (CISC) microprocessors in common use in

What is memory?

The part of a computer system used to store data and programs either permanently or temporarily is called **memory.** There are two main types: immediate access memory and backing storage. Memory capacity is measured in bytes or, more conveniently, in kilobytes (units of 1,024 bytes) or megabytes (units of 1,024 kilobytes).

Immediate access memory, or **internal memory,** describes the memory locations that can be addressed directly and individually by the central processing unit. It is either read-only (stored in ROM, PROM, and EPROM chips) or read/write (stored in RAM chips). Read-only memory stores information that must be constantly available and is unlikely to be changed. It is nonvolatile – that is, it is not lost when the computer is switched off. Read/write memory is volatile – it stores programs and data only while the computer is switched on.

Backing storage, or **external memory,** is nonvolatile memory, located outside the central processing unit, used to store programs and data that are not in current use. Backing storage is provided by such devices as magnetic disks (floppy and hard disks), magnetic tape (tape streamers and cassettes), optical disks (such as CD-ROM), and bubble memory. By rapidly switching blocks of information between the backing storage and the immediate-access memory, the limited size of the immediate-access memory may be increased artificially. When this technique is used to give the appearance of a larger internal memory than physically exists, the additional capacity is referred to as **virtual memory.**

the 1990s. Because of the low number and the regularity of machine code instructions, the processor carries out those instructions very quickly.

ROM acronym for **read-only memory** memory device in the form of a collection of integrated circuits (chips), frequently used in microcomputers. ROM chips are loaded with data and programs during manufacture and, unlike RAM (random-access memory) chips, can subsequently only be read, not written to, by computer. However, the contents of the chips are not lost when the power is switched off, as happens in RAM.

Squeezed on to silicon

■ The number of transistors on a single silicon chip increased by a factor of 16,000 in the period 1974–98.

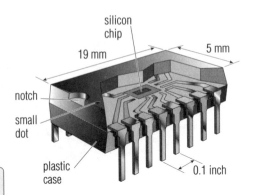

silicon chip A silicon chip, or integrated circuit (IC), is a piece of silicon, about the size of a child's fingernail, on which the components of an electrical circuit are etched. The IC is packed in a plastic container with metal legs that connect it to the circuit board.

silicon chip miniaturized electronic circuit produced on a single crystal, or chip, of a semiconducting material – usually silicon. It may contain many millions of components and yet measure only 5 mm/0.2 in square and 1 mm/0.04 in thick. The silicon chip is encapsulated within a plastic or ceramic case, and linked via gold wires to metal pins with which it is connected to a printed circuit board and the other components that make up such electronic devices as computers and calculators.

smart card plastic card with an embedded microprocessor and memory. It can store, for example, personal data, identification, and bank-account details, to enable it to be used as a credit or debit card. The card can be loaded with credits, which are then spent electronically, and reloaded as needed. Possible other uses range from hotel door 'keys' to passports.

spreadsheet program that mimics a sheet of ruled paper, divided into columns down the page, and rows across. The user enters values into cells within the sheet, then instructs the program to perform some operation on them, such as totalling a column or finding the average of a series of numbers. Highly complex numerical analyses may be built up from these simple steps.

software see **software** feature.

supercomputer fastest, most powerful type of computer, capable of performing its basic operations in picoseconds (thousand-billionths of a second), rather than nanoseconds (billionths of a second), like most other computers.

systems analysis investigation of a business activity or clerical procedure, with a view to deciding if and how it can be computerized. The analyst discusses the existing procedures with the people involved, observes the flow of data through the business, and draws up an outline specification of the required computer system. The next step is systems design.

systems design detailed design of an applications package. The designer breaks the system down into component programs, and designs the required input forms, screen layouts, and

---

Software

The collection of programs and procedures for making a computer perform a specific task is called **software.** A computer's hardware, on the other hand, is its physical components. No computer can function without some form of software. Software is created by programmers and is either distributed on a suitable medium, such as the floppy disk, or built into the computer in the form of firmware. Examples of software include operating systems, compilers, and applications programs such as payrolls or word processors.

To function, computers need two types of software: application software and systems software. **Application software,** such as a payroll system or a word processor, is designed for the benefit of the end user. **Systems software** performs tasks related to the operation and performance of the computer system itself. For example, a systems program might control the operation of the display screen, or control and organize backing storage.

printouts. Systems design forms a link between systems analysis and programming.

terminal device consisting of a keyboard and display screen (VDU) to enable the operator to communicate with the computer. The terminal may be physically attached to the computer or linked to it by a telephone line (remote terminal). A 'dumb' terminal has no processor of its own, whereas an 'intelligent' terminal has its own processor and takes some of the processing load away from the main computer.

UNIX multiuser operating system designed for minicomputers but becoming increasingly popular on microcomputers, workstations, mainframes, and supercomputers.

user interface procedures and methods through which the user operates a program. These might include menus, input forms, error messages, and keyboard procedures. A graphical user interface (GUI or WIMP) is one that makes use of icons (small pictures) and allows the user to make menu selections with a mouse.

VDU abbreviation for **visual display unit.**

virus piece of software that can replicate and transfer itself from one computer to another, without the user being aware of it. Some viruses are relatively harmless, but others can damage or destroy data.

visual display unit (VDU) computer terminal consisting of a keyboard for input data and a screen for displaying output. The oldest and most popular type of VDU screen is the cathode-ray tube (CRT), which uses essentially the same technology as a television screen. Other types use plasma display technology and liquid-crystal displays.

Windows originally Microsoft's graphical user interface (GUI) for IBM PCs and clones running MS-DOS. Windows has developed into a family of operating systems that run on a wide variety of computers from pen-operated palmtop organizers to large, multi-processor computers in corporate data centres.

Computer Programming

Computers have no intelligence of their own. They require a detailed set of instructions provided by a **programmer**. A **programming language** is a special notation in which instructions for controlling a computer are written. Programming languages are designed to be easy for people to write and read, but must be capable of being mechanically translated (by a compiler or an interpreter) into the machine code that the computer can execute. Programming languages may be classified as high-level languages or low-level languages.

algorithm procedure or series of steps that can be used to solve a problem. In computer science, it describes the logical sequence of operations to be performed by a program. A flow chart is a visual representation of an algorithm.

ASCII acronym for **American standard code for information interchange** coding system in which numbers are assigned to letters, digits, and punctuation symbols. Although computers work in code based on the binary number system, ASCII numbers are usually quoted as decimal or hexadecimal numbers. For example, the decimal number 45 (binary 0101101) represents a hyphen, and 65 (binary 1000001) a capital A. The first 32 codes are used for control functions, such as carriage return and backspace.

assembly language low-level computer-programming language closely related to a computer's internal codes. It consists chiefly of a set of short sequences of letters (mnemonics), which are translated, by a program called an assembler, into machine code for the computer's central processing unit (CPU) to follow directly. In assembly language, for example, 'JMP' means 'jump' and 'LDA' means 'load accumulator'. Assembly code is used by programmers who need to write very fast or efficient programs.

CAD acronym for **computer-aided design** the use of computers in creating and editing design drawings. CAD also allows such things as automatic testing of designs and multiple or animated three-dimensional views of designs. CAD systems are widely used in architecture, electronics, and engineering, for example in the motor-vehicle industry, where cars designed with the assistance of computers are now commonplace.

Computer Graphics

Computer graphics utilize computers to display and manipulate information in pictorial form. Input may be achieved by scanning an image, by drawing with a mouse or stylus on a graphics tablet, or by drawing directly on the screen with a light pen. The output may be as simple as a pie chart, or as complex as an animated sequence in a science-fiction film, or a seemingly three-dimensional engineering blueprint. The drawing is stored in the computer as vector graphics or raster graphics.

Vector graphics are stored in the computer memory by using geometric formulas. They can be transformed (enlarged, rotated, stretched, and so on) without loss of picture resolution. It is also possible to select and transform any of the components of a vector-graphics display because each is separately defined in the computer memory. In these respects vector graphics are superior to raster graphics. They are typically used for drawing applications, allowing the user to create and modify technical diagrams such as designs for houses or cars.

Raster graphics are stored in the computer memory by using a map to record data (such as colour and intensity) for every pixel that makes up the image. When transformed (enlarged, rotated, stretched, and so on), raster graphics become ragged and suffer loss of picture resolution, unlike vector graphics. They are typically used for painting applications, which allow the user to create artwork on a computer screen much as if they were painting on paper or canvas.

Computer graphics are increasingly used in computer-aided design (CAD), and to generate models and simulations in engineering, meteorology, medicine and surgery, and other fields of science. Recent developments in software mean that designers on opposite sides of the world soon will be able to work on complex three-dimensional computer models using ordinary personal computers (PCs) linked by telephone lines rather than powerful graphics workstations.

ASCII Codes

Character	Binary (base 2)	Decimal (base 10)	Hexadecimal (base 16)	Character	Binary (base 2)	Decimal (base 10)	Hexadecimal (base 16)
Space	00100000	32	20	P	01010000	80	50
!	00100001	33	21	Q	01010001	81	51
'	00100010	34	22	R	01010010	82	52
#	00100011	35	23	S	01010011	83	53
$	00100100	36	24	T	01010100	84	54
%	00100101	37	25	U	01010101	85	55
&	00100110	38	26	V	01010110	86	56
`	00100111	39	27	W	01010111	87	57
(	00101000	40	28	X	01011000	88	58
)	00101001	41	29	Y	01011001	89	59
*	00101010	42	2A	Z	01011010	90	5A
+	00101011	43	2B	[	01011011	91	5B
,	00101100	44	2C	\	01011100	92	5C
-	00101101	45	2D	]	01011101	93	5D
.	00101110	46	2E	^	01011110	94	5E
/	00101111	47	2F	_	01011111	95	5F
0	00110000	48	30	`	01100000	96	60
1	00110001	49	31	a	01100001	97	61
2	00110010	50	32	b	01100010	98	62
3	00110011	51	33	c	01100011	99	63
4	00110100	52	34	d	01100100	100	64
5	00110101	53	35	e	01100101	101	65
6	00110110	54	36	f	01100110	102	66
7	00110111	55	37	g	01100111	103	67
8	00111000	56	38	h	01101000	104	68
9	00111001	57	39	i	01101001	105	69
:	00111010	58	3A	j	01101010	106	6A
;	00111011	59	3B	k	01101011	107	6B
<	00111100	60	3C	l	01101100	108	6C
=	00111101	61	3D	m	01101101	109	6D
>	00111110	62	3E	n	01101110	110	6E
?	00111111	63	3F	o	01101111	111	6F
@	01000000	64	40	p	01110000	112	70
A	01000001	65	41	q	01110001	113	71
B	01000010	66	42	r	01110010	114	72
C	01000011	67	43	s	01110011	115	73
D	01000100	68	44	t	01110100	116	74
E	01000101	69	45	u	01110101	117	75
F	01000110	70	46	v	01110110	118	76
G	01000111	71	47	w	01110111	119	77
H	01001000	72	48	x	01111000	120	78
I	01001001	73	49	y	01111001	121	79
J	01001010	74	4A	z	01111010	122	7A
K	01001011	75	4B	{	01111011	123	7B
L	01001100	76	4C			01111100	124	7C
M	01001101	77	4D	}	01111101	125	7D
N	01001110	78	4E	~	01111110	126	7E
O	01001111	79	4F	Delete	01111111	127	7F

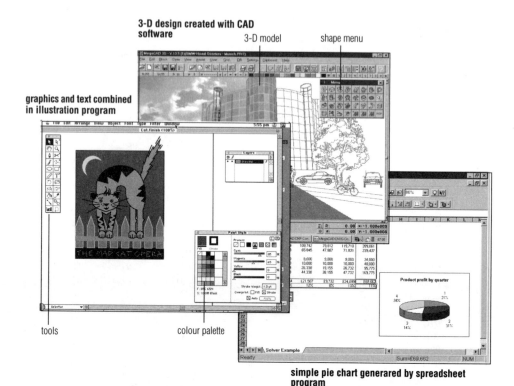

3-D design created with CAD software

3-D model

shape menu

graphics and text combined in illustration program

tools

colour palette

simple pie chart generared by spreadsheet program

computer graphics Some examples of the kinds of graphic design that can be achieved using computers. Text and graphics may be combined within an illustration package, and sophisticated three-dimensional drawings can be created using a computer-aided design (CAD) system.

With a CAD system, picture components are accurately positioned using grid lines. Pictures can be resized, rotated, or mirrored without loss of quality or proportion.

A related development is CAM (computer-assisted manufacturing).

CAM acronym for **computer-aided manufacturing** the use of computers to control production processes; in particular, the control of machine tools and robots in factories. In some factories, the whole design and production system has been automated by linking CAD (computer-aided design) to CAM.

command language set of commands and the rules governing their use, by which users control a program. For example, an operating system may have commands such as SAVE and DELETE, or a payroll program may have commands for adding and amending staff records.

computer-aided design use of computers to create and modify design drawings; see CAD.

computer-aided manufacturing use of computers to regulate production processes in industry; see CAM.

computer program coded instructions for a computer; see program.

computer simulation representation of a real-life situation in a computer program. For example, the program might simulate the flow of customers arriving at a bank. The user can alter variables, such as the number of cashiers on duty, and see the effect.

fuzzy logic form of knowledge representation suitable for notions (such as 'hot' or 'loud') that cannot be defined precisely but depend on their context. For example, a jug of water may be described as too hot or too cold, depending on whether it is to be used to wash one's face or to make tea.

hacking unauthorized access to a computer, either for fun or for malicious or fraudulent purposes. Hackers generally use microcomputers and telephone lines to obtain access. In computing, the term is used in a wider sense to mean using software for enjoyment or self-education, not necessarily involving unauthorized access. The most destructive form of hacking is the introduction of a computer virus.

Millennium Bug crisis facing some computer systems in the year 2000 that will arise because computers may be unable to operate normally when faced with the unfamiliar date format. Information about the year has typically been stored in a two-digit instead of a four-digit field in order to save memory space, which may mean that after the year 1999 ends the year will appear as '00'. Systems may consider this to mean 1900, or they may not recognize it at all and will crash, resulting in data corruption.

multitasking or **multiprogramming** system in which one processor appears to run several different programs (or different parts of the same program) at the same time. All the programs are held in memory together and each is allowed to run for a certain period.

neural network artificial network of processors that attempts to mimic the structure of nerve cells (neurons) in the human brain. Neural networks may be electronic, optical, or simulated by computer software.

program set of instructions that controls the operation of a computer. There are two main kinds: applications programs, which carry out tasks for the benefit of the user – for example, word processing; and systems programs, which control the internal workings of the computer. A utility program is a systems program that carries out specific tasks for the user. Programs can be written in any of a number of programming languages but are always translated into machine code before they can be executed by the computer.

Programming Languages

Language	Main uses	Description
Ada	defence applications	high-level
assembly languages	jobs needing detailed control of the hardware, fast execution, and small program size	fast and efficient but require considerable effort and skill
ALGOL (algorithmic language)	mathematical work	high-level with an algebraic style; no longer in current use, but has influenced languages such as Ada and PASCAL
BASIC (beginners' all-purpose symbolic instruction code)	mainly in education, business, and the home, and among non-professional programmers, such as engineers	easy to learn; early versions lacked the features of other languages
C	systems and general programming	fast and efficient; widely used as a general-purpose language; especially popular among professional programmers
C++	systems and general programming; commercial software development	developed from C, adding the advantages of object-oriented programming
COBOL (common business-oriented language)	business programming	strongly oriented towards commercial work; easy to learn but very verbose; widely used on mainframes
FORTH	control applications	reverse Polish notation language
FORTRAN (formula translation)	scientific and computational work	based on mathematical formulae; popular among engineers, scientists, and mathematicians
Java	developed for consumer electronics; used for many interactive Web sites	multipurpose, cross-platform, object-oriented language with similar features to C and C++ but simpler
LISP (list processing)	artificial intelligence	symbolic language with a reputation for being hard to learn; popular in the academic and research communities *(continued)*

Programming Languages (continued)

LOGO	teaching of mathematical concepts	high-level; popular with schools and home computer users
Modula-2	systems and real-time programming; general programming highly-structured	intended to replace PASCAL for 'real-world' applications
OBERON	general programming	small, compact language incorporating many of the features of PASCAL and Modula-2
PASCAL (program appliqué à la sélection et la compilation automatique de la littérature)	general-purpose language	highly-structured; widely used for teaching programming in universities
Perl (pathological eclectic rubbish lister)	systems programming and Web development	easy manipulation of text, files, and processes, especially in UNIX environment
PROLOG (programming in logic)	artificial intelligence	symbolic-logic programming system, originally intended for theorem solving but now used more generally in artificial intelligence

Pioneers in computing

Aiken, Howard Hathaway (1900–1973) US mathematician and computer pioneer. In 1939, in conjunction with engineers from IBM, he started work on the design of an automatic calculator using standard business-machine components. In 1944 the team completed one of the first computers, the Automatic Sequence Controlled Calculator (known as the Harvard Mark I), a programmable computer controlled by punched paper tape and using punched cards.

Andreessen, Marc (1972–) US systems developer and co-author of the first widely available graphical browser for the World Wide Web, Mosaic, which he wrote with fellow researcher Eric Bina. In 1994 both worked on the next generation of browser software including Netscape Navigator, which was made freely available on the Internet and contributed to the explosive growth of the World Wide Web in the mid-1990s.

Babbage, Charles (1792–1871) English mathematician who devised a precursor of the computer. He designed an analytical engine, a general-purpose mechanical computing device for performing different calculations according to a program input on punched cards (an

idea borrowed from the Jacquard loom). This device was never built, but it embodied many of the principles on which digital computers are based.

Barlow, John Perry (1948–) US writer and cofounder of the Electronic Frontier Foundation in 1991. His writings about cyberspace issues, such as 'Crime and Puzzlement' (1991) and 'A Declaration of the Independence of Cyberspace' (1996), have circulated widely and influentially on the Net. He was formerly a lyricist for the US psychedelic rock group the Grateful Dead.

Berners-Lee, Tim(othy) (1955–) English inventor of the World Wide Web in 1990. He developed the Web whilst working as a consultant at CERN. He currently serves as director of the W3 Consortium, a neutral body that manages the Web.

Boole, George (1815–1864) English mathematician. His work *The Mathematical Analysis of Logic* (1847) established the basis of modern mathematical logic, and his **Boolean algebra** can be used in designing computers. Boole's system is essentially two-valued. By subdividing objects into separate classes, each with a given property, his algebra makes it possible to treat different

classes according to the presence or absence of the same property. Hence it involves just two numbers, 0 and 1 – the binary system used in the computer.

Byron, (Augusta) Ada, Countess of Lovelace (1815–1852) English mathematician, a pioneer in writing programs for Charles Babbage's analytical engine. In 1983 a new, high-level computer language, Ada, was named after her. She was the daughter of the poet Lord Byron.

Cerf, Vinton (1943–) US inventor of part of the TCP/IP protocols on which the Internet is based. Known throughout the industry as the 'Father of the Internet', Cerf is president of the Internet Society and was a principal developer of the ARPANET.

Cray, Seymour Roger (1925–1996) US computer scientist and pioneer in the field of supercomputing. He designed one of the earliest computers to contain transistors in 1960. In 1972 he formed Cray Research to build the first popular supercomputer, the Cray-1, released in 1976. Its success led to the production of further supercomputers, including the Cray-2 in 1985, the Cray Y-MP, a multiprocessor design in 1988, and the Cray-3 in 1989.

Pioneers in computing (continued)

Eckert, John Presper Jr (1919– 1995) US electronics engineer and mathematician who collaborated with John Mauchly on the development of the early ENIAC (1946) and UNIVAC 1 (1951) computers.

Gates, Bill (William) Henry, III (1955–) US entrepreneur and computer programmer. He co-founded Microsoft Corporation in 1975 and was responsible for supplying MS-DOS, the operating system and the BASIC language that IBM used in the IBM PC.

Hollerith, Herman (1860–1929) US inventor of a mechanical tabulating machine, the first device for high-volume data processing. Hollerith's tabulator was widely publicized after being successfully used in the 1890 census. The firm he established, the Tabulating Machine Company, was later one of the founding companies of IBM.

Hopper, Grace (1906–1992) US computer pioneer and mathematician who created the first compiler and helped invent the computer language COBOL. She also coined the term 'debug'.

Jacquard, Joseph Marie (1752– 1834) French textile manufacturer. He invented a punched-card system for programming designs on a carpetmaking loom (the **Jacquard loom**).

Jobs, Steven Paul (1955–) US computer entrepreneur. He cofounded Apple Computer Inc with Stephen Wozniak in 1976, and founded NeXT Technology Inc in 1985. Jobs has been involved with the creation of the Apple II personal computer in 1977, the Apple Macintosh in 1984 – marketed as 'the computer for the rest of us' – and the NeXT workstation in 1988. Jobs returned to Apple in 1996 and became chief executive officer in 1997.

Kahle, Brewster (1960–) US computing entrepreneur who is best known for inventing the software tool WAIS system for publishing material on the Internet. In 1996 he set up an Internet archive which aims to keep a copy of every item on the Net.

Kapor, Mitchell (1951–) US entrepreneur and software designer who founded Lotus Development Corporation, a leading business software company, in 1982. Eight years later, he co-founded the Electronic Frontier Foundation, a non-profit-making organization concerned with protecting civil liberties, in particular freedom of speech on the Internet.

Mauchly, John William (1907– 1980) US physicist and engineer who, in 1946, constructed the first general-purpose computer, the ENIAC, in collaboration with John Eckert. Their company was bought by Remington Rand in 1950, and they built the UNIVAC 1 computer in 1951 for the US census. The work on ENIAC was carried out by the two during World War II, and was commissioned to automate the calculation of artillery firing tables for the US Army. In 1949 Mauchly and Eckert designed a small-scale binary computer, BINAC, which was faster and cheaper to use. Punched cards were replaced with magnetic tape, and the computer stored programs internally.

Mitnick, Kevin (1963–) US computer criminal known as 'the world's most wanted hacker' during the three years he spent on the run before being caught in 1994.

Moore, Gordon (1928–) US cofounder, with Robert Noyce, of microchip manufacturer Intel in 1968. In 1965, when writing an article for the 35th anniversary edition of *Electronics* magazine, Moore formulated what has since been named **Moore's Law**: the number of components that could be squeezed onto a silicon chip would double every year. Moore updated this prediction in 1975 from doubling every year to doubling every two years. These observations proved remarkably accurate – the processing technology of 1996, for example, was some 8 million times more powerful than that of 1966 – partly because chip manufacturers tried to keep up with Moore's Law so as to avoid falling behind their rivals.

Noyce, Robert Norton (1927–1990) US scientist and inventor, with Jack Kilby, of the integrated circuit (microchip), which revolutionized the computer and electronics industries in the 1970s and 1980s. In 1968 he and six colleagues founded the Intel Corporation, which became one of the USA's leading semiconductor manufacturers.

Sinclair, Clive Marles (1940–) British electronics engineer. He produced the first widely available pocket calculator, pocket and wristwatch televisions, a series of home computers, and the innovative but commercially disastrous C5 personal transport (a low cyclelike three-wheeled vehicle powered by a washing-machine motor). Knighted 1983.

Turing, Alan Mathison (1912–1954) English mathematician and logician. In 1936 he described a 'universal computing machine' that could theoretically be programmed to solve any problem capable of solution by a specially designed machine. This concept, now called the **Turing machine,** foreshadowed the digital computer.

Von Neumann, John (1903–1957) originally Johann Hungarian-born US scientist and mathematician, a pioneer of computer design. He invented his 'rings of operators' (called Von Neumann algebras) in the late 1930s, and also contributed to set theory, game theory, quantum mechanics, cybernetics (with his theory of self-reproducing automata, called **Von Neumann machines**), and the development of the atomic and hydrogen bombs.

Wang, An (1920–1990) Chinese-born US engineer, founder of Wang Laboratories (1951), one of the world's largest computer companies in the 1970s. In 1948 he invented the computer memory core, the most common device used for storing computer data before the invention of the integrated circuit (chip).

Wilkes, Maurice Vincent (1913–) English mathematician who led the team at Cambridge University that built the EDSAC (electronic delay storage automatic calculator) in 1949, one of the earliest of the British electronic computers.

INTERNET

Dynamic HTML fourth version of hypertext markup language (HTML), the language used to create Web pages. It is called Dynamic HTML because it enables dynamic effects to be incorporated in pages without the delays involved in downloading Java applets and without referring back to the server.

electronic mail or **e-mail** messages sent electronically from computer to computer via network connections such as Ethernet or the Internet, or via telephone lines to a host system. Messages once sent are stored on the network or by the host system until the recipient picks them up. As well as text, messages may contain enclosed text files, artwork, or multimedia clips).

e-mail abbreviation for electronic mail.

hypertext system for viewing information (both text and pictures) on a computer screen in such a way that related items of information can easily be reached. For example, the program might display a map of a country; if the user clicks (with a mouse) on a particular city, the program will display information about that city.

Internet global computer network connecting governments, companies, universities, and many other networks and users. Electronic mail, electronic conferencing, educational and chat services are all supported across the network, as is the ability to access remote computers and send and retrieve files. In the late 1990s around 60 million adults had access to the Internet in the USA alone.

Acronyms and Abbreviations in Common Use Online

Acronym/ Abbreviation	Meaning	Acronym/ Abbreviation	Meaning
AFAICR	As Far As I Can Recall	NALOPKT	Not A Lot Of People Know That
AFAICT	As Far As I Can Tell	NIMBY	Not In My Back Yard
AIUI	As I Understand It	OIC	Oh I See
ATM	At The Moment	OLR	Off Line Reader
BTDT	Been There Done That	OTOH	On The Other Hand
BTW	By The Way	OTT	Over The Top
CUL	See You Later	OTTH	On The Third Hand
DQM	Don't Quote Me	PIM	Personal Information Manager
DWIM	Do What I Mean	PMFJI	Pardon Me For Jumping In
FAQ	Frequently Asked Question	PMJI	Pardon Me Jumping In
FOAF	Friend Of A Friend	POV	Point Of View
FOC	Free Of Charge	ROTFL	Rolling On The Floor Laughing
FOCL	Falls Off Chair Laughing	RSN	Real Soon Now
FUD	Fear, Uncertainty, and Doubt	SO	Significant Other
FWIW	For What It's Worth	SOTA	State Of The Art
FYI	For Your Information	TIA	Thanks In Anticipation
IIRC	If I Recall/Remember Correctly	TIC	Tongue In Cheek
IKWYM	I Know What You Mean	TLA	Three Letter Abbreviation/Acronym
IMO	In My Opinion	TPTB	The Powers That Be
IOW	In Other Words	TTBOMK	To The Best of My Knowledge
IRL	In Real Life	TTFN	Ta Ta For Now
ISTM	It Seems To Me	TTYL	Talk To You Later
ISTR	I Seem To Recall/Remember	TYVM	Thank You Very Much
IYKWIM	If You Know What I Mean	UKP	United Kingdom Pounds (sterling)
IYSWIM	If You See What I Mean	WRT	With Respect To
LCW	Loud, Confident, and Wrong	WYSIWYG	What You See Is What You Get
LOL	Lots Of Luck/Laughing Out Loud	YHM	You Have Mail
NAFAIK	Not As Far As I Know	YKWIM	You Know What I Mean

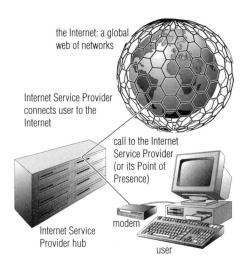

the Internet: a global web of networks

Internet Service Provider connects user to the Internet

call to the Internet Service Provider (or its Point of Presence)

Internet Service Provider hub

modem

user

Internet The Internet is accessed by users via a modem to the service provider's hub, which handles all connection requests. Once connected, the user can access a whole range of information from many different sources, including the World Wide Web.

Common Internet Domain Names

Generic Top-Level Domains

.com	commercial business
.edu	academic
.gov	government
.int	organization established by international treaty
.mil	military
.net	Internet network
.org	non-commercial business

New Generic Top-Level Domains (from 1998)

.arts	arts-related
.info	information services
.nom	individuals
.rec	recreation-related
.store	shopping services
.web	Web-related

UK Domains

.ac.uk	academic
.co.uk	commercial business
.gov.uk	government
.lea.sch.uk	Local Education Authority
.ltd.uk	limited company
.mod.uk	Ministry of Defence
.net.uk	Internet network
.nhs.uk	National Health Service
.org.uk	non-commercial business
.plc.uk	public limited company

Selected Other Country Domains

.au	Australia
.ca	Canada
.cn	China
.de	Germany
.fr	France
.jp	Japan
.nl	Netherlands
.us	USA

network in computing, a method of connecting computers so that they can share data and peripheral devices, such as printers. The main types are classified by the pattern of the connections – star or ring network, for example – or by the degree of geographical spread allowed; for example, local area networks (LANs) for communication within a room or building, and wide area networks (WANs) for more remote systems. Internet is the computer network that connects major English-speaking institutions throughout the world, with around 12 million users.

virtual reality advanced form of computer simulation, in which a participant has the illusion of being part of an artificial environment. The participant views the environment through two tiny television screens (one for each eye) built into a visor. Sensors detect movements of the participant's head or body, causing the apparent viewing position to change. Gloves (datagloves) fitted with sensors may be worn, which allow the participant seemingly to pick up and move objects in the environment.

Major Search Engines

Search engine	Web address	Description
AltaVista	http://www.altavista.digital.com	funded by DEC; select word search
Infoseek	http://www.infoseek.com	powerful engine searches whole Web or focuses on 9 major topic sections; provides related sites
Lycos	http://www.lycos.com	extensive index of documents, including by words in title, headings, subheadings and hyperlinks
UK Index	http://www.ukindex.co.uk	database of almost exclusively UK sites with vetted selection
WebCrawler	http://www.webcrawler.com	database created using spider (automated search routine)
Yahoo	http://www.yahoo.com	search-tree offering constant refinement of choice

Some Internet Terms

acceptable use set of rules enforced by a service provider or backbone network restricting the use to which their facilities may be put

access provider another term for Internet Service Provider

ack radio-derived term for 'acknowledge', used on the Internet as a brief way of indicating agreement with or receipt of a message or instruction

alt hierarchy 'alternative' set of newsgroups on USENET, set up so that anyone can start a newsgroup on any topic

anonymous remailer service that allows Internet users to post to USENET and send e-mail without revealing their true identity or e-mail address

Archie software tool for locating information on the Internet

bang path list of routing that appears in the header of a message sent across the Internet, showing how it travelled from the sender to its destination

Big Seven hierarchies original seven hierarchies of newsgroups on USENET. They are:

comp. – computing;
misc. – miscellaneous;
news. – newsgroups;
rec. – recreation;
sci. – science;
soc. – social issues; and
talk. – debate

blocking software any of various software programs that work on the World Wide Web to block access to categories of information considered offensive or dangerous

blue-ribbon campaign campaign for free speech launched to protest against moves towards censorship on the Internet

'bot (short for robot) automated piece of software that performs specific tasks on the Internet. 'Bots are commonly found on multi-user dungeons (MUDs) and other multi-user role-playing game sites, where they maintain a constant level of activity even when few human users are logged on

bozo filter facility to eliminate messages from irritating users

browser any program that allows the user to search for and view data; Web browsers allow access to the World Wide Web

bulletin board centre for the electronic storage of messages; bulletin board systems are usually dedicated to specific interest groups, and may carry public and private messages, notices, and programs

cancelbot automated software program that cancels messages on USENET; Cancelbot is activated by the CancelMoose, an anonymous individual who monitors newsgroups for complaints about spamming

crawler automated indexing software that scours the Web for new or updated sites

crossposting practice of sending a message to more than one newsgroup on USENET

cybersex online sexual fantasy spun by two or more participants via live, online chat

cyberspace the imaginary, interactive 'worlds' created by networked computers; often used interchangeably with 'virtual world'

cypherpunk passionate believer in the importance of free access to strong encryption on the Internet, in the interests of guarding privacy and free speech

digital city area in cyberspace, either text-based or graphical, that uses the model of a city to make it easy for visitors and residents to find specific types of information

e-zine (contraction of **electronic magazine**) periodical sent by e-mail. E-zines can be produced very cheaply as there are no production costs for design and layout, and minimal costs for distribution

FAQ (abbreviation for **frequently asked questions**) file of answers to commonly asked questions on any topic

firewall security system built to block access to a particular computer or network while still allowing some types of data to flow in and out on to the Internet

flame angry public or private electronic mail message used to express disapproval of breaches of netiquette or the voicing of an unpopular opinion

follow-up post publicly posted reply to a USENET message; unlike a personal e-mail reply, follow-up post can be read by anyone

FurryMUCK popular MUD site where the players take on the imaginary shapes and characters of furry, anthropomorphic animals

Gopher menu-based server on the Internet that indexes resources and retrieves them according to user choice via any one of several built-in methods such as FTP or Telnet. Gopher servers can also be accessed via the World Wide Web and searched via special servers called Veronicas

Gopherspace name for the knowledge base composed of all the documents indexed on all the Gophers in the world

hit request sent to a file server. Sites on the World Wide Web often measure their popularity in numbers of hits

home page opening page on a particular site on the World Wide Web

hop intermediate stage of the journey taken by a message travelling from one site to another on the Internet

HTTP (abbreviation for **Hypertext Transfer Protocol**) protocol used for communications between client (the Web browser) and server on the World Wide Web

hypermedia system that uses links to lead users to related graphics, audio, animation, or video files in the same way

(continued)

Some Internet Terms (continued)

that hypertext systems link related pieces of text

in-line graphics images included in Web pages that are displayed automatically by Web browsers without any action required by the user

Internet Relay Chat (IRC) service that allows users connected to the Internet to chat with each other over many channels

Internet Service Provider (ISP) any company that sells dial-up access to the Internet

Jughead (acronym for **Jonzy's Universal Gopher Hierarchy Excavation and Display)** search engine enabling users of the Internet server Gopher to find keywords in Gopherspace directories

killfile file specifying material that you do not wish to see when accessing a newsgroup. By entering names, subjects or phrases into a killfile, users can filter out tedious threads, offensive subject headings, spamming, or contributions from other subscribers

link image or item of text in a World Wide Web document that acts as a route to another Web page or file on the Internet

lurk read a USENET newsgroup without making a contribution

MBONE (contraction of **multicast backbone**) layer of the Internet designed to deliver packets of multimedia data, enabling video and audio communication

MIME (acronym for **Multipurpose Internet Mail Extensions**) standard for transferring multimedia e-mail messages and World Wide Web hypertext documents over the Internet

moderator person or group of people that screens submissions to certain newsgroups and mailing lists before passing them on for wider circulation

MUD (acronym for **multi-user dungeon**) interactive multi-player game, played via the Internet or modem connection to one of the participating computers. MUD players typically have to solve puzzles, avoid traps, fight other participants, and carry out various tasks to achieve their goals

MUSE (abbreviation for **multi-user shared environment**) type of MUD

MUSH (acronym for **multi-user shared hallucination**) a MUD (multi-user dungeon) that can be altered by the players

netiquette behaviour guidelines evolved by users of the Internet including: no messages typed in upper case (considered to be the equivalent of shouting); new users, or new members of a newsgroup, should read the frequently asked questions (FAQ) file before asking a question; and no advertising via USENET newsgroups

net police USENET readers who monitor and 'punish' postings which they find offensive or believe to be in breach of netiquette. Many newsgroups are policed by these self-appointed guardians

newbie insulting term for a new user of a USENET newsgroup

newsgroup discussion group on the Internet's USENET. Newsgroups are organized in seven broad categories: **comp.** – computers and programming; **news.** – newsgroups themselves; **rec.** – sports and hobbies; **sci.** – scientific research and ideas; **talk.** – discussion groups; **soc.** – social issues and **misc.** – everything else. In addition, there are alternative hierarchies such as the wide-ranging and anarchic **alt.** (alternative). Within these categories there is a hierarchy of subdivisions

newsreader program that gives access to USENET newsgroups, interpreting the standard commands understood by news servers in a simple, user-friendly interface

news server computer that stores USENET messages for access by users. Most Internet Service Providers (ISPs) offer a news server as part of the service

off-line browser program that downloads and copies Web pages onto a computer so that they can be viewed without being connected to the Internet

off-line reader program that downloads information from newsgroups, FTP servers, or other Internet resources, storing it locally on a hard disk so that it can be read without running up a large phone bill

Pretty Good Privacy (PGP) strong encryption program that runs on personal computers and is distributed on the Internet free of charge

proxy server server on the World Wide Web that 'stands in' for another server, storing and forwarding files on behalf of a computer which might be slower or too busy to deal with the request itself

pseudonym name adopted by someone on the Internet, especially to participate in USENET or discussions using IRC (Internet Relay Chat)

signature (or **.sig**) personal information appended to a message by the sender of an e-mail message or USENET posting in order to add a human touch

spamming advertising on the Internet by broadcasting to many or all newsgroups regardless of relevance

spider program that combs the Internet for new documents such as Web pages and FTP files. Spiders start their work by retrieving a document such as a Web page and then following all the links and references contained in it

surfing exploring the Internet. The term is rather misleading: the glitches, delays, and complexities of the system mean the experience is more like wading through mud

sysop (contraction of **system operator**) the operator of a bulletin board system (BBS)

trolling mischievously posting a deliberately erroneous or obtuse message to a newsgroup in order to tempt others to

(continued)

Some Internet Terms (continued)

reply – usually in a way that makes them appear gullible, intemperate, or foolish

URL (abbreviation for **Uniform Resource Locator**) series of letters and/or numbers specifying the location of a document on the World Wide Web. Every URL consists of a domain name, a description of the document's location within the host computer, and the name of the document itself, separated by full stops and backslashes

USENET (acronym for **users' network**) the world's largest bulletin board system, which brings together people with common interests to exchange views and information. It consists of e-mail messages and articles organized into newsgroups

vertical spam on USENET, spam which consists of many, often repetitive, messages per day posted to the same newsgroup or small set of newsgroups. The effect is to drown out other, more useful, conversation in the newsgroup

wAreZ slang for pirated games or other applications that can be downloaded using FTP

Web authoring tool software for creating Web pages. The basic Web authoring tool is HTML, the source code that determines how a Web page is constructed and how it looks

Web browser client software that allows you to access the World Wide Web

Webmaster system administrator for a server on the World Wide Web

Web page hypertext document on the World Wide Web

webzine magazine published on the World Wide Web, instead of on paper

World Wide Web (WWW) hypertext system for publishing information on the Internet. World Wide Web documents ('Web pages') are text files coded using HTML to include text and graphics, stored on a special computer (a Web server) connected to the Internet. Web pages may also contain Java applets for enhanced animation, video, sound, and interactivity

WWW address (URL)

icons link to required audio and video plug-ins

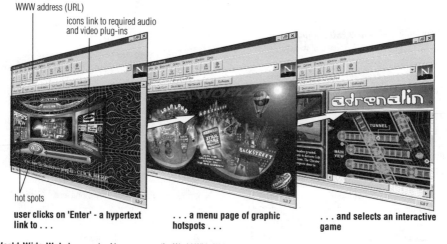

hot spots

user clicks on 'Enter' - a hypertext link to . . .

. . . a menu page of graphic hotspots . . .

. . . and selects an interactive game

World Wide Web An example of how pages on the World Wide Web may be linked to take the user to additional pages of information.

Computing: Chronology

1614 John Napier invents logarithms.

1615 William Oughtred invents the slide rule.

1623 Wilhelm Schickard (1592–1635) invents the mechanical calculating machine.

1645 Blaise Pascal produces a calculator.

1672–74 Gottfried Leibniz builds his first calculator, the Stepped Reckoner.

1801 Joseph-Marie Jacquard develops an automatic loom controlled by punch cards.

1820 The first mass-produced calculator, the Arithometer, is developed by Charles Thomas de Colmar (1785–1870).

1822 Charles Babbage completes his first model for the difference engine.

1830s Babbage creates the first design for the analytical engine.

1890 Herman Hollerith develops the punched-card ruler for the US census.

1936 Alan Turing publishes the mathematical theory of computing.

1938 Konrad Zuse constructs the first binary calculator, using Boolean algebra.

1939 US mathematician and physicist J V Atanasoff (1903–1995) becomes the first to use electronic means for mechanizing arithmetical operations.

1943 The Colossus electronic code-breaker is developed at Bletchley Park, England. The Harvard University Mark I or Automatic Sequence Controlled Calculator (partly financed by IBM) becomes the first program-controlled calculator.

1946 ENIAC (acronym for electronic numerator, integrator, analyzer, and computer), the first general purpose, fully electronic digital computer, is completed at the University of Pennsylvania, USA.

1948 Manchester University (England) Mark I, the first stored-program computer, is completed. William Shockley of Bell Laboratories invents the transistor.

1951 Launch of Ferranti Mark I, the first commercially produced computer. Whirlwind, the first real-time computer, is built for the US air-defence system. Grace Murray Hopper of Remington Rand invents the compiler computer program.

1952 EDVAC (acronym for electronic discrete variable computer) is completed at the Institute for Advanced Study, Princeton, USA (by John Von Neumann and others).

1953 Magnetic core memory is developed.

1958 The first integrated circuit is constructed.

1963 The first minicomputer is built by Digital Equipment (DEC). The first electronic calculator is built by Bell Punch Company.

1964 Launch of IBM System/360, the first compatible family of computers. John Kemeny and Thomas Kurtz of Dartmouth College, USA, invent BASIC (Beginner's All-purpose Symbolic Instruction Code), a computer language similar to FORTRAN.

1965 The first supercomputer, the Control Data CD6600, is developed.

1971 The first microprocessor, the Intel 4004, is announced.

1974 CLIP–4, the first computer with a parallel architecture, is developed by John Backus at IBM.

1975 Altair 8800, the first personal computer (PC), or microcomputer, is launched.

1981 The Xerox Star system, the first WIMP system (acronym for windows, icons, menus, and pointing devices), is developed. IBM launches the IBM PC.

1984 Apple launches the Macintosh computer.

1985 The Inmos T414 transputer, the first 'off-the-shelf' microprocessor for building parallel computers, is announced.

1988 The first optical microprocessor, which uses light instead of electricity, is developed.

1989 Wafer-scale silicon memory chips, able to store 200 million characters, are launched.

1990 Microsoft releases Windows 3, a popular windowing environment for PCs.

(continued)

Computing: Chronology (continued)

1992 Philips launches the CD-I (Compact-Disc Interactive) player, based on CD audio technology, to provide interactive multimedia programs for the home user.

1993 Intel launches the Pentium chip containing 3.1 million transistors and capable of 100 MIPs (millions of instructions per second). The Personal Digital Assistant (PDA), which recognizes users' handwriting, goes on sale.

1995 Intel launches the Pentium Pro microprocessor (formerly codenamed P6).

1996 IBM's computer Deep Blue beats grand master Gary Kasparov at chess, the first time a computer has beaten a human grand master.

1997 In the USA, an attempt to bring legislation to control the Internet, intended to prevent access to sexual material, is rejected as unconstitutional.

1997 The US Justice Department rules that Microsoft's bundling of its web browser with its operating system is unfair trading and an attempt to dominate the market. Microsoft is ordered to sell the browser separately to prevent it from building a monopoly.

1997 A computer employee in Virginia ignores malfunction warnings and causes seven of the world's nine root servers to corrupt all the data sent to them, causing the Internet to break down. Millions of e-mail messages are returned all over the world, prompting speculation about the dangers of the over-centralization of information.

1998 Plans are announced in the USA for Internet2, a high-speed data communications backbone, that will run on a second network Abilene. Serving the main US research universities, it will enable them to bypass congestion on the Internet and should be operational by 1999.

MEDICINE AND HEALTH

M edical science has developed by gradual steps from very early times. In the earliest societies, medical practice was part of the duties of the priests; it relied more on the influence of the gods than on the value of the methods adopted. In ancient Greece, even the priests of Aesculapius, the god of healing, relied mainly on religious exercises to effect a cure. The main advances in medical practice came in the 1800s and 1900s, and today physicians and surgeons have a record of some success in treating and curing disease and injuries.

HUMAN BODY

All human beings develop from the single cell of the fertilized ovum, are born at 40 weeks, and usually reach sexual maturity between 11 and 18 years of age. The bony framework (skeleton) consists of more than 200 bones, over half of which are in the hands and feet. Bones are held together by joints, some of which allow movement. The circulatory system supplies muscles and organs with blood, which provides oxygen and food and removes carbon dioxide and other waste products. Body functions are controlled by the nervous system and hormones.

abdomen part of the body below the thorax, containing the digestive organs. The abdomen is separated from the thorax by the diaphragm, a sheet of muscular tissue. The female reproductive organs are in the abdomen.

Achilles tendon tendon at the back of the ankle attaching the calf muscles to the heel bone. It is one of the largest tendons in the human body, and can resist great tensional strain, but is sometimes ruptured by contraction of the muscles in sudden extension of the foot.

adenoids masses of lymphoid tissue, similar to tonsils, located in the upper part of the throat, behind the nose. They are part of a child's natural defences against the entry of germs but usually shrink and disappear by the age of ten.

adipose tissue type of connective tissue that serves as an energy reserve, and also pads some organs. It is commonly called fat tissue, and consists of large spherical cells filled with fat. Major layers are in the inner layer of skin and around the kidneys and heart.

adrenal gland or **suprarenal gland** triangular gland situated on top of the kidney. The adrenals are soft and yellow, and consist of two parts: the cortex and medulla. The **cortex** (outer part) secretes various steroid hormones and other hormones that control salt and water metabolism and regulate the use of carbohydrates, proteins, and fats. The **medulla** (inner part) secretes the hormones adrenaline and noradrenaline which, during times of stress, cause the heart to beat faster and harder, increase blood flow to the heart and muscle cells, and dilate airways in the lungs, thereby delivering more oxygen to cells throughout the body and in general preparing the body for 'fight or flight'.

antigen any substance that causes the production of antibodies by the body's immune system. Common antigens include the proteins carried on the surface of bacteria, viruses, and pollen grains. The proteins of incompatible blood groups or tissues also act as antigens, which has to be taken into account in medical procedures such as blood transfusions and organ transplants.

aorta the body's main artery, arising from the left ventricle of the heart. Carrying freshly oxygenated blood, it arches over the top of the heart and descends through the trunk, finally splitting in the lower abdomen to form the two iliac arteries. Loss of elasticity in the aorta provides evidence of atherosclerosis, which may lead to heart disease.

artery vessel that carries blood from the heart to the rest of the body. It is built to withstand considerable pressure, having thick walls which contain smooth muscle fibres. During contraction of the heart muscle, arteries expand in diameter to allow for the sudden increase in pressure that occurs; the resulting pulse or pressure wave can be felt at the wrist. Not all arteries carry oxygenated (oxygen-rich) blood; the pulmonary arteries convey deoxygenated (oxygen-poor) blood from the heart to the lungs.

axon long threadlike extension of a nerve cell that conducts electrochemical impulses away from the cell body towards other nerve cells, or towards an effector organ such as a muscle. Axons terminate in synapses, junctions with other nerve cells, muscles, or glands.

ball-and-socket joint joint allowing considerable movement in three dimensions, for instance the joint between the pelvis and the femur. To facilitate movement, such joints are rimmed with cartilage and lubricated by synovial fluid. The bones are kept in place by ligaments and moved by muscles.

bile brownish alkaline fluid produced by the liver. Bile is stored in the gall bladder and is intermittently released into the duodenum (small intestine) to aid digestion. Bile consists of bile salts, bile pigments, cholesterol, and lecithin. **Bile salts** assist in the breakdown and absorption of fats; **bile pigments** are the breakdown products of old red blood cells that are passed into the gut to be eliminated with the faeces.

bladder hollow elastic-walled organ which stores the urine produced in the kidneys. Urine enters the bladder through two ureters, one leading from each kidney, and leaves it through the urethra.

blood fluid circulating in the arteries, veins, and capillaries. Blood carries nutrients and oxygen to each body cell and removes waste products, such as carbon dioxide. It is also important in the immune response and in the distribution of heat throughout the body.

blood clotting complex series of events (known as the blood clotting cascade) that prevents excessive bleeding after injury. The result is the formation of a meshwork of protein fibres (fibrin) and trapped blood cells over the cut blood vessels.

blood group any of the types into which blood is classified according to the presence or otherwise of certain antigens on the surface of its red cells. Red blood cells of one individual may carry molecules on their surface that act as antigens in another individual whose red blood cells lack these molecules. The two main antigens are designated A and B. These give rise to four blood

---

Artificial bladder

■ US urologists succeeded in growing a whole bladder in 1998. The bladder was grown over 6 weeks from 1cm of bladder tissue which had been separated into muscle and epithelial tissue. The cells were then 'painted' onto a bladder-shaped biodegradable polymer (muscle outside, epithelial cells inside). The research was carried out on dogs and the engineered bladders were found to function normally with almost the same capacity as a natural bladder.

---

groups: having A only (A), having B only (B), having both (AB), and having neither (O). Each of these groups may or may not contain the rhesus factor. Correct typing of blood groups is vital in transfusion, since incompatible types of donor and recipient blood will result in coagulation, with possible death of the recipient.

bone hard connective tissue comprising the skeleton. Bone is composed of a network of collagen fibres impregnated with mineral salts (largely calcium phosphate and calcium carbonate), a combination that gives it great density and strength, comparable in some cases with that of reinforced concrete. Enclosed within this solid matrix are bone cells, blood vessels, and nerves. The interior of the long bones of the limbs consists of a spongy matrix filled with a soft marrow that produces blood cells.

bone marrow substance found inside the cavity of bones. In early life it produces red blood cells but later on lipids (fat) accumulate and its colour changes from red to yellow.

Compatibility of Blood Groups

Blood group	Antigen on red blood cell	Antibody in plasma	Blood groups that can be received by this individual	Blood groups that can receive donations from this individual
A	A	anti-B	A, O	A, AB
B	B	anti-A	B, O	B, AB
AB	A and B	none	any	AB
O	neither A nor B	anti-A and anti-B	O	any

What are we made of?

organs

In the upper part of the trunk is the thorax, which contains the lungs and heart. Below this is the abdomen, containing the digestive system (stomach and intestines); the liver, spleen, and pancreas; the urinary system (kidneys, ureters, and bladder); and, in women, the reproductive organs (ovaries, uterus, and vagina). In men, the prostate gland and seminal vesicles only of the reproductive system are situated in the abdomen, the testes being in the scrotum, which, with the penis, is suspended in front of and below the abdomen. The bladder empties through a small channel (urethra); in the female this opens in the upper end of the vulval cleft, which also contains the opening of the vagina, or birth canal; in the male, the urethra is continued into the penis. In both sexes, the lower bowel terminates in the anus, a ring of strong muscle situated between the buttocks.

skeleton

The skull is mounted on the spinal column, or spine, a chain of 24 vertebrae. The ribs, 12 on each side, are articulated to the spinal column behind, and the upper seven meet the breastbone (sternum) in front. The lower end of the spine rests on the pelvic girdle, composed of the triangular sacrum, to which are attached the hipbones (ilia), which are fused in front. Below the sacrum is the tailbone (coccyx). The shoulder blades (scapulae) are held in place behind the upper ribs by muscles, and connected in front to the breastbone by the two collarbones (clavicles).

Each shoulder blade carries a cup (glenoid cavity) into which fits the upper end of the armbone (humerus). This articulates below with the two forearm bones (radius and ulna). These are articulated at the wrist (carpals) to the bones of the hand (metacarpals and phalanges). The upper end of each thighbone (femur) fits into a depression (acetabulum) in the hipbone; its lower end is articulated at the knee to the shinbone (tibia) and calf bone (fibula), which are articulated at the ankle (tarsals) to the bones of the foot (metatarsals and phalanges). At a moving joint, the end of each bone is formed of tough, smooth cartilage, lubricated by synovial fluid. Points of special stress are reinforced by bands of fibrous tissue (ligaments).

skin

The exterior surface of the body is covered with skin. Within the skin are the sebaceous glands, which secrete sebum, an oily fluid that makes the skin soft and pliable, and the sweat glands, which secrete water and various salts. From the skin grow hairs, chiefly on the head, in the armpits, and around the sexual organs; and nails shielding the tips of the fingers and toes; both hair and nails are modifications of skin tissue. The skin also contains nerve receptors for sensations of touch, pain, heat, and cold.

Human Body: Composition

Chemical element or substance	Body weight (%)	Chemical element or substance	Body weight (%)
Pure elements		magnesium, iron, manganese, copper,	
oxygen	65	iodine, cobalt, zinc	traces
carbon	18	**Water and solid matter**	
hydrogen	10	water	60–80
nitrogen	3	total solid material	20–40
calcium	2		
phosphorus	1.1	**Organic molecules**	
potassium	0.35	protein	15–20
sulphur	0.25	lipid	3–20
sodium	0.15	carbohydrate	1–15
chlorine	0.15	other	0–1

What are we made of? (continued)

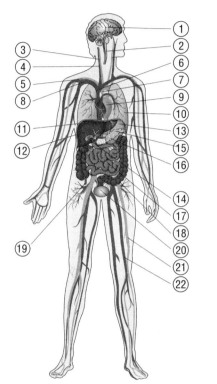

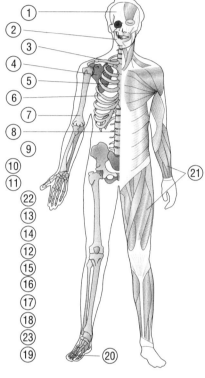

Major organs and blood vessels

1. brain
2. spinal cord
3. carotid artery
4. jugular vein
5. subclavian artery
6. superior vena cava
7. aorta
8. subclavian vein
9. heart
10. lungs
11. diaphragm
12. liver
13. stomach
14. gall bladder
15. kidney
16. pancreas
17. small intestine or ileum
18. large intestine or colon
19. appendix
20. bladder
21. popliteal artery
22. popliteal vein

Musculosketetal System

1. cranium (skull)
2. mandible
3. clavicle
4. scapula
5. sternum
6. rib cage
7. humerus
8. vertebra
9. ulna
10. radius
11. pelvis
12. sacrum
13. metacarpals
14. phalanges
15. femur
16. patella
17. fibula
18. tibia
19. metatarsals
20. phalanges
21. superficial (upper) layer of muscles
22. carpals
23. tarsals

human body The adult human body has approximately 650 muscles, 100 joints, 100,000 km/60,000 mi of blood vessels and 13,000 nerve cells. There are 206 bones in the adult body, nearly half of them in the hands and feet.

brain mass of interconnected nerve cells forming the anterior part of the central nervous system, whose activities it coordinates and controls. In vertebrates, the brain is contained by the skull. At the base of the brainstem, the **medulla oblongata** contains centres for the control of respiration, heartbeat rate and strength, and blood pressure. Overlying this is the **cerebellum,** which is concerned with coordinating complex muscular processes such as maintaining posture and moving limbs.

The cerebral hemispheres (**cerebrum**) are paired outgrowths of the front end of the forebrain greatly developed and involved in the integration of all sensory input and motor output, and in thought, emotions, memory, and behaviour.

bronchus one of a pair of large tubes (bronchi) branching off from the windpipe and passing into the vertebrate lung. Apart from their size, bronchi differ from the bronchioles in possessing cartilaginous rings, which give rigidity and prevent collapse during breathing movements.

cilia singular **cilium** small hairlike organs on the surface of some cells, particularly the cells lining the upper respiratory tract. Their wavelike

How we hear

The ear responds to the vibrations that constitute sound, which are translated into nerve signals and passed to the brain. The human ear consists of three parts: outer ear, middle ear, and inner ear. The **outer ear** is a funnel that collects sound, directing it down a tube to the **ear drum** (tympanic membrane), which separates the outer and **middle ear**s. Sounds vibrate this membrane, the mechanical movement of which is transferred to a smaller membrane leading to the **inner ear** by three small bones, the auditory ossicles. Vibrations of the inner ear membrane move fluid contained in the snail-shaped cochlea, which vibrates hair cells (**stereocilia)** that stimulate the auditory nerve connected to the brain. Exposure to loud noise and the process of ageing damages the stereocilia, resulting in hearing loss. Three fluid-filled canals of the inner ear detect changes of position; this mechanism, with other sensory inputs, is responsible for the sense of balance.

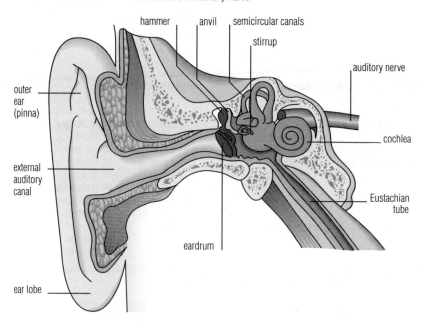

hammer · anvil · semicircular canals · stirrup · auditory nerve · outer ear (pinna) · cochlea · external auditory canal · Eustachian tube · eardrum · ear lobe

ear The structure of the ear. The three bones (auditory ossicles) of the middle ear – hammer, anvil, and stirrup – vibrate in unison and magnify sounds about 20 times. The spiral-shaped cochlea is the organ of hearing. As sound waves pass down the spiral tube, they vibrate fine hairs lining the tube, which activate the auditory nerve connected to the brain. The semicircular canals are the organs of balance, detecting movements of the head.

movements waft particles of dust and debris towards the exterior and keep lubricated surfaces clear of debris.

circulatory system system of vessels that transports blood to and from the different parts of the body. It was first discovered and described by English physician, William Harvey. It consists principally of a pumping organ – the heart – and a network of blood vessels.

coccyx lowermost component of the spine. It consists of four vestigial vertebrae fused to form a single triangular bone.

cochlea part of the inner ear. It is equipped with approximately 10,000 hair cells, which move in response to sound waves and thus stimulate nerve cells to send messages to the brain. In this way they turn vibrations of the air into electrical signals.

collagen protein that is the main constituent of connective tissue. Collagen is present in skin, cartilage, tendons, and ligaments. Bones are made up of collagen, with the mineral calcium phosphate providing increased rigidity.

connective tissue tissue made up of a noncellular substance, the extracellular matrix, in which some

How we see

Light entering the eye is focused by the combined action of the curved **cornea,** the internal fluids, and the **lens.** The eye is a roughly spherical structure contained in a bony socket. Light enters it through the cornea,

and passes through the circular opening (**pupil**) in the iris (the coloured part of the eye). The ciliary muscles act on the lens (the rounded transparent structure behind the iris) to change its shape, so that images

of objects at different distances can be focused on the **retina.** This is at the back of the eye, and is packed with light-sensitive cells (rods and cones), connected to the brain by the optic nerve.

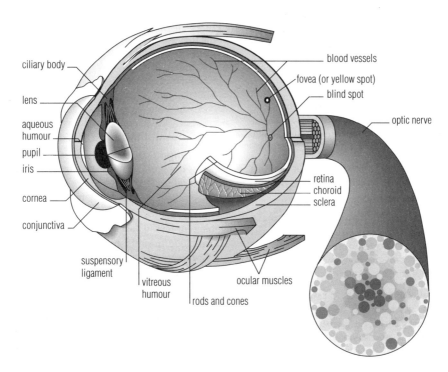

eye The human eye. The retina of the eye contains about 137 million light-sensitive cells in an area of about 650 sq mm/1 sq in. There are 130 million rod cells for black and white vision and 7 million cone cells for colour vision. The optic nerve contains about 1 million nerve fibres. The focusing muscles of the eye adjust about 100,000 times a day. To exercise the leg muscles to the same extent would need an 80 km/50 mi walk.

cells are embedded. Skin, bones, tendons, cartilage, and adipose tissue (fat) are the main connective tissues. There are also small amounts of connective tissue in organs such as the brain and liver, where they maintain shape and structure.

cornea transparent front section of the vertebrate eye. The cornea is curved and behaves as a fixed lens, so that light entering the eye is partly focused before it reaches the lens.

duodenum short length of alimentary canal found between the stomach and the small intestine. Its role is in digesting carbohydrates, fats, and proteins. The smaller molecules formed are then absorbed, either by the duodenum or the ileum.

ear see **how we hear** feature.

eye see **how we see** feature.

Fallopian tube or **oviduct** one of two tubes that carry eggs from the ovary to the uterus. An egg is fertilized by sperm in the Fallopian tubes, which are lined with cells whose cilia move the egg towards the uterus.

fibrin insoluble protein involved in blood clotting. When an injury occurs fibrin is deposited around the wound in the form of a mesh, which dries and hardens, so that bleeding stops. Fibrin is developed in the blood from a soluble protein, fibrinogen.

gall bladder small muscular sac, part of the digestive system situated on the underside of the liver and connected to the small intestine by the bile duct. It stores bile from the liver.

ganglion plural **ganglia** solid cluster of nervous tissue containing many cell bodies and synapses, usually enclosed in a tissue sheath.

gonad the part of the body that produces the sperm or egg cells (ova) required for sexual reproduction. The sperm-producing gonad is called a testis, and the egg-producing gonad is called an ovary.

Graafian follicle fluid-filled capsule that surrounds and protects the developing egg cell inside the ovary during the menstrual cycle. After the egg cell has been released, the follicle remains and is known as a corpus luteum.

gut or **alimentary canal** in the digestive system, the part responsible for processing food and preparing it for entry into the blood.

haemoglobin protein used for oxygen transport because the two substances combine reversibly. It occurs in red blood cells (erythrocytes), giving them their colour.

hair fine filament growing from the skin. Each hair grows from a pit-shaped follicle embedded in the second layer of the skin, the dermis. It consists of dead cells impregnated with the protein keratin.

heart muscular organ that rhythmically contracts to force blood around the body. It consists of four chambers, two atria and two ventricles. The beating of the heart is controlled by the autonomic nervous system and an internal control centre or pacemaker, the **sinoatrial node.**

ileum part of the small intestine of the digestive system, between the duodenum and the colon, that absorbs digested food.

intestine the digestive tract from the stomach outlet to the anus. The **small intestine** is 6 m/20 ft long, 4 cm/1.5 in in diameter, and consists of the duodenum, jejunum, and ileum; the **large intestine** is 1.5 m/5 ft long, 6 cm/2.5 in in diameter, and includes the caecum, colon, and rectum. Both are muscular tubes comprising an inner lining that secretes alkaline digestive juice, a submucous coat containing fine blood vessels and nerves, a muscular coat, and a serous coat covering all, supported by a strong peritoneum, which carries the blood and lymph vessels, and the nerves. The contents are passed along slowly by peristalsis (waves of involuntary muscular action).

islets of Langerhans groups of cells within the pancreas responsible for the secretion of the hormone insulin. They are sensitive to the blood sugar, producing more hormone when glucose levels rise.

jugular vein one of two veins in the necks; they return blood from the head to the superior (or anterior) vena cava and thence to the heart.

kidney one of a pair of organs responsible for fluid regulation, excretion of waste products, and maintaining the ionic composition of the blood. The kidneys are situated on the rear wall of the abdomen. Each one consists of a number of long tubules; the outer parts filter the aqueous components of blood, and the inner parts selectively reabsorb vital salts, leaving waste products in the remaining fluid (urine), which is passed through the ureter to the bladder.

What is a hormone?

A hormone is a chemical secretion of the ductless endocrine glands and specialized nerve cells concerned with control of body functions. The major glands are the thyroid, parathyroid, pituitary, adrenal, pancreas, ovary, and testis. There are also hormone-secreting cells in the kidney, liver, gastrointestinal tract, thymus (in the neck), pineal (in the brain), and placenta. Hormones bring about changes in the functions of various organs according to the body's requirements. The hypothalamus, which adjoins the pituitary gland at the base of the brain, is a control centre for overall coordination of hormone secretion; the thyroid hormones determine the rate of general body chemistry; the adrenal hormones prepare the organism during stress for 'fight or flight'; and the sexual hormones such as oestrogen and testosterone govern reproductive functions.

Hormones and their functions

Gland	Hormone	Functions
posterior pituitary gland	anti-diuretic hormone (ADH)	water reabsorption from kidney tubules
	oxytocin	contraction of the uterus during birth
anterior pituitary gland	growth hormone (GH)	growth
	prolactin	milk production and secretion
	follice-stimulating hormone (FSH)	in females, maturation of the Graafian follicle; in males, sperm production
	luteininzing hormone (LH)	in females, ovulation, formation of the corpus luteum; in males, testosterone synthesis
	thyroid stimulating hormone (TSH)	stimulates the thyroid to release thyroid hormones
	adrenocorticotrophic hormone (ACTH)	stimulates the adrenal cortext to produce corticosteroid hormones
ovary	oestrogen	female secondary sexual characteristics
ovary and placenta	progesterone	prepares uterus for pregnancy; maintains it during pregnancy
testis	testosterone	male secondary sexual characteristics
adrenal gland (cortex)	corticosteroid hormones	controls salt and water metabolism; regulates use of carbohydrates, proteins, and fats
adrenal gland (medulla)	adrenaline	'fright, flight, or fight': increases heart activity, rate and depth of breathing, blood flow to muscles; inhibits digestion and excretion
thyroid	thyroxine	regulates metabolism and growth
	calcitonin	regulates blood calcium levels by reducing release of calcium from bones
parathyroid	parathormone	regulates blood calcium levels by stimulating release of calcium from bones
pancreas (islets of Langerhans)	insulin	regulates blood glucose levels by stimulating conversion of glucose to glycogen
	glucagon	regulates blood glucose levels by stimulating conversion of glycogen to glucose

larynx cavity at the upper end of the trachea (windpipe) containing the vocal cords. It is stiffened with cartilage and lined with mucous membrane. Amphibians and reptiles have much simpler larynxes, with no vocal cords.

liver large organ which has many regulatory and storage functions. The human liver is situated in the upper abdomen, and weighs about 2 kg/4.5 lb. It is divided into four lobes. The liver receives the products of digestion, converts glucose to glycogen (a long-chain carbohydrate used for storage), and then back to glucose when needed. In this way the liver regulates the level of glucose in the blood. It removes excess amino acids from the blood, converting them to urea, which is excreted by the kidneys. The liver also synthesizes vitamins, produces bile and blood-clotting factors, and removes damaged red cells and toxins such as alcohol from the blood.

lung large cavity in the thorax, used for gas exchange. It is essentially a sheet of thin, moist membrane that is folded so as to occupy less space. The lung tissue, consisting of multitudes of air sacs and blood vessels, is very light and spongy, and functions by bringing inhaled air into close contact with the blood so that oxygen can pass into the organism and waste carbon dioxide can be passed out. The efficiency of lungs is enhanced by breathing movements, by the thinness and moistness of their surfaces, and by a constant supply of circulating blood.

lymph fluid found in the lymphatic system of vertebrates.

lymph nodes small masses of lymphatic tissue in the body that occur at various points along the major lymphatic vessels. Tonsils and adenoids are large lymph nodes. As the lymph passes through them it is filtered, and bacteria and other microorganisms are engulfed by cells known as macrophages.

lymphocyte type of white blood cell with a large nucleus, produced in the bone marrow. Most occur in the lymph and blood, and around sites of infection. **B lymphocytes** or B cells are responsible for producing antibodies. **T lymphocytes** or T cells have several roles in the mechanism of immunity.

Long-lasting lymphocytes
■ Fetal lymphocytes can persist in the mother's blood for up to 27 years.

---

macrophage type of white blood cell. Macrophages specialize in the removal of bacteria and other microorganisms, or of cell debris after injury. Like phagocytes, they engulf foreign matter, but they are larger than phagocytes and have a longer life span. They are found throughout the body, but mainly in the lymph and connective tissues, and especially the lungs, where they ingest dust, fibres, and other inhaled particles.

medulla central part of an organ. In the kidney, the medulla lies beneath the outer cortex and is responsible for the reabsorption of water from the filtrate. In plants, it is a region of packing tissue in the centre of the stem. In the vertebrate brain, the medulla is the posterior region responsible for the coordination of basic activities, such as breathing and temperature control.

molar one of the large teeth found towards the back of the mouth. The structure of the jaw, and the relation of the muscles, allows a massive force to be applied to molars.

monoclonal antibody (MAB) antibody produced by fusing an antibody-producing lymphocyte with a cancerous myeloma (bone-marrow) cell. The resulting fused cell, called a hybridoma, is immortal and can be used to produce large quantities of a single, specific antibody. By choosing antibodies that are directed against antigens found on cancer cells, and combining them with cytotoxic drugs, it is hoped to make so-called magic bullets that will be able to pick out and kill cancers.

motor nerve any nerve that transmits impulses from the central nervous system to muscles or organs. Motor nerves cause voluntary and involuntary muscle contractions, and stimulate glands to secrete hormones.

mouth cavity forming the entrance to the digestive tract enclosed by the jaws, cheeks, and palate. Air from the nostrils enters the mouth cavity to pass down the trachea.

mucous membrane thin skin lining all body cavities and canals that come into contact with the air (for example, eyelids, breathing and digestive passages, genital tract). It secretes mucus, a moistening, lubricating, and protective fluid.

muscle contractile tissue that produces locomotion and power, and maintains the movement of body substances. Muscle is made of long cells that can contract to between one-half and one-third of their relaxed length.

myoglobin globular protein, closely related to haemoglobin and located in vertebrate muscle. Oxygen binds to myoglobin and is released only when the haemoglobin can no longer supply adequate oxygen to muscle cells.

nephron microscopic unit in the kidneys that forms **urine.** A human kidney is composed of over a million nephrons. Each nephron consists of a knot of blood capillaries called a glomerulus, contained in the Bowman's capsule, and a long narrow tubule enmeshed with yet more capillaries. Waste materials and water pass from the bloodstream into the tubule, and essential minerals and some water are reabsorbed from the tubule back into the bloodstream. The remaining filtrate (urine) is passed out from the body.

nerve bundle of nerve cells enclosed in a sheath of connective tissue and transmitting nerve impulses to and from the brain and spinal cord. A single nerve may contain both motor and sensory nerve cells, but they function independently.

nerve cell or **neuron** elongated cell, the basic functional unit of the nervous system that transmits information rapidly between different parts of the body. Each nerve cell has a cell body, containing the nucleus, from which trail processes called dendrites, responsible for receiving incoming signals. The unit of information is the **nerve impulse,** a travelling wave of chemical and electrical changes involving the membrane of the nerve cell. The cell's longest process, the axon, carries impulses away from the cell body.

nervous system the system of interconnected nerve cells composed of the central and autonomic nervous systems. The central nervous system comprises of a brain and spinal cord with the peripheral nervous system connecting up with sensory organs, muscles, and glands.

neuron another name for a nerve cell.

oesophagus muscular tube by which food travels from mouth to stomach. The human oesophagus is about 23 cm/9 in long. Its extends downwards from the pharynx, immediately behind the windpipe. It is lined with a mucous membrane which secretes lubricant fluid to assist the downward movement of food (peristalsis).

optic nerve large nerve passing from the eye to the brain, carrying visual information. It may contain up to a million nerve fibres, connecting the sensory cells of the retina to the optical centres in the brain. Embryologically, the optic nerve develops as an outgrowth of the brain.

ovary organ that generates the ovum. The ovaries are two whitish rounded bodies about 25 mm/ 1 in by 35 mm/1.5 in, located in the lower abdomen to either side of the uterus. Every month, from puberty to the onset of the menopause, an ovum is released from the ovary. This is called ovulation, and forms part of the menstrual cycle.

pancreas an accessory gland of the digestive system located close to the duodenum. When stimulated by the hormone secretin, it releases enzymes into the duodenum that digest starches, proteins, and fats. It is about 18 cm/7 in long, and lies behind and below the stomach. It contains groups of cells called the **islets of Langerhans,** which secrete the hormones insulin and glucagon that regulate the blood sugar level.

pectoral relating to the upper area of the thorax associated with the muscles and bones used in moving the arms or forelimbs.

pelvis lower area of the abdomen featuring the bones and muscles used to move the legs. The **pelvic girdle** is a set of bones that allows movement of the legs in relation to the rest of the body and provides sites for the attachment of relevant muscles.

penis male reproductive organ containing the urethra, the channel through which urine and semen are voided. It transfers sperm to the female reproductive tract to fertilize the ovum. The penis is made erect by vessels that fill with blood.

pharynx muscular cavity behind the nose and mouth, extending downwards from the base of the skull. Its walls are made of muscle strengthened with a fibrous layer and lined with mucous membrane. The internal nostrils lead backwards into the pharynx, which continues downwards into the oesophagus and (through the epiglottis) into the windpipe. On each side, a Eustachian tube enters the pharynx from the middle ear cavity.

pituitary gland major endocrine gland situated in the centre of the brain. It is attached to the hypothalamus by a stalk. The pituitary consists of two lobes. The posterior lobe is an extension of the hypothalamus, and is in effect nervous tissue. It stores two hormones synthesized in the hypothalamus: ADH and oxytocin. The anterior lobe secretes six hormones, some of which control the activities of other glands (thyroid, gonads, and adrenal cortex); others are direct-acting hormones affecting milk secretion and controlling growth.

platelet tiny disc-shaped structure found in the blood, which helps it to clot. Platelets are not true cells, but membrane-bound cell fragments without nuclei that bud off from large cells in the bone marrow.

prostate gland gland surrounding and opening into the urethra at the base of the bladder in males.

retina light-sensitive area at the back of the eye connected to the brain by the optic nerve. It has several layers and in humans contains over a million rods and cones, sensory cells capable of converting light into nervous messages that pass down the optic nerve to the brain.

saliva alkaline secretion from the salivary glands that aids the swallowing and digestion of food in the mouth. In mammals, it contains the enzyme amylase, which converts starch to sugar.

sense organ any organ used to gain information about surroundings. All sense organs have specialized receptors (such as light receptors in the eye) and some means of translating their response into a nerve impulse that travels to the brain. The main human sense organs are the eye, which detects light and colour (different

Bones of the Human Body

Bone	Number	Bone	Number	Bone	Number
Cranium (Skull)		**Sternum (Breastbone)**		**Pelvic Girdle**	
Occipital	1	Manubrium	1	Ilium, ischium, and pubis	
Parietal: 1 pair	2	Sternebrae	1	(combined): 1 pair of hip bones,	
Sphenoid	1	Xiphisternum	1	innominate	2
Ethmoid	1	**Total**	3	**Total**	2
Inferior nasal conchae	2				
Frontal: 1 pair, fused	1	**Throat**		**Lower Extremity (Each Leg)**	
Nasal: 1 pair	2	Hyoid	1	**Leg**	
Lacrimal: 1 pair	2	**Total**	1	Femur (thighbone)	1
Temporal: 1 pair	2			Tibia (shinbone)	1
Maxilla: 1 pair, fused	1	**Pectoral Girdle**		Fibula	1
Zygomatic: 1 pair	2	Clavicle: 1 pair (collar-bone)	2	Patella (kneecap)	1
Vomer	1	Scapula (including coracoid): 1 pair			
Palatine: 1 pair	2	(shoulder blade)	2	**Tarsus (Ankle)**	
Mandible (jawbone): 1 pair, fused	1	**Total**	4	Talus	1
Total	21			Calcaneus	1
		Upper Extremity (Each Arm)		Navicular	1
Ears		**Forearm**		Cuneiform, medial	1
Malleus (hammer)	2	Humerus	1	Cuneiform, intermediate	1
Incus (anvil)	2	Radius	1	Cuneiform, lateral	1
Stapes (stirrups)	2	Ulna	1	Cuboid	1
Total	6			Metatarsals (foot bones)	5
		Carpus (Wrist)			
Vertebral Column (Spine)		Scaphoid	1	**Phalanges (Toes)**	
Cervical vertebrae	7	Lunate	1	First digit	2
Thoracic vertebrae	12	Triquetral	1	Second digit	3
Lumbar vertebrae	5	Pisiform	1	Third digit	3
Sacral vertebrae: 5, fused to form the		Trapezium	1	Fourth digit	3
sacrum	1	Trapezoid	1	Fifth digit	3
Coccygeal vertebrae: between 3 and 5,		Capitate	1	**Total**	30
fused to form the coccyx	1	Hamate	1		
Total	26	Metacarpals	5	**TOTAL**	207
Ribs		**Phalanges (Fingers)**			
Ribs, 'true': 7 pairs	14	First digit	2		
Ribs, 'false': 5 pairs, of which		Second digit	3		
2 pairs are floating	10	Third digit	3		
Total	24	Fourth digit	3		
		Fifth digit	3		
		Total	30		

wavelengths of light); the ear, which detects sound (vibrations of the air) and gravity; the nose, which detects some of the chemical molecules in the air; and the tongue, which detects some of the chemicals in food, giving a sense of taste. There are also many small sense organs in the skin, including pain, temperature, and pressure sensors, contributing to our sense of touch.

skeleton the rigid or semirigid framework that supports and gives form to the body, protects its internal organs, and provides anchorage points for its muscles. The skeleton is composed of bone and cartilage. The human skeleton has 206 bones, with the vertebral column (spine) forming the central supporting structure.

spleen organ in vertebrates, part of the reticulo-endothelial system, which helps to process lymphocytes. It also regulates the number of red blood cells in circulation by destroying old cells, and stores iron. It is situated on the left side of the body, behind the stomach.

stomach the first cavity in the digestive system. It is a bag of muscle situated just below the diaphragm. Food enters it from the oesophagus, is digested by the acid and enzymes secreted by the stomach lining, and then passes into the duodenum.

What is skin?

Skin is the covering of the body. The outer layer (epidermis) is dead and its cells are constantly being rubbed away and replaced from below; it helps to protect the body from infection and to prevent dehydration. The lower layer (dermis) contains blood vessels, nerves, hair roots, and sweat and sebaceous glands, and is supported by a network of fibrous and elastic cells. The medical speciality concerned with skin diseases is called dermatology.

> **Shedding skin**
> ■ Each person sheds an average of 18 kg/40 lb of skin in a lifetime.

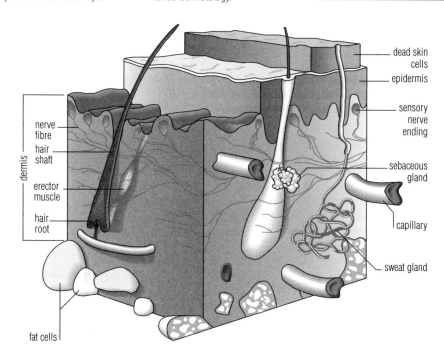

skin The skin of an adult man covers about 1.9 sq m/20 sq ft; a woman's skin covers about 1.6 sq m/17 sq ft. During our lifetime, we shed about 18 kg/40 lb of skin.

synapse junction between two nerve cells, or between a nerve cell and a muscle (a neuro-muscular junction), across which a nerve impulse is transmitted. The two cells are separated by a narrow gap called the **synaptic cleft.** The gap is bridged by a chemical neurotransmitter, released by the nerve impulse.

synovial fluid viscous colourless fluid that bathes movable joints between the bones of vertebrates. It nourishes and lubricates the cartilage at the end of each bone.

tendon or **sinew** cord of very strong, fibrous connective tissue that joins muscle to bone. Tendons are largely composed of bundles of fibres made of the protein collagen, and because of their inelasticity are very efficient at transforming muscle power into movement.

testis plural **testes** the organ that produces sperm in males. It is one of a pair of oval structures that descend from the body cavity during development, to hang outside the abdomen in a scrotal sac. The testes also secrete the male sex hormone androgen.

thorax part of the body containing the heart and lungs, and protected by the ribcage.

thymus organ situated in the upper chest cavity. The thymus processes lymphocyte cells to produce T-lymphocytes (T denotes 'thymus-derived'), which are responsible for binding to specific invading organisms and killing them or rendering them harmless.

thyroid endocrine gland situated in the neck in front of the trachea. It secretes several hormones, principally thyroxine, an iodine-containing hormone that stimulates growth, metabolism, and other functions of the body. The thyroid gland may be thought of as the regulator gland of the body's metabolic rate. If it is overactive, as in hyperthyroidism, the sufferer feels hot and sweaty, has an increased heart rate, diarrhoea, and weight loss. Conversely, an underactive thyroid leads to **myxoedema,** a condition characterized by sensitivity to the cold, constipation, and weight gain. In infants, an underactive thyroid leads to **cretinism,** a form of mental retardation.

tooth one of a set of hard, bonelike structures in the mouth, used for biting and chewing food. The first set (20 milk teeth) appear from age six months to two and a half years. The permanent

Born with teeth
■ About one in every 2,000 babies is born with a tooth. Louis XIV of France was born with two teeth, which may explain why he had had eight wet-nurses by the time he moved on to solid foods.

dentition replaces these from the sixth year onwards, the wisdom teeth (third molars) sometimes not appearing until the age of 25 or 30. Adults have 32 teeth: two incisors, one canine (eye tooth), two premolars, and three molars on each side of each jaw. Each tooth consists of an enamel coat (hardened calcium deposits), dentine (a thick, bonelike layer), and an inner pulp cavity, housing nerves and blood vessels.

trachea or **windpipe** tube that forms an airway and runs from the larynx to the upper part of the chest. Its diameter is about 1.5 cm/0.6 in and its length 10 cm/4 in. It is strong and flexible, and reinforced by rings of cartilage. In the upper chest, the trachea branches into two tubes: the left and right bronchi, which enter the lungs.

ureter tube connecting the kidney to the bladder. Its wall contains fibres of smooth muscle whose contractions aid the movement of urine out of the kidney.

urethra tube connecting the bladder to the exterior. It carries urine and, in males, semen.

urinary system system of organs that removes nitrogenous waste products and excess water from the body. It consists of a pair of kidneys, which produce urine; ureters, which drain the kidneys; and a bladder that stores the urine before its discharge. The urine is expelled through the urethra.

urine amber-coloured fluid filtered out by the kidneys from the blood. It contains excess water, salts, proteins, waste products in the form of urea, a pigment, and some acid.

uterus hollow muscular organ located between the bladder and rectum in females, and connected to the Fallopian tubes above and the vagina below. The embryo develops within the uterus, and is attached to it after implantation via the placenta and umbilical cord. The lining of the uterus changes during the menstrual cycle.

vagina the lower part of the reproductive tract in females, linking the uterus to the exterior. It admits the penis during sexual intercourse, and is the birth canal down which the baby passes during delivery.

vas deferens in males, a tube conducting sperm from the testis to the urethra. The sperm is carried in a fluid secreted by various glands, and can be transported very rapidly when the smooth muscle in the wall of the vas deferens undergoes rhythmic contraction, as in sexual intercourse.

vein any vessel that carries blood from the body to the heart. Veins contain valves that prevent the blood from running back when moving against gravity. They carry blood at low pressure, so their walls are thinner than those of arteries. They always carry deoxygenated blood, with the exception of the **pulmonary vein,** leading from the lungs to the heart, which carries newly oxygenated blood.

vena cava either of the two great veins of the trunk, returning deoxygenated blood to the right atrium of the heart. The **superior vena cava,** beginning where the arches of the two innominate veins join high in the chest, receives blood from the head, neck, chest, and arms; the **inferior vena cava,** arising from the junction of the right and left common iliac veins, receives blood from all parts of the body below the diaphragm.

vertebral column the backbone, giving support to an animal and protecting its spinal cord. It is made up of a series of 26 bones or vertebrae running from the skull to the tail, with a central canal containing the nerve fibres of the spinal cord. The vertebrae show some specialization with the shape of the bones varying according to position. In the chest region the upper or thoracic vertebrae are shaped to form connections to the ribs.

villus plural **villi** small fingerlike projection extending into the interior of the small intestine and increasing the absorptive area of the intestinal wall. Digested nutrients, including sugars and amino acids, pass into the villi and are carried away by the circulating blood.

vocal cords the paired folds, ridges or cords of tissue within the larynx. Air constricted between the folds or membranes makes them vibrate, producing sounds. Muscles in the larynx change the pitch of the sounds produced, by adjusting the tension of the vocal cords.

white blood cell or **leucocyte** one of a number of different cells that play a part in the body's defences and give immunity against disease. Some (neutrophils and macrophages) engulf invading microorganisms, others kill infected cells, while lymphocytes produce more specific immune responses. White blood cells are colourless, with clear or granulated cytoplasm, and are capable of independent amoeboid movement. They occur in the blood, lymph, and elsewhere in the body's tissues.

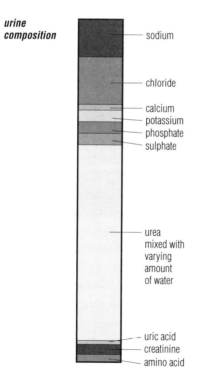

urine composition

sodium
chloride
calcium
potassium
phosphate
sulphate
urea mixed with varying amount of water
uric acid
creatinine
amino acid

urine Urine consists of excess water and waste products that have been filtered from the blood by the kidneys; it is stored in the bladder until it can be expelled from the body via the urethra. Analysing the composition of an individual's urine can reveal a number of medical conditions, such as poorly functioning kidneys, kidney stones, and diabetes.

Medical Abbreviations and Acronyms

A & E accident and emergency department

ABP arterial blood pressure

ADLs activities of daily living

adm. admission

aet. aetiology

AI artificial insemination

AIDS acquired immune deficiency syndrome

ALG antilymphocyte globulin

ALS antilymphocyte serum

ARM artificial rupture of membranes (for delivery)

BCG bacille Calmette-Guérin (TB vaccine)

BMI body mass index

BMR basal metabolic rate

BP blood pressure

BPD bronchopulmonary dysplasia

CA cancer

CABG coronary artery bypass graft

CAPD continuous ambulatory peritoneal dialysis

CAT computerized axial tomography

CCU coronary care unit

CJD Creutzfeldt-Jakob disease

CMV cytomegalovirus

CNS central nervous system

COAD chronic obstructive airways disease

CPAP continuous positive airways pressure

CPR cardiopulmonary resuscitation

CSF cerebrospinal fluid

CT computerized tomography

CV cardiovascular

CVA cardiovascular accident

CVP central venous pressure

CVS chorionic villus sampling

CXR chest X-ray

D & C dilation and curettage

DHA district health authority

DI donor insemination

DIC disseminated intravascular coagulation

disch. discharge

DL danger list

DMD Duchenne's muscular dystrophy

DNA deoxyribonucleic acid

DOA dead on arrival

DPT combined vaccine against diphtheria, pertussis (whooping cough), and tetanus

Dr doctor

DRG diagnostic related group

DTs delirium tremens

DVT deep vein thrombosis

ECG electrocardiogram

ECT electroconvulsive therapy

EEG electroencephalograph

EMG electromyograph

ENT ear, nose, and throat

EPO erythropoietin

ET endotracheal tube (used for patient on ventilator)

GH growth hormone

GIFT gamete intrafallopian transfer

GP general practitioner

GVHD graft-versus-host disease

HBIG hepatitis B immunoglobulin

HCG human chorionic gonadotrophin

HIV human immunodeficiency virus

HLA human leucocyte antigen system

HMO health maintenance organization

HRT hormone replacement therapy

IBS irritable bowel syndrome

ICD international classification of diseases

ICP intracranial pressure

ICU intensive care unit

IHD ischaemic heart disease

IMR infant mortality rate

IMV intermittent mandatory ventilation

IOP intraocular pressure

IPPV intermittent positive pressure ventilation

IQ intelligence quotient

IUD intrauterine device

IV intravenous

Medical Abbreviations and Acronyms (continued)

IVP intravenous pyelogram

IZS insulin zinc suspension

K & M kaolin and morphine

LBW low birth weight

LP lumbar puncture

LSD lysergic acid diethylamide

MAB monoclonal antibody

MAOI monoamine oxidase inhibitor

MAP mean arterial pressure

MBD minimal brain dysfunction

MD doctor of medicine

ME myalgic encephalomyelitis

MHC major histocompatibility complex

MI myocardial infarction

MLD minimum lethal dose

MMR combined vaccine against measles, mumps, and rubella (German measles)

MND motor neurone disease

MO medical officer

MRI magnetic resonance imaging

MRS magnetic resonance spectroscopy

MRSA methicillin-resistant Staphylococcus aureus

MS multiple sclerosis

MSU mid-stream urine specimen

NHS National Health Service (in the UK)

NPO nil per orem (nothing by mouth)

NTD neural tube defect

O & G obstetrics and gynaecology

OA osteoarthritis

OD overdose

OP outpatient

ORT oral rehydration therapy

OT occupational therapy

PA physician's assistant

paed. paediatrics

path. pathology

PCOD polycystic ovary disease

PE pleural effusion

PET positron-emission tomography

PICU paediatric intensive care unit

PID pelvic inflammatory disease

PIH pregnancy-induced hypertension

PKU phenylketonuria

PM postmortem

PMS premenstrual stress disorder

PO per orem (by mouth)

PoP plaster of Paris

pre-op pre-operative

PTA post-traumatic amnesia

RA rheumatoid arthritis

RDS respiratory distress syndrome

REM sleep rapid eye movement sleep

RES reticuloendothelial system

RN registered nurse

RNA ribonucleic acid

RQ respiratory quotient

RSI repetitive strain injury

RSV respiratory syncytial virus

Rx treatment/prescription

SAD seasonal affective disorder

SAH subarachnoid haemorrhage

SIDS sudden infant death syndrome

SLE systemic lupus erythematous

STD sexually transmitted disease

TAB combined vaccine against typhoid, paratyphoid A, and paratyphoid B

TAT thematic apperception test

TATT tired all the time

TB tuberculosis

TENS transcutaneous electrical nerve stimulation

TIA transient ischaemic attack

tPA tissue plasminogen activator (heart drug)

TPR temperature, pulse, and respiration

TS Tourette's syndrome

TSH thyroid-stimulating hormone

Tx transfusion, transplant

URTI upper respiratory tract infection

UTI urinary tract infection

VA visual acuity

VD venereal disease

VF ventricular fibrillation

WHO World Health Organization

PSYCHOLOGY AND PSYCHIATRY

Psychology is the systematic study of human and animal behaviour. The first psychology laboratory was founded in 1879 by Wilhelm Wundt at Leipzig, Germany. The subject includes diverse areas of study and application, among them the roles of instinct, heredity, environment, and culture; the processes of sensation, perception, learning, and memory; the bases of motivation and emotion; and the functioning of thought, intelligence, and language. Significant psychologists have included Gustav Fechner, founder of psychophysics; Wolfgang Köhler, one of the Gestalt or 'whole' psychologists; Sigmund Freud and his associates Carl Jung and Alfred Adler, psychoanalysts; Jean Piaget, developmental psychologist; J B Watson, founder of behaviourism; and B F Skinner, radical behaviourist.

Experimental psychology emphasizes the application of rigorous and objective scientific methods to the study of a wide range of mental processes and behaviour, whereas **social psychology** concerns the study of individuals within their social environment; for example, within groups and organizations. This has led to the development of related fields such as **occupational psychology,** which studies human behaviour at work, and **educational psychology.**

Clinical psychology concerns the understanding and treatment of mental health disorders, such as anxiety, phobias, or depression; treatment may include behaviour therapy, cognitive therapy, counselling, psychoanalysis, or some combination of these. Modern psychological studies have been diverse; for example, the psychological causes of obesity; the nature of religious experience; and the underachievement of women seen as resulting from social pressures. Other related subjects are the nature of sleep and dreams, and the possible extensions of the senses, which leads to the more contentious ground of parapsychology.

anorexia lack of desire to eat, or refusal to eat, especially the pathological condition of **anorexia nervosa,** most often found in adolescent girls and young women. Compulsive eating, or bulimia, distortions of body image, and depression often accompany anorexia.

anxiety unpleasant, distressing emotion usually to be distinguished from fear. Fear is aroused by the perception of actual or threatened danger; anxiety arises when the danger is imagined or cannot be identified or clearly perceived. It is a normal response in stressful situations, but is frequently experienced in many mental disorders.

attention-deficit hyperactivity disorder (ADHA) psychiatric condition occurring in young children characterized by impaired attention and hyperactivity. The disorder, associated with disruptive behaviour, learning difficulties, and under-achievement, is more common in boys. It is treated with methylphenidate (Ritalin).

autism, infantile rare disorder, generally present from birth, characterized by a withdrawn state and a failure to develop normally in language or social behaviour. Although the autistic child may, rarely, show signs of high intelligence (in music or with numbers, for example), many have impaired intellect. The cause is unknown, but is thought to involve a number of factors, possibly including an inherent abnormality of the child's brain. Special education may bring about some improvement.

behaviour therapy application of behavioural principles, derived from learning theories, to the treatment of clinical conditions such as phobias, obsessions, and sexual and interpersonal problems.

bulimia eating disorder in which large amounts of food are consumed in a short time ('binge'), usually followed by depression and self-criticism. The term is often used for **bulimia nervosa,** an emotional disorder in which eating is followed by deliberate vomiting and purging. This may be a chronic stage in anorexia nervosa.

cognitive therapy or **cognitive behaviour therapy** treatment for emotional disorders such as depression and anxiety states. It encourages the patient to challenge the distorted and unhelpful thinking that is characteristic of depression, for example. The treatment may include behaviour therapy.

delusion false belief that is unshakeably held. Delusions are a prominent feature of schizophrenia and paranoia, but may also occur in other psychiatric states.

depression emotional state characterized by sadness, unhappy thoughts, apathy, and dejection. Sadness is a normal response to major losses such as bereavement or unemployment. After childbirth, postnatal depression is common. Clinical depression, which is prolonged or unduly severe, often requires treatment, such as antidepressant medication, cognitive therapy, or, in very rare cases, electroconvulsive therapy (ECT), in which an electrical current is passed through the brain.

hyperactivity condition of excessive activity in young children, combined with restlessness, inability to concentrate, and difficulty in learning. There are various causes, ranging from temperamental predisposition to brain disease. In some cases food additives have come under suspicion; in such instances modification of the diet may help. Mostly there is improvement at puberty, but symptoms may persist in the small proportion diagnosed as having attention-deficit hyperactivity disorder.

libido in Freudian psychology, the energy of the sex instinct, which is to be found even in a newborn child. The libido develops through a number of phases, described by Sigmund Freud in his theory of infantile sexuality. The source of the libido is the id.

mania term used to describe high mood. The affected individual can appear cheerful and optimistic or irritable and angry. Sleep is reduced and the sufferer can be overactive to the point of physical exhaustion. Speech is rapid and can convey grandiose delusions. Mania often occurs as part of manic depression. It is treated with an antipsychotic drug to control the mood and, in the long term, with lithium.

manic depression or **bipolar disorder** mental disorder characterized by recurring periods of either depression or mania (inappropriate elation, agitation, and rapid thought and speech) or both. Sufferers may be genetically predisposed to the condition. Some cases have been improved by taking prescribed doses of lithium.

mental illness disordered functioning of the mind. Since normal working cannot easily be defined, the borderline between mild mental illness and normality is a matter of opinion (not to be confused with normative behaviour. It is broadly divided into two categories: neurosis, in which the patient remains in touch with reality; and psychosis, in which perception, thought, and belief are disordered.

nervous breakdown popular term for a reaction to overwhelming psychological stress. There is no equivalent medical term. People said to be suffering from a nervous breakdown may be suffering from a neurotic illness, such as depression or anxiety, or a psychotic illness, such as schizophrenia.

neurosis general term referring to emotional disorders, such as anxiety, depression, and phobias. The main disturbance tends to be one of mood; contact with reality is relatively unaffected, in contrast to psychosis.

obsession persistently intruding thought, emotion, or impulse, often recognized by the sufferer as irrational, but nevertheless causing distress. It may be a brooding on destiny or death, or chronic doubts interfering with everyday life (such as fear-ing the gas is not turned off and repeatedly checking), or an impulse leading to repetitive action, such as continually washing one's hands.

paranoia mental disorder marked by delusions of grandeur or persecution. In popular usage, paranoia means baseless or exaggerated fear and suspicion.

phobia excessive irrational fear of an object or situation – for example, agoraphobia (fear of open spaces and crowded places), acrophobia (fear of heights), and claustrophobia (fear of enclosed places). Behaviour therapy is one form of treatment.

psychiatry branch of medicine dealing with the diagnosis and treatment of mental disorder, normally divided into the areas of **neurotic conditions,** including anxiety, depression, and hysteria, and **psychotic disorders,** such as schizophrenia. Psychiatric treatment consists of drugs, analysis, or electroconvulsive therapy.

psychoanalysis theory and treatment method for neuroses, developed by Sigmund Freud in the 1890s. Psychoanalysis asserts that the impact of early childhood sexuality and experiences, stored in the unconscious, can lead to the development of adult emotional problems. The main treatment method involves the free association of ideas, and their interpretation by patient and analyst, in order to discover these long-buried events and to grasp their significance to the patient, linking aspects of the patient's historical past with the present relationship to the analyst. Psychoanalytic treatment aims to free the patient from specific symptoms and from irrational inhibitions and anxieties.

psychosis or **psychotic disorder** general term for a serious mental disorder where the individual commonly loses contact with reality and may experience hallucinations (seeing or hearing things that do not exist) or delusions (fixed false beliefs). For example, in a paranoid psychosis, an individual may believe that others are plotting against him or her. A major type of psychosis is schizophrenia.

schizophrenia mental disorder, a psychosis of unknown origin, which can lead to profound changes in personality, behaviour, and perception, including delusions and hallucinations. It is more common in males and the early-onset form is more severe than when the illness develops in later life. Modern treatment approaches include drugs, family therapy, stress reduction, and rehabilitation.

Schizophrenia
■ Schizophrenics hardly ever yawn.

---

senile dementia dementia associated with old age, often caused by Alzheimer's disease.

stress event or situation that makes heightened demands on a person's mental or emotional resources. Stress can be caused by overwork, anxiety about exams, money, job security, unemployment, bereavement, poor relationships, marriage breakdown, sexual difficulties, poor living or working conditions, and constant exposure to loud noise.

Phobias

Fear	Name of phobia	Fear	Name of phobia
Animals	zoophobia	Fever	febriphobia
Bacteria	bacteriophobia, bacillophobia	Fire	pyrophobia
Beards	pogonophobia	Fish	ichthyophobia
Bees	apiphobia, melissophobia	Flying, the air	aerophobia
Being alone	monophobia, autophobia, eremophobia	Fog	homichlophobia
Being buried alive	taphophobia	Food	sitophobia
Being seen by others	scopophobia	Foreign languages	xenoglossophobia
Being touched	haphephobia, aphephobia	Freedom	eleutherophobia
Birds	ornithophobia	Fun	cherophobia
Blood	h(a)ematophobia, hemophobia	Germs	spermophobia, bacillophobia
Blushing	ereuthrophobia, erythrophobia	Ghosts	phasmophobia
Books	bibliophobia	Glass	hyalophobia
Cancer	cancerophobia, carcinophobia	God	theophobia
Cats	ailurophobia, gatophobia	Going to bed	clinophobia
Chickens	alektorophobia	Graves	taphophobia
Childbirth	tocophobia, parturiphobia	Hair	chaetophobia, trichophobia,
Children	paediphobia		hypertrichophobia
Cold	cheimatophobia, frigophobia	Heart conditions	cardiophobia
Colour	chromatophobia, chromophobia,	Heat	thermophobia
	psychrophobia	Heaven	ouranophobia
Comets	cometophobia	Heights	acrophobia, altophobia
Computers	computerphobia, cyberphobia	Hell	hadephobia, stygiophobia
Contamination	misophobia, coprophobia	Home	domatophobia, oikophobia
Criticism	enissophobia	Horses	hippophobia
Crossing bridges	gephyrophobia	Human beings	anthrophobia
Crossing streets	dromophobia	Ice, frost	cryophobia
Crowds	demophobia, ochlophobia	Ideas	ideophobia
Darkness	achulophobia, nyctophobia,	Illness	nosemaphobia, nosophobia
	scotophobia	Imperfection	atelophobia
Dawn	eosophobia	Infection	mysophobia
Daylight	phengophobia	Infinity	apeirophobia
Death, corpses	necrophobia, thanatophobia	Injustice	dikephobia
Defecation	rhypophobia	Inoculations, injections	trypanophobia
Deformity	dysmorphophobia	Insanity	lyssophobia, maniaphobia
Demons	demonophobia	Insects	entomophobia
Dirt	mysophobia	Itching	acarophobia, scabiophobia
Disease	nosophobia, pathophobia	Jealousy	zelophobia
Disorder	ataxiophobia	Knowledge	epistemophobia
Dogs	cynophobia	Lakes	limnophobia
Draughts	anemophobia	Large objects	macrophobia
Dreams	oneirophobia	Leaves	phyllophobia
Drinking	dipsophobia	Left side	levophobia
Drugs	pharmacophobia	Leprosy	leprophobia
Duration	chronophobia	Lice	pediculophobia
Dust	amathophobia, koniphobia	Lightning	astraphobia
Eating	phagophobia	Machinery	mechanophobia
Enclosed spaces	claustrophobia	Many things	polyphobia
Everything	pan(t)ophobia	Marriage	gamophobia
Facial hair	trichopathophobia	Meat	carnophobia
Faeces	coprophobia	Men	androphobia
Failure	kakorrhaphiaphobia	Metals	metallophobia
Fatigue	kopophobia, ponophobia	Meteors	meteorophobia
Fears	phobophobia	Mice	musophobia

(continued)

Phobias (continued)

Fear	Name of phobia	Fear	Name of phobia
Mind	psychophobia	Small objects	microphobia
Mirrors	eisoptrophobia, catotrophobia	Smell	olfactophobia
Money	chrometophobia	Smothering, choking	pnigerophobia
Monsters,	teratophobia	Snakes	ophidiophobia, ophiophobia
monstrosities		Snow	chionophobia
Motion	kinesophobia, kinetophobia	Soiling	rhypophobia
Music	musicophobia	Solitude	eremitophobia, eremophobia
Names	onomatophobia	Sound	akousticophobia
Narrowness	anginaphobia	Sourness	acerophobia
Needles	belonephobia	Speaking aloud	phonophobia
Night, darkness	achluophobia	Speed	tachophobia
Noise	phonophobia	Spiders	arachn(e)ophobia
Novelty	cainophobia, cenotophobia, neophobia	Standing	stasiphobia
Nudity	gymnotophobia	Standing erect	stasibasiphobia
Number 13	triskaidekaphobia, terdekaphobia	Stars	siderophobia
Odours	osmophobia	Stealing	kleptophobia
Open spaces	agoraphobia	Stillness	eremophobia
Pain	algophobia, odynophobia	Stings	cnidophobia
Parasites	parasitophobia	Strangers	xenophobia
Physical love	erotophobia	Strong light	photophobia
Pins	enetophobia	Stuttering	laliophobia, lalophobia
Places	topophobia	Suffocation	anginophobia
Pleasure	hedonophobia	Sun	heliophobia
Pointed instruments	aichmophobia	Symbols	symbolophobia
Poison	toxiphobia, toxophobia, iophobia	Taste	geumaphobia
Poverty	peniaphobia	Teeth	odontophobia
Precipices	cremnophobia	Thinking	phronemophobia
Pregnancy	maieusiophobia	Thrown objects	ballistophobia
Punishment	poinephobia	Thunder	astraphobia, brontophobia,
Rain	ombrophobia		keraunophobia
Reptiles	batrachophobia	Touch	aphephobia, haptophobia,
Responsibility	hypegiaphobia		haphephobia
Ridicule	katagalophobia	Travel	hodophobia
Rivers	potamophobia	Travelling by train	siderodromophobia
Robbery	harpaxophobia	Trees	dendrophobia
Ruin	atephobia	Trembling	tremophobia
Rust	iophobia	Vehicles	amaxophobia, ochophobia
Sacred things	hierophobia	Venereal disease	cypridophobia
Satan	satanophobia	Void	kenophobia
School	scholionophobia	Vomiting	emetophobia
Sea	thalassophobia	Walking	basiphobia
Semen	spermatophobia	Wasps	spheksophobia
Sex	genophobia	Water	hydrophobia, aquaphobia
Sexual intercourse	coitophobia	Weakness	asthenophobia
Shadows	sciophobia	Wind	ancraophobia
Sharp objects	belonephobia	Women	gynophobia
Shock	hormephobia	Words	logophobia
Sin	hamartiophobia	Work	ergophobia, ergasiophobia
Sinning	peccatophobia	Worms	helminthophobia
Skin	dermatophobia	Wounds, injury	traumatophobia
Sleep	hypnophobia	Writing	graphophobia

DISEASES AND DISORDERS

A disease is any condition that disturbs or impairs the normal state of an organism. Diseases can occur in all life forms, and normally affect the functioning of cells, tissues, organs, or systems. Diseases are usually characterized by specific symptoms and signs, and can be mild and short-lasting – such as the common cold – or severe enough to decimate whole communities – such as the 1918–19 flu pandemic that killed 20 million people worldwide. Diseases can be classified as infectious or noninfectious. **Infectious diseases** are caused by microorganisms, such as bacteria and viruses, invading the body; they can be spread across a species, or transmitted between one or more species. All other diseases can be grouped together as **noninfectious diseases.** These can have many causes: they may be inherited (congenital diseases); they may be caused by the ingestion or absorption of harmful substances, such as toxins; they can result from poor nutrition or hygiene; or they may arise from injury or ageing. The causes of some diseases are still unknown.

acne skin eruption, mainly occurring among adolescents and young adults, caused by inflammation of the sebaceous glands which secrete an oily substance (sebum), the natural lubricant of the skin. Sometimes the openings of the glands become blocked, causing the formation of pus-filled swellings. Teenage acne is seen mainly on the face, back, and chest.

AIDS acronym for **acquired immune deficiency syndrome** the gravest of the sexually transmitted diseases, or STDs. It is caused by the human immunodeficiency virus (HIV), now known to be a retrovirus, an organism first identified in 1983. HIV is transmitted in body fluids, mainly blood and genital secretions.

Alzheimer's disease common manifestation of dementia, thought to afflict one in 20 people over 65. After heart disease, cancer, and strokes it is the most common cause of death in the Western world. Attacking the brain's 'grey matter', it is a disease of mental processes rather than physical function, characterized by memory loss and progressive intellectual impairment. It was first described by Alois Alzheimer 1906. It affects up to 4 million people in the USA and around 600,000 in Britain.

anaemia condition caused by a shortage of haemoglobin, the oxygen-carrying component of red blood cells. The main symptoms are fatigue, pallor, breathlessness, palpitations, and poor resistance to infection. Treatment depends on the cause.

angina or **angina pectoris** severe pain in the chest due to impaired blood supply to the heart muscle because a coronary artery is narrowed. Faintness and difficulty in breathing accompany the pain. Treatment is by drugs or bypass surgery.

appendicitis inflammation of the appendix, a small, blind extension of the bowel in the lower right abdomen. In an acute attack, the pus-filled appendix may burst, causing a potentially lethal spread of infection. Treatment is by removal (appendicectomy).

arteriosclerosis hardening of the arteries, with thickening and loss of elasticity. It is associated with smoking, ageing, and a diet high in saturated fats.

arthritis inflammation of the joints, with pain, swelling, and restricted motion. Many conditions may cause arthritis, including gout, infection, and trauma to the joint. There are three main forms of arthritis: rheumatoid arthritis; osteoarthritis; and septic arthritis.

asthma chronic condition characterized by difficulty in breathing due to spasm of the bronchi (air passages) in the lungs. Attacks may be provoked by allergy, infection, and stress. The incidence of asthma may be increasing as a result of air pollution and occupational hazard. Treatment is with bronchodilators to relax the bronchial muscles and thereby ease the breathing, and in severe cases by inhaled steroids that reduce inflammation of the bronchi.

back pain aches in the region of the spine. Low back pain can be caused by a very wide range of medical conditions. About half of all episodes of back pain will resolve within a week, but severe back pain can be chronic and disabling. The causes include muscle sprain, a prolapsed intervertebral disc, and vertebral collapse due to osteoporosis or cancer. Treatment methods include rest, analgesics, physiotherapy, osteopathy, and exercises.

blood poisoning presence in the bloodstream of quantities of bacteria or bacterial toxins sufficient to cause serious illness.

bronchitis inflammation of the bronchi (air passages) of the lungs, usually caused initially by a viral infection, such as a cold or flu. It is aggravated by environmental pollutants, especially smoking, and results in a persistent cough, irritated mucus-secreting glands, and large amounts of sputum.

cancer group of diseases characterized by abnormal proliferation of cells. Cancer (malignant) cells are usually degenerate, capable only of reproducing themselves (tumour formation). Malignant cells tend to spread from their site of origin by travelling through the bloodstream or lymphatic system. Cancer kills about 6 million people a year worldwide.

cataract eye disease in which the crystalline lens or its capsule becomes cloudy, causing blindness. Fluid accumulates between the fibres of the lens and gives place to deposits of albumin. These coalesce into rounded bodies, the lens fibres break down, and areas of the lens or the lens capsule become filled with opaque products of degeneration. The condition is estimated to have blinded more than 25 million people worldwide.

Recommendations for Early Detection of Cancer in People with No Symptoms

Source: American Cancer Society

Test	Sex	Age	Frequency
Sigmoidoscopy, preferably flexible	both	>50	every 3–5 years
Faecal occult blood test	both	>50	every year
Digital rectal examination	both	>40	every year
Prostate examination[1]	male	>50	every year
Breast self-examination	female	>20	every month
Breast clinical examination	female	20–40	every 3 years >40 every year
Mammography[2]	female	40–49	every 1–2 years >50 every year
Pap test (cervical smear)	female	all women who are, or who have been, sexually active, or have reached age 18, should have an annual Pap test and pelvic examination. After a woman has had 3 or more consecutive satisfactory normal annual examinations, the Pap test may be performed less frequently at the discretion of her physician	

[1] Annual digital rectal examination and prostate-specific antigen should be performed on men 50 years and older. If either result is abnormal, further evaluation should be considered.

[2] Screening mammography should begin by age 40.

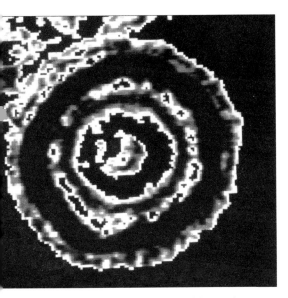

chickenpox An electron micrograph of the chickenpox virus *Varicella zoster*. Viruses are minute infectious particles that can only multiply if they invade a living cell and use its genetic machinery. It is therefore difficult to find a treatment that attacks the virus itself but leaves the host cell unharmed. A healthy body produces antiviral proteins to prevent the infection from spreading to adjacent cells. Though highly contagious, chickenpox usually creates a lifelong immunity. The chickenpox virus is part of the herpes family of viruses. *SmithKline Beecham Plc*

chickenpox or **varicella** common, usually mild disease, caused by a virus of the herpes group and transmitted by airborne droplets. Chickenpox chiefly attacks children under the age of ten. The incubation period is two to three weeks. One attack normally gives immunity for life.

cirrhosis any degenerative disease in an organ of the body, especially the liver, characterized by excessive development of connective tissue, causing scarring and painful swelling. Cirrhosis of the liver may be caused by an infection such as viral hepatitis, chronic obstruction of the common bile duct, chronic alcoholism or drug use, blood disorder, heart failure, or malnutrition. However, often no cause is apparent. If cirrhosis is diagnosed early, it can be arrested by treating the cause; otherwise it will progress to coma and death.

coeliac disease disease in which the small intestine fails to digest and absorb food. The disease can appear at any age but has a peak incidence in the 30–50 age group; it is more common in women. It is caused by an intolerance to gluten (a constituent of wheat, rye, and barley) and characterized by diarrhoea and malnutrition. Treatment is by a gluten-free diet.

colour blindness hereditary defect of vision that reduces the ability to discriminate certain colours, usually red and green. The condition is sex-linked, affecting men more than women.

coronary artery disease condition in which the fatty deposits of atherosclerosis form in the coronary arteries that supply the heart muscle, narrowing them and restricting the blood flow.

Creutzfeldt–Jakob disease (CJD) rare brain disease that causes progressive physical and mental deterioration, leading to death usually within a year of onset. It claims one person in every million and is universally fatal. It has been linked with bovine spongiform encephalopathy (BSE), and there have also been occurrences in people treated with pituitary hormones derived from cows for growth or fertility problems.

croup inflammation of the larynx in small children, with harsh, difficult breathing and hoarse coughing. Croup is most often associated with viral infection of the respiratory tract.

cystic fibrosis hereditary disease involving defects of various tissues, including the sweat glands, the mucous glands of the bronchi (air passages), and the pancreas. The sufferer experiences repeated chest infections and digestive disorders and generally fails to thrive. In 1989 a gene for cystic fibrosis was identified by teams of researchers in Michigan, USA, and Toronto, Canada. This discovery enabled the development of a screening test for carriers; the disease can also be detected in the unborn child.

cystitis inflammation of the bladder, usually caused by bacterial infection, and resulting in frequent and painful urination. It is more common in women. Treatment is by antibiotics and copious fluids with vitamin C.

diabetes disease *diabetes mellitus* in which a disorder of the islets of Langerhans in the pancreas prevents the body producing the hormone insulin, so that sugars cannot be used properly. Treatment is by strict dietary control and oral or injected insulin, depending on the type of diabetes.

diarrhoea frequent or excessive action of the bowels so that the faeces are liquid or semiliquid. It is caused by intestinal irritants (including some drugs and poisons), infection with harmful organisms (as in dysentery, salmonella, or cholera), or allergies.

diverticulitis inflammation of diverticula (pockets of herniation) in the large intestine. It is usually triggered by infection and causes diarrhoea or constipation, and lower abdominal pain. Usually it can be controlled by diet and antibiotics.

eczema inflammatory skin condition, a form of dermatitis, marked by dryness, rashes, itching, the formation of blisters, and the exudation of fluid. It may be allergic in origin and is sometimes complicated by infection.

epilepsy medical disorder characterized by a tendency to develop fits, which are convulsions or abnormal feelings caused by abnormal electrical discharges in the cerebral hemispheres of the brain. Epilepsy can be controlled with a number of anticonvulsant drugs.

gastroenteritis inflammation of the stomach and intestines, giving rise to abdominal pain, vomiting, and diarrhoea. It may be caused by food or other poisoning, allergy, or infection. Dehydration may be severe and it is a particular risk in infants.

genetic disease any disorder caused at least partly by defective genes or chromosomes. In humans there are some 3,000 genetic diseases, including cystic fibrosis, Down's syndrome, haemophilia, Huntington's chorea, some forms of anaemia, spina bifida, and Tay-Sachs disease.

German measles or **rubella** mild, communicable virus disease, usually caught by children. It is marked by a sore throat, pinkish rash, and slight fever, and has an incubation period of two to three weeks. If a woman contracts it in the first three months of pregnancy, it may cause serious damage to the unborn child.

glandular fever or **infectious mononucleosis** viral disease characterized at onset by fever and painfully swollen lymph nodes; there may also be digestive upset, sore throat, and skin rashes. Lassitude persists for months and even years, and recovery can be slow. It is caused by the Epstein–Barr virus.

glaucoma condition in which pressure inside the eye (intraocular pressure) is raised abnormally as excess fluid accumulates. It occurs when the normal outflow of fluid within the chamber of the eye (aqueous humour) is interrupted. As pressure rises, the optic nerve suffers irreversible damage, leading to a reduction in the field of vision and, ultimately, loss of eyesight.

goitre enlargement of the thyroid gland seen as a swelling on the neck. It is most pronounced in simple goitre, which is caused by iodine deficiency. More common is toxic goitre or hyperthyroidism, caused by overactivity of the thyroid gland.

gonorrhoea common sexually transmitted disease arising from infection with the bacterium *Neisseria gonorrhoeae*, which causes inflammation of the genito-urinary tract. After an incubation period of two to ten days, infected men experience pain while urinating and a discharge from the penis; infected women often have no external symptoms.

haemophilia any of several inherited diseases in which normal blood clotting is impaired. The sufferer experiences prolonged bleeding from the slightest wound, as well as painful internal bleeding without apparent cause.

haemorrhoids distended blood vessels (varicose veins) in the area of the anus, popularly called **piles.**

hay fever allergic reaction to pollen, causing sneezing, with inflammation of the nasal membranes and conjunctiva of the eyes. Symptoms are due to the release of histamine. Treatment is by antihistamine drugs.

heart attack or **myocardial infarction** sudden onset of gripping central chest pain, often accompanied by sweating and vomiting, caused by death of a portion of the heart muscle following obstruction of a coronary artery by thrombosis (formation of a blood clot). Half of all heart attacks result in death within the first two hours, but in the remainder survival has improved following the widespread use of thrombolytic (clot-buster) drugs.

herpes any of several infectious diseases caused by viruses of the herpes group. **Herpes simplex I** is the causative agent of a common inflammation, the cold sore. **Herpes simplex II** is responsible for genital herpes, a highly contagious, sexually transmitted disease characterized by painful blisters in the genital area. It can be transmitted in the birth canal from mother to newborn. **Herpes zoster** causes shingles; another herpes virus causes chickenpox.

hypertension abnormally high blood pressure due to a variety of causes, leading to excessive contraction of the smooth muscle cells of the walls of the arteries. It increases the risk of kidney disease, stroke, and heart attack.

impotence in medicine, a physical inability to perform sexual intercourse (the term is not usually applied to women). Impotent men fail to achieve an erection, and this may be due to illness, the effects of certain drugs, or psychological factors. Treatment is by sexual therapy or the drug Viagra.

irritable bowel syndrome condition characterized by episodes of lower abdominal pain with constipation or diarrhoea. The symptoms are caused by spasming of the colon but there is no underlying disease. The condition is often associated with stress or anxiety. It responds to antispasmodic drugs and measures to reduce stress.

jaundice yellow discoloration of the skin and whites of the eyes caused by an excess of bile pigment in the bloodstream. Approximately 60% of newborn babies exhibit some degree of jaundice, which is treated by bathing in white, blue, or green light that converts the bile pigment bilirubin into a water-soluble compound that can be excreted in urine. A serious form of jaundice occurs in rhesus disease.

laryngitis inflammation of the larynx, causing soreness of the throat, a dry cough, and hoarseness. The acute form is due to a virus or other infection, excessive use of the voice, or inhalation of irritating smoke, and may cause the voice to be completely lost. With rest, the inflammation usually subsides in a few days.

leukaemia any one of a group of cancers of the blood cells, with widespread involvement of the bone marrow and other blood-forming tissue. The central feature of leukaemia is runaway production of white blood cells that are immature or in some way abnormal. These rogue cells, which lack the defensive capacity of healthy white cells, overwhelm the normal ones,

leaving the victim vulnerable to infection. Treatment is with radiotherapy and cytotoxic drugs to suppress replication of abnormal cells, or by bone-marrow transplantation.

lumbago pain in the lower region of the back, usually due to strain or faulty posture. If it occurs with sciatica, it may be due to pressure on spinal nerves by a slipped disc. Treatment includes rest, application of heat, and skilled manipulation. Surgery may be needed in rare cases.

malaria see **malaria** feature.

measles acute virus disease (rubeola), spread by airborne infection. Symptoms are fever, severe catarrh, small spots inside the mouth, and a raised, blotchy red rash appearing for about a week after two weeks' incubation. Prevention is by vaccination.

meningitis inflammation of the meninges (membranes) surrounding the brain, caused by bacterial or viral infection. Bacterial meningitis, though treatable by antibiotics, is the more serious threat. Diagnosis is by lumbar puncture.

multiple sclerosis (MS) or **disseminated sclerosis** incurable chronic disease of the central nervous system, occurring in young or middle adulthood. Most prevalent in temperate zones, it affects more women than men. It is characterized by degeneration of the myelin sheath that surrounds nerves in the brain and spinal cord.

mumps or **infectious parotitis** virus infection marked by fever, pain, and swelling of one or both parotid salivary glands (situated in front of the ears). It is usually shortlived in children, although meningitis is a possible complication. In adults the symptoms are more serious and it may cause sterility in men.

osteoporosis disease in which the bone substance becomes porous and brittle. It is common in older people, affecting more women than men. It may be treated with calcium supplements and etidronate. Approximately 1.7 million people worldwide, mostly women, suffer hip fractures, mainly due to osteoporosis. A single gene was discovered in 1993 to have a major influence on bone thinning.

pneumonia inflammation of the lungs, generally due to bacterial or viral infection but also to particulate matter or gases. It is characterized

The threat of malaria

Malaria is an iinfectious parasitic disease of the tropics transmitted by mosquitoes, marked by periodic fever and an enlarged spleen. When a female mosquito of the *Anopheles* genus bites a human who has malaria, it takes in with the human blood one of four malaria protozoa of the genus *Plasmodium*. This matures within the insect and is then transferred when the mosquito bites a new victim. Malaria affects about 267 million people in 103 countries. In sub-Saharan Africa alone between 1.5 and 2 million children die from malaria and its consequences each year. In November 1998, an agreement was reached to establish a multiagency programme for research and control of the disease. The agencies involved include the World Health Organization (WHO), the World Bank, the United Nations Children's Fund, and the United Nations Development Programme. The Roll Back Malaria campaign aims to halve deaths from malaria by 2010.

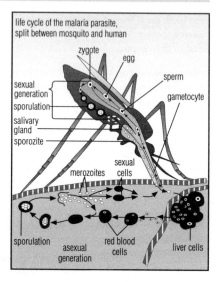

life cycle of the malaria parasite, split between mosquito and human

malaria The life cycle of the malaria parasite is split between mosquito and human hosts. The parasites are injected into the human bloodstream by an infected *Anopheles* mosquito and carried to the liver. Here they attack red blood cells, and multiply asexually. The infected blood cells burst, producing spores, or merozoites, which reinfect the bloodstream. After several generations, the parasite develops into a sexual form. If the human host is bitten at this stage, the sexual form of the parasite is sucked into the mosquito's stomach. Here fertilization takes place, the zygotes formed reproduce asexually and migrate to the salivary glands ready to be injected into another human host, completing the cycle.

by a build-up of fluid in the alveoli, the clustered air sacs (at the ends of the air passages) where oxygen exchange takes place.

premenstrual tension (PMT) or **premenstrual syndrome** medical condition caused by hormone changes and comprising a number of physical and emotional features that occur cyclically before menstruation and disappear with its onset. Symptoms include mood changes, breast tenderness, a feeling of bloatedness, and headache.

psoriasis chronic, recurring skin disease characterized by raised, red, scaly patches, on the scalp, elbows, knees, and elsewhere. Tar preparations, steroid creams, and ultraviolet light are used to treat it, and sometimes it disappears spontaneously. Psoriasis may be accompanied by a form of arthritis (inflammation of the joints).

rabies or **hydrophobia** viral disease of the central nervous system that can afflict all warm-blooded creatures. It is caused by a lyssavirus. It is almost invariably fatal once symptoms have developed.

Rabid vampires

■ Rabies may be responsible for the vampire legend. Symptoms can include facial muscle spasms and inability to swallow combined with the vomiting of blood, which can be triggered by bright light and mirrors as well as water. Some victims attack and bite people and male sufferers may suffer prolonged erections and engage in repeated sexual activity. Rabies affects seven times as many men as women and there was a rabies epidemic in Hungary at around the time that the vampire legends became popular.

Its transmission to humans is generally by a bite from an infected animal. Rabies continues to kill hundreds of thousands of people every year; almost all these deaths occur in Asia, Africa, and South America.

repetitive strain injury (RSI) inflammation of tendon sheaths, mainly in the hands and wrists, which may be disabling. It is found predominantly in factory workers involved in constant repetitive movements, and in those who work with computer keyboards. The symptoms include aching muscles, weak wrists, tingling fingers and in severe cases, pain and paralysis. Some victims have successfully sued their employers for damages.

rickets defective growth of bone in children due to an insufficiency of calcium deposits. The bones, which do not harden adequately, are bent out of shape. It is usually caused by a lack of vitamin D and insufficient exposure to sunlight. Renal rickets, also a condition of malformed bone, is associated with kidney disease.

ringworm any of various contagious skin infections due to related kinds of fungus, usually resulting in circular, itchy, discoloured patches covered with scales or blisters. The scalp and feet (athlete's foot) are generally involved. Treatment is with antifungal preparations.

rubella technical term for German measles.

scabies contagious infection of the skin caused by the parasitic itch mite *Sarcoptes scabiei*, which burrows under the skin to deposit eggs. Treatment is by antiparasitic creams and lotions.

sciatica persistent pain in the back and down the outside of one leg, along the sciatic nerve and its branches. Causes of sciatica include inflammation of the nerve or pressure of a displaced disc on a nerve root leading out of the lower spine.

septicaemia general term for any form of blood poisoning.

sexually transmitted disease (STD) any disease transmitted by sexual contact, involving transfer of body fluids. STDs include not only traditional venereal disease, but also a growing list of conditions, such as AIDS and scabies, which are known to be spread primarily by sexual contact. Other diseases that are transmitted sexually include viral hepatitis. The WHO estimate that there are 356,000 new cases of STDs daily worldwide.

sickle-cell disease hereditary chronic blood disorder common among people of black African descent; also found in the eastern Mediterranean, parts of the Persian Gulf, and in northeastern India. It is characterized by distortion and fragility of the red blood cells, which are lost too rapidly from the circulation. This often results in anaemia.

sinusitis painful inflammation of one of the sinuses, or air spaces, that surround the nasal passages. Most cases clear with antibiotics and nasal decongestants, but some require surgical drainage.

stroke or **cerebrovascular accident** or **apoplexy** interruption of the blood supply to part of the brain due to a sudden bleed in the brain (cerebral haemorrhage) or embolism or thrombosis. Strokes vary in severity from producing almost no symptoms to proving rapidly fatal. In between are those (often recurring) that leave a wide range of impaired function, depending on the size and location of the event.

thrombosis condition in which a blood clot forms in a vein or artery, causing loss of circulation to the area served by the vessel. If it breaks away, it often travels to the lungs, causing pulmonary embolism.

thrush infection usually of the mouth (particularly in infants), but also sometimes of the vagina, caused by a yeastlike fungus (*Candida*). It is seen as white patches on the mucous membranes.

tonsillitis inflammation of the tonsils.

tuberculosis (TB) formerly known as **consumption** or **phthisis,** infectious disease caused by the bacillus *Mycobacterium tuberculosis.* It takes several forms, of which pulmonary tuberculosis is by far the most common. A vaccine, BCG, was developed around 1920 and the first antituberculosis drug, streptomycin, in 1944. The bacterium is mostly kept in check by the body's immune system; about 5% of those infected develop the disease. Treatment of patients with a combination of anti-TB medicines for 6–8 months produces a cure rate of 80%. There are 7 million new cases of TB annually worldwide (1998) and 3 million deaths.

ulcer any persistent breach in a body surface (skin or mucous membrane). It may be caused by infection, irritation, or tumour and is often inflamed. Common ulcers include aphthous (mouth), gastric (stomach), duodenal, decubitus ulcers (pressure sores), and those complicating varicose veins.

varicose veins or **varicosis** condition where the veins become swollen and twisted. The veins of the legs are most often affected; other vulnerable sites include the rectum (haemorrhoids) and testes.

whooping cough or **pertussis** acute infectious disease, seen mainly in children, caused by colonization of the air passages by the bacterium *Bordetella pertussis*. There may be catarrh, mild fever, and loss of appetite, but the main symptom is violent coughing, associated with the sharp intake of breath that is the characteristic 'whoop', and often followed by vomiting and severe nose bleeds. The cough may persist for weeks.

Antibacterial bugs
- Headless bedbugs were applied to ulcers in the 16th century, and crushed bedbugs were still believed to be effective in treating ulcers in 18th-century China. It was not until this century that positive evidence was found of the antibacterial properties of insect haemolymph.

DRUGS

A drug is any of a range of substances, natural or synthetic, administered to humans and animals as therapeutic agents: to diagnose, prevent, or treat disease, or to assist recovery from injury. Traditionally many drugs were obtained from plants or animals; some minerals also had medicinal value. Today, increasing numbers of drugs are synthesized in the laboratory. Drugs are administered in various ways, including: orally, by injection, as a lotion or ointment, as a pessary, by inhalation, or by transdermal patch.

Drugs generally have three names. The first is the **chemical** name, which is often too complicated to remember. Every new drug, if it is likely to have a medical application, also is given an **approved** (generic or non-proprietary) name. Such a drug may have BP (British Pharmacopoeia); BPC (British Pharmaceutical Codex); or USP (United States Pharmacopoeia) after its name. Drugs may be marketed under their approved name, but more often they are known by the **proprietary**, or trade, names given to them by the manufacturing company which initially takes out a patent on their synthesis. One compound may have a large number of proprietary names.

anabolic steroid any hormone of the steroid group that stimulates tissue growth. Its use in medicine is limited to the treatment of some anaemias and breast cancers; it may help to break up blood clots. Side effects include aggressive behaviour, masculinization in women, and, in children, reduced height.

antacid any substance that neutralizes stomach acid, such as sodium bicarbonate or magnesium hydroxide ('milk of magnesia'). Antacids are weak bases, swallowed as solids or emulsions. They may be taken between meals to relieve symptoms of hyperacidity, such as pain, bloating, nausea, and 'heartburn'. Excessive or prolonged need for antacids should be investigated medically.

antibiotic drug that kills or inhibits the growth of bacteria and fungi. It is derived from living organisms such as fungi or bacteria, which distinguishes it from synthetic antimicrobials.

anticoagulant substance that inhibits the formation of blood clots. Common anticoagulants are heparin, produced by the liver and some white blood cells, and derivatives of coumarin. Anticoagulants are used medically in the prevention and treatment of thrombosis and heart attacks. Anticoagulant substances are also produced by blood-feeding animals, such as mosquitoes, leeches, and vampire bats, to keep the victim's blood flowing.

antidepressant any drug used to relieve symptoms in depressive illness. The main groups are the selective serotonin-reuptake inhibitors (SSRIs), the tricyclic antidepressants (TCADs), and the monoamine oxidase inhibitors (MAOIs). They all act by altering chemicals available to the central nervous system. All may produce serious side effects.

anti-emetic any substance that counteracts nausea or vomiting.

antifungal any drug that acts against fungal infection, such as ringworm and athlete's foot.

antihistamine any substance that counteracts the effects of histamine. Antihistamines may occur naturally or they may be synthesized.

anti-inflammatory any substance that reduces swelling in soft tissues. Antihistamines relieve allergic reactions; aspirin and NSAIDs are effective in joint and musculoskeletal conditions; and rubefacients (counterirritant liniments) ease painful joints, tendons, and muscles.

antiviral any drug that acts against viruses, usually preventing them from multiplying. Most viral

Common Drugs Derived from Plants

These plants are poisonous and if swallowed can cause serious illness or unconsciousness. They should only be used if administered by a medically trained professional.

Plant	Drug	Use
Amazonian liana	curare	muscle relaxant
Annual mugwort	artemisinin	antimalarial
Autumn crocus	colchicine	antitumour agent
Coca	cocaine	local anaesthetic
Common thyme	thymol	antifungal
Deadly nightshade (belladonna)	atropine	anticholinergic
Dog button (nux-vomica)	strychnine	central nervous system stimulant
Ergot fungus	ergotamine	analgesic
Foxglove	digitoxin, digitalis	cardiotonic
Indian snakeroot	reserpine	antihypertensive
Meadowsweet	salicylate	analgesic
Mexican yam	diosgenin	birth control pill
Opium poppy	codeine, morphine	analgesic (and antitussive)
Pacific yew	taxol	antitumour agent
Recured thornapple	scopolamine	sedative
Rosy periwinkle	vincristine, vinblastine	antileukaemia
Velvet bean	L-dopa	antiparkinsonian
White willow	salicylic acid	topical analgesic
Yellow cinchona	quinine	antimalarial, antipyretic

infections are not susceptible to antibiotics. Antivirals have been difficult drugs to develop, and do not necessarily cure viral diseases.

aspirin acetylsalicylic acid, a popular pain-relieving drug (analgesic) developed in the late 19th century as a household remedy for aches and pains. It relieves pain and reduces inflammation and fever. It is derived from the white willow tree *Salix alba*, and is the world's most widely used drug.

beta-blocker any of a class of drugs that block impulses that stimulate certain nerve endings (beta receptors) serving the heart muscle. This reduces the heart rate and the force of contraction, which in turn reduces the amount of oxygen (and therefore the blood supply) required by the heart. Beta-blockers may be useful in the treatment of angina, arrhythmia (abnormal heart rhythms), and raised blood pressure, and

following heart attacks. They must be withdrawn from use gradually.

clot-buster popular term for a small group of thrombolytic (clot-dissolving) drugs used in the treatment of heart attack.

cocaine alkaloid $C_{17}H_{21}NO_4$ extracted from the leaves of the coca tree. It has limited medical application, mainly as a local anaesthetic agent that is readily absorbed by mucous membranes (lining tissues) of the nose and throat. It is both toxic and addictive. Its use as a stimulant is illegal. Crack is a derivative of cocaine.

codeine opium derivative that provides analgesia in mild to moderate pain. It also suppresses the cough centre of the brain. It is an alkaloid, derived from morphine but less toxic and addictive.

corticosteroid any of several steroid hormones secreted by the cortex of the adrenal glands; also synthetic forms with similar properties. Corticosteroids have anti-inflammatory and immunosuppressive effects and may be used to treat a number of conditions, including rheumatoid arthritis, severe allergies, asthma, some skin diseases, and some cancers. Side effects can be serious, and therapy must be withdrawn very gradually.

cytotoxic drug any drug used to kill the cells of a malignant tumour; it may also damage healthy cells. Side effects include nausea, vomiting, hair loss, and bone-marrow damage. Some cytotoxic drugs are also used to treat other diseases and to suppress rejection in transplant patients.

diazepam tranquillizer in the benzodiazepine group that is also useful for its muscle-relaxant and anticonvulsant effects. Besides being prescribed for anxiety, it is used in premedication or sedation for surgery, as a hypnotic, to treat muscle spasm and for some epileptic conditions, including status epilepticus. Side effects include drowsiness, disorientation and dependence. It is better known by the trade name Valium.

digitalis drug that increases the efficiency of the heart by strengthening its muscle contractions and slowing its rate. It is derived from the leaves of the common European woodland plant *Digitalis purpurea* (foxglove).

enema infusion of liquid into the rectum to evacuate faecal obstruction or to introduce drugs for treatment, or radio-opaque material (barium sulphate) in order to define the colon on X-ray.

fertility drug any of a range of drugs taken to increase a female's fertility, developed in Sweden in the mid-1950s. They increase the chances of a multiple birth.

heroin or **diamorphine** powerful opiate analgesic, an acetyl derivative of morphine. It is more addictive than morphine but causes less nausea. It has an important place in the control of severe pain in terminal illness, severe injuries, and heart attacks, but is widely used illegally.

histamine inflammatory substance normally released in damaged tissues, which also accounts for many of the symptoms of allergy. It is an amine, $C_5H_9N_3$. Substances that neutralize its activity are known as antihistamines.

ibuprofen non-steroidal anti-inflammatory drug (NSAID) that is used to relieve pain and inflammation.

insulin protein hormone, produced by specialized cells in the islets of Langerhans in the pancreas, that regulates the metabolism (rate of activity) of glucose, fats, and proteins. Insulin was discovered by Canadian physician Frederick Banting and Canadian physiologist Charles Best, who pioneered its use in treating diabetes.

laxative substance used to relieve constipation (infrequent bowel movement). Current medical opinion discourages regular or prolonged use. Regular exercise and a diet high in vegetable fibre are believed to be the best means of preventing and treating constipation.

L-dopa chemical, normally produced by the body, which is converted by an enzyme to dopamine in the brain. It is essential for integrated movement of individual muscle groups.

lignocaine short-term local anaesthetic injected into tissues or applied to skin. It is effective for brief, invasive procedures such as dental care or insertion of a cannula (small tube) into a vein. Temporary paralysis (to prevent involuntary movement during eye surgery, for example) can be achieved by injection directly into the nerve serving the region.

lysergic acid diethylamide full name of the hallucinogenic drug LSD.

marijuana dried leaves and flowers of the hemp plant cannabis, used as a drug; it is illegal in most countries. Mexico is the world's largest producer.

mescaline psychedelic drug derived from a small, spineless cactus *Lophophora williamsii* of northern Mexico and the southwest USA, known as peyote. The tops (called mescal buttons), which scarcely appear above ground, are dried and chewed, or added to alcoholic drinks. Mescaline is a crystalline alkaloid $C_{11}H_{17}NO_3$. It is used by some North American Indians in religious rites.

methadone narcotic drug used to relieve severe pain, or in linctus to suppress coughing. It is also used to treat heroin addiction by acting as a controlled substitute; however, it too is addictive.

mifepristone (RU486) anti-progesterone drug used, in combination with a prostaglandin, to procure early abortion (up to the tenth week in pregnancy). It is administered only in hospitals or recognized clinics and a success rate of 95% is claimed.

narcotic pain-relieving and sleep-inducing drug. The term is usually applied to heroin, morphine, and other opium derivatives, but may also be used for other drugs which depress brain activity, including anaesthetic agents and hypnotics.

NSAID (abbreviation for **nonsteroidal anti-inflammatory drug**) any of a class of drugs used in the long-term treatment of rheumatoid arthritis and osteoarthritis; they act to reduce swelling and pain in soft tissues. Bleeding into the digestive tract is a serious side effect: NSAIDs should not be taken by persons with peptic ulcers.

opium drug extracted from the unripe seeds of the opium poppy (*Papaver somniferum*) of southwestern Asia. An addictive narcotic, it contains several alkaloids, including **morphine,** one of the most powerful natural painkillers and addictive narcotics known, and **codeine,** a milder painkiller.

oral contraceptive synthetic female hormones that are taken by mouth for contraception and commonly referred to as the pill.

painkiller agent for relieving pain. Types of painkiller include analgesics such as aspirin and aspirin substitutes, morphine, codeine, paracetamol, and synthetic versions of the natural inhibitors, the encephalins and endorphins, which avoid the side effects of the others.

paracetamol analgesic, particularly effective for musculoskeletal pain. It is as effective as aspirin in reducing fever, and less irritating to the stomach, but has little anti-inflammatory action. An overdose can cause severe, often irreversible or even fatal, liver and kidney damage.

penicillin any of a group of antibiotic (bacteria killing) compounds obtained from filtrates of moulds of the genus *Penicillium* (especially *P. notatum*) or produced synthetically. Penicillin was the first antibiotic to be discovered (by Alexander Fleming); it kills a broad spectrum of bacteria, many of which cause disease in humans.

Pill, the commonly used term for the contraceptive pill, based on female hormones. The combined pill, which contains synthetic hormones similar to oestrogen and progesterone, stops the production of eggs, and makes the mucus produced by the cervix hostile to sperm. It is the most effective form of contraception apart from sterilization, being more than 99% effective.

prostaglandin any of a group of complex fatty acids present in the body that act as messenger substances between cells. Effects include stimulating the contraction of smooth muscle (for example, of the womb during birth), regulating the production of stomach acid, and modifying hormonal activity. In excess, prostaglandins may produce inflammatory disorders such as arthritis. Synthetic prostaglandins are used to induce labour in humans and domestic animals.

Prozac or **fluoxetine** antidepressant drug that functions mainly by boosting levels of the neurotransmitter serotonin in the brain. Side effects include nausea and loss of libido. It is also used to treat some eating disorders, such as bulimia. It is one of a class of drugs known as selective serotonin-reuptake inhibitors (SSRIs).

> **Synchronized spawning**
> ■ Prozac added to the water induces spawning in molluscs and is therefore useful to aquafarmers, who find it easier to produce a single crop when spawning is in unison than if reproduction and development are occurring at different rates.

smart drug any drug or combination of nutrients (vitamins, amino acids, minerals, and sometimes herbs) said to enhance the functioning of the brain, increase mental energy, lengthen the span of attention, and improve the memory. As yet there is no scientific evidence to suggest that these drugs have any significant effect on healthy people.

tranquillizer common name for any drug for reducing anxiety or tension (anxiolytic), such as benzodiazepines, barbiturates, antidepressants, and beta-blockers. The use of drugs to control anxiety is becoming much less popular, because most of the drugs available are capable of inducing dependence.

Valium trade name for the tranquillizer diazepam.

Viagra drug used to treat impotence, approved by the US Food and Drug Administration (FDA) in March 1998. Viagra works by dilating the blood vessels of the penis and must be taken about an hour before intercourse. Side effects include headaches and fainting (due to dilation of blood vessels), and blue tinted vision.

warfarin poison that induces fatal internal bleeding in rats; neutralized with sodium hydroxide, it is used in medicine as an anticoagulant in the treatment of thrombosis: it prevents blood clotting by inhibiting the action of vitamin K. It can be taken orally and begins to act several days after the initial dose.

DIET AND NUTRITION

For a balanced diet, humans require seven kinds of food in their diet: proteins, carbohydrates, fats, vitamins, minerals, water, and roughage. The amounts and proportions required of each varies according to size, age, and lifestyle. **Dietetics** is the science of feeding individuals or groups; a dietition is a specialist in this science. The average daily requirement for men is 2,500 calories, but this will vary with age, occupation, and weight; in general, women need fewer calories than men. The energy requirements of active children increase steadily with age, reaching a peak in the late teens.

beriberi nutritional disorder occurring mostly in the tropics and resulting from a deficiency of vitamin B_1 (thiamine). The disease takes two forms: in one oedema (waterlogging of the tissues) occurs; in the other there is severe emaciation. There is nerve degeneration in both forms and many victims succumb to heart failure.

carbohydrate see **balanced diet** feature.

casein main protein of milk, from which it can be separated by the action of acid, the enzyme rennin, or bacteria (souring); it is also the main protein in cheese. Casein is used as a protein supplement in the treatment of malnutrition. It is used commercially in cosmetics, glues, and as a sizing for coating paper.

cholesterol white, crystalline sterol found throughout the body, especially in fats, blood, nerve tissue, and bile; it is also provided in the diet by foods such as eggs, meat, and butter. A high level of cholesterol in the blood is thought to contribute to atherosclerosis (hardening of the arteries).

deficiency disease any disease arising from the lack of an essential nutrient in the diet. For example, beriberi is due to a deficiency of vitamin B_1 (thiamine); rickets is due to a lack of vitamin D.

food poisoning any acute illness characterized by vomiting and diarrhoea and caused by eating food contaminated with harmful bacteria (for example, listeriosis), poisonous food (for example, certain mushrooms, puffer fish), or poisoned food (such as lead or arsenic introduced accidentally during processing). A frequent cause of food poisoning is *Salmonella* bacteria. *Salmonella* comes in many forms, and strains are found in cattle, pigs, poultry, and eggs.

gluten protein found in cereal grains, especially wheat and rye. Gluten enables dough to expand during rising. Sensitivity to gliadin, a type of gluten, gives rise to coeliac disease.

kwashiorkor severe protein deficiency in children under five years, resulting in retarded growth, lethargy, oedema, diarrhoea, and a swollen abdomen. It is common in Third World countries with a high incidence of malnutrition.

malnutrition condition resulting from a defective diet where certain important food nutrients (such as protein, vitamins, or carbohydrates) are absent. It can lead to deficiency diseases.

A related problem is undernourishment. In 1998 there was an estimated 180 million malnourished children in the world and malnutrition contributed to 6 million deaths annually, mainly amongst children.

mineral salt simple inorganic chemical that is required by living organisms. Plants usually obtain their mineral salts from the soil, while animals get theirs from their food. Important mineral salts include iron salts (needed by both plants and animals), magnesium salts (needed mainly by plants, to make chlorophyll), and calcium salts (needed by animals to make bone or shell). A trace element is required only in tiny amounts.

scurvy disease caused by deficiency of vitamin C (ascorbic acid), which is contained in fresh vegetables and fruit. The signs are weakness and aching joints and muscles, progressing to bleeding of the gums and other spontaneous haemorrhage, and drying-up of the skin and hair. It is reversed by giving the vitamin.

tartrazine (E102) yellow food colouring produced synthetically from petroleum. Many people are allergic to foods containing it. Typical effects are skin disorders and respiratory problems. It has been shown to have an adverse effect on hyperactive children.

Rules for Safe Food Production

Source: World Health Organization

The World Health Organization (WHO) regards illness due to contaminated food as one of the most widespread health problems in the contemporary world. For infants, immunocompromised people, pregnant women, and the elderly, the consequences of such an illness can be fatal. WHO data indicate that a small number of factors related to food handling are responsible for a large proportion of food-borne disease episodes everywhere. Common errors include:

preparation of food several hours prior to consumption, combined with storage of that food at temperatures that favour growth of bacteria and/or formation of toxins; insufficient cooking or reheating of food and so failing to reduce or eliminate pathogens; cross-contamination; handling of the food by people with poor personal hygiene.

The WHO has devised Ten Golden Rules in response to these errors, offering advice that can reduce the risk of food-borne pathogens being able to contaminate, survive, or multiply. By following these basic rules, the risk of food-borne disease will be significantly reduced.

1. Choose foods processed for safety
While many foods, such as fruits and vegetables, are best in their natural state, others simply are not safe unless they have been processed. For example, always buy pasteurized as opposed to unpasteurized milk, and if you have the choice, select fresh or frozen poultry treated with ionizing radiation. When shopping, keep in mind that food processing was invented to improve safety as well as to prolong shelf-life. Certain foods eaten raw, such as lettuce, need thorough washing.

2. Cook food thoroughly
Many raw foods, most notably poultry, meats, eggs, and unpasteurized milk, may be contaminated with disease-causing organisms. Thorough cooking will kill the bacteria, but remember that the temperature of all parts of the food must reach at least 70°C/158°F. If cooked chicken is still raw, put it back in the oven until it is done – all the way through. Frozen meat, fish, and poultry must be thoroughly thawed before cooking.

3. Eat cooked foods immediately
When cooked foods cool to room temperature, microbes begin to proliferate. The longer the wait, the greater the risk. To be on the safe side, eat cooked foods just as soon as they come off the heat.

4. Store cooked foods carefully
If you must prepare foods in advance or want to keep leftovers, be sure to store them under either hot (near or above 60°C/140°F) or cool (near or below 10°C/50°F) conditions. This rule is of vital importance if you plan to store foods for more than four or five hours. Foods for infants should preferably not be stored at all. A common error, responsible for countless cases of food-borne disease, is putting too large a quantity of warm food in the refrigerator. In an overburdened refrigerator, cooked foods cannot cool to the core as quickly as they must. When the centre of food remains warm (above 10°C/50°F) for too long, microbes thrive, quickly proliferating to disease-causing levels.

5. Reheat cooked foods thoroughly
This is your best protection against microbes that may have developed during storage (proper storage slows down microbial growth but does not kill the organisms). Once again, thorough reheating means that all parts of the food must reach at least 70°C/158°F.

6. Avoid contact between raw foods and cooked foods
Safely cooked food can become contaminated through even the slightest contact with raw food. This cross-contamination can be direct, as when raw poultry meat comes into contact with cooked foods. It can also be more subtle. For example, do not prepare a raw chicken and then use the same unwashed cutting board and knife to carve the cooked bird. Doing so can reintroduce the disease-causing organisms.

7. Wash hands repeatedly
Wash hands thoroughly before you start preparing food and after every interruption – especially if you have to change a baby or have been to the toilet. After preparing raw foods such as fish, meat, or poultry, wash again before you start handling other foods. And if you have an infection on your hand, be sure to bandage or cover it before preparing food. Remember too that household pets – dogs, cats, birds, and especially turtles – often harbour dangerous pathogens that can pass from your hands into food.

8. Keep all kitchen surfaces meticulously clean
Since foods are so easily contaminated, any surface used for food preparation must be kept absolutely clean. Think of every food scrap, crumb, or spot as a potential reservoir of germs. Cloths that come into contact with dishes and utensils should be changed frequently and boiled before re-use. Separate cloths for cleaning the floors also require frequent washing.

9. Protect foods from insects, rodents, and other animals
Animals frequently carry pathogenic micro-organisms that cause food-borne disease. Storing foods in closed containers is your best protection against contamination against animals.

10. Use safe water
Safe water is just as important for food preparation as for drinking. If you have any doubts about the water supply, boil water before adding it to food or making ice for drinks. Be especially careful with any water used to prepare an infant's meal.

Foods for a balanced diet

carbohydrates and fibre The carbohydrates include starches and sugars, which are the major source of metabolic energy. Chemically they are made up of carbon, hydrogen, and oxygen. The basic carbohydrates are the simple sugars, or monosaccharides, and nutritionally glucose, fructose, and galactose are the most important of these. The complex sugars, or disaccharides, include sucrose and maltose. Both monosaccharides and disaccharides are water-soluble. Cellulose and starches, which are found in plant cells, are molecules of simple sugars that have combined to produce polysaccharides. Unlike the sugars they are insoluble. Starches and sugars are present in grains, fruits, pulses (peas and beans), nuts, vegetables, and milk. In a balanced diet, starch-rich food, such as whole grains, root vegetables, pulses, and bananas, should provide half the calorie intake. The fibre content of these foods helps to keep the bowel healthy and protects from high cholesterol levels, some cancers, gallstones, and obesity.

proteins Proteins are composed of long chains of amino acids of which there are about twenty different kinds. In addition to carbon, hydrogen, and oxygen, they also contain nitrogen and small amounts of sulphur. Some proteins, such as haemoglobin – the red pigment in blood – are soluble; others, such as keratin, found in hair and fingernails, are insoluble. Unlike carbohydrates, proteins are not normally used to provide energy. They are used by the body to build and repair cells and to regulate metabolism. Proteins are also needed by the white cells in the blood to produce antibodies; these assist the body's immune system to ward off attacks by bacteria and viruses. All fruits and vegetables contain some protein; good sources include peas, beans, lentils, grains, nuts, seeds, and potatoes. Animal proteins include milk, cheese, meat, eggs, and fish.

fats Fats are composed of glycerol and fatty acids and, like carbohydrates, contain carbon, hydrogen, and oxygen atoms. There are two types of fatty acids: saturated and unsaturated. Unsaturated fatty acids are found in fish oils and vegetable oils – coconut oil and palm oil are the only saturated vegetable oils. Most saturated fats are animal fats, and are solid, such as lard and butter. Margarine is saturated by the process of hydrogenation which forces hydrogen gas through vegetable oil. Fats provide the most concentrated form of energy: in other words, when they are burned in the body, they supply more than twice the number of calories per gram available from carbohydrates. They are also high in cholesterol. Hence the need to control fat intake where obesity and cholesterol levels present a health problem. Heart disease has been linked to the consumption of hydrogenated fats. However, fats are a necessary part of any well-balanced diet. They provide insulation, build cells, and facilitate metabolism. Unsaturated fatty acids are essential for healthy skin, circulation, bone, brain, and nerves.

Most fatty acids can be synthesized by the body, with the exception of three, the **essential fatty acids** (EFAs): linoleic acid, linolenic acid, and arachidonic acid. These have to be supplied from food; vegetable oils, particularly if they are unrefined and cold pressed, are the best sources of EFAs. Sunflower and safflower oils are among the richest sources, containing up to 90%. EFAs are vital for the maintenance of good health. Among their many uses, they help to prevent atheroschlerosis (coronary heart disease) and the formation of blood clots in arteries, and they regulate such diverse reactions as stomach secretions, hormone release, and pancreatic function.

minerals These are inorganic substances, such as calcium, phosphorus, and iron, and although only very small amounts are needed, they play an important part in a balanced diet. Minerals build and maintain bones and teeth, control the composition of body fluids and cells, and release energy. For instance, calcium, which is found in milk, cheese, and bread, is necessary for healthy bones and teeth. A deficiency of this mineral can result in brittle bones and teeth. Similarly, phosphorus, which is contained in milk, is also needed in the formation of bones and teeth. Iron, which is present in liver and egg yolk, is used by the body in the manufacture of haemoglobin; a deficiency of this mineral can result in various forms of anaemia.

vitamins These are organic substances which, like minerals, are used by the body in very small amounts but are vital for normal body chemistry. They are all obtained from food, but vitamin D is also produced by the action of daylight on the skin, and vitamin K is produced by microorganisms in the bowel. Again, like minerals, an insufficient intake of one or more vitamins can result in a wide range of deficiency diseases. For instance, vitamin A, which can be found in eggs, milk, dairy products, fish liver oil, and animal liver, helps to maintain the cells lining the respiratory system and the mucous membranes of the eyes, ear, nose throat, and bladder; it helps to fight colds and a deficiency of the vitamin can lead to respiratory infections.

Some sixteen different B vitamins have been isolated, and as they usually occur together, they are known as vitamin B complex. They can be found in vegetables and animal foods, such as organ meats (particularly liver), wholemeal bread, yeast extract, and brown rice, and are vital for converting carbohydrates to glucose and food into energy. When B vitamins are lacking in the body, carbohydrates are not fully utilized and this can result in stress, nervousness, constipation, fatigue, and indigestion. Most of the complex are concerned with various processes in the liver, eyes, skin, and hair, and have a wide range of effects from alleviating stress to preventing atherosclerosis.

Vitamin C is a very unstable, water-soluble vitamin, which is easily lost in food preparation – not only in cooking, but also in peeling, stoning, and soaking fruits and vegetables. Among its best natural sources are citrus fruits, peppers, broccoli, tomatoes, cabbage, green leafy vegetables, and potatoes. Vitamin C has many functions in the body, among the best known of which are the prevention of scurvy, a skin condition, and fighting the symptoms of the common cold. In addition, it

Foods for a balanced diet (continued)

helps to form collagen (a sub-skin 'cement'), increases immune responses to infectious diseases, and has been found to lower the risk of cancers of the mouth, oesophagus, lung, stomach, colon, cervix, and breast. It has also been shown by several studies to lower cholesterol levels. Human beings are one of very few mammals that cannot synthesize vitamin C, and a regular daily intake from a food source is necessary.

Vitamin D is a fat-soluble vitamin which is supplied from both food, especially milk and dairy foods, and exposure to the sun. It is stored mainly in the liver, but also in smaller quantities in the skin, brain, and bones. Vitamin D promotes absorption of calcium and phosphorus which are both vital for strong teeth and bones, and for the prevention of rickets in children. It also helps to maintain a healthy nervous system, normal

heartbeat, and efficient blood clotting. Since vitamin D is scarce in vegetables, people who do not drink milk may need to supplement their diet with cod liver oil and fish such as sardines, herring, salmon, and tuna. Overdoses of the vitamin can lead to toxicity symptoms such as diarrhoea, nausea, excessive urination, and kidney damage.

Vitamins

Vitamin	Name	Main dietary sources	Established benefit	Deficiency symptoms
A	retinol	dairy products, egg yolk, liver; also formed in body from ß-carotene, a pigment present in some leafy vegetables	aids growth; prevents night blindness and xerophthalmia (a common cause of blindness among children in developing countries); helps keep the skin and mucous membranes resistant to infection	night blindness; rough skin; impaired bone growth
B_1	thiamin	germ and bran of seeds and grains, yeast	essential for carbohydrate metabolism and health of nervous system	beriberi; Korsakov's syndrome
B_2	riboflavin	eggs, liver, milk, poultry, broccoli, mushrooms	involved in energy metabolism; protects skin, mouth, eyes, eyelids, mucous membranes	inflammation of tongue and lips; sores in corners of the mouth
B_6	pyridoxine/ pantothenic acid/biotin	meat, poultry, fish, fruits, nuts, whole grains, leafy vegetables, yeast extract	important in the regulation of the central nervous system and in protein metabolism; helps prevent anaemia, skin lesions, nerve damage	dermatitis; neurological problems; kidney stones
B_{12}	cyanoco-balamin	liver, meat, fish, eggs, dairy products, soybeans	involved in synthesis of nucleic acids, maintenance of myelin sheath around nerve fibres; efficient use of folic acid	anaemia; neurological disturbance
folic acid		green leafy vegetables, liver, peanuts; cooking and processing can cause serious losses in food	involved in synthesis of nucleic acids; helps protect against cervical dysplasia (precancerous changes in the cells of the uterine cervix)	megaloblastic anaemia
nicotinic acid	niacin	meat, yeast extract, some cereals; also formed in the body from the amino acid tryptophan	maintains the health of the skin, tongue, and digestive system	pellagra
C	ascorbic acid	citrus fruits, green vegetables, tomatoes, potatoes; losses occur during storage and cooking	prevents scurvy, loss of teeth; fights haemorrhage; important in synthesis of collagen (constituent of connective tissue); aids in resistance to some types of virus and bacterial infections	scurvy
D	calciferol, cholecalciferol	liver, fish oil, dairy products, eggs; also produced when skin is exposed to sunlight	promotes growth and mineralization of bone	rickets in children; osteomalacia in adults
E	tocopherol	vegetable oils, eggs, butter, some cereals, nuts	prevents damage to cell membranes	anaemia
K	phytomenadione, menaquinone	green vegetables, cereals, fruits, meat, dairy products	essential for blood clotting	haemorrhagic problems

Main Dietary Minerals

Mineral	Main dietary sources	Major functions in the body	Deficiency symptoms
Calcium	milk, cheese, green vegetables, dried legumes	constituent of bones and teeth; essential tetany for nerve transmission, muscle contraction, and blood clotting	
Chromium	vegetable oils, meat	involved in energy metabolism	impaired glucose metabolism
Copper	drinking water, meat	associated with iron metabolism	anaemia
Fluoride	drinking water, tea, seafoods	helps to keep bones and teeth healthy	increased rate of tooth decay
Iodine	seafoods, dairy products, many vegetables, iodized table salt	essential for healthy growth and development	goitre
Iron	meat (especially liver), legumes, green vegetables, whole grains, eggs	constituent of haemoglobin; involved in energy metabolism	anaemia
Magnesium	whole grains, green vegetables	involved in protein synthesis	growth failure, weakness, behavioural disturbances
Manganese	widely distributed in foods	involved in fat synthesis	not known in humans
Molybdenum	legumes, cereals, offal	constituent of some enzymes	not known in humans
Phosphorus	milk, cheese, meat, legumes, cereals	formation of bones and teeth, maintenance of acid–base balance	weakness, demineralization of bone
Potassium	milk, meat, fruits	maintenance of acid–base balance, fluid balance, nerve transmission	muscular weakness, paralysis
Selenium	seafoods, meat, cereals, egg yolk	role associated with that of vitamin E	not known in humans
Sodium	widely distributed in foods	as for potassium	cramp, loss of appetite, apathy
Zinc	widely distributed in foods	involved in digestion	growth failure, underdevelopment of reproductive organs

Nutritive Value of Foods

Source: UK Ministry of Agriculture, Fisheries and Food

The energy value of each food is given in kilojoules (kJ) and kilocalories (kcal), and both have been calculated from the protein, fat, and carbohydrate content per 100 g of edible portion.

Food	Energy	Protein (g)	Fat (g)	Saturated fat (g)	Carbohydrate (g) kJ	kcal
Cereal and Cereal Products						
Bread, brown	927	218	8.5	2.0	0.4	44.3
Bread, white	1,002	235	8.4	1.9	0.4	49.3
Flour, plain, white	1,450	341	9.4	1.3	0.2	77.7
Flour, wholemeal	1,318	310	12.7	2.2	0.3	63.9
Oats, porridge, raw	1,587	375	11.2	9.2	1.6	66.0
Rice, brown, boiled	597	141	2.6	1.1	0.3	32.1
Rice, white, boiled	587	138	2.6	1.3	0.3	30.9
Spaghetti, white, boiled	442	104	3.6	0.7	0.1	22.2

Nutritive Value of Foods (continued)

Food	Energy	Protein (g)	Fat (g)	Saturated fat (g)	Carbohydrate (g) kJ	kcal
Dairy Products						
Butter	3,031	737	0.5	81.7	54.0	0.0
Cheddar cheese	1,708	412	25.5	34.4	21.7	0.1
Cottage cheese	413	98	13.8	3.9	2.4	2.1
Cream, fresh, heavy	1,849	449	1.7	48.0	30.0	2.7
Cream, fresh	817	198	2.6	19.1	11.9	4.1
Eggs, boiled	612	147	12.5	10.8	3.1	0.0
Low-fat spread	1,605	390	5.8	40.5	11.2	0.5
Margarine, polyunsaturated	3,039	739	0.2	81.6	16.2	1.0
Milk, semi-skimmed	195	46	3.3	1.6	1.0	5.0
Milk, skimmed	140	33	3.3	0.1	0.1	5.0
Milk, whole	275	66	3.2	3.9	2.4	4.8
Yoghurt, whole milk, plain	333	79	5.7	3.0	1.7	7.8
Fish						
White fish, steamed, flesh only	417	98	22.8	0.8	0.2	0.0
Shrimps, boiled	451	107	22.6	1.8	0.4	0.0
Fruit						
Apples	199	47	0.4	0.1	0.0	11.8
Apricots	674	158	4.0	0.6	0.0	36.5
Avocados	784	190	1.9	19.5	4.1	1.9
Bananas	403	95	1.2	0.3	0.1	23.2
Cherries	203	48	0.9	0.1	0.0	11.5
Grapefruit	126	30	0.8	0.1	0.0	6.8
Grapes	257	60	0.4	0.1	0.0	15.4
Mangoes	245	57	0.7	0.2	0.1	14.1
Melon	119	28	0.6	0.1	0.0	6.6
Oranges	158	37	1.1	0.1	0.0	8.5
Peaches	142	33	1.0	0.1	0.0	14.0
Pears	169	40	0.3	0.1	0.0	10.0
Plums	155	36	0.6	0.1	0.0	8.8
Raspberries	109	25	1.4	0.3	0.1	4.6
Strawberries	113	27	0.8	0.1	0.0	6.0
Meat						
Beef, lean only, raw	517	123	20.3	4.6	1.9	0.0
Chicken, meat and skin, raw	954	230	17.6	17.7	5.9	0.0
Lamb, lean only, raw	679	162	20.8	8.8	4.2	0.0
Pork, lean only, raw	615	147	20.7	7.1	2.5	0.0
Vegetables						
Aubergine	64	15	0.9	0.4	0.1	2.2
Beetroot	195	46	2.3	0.0	0.0	9.5
Cabbage	109	26	1.7	0.4	0.1	4.1
Celery	32	7	0.5	0.2	0.0	0.9
Courgettes	74	18	1.8	0.4	0.1	1.8
Cucumber	40	10	0.7	0.1	0.0	1.5
Lettuce	59	14	0.8	0.5	0.1	1.7
Mushrooms	55	13	1.8	0.5	0.1	0.4
Onions	150	36	1.2	0.2	0.0	7.9
Parsnips	278	66	1.6	1.2	0.2	12.9
Peas	291	69	6.0	0.9	0.2	9.7
Peppers	65	15	0.8	0.3	0.1	2.6
Potatoes, new, flesh only	298	70	1.7	0.3	0.1	16.1
Potatoes, old, flesh only	318	75	2.1	0.2	0.0	17.2
Spinach	90	21	301	0.8	0.1	0.5
Sweetcorn kernels	519	122	2.9	1.2	0.2	26.6
Sweet potatoes	358	84	1.1	0.3	0.1	20.5
Tofu, soya bean, steamed	304	73	8.1	4.2	0.5	0.7
Watercress	94	22	3.0	1.0	0.3	0.4

Medical terms

abortion ending of a pregnancy before the fetus is developed sufficiently to survive outside the uterus. Loss of a fetus at a later gestational age is termed premature stillbirth. Abortion may be accidental (miscarriage) or deliberate (termination of pregnancy).

abrasion term for a graze or other minor lesion where the skin surface is worn away by friction.

acute term used to describe a disease of sudden and severe onset which resolves quickly; for example, pneumonia and meningitis. In contrast, a **chronic** condition develops and remains over a long period.

afterbirth placenta, umbilical cord, and ruptured membranes, which become detached from the uterus and expelled soon after birth.

amniocentesis sampling the amniotic fluid surrounding a fetus in the womb for diagnostic purposes. It is used to detect Down's syndrome and other genetic abnormalities. The procedure carries a 1 in 200 risk of miscarriage.

anaesthetic drug that produces loss of sensation or consciousness; the resulting state is **anaesthesia,** in which the patient is insensitive to stimuli. Anaesthesia may also happen as a result of nerve disorder.

> **Fatal anaesthetics**
> ■ Although the science of anaesthetics is 150 years old, it is only comparatively recently that safe doses have begun to be calculated correctly. It is said that when the Japanese bombed Pearl Harbor in 1941, more US servicemen were killed by anaesthetists than by bombs.

analgesic agent for relieving pain. Opiates alter the perception or appreciation of pain and are effective in controlling 'deep' visceral (internal) pain. Non-opiates, such as aspirin, paracetamol, and NSAIDs (nonsteroidal anti-inflammatory drugs), relieve musculoskeletal pain and reduce inflammation in soft tissues.

anatomy study of the structure of the body and its component parts, especially the human body, as distinguished from physiology, which is the study of bodily functions.

antenatal before birth. Antenatal care refers to health services provided to ensure the health of pregnant women and their babies.

antibody protein molecule produced in the blood by lymphocytes in response to the presence of foreign or invading substances (antigens); such substances include the proteins carried on the surface of infecting microorganisms. Antibody production is only one aspect of immunity in vertebrates.

antiseptic any substance that kills or inhibits the growth of microorganisms. The use of antiseptics was pioneered by Joseph Lister. He used carbolic acid (phenol), which is a weak antiseptic; antiseptics such as TCP are derived from this.

antitoxin antibody produced by the immune system to counteract a toxin.

Apgar score score achieved on a system devised to evaluate the well-being of a baby immediately after birth. Five parameters are measured: heart rate, skin colour, breathing, response to stimulus and muscle tone. A maximum of two points is awarded for each observation. A newborn with an Apgar score of ten is said to be perfectly fit and robust. A baby scoring less than seven requires resuscitation and support; the test is repeated at intervals to monitor progress.

artificial respiration emergency procedure to restart breathing once it has stopped; in cases of electric shock or apparent drowning, for example, the first choice is the expired-air method, the **kiss of life** by mouth-to-mouth breathing until natural breathing is restored.

bacteria singular **bacterium** microscopic single-celled organisms lacking a nucleus. Bacteria are widespread, present in soil, air, and water, and as parasites on and in other living things. Some parasitic bacteria cause disease by producing toxins, but others are harmless and may even benefit their hosts. Bacteria usually reproduce by binary

> **All over bacteria**
> ■ Bacteria on and in the human body outnumber the number of cells that constitute the body.

fission (dividing into two equal parts), and this may occur approximately every 20 minutes.

biopsy removal of a living tissue sample from the body for diagnostic examination.

blood pressure pressure, or tension, of the blood against the inner walls of blood vessels, especially the arteries, due to the muscular pumping activity of the heart. Abnormally high blood pressure (hypertension) may be associated with various conditions or arise with no obvious cause; abnormally low blood pressure (hypotension) occurs in shock and after excessive fluid or blood loss from any cause.

blood test laboratory evaluation of a blood sample. There are numerous blood tests, from simple typing to establish the blood group to sophisticated biochemical assays of substances, such as hormones, present in the blood only in minute quantities.

Caesarean section surgical operation to deliver a baby by way of an incision in the mother's abdominal and uterine walls. It may be recommended for almost any obstetric complication implying a threat to mother or baby.

catheter fine tube inserted into the body to introduce or remove fluids. The urinary catheter, passed by way of the urethra (the duct that leads urine away from the bladder) was the first to be used. In today's practice, catheters can be inserted into blood vessels, either in the limbs or trunk, to provide blood samples and local pressure measurements, and to deliver drugs and/or nutrients directly into the bloodstream.

CAT scan or **CT scan** (acronym for **computerized axial tomography scan**) sophisticated method of X-ray imaging. Quick and noninvasive, CAT scanning is used as an aid to diagnosis, helping to pinpoint problem areas without the need for exploratory surgery.

cervical smear removal of a small sample of tissue from the cervix (neck of the womb) to screen for changes implying a likelihood of cancer. The procedure is also known as the **Pap test** after its originator, George Papanicolau.

chemotherapy any medical treatment with chemicals. It usually refers to treatment of cancer with cytotoxic and other drugs. The term was coined by the German bacteriologist Paul Ehrlich for the use of synthetic chemicals against infectious diseases.

chiropody care and treatment of feet.

chorionic villus sampling (CVS) biopsy of a small sample of placental tissue, carried out in early pregnancy at 10–12 weeks' gestation. Since the placenta forms from embryonic cells, the tissue obtained can be tested to reveal genetic abnormality in the fetus. The advantage of CVS over amniocentesis is that it provides an earlier diagnosis, so that if any abnormality is discovered, and the parents opt for an abortion, it can be carried out more safely.

chronic fatigue syndrome a common debilitating condition also known as myalgic encephalomyelitis (ME), postviral fatigue syndrome. It is characterized by a diffuse range of symptoms present for at least six months including extreme fatigue, muscular pain, weakness, depression, poor balance and coordination, joint pains, and gastric upset. It is usually diagnosed after exclusion of other diseases and frequently follows a flulike illness.

clinical ecology ascertaining environmental factors involved in illnesses, particularly those manifesting nonspecific symptoms such as fatigue, depression, allergic reactions, and immune-system malfunctions, and prescribing means of avoiding or minimizing these effects.

clinical trial evaluation of the effectiveness of medical treatment in a systematic fashion. Clinical trials compare new treatments with established treatments or placebos under standardized conditions. Such treatments may be drugs or surgical procedures. Ethical standards are maintained by ethics committees and they also ensure that the clinical trial procedure is explained to patients. The system was established with the development of new medicines in the 1940s and 1950s.

cocktail effect the effect of two toxic, or potentially toxic, chemicals when taken together rather than separately. Such effects are known to occur with some mixtures of drugs, with the active ingredient of one making the body more sensitive to the other. This sometimes occurs because both drugs require the same enzyme to break them down.

colonoscopy medical procedure involving the insertion of a **colonoscope** (fibre-optic viewing instrument) into the rectum, to detect abnormalities within the colon. Patients undergoing colonoscopy are given an enema to empty the bowel, before being sedated. Colonoscopies detect cancerous tumours and precancerous polyps.

communicable disease any disease that can be passed from one person to another, either by direct or indirect contact, including droplet infection (as in sneezing, for example).

convulsion series of violent contractions of the muscles over which the patient has no control. It may be associated with loss of consciousness. Convulsions may arise from any one of a number of causes, including brain disease (such as epilepsy), injury, high fever, poisoning, and electrocution.

dermatology medical speciality concerned with the diagnosis and treatment of skin disorders.

dilatation and curettage (D and C) common gynaecological procedure in which the cervix (neck of the womb) is widened, or dilated, giving access so that the lining of the womb can be scraped away (curettage). It may be carried out to terminate a pregnancy, treat an incomplete miscarriage, discover the cause of heavy menstrual bleeding, or for biopsy.

electrocardiogram (ECG) graphic recording of the electrical activity of the heart, as detected by electrodes placed on the skin. Electro-cardiography is used in the diagnosis of heart disease.

electroconvulsive therapy (ECT) or **electroshock therapy** treatment mainly for severe depression, given under anaesthesia and with a muscle relaxant. An electric current is passed through one or both sides of the brain to induce alterations in its electrical activity. The treatment can cause distress and loss of concentration and memory, and so there is much controversy about its use and effectiveness.

electroencephalogram (EEG) graphic record of the electrical discharges of the brain, as detected by electrodes placed on the scalp. The pattern of electrical activity revealed by electroencephalography is helpful in the diagnosis of some brain disorders, in particular epilepsy.

endocrinology medical speciality devoted to the diagnosis and treatment of hormone disorders.

endoscopy examination of internal organs or tissues by an instrument allowing direct vision. An endoscope is equipped with an eyepiece, lenses, and its own light source to illuminate the field of vision. The endoscope used to examine the digestive tract is a flexible fibreoptic instrument swallowed by the patient.

epidemiology study of patterns and occurrence of disease with the aim of improving control and prevention.

forensic medicine branch of medicine concerned with the resolution of crimes. Examples of forensic medicine include the determination of the cause of death in suspicious circumstances or the identification of a criminal by examining tissue found at the scene of a crime. Forensic psychology involves the establishment of a psychological profile of a criminal that can assist in identification.

gallstone pebblelike, insoluble accretion formed in the human gall bladder or bile ducts from cholesterol or calcium salts present in bile. Gallstones may be symptomless or they may cause pain, indigestion, or jaundice. They can be dissolved with medication or removed, either by means of an endoscope or, along with the gall bladder, in an operation known as cholecystectomy.

gastroenterology medical speciality concerned with disorders of the digestive tract and associated organs such as the liver, gall bladder, and pancreas.

gastroscope instrument for viewing the interior of the stomach. It consists of a tube with a light and mirrors attached that is introduced into the stomach via the mouth and the oesophagus. A camera attachment allows photographs to be taken of the stomach interior.

gene therapy medical technique for curing or alleviating inherited diseases or defects; certain infections, and several kinds of cancer in which affected cells from a sufferer would be removed from the body, the DNA repaired in the laboratory (genetic engineering), and the functioning cells reintroduced.

genetic screening determination of the genetic make-up of an individual to determine if he or she is at risk of developing a hereditary disease later in life. Genetic screening can also be used to determine if an individual is a carrier for a particular genetic disease and, hence, can pass the disease on to any children. Genetic counselling should be undertaken at the same time as genetic screening of affected individuals. Diseases that can be screened for include cystic fibrosis, Huntington's chorea, and certain forms of cancer.

geriatrics medical speciality concerned with diseases and problems of the elderly.

gerontology the study of the normal physiological, social, and psychological process of ageing. It is distinct from geriatrics which is concerned with the diseases of the elderly.

haematology medical speciality concerned with disorders of the blood.

haemorrhage loss of blood from the circulatory system. It is 'manifest' when the blood can be seen, as when it flows from a wound, and 'occult' when the bleeding is internal, as from an ulcer or internal injury.

histology laboratory study of cells and tissues.

hormone-replacement therapy (HRT) use of oestrogen and progesterone to help limit the unpleasant effects of the menopause in women.

hysterectomy surgical removal of all or part of the uterus (womb). The operation is performed to treat fibroids (benign tumours growing in the uterus) or cancer; also to relieve heavy menstrual bleeding. A woman who has had a hysterectomy will no longer menstruate and cannot bear children.

immunization conferring immunity to infectious disease by artificial methods. The most widely used technique is vaccination.

Immunization is an important public health measure. If most of the population has been immunized against a particular disease, it is impossible for an epidemic to take hold.

inflammation defensive reaction of the body tissues to disease or damage, including redness, swelling, and heat. Denoted by the suffix -*itis* (as in appendicitis), it may be acute or chronic, and may be accompanied by the formation of pus. This is an essential part of the healing process.

intensive care unit (ICU) or **intensive therapy unit** (ITU) high-technology medical facility concerned with the care of patients with acute life-threatening conditions. It is characterized by the

Immunization for Travel

Although immunization against infectious diseases is rarely an essential legal requirement to enter a country, immunization is often advisable to protect the traveller from diseases not encountered at home. It is necessary to plan ahead for immunizations as some require more than one dose of vaccine and some cannot be given at the same time. General practitioners and travel health centres provide the most up-to-date advice on the immunizations recommended for travelling.
In general, travellers to all countries should have immunity to tetanus and poliomyelitis and childhood immunizations should be up to date. Additional immunizations are required in non-European areas surrounding the Mediterranean, in Africa, the Middle East, Asia, and South America.

typhoid Typhoid vaccine is indicated for travellers to areas where typhoid is endemic, such as Asia and South

America. However, vaccination is no substitution for good hygiene. Food should be freshly prepared and hot and uncooked vegetables, including salads, should be avoided. Fruit should be peeled. Drinking water should be bottled, boiled or treated with water sterilizing tablets.

cholera Cholera vaccine provides little protection against this disease and good hygiene is particularly important in countries where cholera is endemic.

meningitis There is a high incidence of meningococcal meningitis in some Asian countries and in southern sub-Saharan Africa and vaccination is recommended for these areas.

hepatitis A Immunization against hepatitis A is advisable for people visiting Asia and Africa.

yellow fever International certificates of vaccination against yellow fever are still required for

travel to many countries in Africa and South America.

malaria In addition to vaccination, travellers should take a course of antimalarial tablets if they are visiting areas in which malaria is endemic. Resistance to older antimalarial drugs has developed in some areas, such as central Africa, and it is essential to take this into account when requesting drugs for malaria prophylaxis.
The risks of being in contact with diseases such as hepatitis and typhoid are reduced for people staying for a short time in first-class accommodation. Immunization is especially important for people who are planning long backpacking trips or for those who are intending to work in rural areas of the countries visited. Additional immunizations, such as rabies vaccine and Japanese encephalitis vaccine, may be needed for people visiting very remote areas.

Immunizations for Travellers

Disease	Immunization	Timing	Reaction	Protection	Duration of protection	Other precautions	Notes
cholera	2 injections not less than 1 week apart	1 week to 1 month before departure	soreness where injected, fever, headache	50–60%	6 months	avoid food or water that may be dirty	low risk in reasonable tourist accommodation; not recommended for children under 1 year
hepatitis A	(a) injection of immunoglobulin or (b) a vaccine consisting of 2 injections 1 month apart, then a 3rd injection 6–12 months later	(a) just before travel (b) 2 months before	(a) possible soreness where injected and in some cases, hives (b) soreness and possible headache and fatigue	(a) prevents illness (b) lessens its severity	(a) 3 months (b) 10 years	as typhoid	vaccine is not recommended for children under 10 years
hepatitis B	2 injections of vaccine 1 month apart, then booster 4 months later	last injection 1 month before travel	soreness where injected	80–95%	perhaps 5 years	–	usually only given to those at high risk, such as health workers
malaria	none; take preventative tablets from 1 week before to 4 weeks after leaving malaria area	order tablets 2 weeks before travel		90%	only while tablets are taken	use anti-mosquito sprays, mosquito nets; keep arms and legs covered after sunset	some antimalarial drugs are not recommended for pregnant mothers or children under 1 year
polio	unimmunized adults: 3 doses each 1 month apart; immunized adults: 1 booster dose	up to 7 months if first time; only days if booster	very rare cases develop polio	95+%	10 years	–	not usually given in first months of pregnancy
rabies	3 dose series of injections, usually given on days, 0, 7, and 21 or 28	5 weeks before travel	soreness where injected, headache, muscle pains, vomiting possible within 48 hours	opinion divided as to whether vaccine prevents rabies or promotes a faster response to treatment	3 months	avoid bites, scratches, or licks from any animal; wash any bite or scratch with antiseptic or soap as quickly as possible and get immediate medical treatment	
tetanus	normally given in childhood with booster every 10 years; unimmunized adults: 2 injections 1 month apart then 3rd injection 6 months later	not critical	headache, lethargy in rare cases	90+%	about 10 years	wash any wounds with antiseptic	
typhoid	3 types of vaccine: (a) 1–2 injections 4–6 weeks apart (b) single injection (c) 4 daily oral doses	5–7 weeks before departure	soreness where injected, nausea, headache (worst in those over 35 and on repeat immunizations) may last 36 hours	70–90%	(a) 1–3 years (b) 3 years (c) 1 year	avoid food, milk, or water that may be contaminated by sewage or by flies	
yellow fever	1 injection	at least 10 days before departure	possible slight headache and low fever 5–10 days later	almost 100%	10 years	against mosquitoes, as for malaria	may only be available from special centres

details correct at end August 1998

use of the most advanced medical technology – electronic monitoring, mechanical ventilation, and other life-support measures – combined with skilled nursing and drugs.

in vitro fertilization (IVF) 'fertilization in glass', allowing eggs and sperm to unite in a laboratory to form embryos. The embryos (properly called pre-embryos in their two- to eight-celled state) are stored by cooling to the temperature of liquid air (cryopreservation) until they are implanted into the womb of the otherwise infertile mother (an extension of artificial insemination). The first baby to be produced by this method was born in 1978 in the UK. In cases where the Fallopian tubes are blocked, fertilization may be carried out by **intra-vaginal culture,** in which egg and sperm are incubated (in a plastic tube) in the mother's vagina, then transferred surgically into the uterus.

keyhole surgery or **minimally invasive surgery** term used to describe operations that do not involve cutting into the body in the traditional way. These procedures are performed either by means of endoscopy or by passing fine instruments through catheters inserted into the body by way of large blood vessels.

laser surgery use of intense light sources to cut, coagulate, or vaporize tissue. Less invasive than normal surgery, it destroys diseased tissue gently and allows quicker, more natural healing. It can be used by way of a flexible endoscope to enable the surgeon to view the diseased area at which the laser needs to be aimed.

lobotomy another name for the former brain operation, leucotomy.

local anaesthetic anaesthetic that is applied only to the specific area under treatment.

mammography X-ray procedure used to screen for breast cancer. It can detect abnormal growths at an early stage, before they can be seen or felt.

microsurgery part or all of an intricate surgical operation – rejoining a severed limb, for example – performed with the aid of a binocular microscope, using miniaturized instruments. Sewing of the nerves and blood vessels is done with a nylon thread so fine that it is only just visible to the naked eye.

neurology medical speciality concerned with the study and treatment of disorders of the brain, spinal cord, and peripheral nerves.

nuclear medicine use of radioactive isotopes in the diagnosis, investigation, and treatment of disease.

obstetrics medical speciality concerned with the management of pregnancy, childbirth, and the immediate postnatal period.

oncology medical speciality concerned with the diagnosis and treatment of neoplasms, especially cancer.

ophthalmology medical speciality concerned with diseases of the eye and its surrounding tissues.

orthodontics branch of dentistry concerned with dentition, and with treatment of any irregularities, such as correction of malocclusion (faulty position of teeth).

orthopaedics medical speciality concerned with the correction of disease or damage in bones and joints.

osteology part of the science of anatomy, dealing with the structure, function, and development of bones.

paediatrics medical speciality concerned with the care of children.

paraplegia paralysis of the lower limbs, involving loss of both movement and sensation; it is usually due to spinal injury.

patch test placing of small amounts of possible allergens on to the skin, usually on the arm or back, to identify the cause of an allergic reaction. A red flare and swelling will appear in the area of application if the individual is allergic to that substance. Patch tests can achieve very quick results, but in some cases the patch must remain in place for several days.

pathogen any microorganism that causes disease. Most pathogens are parasites, and the diseases they cause are incidental to their search for food or shelter inside the host. Nonparasitic organisms, such as soil bacteria or those living in the human gut and feeding on waste foodstuffs, can also become pathogenic to a person whose immune system or liver is damaged. The larger parasites that can cause disease, such as nematode worms, are not usually described as pathogens.

pathology medical speciality concerned with the study of disease processes and how these provoke structural and functional changes in the body.

pharmacology study of the properties of drugs and their effects on the human body.

physiotherapy treatment of injury and disease by physical means such as exercise, heat, manipulation, massage, and electrical stimulation.

placebo any harmless substance, often called a 'sugar pill', that has no active ingredient, but may nevertheless bring about improvement in the patient's condition.

plastic surgery surgical speciality concerned with the repair of congenital defects and the reconstruction of tissues damaged by disease or injury, including burns. If a procedure is undertaken solely for reasons of appearance, for example, the removal of bags under the eyes or a double chin, it is called **cosmetic surgery.**

polyp or **polypus** small 'stalked' benign tumour, usually found on mucous membrane of the nose or bowels. Intestinal polyps are usually removed, since some have been found to be precursors of cancer.

postmortem or **autopsy** dissection of a dead body to determine the cause of death.

postpartum any events occurring immediately after childbirth.

premedication combination of drugs given before surgery to prepare a patient for general anaesthesia.

prognosis prediction of the course or outcome of illness or injury, particularly the chance of recovery.

prolapse displacement of an organ due to the effects of strain in weakening the supporting tissues. The term is most often used with regard to the rectum (due to chronic bowel problems) or the uterus (following several pregnancies).

prophylaxis any measure taken to prevent disease, including exercise and vaccination. Prophylactic (preventive) medicine is an aspect of public-health provision that is receiving increasing attention.

prostatectomy surgical removal of the prostate gland. In many men over the age of 60 the prostate gland enlarges, causing obstruction to the urethra. This causes the bladder to swell with retained urine, leaving the sufferer more prone to infection of the urinary tract.

psychosomatic of a physical symptom or disease thought to arise from emotional or mental factors.

pulse impulse transmitted by the heartbeat throughout the arterial system. When the heart muscle contracts, it forces blood into the aorta (the chief artery). Because the arteries are elastic, the sudden rise of pressure causes a throb or sudden swelling through them. The actual flow of the blood is about 60 cm/2 ft a second in humans. The average adult pulse rate is generally about 70 per minute. The pulse can be felt where an artery is near the surface, for example in the wrist or the neck.

radiotherapy treatment of disease by radiation from X-ray machines or radioactive sources. Radiation, which reduces the activity of dividing cells, is of special value for its effect on malignant tissues, certain nonmalignant tumours, and some diseases of the skin.

retrovirus any of a family of viruses (Retroviridae) containing the genetic material RNA rather than the more usual DNA.

rhesus factor group of antigens on the surface of red blood cells of humans which characterize the rhesus blood group system. Most individuals possess the main rhesus factor (Rh+), but those without this factor (Rh−) produce antibodies if they come into contact with it. The name comes from rhesus monkeys, in whose blood rhesus factors were first found.

squint or **strabismus** common condition in which one eye deviates in any direction. A squint may be convergent (with the bad eye turned inwards), divergent (outwards), or, in rare cases, vertical. A convergent squint is also called **cross-eye.**

suppository drug or other therapeutic preparation manufactured in solid form for insertion into the vagina or rectum.

tomography the technique of using X-rays or ultrasound waves to procure images of structures deep within the body for diagnostic purposes. In modern medical imaging there are several techniques, such as the CAT scan (computerized axial tomography).

toxicology branch of medicine dealing with the study of poisons. This includes the chemical

Medical prefixes and suffixes

prefix	meaning	prefix	meaning	suffix	meaning
a(n)-	lacking	laryng(o)-	larynx	-aemia	condition of blood
ab-	away from	mal-	abnormal, diseased	-algia	pain
abdomin(o)-	abdominal	mast-	breast	-ase	enzyme
ad-	towards, near	muco-	mucus	-blast	formative cell
andr(o)-	male	my(o)-	muscle	-cele	tumour, swelling
angi(o)-	blood or lymph vessel	necro-	death	-centesis	puncture
ant(i)-	against, counteracting	neo-	new	-cide	destructive, killing
ante-	before	nephr(o)-	kidney	-coccus	spherical bacterium
arthr(o)-	joint	neur(o)-	nerve	-cyte	cell
aut(o)-	self	noct-	night	-derm	skin
bi-	twice, two	oculo-	eye	-dynia	pain
brachi(o)-	arm	olig(o)-	deficiency, few	-ectasis	dilation, extension
brachy-	shortness	ophthalm(o)-	eye	-ectomy	surgical removal of
brady-	slowness	oro-	mouth	-facient	making, causing
bronch(o)-	bronchial tube	ortho-	straight, normal	-fuge	expelling
carcin(o)-	cancer	osteo-	bone	-genesis	origin, development
cardi(o)-	heart	ot(o)-	ear	-genic	causing, produced by
cerebr(o)-	brain	paed-	children	-gram	tracing, record
cholecyst-	gall bladder	path(o)-	disease	-iasis	diseased condition
circum-	surrounding	peri-	around, enclosing	-iatric	practice of healing
colp(o)-	vagina	pharmac(o)-	drugs	-itis	inflammation of
contra-	against	phleb(o)-	vein	-kinesis	movement
crani(o)-	skull	phot(o)-	light	-lith	calculus, stone
cry(o)-	cold	pneumon-	lung	-lysis	breaking down, dissolution
crypt-	hidden, concealed	poly-	many, excessive	-malacia	softening
cyst(o)-	bladder	post-	after	-megaly	enlargement
cyt(o)-	cell	pre-(pro-)	before	-oid	likeness, resemblance
dent-	tooth	ren-	kidney	-oma	tumour
derm-	skin	retro-	behind	-opia	eye defect
di-	double	rhin-	nose	-osis	disease, condition
dys-	difficult, painful, abnormal	sclero-	thickening	-ostomy	surgical opening or outlet
end(o)-	within, inner	ser(o)-	serum	-otomy	surgical incision into an organ or part
enter(o)-	intestine	spondyl-	vertebra, spine	-pathy	disease
epi-	above, upon	supra-	above	-penia	lack of, deficiency
ex(o)-	outside, outer	syn-	together, union	-pexy	surgical fixation
extra-	outside, beyond	tachy-	fast	-phage	ingesting
gastr(o)-	stomach	tetra-	four	-philia	affinity for, morbid attraction
gyn-	female	therm(o)-	heat, temperature	-phobia	fear
haem-	blood	trache(o)-	trachea	-plasty	reconstructive surgery
hepat(o)-	liver	uni-	one	-plegia	paralysis
hist(o)-	tissue	urin-	urine, urinary system	-pnoea	condition of breathing
hyper-	above	utero-	uterus	-poiesis	formation
hypno-	sleep	vaso-	vessel	-ptosis	prolapse
hypo-	below	vesico-	bladder	-scopy	visual examination
hyster(o)-	uterus			-stasis	stagnation, stoppage of flow
immuno-	immunity			-tome	cutting instrument
infra-	below			-uria	condition of urine
intra-	within				

nature of poisons, their origin and preparation, their physiological action, tests to recognize them, pathological changes due to their presence, their antidotes, and the recognition of them by post-mortem evidence.

tropical disease any illness found mainly in hot climates. The most important tropical diseases worldwide are malaria, leishmaniasis, sleeping sickness, lymphatic filiarasis, and schistosomiasis. Other major scourges are Chagas's disease, leprosy, and river blindness. Malaria kills about 1.5 million people each year, and produces chronic anaemia and tiredness in 100 times as many, while schistosomiasis is responsible for 1 million deaths a year. All the main tropical diseases are potentially curable, but the facilities for diagnosis and treatment are rarely adequate in the countries where they occur.

tumour overproduction of cells in a specific area of the body, often leading to a swelling or lump. Tumours are classified as **benign** or **malignant.** Benign tumours grow more slowly, do not invade surrounding tissues, do not spread to other parts of the body, and do not usually recur after removal. However, benign tumours can be dangerous in areas such as the brain. The most familiar types of benign tumour are warts on the skin. In some cases, there is no sharp dividing line between benign and malignant tumours.

urology medical speciality concerned with diseases of the urinary tract.

Medicine, Western: Chronology

c. **400 BC** Hippocrates recognizes that disease had natural causes.

c. **AD 200** Galen consolidates the work of the Alexandrian doctors.

1543 Andreas Vesalius gives the first accurate account of the human body.

1628 William Harvey discovers the circulation of the blood.

1768 John Hunter begins the foundation of experimental and surgical pathology.

1785 Digitalis is used to treat heart disease; the active ingredient is isolated in 1904.

1798 Edward Jenner publishes his work on vaccination.

1877 Patrick Manson studies animal carriers of infectious diseases.

1882 Robert Koch isolates the bacillus responsible for tuberculosis.

1884 Edwin Klebs isolates the diphtheria bacillus.

1885 Louis Pasteur produces a vaccine against rabies.

1890 Joseph Lister demonstrates antiseptic surgery.

1895 Wilhelm Röntgen discovers X-rays.

1897 Martinus Beijerinck discovers viruses.

1899 Felix Hoffman develops aspirin; Sigmund Freud founded psychiatry.

1900 Karl Landsteiner identifies the first three blood groups, later designated A, B, and O.

1910 Paul Ehrlich develops the first specific antibacterial agent, Salvarsan, a cure for syphilis.

Medicine, Western: Chronology (continued)

1922 Insulin is first used to treat diabetes.

1928 Alexander Fleming discovers penicillin.

1932 Gerhard Domagk discovers the first antibacterial sulphonamide drug, Prontosil.

1937 Electro-convulsive therapy (ECT) is developed.

1940s Lithium treatment for manic-depressive illness is developed.

1950s Antidepressant drugs and beta-blockers for heart disease are developed. Manipulation of the molecules of synthetic chemicals becomes the main source of new drugs. Peter Medawar studies the body's tolerance of transplanted organs and skin grafts.

1950 Proof of a link between cigarette smoking and lung cancer is established.

1953 Francis Crick and James Watson announce the structure of DNA. Jonas Salk develops a vaccine against polio.

1958 Ian Donald pioneers diagnostic ultrasound.

1960s A new generation of minor tranquillizers called benzodiazepines is developed.

1967 Christiaan Barnard performs the first human heart transplant operation.

1971 Viroids, disease-causing organisms even smaller than viruses, are isolated outside the living body.

1972 The CAT scan, pioneered by Godfrey Hounsfield, is first used to image the human brain.

1975 César Milstein develops monoclonal antibodies.

1978 World's first 'test-tube baby' is born in the UK.

1980s AIDS (acquired immuno-deficiency syndrome) is first recognized in the USA. Barbara McClintock's discovery of the transposable gene is recognized.

1980 The World Health Organization reports the eradication of smallpox.

1983 The virus responsible for AIDS, now known as human immunodeficiency virus (HIV), is identified by Luc Montagnier at the Institut

Pasteur, Paris; Robert Gallo at the National Cancer Institute, Maryland, USA discovers the virus independently in 1984.

1984 The first vaccine against leprosy is developed.

1987 The world's longest-surviving heart-transplant patient dies in France, 18 years after his operation.

1989 Grafts of fetal brain tissue are first used to treat Parkinson's disease.

1990 Gene for maleness is discovered by UK researchers.

1991 First successful use of gene therapy (to treat severe combined immune deficiency) is reported in the USA.

1993 First trials of gene therapy against cystic fibrosis take place in the USA.

1996 An Australian man, Ben Dent, is the first person to end his life by legally sanctioned euthanasia.

1998 The US manufacturing company Pfizer gets approval for its impotence treatment Viagra. It becomes the fastest-selling prescription drug in US history.

Noteworthy Medical Pioneers

Alzheimer Alois (1864–1915) German psychiatrist and neuropathologist who studied presenile dementia, now known as Alzheimer's disease

Anderson Elizabeth Garrett (1836–1917) English physician and the first English woman to qualify in medicine

Avicenna (Arabic name Ibn Sina) (979–1037) Arabian philosopher and physician whose *Canon Medicinae* was a standard work for many centuries

Banting Frederick Grant (1891–1941) Canadian physician whose research resulted in a treatment for diabetes

Barnard Christiaan Neethling (1922–) South African surgeon who performed the first successful human heart transplant

Beaumont William (1785–1853) US surgeon who conducted pioneering experiments on the digestive system

Behring Emil von (1854–1917) German physician who discovered that the body produces antitoxins, substances able to counteract poisons released by bacteria, and developed new treatments for such diseases as diphtheria

Bell Charles (1774–1842) Scottish anatomist who pioneered research on the human nervous system

Bichat Marie Francois Xavier (1771–1802) French physician and founder of histology

Black James Whyte (1924–) Scottish pharmacologist who developed the first beta-blocker drugs as well as anti-ulcer drugs

Blackwell Elizabeth (1821–1910) English-born US physician who was the first woman to qualify in medicine in the USA

Bright Richard (1789–1858) British physician who described many conditions and linked oedema to kidney disease

Burnet (Frank) Macfarlane (1899–1985) Australian physician who was an authority on immunology and viral diseases, such as influenza, poliomyelitis, and cholera

Cairns Hugh William Bell (1896–1952) Australian surgeon who pioneered work on head injuries and was a campaigner for the motorcycle crash helmet

Cardozo William Warrick (1905–1962) US physician who pioneered work on sickle-cell anaemia

Carrel Alexis (1873–1944) French-born US surgeon who contributed to the development of organ transplants

Chain Ernst Boris (1906–1979) German-born British biochemist who worked with Florey and Fleming on the purification of penicillin

Cushing Harvey Williams (1869–1939) US neurologist who pioneered neurosurgery

Doll (William) Richard Shaboe (1912–) British physician who helped provide the first statistical proof of the link between smoking and cancer

Domagk Gerhard Johannes Paul (1895–1964) German biochemist who discovered the antibacterial sulphonamide drugs

Edelman Gerald Maurice (1929–) US biochemist who established the sequence of amino acids in human immunoglobulin

Ehrlich Paul (1854–1915) German bacteriologist who produced the first cure for syphilis

Eijkman Christiaan (1858–1930) Dutch bacteriologist who pioneered the recognition of vitamins as essential to health and identified vitamin B_1 deficiency as the cause of the disease beriberi

Enders John Franklin (1897–1985) US microbiologist who contributed to the development of vaccines against polio and measles

Fleming Alexander (1881–1955) Scottish bacteriologist who discovered the first antibiotic drug, penicillin

Florey Howard Walter (1898–1968) Australian pathologist who purified and developed the antibiotic penicillin

Freud Sigmund (1856–1939) Austrian physician who pioneered psychoanalysis

Galen (c. 130–c. 200) Greek physician and anatomist whose thinking dominated Western medicine for almost 1,500 years

Gallo Robert Charles (1937–) US scientist credited with identifying the human immuno-

Noteworthy Medical Pioneers (continued)

deficiency virus (HIV), the virus responsible for AIDS

Gray Henry (*c.* 1827–1861) British anatomist who wrote the definitive work on anatomy

Haller (Viktor) Albrecht von (1708–1777) Swiss physician and scientist who was the founder of neurology

Harvey William (1578–1657) English physician who discovered the circulation of the blood

Hippocrates (*c.* 460–377 BC) Greek physician called the founder of medicine and associated with the 'Hippocratic oath' of the medical profession

Hunter John (1728–1793) Scottish physiologist and surgeon who pioneered research in the fields of comparative anatomy and pathology

Issacs Alick (1921–1967) Scottish virologist who helped discover interferon

Jenner Edward (1749–1823) English physician who pioneered vaccination

Jung Carl Gustav (1875–1961) Swiss psychiatrist who pioneered analytical psychology

Kitasato Shibasaburō (1852–1931) Japanese bacteriologist who discovered the plague bacillus and was the first to grow the tetanus bacillus in pure culture

Koch (Heinrich Hermann) Robert (1843–1910) German bacteriologist who devised techniques for culturing bacteria outside the body and formulated the rules for showing whether or not a bacterium is the cause of a disease

Laênnec René Théophile Hyacinthe (1781–1826) French physician who invented the stethoscope

Landsteiner Karl (1868–1943) US pathologist who discovered the four major human blood groups

Lister Joseph (1827–1912) English surgeon and founder of antiseptic surgery

Malpighi Marcello (1628–1694) Italian physiologist who discovered blood capillaries

Manson Patrick (1844–1922) Scottish physician who showed that insects are responsible for the spread of diseases like elephantiasis and malaria

Mechnikov Ilia Ilich (1845–1916) Russian-born French zoologist who discovered the function of white blood cells and phagocytes

Medawar Peter Brian (1915–1987) British zoologist and immunologist who studied skin grafting for burn victims

Menninger Karl Augustus (1893–1990) US psychiatrist who was instrumental in reforming public mental health facilities

Paget James (1814–1899) English surgeon who was one of the founders of pathology

Paracelsus (adopted name of **Philippus Aureolus Theophrastus Bombastus von Hohenheim**) (1493–1541) Swiss physician, alchemist, and scientist who developed the idea that minerals and chemicals might have medical uses and introduced the use of laudanum for pain relief

Paré Ambroise (*c.* 1509–1590) French military surgeon who introduced modern principles to the treatment of wounds

Pasteur Louis (1822–1895) French chemist and microbiologist who developed the germ theory of disease

Reed Walter (1851–1902) US physician and medical researcher who identified the *Aedes* mosquito as the carrier of yellow fever

Ross Ronald (1857–1932) British physician and bacteriologist who identified mosquitoes of the genus *Anopheles* as being responsible for the spread of malaria

Sabin Albert Bruce (1906–1993) Russian-born US microbiologist who developed a highly effective live vaccine against polio

Salk Jonas Edward (1914–1995) US physician and microbiologist who developed the original vaccine for polio

Sanger Margaret Louise (born **Higgins**) (1883–1966) US health reformer and crusader for birth control

Sharpey-Schafer Edward Albert (born **Schäfer**) (1850–1935) English physiologist, one of the founders of endocrinology

Vesalius Andreas (1514–1564) Belgian physician who revolutionized anatomy by performing postmortem dissections

Virchow Rudolf Carl (1821–1902) German pathologist who founded cellular pathology

HISTORY

———— ✳ ————

History is the record of the events of human societies. The earliest surviving historical records are inscriptions concerning the achievements of Egyptian and Babylonian kings. As a literary form in the Western world, historical writing, or **historiography,** began in the 5th century BC with the Greek Herodotus, who was first to pass beyond the limits of a purely national outlook. History from the point of view of ordinary people is now recognized as an important element in historical study. Associated with this is the collection of spoken records known as **oral history.** Contemporary historians also make extensive use of statistics, population figures, and primary records to justify historical arguments. Historians make a distinction between historical evidence or records, historical writing, and historical method or approaches to the study of history.

ANCIENT HISTORY

Prehistory and the Three Age System

Prehistory refers to human cultures before the use of writing. Human prehistory begins with the emergence of early modern hominids approximately 3,500,000 years ago. The first tool user, *Homo habilis* – found at such sites as Koobi Fora, Kenya, and Olduvai Gorge, Tanzania – was in evidence around 2 million years ago. Prehistory extends until the end of the Iron Age, but general chronological dividing lines between history and prehistory, as well as between prehistoric eras, are difficult to determine because communities have developed at differing rates. The study of prehistory is mainly dependent on archaeology. Prehistory is broadly divided into three ages. This 'Three Age System' of classification (published in 1836 by the Danish archaeologist Christian Thomsen) is based on the predominant materials used by early humans for tools and weapons: Stone Age, Bronze Age, and Iron Age.

Stone Age The Stone Age is the developmental stage of humans in prehistory before the use of metals, when tools and weapons were made chiefly of stone, especially flint. The Stone Age is subdivided into the Old or **Palaeolithic** (3,500,000–8500 BC), when flint implements were simply chipped into shape; the Middle or **Mesolithic**; and the New or **Neolithic,** when implements were ground and polished. Palaeolithic people were hunters and gatherers; by the Neolithic period people were taking the first steps in agriculture, the domestication of animals, weaving, and pottery.

Old Stone Age or Palaeolithic
Palaeolithic people were hunters and their remains have been found in the caves in which they lived, and in the sedimentary deposits of river gravel. The early Palaeolithic is divided into the cultures of **Chelles** and **St-Acheul.**

The Middle Palaeolithic is characterized by Mousterian flake flint technology, and in geological time existed during the period of the Würm glacial advance (fourth stage of glaciation in the Alps). Neanderthal people of this era lived with a 'cold' fauna which included the mammoth, horse, ox, and reindeer.

The Upper Palaeolithic includes the Aurignacian, **Solutrean,** and Magdalenian cultures, and in geological time covered the retreat of the Würm glaciation and a dry, rather cold, subsequent period. The fauna changed when, with the onset of colder conditions, the steppe became tundra. The walls of some caves inhabited by Palaeolithic peoples were decorated with sketches and paintings of possibly magic and religious significance. Prehistoric art is often found in the Magdalenian culture of southwestern France and northwestern Spain, and its association with a hunting economy is unmistakable. An impressive series of paintings are in a cave at Lascaux, France.

Neanderthal The Neanderthal is a hominid of the Mid-Late Palaeolithic. *Homo sapiens neanderthalensis* lived from about 150,000 to 35,000 years ago and was similar in build to present-day people, but slightly smaller, stockier, and heavier-featured with a strong jaw and prominent brow ridges on a sloping forehead.

Neanderthals lived in Europe, the Middle East, and Africa. They looked after their disabled and buried their dead ritualistically. Recent evidence suggests their physical capacity for the sounds of speech. They were replaced throughout Europe by, or possibly interbred with, *Homo sapiens sapiens,* newly arrived from Africa. A genetic analysis carried out on mitochondrial DNA extracted from fossil Neanderthal bones indicated in 1997 that Neanderthals shared a common ancestor with

modern humans no later than 600,000 years ago, suggesting that they are not direct ancestors.

Middle Stone Age or Mesolithic There are several distinct cultures in the Mesolithic period, all of them based on a food-gathering economy. The climate had greatly improved, and hunting and fishing are indicated by the presence of **microliths** (small flints fashioned and mounted to form a composite tool such as a saw) and fish-spear barbs. In Britain there seem to have been four cultures, one having affinities with the Baltic.

New Stone Age or Neolithic The Neolithic period, with its colonization of mainland Europe and Atlantic coast routes, saw an advance in development based upon agriculture and stockrearing. There was wide trade in flint and stone axes, particularly from flint mines such as Grimes Graves in Norfolk, England; and the period was also marked by the spread of megaliths as tombs in long barrow (burial mounds), and the construction of **causewayed camps**: earthwork camps with causeways or interrupted ditches. Plants, both cereal and textile, were cultivated, and sheep, oxen, goats, and pigs were domesticated.

Bronze Age The Bronze Age was the stage of prehistory and early history when copper and bronze (an alloy of tin and copper) became the first metals worked extensively and used for tools and weapons. Bronze tools and weapons appeared approximately 5000 BC in the Far East, and continued in the Middle East until about 1200 BC; in Europe this period lasted from about 2000 to 500 BC. In some areas, including most of Africa, there was no Bronze Age, and ironworking was introduced directly into the Stone Age economy.

Mining and metalworking were the first specialized industries of the

Prehistory and the Three Age System (continued)

Bronze Age, and the invention of the wheel during this time revolutionized transport. Agricultural productivity (which began during the New Stone Age, or Neolithic period, about 6000 BC) was transformed by the ox-drawn plough, increasing the size of the population that could be supported by farming.

The earliest use of bronze has been found in the Far East and was originally assumed to have spread, through diffusion of culture, westwards and throughout Europe. However, absolute dating techniques now suggest that metalworking may have been independently invented in other areas, including the Aegean. Some regions, such as Denmark, became important manufacturing centres although they had no native copper or tin ores, indicating the importance of long-distance trade in the European Bronze Age. Tin ore is particularly restricted in its distribution – found, for example, in Cornwall, England; Bohemia, Germany; and Anatolia, Turkey – and must have been carried great distances. The other chief metal used during the Bronze Age was gold, which occurs widely in the pure state and was used for ornament.

In Europe the burials of the Bronze Age peoples have produced a great range of pottery vessels and other objects which provide clues to the way of life and ritual beliefs of the ordinary and the elite. This material can also be used in conjunction with metal artefacts to describe, distinguish, and observe the spread of local cultures, such as that of the Beaker people. In general, Bronze Age society in temperate Europe was based on farming, in which stockrearing continued to play a large part, but the Bronze Age also saw the rise of urbanization in the Middle East and palace economies, such as those of the Minoan civilization and Mycenaean civilization, which were based almost as much on manufacturing and service industries as on the rural hinterland. Interrelationships of

cultures joined by maritime trade routes are important, in particular with regard to the Mediterranean.

The evidence of Bronze Age weapons in graves suggests the symbolic importance as well as the prestige value of such artefacts. Palace economies, such as Knossos on Crete, epitomized organized systems based on hierarchical structure and the trade in prestige goods, sometimes manufactured on site, as evidenced by workshops. This complex system may be seen in prestige burials and trade goods in a network of long-distance exchange. Early Bronze Age burial mounds in areas such as Wessex, southern England, were either simple mounds or elaborate forms with ditches and banks, which may differentiate the ruling elite.

Iron Age The Iron Age was the developmental stage of human technology when weapons and tools were made from iron. Iron was produced in Thailand about 1600 BC, but was considered inferior in strength to bronze until about 1000 BC, when metallurgical techniques improved, and the alloy steel was produced by adding carbon during the smelting process. From 1600, ironworking was introduced into different regions over a wide time span, appearing in Asia Minor about 1200 BC, central Europe about 900 BC, China about 600 BC, and in remoter areas during exploration and colonization by the Old World. It reached the Fiji Islands with an expedition in the late 19th century.

Iron Age cultures include Hallstatt (named after a site in Austria) and La Tène (named after a site in Switzerland). The economic working of iron, particularly for use in agricultural tools and weapons, was a great step forward in material culture. Unlike copper and tin used in bronze, iron ores are widely available and this enabled the spread of cheap, durable metal tools.

The Iron Age saw the

development of hierarchical systems, with tribes and chiefs, and the strengthening of defences, such as hillforts and enclosures. Complex trade routes were established between the Mediterranean and northern Europe, especially using rivers. Conspicuous consumption increased among chiefs, particularly of alcohol, and intense competition increased the output of prestige goods.

The salt industry played a major part in the economy of the **Hallstatt** peoples, the earliest Iron Age culture in central Europe. Late Hallstatt chiefdoms are regarded as precursors of the Celtic hierarchical systems.

La Tène culture Lake Neuchâtel, Switzerland. The various La Tène cultures, regarded as Celtic, grew from trading contacts made between the advanced urban civilizations of the Mediterranean and the Hallstatt farming communities north of the Alps. La Tène peoples used iron extensively for military and general metalware, and bronze and gold mainly for ornaments.Objects decorated in the La Tène style, often found as grave objects, appear throughout Europe, from Greece and Asia Minor to Ireland, and from Denmark to southern Italy, indicating the great expansion of the Celts of central Europe in the later 1st millennium BC. The source of the Celts is an unanswered question in archaeology, as their migrations drew together peoples from a number of areas. Attempts have been made to distinguish them linguistically; otherwise they are known as the 'barbarians' to the classical world of the Romans.

End of the Iron Age In areas that became part of the Roman Empire, the Iron Age is succeeded in archaeological terminology by a Roman period, but elsewhere the Iron Age continues until some other literate culture, often Christianity, becomes dominant.

Achaea or **Achaia** in ancient Greece, an area of the northern Peloponnese. The **Achaeans** were the predominant society during the Mycenaean period and are said by Homer to have taken part in the siege of Troy.

Achaean League union 280 BC of most of the cities of the northern Peloponnese, which managed to defeat Sparta, but was itself defeated by the Romans 146 BC.

Aegean civilization the cultures of Bronze Age Greece, including the **Minoan civilization** of Crete and the **Mycenaean civilization** of the Peloponnese and mainland Greece.

Alexandria or **Al Iskandariya** Egyptian port founded in 331 BC by Alexander the Great. It was the capital of Egypt for over 1,000 years.

Augustan Age golden age of the Roman emperor Augustus (31 BC–AD 14), during which art and literature flourished.

Babylon capital of ancient Babylonia, on the bank of the lower Euphrates River. The Hanging Gardens of Babylon, one of the Seven Wonders of the World, were probably erected on a vaulted stone base, the only stone construction in the mud-brick city. They formed a series of terraces, irrigated by a hydraulic system. The site is now in Iraq.

Alexandria The 15th century fort of Qait Bay, now a naval museum, dominates the eastern harbour of Alexandria, Egypt. Built on a narrow strip of land between the Mediterranean and Lake Maryut, Alexandria has been a major port for centuries. It has been fought over and occupied many times since it was founded by Alexander the Great in 331 BC. *Egyptian Tourist Board*

Britain, ancient period in the British Isles (excluding Ireland) extending through prehistory to the Roman occupation (1st century AD). Settled agricultural life evolved in Britain during the 3rd millennium BC. A peak was reached in Neolithic society in southern England early in the 2nd millennium BC, with the construction of the great stone circles of Avebury and Stonehenge. It was succeeded in central southern Britain by the Early Bronze Age Wessex culture, with strong trade links across Europe. The Iron Age culture of the Celts was predominant in the last few centuries BC, and the Belgae (of mixed Germanic and Celtic stock) were partially Romanized in the century between the first Roman invasion of Britain under Julius Caesar (54 BC) and the Roman conquest (AD 43).

Carthage ancient Phoenician port in North Africa founded by colonists from Tyre in the late 9th century BC; it lay 16 km/10 mi north of Tunis, Tunisia. A leading trading centre, it was in conflict with Greece from the 6th century BC, and then with Rome, and was destroyed by Roman forces 146 BC at the end of the **Punic Wars**. About 45 BC, Roman colonists settled in Carthage, and it became the wealthy capital of the province of Africa. After its capture by the Vandals AD 439 it was little more than a pirate stronghold. From 533 it formed part of the Byzantine Empire until its final destruction by Arabs 698, during their conquest in the name of Islam.

colonies, Greek overseas territories of the ancient Greek city-states. Greek colonization was mostly concerned with land, not trade. Greek cities on the west coast of modern Turkey may have been founded as early as 1000 BC. From the late 8th century BC population expansion prompted settlements in southern Italy (Taranto, by settlers from Sparta) and Sicily (Syracuse, by settlers from Corinth), followed by others in southern France (Marseille), North Africa (Cyrenaica) and on the Black Sea coast.

colonies, Roman territories of the Roman empire. The earliest Roman citizen settlements guarded the local coast (Ostia) from the 4th century BC. In contrast, Latin colonies were independent and helped to secure Italy. In the later Republic, colonies were founded to distribute land to army veterans or the poor. Overseas colonies were supported by Julius Caesar and Augustus in Spain, Gaul (France and Belgium), Africa and Asia. Imperial colonization continued to the end of the 1st century AD.

Constantinople former name (330–1453) of Istanbul, Turkey. It was named after the Roman emperor Constantine the Great when he enlarged the Greek city of Byzantium 328 and declared it the capital of the Byzantine Empire 330. Its elaborate fortifications enabled it to resist a succession of sieges, but it was captured by crusaders 1204, and was the seat of a Latin (Western European) kingdom until recaptured by the Greeks 1261. An attack by the Turks 1422 proved unsuccessful, but it was taken by another Turkish army 29 May 1453, after nearly a year's siege, and became the capital of the Ottoman Empire.

Corinth Greek **Kórinthos** site of the ancient city-state of Corinth, which lies 7 km/4.5 mi southwest of the present-day port. Corinth was already a place of some commercial importance in the 9th century BC. At the end of the 6th century BC it joined the Peloponnesian League, and took a prominent part in the Persian and the Peloponnesian Wars. In 146 BC it was destroyed by the Romans. It was established as a Roman colony by Julius Caesar in 44 BC, and became the capital of the Roman province of Achaea. St Paul visited Corinth in AD 51 and addressed two epistles to its churches. After many changes of ownership it became part of independent Greece in 1822. Corinth's ancient monuments include the ruined temple of Apollo (6th century BC).

Egypt, ancient ancient civilization, based around the River Nile in Egypt, which emerged 5,000 years ago and reached its peak in the 16th century

Egyptian Dynasties

Period	Description	Name	Period	Description	Name
Early Dynastic Period			**New Kingdom**		
c. 3100–c. 2905 BC	First Dynastic Period	Thinite	c. 1570–c. 1293 BC	Eighteenth Dynasty	Theban
c. 2905–c. 2755 BC	Second Dynasty	Thinite	c. 1293–c. 1185 BC	Nineteenth Dynasty	Theban
Old Kingdom			c. 1185–c. 1070 BC	Twentieth Dynasty	Theban
c. 2755–c. 2680 BC	Third Dynasty	Memphite	**Third Intermediate Period**		
c. 2680–c. 2544 BC	Fourth Dynasty	Memphite	c. 1070–c. 946 BC	Twenty-first Dynasty	Theban
c. 2544–c. 2407 BC	Fifth Dynasty	Memphite	c. 946–c. 712 BC	Twenty-second Dynasty	Bubastite
c. 2407–c. 2255 BC	Sixth Dynasty	Memphite	c. 828–c. 720 BC	Twenty-third Dynasty	Tanite
First Intermediate Period			c. 740–c. 712 BC	Twenty-fourth Dynasty	Saite
c. 2255–c. 2235 BC	Seventh–Eighth Dynasties	Memphite	c. 767–c. 656 BC	Twenty-fifth Dynasty	Nubian
c. 2235–c. 2035 BC	Ninth–Tenth Dynasties	Heracleopolitan	**Saite Period**		
Middle Kingdom			c. 664–c. 525 BC	Twenty-sixth Dynasty	Nubian
c. 2134–c. 1991 BC	Eleventh Dynasty	Theban	**Later Dynastic Period**		
c. 1991–c. 1786 BC	Twelfth Dynasty	Theban	c. 525–c. 405 BC	Twenty-seventh Dynasty	Persian Kings
Second Intermediate Period			c. 405–c. 399 BC	Twenty-eighth Dynasty	Saite
c. 1786–c. 1668 BC	Thirteenth Dynasty	Theban	c. 399–c. 380 BC	Twenty-ninth Dynasty	Mendesian
c. 1720–c. 1665 BC	Fourteenth Dynasty	Xoite	c. 380–c. 343 BC	Thirtieth Dynasty	Sebennytic
c. 1668–c. 1560 BC	Fifteenth Dynasty	Hyksos	c. 343–332 BC	Thirty-first Dynasty	Persian Kings
c. 1665–c. 1565 BC	Sixteenth Dynasty	Hyksos	**Conquest of Egypt by Alexander the Great**		
c. 1668–c. 1570 BC	Seventeenth Dynasty	Theban	332–323 BC	Alexander the Great	
			Ptolemaic Period		
			323–30 BC	Ptolemaic Dynasty	Ptolemies
			Conquest of Egypt by Octavian (Augustus) in 30 BC		

Egypt, Ancient: Chronology

5000 BC Egyptian culture already well established in the Nile Valley, with Neolithic farming villages.

c. **3050** Menes unites Lower Egypt (the delta) with his own kingdom of Upper Egypt.

c. **2630** The architect Imhotep builds the step pyramid at Sakkara.

c. **2550** Old Kingdom reaches the height of its power and the kings of the 4th dynasty build the pyramids at El Gîza.

c. **2040–1640** Middle Kingdom, under which the unity lost towards the end of the Old Kingdom is restored.

c. **1750** Infiltrating Asian Hyksos people establish their kingdom in the Nile Delta.

c. **1550** New Kingdom established by the 18th dynasty following the eviction of the Hyksos, with its capital at Thebes. The high point of ancient Egyptian civilization under the pharaohs Thothmes, Hatshepsut, Amenhotep, Akhenaton (who moves the capital to Akhetaton), and Tutankhamen.

c. **1307–1196** 19th dynasty: Major building works by Seti I and Ramses II at Thebes, Abydos and Abu Simbel.

1191 Ramses III defeats the Indo-European Sea Peoples, but after him there is decline, and power within the country passes from the pharaohs to the priests of Amen.

1070–664 Third Intermediate Period: during this period Egypt is often divided between two or more dynasties; the nobles become virtually independent.

8th–7th centuries Brief interlude of rule by kings from Nubia.

666 The Assyrians under Ashurbanipal occupy Thebes.

663–609 Psammetichus I restores Egypt's independence and unity.

525 Egypt is conquered by Cambyses and becomes a Persian province.

c. **405–340** Period of independence.

332 Conquest by Alexander the Great. On the division of his empire, Egypt goes to one of his generals, Ptolemy I, and his descendants, the Macedonian dynasty.

30 Death of Cleopatra, last of the Macedonians, and conquest by the Roman emperor Augustus; Egypt becomes a province of the Roman empire.

AD **641** Conquest by the Arabs; the Christianity of later Roman rule is for the most part replaced by Islam.

Abu Simbel One of the two vast temples built into the cliffs by Ramses II at Abu Simbel on the Upper Nile in the 13th century BC. Ramses II was one of the few Egyptian pharaohs who aggressively sought to extend his authority beyond the Nile Valley. This temple was dedicated to his wife Nefertari and to Hathur, the goddess of love and beauty. The façade is adorned with six statues, two of Nefertari and four of Ramses. The temple consists of halls carved many metres into the sandstone cliff. *Egyptian Tourist Board*

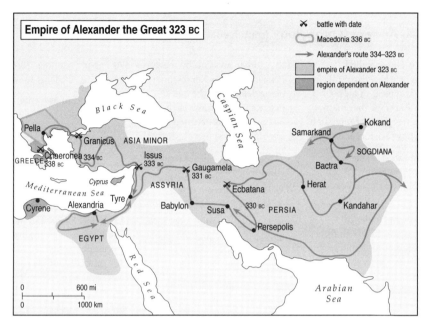

Alexander the Great

BC. Ancient Egypt was famed for its great power and wealth, due to the highly fertile lands of the Nile delta, which were rich sources of grain for the whole Mediterranean region. Egyptians were advanced in agriculture, engineering, and applied sciences. Many of their monuments, such as the pyramids and the sphinx, survive today.

Greece, ancient ancient civilization that flourished 2,500 years ago on the shores of the Ionian and Aegean Seas (modern Greece and the west coast of Turkey). Although its population never exceeded 2 million, ancient

Egyptians on strike

■ The earliest industrial dispute on record occurred in 1160 BC. Workers building the tomb of Pharaoh Ramses III went on strike for higher wages.

Greece made great innovations in philosophy, politics, science, architecture, and the arts, and Greek culture forms the basis of western civilization to this day.

Greece, Ancient: Chronology

c. **1550–1050 BC** The first Greek civilization, known as Mycenaean, owes much to the Minoan civilization of Crete and may have been produced by the intermarriage of Greek-speaking invaders with the original inhabitants.

c. **1300** A new wave of invasions begins. The Achaeans overrun Greece and Crete, destroying the Minoan and Mycenaean

civilizations and penetrating Asia Minor.

1000 Aeolians, Ionians, and Dorians have settled in the area that is now Greece. Many independent city states, such as Sparta and Athens, have developed.

c. **800–500** During the Archaic Period, Ionian Greeks lead the development of philosophy,

science, and lyric poetry. The Greeks become great sea traders, and found colonies around the coasts of the Mediterranean and the Black Sea, from Asia Minor in the east to Spain in the west.

776 The first Olympic games are held.

594 The laws of Solon take the first step towards a more democratic society.

(continued)

Greece, Ancient: Chronology (continued)

*c.*560–510 The so-called 'tyranny' of the Pisistratids in Athens is typical of a pre-democratic stage that many Greek cities pass through after overturning aristocratic rule.

545 From this date the Ionian cities in Asia Minor fall under the dominion of the Persian Empire.

507 Cleisthenes, ruler of Athens, is credited with the establishment of democracy. Other cities follow this lead, but Sparta remains unique, a state in which a ruling race, organized on military lines, dominates the surrounding population.

499–494 The Ionian cities, aided by Athens, revolts unsuccessfully against the Persians.

490 Darius of Persia invades Greece only to be defeated by the Athenians at Marathon and forced to withdraw.

480 Another invasion by the Persian emperor Xerxes, after being delayed by the heroic defence of Thermopylae by 300 Spartans, is defeated at sea off Salamis.

480–323 The Classical Period in ancient Greece.

479 The Persians are defeated on land at Plataea.

478 The Ionian cities, now liberated, form a naval alliance with Athens, the Delian League.

455–429 Under Pericles, the democratic leader of Athens, drama, sculpture, and architecture are at their peak.

433 The Parthenon in Athens is completed.

431–404 The Peloponnesian War destroys the political power of Athens, but Athenian thought and culture remain influential. Sparta becomes the leading Greek power.

370 The philosopher Plato opens his Academy in Athens.

338 Philip II of Macedon (359–336 BC) takes advantage of the wars between the city states and conquers Greece.

336–323 Rule of Philip's son, Alexander the Great. Alexander overthrows the Persian Empire, conquers Syria and Egypt, and invades the Punjab. After his death, his empire is divided among his generals, but his conquests have spread Greek culture across the known world.

280 Achaean League of 12 Greek city states formed in an attempt to maintain their independence against Macedon, Egypt, and Rome.

146 Destruction of Corinth. Greece becomes part of the Roman Empire. Under Roman rule Greece remains a cultural centre and Hellenistic culture remains influential.

Hebrew member of the Semitic people who lived in Palestine at the time of the Old Testament and who traced their ancestry to Abraham of Ur, a city of Sumer.

Hellenic period classical period of ancient Greek civilization, from the first Olympic Games 776 BC until the death of Alexander the Great 323 BC.

Hittite member of any of a succession of peoples who inhabited Anatolia and northern Syria from the 3rd millennium to the 1st millennium BC. The city of Hattusas (now Boğazköy in central Turkey) became the capital of a strong kingdom which overthrew the Babylonian Empire. After a period of eclipse the Hittite New Empire became a great power (about 1400–1200 BC), which successfully waged war with Egypt. The Hittite language is an Indo-European language.

Judaea name used in Graeco-Roman times for the southernmost region of Palestine, now divided

between Israel and Jordan. The area takes the form of a long zigzag central spine which has a series of steep spurs to the east and west.

Judah or **Judaea,** district of southern Palestine. After the death of King Solomon 922 BC, Judah adhered to his son Rehoboam and the Davidic line, whereas the rest of Israel elected Jeroboam as ruler of the northern kingdom. In New Testament times, Judah was the Roman province of Judaea, and in current Israeli usage it refers to the southern area of the West Bank.

Knossos chief city of Minoan Crete, near present-day Irákleion, 6 km/4 mi southeast of Candia. The archaeological site, excavated by Arthur Evans 1899–1935, dates from about 2000–1400 BC, and includes the palace throne room, the remains of frescoes, and construction on more than one level.

Mesopotamia the land between the Tigris and Euphrates rivers, now part of Iraq. The

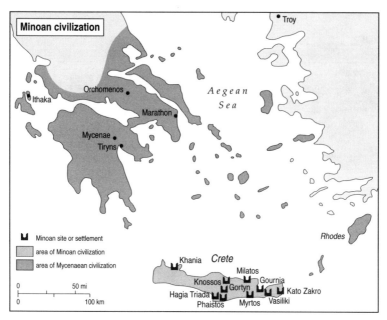

Minoan civilization

civilizations of Sumer and Babylon flourished here. The Sumerian civilization (3500 BC) may have been the earliest urban civilization.

Middle Kingdom period of Egyptian history embracing the 11th and 12th dynasties (roughly 2040–1640 BC); Chinese term for China and its empire until 1912, describing its central position in the Far East.

Minoan civilization Bronze Age civilization on the Aegean island of Crete. The name is derived from Minos, the legendary king of Crete. The

civilization is divided into three main periods: early Minoan, about 3000–2000 BC; middle Minoan, about 2000–1550 BC; and late Minoan, about 1550–1050 BC.

Mycenaean civilization Bronze Age civilization that flourished in Crete, Cyprus, Greece, the Aegean Islands, and western Anatolia about 3000–1000 BC. During this period, magnificent architecture and sophisticated artefacts were produced.

Persia, ancient kingdom in southwestern Asia. The early Persians were a nomadic Aryan people

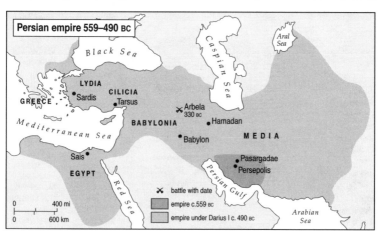

Persia

Roman history

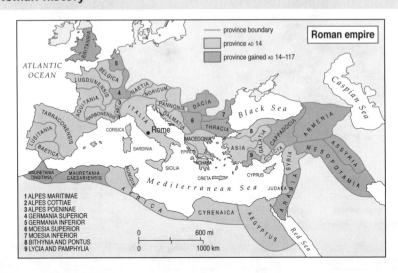

Roman empire

— province boundary
▢ province AD 14
▨ province gained AD 14–117

ATLANTIC OCEAN

BRITANNIA

BELGICA
LUGDUNENSIS
AQUITANIA
TARRACONENSIS
NARBONENSIS
LUSITANIA
BAETICA

RAETIA
NORICUM
ITALIA
DALMATIA
PANNONIA
DACIA

Rome
CORSICA
SARDINIA
SICILIA

MACEDONIA
EPIRUS
ACHAEA
CRETA

Black Sea

THRACIA
ASIA
GALATIA
CAPPADOCIA
ARMENIA
CILICIA
SYRIA
ASSYRIA
MESOPOTAMIA
ARABIA
CYPRUS
JUDAEA

Caspian Sea

Mediterranean Sea

MAURETANIA TINGITANA
MAURETANIA CAESARIENSIS
NUMIDIA
AFRICA
CYRENAICA
AEGYPTUS
Red Sea

1 ALPES MARITIMAE
2 ALPES COTTIAE
3 ALPES POENINAE
4 GERMANIA SUPERIOR
5 GERMANIA INFERIOR
6 MOESIA SUPERIOR
7 MOESIA INFERIOR
8 BITHYNIA AND PONTUS
9 LYCIA AND PAMPHYLIA

0   600 mi
0   1000 km

Roman Empire

Ancient Rome was a civilization based on the city of Rome. It lasted for about 800 years. Traditionally founded as a kingdom in 753 BC, Rome became a republic in 510 BC following the expulsion of its last king, Tarquinius Superbus. From then, its history is one of almost continual expansion until the murder of Julius Caesar and the foundation of the empire in 27 BC under Augustus and his successors. At its peak under Trajan, the Roman Empire stretched from Britain to Mesopotamia and the Caspian Sea. A long line of emperors ruling by virtue of military, rather than civil, power marked the beginning of Rome's long decline; under Diocletian the empire was divided into two parts – East and West – although it was temporarily reunited under Constantine, the first emperor to formally adopt Christianity. The end of the Roman Empire is generally dated by the deposition of the last emperor in the west in AD 476. The Eastern Empire continued until 1453 with its capital at Constantinople (modern Istanbul).

Roman Emperors

Reign	Name	Reign	Name	Reign	Name
Julio-Claudian Emperors		**Despotic Emperors**		238–44	Gordian III
27 BC–AD 14	Augustus	161–80	Marcus Aurelius	244–49	Philip (I) the Arab
14–37	Tiberius I	180–92	Commodus[2]	249–51	Trajan Decius
37–41	Caligula (Gaius Caesar)	193	Pertinax	251–53	Trebonianus Gallus
41–54	Claudius I	193	Didius Julianus	251–53	Volusianus
54–68	Nero			253–60	Valerian
		The Severi		253–68	Gallienus
Civil Wars		193–211	Septimus Severus	268–70	Claudius II
68–69	Galba	193–97	Clodius Albinus	270	Quintillus
69	Otho	193–94	Pescennius Niger	270–75	Aurelian
69	Vitellius	211–217	Caracalla	275–76	Tacitus
		209–12	Geta	276	Florianus
Flavian Emperors		217–18	Macrinus	276–82	Probus
69–79	Vespasian	218	Diadumenianus	282–83	Carus
79–81	Titus	218–22	Elagabalus	283–85	Carinus
81–96	Domitian	222–35	Alexander Severus	283–84	Numerianus
96–98	Nerva			284–305	Diocletian[3]
98–117	Trajan	**The Soldier Emperors**		286–305	Maximianus
117–38	Hadrian	235–38	Maximinus	293–306	Constantius I
		238	Gordian I	293–311	Galerius
Antonine Emperors		238	Gordian II	305–337	Constantine I
138–61[1]	Antoninus Pius	238	Balbinus		
161–69[1]	Lucius Verus	238	Pupienus		

[1] Divided voluntarily between two brothers.
[2] Between 180 and 284 there was a succession of emperors placed on the throne by their respective armies or factions. Therefore, dates of emperors' reigns in this period often overlap.

[3] The end of Diocletian's reign marked the split of the Roman empire. Whereas Diocletian retained supreme power, Maximianus ruled Italy and Africa, Constantius I ruled Gaul and Spain, and Galerius ruled Thrace.

Rome, Ancient: Chronology

753 BC According to tradition, Rome is founded.

510 The Etruscan dynasty of the Tarquins is expelled and a republic established, with power concentrated in patrician hands.

450 Publication of the law code contained in the Twelve Tables.

396 Capture of Etruscan Veii, 15 km/9 mi north of Rome.

387 Rome is sacked by Gauls.

367 Plebeians gain the right to be consuls (the two chief magistrates, elected annually).

343–290 Sabines to the north, and the Samnites to the southeast, are conquered.

338 Cities of Latium form into a league under Roman control.

280–272 Greek cities in southern Italy are subdued.

264–241 First Punic War against Carthage, ending in a Roman victory and the annexation of Sicily.

238 Sardinia is seized from Carthage.

226–222 Roman conquest of Cisalpine Gaul (Lombardy, Italy). More conflict with Carthage, which is attempting to conquer Spain.

218 Second Punic War. Hannibal crosses the Alps and invaded Italy, winning a series of brilliant victories.

202 Victory of General Scipio Africanus Major over Hannibal at Zama is followed by the surrender of Carthage and relinquishing of its Spanish colonies.

188 Peace of Apamea confines the rule of the Seleucid king Antiochus the Great to Asia.

168 Final defeat of Macedon by Rome.

146 After a revolt, Greece becomes in effect a Roman province. Carthage is destroyed and its territory annexed.

133 Tiberius Gracchus suggests agrarian reforms and is murdered by the senatorial party. Roman province of Asia is formed from the kingdom of Pergamum, bequeathed to Rome by the Attalid dynasty.

123 Tiberius' policy is adopted by his brother Gaius Gracchus, who is likewise murdered.

91–88 Social War: revolt by the Italian cities forces Rome to grant citizenship to all Italians.

87 While Sulla is repelling an invasion of Greece by King Mithridates of Pontus (in Asia Minor), Marius seizes power.

82–79 Sulla returns and establishes a dictatorship ruled by terror.

70 Sulla's constitutional changes are reversed by Pompey and Crassus.

66–63 Pompey defeats Mithridates and annexes Syria.

60 The First Triumvirate is formed, an alliance between Pompey and the democratic leaders Crassus and Caesar.

51 Caesar conquers Gaul as far as the Rhine.

49 Caesar crosses the Rubicon and returns to Italy, and a civil war between him and Pompey's senatorial party begins.

48 Pompey is defeated at Pharsalus.

44 Caesar's dictatorship is ended by his assassination.

43 Second Triumvirate formed by Octavian, Mark Antony, and Lepidus.

32 War between Octavian and Mark Antony.

31 Mark Antony is defeated at Actium.

30 Egypt is annexed after the deaths of Mark Antony and Cleopatra.

27 Octavian takes the name Augustus. He is by now absolute ruler, though in title he is only 'princeps' (first citizen).

AD **14** Augustus dies. Tiberius is proclaimed as his successor.

43 Claudius adds Britain to the empire.

70 Jerusalem is sacked by Titus.

96–180 The empire enjoys a golden age under the Flavian and Antonine emperors Nerva, Trajan, Hadrian, Antoninus Pius, and Marcus Aurelius Antoninus.

115 Trajan conquers Parthia, achieving the peak of Roman territorial expansion.

180 Marcus Aurelius dies, and a century of war and disorder follows, with a succession of generals being put on the throne by their armies.

212 Caracalla grants citizenship to the communities of the empire.

284–305 Diocletian reorganizes the empire, dividing power between himself and three others (the Tetrarchy).

Rome, Ancient: Chronology (continued)

313 Constantine the Great recognizes the Christians' right to freedom of worship by the Edict of Milan.

330 Constantine makes Constantinople his new

imperial capital.

395 The empire is divided into eastern and western parts.

410 Visigoths sack Rome. Roman legions withdraw from Britain.

451–52 Huns raid Gaul and Italy.

455 Vandals sack Rome.

476 Last Western emperor, Romulus Augustulus, is deposed.

who migrated through the Caucasus to the Iranian plateau. Cyrus organized the empire into provinces which were each ruled by Satraps. The royal house is known as the Achaemenids after the founder of the line. The administrative centre was Susa, with the royal palace at Persepolis.

Expansion led the Persians into conflicts with Greek cities, notably in the Ionian Revolt, Darius I's campaign that ended at the Athenian victory of Marathon (490 BC), and Xerxes I's full-blown invasion of the Greek mainland 480.

Rome, ancient see **Roman history** feature.

Sparta ancient Greek city-state in the southern Peloponnese (near Sparte), developed from Dorian settlements in the 10th century BC. The Spartans, known for their military discipline and austerity, took part in the Persian and Peloponnesian Wars.

Sumerian civilization the world's earliest civilization, dating from about 3500 BC and located at the confluence of the Tigris and Euphrates rivers in lower Mesopotamia (present-day Iraq). It was a city-state with priests as secular rulers. After 2300 BC, Sumer declined.

Troy *Latin* **Ilium,** ancient city (now Hissarlik or Hisarlih in Turkey) of Asia Minor, just south of the Dardanelles, besieged in the legendary ten-year Trojan War (mid-13th century BC), as described in Homer's *Iliad.* According to the legend, the city fell to the Greeks, who first used the stratagem of leaving behind, in a feigned retreat, a large wooden horse containing armed

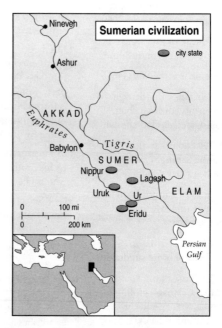

Sumerian civilization

infiltrators to open the city's gates. Believing it to be a religious offering, the Trojans took it within the walls.

Ur ancient city of the Sumerian civilization, in modern Iraq. Excavations by the British archaeologist Leonard Woolley show that it was inhabited from about 3500 BC. He discovered evidence of a flood that may have inspired the *Epic of Gilgamesh* as well as the biblical account, and remains of ziggurats, or step pyramids.

The Middle Ages

The Middles Ages (or **the Medieval period)** is a term used by Europeans to describe the period between ancient history and modern history. It is not a precise term, but is often taken to cover the time from the fall of the Western Roman Empire in AD 476 to the fall of Constantinople (Istanbul) and the end of the Eastern Roman Empire in 1453. The term Dark Ages is sometimes used to cover the period from AD 476 to AD 1000, because it was a time when learning and the rule of law were at a low ebb in Europe. During the Middle Ages Germanic tribes overran Europe, bringing with them changes in language and culture.

The early Middle Ages saw the development of nation states in Europe, particularly England, Scotland, France, Norway, Sweden, Hungary, and Poland. At the heart of Europe was the Holy Roman Empire, a loose confederation of German states, some large, some very small. Over all was the power of the church, with the pope, based in Rome, as its head. Religion played a large part in people's lives. Communities spent large amounts of time and money in building religious buildings, from the humblest parish churches to magnificent cathedrals.

The feudal system prevailed as a form of government and society during the Middle Ages. Great barons held land from the monarch of each state, and in turn lesser people held lands from them. At the bottom of this pyramid were the peasants, very small landholders, and the serfs, landless people who worked as labourers or servants.

The later Middle Ages saw many changes. Some were brought about by the Black Death, an epidemic of bubonic plague that ravaged Europe in 1347–51, killing about a third of the population. This resulted for the first time in a labour shortage, caused inflation, and eventually led to the end of the feudal system. Other changes were due to the growing power of individual rulers, and from time to time splits in the church. In 1309–77 the popes moved from Rome to Avignon in France. This was followed by a period of rival popes, some based in Rome, others at Avignon (1378–1417).

pope versus emperor The 1100s and 1200s saw a series of clashes between popes and emperors over the issue of sovereignty, which dismayed rulers of many European lands who looked to cooperation between the two powers as a guarantee of stability, with the pope as supreme spiritual authority and the emperor as his temporal protector. Popes and emperors had different views as to the meaning of the concept of protection. The pope, who crowned the emperor, could, and sometimes did, withhold coronation. Nor were the emperors, associated territorially with Germany and occasionally with north and central Italy, ever able to exercise any effective authority over the kings of France, England, or the Iberian Peninsula.

cultural achievements While attempts to ensure unified political leadership in western Europe failed, the highest human and cultural achievements of the Middle Ages in Romanesque and Gothic art and architecture were made, and Arabic learning, and with it the learning of the ancient Greeks, spread through the Muslim-occupied areas of Spain and Sicily.

science and religion Scientific knowledge came back to Europe from the Arabs. Aristotelian science, with its emphasis on humans as political beings and as the basis of political organization, threatened the papal view of power as deriving from God through the pope, and represented a challenge to traditional notions, which even the attempts of the Italian philosopher and theologian St Thomas Aquinas, who argued that reason and faith were compatible, failed to silence.

language and literature Latin was the international language of diplomacy and scholarship, while literature in local languages was developed by, among others, Dante Alighieri in Italy and Geoffrey Chaucer in England. The period also saw the rise of the universities, notably those of Bologna, Paris, Oxford, and Cambridge.

seeds of destruction The Crusades to free the Holy Land (Palestine) from Islam were effectively western Europe's first colonial venture, sustained by a rising population, a trend which continued into the early 1300s. Elements of this flourishing culture, however, carried the seeds of medieval Europe's destruction. National kings grew in power, while the Holy Roman Empire declined after the death of Frederick II in 1250. These threats to the structure of medieval Europe coincided with other events such as the loss of the last Crusader foothold in the Holy Land in 1291; the Black Death; constant warfare, especially the Hundred Years' War between England and France; the Great Schism in the church. Everything suggested decay and collapse, a theme with which writers were increasingly obsessed. In the 1400s the leaders of the Italian Renaissance and the Dutch scholar Desiderius Erasmus in northern Europe looked to antiquity for a new order, helping to give the Middle Ages a reputation for darkness and obscurantism which its earlier great achievements did not merit.

EUROPEAN HISTORY

abdication crisis in British history, the constitutional upheaval of the period between 16 November 1936 and 10 December 1936, brought about by the British king Edward VIII's decision to marry Wallis Simpson, a US divorcee. The marriage of the 'Supreme Governor' of the Church of England to a divorced person was considered unsuitable and the king abdicated on 10 December and left for voluntary exile in France. He was created Duke of Windsor and married Mrs Simpson on 3 June 1937.

Alliance, the in UK politics, a loose union 1981–87 formed by the Liberal Party and Social Democratic Party (SDP) for electoral purposes.

Anglo-Saxon one of several groups of Germanic invaders (including Angles, Saxons, and Jutes) that conquered much of Britain between the 5th and 7th centuries. Initially they established conquest kingdoms, commonly referred to as the **Heptarchy**; these were united in the early 9th century under the overlordship of Wessex. The Norman invasion in 1066 brought Anglo-Saxon rule to an end.

Anglo-Saxon Chronicle a history of England from the Roman invasion to the 11th century, consisting of a series of chronicles written in Old English by monks, begun in the 9th century (during the reign of King Alfred), and continuing until 1154.

Anti-Corn Law League extra-parliamentary pressure group formed in September 1838 by Manchester industrialists, and led by Liberals Richard Cobden and John Bright. It argued for free trade and campaigned successfully against duties on the import of foreign corn to Britain imposed by the Corn Laws, which were repealed in 1846.

assassination murder, usually of a political, royal, or public person. The term derives from the order of the Assassins, a Muslim sect that, in the 11th and 12th centuries, murdered officials to further its political ends.

Balfour Declaration letter, dated 2 November 1917, from British foreign secretary A J Balfour to Lord Rothschild (chair, British Zionist Federation) stating: 'HM government view with favour the establishment in Palestine of a national home for the Jewish people. It helped form the basis for the foundation of Israel in 1948.

Bill of Rights in Britain, an act of Parliament of 1689 which established Parliament as the primary governing body of the country. It made provisions limiting royal prerogative with respect to legislation, executive power, money levies, courts, and the army, and stipulated Parliament's consent to many government functions.

British Empire empire covering, at its height in the 1920s, about a sixth of the landmass of the Earth, all of its lands recognizing the United Kingdom (UK) as their leader. It consisted of the Empire of India, four self-governing countries known as dominions, and dozens of colonies and territories. After World War II it began to dissolve as colony after colony became independent, and today the UK has only 13 small dependent territories. With 52 other independent countries, it forms the Commonwealth. Although Britain's monarch is accepted as head of the Commonwealth, most of its member states are republics.

Castile kingdom founded in the 10th century, occupying the central plateau of Spain. Its union with Aragón in 1479, based on the marriage of Ferdinand and Isabella, effected the foundation of the Spanish state, which at the time was occupied and ruled by the Moors. Castile comprised the two great basins separated by the Sierra de Gredos and the Sierra de Guadarrama, known traditionally as Old and New Castile. The area now forms the regions of Castilla–León and Castilla–La Mancha.

Catholic Emancipation in British history, acts of Parliament passed 1780–1829 to relieve Roman Catholics of civil and political restrictions imposed from the time of Henry VIII and the Reformation.

cavalier horseman of noble birth, but mainly used as a derogatory nickname to describe a male supporter of Charles I in the English Civil War (Cavalier), typically with courtly dress and long hair (as distinct from a Roundhead); also a supporter of Charles II after the Restoration.

Chartism radical British democratic movement, mainly of the working classes, which flourished around 1838–48. It derived its name from the People's Charter, a six-point programme comprising universal male suffrage, equal electoral districts, secret ballot, annual parliaments, and abolition of the property qualification for, and payment of, members of Parliament.

chivalry code of gallantry and honour that medieval knights were pledged to observe. Its principal virtues were piety, honour, valour, courtesy, chastity, and loyalty. The word originally meant the knightly class of the feudal Middle Ages. Modern orders of chivalry such as the Order of the Garter are awarded as a mark of royal favour or as a reward for public services.

Civil War, English conflict between King Charles I and the Royalists (also called Cavaliers) on one side and the Parliamentarians (also called Roundheads) under Oliver Cromwell on the other. Their differences centred initially on the king's unconstitutional acts, but later became a struggle over the relative powers of crown and Parliament. Hostilities began in 1642 and a series of Royalist defeats (at Marston Moor in 1644, and then at Naseby in 1645) culminated in Charles's capture in 1647, and execution in 1649. The war continued until the final defeat of Royalist forces at Worcester in 1651. Cromwell then became Protector (ruler) from 1653 until his death in 1658.

Combination Acts laws passed in Britain in 1799 and 1800 making trade unionism illegal. They were introduced after the French Revolution for fear that the unions would become centres of political agitation. The unions continued to exist, but claimed to be friendly societies or went underground, until the acts were repealed in 1824, largely owing to the radical Francis Place.

Cromwell's head

■ Oliver Cromwell's head is buried in the grounds of Sidney Sussex College, Cambridge, but his body is interred on the site of the Tyburn gallows in London.

Corn Laws in Britain until 1846, laws used to regulate the export or import of cereals in order to maintain an adequate supply for consumers and a secure price for producers. For centuries the Corn Laws formed an integral part of the mercantile system in England; they were repealed because they became an unwarranted tax on food and a hindrance to British exports.

Danelaw 11th-century name for the area of north and east England settled by the Vikings in the 9th century. It occupied about half of England, from the River Tees to the River Thames. Within its bounds, Danish law, customs, and language prevailed. Its linguistic influence is still apparent.

Danelaw

Declaration of Rights in Britain, the statement issued by the Convention Parliament in February 1689, laying down the conditions under which the crown was to be offered to William III and Mary. Its clauses were later incorporated in the Bill of Rights.

Defender of the Faith one of the titles of the English sovereign, conferred on Henry VIII in 1521 by Pope Leo X in recognition of the king's treatise against the Protestant Martin Luther. It appears on coins in the abbreviated form F.D. (Latin *Fidei Defensor*).

doge chief magistrate in the ancient constitutions of Venice and Genoa. The first doge of Venice was appointed in 697 with absolute power

Crusade (French *croisade*)

The term **crusade** refers to any European war against non-Christians and heretics, sanctioned by the pope. The Crusades, in particular, were a series of wars undertaken 1096–1291 by European rulers to recover Palestine from the Muslims. Motivated by religious zeal, the desire for land, and the trading ambitions of the major Italian cities, the Crusades were varied in their aims and effects. The Crusades ostensibly began to ensure the safety of pilgrims visiting the Holy Sepulchre in Jerusalem, and to establish Christian rule in Palestine. They continued for more than 200 years, with hardly a decade passing without one or more expeditions. Later they were extended to include most of the Middle East, and attacks were directed against Egypt and even against Constantinople (Istanbul).

the first Crusades In Palestine the mild rule of the Saracens – the first Muslim conquerors – had for centuries allowed a Christian protectorate (first established under Charlemagne) to exist in Jerusalem, and Christian pilgrims were allowed to come and go quite freely. However, peaceful coexistence was shattered in 1010 when the Caliph Hakim destroyed the sanctuary. After 1071, the Saracens were driven out by the Seljuk Turks and Christian pilgrimage became difficult and dangerous.

In 1095 Pope Urban II appealed for protection for the pilgrims, and the first Crusades were launched. They gave the turbulent feudal knights of Europe a new outlet for their energies.

1095–1148 In 1095 several undisciplined hosts, such as those led by Walter the Penniless and Peter the Hermit, set out for the East, but perished on the way. A more serious expedition was mounted in 1096–97, when a great army whose leaders included Godfrey of Bouillon, Bohemund of Otranto, and Raymond of Toulouse, fought its way through Asia Minor (modern Turkey), capturing Antioch

in 1098 and Jerusalem in 1099. A Christian kingdom of Jerusalem was established, with Godfrey as its first king, his brother Baldwin as Count of Edessa (Upper Mesopotamia), and Bohemund as Prince of Antioch. Godfrey died in 1100 and was succeeded by Baldwin. During the next half-century, in spite of reinforcements, including fleets from Genoa, Norway, and Venice, the Christians in Syria were hard-pressed. Two religious orders of knights, the Knights Hospitallers and Knights Templars were formed to assist in the defence of Jerusalem.

Edessa was lost in 1144, and the Second Crusade (1147–49), under Louis VII of France and Conrad III of Germany, ended disastrously. Its failure for a time discouraged any similar ventures, while Muslim pressure increased on all sides.

Saladin's conquests and European reaction The crusading spirit was revived toward the end of the 1100s in response to the conquests of Saladin, Sultan of Egypt. Having captured Damascus in 1174 and Aleppo in 1183, he swept down through Galilee with an immense force, defeated a Christian army at the Horns of Hattin, and took Jerusalem in October 1187.

The news was received in Europe with consternation and rage. Several fresh expeditions were mounted, of which the most important was the Third Crusade led by Philip II of France, Frederick I Barbarossa of Germany, and Richard I of England in 1189. The Germans travelled through Asia Minor, losing their emperor on the way; the French and English went by sea to Acre, which had already been besieged for nearly two years by Guy de Lusignan. Richard distinguished himself in the capture of the city, but quarrelled with his allies, who left him to carry on the war alone. After a year of brilliant but useless exploits, he made a truce with Saladin, and returned to Europe.

13th-century crusades The Fourth Crusade, starting from Venice in 1202, became involved in Venetian

and Byzantine intrigues. Instead of reaching Jerusalem, the Crusaders helped the deposed Byzantine emperor Isaac Angelus to recapture his throne. A few months later the Crusaders stormed and sacked Constantinople, and established a Latin empire there under Baldwin of Flanders in 1204.

Perhaps the most tragic of these expeditions was the Children's Crusade. In 1212 several thousand children were allowed to go on a crusade; many died on their way from France and Germany to the Italian coast. The rest embarked on ships there, but those who reached Alexandria in Egypt were captured and sold into slavery.

Andrew of Hungary led a failed crusade 1218–21 against the Muslims in Egypt. Emperor Frederick II of Germany undertook a more successful crusade, the sixth, in 1228. He regained Jerusalem and the south of Palestine by diplomacy, rather than by fighting, and it remained in Christian hands until 1244. The Seventh Crusade of Louis IX of France (St Louis) in 1249 was, like that of 1217, directed against Egypt, and proved even more disastrous. Louis was captured along with the greater part of his army, and had to pay 800,000 pieces of gold as a ransom. Even after this, he headed the Eighth Crusade in 1270, but died at Carthage in Tunisia on the way to Egypt. A few months later Prince Edward of England (who later became Edward I), led his own followers to Acre, but achieved no results.

diminishing enthusiasm Understandably, after so many failures and only temporary successes, the enthusiasm for crusades died down. In the 14th century several crusades were mounted against the Ottoman Turks, but these were more defensive movements designed to stop the rapid advances of the Turks, who were encroaching on the eastern borders of Europe. Several popes continued to preach about the need for a united Christian holy war

Crusade (French *croisade*) (continued)

against the infidels, but to no avail. Even when Constantinople was captured by Mohammed II in 1453, and the Byzantine Empire came to an inglorious end, Pope Pius II failed to raise a crusade for its recovery.

failure and benefits Although the Crusades failed to achieve the spiritual objects for which they were intended, and led to much needless slaughter, they benefited Europe indirectly in a number of ways. Trade between Europe and Asia Minor was greatly stimulated; the merchants and mariners of the Mediterranean, especially those of Venice and Genoa, found the demand for their shipping greatly increased, both for the transport of armies and for bringing new and rare commodities from east European craftsmen. The Crusaders learned valuable lessons from Saracen skills in art and in war. Sugar, cotton, and many other articles now in everyday use first became known Europe through the Crusades. The cultural contacts that were established between Europe and the East in this period had a stimulating effect on learning in medieval Europe, and to some extent anticipated and paved the way for the Renaissance.

Crusades: Chronology

1076 Seljuk Turks capture Jerusalem and begin to restrict access of Christian pilgrims to the holy places.

1095 Byzantine emperor Alexius Comnenus, threatened by Muslim advances in Anatolia, appeals to the pope for help against the Seljuk Turks. Pope Urban II proclaims a holy war.

1096–99 First Crusade, led by Baldwin of Boulogne, Godfrey of Bouillon, and Peter the Hermit. Motivated by occupation of Anatolia and Jerusalem by Seljuk Turks.

1099 Capture of Jerusalem by the crusaders, accompanied by looting and massacre. A number of small crusader states established on the Syrian coast.

1147–49 Second Crusade, led by Louis VII of France and

Emperor Conrad III, fails to capture Damascus and Edessa.

1187 Jerusalem seized by Saladin, sultan of Egypt and Syria and leader of the Muslims against the crusaders.

1189–92 Third Crusade, led by Philip II Augustus of France and Richard I the Lion-Heart of England, fails to recapture Jerusalem.

1202–04 Fourth Crusade, led by William of Montferrata and Baldwin of Hainault. Originally intended to recover the holy places, it is diverted by its Venetian financial backers to sack and divide Constantinople.

1212 Children's Crusade. Thousands of children cross Europe on their way to Palestine but many are sold

into slavery or die of disease and hunger.

1218–21 Fifth Crusade, led by King Andrew of Hungary, Cardinal Pelagius, King John of Jerusalem, and King Hugh of Cyprus. Captures and then loses Damietta, Egypt.

1228–29 Sixth Crusade, led by the Holy Roman emperor Frederick II. Jerusalem recovered by negotiation with the sultan of Egypt.

1244 Jerusalem finally lost, to remain in Turkish hands until liberated by the British general Allenby in 1917.

1249–54 Seventh Crusade led by Louis IX of France.

1270–72 Eighth Crusade, also led by Louis IX of France.

1291 Acre, the last Christian fortress in Syria, falls to the Turks.

(modified in 1297), and from his accession dates Venice's prominence in history. The last Venetian doge, Lodovico Manin, retired in 1797 and the last Genoese doge in 1804.

Domesday Book record of the survey of England carried out in 1086 by officials of William the Conqueror in order to assess land tax and other dues, ascertain the value of the crown lands, and enable the king to estimate the power of his vassal barons. The name is derived from the belief that its judgement was as final as that of Doomsday.

English Sovereigns From 899

Reign	Name	Relationship	Reign	Name	Relationship
West Saxon Kings			*House of York*		
899–924	Edward the Elder	son of Alfred the Great	1461–70,	Edward IV	son of Richard, Duke of
924–39	Athelstan	son of Edward the Elder	1471–83		York
939–46	Edmund	half-brother of Athelstan	1483	Edward V	son of Edward IV
946–55	Edred	brother of Edmund	1483–85	Richard III	brother of Edward IV
955–59	Edwy	son of Edmund			
959–75	Edgar	brother of Edwy	*House of Tudor*		
975–78	Edward the Martyr	son of Edgar	1485–1509	Henry VII	son of Edmund Tudor, Earl
978–1016	Ethelred (II) the Unready	son of Edgar			of Richmond
			1509–47	Henry VIII	son of Henry VII
1016	Edmund Ironside	son of Ethelred (II) the Unready	1547–53	Edward VI	son of Henry VIII
			1553–58	Mary I	daughter of Henry VIII
			1558–1603	Elizabeth I	daughter of Henry VIII
Danish Kings			*House of Stuart*		
1016–35	Canute	son of Sweyn I of Denmark who conquered England in 1013	1603–25	James I	great-grandson of Margaret (daughter of Henry VII)
1035–40	Harold I	son of Canute	1625–49	Charles I	son of James I
1040–42	Hardicanute	son of Canute	1649–60	the Commonwealth	
West Saxon Kings (restored)			*House of Stuart (restored)*		
1042–66	Edward the Confessor	son of Ethelred (II) the Unready	1660–85	Charles II	son of Charles I
1066	Harold II	son of Godwin	1685–88	James II	son of Charles I
			1689–1702	William III and Mary	son of Mary (daughter of Charles I); daughter of James II
Norman Kings					
1066–87	William I	illegitimate son of Duke Robert the Devil	1702–14	Anne	daughter of James II
1087–1100	William II	son of William I	*House of Hanover*		
1100–35	Henry I	son of William I	1714–27	George I	son of Sophia (granddaughter of James I)
1135–54	Stephen	grandson of William II	1727–60	George II	son of George I
House of Plantagenet			1760–1820	George III	son of Frederick (son of George II)
1154–89	Henry II	son of Matilda (daughter of Henry I)	1820–30	George IV (regent 1811–20)	son of George III
1189–99	Richard I	son of Henry II	1830–37	William IV	son of George III
1199–1216	John	son of Henry II	1837–1901	Victoria	daughter of Edward (son of George III)
1216–72	Henry III	son of John			
1272–1307	Edward I	son of Henry III	*House of Saxe-Coburg*		
1307–27	Edward II	son of Edward I	1901–10	Edward VII	son of Victoria
1327–77	Edward III	son of Edward II			
1377–99	Richard II	son of the Black Prince	*House of Windsor*		
House of Lancaster			1910–36	George V	son of Edward VII
1399–1413	Henry IV	son of John of Gaunt	1936	Edward VIII	son of George V
1413–22	Henry V	son of Henry IV	1936–52	George VI	son of George V
1422–61, 1470–71	Henry VI	son of Henry V	1952–	Elizabeth II	daughter of George VI

estate in European history, an order of society that enjoyed a specified share in government. In medieval theory, there were usually three estates – the **nobility,** the **clergy,** and the **commons** – with the functions of, respectively, defending society from foreign aggression and internal dis-order, attending to its spiritual needs, and working to produce the base with which to support the other two orders.

feudalism (Latin *feudem* 'fief', coined 1839) main form of social organization in medieval Europe.

French Revolution: Chronology 1789–99

1789 (May) Meeting of States General called by Louis XVI to discuss reform of state finances. Nobility opposes reforms.

(June) Third (commoners) estate demands end to system where first (noble) estate and second (church) estate can outvote them; rejected by Louis. Third estate declares itself a national assembly and 'tennis-court oath' pledges them to draw up new constitution.

(July) Rumours of royal plans to break up the assembly lead to riots in Paris and the storming of the Bastille. Revolutionaries adopt the tricolour as their flag. Peasant uprisings occur throughout the country.

1789–91 National-assembly reforms include abolition of noble privileges, dissolution of religious orders, appropriation of church lands, centralization of governments, and limits on the king's power.

1791 (June) King Louis attempts to escape from Paris in order to unite opposition to the assembly, but is recaptured.

(September) The king agrees to a new constitution.

(October) New legislative assembly meets, divided between moderate Girondists and radical Jacobins.

1792 (January) Girondists form a new government but their power in Paris is undermined by the Jacobins. Foreign invasion leads to the breakdown of law and order. Hatred of the monarchy increases.

(August) The king is suspended from office and the government dismissed.

(September) National Convention elected on the basis of universal suffrage; dominated by Jacobins. A republic is proclaimed.

(December) The king is tried and condemned to death.

1793 (January) The king is guillotined.

(April) The National Convention delegates power to the Committee of Public Safety, dominated by Maximilien Robespierre. The Reign of Terror begins.

1794 (July) Robespierre becomes increasingly unpopular, is deposed and executed.

1795 Moderate Thermidoreans take control of the convention and create a new executive Directory of five members.

1795–99 Directory fails to solve France's internal or external problems and becomes increasingly unpopular.

1799 Coup d'état overthrows the Directory and a consulate of three is established, including Napoleon Bonaparte as First Consul with special powers.

A system based primarily on land, it involved a hierarchy of authority, rights, and power that extended from the monarch downwards. An intricate network of duties and obligations linked royalty, nobility, lesser gentry, free tenants, villeins, and serfs. Feudalism was reinforced by a complex legal system and supported by the Christian church. With the growth of commerce and industry from the 13th century, feudalism gradually gave way to the class system as the dominant form of social ranking.

Fidei Defensor see **Defender of the Faith.**

fief estate of lands granted to a vassal by his lord after the former had sworn homage, or fealty, promising to serve the lord. As a noble tenure, it carried with it rights of jurisdiction.

Frank member of a group of Germanic peoples prominent in Europe in the 3rd to 9th centuries. Believed to have originated in Pomerania on the Baltic Sea, they had settled on the Rhine by the 3rd century, spread into the Roman Empire by the 4th century, and gradually conquered most of Gaul, Italy, and Germany under the Merovingian and Carolingian dynasties. The kingdom of the western Franks became France; the kingdom of the eastern Franks became Germany.

French Revolution period 1789–99 that saw the end of the monarchy in France.

Golden Horde invading Mongol-Tatar army that first terrorized Europe from 1237 under the leadership of Batu Khan, a grandson of Genghis Khan. Tamerlane broke their power in 1395, and Ivan III ended Russia's payment of tribute to them in 1480.

Goth East Germanic people who settled near the Black Sea around AD 2nd century. There are two branches, the eastern Ostrogoths and the western Visigoths. The **Ostrogoths** were conquered by the Huns 372. They regained their independence 454 and under Theodoric the Great conquered Italy 488–93; they disappeared as a nation after the Byzantine emperor Justinian I reconquered Italy 535–55.

The **Visigoths** migrated to Thrace. Under Alaric they raided Greece and Italy 395–410, sacked Rome, and established a kingdom in southern France. Expelled from there by the Franks, they established a Spanish kingdom which lasted until the Moorish conquest of 711.

Grand Remonstrance petition passed by the English Parliament in November 1641 that listed all the alleged misdeeds of Charles I and demanded parliamentary approval for the king's ministers and the reform of the church. Charles refused to accept the Grand Remonstrance and countered by trying to arrest five leading members of the House of Commons. The worsening of relations between king and Parliament led to the outbreak of the English Civil War in 1642.

Gunpowder Plot In British history, the Catholic conspiracy to blow up James I and his parliament on 5 November 1605. It was discovered through an anonymous letter. Guy Fawkes was found in the cellar beneath the Palace of Westminster, ready to fire a store of explosives. Several of the conspirators were killed as they fled, and Fawkes and seven others were captured and executed.

Hanseatic League (German *Hanse* 'group, society') confederation of northern European trading cities from the 12th century to 1669. At its height in the late 14th century the Hanseatic League included over 160 cities and towns, among them Lübeck, Hamburg, Cologne, Wrocław (Breslau), and Kraków. The basis of the league's power was its

Holy Roman Emperors

Reign	Name	Reign	Name	Reign	Name
Carolingian Kings and Emperors		1081–93	Hermann of Luxembourg (rival)	1298–1308	Albert I, Habsburg
				1308–13	Henry VII, Luxembourg
800–14	Charlemagne (Charles the Great)	1093–1101	Conrad of Franconia (rival)	1314–47	Louis IV of Bavaria
				1314–25	Frederick of Habsburg (co-regent)
814–40	Louis the Pious	1106–25	Henry V		
840–55	Lothair I	1126–37	Lothair II	1347–78	Charles IV, Luxembourg
855–75	Louis II			1378–1400	Wenceslas of Bohemia
875–77	Charles (II) the Bald	*Hohenstaufen Kings and Emperors*		1400	Frederick III of Brunswick
881–87	Charles (III) the Fat			1400–10	Rupert of the Palatinate
891–94	Guido of Spoleto	1138–52	Conrad III	1411–37	Sigismund, Luxembourg
892–98	Lambert of Spoleto (co-emperor)	1152–90	Frederick Barbarossa		
		1190–97	Henry VI	*Habsburg Emperors*	
896–901	Arnulf (rival)	1198–1215	Otto IV	1438–39	Albert II
901–05	Louis III of Provence	1198–1208	Philip of Swabia (rival)	1440–93	Frederick III
905–24	Berengar	1215–50	Frederick II	1493–1519	Maximilian I
911–18	Conrad (I) of Franconia (rival)	1246–47	Henry Raspe of Thuringia (rival)	1519–56	Charles V
				1556–64	Ferdinand I
		1247–56	William of Holland (rival)	1564–76	Maximilian II
Saxon Kings and Emperors		1250–54	Conrad IV	1576–1612	Rudolf II
918–36	Henry I the Fowler	1254–73	no ruler (the Great Interregnum)	1612–19	Matthias
936–73	Otto (I) the Great			1619–37	Ferdinand II
973–83	Otto II			1637–57	Ferdinand III
983–1002	Otto III	*Rulers from Various Noble Families*		1658–1705	Leopold I
1002–24	Henry (II) the Saint			1705–11	Joseph I
		1257–72	Richard of Cornwall (rival)	1711–40	Charles VI
Franconian (Salian) Emperors				1742–45	Charles VII of Bavaria
1024–39	Conrad II	1257–73	Alfonso X of Castile (rival)		
1039–56	Henry (III) the Black			*Habsburg-Lorraine Emperors*	
1056–1106	Henry IV	1273–91	Rudolf I, Habsburg	1745–65	Francis I of Lorraine
1077–80	Rudolf of Swabia (rival)	1292–98	Adolf I of Nassau	1765–90	Joseph II
				1790–92	Leopold II
				1792–1806	Francis I

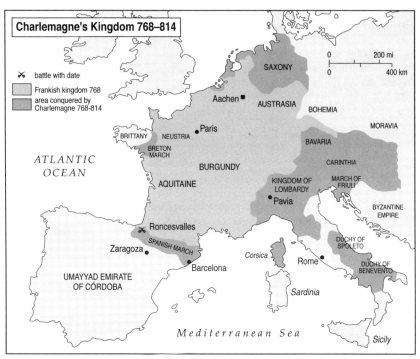

Charlemagne

monopoly of the Baltic trade and its relations with Flanders and England. The decline of the Hanseatic League from the 15th century was caused by the closing and moving of trade routes and the development of nation states.

Holy Roman Empire empire of Charlemagne and his successors, and the German Empire 962–1806, both being regarded as the Christian (hence 'holy') revival of the Roman Empire. At its height it comprised much of western and central Europe.

Home Rule, Irish movement to repeal the Act of Union of 1801 that joined Ireland to Britain, and to establish an Irish Parliament responsible for internal affairs. In 1870 Isaac Butt (1813–1879) formed the Home Rule Association and the movement was led in Parliament from 1880 by Charles Parnell. After 1918 the demand for an independent Irish republic replaced that for home rule.

Industrial Revolution sudden acceleration of technical and economic development that began in Britain in the second half of the 18th century. *See chronology on page 360.*

Irish Republican Army (IRA), militant Irish nationalist organization formed in 1919, the paramilitary wing of Sinn Féin. Its aim is to create a united Irish socialist republic including Ulster. To this end, the IRA habitually carries out bombings and shootings. Despite its close association with Sinn Féin, it is not certain that the politicians have direct control of the military, the IRA usually speaking as a separate, independent organization. The chief common factor shared by Sinn Féin and the IRA is the aim of a united Ireland.

Italian Kings from 1861

Reign	Name
1861–78	Victor Emmanuel II
1878–1900	Umberto I
1900–46	Victor Emmanuel III
1946	Umberto II (abdicated)

Land League Irish peasant-rights organization, formed in 1879 by Michael Davitt and Charles Parnell to fight against tenant evictions. Through

Industrial Revolution: Chronology

1709 Abraham Darby introduces coke smelting to his ironworks at Coalbrookdale in Shropshire.

1712 The first workable steam-powered engine is developed by Thomas Newcomen.

1730 The seed drill is invented by Jethro Tull. This is a critical point of the agricultural revolution which frees labour from the fields and lowers crop prices.

1740 Crucible steelmaking is discovered by Benjamin Huntsman, a clockmaker of Doncaster.

1759 The first Canal Act is passed by the British Parliament; this leads to the construction of a national network of inland waterways for transport and industrial supplies. By 1830 there are 6,500 km/4,000 mi of canals in Britain.

1763 The spinning jenny, which greatly accelerates cotton spinning, is invented by James Hargreaves in Blackburn.

1764 Pierre Trosanquet, a French engineer, develops a new method of road building. Similar techniques are used by Thomas Telford in Britain to build modern roads from 1803.

1765 James Watt produces a more reliable and efficient version of the Newcomen engine.

1779 The spinning mule, which makes the production of fine yarns by machine possible, is developed in Bolton by Samuel Crompton.

1785 The power loom marks the start of the mechanised textile industry.

1785–99 Techniques of mass production of interchangeable parts are developed by the arms industry in the USA, led by Eli Whitney.

1793 The problem of supplying cotton fast enough for the textile industry is solved by Eli Whitney's cotton gin.

1797 The first true industrial lathe is invented, virtually simultaneously, by Henry Maudslay in England and David Wilkinson in the USA.

1802 The first electric battery capable of mass production is designed by William Cruickshank in England.

1811–16 Textile workers known as Luddites stage widespread protests against low pay and unemployment in Nottinghamshire, which involve destroying new machines.

c. **1813** Industrial employment overtakes agricultural employment in England for the first time.

1825 The first regular railway services start between Stockton and Darlington in northeast England.

1826 The Journeymen Steam Engine Fitters, the first substantial industrial trade union, is established in Manchester.

1829 With his steam locomotive *Rocket,* English engineer George Stephenson wins a contest to design locomotives

for the new Manchester–Liverpool railway.

1831–52 British industrial production doubles.

1832 Hippolyte Pixii of France produces a prototype electricity generator using magnets.

1832 The Reform Act concerning elections to the British Parliament gives representation to the industrial cities.

1833 The first effective Factory Act is passed in Britain regulating child labour in cotton mills.

c. **1840** The USA becomes the world leader for railroads, with over 5,000 km/3,000 mi laid. By 1860 this will rise to 50,000 km/30,000 mi.

1840s Cornelius Vanderbilt and John Jacob Astor become the most prominent millionaires of the industrial age.

1842 Cotton-industry workers in England stage a widespread strike.

1846 Repeal of the Corn Law in Britain reduces agricultural prices, thereby helping industry.

1851 Britain celebrates its industrial achievements in the Great Exhibition.

1852–80 British industrial production doubles again.

1858 The 'great stink' of London dramatizes the increasing pollution in the cities.

c. **1860** New York City becomes the first US city with over 1 million inhabitants.

its skilful use of the boycott against anyone who took a farm from which another had been evicted, it forced Gladstone's government to introduce a law in 1881 restricting rents and granting tenants security of tenure.

Long Parliament English Parliament 1640–53 and 1659–60, which continued through the Civil War. After the Royalists withdrew in 1642 and the Presbyterian right was excluded in 1648, the remaining Rump ruled England until expelled by Oliver Cromwell in 1653. Reassembled in 1659–60, the Long Parliament initiated the negotiations for the restoration of the monarchy.

Magna Carta (Latin 'great charter') in English history, charter granted by King John at Runnymede on 15 June 1215. It was originally proposed to the English barons in 1213 by the Archbishop of Canterbury, Stephen Langton, as a reply to the King's demands for excessive feudal dues and attacks on the privileges of the church. The charter defined the barons' obligations to the monarch, confirmed the liberties of the English church, and opposed the arbitrary application of justice. The charter was reissued with changes in 1216, 1217, and 1225. As feudalism declined the Magna Carta lost its significance, and under the Tudors was almost forgotten. During the 17th century it was rediscovered and reinterpreted by the Parliamentary party as a democratic document. Four original copies exist: one each in Salisbury and Lincoln cathedrals and two in the British Library in London.

Model Parliament English parliament set up in 1295 by Edward I; it was the first to include representatives from outside the clergy and aristocracy, and was established because Edward needed the support of the whole country against his opponents: Wales, France, and Scotland. His sole aim was to raise money for military purposes, and the parliament did not pass any legislation.

William the Conqueror

■ The funeral of the English king William the Conqueror at Caen in 1087 was marred by the king's overweight corpse exploding as attendants tried to squeeze it into a stone coffin.

Norman any of the descendants of the Norsemen (to whose chief, Rollo, Normandy was granted by Charles III of France in 911) who adopted French language and culture. During the 11th and 12th centuries they conquered England in 1066 (under William the Conqueror), Scotland in 1072, parts of Wales and Ireland, S Italy, Sicily, and Malta, and took a prominent part in the Crusades.

Norman Conquest invasion and settlement of England by the Normans, following the victory of William the Conqueror at the Battle of Hastings in 1066.

Palatinate (German 'Pfalz') historic division of Germany, dating from before the 8th century. It was ruled by a **count palatine** (a count with royal prerogatives) and varied in size.

parliament (French 'speaking') legislative body of a country. The world's oldest parliament is the Icelandic Althing, which dates from about 930. The UK Parliament is usually dated from 1265.

Reform Acts UK acts of Parliament in 1832, 1867, and 1884 that extended voting rights and redistributed parliamentary seats; also known as Representation of the People Acts.

Russian Revolution two revolutions in 1917 that began with the overthrow of the Romanov dynasty and ended with the establishment of a communist soviet (council) state, the Union of Soviet Socialist Republics (USSR). *See chronology on page 362.*

Saracen ancient Greek and Roman term for an Arab, used in the Middle Ages by Europeans for all Muslims. The equivalent term used in Spain was Moor.

Saxon member of a Germanic tribe once inhabiting the Danish peninsula and northern Germany. The Saxons migrated from their homelands in the early Middle Ages, under pressure from the Franks, and spread into various parts of Europe, including Britain. They also undertook piracy in the North Sea and the English Channel.

Short Parliament English Parliament that was summoned by Charles I on 13 April 1640 to raise funds for his war against the Scots. It was succeeded later in the year by the Long Parliament.

sovereignty absolute authority within a given territory. The possession of sovereignty is taken to

Russian Revolution: Chronology (Western Calendar)

1894 Beginning of the reign of Tsar Nicholas II.

1898 Formation of the Social Democratic Party among industrial workers under the influence of Georgi Plekhanov and Vladimir Lenin.

1901 Formation of the Socialist Revolutionary Party.

1903 Split in Social Democratic Party at the party's second congress (London Conference) into Bolsheviks and Mensheviks.

1905 (January) 'Bloody Sunday', where repression of workers in St Petersburg leads to widespread strikes and the '1905 Revolution'.
   (October) Strikes and the first 'soviet' (local revolutionary council) in St Petersburg. October constitution provides for new parliament (Duma).
   (December) Insurrection of workers in Moscow. Punitive repression by the 'Black Hundreds'.

1914 (July) Outbreak of war between Russia and the Central Powers.

1917 (March) Outbreak of riots in Petrograd (St Petersburg). Tsar Nicholas abdicates. Provisional government is established under Prince Lvov. Power struggles between government and Petrograd soviet.
   (April) Lenin arrives in Petrograd. He demands the transfer of power to soviets; an end to the war; the seizure of land by the peasants; control of industry by the workers.
   (July) Bolsheviks attempt to seize power in Petrograd. Leon Trotsky is arrested and Lenin is in hiding. Aleksandr Kerensky becomes head of a provisional government.
   (September) Lavr Kornilov coup fails owing to strike by workers. Kerensky's government weakens.
   (November) Bolshevik Revolution. Military revolutionary committee and Red Guards seize government offices and the Winter Palace, arresting all the members of the provisional government. Second All-Russian Congress of Soviets creates the Council

of Peoples Commissars as new governmental authority. It is led by Lenin, with Trotsky as commissar for war and Joseph Stalin as commissar for national minorities. Land Decree orders immediate distribution of land to the peasants. Banks are nationalized and national debt repudiated. Elections to the Constituent Assembly give large majority to the Socialist Revolutionary Party. Bolsheviks a minority.

1918 (January) Constituent Assembly meets in Petrograd but is almost immediately broken up by Red Guards.
   (March) Treaty of Brest-Litovsk marks the end of the war with the Central Powers but with massive losses of territory.
   (July) Murder of the tsar and his family.

1918–20 Civil War in Russia between Red Army and White Russian forces. Red Army ultimately victorious.

1923 (6 July) Constitution of USSR adopted.

---

be the distinguishing feature of the state, as against other forms of community. The term has an internal aspect, in that it refers to the ultimate source of authority within a state, such as a parliament or monarch, and an external aspect, where it denotes the independence of the state from any outside authority.

Stamp Act UK act of Parliament in 1765 that sought to raise enough money from the American colonies to cover the cost of their defence. Refusal to use the required tax stamps and a blockade of British merchant shipping in the colonies forced repeal of the act the following

year. It helped to precipitate the American Revolution.

Suez Crisis military confrontation from October to December 1956 following the nationalization of the Suez Canal by President Nasser of Egypt. In an attempt to reassert international control of the canal, Israel launched an attack, after which British and French troops landed. Widespread international censure forced the withdrawal of the British and French. The crisis resulted in the resignation of British prime minister Eden.

Union, Acts of act of Parliament of 1707 that brought about the union of England and

Scotland; that of 1801 united England and Ireland. The latter was revoked when the Irish Free State was constituted in 1922.

Vandal member of a Germanic people related to the Goths. In the 5th century AD the Vandals invaded Roman Gaul and Spain, many settling in Andalusia (formerly Vandalitia) and others reaching North Africa 429. They sacked Rome 455 but were defeated by Belisarius, general of the emperor Justinian, in the 6th century.

Viking or **Norseman** the inhabitants of Scandinavia in the period 800–1100. They traded with, and raided, much of Europe, and often settled there. In their narrow, shallow-draught, highly manoeuvrable longships, the Vikings penetrated far inland along rivers. They plundered for gold and land, and were equally energetic as colonists – with colonies stretching from North America to central Russia – and as traders, with main trading posts at Birka (near Stockholm) and Hedeby (near Schleswig). The Vikings had a sophisticated literary culture, with sagas and runic inscriptions, and an organized system of government with an assembly ('thing'). Their kings and chieftains were buried with their ships, together with their possessions.

AMERICAN HISTORY

abolitionism movement culminating in the late 18th and early 19th centuries that aimed first to end the slave trade, and then to abolish the institution of slavery and emancipate slaves.

affirmative action government policy of positive discrimination by the use of legal measures and moral persuasion that favours women and members of minority ethnic groups in such areas as employment and education.

Alamo, the mission fortress in San Antonio, Texas, USA. It was besieged 23 February–6 March 1836 by Santa Anna and 4,000 Mexicans; they killed the garrison of about 180, including Davy Crockett and Jim Bowie.

American Independence, War of alternative name of the American Revolution, the revolt 1775–83 of the British North American colonies that resulted in the establishment of the United States of America.

Appomattox Court House former village in Virginia, USA, scene of the surrender 9 April 1865 of the Confederate army under Robert E Lee to the Union army under Ulysses S Grant, which ended the American Civil War.

Aztec member of an American Indian people who migrated south into the valley of Mexico in the AD 1100s, and in 1325 began reclaiming lake marshland to build their capital, Tenochtitlán, on the site now occupied by Mexico City. Under their emperor Montezuma I, who reigned from 1440, the Aztecs created an empire in central Mexico. After the Spanish conquistador Hernán Cortés landed in 1519, Montezuma II, who reigned from 1502, was killed and Tenochtitlańn was destroyed.

Nahuatl is the Aztec language; it belongs to the Uto-Aztecan family of languages, and is still spoken by some Mexicans.

Bill of Rights in the USA, the first ten amendments to the US Constitution, incorporated in 1791: **1** guarantees freedom of worship, of speech, of the press, of assembly, and to petition the government; **2** grants the right to keep and bear arms; **3** prohibits billeting of soldiers in private homes in peacetime; **4** forbids unreasonable search and seizure; **5** guarantees none be 'deprived of life, liberty or property without due process of law' or compelled in any criminal case to be a witness against himself or herself; **6** grants the right to speedy trial, to call witnesses, and to have defence counsel; **7** grants the right to trial by jury of one's peers; **8** prevents the infliction of excessive bail or fines, or 'cruel and unusual punishment'; **9, 10** provide a safeguard to the states and people for all rights not specifically delegated to the central government.

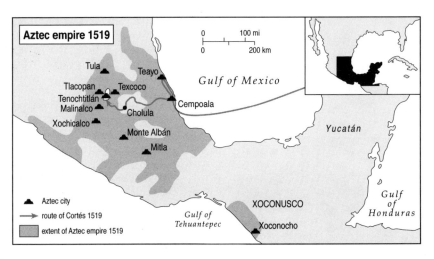

Aztec

black nationalism movement towards black separatism in the USA during the 1960s.

Boston Tea Party protest in 1773 by colonists in Massachusetts, USA, against the tea tax imposed on them by the British government before the American Revolution.

Chichen Itzá Toltec city situated among the Maya city-states of Yucatán, Mexico. It flourished AD 900–1200 and displays Classic and Post-Classic architecture of the Toltec style. The site has temples with sculptures and colour reliefs, an observatory, and a sacred well into which sacrifices, including human beings, were cast.

civil-rights movement general term for efforts by African-American people to affirm their constitutional rights and improve their status in society after World War II. Having made a significant contribution to the national effort in wartime, they began a sustained campaign for full civil rights which challenged racial discrimination and segregation; the Civil Rights Commission was created by the Civil Rights Act of 1957. Further favourable legislation followed, such as the Civil Rights Act of 1964 and the 1965 Voting Rights Act.

Civil War, American also called the **War Between the States,** war 1861–65 between the Southern or Confederate States of America and the Northern or Union states. The former wished to maintain certain 'states' rights', in particular the right to determine state law on the institution of slavery, and claimed the right to secede from the Union; the latter fought primarily to maintain the Union, with slave emancipation (proclaimed in 1863) a secondary issue.

Confederacy popular name for the **Confederate States of America,** the government established by 7 (later 11) Southern states in February 1861 when they seceded from the Union, precipitating the American Civil War. Richmond, Virginia, was the capital, and Jefferson Davis the president. The Confederacy fell after its army was defeated in 1865 and General Robert E Lee surrendered.

Confederation, Articles of initial means by which the 13 former British colonies created a form of national government. Ratified in 1781, the articles established a unicameral legislature, Congress, with limited powers of raising revenue, regulating currency, and conducting

Union general
US general William Tecumseh Sherman who, as a leader of the Union forces in the American Civil War, was second only to Ulysses Grant. Attempting to destroy Confederate supplies and morale, he waged an economic campaign against the civilian population of Georgia and the Carolinas, laying waste the countryside. After the war there was an attempt to nominate him for president, but he announced that he would not run if nominated, and would not serve if selected. *Library of Congress*

foreign affairs. But because the individual states retained significant autonomy, the confederation was unmanageable. The articles were superseded by the US Constitution in 1788.

Continental Congress in US history, the federal legislature of the original 13 states, acting as a provisional government during the American Revolution. It was responsible for drawing up the Declaration of Independence in July 1776, and the Articles of Confederation in 1777.

Contra member of a Central American right-wing guerrilla force attempting to overthrow the democratically elected Nicaraguan Sandinista government 1979–90. The Contras, many of them mercenaries or former members of the deposed dictator Somoza's guard (see **Nicaraguan Revolution**), operated mainly from bases outside Nicaragua, mostly in Honduras, with covert US funding, as revealed by the Irangate hearings 1986–87.

Declaration of Independence historic US document stating the theory of government on which the USA was founded, based on the right 'to life, liberty, and the pursuit of happiness'. The statement was issued by the Continental Congress on 4 July 1776, renouncing all allegiance to the British crown and ending the political connection with Britain.

El Dorado fabled city of gold believed by the 16th-century Spanish and other Europeans to exist somewhere in the area of the Orinoco and Amazon rivers.

Ellis Island island in New York harbour, USA, 1.5 km/1 mi from Manhattan Island; area 110 sq km/42 sq mi. A former reception centre for immigrants during the immigration waves between 1892 and 1943 (12 million people passed through it 1892–1924), it was later used (until 1954) as a detention centre for nonresidents without documentation, or for those who were being deported. Ellis Island is now a national historic site (1964) and contains the Museum of Immigration (1989).

Emancipation Proclamation President Lincoln's Civil War announcement, 22 September 1862, stating that from the beginning of 1863 all black slaves in states still engaged in rebellion against the federal government would be emancipated. Slaves in border states still remaining loyal to the Union were excluded.

Gettysburg site of one of the decisive battles of the American Civil War: a Confederate defeat by Union forces 1–3 July 1863, at Gettysburg, Pennsylvania, 80 km/50 mi northwest of Baltimore. The site is now a national cemetery, at the dedication of which President Lincoln delivered the **Gettysburg Address** on 19 November 1863, a speech in which he reiterated the principles of freedom, equality, and democracy embodied in the US Constitution.

Great Depression period following the Wall Street crash of 29 October 1929 when millions of dollars were wiped off US share values in a matter of hours. This forced the closure of many US banks involved in stock speculation and led to the recall of US overseas investments. This loss of US credit had serious repercussions on the European economy, especially that of Germany, and led to a steep fall in the levels of international trade as countries attempted to protect their domestic economies. Although most European countries experienced a slow recovery during the mid-1930s, the main impetus for renewed economic growth was provided by rearmament programmes later in the decade.

Hudson's Bay Company chartered company founded by Prince Rupert in 1670 to trade in furs with North American Indians. In 1783 the rival North West Company was formed, but in 1851 this became amalgamated with the Hudson's Bay Company. It is still Canada's biggest fur company, but today also sells general merchandise through department stores and has oil and natural gas interests.

Inca member of an ancient Peruvian civilization of Quechua-speaking American Indians that began in the Andean highlands about AD 1200. By the time the Spanish conquered the region in the 1530s, the Inca people ruled an area that stretched from Ecuador in the north to Chile in the south. Inca means 'king', and was the title of the ruler as well as the name of the people.

Independence Day public holiday in the USA, commemorating the adoption of the Declaration of Independence on 4 July 1776.

Irangate US political scandal in 1987 involving senior members of the Reagan administration (the name echoes the Nixon administration's Watergate). Congressional hearings 1986–87 revealed that the US government had secretly sold weapons to Iran in 1985 and traded them for hostages held in Lebanon by pro-Iranian militias, and used the profits to supply right-wing Contra guerrillas in Nicaragua with arms. The attempt to get around the law (Boland amendment) specifically prohibiting military assistance to the Contras also broke other laws in the process.

Louisiana Purchase purchase by the USA from France in 1803 of an area covering about 2,144,000 sq km/828,000 sq mi, including the present-day states of Louisiana, Missouri, Arkansas, Iowa, Nebraska, North Dakota, South Dakota, and Oklahoma.

COLOMBIA	**Inca civilization**

Quito
ECUADOR
Huancabamba
PERU
Chan Chan
Huanuco
Machu Picchu
Andahuaylas
Cuzco
Lake Titicaca
Tiahuanaco
PACIFIC OCEAN
Pica
CHILE
La Paya
Santiago
Talca

BRAZIL
BOLIVIA
ARGENTINA

- Inca city
- Inca empire c.1203
- Inca empire c.1525
- modern area of Quechua language

0 — 400 mi
0 — 800 km

Inca

Inca Emperors *c.* 1200–1572

Reign	Name
The Kingdom of Cuzco	
c. 1200–1400	Manco Capac[1]
	Sinchi Roca[1]
	Lloque Yupanqui[1]
	Mayta Capac[1]
	Capac Yupanqui[2]
	Inca Roca[2]
	Yahuar Huacadc[2]
until 1438	Viracocha Inca
The Empire	
1438–71	Pachacuti
1471–93	Topa Inca
1493–1528	Huayna Capac
1528–32	Huascar
1532–33	Atahualpa
The Vilcabamba State	
1533	Topa Hualpa
1533–45	Manco Inca
1545–60	Sayri Tupac
1560–71	Titu Cusi Yupanqui
1571–72	Tupac Amaru

[1] This is a mythical figure.
[2] The dates of his reign are unknown.

Mason–Dixon Line in the USA, the boundary line between Maryland and Pennsylvania (latitude 39° 43' 26.3' N), named after Charles Mason (1730–1787) and Jeremiah Dixon (died 1777), English astronomers and surveyors who surveyed it 1763–67. It is popularly seen as dividing the North from the South.

Maya member of an American Indian civilization originating in the Yucatán Peninsula in Central America about 2600 BC, with later sites in Mexico, Guatemala, and Belize, and enjoying a classical period AD 325–925, after which it declined. Today they are Roman Catholic, and number 8–9 million (1994 est). They live in Yucatán, Guatemala, Belize, and western Honduras. Many still speak Maya, a member of the Totonac-Mayan (Penutian) language family, as well as Spanish. In the 1980s more than 100,000 Maya fled from Guatemala to Mexico.

Mayflower ship in which the Pilgrims sailed in 1620 from Plymouth, England, to found Plymouth plantation and Plymouth colony in present-day Massachusetts.

Mexican Empire short-lived empire 1822–23 following the liberation of Mexico from Spain. The empire lasted only eight months, under the revolutionary leader Agustín de Iturbide.

Monroe Doctrine declaration by US president James Monroe in 1823 that any further European colonial ambitions in the western hemisphere would be regarded as threats to US peace and security, made in response to proposed European intervention against newly independent former Spanish colonies in South America. In return for the quietening of such European ambitions, the USA would not interfere in European affairs. The doctrine, subsequently broadened, has been a recurrent theme in US foreign policy, although it has no basis in US or international law.

New World the Americas, so called by the first Europeans who reached them. The term also describes animals and plants of the western hemisphere.

Pilgrims emigrants who sailed from Plymouth, Devon, England, in the *Mayflower* on 16 September 1620 to found the first colony in New England at New Plymouth, Massachusetts. Of the 102 passengers fewer than a quarter were Puritan refugees.

Prohibition the period 1920–33 when alcohol was illegal. This led to bootlegging (the illegal distribution of liquor, often illicitly distilled), to the financial advantage of organized crime.

Reconstruction in US history, the period 1865–77 after the Civil War during which the nation was reunited under the federal government after the defeat of the Southern Confederacy.

slavery enforced servitude of one person (a slave) to another or one group to another. A slave has no personal rights and is the property of another person through birth, purchase, or capture. In the American South in the 17th to 19th centuries, slavery became a mainstay of an agricultural factory economy, with millions of Africans sold to work on plantations in North and South America. Millions more died in the process, but the profits from this trade were enormous. Slavery was abolished in the British Empire in 1833 and in the USA at the end of the Civil War (1863–65), but continues illegally in some countries.

South America, ancient until recently archaeological research in South America has been restricted to areas with good preservation or fine artefacts. Today each country is subject to extensive investigation. For some, such as Peru and Bolivia, a great deal was already known, if not fully understood, but for others, such as Brazil and Uruguay, prehistoric knowledge was lacking. The new information has changed the overall perspective significantly. Furthermore, in the absence of pre-European documents, colonial records have provided much information about socio-political organization, religion, economy, and agriculture of the ancient cultures.

Thirteen Colonies 13 American colonies that signed the Declaration of Independence from Britain in 1776. Led by George Washington, the Continental Army defeated the British army in the American Revolution 1776–81 to become the original 13 United States of America: Connecticut, Delaware, Georgia, Maryland, Massachusetts, New Hampshire, New Jersey, New York, North Carolina, Pennsylvania, Rhode Island, South Carolina, and Virginia. They were united first under the Articles of Confederation and from 1789, the US constitution.

Watergate US political scandal, named after the building in Washington, DC, which housed the headquarters of the Democratic National Committee in the 1972 presidential election. Five men, hired by the Republican Committee for the Re-election of the President (popularly known as CREEP), were caught after breaking into the Watergate with complex electronic surveillance equipment. Investigations revealed that the White House was implicated in the break-in, and that there was a 'slush fund', used to finance unethical activities, including using the CIA and the Internal Revenue Service for political ends, setting up paramilitary operations against opponents, altering and destroying evidence, and bribing defendants to lie or remain silent. In August 1974, President Nixon was forced by the Supreme Court to surrender to Congress tape recordings of conversations he had held with administration officials, which indicated his complicity in a cover-up. Nixon resigned rather than face impeachment for obstruction of justice and other charges

American Revolution: Chronology

1773 A government tax on tea leads Massachusetts citizens disguised as North American Indians to board British ships carrying tea and throw it into Boston harbour, the Boston Tea Party.

1774–75 The First Continental Congress is held in Philadelphia to call for civil disobedience in reply to British measures such as the Intolerable Acts, which closes the port of Boston and quarters British troops in private homes.

1775 19 April: Hostilities begin at Lexington and Concord, Massachusetts. The first shots are fired when British troops, sent to seize illegal military stores and arrest rebel leaders John Hancock and Samuel Adams, are attacked by the local militia (minutemen).

1775 10 May: Fort Ticonderoga, New York, is captured from the British.

1775 17 June: The colonists are defeated in the first battle of the Revolution, the Battle of Bunker Hill (which actually takes place on Breed's Hill, nearby); George Washington is appointed colonial commander in chief soon afterwards.

1776 4 July: The Second Continental Congress issues the Declaration of Independence, which specifies some of the colonists' grievances and proclaims an independent government.

1776 27 August: Washington is defeated at Long Island and is forced to evacuate New York and retire to Pennsylvania.

1776 26 December: Washington recrosses the Delaware River and defeats the British at Trenton, New Jersey.

1777 3 January: Washington defeats the British at Princeton, New Jersey.

1777 11 September–4 October: British general William Howe defeats Washington at Brandywine and Germantown, and occupies Philadelphia.

1777 17 October: British general John Burgoyne surrenders at Saratoga, New York, and is therefore unable to link up with Howe.

1777–78 Washington winters at Valley Forge, Pennsylvania, enduring harsh conditions and seeing many of his troops leave to return to their families.

1778 France, with the support of its ally Spain, enters the war on the US side (John Paul Jones leads a French-sponsored naval unit).

1780 12 May: The British capture Charleston, South Carolina, one of a series of British victories in the South, but alienate support by enforcing conscription.

1781 19 October: British general Charles Cornwallis, besieged in Yorktown, Virginia, by Washington and the French fleet, surrenders.

1782 Peace negotiations open.

1783 3 September: The Treaty of Paris recognizes American independence.

WARFARE AND THE MILITARY

—————————— ✳ ——————————

War is an act of force, usually on behalf of the state, intended to compel a declared enemy to obey the will of the other. The aim is to render the opponent incapable of further resistance by destroying its capability and will to bear arms in pursuit of its own aims. War is therefore a continuation of politics carried on with violent and destructive means, as an instrument of policy.

The extent and intensity of war varies. **Limited war**, such as the Korean War (1950–53), is a war which may be limited in both geographical extent and levels of force exerted and has aims that stop short of achieving the destruction of the enemy. **Total war** is war waged against both combatants and noncombatants, taking the view that no distinction should be made between them. The Spanish Civil War marked the beginning of this type of warfare, in which bombing from the air included both civilian and military targets. In **absolute war** there would be no limitations, such as law, compassion, or prudence, in the application of force, the sole aim being to achieve the complete annihilation of one's opponent. It has been claimed that nuclear warfare would assume such proportions.

Wars and Battles

Actium, Battle of naval battle in which Octavian defeated the combined fleets of Mark Antony and Cleopatra on 2 September 31 BC to become the undisputed ruler of the Roman world (as the emperor Augustus). The site of the battle is at Akri, a promontory in western Greece.

Agincourt, Battle of battle of the Hundred Years' War in which Henry V of England defeated the French on 25 October 1415, mainly through the overwhelming superiority of the English longbow. The French lost more than 6,000 troops to about 1,600 English casualties.

As a result of the battle, Henry gained France and the French princess Catherine of Valois as his wife. The village of Agincourt (modern **Azincourt**) is south of Calais, in northern France.

Alamein, El, Battles of two decisive battles of World War II in the western desert of northern Egypt. In the first (1–27 July 1942), the British 8th Army under Auchinleck held off the German and Italian forces under Rommel; in the second (23 October–4 November 1942), Montgomery defeated Rommel.

American Independence, War of alternative name of the American Revolution, the revolt 1775–83 of the British North American colonies that resulted in the establishment of the United States of America. It was caused by colonial opposition to British economic exploitation and by the unwillingness of the colonists to pay for a standing army. It was also fuelled by the colonists' antimonarchist sentiment and their desire to participate in the policies affecting them.

Major Battles in the American Civil War

Major battles fought between the North and the secessionist South, 1861–65.

Battles

Battle	Date	Site
First Battle of Bull Run (or the First Battle of Manassas)	21 July 1861	Manassas, Virginia
Fort Henry	6 February 1862	western Tennessee
Fort Donelson	16 February 1862	western Tennessee
Shiloh (also called the Battle of Pittsburg Landing)	6–7 April 1862	near Pittsburg Landing, Tennessee
Battles of the Seven Days	25 June–1 July 1862	Virginia
Second Battle of Bull Run (or the Second Battle of Manassas)	27–30 August 1862	Manassas, Virginia
Antietam	17 September 1862	Antietam Creek, Maryland
Fredericksburg	13 December 1862	Fredericksburg, Virginia
Chancellorship	1–4 May 1863	Chancellorship, Virginia
Siege of Vicksburg	19 May–4 July 1863	Vicksburg, Virginia
Gettysburg	1–3 July 1863	near Gettysburg, Pennsylvania
Chickamauga	19–20 September 1863	Chickamauga, Georgia
Chattanooga	23–25 November 1863	Chattanooga, Tennessee
Battle of the Wilderness	5–9 May 1864	northern Virginia
Spotsylvania	May 1864	Spotsylvania Court House, Virginia
Cold Harbor	3 June 1864	Virginia
Siege of Petersburg	20 June 1864–2 April 1865	Petersburg, Virginia
Mobile Bay	5 August 1864	Alabama
Atlanta	2 September 1864	Georgia
Nashville	15–16 December 1864	Tennessee

Surrenders

Surrender	Date	Site
General Lee surrendered to General Grant	9 April 1865	Appomattox Court House, Virgina
General Johnson surrendered to General Sherman	17 April 1865	Raleigh, North Carolina

The American Civil War also called the War Between the States

The American Civil War, the war between the Southern or Confederate States of America and the Northern or Union states, lasted from 1861–65. The Southern states wished to maintain certain 'states' rights', in particular the right to determine state law on the institution of slavery, and claimed the right to secede from the Union; the North fought primarily to maintain the Union, with slave emancipation (proclaimed 1863) a secondary issue.

The issue of slavery had brought to a head long-standing social and economic differences between the two oldest sections of the country. A series of political crises was caused by the task of determining whether newly admitted states, such as California, should permit or prohibit slavery in their state constitutions. The political parties in the late 1850s came to represent only sectional interests – Democrats in the South, Republicans in the North. This breakdown of an underlying national political consensus (which had previously sustained national parties) led to the outbreak of hostilities, only a few weeks after the inauguration of the first Republican president, Abraham Lincoln.

The war, and in particular its aftermath, when the South was occupied by Northern troops in the period known as the Reconstruction, left behind much bitterness. Industry prospered in the North, while the economy of the South, which had been based on slavery, stagnated for some time.

outbreak of war Upon Abraham Lincoln's inauguration as president March 1861, he affirmed that he did not propose to interfere with slavery where it already existed but he also asserted that no state could withdraw from the Union, and that he regarded it at his duty to preserve, protect, and defend the Union. Rebel Confederate forces began bombarding the federal garrison at Fort Sumter, South Carolina, 12 April and 34 hours later the fort was surrendered. With the fall of Fort Sumter the Civil War began.

balance of power The North had certain advantages in the forthcoming war which were ultimately to weigh decisively in the balance. Its white population, and hence its fighting strength, was four times as large as that of the South – if there was to be a lengthy war, the North's numerical superiority would enable it to sustain casualties far better. It was also far more advanced industrially and could meet all its own needs and those of its armies, whereas the Southern states were mainly agricultural and dependent for most nonagricultural produce on purchases from the North and Europe. The Union states also had the stronger navy and soon had command of the sea, enabling them to blockade Confederate ports.

Two days after the fall of Fort Sumter, Lincoln called for 75,000 troops to join a militia to fight for the Union; the Confederate commander Jefferson Davis asked for 100,000. In the South, Virginia, which had at first been against secession, now joined South Carolina, Mississippi, Florida, Alabama, Georgia, Louisiana, and Texas in the Confederacy, together with Arkansas, Tennessee, and North Carolina. The Confederate capital was moved to Richmond, Virginia. There were four border slave states – Delaware, Maryland, Kentucky, and Missouri – and the Confederates put much effort in trying to win over Missouri and Kentucky, but although their governors favoured secession, their legislatures overruled them.

There was dismay in the North when Britain issued a declaration of neutrality on 13 May 1861 which recognized the Confederacy was entitled to the belligerent rights of a sovereign nation; most European nations soon followed suit. However, the Union army was beginning to gather strength, with nearly half a million recruits compared to only about half that number who had responded in the South.

1861–62 The first real clash of arms came at the Battle of Bull Run 21 July 1861 between the Union army under Irvin McDowell and the Confederates under P G T Beauregard and Joseph E Johnston. The Union forces were routed, retreating as far as Washington. Federal strength first began to show in 1862. In the West,

Ulysses S Grant captured Fort Donelson on the Cumberland River on 15 February 1862; the Confederate general Simon Buckner was forced to accept Grant's stipulation of unconditional surrender, and surrendered an army of 14,000. The two armies next met in battle at Shiloh on 6 April. The first day's fighting favoured the Confederates, but Albert S Johnston, one of the best of the Confederate commanders, was killed. In the second day's fighting the Union forces won and the Confederates retreated to Corinth. The Confederates suffered a further blow with the Union capture of New Orleans.

The principal Union advance against Richmond began in March 1862 as George McClellan led the Army of the Potomac up the Virginia Peninsula, first coming upon the Confederates at Yorktown. His army had been weakened by the sudden withdrawal of 25,000 troops to defend Washington, and he settled down for a siege, only to find that the enemy had retreated. He met them in battle at Williamsburg, where once more the enemy retreated toward Richmond. McClellan was unable to pursue as he was then ordered to march on Thomas 'Stonewall' Jackson in the Shenandoah Valley. Davis sent reinforcements to Jackson, who defeated Banks at Winchester, evaded the other two Union armies which were seeking him, and triumphantly led his troops back to join the forces in line near Richmond.

In the meantime McClellan's army fought a great battle at Fair Oaks 31 May–1 June. At first it seemed as if the Union force had lost the day but the timely arrival of a new corps put the Confederates to flight. Davis now appointed General Robert E Lee as commander in chief of the Southern armies. Lee was quick to take advantage of the pause in McClellan's movement. He rushed up reinforcements from all over the South until he had an effective fighting force of 90,000 troops against his enemy's 100,000 and drove the Union forces back in the Seven Days' campaign.

McClellan was soon ready to attempt the capture of Richmond again, but the Union government

(continued)

The American Civil War also called the War Between the States (continued)

ordered him to return with his army to cover Washington. Henry Halleck was appointed commander in chief of the Union forces and General John Pope was given the best part of McClellan's army. The Union defeat at the second Battle of Bull Run 29 August and at Chantilly shortly after completely destroyed Pope's reputation as a general; Lincoln called on McClellan to resume command of the Army of the Potomac once more.

Lee had moved into Maryland, hoping to win the state to the Confederacy, capture Baltimore, and then advance into Pennsylvania, carrying the war into Union territory. McClellan met him in the great struggle at Antietam on 17 September. Lee was forced to retreat across the Potomac. McClellan, however, did not follow his victory through and was then relieved of his command for good.

proclamation of emancipation
Lincoln now took a bold step. He had until this point merely struggled to preserve the Union intact, holding the issue of slavery in abeyance for fear of alienating the Democrats in the North and the border states. But on 22 September 1862, he issued his proclamation of emancipation, declaring that the slaves in all states in rebellion against the government should be free as from 1 January 1863. In Europe, the declaration was well received as most nations were already abolitionist. But the reaction in the USA itself was mixed. The Democrats made big gains in the elections held in November, and it was only New England and the border states that kept the House of Representatives Republican.

In the autumn of 1862, Union victories at Corinth and Murfreesboro left most of Tennessee held by General William Rosecrans while in the East Lee severely defeated Ambrose Burnside in the Battle of Fredericksburg on 13 December 1862.

1863 The Confederates won a great victory at Chancellorsville 1 May 1863 but at the cost of Stonewall Jackson. In the West, Grant took Vicksburg 4 July 1863 after a siege lasting six weeks. While this siege was still in

progress, the Confederates were decisively defeated 1–3 July 1863 at Gettysburg, Pennsylvania, in probably the greatest battle of the war, and Lee retreated into Virginia. This victory, the turning point of the war, was followed by success in the West. Initially, Braxton Bragg beat Union forces under Rosecrans at Chickamauga, Tennessee, September 1863 but the Confederates suffered heavily at the subsequent battle of Chattanooga in November, forcing them back into Georgia. This was one of the most important actions in the war, ensuring ultimate Federal success in the West.

1864 Ulysses S Grant's success as commander in chief in late 1863 led Lincoln to appoint him lieutenant general in charge of all the armies in February 1864. Grant now planned to end the war. He set out to face Lee in Virginia, intending to destroy his army and take Richmond. At the same time he dispatched Sherman to face General J E Johnston in Georgia. After the indecisive Battle of the Wilderness in May 1864 there was a further clash at Spotsylvania, Virginia, with similar results. At the Battle of Cold Harbor on 3 June 1864, over 12,000 Union soldiers were killed or wounded in less than an hour. Grant had lost 60,000 troops in his campaign by this time, compared with Confederate losses of

American Civil War
Union soldiers in trenches before a battle, Petersburg, Virginia, 1865. Petersburg, a port on the Appomattox River, was under siege for ten months. Its fall in April 1865 helped to hasten the end of the war.
Library of Congress

40,000. However, he knew that the South could not replace its losses as easily as the North could.

The Confederate fleet was destroyed at the Battle of Mobile Bay in August 1864 and in the early autumn Sheridan won victories at Winchester and Cedar Creek and then laid waste the entire Shenandoah Valley. Sherman entered Atlanta on 2 September 1864 and in November set out on a march to the sea from Atlanta with an army of 62,000 leaving destruction in its wake. He entered Savannah unopposed on 21 December 1864. In Tennessee, General George Thomas defeated the Confederates at the Battle of Nashville in December 1864, driving them out of the state.

1865 With the capture of Wilmington, North Carolina, January 1865, the last remaining port of the Confederacy was closed and Sherman began his march back from the sea. Columbia was burned down, and Charleston was deserted by the Confederates. Union forces captured Petersburg April 1865 and entered Richmond 3 April. Lee was completely surrounded and he surrendered at Appomattox Court House on 9 April. Johnston surrendered to Sherman on 26 April, and by the end of May all organized Confederate forces in the South had laid down their arms. Five days after Lee's surrender, Lincoln was assassinated by a Confederate sympathizer, the actor John Wilkes Booth.

reconstruction The civil war was enormously costly: over 620,000 lives had been lost, and tens of thousands of soldiers returned with their health permanently impaired. The Union's debt had risen to nearly $3,000 million: the cost to the Confederacy has never been definitely estimated. Despite all this, the North was stronger than ever; the South, on the other hand, was ruined. The victory of the Union did not bring real reconciliation between the sections. Reconstruction was finally achieved only at tremendous social and political cost, and many of the problems of 20th-century America stem from the post–Civil War period.

Arab–Israeli Conflict series of wars and territorial conflicts between Israel and various Arab states in the Middle East since the founding of the state of Israel in May 1948. These include the war of 1948–49; the 1956 Suez War between Israel and Egypt; the Six-Day War of 1967, in which Israel captured territory from Syria and Jordan; the October War of 1973; and the 1982–85 war between Israel and Lebanon. In the times between the wars tension remained high in the area, and resulted in skirmishes and terrorist activity taking place on both sides.

Arnhem, Battle of in World War II, airborne operation by the Allies, 17–26 September 1944, to secure a bridgehead over the Rhine, thereby opening the way for a thrust towards the Ruhr and a possible early end to the war. It was only partially successful, with 7,600 casualties.

Arras, Battle of battle of World War I, April–May 1917; an effective but costly British attack on German forces in support of a French offensive, which was only partially successful, on the Siegfried Line. British casualties totalled 84,000 as compared to 75,000 German casualties.

Atlantic, Battle of the during World War II, continuous battle fought in the Atlantic Ocean by the sea and air forces of the Allies and Germany, to control the supply routes to the UK. The Allies destroyed nearly 800 U-boats during the war and at least 2,200 convoys of 75,000 merchant ships crossed the Atlantic, protected by US naval forces.

Balaclava, Battle of Russian attack on 25 October 1854, during the Crimean War, on British positions, near a town in Ukraine, 10 km/6 mi southeast of Sevastopol. It was the scene of the ill-timed **Charge of the Light Brigade** of British cavalry against the Russian entrenched artillery. Of the 673 soldiers who took part, there were 272 casualties. **Balaclava helmets** were knitted hoods worn here by soldiers in the bitter weather.

Bannockburn, Battle of battle on 23–24 June 1314 in which Robert (I) the Bruce of Scotland defeated the English under Edward II, who had come to relieve the besieged Stirling Castle. The battle is named after the town of Bannockburn, south of Stirling, central Scotland.

Bataan peninsula in Luzon, the Philippines, which was defended against the Japanese in World War II by US and Filipino troops under General MacArthur 1 Jan–9 April 1942. MacArthur was evacuated, but some 67,000 Allied prisoners died on the **Bataan Death March** to camps in the interior.

Boer War second of the South African Wars 1899–1902, waged between Dutch settlers in South Africa and the British.

Boyne, Battle of the battle fought on 1 July 1690 in eastern Ireland, in which the exiled king James II was defeated by William III and fled to France. It was the decisive battle of the War of English Succession, confirming a Protestant monarch. It took its name from the River Boyne which rises in County Kildare and flows 110 km/69 mi northeast to the Irish Sea.

Britain, Battle of World War II air battle between German and British air forces over Britain from 10 July–31 October 1940.

Bulge, Battle of the or **Ardennes offensive** in World War II, Hitler's plan (code-named 'Watch on the Rhine') for a breakthrough by his field marshal Gerd von Rundstedt, aimed at the US line in the Ardennes from 16 December 1944–28 January 1945. Hitler aimed to isolate the Allied forces north of a corridor that would be created by a drive through the Ardennes, creating a German salient (prominent part of a line of attack, also known as a 'bulge'). There were 77,000 Allied casualties and 130,000 German, including Hitler's last powerful reserve of elite Panzer units. Although US troops were encircled for some weeks at Bastogne, the German counteroffensive failed.

Bunker Hill, Battle of the significant engagement in the American Revolution, 17 June 1775, near a small hill in Charlestown (now part of Boston), Massachusetts; the battle actually took place on Breed's Hill, but is named after Bunker Hill as this was the more significant of the two. Although the colonists were defeated, they were able to retreat to Boston in good order.

Carthage, Battle of battle fought in AD 238 at Carthage, North Africa, between Gordian I, the Roman governor of Africa, and Capellianus, governor of the neighbouring Roman province of Numidia. Gordian had proclaimed himself emperor, but was defeated by Capellianus's small army, which was supported by a large number of irregular troops.

Charge of the Light Brigade disastrous attack by the British Light Brigade of cavalry against the

Russian entrenched artillery on 25 October 1854 during the Crimean War at the Battle of Balaclava. Of the 673 soldiers who took part, there were 272 casualties.

Civil War, Spanish war 1936–39 precipitated by a military revolt led by General Franco against the Republican government. Inferior military capability led to the gradual defeat of the Republicans by 1939, and the establishment of Franco's dictatorship.

Crimean War war 1853–56 between Russia and the allied powers of England, France, Turkey, and Sardinia. The war arose from British and French mistrust of Russia's ambitions in the Balkans. It began with an allied Anglo-French expedition to the Crimea to attack the Russian Black Sea city of Sevastopol. The battles of the River Alma, Balaclava (including the Charge of the Light Brigade), and Inkerman 1854 led to a siege which, owing to military mismanagement, lasted for a year until September 1855. The war was ended by the Treaty of Paris in 1856. The scandal surrounding French and British losses through disease led to the organization of proper military nursing services by Florence Nightingale.

crusade (French '*croisade*') European war against non-Christians and heretics, sanctioned by the pope; in particular, the Crusades, a series of wars undertaken 1096–1291 by European rulers to recover Palestine from the Muslims. Motivated by religious zeal, the desire for land, and the trading ambitions of the major Italian cities, the Crusades were varied in their aims and effects.

Culloden, Battle of defeat in 1746 of the Jacobite rebel army of the British prince Charles Edward Stuart (the 'Young Pretender') by the Duke of Cumberland on a stretch of moorland in Inverness-shire, Scotland. This battle effectively ended the military challenge of the Jacobite rebellion.

Dacian War campaign fought by the Roman emperor Domitian in AD 89 against the Dacians, who threatened the Roman frontier on the central Danube.

D-day 6 June 1944, the day of the Allied invasion of Normandy under the command of General Eisenhower to commence Operation Overlord, the liberation of Western Europe from German occupation. The Anglo-US invasion fleet landed on the Normandy beaches on the stretch of coast

Caring in the Crimean War
Although nursing was thought to be totally unsuitable work for a woman of the Victorian middle classes, Florence Nightingale (seen in this 1859 photograph) was unwavering in her determination to transform both the standard of care that nurses provided and their professional status. The publicity surrounding her work in the Crimean War as 'the Lady with the Lamp' allowed her to achieve both aims.
St Thomas's Library

D-day US soldiers landing on the Normandy coast on D-day, 6 June 1944, the beginning of the Allied invasion of Europe. It was one of the largest and most complex movements of men and equipment in history. More than 5,000 ships were used, transporting 90,000 British, US, and Canadian troops (a further 20,000 were taken by air). *Library of Congress*

between the Orne River and St Marcouf. Artificial harbours known as 'Mulberries' were constructed and towed across the Channel so that equipment and armaments could be unloaded on to the beaches. After overcoming fierce resistance the allies broke through the German defences; Paris was liberated on 25 August, and Brussels on 2 September. D-day is also military jargon for any day on which a crucial operation is planned. D+1 indicates the day after the start of the operation.

Desert Storm, Operation code-name of the military action to eject the Iraqi army from Kuwait 1991. The build-up phase was code-named **Operation Desert Shield** and lasted from August 1990, when Kuwait was first invaded by Iraq, to January 1991 when Operation Desert Storm was unleashed, starting the Gulf War. Desert Storm ended with the defeat of the Iraqi army in the Kuwaiti theatre of operations late February 1991. The cost of the operation was $53 billion.

Falklands War war between Argentina and Britain over disputed sovereignty of the Falkland Islands initiated when Argentina invaded and occupied the islands on 2 April 1982. On the following day, the United Nations Security Council passed a resolution calling for Argentina to withdraw. A British task force was immediately dispatched and, after a fierce conflict in which more than 1,000 Argentine and British lives were lost, 12,000 Argentine troops surrendered and the islands were returned to British rule 14–15 June 1982.

First World War another name for World War I, 1914–18.

Franco-Prussian War war between France and Prussia 1870–71. The Prussian chancellor Otto

The English Civil War

The English Civil War was the 17th-century conflict between King Charles I and the Royalists (also called Cavaliers) on one side and the Parliamentarians (also called Roundheads) under Oliver Cromwell on the other. Their differences centred initially on the king's unconstitutional acts, but later became a struggle over the relative powers of crown and Parliament. Hostilities began in 1642 and a series of Royalist defeats (at Marston Moor in 1644, and then at Naseby in 1645) culminated in Charles's capture in 1647, and execution in 1649. The war continued until the final defeat of Royalist forces at Worcester in 1651. Cromwell then became Protector (ruler) from 1653 until his death in 1658.

causes Charles I became the king of Great Britain and Ireland in 1625, and quickly became involved in a number of disputes with Parliament over taxation. These led to the latter's dissolution in 1629, after which Charles ruled absolutely for 11 years. In 1639, however, war was declared with Scotland and, in 1640, Charles called the Short Parliament in order to raise funds. His request for

war taxes was refused, and the Parliament was quickly dissolved, but, after a second war with Scotland (known as the Second Bishop's War) began in 1640, and ended with the defeat of the English, Charles then called the Long Parliament of 1640. The Long Parliament imprisoned Charles's deputy, Archbishop Laud, declared extra-parliamentary taxation illegal, and voted that Parliament could not be dissolved without its own assent. Charles tried unsuccessfully to arrest the parliamentary leaders in January 1642, and then fled north to Nottingham, where he declared war against Parliament on 22 August.

first phase of the war The Royalist and Parliamentarian armies first met at the Battle of Edgehill, South Warwickshire, in October 1642, which had no conclusive outcome. After this initial battle, a series of victories followed for both sides, with the Royalists taking control of most of Yorkshire after the Battle of Adwalton Moor in June 1643, while the Parliamentarians won the Battle of Marston Moor in July 1644. The main turning point in the war came with the formation of

the Parliamentarian New model Army in February 1645. The army was nationally organized and regularly paid, was commanded by Thomas Cromwell and Sir Thomas Fairfax, and won a resounding victory at the Battle of Naseby, near Leicester, which brought the first stage of the war to an end in June 1645.

second phase of the war The Royalist army was disbanded in 1646 and King Charles took refuge with the Scottish army based in the north of England, but was handed over as a prisoner to the Parliamentarians in January 1647. During 1647, however, he was kidnapped by the Roundhead army (which was increasingly at odds with Parliament), and then escaped to the Isle of Wight, where he negotiated with a Scottish group for assistance to continue the war. Royalist rebellions and a further Scottish invasion of England in July 1648 followed, but both were suppressed, with Cromwell leading the New Model Army to victory against the Scots at Preston in August 1648. King Charles was tried for treason in January 1649, and was found guilty and executed.

von Bismarck put forward a German candidate for the vacant Spanish throne with the deliberate, and successful, intention of provoking the French emperor Napoleon III into declaring war. The Prussians defeated the French at Sedan, then besieged Paris. The Treaty of Frankfurt May 1871 gave Alsace, Lorraine, and a large French indemnity to Prussia. The war established Prussia, at the head of a newly established German empire, as Europe's leading power.

Fredericksburg, Battle of in the American Civil War, Confederate victory 11–15 December 1862 over Union forces on the Rapahannock River close to Fredericksburg, Virginia. Although the Confederates halted the Union march on Richmond, losses on both sides were heavy: Union casualties were 13,000 dead and wounded; Confederate casualties 5,000, although many of them were lightly wounded.

Gallic Wars series of military campaigns 58–51 BC in which Julius Caesar, as proconsul of Gaul, annexed Transalpine Gaul (the territory that formed the geographical basis of modern-day France). His final victory over the Gauls led by Vercingetorix 52 BC left him in control of the land area from the Rhine to the Pyrenees and from the Alps to the Atlantic. The final organization of the provinces followed under Augustus.

Gallipoli port in European Turkey, giving its name to the peninsula on which it stands. In World War I, at the instigation of Winston Churchill, an unsuccessful attempt was made February 1915–January 1916 by Allied troops to force their way through the Dardanelles and link up with Russia. The campaign was fought mainly by Australian and New Zealand (ANZAC) forces, who suffered heavy losses. An estimated 36,000 Commonwealth troops died during the nine-month campaign.

Gulf War war 16 Jan–28 February 1991 between Iraq and a coalition of 28 nations led by the USA. The invasion and annexation of Kuwait by Iraq on 2 August 1990 provoked a build-up of US troops in Saudi Arabia, eventually totalling over 500,000. The UK subsequently deployed 42,000 troops, France 15,000, Egypt 20,000, and other nations smaller contingents.

An air offensive lasting six weeks, in which 'smart' weapons came of age, destroyed about one-third of Iraqi equipment and inflicted massive casualties. A 100-hour ground war followed, which effectively destroyed the remnants of the 500,000-strong Iraqi army in or near Kuwait.

Hastings, Battle of battle 14 October 1066 at which William, Duke of Normandy ('the Conqueror') defeated Harold, King of England, and himself took the throne. The site is 10 km/6 mi inland from Hastings, at Senlac, Sussex; it is marked by Battle Abbey.

Hundred Years' War series of conflicts between England and France 1337–1453. Its origins lay with the English kings' possession of Gascony (southwest France), which the French kings claimed as their fief, and with trade rivalries over Flanders. The two kingdoms had a long history of strife before 1337, and the Hundred Years' War has sometimes been interpreted as merely an intensification of these struggles. It was caused by fears of French intervention in Scotland, which the English were trying to subdue, and by the claim of England's Edward III (through his mother Isabella, daughter of Philip IV of France) to the crown of France.

Indochina War war of independence 1946–54 between the nationalist forces of what was to become Vietnam and France, the occupying colonial power.

Iran–Iraq War war between Iran and Iraq 1980–88, claimed by the former to have begun

Iran–Iraq War

with the Iraqi offensive 21 September 1980, and by the latter with the Iranian shelling of border posts 4 September 1980. Occasioned by a boundary dispute over the Shatt-al-Arab waterway, it fundamentally arose because of Saddam Hussein's fear of a weakening of his absolute power base in Iraq by Iran's encouragement of the Shi'ite majority in Iraq to rise against the Sunni government. An estimated 1 million people died in the war.

Italian Wars a series of conflicts 1494–1559 between the leading European powers for control of the Italian states. The wars involved most of the Italian states, the papacy, Spain, the Holy Roman Empire, France, and Switzerland. Principally, the conflict was between France and Spain, with the changing allegiance of the rival Italian states and of the pope being determined by their own immediate interests. The final outcome was the victory of Spain. Culturally, the wars were significant for spreading the influence of the Italian Renaissance throughout Europe.

Iwo Jima, Battle of intense fighting between Japanese and US forces 19 February–17 March 1945 during World War II. In February 1945, US marines landed on the island of Iwo Jima, a Japanese air base, intending to use it to prepare for a planned final assault on mainland Japan. The 22,000 Japanese troops put up a fanatical resistance but the island was finally secured 16 March. US casualties came to 6,891 killed and 18,700 wounded, while only 212 of the Japanese garrison survived.

Jutland, Battle of World War I naval battle between British and German forces 31 May 1916, off the west coast of Jutland. Its outcome was indecisive, but the German fleet remained in port for the rest of the war.

Khe Sanh in the Vietnam War, US Marine outpost near the Laotian border and just south of the demilitarized zone between North and South Vietnam. Garrisoned by 4,000 Marines, it was attacked unsuccessfully by 20,000 North Vietnamese troops 21 January–7 April 1968.

Korean War war 1950–1953 between North Korea (supported by China) and South Korea, aided by the United Nations (the troops were mainly US). North Korean forces invaded South Korea on 25 June 1950, and the Security Council of the United Nations, owing to a walk-out by the USSR, voted to oppose them. The North Koreans held most of the South when US reinforcements arrived in September 1950 and forced their way through to the North Korean border with China. The Chinese retaliated, pushing them back to the original boundary by October 1950; truce negotiations began in 1951, although the war did not end until 1953.

Lexington and Concord, Battle of first battle of the American Revolution on 19 April 1775 at Lexington, Massachusetts, USA. The first shots were fired when British troops, sent to seize illegal military stores and arrest rebel leaders John Hancock and Samuel Adams, were attacked by the local militia (minutemen). Although a somewhat inconclusive action in itself, it sparked wider rebellion and so precipitated the revolution.

Little Bighorn river in Montana, USA, a tributary of the Bighorn. It was the site of Lt-Col George Custer's defeat by the Sioux Indians 25 June 1876 under their chiefs Crazy Horse and Sitting Bull, known as **Custer's last stand.**

Custer at Little Bighorn
US general George A Custer (centre) during a Black Hills expedition in 1874. Custer was then engaged in the campaign against the Sioux Indians that would lead to his famous 'last stand' at the Battle of Little Big Horn in 1876.
Library of Congress

Marne, Battles of the in World War I, two unsuccessful German offensives in northern France. In the **First Battle** from 6–9 September 1914 German advance was halted by French and British troops under the overall command of the French general Jospeh Joffre; in the **Second Battle** from 15 July–4 August 1918, the German advance was defeated by British, French, and US troops under the French general Henri Pétain, and German morale crumbled.

Marston Moor, Battle of battle fought in the English Civil War on 2 July 1644 on Marston Moor, 11 km/7 mi west of York. The Royalists were conclusively defeated by the Parliament arians and Scots.

Mexican War war between the USA and Mexico 1846–48, begun in territory disputed between Texas (annexed by the USA in 1845 but claimed by Mexico) and Mexico. It began when General Zachary Taylor invaded New Mexico after efforts to purchase what are now California and New Mexico failed. Mexico City was taken 1847, and under the Treaty of Guadaloupe Hidalgo that ended the war, the USA acquired New Mexico and California, as well as clear title to Texas in exchange for $15 million.

Naseby, Battle of decisive battle of the English Civil War on 14 June 1645, when the Royalists, led by Prince Rupert, were defeated by the Parliamentarians ('Roundheads') under Oliver Cromwell and General Fairfax. It is named after the nearby village of Naseby, 32 km/20 mi south of Leicester.

Opium Wars two wars, the First Opium War 1839–42 and the Second Opium War 1856–60, waged by Britain against China to enforce the opening of Chinese ports to trade in opium. Opium from British India paid for Britain's imports from China, such as porcelain, silk, and, above all, tea.

Pacific War war 1879–83 fought by an alliance of Bolivia and Peru against Chile. Chile seized Antofagasta and the coast between the mouths of the rivers Loa and Paposo, rendering Bolivia landlocked, and also annexed the south Peruvian coastline from Arica to the mouth of the Loa, including the nitrate fields of the Atacama Desert.

Pearl Harbor US Pacific naval base in Oahu, Hawaii, USA, the scene of a Japanese aerial attack

Pearl Harbor USS *West Virginia* after the surprise Japanese attack on the US naval base at Pearl Harbor in Hawaii 7 Dec 1941. Despite its devastating impact, the attack was not the success it might have been since most of the US aircraft carriers, of vital importance in a Pacific war, were out of the harbour on manoeuvres. *Library of Congress*

on 7 December 1941, which brought the USA into World War II. The attack took place while Japanese envoys were holding so-called peace talks in Washington. More than 2,000 members of the US armed forces were killed, and a large part of the US Pacific fleet was destroyed or damaged.

Peloponnesian War conflict between Athens and Sparta, backed by their respective allies, 431–404 BC, originating in suspicions about the ambitions of the Athenian leader Pericles. It was ended by the Spartan general Lysander's capture of the Athenian fleet in 405, and his starving the Athenians into surrender in 404. Sparta's victory meant the destruction of the political power of Athens.

Pigs, Bay of inlet on the south coast of Cuba about 145 km/90 mi southwest of Havana. It was the site of an unsuccessful invasion attempt by 1,500 US-sponsored Cuban exiles 17–20 April 1961; 1,173 were taken prisoner.

Punic Wars three wars between Rome and Carthage: **First Punic War** 264–241 BC, resulted in the defeat of the Carthaginians under Hamilcar Barca and the cession of Sicily to Rome; **Second Punic War** 218–201 BC, Hannibal invaded Italy, defeated the Romans at Trebia, Trasimene, and at Cannae (under Fabius Maximus), but was finally defeated himself by Scipio Africanus Major at Zama (now in Algeria); **Third Punic War** 149–146 BC, ended in the destruction of Carthage, and its possessions becoming the Roman province of Africa.

Roses, Wars of the civil wars in England from 1455 to 1485 between the houses of Lancaster (badge, red rose) and York (badge, white rose), both of whom claimed the throne through descent from the sons of Edward III. As a result of Henry VI's lapse into insanity in 1453, Richard, Duke of York, was installed as protector of the realm. Upon his recovery, Henry forced York to take up arms in self-defence. The name Wars of the Roses was given in the 19th century by novelist Walter Scott.

Salamis, Battle of in the Persian Wars, Greek naval victory over the Persians in 480 BC in the Strait of Salamis west of Athens. Despite being heavily outnumbered, the Greeks inflicted a crushing defeat on the invading Persians which effectively destroyed their fleet.

Sikh Wars two wars in India between the Sikhs and the British:

The **First Sikh War 1845–46** followed an invasion of British India by Punjabi Sikhs. The Sikhs were defeated and part of their territory annexed.

The **Second Sikh War 1848–49** arose from a Sikh revolt in Multan. They were defeated, and the British annexed the Punjab.

Sino-Japanese Wars two wars waged by Japan against China 1894–95 and 1931–45 to expand to the mainland. Territory gained in the First Sino-Japanese War (Korea) and in the 1930s (Manchuria, Shanghai) was returned at the end of World War II.

Somme, Battle of the Allied offensive in World War I during July–November 1916 on the River Somme in northern France, during which severe losses were suffered by both sides. It was planned by the Marshal of France, Joseph Joffre, and UK commander in chief Douglas Haig; the Allies lost over 600,000 soldiers and advanced 13 km/8 mi. It was the first battle in which tanks were used. The German offensive around St Quentin during

March–April 1918 is sometimes called the Second Battle of the Somme.

Spanish Civil War 1936–39. See Civil War, Spanish.

Thirty Years' War major war 1618–48 in central Europe. Beginning as a German conflict between Protestants and Catholics, it was gradually transformed into a struggle to determine whether the ruling Austrian Habsburg family could gain control of all Germany. The war caused serious economic and demographic problems in central Europe. Under the **Peace of Westphalia** the German states were granted their sovereignty and the emperor retained only nominal control.

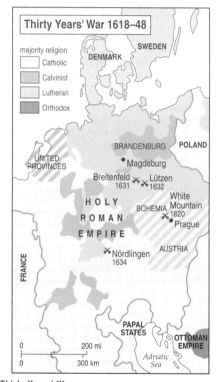

Thirty Years' War

Vicksburg, Battle of in the American Civil War, Union victory over Confederate forces May–July 1863, at Vicksburg, Mississippi, 380 km/235 mi north of New Orleans. Vicksburg was a well-fortified communications hub of great importance on the Mississippi and the Union capture of the town virtually split the Confederacy in

Football on the battlefield

■ On the first day of the Battle of the Somme, 1 July 1916, some British officers were so confident of easily breaching the German lines that they gave their men footballs to kick as they advanced across no-man's land towards the German trenches.

two. It also brought Ulysses S Grant to public prominence, eventually leading to him being given command of all Union forces.

Vietnam War 1954–75, war between communist North Vietnam and US-backed South Vietnam. 200,000 South Vietnamese soldiers, 1 million North Vietnamese soldiers, and 500,000 civilians were killed. 56,555 US soldiers were killed 1961–75, a fifth of them by their own troops. The war destroyed 50% of the country's forest cover and 20% of agricultural land. Cambodia, a neutral neighbour, was bombed by the US 1969–75, with 1 million killed or wounded.

Vietnam War: Chronology

1945 Japanese surrender in French Indochina. Northern zone under Chinese control allows establishment of Democratic Republic of Vietnam under Ho Chi Minh.

1946 French reoccupy southern zone but fail to defeat nationalist Vietminh forces under General Giap.

1948 Attempt to form alternative government under Bao Dai fails to halt civil war.

1953 Vietminh forces invade Laos.

1954 French suffer colossal military defeat at Dien Bien Phu. Geneva Conference of foreign ministers agrees partition of Indochina into four states: Laos, Cambodia, North Vietnam, and South Vietnam.

1955 Bao Dai is deposed and replaced by US-backed Ngo Dinh Diem, who uses dictatorial methods and refuses a referendum on government in South Vietnam.

1957 Insurgent communist Vietcong begin an offensive against the south. USA provides limited amounts of indirect aid to South Vietnamese government.

1963 Military coup overthrows and kills Diem.

1964 Tonkin Gulf incident, when US destroyers are reportedly attacked by North Vietnamese, triggers US entry into the war.

1965 January Major defeat of government forces at Binh-Gia, east of Saigon, by communists.

March USA begins regular bombing of North Vietnam (Operation Rolling Thunder).

July USA begins to send in combat troops.

1966 President Johnson increases numbers of US ground forces. The USA admits using defoliants to destroy the rainforest.

1967 US troops invade the Demilitarized Zone (DMZ).

1968 January Vietcong begin Tet Offensive with attacks around Saigon, Hue, and Khe Sanh.

March My Lai massacre by US troops.

May Peace talks between USA and North Vietnam begin in Paris.

November US bombing of North Vietnam is halted.

1969 January Paris peace talks include Vietcong and South Vietnam.

September President Nixon announces phased withdrawal of 550,000 American troops in an attempt to 'Vietnamize' the war. Death of Ho Chi Minh, succeeded by Ton Duc Thang.

November–December Widespread anti-Vietnam War demonstrations in USA.

1970 Fighting extended to Cambodia in an attempt to eliminate communist bases. Government of Prince Sihanouk is overthrown and a republic proclaimed.

1971 South Vietnamese forces move into Laos with US air support, in a further bid to cut off communist supply lines. USA breaks off peace talks in Paris.

1972 March Major North Vietnamese offensive only halted by US bombing campaign and shelling of North Vietnam. US ground forces do not participate.

1973 January Ceasefire agreement and withdrawal of remaining US forces.

1973–74 South Vietnamese forces are gradually overwhelmed.

1975 North Vietnamese capture Saigon (renamed Ho Chi Minh City).

World War I war 1914–18, between the Central European Powers (Germany, Austria-Hungary, and allies) on one side and the Triple Entente (Britain and the British Empire, France, and Russia) and their allies, including the USA (which entered 1917), on the other side. An estimated 10 million lives were lost and twice that number were wounded. It was fought on the eastern and western fronts, in the Middle East, in Africa, and at sea.

World War II war 1939–45, between Germany, Italy, and Japan (the Axis powers) on one side, and Britain, the Commonwealth, France, the USA, the USSR, and China (the Allied powers) on the other. An estimated 55 million lives were lost (20 million of them citizens of the USSR), and 60 million people in Europe were displaced because of bombing raids. The war was fought in the Atlantic and Pacific theatres.

Military Casualties in World War I

World War I casualty statistics vary greatly from source to source. Official records are often lacking and based on differing criteria and these figures remain open to interpretation and debate. Figures are for 1914–18 and are rounded to the nearest 250. (N/A = not available.)

Country	Mobilized	Deaths	Wounded	Total casualties	Prisoners/ missing
Allied Powers					
Belgium	207,000	13,750	44,000	57,750	67,750
British Empire[1]					
UK	5,397,000	702,500	1,662,750	2,365,250	170,500
Australia	330,000	59,250	152,250	211,500	4,000
Canada	552,000	56,750	149,750	206,500	3,750
India[2]	1,216,000	64,500	69,250	133,750	11,250
Newfoundland	N/A	1,250	2,250	3,500	250
New Zealand	N/A	16,750	41,250	58,000	500
South Africa	N/A	7,000	12,000	19,000	1,500
Other colonies	N/A	500	750	1,250	N/A
Total British Empire	>7,495,000	908,500	2,090,250	2,998,750	191,750
France (including colonial territories)	7,500,000	1,385,250	2,675,000– 4,266,000[3]	4,060,250– 5,651,250	446,250
Greece	230,000	5,000	21,000	26,000	1,000
Italy	5,500,000	460,000	947,000	1,407,000	530,000
Japan	800,000	250	1,000	1,250	0
Montenegro	50,000	3,000	10,000	13,000	7,000
Portugal	100,000	7,250	15,000	22,250	12,250
Romania	750,000	200,000	120,000	320,000	80,000
Russia	12,000,000	1,700,000	4,950,000	6,650,000	2,500,000
Serbia	707,250	127,500	133,250	260,750	153,000
USA	4,272,500	116,750	204,000	320,750	4,500
Central Powers					
Austria-Hungary	6,500,000	1,200,000	3,620,000	4,820,000	2,200,000
Bulgaria	400,000	101,250	152,500	253,750	11,000
Germany	11,000,000	1,718,250	4,234,000	5,952,250	1,073,500
Turkey[4]	1,600,000	>335,750	>400,000	>735,750	>200,000

[1] Figures for the British Empire and constituent countries are for 1914–20.

[2] Includes 4,912 British casualties: British drafts and units serving with the Indian Army.

[3] Official records for the number of French wounded are not available.

[4] There are no official records available for Turkish casualties.

World War II Casualties

Figures are for 1939–45 and are rounded to the nearest 250. (– = not applicable. N/A = not available.)

Country	Personnel[1]	Military killed	Military wounded	Prisoners of war	Civilian dead
Allied Powers					
Australia	680,000	23,250	39,750	26,250	–
Belgium	800,000	7,750	14,500	N/A	75,000[2]
Brazil	200,000	1,000	4,250	–	–
Canada	780,000	37,500	53,250	9,750	–
China	5,000,000	1,324,500[3]	1,762,000	N/A	N/A[4]
Czechoslovakia	180,000	6,750	8,000	–	310,000[5]
Denmark	15,000	4,250	N/A	–	–
Estonia	–	–	–	–	140,000
France	5,000,000	205,750	390,000	765,000	300,000
Greece	150,000	16,250	50,000	N/A	337,000[6]
India	2,394,000	24,250	64,250	79,500	–
Latvia	–	–	–	–	120,000
Lithuania	–	–	–	–	170,000
Netherlands	500,000	13,750	2,750	N/A	236,250[7]
New Zealand	157,000	12,250	19,250	8,500	–
Norway	25,000	4,750	N/A	N/A	5,500[8]
Poland	1,000,000	320,000	530,000	–	6,028,000[9]
South Africa	140,000	8,750	14,250	14,500	–
UK	4,683,000	264,500	277,000	172,500[10]	60,500
USA	16,353,750	405,500	671,750	105,000	–
USSR	20,000,000	13,600,000	5,000,000	N/A	7,720,000
Yugoslavia	3,741,000	305,000	425,000	–	1,355,000[11]
Axis Powers					
Austria	800,000	380,000	N/A	N/A	145,000[12]
Finland	250,000	79,000	N/A	–	–
Germany	10,000,000	3,300,000	N/A	630,000[13]	3,063,000[14]
Hungary	350,000	147,500	N/A	–	280,000[15]
Italy	4,500,000	262,500	N/A	1,478,000	93,000[16]
Japan	N/A	1,140,500	N/A	11,600[17]	953,000[18]
Romania	600,000	300,000	N/A	N/A	145,000[19]

[1] Peak strength of armed forces during World War II.

[2] Includes approximately 25,000 Jews.

[3] Estimates vary for Chinese military killed.

[4] Estimates for Chinese civilian dead vary very widely, from 700,000 to 10,000,000.

[5] Includes approximately 250,000 Jews.

[6] Includes approximately 260,000 deaths due to starvation.

[7] Includes approximately 104,000 Jews, 25,000 civilian underground workers, and 15,000 deaths due to starvation.

[8] Includes approximately 2,000 resistance fighters and 750 Norwegians serving in the German army.

[9] Includes approximately 3,200,000 Jews.

[10] 7,250 British prisoners of war died while in German captivity; 12,500 died while in Japanese captivity.

[11] Includes approximately 55,000 Jews.

[12] Includes approximately 60,000 Jews.

[13] Excludes those in the USSR.

[14] Includes approximately 170,000 Jews.

[15] Includes approximately 200,000 Jews.

[16] Includes approximately 8,000 Jews.

[17] Excludes those in the USSR.

[18] Includes approximately 668,000 killed in air raids on home islands.

[19] Includes approximately 60,000 Jews.

World War II

It is estimated that, during the course of the war, for every tonne of bombs dropped on the UK, 315 fell on Germany.

In May 1945, Germany surrendered but Japan fought on until the USA dropped atomic bombs on Hiroshima and Nagasaki (August).

Yom Kippur War the surprise attack on Israel in October 1973 by Egypt and Syria. It is named after the Jewish national holiday on which it began, the holiest day of the Jewish year.

Ypres, Battles of in World War I, three major battles 1914–17 between German and Allied forces near Ypres, a Belgian town in western Flanders, 40 km/25 mi south of Ostend. Neither side made much progress in any of the battles, despite heavy casualties, but the third battle in particular (also known as Passchendaele) July–November 1917 stands out as an enormous waste of life for little return. The Menin Gate (1927) is a memorial to British soldiers lost in these battles.

World War I: Chronology

1914 June Assassination of Archduke Franz Ferdinand of Austria, 28 June.

July German government issues 'blank cheque' to Austria, offering support in war against Serbia. Austrian ultimatum to Serbia. Serbs accepts all but two points. Austria refuses to accept compromise and declares war. Russia begins mobilization to defend Serbian ally. Germany demands Russian demobilization.

August Germany declares war on Russia. France mobilizes to assist Russian ally. Germans occupies Luxembourg and demands access to Belgian territory, which is refused. Germany declares war on France and invades Belgium. Britain declares war on Germany, then on Austria. Dominions within the British Empire, including Australia, are automatically involved. Battle of Tannenburg between Central Powers and Russians. Russian army encircled.

September British and French troops halt German advance just short of Paris, and drive them back. First Battle of the Marne, and of the Aisne. Beginning of trench warfare.

October–November First Battle of Ypres. Britain declares war on Turkey.

1915 April–May Gallipoli offensive launched by British and dominion troops against Turkish forces. Second Battle of Ypres. First use of poison gas by Germans. Italy joins war against Austria. German submarine sinks ocean liner *Lusitania* on 7 May, later

helping to bring USA into the war.

August–September Warsaw is evacuated by the Russians. Battle of Tarnopol. Vilna is taken by the Germans. Tsar Nicholas II takes supreme control of Russian forces.

1916 January Final evacuation of British and dominion troops from Gallipoli.

February German offensive against Verdun begins, with huge losses for small territorial gain.

May Naval Battle of Jutland between British and German imperial fleets ends inconclusively, but puts a stop to further German naval participation in the war.

June Russian (Brusilov) offensive against the Ukraine begins.

July–November First Battle of the Somme, a sustained Anglo-French offensive which wins little territory and costs a huge number of lives.

August Hindenburg and Ludendorff take command of the German armed forces. Romania enters the war against Austria but is rapidly overrun.

September Early tanks are used by British on Western Front.

November Nivelle replaces Joffre as commander of French forces. Battle of the Ancre on the Western Front.

December French complete recapture of Verdun fortifications. Austrians occupy Bucharest.

1917 February Germany declares unrestricted submarine warfare. Russian Revolution begins and tsarist rule is overthrown.

March British seizure of Baghdad and occupation of Persia.

March–April Germans retreat to Siegfried Line (Arras-Soissons) on Western Front.

April–May USA enters the war against Germany. Unsuccessful British and French offensives. Mutinies among French troops. Nivelle replaced by Pétain.

July–November Third Ypres offensive including Battle of Passchendaele.

September Germans occupy Riga.

October–November Battle of Caporetto sees Italian troops defeated by Austrians.

December Jerusalem taken by British forces under Allenby.

1918 January US President Woodrow Wilson proclaims 'Fourteen Points' as a basis for peace settlement.

March Treaty of Brest-Litovsk with Central Powers ends Russian participation in the war, with substantial concessions of territory and reparations. Second Battle of the Somme begins with German spring offensive.

July–August Allied counter-offensive, including tank attack at Amiens, drives Germans back to the Siegfried Line.

September Hindenburg and Ludendorff call for an armistice.

World War I: Chronology (continued)

October Armistice offered on the basis of the 'Fourteen Points'. German naval and military mutinies at Kiel and Wilhelmshaven.

November Austria-Hungary signs armistice with Allies. Kaiser Wilhelm II of Germany goes into exile. Provisional government under social democrat Friedrich Ebert is formed. Germany agrees armistice. Fighting on Western Front stops.

1919 January Peace conference opens at Versailles.

May Demands are presented to Germany.

June Germany signs peace treaty at Versailles, followed by other Central Powers: Austria (Treaty of St Germain-en-Laye, September), Bulgaria (Neuilly, November), Hungary (Trianon, June 1920), and Turkey (Sèvres, August 1920).

World War II: Chronology

1939 September German invasion of Poland; Britain and France declare war on Germany; the USSR invades Poland; fall of Warsaw (Poland divided between Germany and USSR).

November The USSR invades Finland.

1940 March Soviet peace treaty with Finland.

April Germany occupies Denmark, Norway, the Netherlands, Belgium, and Luxembourg. In Britain, a coalition government is formed under Churchill.

May Germany outflanks the defensive French Maginot Line.

May–June Evacuation of 337,131 Allied troops from Dunkirk, France, across the Channel to England.

June Italy declares war on Britain and France; the Germans enter Paris; the French Prime Minister Pétain signs an armistice with Germany and moves the seat of government to Vichy.

July–October Battle of Britain between British and German air forces.

September Japanese invasion of French Indochina.

October Abortive Italian invasion of Greece.

1941 April Germany occupies Greece and Yugoslavia.

June Germany invades the USSR; Finland declares war on the USSR.

July The Germans enter Smolensk, USSR.

December The Germans come within 40 km/25 mi of Moscow, with Leningrad (now St Petersburg) under siege. First Soviet counteroffensive. Japan bombs Pearl Harbor, Hawaii, and declares war on the USA and Britain. Germany and Italy declare war on the USA.

1942 January Japanese conquest of the Philippines.

June Naval battle of Midway, the turning point of the Pacific War.

August German attack on Stalingrad (now Volgograd), USSR.

October–November Battle of El Alamein in North Africa, turn of the tide for the Western Allies.

November Soviet counteroffensive on Stalingrad.

1943 January The Casablanca Conference issues the Allied demand of unconditional surrender; the Germans retreat from Stalingrad.

March The USSR drives the Germans back to the River Donetz.

May End of Axis resistance in North Africa.

July A coup by King Victor Emmanuel and Marshal Badoglio forces Mussolini to resign.

August Beginning of the campaign against the Japanese in Burma (now Myanmar); US Marines land on Guadalcanal, Solomon Islands.

September Italy surrenders to the Allies; Mussolini is rescued by the Germans who set up a Republican Fascist government in northern Italy; Allied landings at Salerno; the USSR retakes Smolensk.

World War II: Chronology (continued)

October Italy declares war on Germany.

November The US Navy defeats the Japanese in the Battle of Guadalcanal.

November–December The Allied leaders meet at the Tehran Conference.

1944 January Allied landing in Nazi-occupied Italy: Battle of Anzio.

March End of the German U-boat campaign in the Atlantic.

May Fall of Monte Cassino, southern Italy.

6 June D-day: Allied landings in Nazi-occupied and heavily defended Normandy.

July The bomb plot by German generals against Hitler fails.

August Romania joins the Allies.

September Battle of Arnhem on the Rhine; Soviet armistice with Finland.

October The Yugoslav guerrilla leader Tito and Soviets enter Belgrade.

December German counteroffensive, Battle of the Bulge.

1945 February The Soviets reach the German border; Yalta conference; Allied bombing campaign over Germany (Dresden destroyed); the US reconquest of the Philippines is completed; the Americans land on Iwo Jima, south of Japan.

April Hitler commits suicide; Mussolini is captured by Italian partisans and shot.

May Germany surrenders to the Allies.

June US troops complete the conquest of Okinawa (one of the Japanese Ryukyu Islands).

July The Potsdam Conference issues an Allied ultimatum to Japan.

August Atom bombs are dropped by the USA on Hiroshima and Nagasaki; Japan surrenders.

WEAPONS AND EQUIPMENT

A weapon is any implement used for attack and defence, from simple clubs, spears, and bows and arrows in prehistoric times to machine guns and nuclear bombs in modern times. The first revolution in warfare came with the invention of gunpowder and the development of cannons and shoulder-held guns. Many other weapons now exist, such as grenades, shells, torpedoes, rockets, and guided missiles. The ultimate in explosive weapons are the atomic (fission) and hydrogen (fusion) bombs. They release the enormous energy produced when atoms split or fuse together. There are also chemical and bacteriological weapons, which release poisons or disease.

acoustic weapons in World War II, underwater weapons fitted with a sensor which would detect the sound of a ship's propellers. The sensor would steer a torpedo towards the ship or, if fitted to a mine, detonate it when it was close enough to the ship's hull.

Agent Orange selective weedkiller, notorious for its use in the 1960s during the Vietnam War by US forces to eliminate ground cover which could protect enemy forces. It was subsequently revealed that it contained highly poisonous dioxin. Thousands of US troops who had handled it, along with many Vietnamese people who came into contact with it, later developed cancer or went on to have deformed babies.

aircraft carrier ocean-going naval vessel with a broad, flat-topped deck for launching and landing military aircraft; a floating military base for warplanes too far from home for refuelling, repairing, reconnaissance, escorting, and attack and defence operations. Aircraft are catapult-launched or take off and land on the flight-deck, a large expanse of unobstructed deck, often fitted with barriers and restraining devices to halt the landing aircraft.

armoured fighting vehicle (AFV) powered vehicle using wheels or chain tracks for motion, and mounting armour plate for protection against small arms and artillery fire, mines, and grenades. A weapons system incorporating machine guns or automatic cannon, missiles, or main-armament artillery is usually an integral part of the vehicle.

AFVs can be divided into four main types: tanks, armoured cars, armoured personnel carriers, and self-propelled artillery.

armoured personnel carrier (APC) wheeled or tracked military vehicle designed to transport up to ten people. Armoured to withstand small-arms fire and shell splinters, it is used on battlefields.

atom bomb bomb deriving its explosive force from nuclear fission as a result of a neutron chain reaction, developed in the 1940s in the USA into a usable weapon.

atom bomb The atomic explosion over the Japanese city of Nagasaki, in 9 Aug 1945. Known as 'Fat Man', the Nagasaki bomb exploded at about 245 m/800 ft above the city, its 1.13 kg/2.5 lb of plutonium producing an explosion equivalent to some 200,000 metric tons of TNT. *Library of Congress*

battleship class of large warships with the biggest guns and heaviest armour. In 1991, four US battleships were in active service. They are now all decommissioned.

bayonet short sword attached to the muzzle of a firearm. The bayonet was placed inside the barrel of the muzzleloading muskets of the late 17th century. The **sock** or ring bayonet, invented 1700, allowed a weapon to be fired without interruption, leading to the demise of the pike.

bazooka US 2.36 in calibre rocket launcher fired from the shoulder. A lightweight tube with simple sights, it fires a fin-stabilized rocket containing a shaped charge warhead.

binary weapon in chemical warfare, weapon consisting of two substances that in isolation are harmless but when mixed together form a poisonous nerve gas. They are loaded into the delivery system separately and combine after launch.

bomb container filled with explosive or chemical material and generally used in warfare. There are also incendiary bombs and nuclear bombs and missiles. Any object designed to cause damage by explosion can be called a bomb (car bombs, letter bombs). Initially dropped from aeroplanes (from World War I), bombs were in World War II also launched by rocket (V1, V2). The 1960s saw the development of missiles that could be launched from aircraft, land sites, or submarines. In the 1970s laser guidance systems were developed to hit small targets with accuracy.

Browning automatic rifle US light machine gun used for infantry support, adopted by the US Army in 1917 and standard issue until the early 1950s. It used a 20-shot magazine and fired at 500 rounds per minute.

crossbow bow with a mechanism to draw back the string and a trigger to release it, used in medieval European warfare. The bow was fixed to a stock fitted with a catch to hold the string in place. There was usually a projecting nut on the stock over which the string was drawn, the nut being retracted to release the string by a trigger.

destroyer small, fast warship designed for anti-submarine work. Destroyers played a critical role in the convoy system in World War II.

enhanced radiation weapon another name for the neutron bomb.

explosive any material capable of a sudden release of energy and the rapid formation of a large volume of gas, leading, when compressed, to the development of a high-pressure wave (blast).

firearm weapon from which projectiles are discharged by the combustion of an explosive. Firearms are generally divided into two main sections: **artillery** (ordnance or cannon), with a bore greater than 2.54 cm/1 in, and **small arms,** with a bore of less than 2.54 cm/1 in.

Although gunpowder was known in Europe 60 years previously, the invention of guns dates from 1300 to 1325, and is attributed to Berthold Schwartz, a German monk.

frigate escort warship smaller than a destroyer. Before 1975 the term referred to a warship larger than a destroyer but smaller than a light cruiser. In the 18th and 19th centuries a frigate was a small, fast sailing warship.

fuel-air explosive warhead containing a highly flammable petroleum and oxygen mixture; when released over a target, this mixes with the oxygen in the atmosphere and produces a vapour which, when ignited, causes a blast approximately five times more powerful than conventional high explosives.

gas shell artillery projectile carrying a chemical agent, first used during World War I. The explosive is contained in a central cylinder and the remaining space filled with liquefied gas so that the explosion is sufficient to release the gas and allow it to disperse without disintegrating it.

grenade small missile, containing an explosive or other charge, usually thrown (hand grenade) but sometimes fired from a rifle. Hand grenades are generally fitted with a time fuse of about four seconds: a sufficient amount of time for the grenade to reach the target but not enough for the enemy to pick it up and throw it back.

howitzer cannon, in use since the 16th century, with a particularly steep angle of fire. It was much developed in World War I for demolishing the fortresses of the trench system. The multinational NATO FH70 field howitzer is mobile and fires, under computer control, three 43 kg/95 lb shells at 32 km/20 mi range in 15 seconds.

hydrogen bomb bomb that works on the principle of nuclear fusion. Large-scale explosion results from the thermonuclear release of energy when hydrogen nuclei are fused to form helium nuclei. The first hydrogen bomb was exploded at Enewetak Atoll in the Pacific Ocean by the USA in 1952.

incendiary bomb bomb containing inflammable matter. Usually dropped by aircraft, incendiary bombs were used in World War I and incendiary shells were used against Zeppelin aircraft. Incendiary bombs were a major weapon in attacks on cities in World War II, causing widespread destruction. To hinder firefighters, delayed-action high-explosive bombs were usually dropped with them. In the Vietnam War, US forces used napalm in incendiary bombs.

longbow longer than standard bow, made of yew, introduced in the 12th century. They were favoured by English archers in preference to the cross bow, as the longer bow allowed arrows of greater weight to be fired further and more accurately. They were highly effective in the Hundred Years' War, to the extent that the French took to removing the first two fingers of prisoners so that they would never again be able to draw a bow.

machine gun rapid-firing automatic gun. The Maxim (named after its inventor, US-born British engineer H S Maxim (1840–1916)) of 1884 was recoil-operated, but some later types have been gas-operated (Bren) or recoil assisted by gas (some versions of the Browning).

magnetic mine naval mine detonated by the magnetic field of a ship passing over or alongside.

mine explosive charge on land or sea, or in the atmosphere, designed to be detonated by contact, vibration (for example, from an enemy engine), magnetic influence, or a timing device. Countermeasures include metal detectors (useless for plastic types), specially equipped helicopters, and (at sea) minesweepers. Mines were first used at sea in the early 19th century, during the Napoleonic Wars; landmines came into use during World War I to disable tanks.

minesweeper small naval vessel for locating and destroying mines at sea. A typical minesweeper weighs about 725 tonnes, and is built of reinforced plastic (immune to magnetic and acoustic mines). Remote-controlled miniature submarines may be used to lay charges next to the mines and destroy them.

missile rocket-propelled weapon, which may be nuclear-armed. Modern missiles are often classified as surface-to-surface missiles (SSM), air-to-air missiles (AAM), surface-to-air missiles (SAM), or air-to-surface missiles (ASM). A **cruise missile** is in effect a pilotless, computer-guided aircraft; it can be sea-launched from submarines or surface ships, or launched from the air or the ground.

Molotov cocktail or **petrol bomb** home-made weapon consisting of a bottle filled with petrol, plugged with a rag as a wick, ignited, and thrown as a grenade. Resistance groups during World War II named them after the Soviet foreign minister Molotov.

napalm fuel used in flamethrowers and incendiary bombs. Produced from jellied petrol, it is a mixture of **na**phthenic and **palm**itic acids. Napalm causes extensive burns because it sticks to the skin even when aflame. It was widely used by the US Army during the Vietnam War, and by Serb forces in the civil war in Bosnia-Herzegovina.

neutron bomb small hydrogen bomb for battlefield use that kills by radiation, with minimal damage to buildings and other structures.

howitzer A 240 mm/9.4 in howitzer being used by the US army in Italy 1944. Historically, a howitzer fired shells with a high, arching trajectory, but in this century many designs have fired high-speed shells with a low trajectory. *Library of Congress*

Patriot missile ground-to-air medium-range missile system used in air defence.

It has high-altitude coverage, electronic jamming capability, and excellent mobility. US Patriot missiles were tested in battle against Scud missiles fired by the Iraqis in the 1991 Gulf War. They successfully intercepted 24 Scud missiles out of about 85 attempts.

remotely piloted vehicle (RPV) crewless mini-aircraft used for military surveillance and to select targets in battle. RPVs barely show up on radar, so they can fly over a battlefield without being shot down, and they are equipped to transmit TV images to an operator on the ground. RPVs were used by Israeli forces in 1982 in Lebanon and by the Allies in the 1991 Gulf War. The US system is called Aquila and the British system Phoenix.

rifle firearm that has spiral grooves (rifling) in its barrel. When a bullet is fired, the rifling makes it spin, thereby improving accuracy. Rifles were first introduced in the late 18th century.

scorpio name given to a small, rapid-fire *ballista* (stone-shooting machine), used, mainly by the Romans, in the 1st and 2nd centuries BC.

Scud Soviet-produced surface-to-surface missile that can be armed with a nuclear, chemical, or conventional warhead. The **Scud-B,** deployed on a mobile launcher, was the version most commonly used by the Iraqi army in the Gulf War 1991. It is a relatively inaccurate weapon.

Semtex plastic explosive, manufactured in the Czech Republic. It is safe to handle (it can only be ignited by a detonator) and difficult to trace, since it has no smell. It has been used by extremist groups in the Middle East and by the IRA in Northern Ireland.

siphon weapon used on medieval Byzantine ships to shoot inflammable Greek fire against enemy vessels. No examples survive, but it was apparently a brass tube into which the fuel was sucked and then expelled by a pair of bellows.

smart weapon programmable bomb or missile that can be guided to its target by laser technology, TV homing technology, or terrain-contour matching (TERCOM). A smart weapon relies on its pinpoint accuracy to destroy a target rather than on the size of its warhead.

stealth technology methods used to make an aircraft as invisible as possible, primarily to radar detection but also to detection by visual means

and heat sensors. This is achieved by a combination of aircraft-design elements: smoothing off all radar-reflecting sharp edges; covering the aircraft with radar-absorbent materials; fitting engine coverings that hide the exhaust and heat signatures of the aircraft; and other, secret technologies.

tank armoured fighting vehicle that runs on tracks and is fitted with weapons systems capable of defeating other tanks and destroying life and property. The term was originally a code name for the first effective tracked and armoured fighting vehicle, invented by the British soldier and scholar Ernest Swinton, and first used in the Battle of the Somme 1916.

TASM abbreviation for **tactical air-to-surface missile** missile with a range of under 500 km/300 mi and a nuclear warhead. TASMs are being developed independently by the USA and France to replace the surface-to-surface missiles being phased out by NATO from 1990.

torpedo self-propelled underwater missile, invented 1866 by British engineer Robert Whitehead. Modern torpedoes are homing missiles; some resemble mines in that they lie on the seabed until activated by the acoustic signal of a passing ship. A television camera enables them to be remotely controlled, and in the final stage of attack they lock on to the radar or sonar signals of the target ship.

U-boat (German *Unterseeboot* 'undersea boat') German submarine. The term was used in both world wars when U-boat attacks posed a great threat to Allied shipping.

V1, V2 (German *Vergeltungswaffe* 'revenge weapons') German flying bombs of World War II, launched against Britain in 1944 and 1945. The V1, also called the doodlebug and buzz bomb, was an uncrewed monoplane carrying a bomb, powered by a simple kind of jet engine called a pulse jet. The V2, a rocket bomb with a preset guidance system, was the first long-range ballistic missile. It was 14 m/47 ft long, carried a 1-tonne warhead, and hit its target at a speed of 5,000 kph/3,000 mph.

warship fighting ship armed and crewed for war. The supremacy of the battleship at the beginning of the 20th century was rivalled during World War I by the development of submarine attack, and was rendered obsolescent in World War II with the advent of long-range air attack. Today the largest and most important surface warships are the aircraft carriers.

CONFERENCES AND TREATIES

Treaties have played a significant role in the development of international law since the advent of the International Law Commission of the United Nations Organization. The function of this body is to develope and codify the law. In so doing the commission has put forward to diplomatic conferences important treaties to clarify law in such fields as the law of the sea (Geneva Conventions 1958), the law of diplomatic relations (Vienna Convention 1961), and the Law of treaties itself (Vienna Convention 1969). Treaties as a source of rules of international law have also been given an added importance. A large number of new subjects of international law have been created since the birth of the United Nations, many of which are socialist states. The fact that existing international law created largely in an era of *laissez-faire* capitalism is to some extent unacceptable to such socialist states, makes the agreed codification of a mutually acceptable system of rules established by treaties most important.

Aigun, Treaty of treaty between Russia and China signed 1858 at the port of Aigun in China on the Amur River. The left bank was ceded to Russia, but this has since been repudiated by China.

Anzam Treaty Australia, New Zealand, and Malaya, 1948 arrangement to coordinate service planning in defending air and sea communications in the region. Cover was extended to the defence of Malaya 1954–55, but this was incorporated into the Anglo-Malayan Defence Agreement shortly after Malayan independence 1957.

Arras, Congress and Treaty of meeting in northern France 1435 between representatives of Henry VI of England, Charles VII of France, and Philip the Good of Burgundy to settle the Hundred Years' War. The outcome was a diplomatic victory for France. Although England refused to compromise on Henry VI's claim to the French crown, France signed a peace treaty with Burgundy, England's former ally.

Brétigny, Treaty of treaty made between Edward III of England and John II of France in 1360 at the end of the first phase of the Hundred Years' War, under which Edward received Aquitaine and its dependencies in exchange for renunciation of his claim to the French throne.

Central Treaty Organization (CENTO) military alliance that replaced the Baghdad Pact 1959; it collapsed when the withdrawal of Iran, Pakistan, and Turkey in 1979 left the UK as the only member.

Geneva Convention international agreement 1864 regulating the treatment of those wounded in war, and later extended to cover the types of weapons allowed, the treatment of prisoners and the sick, and the protection of civilians in wartime. The rules were revised at conventions held 1906, 1929, and 1949, and by the 1977 Additional Protocols.

Georgetown, Declaration of call, at a conference in Guyana of nonaligned countries in 1972, for a multipolar system to replace the two world power blocs, and for the Mediterranean Sea and Indian Ocean to be neutral.

Helsinki Conference international meeting 1975 at which 35 countries, including the USSR and the USA, attempted to reach agreement on cooperation in security, economics, science, technology, and human rights. This established the Conference on Security and Cooperation in Europe.

Intermediate Nuclear Forces Treaty agreement signed 8 December 1987 between the USA and the USSR to eliminate all ground-based nuclear missiles in Europe that were capable of hitting only European targets (including European Russia). It reduced the countries' nuclear arsenals by some 2,000 (4% of the total). The treaty included provisions for each country to inspect the other's bases.

Paris, Treaty of any of various peace treaties signed in Paris, including: **1763** ending the Seven

Years' War; **1783** recognizing American independence; **1814** and **1815** following the abdication and final defeat of Napoleon I; **1856** ending the Crimean War; **1898** ending the Spanish-American War; **1919–20** the conference in Paris preparing the Treaty of Versailles at the end of World War I; **1947** after World War II, the peace treaties between the Allies and Italy, Romania, Hungary, Bulgaria, and Finland; **1951** treaty signed by France, West Germany, Italy, Belgium, Netherlands, and Luxembourg, embodying the Schuman Plan to set up a single coal and steel authority; **1973** ending US participation in the Vietnam War.

Potsdam Conference conference held in Potsdam, Germany, 17 July–2 August 1945, between representatives of the USA, the UK, and the USSR. They established the political and economic principles governing the treatment of Germany in the initial period of Allied control at the end of World War II, and sent an ultimatum to Japan demanding unconditional surrender on pain of utter destruction.

Southeast Asia Treaty Organization (SEATO) collective military system 1954–77 established by Australia, France, New Zealand, Pakistan, the Philippines, Thailand, the UK, and the USA, with Vietnam, Cambodia, and Laos as protocol states.

After the Vietnam War, SEATO was phased out.

Strategic Arms Limitation Talks (SALT) series of US-Soviet discussions 1969–79 aimed at reducing the rate of nuclear-arms build-up (as opposed to disarmament, which would reduce the number of weapons, as discussed in Strategic Arms Reduction Talks [START]). Treaties in the 1970s sought to prevent the growth of nuclear arsenals.

Strategic Arms Reduction Talks (START) phase in peace discussions dealing with disarmament, initially involving the USA and the Soviet Union, from 1992 the USA and Russia, and from 1993 Belarus and the Ukraine.

It began with talks in Geneva 1983, leading to the signing of the Intermediate Nuclear Forces (INF) Treaty 1987. Reductions of about 30% in strategic nuclear weapons systems were agreed in 1991 (START) and more significant cuts January in 1993 (START II); the latter treaty was ratified by the US Senate January 1996.

Tianjin, Treaty of agreement in 1858 between China and Western powers, signed at the end of the Second Opium (Arrow) War. It was one of the unequal treaties forced on China by the West. A further ten treaty ports, mainly along the Chang Jiang, were opened to Britain, France, Russia, and the USA.

Tlatelolco, Treaty of international agreement signed 1967 in Tlatelolco, Mexico, prohibiting nuclear weapons in Latin America.

Tordesillas, Treaty of agreement reached in 1494 when Castile and Portugal divided the uncharted world between themselves. An imaginary line was drawn 370 leagues west of the Azores and the Cape Verde Islands, with Castile receiving all lands discovered to the west, and Portugal those to the east.

Versailles, Treaty of peace treaty after World War I between the Allies and Germany, signed on 28 June 1919. It established the League of Nations. Germany surrendered Alsace-Lorraine to France, and large areas in the east to Poland, and made smaller cessions to Czechoslovakia, Lithuania, Belgium, and Denmark. The Rhineland was demilitarized, German rearmament was restricted, and Germany agreed to pay reparations for war damage. The treaty was never ratified by the USA, which made a separate peace with Germany and Austria in 1921.

Yalta Conference in 1945, a meeting at which the Allied leaders Churchill (UK), Roosevelt (USA), and Stalin (USSR) completed plans for the defeat of Germany in World War II and the foundation of the United Nations. It took place in Yalta, a Soviet holiday resort in the Crimea.

Disarmament

Disarmament is the reduction of a country's weapons of war. Most disarmament talks since World War II have been concerned with nuclear-arms verification and reduction, but biological, chemical, and conventional weapons have also come under discussion at the United Nations and in other forums. Attempts to limit the arms race (initially between the USA and the USSR and since 1992 between the USA and Russia) have included the Strategic Arms Limitation Talks (SALT) of the 1970s and the Strategic Arms Reduction Talks (START) of the 1980s–90s.

before 1914 The enormous cost in lives and materials of World War I provided a considerable stimulus to efforts to reduce the arms race which had played a crucial role before 1914. International principles were laid down in the covenant of the League of Nations to that end, attempts were made by the League to secure a limitation on armaments, and limited disarmament treaties were made between some states (for example by Britain, the USA, and Japan on naval forces in 1930). The rise of the fascist dictatorships in Europe and the aggressive role of Japan in Asia effectively destroyed further attempts at general disarmament and the international situation steadily deteriorated, culminating in the outbreak of war in 1939.

after 1945 At the conclusion of World War II the world was confronted with the problem of controlling nuclear weapons and the related question of disarmament again came to the fore. The situation was made more serious by the increasingly sophisticated means of delivery, especially by nuclear submarines, and by other technological advances, such as satellites. The main problem was the lack of mutual trust between the Soviet bloc and the Western allies and, after the failure to limit armaments in the early post-war period through the establishment at the United Nations of a Conventional Arms Commission and an Atomic Energy Commission, attempts were made to impose unilateral disarmament on the states defeated in 1945.

the Cold War As the Cold War developed, attempts to impose unilateral disarmament were abandoned and the Soviet Union and the Western allies assisted in the rearming of the former enemy countries. In 1952 the two UN Commissions were merged into a new Disarmament Commission, but deadlock continued throughout most of the 1950s, with particular difficulty arising over the creation of reliable and mutually acceptable systems of inspection to enforce any agreements that might be reached. In 1958, however, it was agreed that it was possible to detect and identify certain types of nuclear explosions and this made possible the partial nuclear test-ban treaty signed by the USA, the USSR, and the UK in 1963.

In the meantime, in 1959 the first of a series of treaties declaring nuclear-free zones of the world was signed. This first treaty banned nuclear weapons from Antarctica and was signed by 12 nations, including the USA, the USSR, the UK, and France. This was followed in 1966 by a treaty signed by 21 Latin American states banning nuclear weapons from Latin America and in 1967 by a treaty signed by the USA, the USSR, and the UK banning nuclear weapons from outer space. Also in 1967 a nuclear non-proliferation treaty was signed by 59 states, including the 3 principal nuclear powers. By mid-1976 this had been signed by 100 states.

Further progress was made in the 1970s with an agreement in 1972 between the USA and the USSR to limit their antiballistic missile systems and in 1974 a limit on underground nuclear tests was agreed. A further agreement on underground tests allowing for the inspection of sites was signed by the USA and the USSR in 1976. These agreements between the USA and the USSR arose out of the continuing Strategic Arms Limitation Talks (SALT), which began in the early 1970s.

conventional armaments The agreements on nuclear weapons were facilitated by the fear of nuclear war, a desire to limit military expenditure, and by technological developments, but the control of conventional armaments has proved more difficult, although some progress has been made. Many years of discussion resulted in the holding of a three-stage European Security Conference between 1973 and 1975. The final stage in September 1975, in which 35 countries (the USA, the USSR, Canada, and all European countries except Albania) took part, reached agreement on a wide range of matters, including agreements to respect each other's sovereignty and frontiers, to refrain from intervention in each other's internal affairs, and to respect human rights and the right of self-determination. Apart from a general agreement to refrain from the threat of or use of force as a means of settling disputes, and to give prior notice of and exchange observers at manoeuvres, no specific agreement on disarmament was reached.

Following a recommendation of the UN General Assembly, the Conference on Disarmament (CD) was set up in 1978. Its objective is to promote the attainment of general and complete disarmament under effective international control. It held its first meeting in 1979, building on the 1963 Test Ban Treaty, the 1970 Non-proliferation Treaty, the 1972 Seabed Arms Control Treaty, and the 1972 Biological and Toxin Weapons Convention. In 1992 it introduced its own Chemical Weapons Convention, and is now the world's principal multilateral disarmament negotiating forum. It is based in Geneva.

Military terms

admiral highest-ranking naval officer.

aerial reconnaissance technique used primarily for the recording and interpretation of archaeological sites from the air, though at times it can also be useful in discovering new sites.

anti-submarine warfare all methods used to deter, attack, and destroy enemy submarines: missiles, torpedoes, depth charges, bombs, and direct-fire weapons from ships, other submarines, or aircraft.

Frigates are the ships most commonly used to engage submarines in general. Submarines carrying nuclear missiles are tracked and attacked with 'hunter-killer', or attack, submarines, usually nuclear-powered.

appeasement historically, the conciliatory policy adopted by the British government, in particular under Neville Chamberlain, towards the Nazi and Fascist dictators in Europe in the 1930s in an effort to maintain peace. It was strongly opposed by Winston Churchill, but the Munich Agreement of 1938 was almost universally hailed as its justification. Appeasement ended when Germany occupied Bohemia–Moravia in March 1939.

arms trade sale of weapons from a manufacturing country to another nation. Nearly 56% of the world's arms exports end up in Third World countries. Iraq, for instance, was armed in the years leading up to the 1991 Gulf War mainly by the USSR but also by France, Brazil, and South Africa.

artillery collective term for military firearms too heavy to be carried. Artillery can be mounted on tracks, wheels, ships, or aeroplanes and includes cannons and rocket launchers.

AWACS (acronym for **Airborne Warning And Control System**) surveillance system that

Armed Forces: Top 60 Countries

Source: US Arms Control and Disarmament Agency

(N/A = not available.)

(1995)

Rank	Country	Rate per 1,000 members of population	Rank	Country	Rate per 1,000 members of population	Rank	Country	Rate per 1,000 members of population
1	Korea, North	44.3	22	Cyprus	13.6	42	Portugal	7.9
2	Israel	34.9	23	Turkey	13.1	43	Uruguay	7.8
3	Jordan	27.3	24	Serbia and Montenegro	12.3	44	Macedonia, Former	
4	São Tomé and Principe	N/A	25	Croatia	12.1		Yugoslav Republic of	7.6
5	Syria	21.2	26	Azerbaijan	11.4	45	Italy	7.6
6	United Arab Emirates	20.5	27	Belarus	11.1	46	Vietnam	7.6
7	Greece	20.3	28	Kuwait	11.0	47	Chile	7.2
8	China (Taiwan)	20.0	29	Laos	10.3	48	Poland	7.2
9	Djibouti	19.0	30	Bulgaria	10.0	49	Myanmar	7.1
10	Iraq	18.9	31	Slovakia	9.7	50	Hungary	7.1
11	Qatar	18.7	32	Romania	9.5	51	Egypt	6.9
12	Singapore	18.0	33	Russia	9.4	52	Iran	6.8
13	Bosnia-Herzegovina	18.0	34	Saudi Arabia	9.3	53	Morocco	6.7
14	Armenia	17.3	35	Ukraine	9.3	54	Czech Republic	6.6
15	Brunei	17.1	36	Norway	8.7	55	Cuba	6.4
16	Oman	17.1	37	France	8.7	56	Finland	6.3
17	Albania	16.2	38	Mongolia	8.6	57	Malaysia	6.2
18	Lebanon	14.9	39	Cambodia	8.5	58	Guinea-Bissau	6.2
19	Korea, South	14.6	40	Gabon	8.2	59	USA	6.2
20	Libya	14.5	41	Angola	8.1	60	Sri Lanka	6.0
21	Bahrain	13.9						

incorporates a long-range surveillance and detection radar mounted on a Boeing E-3 sentry aircraft. It was used with great success in the 1991 Gulf War.

battalion or **unit** basic personnel unit in the military system, usually consisting of four or five companies. A battalion is commanded by a lieutenant colonel. Several battalions form a brigade.

biological warfare the use of living organisms, or of infectious material derived from them, to bring about death or disease in humans, animals, or plants. At least ten countries have this capability.

brigade military formation consisting of a minimum of two battalions, but more usually three or more, as well as supporting arms. There are typically about 5,000 soldiers in a brigade, which is commanded by a brigadier. Two or more brigades form a division.

carrier warfare naval warfare involving aircraft carriers. Carrier warfare was conducted during World War II in the battle of the Coral Sea in May 1942, which stopped the Japanese advance in the South Pacific, and in the battle of Midway Islands in June 1942, which weakened the Japanese navy through the loss of four aircraft carriers. The US Navy deployed six aircraft carriers during the Gulf War 1991.

Central Command military strike force consisting of units from the US army, navy, and air force, which operates in the Middle East and North Africa. Its headquarters are in Fort McDill, Florida. It was established in 1979, following the Iranian hostage crisis and the Soviet invasion of Afghanistan, and was known as the Rapid Deployment Force until 1983. It commanded coalition forces in the Gulf War in 1991.

chemical warfare use in war of gaseous, liquid, or solid substances intended to have a toxic effect on humans, animals, or plants. Together with biological warfare, it was banned by the Geneva Protocol in 1925, and the United Nations in 1989 also voted for a ban. In June 1990, the USA and USSR agreed bilaterally to reduce their stockpile to 5,000 tonnes each by 2002. The USA began replacing its stocks with new nerve-gas binary weapons. In 1993, over 120 nations, including the USA and Russia, signed a treaty outlawing the manufacture, stockpiling, and use of chemical weapons. However, it was not until 1997 that the Russian parliament ratified the treaty.

civil defence or **civil protection,** organized activities by the civilian population of a state to mitigate the effects of enemy attack.

civil war war between rival groups within the same country.

COIN (acronym for **counter insurgency**) the suppression by a state's armed forces of uprisings against the state. Also called internal security (IS) operations of counter-revolutionary warfare (CRW).

colours, military flags or standards carried by military regiments, so called because of the various combinations of colours employed to distinguish one country or one regiment from another.

commando member of a specially trained, highly mobile military unit. The term originated in South Africa in the 19th century, where it referred to Boer military reprisal raids against Africans and, in the South African Wars, against the British. Commando units have often carried out operations behind enemy lines.

company in the army, a subunit of a battalion. It consists of about 120 soldiers, and is commanded by a major in the British army, a captain in the US army. Four or five companies make a battalion.

conscription legislation for all able-bodied male citizens (and female in some countries, such as Israel) to serve with the armed forces. It originated in France in 1792, and in the 19th and 20th centuries became the established practice in almost all European states. Modern conscription systems often permit alternative national service for conscientious objectors.

corps military formation consisting of two to five divisions. Its strength is between 50,000 and 120,000 people. All branches of the army are represented. A corps is commanded by a lieutenant general or, in the USA, a three-star general. Two or more corps form an army group.

Delta Force US antiguerrilla force, based at Fort Bragg, North Carolina, and modelled on the British Special Air Service.

division military formation consisting of two or more brigades. A major general at divisional headquarters commands the brigades and also additional artillery, engineers, attack helicopters, and other logistic support. There are 10,000 or more soldiers in a division. Two or more divisions form a corps.

early warning in war, advance notice of incoming attack, often associated with nuclear attack. There are early-warning radar systems in the UK (Fylingdales), Alaska, and Greenland. **Airborne early warning** (AEW) is provided by reconnaissance planes; NATO has such a system.

field marshal the highest rank in many European armies. A British field marshal is equivalent to a US general (of the army).

fifth column group within a country secretly aiding an enemy attacking from without. The term originated in 1936 during the Spanish Civil War, when General Mola boasted that Franco supporters were attacking Madrid with four columns and that they had a 'fifth column' inside the city.

gas warfare military use of gas to produce a toxic effect on the human body. See chemical warfare.

Chlorine gas

■ Fritz Haber developed chlorine gas for use by the Germans in World War I. Unable to live with this, his wife committed suicide in 1915.

---

general senior military rank, the ascending grades being major general, lieutenant general, and general. The US rank of general of the army is equivalent to the British field marshal.

Gestapo (contraction of **Geheime Staatspolizei**) Nazi Germany's secret police, formed 1933, and under the direction of Heinrich Himmler from 1934.

GI (abbreviation for **government issue**), hence (in the USA) a common soldier.

guerrilla (Spanish 'little war') irregular soldier fighting in a small, unofficial unit, typically against an established or occupying power, and engaging in sabotage, ambush, and the like, rather than pitched battles against an opposing army. Guerrilla tactics have been used both by resistance armies in wartime (for example, the Vietnam War) and in peacetime by national liberation groups and militant political extremists (for example, the Tamil Tigers).

home front the organized sectors of domestic activity in wartime, mainly associated with

World Wars I and II. Features of the UK home front in World War II included the organization of the black-out, evacuation, air-raid shelters, the Home Guard, rationing, and distribution of gas masks. With many men on active military service, women were called upon to carry out jobs previously undertaken only by men.

kamikaze (Japanese 'wind of the gods') pilots of the Japanese air force in World War II who deliberately crash-dived their planes, loaded with bombs, usually on to ships of the US Navy.

Luftwaffe German air force used both in World War I and (as reorganized by the Nazi leader Hermann Goering in 1933) in World War II. The Luftwaffe also covered anti-aircraft defence and the launching of the flying bombs V1 and V2.

major-general after the English Civil War, one of the officers appointed by Oliver Cromwell 1655 to oversee the 12 military districts into which England had been divided. Their powers included organizing the militia, local government, and the collection of some taxes.

marines fighting force that operates both on land and at sea. The **US Marine Corps** (1775) is constituted as an arm of the US Navy. It is made up of infantry and air support units trained and equipped for amphibious landings under fire.

marines US marines in the S Pacific in 1943. Because there were so many islands to invade, marines played a vital role in the capture of the Pacific Islands from the Japanese during World War II. The dogs seen here were used for scouting and for running messages. *Library of Congress*

Medals and Decorations

Armada medal	Issued by Elizabeth I following the defeat of the Armada; the first English commemorative medal
George Cross	1940 highest British civilian award for bravery, the medallion in the centre of the cross depicting St George and the Dragon
Iron Cross	German, instituted 1813 by Frederick William III and granted to civil as well as military personnel
Légion d'honneur	French, established 1802 and is divided into five ranks: knights of the grand cross, grand officers, commanders, officers, and knights
Medal of Honor	highest award given in the USA for the navy (1861) and army (1862) for gallantry in action
Medal for Merit	US civilian, 1942; recognizes exceptional conduct in the performance of outstanding service
Ordre National du Mérite	French, civil and military, 1963, replacing earlier merit awards
Order of Merit	British order instituted 1902 and limited in number to 24 people
Order of the Purple Heart	US military, established by Washington 1782, when it was of purple cloth (now made of bronze and enamel); revived by Hoover 1932, when it was issued to those wounded in action from World War I onwards
Pour le Mérite	German, instituted by Frederick the Great, military in 1740, and since 1842 for science and art
Presidential Medal of Freedom	USA, highest peacetime civilian award since 1963
Gold Star Medal	former Soviet Union, civilian and military
Victoria Cross	British military, 1856
Waterloo Medal	British, established 1816; until the 19th century medals were awarded only to officers; this was the first to be issued to all ranks.

marshal highest military rank in the British Royal Air Force.

midshipman trainee naval officer.

military law articles or regulations that apply to members of the armed forces of most western nations in addition to civil law.

Military Order European orders of warrior monks who fought to defend and expand Christendom in the context of the Crusades. Their heyday was from the mid-12th century to 1291 in the Holy Land, but they survived and flourished in Spain and on the German frontiers until the end of the Middle Ages. The Knights Hospitaller became the rulers of Rhodes (until 1480) and Malta (until 1798) and maintained religious warfare against the Ottoman Turks.

ninja (Japanese, from ninjutsu 'the art of invisibility') member of a body of trained assassins in feudal Japan, whose martial-arts skills were greatly feared. Popular legend had it that they were able to make themselves invisible.

nuclear warfare war involving the use of nuclear weapons. Nuclear-weapons research began in Britain in 1940, but was transferred to the USA after it entered World War II. The research programme, known as the Manhattan Project, was directed by J Robert Oppenheimer. The worldwide total of nuclear weapons in 1990 was about 50,000, and the number of countries possessing nuclear weapons stood officially at five – USA, USSR, UK, France, and China.

platoon in the army, the smallest infantry subunit. It contains 30–40 soldiers and is commanded by a lieutenant or second lieutenant. There are three or four platoons in a company.

prisoner of war (POW) person captured in war, who has fallen into the hands of, or surrendered to, an opponent. Such captives may be held in prisoner-of-war camps. The treatment of POWs is governed by the Geneva Convention.

Rapid Deployment Force former name (to 1983) of US Central Command, a military strike force.

rearmament re-equipping a country with new weapons and other military hardware. The Nazi dictator Adolf Hitler concentrated on rearmament in Germany after he achieved power in 1934.

prisoner of war German prisoners of war captured at the fall of Aachen in Oct 1944. According to the Geneva Conventions of 1929, a prisoner of war must be a combatant who takes orders from a commander, wears a recognized uniform, and fights according to the 'laws and customs of war'. *Library of Congress*

Red Army the army of the USSR until 1946; later known as the **Soviet Army.** It developed from the Red Guards, volunteers who carried out the Bolshevik revolution, and received its name because it fought under the red flag. The Chinese revolutionary army was also called the Red Army.

regiment military formation equivalent to a battalion in parts of the British army, and to a brigade in the armies of many other countries. In the British infantry, a regiment may include more than one battalion, and soldiers belong to the same regiment throughout their career.

Royal Air Force (RAF) the air force of Britain. The RAF was formed 1918 by the merger of the Royal Naval Air Service and the Royal Flying Corps.

Royal Marines British military force trained for amphibious warfare.

SAS abbreviation for **Special Air Service.**

scorched earth policy of burning and destroying everything that might be of use to an invading army, especially the crops in the fields. It was used to great effect in Russia in 1812 against the invasion of the French emperor Napoleon and again during World War II to hinder the advance of German forces in 1941.

sergeant in the medieval period, term for an ordinary soldier, commonly a cavalryman who was not a knight, but also used for infantry. A sergeant was also a tenant owing military service to a lord, but sergeanty tenure, not always military, was an inferior form of tenure. A sergeant might also be an officer with police duties.

Special Air Service (SAS), specialist British regiment recruited from regiments throughout the army. It has served in Malaysia, Oman, Yemen, the Falklands, Northern Ireland, and during the 1991 Gulf War, as well as against international urban guerrillas, as in the siege of the Iranian embassy in London 1980.

Strategic Defense Initiative (SDI) also called **Star Wars** attempt by the USA to develop a defence system against incoming nuclear missiles, based in part outside the Earth's atmosphere. It was announced by President Reagan in March 1983, and the research had by 1990 cost over $16.5 billion. In 1988, the Joint Chiefs of Staff announced that they expected to be able to intercept no more than 30% of incoming missiles.

Strategy and Tactics

War is generally divided into strategy, the planning and conduct of a war, and tactics, the deployment of forces in battle.

SALT abbreviation for Strategic Arms Limitation Talks, a series of US–Soviet negotiations 1969–79.

strategy, military the planning of warfare. **Grand strategy** requires both political and military input and designs the overall war effort at national level. Planning for a campaign at army-group level or above is **strategy** proper. **Operational strategy** involves military planning at corps, divisional, and brigade level. **Tactics** is the art of warfare at unit level and below; that is, the disposition of relatively small numbers of soldiers over relatively small distances.

unit another name for a battalion.

war crime offence (such as murder of a civilian or a prisoner of war) that contravenes the internationally accepted laws governing the conduct of wars, particularly the Hague Convention of 1907 and the Geneva Convention of 1949. A key principle of the law relating to such crimes is that obedience to the orders of a superior is no defence. In practice, prosecutions are generally brought by the victorious side.

warlord in China, any of the provincial leaders who took advantage of central government weakness, after the death of the first president of republican China in 1912, to organize their own private armies and fiefdoms. They engaged in civil wars until the nationalist leader Jiang Jie Shi's (Chiang Kai-shek's) Northern Expedition against them in 1926, and they exerted power until the communists seized control under Mao Zedong in 1949.

SOCIETY

———— ✳ ————

Sociology is the systematic study of the origin and constitution of human **society** and the organization of people into communities or groups. In particular, sociology is concerned with social order and social change, social conflict, and social problems. By studying institutions such as the family, law, and the church, as well as concepts such as norm, role, culture, values, symbols, and ritual, sociology attempts to study people in their social environment according to certain underlying moral, philosophical, and political codes of behaviour.

Sociology arose in the 19th century in an attempt to understand the far-reaching changes in human society due to industrialization, urbanization, and the development of new types of political systems. Although its primary focus is still on contemporary society, it makes comparisons with pre-industrial societies and draws on such related disciplines as history, politics, economics, psychology, philosophy, and anthropology.

Since the 1970s, sociology has played an increasing role in the development of evaluation of government policies in such areas as health, education, and social welfare. Today, issues of class, ethnicity and race, gender, poverty, politics, aggression, marriage, education, communication, work, social change, urbanism, health, and social movements influence public policy.

Society and Sociology

birth rate the number of live births per thousand of the population over a period of time, usually a year (sometimes it is also expressed as a percentage). For example, a birth rate of 20 per thousand (or 2%) would mean that 20 babies were being born per thousand of the population. It is sometimes called **crude birth rate** because it takes in the whole population, including men and women who are too old to bear children.

bourgeoisie (French 'the freemen of a borough') the social class above the workers and peasants, and below the nobility; the middle class. 'Bourgeoisie' (and **bourgeois**) has also acquired a contemptuous sense, implying commonplace, philistine respectability. By socialists it is applied to the whole propertied class, as distinct from the proletariat.

capital punishment punishment by death. Capital punishment is retained in 92 countries and terri-

Birth and Death Rates Worldwide

Source: UNICEF

(Birth rate data are for live births; selected countries.)

1996

Region/country	Birth rate (per thousand)	Death rate (per thousand)	Region/country	Birth rate (per thousand)	Death rate (per thousand)
Africa			*Europe*		
Average	40	15	Greece	10	10
Algeria	30	6	Hungary	11	15
Angola	49	19	Russia	10	14
Burundi	44	18	Sweden	12	11
Congo, Democratic Republic of	46	14	UK	12	11
Côte d'Ivoire	38	14			
Ethiopia	48	17	*Latin America*		
Ghana	39	11	Average	23	6
Kenya	37	11	Argentina	20	8
Lesotho	36	11	Bolivia	34	9
Nigeria	43	14	Brazil	20	7
Sudan	34	12	Colombia	24	6
			Cuba	14	7
Asia			Mexico	25	5
Average	28	7	Venezuela	26	5
Afghanistan	52	21			
Bangladesh	27	10	*North America*		
China	17	7	Average	14	8
India	26	9	Canada	13	7
Indonesia	24	8	USA	14	9
Iran	35	6			
Iraq	37	9	*Oceania*		
Japan	10	8	Average	27	7
Korea, North	21	6	Australia	14	7
Korea, South	15	6	New Zealand	16	8
Pakistan	37	8	Papua New Guinea	33	10
Philippines	29	6			
			World		
Europe			Average	23	9
Average	11	12	More developed regions	12	9
France	12	9	Less developed regions	26	9
Germany	9	11	Least developed regions	40	14

tories (1990), including the USA (38 states), China, and Islamic countries. It was abolished in the UK in 1965 for all crimes except treason. Methods of execution include electrocution, lethal gas, hanging, shooting, lethal injection, garrotting, and decapitation.

census official count of the population of a country, originally for military call-up and taxation, later for assessment of social trends as other information regarding age, sex, and occupation of each individual was included. They may become unnecessary as computerized databanks are developed. The data collected are used by government departments in planning for the future in such areas as health, education, transport, and housing.

city generally, a large and important town. In the Middle East and ancient Europe, and in the

Countries that have Abolished the Death Penalty for all Crimes

Source: Amnesty International

(N/A = not available.)

Country	Date of abolition	Date of last execution	Country	Date of abolition	Date of last execution
Andorra	1990	1943	Marshall Islands	N/A[4]	
Angola	1992	N/A	Mauritius	1995	1987
Australia	1985	1967	Micronesia	N/A[4]	
Austria	1968	1950	Moldova	1995	N/A
Belgium	1996	1950	Monaco	1962	1847
Cambodia	1989	N/A	Mozambique	1990	1986
Cape Verde	1981	1835	Namibia	1990	1988[3]
Colombia	1910	1909	Netherlands, the	1982	1952
Costa Rica	1877	N/A	New Zealand	1989	1957
Croatia	1990	N/A	Nicaragua	1979	1930
Czech Republic	1990[1]	N/A	Norway	1979	1948
Denmark	1978	1950	Palau	N/A	N/A
Dominican Republic	1966	N/A	Panama	N/A	1903[3]
Ecuador	1906	N/A	Portugal	1976	1849[3]
Finland	1972	1944	Romania	1989	1989
France	1981	1977	San Marino	1865	1468[3]
Germany	1949/1987[2]	1949[2]	São Tomé and Príncipe	1990[4]	
Greece	1993	1972	Slovak Republic	1990[1]	N/A
Guinea-Bissau	1993	1986[3]	Slovenia	1989	N/A
Haiti	1987	1972[3]	Solomon Islands	N/A[4]	
Honduras	1956	1940	Spain	1995	1975
Hungary	1990	1988	Sweden	1972	1910
Iceland	1928	1830	Switzerland	1992	1944
Ireland, Republic of	1990	1954	Tuvalu	N/A[4]	
Italy	1994	1947	UK	1965[5]	1964
Kiribati	N/A[4]		Uruguay	1907	N/A
Liechtenstein	1987	1785	Vanuatu	N/A[4]	
Luxembourg	1979	1949	Vatican City State	1969	N/A
Macedonia, Former Yugoslav			Venezuela	1863	N/A
Republic of	N/A	N/A			

[1] The death penalty was abolished in the Czech and Slovak Federal Republic in 1990. On 1 January 1993 the Czech and Slovak Federal Republic divided into two states, the Czech Republic and the Slovak Republic. The last execution in the Czech and Slovak Federal Republic was in 1988.

[2] The death penalty was abolished in the Federal Republic of Germany (FRG) in 1949 and in the German Democratic Republic (GDR) in 1987. The last execution in the FRG was in 1949; the date of the last execution in the GDR is not known. The FRG and the GDR were unified in October 1990.

[3] Date of last known execution.

[4] No executions since independence.

[5] The death penalty was abolished for all crimes except treason.

Largest Cities in the World 1950–2015

Source: UN Population Division

Rank	City	Population (millions)	Rank	City	Population (millions)
1950			*2000*		
1	New York (NY), USA	12.30	1	Tokyo, Japan	27.90
2	London, UK	8.70	2	Bombay, India	18.10
3	Tokyo, Japan	6.90	3	São Paulo, Brazil	17.80
4=	Paris, France	5.40	4	Shanghai, China	17.20
4=	Moscow, Russia	5.40	5	New York (NY), USA	16.60
6=	Shanghai, China	5.30	6	Mexico City, Mexico	16.40
6=	Essen, Germany	5.30	7	Beijing, China	14.20
8	Buenos Aires, Argentina	5.00	8	Jakarta, Indonesia	14.10
9	Chicago (IL), USA	4.90	9	Lagos, Nigeria	13.50
10	Calcutta, India	4.40	10	Los Angeles (CA), USA	13.10
1980			*2010*		
1	Tokyo, Japan	21.90	1	Tokyo, Japan	28.70
2	New York (NY), USA	15.60	2	Bombay, India	24.30
3	Mexico City, Mexico	13.90	3	Shanghai, China	21.50
4	São Paulo, Brazil	12.10	4	Lagos, Nigeria	20.80
5	Shanghai, China	11.70	5	São Paulo, Brazil	20.10
6	Osaka, Japan	10.00	6	Jakarta, Indonesia	19.20
7	Buenos Aires, Argentina	9.90	7	Mexico City, Mexico	18.20
8	Los Angeles (CA), USA	9.50	8	Beijing, China	17.80
9=	Calcutta, India	9.00	9	Karachi, Pakistan	17.60
9=	Beijing, China	9.00	10	New York (NY), USA	17.30
1995			*2015*		
1	Tokyo, Japan	26.84	1	Tokyo, Japan	28.70
2	São Paulo, Brazil	16.42	2	Bombay, India	27.40
3	New York (NY), USA	16.33	3	Lagos, Nigeria	24.40
4	Mexico City, Mexico	15.64	4	Shanghai, China	23.40
5	Bombay, India	15.09	5	Jakarta, Indonesia	21.20
6	Shanghai, China	15.08	6	São Paulo, Brazil	20.80
7	Los Angeles (CA), USA	12.41	7	Karachi, Pakistan	20.60
8	Beijing, China	12.36	8	Beijing, China	19.40
9	Calcutta, India	11.67	9	Dhaka, Bangladesh	19.00
10	Seoul, South Korea	11.64	10	Mexico City, Mexico	18.80

ancient civilizations of Mexico and Peru, cities were states in themselves. In the early Middle Ages, European cities were usually those towns that were episcopal sees (seats of bishops).

clan social grouping based on kinship. Some traditional societies are organized by clans, which are either matrilineal or patrilineal, and whose members must marry into another clan in order to avoid in-breeding.

class main grouping of social stratification in industrial societies, based primarily on economic and occupational factors, but also referring to people's style of living or sense of group identity.

commune group of people or families living together, sharing resources and responsibilities. There have been various kinds of commune through the ages, including a body of burghers or burgesses in medieval times, a religious community in America, and a communal division in communist China.

community in the social sciences, the sense of identity, purpose, and companionship that comes from belonging to a particular place, organization, or social group. The concept dominated sociological thinking in the first half of the 20th century, and inspired the academic discipline of **community studies.**

conspicuous consumption selection and purchase of goods for their social rather than their inherent value. These might include items with an obviously expensive brand-name tag. The term was coined by US economist Thorsten Veblen.

conurbation or **metropolitan area** large continuous built-up area formed by the joining together of several urban settlements. Conurbations are often formed as a result of urban sprawl. Typically, they have populations in excess of 1 million and some are many times that size; for example, the Osaka–Kobe conurbation in Japan, which contains over 16 million people.

counterurbanization movement of people and employment away from urban areas to smaller towns and villages in rural locations. Push factors within urban regions may be responsible – for example, congestion, high land prices, and population pressure – together with pull factors such as the perceived environmental quality of the countryside and improvements in transport systems.

crime see **crime** feature on page 400.

culture way of life of a particular society or group of people, including patterns of thought, beliefs, behaviour, customs, traditions, rituals, dress, and language, as well as art, music, and literature. Archaeologists use the word to mean the surviving objects or artefacts that provide evidence of a social grouping.

demographic transition any change in birth and death rates; over time, these generally shift from a situation where both are high to a situation where both are low. This may be caused by a variety of social factors (among them education and the changing role of women) and economic factors (such as higher standard of living and improved diet). The **demographic transition model** suggests that it happens in four stages:
1) high birth rate, fluctuating but high death rate;
2) birth rate stays high, death rate starts to fall, giving maximum population growth;
3) birth rate starts to fall, death rate continues falling;
4) birth rate is low, death rate is low.

demography see **demography** feature on page 402.

depressed area region with substandard economic performance, perhaps as a result of a change in industrial structure, such as a decline in manufacturing industry. Depressed areas may be characterized by high unemployment, low-quality housing, and poor educational standards. Government aid may be needed to reverse such decline.

family group of people related to each other by blood or by marriage. Families are usually described as either **extended** (a large group of relations living together or in close contact with each other) or **nuclear** (a family consisting of two parents and their children).

functionalism view of society as a system made up of a number of interrelated parts, all interacting on the basis of a common value system or consensus about basic values and common goals. Every social custom and institution is seen as having a function in ensuring that society works efficiently; deviance and crime are seen as forms of social sickness.

gentrification the movement of higher social or economic groups into an area after it has been renovated and restored. This may result in the outmigration of the people who previously occupied the area. Often the classification of an area as a conservation area encourages gentrification. It is one strategy available to planners in urban renewal schemes within the inner city.

ghetto any deprived area occupied by a minority group, whether voluntarily or not. Originally a ghetto was the area of a town where Jews were compelled to live, decreed by a law enforced by papal bull 1555. The term came into use 1516 when the Jews of Venice were expelled to an island within the city which contained an iron foundry. Ghettos were abolished, except in Eastern Europe, in the 19th century, but the concept and practice were revived by the Germans and Italians 1940–45.

health service government provision of medical care on a national scale.

government see **government** feature on page 403.

immigration and emigration movement of people from one country to another. Immigration is movement to a country; emigration is movement from a country. Immigration or emigration on a large scale is often for economic reasons or because of religious, political, or social persecution (which may create refugees), and often prompts restrictive legislation by individual countries. The USA has received immigrants on a larger scale than any other country, more than 50 million during its history.

Crime

A crime is any behaviour or action that is punishable by criminal law. It is a public, as opposed to a moral, wrong; an offence committed against (and hence punishable by) the state or the community at large. Many crimes are immoral, but not all actions considered immoral are illegal.

what constitutes a crime The laws of each country specify which actions or omissions are criminal. These include serious moral wrongs and offences against the person, such as murder and rape; offences against the state, such as treason or tax evasion (which affect state security and social order); wrongs perpetrated against the community, such as littering; and offences against property, such as theft and the handling of stolen goods.

Because crime is socially determined, the definition of what constitutes a crime may vary geographically and over time. Thus, an action may be considered a crime in one society but not in another; for example, drinking alcohol is not generally prohibited in the West, but is a criminal offence in many Islamic countries. Certain categories of crime, however, such as violent crime and theft, are recognized almost universally.

penalties Crime is dealt with in most societies by the judicial system, comprising the police, the courts, and so on. These may impose penalties ranging from a fine to imprisonment to, in some instances, death, depending upon the severity of the offence and the penalty laid down by the country where the offence was committed. Most

European countries have now abolished the death penalty, though it is still retained by a number of African and Asian countries as well as some US states. Non-capital and minor offences are also punished in some countries, such as Britain and the USA, by the granting of suspended sentences, where an offender's prison sentence is waived on condition that they do not reoffend during a set period of time. Other common elements in sentencing in Britain and the USA include the provision of probation periods, where offenders are released into the community, but are regularly supervised by probation officers; and community service, where offenders are required, in lieu of a prison sentence, to perform a certain amount of unpaid work for the good of the community.

World Murder Rates (Selected Countries)

Source: International Crime Statistics (Interpol) 1994

Country	Population[1]	Total offences	Country	Population[1]	Total offences
Andorra	63,000	1	Estonia	1,500,000	365
Angola	10,700,000	362	Ethiopia	60,500,000	8,757
Argentina	33,000,000	93	Fiji Islands	784,000	90
Armenia	3,750,500	201	Finland	5,000,000	32
Austria	8,000,000	198	France	58,000,000	2,696
Azerbaijan	7,500,000	605	Gambia	1,100,000	4
Bahrain	560,000	10	Georgia	5,500,000	578
Bangladesh	117,000,000	2,222	Germany	81,300,000	3,751
Barbados	263,500	18	Greece	10,300,000	264
Belgium	1,000,000	315	Grenada	90,000	7
Brunei	260,000	4	Guyana	761,000	151
Bulgaria	8,500,000	499	Honduras	4,500,000	2,861
Cameroon	12,000,000	17	Hong Kong	6,100,000	98
Canada	29,500,000	1,514	Hungary	10,300,000	439
Chile	14,000,000	1,545	Indonesia	192,000,000	1,457
China	1,300,000,000	2,553	Ireland, Republic of	3,500,000	25
Croatia	4,800,000	354	Israel	5,500,000	114
Cyprus	726,000	12	Italy	57,000,000	2,691
Denmark	5,200,000	255	Jamaica	2,500,000	692
Ecuador	11,500,000	1,199	Japan	125,000,000	1,279

Crime (continued)

theories of punishment There are a number of different theories of punishment, ranging from those which place most emphasis upon the aspect of retribution, where the criminal's punishment is seen as an end in itself (though the punishment's severity may still be linked to that of the crime), to theories which stress the deterrent and reformative aspects of punishment. However, the theory that punishment is intended merely as expiation is not subscribed to by most modern penologists, and in practice the different theories are frequently combined. The most positive theory of penology is aimed at the reform or rehabilitation of the criminal, and stresses the importance of training and educating criminals in preparation for their return to the community as law-abiding citizens.

The most optimistic criminologists are forced to admit, however, that modern methods have so far failed to influence persistent offenders.

organized crime In the 20th century a number of different forms of organized crime have developed. Offences committed by organized crime groups include fraud, kidnapping, and the extraction of 'protection money', and may be politically or simply financially motivated. In countries such as the USA, Russia, and China, the main source of income for organized crime groups is the trade in 'contraband' products such as drugs and prostitution. Chinese triads, in particular, play an important role in drug-smuggling to Europe, and in Colombia and other South American countries organized drug trafficking

is a major social problem. Other forms of organized crime include 'white-collar' crime, which involves offences committed by business people or politicians either for personal, corporate, or political gain; and international terrorism, which may take the form of hijacking, political kidnapping and assassination, or bombing campaigns directed against civilian or military targets. In the 1990s organized crime has also developed in new directions following the widespread popularity of the computer Internet: criminals have not only begun to use the Internet for communications purposes, but have also found that it provides new possibilities for organized fraud and the supply of illegal pornography.

World Murder Rates (Selected Countries) (continued)

Country	Population[1]	Total offences	Country	Population[1]	Total offences
Kiribati	77,800	4	Poland	38,500,000	1,212
Kuwait	1,600,000	27	Portugal	9,000,000	415
Latvia	2,500,000	375	Qatar	600,000	11
Lebanon	5,000,000	216	Romania	23,000,000	749
Libya	4,750,000	63	Russia	148,000,000	32,286
Luxembourg	400,000	6	Rwanda	8,000,000	1,000,000
Macedonia, Former Yugoslav			Samoa	50,000	4
Republic of	1,940,000	75	Saudi Arabia	17,000,000	150
Madagascar	12,000,000	73	Seychelles	74,000	2
Malaysia	19,800,000	418	Singapore	2,900,000	51
Malta	370,000	11	Slovak Republic	5,300,000	129
Mauritius	1,120,000	36	Slovenia	1,975,000	96
Monaco	30,000	0	Spain	39,500,000	1,015
Mongolia	2,250,000	429	Swaziland	900,000	799
Namibia	1,200,000	869	Sweden	8,800,000	837
Nepal	19,700,000	491	Switzerland	7,000,000	161
New Zealand	3,500,000	139	Thailand	58,340,000	4,499
Nicaragua	4,400,000	1,128	Trinidad and Tobago	1,347,000	157
Oman	2,000,000	16	Ukraine	52,200,000	4,571
Panama	2,300,000	323	USA	260,300,000	23,310
Paraguay	4,700,000	735	Venezuela	21,380,000	4,733
			Zimbabwe	11,000,000	549

[1] Figures have been rounded up or down.

Demography

Demography is the study of the size, structure, dispersement, and development of human populations – the number of people living in a specific area or region, such as a town or country, at any one time. Demography aims to establish reliable statistics on such factors as birth and death rates, marriages and divorces, life expectancy, and migration. Demography is significant in the social sciences as the basis for industry and for government planning in such areas as education, housing, welfare, transport, and taxation. Demographic changes are important for many businesses. For example, the forecast rise in the number of people aged 75+ over the next 20 years will lead to an expansion of demand for accommodation for the elderly.

Information on population is obtained in a number of ways, such as through the registration of births and deaths. These figures are known as 'vital statistics'. However, more detailed information on population distribution, density, and change is necessary to enable governments to plan for education, health, housing, and transport on local and national levels. This information is usually obtained from censuses (population counts), which provide data on sex, age, occupation, and nationality.

The word 'census' comes from a Latin word meaning to count or assess, and the censuses conducted by the Romans were mainly for purposes of tax and the recruitment of armies. Nowadays, censuses are carried out by most countries on a regular basis; in the USA a census has been taken every ten years since 1790. In Europe the first national censuses were taken in 1800 and 1801 and provided population statistics for Ireland, Italy, Spain, and the UK, and for the cities of Berlin, London, Paris, and Vienna. Most countries in the world have taken at least one census within the last decade.

Serious population studies date from the end of the 18th century, and demography as a discipline is considered to have begun with the development by the British economist Thomas Malthus of his theory of population growth, and the publication in 1798 of his pamphlet 'Essay on the Principle of Population'. The growth of the behavioural sciences in the 20th century, and the development of computer sciences, have stimulated and aided demographic research.

As the 21st century approaches, the key issues for demographers, economists, and governments are the limiting and stabilization of growth in the world population.

urban population growth The increasing industrialization of Europe and North America in the 19th and 20th centuries, together with the mechanization of agriculture, has caused large numbers of people to move from rural areas to the ever-expanding cities in search of work. This migration of people to urban areas has created vast changes in population distribution and population density. At the beginning of the 19th century, only 20% of the population of England lived in cities. Today, the majority of Western populations live in cities and only about 5% in rural areas.

shifting population patterns Improvements in living standards, education, health care, and social welfare have resulted in a fall in birth rate and a fall in death rate, particularly infant mortality rate. One of the most significant trends in modern industrialized nations has been the decline in fertility, which is explained in socioeconomic terms by the theory of demographic transition. The combined effect of the decrease in fertility and the decline in mortality rates has resulted in a state of population equilibrium similar to that existing in pre-industrialized populations.

increased global population In the less industrialized nations of Africa, Asia, and South America, a decline in death rates did not come about until the mid-20th century and, since this was not matched by a corresponding decrease in birth rates, the overall population of low-income countries has increased rapidly in the latter part of the 20th century. Since the poorer nations also tend to be the most highly populated to begin with, this has caused the global population to soar. Between 1990 and 1995 world population increased by 1.7% a year, and the elderly population by 2.7%. In mid-1994 world population was 5.7 billion and increasing at the rate of 86 million per year. According to a UN low variant projection, the world population will be at least 7.9 billion by 2050, 9.8 billion by a mid-range projection, or 13 billion by high-range forecasts.

population control By 1990, the population of the developed nations was 1.2 billion people, compared to 4.1 billion people in the developing countries. In September 1994 a UN international conference on population and development was attended by politicians from 150 countries. It emphasized the importance of improving the position of women for effective population control, and of improving sex education and contraception, particularly in the less industrialized countries. Since the early 1950s, India has taken the lead among developing nations to control its population growth with government-sponsored family planning programmes. China, with its one-child family policy, is struggling to control the rising numbers of its huge population. The majority of developing nations now have governments that support some form of family planning programme.

Government

A government is any system whereby political authority is exercised. Modern systems of government distinguish between liberal democracies, totalitarian (one-party) states, and autocracies (authoritarian, relying on force rather than ideology). The Greek philosopher Aristotle was the first to attempt a systematic classification of governments. His main distinctions were between government by one person, by few, and by many (monarchy, oligarchy, and democracy), although the characteristics of each may vary between states and each may degenerate into tyranny (rule by an oppressive elite in the case of oligarchy or by the mob in the case of democracy).

types of government The French philosopher Montesquieu distinguished between **constitutional governments** – whether monarchies or republics – which operated under various legal and other constraints, and **despotism,** which was not

constrained in this way. Many of the words used (dictatorship, tyranny, totalitarian, democratic) have acquired negative or positive connotations that make it difficult to use them objectively.

The term **liberal democracy** was coined to distinguish Western types of democracy from the many other political systems that claimed to be democratic. Its principal characteristics are the existence of more than one political party, relatively open processes of government and political debate, and a separation of powers.

Totalitarian has been applied to both fascist and communist states and denotes a system where all power is centralized in the state, which in turn is controlled by a single party that derives its legitimacy from an exclusive ideology.

Autocracy describes a form of government that has emerged in a number of Third World countries, where state power is in the hands either of an individual or of the army;

normally ideology is not a central factor, individual freedoms tend to be suppressed where they may constitute a challenge to the authority of the ruling group, and there is a reliance upon force.

Other useful distinctions are between **federal** governments (where powers are dispersed among various regions which in certain respects are self-governing) and **unitary** governments (where powers are concentrated in a central authority); and between **presidential** (where the head of state is also the directly elected head of government, not part of the legislature) and **parliamentary** systems (where the government is drawn from an elected legislature that can dismiss it).

distribution In 1995, 73 of the world's 192 sovereign states were liberal democracies and 72 were emergent democracies, 13 had authoritarian nationalist regimes, 12 absolutist, 8 nationalistic-socialist, 7 military, 5 communist, and 2 Islamic-nationalist.

inner city the area in or near the central business district of a town or city. In many cities this is one of the older parts and may suffer from decay and neglect, leading to social problems.

kinship in anthropology, human relationship based on blood or marriage, and sanctified by law and custom. Kinship forms the basis for most human societies and for such social groupings as the family, clan, or tribe.

World Illiteracy Rates: Highest 25 Countries

Source: UNESCO
The percentages in this table are all estimates. Figures for 1995.

Rank	Country	Illiterates (%)	Rank	Country	Illiterates (%)	Rank	Country	Illiterates (%)
1	Niger	86.4	10	Guinea	64.1	19	Angola	59.0[1]
2	Burkina Faso	80.8	11	Benin	63.0	20	Bhutan	57.8
3	Nepal	72.5	12	Mauritania	62.3	21	Morocco	56.3
4	Mali	69.0	13	Pakistan	62.2	22	Haiti	55.0
5	Sierra Leone	68.6	14	Bangladesh	61.9	23	Madagascar	54.3
6	Afghanistan	68.5	15	Liberia	61.7	24	Sudan	53.9
7	Senegal	66.9	16	Gambia, the	61.4	25	Chad	51.9
8	Burundi	64.7	17=	Côte d'Ivoire	59.9			
9	Ethiopia	64.5	17=	Mozambique	59.9	[1] This is a 1985 estimate.		

life expectancy average lifespan that can be presumed of a person at birth. It depends on nutrition, disease control, environmental contaminants, war, stress, and living standards in general.

literacy ability to read and write. The level at which functional literacy is set rises as society becomes more complex, and it becomes increasingly difficult for an illiterate person to find work and cope with the other demands of everyday life.

marriage legally or culturally sanctioned union of one man and one woman (monogamy); one man and two or more women (polygamy); one woman

Life Expectancy Worldwide

Source: UN Population Fund

1995–2000

Region/ Country	Life expectancy at birth (years) Male	Female	Region/ Country	Life expectancy at birth (years) Male	Female	Region/ Country	Life expectancy at birth (years) Male	Female
Africa			**Europe**			**North America**		
Average	52.3	55.3	*Average*	68.3	77.0	*Average*	73.6	80.3
Algeria	67.5	70.3	Austria	73.7	80.1	Canada	76.1	81.8
Angola	44.9	48.1	Croatia	68.1	76.5	USA	73.4	80.1
Ethiopia	48.4	51.6	Czech Republic	69.8	76.0	**Oceania**		
Ghana	56.2	59.9	Estonia	63.9	75.0	*Average*	71.5	76.4
Kenya	52.3	55.7	Finland	73.0	80.1	Australia	75.4	81.2
Madagascar	57.0	60.0	France	74.6	82.9	Micronesia	67.2	70.9
Mauritius	68.3	75.0	Germany	73.4	79.9	New Zealand	74.7	79.7
Nigeria	50.8	54.0	Greece	75.5	80.6	Papua New Guinea	57.2	58.7
Rwanda	40.8	43.4	Hungary	64.5	73.8	Vanuatu	65.5	69.5
Sierra Leone	36.0	39.1	Ireland, Republic of	74.0	79.4			
South Africa	62.3	68.3	Italy	75.1	81.4	**Selected Countries of the Former USSR**		
Sudan	53.6	56.4	Norway	74.8	80.6			
Tunisia	68.4	70.7	Romania	66.0	73.2	Armenia	67.2	74.0
Uganda	40.4	42.3	Sweden	76.2	80.8	Belarus	64.4	74.8
Asia			Switzerland	75.3	81.8	Georgia	68.5	76.7
Average	64.8	67.7	UK	74.5	79.8	Kazakhstan	62.8	72.4
Afghanistan	45.0	46.0	**Latin America and Caribbean**			Russia	58.0	71.5
Bhutan	51.6	54.9	*Average*	66.4	72.9	Turkmenistan	61.2	68.0
Cambodia	52.6	55.4	Argentina	69.6	76.8	Ukraine	63.6	74.0
China	68.2	71.7	Bolivia	59.8	63.2			
India	62.1	62.7	Brazil	63.4	71.2	**World**		
Iraq	66.9	63.9	Chile	72.3	78.3	More developed regions[1]	70.6	78.4
Israel	75.7	79.5	Colombia	68.2	73.7	Less developed regions[2]	62.1	65.2
Japan	76.9	82.9	Costa Rica	74.5	79.2	Least developed countries[3]	50.9	53.0
Korea, North	68.9	75.1	Cuba	74.2	78.0			
Korea, South	68.8	76.0	Dominican Republic	68.9	73.1	**Total**	63.4	67.7
Laos	52.0	55.0	Guatemala	64.7	69.8			
Philippines	66.6	70.2	Haiti	52.8	56.0			
Singapore	75.1	79.5	Jamaica	72.4	76.8			
Syria	66.7	71.2	Mexico	69.5	75.5			
Yemen	57.4	58.4	Nicaragua	65.8	70.6			
			Peru	65.9	70.9			

[1] More developed regions comprise Northern America, Japan, Europe, and Australia and New Zealand.

[2] Less developed regions comprise all regions of Africa, Asia (excluding Japan), Latin America and the Caribbean, Melanesia, Micronesia, and Polynesia.

[3] Least developed countries according to standard UN designation.

Marriage and Divorce Rates

Source: Office for Official Publications of the European Communities, Luxembourg
(– = not applicable.)

Country	Marriages (per thousand people)		Divorces (per thousand people)		Country	Marriages (per thousand people)		Divorces (per thousand people)	
	1985	1995	1985	1995		1985	1995	1985	1995
Austria	5.9	5.3	2.0	2.3	Italy	5.3	4.9	0.3	0.5[2]
Belgium	5.8	5.1	1.9	3.5	Japan	6.1	6.3[2]	1.4	1.6[2]
Canada	7.1	5.5[1]	2.4	2.7[1]	Luxembourg	5.4	5.1	1.8	1.8
Denmark	5.7	6.7	2.8	2.5	Netherlands	5.7	5.2	2.3	2.2
Finland	5.3	4.6	1.8	2.7	Norway	4.9	4.8[2]	2.0	2.5[2]
France	4.9	4.4	1.9	2.0[2]	Portugal	6.8	6.7[2]	0.9	1.4[2]
Germany	6.4	5.3	2.3	2.0[2]	Spain	5.2	5.0	0.5	2.0[2]
Greece	6.4	6.2	0.8	0.7	Sweden	4.6	3.8	2.4	2.5
Iceland	5.2	4.5	2.2	1.9	Switzerland	6.0	5.8	1.8	2.2
Ireland, Republic of	5.3	4.6[2]	–[3]	–[3]	UK	6.9	5.9[1]	3.1	3.0[2]
					USA	10.1	9.1[2]	5.0	4.6[2]

[1] 1993.

[2] 1994.

[3] Divorce was not allowed in the Republic of Ireland until 1997.

and two or more men (polyandry). The basis of marriage varies considerably in different societies (romantic love in the West; arranged marriages in some other societies), but most marriage ceremonies, contracts, or customs involve a set of rights and duties, such as care and protection, and there is generally an expectation that children will be born of the union to continue the family line and maintain the family property.

In the 1990s the concept of marriage was extended in some countries to include the blessing or registration of homosexual relationships.

matriarchy theoretical form of society where domestic and political life is dominated by women, where kinship is traced exclusively through the female line, and where religion is centred around the cult of a mother goddess. Its opposite concept is that of **patriarchy.**

metropolitan area another term for conurbation.

middle class those members of society who earn their living by nonmanual labour. Their income is usually higher than that of the working class in recognition of greater skills. The subdivisions **upper middle class** and **lower middle class** refer respectively to the more skilled professions (doctors, lawyers, and so on) and white-collar workers (lower management, shopkeepers, and so on).

migration movement of population away from its home, either occurring from one country to another (**international** migration) or from one region in a country to another (**internal** migration). Migrations may be temporary (for example, holidaymakers), seasonal (transhumance), or permanent (people moving to cities to find employment); local, national, or international.

monogamy practice of having only one husband or wife at a time in marriage.

Monogamy is rare
■ Only 5% of all species of mammal are monogamous.

nuclear family the basic family unit of mother, father, and children. This is the familial norm of industrial societies, in contrast to countries with traditional economies, where the extended family (nuclear family plus assorted kin) is more common.

patriarchy form of social organization in which a man heads and controls the family unit. By extension, in a patriarchal society men also control larger social and working groups as well as government. The definition has been broadened by feminists to describe the dominance of male values throughout society.

philanthropy love felt by an individual towards humankind. It is expressed through acts of generosity and charity and seeks to promote the greater happiness and prosperity of humanity.

polygamy the practice of having more than one spouse at the same time. It is found among many peoples. Normally it has been confined to the wealthy and to chiefs and nobles who can support several women and their offspring, as among ancient Egyptians, Teutons, Irish, and Slavs. Islam limits the number of legal wives a man may have to four. Certain Christian sects – for example, the Anabaptists of Münster, Germany, and the Mormons – have practised polygamy because it was the norm in the Old Testament.

philanthropy US industrialist Andrew Carnegie. On his retirement, he devoted his life to the philanthropic distribution of his vast fortune. *Sachem*

Population: Growth in World Population	
Date	Estimated world population
2000 BC	100,000,000
1000	120,000,000
AD 1	180,000,000
1000	275,000,000
1250	375,000,000
1500	420,000,000
1650	500,000,000
1700	615,000,000
1750	750,000,000
1800	900,000,000
1850	1,260,000,000
1900	1,620,000,000
1950	2,500,000,000
1960	3,050,000,000
1970	3,700,000,000
1980	4,450,000,000
1990	5,245,000,000
2000	6,100,000,000

population control measures taken by some governments to limit the growth of their countries' populations by trying to reduce birth rates. Propaganda, freely available contraception, and tax disincentives for large families are some of the measures that have been tried.

population density the number of people living in a given area, usually expressed as people per square kilometre. It is calculated by dividing the population of a region by its area.

population explosion the rapid and dramatic rise in world population that has occurred over the last few hundred years. Between 1959 and 1995, the world's population increased from 2.5 billion to 5.6 billion people. It is estimated that it will be at least 6 billion by the end of the century.

poverty condition where the basic needs of human beings (shelter, food, and clothing) are not being met. Over one-fifth of the world's population was living in extreme poverty in 1995, of which around 70% were women. Nearly 13.5 million children under five die each year from poverty-related illness (measles, diarrhoea, malaria, pneumonia, and malnutrition). There are different definitions of the standard of living considered to be the minimum adequate level (known as the **poverty level**).

proletariat (Latin *proletarii* 'the class possessing no property') in Marxist theory, those classes in society that possess no property, and therefore depend on the sale of their labour or expertise (as opposed to the capitalists or bourgeoisie, who own the means of production, and the petty bourgeoisie, or working small-property owners). They are usually divided into the industrial, agricultural, and intellectual proletariat.

secularization the process through which religious thinking, practice, and institutions lose their religious and/or social significance. The

concept is based on the theory, held by some sociologists, that as societies become industrialized their religious morals, values, and institutions give way to secular ones and some religious traits become common secular practices.

slum area of poor-quality housing. Slums are typically found in parts of the inner city in rich countries and in older parts of cities in poor countries. Slum housing is usually densely populated, in a bad state of repair, and has inadequate services (poor sanitation, for example). Its occupants are often poor with low rates of literacy.

socialization process, beginning in childhood, by which a person becomes a member of a society, learning its norms, customs, laws, and ways of living. The main agents of socialization are the family, school, peer groups, work, religion, and the mass media. The main methods of socialization are direct instruction, rewards and punishment, imitation, experimentation, role play, and interaction.

social mobility movement of groups and individuals up and down the social scale in a classed society. The extent or range of social mobility varies in different societies. Individual social mobility may occur through education, marriage, talent, and so on; group mobility usually occurs through change in the occupational structure caused by new technological or economic developments.

suicide the act of intentionally killing oneself; also someone who does this. The frequency of attempted suicide is 20 times higher than actual suicide. Three times more women than men attempt suicide, and three times more men succeed. Men tend to use more violent methods like gunshot wounds to the head; women are more likely to take an overdose. Over 6,000 people in the USA use handguns to kill themselves each year. The highest suicide rate for both sexes is in the over-75 age group. Suicide among people aged 18–24, although relatively infrequent, is the third leading cause of death, after accidents and homicides, in the USA and UK.

urbanization process by which the proportion of a population living in or around towns and cities increases through migration and natural increase as the agricultural population decreases. The growth of urban concentrations in the USA and Europe is a relatively recent phenomenon, dating back only about 150 years to the beginning of the Industrial Revolution (although the world's first cities were built

Highest and Lowest Urban Populations

Source: UNICEF (Figures for 1996.)

Rank	Country	Population living in urban areas (%)	Rank	Country	Population living in urban areas (%)
Highest Urban Population			*Lowest Urban Population*		
1=	Kuwait	100	1=	Bhutan	6
1=	Monaco	100	1=	Rwanda	6
1=	Nauru	100	3	Burundi	8
1=	Singapore	100	4	Nepal	11
5	Belgium	97	5	Uganda	13
6	San Marino	96	6	Malawi	14
7=	Iceland	92	7=	Burkina Faso	16
7=	Qatar	92	7=	Ethiopia	16
9	Bahrain	91	7=	Papua New Guinea	16
10=	Israel	90	10=	Eritrea	18
10=	Luxembourg	90	10=	Solomon Islands	18
10=	Uruguay	90	12=	Bangladesh	19
13=	Malta	89	12=	Niger	19
13=	Netherlands	89	12=	Vanuatu	19
13=	UK	89	12=	Vietnam	19

more than 5,000 years ago). The UN Population Fund reported that by 2006 the majority of the world's population would be living in urban conglomerations. Almost all urban growth will occur in the developing world, spawning ten large cities a year.

wage, minimum the lowest wage that an employer is allowed to pay its employees by law or union contract.

white-collar worker non-manual employee, such as an office worker or manager. With more mechanized production methods, the distinction between white- and blue-collar (manual) workers is becoming increasingly blurred.

working class term applied to those members of an industrial society who earn their living through manual labour, known in the USA as **blue-collar workers.** The cultural and political identity of the working class has been eroded since World War II by the introduction of new technology and the break-up of traditional communities through urban redevelopment.

PRESIDENTS AND PRIME MINISTERS

Argentine Presidents from 1944

Term	Name	Party
1944–46	Edelmiro Farrell	military
1946–55	Juan Perón	Justice Front of Liberation
1955	Eduardo Lonardi	military
1955–58	Pedro Aramburu	military
1958–62	Arturo Frondizi	Civic Radical Union-Intransigent
1962–63	José Guido	acting: independent
1963–66	Arturo Illía	Civic Radical Union of the People
1966–70	Juan Onganía	military
1970–71	Roberto Levingston	military
1971–73	Alejandro Lanusse	military
1973	Héctor Cámpora	Justice Front of Liberation
1973	Raúl Lastiri	acting: independent
1973–74	Juan Perón	Justice Front of Liberation
1974–76	Maria Estela de Perón	Justice Front of Liberation
1976–81	Jorge Videla	military
1981	Roberto Viola	military
1981–82	Leopoldo Galtieri	military
1982	Alfredo Saint-Jean	acting: military
1982–83	Reynaldo Bignone	military
1983–89	Raúl Alfonsín	Civic Radical Union
1989–	Carlos Saúl Menem	Justice Party

Brazilian Presidents from 1945

Term	Name	Party
1945–46	José Linhares	independent
1946–51	Eurico Dutra	Social Democratic Party
1951–54	Getúlio Vargas	Brazil Labour Party
1954–55	João Café	Social Progressive Party
1955	Carlos da Luz	independent
1955–56	Nereu Ramos	independent
1956–61	Juscelino Kubitschek	Social Democratic Party
1961	Jânio Quadros	Christian Democratic Party/Democratic National Union
1961–64	João Goulart	Brazil Labour Party
1964	Ranieri Mazzili	independent
1964–67	Humberto Branco	military
1967–69	Arthur da Costa e Silva	military
1969–74	Emilio Medici	military
1974–79	Ernesto Geisel	military
1979–85	João Figueiredo	military
1985–89	José Sarney	Social Democratic Party
1989–92	Fernando Collor de Mello	National Reconstruction Party
1992–94	Itamar Franco	National Reconstruction Party
1995–	Fernando Henrique Cardoso	Social Democratic Party

Chinese Prime Ministers and Communist Party Leaders

Term	Name	Term	Name
Prime Ministers		*Communist Party Leaders*	
1949–76	Zhou Enlai	1935–76	Mao Zedong
1976–80	Hua Guofeng	1976–81	Hua Guofeng
1980–87	Zhao Ziyang	1981–87	Hu Yaobang
1987–98	Li Peng	1987–89	Zhao Ziyang
1998–	Zhu Rongji	1989–	Jiang Zemin

French Presidents and Prime Ministers from 1959 (the Fifth Republic)

Term	Name	Party	Term	Name	Party
Presidents			1972–74	Pierre Messmer	Gaullist
1959–69	General Charles de Gaulle	Gaullist	1974–76	Jacques Chirac	Gaullist
1969–74	Georges Pompidou	Gaullist	1976–81	Raymond Barre	Union of French
1974–81	Valéry Giscard d'Estaing	Republican/Union of			Democracy
		French Democracy	1981–84	Pierre Mauroy	Socialist
1981–95	François Mitterand	Socialist	1984–86	Laurent Fabius	Socialist
1995–	Jacques Chirac	Neo-Gaullist RPR	1986–88	Jacques Chirac	Neo-Gaullist RPR
			1988–91	Michel Rocard	Socialist
Prime Ministers			1991–92	Edith Cresson	Socialist
1959–62	Michel Debré	Gaullist	1992–93	Pierre Bérégovoy	Socialist
1962–68	Georges Pompidou	Gaullist	1993–95	Edouard Balladur	Neo-Gaullist RPR
1968–69	Maurice Couve de Murville	Gaullist	1995–97	Alain Juppé	Neo-Gaullist RPR
1969–72	Jacques Chaban-Delmas	Gaullist	1997–	Lionel Jospin	Socialist

German Political Leaders from 1949

Term	Name	Party	Term	Name	Party
Federal Republic			**Democratic Republic**		
Chancellors			*Communist Party leaders*		
1949–63	Konrad Adenauer	Christian Democrat	1949–50	Wilhelm Pieck	
1963–66	Ludwig Erhard	Christian Democrat	1950–71	Walter Ulbricht	
1966–69	Kurt Kiesinger	Christian Democrat	1971–89	Erich Honecker	
1969–74	Willy Brandt	Social Democrat	1989	Egon Krenz	
1974–82	Helmut Schmidt	Social Democrat			
1982–98[1]	Helmut Kohl	Christian Democrat	*Prime Ministers*		
			1989–90	Hans Modrow	
Germany			1990–91	Lothar de Maizière	
Chancellors					
1998–	Gerhard Schroeder	Social Democrat			

[1] The official reunification of the two countries, with Kohl as chancellor, took place in 1990.

Prime Ministers of Great Britain and the UK

Term	Name	Party
1721–42	Robert Walpole[1]	Whig
1742–43	Spencer Compton, Earl of Wilmington	Whig
1743–54	Henry Pelham	Whig
1754–56	Thomas Pelham-Holles, 1st Duke of Newcastle	Whig
1756–57	William Cavendish, 4th Duke of Devonshire	Whig
1757–62	Thomas Pelham-Holles, 1st Duke of Newcastle	Whig
1762–63	John Stuart, 3rd Earl of Bute	Tory
1763–65	George Grenville	Whig
1765–66	Charles Watson Wentworth, 2nd Marquess of Rockingham	Whig
1766–68	William Pitt, 1st Earl of Chatham	Tory
1768–70	Augustus Henry Fitzroy, 3rd Duke of Grafton	Whig
1770–82	Frederick North, Lord North[2]	Tory
1782	Charles Watson Wentworth, 2nd Marquess of Rockingham	Whig
1782–83	William Petty-Fitzmaurice, 2nd Earl of Shelburne[3]	Whig
1783	William Henry Cavendish-Bentinck, 3rd Duke of Portland	Whig
1783–1801	William Pitt, The Younger	Tory

Prime Ministers of Great Britain and the UK (continued)

Term	Name	Party
1801–04	Henry Addington	Tory
1804–06	William Pitt, The Younger	Tory
1806–07	William Wyndham Grenville, 1st Baron Grenville	Whig
1807–09	William Henry Cavendish-Bentinck, 3rd Duke of Portland	Whig
1809–12	Spencer Perceval	Tory
1812–27	Robert Banks Jenkinson, 2nd Earl of Liverpool	Tory
1827	George Canning	Tory
1827–28	Frederick John Robinson, 1st Viscount Goderich	Tory
1828–30	Arthur Wellesley, 1st Duke of Wellington	Tory
1830–34	Charles Grey, 2nd Earl Grey	Whig
1834	William Lamb, 2nd Viscount Melbourne	Whig
1834	Arthur Wellesley, 1st Duke of Wellington	Tory
1834–35	Sir Robert Peel, 2nd Baronet	Tory
1835–41	William Lamb, 2nd Viscount Melbourne	Whig
1841–46	Sir Robert Peel, 2nd Baronet	Conservative
1846–52	John Russell, Lord Russell	Whig-Liberal
1852	Edward Geoffrey Stanley, 14th Earl of Derby	Conservative
1852–55	George Hamilton-Gordon, 4th Earl of Aberdeen	Peelite
1855–58	Henry John Temple, 3rd Viscount Palmerston	Liberal
1858–59	Edward Geoffrey Stanley, 14th Earl of Derby	Conservative
1859–65	Henry John Temple, 3rd Viscount Palmerston	Liberal
1865–66	John Russell, 1st Earl Russell	Liberal
1866–68	Edward Geoffrey Stanley, 14th Earl of Derby	Conservative
1868	Benjamin Disraeli	Conservative
1868–74	William Ewart Gladstone	Liberal
1874–80	Benjamin Disraeli[4]	Conservative
1880–85	William Ewart Gladstone	Liberal
1885–86	Robert Cecil, 3rd Marquess of Salisbury	Conservative
1886	William Ewart Gladstone	Liberal
1886–92	Robert Cecil, 3rd Marquess of Salisbury	Conservative
1892–94	William Ewart Gladstone	Liberal
1894–95	Archibald Philip Primrose, 5th Earl of Rosebery	Liberal
1895–1902	Robert Cecil, 3rd Marquess of Salisbury	Conservative
1902–05	Arthur James Balfour	Conservative
1905–08	Sir Henry Campbell-Bannerman	Liberal
1908–16	H H Asquith	Liberal
1916–22	David Lloyd George	Liberal
1922–23	Bonar Law	Conservative
1923–24	Stanley Baldwin	Conservative
1924	Ramsay Macdonald	Labour
1924–29	Stanley Baldwin	Conservative
1929–35	Ramsay Macdonald	Labour
1935–37	Stanley Baldwin	Conservative
1937–40	Neville Chamberlain	Conservative
1940–45	Winston Churchill	Conservative
1945–51	Clement Attlee	Labour
1951–55	Winston Churchill[5]	Conservative
1955–57	Sir Anthony Eden	Conservative
1957–63	Harold Macmillan	Conservative
1963–64	Sir Alec Douglas-Home	Conservative
1964–70	Harold Wilson	Labour
1970–74	Edward Heath	Conservative
1974–76	Harold Wilson	Labour
1976–79	James Callaghan	Labour
1979–90	Margaret Thatcher	Conservative
1990–97	John Major	Conservative
1997–	Tony Blair	Labour

[1] From 1725, Sir Robert Walpole.

[2] From 1790, 2nd Earl of Guilford.

[3] From 1784, 1st Marquess of Lansdowne.

[4] From 1876, Earl of Beaconsfield.

[5] From 1953, Sir Winston Churchill.

Indian Prime Ministers

Term	Name	Party
1947–64	Jawaharlal Nehru	Congress
1964–66	Lal Bahadur Shastri	Congress
1966–77	Indira Gandhi	Congress (I)
1977–79	Morarji Desai	Janata
1979–80	Charan Singh	Janata/Lok Dal
1980–84	Indira Gandhi	Congress (I)
1984–89	Rajiv Gandhi	Congress (I)
1989–90	Viswanath Pratap Singh	Janata Dal
1990–91	Chandra Shekhar	Janata Dal (Socialist)
1991–96	P V Narasimha Rao	Congress (I)
1996	Atal Behari Vaj Payee	Bharatiya Janata Party
1996–97	H D Deve Gowda	Janata Dal
1997–98	Inder Kumar Gujral	Janata Dal
1998–	Atal Bihari Vaijpayee	Bharatiya Janata Party

Irish Prime Ministers from 1922

Term	Name	Party
1922	Michael Collins	Sinn Féin
1922–32	William T Cosgrave	Fine Gael
1932–48	Eamon de Valera	Fianna Fáil
1948–51	John A Costello	Fine Gael
1951–54	Eamon de Valera	Fianna Fáil
1954–57	John A Costello	Fine Gael
1957–59	Eamon de Valera	Fianna Fáil
1959–66	Sean Lemass	Fianna Fáil
1966–73	Jack Lynch	Fianna Fáil
1973–77	Liam Cosgrave	Fine Gael
1977–79	Jack Lynch	Fianna Fáil
1979–81	Charles Haughey	Fianna Fáil
1981–82	Garrett Fitzgerald	Fine Gael
1982	Charles Haughey	Fianna Fáil
1982–87	Garrett Fitzgerald	Fine Gael
1987–92	Charles Haughey	Fianna Fáil
1992–94	Albert Reynolds	Fianna Fáil
1994–97	John Bruton	Fine Gael
1997–	Patrick 'Bertie' Ahern	Fianna Fáil

Israeli Prime Ministers from 1948

Term	Name	Party	Term	Name	Party
1948–53	David Ben-Gurion	Mapai	1983–84	Yitzhak Shamir	Likud
1953–55	M Sharett	Mapai	1984–86	Shimon Peres	Labour
1955–63	David Ben-Gurion	Mapai	1986–92	Yitzhak Shamir	Likud
1963–69	Levi Eshkol	Mapai/Labour	1992–95	Yitzhak Rabin	Labour
1969–74	Golda Meir	Labour	1995–96	Shimon Peres	Labour
1974–77	Yitzhak Rabin	Labour	1996–	Binyamin Netanyahu	Likud
1977–83	Menachem Begin	Likud			

Italian Prime Ministers from 1945

Term	Name	Party	Term	Name	Party
1945–53	Alcide de Gasperi	Christian Democratic Party	1976–79	Giulio Andreotti	Christian Democratic Party
1953–54	Giuseppe Pella	Christian Democratic Party	1979–80	Francesco Cossiga	Christian Democratic Party
1954	Amintore Fanfani	Christian Democratic Party	1980–81	Arnaldo Forlani	Christian Democratic Party
1954–55	Mario Scelba	Christian Democratic Party	1981–82	Giovanni Spadolini	Republican Party
1955–57	Antonio Segni	Christian Democratic Party	1982–83	Amintore Fanfani	Christian Democratic Party
1957–58	Adone Zoli	Christian Democratic Party	1983–87	Benedetto (Bettino) Craxi	Socialist Party
1958–59	Amintore Fanfani	Christian Democratic Party	1987	Amintore Fanfani	Christian Democratic Party
1959–60	Antonio Segni	Christian Democratic Party	1987–88	Giovanni Goria	Christian Democratic Party
1960	Fernando Tambroni	Christian Democratic Party	1988–89	Ciriaco de Mita	Christian Democratic Party
1960–63	Amintore Fanfani	Christian Democratic Party	1989–92	Giulio Andreotti	Christian Democratic Party
1963	Giovanni Leone	Christian Democratic Party	1992–93	Giuliano Amato	Socialist Party
1963–68	Aldo Moro	Christian Democratic Party	1993–94	Carlo Azeglio Ciampi	Christian Democratic Party
1968	Giovanni Leone	Christian Democratic Party	1994–95	Silvio Berlusconi	Freedom Alliance
1968–70	Mariano Rumor	Christian Democratic Party	1995–96	Lamberto Dini	independent
1970–72	Emilio Colombo	Christian Democratic Party	1996–98	Romano Prodi	Olive Tree Alliance
1972–73	Giulio Andreotti	Christian Democratic Party	1998–	Massimo D'Alema	Democrats of the Left
1973–74	Mariano Rumor	Christian Democratic Party			
1974–76	Aldo Moro	Christian Democratic Party			

Japanese Prime Ministers from 1945

Term	Name	Party	Term	Name	Party
1945–46	Kijurō Shidehara	coalition	1978–80	Masayoshi Ohira	LDP
1946–47	Shigeru Yoshida	Liberal	1980–82	Zenkō Suzuki	LDP
1947–48	Tetsu Katayama	coalition	1982–87	Yasuhiro Nakasone	LDP
1948	Hitoshi Ashida	Democratic	1987–89	Noboru Takeshita	LDP
1948–54	Shigeru Yoshida	Liberal	1989	Sōsuke Uno	LDP
1954–56	Ichirō Hatoyama	Liberal[1]	1989–91	Toshiki Kaifu	LDP
1956–57	Tanzan Ishibashi	LDP	1991–93	Kiichi Miyazawa	LDP
1957–60	Nobusuke Kishi	LDP	1993–94	Morohiro Hosokawa	JNP-led coalition
1960–64	Hayato Ikeda	LDP	1994	Tsutoma Hata	Shinseito-led coalition
1964–72	Eisaku Satō	LDP	1994–96	Tomiichi Murayama	SDPJ-led coalition
1972–74	Kakuei Tanaka	LDP	1996–98	Ryutaro Hashimoto	LDP
1974–76	Takeo Miki	LDP	1998–	Keizo Obuchi	LDP
1976–78	Takeo Fukuda	LDP			

[1] The conservative parties merged in 1955 to form the Liberal Democratic Party (LDP, Jiyū-Minshutō).

Kenyan Presidents from 1963

Term	Name	Party
1963–78	Jomo Kenyatta	Kenya African National Union (KANU)
1978–	Daniel arap Moi	KANU

Mexican Presidents from 1946

Term	Name	Party
1946–52	Miguel Alemán Valdés	Institutional Revolutionary Party
1952–58	Adolfo Ruiz Cortines	Institutional Revolutionary Party
1958–64	Adolfo López Mateos	Institutional Revolutionary Party
1964–70	Gustavo Díaz Ordaz	Institutional Revolutionary Party
1970–76	Luís Echeverría Alvarez	Institutional Revolutionary Party
1976–82	José López Portillo y Pacheco	Institutional Revolutionary Party
1982–88	Miguel de la Madrid Hurtado	Institutional Revolutionary Party
1988–94	Carlos Salinas de Gortari	Institutional Revolutionary Party
1994–	Ernesto Zedillo Ponce de Léon	Institutional Revolutionary Party

Netherlands Prime Ministers from

Term	Name	Party
1945	Pieter Gerbrandy	Anti-Revolutionary Party
1945–46	Willem Schermerhorn	Socialist Party
1946–48	Louis Beel	Catholic Party
1948–58	Willem Drees	Socialist Party
1958–59	Louis Beel	Catholic Party
1959–63	Jan de Quay	Catholic Party
1963–65	Victor Marijnen	Catholic Party
1965–66	Joseph Cals	Catholic Party
1966–67	Jelle Zijlstra	Anti-Revolutionary Party
1967–71	Petrus de Jong	Catholic Party
1971–73	Barend Biesheuvel	Anti-Revolutionary Party
1973–77	Johannes (Joop) den Uyl	Labour Party
1977–82	Andreas van Agt	Christian Democratic Appeal Party
1982–94	Rudolphus (Ruud) Lubbers	Christian Democratic Appeal Party
1994–	Wim Kok	Labour Party

Nigerian Leaders from 1960

Term	Name	Party
Governor-Generals		
1960	James Robertson	independent
1960–63	Nnamdi Azikiwe	Nigerian National Democratic Party
Presidents[1]		
1963–66	Nnamdi Azikiwe	Nigerian National Democratic Party
1966	Johnson Aguiyi-Ironsi	military
1966–75	Colonel Yakubu Gowon	military
1975–76	Murtala Mohammed	military
1976–79	General Olusegun Obasanjo	military
1979–83	Shehu Shagari	National Party of Nigeria
1983–85	Major General Mohammed Buhari	military
1985–93	Major General Ibrahim Babangida	military
1993	Ernest Shonekan	independent
1993–98	General Sani Abacha	military
1998–	General Abdusalam Abubakar	military

[1] Heads of state from January 1966 until October 1979 and from December 1983 did not officially use the title of president.

Norwegian Prime Ministers from 1945

Term	Name	Party	Term	Name	Party
1945–51	Einar Gerhardsen	Labour Party	1976–81	Odvar Nordli	Labour Party
1951–55	Oscar Torp	Labour Party	1981	Gro Harlem Brundtland	Labour Party
1955–63	Einar Gerhardsen	Labour Party	1981–86	Kaare Willoch	Conservative Party
1963	John Lyng	Conservative Party	1986–89	Gro Harlem Brundtland	Labour Party
1963–65	Einar Gerhardsen	Labour Party	1989–90	Jan Syse	Conservative Party
1965–71	Per Borten	Centre Party	1990–96	Gro Harlem Brundtland	Labour Party
1971–72	Trygve Bratteli	Labour Party	1996–97	Thorbjoern Jagland	Labour Party
1972–73	Lars Korvald	Christian People's Party	1997–	Kjell Magne Bondevik	Christian People's Party
1973–76	Trygve Bratteli	Labour Party			

Polish Political Leaders from 1945

Term	Name	Party	Term	Name	Party
Communist Party Leaders[1]			1980–81	Stanisław Kania	
1945–48	Władysław Gomułka		1981–89	Wojciech Jaruzelski	
1948–56	Bolesław Bierut				
1956	Edward Ochab		*Presidents*		
1956–70	Władysław Gomułka		1990–95	Lech Wałesa	Solidarity/independent
1970–80	Edward Gierek		1995–	Aleksander Kwaśniewski	Democratic Left Alliance

[1]From 1945–90 the political leaders were the Communist Party leaders.

South African Prime Ministers and Presidents from 1910

Term	Name
Prime Ministers	
1910–19	L Botha
1919–24	Jan Smuts
1924–39	James Hertzog
1939–48	Jan Smuts
1948–54	Daniel Malan
1954–58	J Strijdon

Term	Name
1958–66	Hendrik Verwoerd
1966–78	Balthazar Johannes Vorster
1978–84	Pieter Botha
Presidents[1]	
1984–89	Pieter Botha
1989–94	F W de Klerk
1994–	Nelson Mandela

[1] The post of prime minister was abolished in 1984 and combined with that of president.

Soviet and Russian Presidents and Communist Party Leaders

Term	Name USSR
Communist Party Leaders	
1917–22	Vladimir Ilich Lenin
1922–53	Joseph Stalin
1953–64	Nikita Khrushchev
1964–82	Leonid Brezhnev
1982–84	Yuri Andropov
1984–85	Konstantin Chernenko
1985–91	Mikhail Gorbachev
Presidents	
1917–22	Vladimir Ilich Lenin[1]
1919–46	Mikhail Kalinin[2]
1946–53	Nikolai Shvernik
1953–60	Marshal Kliment Voroshilov

1960–64	Leonid Brezhnev
1964–65	Anastas Mikoyan
1965–77	Nikolai Podgorny
1977–82	Leonid Brezhnev
1982–83	Valery Kuznetsov (acting)
1983–84	Yuri Andropov
1984	Valery Kuznetsov (acting)
1984–85	Konstantin Chernenko
1985	Valery Kuznetsov (acting)
1985–88	Andrei Gromyko
1988–91	Mikhail Gorbachev
Russia	
Presidents	
1991–	Boris Yeltsin

[1] In 1917 Lenin was elected chairman of the Council of People's Commisars, that is, head of government. He held that post until 1922.

[2] In 1919, Kalinin became head of state (president of the Central Executive Committee of the Soviet government until 1937; president of the Presidium of the Supreme Soviet until 1946.)

Spanish Presidents, Chiefs of State, and Prime Ministers from 1931

Term	Name	Party
Presidents		
1931–36	Niceto Alcala Zamora	Liberal Republicans
1936	Diego Martinez y Barro	Radical Party
1936–39	Manuel Azaña y Diéz	Left Republican Party
Chiefs of State		
1939–75	Francisco Franco y Bahamonde	National Movement/Falange
Prime Ministers		
1931–33	Manuel Azaña y Diéz	Left Republican Party
1933	Alejandro Lerroux y García	Radical Republican Party
1933	Diego Martínez y Barro	Radical Republican Party
1933–34	Alejandro Lerroux y García	Radical Republican Party
1934	Ricardo Samper Ibañez	Radical Republican Party–Valencian branch

Spanish Presidents, Chiefs of State, and Prime Ministers from 1931 (continued)

Term	Name	Party
1934–35	Alejandro Lerroux y García	Radical Republican Party
1935	Joaquín Chapaprieta y Terragosa	independent
1935–36	Manuel Portela Valladares	Radical Republican Party
1936	Manuel Azaña y Diéz	Left Republican Party
1936	Santiago Cásares Quiroga	Left Republican Party
1936	José Giral y Pereira	Left Republican Party
1936–37	Francisco Largo Caballero	Socialist Party
1937–39	Juan Negrin	Socialist Party
1939–73	Francisco Franco Bahamonde	National Movement
1973	Luis Carrero Blanco	National Movement
1973–74	Torcuato Fernández Miranda	National Movement
1974–76	Carlos Arias Navarro	National Movement
1976–81	Adolfo Suárez González	Union of the Democratic Centre
1981–82	Leopoldo Calvo-Sotelo y Bustelo	Union of the Democratic Centre
1982–96	Felipe González Márquez	Socialist Workers' Party
1996–	José María Aznar	Popular Party

Swedish Prime Ministers from 1946

Term	Name	Party	Term	Name	Party
1946–69	Tage Erlander	Social Democratic Labour Party	1982–86	Olof Palme	Social Democratic Labour Party
1969–76	Olof Palme	Social Democratic Labour Party	1986–91	Ingvar Carlsson	Social Democratic Labour Party
1976–78	Thorbjörn Fälldin	Centre Party	1991–94	Carl Bildt	Moderate Party
1978–79	Ola Ullsten	Liberal Party	1994–96	Ingvar Carlsson	Social Democratic Labour Party
1979–82	Thorbjörn Fälldin	Centre Party	1996–	Göran Persson	Social Democratic Labour Party

US Presidents

Year elected/ took office	President	Party	Losing candidate(s)	Party
1789	1. George Washington	Federalist	no opponent	
1792	re-elected		no opponent	
1796	2. John Adams	Federalist	Thomas Jefferson	Democrat–Republican
1800	3. Thomas Jefferson	Democrat–Republican	Aaron Burr	Democrat–Republican
1804	re-elected		Charles Pinckney	Federalist
1808	4. James Madison	Democrat–Republican	Charles Pinckney	Federalist
1812	re-elected		DeWitt Clinton	Federalist
1816	5. James Monroe	Democrat–Republican	Rufus King	Federalist
1820	re-elected		John Quincy Adams	Democrat–Republican
1824	6. John Quincy Adams	Democrat–Republican	Andrew Jackson	Democrat–Republican
			Henry Clay	Democrat–Republican
			William H Crawford	Democrat–Republican
1828	7. Andrew Jackson	Democrat	John Quincy Adams	National Republican
1832	re-elected		Henry Clay	National Republican
1836	8. Martin Van Buren	Democrat	William Henry Harrison	Whig
1840	9. William Henry Harrison	Whig	Martin Van Buren	Democrat
1841	10. John Tyler[1]	Whig		
1844	11. James K Polk	Democrat	Henry Clay	Whig
1848	12. Zachary Taylor	Whig	Lewis Cass	Democrat
1850	13. Millard Fillmore[2]	Whig		
1852	14. Franklin Pierce	Democrat	Winfield Scott	Whig
1856	15. James Buchanan	Democrat	John C Fremont	Republican
1860	16. Abraham Lincoln	Republican	Stephen Douglas	Democrat
			John Breckinridge	Democrat
			John Bell	Constitutional Union
1864	re-elected		George McClellan	Democrat
1865	17. Andrew Johnson[3]	Democrat		
1868	18. Ulysses S Grant	Republican	Horatio Seymour	Democrat
1872	re-elected		Horace Greeley	Democrat–Liberal Republican
1876	19. Rutherford B Hayes	Republican	Samuel Tilden	Democrat
1880	20. James A Garfield	Republican	Winfield Hancock	Democrat
1881	21. Chester A Arthur[4]	Republican		
1884	22. Grover Cleveland	Democrat	James Blaine	Republican
1888	23. Benjamin Harrison	Republican	Grover Cleveland	Democrat
1892	24. Grover Cleveland	Democrat	Benjamin Harrison	Republican
			James Weaver	People's
1896	25. William McKinley	Republican	William J Bryan	Democrat–People's
1900	re-elected		William J Bryan	Democrat
1901	26. Theodore Roosevelt[5]	Republican		
1904	re-elected		Alton B Parker	Democrat
1908	27. William Howard Taft	Republican	William J Bryan	Democrat
1912	28. Woodrow Wilson	Democrat	Theodore Roosevelt	Progressive
			William Howard Taft	Republican
1916	re-elected		Charles E Hughes	Republican
1920	29. Warren G Harding	Republican	James M Cox	Democrat
1923	30. Calvin Coolidge[6]	Republican		
1924	re-elected		John W Davis	Democrat
			Robert M LaFollette	Progressive
1928	31. Herbert Hoover	Republican	Alfred E Smith	Democrat
1932	32. Franklin D Roosevelt	Democrat	Herbert C Hoover	Republican
			Norman Thomas	Socialist

US Presidents (continued)

Year elected/ took office	President	Party	Losing candidate(s)	Party
1936	re-elected		Alfred Landon	Republican
1940	re-elected		Wendell Willkie	Republican
1944	re-elected		Thomas E Dewey	Republican
1945	33. Harry S Truman[7]	Democrat		
1948	re-elected		Thomas E Dewey	Republican
			J Strom Thurmond	States' Rights
			Henry A Wallace	Progressive
1952	34. Dwight D Eisenhower	Republican	Adlai E Stevenson	Democrat
1956	re-elected		Adlai E Stevenson	Democrat
1960	35. John F Kennedy	Democrat	Richard M Nixon	Republican
1963	36. Lyndon B Johnson[8]	Democrat		
1964	re-elected		Barry M Goldwater	Republican
1968	37. Richard M Nixon	Republican	Hubert H Humphrey	Democrat
			George C Wallace	American Independent
1972	re-elected		George S McGovern	Democrat
1974	38. Gerald R Ford[9]	Republican		
1976	39. James Earl Carter	Democrat	Gerald R Ford	Republican
1980	40. Ronald Reagan	Republican	James Earl Carter	Democrat
			John B Anderson	Independent
1984	re-elected		Walter Mondale	Democrat
1988	41. George Bush	Republican	Michael Dukakis	Democrat
			Ross Perot	Independent
1992	42. Bill Clinton	Democrat	George Bush	Republican
1996	re-elected		Bob Dole	Republican
			Ross Perot	Reform

[1] Became president on death of Harrison.

[2] Became president on death of Taylor.

[3] Became president on assassination of Lincoln.

[4] Became president on assassination of Garfield.

[5] Became president on assassination of McKinley.

[6] Became president on death of Harding.

[7] Became president on death of F D Roosevelt.

[8] Became president on assassination of Kennedy.

[9] Became president on resignation of Nixon.

ECONOMICS

balance of payments account of a country's debit and credit transactions with other countries. Items are divided into the **current account,** which includes both visible trade (imports and exports of goods) and invisible trade (services such as transport, tourism, interest, and dividends), and the **capital account,** which includes investment in and out of the country, international grants, and loans. Deficits or surpluses on these accounts are brought into balance by buying and selling reserves of foreign currencies.

balance of trade the balance of trade transactions of a country recorded in its current account; it forms one component of the country's balance of payments.

bank financial institution that uses funds deposited with it to lend money to companies or individuals, and also provides financial services to its customers. The first banks opened in Italy and Cataluña around 1400.

capital stock of goods used in the production of other goods. **Financial capital** is accumulated or inherited wealth held in the form of assets, such as stocks and shares, property, and bank deposits.

comparative advantage law of international trade first elaborated by English economist David Ricardo showing that trade becomes worthwhile if the cost of production of particular items differs between one country and another.

consumption purchase of goods and services for final use, as opposed to spending by firms on capital goods, known as capital formation.

cost of living cost of goods and services needed for an average standard of living.

cost-push inflation theory of inflation which states that inflation is caused by increases in the costs of production. A rise in wages, profit levels, or product inputs to the firm will push up its costs. It responds by increasing its prices. This

Merchandise Trade Balance by Country

Source: International Monetary Fund
(N/A = not available. In millions of dollars.) Figures for 1995.

Country	Surplus/deficit	Country	Surplus/deficit	Country	Surplus/deficit
Algeria	N/A	Ghana	N/A	Peru	−2,111
Argentina	2,237	Greece	−14,425	Philippines	−8,944
Australia	−4,166	Hungary	−2,433	Poland	−3,224
Austria	−5,103	India	N/A	Portugal	−8,484
Bangladesh	−2,324	Indonesia	5,710	Romania	−1,231
Belgium	10,206	Ireland, Republic of	13,125	Saudi Arabia	24,390
Brazil	−3,157	Israel	−7,694	Singapore	1,625
Burma	N/A	Italy	44,082	South Africa	1,610
Cameroon	N/A	Japan	131,790	Spain	−17,661
Canada	22,341	Kenya	−738	Sri Lanka	−880
Chile	1,383	Korea, South	−4,746	Sudan	−510
China	18,050	Kuwait	5,478	Sweden	15,973
Colombia	−2,548	Libya	N/A	Switzerland	3,237
Congo, Democratic Republic of	N/A	Malaysia	−100	Syria	−143
Côte d'Ivoire	1,345	Mexico	7,089	Thailand	−7,968
Denmark	6,820	Morocco	−2,397	Trinidad and Tobago	588
Ecuador	354	Nepal	−961	Turkey	−13,212
Egypt	−7,597	Netherlands	20,979	UK	−18,390
Finland	12,346	Nigeria	N/A	USA	−171,990
France	11,175	Norway	N/A	Venezuela	7,290
Germany	66	Pakistan	N/A		

then contributes to inflation in the economy. The world oil price increase in 1974 was a major cause of cost-push inflation.

credit means by which goods or services are obtained without immediate payment, usually by agreeing to pay interest. The three main forms are **consumer credit** (usually extended to individuals by retailers), **bank credit** (such as overdrafts or personal loans), and **trade credit** (common in the commercial world both within countries and internationally).

crowding out situation in which an increase in government expenditure results in a fall in private-sector investment, either because it causes inflation or a rise in interest rates (as a result of increased government borrowing) or because it reduces the efficiency of production as a result of government intervention. Crowding out has been used in recent years as a justification of supply-side economics such as the privatization of state-owned industries and services.

debt crisis any situation in which an individual, company, or country owes more to others than it can repay or pay interest on; more specifically, the massive indebtedness of many Third World countries that became acute in the 1980s, threatening the stability of the international banking system as many debtor countries became unable to service their debts.

deficit financing planned excess of expenditure over income, dictated by government policy, creating a shortfall of public revenue which is met by borrowing. The decision to create a deficit is made to stimulate an economy by increasing consumer purchasing and at the same time to create more jobs.

demand-pull inflation rise in prices (inflation) caused by excess aggregate demand (total demand for goods and services) in the economy. For example, when the economy is in boom, aggregate demand tends to be rising quickly, but inflation also rises quickly.

depression period of low output and investment, with high unemployment. Specifically, the term describes two periods of crisis in world economy: 1873–96 and 1929 to the mid-1930s.

deregulation action to abolish or reduce government controls and supervision of private economic activities, with the aim of improving competitiveness. In Britain, the major changes in

the City of London 1986 (the Big Bang) were in part deregulation. Another UK example was the Building Societies Act 1985 that enabled building societies to compete in many areas with banks.

devaluation lowering of the official value of a currency against other currencies, so that exports become cheaper and imports more expensive. Used when a country is badly in deficit in its balance of trade, it results in the goods the country produces being cheaper abroad, so that the economy is stimulated by increased foreign demand.

disinvestment withdrawal of investments in a country for political reasons. The term is also used in economics to describe non-replacement of stock as it wears out.

economic growth rate of growth of output of all goods and services in an economy, usually measured as the percentage increase in gross domestic product or gross national product from one year to the next. It is regarded as an indicator of the rate of increase or decrease (if economic growth is negative) in the standard of living.

exchange rate the price at which one currency is bought or sold in terms of other currencies, gold, or accounting units such as the special drawing right (SDR) of the International Monetary Fund. Exchange rates may be fixed by international agreement or by government policy; or they may be wholly or partly allowed to 'float' (that is, find their own level) in world currency markets.

exchange rate policy policy of government towards the level of the exchange rate of its cur-

depression During the 1930s, soup kitchens like this one in Chicago sprang up all over the USA to help those worst affected by the world economic recession. *Library of Congress*

rency. It may want to influence the exchange rate by using its gold and foreign currency reserves held by its central bank to buy and sell its currency. It can also use interest rates (monetary policy) to alter the value of the currency.

excise duty indirect tax levied on certain goods produced within a country, such as petrol, alcohol, and tobacco. It is collected by the government's Customs and Excise department.

export goods or service produced in one country and sold to another. Exports may be visible (goods such as cars physically exported) or invisible (services such as banking and tourism, that are provided in the exporting country but paid for by residents of another country).

fiscal policy that part of government policy concerning taxation and other revenues, public spending, and government borrowing (the public sector borrowing requirement).

free-enterprise economy another term for free-market economy.

free market or **free enterprise,** another term for capitalism.

gross domestic product (GDP) value of the output of all goods and services produced within a nation's borders, normally given as a total for the year. It thus includes the production of foreign-owned firms within the country, but excludes the income from domestically owned firms located abroad.

Countries with the Highest Per Capita GDP

Source: UN Statistics Division

Data are for most recent figures available for all countries shown (1995). There are different systems for calculating GDO per capita. The rates below are based on official exchange rates for the year shown, and not on the purchasing power parity (PPP) system. (The latter system converts the GDP per capita of a country into US dollars on the basis of the purchasing power parity of the country's currency; this system allows for more accurate international comparisons of GDP and its components, and is the one used in the articles for individual countries in this book.)

Rank	Country/Region	Per capita GDP ($)	Rank	Country/Region	Per capita GDP ($)
1	Switzerland	42,416	26	Brunei	16,683
2	Japan	41,718	27	Kuwait	15,757
3	Luxembourg	35,109	28	Spain	14,111
4	Norway	33,734	29	Qatar	14,013
5	Denmark	33,191	30	Bahamas	12,545
6	Bermuda	32,495	31	Taiwan	12,359
7	Germany	29,632	32	Puerto Rico	12,213
8	Austria	29,006	33	Cyprus	11,459
9	Belgium	26,582	34	Iraq	11,308
10	France	26,444	35	Portugal	10,428
11	Sweden	26,253	36	Korea, South	9,736
12	Iceland	26,217	37	Slovenia	9,652
13	USA	26,037	38	Bahrain	9,073
14	Netherlands	25,635	39	Netherlands Antilles	9,039
15	Singapore	25,581	40	Malta	8,793
16	Finland	24,453	41	Greece	8,684
17	Hong Kong	22,898	42	Argentina	8,055
18	Australia	20,046	43	Seychelles	7,272
19	Italy	19,121	44	Barbados	7,173
20	Canada	18,943	45	Antigua and Barbuda	6,966
21	UK	18,913	46	Saudi Arabia	6,583
22	United Arab Emirates	17,690	47	Oman	6,232
23	Ireland, Republic of	17,419	48	Uruguay	5,602
24	New Zealand	16,866	49	Libya	5,498
25	Israel	16,738	50	Cook Islands	5,432

Countries with the Lowest Per Capita GDP

Source: UN Statistics Division (figures for 1995.)

Rank	Country	Per capita GDP ($)	Rank	Country	Per capita GDP ($)
1	Sudan	36	11	Tanzania	139
2	São Tomé and Príncipe	49	12	Malawi	142
3	Mozambique	77	13	Burkina Faso	165
4=	Ethiopia	96	14	Bhutan	166
4=	Eritrea	96	15	Chad	187
6	Congo, Democratic Republic of	117	16	Nepal	203
7	Somalia	119	17	Burundi	205
8	Tajikistan	122	18	Niger	207
9	Cambodia	130	19	Madagascar	215
10	Guinea-Bissau	131	20	Mali	223

gross national product (GNP) the most commonly used measurement of the wealth of a country. GNP is defined as the total value of all goods and services produced by firms owned by the country concerned. It is measured as the gross domestic product plus income from abroad, minus income earned during the same period by foreign investors within the country.

hyperinflation rapid and uncontrolled inflation, or increases in prices, usually associated with political and/or social instability (as in Germany in the 1920s).

import product or service that one country purchases from another for domestic consumption, or for processing and re-exporting (Hong Kong, for example, is heavily dependent on imports for its export business). Imports may be visible (goods) or invisible (services). If an importing country does not have a counterbalancing value of exports, it may experience balance-of-payments difficulties and accordingly consider restricting imports by some form of protectionism (such as an import tariff or import quotas).

Gross National Product

countries with the highest GNP per head

Country	GNP per head (US $)	Country	GNP per head (US $)
Switzerland	35,500	Singapore	18,143
Japan	32,018	Australia	17,320
Luxembourg	31,080	UK	17,300
Sweden	29,600		
Denmark	28,200		

countries with the lowest GNP per head

Country	GNP per head (US $)
Norway	28,200
Finland	24,400
Belgium	22,600

Country	GNP per head (US $)
Mozambique	80
Ethiopia	120

Country	GNP per head (US $)
Iceland	22,580
USA	22,520
Canada	21,170
Netherlands	21,400
Liechtenstein	21,020
Italy	20,200
United Arab Emirates	19,680

Country	GNP per head (US $)
Tanzania	120
Somalia	150
Nepal	170
Guinea-Bissau	180
Chad	190
Bhutan	190

based on 1990–92 estimates

import control control that limits the number of imports entering the country. One type of import control is an import quota.

incomes policy government-initiated exercise to curb inflation by restraining rises in incomes, on either a voluntary or a compulsory basis; often linked with action to control prices, in which case it becomes a prices and incomes policy.

income tax direct tax levied on personal income, mainly wages and salaries, but which may include the value of receipts other than in cash. It is one of the main instruments for achieving a government's income redistribution objectives. In contrast, **indirect taxes** are duties payable whenever a specific product is purchased; examples include VAT and customs duties.

industrial sector any of the different groups into which industries may be divided: primary, secondary, tertiary, and quaternary. **Primary** industries extract or use raw materials; for example, mining and agriculture. **Secondary** industries are manufacturing industries, where raw materials are processed or components are assembled. **Tertiary** industries supply services such as retailing. The **quaternary** sector of industry is concerned with the professions and those services that require a high level of skill, expertise, and specialization. It includes education, research and development, administration, and financial services such as accountancy.

inflation rise in the general level of prices. The many causes include cost-push inflation, which results from rising production costs. **Demand-pull inflation** occurs when overall demand exceeds supply. **Suppressed inflation** occurs in controlled economies and is reflected in rationing, shortages, and black-market prices. **Hyperinflation** is inflation of more than 50% in one month. **Deflation,** a fall in the general level of prices, is the reverse of inflation.

interest in finance, a sum of money paid by a borrower to a lender in return for the loan, usually expressed as a percentage per annum. **Simple interest** is interest calculated as a straight percentage of the amount loaned or invested. In **compound interest,** the interest earned over a period of time (for example, per annum) is added to the investment, so that at the end of the next period interest is paid on that total.

labour one of the factors of production, used to produce goods and provide services. Wages are the reward for labour. The quantity of labour in a modern economy is determined by the size of the population and the extent to which young and old people and women are prepared to take paid work.

The size of the labour force in some countries has gone down over the past 30 years because more and more young people are staying longer in education and because workers are tending to retire earlier. However, this has been more than offset by an increase in the total population of working age and by a growth in the number of women taking paid jobs rather than staying at home. The quality of the labour force is determined by education and training. The more highly trained and educated the labour force is, the more productive it will be. Division of labour indicates a system of work where a task is split into several parts and done by different workers. For example, on a car assembly line, one worker will fit doors, another will make the engine block, and another will work in the paint shop. The division of labour is an example of specialization.

labour turnover the frequency with which workers have to be replaced in a job over a period of time. For example, in a fast food outlet the rate of staff turnover could be six times a year, meaning that the average worker only stays with the company for two months. High labour turnover can be costly for a business organization if it has to train new workers to any extent and because recruitment of new staff is costly. It is also likely to be an indicator of poor worker morale or low wages.

laissez faire (French 'let alone') theory that the state should not intervene in economic affairs, except to break up a monopoly. The phrase originated with the Physiocrats, 18th-century French economists whose maxim was *laissez faire et laissez passer* (literally, 'let go and let pass' – that is, leave the individual alone and let commodities circulate freely). The degree to which intervention should take place is still one of the chief problems of economics. The Scottish economist Adam Smith justified the theory in *The Wealth of Nations* 1776.

market any situation where buyers and sellers are in contact with each other. This could be a street market or it could be a world market where buyers and sellers communicate via letters, faxes, telephones, and representatives.

market economy economy in which most resources are allocated through markets rather than through state planning.

Macroeconomics

Macroeconomics is a division of economics concerned with the study of whole (aggregate) economies or systems, including such aspects as government income and expenditure, the balance of payments, fiscal policy, investment, inflation, and unemployment. It seeks to understand the influence of all relevant economic factors on each other and thus to quantify and predict aggregate national income. Modern macroeconomics takes much of its inspiration from the work of Maynard Keynes, whose *General Theory of Employment, Interest, and Money* 1936 proposed that governments could prevent financial crises and unemployment by adjusting demand through control of credit and currency. **Keynesian macroeconomics** thus analyzes aggregate supply and demand and holds that markets do not

continuously 'clear' (quickly attain equilibrium between supply and demand) and may require intervention if objectives such as full employment are thought desirable.

Keynesian macroeconomic formulations were generally accepted well into the postwar era and have been refined and extended by the **neo-Keynesian school**, which contends that in a recession the market will clear only very slowly and that full employment equilibrium may never return without significant demand management (by government). At the same time, however, **neoclassical economics** has experienced a resurgence, using tools from microeconomics to challenge the central Keynesian assumption that resources may be underemployed and that full employment equilibrium requires state intervention.

Another important school is **new classical economics**, which seeks to show the futility of Keynesian demand-management policies and stresses instead the importance of **supply-side economics**, believing that the principal factor influencing growth of national output is the efficient allocation and use of labour and capital. A related school is that of the **Chicago monetarists**, led by Milton Friedman, who have revived the old idea that an increase in money supply leads inevitably to an increase in prices rather than in output; however, whereas the new classical school contends that wage and price adjustment are almost instantaneous and so the level of employment at any time must be the natural rate, the Chicago monetarists are more gradualist, believing that such adjustment may take some years.

market forces the forces of demand (a want backed by the ability to pay) and supply (the willingness and ability to supply).

monetarism economic policy that proposes control of a country's money supply to keep it in step with the country's ability to produce goods, with the aim of curbing inflation. Cutting government spending is advocated, and the long-term aim is to return as much of the economy as possible to the private sector, allegedly in the interests of efficiency. Monetarism was first advocated by the US economist Milton Friedman and the Chicago school of economists.

monetary policy economic policy aimed at controlling the amount of money in circulation, usually through controlling the level of lending or credit. Increasing interest rates is an example of a contractionary monetary policy, which aims to reduce inflation by reducing the rate of growth of spending in the economy.

money supply quantity of money in circulation in an economy at any given time. It can include notes, coins, and clearing-bank and other deposits used for everyday payments. Changes in the quantity of lending are a major determinant of changes in the money supply. One of the main

principles of monetarism is that increases in the money supply in excess of the rate of economic growth are the chief cause of inflation.

monopoly the domination of a market for a particular product or service by a single company, which can therefore restrict competition and keep prices high. In practice, a company can be said to have a monopoly when it controls a significant proportion of the market (technically an oligopoly). In communist countries the state itself has the overall monopoly; in capitalist ones some services, such as transport or electricity supply, may be state monopolies.

multiplier theoretical concept, formulated by John Maynard Keynes, of the effect on national income or employment by an adjustment in overall demand. For example, investment by a company in a new plant will stimulate new income and expenditure, which will in turn generate new investment, and so on, so that the actual increase in national income may be several times greater than the original investment.

national debt debt incurred by the central government of a country to its own people and institutions and also to overseas creditors. A government can borrow from the public by means of selling interest-bearing bonds, for example, or from abroad. Traditionally, a major cause of national debt was the cost of war but in recent decades governments have borrowed heavily in order to finance development or nationalization, to support an ailing currency, or to avoid raising taxes.

newly industrialized country (NIC) country that has in recent decades experienced a breakthrough into manufacturing and rapid export-led economic growth. The prime examples are Taiwan, Singapore, and South Korea. Their economic development during the 1970s and 1980s was partly due to a rapid increase of manufactured goods in their exports.

oligopoly in economics, a situation in which a few companies control the major part of a particular market.

productivity output produced by a given quantity of labour, usually measured as output per person employed in the firm, industry, sector, or economy concerned. Productivity is determined by the quality and quantity of the fixed capital used by labour, and the effort of the workers concerned.

public sector borrowing requirement (PSBR) amount of money needed by a government to cover any deficit in financing its own activities.

public sector debt repayment (PSDR) amount left over when government expenditure (public spending) is subtracted from government receipts. This occurs only when government spending is less than government receipts. A PSDR enables a government to repay some of the national debt. A PSDR enables a government to repay some of the national debt.

public spending expenditure by government, covering the military, health, education, infrastructure, development projects, and the cost of servicing overseas borrowing.

quantity theory of money economic theory claiming that an increase in the amount of money in circulation causes a proportionate increase in prices.

recession a fall in business activity lasting more than a few months, causing stagnation in a country's output.

reserve currency country's holding of internationally acceptable means of payment (major

foreign currencies or gold); central banks also hold the ultimate reserve of money for their domestic banking sector. On the asset side of company balance sheets, undistributed profits are listed as reserves.

retail-price index (RPI) indicator of variations in the cost of living, superseded in the USA by the consumer price index.

savings unspent income, after deduction of tax. In economics a distinction is made between investment, involving the purchase of capital goods, such as buying a house, and saving (where capital goods are not directly purchased; for example, buying shares).

Say's law 'law of markets' formulated by Jean-Baptiste Say (1767–1832) to the effect that supply creates its own demand and that resources can never be underused.

self-sufficiency situation where an individual or group does not rely on outsiders. Economic self-sufficiency means that no trade takes place between the individual or group and others. If an economy were self-sufficient, it would not export or import. For a family to be self-sufficient, for example, it would have to grow all its own food, make its own clothes, and provide all its own services. In a modern economy, there is very little self-sufficiency because specialization enables individuals to enjoy a much higher standard of living than if they were self-sufficient.

slump in the business or trade cycle, the period of time when the economy is in depression, unemployment is very high, and national income is well below its full employment level. In the UK, the economy experienced a slump in the 1930s (the Great Depression), in 1980–81, and 1990–92.

social costs and benefits costs and benefits to society as a whole that result from economic decisions. These include private costs (the financial cost of production incurred by firms) and benefits (the profits made by firms and the value to people of consuming goods and services) and external costs and benefits (affecting those not directly involved in production or consumption); pollution is one of the external costs.

stagflation economic condition (experienced in Europe in the 1970s) in which rapid inflation is accompanied by stagnating, even declining, output and by increasing unemployment. Its cause is often sharp increases in costs of raw materials and/or labour.

stock exchange institution for the buying and selling of stocks and shares (securities). The world's largest stock exchanges are London, New York (Wall Street), and Tokyo. The oldest stock exchanges are Antwerp 1460, Hamburg 1558, Amsterdam 1602, New York 1790, and London 1801. The former division on the London Stock Exchange between brokers (who bought shares from jobbers to sell to the public) and jobbers (who sold them only to brokers on commission, the 'jobbers' turn') was abolished in 1986.

stocks and shares investment holdings (securities) in private or public undertakings. Although distinctions have become blurred, in the UK stock usually means fixed-interest securities – for example, those issued by central and local government – while shares represent a stake in the ownership of a trading company which, if they are ordinary shares, yield to the owner dividends reflecting the success of the company. In the USA the term stock generally signifies what in the UK is an ordinary share.

trade cycle or **business cycle** period of time that includes a peak and trough of economic activity, as measured by a country's national income. In Keynesian economics, one of the main roles of the government is to smooth out the peaks and troughs of the trade cycle by intervening in the economy, thus minimizing 'overheating' and 'stagnation'. This is accomplished by regulating interest rates and government spending.

unemployment lack of paid employment. The unemployed are usually defined as those out of work who are available for and actively seeking work. Unemployment is measured either as a total or as a percentage of those who are available for work, known as the working population, or labour force. Periods of widespread unemployment in Europe and the USA in the 20th century include 1929–1930s, and the years since the mid-1970s.

Unemployment Rates by Selected Countries

Source: Organization for Economic Cooperation and Development

Data are annual averages. The standardized unemployment rates shown here are calculated as the number of unemployed persons as a percentage of the civilian labour force. The unemployed are persons of working age who, in the reference period, are without work, available for work, and have taken specific steps to find work. (N/A = not available.)

Country	1994	1995	1996	Country	1994	1995	1996
European Union	11.1	10.8	10.9	Japan	2.9	3.1	3.4
OECD	7.9	7.5	7.6	Luxembourg	3.2	2.9	3.1
Australia	9.8	8.6	8.6	Netherlands	7.1	6.9	6.3
Austria	N/A	3.9	4.4	New Zealand	8.1	6.3	6.1
Belgium	10.0	9.9	9.8	Norway	5.5	5.0	4.9
Canada	10.4	9.5	9.7	Portugal	7.0	7.3	7.3
Denmark	8.2	7.1	6.0	Spain	24.1	22.9	22.2
Finland	17.9	16.6	15.7	Sweden	9.8	9.2	10.0
France	12.3	11.7	12.4	Switzerland	3.6	3.3	3.3
Germany	8.4	8.2	9.0	UK	9.6	8.8	8.2
Ireland, Republic of	14.3	12.4	12.3	USA	6.1	5.6	5.4
Italy	11.4	11.9	12.0				

Glossary of Stock Market Terms

Source: The Stock Exchange

After hours dealing dealing done after the mandatory quote period which is treated as dealing done on the following business day

AGM Annual General Meeting of shareholders which a company must call every year

AIM Alternative Investment Market – the Exchange's new market which began trading in June 1995 for smaller and growing companies

Allotment letter see renounceable documents

APCIMS Association of Private Client Investment Managers and Stockbrokers

Arbitrage buying securities in one country, currency, or market, and selling in another to take advantage of price differences

Bear an investor who has sold a security in the hope of buying it back at a lower price as he thinks the market will go down

Bear market a falling market in which bears would prosper

Bed and breakfast deal selling shares one day and buying them back the next for tax purposes at the end of the financial year

Best execution brokers are advised to take reasonable care to find out the price which is the best available for their customers

Bid (1) the price at which the market maker will buy shares; (2) an approach made by one company wishing to buy the majority of another company's shares

Big Bang 27 October 1986, when the Exchange's new regulations took effect and the new automated price quotation system was introduced

Blue chip term for the most highly regarded shares; originally an American term, from the highest value poker chip

Bonus issue see Capitalization issue

Broker/dealer a London Stock Exchange member firm which provides advice and dealing services to the public and which can deal on its own account

Bull an investor who has bought a security in the hope of selling it at a higher price as he thinks the market will go up

Bull market a rising market in which bulls would prosper

Call the amount due to be paid to a company by the buyer of new or partly-paid shares

Call option the right (but not the obligation) to buy stock or shares at an agreed price up to a date in the future

Capital adequacy requirement for firms conducting investment business to have sufficient funds

Capitalization issue money from a company's reserves is converted into issued capital, which is then distributed to shareholders in place of a cash dividend; also known as a bonus or scrip issue

Commission the fee that a broker may charge clients for dealing on their behalf

Commodity any item that can be bought and sold; taken to refer to Exchange-traded items, including sugar, wheat, coffee, tin, etc

Consideration the money value of a transaction (number of shares multiplied by the price) before adding or deducting commission, stamp duty, etc

Contract note on the same day as a transaction takes place a member firm sends to the client a contract note detailing the transaction, including full title of the stock, price, stamp duty (if applicable), consideration, commission, time of deal, etc

Coupon (1) on bearer stocks, the detachable part of the certificate exchangeable for dividends; (2) denotes the rate of interest on a fixed interest security – a 10 percent coupon pays interest of 10 percent on the face value of the stock

Covered warrants covered warrants allow the buyer the right – but not the obligation – to buy or sell an asset at a specified price on, or before, a specified date

CREST the new paperless share settlement system, introduced by CRESTCo in 1996

Cum Latin for 'with', used in the abbreviations cum cap, cum div, cum rights, etc to indicate that the buyer of a security is entitled to participate in the forthcoming capitalization issue, dividend, or rights issue

Daily Official List the Daily Official List is the register of listed securities and gives the prices at which all stocks were traded on the previous day; it is produced by Extel

Debenture a loan raised by a company, paying a fixed rate of interest and secured on the assets of the company

Depositary receipts marketed internationally to sophisticated investors, these are negotiable certificates that give evidence of ownership of a company's shares. They are a good medium for international investors because they may be more liquid and more easily traded than the shares they represent

Discount when the market price of a newly issued security is lower than the issue price

Dividend that part of a company's profits after tax distributed to shareholders, usually expressed in pence per share; see final dividend and interim dividend

EDS Electronic Data Services – an historical turnover information service representing trading on the London Stock Exchange

EGM Extraordinary General Meeting – any meeting of a company's shareholders other than its AGM

Equity the risk sharing part of a company's capital, usually referred to as ordinary shares

Eurobond a long-term loan issued in a currency other than that of the country or market in which it is issued; interest is paid without the deduction of tax

Glossary of Stock Market Terms (continued)

Ex the opposite of *cum,* and used to indicate that the buyer is not entitled to participate in whatever forthcoming event is specified. Ex cap, ex dividend, ex rights, etc

FESE Federation of European Stock Exchanges

FIBV Fédération Internationale des Bourses de Valeurs (World Federation of Stock Exchanges)

Final dividend the dividend paid by a company at the end of the financial year

Fixed interest loans issued by a company, the government (gilts or gilt-edged), or a local authority, where the amount of interest to be paid each year is set on issue; usually the date of repayment is included in the title

Flotation the occasion on which a company's shares are offered on the market for the first time

FTSE indices figures that show the performance of the UK and the European markets over a period of time, the FTSE indices are run by FTSE International Ltd; they are:

FTSE 100	FTSE 250
FTSE Small Cap	FTSE 350 Yield
FTSE All-Share	FTSE Fledgling
FTSE Eurotrack 100	FTSE Eurotrack 200

Futures securities or goods bought or sold at a fixed price for future delivery; there may be no intention to take them up but to rely upon price changes in order to sell at a profit before delivery

Gearing a company's debts expressed as a percentage of its equity capital. High gearing means debts are high in relation to equity capital

GDRs Global Depositary Receipts are negotiable certificates that give evidence of ownership of a company's shares; they are marketed internationally, mainly to financial institutions

GEMMS Gilt-Edged Market Makers

Gilts or gilt-edged securities loans issued on behalf of the government to fund its spending; they fall into the following categories:

'longs': those with a redemption date greater than 15 years
'mediums': those with a redemption date between 5 and 15 years
'shorts': those with a redemption date within five years

Gross before deduction of tax

Index linked gilt a gilt whose interest and capital change in line with the retail price index

Insider dealing the purchase or sale of shares by someone who possesses 'inside' information about the company. This is the information on the company's performance and prospects which has not yet been made available to the market as a whole, and which, if available, might affect the share price. In the UK such deals are a criminal offence

Interim dividend a dividend declared part-way through a company's financial year, authorized solely by the directors

Investment Trust company whose sole business consists of buying, selling, and holding shares

IOSCO International Organization of Securities Commissions

Issuing house an organization, usually a merchant bank, that arranges the details of an issue of stocks or shares; it will also make sure the listing of that issue complies with Exchange regulations

LCAC Listed Companies Advisory Committee

Letter of renunciation this applies to a rights issue and is the form attached to an allotment letter which is completed should the original holder wish to pass entitlement to someone else, or to renounce rights absolutely

LIFFE London International Financial Futures and Options Exchange

Liquidity ease with which an item can be traded on the market

Listed company a company whose shares have been admitted to the Daily Official List; it has had to comply with the Exchange's listing regulations

Listing particulars the details a company must publish about itself and any securities it issues before these can be listed in the Daily Official List; often called a prospectus

Loan stock stock bearing a fixed rate of interest; unlike a debenture, loan stocks may be unsecured

London Market Information Link the Exchange's new main source of UK financial data for market professionals and information vendors; it is part of the Exchange's Sequence programme

Mandatory quote period the period of time from Monday to Friday when all registered market makers in a security must display their prices; for SEAQ the period is from 8.30 a.m.–4.30 p.m., and for SEAQ International, 9.30 a.m.–4.00 p.m.

Market maker an Exchange member firm which is obliged to offer to buy and sell securities in which it is registered throughout the mandatory quote period

Member firm a trading firm of the London Stock Exchange which may deal in shares on behalf of its clients or on behalf of the firm itself

Mid-price the price half-way between the two prices shown in the Daily Official list under 'Quotation', or the average of both buying and selling prices offered by the market makers; the prices found in newspapers are normally the mid-prices

Minimum quote size (MQS) the minimum number of shares in which market makers are obliged to display prices on SEAQ for securities in which they are registered

Net asset value the value of a company after all debts have been paid, expressed in pence per share

New issue a company coming to the market for the first time or issuing extra shares

Glossary of Stock Market Terms (continued)

Nil paid a new issue of shares, usually as the result of a rights issue, on which no payment has yet been made

Nil value shares shares newly issued by a company; these shares can usually be transferred on renounceable documents

Nominated adviser a London Stock Exchange approved adviser for AIM companies

Nominee name name in which a security is registered and held in trust on behalf of the rightful owner

Normal market size (NMS) the SEAQ classification system that replaced the old alpha, beta, gamma system; NMS is a value expressed as a number of shares used to calculate the minimum quote size for each security

Offer the price at which the market maker will sell shares to investors

Offer for sale a method of bringing a company to the market. The public can apply for shares directly at a fixed price; a prospectus containing details of the sale must be printed in a national newspaper

Option the right (but not the obligation) to buy or sell securities at a fixed price within a specified period

Ordinary shares the most common form of share; holders receive dividends which vary in amount in line with the profitability of the company and recommendation of directors; the holders are the owners of the company

Par the nominal value of a security

PEP a Personal Equity Plan, allowing investment in a number of shares. It carries various tax benefits including receiving dividends without paying income tax on the income, and sales free from capital gains tax on the profit

PIA Personal Investment Authority – the self-regulating organization responsible for personal pensions and unit trusts

Portfolio a collection of securities owned by an investor

POTAM or **Panel on Take-Overs and Mergers** regulates conduct of take-overs and is non-statutory

Preference shares these are normally fixed-income shares whose holders have the right to receive dividends before ordinary shareholders but after debenture and loan stock holders have received their interest

Preferential form the London Stock Exchange allows companies offering shares to the public to set aside up to 10 percent of the issue for application from employees and, where a parent company is floating off a subsidiary, from shareholders of the parent company; separate application forms, usually pink (hence the nickname pink forms), are used for this

Premium (1) if the market price of a new security is higher than the usual price, the difference is the premium; if it is lower, the difference is called the discount; (2) the cost of purchasing a trading option

Price/Earnings ratio (P/E ratio) a measure of the level of confidence investors have in a company (rightly or wrongly);

generally, the higher the figure, the higher the confidence. It is worked out by dividing the current share price by the last published earnings per share which is net profit divided by the number of ordinary shares

Price sensitive information information that has to be reported to the Exchange's Regulatory News Service, that may have an effect on a company's share price

Primary market the function of a stock exchange in bringing securities to the market for the first time; money is being raised either for the founders of the company or to fund future growth

Private company a company that is not a public company and which is not allowed to offer its shares to the general public

Privatization conversion of a state run company to a public limited company status often accompanied by a sale of its shares to the public

ProShare an independent organization that promotes share ownership among individual investors, including employees

Prospectus document giving the details that a company is required to make public to support a new issue of shares; see listing particulars

Proxy a person empowered by a shareholder to vote on his behalf at company meetings

Public limited company (plc) A company whose shares may be purchased by the public and traded freely on the open market and whose share capital is not less than a statutory minimum

Put option the right (but not the obligation) to sell at an agreed price at or within a stated future time

Quote vendors screen-based computer system providing instant information on prices of shares, foreign exchanges, and commodities

Redemption date the date on which a security (usually a fixed interest stock) is due to be repaid by the issuer at its full face value; the year is included in the title of the security; the actual redemption date is that on which the last interest is due to be paid

Registrar an organization that takes responsibility for maintaining a company's share register

Regulatory News Service (RNS) a service operated by the Exchange, in its role as competent authority for listing, which ensures that price-sensitive information from listed companies is collected and then disseminated to all RNS subscribers at the same time

Renounceable documents temporary evidence of ownership, of which there are three main types: when a company offers shares to the public, it sends an allotment letter to the successful applicants; if it makes a rights issue, it sends a provisional allotment letter to its shareholders; in the case of a capitalization issue, it sends a renounceable

Glossary of Stock Market Terms (continued)

certificate. All of these are in effect bearer securities, and are valuable. Each includes full instructions on what should happen if the holder wishes to have the newly issued shares registered in their own name, or if they wish to renounce them in favour of somebody else

RIE Recognized Investment Exchange – an investment exchange that meets the Security and Investments Board's requirements for recognition

Rights issue an invitation to existing shareholders to purchase additional shares in the company

SAEF SEAQ Automated Execution Facility – this enables small trades in UK shares to be carried out automatically at a computer terminal instead of over the telephone

Scrip issue see capitalization issue

SEAQ The Stock Exchange Automated Quotations system for UK securities; this is a continuously updated computer database containing price quotations and trade reports in UK securities. SEAQ carries the market makers' bids and offers for the UK securities and is part of the Exchange's Sequence programme

SEAQ International the Exchange's electronic price quotation system for non-UK equities; similar to SEAQ, it is part of the Exchange's Sequence programme

SEATS PLUS a service which supports the trading of listed UK equities in which turnover is insufficient for the market making system. It is distributed via a number of screen-based information services; it shows current orders, company information, historical trading activity for each stock and the sole market maker, where only one is registered; it is part of the Exchange's Sequence programme

Secondary market marketplace for trading in securities that are not new issues

Securities general name for stocks and shares of all types; in common usage, stocks are fixed interest securities and shares are the rest

Securities and Futures Authority (SFA) the self-regulating organization (previously known as the Securities Association) responsible for regulating the conduct of brokers and dealers in securities, options, and futures, including most member firms of the Exchange

Securities and Investments Board (SIB) agency appointed by the government under the Financial Services Act to oversee the regulation of the investment industry, including the SROs, RIEs, and clearing houses

Self-Regulating Organization (SRO) an organization recognized by the SIB and responsible for monitoring the conduct of business by, and capital adequacy of, investment firms

SEPON the Stock Exchange Pool Nominee – an account into which stock is registered during the course of settlement

Sequence an integrated, reliable computer system developed by the Exchange to deliver a wider range of better quality trading and information services to market participants; the SEAQ, SEATS, PLUS, and SEAQ International trading services operate on the new system

SETS Stock Exchange Electronic Trading Service

Settlement once a deal has been made, the settlement process transfers stock from seller to buyer and arranges the corresponding movement of money between buyer and seller (see Talisman)

Settlement day day on which bought stock is due for delivery to the buyer and the appropriate payment to the seller

Shares see Securities

Shorts See Gilts or gilt-edged securities

Stag one who applies for a new issue in the hope of being able to sell the shares allotted to him/her at a profit as soon as dealing starts

Stamp duty a UK tax currently levied on the purchase of shares

Stocks see Securities

Talisman the computerized settlement system used by the Exchange until April 1997, which acted as a central clearing house for transactions in equities (see CREST)

Tender offer in an offer by tender, buyers of shares specify the price at which they are willing to buy

Touch the best buying and selling prices available from a market maker on SEAQ and SEAQ International in a given security at any one time

Traded Options transferable options with the right to buy and sell a standardized amount of a security at a fixed price within a specified period

Transaction a deal made on the Exchange or subject to the rules of the Exchange

Transfer the form signed by the seller of a security authorizing the company to remove his/her name from the register, and substitute that of the buyer

Underwriting an arrangement by which a company is guaranteed that an issue of shares will raise a given amount of cash; the underwriters undertake to subscribe for any of the issue not taken up by the public; they charge commission for this service

Unit trust a portfolio of holdings in various companies, divided into units and managed by professionals

White knight a company that rescues another company which is in financial difficulty, especially one which saves a company from an unwelcome take-over bid

Yield the return earned on an investment taking into account the annual income and its present capital value; there are a number of different types of yield, and in some cases different methods of calculating each type

BELIEFS AND IDEAS

*

Religion is a code of belief or philosophy that often involves the worship of a God or gods. Belief in a supernatural power is not essential (absent in, for example, Buddhism and Confucianism), but faithful adherence is usually considered to be rewarded; for example, by escape from human existence (Buddhism), by a future existence (Christianity, Islam), or by worldly benefit (Sōka Gakkai Buddhism). A common factor in religions is the ascription to the God or gods of an interest in the behaviour of humans and their judgement of it as right or wrong, although the standards of morality attributed to gods vary enormously. From this follows the idea that a deity is to be obeyed, or at least placated, or retribution will follow. Assistance from a divine being can usually be obtained on certain terms. Most religions also have the idea of reward and punishment after death. In addition to each of these general ideas are a large number of ritual practices, such as penances, prayer, healing, festivities, and sacrifices; there are usually also teachings on morals and the afterlife.

RELIGIONS AND RELIGIOUS MOVEMENTS

Major World Faiths

Note: for religions other than Christianity, the abbreviations CE and BCE have been used for dates instead of AD and BC. in accordance with multi-faith practice.

Baha'i

The Baha'i faith originated in the mid-19th century in the area of present-day Iran. It is based on the belief that the man born as Mirza Husayn Ali in 1817 was the prophet sent by God to the present age. He is now known as Baha'u'llah – 'the Glory of God'. Baha'is believe that there have been revelations from God appropriate to each era, including the Torah, the New Testament, the Koran, and the words of the Buddha and the Hindu god Krishna. Baha'is maintain that these revelations have been superseded, although not contradicted, by the writings of Baha'u'llah and his successor Abdul Baha. These writings form the main body of Baha'i scripture. Baha'is believe that humanity is constantly evolving and growing more adult in its understanding and behaviour, and thus gradually becoming capable of forming one world rather than diverse nations, races, and religions. Baha'is also believe in One God, creator of all, and that humanity is a special creation, essentially good. The Baha'i teachings stress economic justice, equal rights, and education for all, and the breaking down of traditional barriers of race, class, and creed. These are seen as flaws that will disappear as the Baha'i faith becomes universal. The Baha'i international headquarters is in Haifa, Israel, and includes an International House of Justice in preparation for the time when there will be one world government, guided by the Baha'i faith. The Baha'i community meet in local spiritual assemblies whose structure is democratic and participatory, intended as a model for universal government. There are 5 million Baha'is worldwide in more than 175 countries, with the largest concentrations in the USA (approximately 300,000) and Africa (approximately 1 million). The claim that the Baha'i sacred texts are the successor to the Koran has led to criticism of Baha'i in many Muslim lands, including Iran, where the faith began. Most Baha'is today are not from Iran.

Buddhism

Buddhists follow the teachings of Siddhartha Gautama, given the title of the Buddha – the 'enlightened' or 'awakened' one. He was born the son of a nobleman in northern India in the 6th century BCE. He grew up in a palace protected from the harsh realities of life, but when he eventually encountered suffering, old age, and death, he left the palace to search for understanding of suffering and the way to end it. When he reached enlightenment, he began to teach the Four Noble Truths: Suffering exists; There is a reason for suffering; There is a way to end suffering; The way to end suffering is through the Eightfold Path. The Eightfold Path consists of Right Views, Right Thoughts, Right Speech, Right Action, Right Livelihood, Right Effort, Right Mindfulness, and Right Concentration. By learning and practising this path one can eventually escape the cycle of birth and death. Buddhists believe that all beings are reborn into many different forms because of the ties of desire. When desire is allowed to cool like a fire going out, the attachment to the cycle of birth and death is loosened. Buddhists try to perfect the qualities of wisdom, compassion, and harmlessness in order to achieve enlightenment, or Buddhahood, leading to the highest peace and freedom, which is nirvana. According to Buddhist tradition, there have been other Buddhas both before and since Siddhartha Gautama.

The teachings of the Buddha were handed down orally and eventually written in the first century BCE in a collection of writings called the *Tripitaka* – 'three baskets'. Different versions survive in Chinese, Tibetan, and Pali (an ancient south Indian language), and they are now translated into hundreds of languages worldwide. There are also important Buddhist scriptures written by later sages and scholars, many of them in the ancient Indian language Sanskrit. There are three main branches of Buddhism: Theravada, found mainly in southeast Asia, Sri Lanka, and India; Tibetan Mahayana; and Chinese/Japanese Mahayana. There is also a wide variety of new Buddhist movements. Each branch of Buddhism has its own festivals. The most common is Wesak (May/June), which celebrates the birth, enlightenment, and death of the Buddha, all of which happened on the same day in different years. It is impossible to estimate the number of Buddhists worldwide, as there is no central organization. The majority of Buddhists live in Asia, although Buddhism is growing rapidly beyond Asia, particularly in the USA and UK. More than 85% of the population of Myanmar (Burma) and Thailand are Buddhists, and more than 70% in Cambodia, Laos, and Japan. Buddhism is the state religion in Thailand and Bhutan. There is no central authority in Buddhism, each school having its own teachers and spiritual guides, although figures such as the Dalai Lama have raised the worldwide profile of Buddhism and voiced a Buddhist viewpoint on world affairs.

Christianity

Christians believe in one God who created the universe, and created human beings to have a special relationship with him. Through human wilfulness, exemplified in the story of Adam and Eve, this relationship was broken. Christians believe that because of his love for humanity, God took on the form of a man, Jesus, in order to bring them back into a relationship with him. The Gospels relate that Jesus was conceived by a virgin, Mary, through the power of God, and was born as a baby in Bethlehem. Modern scholarship now puts his birth around 4 BC. Christians take their name from the title given to Jesus: 'the Christ', meaning the anointed one of God. After three years of teaching, Jesus was crucified and died, but Christians believe that through the power of

Major World Faiths (continued)

God he came to life again. This belief was spread by Jesus's closest followers, the Apostles, and Christianity grew rapidly in the first three centuries AD. The Christian Bible consists of the Old Testament, originally written in Hebrew (the same book as the Hebrew Bible read by Jews), and the New Testament, originally written in Greek, which contains accounts of the life and teachings of Jesus, and letters from early Christians. The Bible is translated into many different languages. Major festivals are Christmas (December 25), which celebrates the birth of Jesus, and Easter (March/April), which celebrates his resurrection from death. There are nearly two billion Christians worldwide, especially in Europe, North and South America, southern Africa, and Australasia. Christianity has many different branches, referred to as churches or denominations. Catholicism is the largest with 900 million followers under the leadership of the Pope, who is based in Rome. Other major branches are Orthodox and Protestant. The Orthodox churches are self-governing, each led by a Patriarch. There is a large number of Protestant denominations, each with a different organization and authority. The World Council of Churches provides a forum for dialogue amongst the major Protestant Churches.

Hinduism

Hinduism encompasses a wide variety of beliefs originating in India, and is regarded by some as not constituting a formal religion at all. No precise dates can be given for its origins, although the Vedas, the earliest texts of Hinduism, arose from a culture that was probably established in India during the second millennium BCE. Most Hindus believe that God takes many forms and is worshipped by many different names, so the multitude of gods and goddesses in Hindu belief are aspects of the same godhead. God has three main male forms, Brahma the Creator, Vishnu the Preserver, and Shiva the Destroyer. Each of these has a female counterpart: respectively Sarasvati, Lakshmi, and Parvati. God may also come to earth in human form: the best known of these are Krishna and Rama, both incarnations of Vishnu. Each person and each animal embodies a spark (atman) of the universal soul, which is God. After death the atman is reborn in a new body. Therefore God is in every object in the universe, and everything that exists is part of God. Hindus believe that every action, good or bad, has an effect (karma) on this life and on future lives. By accumulating positive karma one can eventually break free from the cycles of birth and death to achieve liberation or moksha, which is complete union with God. There are many sacred books, all written in the ancient Indian language Sanskrit. The oldest are the Vedas, first written in the second millennium BCE, followed by the Upanishads, more philosophical writings. Two great epics, the Mahabharata and the Ramayana, existed in oral form long before they were written around 2,000 years ago. The Mahabharata contains the best-loved Hindu scripture, the Bhagavad Gita, or 'Song of the Lord', about the god Krishna. Festivals vary in different parts of India. Two almost universally celebrated festivals are Holi (March/April), a time of games and pranks with several different associated stories, and Divali (October), a new-year festival that celebrates the story of the god Rama and his wife Sita.

There are nearly 750 million Hindus worldwide, almost all living in south Asia. In India there are 650 million Hindus, and other large Hindu communities live in countries where colonial or trading ties encouraged migration from India: the UK, Guyana, Kenya, South Africa, and Indonesia.

Islam

The beliefs of Islam are summed up in the Declaration of Faith: 'There is no god but God, and Muhammad is the Prophet of God'. Islam means 'peace' or 'submission', and a Muslim is 'one who submits' (to the will of God). In Islam there is one God (Arabic Allah), who is creator of the universe and the only absolute power. According to Muslim belief, God has sent many prophets, from Adam onwards, to give his message to humanity, but their message was partially lost or misunderstood. The complete message is believed to have been given by the Prophet Muhammad, who lived in Arabia in the 6th century CE. Although this message marked the beginning of a formal religion, Muslims believe that all previous prophets were Muslims, and that Islam is the primordial faith. Muslims regard Muhammad with deep love and respect as God's final prophet, and seek to follow his example, but worship is due only to God.

Muslims believe that the Koran was dictated to the Prophet Muhammad by the angel Jibra'il, a messenger from God, and, because it was committed to memory and written down almost immediately, that it is the final and complete revelation from God. The Koran is believed to have been written by God, in Arabic, before time began. Muslims point to the beauty of the language as evidence of its divine origin, and it is always recited in Arabic. Muslim festivals are dated according to the lunar calendar. The main festivals are Eid-Lul-Fitr, celebrating the end of the month of fasting, and Eid-ul-Adha, celebrating the obedience of the prophet Ibrahim (Abraham), and the culmination of the annual pilgrimage to Mecca (Arabic Makkah). There are over a billion Muslims worldwide, especially in the Middle East, North and West Africa, southeastern Europe, Indonesia, and Malaysia. In 19 countries of the Middle East and North Africa, more than 90% of the population is Muslim. There are two main branches of Islam: Sunni who make up 80% of all Muslims, and Shi'a, who are found mainly in Iran, Iraq, Yemen, and Bahrain. There is no overall world organization of Islam, but several bodies have been set up to promote contact and to give Islam a voice in international affairs. These bodies include the World Muslim Congress, the Muslim World League, and the Organization of the Islamic Conference.

(continued)

Major World Faiths (continued)

Jainism

The word Jain means follower of the Jinas – 'those who overcome', in the sense of achieving discipline over one's own desires, thoughts, and actions. There were 24 Jinas, also known as Tirthankaras ('bridge-builders'), the last of whom was Mahavira who lived in India in the 5th century BCE. The first is believed to have lived millions of years ago and to have invented human culture. The example of the Jinas helps others to achieve freedom from reincarnation. The belief in non-violence, ahimsa, is central to the Jain tradition, and Jains try to avoid violence to life in every form, including animals and plants as well as humans. Jain monks and nuns wear a cloth over the mouth and nose to avoid harming any flying insects, and sweep the ground in front of them to avoid treading on any creature. This central teaching of non-violence has had a powerful effect on Indian culture and thought and was highlighted by the teachings of Mahatma Gandhi. The main festival is Paryushana (August/September), an eight-day period of confession and fasting. There are

8 million Jains worldwide, over 98% of them in India. The two largest Jain communities outside India are in the UK and the USA. The Jain tradition is divided into two groups: Svetambaras, who are concentrated in northeast India, and Digambaras, who mainly live in southern India. There are Jain temples in all the main Indian cities.

Judaism

Jews believe in one God, the Creator and Ruler of the universe. They believe that God made a Covenant, or agreement, with Abraham, who is regarded as the father of the Jewish people, and is believed by some scholars to have lived around 1900 BCE. Keeping the law is the Jewish people's part in this Covenant. Jews look forward to the coming of the Messiah, a leader from God, who will bring peace, fruitfulness, and security to the whole world. At the Messiah's coming, the dead will be brought back to life and judged by God. The Hebrew Bible consists of the Torah (Five Books of Moses), the Prophets, and other writings, including the Psalms. It was originally written in Hebrew, and is still read in Hebrew. The Torah tells the early history of the Jewish people, and contains laws and guidance on one's way of life. Study of the law is an important part of Jewish life. The fifth commandment lays down that no work must be done on the seventh day of the week, the Sabbath, or Shabbat. Since Jewish days are reckoned from nightfall to nightfall, the Sabbath begins as it gets dark on Friday evening, and ends at dusk on Saturday evening. Jewish food laws (called kashrut) relate to what is eaten, and how it is slaughtered, prepared, cooked, and eaten. Food is either kosher (permitted) or terefah (forbidden). Major festivals are Rosh Hashanah (New Year – September/October), Yom Kippur (the Day of Atonement) which is a major fast within the new-year period, and Pesach (Passover – March/April), which celebrates the escape of the Hebrews from slavery in Egypt. Jews have no overall religious authority, but questions of belief and practice are debated by Rabbis who are trained in Jewish law and its interpretation. The most traditional form of Judaism is known as Orthodox. Orthodox Jews use only Hebrew in services, and interpret the laws quite strictly. Conservative Judaism, mainly found in the USA, seeks to interpret the law in the light of changing circumstances, while remaining true to tradition. Reform, or Liberal, Judaism arose in the 19th century and observes fewer dietary laws,; services are held in the vernacular rather than in Hebrew. Bodies such as the World Jewish Congress, which represents around 70%t of all Jews, provide a forum for debate and a Jewish voice in world affairs. There are approximately 12.8 million Jews worldwide, in the sense that a Jew is the child of a Jewish mother, although not all are religious Jews who follow the laws given by God to Moses. Approximately 48% live in North America, 30% in Israel, and 20% in Europe and Russia.

Shintoism

Shinto is the traditional religion of Japan, and means 'the way of the gods'. Shinto religion is closely tied up with the landscape of Japan and with family ancestors. Shinto ceremonies appeal to kami, the mysterious powers of nature, for protection and benevolent treatment. Kami are associated with natural features such as caves, rocks, streams, trees, and particularly mountains. Communal festivals and personal landmarks are celebrated at Shinto shrines, some of which are linked to particular aspects of life such as a trade or old age.

Major festivals are New Year's Day and the Cherry Blossom Festival in early spring. It is difficult to estimate numbers of Shinto followers, since the majority of Japanese follow Shinto ceremonies and practices for particular occasions or because of a family tradition, but many combine this with another religion, especially Buddhism. Since Shinto worship is so intimately linked with the land of Japan, it is only found there or in émigré communities.

Sikhism

The Sikh faith began in the Punjab in India in the 15th century. Guru Nanak, the founder of Sikhism, taught this new faith that rejected both Hindu and Muslim religious and social practices of the time. The Punjabi word Sikh means 'follower' or 'disciple'. Guru Nanak was succeeded by nine further Gurus, or teachers, each of whom was chosen by his predecessor, and each of whom made a distinctive contribution to the development of the Sikh faith. In 1708 the collection of Sikh writings was instituted as the Guru for all time to come. Sikhs revere their scripture, the Guru Granth Sahib, as they would a living teacher. The Guru Granth Sahib contains hymns written by some of the Sikh Gurus. These were collected by Guru Arjan, the fifth Guru, who also added hymns and poems written by

Major World Faiths (continued)

devout Muslims and Hindus, saying that God's revelation is not confined to Sikhs. This collection was known as the Adi Granth, or 'first book'. Guru Gobind Singh, the tenth Guru, instituted this collection as the Guru for the Sikhs for all time. It is written in Gurmukhi, a form of written Punjabi. Sikhs believe in one God, described as 'timeless and without form', creator and director of the universe. He cannot be found by religious practices, but makes himself known to those who are ready, as they seek him through prayer and service to others. Sikh teachings emphasize equality, service, and protection of the weak against injustice. Sikhs wear five distinctive marks of their faith, known as the 'five Ks' because their names in Punjabi all begin with K:

Kesh – uncut hair. Devout Sikhs do not cut their hair or beard at any time.
Kanga – a comb to keep the hair in place. The hair is also kept tidy under a turban in imitation of the great Sikh Guru, Gobind Singh.
Kara – a steel bangle, a complete circle symbolizing one God and one truth.
Kirpan – a small sword or dagger, a reminder of the need to fight injustice.
Kacchera – short trousers or breeches, indicating readiness to ride into battle.

The main festivals are Baisakhi (April) which celebrates the founding of the Khalsa, the community of committed Sikhs, and the birthday of Guru Nanak (November). There are approximately 15 million Sikhs worldwide. Most of them (around 13 million) live in India, mainly in the Punjab in northwest India, but Sikhs have migrated to many parts of the world, and there are sizeable communities in the UK (up to half a million), the USA (over 250,000) and Canada (50,000), and smaller ones in East Africa, Europe, Malaysia, Indonesia, Australia, and New Zealand. The Sikh World Council was formed in 1995 to provide a forum and an international voice for Sikhs.

Taoism
Taoism emerged in China around the first century CE, and is named after the Chinese word *Tao* (Way or Path). The Tao is a natural force, the Way of the Universe, which guides all life. Living in harmony with the Tao brings peace and happiness; struggling against it brings suffering. The balance of the universe is created by the forces of yin and yang – opposite forces in continual interaction and change, giving order to all life. Yin is heavy, dark, moist, earthy, and is associated with the feminine. Yang is airy, light, dry, hot, heavenly, and associated with the masculine. All forms of life are either predominantly yin or yang, but never exclusively so. The yin/yang symbol represents the two forces in balance, but each containing a speck of the other. From the 5th to the 3rd century BCE, much was written on the significance of the Tao, most significantly the *Tao Te Ching* of Lao Tzu, the book of the sage Chuang Tzu, and the writings of Kung Fu Tzu (Confucius). They are still influential to this day, but there are also hundreds of other Taoist texts. By the 14th century CE, over 1,440 of these had been collected together to form the Taoist Canon. Traditional Taoist practices include the exorcism of evil spirits and ghosts, divination in various forms, and the worship of deities, many of whom have specific roles such as help in childbirth or different illnesses. The art of *feng shui*, or geomancy, is also practised in order to build in accordance with the Tao of the landscape. Major festivals are Chinese New Year (January/February) and the mid-autumn Moon festival. Because of the repression of religion in China, it is impossible to estimate the number of Taoists. However, the number of male and female Taoist priests in China is growing rapidly, and now stands at around 15,000. New temples are being opened and old ones restored. Taoist traditions are followed by members of Chinese communities throughout the world, and Taoist thought, literature, and philosophy is becoming increasingly popular with non-Chinese followers. The China Taoist Association promotes Taoism in China, although its function is partly political rather than religious.

Adventist person who believes that Jesus will return to make a second appearance on Earth. Expectation of the Second Coming of Christ is found in New Testament writings generally. Adventist views are held by the Seventh-Day Adventists, Christadelphians, and the Four Square Gospel Alliance.

American Indian religions religious beliefs of American Indians from Alaska to the tip of

totemism Totem poles in Stanley Park, Vancouver, Canada. Among the American Indians of the NW coast of America, images of totems – the animals with which a tribe or group within a tribe felt a special affinity – were often carved out of tall trees. In declaring the totem animal, totem poles often also announced the status, wealth, and family history of the owners.

Gods: Celtic

Celtic mythology has three traditions originating from Britain (including Wales), Gaul, and Ireland.

Alisanos god of the rock

Anoniredi (Gaul), **Anna** (Britain), **Anu** (Ireland) goddess of plenty; one aspect of the divine mother

Arianrhod in Welsh mythology, mother of Llew and Dylan

Badhbh war goddess, often portrayed as a crow or raven, also associated with divine metamorphosis

Banbha in Irish mythology, one of the three sisters who – together with Fodla and Eriu – formed the goddess of sovereignty, or the spirit of Ireland

Boann river goddess; mother of Oenghus

Belenus (Gaul), **Bel, Beli,** or **Belinus** (Britain), **Bíle** (Ireland) god associated mostly with solar symbolism and light, sometimes compared to the Greek Apollo; his other major aspects were Mabon and Oenghus, perhaps also Merlin. His cult was later replaced with the worship of the Archangel Michael in the Christian church

Blodeuwedd ('the flower maiden') deity associated with love and giving

Borvo, Bormo, or **Bormanus** (Gaul) god associated with thermal waters

Brigantu (Gaul), **Brigantia** or **Brighid** (Britain), **Brigit** (Ireland) goddess often associated with the Roman goddess Minerva; she was the patron of livestock and the produce of the earth; also goddess of crafts, therapy, and poetic inspiration. Later worshipped as St Brigit or St Bride in the Christian church

Cernunnos ('the Horned (or Peaked) One') ruler and protector of the animal kingdom, often portrayed in a zoomorphic manner, or accompanied by powerful animals (such as serpents or bulls); also the Lord of the Underworld. Early Christianity targeted him as the Devil; modern paganism endeavours to revive the worship of this deity

Cerridwen Welsh goddess of the Underworld and of dark prophetic powers, represented by a sow

Cliodna goddess of beauty and peace

Condatis god of confluence

Dea Arduinna one of many goddesses associated with wild animals, often portrayed with a wild boar

Dea Artio goddess associated with the bear, often connected to the Irish goddess Flidhais

Daghdha, Dagda, Dana, or **Donn** (Ireland), **Don** (Britain) the ancestor deity, often perceived to be the lord of the Otherworld, similar to the Roman god of the dead, Dis; sometimes associated with Cernunnos, father of Oenghus (the Irish Maponos); he was the greatest of Irish gods worshipped in Druidism as a god of wisdom and power

Dunatis god of fortified places

Dylan Welsh god associated with the sea; son of Arianrhod

Édain or **Étain** goddess of the Otherworld, maiden of joy and sorrow who was parted from, and then won back by, her divine husband Midhir

Epona (Gaul and Britain) the horse goddess, patroness of cavalry; sometimes associated with the Irish Édain and the Welsh Rhiannon

Flidhais Irish goddess who ruled the wild animals of the forests

Goibhniu (Ireland), **Gofannon** (Britain) god equivalent to the Roman Vulcan, he was thought to be a smith, a patron of crafts, but also of strength; often portrayed as the host of the Otherworld, accompanied by two further aspects, Creidhne (god of metal-working) and Luchtaine (divine wheelwright)

Grannos (Gaul and Britain) god associated primarily with curative powers and healing; similar to the Greek god Apollo

Ialonus god of the clearing of cultivated fields

Llew Welsh god associated with sacred kingship and Threefold Death; son of Arianrhod; sometimes associated with the Irish Lugh (equivalent of the Roman Mercury)

Lugh (Ireland), **Lugos** (Gaul), **Lleu** (Britain) god of skill, arts, crafts, and commerce; in the Gaulish tradition, portrayed like the Roman god Mercury; in the Irish tradition, his images are associated with youth, athleticism, and victory of light over darkness

Macha horse goddess associated with war, battle, and valour; linked also to festivals and ritual games

Maponos or **Maponus** (Gaul), **Mabon** (Britain), **Oenghus** (Ireland) god associated with music, healing, and youth; sometimes portrayed as a hunter; the 'Celtic Apollo'

Manannán (Ireland), **Manawydan** (Britain) deity of patience, wisdom, and counsel; also god of the sea, portrayed riding his chariot across the waves

Matres or **Matronae** (Gaul and Britain) goddesses and divine consorts, usually appearing in groups of three, symbolizing the concept of Earth as a divine mother; also associated with fertility, childbirth, and earthly fecundity

Medhbh of Connacht goddess of sexuality and physical love; a woman-warrior

Merlin one of the aspects of the 'Son of Light', a guardian god of the land; there are certain parallels between his mythical biography and the life of Christ as documented in the New Testament of the Christian church

Modron supreme divine 'Mother'; her divine child was known as Mabon ('Son')

Morríghan ('Phantom Queen') one of the goddesses of war and destruction; often appears in triple form together with Nemhain and Badhbh

Gods: Celtic (continued)

Nantosvelta goddess associated with water

Nemhain ('Frenzy') one of the goddesses of war and devastation

Nudd or **Nodons** (Britain), **Nuada** or **Nuadha** (Ireland) god associated with the protection of the kingship and with the sovereignty of the land

Ogmios (Gaul), **Ogmia** (Britain), **Ogma** or **Oghma** (Ireland) a giver of eloquence and strength; often associated with the Roman hero Hercules

Rhiannon Welsh goddess, the 'Great Queen', associated with the horse and totem birds

Silvanus (Gaul and Britain), **Sucellus** (Britain) god associated with the underworld, but also, probably, with the fertility of the earth; he is often portrayed with a mallet, a drinking jar, and, on occasion, with a dog; his companion was the goddess Nantosvelta

Taranis (Gaul), **Taran** (Britain) god of war and of leadership; often portrayed as a fearsome soldier; in Gaulish tradition associated with the Roman gods Mars and Jupiter

---

South America. They are numerous and often vastly different, and include **Shamanism,** new forms of **Christianity,** and **Peyotism.**

Armenian Church form of Christianity adopted in Armenia in the 3rd century. The Catholicos, or exarch, is the supreme head, and Echmiadzin (near Yerevan) is his traditional seat. Believers number about 2 million.

Babi faith faith from which the Baha'i faith grew.

Babism religious movement founded during the 1840s by Mirza Ali Mohammad ('the Bab'). An offshoot of Islam, it differs mainly in the belief that Muhammad was not the last of the prophets. The movement split into two groups after the death of the Bab; Baha'u'llah, the leader of one of these groups, founded the Baha'i faith.

Baha'i see **major world faiths** feature on pages 434–37.

Baptist member of any of several Protestant and evangelical Christian sects that practise baptism by immersion only upon profession of faith. Baptists seek their authority in the Bible. They originated among English Dissenters who took refuge in the Netherlands in the early 17th century, and spread by emigration and, later, missionary activity. Of the world total of approximately 31 million, some 26.5 million are in the USA and 265,000 in the UK.

Benedictine order religious order of monks and nuns in the Roman Catholic Church, founded by St Benedict at Subiaco, Italy, in the 6th century. It had a strong influence on medieval learning and reached the height of its prosperity in the early 14th century.

Black Muslims religious group founded in 1930 in the USA. Members adhere to Muslim values and believe in economic independence for black Americans. Under the leadership of Louis Farrakhan and the group's original name of the **Nation of Islam**, the movement has undergone a resurgence of popularity in recent years. In October 1995 more than 400,000 black males attended a 'Million Man March' to Washington, DC. Organized by the Nation of Islam, it was the largest ever civil-rights demonstration in US history.

Buddhism see **major world faiths** feature on pages 434–37.

Buddhism The Borobudur Buddhist monument, Java, built about AD 800. It consists of a hill covered in a terraced structure of five rectangular and four circular levels. The building is a mandala in which the visitor symbolically climbs levels of enlightenment. It was restored in the early 1980s. The restoration work involved reconstructing the entire edifice (which involved moving 1 million blocks of stone), laying new concrete foundations, and installing a new drainage system. *UNESCO*

Calvanism Christian doctrine as interpreted by John Calvin and adopted in Scotland, parts of Switzerland and the Netherlands; by the Puritans in England and New England, USA; and by the subsequent Congregational and Presbyterian churches in the USA. Its central doctrine is predestination, under which certain souls (the elect) are predestined by God through the sacrifice of Jesus to salvation, and the rest to damnation. Although Calvanism is rarely accepted today in its strictest interpretation, the 20th century has seen a neo-Calvanist revival through the work of Karl Barth.

Carmelite order mendicant order of friars in the Roman Catholic Church. The order was founded on Mount Carmel in Palestine by Berthold, a crusader from Calabria, about 1155, and spread to Europe in the 13th century. The Carmelites have devoted themselves largely to missionary work and mystical theology. They are known as **White Friars** because of the white overmantle they wear (over a brown habit).

Carthusian order Roman Catholic order of monks and, later, nuns, founded by St Bruno 1084 at Chartreuse, near Grenoble, France. Living chiefly in unbroken silence, they ate one vegetarian meal a day and supported themselves by their own labours; the rule is still one of severe austerity.

Catholic church whole body of the Christian church, though usually referring to the Roman Catholic Church.

Christianity see **major world faiths** feature on pages 434–37.

Christian Science or the Church of Christ **Scientist,** sect established in the USA by Mary Baker Eddy in 1879. Christian Scientists believe that since God is good and is a spirit, matter and evil are not ultimately real. Consequently they refuse all medical treatment. The church has publishes a daily newspaper, the *Christian Science Monitor,* which reports on international news.

Christians of St Thomas sect of Indian Christians on the Malabar Coast, named after the apostle who is supposed to have carried his mission to India. In fact the Christians of St Thomas were established in the 5th century by Nestorians from Persia. They now form part of the Assyrian church and have their own patriarch.

Church of England established form of Christianity in England, a member of the Anglican Communion. It was dissociated from the Roman Catholic Church in 1534 under Henry VIII; the British monarch is still the supreme head of the Church of England today. The service book is the Book of Common Prayer.

Church of Scotland established form of Christianity in Scotland, first recognized by the state in 1560. It is based on the Protestant doctrines of the reformer Calvin and governed on Presbyterian lines.

Cistercian order Roman Catholic monastic order established at Cîteaux in 1098 by St Robert de Champagne, abbot of Molesmes, as a stricter form of the Benedictine order. Living mainly by agricultural labour, the Cistercians made many advances in farming methods in the Middle Ages. The **Trappists,** so called from the original house at La Trappe in Normandy (founded by Dominique de Rancé in 1664), followed a particularly strict version of the rule.

Confucianism body of beliefs and practices based on the Chinese classics and supported by the authority of the philosopher Kung Fu Thi (Confucius). The origin of things is seen in the union of **yin** and **yang,** the passive and active principles. Human relationships follow the patriarchal pattern. For more than 2,000 years Chinese political government, social organization, and individual conduct was shaped by Confucian principles. In 1912, Confucian philosophy, as a basis for government, was dropped by the state.

Congregationalism form of church government adopted by those Protestant Christians known as Congregationalists, who let each congregation manage its own affairs. The first Congregationalists were the Brownists, named after Robert Browne, who defined the congregational principle jn 1580.

Copt descendant of those ancient Egyptians who adopted Christianity in the 1st century and refused to convert to Islam after the Arab conquest. They now form a small minority (about 5%) of Egypt's population. **Coptic** is a member of the Hamito-Semitic language family. It is descended from the language of the ancient

Egyptians and is the ritual language of the Coptic Christian church. It is written in the Greek alphabet with some additional characters derived from demotic script.

Dinka religion beliefs of the Dinka, a pastoral people of southern Sudan. It is dominated by Nhialic ('Sky'), who is God and speaks through a number of spirits who take possession of individuals in order to speak through them. The sacrificing of oxen forms a central component of the faith, carried out by leaders known as the Spear-Masters. These powerful figures guide the destiny of the people.

Dominican order Roman Catholic order of friars founded in 1215 by St Dominic. The Dominicans are also known as Friars Preachers, Black Friars, or Jacobins. The order is worldwide and there is also an order of contemplative nuns; the habit is black and white.

Dreamtime or **Dreaming** mythical past of the Australian Aborigines, the basis of their religious beliefs and creation stories. In the Dreamtime, spiritual beings shaped the land, the first people were brought into being and set in their proper territories, and laws and rituals were established. Belief in a creative spirit in the form of a huge snake, the Rainbow Serpent, occurs over much of Aboriginal Australia, usually associated with waterholes, rain, and thunder. A common feature of religions across the continent is the Aborigines' bond with the land.

Druse or **Druze** religious sect in the Middle East of some 300,000 people. It began as a branch of Shi'ite Islam, based on a belief in the divinity of the Fatimid caliph al-Hakim (996–1021) and that he will return at the end of time. Their particular doctrines are kept secret, even from the majority of members.

Eastern Orthodox Church see **Orthodox Church.**

Egyptian religion in the civilization of ancient Egypt, totemic animals, believed to be the ancestors of the clan, were worshipped. Totems later developed into gods, represented as having animal heads. One of the main cults was that of Osiris, the god of the underworld. Immortality, conferred by the magical rite of mummification, was originally the sole prerogative of the king, but was extended under the New Kingdom to all who could afford it; they were buried with the *Book of the Dead.*

Evangelical Movement in Britain, a 19th-century group that stressed basic Protestant beliefs and the message of the four Gospels. The movement was associated with the cleric Charles Simeon (1783–1836). It aimed to raise moral enthusiasm and ethical standards among Church of England clergy.

Franciscan order Catholic order of friars, **Friars Minor** or **Grey Friars,** founded in 1209 by Francis of Assisi. Subdivisions were the strict

---

Gods of Ancient Egypt

Ammon (Amen, Amun, or Amon; 'the hidden one') king of the gods, a sun god identified by the Greeks with Zeus (Roman Jupiter), portrayed with a ram's head or wearing a headdress bearing two goose plumes

Anubis (Anpu) jackal-headed god of the dead who oversaw the weighing of hearts; son of Osiris

Apis bull god, believed to be the personification of the creator god Ptah

Aton (Aten) sun god, supreme deity, worshipped as the one true god in the monotheistic religion introduced by the pharaoh Akhenaten

Atum a sun god and creator of the universe, the original god of Heliopolis, preceding Ra, shown wearing the double crown of united Egypt, often associated with a serpent

Batet (Bast, Pasht) a goddess identified by the Greeks with Artemis, portrayed originally as a lioness, later as a cat-headed woman, associated with sexual pleasure

Bes god of music and dance, usually shown as a grotesque dwarf

Geb god of earth; son of Shu and Tefnet

Hapi god of the Nile, shown as an overweight man with the breasts of a woman, symbolizing abundance and nourishment

Hathor (temenos [dwelling] of Horus) sky goddess, wife or mother of Horus, also goddess of dance, music, and love, corresponding to the Greek Aphrodite; she is depicted as a cow, or wearing a helmet in the shape of a sun-disc with cow's horns

(continued)

Gods of Ancient Egypt (continued)

Horus hawk-headed sun god, son of Isis and Osiris, of whom the pharaohs were declared to be the incarnation

Isis principal goddess of ancient Egypt; daughter of Geb and Nut (Earth and Sky), and sister-wife of Osiris

Khepre (Khepera) god of the rising sun, portrayed as a scarab beetle

Khonsu (Khons) moon god, sometimes portrayed with a falcon's head

Maat (Maut) goddess of order, justice, and truth; wore an ostrich feather on her head against which the hearts of the dead were weighed to estimate their purity

Min an aspect of the god Ammon, one of the oldest Egyptian deities

Montu a god of war and a solar god in Upper Egypt, portrayed as a man with a bull's or a hawk's head

Mut upper Egyptian counterpart of Sekhmet; the vulture was her sacred bird

Neferten son of Ptah and Sekhmet, representing the divine lotus and associated with the sun

Nephthys goddess of the dead; sister and wife of Set

Nu (Nun) personification of the primal waters, the chaos existing before form

Nut creator goddess, the fundamental female principle; portrayed as a cow

Osiris god who ruled the underworld after being killed by Set; the embodiment of goodness

Ptah the divine potter, a personification of the creative force; said to have brought both genders into existence from himself

Ra (Re) ancient sun god, often portrayed with a falcon's head

Sebek a crocodile god

Sekhmet 'the powerful she' goddess of war, portrayed as a lioness

Set god of night, the desert, and of all evils, portrayed as a grotesque animal; Set was the murderer of Osiris

Shu air god, portrayed in human form wearing an ostrich feather on his head

Tefnet (Tefnut) water goddess, portrayed as a lioness or lioness-headed

Thoth (Tehnuti) god of wisdom and learning, represented as a scribe with the head of an ibis, the bird sacred to him

---

Observants; the Conventuals, who were allowed to own property corporately; and the Capuchins, founded in 1529.

Free Church the Protestant denominations in England and Wales that are not part of the Church of England; for example, the Methodist Church, Baptist Union, and United Reformed Church (Congregational and Presbyterian). These churches joined for common action in the Free Church Federal Council in 1940.

Free Church of Scotland the body of Scottish Presbyterians who seceded from the Established Church of Scotland in the Disruption of 1843. In 1900 all but a small section that retains the old name (known as the **Wee Frees**) combined with the United Presbyterian Church to form the United Free Church of Scotland. Most of this reunited with the Church of Scotland in 1929, although there remains a continuing United Free Church of Scotland.

Gnosticism esoteric cult of divine knowledge (a synthesis of Christianity, Greek philosophy, Hinduism, Buddhism, and the mystery cults of the Mediterranean), which flourished during the 2nd and 3rd centuries and was a rival to, and influence on, early Christianity. The medieval French Cathar heresy and the modern Mandean sect (in southern Iraq) descend from Gnosticism.

Greek Orthodox Church see **Orthodox Church**.

Hasid or **Hassid, Chasid** (plural Hasidim, Hassidim, Chasidim), member of a sect of Orthodox Jews, originating in 18th-century Poland under the leadership of Israel Ba'al Shem Tov (c. 1700–1760). Hasidic teachings encourage prayer, piety, and 'serving the Lord with joy'. Many of their ideas are based on the kabbala.

Hinduism see **major world faiths** feature on pages 434–37.

Islam see **major world faiths** feature on pages 434–37.

Jainism see **major world faiths** feature on pages 434–37.

Japanese religions Japan is dominated by two religions: Shinto and various forms of Japanese

Gods of Ancient Greece

Aeolus god of the winds, who kept them imprisoned in a cave on the Lipari (Aeolian) Islands

Aphrodite goddess of love; unfaithful wife of Hephaestus, and mother of Eros

Apollo god of the sun, music, poetry, prophecy, agriculture, and pastoral life; the twin child (with Artemis) of Zeus and Leto

Ares god of war; the son of Zeus and Hera

Artemis goddess of chastity, the young of all creatures, the Moon, and the hunt; also associated with childbirth; twin sister of Apollo

Asclepius god of medicine whose emblem was the caduceus, a winged staff with two snakes coiled around it; son of Apollo

Athene (Athena, Pallas Athene) goddess of war, wisdom, and the arts and crafts, who was supposed to have sprung fully grown from the head of Zeus; she was the patron of Athens

Boreas god of the north wind

Cronos (Kronus) ancient fertility god who castrated his father and protected himself from a similar fate by eating his children; son of Gaia and Uranus and husband of Rhea

Demeter goddess of agriculture; daughter of Kronos and Rhea, and mother of Persephone by Zeus

Dione goddess worshipped alongside Zeus at his most ancient shrine at Dodona; said to be the daughter of Okeanos and Tethys and mother of Aphrodite

Dionysus (Bakkhos) god of wine, orgiastic excess, and mystic ecstasy; son of Semele and Zeus

Eos goddess of the dawn; daughter of Hyperion and Thea

Erebos primordial god of darkness who sprang from Chaos; father of Aither (upper air) and Hemera (day)

Eros boy-god of love who fell in love with Psyche, traditionally armed with bow and arrows; the son of Aphrodite

Erinyes (the Furies) goddesses with fearsome faces and serpents twisted in their hair, who visited retribution upon those who had committed crimes, such as filial disobedience, murder, inhospitality and oath-breaking, but who were also associated with fertility; their names were Alecto (relentless), Megara (resentful), and Tisiphone (avenger of murder)

Gaia (Ge) goddess of the Earth; she sprang from primordial Chaos and herself produced Uranus, by whom she was the mother of the Cyclopes and Titans

Graces (Charities) goddesses who personified beauty, grace, and good nature; named Aglaia (splendour), Euphrosyne (rejoicing of the heart), and Thaleia (blossom)

Hades god of the underworld (which bore his name); brother of Zeus and Poseidon

Hebe goddess of youth, who served nectar and ambrosia at Olympian banquets; dutiful daughter of Zeus and Hera

Hecate goddess of the underworld and magic, sometimes identified with Artemis and the Moon

Helios the sun god, thought to make his daily journey across the sky in a chariot; father of Phaethon

Hephaestus god of fire and metalcraft; son of Zeus and Hera, and husband of Aphrodite

Hera goddess of women and marriage; queen of the gods, sister and consort of Zeus, mother of Hephaestus, Hebe, and Ares

Hermes god of merchants, thieves, and travellers, and messenger of the gods who carried a staff around which serpents coiled; son of Zeus and Maia

Hestia goddess of the hearth

Hygieia goddess of health, whose sacred creature was a snake; daughter of Asclepius

Hypnos god of sleep, often depicted carrying a poppy; son of Nyx, brother of Thanatos, and father of Morpheus

Irene goddess of peace and wealth, sometimes regarded as one of the Horae, who presided over the seasons and the order of nature, and were the daughters of Zeus and Themis

Iris virgin rainbow goddess, messenger of the gods, depicted with wings and a staff

Kybele great mother goddess, originally from Phrygia and later identified with Rhea

Metis goddess of wisdom who helped Zeus to overcome his father Cronos; daughter of Okeanos and Tethys

Mnemosyne goddess of memory; the Titan mother, by Zeus, of the nine muses

Moirai (the Fates) the three goddesses who controlled human life: Klotho (spinner) who spun the thread of life, Lachesis (caster of lots) who tended the thread, and Atropos (death's inevitability) who cut the thread

Muses nine daughters of Zeus, who were each associated with a particular art or science: Calliope, epic poetry; Clio, history; Erato, love poetry; Euterpe, lyric poetry; Melpomene, tragedy; Polyhymnia, sacred song; Terpsichore, dance; Thalia, comedy; and Urania, astronomy

Nemesis goddess of justice and retribution

Nike goddess of victory, sometimes represented as winged

Nereus god of water, the sea in particular; older than Poseidon, he was called 'the old man of the sea'; his fifty daughters by the sea nymph Doris were the Nereids (divine sea nymphs)

Okeanos god who embodied the ocean, believed to be a great river encircling the earth

Pan god of flocks and herds, shown as a man with the horns, ears, and hoofed legs of a goat, and playing a shepherd's panpipe

Persephone (Kore) goddess and queen of the underworld: daughter of Zeus and Demeter

Phaethon son of Helios, the sun god, who was allowed to drive his father's chariot of the sun across the sky for one day; he lost control and plunged too close to the Earth, scorching parts of it

(continued)

Gods of Ancient Greece (continued)

and blackening the skin of some humans; he was killed by Zeus with a thunderbolt

Plutos (Pluto) a god of wealth, sometimes identified with the underworld

Pontos ancient embodiment of the sea

Poseidon chief god of the sea, also worshipped as god of earthquakes; brother of Zeus and Hades

Priapus god of fertility, represented as grotesquely ugly with an exaggerated phallus; son of Dionysus and Aphrodite; he was later a Roman god of gardens

Proteus a sea god with oracular powers; he could assume any shape and would do so to avoid answering questions

Rhea a fertility goddess, one of the Titans; wife of Cronos and mother of several gods, including Zeus

Selene goddess of the Moon; daughter of a Titan, and sister of Helios

Tethys sea goddess; daughter of Uranus and Gaia

Triton a merman sea god; son of Poseidon and the sea goddess Amphitrite

Uranus ('Heaven') the primeval sky god; son and husband of the Earth goddess Gaia, and father of Cronos and the Titans

Zephyrus god of the west wind; husband of Iris

Zeus chief of the gods who dispensed good and evil, he was the father and ruler of all; son of Cronos

Greek Religion

The religion of ancient Greece from the 8th to the 3rd century BC consisted of a pantheon of gods including Zeus; his consort Hera; Athena, the goddess of wisdom; Ares, the god of war; and many others, who lived on Mount Olympus/Greek religion, as a discernible form, emerged in the 8th century BC from what was formerly a collection of local or tribal deities. Greek religion was based upon a network of **mysteries** and sacred sites without a full-time professional priesthood. The mysteries were often associated with women, and appear to represent a very old strand in Greek religion. The oracles, such as that at Delphi and the healing centres associated with the god of medicine, Aesculapius, formed centres for Greek worship, as did the civic gods of each town who were honoured through plays and performances.

Under the influence of Plato, Greek religion of the last three centuries BC veered away from the pantheon of gods towards a more abstract notion of God as mind and as ultimate meaning, and a rejection of the notion, found in Homer, that human beings were the playthings of the gods of Mount Olympus.

Ephesus A marble statue of Artemis, Greek goddess of chastity, childbirth, the Moon, and the hunt, dating from the 2nd century AD, found in Ephesus, an ancient Greek seaport in Asia Minor (now Turkey). Ephesus was the centre of the Artemis cult, and her temple there was one of the Seven Wonders of the World.

Buddhism. Most Japanese, while saying they are not religious, will practise elements of both religions at appropriate times during the year and during central moments of their life. For example, birth is seen as the province of Shinto whereas most funerals are Buddhist.

Jehovah's Witness member of a religious organization originating in the USA in 1872 under Charles Taze Russell (1852–1916). Jehovah's Witnesses attach great importance to Christ's second coming, which Russell predicted would occur 1914, and which Witnesses still believe is

Hindu Gods

The Hindu pantheon is dominated by the primary gods Shiva and Vishnu, and, to a lesser extent, Brahma, the creator, who control the powers of destruction and preservation. Throughout India, Hinduism is organized around the two main sects, Vaishnavism and Shaivism, whose followers regard either Vishnu or Shiva as the pre-eminent deity. Vishnu is also worshipped in up to 22 earthly incarnations. The best-known deities and their aspects or incarnations are listed below.

Agni god of fire; a three-headed god who rides on a ram

Balarama brother of Krishna

Bhairava incarnation of Shiva

Brahma god of creation

Durga wife of Shiva, the inaccessible

Ganesh elephant-headed son of Shiva

Garuda bird on which Shiva rides

Hanuman monkey god

Indra storm god, bringer of rain

Iswara collectively represented as Trimurti by Brahma, Vishnu, and Shiva; Iswara corresponds to nature and the human soul

Kali goddess of destruction; evil wife of Shiva

Kalkin incarnation of Vishnu as a giant with a horse's head

Kama god of desire and sexual lust

Karaikkal-Ammaiyar mother goddess and teacher, often shown playing the cymbals

Karrttikeya six-headed, twelve-armed god who rides on a peacock

Krishna incarnation of Vishnu which corresponds to the perfect deification of life

Kurma incarnation of Vishnu as a tortoise

Lakshmana half-brother of Rama

Lakshmi (Sri) goddess of wealth and good fortune; wife of Vishnu

Mahadevi Shakti (Mahasakti) supreme goddess; corresponds to the Absolute (Brahman) and facilitates its self-manifestation

Mahishasuramardini consort of Shiva

Matsya incarnation of Vishnu as a fish

Nandin bull vehicle of Shiva

Narada incarnation of Vishnu

Narasimha incarnation of Vishnu as a man-lion

Nataraja aspect of Shiva as the lord of dance and rhythm

Parashurama incarnation of Vishnu

Parvati good wife of Shiva; opposite of Kali

Pidari consort of Shiva

Pushan the enhancer, prosperer, and enlightener

Radha consort of Krishna; represents romantic love

Rama incarnation of Vishnu

Rudra the violent, terrifying aspect of Shiva

Sarasvati mother goddess of art, music, and learning; female counterpart of Brahma

Savitri creator of the true and the just

Shakti female symbol of power or energy

Shani astral god and bringer of ill-luck

Shiva god of creation and destruction; lord of the dance

Shatrughna half brother of Rama

Sita wife of Rama

Skanda formed from the discarded semen of Shiva

Surya sun god; the illuminator

Uma the gracious; ascetic goddess

Vamana incarnation of Vishnu as a dwarf

Varaha incarnation of Vishnu as a boar

Virabhadra incarnation of Shiva

Vishnu god of creation

Yashoda foster mother of Krishna

imminent. All Witnesses are expected to take part in house-to-house preaching; there are no clergy.

Jesuit member of the largest and most influential Roman Catholic religious order (also known as the **Society of Jesus**) founded by Ignatius Loyola in 1534, with the aims of protecting Catholicism against the Reformation and carrying out missionary work. During the 16th and 17th centuries Jesuits were missionaries in Japan, China, Paraguay, and among the North American Indians. The order had (1991) about 29,000 members (15,000 priests plus students and lay members). Jesuits run schools and universities.

Judaism see **major world faiths** fatures on pages 434–37.

Lamaism Buddhism of Tibet and Mongolia, a form of Mahāyāna Buddhism. Buddhism was introduced into Tibet in AD 640, but the real founder of Tibetan Buddhism was the Indian missionary Padma Sambhava, who was active about 750. Tibetan Buddhism developed several orders, based on lineages of teachings transmitted by reincarnated lamas (teachers). In the 14th–15th centuries Tsong-kha-pa founded the sect of Geluk-Pa ('virtuous'), which became the most powerful order in the country. Its head is the Dalai Lama, who

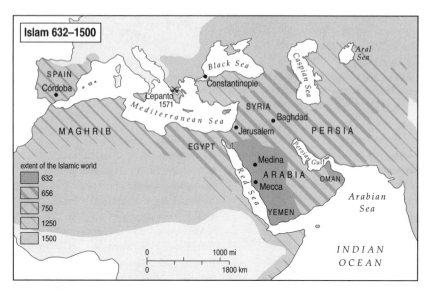

Islam The spread of Islam from the death of the prophet Muhammad till the Battle of Lepanto, after which Ottoman power declined.

is considered an incarnation of the Bodhisattva Avalokiteśvara.

Lutheranism form of Protestant Christianity derived from the life and teaching of Martin Luther; it is sometimes called Evangelical to distinguish it from the other main branch of European Protestantism, the Reformed. The most generally accepted statement of Lutheranism is that of the **Confession of Augsburg** in 1530 but Luther's *Shorter Catechism* also carries great weight. It is the largest Protestant body, including some 80 million persons, of whom 40 million are in Germany, 19 million in Scandinavia, 8.5 million in the USA and Canada, with most of the remainder in central Europe.

Maori religion religion of the original inhabitants of New Zealand, having the god Io at its peak, who acts through an array of gods, spirits, and ancestors. The world of the dead is seen as the most dangerous because it overlaps with this world. It is filled with *mana,* a dynamic holy power which can spill over into this world, causing great troubles or, conversely, endowing great powers. Nature is imbued with great power and sanctity and it is essential for human wellbeing that the land is content and cared for.

Mayan religion religion of the Maya people of Central America. The religion of pre-conquest

Central America has survived almost unchanged in some rural areas, whereas in other areas there are heavy influences from Catholicism, which in its turn is influenced by Mayan traditions. In pre-conquest times, the main deities were the Earth Lord, who protected the crops, the Father Sun, the Mother Moon, and the Morning Star, who was the warriors' god. Today the Mother Moon is often linked to the Virgin Mary but the Earth Lord is to be found worshipped as before, though local saints also have a role in crop protection. The Mayans believe that each person has an animal spirit which inhabits a creature born at the same time. Should the animal be killed, the person also dies. Like most Central American traditional religions, it is shamanistic in basis.

megalithic religions the beliefs of the cultures that raised the megalithic monuments such as Stonehenge, the stone circles found across Ireland and Scotland, and the great sacred sites such as Avebury in England. Probably the megalithic monuments were related to the movement of the Sun and acted as centres of calculation for the seasons of the year. There are approximately 50,000 megalithic monuments across Europe; they were clearly focal points for considerable numbers of communities and may have had a social as well as specifically religious function.

Methodism evangelical Protestant Christian movement that was founded by John Wesley in 1739

Gods of Nordic Mythology

Aegir god of the sea, married to Ran; their nine daughters were waves of the sea

Aesir a race of gods belonging to the sky, warlike in nature, and including most of the more familiar deities

Balder (Beldur) the best, wisest, and most loved of all the gods; son of Odin and Freya and husband of Nanna; he was killed, at Loki's instigation, by a twig of mistletoe shot by the blind god Hoder

Eostre (Ostara) an Anglo-Saxon goddess of spring; identified with the rising sun

Frey (Freyr) fertility god; brother of Freya

Freya (Freyja, Gefn) goddess of married love and the hearth; wife of Odin and mother of Thor

Frigg (Friga) the chief goddess, often identified with Freya; associated with Venus by the Romans

Gefion goddess of virginity and fertility

Heimdall god of light, who was present at the birth of the world, and who watches over the other gods

Hel (Hela) goddess of the underworld

Hoder (Hodur) blind god who killed Balder

Hoenir creator god who, with Odin and Lodur, made the first humans, endowing them with the senses

Idun goddess, keeper of the golden apples of eternal youth

Lodur creator god who, with Odin and Hoenir, made the first humans, endowing them with life and energy

Loki one of the principal gods, but cause of dissension among the gods, and the slayer of Balder; also known as god of mischief

Mimir guardian of the well of knowledge

Nanna wife of Balder; died of grief after his murder

Njord god of sailors and fishermen

Norn any of three goddesses of fate: the goddess of the past (Urd), the goddess of the present (Verdandi), and the goddess of the future (Skuld)

Odin chief god, the **Woden** or **Wotan** of the Germanic peoples; a sky god, he lives in Asgard (Walhallo), at the top of the world-tree, with his wife Freya; together with Hoenir and Lodur, he created the first humans and endowed them with a soul

Ran storm goddess; wife of Aegir

Sif corn goddess; wife of Thor

Sigyn wife of Loki

Skadi mountain goddess; wife of Njord, mother of Frey and Freya

Sol sun goddess who drove her chariot across the sky

Thor god of thunder (his hammer); son of Odin and Freya

Tyr (Tiw, Tiwaz) god of battles

Ull god of justice and fertility; son of Sif

Vali son of Odin, who avenged Balder's death by killing Hoder

Valkyries female warrior spirits who assisted Odin by training and protecting warriors

Vanir a peaceful race of gods associated with the earth and fertility

Ve (Vili) brother of Odin

Vidar son of Odin who avenged his death by killing the wolf

---

within the Church of England, but became a separate body in 1795. The Methodist Episcopal Church was founded in the USA in 1784. There are over 50 million Methodists worldwide.

Moonie popular name for a follower of the Unification Church, a religious sect founded by Sun Myung Moon.

Mormon or **Latter-day Saint**, member of a Christian sect, the **Church of Jesus Christ of Latter-day Saints,** founded at Manchester, New York, in 1830 by Joseph Smith. According to Smith, Mormon was an ancient prophet in North America whose *Book of Mormon,* of which Smith claimed divine revelation, is accepted by Mormons as part of the Christian

scriptures. It is a missionary church with headquarters in Utah and a worldwide membership of about 6 million.

Orthodox Church or **Eastern Orthodox Church** or **Greek Orthodox Church** federation of self-governing Christian churches mainly found in Eastern Europe and parts of Asia. The centre of worship is the Eucharist. There is a married clergy, except for bishops; the Immaculate Conception is not accepted. The highest rank in the church is that of ecumenical patriarch, or bishop of Istanbul. There are (1990) about 130 million adherents.

Pentecostal movement Christian revivalist movement inspired by the baptism in the Holy Spirit with 'speaking in tongues' experienced by the apostles at the time of Pentecost. It represents a reaction against the rigid theology and formal worship of the traditional churches. Pentecostalists believe in the literal word of the Bible. It is an intensely missionary faith, and recruitment has been rapid since the 1960s: worldwide membership is more than 10 million.

Presbyterianism system of Christian Protestant church government, expounded during the Reformation by John Calvin, which gives its name to the established Church of Scotland, and is also practised in England, Wales, Ireland, Switzerland, North America, and elsewhere. There is no compulsory form of worship and each congregation is governed by presbyters or elders (clerical or lay), who are of equal rank.Congregations are grouped in presbyteries, synods, and general assemblies.

Protestantism one of the main divisions of Christianity, which emerged from Roman Catholicism at the Reformation. The chief denominations are the Anglican Communion (Episcopalian in the USA), Baptists, Lutherans, Methodists, Pentecostals, and Presbyterians, with a total membership of about 300 million.

Puritan from 1564, a member of the Church of England who wished to eliminate Roman Catholic survivals in church ritual, or substitute a presbyterian for an episcopal form of church government. The term also covers the separatists who withdrew from the church altogether. The Puritans were increasingly identified with the parliamentary opposition under James I and Charles I.

Quaker popular name, originally derogatory, for a member of the Society of Friends.

Rastafarianism religion originating in the West Indies, based on the ideas of Marcus Garvey, who called on black people to return to Africa and set up a black-governed country there. When Haile Selassie (**Ras Tafari,** 'Lion of Judah') was crowned emperor of Ethiopia in 1930, this was seen as a fulfilment of prophecy and some Rastafarians acknowledged him as an incarnation of God (**Jah**), others as a prophet. The use of ganja (marijuana) is a sacrament. There are no churches. There were about 1 million Rastafarians by 1990.

Roman Catholicism one of the main divisions of the Christian religion, separate from the Eastern Orthodox Church from 1054, and headed by the pope. Membership in 1995 was about 970 million worldwide, concentrated in southern Europe, Latin America, and the Philippines.

Roman religion religious system that retained early elements of animism (with reverence for stones and trees) and totemism (see Romulus and Remus), and had a strong domestic base in the lares and penates, the cult of Janus and Vesta. It also had a main pantheon of gods derivative from the Greek one, which included Jupiter and Juno, Mars and Venus, Minerva, Diana, Ceres, and many lesser deities (see Gods of Ancient Rome).

Russian Orthodox Church one of the main branches of the **Orthodox Church.**

Scientology 'applied religious philosophy' based on dianetics, founded in California in 1952 by L Ron Hubbard as the **Church of Scientology,** and claiming to 'increase man's spiritual awareness'. Its headquarters from 1984 have been in Los Angeles.

Seventh-Day Adventist, member of the Protestant religious sect of the same name. It originated in the USA in the fervent expectation of Christ's Second Coming, or advent, that swept across New York State following William Miller's prophecy that Christ would return on 22 October 1844. When this failed to come to pass, a number of Millerites, as his followers were called, reinterpreted his prophetic speculations and continued to maintain that the advent was imminent. Adventists observe Saturday as the Sabbath and emphasize healing and diet; many are vegetarians. The sect has 36,920 organized churches and almost 8 million members in 210 countries and territories (1995).

Shi'ite or **Shiah** member of a sect of Islam that believes that Ali was Muhammad's first true successor. The Shi'ites are doctrinally opposed to the Sunni Muslims. They developed their own law differing in certain directions, such as inheritance and the status of women. In Shi'ism, the clergy are empowered to intervene between God and humans, whereas among the Sunni, the relationship with God is direct and the clergy serve as advisers. The Shi'ites are prominent in Iran,

Gods of Ancient Rome

Aesculapius god of medicine, equivalent to the Greek Asclepius

Apollo in Greek and Roman mythology, the god of the sun, music, poetry, prophecy, agriculture, and pastoral life; he was the twin of Diana

Aurora goddess of the dawn; her Greek equivalent is Eos

Bacchus god of fertility and of wine; identified with the Greek Dionysus

Bellona goddess of war

Ceres goddess of agriculture; equivalent to the Greek Demeter

Cupid god of love; identified with the Greek Eros

Diana goddess of chastity, hunting, and the Moon; daughter of Jupiter and twin of Apollo; her Greek equivalent is the goddess Artemis

Dis god of the underworld, also known as Orcus, equivalent to the Greek Hades; Dis is also a synonym for the underworld itself

Faunus god of fertility and prophecy, with goat's ears, horns, tail, and hind legs; identified with the Greek Pan

Flora goddess of flowers, youth, and spring

Fortuna goddess of chance and good fortune; identified with the Greek Tyche

Janus god of doorways and passageways, after whom January is named; he is represented as having two faces, one looking forwards and one back; also god of past, present, and future, considered to be the god who gave agriculture and law to humanity

Juno principal goddess, identified with the Greek Hera; the wife of Jupiter, she was concerned with all aspects of women's lives

Jupiter (Jove) chief god, identified with the Greek Zeus; he was god of the sky, associated with lightning and thunderbolts, the protector in battle, and the bestower of victory

Luna goddess of the moon

Maia earth goddess, sometimes seen as the mother of Mercury

Mars god of war, equivalent to the Greek Ares

Mercury a god, identified with the Greek Hermes, and, like him, represented with winged sandals and a winged staff entwined with snakes; he was the messenger of the gods and was associated particularly with commerce

Minerva goddess of intelligence, and of handicrafts and the arts; equivalent to the Greek Athena

Mithras sun god and god of light

Neptune god of the sea; equivalent to the Greek Poseidon

Ops goddess of harvest and growth of seed; wife of Saturn

Pales goddess of flocks and shepherds

Parcae three goddesses – Decima, Nona, and Morta – equated with the Greek Moirai

Pax goddess of peace; equivalent to the Greek Irene

Pluto god of the underworld

Pomona goddess of fruit trees who is often depicted in art holding a cornucopia, symbolizing the fruits of the earth

Priapus originally a Greek fertility god; later a Roman god of gardens, where his image was frequently used as a scarecrow

Proserpine goddess of the underworld; her Greek equivalent is Persephone

Saturn god of agriculture; identified by the Romans with the Greek god Cronos

Silvanus a woodland god, at times identified with the Greek Pan

Sol sun god

Tellus goddess of the Earth; identified with a number of other agricultural gods and celebrations

Terminus god of land boundaries whose worship was associated with that of Jupiter

Venus goddess of love and beauty, equivalent to the Greek Aphrodite; as mother of Aeneas, she was regarded as guardian of the Roman people, as well as goddess of military victory and patroness of spring

Vertumnus ancient Etruscan god of seasonal change and of fruit; husband of Pomona

Vesta goddess of the hearth; equivalent to the Greek Hestia

Vulcan god of fire and destruction; later identified with the Greek god Hephaestus

---

the Lebanon, and Indo-Pakistan, and are also found in Iraq and Bahrain.

Shintoism see **major world faiths** feature on pages 434–37.

Sikhism see **major world faiths** feature on pages 434–37.

Society of Friends Protestant sect founded by George Fox in England in the 17th century. They were persecuted for their nonviolent activisim and many emigrated to form new communities, such as in Pennsylvania and New England.

Sumerian religion religion of the Sumerian civilization. Sumerian society was ruled by gods – everything belonged to the gods and the kings were their representatives. Humanity's role was to serve the gods and to fulfil their will in their eternal struggles with each other.

Sunni member of the larger of the two main sects of Islam, with about 680 million adherents. Sunni Muslims believe that the first three caliphs were all legitimate successors of the prophet Muhammad, and that guidance on belief and life should come from the Koran and the Hadith, and from the Shari'a, not from a human authority or spiritual leader. Imams in Sunni Islam are educated lay teachers of the faith and prayer leaders.

Tamil Hinduism traditional form of Hinduism found in southern India, particularly in Tamil Nadu, where the invasions and political upheavals of northern India had little influence. The important centres of Tamil Hinduism are Rameshvaram, dedicated to Shiva; Shrirangam, dedicated to Vishnu; and Madurai, dedicated to Meenakshi, the wife of Shiva. Tamil temple architecture is characterized by towering *gopurams*, or temple gateways.

Taoism see **major world faiths** feature on pages 434–37.

Unification Church or **Moonies** church founded in Korea in 1954 by the Reverend Sun Myung Moon. The number of members (often called 'moonies') is about 200,000 worldwide. The theology unites Christian and Taoist ideas and is based on Moon's book *Divine Principle*, which teaches that the original purpose of creation was to set up a perfect family, in a perfect relationship with God.

Unitarianism a Christian denomination that rejects the orthodox doctrine of the Trinity, asserts the fatherhood of God and the brotherhood of humanity, and gives a pre-eminent position to Jesus as a religious teacher, while denying his divinity.

voodoo set of magical beliefs and practices, followed in some parts of Africa, South America, and the West Indies, especially Haiti. It arose in the 17th century on slave plantations as a combination of Roman Catholicism and West African religious traditions; believers claim to retain membership in the Roman Catholic church. It was once practiced in New Orleans and other areas of southern USA by African-Americans. Beliefs include the existence of **loa**, spirits who closely involve themselves in human affairs, and some of whose identities mesh with those of Christian saints. The loa are invoked by the priest (*houngan*) or priestess (*manbo*) at ceremonies, during which members of the congregation become possessed by the spirits and go into a trance.

Zoroastrianism pre-Islamic Persian religion founded by the Persian prophet Zoroaster in the 6th century BC, and still practised by the Parsees in India. The **Zend-Avesta** are the sacred scriptures of the faith. The theology is dualistic, **Ahura Mazda** or **Ormuzd** (the good God) being perpetually in conflict with **Ahriman** (the evil God), but the former is assured of eventual victory. There are approximately 100,000 (1991) Zoroastrians worldwide; membership is restricted to those with both parents belonging to the faith.

HOLY BOOKS

Adi Granth or **Guru Granth Sahib** holy book of Sikhism; see *Guru Granth Sahib.*

Apocrypha (Greek *apokryptein* 'to hide away') appendix to the Old Testament of the Bible, 14 books not included in the final Hebrew canon but recognized by Roman Catholics. There are also disputed New Testament texts known as Apocrypha.

Bardo Thödol or **Book of the Dead** Tibetan Buddhist text giving instructions to the newly dead about the Bardo, or state between death and rebirth.

Bhagavad-Gītā (Hindi 'the Song of the Blessed') religious and philosophical Sanskrit poem, dating from around 300 BC, forming an episode in the sixth book of the *Mahābhārata,* one of the two great Hindu epics. It is the supreme religious work of Hinduism.

Bible (Greek *ta biblia* 'the books') the sacred book of the Jewish and Christian religions. The Hebrew Bible, recognized by both Jews and Christians, is called the **Old Testament** by Christians. The **New Testament** comprises books recognized by the Christian church from the 4th century as canonical. The Roman Catholic Bible also includes the **Apocrypha.**

Books of the Bible

Name of book	Chapters	Date written	Name of book	Chapters	Date written
Books of the Old Testament			Nahum	3	c. 626 BC
Genesis	50	mid-8th century BC	Habakkuk	3	c. 600 BC
Exodus	40	950–586 BC	Zephaniah	3	3rd century BC
Leviticus	27	mid-7th century BC	Haggai	2	c. 520 BC
Numbers	36	850–650 BC	Zechariah	14	c. 520 BC
Deuteronomy	34	mid-7th century BC	Malachi	4	c. 430 BC
Joshua	24	c. 550 BC			
Judges	21	c. 550 BC	*Books of the New Testament*		
Ruth	4	late 3rd century BC	Matthew	28	before AD 70
1 Samuel	31	c. 900 BC	Mark	16	before AD 70
2 Samuel	24	c. 900 BC	Luke	24	AD 70–80
1 Kings	22	550–600 BC	John	21	AD 90–100
2 Kings	25	550–600 BC	Acts	28	AD 70–80
1 Chronicles	29	c. 300 BC	Romans	16	AD 120
2 Chronicles	36	c. 300 BC	1 Corinthians	16	AD 57
Ezra	10	c. 450 BC	2 Corinthians	13	AD 57
Nehemiah	13	c. 450 BC	Galatians	6	AD 53
Esther	10	c. 200 BC	Ephesians	6	AD 140
Job	42	600–400 BC	Philippians	4	AD 63
Psalms	150	6th–2nd century BC	Colossians	4	AD 140
Proverbs	31	350–150 BC	1 Thessalonians	5	AD 50–54
Ecclesiastes	12	c. 200 BC	2 Thessalonians	3	AD 50–54
Song of Solomon	8	3rd century BC	1 Timothy	6	before AD 64
Isaiah	66	late 3rd century BC	2 Timothy	4	before AD 64
Jeremiah	52	604 BC	Titus	3	before AD 64
Lamentations	5	586–536 BC	Philemon	1	AD 60–62
Ezekiel	48	6th century BC	Hebrews	13	AD 80–90
Daniel	12	c. 166 BC	James	5	before AD 52
Hosea	14	c. 732 BC	1 Peter	5	before AD 64
Joel	3	c. 500 BC	2 Peter	3	before AD 64
Amos	9	775–750 BC	1 John	5	AD 90–100
Obadiah	1	6th–3rd century BC	2 John	1	AD 90–100
Jonah	4	600–200 BC	3 John	1	AD 90–100
Micah	7	late 3rd century BC	Jude	1	AD 75–80
			Revelation	22	AD 81–96

Common Prayer, Book service book of the Church of England and the Episcopal Church, based largely on the Roman breviary.

Guru Granth Sahib holy book of Sikhism, a collection of nearly 6,000 hymns by the first five and the ninth Sikh gurus, but also including the writings of some Hindus and Muslims. It is regarded as a living guru and treated with the respect that this implies.

Hebrew Bible sacred writings of Judaism (some dating from as early as 1200 BC), called by Christians the Old Testament. It includes the Torah (the first five books, ascribed to Moses), historical and prophetic books, and psalms, originally written in Hebrew and later translated into Greek (Septuagint) and other languages.

Hours, Book of a collection of liturgical prayers for the use of the faithful in medieval Europe.

I Ching or **Book of Changes** ancient Chinese book of divination based on 64 hexagrams, or patterns of six lines. The lines may be 'broken' or 'whole' (yin or yang) and are generated by tossing yarrow stalks or coins. The enquirer formulates a question before throwing, and the book gives interpretations of the meaning of the hexagrams.

Koran (alternatively transliterated as **Quran**) the sacred book of Islam, written in Arabic. It is said to have been divinely revealed through the angel Gabriel, or Jibra'el, to the prophet Muhammad between about AD 610 and 632. The Koran is the prime source of all Islamic ethical and legal doctrines.

Mahabharata (Sanskrit 'great poem of the Bharatas') Sanskrit Hindu epic consisting of 18 books and 90,000 stanzas, probably composed in its present form about 300 BC. It forms with the *Ramayana* the two great epics of the Hindus. It contains the *Bhagavad-Gita,* or *Song of the Blessed,* an episode in the sixth book.

New Testament second part of the Bible, recognized by the Christian church from the 4th century as sacred doctrine. The New Testament includes the Gospels, which tell of the life and teachings of Jesus, the history of the early church, the teachings of St Paul, and mystical writings. It was written in Greek during the 1st and 2nd centuries AD, and the individual sections have been ascribed to various authors by biblical scholars.

Old Testament Christian term for the Hebrew Bible, which is the first part of the Christian Bible. It contains 39 (according to Christianity) or 24 (according to Judaism) books, which include the origins of the world, the history of the ancient Hebrews and their covenant with God, prophetical writings, and religious poetry. The first five books (*The Five Books of Moses)* are traditionally ascribed to Moses and known as the Pentateuch (by Christians) or the Torah (by Jews).

Ramayana Sanskrit epic of *c.* 300 BC, in which Rama (an incarnation of the god Vishnu) and his friend Hanuman (the monkey chieftain) strive to recover Rama's wife, Sita, abducted by the demon king Ravana.

Talmud two most important works of post-Biblical Jewish literature. The Babylonian and the Palestinian (or Jerusalem) Talmud provide a compilation of ancient Jewish law and tradition. The Babylonian Talmud was edited at the end of the 5th century AD and is the more authoritative version for later Judaism; both Talmuds are written in a mix of Hebrew and Aramaic. They contain the commentary (*gemara)* on the *Mishnah* (early rabbinical commentaries compiled about AD 200), and the material can be generally divided into *halakhah,* consisting of legal and ritual matters, and *aggadah* (or *haggadah),* concerned with ethical, theological, and folklorist matters.

Tao Te Ching the most influential Taoist book, reputedly written down in one night by the 6th-century BC sage Lao Zi as he left China for the West, although it appears in fact to date from the 3rd century BC. The short book is divided into 81 chapters which contain oracle sayings or proverbs with commentary.

Torah in Judaism, the first five books of the Hebrew Bible (Christian Old Testament). It contains a traditional history of the world from the Creation to the death of Moses; it also includes the Hebrew people's covenant with their one God, rules for religious observance, and guidelines for social conduct, including the Ten Commandments.

Tripitaka (Sanskrit 'three baskets') canonical texts of Theravāda Buddhism, divided into three parts: the **Vinaya-pitaka,** containing the rules governing the monastic community; the **Sūtra-**

pitaka, a collection of scriptures recording the teachings of the Buddha; and **Abhidharma-pitaka,** a collection of Buddhist philosophical writings.

Upanishad one of a collection of Hindu sacred treatises, written in Sanskrit, connected with the Vedas but composed later, about 800–200 BC. Metaphysical and ethical, their doctrine equated the atman (self) with the Brahman (supreme spirit) – '*Tat tvam asi*' ('Thou art that') – and developed the theory of the transmigration of souls.

Veda (Sanskrit 'divine knowledge') the most sacred of the Hindu scriptures, hymns written in an old form of Sanskrit; the oldest may date from 1500 or 2000 BC. The four main collections are: the *Rig-veda* (hymns and praises); *Yajur-Veda* (prayers and sacrificial formulae); *Sâma-Veda* (tunes and chants); and *Atharva-Veda,* or Veda of the Atharvans, the officiating priests at the sacrifices.

FESTIVALS

Advent (Latin *adventus* 'coming') in the Christian calendar, the preparatory season for Christmas, including the four Sundays preceding it. It begins with Advent Sunday, the Sunday that falls nearest (before or after) St Andrew's Day (30 November).

Ascension Day or **Holy Thursday,** in the Christian calendar, the feast day commemorating Jesus' ascension into heaven. It is the 40th day after Easter.

Ash Wednesday first day of Lent, the period in the Christian calendar leading up to Easter; in the Roman Catholic Church the foreheads of the congregation are marked with a cross in ash, as a sign of penitence.

Atonement, Day of Jewish holy day (**Yom Kippur**) held on the tenth day of Tishri (September–October), the first month of the Jewish year. It is a day of fasting, penitence, and cleansing from sin, ending the Ten Days of Penitence that follow **Rosh Hashanah,** the Jewish New Year.

auto-da-fé (Portuguese 'act of faith') religious ceremony, including a procession, solemn mass, and sermon, which accompanied the sentencing of heretics by the Spanish Inquisition before they were handed over to the secular authorities for punishment, usually burning.

Christmas Christian religious holiday, observed throughout the Western world on 25 December and traditionally marked by feasting and gift-giving. In the Christian church, it is the day on which the birth of Jesus is celebrated, although his actual birth date is unknown. Many of its customs have a non-Christian origin and were adapted from celebrations of the winter solstice.

Diwali ('garland of lamps') Hindu festival in October/November celebrating Lakshmi, goddess of light and wealth, as well as the New Year and the story of the *Ramayana*. It is marked by the lighting of lamps and candles (inviting the goddess into the house), feasting, and the exchange of gifts. For Sikhs, Diwali celebrates Guru Hargobind's release from prison.

Easter spring feast of the Christian church, commemorating the Resurrection of Jesus. It is a moveable feast, falling on the first Sunday following the full moon after the vernal equinox (21 March); that is, between 22 March and 25 April.

Buddhism: Festivals

Myanmar			*Thailand*	
16–17 April	New Year		13–16 April	New Year
May–June	The Buddha's Birth, Enlightenment and Death		May	The Buddha's Enlightenment
July	The Buddha's First Sermon		May–June	The Buddha's Cremation
July	Beginning of the Rains Retreat		July–October	Rains Retreat
October	End of the Rains Retreat		October	End of the Rains Retreat
November	Kathina Ceremony		November	Kathina Ceremony
			November	Festival of Lights
China			February	All Saints' Day
June–August	Summer Retreat			
August	Festival of Hungry Ghosts		*Tibet*	
August	Gautama Buddha's Birth		February	New Year
August	Kuan-Yin		May	The Buddha's Birth, Enlightenment, and Death
Sri Lanka			June	Dzamling Chisang
13 April	New Year		June–July	The Buddha's First Sermon
May–June	The Buddha's Birth, Enlightenment, and Death		October	The Buddha's Descent from Tushita
June–July	Establishment of Buddhism in Sri Lanka		November	Death of Tsongkhapa
July	The Buddha's First Sermon		January	The Conjunction of Nine Evils and the Conjunction of Ten Virtues
July–August	Procession of the Month of Asala			
September	The Buddha's First Visit to Sri Lanka			
December–January	Arrival of Sanghamitta			

Christianity: Festivals and Holy Days

1 January	the naming of Jesus; The Circumcision of Christ; The Solemnity of Mary Mother of God
6 January	Epiphany
25 January	the Conversion of St Paul
2 February	the Presentation of Christ in the Temple
19 March	St Joseph of Nazareth, Husband of the Blessed Virgin Mary
25 March	tThe Annunciation of Our Lord to the Blessed Virgin Mary
25 April	St Mark the Evangelist
1 May	St Philip and St James, Apostles
14 May	St Matthias the Apostle
31 May	the Visitation of the Blessed Virgin Mary
11 June	St Barnabas the Apostle
24 June	the Birth of St John the Baptist
29 June	St Peter the Apostle
3 July	St Thomas the Apostle
22 July	St Mary Magdalen
25 July	St James the Apostle
6 August	the Transfiguration of our Lord
24 August	St Bartholomew the Apostle
8 September	the Nativity of the Blessed Virgin Mary
14 September	the Exaltation of the Holy Cross
21 September	St Matthew the Apostle
29 September	St Michael and All Angels (Michaelmas)
18 October	St Luke the Evangelist
28 October	St Simon and St Jude, Apostles
1 November	All Saints
21 November	Presentation of the Blessed Virgin Mary in the Temple
30 November	St Andrew the Apostle
8 December	the Immaculate Conception of the Blessed Virgin Mary
25 December	Christmas
26 December	St Stephen the first Martyr
27 December	St John the Evangelist
28 December	The Holy Innocents

Christianity: Movable Feasts 1996–2025

	Ash Wednesday	Easter Day	Ascension Day	Pentecost (Whit Sunday)	Advent Sunday
1996	21 February	7 April	16 May	26 May	1 December
1997	12 February	30 March	8 May	18 May	30 November
1998	25 February	12 April	21 May	31 May	29 November
1999	17 February	4 April	13 May	23 May	28 November
2000	8 March	23 April	1 June	11 June	3 December
2001	28 February	15 April	24 May	3 June	2 December
2002	13 February	31 March	9 May	19 May	1 December
2003	5 March	20 April	29 May	8 June	30 November
2004	25 February	11 April	20 May	30 May	28 November
2005	9 February	27 March	5 May	15 May	27 November
2006	1 March	16 April	25 May	4 June	3 December
2007	21 February	8 April	17 May	27 May	2 December
2008	6 February	23 March	1 May	11 May	30 November
2009	25 February	12 April	21 May	31 May	29 November
2010	17 February	4 April	13 May	23 May	28 November
2011	9 March	24 April	2 June	12 June	27 November
2012	22 February	8 April	17 May	27 May	2 December
2013	13 February	31 March	9 May	19 May	1 December
2014	5 March	20 April	29 May	8 June	30 November
2015	18 February	5 April	14 May	24 May	29 November
2016	10 March	27 March	5 May	15 May	27 November
2017	1 March	16 April	25 May	4 June	3 December
2018	14 February	1 April	10 May	20 May	2 December
2019	6 March	21 April	30 May	9 June	1 December
2020	26 February	12 April	21 May	31 May	29 November
2021	17 February	4 April	13 May	23 May	28 November
2022	2 March	17 April	26 May	5 June	27 November
2023	22 February	9 April	18 May	28 May	3 December
2024	14 February	31 March	9 May	19 May	1 December

Eid ul-Adha Muslim festival that takes place during the *hajj*, or pilgrimage to Mecca, and commemorates Abraham's willingness to sacrifice his son Ishmael at the command of Allah.

Eid ul-Fitr Muslim festival celebrating the end of Ramadan, the month of fasting.

Epiphany festival of the Christian church, held 6 January, celebrating the coming of the Magi (the three Wise Men) to Bethlehem with gifts for the infant Jesus, and symbolizing the manifestation of Jesus to the world. It is the 12th day after Christmas, and marks the end of the Christmas festivities.

Good Friday in the Christian church, the Friday before Easter, which is observed in memory of the Crucifixion (the death of Jesus on the cross).

Hanukkah or **Hanukah** or **Chanukkah** in Judaism, an eight-day festival of lights that takes place at the beginning of December. It celebrates the recapture and rededication of the Temple in Jerusalem by Judas Maccabaeus in 164 BC.

Holy Week in the Christian church, the last week of Lent, when Christians commemorate the events that led up to the crucifixion of Jesus. Holy Week begins on Palm Sunday and includes Maundy Thursday, which commemorates the Last Supper.

Lailat ul-Barah the **Night of Forgiveness** Muslim festival which takes place two weeks before the beginning of the fast of Ramadan (the ninth month of the Islamic year) and is a time for asking and granting forgiveness.

Lailat ul-Isra Wal Mi'raj Muslim festival that celebrates the prophet Muhammad's Night Journey.

Lailat ul-Qadr the **Night of Power** Muslim festival which celebrates the giving of the Koran to Muhammad. It usually falls at the end of Ramadan.

Lent in the Christian church, the 40-day period of fasting that precedes Easter, beginning on Ash Wednesday, but omitting Sundays.

Maundy Thursday in the Christian church, the Thursday before Easter. The ceremony of washing the feet of pilgrims on that day was instituted in commemoration of Jesus' washing of the apostles' feet and observed from the 4th century.

Hinduism: Festivals

January	Makar Sankranti/Til Sankranti/Lohri, Pongal, Kumbha Mela at Prayag (every 12 years)
January–February	Vasanta Panchami/Shri Panchami/Saraswati Puja, Bhogali Bihu, Mahashivratri
20 February	Ramakrishna Utsav
February–March	Holi
March–April	Ugadi, Basora, Rama Navami, Hanuman Jayanti
April	Vaisakhi
April–May	Akshaya Tritiya, Chittrai
May–June	Ganga Dasa-hara, Nirjala Ekadashi, Snan-yatra
June–July	Ratha-yatra/Jagannatha, Ashadhi Ekadashi/Toli Ekadashi
July–August	Teej, Naga Panchami, Raksha Bandhan/Shravana Purnima/Salono/Rakhi Purnima
August–September	Onam, Ganesha Chaturthi, Janamashtami/Krishna Jayanti
September–October	Mahalaya/Shraddha/Pitri Paksha/Kanagat, Navaratri/Durga Puja/Dassehra, Lakshmi Puja
2 October	Gandhi Jayanti
October–November	Diwali/Deepavali, Chhath, Karttika Ekadashi/Devuthna, Ekadashi/Tulsi Ekadashi, Karttika Purnima/Tripuri Purnima, Hoi, Skanda Shasti
November–December	Vaikuntha Ekadashi, Lakshmi Puja (Orissa)

Michaelmas Day in Christian church tradition, the festival of St Michael and All Angels, observed on 29 September.

Palm Sunday in the Christian calendar, the Sunday before Easter and first day of Holy Week, commemorating Jesus' entry into Jerusalem, when the crowd strewed palm leaves in his path.

Passover also called **Pesach** in Judaism, an eight-day spring festival which commemorates the exodus of the Israelites from Egypt and the passing over by the Angel of Death of the Jewish houses, so that only the Egyptian firstborn sons were killed, in retribution for Pharaoh's murdering of all Jewish male infants.

Pentecost in Judaism, the festival of *Shavuot*, celebrated on the 50th day after Passover in commemoration of the giving of the Ten Commandments to Moses on Mount Sinai, and the end of the grain harvest; in the Christian church, Pentecost is the day on which the apostles experienced descent of the Holy Spirit, commemorated on Whit Sunday.

Purim Jewish festival celebrated in February or March (the 14th of Adar in the Jewish calendar), commemorating Esther, who saved the Jews from destruction in 473 BC during the Persian occupation.

Ramadan in the Muslim calendar, the ninth month of the year. Throughout Ramadan a strict fast is observed during the hours of daylight; Muslims are encouraged to read the whole Koran in commemoration of the Night of Power when, it is believed, Muhammad first received his revelations from the angel Gabriel.

Rosh Hashanah two-day holiday that marks the start of the Jewish New Year (first new Moon after the autumn Equinox), traditionally announced by blowing a ram's horn (a shofar).

Shrove Tuesday in the Christian calendar, the day before the beginning of Lent. It is also known as **Mardi Gras.**

Succot or **Sukkoth** in Judaism, a harvest festival celebrated in October, also known as the **Feast of Booths,** which commemorates the time when the Israelites lived in the wilderness during the Exodus from Egypt. As a reminder of the shelters used in the wilderness, huts are built and used for eating and sleeping during the seven days of the festival.

Yom Kippur the Jewish Day of Atonement.

Holy Places

Amritsar industrial city in the Punjab, India, and the holy city of Sikhism, with the Guru Nanak University (named after the first Sikh guru), and the Golden Temple, surrounded by the sacred pool Amrita Saras. The Jallianwala Bagh area of the city was the scene of the Amritsar Massacre in 1919, when the British Gen Dyer ordered troops to fire on a crowd agitating for self-government; 379 were killed and 1,200 wounded. In 1984, armed Sikh demonstrators were evicted from the Golden Temple by the Indian army, in Operation Bluestar, led by Gen Dayal. Over 300 were killed. Later in 1984, Indian prime minister Indira Gandhi was assassinated in reprisal by Sikh extremists wanting an independent Sikh state in Punjab. The whole of Punjab was put under presidential control in 1987 following riots.

Calvary (Aramaic *Golgotha* 'skull') in the New Testament, the site of Jesus' crucifixion at Jerusalem. Two chief locations are suggested: the site where the Church of the Sepulchre now stands, and the hill beyond the Damascus gate.

cathedral (Latin *cathedra* 'seat' or 'throne') principal Christian church of a bishop or archbishop, containing his throne, which is usually situated on the south side of the choir. A cathedral is governed by a dean and chapter.

chapel (from Latin *capella*, diminutive of *cappa* 'a cloak') small or subordinate place of Christian worship other than a parish or cathedral church; also a church subordinate to and dependent on the principal parish church, to which it is in some way supplementary.

church in architecture, a building designed as a Christian place of worship; also the Christian community generally, or a subdivision or denomination of it, such as the Protestant Episcopal Church. Churches were first built in the 3rd century, when persecution ceased under the Roman emperor Constantine.

Hagia Sophia (Greek 'holy wisdom') Byzantine building in Istanbul, Turkey, built 532–37 as a Christian cathedral, replacing earlier churches. From 1453 to 1934 it was an Islamic mosque; in 1934 it became a museum.

Jerusalem (Arabic al-Quds; Hebrew Yerushalayim), ancient city of Palestine, 762 m/ 2,500 ft above sea level, situated in hills 55 km/34 mi from the Mediterranean, divided in 1948 between Jordan and the new republic of Israel; area pre-1967 37.5 sq km/14.5 sq mi, post-1967 108 sq km/42 sq mi, including areas of the West Bank; population (1995) 591,400. In 1950 the western New City was proclaimed as the Israeli capital, and, having captured from Jordan the eastern Old City in 1967, Israel affirmed in 1980 that the united city was the country's capital; the United Nations does not recognize East Jerusalem as part of Israel, and regards Tel Aviv as the capital.

Kaaba (Arabic 'chamber') in Mecca, Saudi Arabia, an oblong building in the quadrangle of the Great Mosque, into the northeastern corner of which is built the Black Stone declared by the prophet Muhammad to have been given to Abraham by the archangel Gabriel, and revered by Muslims.

Mecca (Arabic Makkah) city in Saudi Arabia and, as birthplace of Muhammad, the holiest city of the Islamic world. In the centre of Mecca is the Great Mosque, in the courtyard of which is the Kaaba.

Medina Saudi Arabian city, about 355 km/220 mi north of Mecca. It is the second holiest city in the Islamic world, and contains the tomb of Muhammad.

mosque (Arabic *mesjid*) in Islam, a place of worship. Chief features are: the dome; the minaret, a balconied turret from which the faithful are called to prayer; the *mihrab*, or prayer niche, in one of the interior walls, showing the direction of the holy city of Mecca; and an open court surrounded by porticoes.

temple structure designed for religious worship. In US usage, temple is another name for synagogue.

Varanasi or **Benares** or **Banaras,** city in Uttar Pradesh, India, one of the seven holy cities of Hinduism, on the River Ganges. There are 1,500 golden shrines, and a 5 km/3 mi frontage to the Ganges with sacred stairways (ghats) for purification by bathing. Varanasi is also a sacred centre of Jainism, Sikhism, and Buddhism: Buddha came to Varanasi from Gaya and is believed to have preached in the Deer Park. One-third of its inhabitants are Muslim.

Wailing Wall or (in Judaism) **Western Wall** remaining part of the Temple in Jerusalem, a sacred site of pilgrimage and prayer for Jews. There they offer prayers either aloud ('wailing') or on pieces of paper placed between the stones of the wall.

Religious Terms

angel (Greek *angelos* 'messenger') in Jewish, Christian, and Muslim belief, a supernatural being intermediate between God and humans. The Christian hierarchy has nine orders, from the top down: **Seraphim, Cherubim, Thrones** (who contemplate God and reflect his glory), **Dominations, Virtues, Powers** (who regulate the stars and the universe), **Principalities, Archangels,** and **Angels** (who minister to humanity). In traditional Catholic belief every human being has a guardian angel. The existence of angels was reasserted by Pope John Paul II in 1986.

Antichrist in Christian theology, the opponent of Christ. The appearance of the Antichrist was believed to signal the Second Coming, at which Christ would conquer his opponent. The concept may stem from the idea of conflict between Light and Darkness, present in Persian, Babylonian, and Jewish literature, which influenced early Christian thought.

antipope rival claimant to the elected pope for the leadership of the Roman Catholic Church, for instance in the Great Schism 1378–1417 when there were rival popes in Rome and Avignon.

apocalypse (Greek 'revelation' or 'unveiling') revelation disclosed only to a chosen person. The term is applied to the last book of the New Testament, the Apocalypse of St John, otherwise known as Revelation.

apostle (Greek 'messenger') in the New Testament, any of the chosen 12 disciples sent out by Jesus after his resurrection to preach the Gospel.

archbishop in the Christian church, a bishop of superior rank who has authority over other bishops in his jurisdiction and often over an ecclesiastical province. The office exists in the Roman Catholic, Eastern Orthodox, and Anglican churches.

archdeacon originally an ordained dignitary of the Christian church charged with the supervision of the deacons attached to a cathedral. Today in the Roman Catholic Church the office is purely titular; in the Anglican Church an archdeacon, directly subordinate to the bishop, still has many business duties, such as the periodic inspection of churches. The office is not found in other Protestant churches.

Ark of the Covenant in the Old Testament, the chest that contained the Tablets of the Law as given to Moses. It is now the cupboard in a synagogue in which the Torah scrolls are kept.

ashram Indian community whose members lead a simple life of discipline and self-denial and devote themselves to social service. Noted ashrams are those founded by Mahatma Gandhi at Wardha (near Nagpur, Maharashtra) and by poet Rabindranath Tagore at Santiniketan.

atonement in Christian theology, the doctrine that Jesus suffered on the cross to bring about reconciliation and forgiveness between God and humanity.

avatar in Hindu mythology, the descent of a deity to Earth in a visible form, for example the ten avatars of Vishnu.

ayatollah (Arabic 'sign of God') honorific title awarded to Shi'ite Muslims in Iran by popular consent, as, for example, to Ayatollah Ruhollah Khomeini.

baptism (Greek 'to dip') immersion in or sprinkling with water as a religious rite of initiation. It was practised long before the beginning of Christianity. In the Christian baptism ceremony, sponsors or godparents make vows on behalf of the child, which are renewed by the child at confirmation. It is one of the seven sacraments. The *amrit* ceremony in Sikhism is sometimes referred to as baptism.

bar mitzvah (Hebrew 'son of the commandment') in Judaism, initiation of a boy, which takes place at the age of 13, into the adult Jewish community; less common is the **bat mitzvah** or **bat** for girls aged 12. The child reads a passage from the Torah in the synagogue on the Sabbath and is subsequently regarded as a full member of the congregation.

blasphemy (Greek 'evil-speaking') written or spoken insult directed against religious belief or sacred things with deliberate intent to outrage believers.

bodhisattva in Mahayana Buddhism, someone who seeks enlightenment in order to help other living beings. A bodhisattva is free to enter nirvana but voluntarily chooses to be reborn until all other beings have attained that state. Bodhisattvas are seen as intercessors to whom believers may pray for help.

Brahman in Hinduism, the supreme being, an abstract, impersonal world soul into whom the *atman,* or individual soul, will eventually be absorbed when its cycle of rebirth is ended.

canonization in the Catholic church, the admission of one of its members to the Calendar of Saints. The evidence of the candidate's exceptional piety is contested before the Congregation for the Causes of Saints by the *Promotor Fidei*, popularly known as the **devil's advocate.** Papal ratification of a favourable verdict results in beatification, and full sainthood (conferred in St Peter's basilica, the Vatican) follows after further proof.

canon law rules and regulations of the Christian church, especially the Orthodox, Roman Catholic, and Anglican churches. Its origin is sought in the declarations of Jesus and the apostles. In 1983 Pope John Paul II issued a new canon law code reducing offences carrying automatic excommunication, extending the grounds for annulment of marriage, removing the ban on marriage with non-Catholics, and banning trade-union and political activity by priests.

cantor (Latin *cantare,* 'to sing') in Roman Catholicism and Judaism, the prayer leader and choir master, responsible for singing solo parts of the chant. The position can be held by any lay person. In Protestant churches, the music director is known as the cantor.

cardinal in the Roman Catholic church, the highest rank next to the pope. Cardinals act as an advisory body to the pope and elect him. Their red hat is the badge of office. The number of cardinals varies.

casuistry the application of an ethical theory to particular cases or types of case, especially in theology and dogmatics. Casuistry is contrasted with situationism, which considers each moral situation as it arises and without reference to ethical theory or moral principles.

catechism teaching by question and answer on the Socratic method, but chiefly as a means of instructing children in the basics of the Christian creed. A person being instructed in this way in preparation for baptism or confirmation is called a **catechumen.**

chalice cup, usually of precious metal, used in celebrating the Eucharist in the Christian church.

cherub type of angel in Christian belief, usually depicted as a young child with wings. Cherubim form the second order of angels.

christening Christian ceremony of baptism of infants, including giving a name.

Communion, Holy in the Christian church, another name for the Eucharist.

conclave secret meeting, in particular the gathering of cardinals in Rome to elect a new pope. They are locked away in the Vatican Palace until they have reached a decision. The result of each ballot is announced by a smoke signal – black for an undecided vote and white when the choice is made.

confession confession of sins practised in Roman Catholic, Orthodox, and most Far Eastern Christian churches, and since the early 19th century revived in Anglican and Lutheran churches. The Lateran Council of 1215 made auricular confession (self-accusation by the penitent to a priest, who in Catholic doctrine is divinely invested with authority to give absolution) obligatory once a year.

confirmation rite practised by a number of Christian denominations, including Roman Catholic, Anglican, and Orthodox, in which a previously baptized person is admitted to full membership of the church. In Reform Judaism there is often a confirmation service several years after the bar or bat mitzvah (initiation into the congregation).

creationism theory concerned with the origins of matter and life, claiming, as does the Bible in Genesis, that the world and humanity were created by a supernatural Creator, not more than 6,000 years ago. It was developed in response to Darwin's theory of evolution; it is not recognized by most scientists as having a factual basis.

creed in general, any system of belief; in the Christian church the verbal confessions of faith expressing the accepted doctrines of the church. The different forms are the Apostles' Creed, the Nicene Creed, and the Athanasian Creed. The only creed recognized by the Orthodox Church is the Nicene Creed.

crucifixion death by fastening to a cross, a form of capital punishment used by the ancient Romans, Persians, and Carthaginians, and abolished by the Roman emperor Constantine. Specifically, **the Crucifixion** refers to the execution by the Romans of Jesus in this manner.

deacon in the Roman Catholic and Anglican churches, an ordained minister who ranks immediately below a priest. In the Protestant churches, a deacon is in training to become a minister or is a lay assistant.

deism (Latin *deus* 'god') belief in a supreme being. The term usually refers to a movement in the 17th and 18th centuries characterized by the belief in a rational 'religion of nature' as opposed to the orthodox beliefs of Christianity. Deists believed that God is the source of natural law but does not intervene directly in the affairs of the world, and that the only religious duty of humanity is to be virtuous.

dervish in Iran and Turkey, a religious mendicant; throughout the rest of Islam a member of an Islamic religious brotherhood, not necessarily mendicant in character. The Arabic equivalent is **fakir.** There are various orders of dervishes, each with its rule and special ritual. The 'whirling dervishes' claim close communion with the deity through ecstatic dancing, reaching spiritual awareness with a trance-like state created by continual whirling. The spinning symbolizes the Earth's orbit of the Sun. 'Howling dervishes' gash themselves with knives to demonstrate the miraculous feats possible to those who trust in Allah.

devil in Jewish, Christian, and Muslim theology, the supreme spirit of evil (**Beelzebub, Lucifer, Iblis**), or an evil spirit generally.

disciple follower, especially of a religious leader. The word is used in the Bible for the early followers of Jesus. The 12 disciples closest to him are known as the apostles.

Eightfold Path fourth of the Four Noble Truths of Buddhism. The Eightfold Path outlines a course of discipline and correct behaviour which leads towards freedom from rebirth. The eight elements of the Path are: 1. right understanding; 2. right aspirations; 3. right speech; 4. right bodily action; 5. right livelihood; 6. right endeavour; 7. right mindfulness; 8. right concentration. The Path is also known as the Middle Way, since it describes a course that lies between asceticism and sensual pleasure.

enlightenment in Buddhism, the term used to translate the Sanskrit *bodhi,* awakening: perceiving the true nature of the world, the unreality of the self, and becoming liberated from suffering (Sanskrit *duhkha).* By experience of *bodhi,* nirvana is attained.

Eucharist chief Christian sacrament, in which bread is eaten and wine drunk in memory of the death of Jesus. Other names for it are the **Lord's Supper, Holy Communion,** and (among Roman Catholics, who believe that the bread and wine are transubstantiated, that is, converted to the body and blood of Christ) the **Mass.** The doctrine of transubstantiation was rejected by Protestant churches during the Reformation.

evangelist person travelling to spread the Christian gospel, in particular the authors of the four Gospels in the New Testament: Matthew, Mark, Luke, and John. Proselytizers who appear mainly on television are known as televangelists.

excommunication in religion, exclusion of an offender from the rights and privileges of the Roman Catholic Church. The English monarchs King John, Henry VIII, and Elizabeth I were all excommunicated.

five pillars of Islam the five duties required of every Muslim: repeating the **creed,** which affirms that Allah is the one God and Muhammad is his prophet; daily **prayer** or *salat*; giving **alms; fasting** during the month of Ramadan; and, if not prevented by ill health or poverty, the *hajj,* or **pilgrimage** to Mecca, once in a lifetime.

Four Noble Truths in Buddhism, a summary of the basic concepts: there is suffering (Sanskrit *duhkha)*; suffering has its roots in desire (*tanha,* clinging or grasping); the cessation of desire is the end of suffering, *nirvana;* and this can be reached by the Noble Eightfold Path as taught by the Buddha.

friar a monk of any order, but originally the title of members of the mendicant (begging) orders, the chief of which were the Franciscans or Minors (Grey Friars), the Dominicans or Preachers (Black Friars), the Carmelites (White Friars), and Augustinians (Austin Friars).

fundamentalism in religion, an emphasis on basic principles or articles of faith. **Christian fundamentalism** emerged in the USA just after World War I (as a reaction to theological modernism and the historical criticism of the Bible) and insisted on belief in the literal truth of everything in the Bible. **Islamic fundamentalism** insists on strict observance of Muslim Shari'a law.

God concept of a supreme being, a unique creative entity, basic to several monotheistic religions (for example Judaism, Christianity, Islam); in many polytheistic cultures (for example Norse, Roman, Greek) the term 'god' refers to a supernatural being who personifies the force behind an aspect of life (for example Neptune, Roman god of the sea).

gurdwara Sikh place of worship and meeting. As well as a room housing the *Guru Granth Sahib,* the holy book, the gurdwara contains a kitchen and eating area for the *langar,* or communal meal.

guru Hindi *gurū* Hindu or Sikh leader, or religious teacher.

hajj pilgrimage to Mecca that should be undertaken by every Muslim at least once in a lifetime, unless he or she is prevented by financial or health difficulties. A Muslim who has been on hajj may take the additional name Hajji. Many of the pilgrims on hajj also visit Medina, where the prophet Muhammad is buried.

halal (Arabic 'lawful') conforming to the rules laid down by Islam. The term can be applied to all aspects of life, but usually refers to food permissible under Muslim dietary laws, including meat from animals that have been slaughtered in the correct ritual fashion.

heaven in Christianity and some other religions, the abode of God and the destination of the virtuous after death. In Islam, heaven is seen as a paradise of material delights, though such delights are generally accepted as being allegorical.

hell in various religions, a place of posthumous punishment. In Hinduism, Buddhism, and Jainism, hell is a transitory stage in the progress of the soul, but in Christianity and Islam it is eternal (Christian purgatory is transitory). Judaism does not postulate such punishment.

heresy any doctrine opposed to orthodox belief, especially in religion. Those holding ideas considered heretical by the Christian church have included Gnostics, Arians, Pelagians, Montanists, Albigenses, Waldenses, Lollards, and Anabaptists.

hermit person living in seclusion, generally practising asceticism for religious reasons.

Hijrah or **Hegira** (Arabic 'flight') flight from Mecca to Medina of the prophet Muhammad, which took place in AD 622 as a result of the persecution of the prophet and his followers. The Muslim calendar dates from this event, and the day of the Hijrah is celebrated as the Muslim New Year.

Holy Grail in medieval Christian legend, the dish or cup used by Jesus at the Last Supper, supposed to have supernatural powers. Together with the spear with which he was wounded at the Crucifixion, it was an object of quest by King Arthur's knights in certain stories incorporated in the Arthurian legend.

Holy Spirit third person of the Christian Trinity, also known as the Holy Ghost or the Paraclete, usually depicted as a white dove.

hymn song in praise of a deity. Examples include Akhenaton's hymn to the Aton in ancient Egypt, the ancient Greek Orphic hymns, Old Testament psalms, extracts from the New Testament (such as the 'Ave Maria/Hail Mary'), and hymns by the British writers John Bunyan ('Who would true valour see') and Charles Wesley ('Hark! the herald angels sing'). The earliest sources of modern hymn melodies can be traced to the 11th and 12th centuries, and the earliest polyphonic settings date from the late 14th century. Gospel music and carols are forms of Christian hymn singing.

icon in the Greek or Eastern Orthodox Church, a representation of Jesus, Mary, an angel, or a saint, in painting, low relief, or mosaic. The painted icons were traditionally done on wood. After the 17th century and mainly in Russia, a *riza,* or gold and silver covering that leaves only the face and hands visible (and may be adorned with jewels presented by the faithful in thanksgiving), was often added as protection.

iconoclast (Greek 'image-breaker') literally, a person who attacks religious images, originally in obedience to the injunction of the Second Commandment not to worship 'graven images'. Under the influence of Islam and Judaism, an iconoclastic movement calling for the destruction of religious images developed in the Byzantine Empire, and was endorsed by the Emperor Leo III in 726. Fierce persecution of those who made and venerated icons followed, until iconoclasm was declared a heresy in the

9th century. The same name was applied to those opposing the use of images at the Reformation, when there was much destruction in churches. Figuratively, the term is used for a person who attacks established ideals or principles.

incarnation assumption of living form (plant, animal, human) by a deity; for example, the gods of Greece and Rome, Hinduism, and Christianity (Jesus as the second person of the Trinity).

jihad (Arabic 'conflict') holy war undertaken by Muslims against nonbelievers. In the **Mecca Declaration** of 1981, the Islamic powers pledged a jihad against Israel, though not necessarily military attack.

kabbala or **cabbala** (Hebrew 'tradition') ancient esoteric Jewish mystical tradition of philosophy containing strong elements of pantheism, yet akin to neo-Platonism. Kabbalistic writing reached its peak between the 13th and 16th centuries. It is largely rejected by current Judaic thought as medieval superstition, but is basic to the Hasid sect.

karma (Sanskrit 'action') in Hinduism, the sum of a human being's actions, carried forward from one life to the next, resulting in an improved or worsened fate. Buddhism has a similar belief, except that no permanent personality is envisaged, the karma relating only to volitional tendencies carried on from birth to birth, unless the power holding them together is dispersed in the attainment of nirvana.

liturgy in the Christian church, any written, authorized version of a service for public worship, especially the Roman Catholic Mass.

maharishi (Sanskrit *mahā* 'great', *rishi* 'sage') Hindu guru (teacher), or spiritual leader. The Maharishi Mahesh Yogi influenced the Beatles and other Westerners in the 1960s.

mantra in Hindu or Buddhist belief, a word repeatedly intoned to assist concentration and develop spiritual power; for example, *om,* which represents the names of Brahma, Vishnu, and Siva. Followers of a guru may receive their own individual mantra.

meditation act of spiritual contemplation, practised by members of many religions or as a secular exercise. It is a central practice in Buddhism (the Sanskrit term is *samādhi)* and the movement for transcendental meditation.

monasticism devotion to religious life under vows of poverty, chastity, and obedience, known to Judaism (for example Essenes), Buddhism, and other religions, before Christianity. In Islam, the Sufis formed monastic orders from the 12th century.

nirvana (Sanskrit 'a blowing out') in Buddhism, a religious goal characterized by the attainment of perfect serenity, compassion, and wisdom by the eradication of all desires.

original sin Christian doctrine that the Fall of Man rendered humanity predisposed to sin and unable to achieve salvation except through divine grace and the redemptive power of Jesus.

papal infallibility doctrine formulated by the Roman Catholic Vatican Council in 1870, which stated that the pope, when speaking officially on certain doctrinal or moral matters, was protected from error by God, and therefore such rulings could not be challenged.

pope the bishop of Rome, head of the Roman Catholic Church, which claims he is the spiritual descendant of St Peter. Elected by the Sacred College of Cardinals, a pope dates his pontificate from his coronation with the tiara, or triple crown, at St Peter's Basilica, Rome. Popes had great political power in Europe from the early Middle Ages until the Reformation.

prayer address to divine power, ranging from a ritual formula to attain a desired end, to selfless communication in meditation. Within Christianity, the Catholic and Orthodox churches sanction prayer to the Virgin Mary, angels, and saints as intercessors, whereas Protestantism limits prayer to God alone. Muslims pray only to God.

prophet person thought to speak from divine inspiration or one who foretells the future. Prophets whose words and actions are recorded in the Bible include Moses, Samuel, Elijah, Isaiah, and Jeremiah. In Islam, Muhammad is believed to be the last and greatest of a long line of prophets beginning with Adam and including Moses and Jesus.

psalm sacred poem or song of praise. The Book of Psalms in the Old Testament is divided into five books containing 150 psalms, traditionally ascribed to David, the second king of Israel. In the Christian church they may be sung

Patron Saints

Saint	Occupation	Saint	Occupation
Adam	gardeners	Honoratus	bakers
Albert the Great	scientists	Isidore	farmers
Alphonsus Liguori	theologians	Ivo	lawyers
Amand	brewers, hotelkeepers	James	labourers
Andrew	fisherfolk	Jean-Baptiste Vianney	priests
Angelico	artists	Jerome	librarians
Anne	miners	Joan of Arc	soldiers
Apollonia	dentists	John Baptist de la Salle	teachers
Augustine	theologians	John Bosco	labourers
Barbara	builders, miners	John of God	book trade, nurses, printers
Bernadino (Feltre)	bankers	Joseph	carpenters
Bernadino of Siena	advertisers	Joseph (Arimathea)	gravediggers, undertakers
Camillus de Lellis	nurses	Joseph (Cupertino)	astronauts
Catherine of Alexandria	librarians, philosophers	Julian the Hospitaler	hotelkeepers
Cecilia	musicians, poets, singers	Lawrence	cooks
Christopher	motorists, sailors	Leonard	prisoners
Cosmas and Damian	barbers, chemists, doctors, surgeons	Louis	sculptors
Crispin	shoemakers	Lucy	glassworkers, writers
Crispinian	shoemakers	Luke	artists, butchers, doctors,
David	poets		glassworkers, sculptors, surgeons
Dismas	undertakers	Martha	cooks, housewives, servants, waiters
Dominic	astronomers	Martin of Tours	soldiers
Dorothy	florists	Matthew	accountants, bookkeepers, tax
Eligius	blacksmiths, jewellers, metalworkers		collectors
Erasmus	sailors	Michael	grocers, police
Fiacre	gardeners, taxi drivers	Our Lady of Loreto	aviators
Florian	firefighters	Peter	fisherfolk
Francis de Sales	authors, editors, journalists	Raymond Nonnatus	midwives
Francis of Assisi	merchants	Sebastian	athletes, soldiers
Francis of Paola	sailors	Thérèse of Lisieux	florists
Gabriel	messengers, postal workers, radio	Thomas (Apostle)	architects, builders
	workers, television workers	Thomas Aquinas	philosophers, scholars, students,
Genesius	actors, secretaries		theologians
George	soldiers	Thomas More	lawyers
Gregory	singers	Vitus	actors, comedians, dancers
Gregory the Great	musicians, teachers	Wenceslaus	brewers
Homobonus	tailors	Zita	servants

antiphonally in plainsong or set by individual composers to music in a great variety of styles, from Josquin Desprez's *De profundis* to Igor Stravinsky's *Symphony of Psalms* 1930.

purdah (Persian and Hindu 'curtain') seclusion of women practised by some Islamic and Hindu peoples. It had begun to disappear with the adoption of Western culture, but the fundamentalism of the 1980s revived it; for example, the wearing of the chador (an all-enveloping black mantle) is obligatory in Iran.

purgatory in Roman Catholic belief, a purificatory state or place where the souls of those who have died in a state of grace can expiate their venial sins, with a limited amount of suffering.

rabbi in Judaism, the chief religious leader of a synagogue or the spiritual leader (not a hereditary high priest) of a Jewish congregation; also, a scholar of Judaic law and ritual from the 1st century AD.

reincarnation or **transmigration** or **metempsychosis,** belief that after death the human soul or the spirit of a plant or animal may live again in another human or animal. It is part of the teachings of many religions and philosophies; for example, ancient Egyptian and Greek (the philosophies of Pythagoras and Plato), Buddhism, Hinduism, Jainism, Sikhism, certain Christian heresies (such as the Cathars), and theosophy.

sacrament in Christian usage, observances forming the visible sign of inward grace. In the Roman Catholic Church there are seven sacraments: baptism, Holy Communion (Eucharist), confirmation, rite of reconciliation (confession and penance), holy orders, matrimony, and the anointing of the sick.

Sadducee Hebrew 'righteous', member of the ancient Hebrew political party and sect of Judaism that formed in pre-Roman Palestine in the first century BC. They were the group of priestly aristocrats in Jerusalem until the final destruction of the Temple in AD 70.

saint holy man or woman respected for his or her wisdom, spirituality, and dedication to their faith. Within the Roman Catholic Church a saint is officially recognized through canonization by the pope. Many saints are associated with miracles and canonization usually occurs after a thorough investigation of the lives and miracles attributed to them.

sin transgression of the will of God or the gods, as revealed in the moral code laid down by a particular religion. In Roman Catholic theology, a distinction is made between **mortal sins,** which, if unforgiven, result in damnation, and **venial sins,** which are less serious. In Islam, the one unforgivable sin is **shirk,** denial that Allah is the only god.

soul according to many religions, an intangible part of a human being that survives the death of the physical body. Judaism, Christianity, and Islam all teach that at the end of the world each soul will be judged and assigned to heaven or hell on its merits.

stigmata impressions or marks corresponding to the five wounds Jesus received at his crucifixion, which are said to have appeared spontaneously on St Francis and other saints.

Ten Commandments in the Old Testament, the laws given by God to the Hebrew leader Moses on Mount Sinai, engraved on two tablets of stone. They are: to have no other gods besides Jehovah; to make no idols; not to misuse the name of God; to keep the sabbath holy; to honour one's parents; not to commit murder, adultery, or theft; not to give false evidence; and not to be covetous. They form the basis of Jewish and Christian moral codes; the 'tablets of the Law' given to Moses are also mentioned in the Koran. The giving of the Ten Commandments is celebrated in the Jewish festival of *Shavuot.*

Thirty-Nine Articles set of articles of faith defining the doctrine of the Anglican Church.

Trinity in Christianity, the union of three persons – Father, Son, and Holy Ghost/Spirit – in one godhead. The precise meaning of the doctrine has been the cause of unending dispute, and was the chief cause of the split between the Eastern Orthodox and Roman Catholic churches. **Trinity Sunday** occurs on the Sunday after Pentecost (Whitsun).

Noteworthy Religious Thinkers and Leaders

Abduh Muhammad (1849–1905) Egyptian religious thinker who was the founder of Islamic modernism

Abelard Peter (English form of Pierre Abailard) (1079–1142) French scholastic theologian who worked on logic and perception and whose romantic liaison with his pupil Héloïse created a scandal

Albertus Magnus, St Graf von Bollstädt (1206–1280) German theologian who was known as 'doctor universalis' because of the breadth of his knowledge

Anandamurti Shrii Shrii (Prabhat Rainjan Sarkar; Baba) (1923–1990) Indian religious thinker who founded the Ananda Marga (Path of Bliss) organization

Anselm of Canterbury (1033–1109) French-born British archbishop whose *Cur Deus Homo* is a classic mediaeval text on the theology of the Atonement

Aquinas Thomas, St (1225–1274) Italian scholastic theologian whose writings form the basis for Roman Catholic theology

Augustine of Hippo (Aurelius Augustinus) (354–430) North African bishop whose teachings on sin and predestination influenced both Roman Catholic and Protestant traditions

Averröes or **Averrhoês** (Full Arabic name: Abū al-Walīd Muhammad ibn Ahmad ibn Muhammad ibn Rushd) (1126–1198) Spanish Islamic philosopher who attempted to reconcile Islamic teaching with Greek thought

Baader Benedict Franz von (1765–1841) German Roman Catholic theologian who opposed the claims of ecclesiastic authority in the field of speculation

Barth Karl (1886–1968) Swiss theologian whose *Kirchliche Dogmatik/Church Dogmatics* had a major impact on 20th-century Protestant theology

Bernard of Clairvaux ('the Mellifluous Doctor') (1090–1153) French Cistercian monk whose devotional works encouraged reform in the mediaeval church and monastic movement

Beza Theodorus (properly Théodore de Bèsze) (1519–1605) French-born Swiss theologian and translator who discovered the oldest Greek manuscript of the New Testament (*Codex Bezae*)

Blavatsky Helena Petrovna (born Hahn) (1831–1891) Russian spiritualist and mystic who co-founded the Theosophical Society in 1875 and later became a Buddhist

Boehme Jakob (1575–1624) German mystic who claimed to have found a way to reconcile good and evil

Booth William (1829–1912) British church leader who founded the Salvation Army

Bruno Giordano (born Filippo Bruno) (1548–1600) Italian Dominican monk who was burned at the stake for his opposition to Roman Catholic doctrines

Brunner (Heinrich) Emil (1889–1966) Swiss Protestant theologian whose *Das Gebot und die Ordnungen/The Divine Imperative* influenced the field of Christian ethics

Bryan William Jennings (1860–1925) US Protestant leader and politician who opposed Clarence Darrow in the Scopes monkey trial in Dayton, Tennessee, in 1923

Buber Martin (1878–1965) Austrian-born Jewish philosopher whose *Ich und Du/I and Thou* had a significant impact on Jewish and Christian theology

Bucer or **Butzer** Martin (1491–1551) German Protestant reformer who sought to reconcile the Eucharist views of Martin Luther and Ulrich Zwingli

Buddha (the 'enlightened one' title of Prince Gautama Siddartha) (c. 563–483 BC) Indian religious leader and founder of Buddhism

Calvin John (1509–1564) French-born Swiss theologian whose works formed the basis for Calvinism and Presbyterianism

Camara (Dom) Helder Pessoa (1909–) Brazilian Catholic archbishop who has campaigned for social reform and the establishment of 'base ecclesial communities'

Noteworthy Religious Thinkers and Leaders (continued)

Cartwright Thomas (1535–1603) British Protestant theologian who, in 1603, drew up the Millenary Petition, which initiated reform in the Church of England

Chang Lu (c. 184–220) Chinese Taoist thinker who established the first theocratic state to follow Taoist teachings

Chu Hsi (1130–1200) Chinese religious thinker who significantly influenced the development of the Confucian tradition in East Asia

Cohen Hermann (1842–1912) German Jewish philosopher who thought Judaism was primarily a religion of ethical reason

Colet John (c. 1467–1519) English humanist who founded modern biblical exegesis

Confucius (Latinized form of Kongfuzi or Kung Fu Tzu, 'Kong the Master') (551–479 BC) Chinese thinker who emphasized moral order and obedience to patriarchal authority

Cordovero Moses (1522–1570) Palestinian Jewish mystic whose encyclopedic work on kabbalistic teachings, *Pardes Rimmonium/Pomegranate Orchard*, greatly influenced Jewish mysticism

Cyril of Alexandria (c. 376–444) patriarch of Alexandria who condemned Nestorius (d. c. 457, patriarch of Constantinople 428–31) for his refusal to call Mary the *Theotokos* ('God-bearer')

Dayananda Sarasvati (originally Mula Sankara) (1824–1883) Indian religious thinker who founded the Arya Samaj to promote neo-orthodox Hinduism

Dharmakirti (600–660) Indian Buddhist philosopher whose philosophical writings formed the basis for later Buddhist thought in India and Tibet

Duns Scotus John (c. 1265–1308) Scottish Franciscan monk who was a leading figure in mediaeval scholasticism

Eddy Mary Morse (born Baker) (1821–1910) US religious thinker who founded the Christian Science movement

Edwards Jonathan (1703–1758) US theologian whose writings on predestination and revivalist preaching greatly influenced early US Protestant theology

Emerson Ralph Waldo (1803–1882) US religious thinker who was a major figure in New England transcendentalism

Erasmus Desiderius (c. 1466–1536) Dutch humanist who pioneered the use of the Greek text of the New Testament in biblical exegesis

Erigena Johannes Scotus (also called Scotus Eriugena, or John the Scot) (c. 810–c. 877) Irish religious thinker who attempted to combine Christian thought with neo-Platonism

Francis of Assisi, St (originally Francesco di Pietro di Bernardone) (1181–1226) founder of the Franciscan order; he advocated poverty and chastity, and believed in the unity of creation

Foucauld Charles Eugene de (known as Brother Charles of Jesus) (1858–1916) French-born Trappist monk who formed the orders of the Little Brothers of Jesus and the Little Sisters of Jesus

Fox George (1624–1691) British religious thinker who founded the Society of Friends ('Quakers')

Gandhi Mahatma (originally Mohandas Karamchand Gandhi) (1869–1948) Indian religious thinker whose teaching on nonviolence greatly influenced the Indian independence movement

Geiger Abraham (1810–1874) German Jewish philosopher who was a leading figure in the formation of Reform Judaism

Gershom ben Judah (Rabbeau Gershom) (c. 960–1028) German Rabbinic thinker whose writings influenced the development of Jewish law

Geulincx Arnold (also known as Philaretus) (1624–1669) Belgian religious thinker who formed the theory of occasionalism

Ghazali Abu Hamid Muhammad al- (1058–1111) Iranian Islamic theologian whose writings served as an authoritative reference for later Islamic belief and practice

Noteworthy Religious Thinkers and Leaders (continued)

Gilson Etienne Henry (1884–1978) French philosopher whose work *L'Espirit de la philosophie médiéval/The Spirit of Mediaeval Philosophy* contributed to the development of neo-Thomism

Graham Billy (William Franklin) (1918–) US cleric who revolutionized revivalist techniques in the 20th century with his mass evangelistic crusades

Grotius Hugo (Huig de Groot) (1583–1645) Dutch Protestant jurist whose *De Veritate Religionis Christianae/On the Truth of the Christian Religion* sought to promote Protestant unity

Gutiérrez Gustavo (1928–) Peruvian theologian who was one of the founders of liberation theology in Latin America

Hasan al-Banna (1904–1949) Egyptian Islamic thinker who founded the Muslim Brotherhood in 1928

Herbert Edward (1583–1648) English philosopher who developed deism

Heschel Abraham Joshua (1907–1972) Polish-born US Jewish theologian who sought to combine traditional Hasidic piety with existentialist philosophy

Hooker Richard (1554–1600) British theologian whose *Of the Laws of Ecclesiastical Polity* significantly influenced later Anglican thought

Hubbard L(afayette) Ron(ald) (1911–1986) US religious thinker and writer who founded scientology

Hügel Friedrich von (1852–1925) Italian-born British philosopher who was a leading figure in Roman Catholic mysticism

Huss John (Jan) (c. 1369–1415) Bohemian theologian whose *De ecclesia/The Church* helped initiate the Protestant Reformation in Europe

Ibiam Francis Akanu (1906–) Nigerian church leader who was a leading figure in the creation of the All Africa Conference of Churches in 1958

Ibn Daud Abraham (c. 1110–1180) Spanish Jewish philosopher who attempted to harmonize Judaism with Aristotelianism

Ibn Khaldun (1332–1406) Tunisian-born Islamic thinker who was a pioneer in the study of history and religion

Ignatius Loyola (Iñigo López de Recalde) (1491–1556) Spanish theologian who founded the Society of Jesus (Jesuits)

Jacob ben Asher (c. 1270–1340) German-born Spanish Jewish philosopher whose *Sefer ha-Turim/Book of Rows* is a major text in Rabbinic thought

Jerome, St (Eusebius Hieronymus) (c. 342–420) Christian scholar whose Latin translation of the Bible, *The Vulgate*, became the authoritative text for the mediaeval church

Jesus (Christ) (c. 5 BC–AD 29/30) Hebrew preacher on whose teachings Christianity was founded

al-Jilani Abd al-Qadir (1077–1166) Iranian-born Islamic thinker who founded the Qadiri Sufi order

John of Damascus, St (c. 676–754) Syrian-born Greek theologian whose *De fide orthodoxa/On the Orthodox Faith* was an influential text in the development of Greek Orthodox theology

John of Kronstadt (1829–1908) Russian church leader who promoted liturgical reform in the Russian Orthodox church

John of the Cross, St (Juan de Yepes y Álvarez) (1542–1591) Spanish Carmelite monk whose *Noche obscura del alma/The Dark Night of the Soul* is a major text in Catholic mysticism

John Paul II (Karol Wojtyła) (1920–) Polish-born Roman Catholic Pope since 1978 who has emphasized traditional Catholic values in his leadership

Jones Eli Stanley (1884–1973) US missionary whose *Christ of the Indian Road* encouraged an ecumenical approach to other religions

Khomeini Ruhollah (originally Ruholla Hendi) (1900–1989) Islamic scholar and Iranian ayatollah who, on his return to Iran from exile in 1979, launched the Islamic revolution against

Noteworthy Religious Thinkers and Leaders (continued)

Western influences

Knox John (*c.* 1513–1572) Scottish Protestant theologian and church reformer who founded the Church of Scotland

Krishnamurti Jiddu (1895–1986) Indian religious thinker who taught that an unconditioned state of mind is the goal of religious experience

Lao Zi or **Lao Tzu** (*c.* 604–531 BC) Chinese philosopher whose *Tao Te Ching/Classic of the Way and its Virtue* is the foundation for Taoist thought

Latimer Hugh (*c.* 1485–1555) English churchman who was burned at the stake in Oxford during the reign of Queen Mary for advocating Protestant views

Luther Martin (1483–1546) German Protestant reformer who founded Lutheranism

Maharishi Mahesh Yogi (Mahesh Prasad Varma) (1911–) Indian religious thinker who founded the transcendental meditation movement

Maimonides Moses (Moses ben Maimon or Rambam) (1135–1204) Spanish-born Jewish jurist and philosopher who attempted to reconcile Aristotelianism with Jewish tradition

Moon Sun Myung (1920–) Korean industrialist and founder in 1954 of the Unitarian Church (Moonies)

More Henry (1614–1687) English theologian who opposed Cartesian dualism and was a member of the Cambridge Platonists

Muhammad or **Mohammed** (*c.* 570–*c.* 632) founder of Islam who believed that the words of the Koran were revealed to him by God

Muhammad Elijah (originally Elijah Poole) (1897–1975) US religious thinker who helped found the Nation of Islam

Nanak (1469–1539) Indian guru and founder of Sikhism

Nicholas of Cusa or **Nicolaus Cusanus** (1401–1464) German-born Roman Catholic cardinal whose *De docta ignorantia/Of Learned Ignorance*

offered an alternative to scholastic thought

Occam or **Ockham** William of (*c.* 1285–1349) British Franciscan monk who revived the fundamentals of nominalism in the mediaeval church

Philo Judaeus (*c.* 20 BC–AD 50) Egyptian Jewish philosopher who sought to reconcile Judaism and Platonism

Ram Mohun Roy (or Rájá Rám Mohan Ráj) (1774–1833) Indian religious thinker and mystic who founded the Brahmo Samaj ('Theistic Society') in 1828

Russell Charles Taze (1852–1916) US founder of the Jehovah's Witness sect

Sānusī Sidi Muhammad ibn Ali as- (*c.* 1787–1859) Algerian-born Islamic philosopher who preached a return to the puritanism of early Islam

Savonarola Girolamo (1452–1498) Italian Dominican friar whose crusade against corruption overthrew the ruling Medici family in Florence in 1494

Schweitzer Albert (1875–1965) German theologian whose 'reverence for life' philosophy provided a rationale for humanitarianism

Segundo Juan Luis (1925–) Uruguayan-born theologian who was a pioneer in the liberation movement in Latin America

Smith Joseph (1805–1844) US founder of the Mormon sect (Church of Jesus Christ of Latter-day Saints)

Steiner Rudolf (1861–1925) Austrian religious thinker who founded Anthroposophy

Strauss David Friedrich (1808–1874) German Protestant theologian whose *Das Leben Jesu/Life of Jesus* attempted to dismiss all supernatural elements in the gospel accounts

Tagore Rabindranath (1817–1905) Indian Hindu thinker and poet who attempted a reform of Hinduism and regarded traditional Hindu rituals as idolatrous

Teilhard de Chardin Pierre (1881–1955) French Jesuit theologian, paleontologist, and philoso-

Noteworthy Religious Thinkers and Leaders (continued)

pher who developed a creative synthesis of religion and nature presented in *Le Phénomène humain/The Phenomenon of Man*

Tillich Paul Johannes (1886–1965) German-born US theologian whose *Systematic Theology* greatly influenced 20th-century Protestant theology

Tutu Desmond Mpilo (1931–) South African archbishop who was the primary church spokesperson in the struggle against apartheid in South Africa

Visser `t Hooft Willem Adolph (1900–1985) Dutch Protestant church leader who was a pioneer in the creation of the World Council of Churches

Vivekananda Swami (originally Narendranath Dutt or Datta) (1863–1902) Hindu religious leader who founded the Ramakrishna Order

Watts Alan Wilson (1915–1973) British-born US religious philosopher who popularized Zen teaching for Western audiences

Wesley John (1703–1791) British theologian who founded the Methodist movement

White Ellen Gould (1827–1915) US religious thinker who co-founded the Seventh-Day Adventist Church

Wycliffe John (*c.* 1329–1384) English theologian whose produced the first translation of the Bible into English

Yamazaki Ansai (1618–1682) Japanese thinker who was the founder of Suiga (or Suika) Shinto, which is a mixture of neo-Confucianism and Shinto thought

Yung-ming Yen-shou (Yomyo Enju) (904–975) Chinese thinker who advocated a synthesis of the Ch'an and Pure Land schools of Buddhist thought

Zwingli Ulrich (Latin: Ulricus Zuinglius) (1484–1531) Swiss theologian who was a leader in the Swiss Protestant Reformation

ARTS

---*---

Definitions of art usually reflect aesthetic criteria and the arts may encompass literature, music, drama, painting, and sculpture.

In Western culture, aesthetic criteria introduced by the ancient Greeks still influence our perceptions and judgements of art. Two currents of thought run through our ideas about art. In one, derived from Aristotle, art is concerned with mimesis (imitation), the representation of appearances, and gives pleasure through the accuracy and skill with which it depicts the real world. The other view, derived from Plato, holds that the artist is inspired by the Muses (or by God, or by the inner impulses, or by the collective unconscious) to express that which is beyond appearances – inner feelings, eternal truths, or the essence of the age.

ARCHITECTURE

Architecture is the art of designing structures. The term covers the design of the visual appearance of structures; their internal arrangements of space; selection of external and internal building materials; design or selection of natural and artificial lighting systems, as well as mechanical, electrical, and plumbing systems; and design or selection of decorations and furnishings. Architectural style may emerge from evolution of techniques and styles particular to a culture in a given time period with or without identifiable individuals as architects, or may be attributed to specific individuals or groups of architects working together on a project.

Notable Buildings of the Post-war Era

(All dates given are dates of completion.)

Eames House, Pacific Palisades, Los Angeles, California, USA (Charles and Ray Eames, 1949) Partially engaged to its hillside site and personalized by its owner-builders, this house provided a model to a generation of young architects, showing that modernism could be humanized and still adhere to a strict set of principles. Modernism, or the modern movement, was a conscious attempt to break with the artistic traditions of the 19th century. It was based on a concern with form and the expression of technique, as opposed to content and narrative; functionalism ousted decorativeness as a central objective.

Lever House, New York City, New York, USA (Skidmore, Owings, and Merrill, 1952) The building commercialized the language of the Modern Movement; the design provided the model for buildings throughout the world.

Church of Nôtre-Dame-du-Haut, Ronchamp, Vosges, France (Le Corbusier, 1955) This building was revolutionary for its expressive use of massive concrete walls and a concrete shell roof; for the first time, concrete was used in a sculptural way to create a fluid structure. It was a departure from Le Corbusier's rectilinear work, which had been seen as archetypal of the Modern Movement.

Seagram Building, New York City, New York, USA (Ludwig Mies van der Rohe and Philip Johnson, 1958) This building provided a compelling image for the skyscraper in the urban context that conformed to the new post-war corporate image of sleekness, sophistication, cool elegance, and control.

Guggenheim Museum, New York City, New York, USA (Frank Lloyd Wright, 1959) This was the most important building of Wright's last period, a low-rise circular tower in the high-rise cityscape of New York. The round, spiralling ramp took the visitor and the works of modern art to the full height of the building and provided a revolutionary circulation model for museums.

Richards Medical Research Building, University of Pennsylvania, Philadelphia, Pennsylvania, USA (Louis Kahn, 1960) Stretched the modernist invocation against historicism by evoking vernacular images of an Italian hill town that inspired the architect, whilst also accentuating the function of the various elements of the building in a meaningful way. Historicism is the copying of styles from the past. It implies a detailed imitation, rather than the ironic reference that is common in Post-Modernism (see **House, Chestnut Hill**).

TWA Terminal, John F Kennedy International Airport, New York City, New York, USA (Eero Saarinen, 1962) Served as a model of originality and elegance in concrete construction, showing the fluid possibilities of concrete, in this instance used as a metaphor for flight.

Faculty of Engineering, Leicester University, Leicester, UK (James Stirling and James Gowan, 1963) Refined the language of modernism and reinvigorated the modernist style.

Notable Buildings of the Post-war Era (continued)

House, Chestnut Hill, Philadelphia, USA (Robert Venturi and John Rausch, 1964) Changed perceptions about the principle of form following function, as advocated by modernists. The exterior symbolically expressed a domestic image that was detached from interior use; it is considered to be the first Post-Modern building. Post-Modernism rejects the preoccupation of Modernism with purity of form and techniques. Post-Modernists use an amalgam of style elements from the past, such as Classical and Baroque, and apply them to spare modern forms, often with ironic effect.

Modena Cemetery, Modena, Italy (Aldo Rossi, 1971) A major nationalistic statement using the arcade typology and blending of rationalism (an architecture derived from logic rather than empiricism) with metaphorical symbols.

Willis Faber and Dumas Office Building, Ipswich, Suffolk, UK (Norman Foster and Associates, 1975) A sensitive application of the high-tech approach to an urban environment. Its hung glass façade provided two faces: a slick black covering that reflects its surroundings by day and a transparent skin that seems to disappear when lit from inside by night.

Pompidou Centre, Paris, France (Richard Rogers and Renzo Piano, 1977) With its external escalators snaking up the walls, it brought high-tech architecture at mega-scale into the city. Became a symbol of the museum as a cultural centre and the power of a modern building in regenerating an urban centre.

Abteiburg Museum, Mönchen-Gladbach, Germany (Hans Hollein, 1982) This building helped to define the role of the museum, with its sculptural interior and innovative circulation pattern.

AT&T Building, New York City, New York, USA (Philip Johnson and John Burgee, 1982) The first Post-Modern building that became memorable to the public. The use of a broken pediment defining the building's roof profile provoked controversy about the use and interpretation of traditional and modern forms.

National Commercial Bank Headquarters, Jeddah, Saudi Arabia (Skidmore, Owings, and Merrill, 1982) Two enormous rectangular openings in the plain, monumental exterior walls and a triangular plan gave this skyscraper a dramatic appearance unlike any other high-rise building to date. The building was innovative in its control of glare and air circulation. Removing the elevator and stairs from their usual positions in the middle of the building to the outside walls, the architect created atrium-like courtyards.

Haj Terminal, Jeddah, Saudi Arabia (Skidmore, Owings, and Merrill, 1982) High-technology materials were used – teflon-impregnated fibreglass fabric – to create an elegant tent structure that ameliorated harsh climate conditions and was an appropriate cultural expression using traditional forms. The research on new materials for tent structures formed the basis for works by architects throughout the world.

Public Service Building, Portland, Oregon, USA (Michael Graves, 1983) This building galvanized opinions among architects about Post-Modernism; until the design of this building, Post-Modernism had been considered an exercise in the avant-garde rather than a mainstream movement in architecture.

Staatsgalerie, Stuttgart, Germany (James Stirling and Michael Wilford, 1984) A skilful application of Post-Modern aesthetics to the urban context. Reformed the museum for the 1980s and 1990s by making it a popular playground with plazas and galleries.

Hong Kong and Shanghai Banking Corporation, Hong Kong, Special Administrative Region of China (Norman Foster, 1986) Redefined the skyscraper by using an innovative suspension structure (inspired by the Golden Gate Bridge in San Francisco, USA), allowing for a soaring atrium space inside.

Petronas Towers, Kuala Lumpur, Malaysia (Cesar Pelli, 1996 (main structure)) The tallest building in the world, it expands skyscraper design to the category of megastructure.

Bilbao Guggenheim Museum, Bilbao, Spain (Frank Gehry, 1997) A colossal, shimmering edifice located on a waterfront site, this building was seen as inspirational by many critics. Outside, the building's curving forms, together resembling a boat, are coated with titanium panels. Inside, the fluid spaces include an atrium of glass and flowing white plaster walls. The fluidity of the design and interior spaces might not have been attempted without the latest computer-aided technology; specifically, a program used by a French aeronautical company in designing jet aircraft.

The Tallest Buildings in the World

(N/A = not available.)

Building/structure	City	Height		Storeys
		m	ft	
Inhabited Buildings				
Miglin-Beitler Tower[1]	Chicago (IL), USA	609	1,999	N/A
Chongqing Tower	Chongqing, China	460[2]	1,509[2]	114
Petronas Tower II[3]	Kuala Lumpur, Malaysia	452[2]	1,483[2]	113
Sears Tower	Chicago (IL), USA	442[2]	1,450[2]	110
Jin Mao Building	Shanghai, China	421	1,380	N/A
Two World Trade Center[3]	New York (NY), USA	415[2]	1,362[2]	110
Empire State Building	New York (NY), USA	381[2]	1,250[2]	102
Bank of China	Hong Kong, China	368	1,209	72
Amoco Building	Chicago (IL), USA	346	1,136	80
John Hancock Centre	Chicago (IL), USA	344	1,127	100
Chrysler Building	New York (NY), USA	319	1,046	77
Nations Bank Tower	Atlanta (GA), USA	312	1,023	55
First Interstate World Center	Los Angeles (CA), USA	310	1,017	73
Stratosphere Tower	Las Vegas (NV), USA	308	1,012	114
Texas Commerce Tower	Houston (TX), USA	305	1,002	75
Allied Bank Plaza	Houston (TX), USA	302	992	71
Two Prudential Plaza	Chicago (IL), USA	298	978	64
311 South Waker Drive	Chicago (IL), USA	295	969	65
First Canadian Place	Toronto, Ontario, Canada	290	952	72
American International	New York (NY), USA	290	952	66
Bay/Adelaide Centre	Toronto, Ontario, Canada	288	945	53
One Liberty Place	Philadelphia (PA), USA	288	945	62
Columbia Seafirst Center	Seattle (WA), USA	287	943	76
40 Wall Tower	New York (NY), USA	283	927	70
Nations Bank Plaza	Dallas (TX), USA	281	921	72
Citicorp Center	New York (NY), USA	279	915	59
Scotia Plaza	Toronto, Ontario, Canada	275	902	68
One Peach Tree Center	Atlanta (GA), USA	275	902	60
Transco Tower	Houston (TX), USA	274	901	64
Society Center	Cleveland (OH), USA	271	888	57
Two Union Square	Seattle (WA), USA	270	886	56
AT&T Corporate Center	Chicago (IL), USA	270	885	60
Mellon Bank Center	Philadelphia (PA), USA	268	880	56
Nations Bank Corporate Center	Charlotte (NC), USA	267	875	60
900 North Michigan	Chicago (IL), USA	265	871	66
Canada Trust Tower	Toronto, Ontario, Canada	263	863	51
Water Tower Place	Chicago (IL), USA	262	859	74
First Interstate Bank	Los Angeles (CA), USA	261	858	62
Transamerica Pyramid	San Francisco (CA), USA	260	853	61
G E Building, Rockefeller Center	New York (NY), USA	259	850	70
One First National Plaza	Chicago (IL), USA	259	851	60
Two Liberty Place	Philadelphia (PA), USA	258	845	52
USX Towers	Pittsburgh (PA), USA	256	841	64
One Atlantic Center	Atlanta (GA), USA	251	825	50
Cityspire	New York (NY), USA	248	814	72
One Chase Manhattan	New York (NY), USA	248	813	60
Metlife Building	New York (NY), USA	246	808	59
John Hancock Tower	Boston (MA), USA	244	800	60
Tallest Structures				
Warszawa Radio Maszt[4]	Konstantynów, Poland	646	2,120	–
KTHI-TV Mast	Fargo (ND), USA	629	2,063	–
CN Tower	Toronto, Ontario, Canada	555	1,822	–

[1] Planned; this will become the tallest inhabited building when completed.

[2] Excluding TV antennas.

[3] Tallest tower in building listed.

[4] Collapsed during renovation, August 1991.

Architectural Movements

early architecture Little remains of the earliest forms of architecture, but archaeologists have examined remains of prehistoric sites and documented villages of wooden-post buildings with above-ground construction of organic materials (mud or wattle and daub) from the Upper Palaeolithic, Mesolithic, and Neolithic periods in Asia, the Middle East, Europe, and the Americas. More extensive remains of stone-built structures have given clues to later Neolithic farming communities as well as to the habitations, storehouses, and religious and civic structures of early civilizations. The best documented are those of ancient Egypt, where exhaustive work in the 19th and 20th centuries revealed much about both ordinary buildings and monumental structures, such as the pyramid tombs near modern Cairo and the temple and tomb complexes concentrated at Luxor and Thebes.

Classical The basic forms of Classical architecture evolved in Greece between the 6th and 2nd centuries BC. A hallmark was the post-and-lintel construction of temples and public structures, classified into the Doric, Ionic, and Corinthian orders and defined by simple, scrolled, or acanthus-leaf capitals for support columns. The Romans copied and expanded on Greek Classical forms, notably introducing bricks and concrete and developing the vault, arch, and dome for public buildings and aqueducts.

Byzantine This form of architecture developed primarily in the Eastern Roman Empire from the 4th century, with its centre at Byzantium (later named Constantinople, now Istanbul, modern day Turkey). It is dominated by the arch and dome, with the Classical orders reduced in importance. Its most notable features are churches, some very large, based on the Greek cross plan (Hagia Sophia, Istanbul; St Mark's, Venice), with formalized painted and mosaic decoration. The Byzantine style is characterized by heavy stylization, strong linear emphasis, the use of

rigid artistic stereotypes, and rich colours such as gold.

Islamic Islamic architecture developed from the 8th century, when the Islamic religion spread from its centre in the Middle East west to Spain and east to China and parts of the Philippine Islands. Notable features are the development of the tower with dome and the pointed arch. Islamic architecture, chiefly through Spanish examples such as the Great Mosque at Córdoba and the Alhambra in Granada, profoundly influenced Christian church architecture, for example, the adoption of the pointed arch in Gothic architecture.

Romanesque This style of architecture flourished in Western European Christianity from the 10th to the 12th centuries. It is marked by churches with massive walls for structural integrity, rounded arches, small windows, and resulting dark volumes of interior space. In England the style is generally referred to as Norman architecture (an example is Durham Cathedral). Romanesque enjoyed a renewal of interest in Europe and the USA in the late 19th and early 20th centuries.

Gothic Gothic architecture emerged out of Romanesque. The development of the pointed arch and flying buttress made it possible to change from thick supporting walls to lighter curtain walls with extensive expansion of window areas (and stained-glass artwork) and resulting increases in interior light. Gothic architecture was developed mainly in France from the 12th to 16th centuries. The style is divided into Early Gothic (for example, Sens Cathedral), High Gothic (Chartres Cathedral), and Late or Flamboyant Gothic. In England the corresponding divisions are Early English (Salisbury Cathedral), Decorated (Wells Cathedral), and Perpendicular (Kings College Chapel, Cambridge). Gothic was also developed extensively in Germany and Italy.

Gothic architecture in Pisa
The circular baptistry, marble-clad cathedral, and campanile (Leaning Tower of Pisa, not shown) form the most celebrated complex of Gothic architecture in Italy. In 1993 a team of British engineers succeeded in halting the lean of the Leaning Tower by weighting it with lead. *Italian State Tourist Office*

Renaissance This style of architecture, which began in 15th-century Italy, is based on the revival of Classical, especially Roman, architecture developed by Filippo Brunelleschi. It is characterized by a concern with balance, clarity, and proportion, and by the external use of columns and fluted pilasters. A major source of inspiration for the great Renaissance architects – Andrea Palladio, Leon Battista Alberti, Filippo Brunelleschi, Donato Bramante, and Michelangelo Buonarotti – was the work of the 1st-century BC Roman engineer Marcus Vitruvius Pollio. The Palladian style was later used extensively in England by Inigo Jones; Christopher Wren also worked in the Classical idiom. Classicism, or Neo-Classicism as it is also known, has been popular in the USA from the 18th century, as evidenced in much of the civic and commercial architecture since the time of the early republic (the US Capitol and Supreme Court buildings in Washington; many state capitols).

Baroque European architecture of the 17th and 18th centuries elaborated on Classical models with exuberant and extravagant

(continued)

Architectural Movements (continued)

decoration. In large-scale public buildings, the style is best seen in the innovative works of Giovanni Lorenzo Bernini and Francesco Borromini in Italy and later in those of John Vanbrugh, Nicholas Hawksmoor, and Christopher Wren in England. There were numerous practitioners in France and the German-speaking countries, and notably in Vienna.

Rococo This architecture of 18th-century Europe extends the Baroque style with an even greater extravagance of design motifs, using a new lightness of detail and naturalistic elements, such as shells, flowers, and trees. The term 'Rococo' is derived from the French *rocaille* (rock- or shell-work), a style of interior decoration based on S-curves and scroll-like forms. In the 1730s the movement became widespread in Europe, notably in the churches and palaces of southern Germany and Austria. Chippendale furniture is an English example of the French Rococo style. The architectural and interior design of the Amalienburg pavilion at Nymphenburg near Munich, Germany, and the Hôtel de Soubise pavilion in Paris, France, are typical of the movement. The painters François Boucher and Jean Honoré Fragonard both painted typically decorative Rococo panels for Parisian *hôtels* (town houses).

Neo-Classical European architecture of the 18th and 19th centuries again focused on the more severe Classical idiom (inspired by archaeological finds), producing, for example, the large-scale rebuilding of London by Robert Adam and John Nash and later of Paris by Georges Haussman. Neo-Classicism superseded the Rococo style and was inspired both by the excavation of the Roman towns of Pompeii and Herculaneum and by the theories of the cultural studies of the German art historian Johann J Winckelmann (which revived Greek styles).

Neo-Gothic The late 19th century saw a Gothic revival in Europe and the USA, which was evident in churches and public buildings, such

as the Houses of Parliament in London, designed by Charles Barry and A W Pugin, and Trinity Church, New York, by Richard Upjohn. The growth of Romanticism led some writers, artists, and antiquaries to embrace a fascination with Gothic forms that emphasized the supposedly bizarre and grotesque aspects of the Middle Ages. During the Victorian period, however, a far better understanding of Gothic forms was achieved, and this resulted in some impressive Neo-Gothic architecture, as well as some desecration of genuine Gothic churches in the name of 'restoration'.

Art Nouveau This architectural and design movement, arising at the end of the 19th century, countered Neo-Gothic with sinuous, flowing shapes for buildings, room plans, and interior decoration. The style is characterized by the work of Charles Rennie Mackintosh in Scotland (Glasgow Art School) and Antonio Gaudí in Spain (Church of the Holy Family, Barcelona).

Modern Movement The Modern Movement began in the 1900s with the Vienna School and the German Bauhaus and was also developed in the USA, Scandinavia, and France. With Functionalism as its central precept, its hallmarks are the use of spare line and form, an emphasis on rationalism, and the elimination of ornament. It makes great use of technological advances in materials such as glass, steel, and concrete, and of construction techniques that allow flexibility of design. Notable practitioners include Frank Lloyd Wright, Mies van der Rohe, and Charles Edouard Jeanneret, known as Le Corbusier. Modern architecture has furthered the notion of the planning of extensive multibuilding projects and of whole towns or communities.

International Style Also called **International Modern,** this architectural style was an early and influential phase of the Modern Movement, originating in Western Europe in the 1920s but finding its

fullest expression in the 1930s, notably in the USA. It is characterized by a dominance of geometric, especially rectilinear, forms; emphasis on asymmetrical composition; large expanses of glazing; and white rendered walls. Examples are Walter Gropius's Bauhaus building, Dessau, Germany, (1925–26); Le Corbusier's Villa Savoye, Poissy, France, (1927–31); Alvar Aalto's Viipuri Library, Finland (now in Russia; 1927–35); and Mies van der Rohe's Barcelona Pavilion, Spain (1929).

Philip Johnson and Alfred Barr coined the term 'International Style' in 1932 to describe the work of Le Corbusier, Gropius, and Mies van der Rohe (among others) during the preceding decade. It is sometimes used as another name for the Modern Movement as a whole.

Brutalism This architectural movement of the 1950s and 1960s evolved from the work of Le Corbusier and Mies van der Rohe. Uncompromising in its approach, it stresses functionalism and honesty to materials; steel and concrete are favoured. The term was coined by Alison and Peter Smithson who developed the style in the UK. The Smithsons' design for Hunstanton School, Norfolk, (1949–54) recalls the work of Mies van der Rohe but is more brutally honest, exposing all the services to view. The Park Hill Housing Estate, Sheffield, England (1961), by Jack Lynn and Ivor Smith makes use of the rough concrete (*béton brut*) characteristic of Le Corbusier's later work.

Post-Modernism This late 20th-century movement in architecture rejects the preoccupation of Modernism with purity of form and technique. Emerging in the 1980s in the USA, the UK, and Japan, the style favoured an eclectic mixture of styles and motifs, often Classical. Its use of irony, parody, and illusion is in sharp distinction to the Modernist ideals of truth to materials and form following function. Exponents include Robert Venturi and Michael Graves.

Architectural Movements (continued)

High Tech Originating in the UK in the 1970s, this approach to design concentrates on technical innovation, often using exposed structure and services as a means of creating exciting forms and spaces. The Hong Kong and Shanghai Bank, Hong Kong (1986), designed by Norman Foster, is a masterpiece of High Tech architecture. Other outstanding examples are the Lloyds Building (1986) in the City of London, by Richard Rogers, which dramatically exhibits the service requirements of a large building; and Nicholas Grimshaw's *Financial Times* printing works, London, UK (1988).

High cost High Tech The Hong Kong and Shanghai Banking Corporation Headquarters (1986), designed by English architect Norman Foster. It is reputed to be the most expensive building in the world, having cost $615 million. The floors hang from the external frame, sun scoops reflect light into open central areas, and escalators provide movement as part of a layered and stepped exterior. The building's post-modernist mix of technology, romanticism, and allusion has won widespread acclaim. *Sir Norman Foster and Partners*

Deconstructionism An architectural debate as much as a style, Deconstructionism fragments forms and space by taking the usual building elements of floors, walls, and ceilings and sliding them apart to create a sense of disorientation and movement. Essentially Modernist, it draws inspiration from the optimism of the Soviet avant-garde of the 1920s. Its proponents include Zaha Hadid in the UK, Frank Gehry and Peter Eisenman in the USA, and Coop Himmelbau in Austria.

Noteworthy Architects

Aalto (Hugo) Alvar Henrik (1898–1976) Finnish architect and designer who pioneered the Modern Movement in Finland

Adam William (1689–1748) and son Robert (1728–1792) family of Scottish architects and designers

Alberti Leon Battista (1404–1472) Italian Renaissance architect and theorist who set the principles of Classical style

Asam Cosmas Damian (1686–1739) and his brother Egid Quirin (1692–1750) German architects famous for their churches in flamboyant Late Baroque style

Barragán Luis (1902–1988) Mexican architect who combined Modernism with vernacular South American styles

Barry Charles (1795–1860) English architect whose work includes the Neo-Gothic Houses of Parliament in London, UK

Behrens Peter (1868–1940) German architect who adapted architecture to industry

Belluschi Pietro (1899–1994) Italian-born modernist architect who designed the Juilliard School of Music in New York, New York, and St Mary's Cathedral in San Francisco, California

Bernini Gianlorenzo (Giovanni Lorenzo) (1598–1680) Italian sculptor, architect, and painter who developed the Baroque style and designed the Roman papal monuments

Borromini Francesco (Castelli) (1599–1667) Swiss-born Italian Baroque architect in the Classical style whose work includes the churches of San Carlo alle Quattro Fontane and Sant'Ivo della Sapienza

Bramante Donato (1444–1514) Italian Renaissance artist and architect who designed the circular Tempietto of San Pietro and rebuilt part of the Vatican, both in Rome, Italy

Breuer Marcel Lajos (1902–1981) Hungarian-born architect and designer with an affinity for natural materials who designed the Bijenkorf in Rotterdam, Netherlands

Brunelleschi Filippo (1377–1446) Italian Renaissance architect who pioneered the scientific use of perspective and designed the Florence Cathedral dome, Italy

Bulfinch Charles (1763–1844) American architect who designed the State House in Boston, Massachusetts, and part of the Capitol in Washington, DC

Bunshaft Gordon (1909–1990) US architect who applied the International Style to US glass skyscrapers

Burges William (1827–1881) English Gothic Revival architect and designer, known for sumptuous interiors, who designed Cork Cathedral, Ireland

Butterfield William (1814–1900) English architect who was a leading figure in the Gothic Revival

Callicrates (5th century BC) Athenian architect who designed, with Ictinus, the Parthenon, Athens, Greece

Campbell Colen (1676–1729) Scottish architect, principal figure of British Palladian architecture and author of *Vitruvius Britannicus*

Chambers William (1723–1796) Swedish-born English architect who designed the Chinese-style pagoda in Kew Gardens, London, UK, and the Neo-Palladian Somerset House, also in London

Coates Nigel (1949–) English architect who spurred regeneration of London's derelict areas

Duiker Johannes (1890–1935) Dutch architect whose work demonstrates structural vigour, and who designed the Zonnestraal Sanatorium in Hilversum and the Open Air School in Amsterdam, both in the Netherlands

Eiffel (Alexandre) Gustave (1832–1923) French engineer who constructed the Eiffel Tower in Paris

Esquivel Adolfo (1932–) Argentine sculptor and architect who won the 1980 Nobel Peace Prize

Farrell Terry (1938–) English architect in the Post-Modern style

Fathy Hassan (1900–1989) Egyptian architect who used indigenous building technology and natural materials to solve contemporary housing problems

Fontana Domenico (1543–1607) Italian architect who designed the Lateran Palace and the Vatican Library in Rome, Italy

Foster Norman (Robert) (1935–) English architect of the High Tech school

Fuller (Richard) Buckminster (1895–1983) US architect, engineer, and social philosopher who invented the geodesic dome

Gaudí Antonio (1852–1926) Spanish architect with a flamboyant Art Nouveau style, noted for his unusual materials and technical innovation

Geddes Patrick (1854–1932) Scottish town planner who established the importance of surveys and research work

Gehry Frank Owen (1929–) US architect who designed the Guggenheim Museum, Bilbao, Spain, and, whose use of collage and montage techniques approaches abstract art

Gibbs James (1682–1754) Scottish Neo-Classical architect who designed the Radcliffe Camera in Oxford, England

Gilbert Cass (1859–1934) US architect who designed the Woolworth Building, New York, New York

Graves Michael (1934–) US architect who blends Classical and Modern styles; his works include a commission to design the addition to the Whitney Museum of American Art in Manhattan, New York, New York

Grimshaw Nicholas (Thomas) (1939–) English architect of a distinctly industrial, High Tech style

Gropius Walter Adolf (1883–1969) German-born US architect who was an early exponent of the International style

Haussmann Georges Eugène (1809–1891) French administrator who replanned Paris with long wide boulevards and parks

Hawksmoor Nicholas (1661–1736) English architect who developed a distinctive style incorporating elements from both Gothic and Classical sources

Hoban James C (1762–1831) Irish-born US architect who designed the White House in Washington, DC, and other public buildings

Hood Raymond (Mathewson) (1881–1934) US architect who co-designed the Rockefeller Center, New York, New York

Howard Ebenezer (1850–1928) English town planner who pioneered the garden city ideal

Isozaki Arata (1931–) Japanese architect who blends Western Post-Modernism with elements of traditional Japanese architecture; his designs include the Museum of Contemporary Art, Los Angeles, California

Johnson Philip Cortelyou (1906–) US architect who coined the term International style and designed the AT&T building in New York, New York

Jones Inigo (1573–1652) English Classical architect who introduced the Palladian Style to England, and whose work includes the Banqueting House in Whitehall, London, UK

Kahn Louis Isadore (1901–1974) US architect with a classically Romantic style and imaginative use of concrete and brick, whose work includes the Yale Art Gallery, Connecticut

Kent William (1684–1748) English architect, landscape gardener, and interior designer whose work excelled in richly carved interiors and furnishings, as in Holkham Hall in Norfolk, England; he was also a pioneer in Romantic landscape gardening

Lasdun Denys Louis (1914–) English Modernist architect whose work includes the University of East Anglia, Norwich, and London's National Theatre, both in the UK

Latrobe Benjamin Henry (1764–1820) English-born US architect whose works include the Bank of Pennsylvania, Philadelphia, Pennsylvania, and the Roman Catholic cathedral in Baltimore, Maryland

Le Corbusier (Charles-Edouard Jeanneret) (1887–1965) Swiss-born French architect who was influential in the Modern Movement and advocated 'vertical garden cities' as a solution to urban chaos

L'Enfant Pierre Charles (1754–1825) French-born US architect who is principally remembered for his plan for Washington, DC

Le Vau Louis (1612–1670) French architect of Vaux-le-Vicomte château outside Paris, France, whose work also includes the inspired remodelling of Versailles, France

Libeskind Daniel (1946–) US architect who designed the extension to the Berlin Museum, Germany the Ouzo Observatory in Japan, and the proposed extension to the Victoria & Albert Museum, London, UK

Loos Adolf (1870–1933) Austrian architect who designed private houses on Lake Geneva, Switzerland, and the Steiner House in Vienna, Austria

Lorimer Robert Stodart (1864–1929) Scottish architect in Scotland's Arts and Crafts movement whose work includes Ardkinglas House, Argyll, Scotland, and Rowallan House, Ayrshire, Scotland

Lubetkin Berthold Romanovich (1901–1990) Russian-born English architect whose pioneering designs include Highpoint I, in Highgate, London and the Penguin Pool at London Zoo, both in the UK

Lutyens Edwin Landseer (1869–1944) English architect best known for his country houses in the Arts and Crafts style, and for his work planning New Delhi, in India

McKim Charles Follen (1847–1909) US architect who designed the Boston Public Library, Massachusetts, and co-founded the firm that became McKim, Mead, and White

Mackintosh Charles Rennie (1868–1928) Scottish architect, designer, and painter, and one of the leading figures in Art Nouveau

Michelozzo di Bartolommeo (1396–1472) Italian architect and sculptor of the Early Renaissance

Mies van der Rohe Ludwig (1886–1969) German-born US architect and leading exponent of the International style whose work includes the Seagram building in New York, New York, and the National Gallery in Berlin, Germany

Mills Robert (1781–1855) US architect who designed the Washington Monument, Washington, DC, and other classically inspired works

Nash John (1752–1835) English architect who designed Regent's Park in London, UK, with its grandiose scheme of terraces, crescents, and palatial-style houses; other work includes

Trafalgar Square and St James's Park, also in London

Nervi Pier Luigi (1891–1979) Italian engineer who used steel mesh within concrete to create flowing form; his work includes the cathedral at New Norcia, near Perth, Australia, and the Turin Exhibition Hall, Italy

Neutra Richard Joseph (1892–1970) Austrian-born US architect who was a leading exponent of the International style

Niemeyer (Soares Filho) Oscar (1907–) Brazilian architect and joint designer of the United Nations headquarters in New York, New York, whose work includes the Catholic cathedral in Brasília, Brazil

Nouvel Jean (1945–) French architect in the High Tech style who adapted traditional Islamic motifs to technological ends in the Institut du Monde Arabe in Paris, France

Oud J(acobus) J(ohannes) P(ieter) (1890–1963) Dutch architect and designer, and one of the leading figures of the De Stijl movement

Palladio Andrea (1508–1580) Italian Renaissance architect who used Roman Classical forms, symmetry, and proportion

Paxton Joseph (1801–1865) English architect who designed the Great Exhibition building in London, UK, revolutionary in its structural use of glass and iron

Pei Ieoh Ming (1917–) Chinese-born US Modernist architect known for innovative High Tech structures and glass walls, whose work includes the Bank of China, Hong Kong, and the Pyramid in The Louvre, Paris, France

Piano Renzo (1937–) Italian architect who designed (with Richard Rogers) the Pompidou Centre, Paris, France, and the new Kansai International Airport, Osaka, Japan

Pugin Augustus Welby Northmore (1812–1852) English architect whose work instigated the Gothic Revival in England; he collaborated on the design of the Houses of Parliament in London, UK

Rastrelli Bartolomeo Francesco (1700–1771) Italian architect who became a major figure in the creation of St Petersburg, Russia

Richardson Henry Hobson (1838–1886) US architect who revived the Romanesque style; his works include Trinity Church in Boston, Massachusetts

Rietvelt Gerrit Thomas (1888–1964) Dutch architect associated with the De Stijl group, whose work includes the Schroeder House in Utrecht, Netherlands

della Robbia Italian family of sculptors in Florence during the 15th century: Luca della Robbia (1400–1482) created the marble *cantoria* (singing gallery) in Florence Cathedral, Italy

Rogers Richard George (1933–) English High Tech architect whose work includes the Pompidou Centre, Paris, France, the Lloyd's of London building, and the Reuters building at Blackwell Yard, (RIBA award) both London UK

Rossi Aldo (1931–1997) Italian architect and theorist, leader of Neo-Rationalism, whose design theories offer an alternative to Modernism

Saarinen Eero (1910–1961) Finnish-born US architect renowned for innovative Modernist designs, whose work includes the US Embassy in London, UK, the TWA Kennedy terminal in New York, New York, and Dulles Airport in Washington, DC

Saarinen (Gottlieb) Eliel (1873–1950) Finnish-born US architect and town planner, and founder of the Finnish Romantic school, whose work includes Helsinki railway station, Finland, the Cranbrook Academy of Art in Bloomfield Hills, Michigan, and Christ Church in Minneapolis, Minnesota

Sansovino (Jacopo d'Antonio Tatti) (1486–1570) Italian architect who introduced the High Renaissance style to Venice, Italy

Schinkel Karl Friedrich (1781–1841) German architect and designer noted for his grandiose public buildings in the Neo-Classical style

Scott Gilbert (1880–1960) English architect who designed Liverpool Anglican cathedral, Cambridge University Library, and Waterloo Bridge, London, all in England; he also supervised the rebuilding of the House of Commons, London, after World War II

Sinan (1489–1588) Ottoman architect who designed hundreds of buildings including the

Suleimaniye Mosque complex in Istanbul and Selimiye Mosque in Adrianople, both in Turkey

Soane John (1753–1837) English architect whose Neo-Classical designs anticipated contemporary taste, and whose work includes the Soane Museum, London, UK

Speer Albert (1905–1981) German architect and Nazi minister during World War II who worked as Hitler's architect, and whose overblown Classicism glorified the state

Spence Basil Urwin (1907–1976) Scottish architect whose work includes Coventry Cathedral, England, and the British Embassy in Rome, Italy

Stern Robert (1939–) US architect who is a leading exponent of Post-Modernism

Stirling James Frazer (1926–1992) Scottish architect whose masterpiece, the Staatsgalerie in Stuttgart, Germany, blends Constructivism, Modernism, and strands of Classicism

Sullivan Louis Henry (1856–1924) US architect who was a leader of the Chicago School and an early developer of the skyscraper, including the Wainwright Building, St Louis, Missouri

Tadao Ando (1941–) Japanese architect who combined Modernist techniques with elements of traditional Japanese architecture, and whose work includes the Church of Light, Osaka, Japan

Tange Kenzo (1913–) Japanese architect who helped to introduce Modernism to Japan

Vanbrugh John (1664–1726) English Baroque architect and dramatist who designed Blenheim Palace, Oxfordshire, and Castle Howard, Yorkshire, both in England

Vasari Giorgio (1511–1574) Italian architect and painter who designed the Uffizi Palace, Florence, Italy

Venturi Robert Charles (1925–) US architect who pioneered Post-Modernism and whose work includes the Sainsbury Wing extension to the National Gallery in London, UK

Vignola (Jacopo Barozzi) (1507–1573) Italian architect whose late works (in particular the church of Il Gesù in Rome, Italy) anticipate the Baroque style

Vitruvius (Marcus Vitruvius Pollio) (1st century AD) Roman architect whose book *De Architectural On Architecture* had a profound effect on Renaissance and Neo-Classical architecture

Voysey Charles Francis Annesley (1857–1941) English architect and designer of asymmetrical country houses with massive buttresses, long sloping roofs, and roughcast walls

Wagner Otto (1841–1918) Viennese architect who rejected ornament for Rationalism, and whose work includes the Post Office Savings Bank in Vienna, Austria

Waterhouse Alfred (1830–1905) English architect and leading exponent of the Victorian Neo-Gothic style, whose work includes the National History Museum in London, UK

Webb Philip Speakman (1831–1915) English architect involved in the revival of 19th-century English domestic architecture

White Stanford (1853–1906) US architect who co-founded the firm of McKim, Mead, and White; his designs include the original Madison Square Garden and the Washington Square Arch, both in New York, New York

Wilkins William (1778–1839) English architect who pioneered the Greek Revival in England with his design for Downing College, Cambridge, UK; other work includes the National Gallery, London, UK

Wren Christopher (1632–1723) English architect with a refined and sober Baroque style, whose work includes St Paul's Cathedral, London, UK

Wright Frank Lloyd (1869–1959) US architect known for 'organic architecture', in which buildings reflect their natural surroundings, as in his prairie-house style; he designed the Guggenheim Museum in New York, New York

Yamasaki Minoru (1912–1986) US architect who designed the World Trade Center, New York, New York

Music

Noteworthy Composers of Classical Music

Albinoni Tomasso (1671–1751) Italian composer whose numerous operas and sonatas helped establish the Baroque style

Babbitt Milton (1916–) US composer and theorist who pioneered the application of information theory to music

Bach Johann Sebastian (1685–1750) German musician and one of the world's great composers whose music epitomizes the Baroque polyphonic style

Barber Samuel (1910–1981) US Neo-Classical composer whose compositions include *Adagio for Strings* and the opera *Vanessa*

Bartók Béla (1881–1945) Hungarian composer whose works combine folk elements with mathematical concepts of tonal and rhythmic proportion

Beethoven Ludwig van (1770–1827) German composer and pianist who was the dominant influence on 19th-century music, and whose *Ode to Joy* from the 9th Symphony is the anthem of the European Union

Berg Alban (1885–1935) Austrian composer who developed a personal 12-tone idiom of great emotional and stylistic versatility and wrote the operas *Wozzeck* and *Lulu*

Berio Luciano (1925–) Italian composer whose work combines serial techniques with commedia dell'arte and antiphonal practices

Berlioz (Louis) Hector (1803–1869) French Romantic composer known as the founder of modern orchestration

Bizet Georges (Alexandre César Léopold) (1838–1875) French composer of operas whose operatic masterpiece is *Carmen*

Borodin Aleksander Porfir'yevich (1833–1887) Russian composer of symphonies, songs, and chamber music whose principal work is the opera *Prince Igor*

Boulez Pierre (1925–) French composer who is the founder and director of IRCAM, a music research studio in Paris

Brahms Johannes (1833–1897) German composer who is considered one of the greatest composers of symphonic music and songs

Britten (Edward) Benjamin (1913–1976) English composer whose works include *Young Person's Guide to the Orchestra* and the oratorio *War Requiem*

Bruckner (Josef) Anton (1824–1896) Austrian Romantic composer whose works include numerous choral pieces and 11 symphonies

Busoni Ferruccio Dante Benvenuto (1866–1924) Italian composer and pianist who wrote for the piano and composed several operas, including *Doktor Faust*

Buxtehude Diderik (1637–1707) Danish composer of organ works, cantatas, and trio sonatas for two violins, viola da gamba, and harpsichord

Byrd William (1543–1623) English composer whose sacred and secular choral music exemplifies the English polyphonic style

Cage John (1912–1992) US composer who experimented with randomness and inexactitude to produce ultra-modern sounds

Chopin Frédéric François (1810–1849) Polish composer and pianist who revolutionized the technique of pianoforte playing

Copland Aaron (1900–1990) US composer whose works include the ballets *Billy the Kid* and *Appalachian Spring*

Corelli Arcangelo (1653–1713) Italian composer and one of the first virtuoso exponents of the Baroque violin, whose works include a set of *concerti grossi*

Couperin François le Grand (1668–1733) French composer of numerous chamber concertos and harpsichord suites

Debussy (Achille-)Claude (1862–1918) French composer, traditionally regarded as one of the musical Impressionists, who introduced qualities of melody and harmony based on the whole-tone scale

Delibes (Clement Philibert) Leo (1836–1891) French composer whose works include the ballet *Coppélia* and the opera *Lakmé* songs

Donizetti (Domenico) Gaetano (Maria) (1797–

Noteworthy Composers of Classical Music (continued)

1848) Italian composer who created more than 60 operas, including *Lucrezia Borgia*

Dowland John (*c.* 1563–*c.* 1626) English composer of lute songs who introduced refinements of harmony and ornamentation to English Renaissance style

Dufay Guillaume (*c.* 1400–1474) Flemish composer whose masses and motets were very influential in the Renaissance

Dukas Paul Abraham (1865–1935) French composer whose works include the animated orchestral scherzo *L'Apprenti sorcier/ The Sorcerer's Apprentice*

Dunstable John (*c.* 1385–1453) English composer who was an early exponent of counterpoint

Dvořák Antonin Leopold (1841–1904) Czech composer whose works include the *New World Symphony*

Elgar Edward (William) (1857–1934) English composer who wrote *The Dream of Gerontius* and *Pomp and Circumstance* marches

Falla Manuel de (Manuel Maria de Falla y Matheu) (1876–1946) Spanish composer whose works include *Noches en los jardines de España/Nights in the Gardens of Spain* and *El sombrero de tres picos/The Three-Cornered Hat*

Fauré Gabriel (Urbain) (1845–1924) French composer who wrote songs, chamber music, and a choral *Requiem*

Gershwin George (born Jacob) (1898–1937) US composer whose works include *Rhapsody in Blue* and the opera *Porgy and Bess*

Gluck Christoph Willibald von (1714–1787) German composer who revolutionized opera by giving free scope to dramatic effect, most notably in *Orfeo*

Gounod Charles François (1818–1893) French composer and organist whose operas and songs combine graceful melody and elegant harmonization

Grieg Edvard (Hagerup) (1843–1907) Norwegian national composer whose works include *Piano Concerto in A Minor* and *Peer Gynt*

Handel Georg Friedrich (originally Händel) (1685–1759) German-born British composer whose prolific operas and oratorios include the *Messiah*

Haydn (Franz) Joseph (1732–1809) Austrian composer who was a major exponent of the classical symphony, and who influenced Mozart and Beethoven

Hindemith Paul (1895–1963) German composer of the operas *Cardillac* and *Mathis der Maler/ Matthias the Painter*

Holst Gustav(us) Theodore von (1874–1934) English composer of operas, ballets, choral works, orchestral suites, and songs; his work includes *The Planets*

Honegger Arthur (1892–1955) Swiss composer who was one of the group of composers known as 'Les Six'

Ives Charles Edward (1874–1954) US composer who experimented with atonality, quarter tones, clashing time signatures, and quotations from popular music

Janáček Leoš (1854–1928) Czech national composer whose work was influenced by Moravian folk music

Janequin Clément (*c.* 1472–*c.* 1560) French composer of chansons and psalms

Josquin Desprez (or des Prés) (1440–1521) Franco-Flemish composer whose polyphonic masses and motets mark a peak in Renaissance vocal music

Khachaturian Aram Ilich (1903–1978) Armenian composer who used folk themes in works such as Gayane

Kodály Zoltán (1882–1967) Hungarian composer whose works include the cantata *Psalmus Hungaricus* and a comic opera *Háry János*

Leoncavallo Ruggiero (1858–1919) Italian operatic composer whose works include *I Pagliacci/The Strolling Players*

Ligeti György Sándor (1923–) Hungarian-born Austrian composer who has developed a highly chromatic polyphonic style in his works

Noteworthy Composers of Classical Music (continued)

Liszt Franz (1811–1886) Hungarian keyboard virtuoso and composer who developed the symphonic poem

Lully Jean-Baptiste (adopted name of Giovanni Battista Lulli) (1632–1687) Italian-born French composer who established French opera with such works as *Alceste*

Lutosławski Witold (1913–1994) Polish composer whose works are technically refined, yet remain expressive and lyrical

Mahler Gustav (1860–1911) Austrian composer and conductor whose melancholic style reaches full expression in the *5th Symphony*

Massenet Jules Emile Frédéric (1842–1912) French composer of operas, oratorios, and orchestral suites

Mendelssohn(-Bartholdy) (Jakob Ludwig) Felix (1809–1847) German composer whose works include the *Fingals Höhle/Fingal's Cave* overture and *A Midsummer Night's Dream,* from which comes the famous *Wedding March*

Messiaen Olivier Eugène Prosper Charles (1908–1992) French composer whose works include *Quatuor pour la fin du temps/Quartet for the End of Time*

Morley Thomas (*c.* 1557–1602) English composer who wrote consort music, madrigals, and airs

Mozart (Johann Chrysostom) Wolfgang Amadeus (1756–1791) Austrian composer, child prodigy, and musical genius, whose vast output included over 40 symphonies and operas, including *The Magic Flute*

Mussorgsky Modest Petrovich (1839–1881) Russian national composer whose operatic masterpiece is *Boris Godunov*

Nono Luigi (1924–1990) Italian composer whose works include *Suspended Song* and *Intolerance*

Orff Carl (1895–1982) German composer whose music is characterized by sharp dissonances and percussion

Palestrina Giovanni Pierluigi da (*c.* 1525–1594) Italian composer and papal choirmaster whose many liturgical choral works had a great influence on later composers

Pärt Arvo (1935–   ) Estonian composer resident in Germany whose music fuses traditional and modern styles to express contemporary spirituality

Penderecki Krzysztof (1933–   ) Polish composer whose works include *Magnificat* and *Die schwarze Maske/The Black Mask*

Poulenc Francis Jean Marcel (1899–1963) French composer and pianist whose works include the ballet *The Little Darlings*

Prokofiev Sergei Sergeievich (1891–1953) Russian composer whose works include *Romeo and Juliet* and *Peter and the Wolf*

Puccini Giacomo (Antonio Domenico Michele Secondo Maria) (1858–1924) Italian composer whose popular operas include *La bohème, Tosca,* and *Madam Butterfly*

Purcell Henry (*c.* 1659–1695) English court musician and organist at the Chapel Royal, London, whose works include the opera *Dido and Aeneas* and *The Fairy Queen*

Rachmaninov Sergei Vasilevich (1873–1943) Russian Romantic composer, conductor, and pianist whose works include three symphonies and four piano concertos

Rameau Jean-Philippe (1683–1764) French organist and composer whose *Traité de l'harmonie/Treatise on Harmony* established academic rules for harmonic progression

Ravel (Joseph) Maurice (1875–1937) French composer and pianist whose work is characterized by sensuousness, exotic harmonics, and dazzling orchestral effects, as in *Boléro*

Rimsky-Korsakov Nikolai Andreievich (1844–1908) Russian national composer whose operas include *Pskovitianka/The Maid of Pskov* and *Snegurochka/The Snow Maiden*

Rossini Gioacchino Antonio (1792–1868) Italian composer and 19th century master of the comic opera, particularly noted for long and exciting overtures

Saint-Saëns (Charles) Camille (1835–1921) French composer, pianist, and organist whose works include the orchestral *Le carnaval des animaux/Carnival of the Animals*

Noteworthy Composers of Classical Music (continued)

Satie Erik (Alfred Leslie) (1866–1925) French composer whose piano works include *Gymnopedies* and *Messe des pauvres/Poor People's Mass*

Scarlatti (Pietro) Alessandro (Gaspare) (1660–1725) Italian Baroque composer who wrote more than 100 operas that contributed to the development of the operatic genre, as well as hundreds of liturgical choral works

Schoenberg Arnold Franz Walter (1874–1951) Austro-Hungarian-born US composer who developed the 12-tone system of musical composition

Schubert Franz Peter (1797–1828) Austrian composer who combined Romantic expression of emotion with pure melody and is best known for his Lieder

Schumann Robert Alexander (1810–1856) German composer whose works include four symphonies, a violin concerto, and a piano concerto

Shostakovich Dmitri Dmitrievich (1906–1975) Russian composer whose work includes 15 symphonies

Sibelius Jean Julius Christian (1865–1957) Finnish composer whose works include *En saga* and *Finlandia*

Skriabin (or **Scriabin**) Aleksander Nikolaievich (1872–1915) Russian composer and pianist whose works include *Prometheus* and *Bozhestvennaya poema/Divine Poem*

Stockhausen Karlheinz (1928–) German composer of avant-garde music whose major works include *Gesang de Jünglinge* and *Sirius*

Strauss Johann (Baptist) (1825–1899) Austrian conductor and composer of operettas and waltzes, including *An der schönen blauen Donau/The Blue Danube*

Strauss Richard (1864–1949) German Neo-Romantic composer best known for his symphonic poems, such as *Also sprach Zarathustra/Thus Spake Zarathustra,* and his opera *Der Rosenkavalier/The Knight of the Rose*

Stravinsky Igor (1882–1971) Russian-born French and US composer whose works include *The Firebird* and *The Rite of Spring*

Tallis Thomas (*c.* 1505–1585) English composer whose works include *Tallis's Canon* and the 40-part motet *Spem in alium*

Tavener John Kenneth (1944–) English composer whose works, show the influence of the Greek Orthodox Church

Tchaikovsky Piotr Ilich (1840–1893) Russian composer whose works include *The Nutcracker,* operas, and five symphonies

Telemann Georg Philipp (1681–1767) German Baroque composer whose prolific output includes both instrumental and vocal music

Tippett Michael Kemp (1905–1998) English composer whose works include three operas, four symphonies, and compositions of choral music

Vaughan Williams Ralph (1872–1958) English composer whose work includes nine symphonies and *Fantasia on a Theme of Tallis*

Verdi Giuseppe Fortunino Francesco (1813–1901) master of Italian opera whose works include *Otello* and *Falstaff*

Vivaldi Antonio Lucio (1678–1741) Italian Baroque composer whose prolific number of symphonies, sonatas, concertos, operas, and sacred music includes *The Four Seasons*

Wagner (Wilhelm) Richard (1813–1883) German composer of *The Ring Cycle* opera and founder of the Bayreuth Theatre

Walton William Turner (1902–1983) English composer whose works include *Façade* and *Belshazzar's Feast*

Weber Carl Maria Friedrich Ernst von (1786–1826) German composer who established the Romantic school of opera with *Der Freischütz/The Freeshooter* and other works

Webern Anton (Friedrich Wilhelm von) (1883–1945) Austrian composer whose constructivist aesthetic influenced the post-war generation of advanced composers

Wolf Hugo (Filipp Jakob) (1860–1903) Austrian composer of late-Romantic Lieder whose works include *Mörike-Lieder/Mörike Songs* and *Italienisches Liederbuch/Italian Songbook*

Some Musical Expressions

Expression	Meaning	Expression	Meaning
accelerando	gradually faster	poco, pochissimo	a little, very little
adagio, adagietto	easy-going	portamento	lifting (note to note)
agitato	agitated	presto, prestissimo	at speed, at high speed
alla breve	four beat as two to the bar	quasi	sort of, rather
allargando	spreading out in tempo	ripieno	the accompanying ensemble
allegro, allegretto	with lightness of action	ritardando	gradually coming to a stop
andante, andantino	with movement	ritenuto	pulling back
calando	winding down, slower and softer	ritornello	refrain
cantabile	singing	rubato	borrowed (time)
con brio	with spirit	secco	with a dry tone
con fuoco	with fire	segno	cue sign
concerto	the solo (group)	segue	follow on
crescendo	gradually louder	sempre	always
da capo	from the top (beginning)	sforzato, sforzando	with a forced tone
deciso	firmly	smorzando	smothering, stifling the tone
diminuendo	gradually softer	sotto voce	in an undertone
divisi a 2, 3, etc	divided in 2, 3, etc., parts	spiccato	bounced (of the bow off the string)
dolce, dolcissimo	soft and sweetly	staccato,	short, very short
doloroso	mournfully	staccatissimo	
espressivo	with expression	subito	sudden, suddenly
flatterzunge	(German) fluttertongue	Takt	(German) beat, metre, bar
forte	loud		measure
fortissimo	very loud	tanto	so much
giocoso	with fun	tema	theme
grave	with gravity	tenuto	holding back
largo, larghetto	expansively	tessitura	range of instrument or voice
legato	smoothly	tranquillo	calmly
lento	slowly	troppo	too much
listesso (tempo)	the same (tempo)	via	remove (eg mute)
loco	in (its usual) place	veloce	at speed
lungo, lunga	long	vivo, vivace	with life
mezzo	quite	voce, voci	voice, voices
misterioso	mysteriously	volante	as though flying
molto	much, very	wieder	(German) again
pesante	weightily	Zeitmass	(German) tempo
pianissimo	very soft	zingaresca	gypsy
piano	soft	zu 2	(German) for 2 players; in 2 parts

alto (Italian 'high') voice or musical instrument between tenor and soprano, of approximate range G3–D5. As a prefix to the name of an instrument, for example alto saxophone, it denotes a size larger than soprano.

aria (Italian 'air') melodic solo song of reflective character, often with a contrasting middle section, expressing a moment of truth in the action of an opera or oratorio. Already to be found in Peri's *Euridice* (1600) and Monteverdi's *Orfeo* (1607), it reached its more elaborate form in the work of Alessandro Scarlatti and Handel, becoming a set piece for virtuoso opera singers. An example is Handel's 'Where'er you walk' from the secular oratorio *Semele* (1744) to words by William Congreve. As an instrumental character piece, an aria is melodious and imitative of a vocal line.

atonality music in which the sense of tonality is distorted or obscured; music of no apparent key. It is used by film and television composers for situations of mystery or horror, exploiting dissonance for its power to disturb.

baritone male voice pitched between bass and tenor, of approximate range G2–F4. As a prefix to the name of an instrument, for example baritone saxophone, it indicates that the instrument sounds in approximately the same range.

bass the lowest male voice, of approximate range C2–D4. As the prefix to the name of an instrument, it indicates that the instrument sounds in approximately the same range.

bel canto (Italian 'beautiful song') in music, an 18th-century Italian style of singing with emphasis on perfect technique and beautiful tone. The style reached its peak in the operas of Rossini, Donizetti, and Bellini.

cadenza unaccompanied exhibition passage in the style of an improvisation, inserted by the soloist at the climax of a concerto movement.

cantata an extended work for voices, from the Italian, meaning 'sung', as opposed to sonata ('sounded') for instruments. A cantata can be sacred or secular, sometimes uses solo voices, and usually has orchestral accompaniment. The first printed collection of sacred cantata texts dates from 1670.

chamber music music intended for performance in a small room or chamber, rather than in the concert hall, and usually written for instrumental combinations, played with one instrument to a part, as in the string quartet.

chromatic scale musical scale proceeding by semitones. In theory the inclusion of all 12 notes makes it a neutral scale without the focus provided by the seven-tone diatonic major or minor scale; in practice however, owing to small deviations from equal temperament, it is possible for a trained ear to identify the starting point of a randomly chosen chromatic scale.

chromatic An ascending and descending chromatic scale beginning on C.

clef a symbol prefixed to a five-line stave indicating the pitch range to which the written notes apply. Introduced as a visual aid in plainchant notation, it is based on the letter G (treble clef), establishing middle C (C4) as a prime reference

pitch, G4 a fifth higher for higher voices, and F3 a fifth lower for lower voices.

coloratura a rapid ornamental vocal passage with runs and trills. A **coloratura soprano** is a light, high voice suited to such music.

concerto composition, usually in three movements, for solo instrument (or instruments) and orchestra. It developed during the 18th century from the **concerto grosso** form for string orchestra, in which a group of solo instruments (concerto) is contrasted with a full orchestra (ripieno).

contralto low-register female voice, a high male voice, or a low boy's voice;

counterpoint art of combining different forms of an original melody with apparent freedom while preserving a harmonious effect. Giovanni Palestrina and Johann Sebastian Bach were masters of counterpoint.

diatonic scale scale consisting of the seven notes of any major or minor key.

fugue (Latin 'flight') a contrapuntal form with two or more subjects (principal melodies) for a number of parts, which enter in succession in direct imitation of each other or transposed to a higher or lower key, and may be combined in augmented form (larger note values). It represents the highest form of contrapuntal ingenuity in works such as Johann Sebastian Bach's *Das musikalische Opfer/The Musical Offering* (1747), on a theme of Frederick II of Prussia, and *Die Kunst der Fuge/The Art of the Fugue* (1751), and Beethoven's *Grosse Fuge/Great Fugue* for string quartet (1825–26).

harmonics series of partial vibrations that combine to form a musical tone. The number and relative prominence of harmonics produced determines an instrument's tone colour (timbre). An oboe is rich in harmonics, the flute has few. Harmonics conform to successive divisions of the sounding air column or string: their pitches are harmonious.

key diatonic scale around which a piece of music is written. For example, a passage in the key of C major uses mainly the notes of the C major scale, and harmonies made up of the notes of that scale. The first note of the scale is known as the tonic; it gives the name of the key and is the note on which the music usually starts and finishes.

libretto (Italian 'little book') text of an opera or other dramatic vocal work, or the scenario of a ballet.

Lied (German 'song', plural Lieder) musical dramatization of a poem, usually for solo voice and piano; referring to Romantic songs of Schubert, Schumann, Brahms, and Hugo Wolf.

madrigal form of secular song in four or five parts, usually sung without instrumental accompaniment. It originated in 14th-century Italy. Madrigal composers include Andrea Gabrieli, Carlo Monteverdi, Thomas Morley, and Orlando Gibbons.

melody (Greek *melos* 'song') recognizable series of notes played or sung one after the other, a tune. Melody is one of the three main elements of music, the others being rhythm and harmony. In western music a melody is usually formed from the notes of a scale or mode. A melody, with or without accompaniment, may be a complete piece on its own – such as a simple song. In classical music it is more often used as a theme within a longer piece of music.

metre the timescale represented by the beat. Metre is regular, whereas rhythm is irregular.

mezzo-soprano female singing voice with an approximate range A4–F5, between contralto and soprano.

middle C white note, C4, at the centre of the piano keyboard, indicating the division between left- and right-hand regions and between the treble and bass staves of printed music. Middle C is also the pitch indicated by a C clef, for example, for viola.

minuet French country dance in three time adapted as a European courtly dance of the 17th century. The music was later used as the third movement of a classical four-movement symphony where its gentle rhythm provides a foil to the slow second movement and fast final movement.

modulation movement from one key to another. In classical dance music, modulation is a guide to phrasing rhythm to the step pattern.

movement self-contained composition of specific character, usually a constituent piece of a suite, symphony, or similar work, with its own tempo, distinct from that of the other movements.

nocturne a reflective character piece, often for piano, introduced by John Field (1782–1837) and developed by Chopin.

octave span of eight notes as measured on the white notes of a piano keyboard. It corresponds to the consonance of first and second harmonics.

opera dramatic musical work in which singing takes the place of speech. In opera the music accompanying the action has paramount importance, although dancing and spectacular staging may also play their parts. Opera originated in late 16th-century Florence when the musical declamation, lyrical monologues, and choruses of Classical Greek drama were reproduced in current forms.

Major Operas and their First Performances

Date	Opera	Composer	Librettist	Location[1]
1607	Orfeo	Monteverdi	Striggio	Mantua, Italy
1642	The Coronation of Poppea	Monteverdi	Busenello	Venice, Italy
1689	Dido and Aeneas	Purcell	Tate	London, UK
1724	Julius Caesar in Egypt	Handel	Haym	London, UK
1762	Orpheus and Eurydice	Gluck	Calzabigi	Vienna, Austria
1786	The Marriage of Figaro	Mozart	Da Ponte	Vienna, Austria
1787	Don Giovanni	Mozart	Da Ponte	Prague, Czech Republic
1790	Così fan tutte	Mozart	Da Ponte	Vienna, Austria
1791	The Magic Flute	Mozart	Schikaneder	Vienna, Austria
1805	Fidelio	Beethoven	Sonnleithner	Vienna, Austria
1816	The Barber of Seville	Rossini	Sterbini	Rome, Italy
1821	Der Freischütz	Weber	Kind	Berlin, Germany

Major Operas and their First Performances (continued)

Date	Opera	Composer	Librettist	Location[1]
1831	*Norma*	Bellini	Romani	Milan, Italy
1835	*Lucia di Lammermoor*	Donizetti	Cammarano	Naples, Italy
1836	*Les Huguenots*	Meyerbeer	Scribe	Paris, France
1842	*Ruslan and Lyudmila*	Glinka	Shirkov/Bakhturin	St Petersburg, Russia
1850	*Lohengrin*	Wagner	Wagner	Weimar, Germany
1851	*Rigoletto*	Verdi	Piave	Venice, Italy
1853	*Il Trovatore*	Verdi	Cammarano	Rome, Italy
	La Traviata	Verdi	Piave	Venice, Italy
1859	*Faust*	Gounod	Barbier/Carré	Paris, France
1865	*Tristan und Isolde*	Wagner	Wagner	Munich, Germany
1866	*The Bartered Bride*	Smetana	Sabina	Prague, Czech Republic
1868	*Die Meistersinger von Nürnberg*	Wagner	Wagner	Munich, Germany
1871	*Aida*	Verdi	Ghislanzoni	Cairo, Egypt
1874	*Boris Godunov*	Mussorgsky	Mussorgsky	St Petersburg, Russia
	Die Fledermaus	Johann Strauss II	Haffner/Genée	Vienna, Austria
1875	*Carmen*	Bizet	Meilhac/Halévy	Paris, France
1876	*The Ring of the Nibelung*	Wagner	Wagner	Bayreuth, Germany
1879	*Eugene Onegin*	Tchaikovsky	Tchaikovsky/Shilovsky	Moscow, Russia
1881	*The Tales of Hoffmann*	Offenbach	Barbier	Paris, France
1882	*Parsifal*	Wagner	Wagner	Bayreuth, Germany
1885	*The Mikado*	Sullivan	Gilbert	London, UK
1887	*Otello*	Verdi	Boito	Milan, Italy
1890	*Cavalleria Rusticana*	Mascagni	Menasci/Targioni-Tozzetti	Rome, Italy
	Prince Igor	Borodin	Borodin	St Petersburg, Russia
1892	*I Pagliacci*	Leoncavallo	Leoncavallo	Milan, Italy
	Werther	Massenet	Blau/Milliet/Hartman	Vienna, Austria
1896	*La Bohème*	Puccini	Giacosa/Illica	Turin, Italy
1900	*Tosca*	Puccini	Giacosa/Illica	Rome, Italy
1902	*Pelléas et Mélisande*	Debussy	Maeterlinck	Paris, France
1904	*Jenůfa*	Janáček	Janáček	Brno, Czech Republic
	Madame Butterfly	Puccini	Giacosa/Illica	Milan, Italy
1905	*Salome*	Richard Strauss	Wilde/Lachmann	Dresden, Germany
1909	*The Golden Cockerel*	Rimsky-Korsakov	Bel'sky	Moscow, Russia
1911	*Der Rosenkavalier*	Richard Strauss	Hofmannsthal	Dresden, Germany
1918	*Duke Bluebeard's Castle*	Bartók	Balázs	Budapest, Hungary
1925	*Wozzeck*	Berg	Berg	Berlin, Germany
1935	*Porgy and Bess*	Gershwin	Ira Gershwin/Heyward	Boston, USA
1937	*Lulu*	Berg	Berg	Zürich, Switzerland
1945	*Peter Grimes*	Britten	Slater	London, UK
1946	*War and Peace*	Prokofiev	Prokofiev/Mendelson	St Petersburg, Russia
1951	*The Rake's Progress*	Stravinsky	Auden/Kallman	Venice, Italy
1978	*Paradise Lost*	Penderecki	Fry	Chicago, USA
1984	*Akhnaten*	Glass	Glass	Stuttgart, Germany
1986	*The Mask of Orpheus*	Birtwistle	Zinovieff	London, UK
1989	*New Year*	Tippett	Tippett	Houston, USA
1992	*Dienstag aus Licht*	Stockhausen	Stockhausen	Lisbon, Portugal

[1] Present-day city and country names are given.

operetta light form of opera, with music, dance, and spoken dialogue. The story line is romantic and sentimental, often employing farce and parody. Its origins lie in the 19th-century *opéra comique* and is intended to amuse. Examples of operetta are Jacques Offenbach's *Orphée aux enfers/Orpheus in the Underworld* (1858), Johann Strauss' *Die Fledermaus/The Flittermouse* (1874), and Gilbert and Sullivan's *The Pirates of Penzance* (1879) and *The Mikado* (1885).

opus (Latin 'work') term, used with a figure, to indicate the numbering of a composer's works, usually in chronological order.

oratorio dramatic, nonscenic musical setting of mostly religious texts, scored for orchestra, chorus, and solo voices. Its origins lie in the *laude spirituali* performed by St Philip Neri's Oratory in Rome in the 16th century, followed by the first definitive oratorio in the 17th century by Cavalieri. The form reached perfection in such works as J S Bach's *Christmas Oratorio,* and Handel's *Messiah.*

overture opening piece of a concert or opera, having the dual function of settling the audience and allowing the conductor and musicians to become acquainted with the acoustic of a concert auditorium. See also **prelude.**

pitch indicates how high or low a note is. This depends on the frequency of vibration of the sound and is measured in Hertz (Hz), or cycles per second. It also means the standard to which instruments are tuned, nowadays using the A above middle C (A4 or a') with a frequency of 440Hz as a reference tone. This is often known as **concert pitch.**

Pitch can now be measured accurately by electronic tuning devices, which are beginning to replace the traditional tuning fork, but it is still normal practice for orchestras to tune to an oboe playing a', despite the inherent inaccuracy of this practice.

prelude composition intended as the preface to further music, especially preceding a fugue, forming the opening piece of a suite, or setting the mood for a stage work, as in Wagner's *Lohengrin.* As used by Chopin, a prelude is a short self-contained piano work.

programme music instrumental music that interprets a story, depicts a scene or painting, or illustrates a literary or philosophical idea. The term

---

Drugs and decapitation

■ The French composer Hector Berlioz wrote a *Fantastic Symphony (1830)*, depicting the opium-crazed nightmare of a young artist rejected in love. The orchestra imitates gibbering witches, the fall of the guillotine, and the thud of a severed head. Many other composers have written **programme music** illustrating events in a story.

---

was first used by Franz Liszt in the 19th century, when programme music was especially popular with composers of Romantic music but there had been a great deal of descriptive music before then. Examples include Antonio Vivaldi's *Four Seasons* concertos, Ludwig van Beethoven's *Eroica* and *Pastoral* symphonies, Felix Mendelssohn's *Hebrides Overture* ('Fingal's Cave'), and the symphonic poems of Liszt and Richard Strauss.

recitative in opera and oratorio, sung narration partly modelled on the rhythms and inflections of natural speech. It is usually sparingly accompanied by harpsichord or organ.

requiem in the Roman Catholic Church, a Mass for the dead. Musical settings include those by Palestrina, Mozart, Berlioz, Verdi, Fauré, and Britten.

rhapsody instrumental fantasia, often based on folk melodies, such as Franz Liszt's *Hungarian Rhapsodies* (1853–54).

rondo *or* **rondeau,** antique musical form in which verses alternate with a refrain. Often festive in character, it is a popular final movement of a sonata, concerto, or symphony.

scale sequence of pitches that establishes a key, and in some respects the character of a composition. A scale is defined by its starting note and may be **major** or **minor** depending on the order of intervals. A **chromatic scale** is the full range of 12 notes: it has no key because there is no fixed starting point.

scherzo (Italian 'joke') lively piece, usually in rapid triple (3/4) time; often used for the third movement of a symphony, sonata, or quartet as a substitute for the statelier minuet and trio.

serenade musical piece in several movements for chamber orchestra or wind instruments, originally intended for informal evening enter-tainment, such as Mozart's *Eine kleine Nachtmusik/A Little Night Music. (1787)*

sonata (Italian 'sounded') instrumental composi-tion for a solo player or a small ensemble and consisting of a single movement or series of movements. The name signifies that the work is not beholden to a text or existing dance form, but is self-sufficient.

soprano highest range of the female voice, stretch-ing from around D4 to A6. Some operatic roles require the extended upper range of a coloratura soprano, reaching to around F6. Some instru-ments use the prefix soprano for models that sound in the compass of the soprano voice.

soprano The soprano range has approximately the compass shown, but is often extended further in florid operatic arias requiring dexterity.

suite in Baroque music, a set of contrasting instru-mental pieces based on dance forms, known by their French names as allemande, bourrée, courante, gavotte, gigue, minuet, musette, passepied, rigaudon, sarabande, and others. The term refers in more recent usage to a concert arrangement of set pieces from an extended

ballet or stage composition, such as Tchaikovsky's *Nutcracker Suite* (1891–92). Stravinsky's suite from *The Soldier's Tale* (1920) incorporates a tango, waltz, and ragtime.

symphony abstract musical composition for orchestra, traditionally in four separate but closely related movements. It developed from the smaller sonata form, the Italian overture, and the concerto grosso.

tempo (Italian 'time') in music, the speed at which a piece should be played. One way of indicating the tempo of a piece of music is to give a metronome marking, which states the number of beats per minute; for example, 'crotchet = 60' means that there should be 60 crotchet beats to the minute. Modern electronic metronomes

measure tempo very accurately, but performers often change or even ignore metronome mark-ings, playing at a tempo that suits their interpre-tation of the music.

tenor highest range of adult male singing voice when not using falsetto, approximately C3–A5. It is the preferred voice for operatic heroic roles. Exponents are Luciano Pavarotti and Placido Domingo.

timbre (French 'tone') tone colour, or quality of tone, of a particular sound. Different instru-ments playing a note at the same pitch have dif-ferent sound qualities, and it is the timbre that enables the listener to distinguish the sound of, for example, a trumpet from that of a violin. The tone quality of a sound depends on several things, including its waveform, the strength of its harmonics, and its attack and decay – the 'shape' of the sound. The study of the elements of sound quality is part of the science of acoustics.

tonality sense of key orientation in relation to form, for example the step pattern of a dance as expressed by corresponding changes of direction from a tonic or 'home' key to a related key. Most popular and folk music worldwide recognizes an underlying tonality or reference pitch against which the movement of a melody can be clearly heard. The opposite of tonality is **atonality**

variation form based on constant repetition of a simple theme, each new version being elaborated or treated in a different manner. The theme is eas-ily recognizable; it may be a popular tune or the work of a fellow composer; for example, Chopin's variations *La ci darem la mano*, based on an *aria* from Mozart's *Don Giovanni* The principle of variations has been adopted in larger-scale and orchestral works by modern composers, for exam-ple Elgar's *Enigma Variations* (1899).

waltz ballroom dance in moderate triple time (3/4) that developed in Germany and Austria during the late 18th century from the Austrian *Ländler* (traditional peasants' country dance). Associated particularly with Vienna and the Strauss family, the waltz has remained popular up to the present day and has inspired composers including Chopin, Brahms, and Ravel.

Grammy Awards

US annual music awards which are for outstanding achievement in the record industry for the previous year. The gold-plated disks are presented by the National Academy of Recording Arts and Sciences. The first Grammy Awards were for records released in 1958.

Best Record and Best Album

1980–98

Year	Best Record	Best Album
1980	Christopher Cross 'Sailing'	Christopher Cross *Christopher Cross*
1981	Kim Carnes 'Bette Davis Eyes'	John Lennon, Yoko Ono *Double Fantasy*
1982	Toto 'Rosanna'	Toto *Toto IV*
1983	Michael Jackson 'Beat It'	Michael Jackson *Thriller*
1984	Tina Turner 'What's Love Got to Do With It'	Lionel Richie *Can't Slow Down*
1985	USA for Africa 'We Are the World'	Phil Collins *No Jacket Required*
1986	Steve Winwood 'Higher Love'	Paul Simon *Graceland*
1987	Paul Simon 'Graceland'	U2 *The Joshua Tree*
1988	Bobby McFerrin 'Don't Worry, Be Happy'	George Michael *Faith*
1989	Bette Midler 'Wind Beneath My Wings'	Bonnie Raitt *Nick of Time*
1990	Phil Collins 'Another Day in Paradise'	Quincy Jones *Back on the Block*
1991	Natalie Cole, with Nat 'King' Cole 'Unforgettable'	Natalie Cole, with Nat 'King' Cole *Unforgettable*
1992	Eric Clapton 'Tears in Heaven'	Eric Clapton *Unplugged*
1993	Whitney Houston 'I Will Always Love You'	Whitney Houston *The Bodyguard*
1994	Sheryl Crow 'All I Wanna Do'	Tony Bennett *MTV Unplugged*
1995	Seal 'Kiss from a Rose'	Alanis Morissette *Jagged Little Pill*
1996	Eric Clapton 'Change the World'	Celine Dion *Falling into You*
1997	Shawn Colvin 'Sunny Came Home'	Bob Dylan *Time Out of Mind*
1998	Céline Dion 'My Heart Will Go On'	Lauryn Hill *The Miseducation of Lauryn Hill*

Brit Awards

These are among the UK's most prestigious and popular music awards. They are run by the British Phonographic Industry; other committee members come from major and independent record companies, publishing and retail sectors, the publicity industry, the media, retailers, promoters, the black music industry, and the Music Publishers' Association.

1993–98

Year	Best Group	Best Newcomer	Best Album	Best Single
1993	Simply Red	Tasmin Archer	Annie Lennox *Diva*	Take That 'Could it be Magic'
1994	Stereo MCs	Gabrielle	Stereo MCs *Connected*	Take That 'Pray'
1995	Blur	Oasis	Blur *Parklife*	Blur 'Parklife'
1996	Oasis	Supergrass	Oasis *(What's the Story) Morning Glory?*	Take That 'Back for Good'
1997	Manic Street Preachers	Kula Shaker	Manic Street Preachers *Everything Must Go*	Spice Girls 'Wannabe'
1998	The Verve	Stereophonics	The Verve *Urban Hymn*	All Saints 'Never Ever'

PAINTING AND SCULPTURE

Top Ten Highest Prices Paid for Sculptures Sold at Auction

Source: Art Sales Index

Rank	Work	Artist	Place and date of sale	Price ($)
1	Petite Danseuse de Quatorze Ans	Edgar Degas	Sotheby's, New York, 12 November 1996	10,800,000
2	The Dancing Faun	Adriaen de Vries	Sotheby's, London, 7 December 1989	9,796,000
3	Petite Danseuse de Quatorze Ans (resold later, see above)	Edgar Degas	Christie's, New York, 14 November 1988	9,250,000
4	Petite Danseuse de Quatorze Ans (resold later, see above)	Edgar Degas	Sotheby's, New York, 10 May 1988	9,200,000
5	La Negresse Blonde	Constantin Brancusi	Sotheby's, New York, 16 May 1990	8,000,000
6	La Muse Endormie III	Constantin Brancusi	Christie's, New York, 14 November 1989	7,500,000
7	Mlle Pogany II	Constantin Brancusi	Christie's, New York, 14 May 1997	6,400,000
8	L'Homme Qui Marche I	Alberto Giacometti	Christie's, London, 28 November 1988	6,358,000
9	La Muse Endormie II	Constantin Brancusi	Christie's, New York, 11 November 1997	6,000,000
10	Grande Femme Debout I	Alberto Giacometti	Christie's, New York, 14 November 1989	4,500,000

Top Ten Highest Prices Paid for Paintings Sold at Auction

Source: Art Sales Index

Rank	Work	Artist	Place and date of sale	Price ($)
1	Portrait of Dr Gachet	Vincent van Gogh	Christie's, New York, 15 May 1990	75,000,000
2	Au Moulin de la Galette	Pierre-Auguste Renoir	Sotheby's, New York, 17 May 1990	71,000,000
3	Les Noces de Pierette	Pablo Picasso	Binoche et Godeau, Paris, 30 November 1989	51,671,920
4	Irises	Vincent van Gogh	Sotheby's, New York, 11 November 1987	49,000,000
5	Le Rêve	Pablo Picasso	Christie's, New York, 10 November 1997	44,000,000
6	Self Portrait: Yo Picasso	Pablo Picasso	Sotheby's, New York, 9 May 1989	43,500,000
7	Au Lapin Agile	Pablo Picasso	Sotheby's, New York, 15 November 1989	37,000,000
8	Sunflowers	Vincent van Gogh	Christie's, London, 30 March 1987	36,225,000
9	Acrobate et Jeune Arlequin	Pablo Picasso	Christie's, London, 28 November 1988	35,000,000
10	Portrait of Duke Cosimo I de' Medici	Jacopo Carucci (also known as Pontormo)	Christie's, New York, 31 May 1989	32,000,000[1]

[1] This is the record price for an Old Master.

Top Five Highest Prices Paid for Paintings at Auction by Living Artists

Source: Art Sales Index

Rank	Work	Artist	Place and date of sale	Price ($)
1	False Start	Jasper Johns	Sotheby's, New York, 10 November 1988	15,500,000
2	Two Flags	Jasper Johns	Sotheby's, New York, 8 November 1989	11,000,000
3	Corpse and Mirror	Jasper Johns	Christie's, New York, 10 November 1997	7,600,000
4	White Numbers	Jasper Johns	Christie's, New York, 10 November 1997	7,200,000
5	Rebus	Robert Rauschenberg	Sotheby's, New York, 30 April 1991	6,600,000

Turner Prize

Established in 1984 to encourage discussion about new developments in contemporary British art, this prize has often attracted criticism for celebrating what is not traditionally considered to be art. It is open to any British artist under 50 and has a prize of £20,000.

Year	Winner	Year	Winner	Year	Winner
1984	Malcolm Morley	1989	Richard Long	1994	Antony Gormley
1985	Howard Hodgkin	1990	no award	1995	Damien Hirst
1986	Gilbert and George	1991	Anish Kapoor	1996	Douglas Gordon
1987	Richard Deacon	1992	Grenville Davey	1997	Gillian Wearing
1988	Tony Cragg	1993	Rachel Whiteread	1998	Chris Ofili

Noteworthy Artists

Angelico Fra (originally Guido di Pietro) (*c.* 1400–1455) Italian monk and painter of religious scenes who created the frescoes at the monastery of San Marco, Florence, Italy

Bacon Francis (1909–1992) Irish-born painter of distorted, blurred figures in loosely defined space, including *Study after Velázquez's Portrait of Pope Innocent X*

Balthus (adopted name of Balthazar Klossowski de Rola) (1908–) Polish-born French painter of self-absorbed figures, frequently languid, pubescent girls, clothed or nude, such as *Le nu avec un chat/Nude with Cat*

Bellini Jacopo (*c.* 1400–1470/71) and his sons, Gentile (*c.* 1429–1507) and Giovanni (*c.* 1430–1516) Venetian family of artists, and founders of the Venetian school

Blake William (1757–1827) English poet, artist, engraver, and visionary, and one of the most important figures of English Romanticism

Bosch Hieronymus (Jerome) (*c.* 1460–1516) Netherlandish painter of bizarre, cruel images of a sinful, tormented world, such as the triptych *The Garden of Earthly Delights*

Botticelli Sandro Filipepi (adopted name of Alessandro di Mariano Filipepi) (1445–1510) Florentine painter of religious and mythological subjects, such as *The Birth of Venus*

Braque Georges (1882–1963) French painter decisive in developing Cubism

Brueghel or **Bruegel** Pieter (*c.* 1525–1569) one of a family of Flemish painters who captured peasant life, as in *Hunters in the Snow*

Burne-Jones Edward Coley (1833–1898) English painter associated with the Pre-Raphaelite movement and symbolism

Canaletto Antonio (Giovanni Antonio Canal) (1697–1768) Italian painter of highly detailed views of Venice, London, and the River Thames, such as *Venice: Regatta on the Grand Canal*

Caravaggio Michelangelo Merisi da (1573–1610) Italian early Baroque painter known for dramatic contrasts of light and shade

Carracci Lodovico (1555–1619) and his two cousins, Agostino (1557–1602) and Annibale (1560–1609) three Italian painters who were leaders in developing early Baroque

Cézanne Paul (1839–1906) French Post-Impressionist painter whose paintings include *Cardplayers*

Chagall Marc (1887–1985) Belarusian-born French painter and designer inspired by village life and Jewish and Russian folk traditions, as in *I and the Village*

Cimabue Giovanni (Cenni di Peppi) (*c.* 1240–1302) Italian painter often considered the 'father of Italian painting' whose works include *Crucifix*

Constable John (1776–1837) English landscape artist whose paintings include *The Haywain*

Correggio (Antonio Allegri) (*c.* 1494–1534) Italian painter of the High Renaissance who placed emphasis on movement, soft forms, and contrasts of light and shade

Cranach the Elder Lucas (Lucas Müller) (1472–1553) German painter, etcher, and woodcut

Noteworthy Artists (continued)

artist of religious scenes, allegories, and precise portraits, such as *Martin Luther*

Dalí Salvador (Felippe Jacinto) (1904–1989) Spanish Surrealist painter and designer known for hallucinatory images and distorted figures, such as *The Persistence of Memory*

David Jacques-Louis (1748–1825) French Neo-Classical painter of politically significant works, such as *Death of Marat*

Degas (Hilaire Germain) Edgar (1834–1917) French Impressionist painter, and sculptor, who specialized in informal studies of ballet, horse racing, and young women working

De Kooning Willem (1904–1997) Dutch-born US Abstract Expressionist painter whose works include *Women*

Delacroix (Ferdinand Victor) Eugène (1798–1863) French Romantic painter of historical and literary subjects, such as *The Death of Sardanapalus*

Domenichino (Domenico Zampieri) (1581–1641) Italian Baroque painter and architect who was a pioneer of landscape painting

Dubuffet Jean (Philippe Arthur) (1901–1985) French artist and originator of Art Brut, 'raw' or 'brutal' art

Duchamp Marcel (1887–1968) French-born US artist and exponent of Dada whose paintings include *Nude Descending a Staircase No. 2*

Dürer Albrecht (1471–1528) German graphic artist and painter who perfected a technique of woodcut and engraving; his works include *Apocalypse*

Dyck Anthony van (1599–1641) Flemish painter of religious works and portraits, such as *Charles I on Horseback*

Ernst Max (1891–1976) German artist and major figure in Dada and Surrealism; his paintings include *The Elephant Celebes*

Eyck Jan van (c. 1390–1441) Netherlandish painter of meticulous religious scenes and portraits, such as *The Arnolfini Wedding*

Fragonard Jean-Honoré (1732–1806) French Rococo painter of light-hearted, often erotic works, such as *The Swing*

Freud Lucian (1922–) German-born British figurative artist who combined meticulous accuracy with disquieting intensity, as in *Portrait of Francis Bacon*

Gaddi Italian family of artists: Gaddo (c. 1260–1332) painter and mosaic worker, and his sons Taddeo (c. 1300–1366) painter of frescoes, and Agnola (active 1369–1396) painter of frescoes

Gainsborough Thomas (1727–1788) English landscape and society portrait painter whose paintings include *The Blue Boy*

Gauguin (Eugène Henri) Paul (1848–1903) French Post-Impressionist painter of sensuously coloured, heavily symbolic, and decorative style, such as *The Yellow Christ*

Géricault (Jean Louis André) Théodore (1791–1824) French Romantic painter and graphic artist of energy and emotional intensity, as seen in *The Raft of the Medusa*

Ghirlandaio Domenico (Domenico di Tommaso Bigordi) (c. 1449–1494) Italian fresco painter whose painting was characterized by contemporary domestic detail

Giorgione da Castelfranco (Giorgio Barbarelli) (c. 1475–1510) Italian Renaissance painter who created the Renaissance poetic landscape

Gogh Vincent Willem van (1853–1890) Dutch Post-Impressionist painter who used intense colour and expressive brushwork, as in his *Sunflowers* series

Gorky Arshile (Vosdanig Manoüg Adoian) (1904–1948) Armenian-born US painter who combined organic shapes and vigorous brushwork with a sense of fantasy, as in *The Liver Is the Cock's Comb*

Goya Francisco José de Goya y Lucientes (1746–1828) Spanish painter and engraver who depicted Spanish life with often strange, nightmarish works, such as the *Caprichos*

Greco, El (originally Doménikos Theotokopoulos) (1541–1614) Greek-born Spanish painter of elegant portraits and intensely emotional religious scenes with distorted figures and unearthly light, such as *The Burial of Count Orgaz*

Noteworthy Artists (continued)

Grosz George (1893–1959) German-born US Expressionist painter, graphic artist, and founder of Berlin Dada

Hals Frans (*c*. 1581–1666) Flemish-born painter of vibrant portraits, such as *Laughing Cavalier*

Hamilton Richard (1922–) English pioneer of typically humorous and satirical Pop art, such as *Just What Is It That Makes Today's Homes So Different, So Appealing?*

Hogarth William (1697–1764) English engraver and painter of portraits and moralizing genre scenes, such as *A Rake's Progress*

Hokusai Katsushika (1760–1849) Japanese artist and exponent of ukiyo-e (colour prints depicting scenes from everyday life), such as *36 Views of Mount Fuji*

Holbein the Elder Hans (*c*. 1464–1524) German painter of mainly religious works, such as the altarpiece *St Sebastian*

Holbein the Younger Hans (1497–1543) German Renaissance portrait painter who depicted the court of Henry VIII

Jones Allen (1937–) English Pop artist, painter, sculptor, and printmaker whose works include *Perfect Match*

Kahlo Frida (1907–1954) Mexican surrealist painter who painted a series of frank and disturbing self-portraits

Kandinsky Wasily (1866–1944) Russian-born painter who was a pioneer of abstract art and originator of the Expressionist Blaue Reiter movement

Klee Paul (1879–1940) inventive and playful Swiss painter and graphic artist whose paintings suggest child-like innocence, as in *Twittering Machine*

Klimt Gustav (1862–1918) Austrian painter who created often sensual and erotic works, such as *The Kiss*

Kokoschka Oskar (1886–1980) Austrian Expressionist painter of vivid landscapes and highly charged allegories and portraits, such as *The Bride of the Wind (The Tempest)*

Léger Fernand (1881–1955) French painter and designer associated with Cubism

Leonardo da Vinci (1452–1519) Italian painter, sculptor, architect, engineer, and scientist, perhaps the greatest figure of the Italian Renaissance, whose paintings include *The Last Supper* and *Mona Lisa*

Lippi Filippino (*c*. 1457–1504) Italian painter of religious scenes

Lippi Fra Filippo (*c*. 1406–1469) Italian painter of frescoes depicting religious scenes

Lucas van Leyden (1494–1533) Dutch painter and engraver; he was a pioneer of genre scenes and his paintings include *The Chess Players*

Mabuse Jan (adopted name of Jan Gossaert) (*c*. 1478–*c*. 1533) Flemish painter who started a vogue for Classical detail, as in *Neptune and Amphitrite*

Magritte René François Ghislain (1898–1967) Belgian Surrealist painter who focused on visual paradoxes and everyday objects taken out of context, as in *Golconda*

Malevich Kasimir Severinovich (1878–1935) Russian abstract painter who launched Suprematism, and whose paintings include *White on White*

Manet Édouard (1832–1883) French painter who developed a clear and unaffected Realist style close to that of the Impressionists, as in *A Bar at the Folies-Bergère*

Masaccio (adopted name of Tommaso di Giovanni di Simone Guidi) (1401–*c*. 1428) Florentine early Italian Renaissance painter of frescoes who pioneered the use of perspective

Matisse Henri (1869–1954) French painter, sculptor, and illustrator, and a leading figure in Fauvism; his paintings include *Dance*

Memling or **Memlinc** Hans (*c*. 1430–1494) Flemish painter of religious subjects and portraits, such as *Tommaso Portinari and His Wife* **Modigliani** Amedeo (1884–1920) Italian painter and sculptor of graceful, sensual nudes and portraits

Mondrian Piet (originally Pieter Cornelis Mondriaan) (1872–1944) Dutch abstract painter and exponent of Neo-Plasticism, based on simple geometric forms and pure colours, as seen in *Composition in Red, Yellow, and Blue*

Noteworthy Artists (continued)

Monet Claude (1840–1926) French painter and pioneer of Impressionism whose paintings include *Impression, Sunrise*, and *Water Lilies*

Moses Grandma (adopted name of Anna Mary Robertson) (1860–1961) US primitive painter of colourful scenes depicting rural American life, such as *What a Farmwife Painted*

Mucha Alphonse Maria (1860–1939) Czech Art Nouveau painter and designer who created theatre posters, such as *Gismonda*

Munch Edvard (1863–1944) Norwegian painter and graphic artist who focused on intense emotional states, as in *The Scream*

Murillo Bartolomé Esteban (*c.* 1618–1682) Spanish painter of self-portraits, sentimental pictures depicting the Immaculate Conception, and street urchins

Newman Barnett (1905–1970) US painter who was one of the founders of Abstract Expressionism

O'Keeffe Georgia (1887–1986) US painter of semi-abstract studies of flowers and bones, such as *Black Iris*

Orozco José Clemente (1883–1949) Mexican muralist who painted social and political works in public buildings in the USA and Mexico

Picasso Pablo (Ruiz y) (1881–1973) Spanish artist of inventive and prolific talents whose Blue Period and Rose Period preceded Cubism; his paintings include *Les Demoiselles d'Avignon* and *Guernica*

Piero della Francesca (*c.* 1420–1492) Italian painter of solemn stillness and solid figures in luminous colour, as in *The Flagellation of Christ*

Piero di Cosimo (*c.* 1462–*c.* 1521) Italian painter of inventive pictures of mythological and religious subjects, such as *Mythological Scene*

Pinturicchio or **Pintoricchio** (adopted name of Bernardino di Betto) (*c.* 1454–1513) Italian painter of frescoes in the Borgia Apartments in the Vatican

Pisarro Camille (1830–1903) French Impressionist painter of the French country-side, peasant life, and street scenes, as in *Boulevard Montmartre*

Pollock (Paul) Jackson (1912–1956) US painter who was a pioneer of Abstract Expressionism

Poussin Nicolas (1594–1665) French painter known for mythological and literary scenes done in austere Classical style, such as *Et in Arcadia Ego*

Raphael Sanzio (Raffaello Sanzio) (1483–1520) great Italian High Renaissance painter of portraits and mythological and religious works, such as *The School of Athens*

Rembrandt (Harmensz) van Rijn (1606–1669) Netherlandish painter and etcher of penetrating self-portraits and religious subjects, whose works include *The Night Watch*

Renoir Pierre-Auguste (1841–1919) French Impressionist painter who created a 'rainbow' style, using lively, colourful, and feathery brushwork to depict scenes of everyday life, such as *The Luncheon of the Boating Party*

Reynolds Joshua (1723–1792) English portrait painter in the 'Grand Manner' style, as seen in *Mrs Siddons as the Tragic Muse*

Riley Bridget Louise (1931–   ) English painter and pioneer of Op art, as seen in *Fission*

Rossetti Dante Gabriel (1828–1882) English painter of romantic mediaeval scenes and idealized portraits of women, such as *Beata Beatrix*; he was a founding member of the Pre-Raphaelite Brotherhood

Rothko Mark (adopted name of Marcus Rothkovich) (1903–1970) Russian-born US Abstract Expressionist painter and pioneer of Colour Field painting, as in *Light Red over Black*

Rubens Peter Paul (1577–1640) Flemish painter of the Baroque who created religious and allegorical paintings that revealed a mastery of drama and movement, as in *The Rape of the Daughters of Leucippus*

Rublev or **Rublyov** Andrei (*c.* 1360–*c.* 1430) Russian icon painter whose finest surviving work is *Old Testament Trinity*

Ruisdael Jacob Isaakszoon van (*c.* 1628–1682) Netherlandish landscape painter of

Noteworthy Artists (continued)

atmospheric style who concentrated on dramatic aspects of nature, as in *The Jewish Cemetery*

Sickert Walter (Richard) (1860–1942) English artist who worked in a broadly Impressionist style, depicting shabby music halls, streets, and interiors, as in *Ennui*

Signac Paul (1863–1935) French artist known for landscapes and seascapes painted in mosaic-like blocks of pure colour

intense, emotionally charged landscapes and portraits, such as *Page Boy*

Spencer Stanley (1891–1959) English painter of meticulously detailed, often humorous depictions of everyday life with elaborate religious symbolism, such as *The Resurrection, Cookham*

Steen Jan (Havickszoon) (*c.* 1626–1679) Netherlandish painter of humorous genre scenes, portraits, and landscapes, such as *The Prince's Birthday*

Steer Philip Wilson (1860–1942) Leader of the English Impressionist painters, noted for his landscapes, such as *The Beach at Walberswick*

Tintoretto (adopted name of Jacopo Robusti) (1518–1594) Italian Mannerist painter of portraits and religious works of great intensity and unearthly light, such as *St George and the Dragon*

Titian (adopted name of Tiziano Vecellio) (*c.*1487–1576) Italian High Renaissance painter of portraits and religious and mythological scenes, such as *Venus and Adonis*

Toulouse-Lautrec Henri Marie Raymond de (1864–1901) French artist of brilliant technical skill whose work was vital to the development of poster art

Turner (Joseph Mallord) William (1775–1851) English landscape painter whose paintings anticipated Impressionism; they include *Rain, Steam and Speed*

Uccello Paolo (Paolo di Dono) (1397–1475) Italian painter who experimented with perspective, as in *St George and the Dragon*

Utamaro Kitagawa (1753–1806) Japanese artist who created colour prints of women engaged in everyday activities

Vasarely Victor (1908–1997) Hungarian-born French artist and exponent of Op art

Velázquez Diego Rodríguez de Silva y (1599–1660) Spanish painter of portraits, and religious and genre scenes, such as *The Maids of Honour*

van de Velde Essaias (*c.* 1591–1630), his brother, Willem the Elder (*c.* 1610–1693), and Willem's sons, Willem the Younger (1633–1707) and Adriaen (1636–1672) family of Netherlandish landscape painters

Vermeer Jan (1632–1675) Netherlandish painter of quiet, everyday scenes characterized by his remarkable ability to capture light on objects, as in *Maidservant Pouring Milk*

Veronese Paolo (*c.* 1528–1588) Italian painter of grand decorative themes celebrating the power and splendour of Venice

Vlaminck Maurice de (1876–1958) French artist who was a leading figure in Fauvism

Warhol Andy (adopted name of Andrew Warhola) (1928–1987) US Pop artist and filmmaker known for painting Campbell's soup cans, Coca-Cola bottles, and film stars

Watteau (Jean-)Antoine (1684–1721) French Rococo painter of fanciful outdoor scenes with elegant young people, such as *The Embarkation for Cythera*

Whistler James (Abbott) McNeill (1834–1903) US painter, etcher, and leading figure in the Aesthetic movement whose paintings include *Arrangement in Grey and Black: Portrait of the Painter's Mother*

Yeats Jack Butler (1871–1957) Irish painter of spirited portrayals of Irish life and landscapes, such as *Back from the Races*

Noteworthy Sculptors

Archipenko Alexander (1887–1964) Ukrainian-born US sculptor noted for Cubist sculptures, including *Woman Combing Her Hair*

Arp Hans, or Jean (1887–1966) French abstract painter, poet, and sculptor who was a founder of the Dada movement

Noteworthy Artists (continued)

Bernini Gianlorenzo (Giovanni Lorenzo) (1598–1680) Italian sculptor, architect, and painter who was a leading figure in developing the Baroque style

Borglum (John) Gutzon (de la Mothe) (1867–1941) US sculptor who created the group of giant heads of four US presidents carved into the mountainside at Mount Rushmore

Bourgeois Louise (1911–) French-born US printmaker, sculptor, and performance artist whose early sculptures were among the pioneering examples of American Surrealism

Brancusi Constantin (1876–1957) Romanian pioneer of abstract sculpture who reduced forms to their most essential, simplified nature, as in *Bird in Space*

Canova Antonio (Marquese d'Ischia) (1757–1822) Italian Neo-Classical sculptor of highly-

Cellini Benvenuto (1500–1571) Italian Mannerist sculptor and goldsmith who created the graceful bronze *Perseus*

César (full name César Baldaccini) (1921–1998) French sculptor of imaginary insects and animals from iron, scrap metal, and crushed car bodies

Christo (full name Christo Javacheff) (1935–) Bulgarian-born US sculptor known for wrapping buildings and other large structures in fabric tied down with rope

Donatello (Donato di Niccolo) (*c.* 1386–1466) Italian early Renaissance sculptor who revived the Classical style, as in the bronze *David* and the equestrian statue *Gattamelata*

Epstein Jacob (1880–1959) US-born British sculptor who created monumental figures, including *St Michael and the Devil*, and muscular nudes, such as *Genesis*

Frink Elisabeth (1930–1993) English sculptor of rugged naturalistic bronzes of human and animal forms, such as *Running Man*

Giacometti Alberto (1901–1966) Swiss sculptor of thin, rough-textured, single bronze figures, such as *Man Pointing*

Gormley Anthony (1950–) English sculptor best known for his *Angel of the North* and *Derry Sculpture*

Hepworth (Jocelyn) Barbara (1903–1975) English abstract sculptor of wood or stone whose works feature slender, upright, or round hollowed forms, such as *Pelagos*

Lipchitz Jacques (1891–1973) Lithuanian-born early Cubist sculptor whose works include *Man with Guitar*

Lysippus or **Lysippos** (4th century BC) Greek sculptor of *Apoxyomenos* and the colossal *Hercules* (lost)

Michelangelo (Michelangelo di Lodovico Buonarroti) (1475–1564) dominant Italian High Renaissance sculptor, painter, architect, and poet; his marble *David* set a new standard in nude sculpture

Moore Henry (Spencer) (1898–1986) English sculptor of reclining nudes, mother-and-child groups, warriors, and interlocking abstract forms, such as *Reclining Figure*

Myron (*c.* 500–*c.* 440 BC) Greek sculptor who excelled at representing movement, as in *Discobolus/Discus-Thrower*

Phidias or **Pheidias** (mid-5th century BC) Greek sculptor of the colossal *Zeus* at Olympia

Praxiteles (mid-4th century BC) Greek sculptor of life-size, free-standing female nudes, such as *Aphrodite of Cnidus*

Rodin (René François) Auguste (1840–1917) French sculptor who is considered the greatest of his time; his work includes *The Thinker*

Tatlin Vladimir Yevgrapovich (1885–1953) Russian highly abstract sculptor and co-founder of Constructivism

Verrocchio Andrea del (Andrea di Cione) (*c.* 1435–1488) Italian sculptor, painter, and goldsmith who created the vigorous equestrian statue of *Bartolomeo Colleoni* and the painting *The Baptism of Christ*

Abstract Expressionism movement in US painting that was the dominant force in the country's art in the late 1940s and 1950s. It was characterized by the sensuous use of paint, often on very large canvases, to convey powerful emotions. Some of the artists involved painted pure abstract pictures, but others often retained figurative traces in their work. Most of the leading Abstract Expressionists were based in New York during the heyday of the movement (they are sometimes referred to as the New York School), and their critical and financial success (after initial opposition) helped New York to replace Paris as the world's leading centre of contemporary art, a position it has held ever since.

Conceptual art or **Concept art Conceptualism** type of modern art in which the idea or ideas that a work expresses are considered its essential

Paint Media

acrylic paint Acrylic paints, a range of synthetic substitutes for oil paint that are mostly soluble in water, are used in a variety of painting techniques, from wash to impasto. They dry quicker than oil paint, are waterproof, and remain slightly flexible, but lack the translucency of natural substances.

computer art Since the 1950s the aesthetic use of computers has been increasingly evident in most artistic disciplines, including film animation, architecture, and music. Computer graphics has been the most developed area, with the 'paint-box' computer liberating artists from the confines of the canvas. It is now also possible to programme computers in advance to generate graphics, music, and sculpture, according to 'instructions' which may include a preprogrammed element of unpredictability. In this last function, computer technology has been seen as a way of challenging the elitist nature of art by putting artistic creativity within relatively easy reach of anyone owning a computer.

fresco Fresco is a mural painting technique using water-based paint on wet plaster that has been freshly applied to the wall (*fresco* is Italian for fresh). The technique is ancient and widespread; some of the earliest examples (*c.* 1750–1400 BC) were found in Knossos, Crete (now preserved in the Heraklion Museum). However, fresco reached its finest expression in Italy from the 13th to the 17th centuries. Giotto, Masaccio, Michelangelo, and many other artists worked in the medium. In the 20th century there was an important revival of the technique in Mexico,

most notably in the work of José Orozco, Diego Rivera, and David Siqueiros. Fresco is suitable only for dry climates, as damp causes the plaster to crumble. For this reason, fresco was never as popular in watery Venice as it was in other major Italian art centres such as Florence and Rome.

The advantage of fresco over other wall-painting methods is that it produces an exceptionally permanent result. The colours become incorporated with the substance of the plaster, and, if the process is properly carried out, are as lasting as the plaster itself. The plaster is applied to a brick or stone wall in two basic coatings, the first (*arriccio*), half an inch thick, to the whole wall at once; the second, finer coating (*intonaco*) only to that portion of the wall which it is intended to be painted in any one day so that it may not be dry before receiving the pigments. In drying, a crystal surface of carbonate of lime forms over the plaster, and it is essential that the pigments should be there ready to receive this coating, which is protective to them and gives them clearness.

The artist would earlier have made a full-scale drawing of the picture (called a cartoon) and this was transferred to the *intonaco* by holding it against the wall and either running a stylus around the outlines, indenting the plaster beneath, or dusting charcoal through a series of pin pricks along the outlines (a process known as pouncing). The cartoon was usually cut into sections of varying size, so that each could be used for a day's work. As the joins of each section of plaster remain fairly

clearly perceptible, it is possible for art historians to calculate the number of days the artist spent painting the whole work. The colours, principally earths or minerals, which best resist the chemical action of the lime, are ground and mixed with pure water and applied thinly and transparently, rather darker than the desired effect because they become paler in drying. **Buon fresco,** the true method, is distinguished from **fresco secco** ('dry fresco'), painted on dry plaster. The result of the latter method is far less durable, though *fresco secco* is sometimes employed to add final touches to work carried out in true fresco.

gouache Gouache (or **body colour**) is a painting medium in which watercolour is mixed with white pigment. Applied in the same way as watercolour, gouache gives a chalky finish similar to that of tempera painting. It has long been popular in continental Europe, where Dürer and Boucher were both masters of the technique. Poster paints are usually a form of gouache.

ink Ink is a coloured liquid used for writing, drawing, and printing. Traditional ink (blue, but later a permanent black) was produced from gallic acid and tannic acid, but inks are now based on synthetic dyes.

oil paint Oil paint, a painting medium in which ground pigment is bound with oil, usually linseed, was in decorative use as early as the 5th century, but its artistic application is usually credited to the early-15th-century Flemish painter Jan van Eyck. Passing from Flanders to Italy, it quickly succeeded tempera as the

point, with its visual appearance being of secondary (often negligible) importance. It is a highly controversial type of art. Its supporters think it marks a significant expansion of the boundaries of art, but its detractors believe that it is trite and pretentious.

Constructivism abstract art movement that originated in Russia in about 1914 and subsequently had great influence on Western art. Constructivism usually involves industrial materials such as glass, steel, and plastic in clearly defined arrangements, but the term is difficult to define precisely, as the meaning attached to it has varied according to place and time. Some art historians distinguish between Russian (or Soviet) Constructivism and the more diffuse European (or International) Constructivism.

Paint Media (continued)

standard medium. Capable of the greatest flexibility and luminosity, oil paint has since the 16th century been considered pre-eminent among painting media, although acrylic paint may prove in time to be a rival.

Oil painting first developed in a distinct form in the Netherlands and Germanic lands during the 14th century, and with van Eyck attained a brilliance that led to the belief that he possessed some secret powers. His method, and the **Netherlandish technique** in general, was to paint transparently on a white gesso ground, the picture being smoothly finished piece by piece, with a luminous enamel-like result. The method was taken up in Italy, Antonello da Messina being a pioneer. The **Renaissance techniques,** particularly that of Giovanni Bellini in Venice, rivalled the brilliance of Flemish technique. A combination of a tempera underpainting with a final glaze of oil colour was a Renaissance technique used by Michelangelo. In the 16th and 17th centuries there was a further development of technique, and a desire to obtain greater depth and three-dimensional effect. The transparent method, still in essence that of the tempera painter, was replaced by a more elaborate process. The picture was first painted in monochrome, and on this basis the light parts were painted with thick opaque colour, the shadows being painted thinly. Successive glazes of transparent colour gave richness. The new phase of oil painting flourished in Venice, and Titian led it to perfection. Rembrandt, Rubens, and Velázquez give individual variants of what may

be called the classic method.

A decisive change came with the 19th century, when painters such as the Impressionists abandoned the old-master process of building up a picture in stages in favour of a direct mode of painting. In part this was due to the practice of painting from nature, which made swiftness of execution necessary, but it was also due to the translation of tone into colour, which entailed instant decision in determining and laying down the colour with the desired effect.

Oil painting has remained the most responsive of media to individual treatment. Thus one might contrast the later work of Paul Cézanne, with its application of transparent colour (almost like watercolour) to represent delicate modifications of light on the form of an object, with the heavily loaded paint of Vincent van Gogh, who used the medium with an emotional violence.

tempera Tempera is a painting medium in which powdered pigments are mixed with a water-soluble binding agent such as egg yolk. Tempera is noted for its strong, translucent colours. A form of tempera was used in ancient Egypt, and egg tempera was the foremost medium for panel painting in late Medieval and early Renaissance Europe. It was gradually superseded by oils from the late 15th century onwards. In the 20th century tempera has been used by the US painter Andrew Wyeth.

In **pure egg tempera** well-ground inorganic pigments are mixed with egg yolk and water and painted onto a slightly absorbent gesso panel.

(The yellow of egg yolk bleaches out, whereas white of egg may turn brown.) In early Italian painting, the initial lay-in of a design was often done with *terra-verde*. Colours were then applied to the design in a mixture with flake or zinc white, gradually being strengthened and modelled with glazes or hatches of pure transparent colour. **Casein** is a variant of egg tempera in which the medium is fresh white curd and a little slaked lime, diluted with water. **Tempera emulsion** uses for its medium a well-fused mixture of egg yolk and stand oil, which permits dilution with water. It dries hard sooner and, being more flexible, can be used on canvas prepared with a water ground, that is, with size and gesso.

watercolour painting The method of painting with pigments mixed with water was known in China as early as the 3rd century. The technique requires great skill since its transparency rules out overpainting. The art as practised today began in England in the 18th century with the work of Paul Sandby and was developed by Thomas Girtin, John Sell Cotman, and J M W Turner. Other outstanding watercolourists were Raoul Dufy, Paul Cézanne, and John Marin. Western artists excelling in watercolour painting include J R Cozens, Peter de Wint, John Constable, David Cox, John Singer Sargent, Philip Wilson Steer, Paul Signac, Emil Nolde, Paul Klee, and Paul Nash. More recently, David Hockney and R B Kitaj have made memorable use of the medium.

The Evolution of Sculpture

Sculpture, the artistic shaping of materials (such as wood, stone, clay, or metal), is an ancient art form. The earliest prehistoric human artefacts include sculpted stone figurines, and all ancient civilizations have left behind examples of sculpture. Historically, most sculpture has been religious in intent. Chinese, Japanese, and Indian sculptures are usually Buddhist or Hindu images. African, American Indian, and Oceanic sculptures reflect spirit cults and animist beliefs. Many indigenous cultures have maintained rich traditions of sculpture. Those of Africa, South America, and the Caribbean in particular have been influential in the development of contemporary Western sculpture. There are two main techniques traditionally employed in sculpture: **carving,** involving the cutting away of hard materials such as wood or stone to reveal an image; and

modelling, involving the building up of an image from malleable materials, such as clay or wax, which may then be cast in bronze. In the 20th century various techniques for 'constructing' sculptures have been developed, for example metal welding and assemblage.

ancient sculpture Ancient Egyptian and Mesopotamian sculpture took the form of monumental reliefs in palace and temple decoration. Standing sculptures of the period were intended to be seen only from the front and sides. The first sculptures in the round (to be seen from all sides) were Greek. The development of vigorous poses *(contrapposto)* and emotional expressiveness elevated Greek sculpture to the pinnacle of artistic achievement and much of subsequent Western sculpture has been imitative of Greek ideals.

Lifelike portrait sculpture was introduced by the Romans.

medieval sculpture Sculpture of the medieval period is epitomized by niche figures carved in stone for churches (for example, Chartres Cathedral, France) and by delicate ivory carvings. The work of Nicola Pisano began a great tradition of Italian sculpture.

Renaissance sculpture During the Renaissance, Greek supremacy was challenged by the reintroduction of free-standing sculptures, notably Michelangelo's *David* (1501–04), and by superlative bronze casting, for example, Donatello's equestrian monument of *Gattamelata* (1447–50; Piazza del Santo, Padua). In the work of Lorenzo Ghiberti, Luca della Robbia, and Andrea del Verrocchio, figure sculpture attained a new dignity and power. The work of Benvenuto Cellini and Giovanni

Cubism revolutionary style of painting created by Georges Braque and Pablo Picasso in Paris in 1907–14. It was the most radical of the developments that revolutionized art in the years of unprecedented experimentation leading up to World War I, and it changed the course of painting by introducing a new way of seeing and depicting the world. To the Cubists, a painting was first and foremost a flat object that existed in its own right, rather than a kind of window through which a representation of the world is seen. Cubism also had a marked, though less fundamental, effect on sculpture, and even influenced architecture and the decorative arts.

Dada or **Dadaism,** artistic and literary movement founded in 1915 in a spirit of rebellion and disillusionment during World War I and lasting until about 1922. Although the movement had a fairly short life and was concentrated in only a few centres (New York being the only non-European one), Dada was highly influential, establishing the tendency for avant-garde art movements to question traditional artistic conventions and values. There are several accounts of how the name Dada (French for hobby horse) originated; the most often quoted is that it was chosen at random by inserting a penknife into a dictionary,

symbolizing the antirational nature of the movement.

Expressionism style of painting, sculpture, and literature that expresses inner emotions; in particular, a movement in early 20th-century art in northern and central Europe. Expressionists tended to distort or exaggerate natural appearance in order to create a reflection of an inner world; the Norwegian painter Edvard Munch's *Skriket/The Scream* (1893; National Gallery, Oslo) is perhaps the most celebrated example. Expressionist writers include August Strindberg and Frank Wedekind.

Fauvism (French *fauve*, 'wild beast') movement in modern French painting characterized by the use of very bold, vivid colours. The name is a reference to the fact that the works seemed to many people at the time to be crude and untamed. Although short-lived, lasting only about two years (1905–07), the movement was highly influential. It was the first of the artistic movements that transformed European art between the turn of the century and World War I.

Futurism avant-garde art movement founded in 1909 that celebrated the dynamism of the modern world. It was chiefly an Italian movement

The Evolution of Sculpture (continued)

Bologna (1524–1608) exemplified the Mannerist style. Pedro Berruguete, a pupil of Michelangelo, introduced the Renaissance to Spain. In France, Jean Goujon developed Mannerism. However, it was the High Renaissance style of Michelangelo that was later encouraged by Louis XIV, who commissioned numerous busts and figure groups, notably by François Girardon.

Baroque and Rococo sculpture Relief rather than free-standing sculptures came to the fore. The virtuosity of such sculptors as Giovanni Bernini seemed to defy the nature of the materials they used. The style was represented in France by Etienne Falconet, and in Spain by Alonso Cano.

Neo-Classical sculpture Sculpture of the 18th century concentrated on smooth perfection of form and surface, as in the work of Antonio Canova. The last great exponent of sculpture in the Classical tradition was Auguste Rodin. The work of Aristide Maillol and Antoine Bourdelle (1861–1929) emphasized formal qualities, rejecting both Realism and Impressionism.

20th century Sculptors such as Henry Moore, Barbara Hepworth, and Jacob Epstein used traditional materials and techniques to create forms inspired by 'primitive' art and nature. The work of Amedeo Modigliani and Henri Gaudier-Brzeska also reflects such influences. Abstract sculpture was pioneered by Alexander Archipenko and Ossip Zadkine, both exponents of Cubism, and Constantin Brancusi and Alberto Giacometti, who developed three-dimensional abstract forms from natural materials. Followers of the nonrepresentational school include Jacques Lipchitz, Jean Arp, Naum Gabo and Antoine Pevsner (pioneers of Russian Constructivism), Reg Butler, and Anthony Caro. Among more traditional sculptors whose work powerfully expresses the modern idiom are Marino Marini in Italy and Frank Dobson in England. Other sculptors have broken with the past entirely, rejecting both carving and modelling. Today the term sculpture applies to the mobiles of Alexander Calder, assemblages of various materials, 'environment sculpture' and earthworks (pioneered by Carl André), and 'installations'. Materials such as plastic and other synthetics are used. Another development has been the sculpture garden; for example, Hakore open-air museum in Japan and the Grizedale Forest sculpture project in the Lake District, England.

and was mainly expressed in painting, but it also embraced other arts, including literature and music, and it had extensive influence outside Italy, particularly in Russia. In Italy the movement virtually died during World War I, but in Russia it continued to flourish into the 1920s.

Impressionism movement in painting that originated in France in the 1860s and had enormous influence in European and North American painting in the late 19th century. The Impressionists wanted to depict real life, to paint straight from nature, and to capture the changing effects of light. The term was first used abusively to describe Claude Monet's painting *Impression: Sunrise* (1872). The other leading Impressionists included Paul Cézanne, Edgar Degas, Edouard Manet, Camille Pissarro, Pierre-Auguste Renoir, and Alfred Sisley, but only Monet remained devoted to Impressionist ideas throughout his career.

Minimalism movement in abstract art (mostly sculpture) and music towards severely simplified composition. Minimal art developed in the USA in the 1950s in reaction to Abstract Expressionism, shunning its emotive approach in favour of impersonality and elemental, usually geometric, shapes. It has found its fullest expression in sculpture, notably in the work of Carl Andre, who employs industrial materials in modular compositions.

Op art abbreviation for **Optical art** type of abstract art, mainly painting, in which patterns are used to create the impression that the image is flickering or vibrating. This type of art began to emerge in about 1960 and the name was coined in 1964; it is a pun on Pop art, a dominant style in the art world at the time.

Pop art movement in modern art that took its imagery from the glossy world of advertising and from popular culture such as comic strips, films, and television; it developed in the 1950s and flourished in the 1960s, notably in Britain and the USA. The term was coined by the British critic Lawrence Alloway (1926–1990) in about 1955, to refer to works of art that drew upon popular culture. Richard Hamilton, one of the leading British pioneers and exponents of Pop art, defined it in 1957 as 'popular, transient, expendable, low-cost, mass-produced, young, witty, sexy, gimmicky, glamorous, and Big Business'. In its eclecticism and sense of irony and playfulness, Pop art helped to prepare the way for the Post-Modernism that has been a feature of Western culture since the 1970s.

Post-Impressionism broad term covering various developments in French painting that emerged out of Impressionism in the period from about 1880 to about 1905. Some of these developments built on the achievements of Impressionism, but others were reactions against its concentration on surface appearances, seeking to reintroduce a concern with emotional and symbolic values.

Surrealism movement in art, literature, and film that developed out of Dada around 1922. Led by André Breton, who produced the *Surrealist Manifesto* (1924), the Surrealists were inspired by the thoughts and visions of the subconscious mind. They explored varied styles and techniques,

> **Suffocating surrealists**
> ■ At the International Surrealist Exhibition in 1936, Spanish artist Salvador Dalí gave a lecture wearing a diving suit, accompanied by two wolfhounds. No one could hear what he said, and he was almost asphyxiated.

and the movement became the dominant force in Western art between World Wars I and II.

Symbolism late 19th-century movement in French poetry, which inspired a similar trend in French painting. The Symbolist artists created works to represent their symbolic rather than concrete meaning. Leading exponents include Gustave Moreau, Pierre Puvis de Chavannes, Volilon Predon, Arnold Bocklin, Edward Burne-Jones, and Jan Theodor Toorop.

What is Video Art?

Video art is created by visual artists using video and television equipment. The equipment can be used in any of various ways, for example in installations or as part of performance art. Thus video art often overlaps with other forms of avant-garde expression. The German artist Wolf Vostell (1932–) used television sets as part of sculptural assemblages as early as 1959, but the creator of video art is usually thought to be the Korean-born artist Nam June Paik (1932–), who trained as a musician and has also worked as a sculptor and performance artist. He moved to New York in 1964 and bought a portable video recorder the following year, at a time when such equipment was still a novelty; he is said to have made and showed his first work of video art on the very day he bought the camera. Paik's work usually sets out to entertain; a well-known example is *Bra for Living Sculpture* (1969), in which a female cellist plays her instrument while wearing a bra that incorporates two small television screens (nicknamed 'boob tubes'). Other exponents of video art are much more serious; the work of the US artist Bill Viola (1951–), for example, includes *To Pray Without Ceasing* (1992), a 12-hour sequence of images that he describes as 'a cycle of individual and universal life'. Many critics find such work tedious and pretentious, but video art has made a substantial impression in the world of avant-garde art.

LITERATURE AND LANGUAGE

The role of literature has evolved since ancient times. Literature of the ancient oral traditions had a mainly public function – mythic and religious. As literary works came to be preserved in writing, and, eventually, printed, their role became more private, serving as a vehicle for the exploration and expression of emotion and the human situation. In the development of literature, aesthetic criteria have come increasingly to the fore, although these have been challenged on ideological grounds by some recent cultural critics.

Literature may be broadly categorized as either poetry or prose. The English poet and critic Coleridge defined **prose** as words in their best order, and **poetry** as the 'best' words in the best order. The distinction between poetry and prose is not always clear-cut, but in practice poetry tends to be metrically formal (making it easier to memorize), whereas prose corresponds more closely to the patterns of ordinary speech. Poetry therefore had an early advantage over prose in the days before printing, which it did not relinquish until comparatively recently.

Over the centuries poetry has taken on a wide range of forms, from the lengthy narrative such as the epic, to the lyric, expressing personal emotion in songlike form; from the ballad and the 14-line sonnet, to the extreme conciseness of the 17-syllable Japanese haiku.

Prose came into its own in the West as a vehicle for imaginative literature with the rise of the novel in the 18th century. Fiction has since been divided into various genres such as the historical novel, detective fiction, fantasy, and science fiction.

LITERARY TERMS

alexandrine 12-syllable line of verse known to date from the 12th century, and used for almost all French poetry from the 16th century. It has been variously divided into two groups of six syllables (usually in English poetry) or three groups of four syllables (usually in French poetry).

allegory description or illustration of one thing in terms of another, or the personification of abstract ideas. The term is also used for a work of poetry or prose in the form of an extended metaphor or parable that makes use of symbolic fictional characters.

alliteration use, within a line or phrase, of words beginning with the same sound, as in 'Two tired toads trotting to Tewkesbury'. It was a common device in Old English poetry, and its use survives in many traditional phrases, such as *dead as a doornail* and *pretty as a picture*.

apostrophe figure of speech in which the speaker turns from the main subject to address some absent person or quality, as in 'O Death, where is thy sting' or Hamlet's 'Frailty, thy name is woman'.

assonance matching of vowel (or, sometimes, consonant) sounds in a line, generally in poetry. 'Load' and 'moat', 'farther' and 'harder' are examples of assonance, since they match in vowel sounds and stress pattern, but do not rhyme.

biography account of a person's life. When it is written by that person, it is an autobiography. Biography may consist simply of the factual details of a person's life told in chronological order, but has generally become a matter of interpretation as well as historical accuracy. Unofficial biographies (not sanctioned by the subject) have frequently led to legal disputes over both interpretation and facts.

blank verse unrhymed iambic pentameter or ten-syllable line of five stresses. First used by the Italian Gian Giorgio Trissino in his tragedy *Sofonisba* (1514–15), it was introduced to England in about 1540 by the Earl of Surrey, who used it in his translation of Virgil's *Aeneid*. It was developed by Christopher Marlowe and Shakespeare, quickly becoming the distinctive verse form of Elizabethan and Jacobean drama. It was later used by Milton in *Paradise Lost* (1667) and by Wordsworth in *The Prelude* (1805). More recent exponents of blank verse in English include Thomas Hardy, T S Eliot, and Robert Frost.

caesura natural pause in a line of verse.

Classical complexity
Irish-born English novelist and philosopher Iris Murdoch. Her novels are noted for their complex plots adroitly handled and the subtle, ever changing relationships of the characters. Though their incidents are often comic and bizarre, their underlying concern is how love, freedom, and goodness can survive moral and intellectual blindness. These themes are analysed formally in her philosophical works, which include studies of Sartre and Plato. *Penguin Books Limited*

couplet pair of lines of verse, usually of the same length and rhymed.

essay short piece of nonfiction, often dealing with a particular subject from a personal point of view. The essay became a recognized genre with the French writer Montaigne's *Essais* (1580) and in English with Francis Bacon's *Essays* (1597). Today the essay is a part of journalism: articles in the broadsheet newspapers are in the essay tradition.

fable story, in either verse or prose, in which animals or inanimate objects are given the mentality and speech of human beings to point out a moral. Fables are common in folklore and children's literature, and range from the short fables of the ancient Greek writer Aesop to the modern novel *Animal Farm* (1945) by George Orwell.

fiction any work in which the content is completely or largely invented. The term describes imaginative works of narrative prose (such as the novel or the short story), and is distinguished from **nonfiction** (such as history, biography, or works on practical subjects) and **poetry.**

foot unit of metrical pattern in poetry. The five most common types of foot in English poetry are iamb (v –), trochee (– v), dactyl (– vv), spondee (–), and anapaest (vv –); v stands for an unstressed syllable and – for a stressed one.

hyperbole figure of speech that is an intentional exaggeration or overstatement, used for emphasis or comic effect. Many everyday idioms are hyperbolic: 'waiting for ages' and 'a flood of tears'.

imagery use of metaphor, simile, and other figures of speech that create sensual comparisons; the use of symbols and descriptive language. The aim is to clarify or explain, to enable the reader to see in a different light or from a different angle.

irony literary technique that uses words to convey a meaning opposite to their literal sense, through the use of humour or sarcasm. It can be traced through all periods of literature, from classical Greek and Roman epics and dramas to the subtle irony of Chaucer and the 20th-century writer's method for dealing with despair, as in Samuel Beckett's *Waiting for Godot.*

literary criticism the assessment and interpretation of literary works. The term 'criticism' is often taken to mean exclusively adverse comment, but in fact it refers to all literary assessment, whether positive or negative. Contemporary criticism offers analyses of literary works from structuralist, semiological, feminist, Marxist, and psychoanalytical perspectives, whereas earlier criticism tended to deal with moral or political ideas, or with a literary work as a formal object independent of its creator.

litotes use of understatement for effect ('He is no Einstein' = 'He is a bit dim'). It is the opposite of hyperbole.

magic realism in 20th-century literature, a fantastic situation realistically treated, as in the works of many Latin American writers such as Isabel Allende, Jorge Luis Borges, and Gabriel García Márquez.

metaphor (Greek 'transfer') figure of speech using an analogy or close comparison between two things that are not normally treated as if they had anything in common. Metaphor is a common means of extending the uses and references of words.

metre in poetry, the recurring pattern of stressed and unstressed syllables in a line of verse. The unit of metre is a **foot.** Metre is classified by the number of feet to a line: a minimum of two and a maximum of eight. A line of two feet is a dimeter. They are then named, in order, trimeter, tetrameter, pentameter, hexameter, heptameter, and octameter.

naturalism term referring to a movement in literature and drama that originated in France in the late 19th century with the writings of Emile Zola and the brothers Goncourt. Similar to realism in that it was concerned with everyday life, naturalism also held that people's fates were determined by heredity, environment, and social forces beyond their control.

Oral Literature

Most pre-literate societies have had a tradition of oral literature – stories that are or have been transmitted in spoken form rather than through writing or printing – including short folk tales, legends, myths, proverbs, and riddles. Longer narrative works and most of the ancient epics, such as the Greek *Odyssey* and the Mesopotamian *Gilgamesh,* seem to have been composed and added to over many centuries before they were committed to writing.

Some ancient stories from oral traditions were not written down as literary works until the 19th century, such as the Finnish *Kalevala* (1835–49); many fairy tales, such as those collected in Germany by the Grimm brothers, also come into this category. Much of this sort of **folk literature** may have been consciously embellished and altered, as happened in 19th-century Europe for nationalistic purposes. Oral literatures have continued to influence the development of national written literatures in the 20th century, particularly in Africa, central Asia, and Australia. Russian investigations and studies of Balkan oral literature, originally undertaken to illuminate the oral basis of Homeric narrative, have prompted collections and scientific studies in many other parts of the world.

novel extended fictional prose narrative, usually between 30,000 and 100,000 words, that deals imaginatively with human experience through the psychological development of the central characters and of their relationship with a broader world. The modern novel took its name and inspiration from the Italian *novella*, the short tale of varied character which became popular in the late 13th century. As the main form of narrative fiction in the 20th century, the novel is frequently classified according to genres and subgenres such as the historical novel, detective fiction, fantasy, and science fiction.

parody work that imitates the style of another work, usually with mocking or comic intent; it is related to satire.

personification figure of speech (poetic or imaginative expression) in which animals, plants, objects, and ideas are treated as if they were human or alive ('Clouds chased each other across the face of the Moon'; 'Nature smiled on their work and gave it her blessing'; 'The future beckoned eagerly to them').

plot storyline in a novel, play, film, or other work of fiction. A plot is traditionally a scheme of connected events. Novelists in particular have at times tried to subvert or ignore the reader's expectation of a causally linked story with a clear beginning, middle, and end, with no loose ends. James Joyce and Virginia Woolf wrote novels that explore the minutiae of a character's experience, rather than telling a tale. However, the tradition that the novel must tell a story, whatever else it may do, survives for the most part intact.

Breaking new ground
US poet Walt Whitman, whose breaking away from conventional form made him one of the most influential writers of his generation. The main themes in his poetry include the sacredness of the self, the beauty of death, the equality of all people, brotherly love, and the immortality of the soul. *Sachem*

Poets Laureate of the UK

The Poet of the British royal household is so called because of the laurel wreath awarded to eminent poets in the Greco-Roman world. There is a stipend of £70 a year, plus £27 in lieu of the traditional butt of sack (cask of wine).

Appointed	Poet Laureate	Appointed	Poet Laureate
1668	John Dryden (1631–1700)	1813	Robert Southey (1774–1843)
1689	Thomas Shadwell (c 1642–1692)	1843	William Wordsworth (1770–1850)
1692	Nahum Tate (1652–1715)	1850	Alfred, Lord Tennyson (1809–1892)
1715	Nicholas Rowe (1674–1718)	1896	Alfred Austin (1835–1913)
1718	Laurence Eusden (1688–1730)	1913	Robert Bridges (1844–1930)
1730	Colley Cibber (1671–1757)	1930	John Masefield (1878–1967)
1757	William Whitehead (1715–1785)	1968	Cecil Day Lewis (1904–1972)
1785	Thomas Warton (1728–1790)	1972	Sir John Betjeman (1906–1984)
1790	Henry James Pye (1745–1813)	1984	Ted Hughes (1930–1998)

Poets Laureate of the USA

The post of the Poet Laureate of the USA was created in 1985 with the first appointment made in 1986. The post is for a one-year term, but it is renewable.

Term of appointment	Poet Laureate	Term of appointment	Poet Laureate
1986–87	Robert Penn Warren (1905–1989)	1992–93	Mona Van Duyn (1921–)
1987–88	Richard Wilbur (1921–)	1993–95	Rita Dove (1952–)
1988–90	Howard Nemerov (1920–1991)	1995–97	Robert Hass (1941–)
1990–91	Mark Strand (1934–)	1997–	Robert Pinsky (1940–)
1991–92	Joseph Brodsky (1940–1996)		

poetry imaginative expression of emotion, thought, or narrative, frequently in metrical form and often using figurative language. Poetry has traditionally been distinguished from prose (ordinary written language) by rhyme or the rhythmical arrangement of words (metre), the employment of the line as a formal unit, heightened vocabulary, and freedom of syntax. Poetic images are presented using a variety of techniques, of which the most universal is the use of metaphor and simile to evoke a range of associations through implicit or explicit comparison. Although not frequently encountered in modern verse, alliteration has been used, chiefly for rhetoric or emphasis, in works dating back to Old English.

prosody the rhythm, intonation, and stress patterns of poetry. The term, now rather archaic, may also be applied to the rhythms of prose or speech.

pun figure of speech, a play on words, or double meaning that is technically known as **paronomasia** (Greek 'adapted meaning'). Double meaning can be accidental, often resulting from homonymy, or the multiple meaning of words; puns, however, are deliberate, intended as jokes or as clever and compact remarks.

Realism in the arts and literature generally, an unadorned, naturalistic approach to subject matter. More specifically, the term refers to a movement in mid-19th-century European art and literature, a reaction against Romantic and Classical idealization and a rejection of conventional academic themes (such as mythology, history, and sublime landscapes) in favour of everyday life and carefully observed social settings. The movement was particularly important in France, where it had political overtones; the painters Gustave Courbet and Honoré Daumier, two leading Realists, both used their art to expose social injustice.

rhyme identity of sound, usually in the endings of lines of verse, such as *wing* and *sing*. Avoided in Japanese, it is a common literary device in other Asian and European languages. Rhyme first appeared in Europe in late Latin poetry but was not used in Classical Latin or Greek.

rhythm recurring stress pattern in poetry or prose.

saga prose narrative written down in the 11th–13th centuries in Norway and Iceland. The sagas range from family chronicles, such as the *Landnamabok* of Ari (1067–1148), to legendary and anonymous works such as *Njal's Saga*.

satire literary or dramatic work that ridicules human pretensions or exposes social evils. Satire is related to parody in its intention to mock, but satire tends to be more subtle and to mock an attitude or a belief, whereas parody tends to mock a particular work (such as a poem) by imitating its style, often with purely comic intent.

short story short work of prose fiction, usually consisting of between 500 and 10,000 words, which typically either sets up and resolves a single narrative point or depicts a mood or an atmosphere.

simile (Latin 'likeness') figure of speech that in English uses the conjunctions *like* and *as* to express comparisons between two things of different kinds ('run like the devil'; 'as deaf as a post'). It is sometimes confused with metaphor. The simile makes an explicit comparison, while the metaphor's comparison is implicit.

Poetic Forms

ballad (Latin *ballare* 'to dance')
The ballad is a form of traditional
narrative poetry, widespread in
Europe and the USA. Ballads are
metrically simple, sometimes (as in
Russia) unstrophic and unrhymed or
(as in Denmark) dependent on
assonance. Concerned with some
strongly emotional event, the ballad
is halfway between the lyric and the
epic. Most English ballads date from
the 15th century but may describe
earlier events. Poets of the Romantic
movement both in England and in
Germany were greatly influenced by
the ballad revival, as seen in, for
example, the *Lyrical Ballads* (1798) of
Wordsworth and Coleridge.

Historically, the ballad was
primarily intended for singing at the
communal ring-dance, the refrains
representing the chorus. Opinion is
divided as to whether the authorship
of the ballads may be attributed to
individual poets or to the community.
Later ballads tend to centre on a
popular folk hero, such as Robin
Hood or Jesse James.

Clerihew Clerihew, a humorous
verse form invented by Edmund
Clerihew Bentley, is characterized by a
first line consisting of a person's
name. The four lines rhyme AABB, but
the metre is often distorted for comic
effect. An example, from Bentley's
Biography for Beginners (1905), is: 'Sir
Christopher Wren/Said, I am going to
dine with some men./If anybody calls/
Say I am designing St Paul's'.

dramatic monologue The
dramatic monologue consists of a
speech by a single character, in
which his or her thoughts, character,
and situation are revealed to the
reader. It developed from the
soliloquy, a monologue spoken in a
play. It was a particularly popular
form in the 19th century. Examples
include Robert Browning's 'My Lost
Duchess' and T S Eliot's 'Love Song
of J Alfred Prufrock'.

elegy The elegy, an ancient Greek
verse form originally combining a
hexameter with a shorter line in a
couplet, was used by the Greeks for
epigrams, short narratives, and
discursive poems. It was adopted by
the Roman poets (Ovid, Propertius),
particularly for erotic verse. In
contemporary usage, the term refers
to a nostalgic poem or a lament,
often a funeral poem. Thomas Gray's
'Elegy Written in a Country Church-
Yard' (1751) is one of the best-
known elegies in English. An elegy is
likely to be a personal and private
expression of grief.

epic An epic is a narrative poem or
cycle of poems dealing with some
great deed – often the founding of a
nation or the forging of national
unity – and often using religious or
cosmological themes. The two main
epic poems in the Western tradition
are *The Iliad* and *The Odyssey,*
attributed to Homer, which were
probably intended to be chanted in
sections at feasts. Greek and later
criticism, which considered the
Homeric epic the highest form of
poetry, produced the genre of
secondary epic – such as the
Aeneid of Virgil, Tasso's *Jerusalem
Delivered,* and Milton's *Paradise Lost*
– which attempted to emulate
Homer. The term is also applied to
narrative poems of other traditions:
the Anglo-Saxon *Beowulf* and the
Finnish *Kalevala;* in India the
Ramayana and *Mahabharata;* and
the Babylonian *Gilgamesh.* All of
these evolved in different societies to
suit similar social needs and used
similar literary techniques.

epigram The epigram, a short,
witty, and pithy saying or short
poem, was common among writers
of ancient Rome, including Catullus
and Martial. In English, the epigram
has been used by Ben Jonson,
George Herrick, John Donne,
Alexander Pope, Jonathan Swift, W B
Yeats, and Ogden Nash. An epigram
was originally a religious inscription,
such as that on a tomb, but has
come to mean a miniature poem
summing up a single thought or
situation. The form is often based
on antithesis, as in Pope's line 'For
fools rush in where angels fear to
tread.' Epigrams are often satirical,
as in Wilde's observation: 'Speech
was given us to conceal our
thoughts.' While Greek epigrams
were usually satirical, in Roman
literature satire became the rule.

Among the earliest examples of
epigrams are those of the Greek
Simonides of Ceos, who wrote
epitaphs in elegiac couplets for the
Greeks who died in the Persian wars,
a typical example being his couplet
on the battle of Marathon: 'Fighting

stanza (Italian 'resting or stopping place') group of
lines in a poem. A stanza serves the same function
in poetry as a paragraph in prose. Stanzas are
often of uniform length and separated by a blank
line.

stream of consciousness narrative technique in
which a writer presents directly the uninterrupted
flow of a character's thoughts, impressions, and
feelings, without the conventional devices of dialogue and description. It first came to be widely
used in the early 20th century. Leading exponents
have included the novelists Virginia Woolf, James
Joyce, and William Faulkner.

stress pattern of emphasis in the metre of poetry;
also, the emphasis in any multisyllable word.
Repeated patterns of stressed and unstressed syllables are divided into feet (see foot) and form
the rhythm of the verse.

syllepsis (Greek *sun*, 'together', *lambanein*, 'to
take') figure of speech in which one word acts in
a sentence with two or more others; it applies

Poetic Forms (continued)

for Greece, the Athenians at Marathon laid low the might of the gilded Medes'. The famous *Palatine Anthology* contains about 4,000 Greek epigrams from 700 BC–AD 1000.

The English epigram began with John Heywood, but the poet who employed it to best effect was Pope, as with 'You beat your pate and fancy wit will come: Knock as you please, there's nobody at home.' Prior, Goldsmith, and Garrick all used epigrams effectively, as in the 19th century did Byron, Thomas Hood, Moore, Landor, and Coleridge, who described the epigram itself in a couplet: 'What is an epigram? A dwarfish whole, Its body brevity, and wit its soul'. Later writers who used the form effectively have included Rudyard Kipling, Hilaire Belloc, and George Bernard Shaw.

free verse Poetry without metrical form is called free verse. At the beginning of the 20th century, many poets believed that the 19th century had accomplished most of what could be done with regular metre, and rejected it, in much the same spirit as John Milton in the 17th century had rejected rhyme, preferring irregular metres that made it possible to express thought clearly and without distortion. This was true of T S Eliot and the Imagists; it was also true of poets who, like the Russians Sergey Esenin and Vladimir Mayakovsky, placed emphasis on public performance. The shift to free verse began under the very different

influences of US poet Walt Whitman and French poet Stéphane Mallarmé. Poets including Robert Graves and W H Auden have criticized free verse on the ground that it lacks the difficulty of true accomplishment, but their own metrics would have been considered loose by earlier critics. The freeness of free verse is largely relative.

haiku Haiku, a seventeen-syllable Japanese verse form, is usually divided into three lines of five, seven, and five syllables. Bashō popularized the form in the 17th century. It evolved from the 31-syllable *tanka* form dominant from the 8th century. Traditionally haiku contain a word or expression relating the poem to a particular season; for example, 'the moon' refers to autumn, 'the hazy moon' to spring. Within each season, haiku are subclassified by topic: weather, fields and mountains; temples and shrines; human affairs; birds and other animals; trees and flowers. The stress on simplicity and intuitive perception came to haiku from Zen Buddhism. The two greatest haiku poets after Bashō were Yosa Buson (1716–1783) and Kobayashi Issa (1763–1827).

limerick The limerick is a five-line humorous verse, often nonsensical. It first appeared in England in about 1820 and was popularized by Edward Lear. An example is:
'There was a young lady of Riga,
Who rode with a smile on a tiger;
They returned from the ride
With the lady inside,

And the smile on the face of the tiger.'

lyric poem Lyric poetry is a genre; it does not imply a particular rhyme scheme or technique. Any short, personal, and passionate form of verse can be called a lyric poem. Sonnets, odes, and elegies are lyric poems, for example, since they express strong feeling or ideas. Originally, a lyric was a song sung to a lyre, and song texts are still called lyrics.

ode An ode is a lyric poem of complex form. Odes originated in ancient Greece, where they were chanted to a musical accompaniment. Classical writers of odes include Sappho, Pindar, Horace, and Catullus. English poets who adopted the form include Spenser, Milton, Dryden, and Keats.

sonnet The sonnet is a 14-line poem of Italian origin that was introduced to England by Thomas Wyatt in the form used by Petrarch (rhyming *abba abba cdcdcd* or *cdecde*). The difference in the rhyme scheme of the first eight lines (the octet) and the last six (the sestet) reflected a change in mood or direction of the Petrarchan sonnet. Sonnets of Milton and Wordsworth took this form. Shakespeare used the form *abab cdcd efef gg*. In the final couplet Shakespeare summed up the argument of the sonnet or introduced a new, perhaps contradictory, idea.

properly to each of the other words, but the sense differs in each case. An example taken from Dickens is 'Miss Bolo went home in a flood of tears and a sedan chair'. Syllepsis differs from zeugma, with which it is often identified, by being grammatically correct. In zeugma the single word actually fails to make sense with one of the two to which it is applied.

Symbolism in the arts, the use of symbols as a device for concentrating or intensifying meaning. The Symbolist movement in art flourished during the last two decades of the 19th century.

Symbolist artists rejected Realism and Impressionism, seeking to express moods and psychological states. Their subjects were often mythological, mystical, or fantastic. Leading exponents included Baudelaire, Rimbaud, Mallarmé, Verlaine, and Maeterlinck.

verse arrangement of words in a rhythmic pattern, which may depend on the length of syllables (as in Greek or Latin verse), or on stress, as in English. Classical Greek verse depended upon quantity, a long syllable being regarded as occupying twice the time taken up by a short syllable.

Noteworthy Poets

Akhmatova Anna (adopted name of Anna Andreyevna Gorenko) (1889–1966) Russian poet and member of the Acmeist movement; her works include 'Requiem'

Apollinaire Guillaume (adopted name of Wilhelm Apollinaris de Kostrowitsky) (1880–1918) French avant-garde poet of Polish descent who wrote experimental poems in such volumes as *Alcools/Alcohol* and *Calligrammes/Word Pictures*

Aragon Louis (1897–1982) French poet, novelist, and leading Surrealist whose work includes *Le Crève-coeur/Heartbreak* and *Les Yeux d'Elsa/Elsa's Eyes*

Ariosto Ludovico (1474–1533) Italian poet and author of the epic poem *Orlando Furioso/Orlando Enraged*

Bashō (adopted name of Matsuo Munefusa) (1644–1694) Japanese poet and haiku master; his work *The Narrow Road to the Deep North* combines haiku and prose

Baudelaire Charles (Pierre) (1821–1867) influential French poet who combined rhythmical and musical perfection with morbid romanticism, symbolism, and eroticism, as in *Les Fleurs du Mal/Flowers of Evil*

Betjeman John (1906–1984) English poet laureate and essayist who wrote romantic and nostalgic light verse, such as the collection *New Bats in Old Belfries*

Blake William (1757–1827) English Romantic poet, artist, engraver, and spiritual visionary whose works include *Songs of Innocence*

Boileau-Despréaux Nicolas (1636–1711) French poet and critic whose works include *L'Art poétique/The Art of Poetry*

Brodsky Joseph (Aleksandrovich) (1940–1996) Russian Nobel prizewinning poet and US poet laureate, known for his wit and understatement, as in *A Part of Speech*

Brooke Rupert (Chawner) (1887–1915) English poet and symbol of the 'lost generation' whose war sonnets include 'The Soldier'

Browning Elizabeth (Moulton) Barrett (born Barrett) (1806–1861) English poet whose work includes the poetic novel *Aurora Leigh*

Browning Robert (1812–1889) English poet who specialized in dramatic monologue, as in *Bishop Blougram's Apology*

Burns Robert (1759–1796) Scottish poet who wrote in Scots dialect, as in *Poems, Chiefly in the Scottish Dialect* and 'Tam O'Shanter'

Byron (George Gordon Noel) Lord (1788–1824) English Romantic poet and political liberal who wrote the satirical epic *Don Juan*

Camoêns or Camoes Luis Vaz de (1524–1580) Portuguese poet and soldier whose *Os Lusiades/The Lusiadas* is Portugal's national epic

Carew Thomas (*c.* 1595–*c.* 1640) English Cavalier poet and author of *Coelum Britannicum*

Catullus Caius Valerius (*c.* 84–*c.* 54 BC) Roman lyric poet who wrote in a variety of metres, forms, and styles

Chatterton Thomas (1752–1770) English poet whose medieval style inspired English Romanticism

Chaucer Geoffrey (*c.* 1343–1400) the most influential English poet of the Middle Ages; his *The Canterbury Tales* shows his genius for metre and characterization

Chrétien de Troyes (died *c.* 1183) French poet whose epics introduced the Holy Grail concept, as in *Lancelot, ou le chavalier de la charrette/Lancelot, or the Knight of the Cart*

Coleridge Samuel Taylor (1772–1834) English Romantic poet whose poems include 'The Rime of the Ancient Mariner' and 'Kubla Khan'

cummings e(dward) e(stlin) (1894–1962) US poet whose work incorporates idiosyncratic punctuation and typography, as in *Tulips and Chimneys*

Dafydd ap Gwilym (*c.* 1340–*c.* 1400) Welsh poet concerned with nature whose work contains references to Classical and Italian poetry

Dante Alighieri (1265–1321) Italian poet who wrote *La divina commedia/The Divine Comedy*, an epic journey through Hell, Purgatory, and Paradise

Noteworthy poets (continued)

Day-Lewis C(ecil) (1904–1972) influential left-wing Irish poet of the 1930s and British poet laureate (1968–72)

Dickinson Emily (Elizabeth) (1830–1886) US poet whose poetry is characterized by wit and boldness, as in 'I Could Not Stop for Death'

Donne John (1572–1631) English metaphysical poet and preacher who wrote powerful poems about sexual love and his relationship with God

Dryden John (1631–1700) English poet laureate and dramatist of satiric verse in the form of the heroic couplet whose work includes 'A Song for St Cecilia's Day' and 'Absalom and Achitophel'

Eliot T(homas) S(tearns) (1888–1965) US-born English Nobel prizewinning poet, playwright, and critic whose poem *The Waste Land* is experimental in form and rhythm

Eluard Paul (adopted name of Eugène Grindel) (1895–1952) surrealist French poet who wrote about love and war, as in his collection *Poésie et vérité/Poetry and Truth*

Esenin or **Yesenin** Sergey Aleksandrovich (1895–1925) Russian poet involved in the Symbolist and Imaginist movements

Firdausi (adopted name of Abdul Qasim Mansur) (*c.* 935–*c.* 1020) Persian epic poet; his *The Book of Kings* is a history of Persia

Frost Robert (Lee) (1874–1963) US poet whose verse is flavoured with New England speech patterns and penetrating vision, as in 'The Road Not Taken'

Gautier Théophile (1811–1872) French Romantic poet who emphasized perfect form, beautiful language, and imagery, as in *Emaux et camés/Enamels and Cameos*

Gay John (1685–1732) English poet and dramatist whose *Trivia* depicts London in verse

Ginsberg Allen (1926–1997) US poet whose poetry is informed by politics and Oriental philosophies, and whose 'Howl' shaped the spirit of the Beat Generation

Graves Robert (Ranke) (1895–1985) English poet and writer who first achieved notice for his war poetry, but who later wrote some of the finest of modern love poems

Goethe Johann Wolfgang von (1749–1832) German Romantic poet, dramatist and novelist whose poetry collections include *Roman Elegies*

Gray Thomas (1716–1771) English poet whose poetry was a precursor of Romanticism, and whose 'Elegy Written in a Country Churchyard' is a dignified contemplation of death

Heaney Seamus (Justin) (1939–) Irish Nobel prizewinning poet and critic who writes about Northern Ireland and Ireland's cultural heritage, and whose works include 'Field Work'

Heine Heinrich (1797–1856) German Romantic poet, journalist, and satirist whose work includes *Das Buch der Lieder/Book of Songs*

Herbert George (1593–1633) English poet whose poems embody religious struggles, as in 'The Temple'

Hesiod (8th century BC) Greek poet, the 'father of Greek didactic poetry', whose surviving known works are the epics *Theogony* and *Works and Days*

Homer (9th or 8th century BC) Greek poet, reputed author of the great epic poems *Iliad* and *Odyssey*, originally composed orally, and notable for their vivid imagery and powerful depiction of emotion

Hopkins Gerard Manley (1844–1889) English Jesuit priest and profoundly religious poet whose innovative poems include 'The Wreck of the Deutschland'

Horace (Quintus Horatius Flaccus) (65–8 BC) Roman lyric and satirical poet whose work includes *Odes* and *Epistles*

Housman A(lfred) E(dward) (1859–1936) English poet and classical scholar; his *A Shropshire Lad* is a series of simple ballad-like poems

Hughes Ted (Edward James) (1930–1998) English poet and poet laureate whose poetry reflects on nature's harshness and power, as in 'Crow'

Noteworthy poets (continued)

Iqbal Muhammad (1873–1938) Islamic poet whose poetry urged Muslims to take their place in the modern world

Juvenal (Decimus Junius Juvenalis) (c. 60– c. 130) Roman satirical poet whose vitriolic and politically provocative *Satires* lament the passing of traditional moral and social values

Keats John (1795–1821) English Romantic poet whose works include 'Ode to a Nightingale' and 'La Belle Dame sans Merci'

Kipling (Joseph) Rudyard (1865–1936) Nobel prizewinning, Indian-born English poet and writer who emphasized moral viewpoints, as in 'Gunga Din'

La Fontaine Jean de (1621–1695) French poet of witty and bawdy tales in verse, such as *Contes et nouvelles en vers/Stories and Tales in Verse*

Lamartine Alphonse Marie Louis de (1790–1869) French poet whose work is characterized by personal romantic poems, such as *Méditations poétiques/Poetical Meditations*

Larkin Philip (Arthur) (1922–1985) English poet who wrote perfectionist, pessimistic verse, such as 'The Less Deceived'

Lermontov Mikhail Yurevich (1814–1841) Russian Romantic poet and novelist whose poems include *Demon*

Li Po (c. 705–762) Chinese poet whose poems are characterized by exuberance, bold imagination, and intense feeling

Longfellow Henry Wadsworth (1807–1882) US poet who is known for ballads, such as 'Excelsior', and mythic narrative epics

Mallarmé Stéphane (1842–1898) French Symbolist poet of condensed, hermetic verse and unorthodox syntax, as in *L'Après-midi d'un faune/The Afternoon of a Faun*

Mandelstam Osip Emilievich (1891–1938) Russian poet and literary critic whose poetry includes the collection *Tistia*

Marlowe Christopher (1564–1593) English poet and dramatist whose verse includes *Hero and Leander*

Masefield John (1878–1967) English poet, novelist, and poet laureate; his poetry collections include *Salt Water Ballads*

Mickiewicz Adam Bernard (1798–1855) Polish revolutionary poet whose *Pan Tadeusz/Master Thadeus* is Poland's national epic

Milton John (1608–1674) English poet and writer who wrote the epic *Paradise Lost*

Muir Ewin (1887–1959) Scottish poet who explored dreams, myths, and menaces, as in *Autobiography*

Neruda Pablo (adopted name of Neftali Ricardo Reyes y Basoatto) (1904–1973) Chilean Nobel prizewinning poet and diplomat who wrote epic poems about the American continent, including *Canto General de Chile*

Novalis (Friedrich Leopold, Freiherr von Hardenberg) (1772–1801) pioneer of German Romantic poetry whose work includes *Hymnen an die Nacht/Hymns to the Night*

Ovid (Publius Ovidius Naso) (43 BC–AD 17) Roman poet whose works, such as *Ars Amatoria/The Art of Love* and *Tristia/Sorrows*, are distinguished by technical skill and an ironic, sophisticated style

Owen Wilfred (Edward Salter) (1893–1918) English poet who wrote moving war poetry such as 'Anthem for Doomed Youth'

Pasternak Boris Leonidovich (1890–1960) Russian poet and novelist whose poetry collections include *My Sister, Life*

Paz Octavio (1914–1998) Mexican poet and essayist, influenced by Marxism, Surrealism, and Aztec mythology, whose poetry includes *Piedra del sol/Sun Stone*

Pearse Patrick (Henry) (1879–1916) Irish poet prominent in Irish nationalism

Petrarch or **Petrarca** Francesco (1304–1374) Italian poet and humanist whose influential love poetry was inspired by his beloved Laura

Plath Sylvia (1932–1963) US poet and novelist who wrote highly personal and intense poems expressing desolation; her *Collected Poems* won a Pulitzer prize

Noteworthy poets (continued)

Pope Alexander (1688–1744) English poet and satirist whose works include the mock epic *The Rape of the Lock*

Pound Ezra (Loomis) (1885–1972) US poet and cultural critic who revolutionized modern poetry and promoted Imagism, as in *Cantos*

Pushkin Aleksandr Sergeyevich (1799–1837) Russian romantic poet and writer; *Eugene Onegin* is his novel in verse

Rilke Rainer Maria (1875–1926) Austrian writer of verse characterized by mystic pantheism, notably *Duino Elegies*

Rimbaud (Jean Nicolas) Arthur (1854–1891) French Symbolist poet who wrote most of his verse before the age of 20; *Les Illuminations* is an example

Roethke Theodore (1908–1963) US poet whose collections include *Words for the Wind*

Ronsard Pierre de (1524–1585) French poet with a lightly sensitive style, as in *Amours de Marie/Loves of Marie*

Rossetti Christina (Georgina) (1830–1894) English poet whose work includes *Goblin Market and Other Poems*

Sappho (*c.* 620–*c.* 580 BC) Greek lyric poet, much admired by her contemporaries, whose metrically innovative work, of which only fragments remain, includes poems of love and on natural themes

Sassoon Siegfried (Lorraine) (1886–1967) English writer whose *War Poems* express his generation's disillusionment

Senghor Léopold Sédar (1906–   ) Senegalese politician and poet who founded *négritude,* a black literary and philosophical movement, and whose work includes *Chants d'ombre/ Shadow Songs*

Shelley Percy Bysshe (1792–1822) English Romantic lyric poet who fought against religion and for political freedom; his works include 'Ode to the West Wind' and 'The Skylark'

Sidney Philip (1554–1586) English poet and soldier whose poetry includes *Arcadia*

Spenser Edmund (*c.* 1552–1599) English poet whose poem *The Faerie Queene* is a moral allegory

Tagore Rabindranath (1861–1941) Nobel prizewinning Indian writer whose poetry collections include *Gitanjali*

Tasso Torquato (1544–1595) Italian poet who wrote the romantic epic poem of the First Crusade, *Gerusalem liberata/Jerusalem Delivered*

Tate Nahum (1652–1715) Irish poet and British poet laureate whose poetry includes *While Shepherds Watched*

Tennyson Alfred (1809–1892) English poet laureate of majestic musical verse typified by the poem 'The Lady of Shalott'

Thomas Dylan (Marlais) (1914–1952) Welsh poet of complex imagery and musicality, as in *Poem in October*

Verlaine Paul Marie (1844–1896) French Symbolic lyric poet influenced by Charles Baudelaire and Arthur Rimbaud, as in *Poèmes saturniens/Saturnine Poems*

Villon François (1431–*c.* 1465) French poet of satiric humour, pathos, and lyric power, as in *Petit Testament*

Virgil (Publius Vergilius Maro) (70–19 BC) Roman poet who wrote the great heroic epic poem of Roman history, the *Aeneid*

Walcott Derek (Walton) (1930–   ) St Lucian Nobel prizewinning poet and playwright whose poetry includes *Omeros*

Walther von der Vogelweide (*c.* 1170–1230) German poet who wrote songs about courtly love

Whitman Walt(er) (1819–1892) US poet who used unconventional free verse, as in *Song of Myself*

Wordsworth William (1770–1850) English Romantic poet laureate whose work includes *Lyrical Ballads* and *The Prelude*

Yeats W(illiam) B(utler) (1865–1939) Nobel prizewinning Irish poet and leader of the

---

Noteworthy poets (continued)

Celtic revival whose works include the collections *The Wild Swans at Coole* and *The Winding Stair*

Yevtushenko Yevgeny Aleksandrovich (1933–   ) Soviet poet who wrote *Zima Junction* and *Babi Yar*

Zephaniah Benjamin (Obadiah Iqbal) (1958–   ) British poet, dramatist, and writer who draws his themes from the news, pubs, and streets, and from contemporary British politics, and whose verse includes 'Pen Rhythm' and 'The Dread Affair'

Noteworthy Dramatists

Aeschylus (*c.* 524–*c.* 456 BC) Greek tragic dramatist whose powerful plays include *Seven against Thebes* and the *Oresteia* trilogy

Albee Edward Franklin (1928–   ) US playwright, author of *Who's Afraid of Virginia Woolf?* and Pulitzer prizewinners *A Delicate Balance, Seascape,* and *Three Tall Women*

Anderson Maxwell (1888–1959) US dramatist, author of *What Price Glory?* and Pulitzer prizewinner *Both Your Houses*

Anouilh Jean (1910–1987) French dramatist, author of *Antigone* and *Becket*

Aristophanes (*c.* 450–*c.* 380 BC) Greek comic dramatist whose works include *The Frogs* and *Lysistrata*

Ayckbourn Alan (1939–   ) English playwright, author of *Relatively Speaking* and *The Norman Conquests* trilogy

Barrie J(ames) M(atthew) (1860–1937) Scottish dramatist and novelist, author of the plays *The Admirable Crichton* and *Peter Pan*

Beaumarchais Pierre Augustin Caron de (1732–1799) French comic dramatist, author of *Le Barbier de Séville/The Barber of Séville* and *Le Mariage de Figaro/The Marriage of Figaro*

Beckett Samuel (Barclay) (1906–1989) Irish dramatist and novelist, author of the plays *Waiting for Godot* and *Endgame*

Belasco David (1859–1931) US dramatist and producer, author of *Madame Butterfly* and *The Girl of the Golden West*

Bolt Robert Oxton (1924–1995) English historical dramatist and screenwriter, author of *A Man for All Seasons*

Brecht Bertolt (Eugen Berthold Friedrich) (1898–1956) German dramatist and poet, author of many political dramas, including *Mutter Courage und ihre Kinder/Mother Courage and Her Children* and *Der kaukasische Kreiderkreis/The Caucasian Chalk Circle*

Čapek Karel (1890–1938) Czech writer, author of *RUR,* in which he coined the word 'robot'

Chapman George (*c.* 1559–1634) English dramatist who wrote *Bussy D'Ambois*

Chekhov Anton Pavlovich (1860–1904) Russian dramatist and writer of short stories whose plays include *Uncle Vanya, The Three Sisters,* and *The Cherry Orchard*

Congreve William (1670–1729) English dramatist who wrote *The Way of the World*

Corneille Pierre (1606–1684) French classical dramatist, author of *Cinna, Mélite,* and *Le Cid*

Dekker Thomas (*c.* 1570–1632) English dramatist who wrote *The Shoemaker's Holiday*

Dryden John (1631–1700) English poet and dramatist, author of *Marriage A-La-Mode*

Echegaray y Eizaguirre José (1832–1916) Spanish dramatist, author of *Madman or Saint* and *The World and his Wife*

Eliot T(homas) S(tearns) (1888–1965) US-born English poet and dramatist whose plays include *Murder in the Cathedral*

Euripides (*c.* 480–*c.* 406 BC) Greek tragic dramatist, ranked with Aeschylus and Sophocles, whose plays prefigured the later development of drama in dealing with ordinary people, and include *Andromache* and *The Trojan Women*

Feydeau Georges (1862–1921) French comic dramatist, author of *Le Dame de Chez Maxim/The Lady from Maxim's* and *Occupe-toi d'Amélie/Look after Lulu*

Fletcher John (1579–1625) English dramatist of

broad range, co-author of *Philaster* and *The Maid's Tragedy*

Fo Dario (1926–) Italian Nobel prizewinning dramatist of political satire and author of *Morte accidentale di un anarchico/Accidental Death of an Anarchist* and *Non si paya, no si paya/Can't Pay? Won't Pay!*

Ford John (1586–*c.* 1640) English dramatist who wrote *'Tis Pity She's a Whore*

Friel Brian (1929–) Northern Irish dramatist, author of *Philadelphia, Here I Come!* and *Dancing at Lughnasa*

Fry Christopher (Harris) (1907–) English dramatist, author of *The Lady's Not for Burning* and *Venus Observed*

Fugard Athol (Harold Lanigan) (1932–) South African dramatist, author of *The Blood Knot* and *Hello and Goodbye*

Gelber Jack (1932–) US playwright and novelist, author of *The Connection*

Genet Jean (1910–1986) French dramatist, novelist, and poet, author of *The Maids* and *The Balcony*

Giraudoux Jean (1882–1944) French dramatist and novelist whose plays include *La Guerre du Troie n'aura pas lieu/Tiger at the Gates*

Goethe Johann Wolfgang von (1749–1832) German Romantic poet, novelist, dramatist, and scholar, founder of modern German literature whose masterpiece is *Faust,* a poetic play

Gogol Nikolai (Vasilevich) (1809–1852) Russian novelist and dramatist whose best-known play is *The Inspector General*

Goldsmith Oliver (1728–1774) Irish dramatist who wrote *She Stoops to Conquer*

Gombrowicz Witold (1904–1969) Polish allegorical dramatist and novelist, author of *Ilona, Princess of Burgundy*

Gorky or **Gorki** Maksim (adopted name of Aleksei Maksimovich Peshkov) (1868–1936) Russian writer whose plays include *The Lower Depths*

Hare David (1947–) British satirical dramatist and screenwriter, author of *Slag* and *Pravda*

Hart Moss (1904–1961) US dramatist, author of *The Man Who Came to Dinner*

Hauptmann Gerhart Johann Robert (1862–1946) German Nobel prizewinning dramatist, author of *Die Weben/The Weavers*

Havel Václav (1936–) Czech dramatist and politician, author of *Zahradní slavnost/The Garden Party* and *Vyrozumění/The Memorandum*

Hellman Lillian (Florence) (1907–1984) US political and social dramatist, author of *The Children's Hour* and *Toys in the Attic*

Heywood Thomas (*c.* 1574–1641) English dramatist who wrote *A Woman Killed with Kindness*

Hochhuth Rolf (1931–) Swiss dramatist, author of *Soldaten/Soldiers* and *Der Stellvertreter/The Representative*

Ibsen Henrik Johan (1828–1906) Norwegian dramatist and poet, author of *Et dukkehjem/A Doll's House* and *Gengangere/Ghosts*

Ionesco Eugène (1912–1994) Romanian-born French dramatist, author of *La Cantatrice chauve/The Bald Prima Donna* and *Le Roi se meurt/Exit the King*

Jarry Alfred (1873–1907) French satiric dramatist whose play *King Ubu* foreshadowed the Theatre of the Absurd

Jonson Ben(jamin) (1572–1637) English dramatist, poet, and critic, author of *Every Man in his Humour* and *Volpone*

Kyd Thomas (1558–1594) English dramatist who wrote *The Spanish Tragedy*

Lessing Gotthold Ephraim (1729–1781) German dramatist and critic, author of *Miss Sara Sampson* and *Emilia Galotti*

Lorca Federico Garcia (1899–1936) Spanish poet and dramatist whose plays include *Bodas de sangre/Blood Wedding* and *La casa de Bernarda Alba/The House of Bernarda Alba*

Maeterlinck Maurice (1862–1949) Belgian writer and dramatist whose plays included *L'Oiseau bleu/The Blue Bird*

Marlowe Christopher (1564–1593) English poet and dramatist, author of *Tamburlaine the Great* and *Dr Faustus*

Miller Arthur (1915–) US dramatist, author of *Death of a Salesman* and *The Crucible*

Molière (Jean-Baptiste Poquelin) (1622–1673) French satirical dramatist and actor, author of *Le Tartuffe/The Impostor* and *L'Ecole des femmes/The School for Wives*

Nichols Peter Richard (1927–) English dramatist, author of *A Day in the Death of Joe Egg* and *Passion Play*

O'Casey Sean (adopted name of John Casey) (1884–1964) Irish dramatist, author of *Juno and the Paycock* and *The Plough and the Stars*

O'Neill Eugene Gladstone (1888–1953) US playwright, author of Pulitzer prizewinners *Beyond the Horizon* and *A Long Day's Journey into Night*

Orton Joe (John Kingsley) (1933–1967) English dramatist, author of *Loot* and *What the Butler Saw*

Osborne John (James) (1929–1994) English dramatist, author of *Look Back in Anger* and *The Entertainer*

Ostrovsky Aleksander Nikolaevich (1823–1886) Russian dramatist, author of *The Storm* and *The Snow Maiden*

Pinero Arthur Wing (1855–1934) English dramatist, author of *The Magistrate* and *The Second Mrs Tanqueray*

Pinter Harold (1930–) English dramatist and actor, author of *The Birthday Party* and *The Caretaker*

Pirandello Luigi (1867–1936) Italian Nobel prizewinning dramatist, novelist, and short story writer, author of *Sei personaggi in cerca d'autore/Six Characters in Search of an Author*

Plautus Maccius (*c.* 254–*c.* 184 BC) Roman comic dramatist who took plots from Greek comedy to produce works, such as *Miles Gloriosus/The Boastful Soldier* and *Amphitryon*

Priestley J(ohn) B(oynton) (1894–1984) English dramatist and novelist, author of *An Inspector Calls* and *Dangerous Corner*

Racine Jean Baptiste (1639–1699) French dramatist, author of *Andromaque/Andromache* and *Phèdre/Phaedra*

Rice Elmer Leopold (1892–1967) US dramatist, author of *The Adding Machine* and Pulitzer prizewinner *Street Scene*

Rostand Edmond (1868–1918) French poetic dramatist, author of *Cyrano de Bergerac* and *L'Aiglon*

Schiller Johann Christoph Friedrich von (1759–1805) German poet and dramatist whose plays include *Maria Stuart* and *Wallenstein*

Seneca (Lucius Annaeus) (*c.* 4 BC–AD 65) Roman orator, statesman, and dramatist who wrote *Medea* and other tragedies

Seymour Alan (1927–) Australian dramatist, author of *The One Day of the Year*

Shaffer Peter (1926–) English dramatist, author of *Equus* and *Amadeus*

Shakespeare William (1564–1616) English dramatist and poet, author of *Romeo and Juliet, As You Like It, Henry IV,* and *Hamlet*

Shaw George Bernard (1856–1950) Irish dramatist, critic, and novelist, author of *Man and Superman, Pygmalion,* and *St Joan*

Shepard Sam (adopted name of Samuel Shepard Rogers) (1943–) US dramatist and actor, author of Pulitzer prizewinner *Buried Child*

Sheridan Richard Brinsley (1751–1816) Irish dramatist and politician whose social comedies include *The Rivals* and *School for Scandal*

Sherwood Robert Emmet (1896–1955) US dramatist, author of Pulitzer prizewinners *Idiot's Delight* and *Abe Lincoln in Illinois*

Simon (Marvin) Neil (1927–) US dramatist and screenwriter, author of *The Odd Couple* and Pulitzer prizewinner *Lost in Yonkers*

Sophocles (*c.* 496–406 BC) Greek tragic dramatist whose plays include *Oedipus Rex/Oedipus the King* and *Antigone*

Soyinka Wole (Akinwande Oluwole Soyinka) (1934–) Nigerian novelist, poet, and dramatist whose plays include *Death and the King's Horsemen*

Stoppard Tom (adopted name of Tomas Straussler) (1937–) Czech-born British dramatist, author of *Rosencrantz and Guildenstern are Dead* and *Arcadia*

Strindberg (Johan) August (1849–1912) Swedish dramatist and novelist, author of *Dödsdansen/The Dance of Death* and *Fadren/The Father*

Synge J(ohn) M(illington) (1871–1909) Irish dramatist, author of *Riders to the Sea* and *The Playboy of the Western World*

Terence (Publius Terentius Afer) (*c.* 190–*c.* 159 BC) Roman comic dramatist whose stylish plays, based on Greek dramas, include *Eunuchus* and *Adelphi/The Brothers*

Vega Lope Félix de (Carpio) (1562–1635) Spanish poet and founder of modern Spanish drama whose plays include *Fuenteovejuna/The Sheep-Well*

Webster John (*c.* 1580–*c.* 1625) English dramatist, author of *The White Devil* and *The Duchess of Malfi*

Wedekind Frank (1864–1918) German dramatist, author of *Frühlings Erwachen/The Awakening of Spring* and *Büchse der Pandora/Pandora's Box*

Weiss Peter (Ulrich) (1916–1982) German-born Swedish dramatist, novelist, and film producer, author of *Marat/Sade* and *Die Ermittlung/The Investigation*

Wilde Oscar (Fingal O'Flahertie Wills) (1854–1900) Irish writer and dramatist, famous for a series of sharp comedies, including *The Importance of Being Earnest*

Wilder Thornton (Niven) (1897–1975) US dramatist and novelist, author of Pulitzer prizewinners *Our Town* and *The Skin of Our Teeth*

Williams Tennessee (adopted name of Thomas Lanier Williams) (1911–1983) US dramatist, author of Pulitzer prizewinners *A Streetcar Named Desire* and *Cat on a Hot Tin Roof*

Wilson August (1945–   ) US playwright, author of Pulitzer prizewinners *Fences* and *The Piano Lesson*

Zuckmayer Carl (1896–1977) German dramatist and writer, author of *The Devil's General* and *The Cold Light*

LITERARY PRIZES

Awards for literature are usually annual and for a specific category (poetry, nonfiction, children's, and so on). The Nobel Prize for Literature is international; other prizes are usually for books first published in a particular language or country, such as the Booker Prize (Commonwealth), the Prix Goncourt (France), the Pulitzer prizes (USA), the Miles Franklin Award (Australia), and the Akutagawa Prize (Japan).

Booker Prize

This UK literary prize of £20,000 is awarded annually in October.

Year	Winner	Awarded for	Year	Winner	Awarded for
1969	P H Newby	Something to Answer For	1984	Anita Brookner	Hotel du Lac
			1985	Keri Hulme	The Bone People
1970	Bernice Rubens	The Elected Member	1986	Kingsley Amis	The Old Devils
1971	V S Naipaul	In a Free State	1987	Penelope Lively	Moon Tiger
1972	John Berger	G	1988	Peter Carey	Oscar and Lucinda
1973	J G Farrell	The Siege of Krishnapur	1989	Kazuo Ishiguro	The Remains of the Day
1974	Nadine Gordimer	The Conservationist	1990	A S Byatt	Possession
	Stanley Middleton	Holiday	1991	Ben Okri	The Famished Road
1975	Ruth Prawer Jhabvala	Heat and Dust	1992	Barry Unsworth	Sacred Hunger
1976	David Storey	Saville		Michael Ondaatje	The English Patient
1977	Paul Scott	Staying On	1993	Roddy Doyle	Paddy Clarke Ha Ha Ha
1978	Iris Murdoch	The Sea, The Sea	1994	James Kelman	How Late It Was, How Late
1979	Penelope Fitzgerald	Offshore			
1980	William Golding	Rites of Passage	1995	Pat Barker	The Ghost Road
1981	Salman Rushdie	Midnight's Children	1996	Graham Swift	Last Orders
1982	Thomas Keneally	Schindler's Ark	1997	Arundhati Roy	The God of Small Things
1983	J M Coetzee	The Life and Times of Michael K	1998	Ian McEwan	Amsterdam

Nobel Prize for Literature

Year	Winner(s)[1]	Year	Winner(s)[1]
1901	René Sully-Prodhomme (France)	1914	no award
1902	Theodor Mommsen (Germany)	1915	Romain Rolland (France)
1903	Bjørnsterne Bjørnsen (Norway)	1916	Verver von Heidenstam (Sweden)
1904	Frédéric Mistral (France); José Echegaray (Spain)	1917	Karl Gjellerup (Denmark); Henrik Pontoppidan (Denmark)
1905	Henryk Sienkiewicz (Poland)		
1906	Giosuè Carducci (Italy)	1918	Erik Axel Karlfeldt (Sweden) (declined)
1907	Rudyard Kipling (UK)	1919	Carl Spitteler (Switzerland)
1908	Rudolk Eucken (Germany)	1920	Knut Hamsun (Norway)
1909	Selma Lagerlöf (Sweden)	1921	Anatole France (France)
1910	Paul von Heyse (Germany)	1922	Jacinto Benavente y Martinez (Spain)
1911	Maurice Maeterlinck (Belgium)	1923	William Butler Yeats (Ireland)
1912	Gerhart Hauptmann (Germany)	1924	Władysław Stanisław Reymont (Poland)
1913	Rabindranath Tagore (India)	1925	George Bernard Shaw (Ireland)

Nobel Prize for Literature (continued)

Year	Winner(s)[1]	Year	Winner(s)[1]
1926	Grazia Deledda (Italy)	1963	George Seferis (Greece)
1927	Henri Bergson (France)	1964	Jean-Paul Sartre (France) (declined)
1928	Sigrid Undset (Norway)	1965	Mikhail Sholokhov (USSR)
1929	Thomas Mann (Germany)	1966	Shmuel Yosef Agnon (Israel); Nelly Sachs (Sweden)
1930	Sinclair Lewis (USA)	1967	Miguel Angel Asturias (Guatemala)
1931	Erik Axel Karlfeldt (Sweden) (posthumous award)	1968	Yasunari Kawabata (Japan)
1932	John Galsworthy (UK)	1969	Samuel Beckett (Ireland)
1933	Ivan Bunin (USSR)	1970	Aleksandr Solzhenitsyn (USSR)
1934	Luigi Pirandello (Italy)	1971	Pablo Neruda (Chile)
1935	no award	1972	Heinrich Böll (West Germany)
1936	Eugene O'Neill (USA)	1973	Patrick White (Australia)
1937	Roger Martin du Gard (France)	1974	Eyvind Johnson (Sweden); Harry Martinson (Sweden)
1938	Pearl Buck (USA)	1975	Eugenio Montale (Italy)
1939	Frans Eemil Sillanpää (Finland)	1976	Saul Bellow (USA)
1940	no award	1977	Vicente Aleixandre (Spain)
1941	no award	1978	Isaac Bashevis Singer (USA)
1942	no award	1979	Odysseus Elytis (Greece)
1943	no award	1980	Czesław Miłosz (USA)
1944	Johannes V Jensen (Denmark)	1981	Elias Canetti (Bulgaria)
1945	Gabriela Mistral (Chile)	1982	Gabriel García Márquez (Colombia)
1946	Hermann Hesse (Switzerland)	1983	William Golding (UK)
1947	André Gide (France)	1984	Jaroslav Seifert (Czechoslovakia)
1948	T S Eliot (UK)	1985	Claude Simon (France)
1949	William Faulkner (USA)	1986	Wole Soyinka (Nigeria)
1950	Bertrand Russell (UK)	1987	Joseph Brodsky (USA)
1951	Pär Lagerkvist (Sweden)	1988	Naguib Mahfouz (Egypt)
1952	François Mauriac (France)	1989	Camilo José Cela (Spain)
1953	Winston Churchill (UK)	1990	Octavio Paz (Mexico)
1954	Ernest Hemingway (USA)	1991	Nadine Gordimer (South Africa)
1955	Halldór Laxness (Iceland)	1992	Derek Walcott (Santa Lucia)
1956	Juan Ramón Jiménez (Spain)	1993	Toni Morrison (USA)
1957	Albert Camus (France)	1994	Kenzaburo Oe (Japan)
1958	Boris Pasternak (USSR) (declined)	1995	Seamus Heaney (Ireland)
1959	Salvatore Quasimodo (Italy)	1996	Wisława Szymborska (Poland)
1960	Saint-John Perse (France)	1997	Dario Fo (Italy)
1961	Ivo Andric (Yugoslavia)	1998	José Saramago (Portugal)
1962	John Steinbeck (USA)		

[1] Nationality given is the citizenship of recipient at the time award was made.

Pulitzer Prizes in Letters: Fiction

Year	Winner	Awarded for	Year	Winner	Awarded for
1918	Ernest Poole	*His Family*	1962	Edwin O'Connor	*The Edge of Sadness*
1919	Booth Tarkington	*The Magnificent Ambersons*	1963	William Faulkner	*The Reivers*
1920	no award		1964	no award	
1921	Edith Wharton	*The Age of Innocence*	1965	Shirley Ann Grau	*The Keepers of the House*
1922	Booth Tarkington	*Alice Adams*			
1923	Willa Cather	*One of Ours*	1966	Katherine Anne Porter	*The Collected Stories of Katherine Anne Porter*
1924	Margaret Wilson	*The Able McLaughlins*	1967	Bernard Malamud	*The Fixer*
1925	Edna Ferber	*So Big*	1968	William Styron	*The Confessions of Nat Turner*
1926	Sinclair Lewis	*Arrowsmith*			
1927	Louis Bromfield	*Early Autumn*	1969	N Scott Momaday	*House Made of Dawn*
1928	Thornton Wilder	*The Bridge of San Luis Rey*	1970	Jean Stafford	*Collected Stories*
			1971	no award	
1929	Julia Peterkin	*Scarlet Sister Mary*	1972	Wallace Stegner	*Angle of Repose*
1930	Oliver La Farge	*Laughing Boy*	1973	Eudora Welty	*The Optimist's Daughter*
1931	Margaret Ayer Barnes	*Years of Grace*			
1932	Pearl S Buck	*The Good Earth*	1974	no award	
1933	T S Stribling	*The Store*	1975	Michael Shaara	*The Killer Angels*
1934	Caroline Miller	*Lamb in His Bosom*	1976	Saul Bellow	*Humboldt's Gift*
1935	Josephine Winslow Johnson	*Now in November*	1977	no award	
			1978	James Alan McPherson	*Elbow Room*
1936	Harold L Davis	*Honey in the Horn*	1979	John Cheever	*The Stories of John Cheever*
1937	Margaret Mitchell	*Gone With the Wind*			
1938	John Phillips Marquand	*The Late George Apley*	1980	Norman Mailer	*The Executioner's Song*
1939	Marjorie Kinnan Rawlings	*The Yearling*	1981	John Kennedy Toole	*A Confederacy of Dunces*
1940	John Steinbeck	*The Grapes of Wrath*	1982	John Updike	*Rabbit is Rich*
1942	Ellen Glasgow	*In This Our Life*	1983	Alice Walker	*The Color Purple*
1943	Upton Sinclair	*Dragon's Teeth*	1984	William Kennedy	*Ironweed*
1944	Martin Flavin	*Journey in the Dark*	1985	Alison Lurie	*Foreign Affairs*
1945	John Hersey	*A Bell for Adano*	1986	Larry McMurtry	*Lonesome Dove*
1947	Robert Penn Warren	*All the King's Men*	1987	Peter Taylor	*A Summons to Memphis*
1948	James A Michener	*Tales of the South Pacific*			
			1988	Toni Morrison	*Beloved*
1949	James Gould Cozzens	*Guard of Honor*	1989	Anne Tyler	*Breathing Lessons*
1950	A B Guthrie Jr	*The Way West*	1990	Oscar Hijuelos	*The Mambo Kings Play Songs of Love*
1951	Conrad Richter	*The Town*			
1952	Herman Wouk	*The Caine Mutiny*	1991	John Updike	*Rabbit at Rest*
1953	Ernest Hemingway	*The Old Man and the Sea*	1992	Jane Smiley	*A Thousand Acres*
			1993	Robert Olen Butler	*A Good Scent From a Strange Mountain*
1955	William Faulkner	*A Fable*	1994	E Annie Proulx	*The Shipping News*
1956	MacKinley Kantor	*Andersonville*	1995	Carol Shields	*The Stone Diaries*
1957	no award		1996	Richard A Ford	*Independence Day*
1958	James Agee	*A Death in the Family*	1997	Steven Millhauser	*Martin Dressler: The Tale of an American Dreamer*
1959	Robert Lewis Taylor	*The Travels of Jamie McPheeters*			
1960	Allen Drury	*Advise and Consent*			
1961	Harper Lee	*To Kill a Mockingbird*	1998	Philip Roth	*American Pastoral*

GRAMMAR

All forms of a language, standard or otherwise, have their own grammatical systems, rules for combining words into phrases, clauses, sentences, and paragraphs. People often acquire several overlapping grammatical systems within one language; for example, a formal system for writing and standard communication and a less formal system for everyday and peer-group communication. When compared with Latin, English has been widely regarded as having less grammar or at least a simpler grammar; it would be truer, however, to say that English and Latin have different grammars, each complex in its own way.

Originally 'grammar' was an analytical approach to writing, intended to improve the understanding and the skills of scribes, philosophers, and writers. In the contemporary study of language – linguistics – grammar, or syntax, refers to the arrangement of the elements in a language for the purposes of acceptable communication in speech, writing, and print. The standardizing impact of print has meant that spoken or colloquial language is often perceived as less grammatical than written language.

Not even the most comprehensive grammar book (or grammar) of a language like English, French, Arabic, or Japanese completely covers or fixes the implicit grammatical system that people use in their daily lives. The rules and tendencies of natural grammar operate largely in nonconscious ways but can, for many social and professional purposes, be studied and developed for conscious as well as inherent skills. Recent theories of the way language functions include **phrase structure grammar**, **transformational grammar**, and **case grammar**.

adjective (Latin *adjectivus* 'added') grammatical part of speech for words that describe nouns (for example, *new* and *beautiful*, as in 'a new hat' and 'a beautiful day'). Adjectives generally have three degrees (grades or levels for the description of relationships): the positive degree (*new, beautiful*), the comparative degree (*newer, more beautiful*), and the superlative degree (*newest, most beautiful*).

English language

■ In written English, the ten most common words are: the, of, to, in, and, a, for, was, is, that. In spoken English, however, the top three are: the, and, I.

---

adverb grammatical part of speech for words that modify or describe verbs ('she ran *quickly*'),

adjectives ('a *beautifully* clear day'), and adverbs ('they did it *really* well'). Most adverbs are formed from adjectives or past participles by adding -*ly* (*quick: quickly*) or -*ally* (*automatic: automatically*).

apostrophe mark (') used in written English and some other languages. In English it serves primarily to indicate either a missing letter (*mustn't* for *must not*), number (*'47* for *1947*), or grammatical possession ('*John's* camera', '*women's* dresses'). It is often omitted in proper names (Publishers Association, Consumers Union, Actors Studio, *Collins Dictionary*). Many people otherwise competent in writing have great difficulty with the apostrophe, which has never been stable at any point in its history.

article grammatical part of speech. There are two articles in English: the **definite article** *the*, which

Some Commonly Misspelled Words

accommodation	conscientious	exercise	install	omit	separate
achieve	controversial	exhilarate	instalment	oneself	sergeant
acquittal	definitely	extravagant	jewellery	parallel	siege
address	dependant (noun)	February	league	paraphernalia	sieve
aggressive	dependent	foreign	liaise	permissible	sincerely
amount	(adjective)	friend	library	personnel	soldier
anemone	describe	fulfil	liquefy	Pharaoh	solemn
appearance	desiccate	gauge	literature	poisonous	supersede
asphalt	desperate	gazetteer	longitude	possess	targeted
attach	detach	government	manoeuvre	potatoes	terrestrial
banister	diarrhoea	grammar	Mediterranean	practice (noun)	tomatoes
beautiful	diphtheria	guarantee	millennium	practise (verb)	tranquillity
beginning	disappear	guard	millionaire	precede	traveller
bicycle	disappoint	handkerchief	mischievous	prejudice	unnecessary
biscuit	dissect	harass	mortgage	privilege	until
budgeted	dissipated	height	necessary	profession	unusual
business	ecstasy	hygiene	neither	pronunciation	unwieldy
cemetery	eighth	hypocrisy	niece	publicly	vetoed
cigarette	embarrass	idiosyncrasy	noticeable	questionnaire	vicious
collapsible	exaggerate	immediately	nuisance	receive	videoed
committee	excellent	independent (noun	occasion	repellent	Wednesday
competition	excitement	and adjective)	occurrence	seize	yield

serves to specify or identify a noun (as in 'This is *the* book I need'), and the **indefinite article** *a* or (before vowels) *an,* which indicates a single unidentified noun ('They gave me *a* piece of paper and *an* envelope').

colon punctuation mark (:) commonly used before a direct quotation (She said: 'Leave it out') or a list, or to add detail to a statement ('That is his cat: the fluffy white one').

comma punctuation mark (,) most commonly used to mark off a phrase or noun in apposition, mark off a subordinate clause or phrase, or separate items in a list.

conjunction grammatical part of speech that serves to connect words, phrases, and clauses. Coordinating conjunctions link parts of equal grammatical value; *and, but,* and *or* are the most common. Subordinating conjunctions link subordinate clauses to the main clause in a sentence; among the most common are *if, when,* and *though.*

exclamation mark or **exclamation point** punctuation mark (!) used to indicate emphasis or strong emotion ('That's terrible!'). It is appropriate after interjections ('Rats!'), emphatic greetings ('Yo!'), and orders ('Shut up!'), as well as

those sentences beginning *How* or *What* that are not questions ('How embarrassing!', 'What a surprise!').

hyphen punctuation mark (-) with two functions: to join words, parts of words, syllables, and so on, as an aid to sense; and to mark a word break at the end of a line. Adjectival compounds are hyphenated because they modify the noun jointly rather than separately ('a small-town boy' is a boy from a small town; 'a small town boy' is a small boy from a town). The use of hyphens with adverbs is redundant unless an identical adjective exists (*well, late, long*): 'late-blooming plant' but 'brightly blooming plant'.

infinitive basic form of a verb, the form by which verbs are identified: 'to be', 'to hit', 'to love', and so on. The infinitive form of the verb in English is always preceded by *to.*

inflection or **inflexion** in grammatical analysis, an ending or other element in a word that indicates its grammatical function (whether plural or singular, masculine or feminine, subject or object, and so on).

noun grammatical part of speech that names a person, animal, object, quality, idea, or time. Nouns can refer to objects such as *house, tree* (**concrete nouns**); specific persons and places such as *John Alden,* the *White House* (**proper nouns**); ideas such as *love, anger* (**abstract nouns**). In English many simple words are both noun and verb (*jump, reign, rain*). Adjectives are sometimes used as nouns ('a *local* man', 'one of the *locals*').

participle form of the verb. English has two forms, a **present participle** ending in -*ing* (for example, 'work*ing*' in 'They were *working*', '*working* men', and 'a hard-*working* team') and a **past participle** ending in -*ed* in regular verbs (for example, 'train*ed*' in 'They have been *trained* well', '*trained* soldiers', and 'a well-*trained* team').

part of speech grammatical function of a word, described in the grammatical tradition of the Western world, based on Greek and Latin. The four major parts of speech are the noun, verb, adjective, and adverb; the minor parts of speech vary according to schools of grammatical theory, but include the article, conjunction, preposition, and pronoun.

period in punctuation, another name for full stop.

preposition part of speech coming before a noun or a pronoun to show a location (*in, on*), time (*during*), or some other relationship (for example, figurative relationships in phrases like '*by* heart' or '*on* time').

pronoun part of speech that is used in place of a noun, usually to save repetition of the noun. For example: 'The people arrived around nine o'clock. They behaved as though we were expect-ing them'. Here, 'they' and 'them' are substitutes for repeating 'the people'.

punctuation system of conventional signs (punctuation marks) and spaces employed to organize written and printed language in order to make it as readable, clear, and logical as possible.

question mark punctuation mark (?) used to indicate an enquiry, placed at the end of a direct question ('Who is coming?') or an implied question ('This is my reward?'). A question mark is never needed at the end of an indirect question ('He asked us who was coming'), since this is a statement. To express doubt, a writer or editor may insert a question mark ('born in ? 1235'), often in brackets.

semicolon punctuation mark (;) with a function halfway between the separation of sentence from sentence by means of a period, or full stop, and the gentler separation provided by a comma. It also helps separate items in a complex list: 'pens, pencils, and paper; staples, such as rice and beans; tools, various; and rope'.

verb grammatical part of speech for what someone or something does (*to go*), experiences (*to live*), or is (*to be*). Verbs involve the grammatical categories known as number (singular or plural: 'he *runs;* they *run*'), voice (active or passive: 'she *writes* books; it *is written*'), mood (statements, questions, orders, emphasis, necessity, condition), aspect (completed or continuing action: 'she *danced;* she *was dancing*'), and tense (variation according to time: simple present tense, present progressive tense, simple past tense, and so on).

SPORT

---✳---

There are many different kinds of sport, but most can be grouped into four main categories: these are athletics, which includes swimming competitions, gymnastics, and a wide range of track and field events; racing sports, which involve the use of transportation, such as horse racing, cycling, and motor racing; combat-based sports, such as judo and wrestling; and ball games, such as baseball, tennis, and football.

The origins of many sports can be traced to ancient Egyptian or Greek times. Coursing, for example, was believed to have taken place in Egypt in 3000 BC, using saluki dogs; while wrestling took place in what is now Iraq more than 4,000 years ago. A form of hockey was played in Egypt about 2050 BC; and falconry, boxing, track and field athletics, and fencing were all known more than 4,000 years ago. A number of modern ball games may also be derived from games first played on the European continent during the latter part of the middle ages. In 12th-century France, for example, the game of *la soule* was developed, where two teams competed to move a ball into a goal, and was later followed, in the 14th century, by an ancestor form of baseball and cricket, known as stoolball.

SPORTS A–Z

angling fishing with rod and line. It is widespread and ancient in origin, fish hooks having been found in prehistoric cave dwellings. Competition angling exists and world championships take place for most branches of the sport. The oldest is the World Freshwater Championship, inaugurated 1957.

archery use of the bow and arrow, originally in hunting and warfare, now as a competitive sport. The world governing body is the Fédération Internationale de Tir à l'Arc (FITA) founded in 1931. In competitions, results are based on double FITA rounds; that is, 72 arrows at each of four targets at 90, 70, 50, and 30 metres (70, 60, 50, and 30 for women). The best possible score is 2,880. Archery was reintroduced to the Olympic Games in 1972.

athletics competitive track and field events consisting of running, throwing, and jumping disciplines. **Running events** range from sprint races (100 metres) and hurdles to cross-country running and the marathon (26 miles 385 yards). **Jumping events** are the high jump, long

Athletics: Outdoor World Records

As of 1 February 1998

Event	Record	Record holder	Event	Record	Record holder
men			3,000-metre steeplechase	7 min 55.72 sec	Bernard Barmasai *(Kenya)*
100 metres	9.84 sec	Donovan Bailey *(Canada)*	4 × 100-metre relay	37.40 sec	USA
200 metres	19.32 sec	Michael Johnson *(USA)*	4 × 400-metre relay	2 min 54.20 sec	USA
400 metres	43.29 sec	Butch Reynolds *(USA)*	4 × 800-metre relay	7 min 03.89 sec	Great Britain
800 metres	1 min 41.11 sec	Wilson Kipteker *(Denmark)*	4 × 1,500-metre relay	14 min 38.8 sec	West Germany
1,000 metres	2 min 12.18 sec	Sebastian Coe *(Great Britain)*	high jump	2.45 metres	Javier Sotomayor *(Cuba)*
1,500 metres	3 min 26.00 sec	Hicham El Guerronj *(Morocco)*	pole vault	6.15 metres	Sergey Bubka *(Ukraine)*
mile	3 min 44.39 sec	Noureddine Morceli *(Algeria)*	long jump	8.95 metres	Mike Powell *(USA)*
2,000 metres	4 min 47.88 sec	Noureddine Morceli *(Algeria)*	triple jump	18.29 metres	Jonathan Edwards *(Great Britain)*
3,000 metres	7 min 20.67 sec	Daniel Komen *(Kenya)*	shot	23.12 metres	Randy Barnes *(USA)*
5,000 metres	12 min 39.36 sec	Haile Gebrselassie *(Ethiopia)*	discus	74.08 metres	Jürgen Schult *(East Germany)*
10,000 metres	26 min 22.75 sec	Haile Gebrselassie *(Ethiopia)*	hammer	86.74 metres	Yuriy Sedykh *(USSR)*
20,000 metres	56 min 55.6 sec	Arturo Barrios *(Mexico)*	javelin	98.48 metres	Jan Zelezný *(Czech Republic)*
20,994 metres	1 hr	Jos Hermans *(Holland)*	decathlon	8,891 points	Dan O'Brien *(USA)*
25,000 metres	1 hr 13 min 55.8 sec	Toshihiko Seko *(Japan)*	marathon	2 hr 6 min 05 sec	Ronaldo Da Costa *(Brazil)*
30,000 metres	1 hr 29 min 18.8 sec	Toshihiko Seko *(Japan)*	**women**		
110-metre hurdles	12.91 sec	Colin Jackson *(Great Britain)*	100 metres	10.49 sec	Florence Griffith-Joyner *(USA)*
400-metre hurdles	46.78 sec	Kevin Young *(USA)*	200 metres	21.34 sec	Florence Griffith-Joyner *(USA)*
			400 metres	47.60 sec	Marita Koch *(East Germany)*

Athletics: Outdoor World Records (continued)

Event	Record	Record holder	Event	Record	Record holder
800 metres	1 min 53.28 sec	Jarmila Kratochvilová *(Czechoslovakia)*	4 × 400-metre relay	3 min 15.17 sec	USSR
1,500 metres	3 min 50.46 sec	Qu Yunxia *(China)*	high jump	2.09 metres	Stefka Kostadinova *(Bulgaria)*
mile	4 min 12.56 sec	Svetlana Masterkova *(Russia)*	pole vault	4.60 metres	Emma George *(Australia)*
1,000 metres	2 min 28.98 sec	Svetlana Masterkova *(Russia)*	long jump	7.52 metres	Galina Chistiakova *(Russia)*
2,000 metres	5 min 25.36 sec	Sonia O'Sullivan *(Ireland)*	triple jump	15.5 metres	Inessa Kravets *(Ukraine)*
3,000 metres	8 min 06.11 sec	Wang Junxia *(China)*	shot	22.63 metres	Natalya Lisovskaya *(Russia)*
5,000 metres	14 min 28.09 sec	Jiang Bo *(China)*			
10,000 metres	29 min 31.78 sec	Wang Junxia *(China)*			
25,000 metres	1 hr 29 min 29.2 sec	Karolina Szabo *(Hungary)*	discus	76.80 metres	Gaby Reinsch *(Germany)*
30,000 metres	1 hr 49 min 5.6 sec	Karolina Szabo *(Hungary)*	hammer	73.14 metres	Michaela Melinte *(Romania)*
100-metre hurdles	12.21 sec	Yordanka Donkova *(Bulgaria)*	javelin	80.00 metres	Petra Felke *(Germany)*
400-metre hurdles	52.61 sec	Kim Batten *(USA)*	heptathlon	7,291 points	Jackie Joyner-Kersee *(USA)*
4 × 100-metre relay	41.37 sec	East Germany	marathon	2 hr 20 min 47 sec	Tegla Laroupe *(Kenya)*
4 × 200-metre relay	1 min 28.15 sec	East Germany			

Men's Athletics: Recent Olympic Gold Medallists

Year	Name	Country	Result	Year	Name	Country	Result
100 m				1988	Paul Ereng	Kenya	1:43.45
1980	Allan Wells	Great Britain	10.25	1992	William Tanui	Kenya	1:43.66
1984	Carl Lewis	USA	9.99	1996	Vebjörn Rodal	Norway	1:42.58
1988	Carl Lewis	USA	9.92				
1992	Linford Christie	Great Britain	9.96	**1,500 m**			
1996	Donovan Bailey	Canada	9.84	1980	Sebastian Coe	Great Britain	3:38.40
				1984	Sebastian Coe	Great Britain	3:32.53
200 m				1988	Peter Rono	Kenya	3:35.96
1980	Pietro Mennea	Italy	20.19	1992	Fermin Cacho	Spain	3:40.12
1984	Carl Lewis	USA	19.80	1996	Noureddine Morceli	Algeria	3:35.78
1988	Joe DeLoach	USA	19.75				
1992	Mike Marsh	USA	20.01	**5,000 m**			
1996	Michael Johnson	USA	19.32	1980	Miruts Yitfer	Ethiopia	13:21.00
				1984	Saïd Aouita	Morocco	13:05.59
400 m				1988	John Ngugi	Kenya	13:11.70
1980	Viktor Markin	USSR	44.60	1992	Dieter Baumann	Germany	13:12.52
1984	Alonzo Babers	USA	44.27	1996	Venuste Niyongabo	Burundi	13:07.96
1988	Steve Lewis	USA	43.87				
1992	Quincy Watts	USA	43.50	**10,000 m**			
1996	Michael Johnson	USA	43.49	1980	Miruts Yitfer	Ethiopia	27:42.70
				1984	Alberto Cova	Italy	27:47.54
800 m				1988	Brahim Boutayeb	Morocco	27:21.46
1980	Steve Ovett	Great Britain	1:45.40	1992	Khalid Skah	Morocco	27:46.70
1984	Joaquim Cruz	Brazil	1:43.00	1996	Haile Gebrselassie	Ethiopia	27:07.34

(continued)

Men's Athletics: Recent Olympic Gold Medallists (continued)

Year	Name	Country	Result
Marathon			
1980	Waldemar Cierpinski	East Germany	2h 11:03.00
1984	Carlos Lopes	Portugal	2h 09:21.00
1988	Gelindo Bordin	Italy	2h 10:32.00
1992	Hwang Young-cho	South Korea	2h 13:23.00
1996	Josia Thugwane	South Africa	2h 12:36.00
110 m Hurdles			
1980	Thomas Munkelt	East Germany	13.39
1984	Roger Kingdom	USA	13.20
1988	Roger Kingdom	USA	12.98
1992	Mark McCoy	Canada	13.12
1996	Allen Johnson	USA	12.95
400 m Hurdles			
1980	Volker Beck	East Germany	48.70
1984	Edwin Moses	USA	47.75
1988	Andre Phillips	USA	47.19
1992	Kevin Young	USA	46.78
1996	Derrick Adkins	USA	47.54
20 km Walk			
1980	Maurizio Damilano	Italy	1h 23:35.50
1984	Ernesto Canto	Mexico	1h 23:13.00
1988	Josef Pribilinec	Czechoslovakia	1h 19:57.00
1992	Daniel Plaza	Spain	1h 21:45.00
1996	Jefferson Perez	Ecuador	1h 20.07.00
50 km Walk			
1980	Hartwig Gauder	East Germany	3h 49:24.00
1984	Raul Gonzalez	Mexico	3h 47:26.00
1988	Vyacheslav Ivanenko	USSR	3h 38:29.00
1992	Andrei Perlov	USSR	3h 50:13.00
1996	Robert Korzeniowski	Poland	3h 43:30.00
3,000 m Steeplechase			
1980	Bronisław Malinowski	Poland	8:09.70
1984	Julius Korir	Kenya	8:11.80
1988	Julius Kariuki	Kenya	8:05.51
1992	Matthew Birir	Kenya	8:08.84
1996	Joseph Keter	Kenya	8:07.12
High Jump			
1980	Gerd Wessig	East Germany	2.36 m/7 ft $8\frac{3}{4}$ in
1984	Dietmeir Mögenburg	West Germany	2.35 m/7 ft $8\frac{1}{2}$ in
1988	Gennady Avdeyenko	USSR	2.38 m/7 ft $9\frac{1}{2}$ in
1992	Javier Sotormayor	Cuba	2.34 m/7 ft 8 in
1996	Charles Austin	USA	2.39 m/7 ft 10 in
Pole Vault			
1980	Władisław Kozakiewicz	Poland	5.78 m/18 fr $11\frac{1}{2}$ in

Year	Name	Country	Result
1984	Pierre Quinon	France	5.75 m/18 ft $10\frac{1}{4}$ in
1988	Sergei Bubka	USSR	5.90 m/19 ft $4\frac{1}{4}$ in
1992	Maksim Tarassov	Unified Team[1]	5.80 m/19 ft $\frac{1}{4}$ in
1996	Jean Galfione	France	5.92 m/19 ft 5 in
Long Jump			
1980	Lutz Dombrowski	East Germany	8.54 m/28 ft $\frac{1}{4}$ in
1984	Carl Lewis	USA	8.54 m/28 ft $\frac{1}{4}$ in
1988	Carl Lewis	USA	8.72 m/28 ft $7\frac{1}{4}$ in
1992	Carl Lewis	USA	8.67 m/28 ft $5\frac{1}{2}$ in
1996	Carl Lewis	USA	8.50m/27 ft $10\frac{3}{4}$ in
Triple Jump			
1980	Jaak Udmäe	USSR	17.35 m/56 ft $11\frac{1}{4}$ in
1984	Al Joyner	USA	17.26 m/56 ft $7\frac{1}{2}$ in
1988	Khristo Markov	Bulgaria	17.61 m/57 ft $9\frac{1}{4}$ in
1992	Mike Conley	USA	18.17 m/57 ft $10\frac{1}{4}$ in
1996	Kenny Harrison	USA	18.09 m/59 ft $4\frac{1}{4}$ in
Shot Put			
1980	Vladimir Kiselyev	USSR	21.35 m/70 ft $\frac{1}{2}$ in
1984	Alessandro Andrei	Italy	21.26 m/69 ft 9 in
1988	Ulf Timmermann	East Germany	22.47 m/73 ft $8\frac{3}{4}$ in
1992	Mike Stulce	USA	21.70 m/71 ft $2\frac{1}{4}$ in
1996	Randy Barnes	USA	21.62 m/70 ft $11\frac{1}{4}$ in
Discus			
1980	Viktor Rashchupkin	USSR	66.64 m/218 ft 8 in
1984	Rolf Danneburg	West Germany	66.60 m/218 ft 6 in
1988	Jürgen Schult	East Germany	68.82 m/225 ft $9\frac{1}{4}$ in
1992	Romas Ubartas	Lithuania	65.12 m/213 ft $7\frac{3}{4}$ in
1996	Lars Reidel	Germany	69.40 m/227 ft 8 in
Hammer			
1980	Yuri Sedykh	USSR	81.80 m/268 ft $4\frac{1}{2}$ in
1984	Juha Tiainen	Finland	78.08 m/256 ft 2 in
1988	Sergei Litvinov	USSR	84.80 m/278 ft $2\frac{1}{2}$ in
1992	Andrei Abduvaliyev	Unified Team[1]	82.54 m/270 ft $9\frac{1}{2}$ in
1996	Balazs Kiss	Hungary	81.24 m/266 ft 6 in
Javelin			
1980	Dainis Kula	USSR	91.20 m/299 ft $2\frac{3}{8}$ in

Men's Athletics: Recent Olympic Gold Medallists (continued)

Year	Name	Country	Result	Year	Name	Country	Result
1984	Arto Härkonen	Finland	86.76 m/284 ft 8 in	*Decathlon*			
1988	Tapio Korjus	Finland	84.28 m/276 ft 6 in	1980	Daley Thompson	Great Britain	8495 points
1992	Jan Zelezný	Czechoslovakia	89.66 m/294 ft 2 in	1984	Daley Thompson	Great Britain	8798 points
				1988	Christan Schenk	East Germany	8488[2] points
1996	Jan Zelezný	Czech Republic	88.16 m/289 ft 3 in	1992	Robert Zmelic	Czechoslovakia	8611 points
				1996	Dan O'Brien	USA	8824 points

[1]Commonwealth of Independent States plus Georgia.
[2]New points systems were introduced before the 1988 Games.

Women's Athletics: Recent Olympic Gold Medallists

Year	Name	Country	Result	Year	Name	Country	Result
100 m				*10,000 m*			
1980	Lyudmila Kondratyeva	USSR	11.06	1988	Olga Bondarenko	USSR	31:05.21
1984	Evelyn Ashford	USA	10.97	1992	Derartu Tulu	Ethiopia	31:06.02
1988	Florence Griffith-Joyner	USA	10.54	1996	Fernanda Ribeiro	Portugal	31:01.63
1992	Gail Devers	USA	10.82	*Marathon*			
1996	Gail Devers	USA	10.94	1984	Joan Benoit	USA	2h 24.52
200 m				1988	Rosa Mota	Portugal	2h 25.40
1980	Bärbel Wöckel	East Germany	22.03	1992	Valentina Yegorova	Unified Team[2]	2h 32.41
1984	Valerie Brisco-Hooks	USA	21.81	1996	Fatuma Roba	Ethiopia	2h 26:05
1988	Florence Griffith-Joyner	USA	21.34	*100 m Hurdles*			
1992	Gwen Torrence	USA	21.81	1980	Vera Komisova	USSR	12.56
1996	Marie-José Pérec	France	22.12	1984	Benita Fitzgerald-Brown	USA	12.84
400 m				1988	Yordanka Donkova	Bulgaria	12.38
1980	Marita Koch	East Germany	48.88	1992	Paraskevi Patoulidou	Greece	12.64
1984	Valerie Brisco-Hooks	USA	48.83	1996	Lyudmila Engquist	Sweden	12.58
1988	Olga Brzygina	USSR	48.65	*400 m Hurdles*			
1992	Marie-José Pérec	France	48.83	1984	Nawal El Moutawakel	Morocco	54.61
1996	Marie-José Pérec	France	48.25	1988	Debra Flintoff-King	Australia	53.17
800 m				1992	Sally Gunnell	Great Britain	53.23
1980	Nadyezda Olizarenko	USSR	1:53.42	1996	Deon Hemmings	Jamaica	52.82
1984	Doina Melinte	Romania	1:57.60	*10 km Walk*			
1988	Sigrun Wodars	East Germany	1:56.10	1992	Chen Yueling	China	44:32
1992	Ellen van Langen	Netherlands	1:55.54	1996	Yelena Nikolayeva	Russia	41:49
1996	Svetlana Masterkova	Russia	1:57.73	*Triple Jump*			
1,500 m				1996	Inessa Kravets	Ukraine	15.33 m/50 ft 3½ in
1980	Tatyana Kazankina	USSR	3:56.60	*High Jump*			
1984	Gabriella Dorio	Italy	4:03.25	1980	Sara Simeoni	Italy	1.97 m/6 ft 5½ in
1988	Paula Ivan	Romania	3:53.96	1984	Ulrike Meyfarth	West Germany	2.02 m/6 ft 7½ in
1992	Hassiba Boulmerka	Algeria	3:55.30	1988	Louise Ritter	USA	2.03 m/6 ft 8 in
1996	Svetlana Masterkova	Russia	4:00.83	1992	Heike Henkel	Germany	2.02 m/6 ft 7½ in
3,000 m[1]				1996	Stefka Kostadinova	Bulgaria	2.05 m/6 ft 8¾ in
1984	Maricica Puica	Romania	8:35.96				
1988	Tatyana Samolenko	USSR	8:26.53				
1992	Yelena Romanova	Unified Team[2]	8:46.04				
5,000 m							
1996	Wang Junxia	China	14:59.88				

(continued)

Women's Athletics: Recent Olympic Gold Medallists (continued)

Year	Name	Country	Result		Year	Name	Country	Result
Long Jump					1988	Martina Hellmann	East Germany	72.30 m/237 ft $2\frac{1}{4}$ in
1980	Tatyana Kolpakova	USSR	7.06 m/23 ft 2 in		1992	Martiza Marten	Cuba	70.06 m/222 ft 10 in
1984	Anisoara Stanciu	Romania	6.96 m/22 ft 10 in		1996	Ilke Wyludda	Germany	69.66 m/228 ft 6 in
1988	Jackie Joyner-Kersee	USA	7.40 m/24 ft $3\frac{1}{2}$ in		*Javelin*			
					1980	Maria Colon	Cuba	68.40 m/224 ft 5 in
1992	Heike Dreschler	Germany	7.14 m/23 ft $5\frac{1}{4}$ in		1984	Tessa Sanderson	Great Britain	69.56 m/228 ft 2 in
1996	Chioma Ajunwa	Nigeria	7.12 m/23 ft $4\frac{1}{2}$ in		1988	Petra Felke	East Germany	74.68 m/245 ft 0 in
Shot Put					1992	Silke Renk	Germany	68.34 m/224 ft $2\frac{1}{2}$ in
1980	Ilona Slupianek	East Germany	22.41 m/73 ft $6\frac{1}{4}$ in		1996	Heli Ratanen	Finland	67.94 m/222 ft 11 in
1984	Claudia Losch	West Germany	20.48 m/67 ft $2\frac{1}{4}$ in		*Pentathlon[3]*			
1988	Natalya Lisovskaya	USSR	22.24 m/72 ft $11\frac{1}{2}$ in		1980	Nadyezda Tkachenko	USSR	5083 points
1992	Svetlana Krivelyova	Unified Team[2]	21.06 m/69 ft $1\frac{1}{2}$ in		*Heptathlon*			
1996	Astrid Kumbernuss	Germany	20.56 m/67 ft $5\frac{1}{2}$ in		1984	Glynis Nunn	Australia	6390 points
Discus					1988	Jackie Joyner-Kersee	USA	7291 points
1980	Evelin Jahl	East Germany	69.96 m/229 ft 6 in		1992	Jackie Joyner-Kersee	USA	7044 points
1984	Ria Stalman	Netherlands	65.36 m/214 ft 5 in		1996	Ghada Shouaa	Syria	6780 points

[1] Replaced by 5,000 metres in 1996.
[2] Commonwealth of Independent States plus Georgia.
[3] Replaced by heptathlon in 1984.

jump, triple jump, and pole vault. **Throwing events** are javelin, discus, shot put, and hammer throw.

badminton racket game similar to lawn tennis but played on a smaller court and with a shuttlecock (a half sphere of cork or plastic with a feather or nylon skirt) instead of a ball. The object of the game is to prevent the opponent from being able to return the shuttlecock.

baseball national summer game of the USA, derived in the 19th century from the English game of rounders. Baseball is a bat-and-ball game played between two teams, each of nine players, on a pitch ('field') marked out in the form of a diamond, with a base at each corner. The ball is struck with a cylindrical bat, and the players try to score ('make a run') by circuiting the bases. A 'home run' is a circuit on one hit.

Jane Austen and baseball

■ The first recorded use of the word 'baseball' in English occurs in Jane Austen's *Northanger Abbey*, published in 1803.

Baseball: World Series Results

(AL = American League. NL = National League.)

Year	Winner	Loser	Score
1990	Cincinnati Reds, NL	Oakland Athletics, AL	4–0
1991	Minnesota Twins, AL	Atlanta Braves, NL	4–3
1992	Toronto Blue Jays, AL	Atlanta Braves, NL	4–2
1993	Toronto Blue Jays, AL	Philadelphia Phillies, NL	4–2
1994	no World Series[1]		
1995	Atlanta Braves, NL	Cleveland Indians, AL	4–2
1996	New York Yankees, AL	Atlanta Braves, NL	4–2
1997	Florida Marlins, NL	Cleveland Indians, AL	4–3
1998	New York Yankees, AL	San Diego Padres, NL	4–0

[1] Due to a players' strike.

National Basketball Association Champions (USA)

Year	Winner	Coach	Runner Up	Series
1990	Detroit	Chuck Daly	Portland	4–1
1991	Chicago	Phil Jackson	Los Angeles Lakers	4–1
1992	Chicago	Phil Jackson	Portland	4–2
1993	Chicago	Phil Jackson	Phoenix	4–2
1994	Houston	Rudy Tomjanovich	New York Knicks	4–3
1995	Houston	Rudy Tomjanovich	Orlando	4–0
1996	Chicago	Phil Jackson	Seattle	4–2
1997	Chicago	Phil Jackson	Utah	4–2
1998	Chicago	Phil Jackson	Utah	4–2

basketball ball game between two teams of five players on an indoor enclosed court. The object is, via a series of passing moves, to throw the large inflated ball through a circular hoop and net positioned at each end of the court, 3.05 m/ 10 ft above the ground. The first world championship for men was held in 1950, and in 1953 for women. They are now held every four years.

Basketball: World Champions

The world championship was first held in 1950 for men and 1953 for women. It is contested every four years.

Year	Country	Year	Country
Men		*Women*	
1950	Argentina	1953	USA
1954	USA	1957	USA
1959	Brazil	1959	USSR
1963	Brazil	1964	USSR
1967	USSR	1967	USSR
1970	Yugoslavia	1971	USSR
1974	USSR	1975	USSR
1978	Yugoslavia	1979	USA
1982	USSR	1983	USSR
1986	USA	1986	USA
1990	Yugoslavia	1990	USA
1994	USA	1994	Brazil
1998	Yugoslavia	1998	USA

bobsleighing or **bobsledding** sport of racing steel-bodied, steerable toboggans, crewed by two or four people, down mountain ice chutes at speeds of up to 130 kph/80 mph. It was introduced as an Olympic event in 1924 and world championships have been held every year since 1931.

Basketball: Olympic Medallists

Year	Gold	Silver	Bronze
Men			
1936	USA	Canada	Mexico
1948	USA	France	Brazil
1952	USA	USSR	Uruguay
1956	USA	USSR	Uruguay
1960	USA	USSR	Brazil
1964	USA	USSR	Brazil
1968	USA	Yugoslavia	USSR
1972	USSR	USA	Cuba
1976	USA	Yugoslavia	USSR
1980	Yugoslavia	Italy	USSR
1984	USA	Spain	Yugoslavia
1988	USSR	Yugoslavia	USA
1992	USA	Croatia	Lithuania
1996	USA	Yugoslavia	Lithuania
Women			
1976	USSR	USA	Bulgaria
1980	USSR	Bulgaria	Yugoslavia
1984	USA	South Korea	China
1988	USA	Yugoslavia	USSR
1992	Unified Team[1]	China	USA
1996	USA	Brazil	Australia

[1] Commonwealth of Independent States plus Georgia.

Included among the major bobsleighing events are the Olympic Championships (the four-crew event was introduced at the 1924 Winter Olympics and the two-crew in 1932) and the World Championships, the four-crew championship introduced in 1924 and the two-crew in 1931. In Olympic years winners automatically become world champions.

bowls outdoor and indoor game popular in Commonwealth countries. It has been played in Britain since the 13th century and was popularized by Francis Drake, who is reputed to have played bowls on Plymouth Hoe as the Spanish Armada approached in 1588.

boxing fighting with gloved fists, almost entirely a male sport. The sport dates from the 18th century, when fights were fought with bare knuckles and untimed rounds. Each round ended with a knockdown. Fighting with gloves became the accepted form in the latter part of the 19th century after the formulation of the Queensberry Rules in 1867.

Boxing: Recent World Heavyweight Champions

(Present weight limit: over 86.2 kg/190 lb. Fighters are US nationals unless otherwise stated.)

Year	Name
WBA Champions (Since 1978)	
1978	Leon Spinks
1978–79	Muhammad Ali[1]
1979–80	John Tate
1980–82	Mike Weaver
1982–83	Michael Dokes
1983–84	Gerrie Coetzee (South Africa)
1984–85	Greg Page
1985–86	Tony Tubbs
1986	Tim Witherspoon
1986–87	James 'Bonecrusher' Smith
1987–90	Mike Tyson (& WBC, IBF)
1990	James 'Buster' Douglas (& WBC, IBF)
1990–92	Evander Holyfield (& WBC, IBF)
1992–93	Riddick Bowe (& IBF, WBC)[2]
1993–94	Evander Holyfield (& IBF)
1994	Michael Moorer (& IBF)
1994–95	George Foreman (& IBF)[2]
1995–96	Bruce Seldon
1996	Mike Tyson
1996–	Evander Holyfield (& IBF)
WBC Champions (Since 1978)	
1978	Ken Norton
1978–83	Larry Holmes[3]
1984	Tim Witherspoon

Year	Name
1984–86	Pinklon Thomas
1986	Trevor Berbick (Canada)
1986–90	Mike Tyson (& WBA, IBF 1987–90)
1990	James 'Buster' Douglas (& WBA, IBF)
1990–92	Evander Holyfield (& WBA, IBF)
1992	Riddick Bowe (& IBF, WBC)[2]
1992–94	Lennox Lewis (UK)
1994–95	Oliver McCall
1995–96	Frank Bruno (UK)
1996	Mike Tyson[1]
1997–	Lennox Lewis (UK)
IBF Champions (Since 1983)	
1983–85	Larry Holmes
1985–87	Michael Spinks[1]
1987	Tony Tucker
1987–90	Mike Tyson (& WBA, WBC)
1990	James 'Buster' Douglas (& WBA, WBC)
1990–92	Evander Holyfield (& WBA, WBC)
1992–93	Riddick Bowe (& IBF, WBC)[2]
1993–94	Evander Holyfield (& WBA)
1994	Michael Moorer (& WBA)
1994–95	George Foreman (& WBA)[1]
1996	Michael Moorer
1997–	Evander Holyfield (& WBA)

[1] Relinquished or stripped of title, or retired as champion.
[2] Bowe relinquished his WBC title in December 1992.
[3] Holmes relinquished his WBC title in December 1983 to become the newly formed IBF's first champion.

canoeing sport of propelling a lightweight, shallow boat, pointed at both ends, by paddles or sails. Present-day canoes are made from fibreglass, but original boats were of wooden construction covered in bark or skin. Canoeing was popularized as a sport in the 19th century.

cricket bat-and-ball game between two teams of 11 players each. It is played with a small solid ball and long flat-sided wooden bats, on a round or oval field, at the centre of which is a finely mown pitch, 20 m/22 yd long. At each end of the pitch is a wicket made up of three upright wooden sticks (stumps), surmounted by two smaller sticks (bails). The object of the game is to score more runs than the opposing team. A run is normally scored by the batsman striking the ball and exchanging ends with his or her partner until the ball is returned by a fielder, or by hitting the ball to the boundary line for an automatic four or six runs.

Cricket: World Cup Winners

This competition was first held in 1975.

Year	Winner	Runner-up	Location
1975	West Indies	Australia	England
1979	West Indies	England	England
1983	India	West Indies	England
1987	Australia	England	India
1992	Pakistan	England	Australia
1996	Sri Lanka	Australia	India, Pakistan, and Sri Lanka

Cricket: Recent Winners

English County Championship first held officially in 1890	1991	Nottinghamshire	1994	Worcestershire
	1992	Middlesex	1995	Warwickshire
1990 Middlesex	1993	Glamorgan	1996	Lancashire
1991 Essex	1994	Warwickshire	1997	Essex
1992 Essex	1995	Kent	1998	Lancashire
1993 Middlesex	1996	Surrey	*Benson and Hedges Cup*	
1994 Warwickshire	1997	Warwickshire	*first held in 1972*	
1995 Warwickshire	1998	Lancashire	1990	Lancashire
1996 Leicestershire			1991	Worcestershire
1997 Glamorgan	*NatWest Trophy*		1992	Hampshire
1998 Leicestershire	*formerly the Gillette Cup; first held in 1963*		1993	Derbyshire
			1994	Warwickshire
AXA League	1990	Lancashire	1995	Lancashire
formerly Refuge Assurance	1991	Hampshire	1996	Lancashire
League; first held in 1969	1992	Northamptonshire	1997	Surrey
1990 Derbyshire	1993	Warwickshire	1998	Essex

curling game played on ice with stones; sometimes described as 'bowls on ice'. One of the national games of Scotland, it has spread to many countries. It can also be played on artificial (cement or tarmacadam) ponds. At the 1998 Winter Olympics in Nagano, Japan, curling was included as a medal event for the first time. In 1998 and 1992 it had been a demonstration event. At Nagano, the inaugural men's and women's titles were won by Switzerland and Canada respectively.

cycling riding a bicycle for sport, pleasure, or transport. Cycle racing can take place on oval artificial tracks, on the road, or across country (cyclocross).

Cycling Tour De France: Recent Winners

1990	Greg LeMond *(USA)*
1991	Miguel Indurain *(Spain)*
1992	Miguel Indurain *(Spain)*
1993	Miguel Indurain *(Spain)*
1994	Miguel Indurain *(Spain)*
1995	Miguel Indurain *(Spain)*
1996	Bjarne Riis *(Denmark)*
1997	Jan Ullrich *(Germany)*

diving sport of entering water either from a springboard 1 m/3 ft or 3 m/10 ft above the water, or from a platform, or highboard, 10 m/33 ft above the water. Various differing starts are adopted, facing forwards or backwards, and somersaults, twists, and combinations thereof are performed in midair before entering the water. A minimum pool depth of 5 m/16.5 ft is needed for high or platform diving. Points are awarded and the level of difficulty of each dive is used as a multiplying factor.

equestrianism skill in horse riding, as practised under International Equestrian Federation rules. An Olympic sport, there are three main branches of equestrianism: showjumping, dressage, and three-day eventing. Three other disciplines are under the authority of the International Equestrian Federation (FEI): carriage driving, endurance riding, and vaulting.

fencing sport of fighting with swords including the **foil,** derived from the light weapon used in practice duels; the **épée,** a heavier weapon derived from the duelling sword proper; and the **sabre,** with a curved handle and narrow V-shaped blade. In sabre fighting, cuts count as well as thrusts. Masks and protective jackets are worn, and hits are registered electronically in competitions. Men's fencing has been part of every Olympic programme since 1896; women's fencing was included from 1924 but only using the foil.

football, American contact sport similar to the English game of rugby, played between two teams of 11 players, with an inflated oval ball. Players are well padded for protection and wear protective helmets. The **Super Bowl,** first held in 1967, is now an annual meeting between the

American Football: Super Bowl Results

Super Bowl	Year	Result	Venue
XXIV	1990	San Francisco 49ers 55, Denver Broncos 10	New Orleans
XXV	1991	New York Giants 20, Buffalo Bills 19	Tampa
XXVI	1992	Washington Redskins 37, Buffalo Bills 24	Minneapolis
XXVII	1993	Dallas Cowboys 52, Buffalo Bills 17	Pasadena
XXVIII	1994	Dallas Cowboys 30, Buffalo Bills 13	Atlanta
XXIX	1995	San Francisco 49ers 49, San Diego 26	Miami
XXX	1996	Dallas Cowboys 27, Pittsburgh Steelers 17	Tempe (AZ)
XXXI	1997	Green Bay Packers 35, New England Patriots 21	New Orleans
XXXII	1998	Denver Broncos 31, Green Bay Packers 24	San Diego
XXXIII	1999	Denver Broncos 34, Atlanta Falcons 19	Miami

winners of the National and American Football Conferences.

football, association or **soccer,** form of football originating in the UK, popular throughout the world. Slight amendments to the rules take effect in certain competitions and international matches as laid down by the sport's world governing body, Fédération Internationale de Football Association (FIFA, 1904). FIFA organizes the competitions for the World Cup, held every four years since 1930.

football, Australian rules game that combines aspects of Gaelic football, rugby, and association football; it is played between two teams of 18 players each, with an inflated oval ball. It is unique to Australia.

golf outdoor game in which a small rubber-cored ball is hit with a wooden- or iron-faced club into

Association Football: World Cup Finals

This tournament was not held in 1942 or 1946.

Year	Winner	Runner-up	Score	Venue
1930	Uruguay	Argentina	4–2	Uruguay
1934	Italy	Czechoslovakia	2–1	Italy
1938	Italy	Hungary	4–2	France
1950	Uruguay	Brazil	2–1	Brazil
1954	West Germany	Hungary	3–2	Switzerland
1958	Brazil	Sweden	5–2	Sweden
1962	Brazil	Czechoslovakia	3–1	Chile
1966	England	West Germany	4–2	England
1970	Brazil	Italy	4–1	Mexico
1974	West Germany	Holland	2–1	West Germany
1978	Argentina	Holland	3–1	Argentina
1982	Italy	West Germany	3–1	Spain
1986	Argentina	West Germany	3–2	Mexico
1990	West Germany	Argentina	1–0	Italy
1994	Brazil[1]	Italy	0–0	USA
1998	France	Brazil	3–0	France

[1] Brazil won 3–2 on penalties.

British Open Golf Championship Winners

The competition was played over 36 holes between 1860 and 1891; since 1892 it has been played over 72 holes.

Year	Name	Country	Location	Score
1990	Nick Faldo	UK	St Andrews	270
1991	Ian Baker-Finch	Australia	Royal Birkdale	272
1992	Nick Faldo	UK	Muirfield	272
1993	Greg Norman	Australia	Sandwich	267
1994	Nick Price	Zimbabwe	Turnberry	268
1995	John Daly	USA	St Andrews	282
1996	Tom Lehman	USA	Royal Lytham	271
1997	Justin Leonard	USA	Troon	272
1998	Mark O'Meara	USA	Royal Birkdale	280[2]

[1] Amateur player.
[2] Won after a play-off.

Men's US Open Golf Championship Winners

Year	Name	Country	Location	Score
1990	Hale Irwin	USA	Medinah (IL)	280[2]
1991	Payne Stewart	USA	Hazeltine (MN)	282[2]
1992	Tom Kite	USA	Monterey (CA)	285
1993	Lee Janzen	USA	Baltusrol (NJ)	272
1994	Ernie Els	South Africa	Oakmont (PA)	279
1995	Corey Pavin	USA	Shinnecock Hills (NY)	280
1996	Steve Jones	USA	Oakland Hills (MI)	278
1997	Ernie Els	South Africa	Congressional (MI)	276
1998	Lee Janzen	USA	Olympic Club (CA)	280

[1] Amateur.
[2] Score after play-off.

US Masters Golf Winners

This competition has been held annually at the Augusta National course, Georgia, USA, since 1934.

Year	Name	Country	Score
1990	Nick Faldo	UK	278[1]
1991	Ian Woosnam	UK	277
1992	Fred Couples	USA	275
1993	Bernhard Langer	Germany	277
1994	José-Maria Olazábal	Spain	279
1995	Ben Crenshaw	USA	274
1996	Nick Faldo	UK	276
1997	Tiger Woods	USA	270
1998	Mark O'Meara	USA	279

[1] Score after play-off.

US Women's Open Golf Winners

Players are of US nationality unless otherwise stated.

Year	Winner	Score
1990	Betsy King	284
1991	Meg Mallon	283
1992	Patty Sheehan[1]	280
1993	Lauri Merten	280
1994	Patty Sheehan	277
1995	Annika Sorenstam (Sweden)	278
1996	Annika Sorenstam (Sweden)	272
1997	Alison Nicholas (UK)	274
1998	Se Ri Pak (Korea)	290

[1] Winner after a play-off.

US Professional Golf Association (US PGA) Championship Winners

This competition was first held in 1916. It was contested as a matchplay between 1916 and 1957, and has been contested as strokeplay since 1958. Players are of US nationality unless otherwise stated.

Year	Name	Score
1990	Wayne Grady (Australia)	282
1991	John Daly	276
1992	Nick Price (Zimbabwe)	278
1993	Paul Azinger	272[1]
1994	Nick Price (Zimbabwe)	269
1995	Steve Elkington (Australia)	267
1996	Mark Brooks	277[1]
1997	Davis Love III	269
1998	Vijay Singh (Fiji)	271

[1] Score after play-off.

a series of holes using the least number of shots. On the first shot for each hole, the ball is hit from a tee, which elevates the ball slightly off the ground; subsequent strokes are played off the ground. Most courses have 18 holes and are approximately 5,500 m/6,000 yd in length. Golf developed in Scotland in the 15th century.

greyhound racing spectator sport, invented in the USA in 1919, that has a number of greyhounds pursuing a mechanical hare around a circular or oval track. It is popular in Great Britain and

Gymnastics: Recent Individual Olympic Gold Medallists

Year	Name	Country	Year	Name	Country
Men			*Women*		
1976	Nikolai Andrianov	USSR	1976	Nadia Comaneci	Romania
1980	Aleksandr Ditiatin	USSR	1980	Elena Davidova	USSR
1984	Koji Gushiken	Japan	1984	Mary Lou Retton	USA
1988	Vladimir Artemov	USSR	1988	Elena Chouchounova	USSR
1992	Vitali Shcherbo	Unified Team[1]	1992	Tatiana Gutsu	Unified Team[1]
1996	Li Xiaoshuang	China	1996	Lilia Podkopaieva	Ukraine

[1] Commonwealth of Independent States plus Georgia.

Australia, attracting much on- and off-course betting.

gymnastics physical exercises, originally for health and training (so called from the way in which men of ancient Greece trained: *gymnos* 'naked'). The *gymnasia* were schools for training competitors for public games.

Men's gymnastics includes high bar, parallel bars, horse vault, rings, pommel horse, and floor exercises. Women's gymnastics includes asymmetrical bars, side horse vault, balance beam, and floor exercises. Also popular are **sports acrobatics,** performed by gymnasts in pairs, trios, or fours to music, where the emphasis is on dance, balance, and timing, and **rhythmic gymnastics,** choreographed to music and performed by individuals or six-girl teams, with small hand apparatus such as a ribbon, ball, or hoop.

handball game resembling football but played with the hands instead of the feet. It was popularized in Germany in the late 19th century. The indoor game has 7 players in a team; the outdoor version (field handball) has 11. Indoor handball was introduced as an Olympic event in 1972 for men, and in 1976 for women.

hockey game played with hooked sticks and a small, solid ball, the object being to hit the ball into the goal. It is played between two teams, each of not more than 11 players. Hockey has been an Olympic sport since 1908 for men and since 1980 for women. In North America it is known as 'field hockey', to distinguish it from ice hockey.

horse racing sport of racing mounted or driven horses. Two forms in Britain are **flat racing,** for thoroughbred horses over a flat course, and **National Hunt racing,** in which the horses have to clear obstacles.

ice hockey game played on ice between two teams of six, developed in Canada from hockey or bandy. A rubber disc (puck) is used in place of a ball. Players wear skates and protective clothing.

Ice Hockey World Championship

Year	Country	Year	Country
1990	USSR	1995	Finland
1991	Sweden	1996	Czech Republic
1992	Sweden	1997	Canada
1993	Russia	1998	Sweden
1994	Canada		

American National Hockey League (NHL): Stanley Cup Winners

This tournament was inaugurated in 1927.

Year	Team	Year	Team
1990	Edmonton Oilers	1995	New Jersey Devils
1991	Pittsburgh Penguins	1996	Colorado Avalanche
1992	Pittsburgh Penguins	1997	Detroit Red Wings
1993	Montreal Canadiens	1998	Detroit Red Wings
1994	New York Rangers		

judo (Japanese *judo* 'gentle way') form of wrestling of Japanese origin. The two combatants wear loose-fitting, belted jackets and trousers to facilitate holds, and falls are broken by a square mat; when one has established a painful hold that the other cannot break, the latter signifies surrender by slapping the ground with a free hand. Degrees of proficiency are indicated by the colour of the belt: for novices, white, then yellow, orange (2 degrees), green (2 degrees), blue (2 degrees), brown (2 degrees), then black (Dan grades; 10 degrees, of which 1st to 5th Dan wear black belts, 6th to 9th wear red and white, and 10th wears solid red).

karate (Japanese 'empty hand') one of the martial arts. Karate is a type of unarmed combat derived from *kempo,* a form of the Chinese Shaolin boxing. It became popular in the West in the 1930s.

lacrosse Canadian ball game, adopted from the North American Indians, and named after a fancied resemblance of the lacrosse stick (crosse) to a bishop's crosier. Thongs across the curved end of the crosse form a pocket to carry the small rubber ball. The field is approximately 100 m/110 yd long and a minimum of 55 m/60 yd wide in the men's game, which is played with 10 players per side; the women's field is larger, and there are 12 players per side. The goals are just under 2 m/6 ft square, with loose nets. The world championship was first held in 1967 for men, and in 1969 for women.

motorcycle racing speed contests on motorcycles. It has many different forms: **road racing** over open roads; **circuit racing** over purpose-built tracks; **speedway** over oval-shaped dirt tracks;

Daytona 500 Champions

This championship was first held in 1959.

Year	Driver	Car
1990	Derrike Cope	Chevrolet
1991	Ernie Irvan	Chevrolet
1992	Davey Allison	Ford
1993	Dale Jarrett	Chevrolet
1994	Sterling Marlin	Chevrolet
1995	Sterling Marlin	Chevrolet
1996	Dale Jarrett	Ford
1997	Jeff Gordon	Chevrolet
1998	Dale Earnhardt	Chevrolet

Motorcycle Racing World Champions

1998

Road Racing

125cc	Kazuto Sakata	Japan	Aprilia
250 cc	Loris Capirossi	Italy	Aprilia
500 cc	Michael Doohan	Australia	Honda
Superbike	Carl Fogarty	UK	Ducati
Endurance	Doug Polen and	USA and	Honda
	Christian Lavieille	France	
Sidecar	Steve Webster &	UK	LCR
(World Cup)	David James		Honda

Motocross

125cc	Alessio Chiodi	Italy	
Husqvarna			
250cc	Sebastian Tortelli	France	Kawasaki
500cc	Joel Smets	Belgium	Husaberg
Sidecar	Kristers Sergis &	Latvia	BSU
	Artis Rasmanis		
Trials	Doug Lampkin	UK	Beta

motocross over natural terrain, incorporating hill climbs; and **trials,** also over natural terrain, but with the addition of artificial hazards.

motor racing competitive racing of motor vehicles. It has forms as diverse as hill-climbing, stock-car racing, rallying, sports-car racing, and Formula One Grand Prix racing. The first organized race was from Paris to Rouen in 1894.

Indianapolis 500 Champions

This race was first held in 1911.

Year	Name	Car	Average speed	
			kph	mph
1990	Arie Luyendyk	Lola-Chevrolet	299.229	185.981
1991	Rick Mears	Penske-Chevrolet	283.972	176.457
1992	Al Unser Jr	Galmer-Chevrolet	216.414	134.477
1993	Emerson Fittipaldi	Penske-Chevrolet	252.993	157.207
1994	Al Unser Jr	Penske-Mercedes	258.891	160.872
1995	Jacques Villeneuve	Reynard-Ford	247.214	153.616
1996	Buddy Lazier	Reynard-Ford	238.106	147.956
1997	Arie Luyendyk	G-Force-Aurora	234.679	145.827
1998	Eddie Cheever Jr.	Dallara-Aurora	233.598	145.155

Formula 1 World Drivers' Championship Winners

This championship was inaugurated in 1950.

Year	Name	Country	Car
1990	Ayrton Senna	Brazil	McLaren-Honda
1991	Ayrton Senna	Brazil	McLaren-Honda
1992	Nigel Mansell	Great Britain	Williams-Renault
1993	Alain Prost	France	Williams-Renault
1994	Michael Schumacher	Germany	Benetton-Ford
1995	Michael Schumacher	Germany	Benetton-Renault
1996	Damon Hill	Great Britain	Williams-Renault
1997	Jacques Villeneuve	France	Williams-Renault
1998	Mika Hakkinen	Finland	McLaren-Mercedes

Monte Carlo Rally

This race was first held in 1911.

Year	Name	Country
1990	Didier Auriol	France
1991	Carlos Sainz	Spain
1992	Didier Auriol	France
1993	Didier Auriol	France
1994	François Delecour	France
1995	Carlos Sainz	Spain
1996	Patrick Bernardini	France
1997	Piero Liatti	Italy
1998	Carlos Sainz	Spain

netball game developed from basketball, played by two teams of seven players each on a hard court 30.5 m/100 ft long and 15.25 m/50 ft wide. At each end is a goal, consisting of a post 3.05 m/10 ft high, at the top of which is attached a circular hoop and net. The object of the game is to pass an inflated spherical ball through the opposing team's net. The ball is thrown from player to player; no contact is allowed between players, who must not run with the ball.

orienteering sport of cross-country running and route-finding. Competitors set off at one-minute intervals and have to find their way, using map and compass, to various checkpoints (approximately 0.8 km/0.5 mi apart), where their control cards are marked. World championships have been held since 1966.

polo stick-and-ball game played between two teams of four on horseback. It originated in Iran, spread to India and was first played in England in 1869. Polo is played on the largest field of any game, measuring up to 274 m/300 yd by 182 m/200 yd. A small solid ball is struck with the side of a longhandled mallet through goals at each end of the field. A typical match lasts about an hour, and is divided into 'chukkas' of 7 minutes each. No pony is expected to play more than two chukkas in the course of a day.

real tennis racket and ball game played in France, from about the 12th century, over a central net in an indoor court, but with a sloping roof let into each end and one side of the court, against which the ball may be hit. The term 'real' here means 'royal', not 'genuine'. Basic scoring is as for lawn tennis, but with various modifications.

rock climbing sport originally an integral part of mountaineering. It began as a form of training for Alpine expeditions and is now divided into three categories: the **outcrop climb** for climbs of up to 30 m/100 ft; the **crag climb** on cliffs of 30–300 m/100–1,000 ft, and the **big wall climb,** which is the nearest thing to Alpine climbing, but without the hazards of snow and ice.

rowing propulsion of a boat by oars, either by one rower with two oars (sculling) or by crews (two, four, or eight persons) with one oar each, often with a coxswain. Major events include the world championship, first held in 1962 for men and in 1974 for women, and the Boat Race (between England's Oxford and Cambridge universities), first held in 1829.

rugby contact sport that traditionally believed to have originated at Rugby School, England, 1823

Rugby Union: World Cup

This competition, for the William Webb Ellis Trophy, was first held in 1987.

Year	Country
1987	New Zealand
1991	Australia
1995	South Africa

Olympic Games

The original sporting contests were held in Olympia, ancient Greece, every four years during a sacred truce; records were kept from 776 BC. Women were forbidden to be present, and the male contestants were naked. The ancient Games were abolished in AD 394. The present-day games have been held every four years since 1896. Since 1924 there has been a separate winter Games programme; from 1994 the winter and summer Games are held two years apart.

the modern Games The first modern Games were held in Athens, Greece. They were revived by Frenchman Pierre de Fredi, Baron de Coubertin (1863–1937), and have been held every four years with the exception of 1916, 1940, and 1944, when the two world wars intervened. Special tenth-anniversary Games were held in Athens in 1906. At the first revived Games, 245 competitors represented 14 nations in nine sports. At Atlanta in 1996, over 10,000 athletes represented 197 nations in 29 sports. Athens, host to the first modern Olympic games in 1896, was in 1997 chosen as the venue for the 2004 Games.

the ancient Games Of all the many Games held in Ancient Greece, the Olympic were the oldest and most famous. Claims that certain mythical or even historical characters 'founded' the Olympic Games cannot be taken seriously. The Games were

---

Ladies 100 m won by a man
- The winner of the ladies' 100 metres race at the 1932 Olympic Games was in fact a man. Stella Walsh, a Polish-born American, had beaten the Canadian Hilda Strike by a few centimetres. Her true sex was discovered when 'she' died in 1981, caught in the crossfire in a robbery at Cleveland, Ohio.

---

not suddenly established, but evolved from simple religious ceremonies to become the most grandiose sports festival of antiquity. Thus the origin of the Olympic Games is lost in obscurity, though evidence from excavations suggests that the sanctuary at Olympia dates from at least the 13th century BC.

The first historical mention of the Games at Olympia dates from 776 BC, when a cook named Coroebus from Elis won the 'dromos', a sprint race one length of the stadium, and from this year also dates the four-year period or Olympiad – the interval at which the Games were held.

events The Games expanded over the centuries to include more varied events. In 724 BC the 'diaulos', two stadium lengths, was added; in 720 BC the 'dolichos' was added – 24 lengths of the arena (comparable to the modern 5,000-metre race). All of these races on foot were run up and down, not around, the arena. Boxing, chariot races, the *pancratium* (a mixture of boxing and wrestling)

were added in the 7th century BC, and at various times the following other events were held at Olympia: pentathlon (long jump, discus, javelin, running, and wrestling), boys' events, and events for armed soldiers, heralds, and trumpeters. In addition to these sporting events, artists and sculptors exhibited their works and poets recited their poems. Not every event would be included at each celebration.

development At first the games occupied one day only, but were later extended over 5 days, the final day being devoted to the presentation of prizes (at first a garland), a closing ceremony, and a banquet. The games were also restricted to 'freeborn' Greeks – slaves and foreign competitors were barred, as were women. In the beginning what may be termed an 'amateur' spirit prevailed, but in time professionalism crept in, as eventually considerable money prizes were provided, and the Olympic champion was a national hero, receiving adulation and large material benefits.

---

when a boy, William Webb Ellis, picked up the ball and ran with it while playing football (now soccer). Rugby is played with an oval ball. It is now played in two forms: **Rugby League** and **Rugby Union.**

skating self-propulsion on ice by means of bladed skates, or on other surfaces by skates with small rollers (wheels of wood, metal, or plastic). The chief competitive ice-skating events are figure skating, for singles or pairs, ice-dancing, and simple speed skating. The first world ice-skating championships were held in 1896.

skiing self-propulsion on snow by means of elongated runners (skis) for the feet, slightly bent upward at the tip. It is a popular recreational sport, as cross-country ski touring or as downhill runs on mountain trails; events include downhill; slalom, in which a series of turns between flags have to be negotiated; cross-country racing; and ski jumping, when jumps of over 150 m/490 ft are achieved from ramps up to 90 m/295 ft high. Speed-skiing uses skis approximately one-third longer and wider than normal with which speeds of up to 200 kph/125 mph have been recorded. Recently, **snowboarding** (or

Speed Skating: Olympic Gold Medallists

Year	Category	Name	Country	Year	Category	Name	Country
Men				*Women*			
1994	500 m	Aleksandr Golubiev	Russia	1994	500 m	Bonnie Blair	USA
	1,000 m	Dan Jansen	USA		1,000 m	Bonnie Blair	USA
	1,500 m	Johann-Olav Koss	Norway		1,500 m	Emese Hunyady	Austria
	5,000 m	Johann-Olav Koss	Norway		3,000 m	Svetlana Bazhanova	Russia
	10,000 m	Johann-Olav Koss	Norway		5,000 m	Claudia Pechstein	Germany
1998	500 m	Hiroyasu Shimizu	Japan	1998	500 m	Catriona Lemay-Doan	Canada
	1,000 m	Ids Postma	Netherlands		1,000 m	Marianne Timmer	Netherlands
	1,500 m	Aadne Sondral	Norway		1,500 m	Marianne Timmer	Netherlands
	5,000 m	Gianni Romme	Netherlands		3,000 m	Gunda Niemann-Stirnemann	Germany
	10,000 m	Gianni Romme	Netherlands		5,000 m	Claudia Pechstein	Germany

monoboarding), the use of a single, very broad ski, similar to a surf board, used with the feet facing the front and placed together, has become increasingly popular.

softball bat and ball game, a form of baseball played with similar equipment. The two main differences are the distances between the bases (18.29 m/60 ft) and that the ball is pitched underhand in softball. There are two forms of the game, **fast pitch** and **slow pitch;** in the latter the ball must be delivered to home plate in an arc that must not be less than 2.4 m/8 ft at its height. The fast-pitch world championship was instituted in 1965 for women, in 1966 for men; it is now contested every four years.

squash or **squash rackets** racket-and-ball game usually played by two people on an enclosed court, derived from rackets. Squash became a popular sport in the 1970s and later gained competitive status. There are two forms of squash: the American form, which is played in North and some South American countries, and the English, which is played mainly in Europe and Commonwealth countries such as Pakistan, Australia, and New Zealand.

sumo wrestling national sport of Japan. Fighters of larger than average size (rarely less than 130 kg/21 st or 285 lb) try to push, pull, or throw each other out of a circular ring.

surfing sport of riding on the crest of large waves while standing on a narrow, keeled surfboard, usually of light synthetic material such as fibreglass, about 1.8 m/6 ft long (or about 2.4–7 m/8–9 ft known as the Malibu), as first developed in Hawaii and Australia. Windsurfing is a recent development.

swimming self-propulsion of the body through water. There are four strokes in competitive swimming: freestyle, breaststroke, backstroke, and butterfly. Distances of races vary between 50 and 1,500 metres. Olympic-size pools are 50 m/55 yd long and have eight lanes.

swimming, synchronized aquatic sport that demands artistry as opposed to speed. Competitors, either individual (solo) or in pairs, perform rhythmic routines to music. Points are awarded for interpretation and style. It was introduced into the Olympic swimming programme in 1984.

table tennis or **ping pong** indoor game played on a rectangular table by two or four players. It was developed in Britain about 1880 and derived from lawn tennis. World championships were first held in 1926.

tae kwon do Korean martial art similar to karate, which includes punching and kicking. It was included in the 1988 Olympic Games as a demonstration sport.

tennis or **lawn tennis** racket-and-ball game invented towards the end of the 19th century, derived from real tennis. Although played on different surfaces (grass, wood, shale, clay, concrete), it is also called 'lawn tennis'. The aim of the two or four players is to strike the ball into the prescribed area of the court, with oval-headed rackets (strung with gut or nylon), in such a way that it cannot be returned. Until the

Men's Swimming: Recent Olympic Gold Medallists

Year	Name	Country	Time	Year	Name	Country	Time
50 m Freestyle				*100 m Backstroke*			
1992	Aleksandr Popov	Unified Team[1]	21.91	1992	Mark Tewksbury	Canada	53.98
1996	Aleksandr Popov	Russia	22.13	1996	Jeff Rouse	USA	54.10
100 m Freestyle				*200 m Backstroke*			
1992	Aleksandr Popov	Unified Team[2]	49.02	1992	Martin Lopez-Zubero	Spain	1:58.47
1996	Aleksandr Popov	Russia	48.74	1996	Brad Bridgewater	USA	1:58.54
200 m Freestyle				*100 m Butterfly*			
1992	Yevgeni Sadovyi	Unified Team[2]	1:46.70	1992	Pablo Morales	USA	53.32
1996	Danyon Loader	New Zealand	1:47.63	1996	Denis Pankratov	Russia	52.27
400 m Freestyle				*200 m Butterfly*			
1992	Yevgeni Sadovyi	Unified Team[2]	3:45.00	1992	Mel Stewart	USA	1:56.26
1996	Danyon Loader	New Zealand	3:47.97	1996	Denis Pankratov	Russia	1:56.51
1,500 m Freestyle				*200 m Individual Medley*			
1992	Kieren Perkins	Australia	14:43.48	1992	Tamás Darnyi	Hungary	2:00.76
1996	Kieren Perkins	Australia	14:56.40	1996	Attila Czene	Hungary	1:59.91
100 m Breaststroke				*400 m Individual Medley*			
1992	Nelson Diebel	USA	1:01.50	1992	Tamás Darnyi	Hungary	4:14.23
1996	Fred Deburghgraeve	Belgium	1:00.65	1996	Tom Dolan	USA	4:14.90
200 m Breaststroke							
1992	Mike Barrowman	USA	2:10.16				
1996	Norbert Rozsa	Hungary	2:12.57				

[1] Commonwealth of Independent States plus Georgia.

Women's Swimming: Recent Olympic Gold Medallists

Year	Name	Country	Time	Year	Name	Country	Time
50 m Freestyle				*100 m Backstroke*			
1992	Yang Wenyi	China	24.79	1992	Krisztina Egerszegi	Hungary	1:00.68
1996	Amy Van Dyken	USA	24.87	1996	Beth Botsford	USA	1:01.19
100 m Freestyle				*200 m Backstroke*			
1992	Zhuang Yong	China	54.64	1992	Krisztina Egerszegi	Hungary	2:07.06
1996	Le Jingyi	China	54.50	1996	Krisztina Egerszegi	Hungary	2:07.83
200 m Freestyle				*100 m Butterfly*			
1992	Nicole Haislett	USA	1:57.90	1992	Qian Hong	China	58.62
1996	Claudia Poll	Costa Rica	1:58.16	1996	Amy Van Dyken	USA	59.13
400 m Freestyle				*200 m Butterfly*			
1992	Dagmar Hase	Germany	4:07.18	1992	Summer Sanders	USA	2:08.67
1996	Michelle Smith	Ireland, Republic of	4:07.25	1996	Susan O'Neill	Australia	2:07.76
800 m Freestyle				*200 m Individual Medley*			
				1992	Li Chin	China	2:11.65
1992	Janet Evans	USA	8:25.52	1996	Michelle Smith	Ireland, Republic of	2:13.93
1996	Brooke Bennett	USA	8:27.89				
100 m Breaststroke				*400 m Individual Medley*			
1992	Elena Rudkovskaia	Unified Team[1]	1:08.00	1992	Krisztina Egerszegi	Hungary	4:36.54
1996	Penny Heyns	South Africa	1:07.73	1996	Michelle Smith	Ireland, Republic of	4:39.29
200 m Breaststroke							
1992	Kyoko Iwasaki	Japan	2:26.65				
1996	Penny Heyns	South Africa	2:25.41				

[1] Commonwealth of Independent States plus Georgia.

Tennis: Davis Cup Winners

This international men's team competition was first held in 1900. Until 1972 the winner was decided in a Challenge Round in which the holders of the trophy met the winners of a knockout competition. Since then, the competition has been played entirely on a knockout basis.

Year	Winner	Runner-up	Score	Year	Winner	Runner-up	Score
1990	USA	Australia	3–2	1995	USA	Russia	3–2
1991	France	USA	3–1	1996	France	Sweden	3–2
1992	USA	Switzerland	3–1	1997	Sweden	USA	5–0
1993	Germany	Australia	4–1	1998	Sweden	Italy	4–1
1994	Sweden	Russia	4–1				

Australian Tennis Championship: Singles Champions

Year	Name	Country	Year	Name	Country
Men			*Women*		
1990	Ivan Lendl	Czech Republic	1990	Steffi Graf	West Germany
1991	Boris Becker	Germany	1991	Monica Seles	Yugoslavia
1992	Jim Courier	USA	1992	Monica Seles	Yugoslavia
1993	Jim Courier	USA	1993	Monica Seles	Yugoslavia
1994	Pete Sampras	USA	1994	Steffi Graf	Germany
1995	Andre Agassi	USA	1995	Mary Pierce	France
1996	Boris Becker	Germany	1996	Monica Seles	USA
1997	Pete Sampras	USA	1997	Martina Hingis	Switzerland
1998	Petr Korda	Czech Republic	1998	Martina Hingis	Switzerland
1999	Yevgeny Kafelnikov	Russia	1999	Martina Hingis	Switzerland

French Tennis Championship: Singles Champions

This competition became an open championship in 1968.

Year	Name	Country	Year	Name	Country
Men			*Women*		
1990	Andrés Gómez	Ecuador	1990	Monica Seles	Yugoslavia
1991	Jim Courier	USA	1991	Monica Seles	Yugoslavia
1992	Jim Courier	USA	1992	Monica Seles	Yugoslavia
1993	Sergi Bruguera	Spain	1993	Steffi Graf	Germany
1994	Sergi Bruguera	Spain	1994	Arantxa Sanchez Vicario	Spain
1995	Thomas Muster	Austria	1995	Steffi Graf	Germany
1996	Yevgeny Kafelnikov	Russia	1996	Steffi Graf	Germany
1997	Gustavo Kuerten	Brazil	1997	Iva Majoli	Croatia
1998	Carlos Moya	Spain	1998	Arantxa Sanchez Vicario	Spain

[1] Born Osborne.
[2] Born Haydon.

mid-1970s, tennis rackets were made from wood or moulded from aluminium. In 1976, the Prince racket, made from sandwiched layers of aluminium and glass fibre, doubled the racket area to 130 sq in. Today, rackets are made from graphite and glass fibre.

Major events include the **Davis Cup** first contested 1900 for international men's competition, and the annual All England Tennis Club championships (originating 1877), an open event for players of both sexes at Wimbledon, one of the four **Grand Slam** events; the others are the US Open, the French Championships, and the Australian Championships.

US Tennis Championship: Singles Champions

Winners are from the USA unless otherwise stated. This championship was first held in 1881. In 1968 and 1969, there was a separate Open Champion of professional players. In 1970, the championship became the US Open.

Year	Name
Men	
1990	Pete Sampras
1991	Stefan Edberg (Sweden)
1992	Stefan Edberg (Sweden)
1993	Pete Sampras
1994	Andre Agassi
1995	Pete Sampras
1996	Pete Sampras
1997	Patrick Rafter (Australia)
1998	Patrick Rafter (Australia)
Women	
1990	Gabriela Sabatini (Argentina)
1991	Monica Seles (Yugoslavia)
1992	Monica Seles (Yugoslavia)
1993	Steffi Graf (Germany)
1994	Arantxa Sanchez Vicario (Spain)
1995	Steffi Graf (Germany)
1996	Steffi Graf (Germany)
1997	Martina Hingis (Switzerland)
1998	Lindsay Davenport

Wimbledon Tennis Championship: Singles Champions

The championship was not held during the years 1915–1918 due to World War I, or during the years 1939–1945 due to World War II. Wimbledon became an open championship in 1968.

Year	Name	Country
Men		
1990	Stefan Edberg	Sweden
1991	Michael Stich	Germany
1992	Andre Agassi	USA
1993	Pete Sampras	USA
1994	Pete Sampras	USA
1995	Pete Sampras	USA
1996	Richard Krajicek	Netherlands
1997	Pete Sampras	USA
1998	Pete Sampras	USA
Women		
1990	Martina Navratilova	USA
1991	Steffi Graf	Germany
1992	Steffi Graf	Germany
1993	Steffi Graf	Germany
1994	Conchita Martinez	Spain
1995	Steffi Graf	Germany
1996	Steffi Graf	Germany
1997	Martina Hingis	Switzerland
1998	Jana Novotné	Czech Republic

tenpin bowling indoor sport popular in North America. As in skittles, the object is to bowl a ball down an alley at pins (ten as opposed to nine). The game is usually between two players or teams. A game of tenpins is made up of ten 'frames'. The frame is the bowler's turn to play and in each frame he or she may bowl twice. One point is scored for each pin knocked down, with bonus points for knocking all ten pins down in either one ball or two. The player or team making the greater score wins.

trampolining gymnastics performed on a sprung canvas sheet which allows the performer to reach great heights before landing again. Marks are gained for carrying out difficult manoeuvres. Synchronized trampolining and tumbling are also popular forms of the sport.

volleyball indoor and outdoor team game played on a court between two teams of six players each. A net is placed across the centre of the court, and players hit the ball with their hands over it, the aim being to ground it in the opponents' court.

water polo water sport developed in England 1869, originally called 'soccer-in-water'. The aim is to score goals, as in soccer, at each end of a swimming pool. It is played by teams of seven on each side (from squads of 13).

water skiing water sport in which a person is towed across water on a ski or skis, wider than those used for skiing on snow, by means of a rope (23 m/75 ft long) attached to a speedboat.

Yachting: America's Cup

In 1851 the US schooner *America* of the New York Yacht Club received a 'hundred guinea cup' from the Royal Yacht Squadron for winning a race around the Isle of Wight, England, against 15 British yachts. Renamed The America's Cup, it was offered as a challenge trophy by the New York Yacht Club, with the first challenge taking place in 1870. The yachts are from the USA unless otherwise stated.

Year	Winning yacht	Winning skipper	Series	Challenger
1901	*Columbia*	James Barr	3-0	*Shamrock II* (England)
1903	*Reliance*	James Barr	3-0	*Shamrock III* (England)
1920	*Resolute*	Charles Adams	3-2	*Shamrock IV* (England)
1930	*Enterprise*	Harold Vanderbilt	4-0	*Shamrock V* (England)
1934	*Rainbow*	Harold Vanderbilt	4-2	*Endeavour* (England)
1937	*Ranger*	Harold Vanderbilt	4-0	*Endeavour II* (England)
1958	*Columbia*	Briggs Cunningham	4-0	*Sceptre* (England)
1962	*Weatherly*	Emil Mosbacher Jr	4-1	*Gretel* (Australia)
1964	*Constellation*	Bob Bavier Jr	4-0	*Sovereign* (England)
1967	*Intrepid*	Emil Mosbacher Jr	4-0	*Dame Pattie* (Australia)
1970	*Intrepid*	Bill Ficker	4-1	*Gretel II* (Australia)
1974	*Courageous*	Ted Hood	4-0	*Southern Cross* (Australia)
1977	*Courageous*	Ted Turner	4-0	*Australia* (Australia)
1980	*Freedom*	Dennis Conner	4-1	*Australia* (Australia)
1983	*Australia II* (Australia)	John Bertrand	4-3	*Liberty*
1987	*Stars & Stripes*	Dennis Conner	4-0	*Kookaburra III* (Australia)
1988	*Stars & Stripes*	Dennis Conner	2-0	*New Zealand* (New Zealand)
1992	*America*	Bill Koch	4-1	*Il Moro di Venezia* (Italy)
1995	*Black Magic* (New Zealand)	Russell Coutts	5-0	*Young America*

Competitions are held for overall performances, slalom, tricks, and jumping.

weightlifting sport of lifting the heaviest possible weight above one's head to the satisfaction of judges. In international competitions there are two standard lifts: **snatch** and **jerk.**

wrestling sport popular in ancient Egypt, Greece, and Rome, and included in the Olympics from 704 BC. The two main modern international styles are **Greco-Roman,** concentrating on above-waist holds, and **freestyle,** which allows the legs to be used to hold or trip; in both the aim is to throw the opponent to the ground.

yachting pleasure cruising or racing a small and light vessel, whether sailing or power-driven. At the 1996 Olympic Games there were eight sail-driven categories: Laser, 470, Tornado, Soling, Mistral, Star, Finn, and Europe. The Laser, Mistral, Finn, and Europe are solo events; the Soling class is for three-person crews; all other classes are for crews of two. The International Sailing Federation (ISF) World Sailing Championships were inaugurated in 1994 and are held every four years. Additionally, separate world championships are held annually in each of the Olympic classes and in others such as the Melges 24 or Mumm 30.

COUNTRIES OF THE WORLD

✳

Afghanistan

Republic of

National name: *Islamic Emirate of Afghanistan* **Area:** 652,090 sq km/251,771 sq mi **Capital:** Kabul **Major towns/cities:** Kandahar, Herat, Mazar-i-Sharif, Jalalabad **Physical features:** mountainous in centre and northeast (Hindu Kush mountain range; Khyber and Salang passes, Wakhan salient, and Panjshir Valley), plains in north and southwest, Amu Darya (Oxus) River, Helmand River, Lake Saberi **Head of state and government:** Mohammad Rabbani from 1996 **Political system:** transitional **Political parties:** Hezb-i-Islami, Islamic fundamentalist Mujaheddin, anti-Western; Jamiat-i-Islami, Islamic fundamentalist Mujaheddin; National Liberation Front, moderate Mujaheddin **Currency:** afgháni **Real GDP per capita (PPP):** ($ US) 600 (1995 est) **Exports:** fruit and nuts, carpets, wool, karakul skins, cotton, natural gas. Principal market: Kyrgyzstan 37.3% (1995) **Population:** 20,883,000 (1996 est) **Language:** Pushtu, Dari (Persian), Uzbek, Turkoman, Kirgiz **Religion:** Muslim (85% Sunni, 15% Shi'ite) **Life expectancy:** 45 (men); 46 (women) (1995–2000)

Albania

Republic of

National name: *Republika e Shqipërisë* **Area:** 28,748 sq km/11,099 sq mi **Capital:** Tiranë (Tirana) **Major towns/cities:** Durrës, Shkodër, Elbasan, Vlorë, Korçë **Major ports:** Durrës **Physical features:** mainly mountainous, with rivers flowing east–west, and a narrow coastal plain **Head of state:** Rexhep Mejdani from 1997 **Head of government:** Pandeli Majko from 1997 **Political system:** emergent democracy **Political parties:** Democratic Party of Albania (PDS; formerly the Democratic Party: DP), moderate, market-oriented; Socialist Party of Albania (PSS), ex-communist; Human Rights Union (HMU), Greek minority party **Currency:** lek **Real GDP per capita (PPP):** ($ US) 2,788 (1994) **Exports:** chromium and chrome products, processed foodstuffs, plant and animal products, bitumen, electricity, tobacco. Principal market: Italy 52% (1994) **Population:** 3,401,000 (1996 est) **Language:** Albanian, Greek **Religion:** Muslim, Orthodox, Roman Catholic **Life expectancy:** 70 (men); 76 (women) (1995–2000)

Algeria

Democratic and Popular Republic of

National name: *al-Jumhuriya al-Jazairiya ad-Dimuqratiya ash-Shabiya* **Area:** 2,381,741 sq km/919,590 sq mi **Capital:** Algiers (al-Jaza'ir) **Major towns/cities:** Oran, Annaba, Blida, Sétif, Constantine (Qacentina) **Major ports:** Oran (Ouahran), Annaba (Bône) **Physical features:** coastal plains backed by mountains in north, Sahara desert in south; Atlas mountains, Barbary Coast, Chott Melrhir depression, Hoggar mountains **Head of state:** Liamine Zeroual from 1994 **Head of government:** Ahmed Ouyahia from 1995 **Political system:** military rule **Political parties:** National Liberation Front (FLN), nationalist, socialist; Socialist Forces Front (FSS), Berber-based, left of centre; Islamic Front for Salvation (FIS), Islamic fundamentalist (banned from 1992); National Democratic Rally (RND), left of centre **Currency:** Algerian dinar **Real GDP per capita (PPP):** ($ US) 5,442 (1994) **Exports:** crude oil, gas, vegetables, tobacco, hides, dates. Principal market: Italy 18.8% (1995) **Population:** 28,784,000 (1996 est) **Language:** Arabic (official); Berber, French **Religion:** Sunni

Muslim (state religion) **Life expectancy:** 67 (men); 70
(women) (1995–2000)

Andorra

Principality of

National name: *Principat d'Andorra* **Area:** 468 sq km/
181 sq mi **Capital:** Andorra-la-Vella **Major
towns/cities:** Les Escaldes, Escaldes-Engordany
(suburb of capital) **Physical features:** mountainous,
with narrow valleys; the eastern Pyrenees, Valira
River **Heads of state:** Joan Marti i Alanis (bishop of
Urgel, Spain) and Jacques Chirac (president of
France) **Head of government:** Marc Forne from 1994
Political system: co-principality **Political parties:**
National Democratic Grouping (AND; formerly the
Democratic Party of Andorra: PDA) moderate,
centrist; National Democratic Initiative (IND), left of
centre; New Democracy Party (ND), centrist; National
Andorran Coalition (CNA), centrist; Liberal Union
(UL), right of centre **Currency:** French franc and
Spanish peseta **Real GDP per capita (PPP):** ($ US)
16,200 (1993 est) **Exports:** cigars and cigarettes,
furniture, electricity. Principal market: France 46.7%
(1994) **Population:** 71,000 (1996 est) **Language:**
Catalan (official); Spanish, French **Religion:** Roman
Catholic **Life expectancy:** 70 (men); 73 (women)
(1994 est)

Angola

People's Republic of

National name: *República Popular de Angola* **Area:**
1,246,700 sq km/481,350 sq mi **Capital:** Luanda (and
chief port) **Major towns/cities:** Lobito, Benguela,
Huambo, Lubango, Malange, Namibe (formerly
Moçâmedes) **Major ports:** Huambo, Lubango,
Malange **Physical features:** narrow coastal plain rises
to vast interior plateau with rainforest in northwest;
desert in south; Cuanza, Cuito, Cubango, and
Cunene rivers **Head of state:** José Eduardo dos
Santos from 1979 **Head of government:** Fernando
Franca van Dunem from 1996 **Political system:**

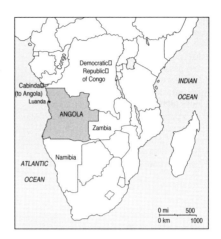

emergent democracy **Political parties:** People's
Movement for the Liberation of Angola–Workers'
Party (MPLA–PT), Marxist-Leninist; National Union for
the Total Independence of Angola (UNITA); National
Front for the Liberation of Angola (FNLA) **Currency:**
kwanza **Real GDP per capita (PPP):** ($ US) 1,600 (1994
est) **Exports:** petroleum and petroleum products,
diamonds, gas. Principal market: USA 65.4% (1995)
Population: 11,185,000 (1996 est) **Language:**
Portuguese (official); Bantu dialects **Religion:** Roman
Catholic 68%, Protestant 20%, animist 12% **Life
expectancy:** 47 (men); 51 (women) (1995–2000)

Antigua and Barbuda

State of

Area: Antigua 280 sq km/108 sq mi, Barbuda 161 sq
km/62 sq mi, plus Redonda 1 sq km/0.4 sq mi (440 sq
km/169 sq mi altogether) **Capital:** St John's (on
Antigua) (and chief port) **Major towns/cities:**
Codrington (on Barbuda) **Physical features:** low-lying
tropical islands of limestone and coral with some
higher volcanic outcrops; no rivers and low rainfall
result in frequent droughts and deforestation.
Antigua is the largest of the Leeward Islands;
Redonda is an uninhabited island of volcanic rock
rising to 305 m/1,000 ft **Head of state:** Elizabeth II

from 1981, represented by governor general James B Carlisle from 1993 **Head of government:** Lester Bird from 1994 **Political system:** liberal democracy **Political parties:** Antigua Labour Party (ALP), moderate left of centre; United Progressive Party (UPP), centrist; Barbuda People's Movement (BPM), left of centre **Currency:** Eastern Caribbean dollar **Real GDP per capita (PPP):** ($ US) 8,977 (1994) **Exports:** petroleum products, food, manufactures, machinery and transport equipment. Principal market: USA (mainly re-exports) **Population:** 66,000 (1996 est) **Language:** English **Religion:** Christian (mostly Anglican) **Life expectancy:** 70 (men); 74 (women) (1994 est)

Argentina

Republic of

National name: *República Argentina* **Area:** 2,780,092 sq km/1,073,393 sq mi **Capital:** Buenos Aires **Major towns/cities:** Rosario, Córdoba, San Miguel de Tucumán, Mendoza, Santa Fé, La Plata **Major ports:** La Plata and Bahía Blanca **Physical features:** mountains in west, forest and savanna in north, pampas (treeless plains) in east-central area, Patagonian plateau in south; rivers Colorado, Salado, Paraná, Uruguay, Río de La Plata estuary; Andes mountains, with Aconcagua the highest peak in western hemisphere; Iguaçu Falls **Territories:** claims Falkland Islands (*Islas Malvinas*), South Georgia, the South Sandwich Islands, and part of Antarctica **Head of state and government:** Carlos Menem from 1989 **Political system:** democratic federal republic **Political parties:** Radical Civic Union Party (UCR), moderate centrist; Justicialist Party (PJ), right-wing Perónist; Movement for Dignity and Independence (Modin), right-wing; Front for a Country in Solidarity (Frepaso), centre left **Currency:** peso = 10,000 australs (which it replaced 1992) **Real GDP per capita (PPP):** ($ US) 8,937 (1994) **Exports:** meat and meat products, prepared animal fodder, cereals, petroleum and petroleum products, soya beans, vegetable oils and fats. Principal market: Brazil 20.8% (1995)

Population: 35,219,000 (1996 est) **Language:** Spanish 95% (official); Italian 3% **Religion:** Roman Catholic (state-supported) **Life expectancy:** 70 (men); 77 (women) (1995–2000)

Armenia

Republic of

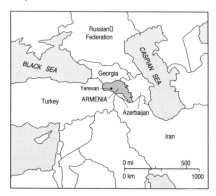

National name: *Haikakan Hanrapetoutioun* **Area:** 29,800 sq km/11,505 sq mi **Capital:** Yerevan **Major towns/cities:** Gyumri (formerly Leninakan), Vanadzor (formerly Kirovakan) **Physical features:** mainly mountainous (including Mount Ararat), wooded **Head of state:** Robert Kocharyan from 1998 **Head of government:** Robert Kocharyan from 1997 **Political system:** authoritarian nationalist **Political parties:** Armenian Pan-National Movement (APM), nationalist, left of centre; Armenian Revolutionary Federation (ARF), centrist (banned in 1994); Communist Party of Armenia (banned 1991–92); National Unity, opposition coalition **Currency:** dram (replaced Russian rouble in 1993) **Real GDP per capita (PPP):** ($ US) 1,737 (1994) **Exports:** machinery and metalworking products, chemical and petroleum products. Principal market: Russia 20% (1995) **Population:** 3,638,000 (1996 est) **Language:** Armenian **Religion:** Armenian Christian **Life expectancy:** 76 (men); 70 (women) (1995–2000)

Australia

Commonwealth of

Area: 7,682,300 sq km/2,966,136 sq mi **Capital:** Canberra **Major towns/cities:** Adelaide, Alice Springs, Brisbane, Darwin, Melbourne, Perth, Sydney, Hobart, Geelong, Newcastle, Townsville, Wollongong **Physical features:** Ayers Rock; Arnhem Land; Gulf of Carpentaria; Cape York Peninsula; Great Australian Bight; Great Sandy Desert; Gibson Desert; Great Victoria Desert; Simpson Desert; the Great Barrier Reef; Great Dividing Range and Australian Alps in the east (Mount Kosciusko, 2,229 m/7,136 ft, Australia's highest peak). The fertile southeast region is watered by the Darling, Lachlan, Murrumbridgee, and Murray rivers. Lake Eyre basin and Nullarbor Plain in the south **Territories:** Norfolk Island, Christmas Island, Cocos (Keeling) Islands, Ashmore and Cartier Islands, Coral Sea Islands, Heard Island and McDonald Islands, Australian Antarctic Territory **Head of state:** Elizabeth II from 1952, represented by governor general William George Hayden from 1989 **Head of government:** John Howard from 1996 **Political system:** federal constitutional monarchy **Political parties:** Australian Labor Party, moderate left of centre; Liberal Party of Australia, moderate, liberal, free enterprise; National Party of Australia (formerly Country Party), centrist non-metropolitan **Currency:** Australian dollar **Real GDP per capita (PPP):** ($ US) 20,368 (1996) **Exports:** major world producer of raw materials: iron ore, aluminium, coal, nickel, zinc, lead, gold, tin, tungsten, uranium, crude oil; wool, meat, cereals, fruit, sugar, wine. Principal markets: Japan 22% (1996) **Population:** 18,057,000 (1996 est) **Language:** English, Aboriginal Languages **Religion:** Anglican 26%, other Protestant 17%, Roman Catholic 26% **Life expectancy:** 75 (men); 81 (women) (1995–2000)

Austria

Republic of

National name: *Republik Österreich* **Area:** 83,500 sq km/32,239 sq mi **Capital:** Vienna **Major towns/cities:** Graz, Linz, Salzburg, Innsbruck, Klagenfurt **Physical features:** landlocked mountainous state, with Alps in west and south (Austrian Alps, including Grossglockner and Brenner and Semmering passes,

Lechtaler and Allgauer Alps north of River Inn, Carnic Alps on Italian border) and low relief in east where most of the population is concentrated; River Danube **Head of state:** Thomas Klestil from 1992 **Head of government:** Franz Vranitzky from 1986 **Political system:** democratic federal republic **Political parties:** Social Democratic Party of Austria (SPÖ), democratic socialist; Austrian People's Party (ÖVP), progressive centrist; Freedom (formerly Freedom Party of Austria: FPÖ), right wing; United Green Party of Austria (VGÖ), conservative ecological; Green Alternative Party (ALV), radical ecological **Currency:** schilling **Real GDP per capita (PPP):** ($ US) 21,120 (1996) **Exports:** dairy products, food products, wood and paper products, machinery and transport equipment, metal and metal products, chemical products. Principal market for exports: EU countries 63.6% (1993) **Population:** 8,106,000 (1996 est) **Language:** German **Religion:** Roman Catholic 78%, Protestant 5% **Life expectancy:** 74 (men); 80 (women) (1995–2000)

Azerbaijan

Republic of

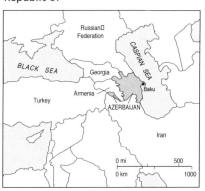

National name: *Azarbaijchan Respublikasy* **Area:** 86,600 sq km/33,436 sq mi **Capital:** Baku **Major towns/cities:** Gyandzha (formerly Kirovabad), Sumgait, Nakhichevan, Stepanakert **Physical features:** Caspian Sea with rich oil reserves; the country ranges from semidesert to the Caucasus Mountains **Head of state:** Geidar Aliyev from 1993 **Head of government:** Artur Rasizade from 1996 **Political system:** authoritarian nationalist **Political parties:** Popular Front of Azerbaijan (FPA), democratic nationalist; New Azerbaijan, ex-communist; Communist Party of Azerbaijan (banned 1991–93); Muslim Democratic Party (Musavat), Islamic, pro-Turkic unity **Currency:** manat (left rouble zone in 1993) **Real GDP per capita (PPP):** ($ US) 1,670 (1994) **Exports:** refined petroleum products, machinery, food products, textiles. Principal market: Iran 30% (1995) **Population:** 7,594,000 (1996 est) **Language:** Azeri **Religion:** Shi'ite Muslim 62%, Sunni Muslim 26%, Orthodox Christian 12% **Life expectancy:** 68 (men); 75 (women) (1995–2000)

Bahamas

Commonwealth of the

Area: 13,864 sq km/5,352 sq mi **Capital:** Nassau (on New Providence Island) **Major towns/cities:** Freeport (on Grand Bahama) **Physical features:** comprises 700 tropical coral islands and about 1,000 cays; the Exumas are a narrow spine of 365 islands; only 30 of the desert islands are inhabited; Blue Holes of Andros, the world's longest and deepest submarine caves **Principal islands** Andros, Grand Bahama, Abaco, Eleuthera, New Providence, Berry Islands, Bimini Islands, Great Inagua, Acklins Island, Exuma Islands, Mayguana, Crooked Island, Long Island, Cat Islands, Rum Cay, Watling (San Salvador) Island, Inagua Islands **Head of state:** Elizabeth II from 1973, represented by governor general Orville Turnquest from 1995 **Head of government:** Hubert Ingraham from 1992 **Political system:** constitutional monarchy **Political parties:** Progressive Liberal Party (PLP), centrist; Free National Movement (FNM), centre left **Currency:** Bahamian dollar **Real GDP per capita (PPP):** ($ US) 15,875 (1994) **Exports:** foodstuffs (fish), oil products and transhipments, chemicals, rum, salt. Principal market: USA 23.7% (1995) **Population:** 284,000 (1996 est) **Language:** English and some Creole **Religion:** Christian 94% (Roman Catholic 26%, Anglican 21%, other Protestant 48%) **Life expectancy:** 70 (men); 79 (women) (1995–2000)

Bahrain

State of

National name: *Dawlat al Bahrayn* **Area:** 688 sq km/266 sq mi **Capital:** Al Manamah on the largest island (also called Bahrain) **Major towns/cities:** Muharraq, Jiddhafs, Isa Town, Hidd, Rifa'a, Sitra **Major ports:** Mina Sulman **Physical features:** archipelago of 35 islands in Arabian Gulf, composed largely of sand-covered limestone; generally poor and infertile soil; flat and hot; causeway linking Bahrain to mainland Saudi Arabia **Head of state:** Sheik Isa bin Sulman al-Khalifa from 1961 **Head of government:** Sheik Khalifa bin Sulman al-Khalifa from 1970 **Political system:** absolute emirate **Political**

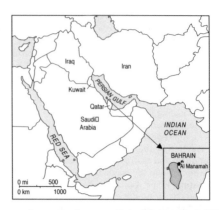

parties: none **Currency:** Bahraini dinar **Real GDP per capita (PPP):** ($ US) 12,000 (1994) **Exports:** petroleum and petroleum products, aluminium. Principal market: India 21.5% (1994) **Population:** 570,000 (1996 est) **Language:** Arabic (official); Farsi, English, Urdu **Religion:** 85% Muslim (Shi'ite 60%, Sunni 40%), Christian; Islam is the state religion **Life expectancy:** 71 (men); 75 (women) (1995–2000)

Bangladesh

People's Republic of (formerly **East Pakistan**)

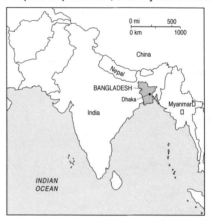

National name: *Gana Prajatantri Bangladesh* **Area:** 144,000 sq km/55,598 sq mi **Capital:** Dhaka (formerly Dacca) **Major towns/cities:** Rajshahi, Khulna, Chittagong, Comilla, Barisal, Sylhet **Major ports:** Chittagong, Khulna **Physical features:** flat delta of rivers Ganges (Padma) and Brahmaputra (Jamuna), the largest estuarine delta in the world; annual rainfall of 2,540 mm/100 in; some 75% of the land is less than 3 m/10 ft above sea level; hilly in extreme southeast and northeast **Head of state:** Abdur Rahman Biswas from 1991 **Head of government:** Sheikha Hasina Wazed from 1996 **Political system:** emergent democracy **Political parties:** Bangladesh Nationalist Party (BNP), Islamic, right of centre; Awami League (AL), secular, moderate socialist; Jatiya Dal (National Party), Islamic nationalist

Currency: taka **Real GDP per capita (PPP):** ($ US)
1,330 (1994) **Exports:** raw jute and jute goods, tea,
clothing, leather and leather products, shrimps and
frogs' legs. Principal market: USA 31.5% (1995)
Population: 120,073,000 (1996 est) **Language:** Bengali
(official); English **Religion:** Sunni Muslim 85%, Hindu
12%; Islam is the state religion **Life expectancy:** 58
(men); 58 (women) (1995–2000)

Barbados

Area: 430 sq km/166 sq mi **Capital:** Bridgetown **Major
towns/cities:** Speightstown, Holetown, Oistins
Physical features: most easterly island of the West
Indies; surrounded by coral reefs; subject to
hurricanes June–November; highest point Mount
Hillaby 340 m/1,115 ft **Head of state:** Elizabeth II
from 1966, represented by Denys Williams from 1995
Head of government: Owen Arthur from 1994
Political system: constitutional monarchy **Political
parties:** Barbados Labour Party (BLP), moderate left
of centre; Democratic Labour Party (DLP), moderate
left of centre; National Democratic Party (NDP),
centrist **Currency:** Barbados dollar **Real GDP per
capita (PPP):** ($ US) 11,051 (1994) **Exports:** sugar,
molasses, syrup-rum, chemicals, electrical
components. Principal market: USA 20% (1995)
Population: 261,000 (1996 est) **Language:** English and
Bajan (Barbadian English dialect) **Religion:** 33%
Anglican, 13% Pentecostalist, 6% Methodist, 4%
Roman Catholic **Life expectancy:** 74 (men); 79
(women) (1995–2000)

Belarus

Republic of

National name: *Respublika Belarus* **Area:** 207,600 sq
km/80,154 sq mi **Capital:** Minsk (Mensk) **Major
towns/cities:** Gomel, Vitebsk, Mogilev, Bobruisk,
Hrodna, Brest **Physical features:** more than 25%
forested; rivers Dvina, Dnieper and its tributaries,
including the Pripet and Beresina; the Pripet Marshes
in the east; mild and damp climate **Head of state:**
Alexandr Lukashenko from 1994 **Head of
government:** Syargey Ling from 1996 **Political**

system: emergent democracy **Political parties:**
Belarus Communist Party (BCP, banned 1991–92);
Belarus Patriotic Movement (BPM), populist;
Belarusian Popular Front (BPF; Adradzhenne),
moderate nationalist; Christian Democratic Union of
Belarus, centrist; Socialist Party of Belarus, left of
centre **Currency:** rouble and zaichik **Real GDP per
capita (PPP):** ($ US) 4,713 (1994) **Exports:** machinery,
chemicals and petrochemicals, iron and steel, light
industrial goods. Principal market: Russia 41.6%
(1996) **Population:** 10,138,000 (1996 est) **Language:**
Belarusian (official); Russian, Polish **Religion:** Russian
Orthodox, Roman Catholic; Baptist, Muslim, and
Jewish minorities **Life expectancy:** 68 (men); 75
(women) (1995–2000)

Belgium

Kingdom of

National name: French *Royaume de Belgique.*
Flemish *Koninkrijk Belgiê* **Area:** 30,510 sq km/11,779
sq mi **Capital:** Brussels **Major towns/cities:** Antwerp,
Ghent, Liège, Charleroi, Bruges, Mons, Namur,
Leuven **Major ports:** Antwerp, Ostend, Zeebrugge
Physical features: fertile coastal plain in northwest,
central rolling hills rise eastwards, hills and forest in
southeast; Ardennes Forest; rivers Schelde and Meuse
Head of state: King Albert from 1993 **Head of**

government: Jean-Luc Dehaene from 1992 **Political system:** federal constitutional monarchy **Political parties:** Flemish Christian Social Party (CVP), centre left; French Social Christian Party (PSC), centre left; Flemish Socialist Party (SP), left of centre; French Socialist Party (PS), left of centre; Flemish Liberal Party (PVV), moderate centrist; French Liberal Reform Party (PRL), moderate centrist; Flemish People's Party (VU), federalist; Flemish Vlaams Blok, right wing; Flemish Green Party (Agalev); French Green Party (Ecolo) **Currency:** Belgian franc **Real GDP per capita (PPP):** ($ US) 21,454 (1996) **Exports:** food, livestock and livestock products, gem diamonds, iron and steel manufacturers, machinery and transport equipment, chemicals and related products. Principal market: Germany 20.6% (1996) **Population:** 10,159,000 (1996 est) **Language:** in the north (Flanders) Flemish (a Dutch dialect, known as *Vlaams*) 55%; in the south (Wallonia) Walloon (a French dialect) 32%; bilingual 11%; German (eastern border) 0.6%. Dutch is official in the north, French in the south; Brussels is officially bilingual **Religion:** Roman Catholic 75%, various Protestant denominations **Life expectancy:** 74 (men); 81 (women) (1995–2000)

Belize

(formerly **British Honduras**)

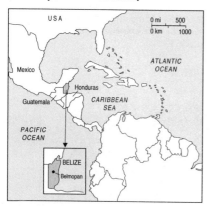

Area: 22,963 sq km/8,866 sq mi **Capital:** Belmopan **Major towns/cities:** Belize City, Dangriga, Orange Walk, Corozal **Major ports:** Belize City, Dangriga, Punta Gorda **Physical features:** tropical swampy coastal plain, Maya Mountains in south; over 90% forested **Head of state:** Elizabeth II from 1981, represented by governor general Dr Norbert Colville Young from 1993 **Head of government:** Manuel Esquivel from 1993 **Political system:** constitutional monarchy **Political parties:** People's United Party (PUP), left of centre; United Democratic Party (UDP), moderate conservative **Currency:** Belize dollar **Real GDP per capita (PPP):** ($ US) 5,590 (1994) **Exports:** sugar, clothes, citrus products, forestry and fish products, bananas. Principal market: UK 40.2% (1994) **Population:** 219,000 (1996 est) **Language:** English (official); Spanish (widely spoken), Creole dialects **Religion:** Roman Catholic 60%, Protestant

35% **Life expectancy:** 73 (men); 76 (women) (1995–2000)

Benin

People's Republic of (formerly known as **Dahomey 1904–75**)

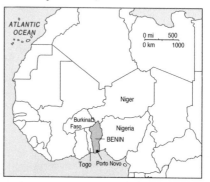

National name: *République Populaire du Bénin* **Area:** 112,622 sq km/43,483 sq mi **Capital:** Porto-Novo (official), Cotonou (de facto) **Major towns/cities:** Abomey, Natitingou, Parakou, Kandi, Ouidah, Djougou, Bohicou **Major ports:** Cotonou **Physical features:** flat to undulating terrain; hot and humid in south; semiarid in north; coastal lagoons with fishing villages on stilts; Niger River in northeast **Head of state and government:** vacant **Political system:** socialist pluralist republic **Political parties:** Union for the Triumph of Democratic Renewal (UTDR); National Party for Democracy and Development (PNDD); Party for Democratic Renewal (PRD); Social Democratic Party (PSD); National Union for Solidarity and Progress (UNSP); National Democratic Rally (RND). The general orientation of most parties is left of centre **Currency:** franc CFA **Real GDP per capita (PPP):** ($ US) 1,696 (1994) **Exports:** cotton, crude petroleum, palm oil and other palm products. Principal market: Morocco 37.6% (1994) **Population:** 5,563,000 (1996 est) **Language:** French (official); Fon 47% and Yoruba 9% in south; six major tribal Languages in north **Religion:** animist 60%, Muslim, Roman Catholic **Life expectancy:** 47 (men); 51 (women) (1995–2000)

Bhutan

Kingdom of

National name: *Druk-yul* **Area:** 46,500 sq km/17,953 sq mi **Capital:** Thimphu (Thimbu) **Major towns/cities:** Paro, Punakha, Mongar, P'sholing, W'phodrang, Bumthang **Physical features:** occupies southern slopes of the Himalayas; Gangkar Punsum (7,529 m/24,700 ft) is one of the world's highest unclimbed peaks; cut by valleys formed by tributaries of the Brahmaputra; thick forests in south **Head of state and government:** Jigme Singye Wangchuk from 1972 **Political system:** absolute monarchy **Political parties:** none officially; illegal Bhutan People's Party (BPP) and Bhutan National Democratic Party (BNDP), both

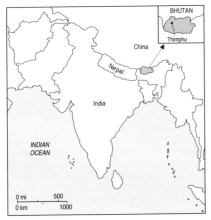

ethnic Nepali **Currency:** ngultrum; also Indian currency**Real GDP per capita (PPP):** ($ US) 730 (1995 est) **Exports:** cardamon, cement, timber, fruit, electricity (to India), precious stones, spices. Principal market: India 94% (1994) **Population:** 1,812,000 (1996 est) **Language:** Dzongkha (official, a Tibetan dialect), Sharchop, Bumthap, Nepali, and English **Religion:** 70% Mahayana Buddhist (state religion), 25% Hindu **Life expectancy:** 52 (men); 55 (women) (1995–2000)

Bolivia

Republic of

National name: *República de Bolivia* **Area:** 1,098,581 sq km/424,162 sq mi **Capital:** La Paz (seat of government), Sucre (legal capital and seat of judiciary) **Major towns/cities:** Santa Cruz, Cochabamba, Oruro, El Alto, Potosí **Physical features:** high plateau (Altiplano) between mountain ridges (cordilleras); forest and lowlands (llano) in east; Andes; lakes Titicaca (the world's highest navigable lake, 3,800 m/12,500 ft) and Poopó **Head of state and government:** Hugo Banzer Suarez from 1997

Political system: emergent democracy **Political parties:** National Revolutionary Movement (MNR), centre right; Movement of the Revolutionary Left (MIR), left of centre; Nationalist Democratic Action Party (ADN), right wing; Solidarity and Civic Union (UCS), populist, free market **Currency:** boliviano **Real GDP per capita (PPP):** ($ US) 2,598 (1994) **Exports:** metallic minerals, natural gas, jewellery, soya beans, wood. Principal market: USA 24.1% (1995). Illegal trade in coca and its derivatives (mainly cocaine) was worth approximately $600 million in 1990 – almost equal to annual earnings from official exports **Population:** 7,593,000 (1996 est) **Language:** Spanish (official); Aymara, Quechua **Religion:** Roman Catholic 95% (state-recognized) **Life expectancy:** 60 (men); 63 (women) (1995–2000)

Bosnia-Herzegovina

Republic of

National name: *Republika Bosna i Hercegovina* **Area:** 51,129 sq km/19,740 sq mi **Capital:** Sarajevo **Major towns/cities:** Banja Luka, Mostar, Prijedor, Tuzla, Zenica **Physical features:** barren, mountainous country, part of the Dinaric Alps; limestone gorges; 20 km/12 mi of coastline with no harbour **Heads of state:** Alija Izetbegović from 1990, Momcilo Krajisnik and Kerismir Zubak from 1996 **Heads of government:** Haris Silajdzic and Boro Bosic from 1997 **Political system:** emergent democracy **Political parties:** Party of Democratic Action (PDA), Muslim-oriented; Serbian Renaissance Movement (SPO), Serbian nationalist; Croatian Christian Democratic Union of Bosnia-Herzegovina (CDU), Croatian nationalist; League of Communists (LC) and Socialist Alliance (SA), left wing **Currency:** dinar **Real GDP per capita (PPP):** ($ US) 300 (1995 est) **Exports:** coal, domestic appliances (industrial production and mining remain low). Principal market: Italy 29.4% (1995) **Population:** 3,628,000 (1996 est) **Language:** Serbian variant of Serbo-Croatian **Religion:** Sunni Muslim, Serbian Orthodox, Roman Catholic **Life expectancy:** 70 (men); 76 (women) (1995–2000)

Botswana

Republic of

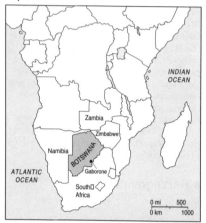

Area: 582,000 sq km/224,710 sq mi **Capital:** Gaborone **Major towns/cities:** Mahalapye, Serowe, Tutume, Bobonong Francistown, Selebi-Phikwe, Lobatse, Molepolol, Kange **Physical features:** Kalahari Desert in southwest (70–80% of national territory is desert), plains (Makgadikgadi salt pans) in east, fertile lands and Okavango Delta in north **Head of state and government:** Festus Mogae from 1998 **Political system:** democracy **Political parties:** Botswana Democratic Party (BDP), moderate centrist; Botswana National Front (BNF), moderate left of centre **Currency:** franc CFA **Real GDP per capita (PPP):** ($ US) 5,367 (1994) **Exports:** diamonds, copper and nickel, beef. Principal market: Europe 86.7% (1994) **Population:** 1,484,000 (1996 est) **Language:** English (official), Setswana (national) **Religion:** Christian 50%, animist, Baha'i, Muslim, Hindu **Life expectancy:** 65 (men); 69 (women) (1995–2000)

Brazil

Federative Republic of

National name: *República Federativa do Brasil* **Area:** 8,511,965 sq km/3,286,469 sq mi **Capital:** Brasília **Major towns/cities:** São Paulo, Belo Horizonte, Nova Iguaçu, Rio de Janeiro, Belém, Recife, Pôrto Alegre, Salvador, Curitiba, Manaus, Fortaleza **Major ports:** Rio de Janeiro, Belém, Recife, Pôrto Alegre, Salvador **Physical features:** the densely forested Amazon basin covers the northern half of the country with a network of rivers; south is fertile; enormous energy resources, both hydroelectric (Itaipú Reservoir on the Paraná, and Tucuruí on the Tocantins) and nuclear (uranium ores); mostly tropical climate **Head of state and government:** Fernando Henrique Cardoso from 1994 **Political system:** democratic federal republic **Political parties:** Workers' Party (PT), left of centre; Social Democratic Party (PSDB), moderate, left of centre; Brazilian Democratic Movement Party (PMDB), centre left; Liberal Front Party (PFL), right wing; National Reconstruction Party (PRN), centre right **Currency:** real **Real GDP per capita (PPP):** ($ US) 5,362 (1994) **Exports:** steel products, transport equipment, coffee, iron ore and concentrates, aluminium, iron, tin, soya beans, orange juice (85% of world's concentrates), tobacco, leather footwear, sugar, beef, textiles. Principal market: USA 18.9% (1995) **Population:** 161,087,000 (1996 est) **Language:** Portuguese (official); 120 Indian Languages **Religion:** Roman Catholic 89%; Indian faiths **Life expectancy:** 65 (men); 70 (women) (1995–2000)

Brunei

State of

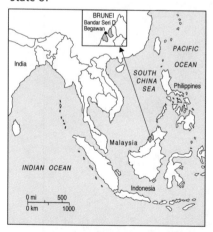

National name: *Negara Brunei Darussalam* **Area:** 5,765 sq km/2,225 sq mi **Capital:** Bandar Seri Begawan **Major towns/cities:** Seria, Kuala Belait, Bangar **Physical features:** flat coastal plain with hilly lowland in west and mountains in east (Mount Pagon 1,850 m/6,070 ft); 75% of the area is forested; the Limbang valley splits Brunei in two, and its cession to Sarawak in 1890 is disputed by Brunei; tropical climate; Temburong, Tutong, and Belait rivers **Head of state and government:** HM Muda Hassanal Bolkiah Mu'izzaddin Waddaulah, Sultan of

Brunei, from 1967 **Political system:** absolute monarchy **Political parties:** Brunei National Democratic Party (BNDP) and Brunei National United Party (BNUP) (both banned since 1988); Brunei People's Party (BPP) (banned since 1962) **Currency:** Brunei dollar (ringgit) **Real GDP per capita (PPP): ($** US) 30,447 (1994) **Exports:** crude petroleum and natural gas (accounting for 91.7% of total export earnings in 1993). Principal market: Japan 50% (1994) **Population:** 300,000 (1996 est) **Language:** Malay (official), Chinese (Hokkien), English **Religion:** Muslim 66%, Buddhist 14%, Christian 10% **Life expectancy:** 73 (men); 77 (women) (1995–2000)

Bulgaria

Republic of

National name: *Republika Bulgaria* **Area:** 110,912 sq km/42,823 sq mi **Capital:** Sofia **Major towns/cities:** Plovdiv, Varna, Ruse, Burgas, Stara Zagora **Major ports:** Black Sea ports Burgas and Varna **Physical features:** lowland plains in north and southeast separated by mountains (Balkan and Rhodope) that cover three-quarters of the country; River Danube in north **Head of state:** Petar Stoyanov from 1997 **Head of government:** Ivan Kostov from 1997 **Political system:** emergent democracy **Political parties:** Union of Democratic Forces (UDF), right of centre; Bulgarian Socialist Party (BSP), left wing, ex-communist; Movement for Rights and Freedoms (MRF), Turkish-oriented, centrist; Civic Alliances for the Republic (CAR), left of centre; Real Reform Movement (DESIR) **Currency:** lev **Real GDP per capita (PPP):** ($ US) 4,533 (1994) **Exports:** base metals, chemical and rubber products, processed food, beverages, tobacco, textiles, footwear. Principal market: EU 38.9% (1995) **Population:** 8,468,000 (1996 est) **Language:** Bulgarian, Turkish **Religion:** Eastern Orthodox Christian, Muslim, Roman Catholic, Protestant **Life expectancy:** 68 (men); 75 (women) (1995–2000)

Burkina Faso

The People's Democratic Republic of (formerly **Upper Volta**)

National name: *République Démocratique Populaire de Burkina Faso* **Area:** 274,122 sq km/105,838 sq mi **Capital:** Ouagadougou **Major towns/cities:** Bobo-Dioulasso, Koudougou **Physical features:** landlocked plateau with hills in west and southeast; headwaters of the River Volta; semiarid in north, forest and farmland in south; linked by rail to Abidjan in Côte d'Ivoire, Burkina Faso's only outlet to the sea **Head of state:** Blaise Compaoré from 1987 **Head of government:** Kadre Desire Ouedraogo from 1996 **Political system:** emergent democracy **Political parties:** Popular Front (FP), centre-left coalition grouping; National Convention of Progressive Patriots–Democratic Socialist Party (CNPP–PSD), left of centre **Currency:** franc CFA **Real GDP per capita (PPP): ($ US)** 796 (1994) **Exports:** cotton, gold, livestock and livestock products. Principal market: France 13.2% (1994) **Population:** 10,780,000 (1996 est) **Language:** French (official); about 50 Sudanic Languages spoken by 90% of population**Religion:** animist 53%, Sunni Muslim 36%, Roman Catholic 11% **Life expectancy:** 45 (men); 48 (women) (1995–2000)

Burundi

Republic of

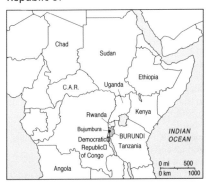

National name: *Republika y'Uburundi* **Area:** 27,834 sq km/10,746 sq mi **Capital:** Bujumbura **Major towns/cities:** Kitega, Bururi, Ngozi, Muhinga, Muramuya **Physical features:** landlocked grassy highland straddling watershed of Nile and Congo; Lake Tanganyika, Great Rift Valley **Head of state:** Pierre Buyoya from 1996 **Head of government:** Pascal-Firmin Ndimira from 1996 **Political system:** authoritarian nationalist **Political parties:** Front for Democracy in Burundi (FRODEBU), left of centre; Union for National Progress (UPRONA), nationalist socialist **Currency:** Burundi franc **Real GDP per capita (PPP):** ($ US) 698 (1994) **Exports:** coffee, tea, glass products, hides and skins. Principal market: UK 28.3% (1995) **Population:** 6,221,000 (1996 est) **Language:** Kirundi (a Bantu Language) and French (both official), Kiswahili **Religion:** Roman Catholic 62%, Pentecostalist 5%, Anglican 1%, Muslim 1%, animist **Life expectancy:** 50 (men); 53 (women) (1995–2000)

Cambodia

State of (**Khmer Republic** 1970–76, **Democratic Kampuchea** 1976–79, **People's Republic of Kampuchea** 1979–89)

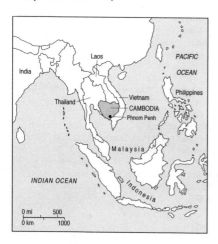

National name: *Roat Kampuchea* **Area:** 181,035 sq km/69,897 sq mi **Capital:** Phnom Penh **Major towns/cities:** Battambang, Kompong Cham **Major ports:** Kompong Cham **Physical features:** mostly flat, forested plains with mountains in southwest and north; Mekong River runs north–south; Lake Tonle Sap **Head of state:** Prince Norodom Sihanouk from 1991 **Head of government:** joint prime ministers Ung Huot and Hun Sen from 1997 **Political system:** limited constitutional monarchy **Political parties:** United Front for an Independent, Neutral, Peaceful, and Cooperative Cambodia (FUNCINPEC), nationalist, monarchist; Liberal Democratic Party (BLDP), republican, anticommunist (formerly the Khmer People's National Liberation Front (KPNLF)); Cambodian People's Party (CPP), reform socialist (formerly the communist Kampuchean People's

Revolutionary Party (KPRP)); Cambodian National Unity Party (CNUP) (political wing of the Khmer Rouge), ultranationalist communist **Currency:** Cambodian riel **Real GDP per capita (PPP):** ($ US) 660 (1995 est) **Exports:** timber, rubber, fishery products. Principal market: Thailand 41.7% (1995) **Population:** 10,273,000 (1996 est) **Language:** Khmer (official), French **Religion:** Theravāda Buddhist 95%, Muslim, Roman Catholic **Life expectancy:** 53 (men); 55 (women) (1995–2000)

Cameroon

Republic of

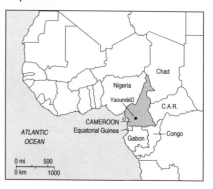

National name: *République du Cameroun* **Area:** 475,440 sq km/183,567 sq mi **Capital:** Yaoundé **Major towns/cities:** Garoua, Douala, Nkongsamba, Maroua, Bamenda, Bafoussam **Major ports:** Douala **Physical features:** desert in far north in the Lake Chad basin, mountains in west, dry savanna plateau in the intermediate area, and dense tropical rainforest in south; Mount Cameroon 4,070 m/13,358 ft, an active volcano on the coast, west of the Adamawa Mountains **Head of state:** Paul Biya from 1982 **Head of government:** Simon Achidi Achu from 1992 **Political system:** emergent democracy **Political parties:** Cameroon People's Democratic Movement (RDPC), nationalist, left of centre; Front of Allies for Change (FAC), centre left **Currency:** franc CFA **Real GDP per capita (PPP):** ($ US) 2,120 (1994) **Exports:** crude petroleum and petroleum products, timber and timber products, coffee, aluminium, cotton, bananas. Principal market: France 22.8% (1995) **Population:** 13,560,000 (1996 est) **Language:** French and English in pidgin variations (official); there has been some discontent with the emphasis on French – there are 163 indigenous peoples with their own African Languages (Sudanic Languages in north, Bantu Languages elsewhere) **Religion:** Roman Catholic 35%, animist 25%, Muslim 22%, Protestant 18% **Life expectancy:** 57 (men); 60 (women) (1995–2000)

Canada

Area: 9,970,610 sq km/3,849,652 sq mi **Capital:** Ottawa **Major towns/cities:** Toronto, Montréal, Vancouver, Edmonton, Calgary, Winnipeg, Québec,

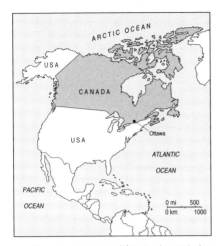

Hamilton, Saskatoon, Halifax, Regina, Windsor, Oshawa, London, Kitchener **Physical features:** mountains in west, with low-lying plains in interior and rolling hills in east; St Lawrence Seaway, Mackenzie River; Great Lakes; Arctic Archipelago; Rocky Mountains; Great Plains or Prairies; Canadian Shield; Niagara Falls; climate varies from temperate in south to arctic in north; 45% of country forested **Head of state:** Elizabeth II from 1952, represented by governor general Roméo A LeBlanc from 1995 **Head of government:** Jean Chrétien from 1993 **Political system:** federal constitutional monarchy **Political parties:** Liberal Party, nationalist, centrist; Bloc Québécois, Québec-based, separatist; Reform Party, populist, right wing; New Democratic Party (NDP), moderate left of centre; Progressive Conservative Party (PCP), free enterprise, right of centre **Currency:** Canadian dollar **Real GDP per capita (PPP):** ($ US) 21,465 (1996) **Exports:** motor vehicles and parts, lumber, wood pulp, paper and newsprint, crude petroleum, natural gas, aluminium and alloys, petroleum and coal products. Principal market: USA 81.4% (1996) **Population:** 29,680,000 (1996 est) **Language:** English, French (both official; 60% English mother tongue, 24% French mother tongue); there are also American Indian Languages and the Inuit Inuktitut **Religion:** Roman Catholic, various Protestant denominations **Life expectancy:** 75 (men); 81 (women) (1995–2000)

Cape Verde

Republic of

National name: *República de Cabo Verde* **Area:** 4,033 sq km/1,557 sq mi **Capital:** Praia **Major towns/cities:** Mindelo **Major ports:** Mindelo **Physical features:** archipelago of ten volcanic islands 565 km/350 mi west of Senegal; the windward (Barlavento) group includes Santo Antão, São Vicente, Santa Luzia, São Nicolau, Sal, and Boa Vista; the leeward (Sotovento) group comprises Maio, São Tiago, Fogo, and Brava; all but Santa Luzia are inhabited **Head of state:** Monteiro Mascarenhas from 1991 **Head of**

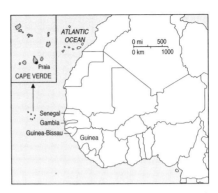

government: Carlos Viega from 1991 **Political system:** emergent democracy **Political parties:** African Party for the Independence of Cape Verde (PAICV), African nationalist; Movement for Democracy (MPD), moderate, centrist **Currency:** Cape Verde escudo **Real GDP per capita (PPP):** ($ US) 1,862 (1994) **Exports:** fish, shellfish and fish products, salt, bananas. Principal market: Portugal 50% (1995) **Population:** 396,000 (1996 est) **Language:** Portuguese (official), Creole **Religion:** Roman Catholic 93%, Protestant (Nazarene Church) **Life expectancy:** 65 (men); 67 (women) (1995–2000)

Central African Republic

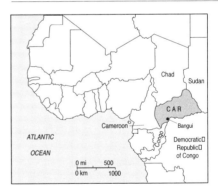

National name: *République Centrafricaine* **Area:** 622,436 sq km/240,322 sq mi **Capital:** Bangui **Major towns/cities:** Berbérati, Bouar, Bambari, Bossangoa, Carnot **Physical features:** landlocked flat plateau, with rivers flowing north and south, and hills in northeast and southwest; dry in north, rainforest in southwest; mostly wooded; Kotto and Mbali river falls; the Oubangui River rises 6 m/20 ft at Bangui during the wet season (June–November) **Head of state:** Ange-Félix Patasse from 1993 **Head of government:** Gabriel Koyambounou from 1995 **Political system:** emergent democracy **Political parties:** Central African People's Liberation Party (MPLC), left of centre; Central African Democratic Rally (RDC), nationalist, right of centre **Currency:** franc CFA **Real GDP per capita (PPP):** ($ US) 1,130 (1994) **Exports:** diamonds, coffee, timber, cotton. Principal market: France 40.1% (1995) **Population:**

3,344,000 (1996 est) **Language:** French (official), Sangho (national), Arabic, Hunsa, and Swahili **Religion:** Protestant, Roman Catholic, Muslim, animist **Life expectancy:** 48 (men); 53 (women) (1995–2000)

Chad

Republic of

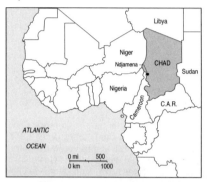

National name: *République du Tchad* **Area:** 1,284,000 sq km/495,752 sq mi **Capital:** N'djaména (formerly Fort Lamy) **Major towns/cities:** Sarh, Moundou, Abéché, Bongor, Doba **Physical features:** landlocked state with mountains (Tibetsi) and part of Sahara Desert in north; moist savanna in south; rivers in south flow northwest to Lake Chad **Head of state:** Idriss Deby from 1990 **Head of government:** Nassour Ouaidou Guelendouksia from 1997 **Political system:** emergent democracy **Political parties:** Patriotic Salvation Movement (MPS), centre left; Alliance for Democracy and Progress (RDP), centre left; Union for Democracy and Progress (UPDT), centre left; Action for Unity and Socialism (ACTUS), centre left; Union for Democracy and the Republic (UDR), centre left **Currency:** franc CFA **Real GDP per capita (PPP):** ($ US) 700 (1994) **Exports:** cotton, live cattle, meat, hides and skins. Principal market: Portugal 16.3% (1995) **Population:** 6,515,000 (1996 est) **Language:** French, Arabic (both official), over 100 African Languages spoken **Religion:** Muslim, Christian, animist **Life expectancy:** 48 (men); 51 (women) (1995–2000)

Chile

Republic of

National name: *República de Chile* **Area:** 756,950 sq km/292,258 sq mi **Capital:** Santiago **Major towns/cities:** Concepción, Viña del Mar, Valparaiso, Talcahuano, San Bernardo, Puente Alto, Chillán, Rancagua, Talca, Temuco **Major ports:** Valparaíso, Antofagasta, Arica, Iquique, Punta Arenas **Physical features:** Andes mountains along eastern border, Atacama Desert in north, fertile central valley, grazing land and forest in south **Territories:** Easter Island, Juan Fernández Islands, part of Tierra del Fuego, claim to part of Antarctica **Head of state:** Eduardo Frei from 1993 **Head of government:** Dante

Cordova from 1995 **Political system:** emergent democracy **Political parties:** Christian Democratic Party (PDC), moderate centrist; National Renewal Party (RN), right wing; Socialist Party of Chile (PS), left wing; Independent Democratic Union (UDI), right wing; Party for Democracy (PPD), left of centre; Union of the Centre-Centre (UCC), right wing; Radical Party (PR), left of centre **Currency:** Chilean peso **Real GDP per capita (PPP):** ($ US) 9,129 (1994) **Exports:** copper, fruits, timber products, fishmeal, vegetables, manufactured foodstuffs and beverages. Principal market: USA 16.6% (1996) **Population:** 14,421,000 (1996 est) **Language:** Spanish **Religion:** Roman Catholic **Life expectancy:** 71 (men); 78 (women) (1995–2000)

China

People's Republic of

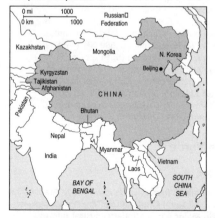

National name: *Zhonghua Renmin Gonghe Guo* **Area:** 9,572,900 sq km/3,696,000 sq mi **Capital:** Beijing (Peking) **Major towns/cities:** Shanghai, Hong Kong, Chongqing (Chungking), Tianjin, Guangzhou (Canton), Shenyang (Mukden), Wuhan, Nanjing (Nanking), Harbin, Chengdu, Xiang, Zibo **Major**

ports: Tianjin (Tientsin), Shanghai, Hong Kong, Qingdao (Tsingtao), Guangzhou (Canton) **Physical features:** two-thirds of China is mountains or desert (north and west); the low-lying east is irrigated by rivers Huang He (Yellow River), Chang Jiang (Yangtze-Kiang), Xi Jiang (Si Kiang) **Head of state:** Jiang Zemin from 1993 **Head of government:** Zhu Rongli from 1998 **Political system:** communist republic **Political party:** Chinese Communist Party (CCP), Marxist-Leninist-Maoist **Currency:** yuan **GDP per capita ($ US):** 2,604 (1994) **Exports:** basic manufactures, miscellaneous manufactured articles (particularly clothing and toys), crude petroleum, machinery and transport equipment, fishery products, cereals, canned food, tea, raw silk, cotton cloth. Principal market: Japan 20.9% (1996) **Population:** 1,232,083,000 (1996 est) **Language:** Chinese, including Mandarin (official), Cantonese, Wu, and other dialects **Religion:** Taoist, Confucianist, and Buddhist; Muslim 20 million; Catholic 3–6 million (divided between the 'patriotic' church established in 1958 and the 'loyal' church subject to Rome); Protestant 3 million **Life expectancy:** 68 (men); 72 (women) (1995–2000)

Colombia

Republic of

National name: *República de Colombia* **Area:** 1,141,748 sq km/440,828 sq mi **Capital:** Bogotá **Major towns/cities:** Medellín, Cali, Barranquilla, Cartagena, Bucaramanga, Buenaventura **Major ports:** Barranquilla, Cartagena, Buenaventura **Physical features:** the Andes mountains run north–south; flat coastland in west and plains (llanos) in east; Magdalena River runs north to Caribbean Sea; includes islands of Providencia, San Andrés, and Mapelo; almost half the country is forested **Head of state and government:** Andres Pastrana from 1998 **Political system:** democracy **Political parties:** Liberal Party (PL), centrist; Conservative Party (PSC), right of centre; M-19 Democratic Alliance (ADM-19), left of centre; National Salvation Movement (MSN), right-of-centre coalition grouping **Currency:** Colombian peso **Real GDP per capita (PPP): ($ US)** 6,107 (1994) **Exports:** coffee, petroleum and petroleum products,

coal, gold, bananas, cut flowers, cotton, chemicals, textiles, paper. Principal market: USA 33.6% (1995). Illegal trade in cocaine in 1995 it was estimated that approximately $3.5 billion (equivalent to about 4% of GDP) was entering Colombia as the proceeds of drug-trafficking **Population:** 36,444,000 (1996 est) **Language:** Spanish **Religion:** Roman Catholic **Life expectancy:** 67 (men); 73 (women) (1995–2000)

Comoros

Federal Islamic Republic of

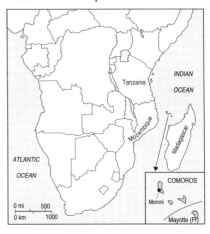

National name: *Jumhurīyat al-Qumur al-Itthādīyah al-Islāmīyah* or *République Fédérale Islamique des Comoros* **Area:** 1,862 sq km/718 sq mi **Capital:** Moroni **Major towns/cities:** Mutsamudu, Domoni, Fomboni, Dzaoudzi **Physical features:** comprises the volcanic islands of Njazídja, Nzwani, and Mwali (formerly Grande Comore, Anjouan, Moheli); at northern end of Mozambique Channel in Indian Ocean between Madagascar and coast of Africa **Head of state:** Muhammad Taki Abdoulkarim from 1996 **Head of government:** Ahmed Abdou from 1996 **Political system:** emergent democracy **Political parties:** National Union for Democracy in the Comoros (UNDC), Islamic, nationalist; Rally for Democracy and Renewal (RDR), left of centre **Currency:** Comorian franc **Real GDP per capita (PPP): ($ US)** 700 (1994 est) **Exports:** vanilla, cloves, ylang-ylang, essences, copra, coffee. Principal market: France 54.6% (1995) **Population:** 632,000 (1996 est) **Language:** Arabic (official), Comorian (Swahili and Arabic dialect), Makua, French **Religion:** Muslim; Islam is the state religion **Life expectancy:** 58 (men); 59 (women) (1995–2000)

Congo

Republic of

National name: *République du Congo* **Area:** 342,000 sq km/132,046 sq mi **Capital:** Brazzaville **Major towns/cities:** Pool, Pointe-Noire, Nkayi, Loubomo, Bouenza, Cuvette, Niari, Plateaux **Major ports:**

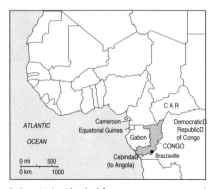

Pointe-Noire **Physical features:** narrow coastal plain rises to central plateau, then falls into northern basin; Congo River on the border with the Democratic Republic of Congo; half the country is rainforest **Head of state:** Denis Sassou-Nguessou from 1997 **Head of government:** Charles David Ganao from 1996 **Political system:** emergent democracy **Political parties:** Pan-African Union for Social Democracy (UPADS), moderate, left of centre; Congolese Movement for Democracy and Integral Development (MCDDI), moderate, left of centre; Congolese Labour Party (PCT), left wing **Currency:** franc CFA **Real GDP per capita (PPP):** ($ US) 2,410 (1994) **Exports:** petroleum and petroleum products, saw logs and veneer logs, veneer sheets. Principal market: Belgium and Luxembourg 24.3% (1995) **Population:** 2,668,000 (1996 est) **Language:** French (official); Kongo Languages; local patois Monokutuba and Lingala **Religion:** animist, Christian, Muslim **Life expectancy:** 48 (men); 52 (women) (1995–2000)

Congo

Democratic Republic of (formerly **Zaire**)

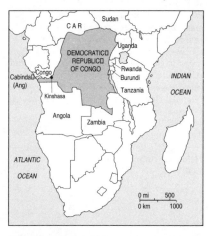

National name: *République Démocratique du Congo* **Area:** 2,344,900 sq km/905,366 sq mi **Capital:** Kinshasa **Major towns/cities:** Lubumbashi, Kananga, Mbuji-Mayi, Kisangani, Bukavu, Kikwit, Matadi **Major**

ports: Matadi, Kalemie **Physical features:** Zaïre/Congo River basin has tropical rainforest (second-largest remaining in world) and savanna; mountains in east and west; lakes Tanganyika, Albert, Edward; Ruwenzori Range; Victoria Falls **Head of state and government:** Laurent Kabila from 1997 **Political system:** transitional **Political parties:** Popular Movement of the Revolution (MPR), African socialist; Democratic Forces of Congo–Kinshasa (formerly Sacred Union, an alliance of some 130 opposition groups), moderate, centrist; Union for Democracy and Social Progress (UPDS), left of centre; Congolese National Movement–Lumumba (MNC), left of centre **Currency:** zaïre **Real GDP per capita (PPP):** ($ US) 429 (1994) **Exports:** mineral products (mainly copper, cobalt, industrial diamonds, and petroleum), agricultural products (chiefly coffee). Principal market: Belgium/Luxembourg 37% (1995) **Population:** 46,812,000 (1996 est) **Language:** French (official); Swahili, Lingala, Kikongo, and Tshiluba are recognized as national Languages; over 200 other Languages **Religion:** Roman Catholic, Protestant, Kimbanguist; also half a million Muslims **Life expectancy:** 50 (men); 53 (women) (1995–2000)

Costa Rica

Republic of

National name: *República de Costa Rica* **Area:** 51,100 sq km/19,729 sq mi **Capital:** San José **Major towns/cities:** Alajuela, Cartago, Limón, Puntarenas **Major ports:** Limón, Puntarenas **Physical features:** high central plateau and tropical coasts; Costa Rica was once entirely forested, containing an estimated 5% of the Earth's flora and fauna **Head of state and government:** Miguel Angel Rodriguez Echeverria, from 1998 **Political system:** liberal democracy **Political parties:** National Liberation Party (PLN), left of centre; Christian Socialist Unity Party (PUSC), centrist coalition; ten minor parties **Currency:** colón **Real GDP per capita (PPP):** ($ US) 5,919 (1994) **Exports:** bananas, coffee, sugar, cocoa, textiles, seafood, meat, tropical fruit. Principal market: USA 38.6% (1995) **Population:** 3,500 ,000 (1996 est) **Language:** Spanish (official) **Religion:** Roman Catholic 90% **Life expectancy:** 76 (men); 79 (women) (1995–2000)

Côte d'Ivoire

Republic of

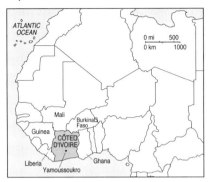

National name: *République de la Côte d'Ivoire* **Area:** 322,463 sq km/124,502 sq mi **Capital:** Yamoussoukro **Major towns/cities:** Abidjan, Bouaké, Daloa, Man, Korhogo **Major ports:** Abidjan, San Pedro **Physical features:** tropical rainforest (diminishing as exploited) in south; savanna and low mountains in north; coastal plain; Vridi canal, Kossou dam, Monts du Toura **Head of state:** Henri Konan Bedie from 1993 **Head of government:** Kablan Daniel Duncan from 1993 **Political system:** emergent democracy **Political parties:** Democratic Party of Côte d'Ivoire (PDCI), nationalist, free enterprise; Rally of Republicans (RDR), nationalist; Ivorian Popular Front (FPI), left of centre; Ivorian Labour Party (PIT), left of centre **Currency:** franc CFA **Real GDP per capita (PPP):** ($ US) 1,668 (1994) **Exports:** cocoa beans and products, petroleum products, timber, coffee, cotton, tinned tuna. Principal market: France 16% (1994) **Population:** 14,015,000 (1996 est) **Language:** French (official); over 60 local Languages **Religion:** animist, Muslim (mainly in north), Christian (mainly Roman Catholic in south) **Life expectancy:** 49 (men); 51 (women) (1995–2000)

Croatia

Republic of

National name: *Republika Hrvatska* **Area:** 56,538 sq km/21,829 sq mi **Capital:** Zagreb **Major towns/cities:** Osijek, Split, Dubrovnik, Rijeka, Zadar, Pula **Major ports:** chief port: Rijeka (Fiume); other ports: Zadar, Sibenik, Split, Dubrovnik **Physical features:** Adriatic coastline with large islands; very mountainous, with part of the Karst region and the Julian and Styrian Alps; some marshland **Head of state:** Franjo Tudjman from 1990 **Head of government:** Zlatko Matesa from 1995 **Political system:** emergent democracy **Political parties:** Croatian Democratic Union (CDU), Christian Democrat, right of centre, nationalist; Croatian Social-Liberal Party (CSLP), centrist; Social Democratic Party of Change (SDP), reform socialist; Croatian Party of Rights (HSP), Croat-oriented, ultranationalist; Croatian Peasant Party (HSS), rural-based; Serbian National Party (SNS), Serb-oriented **Currency:** kuna **Real GDP per capita (PPP):** ($ US) 3,960 (1994) **Exports:** machinery and transport equipment, chemicals, foodstuffs, miscellaneous manufactured items (mainly clothing). Principal market: Germany 22.1% (1994) **Population:** 4,501,000 (1996 est) **Language:** Croatian variant of Serbo-Croatian (official); Serbian variant of Serbo-Croatian also widely spoken, particularly in border areas in east **Religion:** Roman Catholic (Croats); Orthodox Christian (Serbs) **Life expectancy:** 68 (men); 77 (women) (1995–2000)

Cuba

Republic of

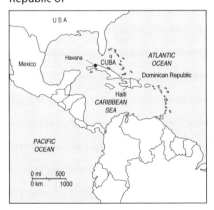

National name: *República de Cuba* **Area:** 110,860 sq km/42,803 sq mi **Capital:** Havana **Major towns/cities:** Santiago de Cuba, Camagüey, Holguín, Guantánamo, Santa Clara, Bayamo, Cienfuegos **Physical features:** comprises Cuba and smaller islands including Isle of Youth; low hills; Sierra Maestra mountains in southeast; Cuba has 3,380 km/2,100 mi of coastline, with deep bays, sandy beaches, coral islands and reefs **Head of state and government:** Fidel Castro Ruz from 1959 **Political system:** communist republic **Political party:** Communist Party of Cuba (PCC), Marxist-Leninist **Currency:** Cuban peso **Real GDP per capita (PPP):** ($ US) 3,000 (1994) **Exports:** sugar,

minerals, tobacco, citrus fruits, fish products.
Principal market: Canada 15.8% (1995 est)
Population: 11,018,000 (1996 est) **Language:** Spanish
Religion: Roman Catholic; also Episcopalians and
Methodists **Life expectancy:** 74 (men); 78 (women)
(1995–2000)

Cyprus

Greek Republic of Cyprus in south, and
Turkish Republic of Northern Cyprus in north

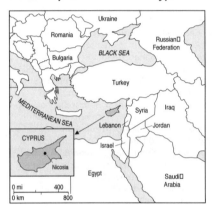

National name: *Kypriakí Dimokratía* (south), and
Kibris Cumhuriyeti (north) **Area:** 9,251 sq km/3,571 sq
mi (3,335 sq km/1,287 sq mi is Turkish-occupied)
Capital: Nicosia (divided between Greek and Turkish
Cypriots) **Major towns/cities:** Morphou, Limassol,
Larnaca, Famagusta, Paphos **Major ports:** Limassol,
Larnaca, and Paphos (Greek); Kyrenia and Famagusta
(Turkish) **Physical features:** central plain between
two east–west mountain ranges **Head of state and
government:** Glafkos Clerides (Greek) from 1993,
Rauf Denktas (Turkish) from 1976 **Political system:**
democratic divided republic **Political parties:** *Greek
zone* : Democratic Party (DEKO), federalist, centre
left; Progressive Party of the Working People (AKEL),
socialist; Democratic Rally (DISY), centrist; Socialist
Party–National Democratic Union of Cyprus
(SK–EDEK), socialist; *Turkish zone* : National Unity
Party (NUP), Communal Liberation Party (CLP),
Republican Turkish Party (RTP), New British Party
(NBP) **Currency:** Cyprus pound and Turkish lira **Real
GDP per capita (PPP):** ($ US) 13,071 (1994) **Exports:**
government-controlled area: clothing, potatoes,
pharmaceutical products. Principal market: UK 27.1%
(1994); TRNC area: citrus fruits, industrial products.
Principal market: UK 46.3% (1994) **Population:**
756,800 (1996 est) **Language:** Greek and Turkish
(official), English **Religion:** Greek Orthodox, Sunni
Muslim **Life expectancy:** 76 (men); 80 (women)
(1995–2000)

Czech Republic

National name: *Česká Republika* **Area:** 78,864 sq
km/30,449 sq mi **Capital:** Prague **Major towns/cities:**
Brno, Ostrava, Olomouc, Liberec, Plzeň, Ustí nad

Labem, Hradec Králové **Physical features:**
mountainous; rivers: Morava, Labe (Elbe), Vltava
(Moldau) **Head of state:** Václav Havel from 1993
Head of government: Miloš Zeman from 1998
Political system: emergent democracy **Political
parties:** Civic Democratic Party (CDP), right of centre,
free-market; Civic Democratic Alliance (CDA), right of
centre, free-market; Civic Movement (CM), liberal,
left of centre; Communist Party of Bohemia and
Moravia (KSCM), reform socialist; Agrarian Party,
centrist, rural-based; Liberal National Social Party
(LNSP; formerly the Czech Socialist Party (SP)), reform
socialist; Czech Social Democratic Party (CSDP),
moderate left of centre; Christian Democratic
Union–Czech People's Party (CDU–CPP), centre right;
Movement for Autonomous Democracy of Moravia
and Silesia (MADMS), Moravian and Silesian-based,
separatist; Czech Republican Party, far right
Currency: koruna (based on Czechoslovak koruna)
Real GDP per capita (PPP): ($ US) 9,201 (1994)
Exports: basic manufactures, machinery and
transport equipment, miscellaneous manufactured
articles, beer. Principal market: EU 37.4% (1995)
Population: 10,251,000 (1996 est) **Language:** Czech
(official) **Religion:** Roman Catholic, Hussite,
Presbyterian Evangelical Church of Czech Brethren,
Orthodox **Life expectancy:** 68 (men); 75 (women)
(1995–2000)

Denmark

Kingdom of

National name: *Kongeriget Danmark* **Area:** 43,075 sq
km/16,631 sq mi **Capital:** Copenhagen **Major
towns/cities:** Århus, Odense, Ålborg, Esbjerg,
Randers **Major ports:** Århus, Odense, Ålborg, Esbjerg
Physical features: comprises the Jutland peninsula
and about 500 islands (100 inhabited) including
Bornholm in the Baltic Sea; the land is flat and
cultivated; sand dunes and lagoons on the west coast
and long inlets on the east; the main island is
Sjælland (Zealand), where most of Copenhagen is
located (the rest is on the island of Amager)
Territories: the dependencies of Faroe Islands and

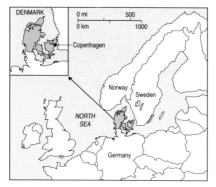

Greenland **Head of state:** Queen Margrethe II from 1972 **Head of government:** Poul Nyrup Rasmussen from 1993 **Political system:** liberal democracy **Political parties:** Social Democrats (SD), left of centre; Conservative People's Party (KF), moderate centre right; Liberal Party (V), centre left; Socialist People's Party (SF), moderate left wing; Radical Liberals (RV), radical internationalist, left of centre; Centre Democrats (CD), moderate centrist; Progress Party (FP), radical antibureaucratic; Christian People's Party (KrF), interdenominational, family values **Currency:** Danish krone **Real GDP per capita (PPP):** ($ US) 22,314 (1996) **Exports:** pig meat and pork products, other food products, fish, industrial machinery, chemicals, transport equipment. Principal market: Germany 35.8% (1995) **Population:** 5,237,000 (1996 est) **Language:** Danish (official); there is a German-speaking minority **Religion:** Lutheran 97% **Life expectancy:** 73 (men); 79 (women) (1995–2000)

Djibouti

Republic of

National name: *Jumhouriyya Djibouti* **Area:** 23,200 sq km/8,957 sq mi **Capital:** Djibouti (and chief port) **Major towns/cities:** Tadjoura, Obock, Dikhil, Ali-Sabieh **Physical features:** mountains divide an inland plateau from a coastal plain; hot and arid **Head of state:** Hassan Gouled Aptidon from 1977 **Head of government:** Barkat Gourad from 1981 **Political system:** emergent democracy **Political parties:** People's Progress Assembly (RPP), nationalist;

Democratic Renewal Party (PRD), moderate left of centre **Currency:** Djibouti franc **Real GDP per capita (PPP):** ($ US) 1,200 (1994 est) **Exports:** hides, cattle, coffee (exports are largely re-exports). Principal market: Kenya 42% (1995) **Population:** 617,000 (1996 est) **Language:** French (official), Somali, Afar, Arabic **Religion:** Sunni Muslim **Life expectancy:** 49 (men); 52 (women) (1995–2000)

Dominica

Commonwealth of

Area: 751 sq km/290 sq mi **Capital:** Roseau, with a deepwater port **Major towns/cities:** Portsmouth, Berekua, Marigot, Rosalie **Major ports:** Roseau, Portsmouth, Berekua, Marigot, Rosalie **Physical features:** second-largest of the Windward Islands, mountainous central ridge with tropical rainforest **Head of state:** Clarence Seignoret from 1983 **Head of government:** Edison James from 1995 **Political system:** liberal democracy **Political parties:** Dominica Freedom Party (DFP), centrist; Labour Party of Dominica (LPD), left-of-centre coalition; Dominica United Workers' Party (DUWP), left of centre **Currency:** Eastern Caribbean dollar; pound sterling; French franc **Real GDP per capita (PPP):** ($ US) 6,118 (1994) **Exports:** bananas, soap, coconuts, grapefruit, galvanized sheets. Principal market: UK 25.3% (1995) **Population:** 71,000 (1996 est) **Language:** English (official), but the Dominican patois reflects earlier periods of French rule **Religion:** Roman Catholic 80% **Life expectancy:** 72 (men); 76 (women) (1994 est)

Dominican Republic

National name: *República Dominicana* **Area:** 48,442 sq km/18,703 sq mi **Capital:** Santo Domingo **Major towns/cities:** Santiago de los Caballeros, La Romana, San Pedro de Macoris, San Francisco de Macoris, Concepcion de la Vega, San Juan **Physical features:** comprises eastern two-thirds of island of Hispaniola; central mountain range with fertile valleys; Pico Duarte 3,174 m/10,417 ft, highest point in Caribbean islands **Head of state and government:** Leoned Fernandez from 1996 **Political system:** democracy **Political parties:** Dominican Revolutionary Party

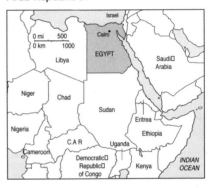

Christian Party (PSC), right wing; Ecuadorian Roldosist Party (PRE), populist, centre left; United Republican Party (PUR), right-of-centre coalition; Democratic Left (ID), moderate socialist; Conservative Party (PC), right wing **Currency:** sucre **Real GDP per capita (PPP):** ($ US) 4,626 (1994) **Exports:** petroleum and petroleum products, bananas, shrimps (a major exporter), coffee, seafood products, cocoa beans and products, cut flowers. Principal market: USA 42.4% (1994) **Population:** 11,699,000 (1996 est) **Language:** Spanish (official), Quechua, Jivaro, and other indigenous Languages **Religion:** Roman Catholic **Life expectancy:** 67 (men); 73 (women) (1995–2000)

Egypt

Arab Republic of

(PRD), moderate, left of centre; Christian Social Reform Party (PRSC), independent socialist; Dominican Liberation Party (PLD), nationalist **Currency:** Dominican Republic peso **Real GDP per capita (PPP):** ($ US) 3,933 (1994) **Exports:** raw sugar, molasses, coffee, cocoa, tobacco, ferro-nickel, gold, silver. Principal market: USA 45.1% (1995) **Population:** 7,961 ,000 (1996 est) **Language:** Spanish (official) **Religion:** Roman Catholic **Life expectancy:** 69 (men); 73 (women) (1995–2000)

Ecuador

Republic of

National name: *República del Ecuador* **Area:** 270,670 sq km/104,505 sq mi **Capital:** Quito **Major towns/cities:** Guayaquil, Cuenca, Machala, Portoviejo, Manta, Ambeto, Esmeraldas **Major ports:** Guayaquil **Physical features:** coastal plain rises sharply to Andes Mountains, which are divided into a series of cultivated valleys; flat, low-lying rainforest in the east; Galápagos Islands; Cotopaxi, the world's highest active volcano. Ecuador is crossed by the equator, from which it derives its name **Head of state and government:** Jamil Mahuad Witt from 1998 **Political system:** emergent democracy **Political parties:** Social

National name: *Jumhuriyat Misr al-Arabiya* **Area:** 1,001,450 sq km/386,659 sq mi **Capital:** Cairo **Major towns/cities:** El Gîza, Shubra Al Khayma, Alexandria, Port Said, El-Mahalla el-Koubra, Tauta, El-Mansoura **Major ports:** Alexandria, Port Said, Suez, Damietta, Shubra Al Khayma **Physical features:** mostly desert; hills in east; fertile land along Nile valley and delta; cultivated and settled area is about 35,500 sq km/ 13,700 sq mi; Aswan High Dam and Lake Nasser; Sinai **Head of state:** Hosni Mubarak from 1981 **Head of government:** Kamal Ahmed Ganzouri from 1996 **Political system:** democracy **Political parties:** National Democratic Party (NDP), moderate, left of centre; Socialist Labour Party (SLP), right of centre; Liberal Socialist Party, free enterprise; New Wafd Party, nationalist; National Progressive Unionist Party, left wing **Currency:** Egyptian pound **Real GDP per capita (PPP):** ($ US) 3,846 (1994) **Exports:** petroleum and petroleum products, textiles, clothing, food, live animals. Principal market: Italy 18.6% (1995) **Population:** 63,271,000 (1996 est) **Language:** Arabic (official); ancient Egyptian survives to some extent in Coptic; English; French **Religion:** Sunni Muslim 90%, Coptic Christian 7% **Life expectancy:** 65 (men); 67 (women) (1995–2000)

El Salvador

Republic of

National name: *República de El Salvador* **Area:** 21,393 sq km/8,259 sq mi **Capital:** San Salvador **Major**

towns/cities: Soyapango, Santa Ana, San Miguel, Nueva San Salvador, Mejicanos **Physical features:** narrow coastal plain, rising to mountains in north with central plateau **Head of state and government:** Armando Calderón Sol from 1994 **Political system:** emergent democracy **Political parties:** Christian Democrats (PDC), anti-imperialist; Farabundo Martí Liberation Front (FMLN), left wing; National Republican Alliance (ARENA), extreme right wing; National Conciliation Party (PCN), right wing **Currency:** Salvadorean colón **Real GDP per capita (PPP):** ($ US) 2,417 (1994) **Exports:** coffee, textiles and garments, sugar, shrimp, footwear, pharmaceuticals. Principal market: USA 53.4% (1996) **Population:** 5,796,000 (1996 est) **Language:** Spanish, Nahuatl **Religion:** Roman Catholic, Protestant **Life expectancy:** 66 (men); 71 (women) (1995–2000)

Equatorial Guinea

Republic of

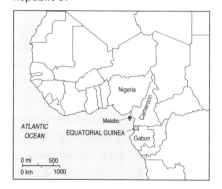

National name: *República de Guinea Ecuatorial* **Area:** 28,051 sq km/10,830 sq mi **Capital:** Malabo **Major towns/cities:** Bata, Evinayong, Ebebiyin, Mongomo **Physical features:** comprises mainland Río Muni, plus the small islands of Corisco, Elobey Grande and Elobey Chico, and Bioko (formerly Fernando Po) together with Annobón (formerly Pagalu); nearly half the land is forested; volcanic mountains on Bioko **Head of state:** Teodoro Obiang

Nguema Mbasogo from 1979 **Head of government:** Angel Serafin Seriche Dougan, from 1996 **Political system:** emergent democracy **Political parties:** Democratic Party of Equatorial Guinea (PDGE), nationalist, right of centre, militarily controlled; People's Social Democratic Convention (CSDP), left of centre; Democratic Socialist Union of Equatorial Guinea (UDSGE), left of centre **Currency:** franc CFA **Real GDP per capita (PPP):** ($ US) 1,673 (1994) **Exports:** timber, re-exported ships and boats, textile fibres and waste, cocoa, coffee. Principal market: USA 34% (1995) **Population:** 410,000 (1995 est) **Language:** Spanish (official); pidgin English is widely spoken, and on Annobón (whose people were formerly slaves of the Portuguese) a Portuguese patois; Fang and other African patois spoken on Río Muni **Religion:** Roman Catholic, Protestant, animist **Life expectancy:** 48 (men); 52 (women) (1995–2000)

Eritrea

State of

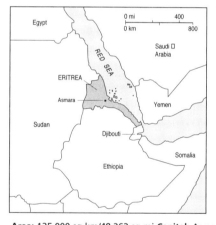

Area: 125,000 sq km/48,262 sq mi **Capital:** Asmara **Major towns/cities:** Asab, Keren, Massawa, Adigrat **Major ports:** Asab, Massawa **Physical features:** coastline along the Red Sea 1,000 km/620 mi; narrow coastal plain that rises to an inland plateau; Dahlak Islands **Head of state and government:** Issaias Afwerki from 1993 **Political system:** emergent democracy **Political parties:** People's Front for Democracy and Justice (PFDJ) (formerly Eritrean People's Liberation Front: EPLF), left of centre; Eritrean National Pact Alliance (ENPA), moderate, centrist **Currency:** Ethiopian birr **Real GDP per capita (PPP):** ($ US) 960 (1994) **Exports:** textiles, leather and leather products, beverages, petroleum products, basic household goods. Principal market: Ethiopia 68.7% (1993) **Population:** 3,280,000 (1996 est) **Language:** Amharic (official), Tigrinya (official), Arabic, Afar, Bilen, Hidareb, Kunama, Nara, Rashaida, Saho, and Tigre **Religion:** Sunni Muslim, Coptic Christian **Life expectancy:** 51 (men); 55 (women) (1995–2000)

Estonia

Republic of

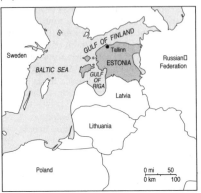

National name: *Eesti Vabariik* **Area:** 45,000 sq km/ 17,374 sq mi **Capital:** Tallinn **Major towns/cities:** Tartu, Narva, Kohtla-Järve, Pärnu **Physical features:** lakes and marshes in a partly forested plain; 774 km/481 mi of coastline; mild climate; Lake Peipus and Narva River forming boundary with Russian Federation; Baltic islands, the largest of which is Saaremaa **Head of state:** Lennart Meri from 1992 **Head of government:** Mart Siimann from 1997 **Political system:** emergent democracy **Political parties:** Coalition Party (KMU), ex-communist, left of centre, 'social market'; Isamaa (National Fatherland Party, or Pro Patria), right wing, nationalist, free market; Estonian Reform Party (ERP), freemarket; Centre Party (CP), moderate nationalist (formerly the Estonian Popular Front (EPF; Rahvarinne); Estonian National Independence Party (ENIP), radical nationalist; Communist Party of Estonia (CPE); Our Home is Estonia; Estonian Social Democratic Party (ESDP) (last three draw much of their support from ethnic Russian community) **Currency:** kroon **Real GDP per capita (PPP):** ($ US) 4,294 (1994) **Exports:** foodstuffs, animal products, textiles, timber products, base metals, mineral products, machinery. Principal market: Finland 19.8% (1996) **Population:** 1,471,000 (1996 est) **Language:** Estonian (official), Russian **Religion:** Lutheran, Russian Orthodox **Life expectancy:** 64 (men); 75 (women) (1995–2000)

Ethiopia

Federal Democratic Republic of (formerly known as **Abyssinia**)

National name: *Hebretesebawit Ityopia* **Area:** 1,096,900 sq km/423,513 sq mi **Capital:** Addis Ababa **Major towns/cities:** Jimma, Dire Dawa, Harar, Nazret, Dessie, Gonder, Mek'elē **Physical features:** a high plateau with central mountain range divided by Rift Valley; plains in east; source of Blue Nile River; Danakil and Ogaden deserts **Head of state:** Negasso Ghidada from 1995 **Head of government:** Meles Zenawi from 1995 **Political system:** transition to democratic federal republic **Political parties:**

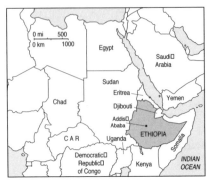

Ethiopian People's Revolutionary Democratic Front (EPRDF), nationalist, left of centre; Tigré People's Liberation Front (TPLF); Ethiopian People's Democratic Movement (EPDM); United Oromo Liberation Front, Islamic nationalist **Currency:** Ethiopian birr **Real GDP per capita (PPP):** ($ US) 427 (1994) **Exports:** coffee, hides and skins, petroleum products, fruit and vegetables. Principal market: Germany 31.7% (1994) **Population:** 58,243,000 (1996 est) **Language:** Amharic (official), Tigrinya, Orominga, Arabic **Religion:** Sunni Muslim, Christian (Ethiopian Orthodox Church, which has had its own patriarch since 1976) 40%, animist **Life expectancy:** 48 (men); 52 (women) (1995–2000)

Fiji Islands

Republic of

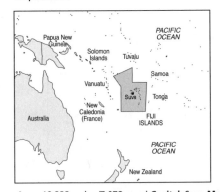

Area: 18,333 sq km/7,078 sq mi **Capital:** Suva **Major towns/cities:** Lautoka, Nadi, Ba, Labasa **Major ports:** Lautoka and Levuka **Physical features:** comprises about 844 Melanesian and Polynesian islands and islets (about 100 inhabited), the largest being Viti Levu (10,429 sq km/4,028 sq mi) and Vanua Levu (5,556 sq km/2,146 sq mi); mountainous, volcanic, with tropical rainforest and grasslands; almost all islands surrounded by coral reefs; high volcanic peaks **Head of state:** Ratu Sir Kamisese Mara from 1994 **Head of government:** Col Sitiveni Rabuka from 1992 **Political system:** democracy **Political parties:** National Federation Party (NFP), moderate left of centre, Indian; Fijian Labour Party (FLP), left of centre, Indian; United Front, Fijian; Fijian Political Party (FPP), Fijian centrist **Currency:** Fiji dollar **Real GDP per capita (PPP):** ($ US) 5,763 (1994) **Exports:** sugar, gold, fish and fish products, clothing, re-exported petroleum products, timber, ginger, molasses. Principal market: Australia 22.4% (1995) **Population:** 797,000 (1996 est) **Language:** English (official), Fijian, Hindi **Religion:** Methodist, Hindu, Muslim, Sikh **Life expectancy:** 71 (men); 75 (women) (1995–2000)

Finland

Republic of

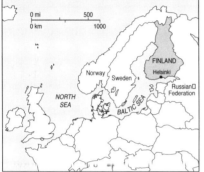

National name: *Suomen Tasavalta* **Area:** 338,145 sq km/130,557 sq mi **Capital:** Helsinki (Helsingfors) **Major towns/cities:** Tampere, Turku, Espoo, Vantaa **Major ports:** Turku, Oulu **Physical features:** most of the country is forest, with low hills and about 60,000 lakes; one-third is within the Arctic Circle; archipelago in south includes Åland Islands; Helsinki is the most northerly national capital on the European continent. At the 70th parallel there is constant daylight for 73 days in summer and 51 days of uninterrupted night in winter. **Head of state:** Martti Ahtisaari from 1994 **Head of government:** Paavo Lipponen from 1995 **Political system:** democracy **Political parties:** Finnish Social Democratic Party (SSDP), moderate left of centre; National Coalition Party (KOK), moderate right of centre; Finnish Centre Party (KESK), radical centrist, rural-oriented; Swedish People's Party (SFP), independent Swedish-oriented; Finnish Rural Party (SMP), farmers and small businesses; Left-Wing Alliance (VL), left wing **Currency:** markka **Real GDP per capita (PPP):** ($ US) 18,657 (1996) **Exports:** metal and engineering products, gold, paper and paper products, machinery, ships, wood and pulp, clothing and footwear, chemicals. Principal market: Germany 12.1% (1996) **Population:** 5,126,000 (1996 est) **Language:** Finnish 93%, Swedish 6% (both official); small Saami- and Russian-speaking minorities **Religion:** Lutheran 90%, Orthodox 1% **Life expectancy:** 73 (men); 80 (women) (1995–2000)

France

French Republic

National name: *République Française* **Area:** (including Corsica) 543,965 sq km/210,024 sq mi

Capital: Paris **Major towns/cities:** Lyon, Lille, Bordeaux, Toulouse, Nantes, Strasbourg, Montpellier, Saint-Etienne, Rennes, Reims, Grenoble **Major ports:** Marseille, Nice, Le Havre **Physical features:** rivers Seine, Loire, Garonne, Rhône; mountain ranges Alps, Massif Central, Pyrenees, Jura, Vosges, Cévennes; Auvergne mountain region; Mont Blanc (4,810 m/15,781 ft); Ardennes forest; Riviera; caves of Dordogne with relics of early humans; the island of Corsica **Territories:** Guadeloupe, French Guiana, Martinique, Réunion, St Pierre and Miquelon, Southern and Antarctic Territories, New Caledonia, French Polynesia, Wallis and Futuna, Mayotte **Head of state:** Jacques Chirac from 1995 **Head of government:** Lionel Jospin from 1997 **Political system:** liberal democracy **Political parties:** Rally for the Republic (RPR), neo-Gaullist conservative; Union for French Democracy (UDF), centre right; Socialist Party (PS), left of centre; Left Radical Movement (MRG), centre left; French Communist Party (PCF), Marxist-Leninist; National Front, far right; Greens, fundamentalist-ecologist; Génération Ecologie, pragmatic ecologist; Movement for France, right wing, anti-Maastricht **Currency:** franc **Real GDP per capita (PPP):** ($ US) 20,534 (1996) **Exports:** machinery and transport equipment, food and live animals, beverages and tobacco, textile yarn, fabrics and other basic manufactures, clothing and accessories, perfumery and cosmetics. Principal market: Germany 17.1% (1996) **Population:** 58,333,000 (1996 est) **Language:** French (regional Languages include Basque, Breton, Catalan, and Provençal) **Religion:** Roman Catholic; also Muslim, Protestant, and Jewish minorities **Life expectancy:** 74 (men); 81 (women) (1995–2000)

Gabon

Gabonese Republic

National name: *République Gabonaise* **Area:** 267,667 sq km/103,346 sq mi **Capital:** Libreville **Major towns/cities:** Port-Gentil, Masuku (Franceville), Lambaréné, Mouanda **Major ports:** Port-Gentil and Owendo **Physical features:** virtually the whole

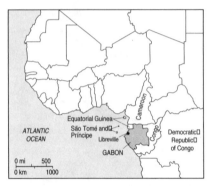

country is tropical rainforest; narrow coastal plain rising to hilly interior with savanna in east and south; Ogooué River flows north–west **Head of state:** Omar Bongo from 1964 **Head of government:** Paulin Obame-Nguema from 1994 **Political system:** emergent democracy **Political parties:** Gabonese Democratic Party (PDG), nationalist; Gabone Progress Party (PGP), left of centre; National Rally of Woodcutters (RNB), left of centre **Currency:** franc CFA **Real GDP per capita (PPP):** ($ US) 3,641 (1994) **Exports:** petroleum and petroleum products, manganese, timber and wood products, uranium. Principal market: USA 49.9% (1994) **Population:** 1,106,000 (1996 est) **Language:** French (official), Bantu **Religion:** Roman Catholic, also Muslim, animist **Life expectancy:** 54 (men); 57 (women) (1995–2000)

Gambia, The

Republic of

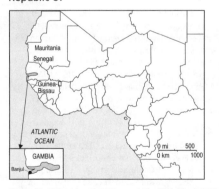

Area: 10,402 sq km/4,016 sq mi **Capital:** Banjul **Major towns/cities:** Serekunda, Birkama, Bakau, Farafenni, Sukuta, Gunjur, Georgetown **Physical features:** consists of narrow strip of land along the River Gambia; river flanked by low hills **Head of state and government:** (interim) Yahya Jameh from 1994 **Political system:** transitional **Political parties:** Progressive People's Party (PPP), moderate centrist; National Convention Party (NCP), left of centre **Currency:** dalasi **Real GDP per capita (PPP):** ($ US) 939 (1994) **Exports:** groundnuts and related products, cotton lint, fish and fish preparations,

hides and skins. Principal market: UK 25% (1995) **Population:** 1,141,000 (1996 est) **Language:** English (official), Mandinka, Fula, and other indigenous tongues **Religion:** Muslim 90%, with animist and Christian minorities **Life expectancy:** 45 (men); 47 (women) (1995–2000)

Georgia

Republic of

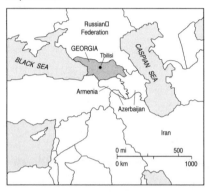

Area: 69,700 sq km/26,911 sq mi **Capital:** Tbilisi **Major towns/cities:** Kutaisi, Rustavi, Batumi, Sukhumi **Physical features:** largely mountainous with a variety of landscape from the subtropical Black Sea shores to the ice and snow of the crest line of the Caucasus; chief rivers are Kura and Rioni **Head of state:** Eduard Shevardnadze from 1992 **Head of government:** Otar Patsatsia from 1993 **Political system:** transitional **Political parties:** Citizens' Union of Georgia (CUG), nationalist, pro-Shevardnadze; National Democratic Party of Georgia (NDPG), nationalist; Round Table/Free Georgia Bloc, nationalist; Georgian Popular Front (GPF), moderate nationalist, prodemocratization; Georgian Communist Party (GCP); National Independence Party (NIP), ultranationalist; Front for the Reinstatement of Legitimate Power in Georgia, strong nationalist **Currency:** lari **Real GDP per capita (PPP):** ($ US) 1,585 (1994) **Exports:** metal products, machinery, tea, beverages. Principal market: Russia 29% (1996) **Population:** 5,442,000 (1996 est) **Language:** Georgian **Religion:** Georgian Orthodox, also Muslim **Life expectancy:** 70 (men); 78 (women) (1995–2000)

Germany

Federal Republic of

National name: *Bundesrepublik Deutschland* **Area:** 357,041 sq km/137,853 sq mi **Capital:** Berlin (government offices moving in phases from Bonn back to Berlin) **Major towns/cities:** Cologne, Hamburg, Munich, Essen, Frankfurt am Main, Dortmund, Stuttgart, Düsseldorf, Leipzig, Dresden, Bremen, Duisburg, Hannover **Major ports:** Hamburg, Kiel, Bremerhaven, Rostock **Physical features:** flat in

north, mountainous in south with Alps; rivers Rhine, Weser, Elbe flow north, Danube flows southeast, Oder and Neisse flow north along Polish frontier; many lakes, including Müritz; Black Forest, Harz Mountains, Erzgebirge (Ore Mountains), Bavarian Alps, Fichtelgebirge, Thüringer Forest **Head of state:** Roman Herzog from 1994 **Head of government:** Gerhard Schröder from 1998 **Political system:** liberal democratic federal republic **Political parties:** Christian Democratic Union (CDU), right of centre, 'social market'; Christian Social Union (CSU), right of centre; Social Democratic Party (SPD), left of centre; Free Democratic Party (FDP), liberal; Greens, environmentalist; Party of Democratic Socialism (PDS), reform-socialist (formerly Socialist Unity Party: SED); German People's Union (DVU), far-right **Currency:** Deutschmark **Real GDP per capita (PPP):** ($ US) 21,116 (1996) **Exports:** road vehicles, electrical machinery, metals and metal products, textiles, chemicals. Principal market: France 10.9% (1996) **Population:** 81,992,000 (1996 est) **Language:** German **Religion:** Protestant (mainly Lutheran) 43%, Roman Catholic 36% **Life expectancy:** 74 (men); 80 (women) (1995–2000)

Ghana

Republic of (formerly the **Gold Coast**)

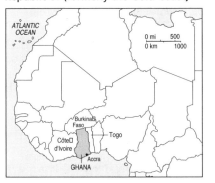

Area: 238,305 sq km/92,009 sq mi **Capital:** Accra **Major towns/cities:** Kumasi, Tamale, Tema, Sekondi-Takoradi,

Cape Coast, Sunyani, Koforidua, Ho, Yendi, Tarkwa, Wa, Bolgatanga **Major ports:** Sekondi, Tema **Physical features:** mostly tropical lowland plains; bisected by River Volta **Head of state and government:** Jerry Rawlings from 1981 **Political system:** emergent democracy **Political parties:** National Democratic Congress (NDC), centrist, progovernment; New Patriotic Party (NPP), left of centre **Currency:** cedi **Real GDP per capita (PPP):** ($ US) 1,960 (1994) **Exports:** gold, cocoa and related products, timber. Principal market: USA 14.6% (1995) **Population:** 17,832,000 (1996 est) **Language:** English (official) and African Languages **Religion:** Christian 62%, Muslim 16%, animist **Life expectancy:** 57 (men); 60 (women) (1995–2000)

Greece

Hellenic Republic

National name: *Elliniki Dimokratia* **Area:** 131,957 sq km/50,948 sq mi **Capital:** Athens **Major towns/cities:** Thessaloníki, Piraeus, Patras, Irákleion, Larissa, Volos **Major ports:** Piraeus, Thessaloníki, Patras, Irákleion **Physical features:** mountainous (Mount Olympus); a large number of islands, notably Crete, Corfu, and Rhodes, and Cyclades and Ionian Islands **Head of state:** Costis Stephanopoulos from 1995 **Head of government:** Costis Simitis from 1996 **Political system:** democracy **Political parties:** Panhellenic Socialist Movement (PASOK), nationalist, democratic socialist; New Democracy Party (ND), centre right; Democratic Renewal (DIANA), centrist; Communist Party (KJKE), left wing; Political Spring, moderate, left of centre **Currency:** drachma **Real GDP per capita (PPP):** ($ US) 12,694 (1996) **Exports:** fruit and vegetables, clothing, mineral fuels and lubricants, textiles, iron and steel, aluminium and aluminium alloys. Principal market: Germany 27.7% (1995) **Population:** 10,490,000 (1996 est) **Language:** Greek (official), Macedonian (100,000– 200,000 est) **Religion:** Greek Orthodox; also Roman Catholic **Life expectancy:** 76 (men); 81 (women) (1995–2000)

Grenada

Area: (including the southern Grenadine Islands, notably Carriacou and Petit Martinique) 344 sq km/

133 sq mi **Capital:** St George's **Major towns/cities:** Grenville, Sauteurs, Victoria, Hillsborough (Carriacou) **Physical features:** southernmost of the Windward Islands; mountainous; Grand-Anse beach; Annandale Falls; the Great Pool volcanic crater **Head of state:** Elizabeth II from 1974, represented by governor general Reginald Palmer from 1992 **Head of government:** Keith Mitchell from 1995 **Political system:** emergent democracy **Political parties:** Grenada United Labour Party (GULP), nationalist, left of centre; National Democratic Congress (NDC), centrist; National Party (TNP), centrist **Currency:** Eastern Caribbean dollar **Real GDP per capita (PPP):** ($ US) 5,137 (1994) **Exports:** cocoa, bananas, cocoa, mace, fresh fruit. Principal market: UK, USA, France 18.5% each (1995) **Population:** 92,000 (1996 est) **Language:** English (official); some French-African patois spoken **Religion:** Roman Catholic 53%, Anglican, Seventh Day Adventist, Pentecostal **Life expectancy:** 68 (men); 73 (women) (1996 est)

Guatemala

Republic of

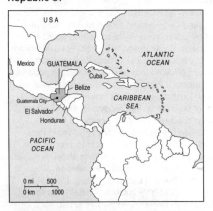

National name: *República de Guatemala* **Area:** 108,889 sq km/42,042 sq mi **Capital:** Guatemala City **Major towns/cities:** Quezaltenango, Escuintla, Puerto Barrios (naval base), Retalhuleu, Chiquimula

Physical features: mountainous; narrow coastal plains; limestone tropical plateau in north; frequent earthquakes **Head of state and government:** Alvaro Arzú from 1996 **Political system:** democracy **Political parties:** Guatemalan Christian Democratic Party (PDCG), Christian, centre left; Centre Party (UCN), centrist; Revolutionary Party (PR), radical; Movement of National Liberation (MLN), extreme right wing; Democratic Institutional Party (PID), moderate conservative; Solidarity and Action Movement (MAS), right of centre; Guatemalan Republican Front (FRG), right wing; National Advancement Party (PAN), right of centre; Social Democratic Party (PSD), right of centre **Currency:** quetzal **Real GDP per capita (PPP):** ($ US) 3,208 (1994) **Exports:** coffee, bananas, sugar, cardamoms, shellfish, tobacco. Principal market: USA 36.6% (1996) **Population:** 10,928,000 (1996 est) **Language:** Spanish (official); 45% speak Mayan Languages **Religion:** Roman Catholic 70%, Protestant 30% **Life expectancy:** 65 (men); 70 (women) (1995–2000)

Guinea

Republic of

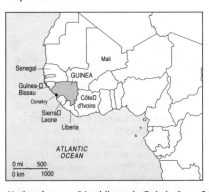

National name: *République de Guinée* **Area:** 245,857 sq km/94,925 sq mi **Capital:** Conakry **Major towns/cities:** Labé, Nzérékoré, Kankan, Kindia **Physical features:** flat coastal plain with mountainous interior; sources of rivers Niger, Gambia, and Senegal; forest in southeast; Fouta Djallon, area of sandstone plateaux, cut by deep valleys **Head of state and government:** Lansana Conté from 1984 **Political system:** emergent democracy **Political parties:** Party of Unity and Progress (PUP), centrist; Rally of the Guinean People (RPG), left of centre; Union of the New Republic (UNR), left of centre; Party for Renewal and Progress (PRP), left of centre **Currency:** Guinean franc **Real GDP per capita (PPP):** ($ US) 1,103 (1994) **Exports:** bauxite, alumina, diamonds, coffee. Principal market: USA 16.1% (1995) **Population:** 7,518,000 (1996 est) **Language:** French (official), African Languages (of which eight are official) **Religion:** Muslim 95%, Christian **Life expectancy:** 46 (men); 47 (women) (1995–2000)

Guinea-Bissau

Republic of (formerly **Portuguese Guinea**)

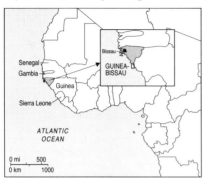

National name: *República da Guiné-Bissau* **Area:** 36,125 sq km/13,947 sq mi **Capital:** Bissau (main port) **Major towns/cities:** Mansôa, São Domingos, Bolama/Bijagós, Catio, Buba, Butata, Farim, Cacine **Physical features:** flat coastal plain rising to savanna in east **Head of state:** João Bernardo Vieira from 1980 **Head of government:** Carlos Correia from 1997 **Political system:** emergent democracy **Political parties:** African Party for the Independence of Portuguese Guinea and Cape Verde (PAIGC), nationalist socialist; Party for Social Renovation (PRS), left of centre; Guinea-Bissau Resistance–Bafata Movement (PRGB-MB), centrist **Currency:** Guinean peso **Real GDP per capita (PPP):** ($ US) 793 (1994) **Exports:** cashew nuts, palm kernels, groundnuts, fish and shrimp, timber. Principal market: Spain 38% (1995) **Population:** 1,091,000 (1996 est) **Language:** Portuguese (official); Crioulo (Cape Verdean dialect of Portuguese), African Languages **Religion:** animist 65%, Muslim 38%, Christian 5% (mainly Roman Catholic) **Life expectancy:** 44 (men); 47 (women) (1995–2000)

Guyana

Cooperative Republic of

Area: 214,969 sq km/82,999 sq mi **Capital:** Georgetown (and port) **Major towns/cities:** Linden, New Amsterdam, Rose Hall, Corriverton **Major ports:** New Amsterdam **Physical features:** coastal plain rises into rolling highlands with savanna in south; mostly tropical rainforest; Mount Roraima; Kaieter National Park, including Kaieter Falls on the Potaro (tributary of Essequibo) 250 m/821 ft **Head of state:** Janet Jagan from 1997 **Head of government:** Samuel Hinds from 1992 **Political system:** democracy **Political parties:** People's National Congress (PNC), Afro-Guyanan, nationalist socialist; People's Progressive Party (PPP), Indian-based, left wing **Currency:** Guyana dollar **Real GDP per capita (PPP):** ($ US) 2,730 (1994) **Exports:** sugar, bauxite, alumina, rice, gold, rum, timber, molasses, shrimp. Principal market: Canada 24.9% (1995) **Population:** 838,000 (1996 est) **Language:** English (official), Hindi, American Indian Languages **Religion:** Hindu 54%, Christian 27%, Sunni Muslim 15% **Life expectancy:** 65 (men); 70 (women) (1995–2000)

Haiti

Republic of

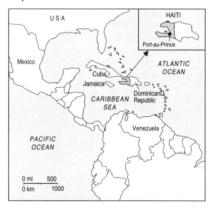

National name: *République d'Haïti* **Area:** 27,750 sq km/10,714 sq mi **Capital:** Port-au-Prince **Major towns/cities:** Cap-Haïtien, Gonaïves, Les Cayes, Port-de-Paix, Jérémie, Jacmée, St Marc **Physical features:** mainly mountainous and tropical; occupies western third of Hispaniola Island in Caribbean Sea **Head of state:** René Preval from 1995 **Head of government:** Herve Denis from 1997 **Political system:** transitional **Political parties:** National Front for Change and Democracy (FNCD), left of centre; Lavalas Political Organization, populist **Currency:** gourde **Real GDP per capita (PPP):** ($ US) 896 (1994) **Exports:** manufactured articles, coffee, essential oils, sisal. Principal market: USA 73.5% (1995) **Population:** 7,259,000 (1996 est) **Language:** French (official, spoken by literate 10% minority), Creole (official) **Religion:** Christian 95% (of which 80% are Roman Catholic), voodoo 4% **Life expectancy:** 57 (men); 60 (women) (1995–2000)

Honduras

Republic of

National name: *República de Honduras* **Area:** 112,100 sq km/43,281 sq mi **Capital:** Tegucigalpa **Major towns/cities:** San Pedro Sula, La Ceiba, El Progreso, Choluteca, Juticalpa, Danlí **Major ports:** La Ceiba, Puerto Cortés **Physical features:** narrow tropical coastal plain with mountainous interior, Bay Islands, Caribbean reefs **Head of state and government:** Carlos Flores from 1997 **Political system:** democracy **Political parties:** Liberal Party of Honduras (PLH), centre left; National Party of Honduras (PNH), right wing **Currency:** lempira **Real GDP per capita (PPP):** ($ US) 2,050 (1994) **Exports:** bananas, lobsters and prawns, zinc, meat. Principal market: USA 68.5% (1995) **Population:** 5,816,000 (1996 est) **Language:** Spanish (official); English, American Indian Languages **Religion:** Roman Catholic **Life expectancy:** 68 (men); 72 (women) (1995–2000)

Hungary

Republic of

National name: *Magyar Köztársaság* **Area:** 93,032 sq km/35,919 sq mi **Capital:** Budapest **Major**

towns/cities: Miskolc, Debrecen, Szeged, Pécs, Gyor, Nyiregyháza, Székesfehérvár, Kecskemét **Physical features:** Great Hungarian Plain covers eastern half of country; Bakony Forest, Lake Balaton, and Transdanubian Highlands in the west; rivers Danube, Tisza, and Raba; more than 500 thermal springs **Head of state:** Arpád Göncz from 1990 **Head of government:** Viktor Orban from 1998 **Political system:** emergent democracy **Political parties:** over 50, including Hungarian Socialist Party (HSP), reform-socialist; Alliance of Free Democrats (AFD), centrist, radical free market; Hungarian Democratic Forum (MDF), nationalist, centre right; Independent Smallholders Party (ISP), right of centre, agrarian; Christian Democratic People's Party (KDNP), right of centre; Federation of Young Democrats, liberal, anticommunist; Fidesz, right of centre **Currency:** forint **Real GDP per capita (PPP):** ($ US) 6,437 (1994) **Exports:** raw materials, semi-finished products, industrial consumer goods, food and agricultural products, transport equipment. Principal market: Germany 29% (1996) **Population:** 10,049,000 (1996 est) **Language:** Hungarian (or Magyar), one of the few Languages of Europe with non-Indo-European origins; it is grouped with Finnish, Estonian, and others in the Finno-Ugric family **Religion:** Roman Catholic 67%, Calvinist 20%, other Christian denominations, Jewish **Life expectancy:** 65 (men); 74 (women) (1995–2000)

Iceland

Republic of

National name: *Lýdveldid Ísland* **Area:** 103,000 sq km/39,768 sq mi **Capital:** Reykjavík **Major towns/cities:** Akureyri, Akranes, Kópavogur, Hafnerfjördur, Vestmannaeyjar **Physical features:** warmed by the Gulf Stream; glaciers and lava fields cover 75% of the country; active volcanoes (Hekla was once thought the gateway to Hell), geysers, hot springs, and new islands created offshore (Surtsey in 1963); subterranean hot water heats 85% of Iceland's homes; Sidujokull glacier moving at 100 metres a day **Head of state:** Olafur Raguar Grimson from 1996 **Head of government:** David Oddsson from 1991 **Political system:** democracy **Political parties:** Independence Party (IP), right of centre; Progressive Party (PP), radical socialist; People's

Alliance (PA), socialist; Social Democratic Party (SDP), moderate, left of centre; Citizens' Party, centrist; Women's Alliance, women- and family-oriented **Currency:** krona **Real GDP per capita (PPP): ($ US)** 23,434 (1996) **Exports:** fish products, aluminium, ferrosilicon, diatomite, fertilizer, animal products. Principal market: UK 19.3% (1995) **Population:** 271,000 (1996 est) **Language:** Icelandic, the most archaic Scandinavian Language **Religion:** Evangelical Lutheran **Life expectancy:** 76 (men); 81 (women) (1995–2000)

India

Republic of

National name: Hindi *Bharat* **Area:** 3,166,829 sq km/ 1,222,713 sq mi **Capital:** Delhi **Major towns/cities:** Bombay, Calcutta, Chennai (Madras), Bangalore, Hyderabad, Ahmadabad, Kanpur, Pune, Nagpur, Bhopal, Jaipur, Lucknow, Surat **Major ports:** Calcutta, Bombay, Chennai (Madras) **Physical features:** Himalaya mountains on northern border; plains around rivers Ganges, Indus, Brahmaputra; Deccan peninsula south of the Narmada River forms plateau between Western and Eastern Ghats mountain ranges; desert in west; Andaman and Nicobar Islands, Lakshadweep (Laccadive Islands) **Head of state:** Kocheril Raman Narayanan from 1997 **Head of government:** Atal Behari Vajpayee from 1998 **Political system:** liberal democratic federal republic **Political parties:** All India Congress Committee, or Congress, cross-caste and cross-religion coalition, left of centre; Janata Dal (People's Party), secular, left of centre; Bharatiya Janata Party (BJP), radical right wing, Hindu-chauvinist; Communist Party of India (CPI), Marxist-Leninist; Communist Party of India–Marxist (CPI–M), West Bengal–based moderate socialist **Currency:** rupee **Real GDP per capita (PPP): ($ US)** 1,348 (1994) **Exports:** tea (world's largest producer), coffee, fish, iron and steel, leather, textiles, clothing, polished diamonds, handmade carpets, engineering goods, chemicals. Principal market: USA 17.4% (1995–96) **Population:** 994,580,000 (1996 est) **Language:** Hindi, English, and 17 other official Languages: Assamese, Bengali,

Gujarati, Kannada, Kashmiri, Konkani, Malayalam, Manipur, Marathi, Nepali, Oriya, Punjabi, Sanskrit, Sindhi, Tamil, Telugu, Urdu; more than 1,650 dialects **Religion:** Hindu 83%, Sunni Muslim 11%, Christian 2.5%, Sikh 2% **Life expectancy:** 63 (men); 63 (women) (1995–2000)

Indonesia

Republic of

National name: *Republik Indonesia* **Area:** 1,904,569 sq km/735,354 sq mi **Capital:** Jakarta **Major towns/cities:** Surabaya, Bandung, Yogyakarta (Java), Medan, Semarang (Java), Banda Aceh, Palembang (Sumatra), Ujung Pandang (Sulawesi), Denpasar (Bali), Kupang (Timor), Padang, Malang **Major ports:** Tanjung Priok, Surabaya, Semarang (Java), Ujung Pandang (Sulawesi) **Physical features:** comprises 13,677 tropical islands (over 6,000 of them are inhabited): the Greater Sundas (including Java, Madura, Sumatra, Sulawesi, and Kalimantan [part of Borneo]), the Lesser Sunda Islands/Nusa Tenggara (including Bali, Lombok, Sumbawa, Flores, Sumba, Alor, Lomblen, Timor, Roti, and Savu), Maluku/Moluccas (over 1,000 islands including Ambon, Ternate, Tidore, Tanimbar, and Halmahera), and Irian Jaya (part of New Guinea); over half the country is tropical rainforest; it has the largest expanse of peatlands in the tropics **Head of state and government:** B J Habibie from 1998 **Political system:** authoritarian nationalist republic **Political parties:** Sekber Golkar, ruling military-bureaucrat- farmers' party; United Development Party (PPP), moderate Islamic; Indonesian Democratic Party (PDI), nationalist Christian **Currency:** rupiah **Real GDP per capita (PPP): ($ US)** 3,740 (1994) **Exports:** petroleum and petroleum products, natural and manufactured gas, textiles, rubber, palm oil, wood and wood products, electrical and electronic products, coffee, fishery products, coal, copper, tin, pepper, tea. Principal market: Japan 27.1% (1995) **Population:** 200,453,000 (1996 est) **Language:** Bahasa Indonesia (official), closely related to Malay; there are 583 regional Languages and dialects; Javanese is the most widely spoken local Language. Dutch is also spoken **Religion:** Muslim 88%, Christian 10%,

Buddhist and Hindu 2% (the continued spread of Christianity, together with an Islamic revival, have led to greater religious tensions) **Life expectancy:** 63 (men); 67 (women) (1995–2000)

Iran

Islamic Republic of (formerly **Persia**)

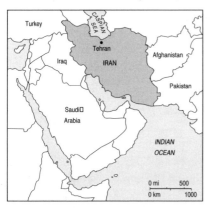

National name: *Jomhori-e-Islami-e-Irân* **Area:** 1,648,000 sq km/636,292 sq mi **Capital:** Tehran **Major towns/cities:** Esfahan, Mashhad, Tabriz, Shiraz, Ahvaz, Bakhtaran, Qom, Kara **Major ports:** Abadan **Physical features:** plateau surrounded by mountains, including Elburz and Zagros; Lake Rezayeh; Dasht-e-Kavir desert; occupies islands of Abu Musa, Greater Tunb and Lesser Tunb in the Gulf **Head of state and government:** Seyyed Mohammad Khatami from 1997 **Leader of the Islamic Revolution** Seyed Ali Khamenei from 1989 **Political system:** authoritarian Islamic republic **Political parties:** none officially recognized **Currency:** rial **Real GDP per capita (PPP):** ($ US) 5,766 (1994) **Exports:** crude petroleum and petroleum products, agricultural goods, metal ores. Principal market: Japan 13.8% (1995) **Population:** 69,975,000 (1996 est) **Language:** Farsi (official), Kurdish, Turkish, Arabic, English, French **Religion:** Shi'ite Muslim (official) 94%, Sunni Muslim, Zoroastrian, Christian, Jewish, Baha'i **Life expectancy:** 69 (men); 70 (women) (1995–2000)

Iraq

Republic of

National name: *al Jumhouriya al `Iraqia* **Area:** 434,924 sq km/167,924 sq mi **Capital:** Baghdad **Major towns/cities:** Mosul, Basra, Kirkuk, Hilla, Najaf, Nasiriya **Major ports:** Basra and Um Qass closed from 1980 **Physical features:** mountains in north, desert in west; wide valley of rivers Tigris and Euphrates running northwest–southeast; canal linking Baghdad and Persian Gulf opened in 1992 **Head of state and government:** Saddam Hussein al-Tikriti from 1979 **Political system:** one-party socialist republic **Political party:** Arab Ba'ath Socialist Party, nationalist socialist **Currency:** Iraqi dinar **Real GDP per capita (PPP):**

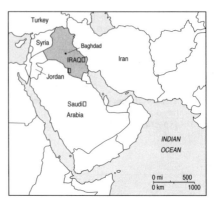

($ US) 3,159 (1994) **Exports:** crude petroleum (accounting for more than 98% of total export earnings (1980–89), dates and other dried fruits. Principal market: Jordan 95% (1995) **Population:** 20,607,000 (1996 est) **Language:** Arabic (official); Kurdish, Assyrian, Armenian **Religion:** Shi'ite Muslim 60%, Sunni Muslim 37%, Christian 3% **Life expectancy:** 67 (men); 70 (women) (1995–2000)

Ireland, Republic of

National name: *Eire* **Area:** 70,282 sq km/27,135 sq mi **Capital:** Dublin **Major towns/cities:** Cork, Limerick, Galway, Waterford, Wexford **Major ports:** Cork, Dun Laoghaire, Limerick, Waterford, Galway **Physical features:** central plateau surrounded by hills; rivers Shannon, Liffey, Boyne; Bog of Allen; Macgillicuddy's Reeks, Wicklow Mountains; Lough Corrib, lakes of Killarney; Galway Bay and Aran Islands **Head of state:** Mary McAleese from 1997 **Head of government:** Bertie Ahern from 1997 **Political system:** democracy **Political parties:** Fianna Fáil (Soldiers of Destiny), moderate centre right; Fine Gael (Irish Tribe or United Ireland Party), moderate centre left; Labour Party, moderate left of centre; Progressive Democrats, radical free-enterprise **Currency:** Irish pound (punt Eireannach) **Real GDP per capita (PPP):** ($ US) 18,784 (1996) **Exports:** beef and dairy products, live animals, machinery and transport equipment, electronic goods, chemicals. Principal market: UK 25.4% (1995) **Population:** 3,554,000 (1996 est) **Language:** Irish Gaelic and English (both official) **Religion:** Roman Catholic 95%, Church of Ireland, other Protestant denominations **Life expectancy:** 73 (men); 79 (women) (1995–2000)

Israel

State of

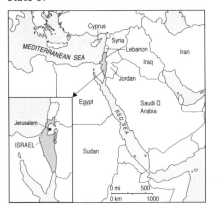

National name: *Medinat Israel* **Area:** 20,800 sq km/ 8,030 sq mi (as at 1949 armistice) **Capital:** Jerusalem (not recognized by United Nations) **Major towns/cities:** Tel Aviv-Yafo, Haifa, Bat-Yam, Holon, Ramat Gan, Petach Tikva, Rishon Leziyyon, Beersheba **Major ports:** Tel Aviv-Yafo, Haifa, 'Akko (formerly Acre), Eilat **Physical features:** coastal plain of Sharon between Haifa and Tel Aviv noted since ancient times for its fertility; central mountains of Galilee, Samaria, and Judea; Dead Sea, Lake Tiberias, and River Jordan Rift Valley along the east are below sea level; Negev Desert in the south; Israel occupies Golan Heights, West Bank, East Jerusalem, and Gaza Strip (the last was awarded limited autonomy, with West Bank town of Jericho, in 1993) **Head of state:** Ezer Weizman from 1993 **Head of government:** Binyamin Netanyahu from 1996 **Political system:** democracy **Political parties:** Israel Labour Party, moderate, left of centre; Consolidation Party (Likud), right of centre; Meretz (Vitality), left-of-centre alliance **Currency:** shekel **Real GDP per capita (PPP):** ($ US) 16,023 (1994) **Exports:** citrus fruits, worked diamonds, machinery and parts, military hardware, food products, chemical products, textiles and clothing. Principal market: USA 30.1% (1995) **Population:** 5,664,000 (1996 est) **Language:** Hebrew and Arabic (official); English, Yiddish, European and western Asian Languages **Religion:** Israel is a secular state, but the predominant faith is Judaism 85%; also Sunni Muslim, Christian, and Druse **Life expectancy:** 75 (men); 79 (women) (1995–2000)

Italy

Republic of

National name: *Repubblica Italiana* **Area:** 301,300 sq km/116,331 sq mi **Capital:** Rome **Major towns/cities:** Milan, Naples, Turin, Palermo, Genoa, Bologna **Major ports:** Naples, Genoa, Palermo, Bari, Catania, Trieste **Physical features:** mountainous (Maritime Alps, Dolomites, Apennines) with narrow coastal lowlands; continental Europe's only active volcanoes: Vesuvius, Etna, Stromboli; rivers Po, Adige, Arno, Tiber, Rubicon; islands of Sicily, Sardinia, Elba, Capri, Ischia, Lipari, Pantelleria; lakes Como, Maggiore, Garda **Head of state:** Oscar Luigi Scalfaro from 1992 **Head of government:** Massimo d'Alema from 1998 **Political system:** democracy **Political parties:** Forza Italia (Go Italy!), free market, right of centre; Northern League (LN), Milan-based, federalist, right of centre; National Alliance (AN), neofascist; Italian Popular Party (PPI), Catholic, centrist; Italian Renewal Party, centrist; Democratic Party of the Left (PDS), pro-European, moderate left wing (ex-communist); Italian Socialist Party (PSI), moderate socialist; Italian Republican Party (PRI), social democratic, left of centre; Democratic Alliance (AD), moderate left of centre; Christian Democratic Centre (CCD), Christian, centrist; Olive Tree alliance, centre left; Panella List, radical liberal; Union of the Democratic Centre (UDC), right of centre; Pact for Italy, reformist; Communist Refoundation (RC), Marxist; Verdi, environmentalist; La Rete (the Network), anti-Mafia **Currency:** lira **Real GDP per capita (PPP):** ($ US) 19,950 (1996) **Exports:** machinery and transport equipment, textiles, clothing, footwear, wine (leading producer and exporter), metals and metal products, chemicals, wood, paper and rubber goods. Principal market: Germany 18.7% (1995) **Population:** 57,226,000 (1996 est) **Language:** Italian; German, French, Slovene, and Albanian minorities **Religion:** Roman Catholic 100% (state religion) **Life expectancy:** 75 (men); 81 (women) (1995–2000)

Jamaica

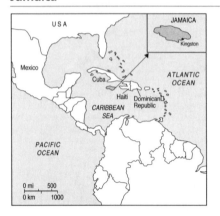

Area: 10,957 sq km/4,230 sq mi **Capital:** Kingston **Major towns/cities:** Montego Bay, Spanish Town, St Andrew, Portmore, May Pen **Physical features:** mountainous tropical island; Blue Mountains (so called because of the haze over them) **Head of state:** Elizabeth II from 1962, represented by governor general Howard Felix Hanlan Cooke from 1991 **Head of government:** Percival Patterson from 1992 **Political system:** constitutional monarchy **Political parties:** Jamaica Labour Party (JLP), moderate, centrist; People's National Party (PNP), left of centre; National Democratic Union (NDM), centrist **Currency:** Jamaican dollar **Real GDP per capita (PPP):** ($ US) 3,816 (1994) **Exports:** bauxite, alumina, gypsum, sugar, bananas, garments, rum. Principal market: USA 45.4% (1995) **Population:** 2,491,000 (1996 est) **Language:** English, Jamaican creole **Religion:** Protestant 70%, Rastafarian **Life expectancy:** 72 (men); 77 (women) (1995–2000)

Japan

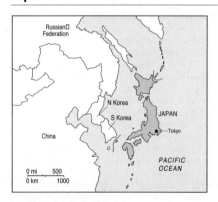

National name: *Nippon* **Area:** 377,535 sq km/145,766 sq mi **Capital:** Tokyo **Major towns/cities:** Yokohama, Osaka, Nagoya, Fukuoka, Kitakyushu, Kyoto, Sapporo, Kobe, Kawasaki, Hiroshima **Major ports:** Osaka, Nagoya, Yokohama, Kobe **Physical features:**

mountainous, volcanic (Mount Fuji, volcanic Mount Aso, Japan Alps); comprises over 1,000 islands, the largest of which are Hokkaido, Honshu, Kyushu, and Shikoku **Head of state:** (figurehead) Emperor Akihito (Heisei) from 1989 **Head of government:** Keizo Obuchi from 1998 **Political system:** liberal democracy **Political parties:** Liberal Democratic Party (LDP), right of centre; Shinshinto (New Frontier Party) opposition coalition, centrist reformist; Social Democratic Party of Japan (SDPJ, former Socialist Party), left of centre but moving towards centre; Shinto Sakigake (New Party Harbinger), right of centre; Japanese Communist Party (JCP), socialist; Democratic Party of Japan (DPJ), Sakigake and SDPJ dissidents **Currency:** yen **Real GDP per capita (PPP):** ($ US) 22,863 (1996) **Exports:** motor vehicles, electronic goods and components, chemicals, iron and steel products, scientific and optical equipment. Principal market: USA 27.2% (1996) **Population:** 125,351,000 (1996 est) **Language:** Japanese; also Ainu **Religion:** Shinto, Buddhist (often combined), Christian **Life expectancy:** 77 (men); 83 (women) (1995–2000)

Jordan

Hashemite Kingdom of

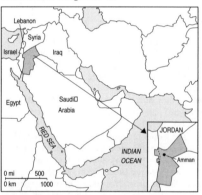

National name: *Al Mamlaka al Urduniya al Hashemiyah* **Area:** 89,206 sq km/34,442 sq mi (West Bank 5,879 sq km/2,269 sq mi) **Capital:** Amman **Major towns/cities:** Zarqa, Irbid, Saet, Ma'an **Major ports:** Aqaba **Physical features:** desert plateau in east; Rift Valley separates east and west banks of River Jordan **Head of state:** King Abdullah ibn Hussein from 1999 **Head of government:** Fayez Tarawneh from 1999 **Political system:** constitutional monarchy **Political parties:** independent groups loyal to the king predominate; of the 21 parties registered since 1992, the most significant is the Islamic Action Front (IAF), Islamic fundamentalist **Currency:** Jordanian dinar **Real GDP per capita (PPP):** ($ US) 4,187 (1994) **Exports:** phosphate, potash, fertilizers, foodstuffs, pharmaceuticals, fruit and vegetables, cement. Principal market: Iraq 18.9% (1995) **Population:** 5,581,000 (1996 est) **Language:** Arabic (official), English **Religion:** Sunni Muslim 80%, Christian 8% **Life expectancy:** 68 (men); 72 (women) (1995–2000)

Kazakhstan

Republic of

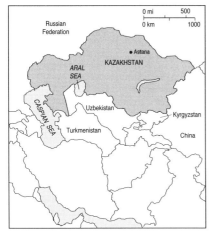

National name: *Kazak Respublikasy* **Area:** 2,717,300 sq km/1,049,150 sq mi **Capital:** Astana (formerly called Akmola) **Major towns/cities:** Karaganda, Pavlodar, Semipalatinsk, Petropavlovsk, Chimkent **Physical features:** Caspian and Aral seas, Lake Balkhash; Steppe region; natural gas and oil deposits in the Caspian Sea **Head of state:** Nursultan Nazarbayev from 1990 **Head of government:** Nurlan Balgimbayev from 1997 **Political system:** authoritarian nationalist **Political parties:** Congress of People's Unity of Kazakhstan, moderate, centrist; People's Congress of Kazakhstan, moderate, ethnic; Socialist Party of Kazakhstan (SPK), left wing; Republican Party, right-of-centre coalition **Currency:** tenge **Real GDP per capita (PPP):** ($ US) 3,284 (1994) **Exports:** ferrous and non-ferrous metals, mineral products (including petroleum and petroleum products), chemicals. Principal market: Russia 42.1% (1995) **Population:** 16,820,000 (1996 est) **Language:** Kazakh (official), related to Turkish; Russian **Religion:** Sunni Muslim **Life expectancy:** 67 (men); 75 (women) (1995–2000)

Kenya

Republic of

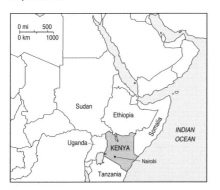

National name: *Jamhuri ya Kenya* **Area:** 582,600 sq km/224,941 sq mi **Capital:** Nairobi **Major towns/cities:** Mombasa, Kisumu, Nakuru, Eldoret, Nyeri **Major ports:** Mombasa **Physical features:** mountains and highlands in west and centre; coastal plain in south; arid interior and tropical coast; semi-desert in north; Great Rift Valley, Mount Kenya, Lake Nakuru (salt lake with world's largest colony of flamingos), Lake Turkana (Rudolf) **Head of state and government:** Daniel arap Moi from 1978 **Political system:** authoritarian nationalist **Political parties:** Kenya African National Union (KANU), nationalist, centrist; Forum for the Restoration of Democracy–Kenya (FORD–Kenya), left of centre; Forum for the Restoration of Democracy–Asili (FORD–Asili), left of centre; Democratic Party (DP), centrist; Safina, centrist **Currency:** Kenya shilling **Real GDP per capita (PPP):** ($ US) 1,404 (1994) **Exports:** coffee, tea, petroleum products, soda ash, horticultural products. Principal market: Uganda 15.8% (1995) **Population:** 27,799,000 (1996 est) **Language:** Kiswahili (official), English; there are many local dialects **Religion:** Roman Catholic, Protestant, Muslim, traditional tribal religions **Life expectancy:** 57 (men); 61 (women) (1995–2000)

Kiribati

Republic of (formerly part of the Gilbert and Ellice Islands)

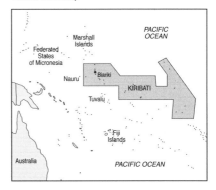

National name: *Ribaberikin Kiribati* **Area:** 717 sq km/277 sq mi **Capital:** Bairiki (on Tarawa Atoll) (and port) **Towns** pricipal atolls: North Tarawa, Gilbert group, Abaiang, Tabiteuea **Major ports:** Betio (on Tarawa) **Physical features:** comprises 33 Pacific coral islands: the Kiribati (Gilbert), Rawaki (Phoenix), Banaba (Ocean Island), and three of the Line Islands including Kiritimati (Christmas Island); island groups crossed by Equator and International Date Line **Head of state and government:** Teburoro Tito from 1994 **Political system:** liberal democracy **Political parties:** Maneaban Te Mauri (MTM), dominant faction; National Progressive Party (NPP), former governing faction 1979–94 **Currency:** Australian dollar **Real GDP per capita (PPP):** ($ US) 860 (1995 est) **Exports:** copra, fish, seaweed, bananas, breadfruit, taro. Principal market: Bangladesh 67% (1993) **Population:** 80,000 (1996 est) **Language:** English (official), Gilbertese

Religion: Roman Catholic, Protestant
(Congregationalist) **Life expectancy:** 51 (men); 56
(women) (1992)

Korea, North

People's Democratic Republic of

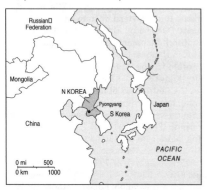

National name: *Chosun Minchu-chui Inmin
Konghwa-guk* **Area:** 120,538 sq km/46,539 sq mi
Capital: Pyongyang **Major towns/cities:** Hamhung,
Chongjin, Nampo, Wonsan, Sinuiji **Physical features:**
wide coastal plain in west rising to mountains cut by
deep valleys in interior **Head of state:** Kim Jong Il
from 1994 **Head of government:** Hong Song Nam
from 1997 **Political system:** communism **Political
parties:** Korean Workers' Party (KWP), Marxist-
Leninist (leads Democratic Front for the
Reunification of the Fatherland, including Korean
Social Democratic Party and Chondoist Chongu
Party) **Currency:** won **Real GDP per capita (PPP):**
($ US) 920 (1995 est) **Exports:** base metals, textiles,
vegetable products, machinery and equipment.
Principal market: Japan 27.9% (1995 est) **Population:**
22,466,000 (1996 est) **Language:** Korean **Religion:**
Chondoist, Buddhist, Christian, traditional beliefs
Life expectancy: 69 (men); 75 (women) (1995–2000)

Korea, South

Republic of Korea

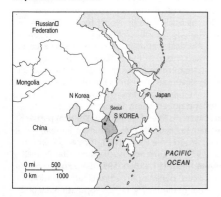

National name: *Daehan Min-kuk* **Area:** 98,799 sq km/
38,146 sq mi **Capital:** Seoul **Major towns/cities:**
Pusan, Taegu, Inchon, Kwangju, Taejon **Major ports:**
Pusan, Inchon **Physical features:** southern end of a
mountainous peninsula separating the Sea of Japan
from the Yellow Sea **Head of state:** Kim Dae Jung
from 1998 **Head of government:** Kim Jong Pil from
1998 **Political system:** emergent democracy **Political
parties:** New Korea Party (NKP, formerly Democratic
Liberal Party (DLP)), right of centre; National
Congress for New Politics (NCNP), centre left;
Democratic Party (DP), left of centre; New
Democratic Party (NDP), centrist, pro-private
enterprise; United Liberal Democratic Party (ULD),
ultra-conservative, pro-private enterprise **Currency:**
won **Real GDP per capita (PPP):** ($ US) 10,656 (1994)
Exports: electrical machinery, textiles, clothing,
footwear, telecommunications and sound
equipment, chemical products, ships ('invisible
export' – overseas construction work). Principal
market: USA 16.7% (1996) **Population:** 45,314,000
(1996 est) **Language:** Korean **Religion:** Shamanist,
Buddhist, Confucian, Protestant, Roman Catholic **Life
expectancy:** 69 (men); 76 (women) (1995–2000)

Kuwait

State of

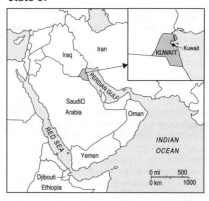

National name: *Dowlat al Kuwait* **Area:** 17,819 sq
km/6,879 sq mi **Capital:** Kuwait (also chief port)
Major towns/cities: as-Salimiya, Hawalli, Faranawiya,
Abraq Kheetan, Jahra, Ahmadi, Fahaheel **Physical
features:** hot desert; islands of Failaka, Bubiyan, and
Warba at northeast corner of Arabian Peninsula
Head of state: Sheikh Jabir al-Ahmad al-Jabir
as-Sabah from 1977 **Head of government:** Crown
Prince Sheikh Saad al-Abdullah as-Salinas as-Sabah
from 1978 **Political system:** absolute monarchy
Political parties: none **Currency:** Kuwaiti dinar **Real
GDP per capita (PPP):** ($ US) 21,630 (1995) **Exports:**
petroleum and petroleum products (accounted for
more than 93% of export revenue in 1994), chemical
fertilizer, gas (natural and manufactured), basic
manufactures. Principal market: Japan 23.5% (1996)
Population: 1,687,000 (1996 est) **Language:** Arabic
(official) 78%, Kurdish 10%, Farsi 4%, English

Religion: Sunni Muslim, Shi'ite Muslim, Christian **Life expectancy:** 74 (men); 78 (women) (1995–2000)

Kyrgyzstan
Republic of

National name: *Kyrgyz Respublikasy* **Area:** 198,500 sq km/76,640 sq mi **Capital:** Bishkek (formerly Frunze) **Major towns/cities:** Osh, Przhevalsk, Kyzyl-Kiya, Tokmak, Djalal-Abad **Physical features:** mountainous, an extension of the Tian Shan range **Head of state:** Askar Akayev from 1990 **Head of government:** Kubanychbek Djumaliev from 1998 **Political system:** emergent democracy **Political parties:** Party of Communists of Kyrgyzstan (banned 1991–92); Ata Meken, Kyrgyz-nationalist; Erkin Kyrgyzstan, Kyrgyz-nationalist; Social Democratic Party, nationalist, pro-Akayev; Democratic Movement of Kyrgyzstan, nationalist reformist **Currency:** som **Real GDP per capita (PPP):** ($ US) 1,930 (1994) **Exports:** wool, cotton yarn, tobacco, electric power, electronic and engineering products, non-ferrous metallurgy, food and beverages. Principal market: Kazakhstan 28% (1994) **Population:** 4,469,000 (1996 est) **Language:** Kyrgyz **Religion:** Sunni Muslim **Life expectancy:** 67 (men); 74 (women) (1995–2000)

Laos
Lao People's Democratic Republic

National name: *Saathiaranagroat Prachhathippatay Prachhachhon Lao* **Area:** 236,790 sq km/91,424 sq mi **Capital:** Vientiane **Major towns/cities:** Louangphrabang (the former royal capital), Pakse, Savannakhet **Physical features:** landlocked state with high mountains in east; Mekong River in west; rainforest covers nearly 60% of land **Head of state:** Gen Khamtay Siphandon from 1998 **Head of government:** Gen Sisavath Keobounphanh from 1998 **Political system:** communist, one-party state **Political party:** Lao People's Revolutionary Party (LPRP, the only legal party) **Currency:** new kip **Real

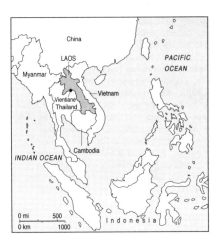

GDP per capita (PPP): ($ US) 2,484 (1994) **Exports:** timber, textiles and garments, motorcycles, electricity, coffee, tin, gypsum. Principal market: Thailand 20.8% (1994) **Population:** 5,035,000 (1996 est) **Language:** Lao (official), French, English **Religion:** Theravāda Buddhist 85%, animist beliefs among mountain dwellers **Life expectancy:** 52 (men); 55 (women) (1995–2000)

Latvia
Republic of

National name: *Latvijas Republika* **Area:** 63,700 sq km/24,594 sq mi **Capital:** Riga **Major towns/cities:** Daugavpils, Leipāja, Jurmala, Jelgava, Ventspils **Major ports:** Ventspils, Leipāja **Physical features:** wooded lowland (highest point 312 m/1,024 ft), marshes, lakes; 472 km/293 mi of coastline; mild climate **Head of state:** Guntis Ulmanis from 1993 **Head of government:** Guntar Krasts from 1997 **Political system:** emergent democracy **Political parties:** Latvian Way, right of centre; Latvian National and Conservative Party (LNNK), right wing, nationalist; Economic-Political Union (formerly known as Harmony for Latvia and Rebirth of the National Economy), centrist; Ravnopravie (Equal Rights), centrist; For the Fatherland and Freedom

(FFF), extreme nationalist; Latvian Peasants' Union (LZS), rural based, centre left; Union of Christian Democrats, centre right; Democratic Centre Party, centrist; Movement for Latvia, pro-Russian, populist; Master in Your Own Home (Saimnieks), ex-communist, populist; Latvian National Party of Reforms, right of centre nationalist coalition **Currency:** lat **Real GDP per capita (PPP):** ($ US) 3,332 (1994) **Exports:** timber and timber products, textiles, food and agricultural products, machinery and electrical equipment, metal industry products. Principal market: Russia 22.8% (1996) **Population:** 2,504,000 (1996 est) **Language:** Latvian **Religion:** Lutheran, Roman Catholic, Russian Orthodox **Life expectancy:** 63 (men); 75 (women) (1995–2000)

Lebanon

Republic of

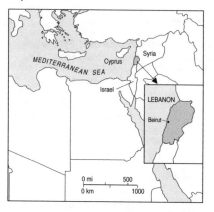

National name: *Jumhouria al-Lubnaniya* **Area:** 10,452 sq km/4,035 sq mi **Capital:** Beirut (and port) **Major towns/cities:** Tripoli, Zahlé, Baabda, Baalbek, Jezzine **Major ports:** Tripoli, Tyre, Sidon, Jounie **Physical features:** narrow coastal plain; fertile Bekka valley running north–south between Lebanon and Anti-Lebanon mountain ranges **Head of state:** Emile Lahoud from 1998 **Head of government:** Rafik al-Hariri from 1992 **Political system:** emergent democracy **Political parties:** Phalangist Party, Christian, radical, nationalist; Progressive Socialist Party (PSP), Druse, moderate, socialist; National Liberal Party (NLP), Maronite, centre left; National Bloc, Maronite, moderate; Lebanese Communist Party (PCL), nationalist, communist; Parliamentary Democratic Front, Sunni Muslim, centrist **Currency:** Lebanese pound **Real GDP per capita (PPP):** ($ US) 4,863 (1994) **Exports:** paper products, textiles, fruit and vegetables, jewellery. Principal market: UAE 28.7% (1995) **Population:** 3,084,000 (1996 est) **Language:** Arabic (official), French, Armenian, English **Religion:** Muslim 58% (Shiite 35%, Sunni 23%), Christian 27% (mainly Maronite), Druse 3%; other Christian denominations including Orthodox, Armenian, and Roman Catholic **Life expectancy:** 68 (men); 72 (women) (1995–2000)

Lesotho

Kingdom of

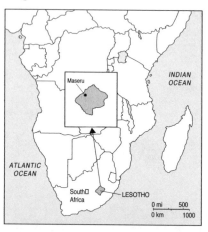

Area: 30,355 sq km/11,720 sq mi **Capital:** Maseru **Major towns/cities:** Qacha's Nek, Teyateyaneng, Mafeteng, Hlotse, Roma, Quthing **Physical features:** mountainous with plateaux, forming part of South Africa's chief watershed **Head of state:** King Letsie III from 1996 **Head of government:** Ntsu Mokhehle from 1993 **Political system:** constitutional monarchy **Political parties:** Basotho National Party (BNP), traditionalist, nationalist, right of centre; Basutoland Congress Party (BCP), left of centre **Currency:** loti **Real GDP per capita (PPP):** ($ US) 1,109 (1994) **Exports:** clothing, footwear, furniture, food and live animals (cattle), hides, wool and mohair, baskets. Principal market: SACU 51.4% (1994) **Population:** 2,078,000 (1996 est) **Language:** Sesotho, English (official), Zulu, Xhosa **Religion:** Protestant 42%, Roman Catholic 38%, indigenous beliefs **Life expectancy:** 61 (men); 66 (women) (1995–2000)

Liberia

Republic of

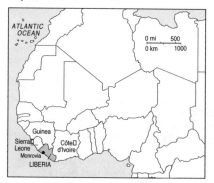

Area: 111,370 sq km/42,999 sq mi **Capital:** Monrovia (and port) **Major towns/cities:** Bensonville, Saniquillie, Gbarnga, Voinjama, Buchanan **Major ports:**

Buchanan, Greenville **Physical features:** forested highlands; swampy tropical coast where six rivers enter the sea **Head of state and government:** Ruth Perry from 1996 **Political system:** emergent democracy **Political parties:** National Democratic Party of Liberia (NDPL), nationalist, left of centre; National Patriotic Front of Liberia (NPFL), left of centre; United Democratic Movement of Liberia for Democracy (Ulimo), left of centre; National Patriotic Party (NPP) **Currency:** Liberian dollar **Real GDP per capita (PPP):** ($ US) 800 (1994 est) **Exports:** iron ore, rubber, timber, coffee, cocoa, palm-kernel oil, diamonds, gold. Principal market: Belgium/Luxembourg 56.3% (1994 est) **Population:** 2,245,000 (1996 est) **Language:** English (official), over 20 Niger-Congo Languages **Religion:** animist, Sunni Muslim, Christian **Life expectancy:** 56 (men); 59 (women) (1995–2000)

Libya

Great Socialist People's Libyan Arab Republic

National name: *Jamahiriya al-Arabiya al-Libya al-Shabiya al-Ishtirakiya al-Uzma* **Area:** 1,759,540 sq km/ 679,358 sq mi **Capital:** Tripoli **Towns and cities** Benghazi, Misurata, Az-Zaiwa, Tobruk, Ajdabiya, Derna **Major ports:** Benghazi, Misurata, Az-Zaiwa, Tobruk, Ajdabiya, Derna **Physical features:** flat to undulating plains with plateaux and depressions stretch southwards from the Mediterranean coast to an extremely dry desert interior **Head of state and government:** Moamer al-Khaddhafi from 1969 **Political system:** one-party socialist state **Political party:** Arab Socialist Union (ASU), radical, left wing **Currency:** Libyan dinar **Real GDP per capita (PPP):** ($ US) 6,125 (1994) **Exports:** crude petroleum (accounted for 94% of 1991 export earnings), chemicals and related products. Principal market: Italy 39.8% (1995) **Population:** 5,593,000 (1996 est) **Language:** Arabic **Religion:** Sunni Muslim **Life expectancy:** 64 (men); 68 (women) (1995–2000)

Liechtenstein

Principality of

National name: *Fürstentum Liechtenstein* **Area:** 160 sq km/62 sq mi **Capital:** Vaduz **Major towns/cities:**

Balzers, Schaan, Ruggell, Triesen, Eschen **Physical features:** landlocked Alpine; includes part of Rhine Valley in west **Head of state:** Prince Hans Adam II from 1989 **Head of government:** Mario Frick from 1993 **Political system:** constitutional monarchy **Political parties:** Patriotic Union (VU), conservative; Progressive Citizens' Party (FBP), conservative **Currency:** Swiss franc **Real GDP per capita (PPP):** ($ US) 23,200 (1992) **Exports:** small machinery, artificial teeth and other material for dentistry, stamps, precision instruments, ceramics. Principal market: Switzerland 14% (1994) **Population:** 31,000 (1996 est) **Language:** German (official); an Alemannic dialect is also spoken **Religion:** Roman Catholic (87%), Protestant **Life expectancy:** 78 (men); 83 (women) (1995–2000)

Lithuania

Republic of

National name: *Lietuvos Respublika* **Area:** 65,200 sq km/25,173 sq mi **Capital:** Vilnius **Major towns/cities:** Kaunas, Klaipeda, Siauliai, Panevezys **Physical features:** central lowlands with gentle hills in west and higher terrain in southeast; 25% forested; some 3,000 small lakes, marshes, and complex sandy coastline; River Nemen **Head of state:** Valdas Adamkus from 1998 **Head of government:**

Gediminas Vagnorius from 1996 **Political system:** emergent democracy **Political parties:** Lithuanian Democratic Labour Party (LDLP), reform-socialist (ex-communist); Homeland Union–Lithuanian Conservatives (Tevynes Santara), right of centre, nationalist; Christian Democratic Party of Lithuania, centre right; Lithuanian Social Democratic Party, left of centre **Currency:** litas **Real GDP per capita (PPP):** ($ US) 4,011 (1994) **Exports:** textiles, machinery and equipment, non-precious metals, animal products, timber. Principal market: Russia 23.8 (1996) **Population:** 3,728,000 (1996 est) **Language:** Lithuanian (official) **Religion:** predominantly Roman Catholic; Lithuanian Lutheran Church **Life expectancy:** 65 (men); 76 (women) (1995–2000)

Luxembourg

Grand Duchy of

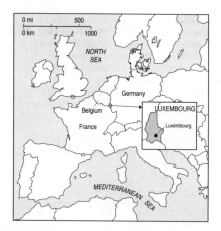

National name: *Grand-Duché de Luxembourg* **Area:** 2,586 sq km/998 sq mi **Capital:** Luxembourg **Major towns/cities:** Esch-Alzette, Differdange, Dudelange, Petange **Physical features:** on the River Moselle; part of the Ardennes (Oesling) forest in north **Head of state:** Grand Duke Jean from 1964 **Head of government:** Jean-Claude Juncker from 1995 **Political system:** liberal democracy **Political parties:** Christian Social Party (PCS), moderate, left of centre; Luxembourg Socialist Workers' Party (POSL), moderate, socialist; Democratic Party (PD), centre left; Communist Party of Luxembourg, pro-European left wing **Currency:** Luxembourg franc **Real GDP per capita (PPP):** ($ US) 32,665 (1996) **Exports:** base metals and manufactures, mechanical and electrical equipment, rubber and related products, plastics, textiles and clothing. Principal market: Germany 28.2% (1993) **Population:** 412,000 (1996 est) **Language:** French, German, local Letzeburgesch (all official) **Religion:** Roman Catholic **Life expectancy:** 73 (men); 80 (women) (1995–2000)

Macedonia

Former Yugoslav Republic of (official international name); Republic of Macedon (official internal name)

National name: *Republika Makedonija* **Area:** 25,700 sq km/9,922 sq mi **Capital:** Skopje **Major towns/cities:** Bitolj, Prilep, Kumanovo, Tetovo **Physical features:** mountainous; rivers: Struma, Vardar; lakes: Ohrid, Prespa, Scutari; partly Mediterranean climate with hot summers **Head of state:** (acting) Stojan Andov from 1995 **Head of government:** Branko Crvenkovski from 1992 **Political system:** emergent democracy **Political parties:** Socialist Party (SP); Social Democratic Alliance of Macedonia (SM) bloc, left of centre; Party for Democratic Prosperity (PDP), ethnic Albanian, left of centre; Internal Macedonian Revolutionary Organization–Democratic Party for Macedonian National Unity (VMRO–DPMNE), radical nationalist; Democratic Party of Macedonia (DPM), nationalist, free market **Currency:** Macedonian denar **Real GDP per capita (PPP):** ($ US) 3,965 (1994) **Exports:** manufactured goods, machinery and transport equipment, miscellaneous manufactured articles, sugar beet, vegetables, cheese, lamb, tobacco. Principal market: Bulgaria 20% (1994) **Population:** 2,174,000 (1996 est) **Language:** Macedonian, closely allied to Bulgarian and written in Cyrillic **Religion:** Christian, mainly Orthodox; Muslim 2.5% **Life expectancy:** 70 (men); 76 (women) (1995–2000)

Madagascar

Democratic Republic of

National name: *Repolika Demokratika n'i Madagaskar* **Area:** 587,041 sq km/226,656 sq mi **Capital:** Antananarivo **Major towns/cities:** Antsirabe, Mahajanga, Fianarantsoa, Toamasina, Ambatondrazaka **Major ports:** Toamasina, Antsiranana, Toliary, Mahajanga **Physical features:** temperate central highlands; humid valleys and tropical coastal plains; arid in south **Head of state:**

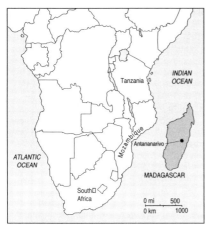

Malawi Congress Party (MCP), multiracial, right wing; United Democratic Front (UDF), left of centre; Alliance for Democracy (AFORD), left of centre **Currency:** Malawi kwacha **Real GDP per capita (PPP):** ($ US) 694 (1994) **Exports:** tobacco, tea, sugar, cotton, groundnuts. Principal market: South Africa 13.8% (1995) **Population:** 9,845,000 (1996 est) **Language:** English, Chichewa (both official) **Religion:** Christian 75%, Muslim 20% **Life expectancy:** 44 (men); 45 (women) (1995–2000)

Malaysia

Federation of (FOM)

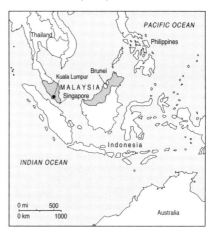

National name: *Persekutuan Tanah Malaysia* **Area:** 329,759 sq km/127,319 sq mi **Capital:** Kuala Lumpur **Major towns/cities:** Johor Baharu, Ipoh, George Town (Penang), Kuala Trengganu, Kuala Baharu, Petalong Jaya, Kelang, Kuching in Sarawak, Kota Kinabalu in Sabah **Major ports:** Kelang **Physical features:** comprises peninsular Malaysia (the nine Malay states – Johore, Kedah, Kelantan, Negri Sembilan, Pahang, Perak, Perlis, Selangor, Trengganu – plus Malacca and Penang); states of Sabah and Sarawak and federal territory of Kuala Lumpur; 75% tropical rainforest; central mountain range (Mount Kinabalu, the highest peak in southeast Asia); swamps in east; Niah caves (Sarawak) **Head of state:** Jaafar bin Abd al-Rahman from 1994 **Head of government:** Mahathir bin Mohamed from 1981 **Political system:** liberal democracy **Political parties:** New United Malays' National Organization (UMNO Baru), Malay-oriented nationalist; Malaysian Chinese Association (MCA), Chinese-oriented, conservative; Gerakan Party, Chinese-oriented, socialist; Malaysian Indian Congress (MIC), Indian-oriented; Democratic Action Party (DAP), multiracial but Chinese-dominated, left of centre; Pan-Malayan Islamic Party (PAS), Islamic; Semangat '46 (Spirit of 1946), moderate, multiracial **Currency:** ringgit **Real GDP per capita (PPP):** ($ US) 8,865 (1994) **Exports:** palm oil, rubber, crude petroleum, machinery and transport equipment, timber, tin, textiles, electronic goods. Principal market: USA 20.7% (1995) **Population:**

Didier Ratsiraka from 1996 **Head of government:** Pascal Rakotomavo from 1997 **Political system:** emergent democracy **Political parties:** National Front for the Defence of the Malagasy Socialist Revolution (FNDR), left-of-centre coalition; Comité des Forces Vives, pro-Zafy, left-of-centre coalition **Currency:** Malagasy franc **Real GDP per capita (PPP):** ($ US) 694 (1994) **Exports:** coffee, shrimps, cloves, vanilla, petroleum products, chromium, cotton fabrics. Principal market: France 29.2% (1995) **Population:** 15,353,000 (1996 est) **Language:** Malagasy (official); French, English **Religion:** traditional beliefs, Roman Catholic, Protestant **Life expectancy:** 58 (men); 61 (women) (1995–2000)

Malawi

Republic of (formerly **Nyasaland**)

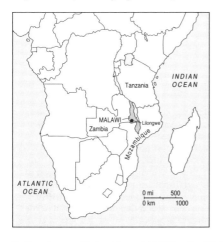

National name: *Malawi* **Area:** 118,000 sq km/45,559 sq mi **Capital:** Lilongwe **Major towns/cities:** Blantyre, Lilongwe, Mzuzu, Zomba **Physical features:** landlocked narrow plateau with rolling plains; mountainous west of Lake Nyasa **Head of state and government:** Bakili Muluzi from 1994 **Political system:** emergent democracy **Political parties:**

20,581,000 (1996 est) **Language:** Malay (official), English, Chinese, Tamil, Iban **Religion:** Muslim (official), Buddhist, Hindu, local beliefs **Life expectancy:** 70 (men); 74 (women) (1995–2000)

Maldives

Republic of the

National name: *Divehi Raajjeyge Jumhooriyaa* **Area:** 298 sq km/115 sq mi **Capital:** Malé **Major towns/cities:** Seenu, Kurehdhu, Kunfunadhoo, Dhiggiri, Anthimatha **Physical features:** comprises 1,196 coral islands, grouped into 12 clusters of atolls, largely flat, none bigger than 13 sq km/5 sq mi, average elevation 1.8 m/6 ft; 203 are inhabited **Head of state and government:** Maumoon Abd al-Gayoom from 1978 **Political system:** authoritarian nationalist **Political parties:** none; candidates elected on basis of personal influence and clan loyalties **Currency:** rufiya **Real GDP per capita (PPP):** ($ US) 1,560 (1994 est) **Exports:** marine products (tuna bonito ('Maldive Fish'), clothing. Principal market: UK 26% (1995) **Population:** 263,000 (1996 est) **Language:** Divehi (Sinhalese dialect), English **Religion:** Sunni Muslim **Life expectancy:** 66 (men); 63 (women) (1995–2000)

Mali

Republic of

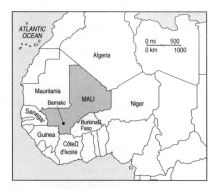

National name: *République du Mali* **Area:** 1,240,142 sq km/478,818 sq mi **Capital:** Bamako **Major towns/cities:** Mopti, Kayes, Ségou, Timbuktu, Sikasso **Physical features:** landlocked state with River Niger and savanna in south; part of the Sahara in north; hills in northeast; Senegal River and its branches irrigate the southwest **Head of state:** Alpha Oumar Konare from 1992 **Head of government:** Ibrahim Boubaker Keita from 1994 **Political system:** emergent democracy **Political parties:** Alliance for Democracy in Mali (ADEMA), left of centre; National Committee for Democratic Initiative (CNID), centre left; Assembly for Democracy and Progress (RDP), left of centre; Civic Society and the Democracy and Progress Party (PDP), left of centre; Malian People's Democratic Union (UDPM), nationalist socialist **Currency:** franc CFA **Real GDP per capita (PPP):** ($ US) 543 (1994) **Exports:** cotton, livestock, gold, miscellaneous manufactured articles. Principal market: Thailand 18.5% (1995) **Population:** 11,134,000 (1996 est) **Language:** French (official), Bambara **Religion:** Sunni Muslim 90%, animist, Christian **Life expectancy:** 46 (men); 50 (women) (1995–2000)

Malta

Republic of

National name: *Repubblika Ta'Malta* **Area:** 320 sq km/124 sq mi **Capital:** Valletta (and port) **Major towns/cities:** Rabat, Birkirkara, Qormi, Sliema, Zetjun, Zabor **Major ports:** Marsaxlokk, Valletta **Physical features:** includes islands of Gozo 67 sq km/26 sq mi and Comino 3 sq km/1 sq mi **Head of state:** Mifsud Bonnici from 1994 **Head of government:** Edward Fenech Adami from 1998 **Political system:** liberal democracy **Political parties:** Malta Labour Party (MLP), moderate, left of centre; Nationalist Party (PN), Christian, centrist, pro-European **Currency:** Maltese lira **Real GDP per capita (PPP):** ($ US) 13,009 (1994) **Exports:** machinery and transport equipment, manufactured articles (including clothing), beverages, chemicals, tobacco. Principal market: Italy 37.5% in 1994 **Population:** 369,000 (1996 est) **Language:** Maltese, English (both official) **Religion:** Roman Catholic

98% **Life expectancy:** 75 (men); 79 (women) (1995–2000)

Marshall Islands

Republic of the (RMI)

Area: 181 sq km/70 sq mi **Capital:** Dalap-Uliga-Darrit (on Majuro atoll) **Major towns/cities:** Ebeye (the only other town) **Physical features:** comprises the Ratak and Ralik island chains in the West Pacific, which together form an archipelago of 31 coral atolls, 5 islands, and 1,152 islets **Head of state and government:** Imata Kabua from 1997 **Political system:** liberal democracy **Political parties:** no organized party system, but in 1991 an opposition grouping, the Ralik Ratak Democratic Party, was founded to oppose the ruling group **Currency:** US dollar **Real GDP per capita (PPP):** ($ US) 1,680 (1995 est) **Exports:** coconut products, trochus shells, copra, handicrafts, fish, live animals. Principal market: USA **Population:** 57,000 (1996 est) **Language:** Marshallese, English (both official) **Religion:** Christian (mainly Protestant) and Baha'i **Life expectancy:** 62 (men); 65 (women) (1995)

Mauritania

Islamic Republic of

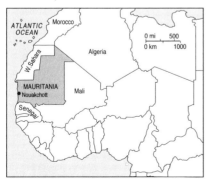

National name: *République Islamique Arabe et Africaine de Mauritanie* **Area:** 1,030,700 sq km/ 397,953 sq mi **Capital:** Nouakchott (port) **Major**

towns/cities: Nouâdhibou, Kaédi, Zouerate, Kiffa, Rosso, Atar **Major ports:** Nouâdhibou **Physical features:** valley of River Senegal in south; remainder arid and flat **Head of state:** Maaoya Sid'Ahmed Ould Taya from 1984 **Head of government:** Cheik el Avia Ould Muhammad Khouna from 1996 **Political system:** emergent democracy **Political parties:** Democratic and Social Republican Party (PRDS), centre left, militarist; Rally for Democracy and National Unity (RDNU), centrist; Mauritian Renewal Party (MPR), centrist; Umma, Islamic fundamentalist **Currency:** ouguiya **Real GDP per capita (PPP):** ($ US) 1,593 (1994) **Exports:** fish and fish products, iron ore. Principal market: Japan 27.2% (1995) **Population:** 2,333,000 (1996 est) **Language:** French and Hasaniya Arabic (both official), African Languages including Pulaar, Soninke, and Wolof **Religion:** Sunni Muslim **Life expectancy:** 52 (men); 55 (women) (1995–2000)

Mauritius

Republic of

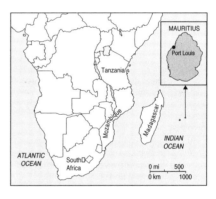

Area: 1,865 sq km/720 sq mi; the island of Rodrigues is part of Mauritius; there are several small island dependencies **Capital:** Port Louis (port) **Major towns/cities:** Beau Bassin-Rose Hill, Curepipe, Quatre Bornes, Vacoas-Phoenix **Physical features:** mountainous, volcanic island surrounded by coral reefs **Head of state:** Cassam Uteem from 1992 **Head of government:** Navim Ramgoolam from 1995 **Political system:** liberal democracy **Political parties:** Mauritius Socialist Movement (MSM), moderate socialist-republican; Mauritius Labour Party (MLP), democratic socialist, Hindu-oriented; Mauritius Social Democratic Party (PMSD), conservative, Francophile; Mauritius Militant Movement (MMM), Marxist-republican; Organization of Rodriguan People (OPR), left of centre **Currency:** Mauritian rupee **Real GDP per capita (PPP):** ($ US) 13,172 (1994) **Exports:** raw sugar, clothing, tea, molasses, jewellery. Principal market: UK 34% (1995) **Population:** 1,129,000 (1996 est) **Language:** English (official), French, Creole, Indian Languages **Religion:** Hindu, Christian (mainly Roman Catholic), Muslim **Life expectancy:** 68 (men); 75 (women) (1995–2000)

Mexico

United States of

Moldova

Republic of

National name: *Estados Unidos Mexicanos* **Area:** 1,958,201 sq km/756,061 sq mi **Capital:** Mexico City **Major towns/cities:** Guadalajara, Monterrey, Puebla, Netzahualcóyotl, Ciudad Juárez, Tijuana **Major ports:** 49 ocean ports **Physical features:** partly arid central highlands; Sierra Madre mountain ranges east and west; tropical coastal plains; volcanoes, including Popocatepetl; Rio Grande **Head of state and government:** Ernesto Zedillo Ponce de Leon from 1994 **Political system:** federal democracy **Political parties:** Institutional Revolutionary Party (PRI), moderate, left wing; National Action Party (PAN), moderate, Christian, centre right; Party of the Democratic Revolution (PRD), centre left **Currency:** Mexican peso **Real GDP per capita (PPP):** ($ US) 7,744 (1996) **Exports:** petroleum and petroleum products, engines and spare parts for motor vehicles, motor vehicles, electrical and electronic goods, fresh and preserved vegetables, coffee, cotton. Principal market: USA 83.9% (1996) **Population:** 92,718,000 (1996 est) **Language:** Spanish (official); Nahuatl, Maya, Zapoteco, Mixteco, Otomi **Religion:** Roman Catholic **Life expectancy:** 69 (men); 75 (women) (1995–2000)

Micronesia

Federated States of (FSM)

Area: 700 sq km/270 sq mi **Capital:** Kolonia, in Pohnpei state **Major towns/cities:** Weno, in Chuuk state; Lelu, in Kosrae state **Major ports:** Teketik, Lepukos, Okak **Physical features:** an archipelago of 607 equatorial, volcanic islands in the West Pacific **Head of state and government:** Jacob Nena from 1997 **Political system:** democratic federal state **Political parties:** no formally organized Political parties: **Currency:** US dollar **Real GDP per capita (PPP):** ($ US) 1,700 (1994 est) **Exports:** copra, pepper, fish **Population:** 126,000 (1996 est) **Language:** English (official) and eight local Languages **Religion:** Christianity (mainly Roman Catholic in Yap state, Protestant elsewhere) **Life expectancy:** 68 (men); 72 (women) (1995–2000)

National name: *Republica Moldoveneasca* **Area:** 33,700 sq km/13,011 sq mi **Capital:** Chişinău (Kishinev) **Major towns/cities:** Tiraspol, Beltsy, Bendery **Physical features:** hilly land lying largely between the rivers Prut and Dniester; northern Moldova comprises the level plain of the Beltsy Steppe and uplands; the climate is warm and moderately continental **Head of state:** Petru Lucinschi from 1997 **Head of government:** Ion Cebuc from 1997 **Political system:** emergent democracy **Political parties:** Agrarian Democratic Party (ADP), nationalist, centrist; Socialist Party and Yedinstvo/Unity Movement, reform-socialist; Peasants and Intellectuals, Romanian nationalist; Christian Democratic Popular Front (CDPF), Romanian nationalist; Gagauz-Khalky (GKPM; Gagauz People's Movement), Gagauz separatist **Currency:** leu **Real GDP per capita (PPP):** ($ US) 1,576 (1994) **Exports:** food and agricultural products, machinery and equipment, textiles, clothing. Principal market: Russia 59.9% (1996) **Population:** 4,444,000 (1996 est) **Language:** Moldovan **Religion:** Russian Orthodox **Life expectancy:** 64 (men); 72 (women) (1995–2000)

Monaco

Principality of

National name: *Principauté de Monaco* **Area:** 1.95 sq km/0.75 sq mi **Capital:** Monaco-Ville **Major towns/cities:** Monte Carlo, La Condamine; heliport Fontvieille **Physical features:** steep and rugged; surrounded landwards by French territory; being expanded by filling in the sea **Head of state:** Prince Rainier III from 1949 **Head of government:** Paul Dijoud from 1994 **Political system:** constitutional monarchy under French protectorate **Political parties:** no formal parties, but lists of candidates: Liste Campora, moderate, centrist; Liste Medecin, moderate, centrist **Currency:** French franc **Real GDP per capita (PPP):** ($ US) 25,000 (1994 est) **Population:** 32,000 (1996 est) **Language:** French (official); English,

Italian **Religion:** Roman Catholic **Life expectancy:** 74 (men); 83 (women) (1995)

Mongolia

State of (**Outer Mongolia** until 1924; **People's Republic of Mongolia** until 1991)

National name: *Mongol Uls* **Area:** 1,565,000 sq km/ 604,246 sq mi **Capital:** Ulaanbaatar (Ulan Bator) **Major towns/cities:** Darhan, Choybalsan, Erdenet **Physical features:** high plateau with desert and steppe (grasslands); Altai Mountains in southwest; salt lakes; part of Gobi desert in southeast; contains both the world's southernmost permafrost and northernmost desert **Head of state:** Natsagiyn Bagabandi from 1997 **Head of government:** Rinchinnyamiin Amarjargal from 1998 **Political system:** emergent democracy **Political parties:** Mongolian People's Revolutionary Party (MPRP), reform-socialist (ex-communist); Mongolian National Democratic Party (MNDP), traditionalist, promarket economy; Union Coalition (UC, comprising the MNPD and the Social Democratic Party (SDP)), democratic, promarket economy **Currency:** tugrik **Real GDP per capita (PPP):** ($ US) 3,766 (1994) **Exports:** minerals and metals (primarily copper concentrate), consumer goods, foodstuffs,

agricultural products. Principal market: Japan 18.7% (1995) **Population:** 2,515,000 (1996 est) **Language:** Khalkha Mongolian (official); Chinese, Russian, and Turkic Languages **Religion:** officially none (Tibetan Buddhist Lamaism suppressed in 1930s) **Life expectancy:** 64 (men); 67 (women) (1995–2000)

Morocco

Kingdom of

National name: *al-Mamlaka al-Maghrebia* **Area:** 458,730 sq km/177,115 sq mi (excluding Western Sahara) **Capital:** Rabat **Major towns/cities:** Casablanca, Marrakesh, Fez, Oujda, Kenitra, Tetouan, Meknès **Major ports:** Casablanca, Tangier, Agadir **Physical features:** mountain ranges, including the Atlas Mountains northeast–southwest; fertile coastal plains in west **Head of state:** Hassan II from 1961 **Head of government:** Abderrahmane Youssoufi from 1998 **Political system:** constitutional monarchy **Political parties:** Constitutional Union (UC), right wing; National Rally of Independents (RNI), royalist; Popular Movement (MP), moderate, centrist; Istiqlal, nationalist, centrist; Socialist Union of Popular Forces (USFP), progressive socialist; National Democratic Party (PND), moderate, nationalist **Currency:** dirham (DH) **Real GDP per capita (PPP):** ($ US) 3,681 (1994) **Exports:** phosphates and phosphoric acid, mineral products, seafoods and seafood products, citrus fruit, tobacco, clothing, hosiery. Principal market: France 29.7% (1995) **Population:** 27,021,000 (1996 est) **Language:** Arabic (official) 75%; Berber 25%, French, Spanish **Religion:** Sunni Muslim **Life expectancy:** 64 (men); 68 (women) (1995–2000)

Mozambique

People's Republic of

National name: *República Popular de Moçambique* **Area:** 799,380 sq km/308,640 sq mi **Capital:** Maputo (and chief port) **Major towns/cities:** Beira, Nampula, Nacala, Chimoio **Major ports:** Beira, Nacala, Quelimane **Physical features:** mostly flat tropical lowland; mountains in west; rivers Zambezi and

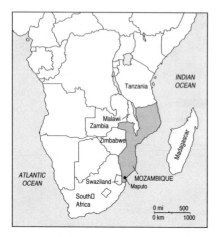

Limpopo **Head of state:** Joaquim Alberto Chissano from 1986 **Head of government:** Pascoal Mocumbi from 1994 **Political system:** emergent democracy **Political parties:** National Front for the Liberation of Mozambique (Frelimo), free market; Renamo, or Mozambique National Resistance (MNR), former rebel movement, right of centre **Currency:** metical **Real GDP per capita (PPP):** ($ US) 986 (1994) **Exports:** shrimps and other crustaceans, cashew nuts, raw cotton, sugar, copra, lobsters. Principal market: Spain 16.1% (1995) **Population:** 17,796,000 (1996 est) **Language:** Portuguese (official); 16 African Languages **Religion:** animist, Roman Catholic, Muslim **Life expectancy:** 45 (men); 48 (women) (1995–2000)

Myanmar

Union of (formerly **Burma** until 1989)

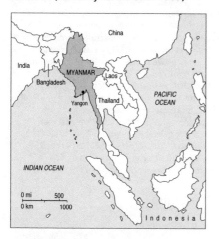

National name: *Thammada Myanmar Naingngandaw* **Area:** 676,577 sq km/261,226 sq mi **Capital:** Yangon (formerly Rangoon) (and chief port) **Major towns/cities:** Mandalay, Mawlamyine, Bago, Bassein, Taunggyi, Sittwe, Manywa **Physical features:**

over half is rainforest; rivers Irrawaddy and Chindwin in central lowlands ringed by mountains in north, west, and east **Head of state and government:** Than Shwe from 1992 **Political system:** military republic **Political parties:** National Unity Party (NUP), military-socialist ruling party; National League for Democracy (NLD), pluralist opposition grouping **Currency:** kyat **Real GDP per capita (PPP):** ($ US) 600 (1994) **Exports:** teak, rice, pulses and beans, rubber, hardwood, base metals, gems, cement. Principal market: Singapore 12.9% (1995) **Population:** 45,922,000 (1996 est) **Language:** Burmese (official), English **Religion:** Hinayāna Buddhist 85%, animist, Christian, Muslim **Life expectancy:** 59 (men); 62 (women) (1995–2000)

Namibia

Republic of (formerly **South West Africa**)

Area: 824,300 sq km/318,262 sq mi **Capital:** Windhoek **Major towns/cities:** Swakopmund, Rehoboth, Rundu **Major ports:** Walvis Bay **Physical features:** mainly desert (Namib and Kalahari); Orange River; Caprivi Strip links Namibia to Zambezi River; includes the enclave of Walvis Bay (area 1,120 sq km/432 sq mi) **Head of state:** Sam Nujoma from 1990 **Head of government:** Hage Geingob from 1990 **Political system:** democracy **Political parties:** South West Africa People's Organization (SWAPO), socialist Ovambo-oriented; Democratic Turnhalle Alliance (DTA), moderate, multiracial coalition; United Democratic Front (UDF), disaffected ex-SWAPO members; National Christian Action (ACN), white conservative **Currency:** Namibia dollar **Real GDP per capita (PPP):** ($ US) 4,027 (1994) **Exports:** diamonds, fish and fish products, live animals and meat, uranium, karakul pelts. Principal market: UK 37% (1994) **Population:** 1,575,000 (1996 est) **Language:** English (official), Afrikaans, German, indigenous Languages **Religion:** mainly Christian (Lutheran, Roman Catholic, Dutch Reformed Church, Anglican) **Life expectancy:** 60 (men); 63 (women) (1995–2000)

Nauru

Republic of

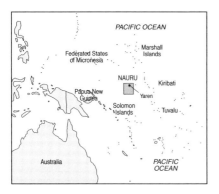

National name: *Naoero* **Area:** 21 sq km/8.1 sq mi
Capital: (seat of government) Yaren District **Physical
features:** tropical coral island in southwest Pacific;
plateau encircled by coral cliffs and sandy beaches
Head of state and government: Bernard Dowiyogo
from 1998 **Political system:** liberal democracy
Political parties: candidates are traditionally elected
as independents, grouped into pro- and
antigovernment factions; Democratic Party of Nauru
(DPN), only formal political party, antigovernment
Currency: Australian dollar **Real GDP per capita
(PPP):** ($ US) 10,000 (1993 est) **Exports:** phosphates.
Principal market: Australia **Population:** 11,000
(1996 est) **Language:** Nauruan (official), English
Religion: Protestant, Roman Catholic **Life
expectancy:** 64 (men); 69 (women) (1996 est)

Nepal

Kingdom of

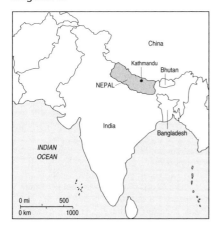

National name: *Nepal Adhirajya* **Area:** 147,181 sq km/
56,826 sq mi **Capital:** Kathmandu **Major towns/cities:**
Pátan, Moráng, Bhádgáon, Biratnagar, Lalitpur,
Bhaktapur, Pokhara **Physical features:** descends from

the Himalayan mountain range in the north through
foothills to the River Ganges plain in the south;
Mount Everest, Mount Kanchenjunga **Head of state:**
King Birendra Bir Bikram Shah Dev from 1972 **Head
of government:** Girija Prasad Koirala from 1998
Political system: constitutional monarchy **Political
parties:** Nepali Congress Party (NCP), left of centre;
United Nepal Communist Party (UNCP; Unified
Marxist–Leninist), left wing; Rashtriya Prajatantra
Party (RPP), monarchist **Currency:** Nepalese rupee
Real GDP per capita (PPP): ($ US) 1,137 (1994)
Exports: woollen carpets, clothing, hides and skins,
food grains, jute, timber, oil seeds, ghee, potatoes,
medicinal herbs, cattle. Principal market: Germany
38.7% (1995) **Population:** 22,021,000 (1996 est)
Language: Nepali (official); 20 dialects spoken
Religion: Hindu 90%; Buddhist, Muslim, Christian
Life expectancy: 57 (men); 57 (women) (1995–2000)

Netherlands, the

Kingdom of (popularly referred to as **Holland**)

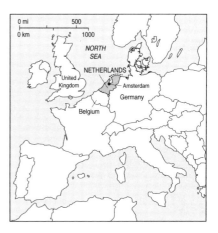

National name: *Koninkrijk der Nederlanden* **Area:**
41,863 sq km/16,163 sq mi **Capital:** Amsterdam **Major
towns/cities:** Rotterdam, The Hague (seat of
government), Utrecht, Eindhoven, Groningen,
Tilburg, Maastricht, Haarlem, Apeldoorn, Nijmegen,
Enschede **Major ports:** Rotterdam **Physical features:**
flat coastal lowland; rivers Rhine, Schelde, Maas;
Frisian Islands **Territories:** Aruba, Netherlands
Antilles (Caribbean) **Head of state:** Queen Beatrix
Wilhelmina Armgard from 1980 **Head of
government:** Wim Kok from 1994 **Political system:**
constitutional monarchy **Political parties:** Christian
Democratic Appeal (CDA), Christian, right of centre;
Labour Party (PvdA), democratic socialist, left of
centre; People's Party for Freedom and Democracy
(VVD), liberal, free enterprise; Democrats 66 (D66),
ecologist, centrist; Political Reformed Party (SGP),
moderate Calvinist; Evangelical Political Federation
(RPF), radical Calvinist; Reformed Political
Association (GPV), fundamentalist Calvinist; Green
Left, ecologist; General League of the Elderly (AOV),

pensioner-oriented **Currency:** guilder **Real GDP per capita (PPP):** ($ US) 20,626 (1996) **Exports:** machinery and transport equipment, foodstuffs, live animals, petroleum and petroleum products, natural gas, chemicals, plants and cut flowers, plant-derived products. Principal market: Germany 28.6% (1995) **Population:** 15,575,000 (1996 est) **Language:** Dutch **Religion:** Roman Catholic, Dutch Reformed Church **Life expectancy:** 75 (men); 81 (women) (1995–2000)

New Zealand

Dominion of

Area: 268,680 sq km/103,737 sq mi **Capital:** Wellington (and port) **Major towns/cities:** Auckland, Hamilton, Palmerston North, Christchurch, Dunedin, Napier-Hastings **Major ports:** Auckland **Physical features:** comprises North Island, South Island, Stewart Island, Chatham Islands, and minor islands; mainly mountainous; Ruapehu in North Island, 2,797 m/9,180 ft, highest of three active volcanoes; geysers and hot springs of Rotorua district; Lake Taupo (616 sq km/238 sq mi), source of Waikato River; Kaingaroa state forest. In South Island are Southern Alps and Canterbury Plains **Territories:** Tokelau (three atolls transferred in 1926 from former Gilbert and Ellice Islands colony); Niue Island (one of the Cook Islands, separately administered from 1903: chief town Alafi); Cook Islands are internally self-governing but share common citizenship with New Zealand; Ross Dependency in Antarctica **Head of state:** Queen Elizabeth II from 1952, represented by governor general Catherine Tizard from 1990 **Head of government:** Jenny Shipley from 1997 **Political system:** constitutional monarchy **Political parties:** Labour Party, moderate, left of centre; New Zealand National Party, free enterprise, centre right; Alliance Party bloc, left of centre, ecologists; New Zealand First Party (NZFP), centrist; United New Zealand Party (UNZ), centrist **Currency:** New Zealand dollar **Real GDP per capita (PPP):** ($ US) 17,264 (1996) **Exports:** meat, dairy products, wool, fish, timber and wood products, fruit and vegetables, aluminium, machinery. Principal market: Australia 20.3% (1995) **Population:** 3,602,000 (1996 est) **Language:** English (official),

Maori **Religion:** Christian **Life expectancy:** 73 (men); 79 (women) (1995–2000)

Nicaragua

Republic of

National name: *República de Nicaragua* **Area:** 127,849 sq km/49,362 sq mi **Capital:** Managua **Major towns/cities:** León, Chinandega, Masaya, Granada **Major ports:** Corinto, Puerto Cabezas, El Bluff **Physical features:** narrow Pacific coastal plain separated from broad Atlantic coastal plain by volcanic mountains and lakes Managua and Nicaragua; one of world's most active earthquake regions **Head of state and government:** Arnoldo Aleman from 1996 **Political system:** emergent democracy **Political parties:** Sandinista National Liberation Front (FSLN), Marxist–Leninist; Opposition Political Alliance (APO, formerly National Opposition Union: UNO), loose US-backed coalition **Currency:** cordoba **Real GDP per capita (PPP):** ($ US) 1,580 (1994) **Exports:** coffee, meat, cotton, sugar, seafood, bananas, chemical products. Principal market: USA 46.7% (1995) **Population:** 4,238,000 (1996 est) **Language:** Spanish (official), Indian, English **Religion:** Roman Catholic 95% **Life expectancy:** 67 (men); 70 (women) (1995–2000)

Niger

Republic of

National name: *République du Niger* **Area:** 1,186,408 sq km/458,072 sq mi **Capital:** Niamey **Major towns/cities:** Zinder, Maradi, Tahoua, Agadez, Birui N'Konui **Physical features:** desert plains between hills in north and savanna in south; River Niger in southwest, Lake Chad in southeast **Head of state:** Ibrahim Barre Mainassara from 1996 **Head of government:** Amadou Boubacar Cisse from 1997 **Political system:** transitional **Political parties:** National Movement for a Development Society (MNSD–Nassara), left of centre; Alliance of the Forces for Change (AFC), left-of-centre coalition; Party for Democracy and Socialism–Tarayya (PNDS–Tarayya), left of centre **Currency:** franc CFA

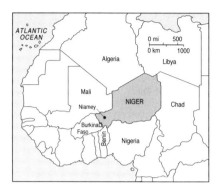

Real GDP per capita (PPP): ($ US) 787 (1994) Exports: uranium ore, live animals, hides and skins, cow-peas, cotton. Principal market: EU 75.2% (1994) Population: 9,465,000 (1996 est) Language: French (official), Hausa, Djerma, and other minority Languages Religion: Sunni Muslim; also Christian, and traditional animist beliefs Life expectancy: 47 (men); 50 (women) (1995–2000)

Nigeria

Federal Republic of

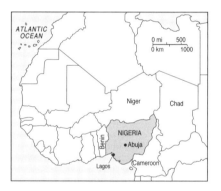

Area: 923,773 sq km/356,668 sq mi Capital: Abuja Major towns/cities: Ibadan, Lagos, Ogbomosho, Kano, Oshogbo, Ilorin, Abeokuta, Zaria, Ouitsha, Iwo, Kaduna Major ports: Lagos, Port Harcourt, Warri, Calabar Physical features: arid savanna in north; tropical rainforest in south, with mangrove swamps along coast; River Niger forms wide delta; mountains in southeast Head of state and government: Abdusalam Abubakar from 1998 Political system: military republic Political parties: Social Democratic Party (SDP), left of centre; National Republican Convention (NRC), right of centre (all parties dissolved on resumption of military rule in 1992) Currency: naira Real GDP per capita (PPP): ($ US) 1,351 (1994) Exports: petroleum, cocoa beans, rubber, palm products, urea and ammonia, fish. Principal market: USA 39.4% (1995) Population: 115,020,000 (1996 est) Language: English (official), Hausa, Ibo, Yoruba Religion: Sunni Muslim 50% (in north), Christian 40% (in south),

local religions 10% Life expectancy: 51 (men); 54 (women) (1995–2000)

Norway

Kingdom of

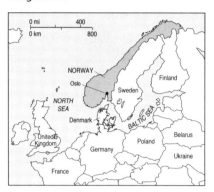

National name: Kongeriket Norge Area: 387,000 sq km/149,420 sq mi (includes Svalbard and Jan Mayen) Capital: Oslo Major towns/cities: Bergen, Trondheim, Stavanger, Kristiansand, Drammen Physical features: mountainous with fertile valleys and deeply indented coast; forests cover 25%; extends north of Arctic Circle Territories: dependencies in the Arctic (Svalbard and Jan Mayen) and in Antarctica (Bouvet and Peter I Island, and Queen Maud Land) Head of state: Harald V from 1991 Head of government: Kjell Magne Bondevik from 1997 Political system: constitutional monarchy Political parties: Norwegian Labour Party (DNA), moderate left of centre; Conservative Party, progressive, right of centre; Christian People's Party (KrF), Christian, centre left; Centre Party (Sp), left of centre, rural-oriented; Progress Party (FrP), right wing, populist Currency: Norwegian krone Real GDP per capita (PPP): ($ US) 24,169 (1996) Exports: petroleum, natural gas, fish products, non-ferrous metals, wood pulp and paper. Principal market: UK 19.8% (1995) Population: 4,348,000 (1996 est) Language: Norwegian (official); there are Saami- (Lapp) and Finnish-speaking minorities Religion: Evangelical Lutheran (endowed by state) Life expectancy: 74 (men); 81 (women) (1995–2000)

Oman

Sultanate of

National name: Saltanat `Uman Area: 272,000 sq km/105,019 sq mi Capital: Muscat Major towns/cities: Salalah, Ibri, Sohar, Al-Buraimi, Nizwa Major ports: Mina Qaboos, Mina Raysut Physical features: mountains to north and south of a high arid plateau; fertile coastal strip; Jebel Akhdar highlands; Kuria Muria Islands Head of state and government: Qaboos bin Said from 1970 Political system: absolute monarchy Political parties: none Currency: Omani rial Real GDP per capita (PPP): ($ US) 10,078 (1994) Exports: petroleum, metals and

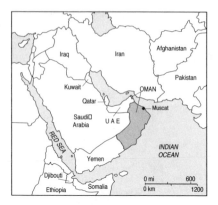

metal goods, textiles, animals and products. Principal market: Japan 32.2% (1995) **Population:** 2,302,000 (1996 est) **Language:** Arabic (official); English, Urdu, other Indian Languages **Religion:** Ibadhi Muslim 75%, Sunni Muslim, Shi'ite Muslim, Hindu **Life expectancy:** 69 (men); 73 (women) (1995–2000)

Pakistan

Islamic Republic of

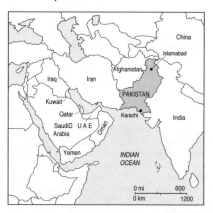

National name: *Islami Jamhuriya e Pakistan* **Area:** 796,100 sq km/307,374 sq mi; one-third of Kashmir under Pakistani control **Capital:** Islamabad **Major towns/cities:** Lahore, Rawalpindi, Faisalabad, Karachi, Hyderabad, Multan, Peshawar, Gujranwala, Sialkot, Sargodha, Quetta, Islamabad **Major ports:** Karachi, Port Qasim **Physical features:** fertile Indus plain in east, Baluchistan plateau in west, mountains in north and northwest; the 'five rivers' (Indus, Jhelum, Chenab, Ravi, and Sutlej) feed the world's largest irrigation system; K2 mountain; Khyber Pass **Head of state:** Rafiq Tarar from 1997 **Head of government:** Nawaz Sharif from 1997 **Political system:** emergent democracy **Political parties:** Islamic Democratic Alliance (IDA), conservative; Pakistan People's Party (PPP), moderate, Islamic, socialist; Pakistan Muslim League (PML), Islamic conservative (contains pro- and anti-government factions); Pakistan Islamic Front (PIF), Islamic

fundamentalist, right wing; Awami National Party (ANP), left wing; National Democratic Alliance (NDA) bloc, left of centre; Mohajir National Movement (MQM), Sind-based *mohajir* settlers (Muslims previously living in India); Movement for Justice, reformative, anti-corruption **Currency:** Pakistan rupee **Real GDP per capita (PPP):** ($ US) 2,154 (1994) **Exports:** cotton, textiles, petroleum and petroleum products, clothing and accessories, leather, rice, food and live animals. Principal market: USA 15% (1995) **Population:** 139,973,000 (1996 est) **Language:** Urdu (official); English, Punjabi, Sindhi, Pashto, Baluchi, other local dialects **Religion:** Sunni Muslim 75%, Shi'ite Muslim 20%; also Hindu, Christian, Parsee, Buddhist **Life expectancy:** 63 (men); 65 (women) (1995–2000)

Palau

Republic of (also known as **Belau**)

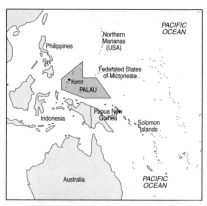

Area: 508 sq km/196 sq mi **Capital:** Koror (on Koror Island) **Major towns/cities:** Melekeiok, Garusuun, Malakal **Physical features:** more than 350 (mostly uninhabited) islands, islets, and atolls in the west Pacific; warm, humid climate, susceptible to typhoons **Head of state and government:** Kuniwo Nakamura from 1992 **Political system:** liberal democracy **Political parties:** there are no formally organized Political parties: **Currency:** US dollar **Real GDP per capita (PPP):** ($ US) 5,000 (1994 est) **Exports:** copra, coconut oil, handicrafts, trochus, tuna **Population:** 17,000 (1996 est) **Language:** Palauan and English **Religion:** Christian, principally Roman Catholic **Life expectancy:** 68 (men); 74 (women) (1994)

Panama

Republic of

National name: *República de Panamá* **Area:** 77,100 sq km/29,768 sq mi **Capital:** Panamá (Panama City) **Major towns/cities:** San Miguelito, Colón, David, La Chorrera, Santiago, Chitré **Major ports:** Colón, Cristóbal, Balboa **Physical features:** coastal plains and mountainous interior; tropical rainforest in east

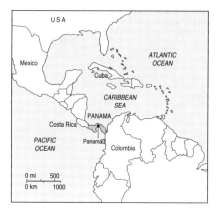

and northwest; Archipelago de las Perlas in Gulf of Panama; Panama Canal **Head of state and government:** Ernesto Pérez Balladares from 1994 **Political system:** emergent democracy **Political parties:** Democratic Revolutionary Party (PRD), right wing; Arnulfista Party (PA), left of centre; Authentic Liberal Party (PLA), left of centre; Nationalist Liberal Republican Movement (MOLIRENA), right of centre; Papa Ego Movement (MPE), moderate, centre left **Currency:** balboa **Real GDP per capita (PPP):** ($ US) 6,104 (1994) **Exports:** bananas, shrimps and lobsters, sugar, clothing, coffee. Principal market: USA 41.9% (1995) **Population:** 2,677,000 (1996 est) **Language:** Spanish (official), English **Religion:** Roman Catholic **Life expectancy:** 72 (men); 76 (women) (1995–2000)

Papua New Guinea

Area: 462,840 sq km/178,702 sq mi **Capital:** Port

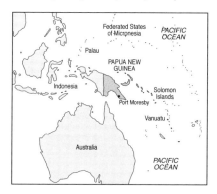

Moresby (on East New Guinea) (also port) **Major towns/cities:** Lae, Madang, Arawa, Wewak, Goroka, Rabaul, Mount Hagen **Major ports:** Rabaul **Physical features:** mountainous; swamps and plains; monsoon climate; tropical islands of New Ireland, New Britain, and Bougainville; Admiralty Islands, D'Entrecasteaux Islands, and Louisiade Archipelago; active volcanoes Vulcan and Tavurvur **Head of state:** Queen Elizabeth II, represented by governor general Silas Atopare from 1997 **Head of government:** Bill Skate from

1997 Political system: liberal democracy **Political parties:** Papua New Guinea Party (Pangu Pati: PP), urban- and coastal-oriented nationalist; People's Democratic Movement (PDM), 1985 breakaway from the PP; National Party (NP), highlands-based, conservative; Melanesian Alliance (MA), Bougainville-based, pro-autonomy, left of centre; People's Progress Party (PPP), conservative; People's Action Party (PAP), right of centre **Currency:** kina **Real GDP per capita (PPP):** ($ US) 2,821 (1994) **Exports:** gold, copper ore and concentrates, crude petroleum, timber, coffee beans, coconut and copra products. Principal market: Australia 32.5% (1995) **Population:** 4,400,000 (1996 est) **Language:** English (official); pidgin English, 715 local Languages **Religion:** Protestant, Roman Catholic, local faiths **Life expectancy:** 57 (men); 59 (women) (1995–2000)

Paraguay

Republic of

National name: *República del Paraguay* **Area:** 406,752 sq km/157,046 sq mi **Capital:** Asunción (and port) **Major towns/cities:** Ciudad del Este, Pedro Juan Caballero, San Lorenzo, Fernando de la Mora, Lambare, Concepción, Villartica, Encaración **Major ports:** Concepción **Physical features:** low marshy plain and marshlands; divided by Paraguay River; Paraná River forms southeast boundary **Head of state and government:** Raul Cubas from 1998 **Political system:** emergent democracy **Political parties:** National Republican Association (Colorado Party), right of centre; Authentic Radical Liberal Party (PLRA), centrist; National Encounter, right of centre; Radical Liberal Party (PLR), centrist; Liberal Party (PL), centrist **Currency:** guaraní **Real GDP per capita (PPP):** ($ US) 3,531 (1994) **Exports:** soya beans (and other oil seeds), cotton, timber and wood manufactures, hides and skins, meat. Principal market: Brazil 46.5% (1996) **Population:** 4,957,000 (1996 est) **Language:** Spanish 6% (official), Guaraní 90% **Religion:** Roman Catholic (official religion);

Mennonite, Anglican **Life expectancy:** 69 (men); 73 (women) (1995–2000)

Peru

Republic of

National name: *República del Perú* **Area:** 1,285,200 sq km/496,216 sq mi **Capital:** Lima **Major towns/ cities:** Arequipa, Iquitos, Chiclayo, Trujillo, Cuzco, Piura, Chimbote **Major ports:** Callao, Chimbote, Salaverry **Physical features:** Andes mountains running northwest–southeast cover 27% of Peru, separating Amazon river-basin jungle in northeast from coastal plain in west; desert along coast north–south (Atacama Desert); Lake Titicaca **Head of state:** Alberto Fujimori from 1990 **Head of government:** Alberto Pandolfi from 1998 **Political system:** democracy **Political parties:** American Popular Revolutionary Alliance (APRA), moderate, left wing; United Left (IU), left wing; Change 90 (Cambio 90), centrist; New Majority (Nueva Mayoria), centrist; Popular Christian Party (PPC), right of centre; Liberal Party (PL), right wing **Currency:** nuevo sol **Real GDP per capita (PPP):** ($ US) 3,645 (1994) **Exports:** copper, fishmeal, zinc, gold, refined petroleum products. Principal market: USA 20.9% (1995) **Population:** 23,944,000 (1996 est) **Language:** Spanish, Quechua (both official), Aymara **Religion:** Roman Catholic (state religion) **Life expectancy:** 66 (men); 69 (women) (1995–2000)

Philippines

Republic of the

National name: *Republika ng Pilipinas* **Area:** 300,000 sq km/115,830 sq mi **Capital:** Manila (on Luzon) (and chief port) **Major towns/cities:** Quezon City (on Luzon), Davao, Caloocan, Cebu, Zamboanga **Major ports:** Cebu, Davao (on Mindanao), Iloilo, Zamboanga (on Mindanao) **Physical features:** comprises over 7,000 islands; volcanic mountain

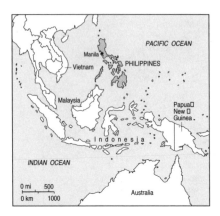

ranges traverse main chain north–south; 50% still forested. The largest islands are Luzon 108,172 sq km/41,754 sq mi and Mindanao 94,227 sq km/36,372 sq mi; others include Samar, Negros, Palawan, Panay, Mindoro, Leyte, Cebu, and the Sulu group; Pinatubo volcano (1,759 m/5,770 ft); Mindanao has active volcano Apo (2,954 m/9,690 ft) and mountainous rainforest **Head of state and government:** Joseph Ejercito Estrada from 1998 **Political system:** emergent democracy **Political parties:** Laban ng Demokratikong Pilipino (Democratic Filipino Struggle Party; LDP–DFSP), centrist, liberal-democrat coalition; Lakas ng Edsa (National Union of Christian Democrats; LNE–NUCD), centrist; Liberal Party, centrist; Nationalist Party (Nacionalista), right wing; New Society Movement (NSM; Kilusan Bagong Lipunan), conservative, pro-Marcos; National Democratic Front, left-wing umbrella grouping, including the Communist Party of the Philippines (CPP); Mindanao Alliance, island-based decentralist body **Currency:** peso **Real GDP per capita (PPP):** ($ US) 2,681 (1994) **Exports:** electronic products (notably semiconductors and microcircuits), garments, agricultural products (particularly fruit and seafood), woodcraft and furniture, lumber, chemicals, coconut oil. Principal market: USA 35.3% (1995) **Population:** 69,282,000 (1996 est) **Language:** Tagalog (Filipino, official); English and Spanish; Cebuano, Ilocano, and more than 70 other indigenous Languages **Religion:** mainly Roman Catholic; Protestant, Muslim, local religions **Life expectancy:** 67 (men); 70 (women) (1995–2000)

Poland

Republic of

National name: *Rzeczpospolita Polska* **Area:** 312,683 sq km/120,726 sq mi **Capital:** Warsaw **Major towns/cities:** Łódź, Kraków (Cracow), Wrocław (Breslau), Poznań (Posen), Gdańsk (Danzig), (Stettin), Katowice (Kattowitz), Bydgoszcz (Bromberg), Lublin **Major ports:** Gdańsk (Danzig), Szczecin (Stettin), Gdynia (Gdingen) **Physical features:** part of the great plain of Europe; Vistula, Oder, and Neisse rivers; Sudeten, Tatra, and Carpathian mountains on

Madeira) **Capital:** Lisbon **Major towns/cities:** Porto, Coimbra, Amadora, Setúbal, Guarde, Portalegre **Major ports:** Porto, Setúbal **Physical features:** mountainous in the north (Serra da Estrêla mountains); plains in the south; rivers Minho, Douro, Tagus (Tejo), Guadiana **Head of state:** Jorge Sampaio from 1996 **Head of government:** Antonio Guterres from 1995 **Political system:** democracy **Political parties:** Social Democratic Party (PSD), moderate left of centre; Socialist Party (PS), centre left; People's Party (PP), right wing, anti-European integration **Currency:** escudo **Real GDP per capita (PPP):** ($ US) 13,059 (1996) **Exports:** textiles, clothing, footwear, pulp and waste paper, wood and cork manufactures, tinned fish, electrical equipment, wine, refined petroleum. Principal market: Germany 21.6% (1995) **Population:** 9,808,000 (1996 est) **Language:** Portuguese **Religion:** Roman Catholic 97% **Life expectancy:** 72 (men); 79 (women) (1995–2000)

southern frontier **Head of state:** Aleksander Kwaśniewski from 1995 **Head of government:** Jerzy Buzek from 1997 **Political system:** emergent democracy **Political parties:** Democratic Left Alliance (SLD), reform socialist (ex-communist); Polish Peasant Party (PSL), moderate, agrarian; Freedom Union (UW), moderate, centrist; Labour Union (UP), left wing; Non-Party Bloc in Support of Reforms (BBWR), Christian Democrat, right of centre, pro-Wałesa; Confederation for an Independent Poland (KPN), right wing; Solidarity Electoral Action (AWS), Christian, right wing **Currency:** ztoty **Real GDP per capita (PPP):** ($ US) 5,002 (1994) **Exports:** machinery and transport equipment, textiles, chemicals, coal, coke, copper, sulphur, steel, food and agricultural products, clothing and leather products, wood and paper products. Principal market: Germany 38.3% (1995) **Population:** 38,601,000 (1996 est) **Language:** Polish (official), German **Religion:** Roman Catholic 95% **Life expectancy:** 67 (men); 76 (women) (1995–2000)

Portugal

Republic of

National name: *República Portuguesa* **Area:** 92,000 sq km/35,521 sq mi (including the Azores and

Qatar

State of

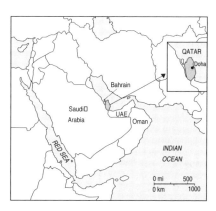

National name: *Dawlat Qatar* **Area:** 11,400 sq km/ 4,401 sq mi **Capital:** Doha (and chief port) **Major towns/cities:** Dukhan, centre of oil production; Halul, terminal for offshore oilfields; Umm Said, Ruwais, Wakra, Al-Khour **Physical features:** mostly flat desert with salt flats in south **Head of state and government:** Sheik Hamad bin Khalifa al-Thani from 1995 **Political system:** absolute monarchy **Political parties:** none **Currency:** Qatari riyal **Real GDP per capita (PPP):** ($ US) 18,403 (1994) **Exports:** petroleum. Principal market: Japan 54.3% (1995) **Population:** 558,000 (1996 est) **Language:** Arabic (official); English **Religion:** Sunni Muslim **Life expectancy:** 70 (men); 75 (women) (1995–2000)

Romania

National name: *România* **Area:** 237,500 sq km/91,698 sq mi **Capital:** Bucharest **Major towns/cities:** Brasov, Timisoara, Cluj-Napoca, Iasl, Constanta, Galati, Craiova, Ploiesti **Major ports:** Galati, Constanta, Brăila **Physical features:** mountains surrounding a

plateau, with river plains in south and east. Carpathian Mountains, Transylvanian Alps; River Danube; Black Sea coast; mineral springs **Head of state:** Emil Constantinescu from 1996 **Head of government:** Radu Vasile from 1998 **Political system:** emergent democracy **Political parties:** Democratic Convention of Romania (DCR), centre-right coalition; Social Democratic Union (SDU), reformist; Social Democracy Party of Romania (PSDR), social democrat; Romanian National Unity Party (RNUP), Romanian nationalist, right wing, anti-Hungarian; Greater Romania Party (Romania Mare), far right, ultranationalist, anti-Semitic; Democratic Party–National Salvation Front (DP–NSF), promarket; National Salvation Front (NSF), centre left; Hungarian Democratic Union of Romania (HDUR), ethnic Hungarian; Christian Democratic–National Peasants' Party (CD–PNC), centre right, promarket; Socialist Labour Party (SLP), ex-communist **Currency:** leu **Real GDP per capita (PPP):** ($ US) 4,037 (1994) **Exports:** base metals and metallic articles, textiles and clothing, machinery and equipment, mineral products, foodstuffs. Principal market: Germany 17.9% (1996) **Population:** 22,655,000 (1996 est) **Language:** Romanian (official), Hungarian, German **Religion:** mainly Romanian Orthodox **Life expectancy:** 67 (men); 73 (women) (1995–2000)

Russian Federation

(formerly to 1991 **Russian Soviet Federal Socialist Republic (RSFSR)**)

National name: *Rossiskaya Federatsiya* **Area:** 17,075,400 sq km/6,592,811 sq mi **Capital:** Moscow **Major towns/cities:** St Petersburg (Leningrad), Nizhniy Novgorod (Gorky), Rostov-na-Donu, Samara (Kuibyshev), Tver (Kalinin), Volgograd, Vyatka (Kirov), Ekaterinburg (Sverdlovsk), Novosibirsk, Chelyabinsk, Kazan, Omsk, Perm, Ufa **Physical features:** fertile Black Earth district; extensive forests; the Ural Mountains with large mineral resources; Lake Baikal, world's deepest lake **Head of state:** Boris Yeltsin from 1991 **Head of government:** Yevgeny Primakov from 1998 **Political system:**

emergent democracy **Political parties:** Russia is Our Home, centrist; Party of Unity and Accord (PRUA), moderate reformist; Communist Party of the Russian Federation (CPRF), left wing, conservative (ex-communist); Agrarian Party, rural-based, centrist; Liberal Democratic Party, far right, ultranationalist; Congress of Russian Communities, populist, nationalist; Russia's Choice, reformist, centre right; Yabloko, gradualist free market; Russian Social Democratic People's Party (Derzhava), communist-nationalist; Patriotic Popular Union of Russia (PPUR), communist-led; Russian People's Republican Party (RPRP) **Currency:** rouble **Real GDP per capita (PPP):** ($ US) 4,828 (1994) **Exports:** mineral fuels, ferrous and non-ferrous metals and derivatives, precious stones, chemical products, machinery and transport equipment, weapons, timber and paper products. Principal market: Ukraine 9% (1996) **Population:** 148,146,000 (1996 est) **Language:** Russian **Religion:** traditionally Russian Orthodox **Life expectancy:** 62 (men); 74 (women) (1995–2000)

Rwanda

Republic of

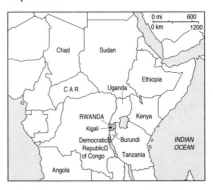

National name: *Republika y'u Rwanda* **Area:** 26,338 sq km/10,169 sq mi **Capital:** Kigali **Major towns/cities:** Butare, Ruhengeri, Gisenyi **Physical**

features: high savanna and hills, with volcanic mountains in northwest; part of lake Kivu; highest peak Mount Karisimbi 4,507 m/14,792 ft; Kagera River (whose headwaters are the source of the Nile) Head of state: Pasteur Bizimungu from 1994 Head of government: Pierre Celestin Rwigema from 1995 Political system: transitional Political parties: National Revolutionary Development Movement (MRND), nationalist-socialist, Hutu-oriented; Social Democratic Party (PSD), left of centre; Christian Democratic Party (PDC), Christian, centrist; Republican Democratic Movement (MDR), Hutu nationalist; Liberal Party (PL), moderate centrist; Rwanda Patriotic Front (FPR), Tutsi-led but claims to be multiethnic Currency: Rwanda franc Real GDP per capita (PPP): ($ US) 352 (1994) Exports: coffee, tea, tin ores and concentrates, pyrethrum, quinquina. Principal market: Brazil 45.5% (1995) Population: 5,397,000 (1996 est) Language: Kinyarwanda, French (official); Kiswahili Religion: Roman Catholic 54%, animist 23%, Protestant 12%, Muslim 9% Life expectancy: 45 (men); 48 (women) (1995–2000)

St Kitts and Nevis

(or St Christopher and Nevis) Federation of

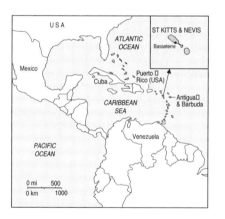

Area: 262 sq km/101 sq mi (St Kitts 168 sq km/ 65 sq mi, Nevis 93 sq km/36 sq mi) Capital: Basseterre (on St Kitts) (and chief port) Major towns/cities: Charlestown (largest on Nevis), Newcastle, Sandy Point Town, Dieppe Bay Town Physical features: both islands are volcanic; fertile plains on coast; black beaches Head of state: Queen Elizabeth II from 1983, represented by governor general Clement Arrindell from 1983 Head of government: Denzil Douglas from 1995 Political system: federal constitutional monarchy Political parties: People's Action Movement (PAM), centre right; Nevis Reformation Party (NRP), Nevis-separatist, centrist; Labour Party (SKLP), moderate left of centre Currency: East Caribbean dollar Real GDP per capita (PPP): ($ US) 9,380 (1995 est) Exports: sugar, manufactures, postage stamps; sugar and sugar products accounted for approximately 40% of export earnings in 1992. Principal market: UK 48.7%

(1992) Population: 41,000 (1996 est) Language: English (official) Religion: Anglican 36%, Methodist 32%, other Protestant 8%, Roman Catholic 10% Life expectancy: 66 (men); 72 (women) (1995 est)

St Lucia

Area: 617 sq km/238 sq mi Capital: Castries Major towns/cities: Soufrière, Vieux-Fort, Laborie Major ports: Vieux-Fort Physical features: mountainous island with fertile valleys; mainly tropical forest; volcanic peaks; Gros and Petit Pitons Head of state: Queen Elizabeth II from 1979, represented by governor general Stanislaus A James from 1992 Head of government: Kenny Anthony from 1997 Political system: constitutional monarchy Political parties: United Workers' Party (UWP), moderate left of centre; St Lucia Labour Party (SLP), moderate left of centre; Progressive Labour Party (PLP), moderate left of centre Currency: East Caribbean dollar Real GDP per capita (PPP): ($ US) 6,182 (1994) Exports: bananas, coconut oil, cocoa beans, copra, beverages, tobacco, miscellaneous articles. Principal market: USA 26.3% (1993) Population: 144,000 (1996 est) Language: English; French patois Religion: Roman Catholic 90% Life expectancy: 68 (men); 75 (women) (1995 est)

St Vincent and the Grenadines

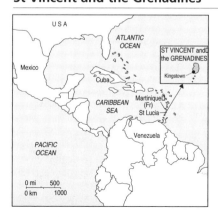

Area: 388 sq km/150 sq mi, including islets of the Northern Grenadines 43 sq km/17 sq mi **Capital:** Kingstown **Major towns/cities:** Georgetown, Châteaubelair, Layon, Baronallie **Physical features:** volcanic mountains, thickly forested; La Soufrière volcano **Head of state:** Queen Elizabeth II from 1979, represented by governor general David Jack from 1989 **Head of government:** James Mitchell from 1984 **Political system:** constitutional monarchy **Political parties:** New Democratic Party (NDP), right of centre; St Vincent Labour Party (SVLP), moderate left of centre **Currency:** East Caribbean dollar **Real GDP per capita (PPP):** ($ US) 5,650 (1994) **Exports:** bananas, eddoes, dasheen, sweet potatoes, flour, ginger, tannias, plantains. Principal market: UK 32% (1994) **Population:** 113,000 (1996 est) **Language:** English; French patois **Religion:** Anglican, Methodist, Roman Catholic **Life expectancy:** 70 (men); 75 (women) (1995 est)

Samoa

Independent State of

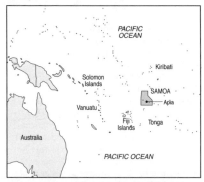

National name: *Malotutu'atasi o Samoa i Sisifo* **Area:** 2,830 sq km/1,092 sq mi **Capital:** Apia (on Upolu island) (and chief port) **Major towns/cities:** Lalomanu, Falevai, Tuasivi, Falealupo **Physical features:** comprises South Pacific islands of Savai'i and Upolu, with two smaller tropical islands and uninhabited islets; mountain ranges on main islands; coral reefs; over half forested **Head of state:** King Malietoa Tanumafili II from 1962 **Head of government:** Tofilau Eti Alesana from 1988 **Political system:** liberal democracy **Political parties:** Human Rights Protection Party (HRPP), led by Tofilau Eti Alesana; Samoa Democratic Party (SDP), led by Le Tagaloa Pita; Samoa National Development Party (SNDP), led by Tupuola Taisi Efi and Va'ai Kolone. All 'parties' are personality-based groupings **Currency:** tala, or Samoa dollar **Real GDP per capita (PPP):** ($ US) 1,900 (1995 est) **Exports:** coconut cream, beer, cigarettes, taro, copra, cocoa, bananas, timber. Principal market: New Zealand 45.5% (1994) **Population:** 166,000 (1996 est) **Language:** English, Samoan (official) **Religion:** Congregationalist; also Roman Catholic, Methodist **Life expectancy:** 68 (men); 71 (women) (1995–2000)

San Marino

Most Serene Republic of

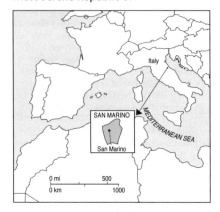

National name: *Serenissima Repubblica di San Marino* **Area:** 61 sq km/24 sq mi **Capital:** San Marino **Major towns/cities:** Serravalle (industrial centre), Faetano, Fiorentino, Monte Giardino **Physical features:** the slope of Mount Titano **Head of state and government:** two captains regent, elected for a six-month period **Political system:** direct democracy **Political parties:** San Marino Christian Democrat Party (PDCS), Christian centrist; Progressive Democratic Party (PDP) (formerly the Communist Party: PCS), moderate left wing; Socialist Party (PS), left of centre **Currency:** Italian lira **Real GDP per capita (PPP):** ($ US) 20,100 (1993 est) **Exports:** wood machinery, chemicals, wine, olive oil, textiles, tiles, ceramics, varnishes, building stone, lime, chestnuts, hides. Principal market: Italy **Population:** 25,000 (1996 est) **Language:** Italian **Religion:** Roman Catholic 95% **Life expectancy:** 75 (men); 81 (women) (1995 est)

São Tomé and Príncipe

Democratic Republic of

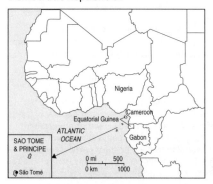

National name: *República Democrática de São Tomé e Príncipe* **Area:** 1,000 sq km/386 sq mi **Capital:** São Tomé **Major towns/cities:** São António, Santana, Porto-Alegre **Physical features:** comprises two main islands and several smaller ones, all volcanic; thickly forested and fertile **Head of state:** Miguel Trovoada from 1991 **Head of government:** Carlos da Graca from 1994 **Political system:** emergent democracy **Political parties:** Movement for the Liberation of São Tomé e Príncipe–Social Democratic Party (MLSTP–PSD), nationalist socialist; Democratic Convergence Party–Reflection Group (PCD–GR), moderate left of centre; Independent Democratic Action (ADI), centrist **Currency:** dobra **Real GDP per capita (PPP):** ($ US) 980 (1994 est) **Exports:** cocoa, copra, coffee, bananas, palm oil. Principal market: the Netherlands 75.7% (1995) **Population:** 135,100 (1996 est) **Language:** Portuguese (official); Fang (a Bantu Language) **Religion:** Roman Catholic 80%, animist **Life expectancy:** 67 (men); 73 (women) (1994 est)

Saudi Arabia

Kingdom of

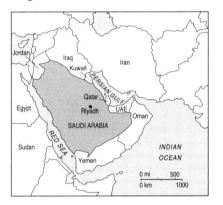

National name: *Mamlaka al-'Arabiya as-Sa'udiya* **Area:** 2,200,518 sq km/849,620 sq mi **Capital:** Riyadh **Major towns/cities:** Jiddah, Mecca, Medina, Taif, Dammam, Hufuf **Major ports:** Jiddah, Dammam, Jubail, Jizan, Yanbu **Physical features:** desert, sloping to the Persian Gulf from a height of 2,750 m/9,000 ft in the west **Head of state and government:** King Fahd Ibn Abdul Aziz from 1996 **Political system:** absolute monarchy **Political parties:** none **Currency:** rial **Real GDP per capita (PPP):** ($ US) 9,338 (1994) **Exports:** crude and refined petroleum, petrochemicals, wheat. Principal market: Japan 17.6% (1995) **Population:** 18,836,000 (1996 est) **Language:** Arabic **Religion:** Sunni Muslim; there is a Shi'ite minority **Life expectancy:** 70 (men); 73 (women) (1995–2000)

Senegal

Republic of

National name: *République du Sénégal* **Area:** 196,200 sq km/75,752 sq mi **Capital:** Dakar (and chief port) **Major towns/cities:** Thiès, Kaolack, Saint-Louis, Ziguinchor, Diourbel **Physical features:** plains rising to hills in southeast; swamp and tropical forest in

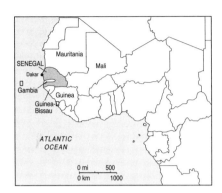

southwest; River Senegal; The Gambia forms an enclave within Senegal **Head of state:** Abdou Diouf from 1981 **Head of government:** Mamadou Lamine Loum from 1998 **Political system:** emergent socialist democracy **Political parties:** Senegalese Socialist Party (PS), democratic socialist; Senegalese Democratic Party (PDS), centrist **Currency:** franc CFA **Real GDP per capita (PPP):** ($ US) 1,596 (1994) **Exports:** fresh and processed fish, refined petroleum products, chemicals, groundnuts and related products, calcium phosphates and related products. Principal market: France 30% (1995) **Population:** 8,532,000 (1996 est) **Language:** French (official); Wolof **Religion:** mainly Sunni Muslim **Life expectancy:** 50 (men); 52 (women) (1995–2000)

Seychelles

Republic of

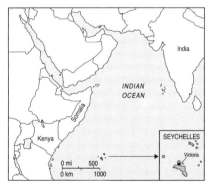

Area: 453 sq km/174 sq mi **Capital:** Victoria (on Mahé island) (and chief port) **Major towns/cities:** Cascade, Port Glaud, Misere **Physical features:** comprises two distinct island groups: one, the Granitic group, concentrated, the other, the Outer or Coralline group, widely scattered; totals over 100 islands and islets **Head of state and government:** France-Albert René from 1977 **Political system:** emergent democracy **Political parties:** Seychelles People's Progressive Front (SPPF), nationalist socialist; Democratic Party (DP), left of centre **Currency:** Seychelles rupee **Real GDP per capita (PPP):** ($ US) 7,891 (1994) **Exports:** fresh and frozen fish, canned tuna, shark fins, cinnamon bark, refined petroleum products. Principal market: UK 16.6% (1995) **Population:** 74,000 (1996 est) **Language:** creole (Asian, African, European mixture) 95%, English, French (all official) **Religion:** Roman Catholic **Life expectancy:** 69 (men); 78 (women) (1994 est)

Sierra Leone

Republic of

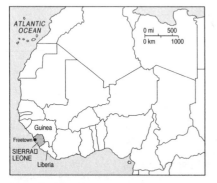

Area: 71,740 sq km/27,698 sq mi **Capital:** Freetown **Major towns/cities:** Koidu, Bo, Kenema, Makeni **Major ports:** Bonthe-Sherbro **Physical features:** mountains in east; hills and forest; coastal mangrove swamps **Head of state and government:** Ahmad Tejan Kabbah from 1998 **Political system:** transitional **Political parties:** All People's Congress (APC), moderate socialist; United Front of Political Movements (UNIFORM), centre left. Party political activity suspended from 1992 **Currency:** leone **Real GDP per capita (PPP):** ($ US) 643 (1994) **Exports:** rutile, diamonds, bauxite, gold, coffee, cocoa beans. Principal market: Belgium/Luxembourg 42% (1995) **Population:** 4,297,000 (1996 est) **Language:** English (official), Krio (a creole Language) **Religion:** animist 52%, Muslim 39%, Protestant 6%, Roman Catholic 2% (1980 est) **Life expectancy:** 40 (men); 43 (women) (1995–2000)

Singapore

Republic of

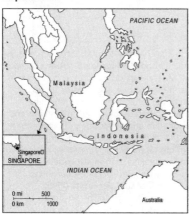

Area: 622 sq km/240 sq mi **Capital:** Singapore City **Major towns/cities:** Jurong, Changi **Physical features:** comprises Singapore Island, low and flat, and 57 small islands; Singapore Island is joined to the mainland by causeway across Strait of Johore **Head of state:** Ong Teng Cheong from 1993 **Head of government:** Goh Chok Tong from 1990 **Political system:** liberal democracy with strict limits on dissent **Political parties:** People's Action Party (PAP), conservative, free market, multi-ethnic; Workers' Party (WP), socialist; Singapore Democratic Party (SDP), liberal pluralist **Currency:** Singapore dollar **Real GDP per capita (PPP):** ($ US) 20,987 (1994) **Exports:** electrical and nonelectrical machinery, transport equipment, petroleum products, chemicals, rubber, foodstuffs, clothing, metal products, iron and steel, orchids and other plants, aquarium fish. Principal market: USA 18.4% (1996) **Population:** 3,384,000 (1996 est) **Language:** Malay (national tongue), Chinese, Tamil, English (all official) **Religion:** Buddhist, Taoist, Muslim, Hindu, Christian **Life expectancy:** 74 (men); 79 (women) (1995–2000)

Slovak Republic

Slovak Republic

National name: *Slovenská Republika* **Area:** 49,035 sq km/18,932 sq mi **Capital:** Bratislava **Major towns/cities:** Košice, Nitra, Prešov, Banská Bystrica, Žilina, Trnava **Physical features:** Western range of Carpathian Mountains, including Tatra and Beskids in north; Danube plain in south; numerous lakes and mineral springs **Head of state:** Ivan Gasparovič from 1998 **Head of government:** Mikulas Dzurinda from 1998 **Political system:** emergent democracy **Political parties:** Movement for a Democratic Slovakia (MDS), centre left, nationalist-populist; Democratic Union of Slovakia (DUS), centrist; Christian Democratic Movement (KSDH), right of centre; Slovak National Party (SNP), nationalist; Party of the Democratic Left (PDL), reform socialist, (ex-communist); Association of Workers of Slovakia, left wing; Hungarian Coalition, ethnic Hungarian **Currency:** Slovak koruna (based on Czechoslovak koruna) **Real GDP per capita**

(PPP): ($ US) 6,389 (1994) **Exports:** basic manufactures, machinery and transport equipment, miscellaneous manufactured articles. Principal market: Czech Republic 35.2% (1995) **Population:** 5,347,000 (1996 est) **Language:** Slovak (official) **Religion:** Roman Catholic (over 50%), Lutheran, Reformist, Orthodox **Life expectancy:** 67 (men); 75 (women) (1995–2000)

Slovenia

Republic of

National name: *Republika Slovenija* **Area:** 20,251 sq km/7,818 sq mi **Capital:** Ljubljana **Major towns/cities:** Maribor, Kranj, Celji, Velenje, Koper (Capodistria) **Major ports:** Koper **Physical features:** mountainous; Sava and Drava rivers **Head of state:** Milan Kučan from 1990 **Head of government:** Janez Drnovšek from 1992 **Political system:** emergent democracy **Political parties:** Slovenian Christian Democrats (SKD), right of centre; Slovenian People's Party (SPP), conservative; Liberal Democratic Party of Slovenia (LDS), centrist; Slovenian Nationalist Party (SNS), right-wing nationalist; Democratic Party of Slovenia (LDP), left of centre; United List of Social Democrats (ZLSD) left of centre, ex-communist **Currency:** tolar **Real GDP per capita (PPP):** ($ US) 10,404 (1994) **Exports:** raw materials, semi-finished goods, machinery, electric motors, transport equipment, foodstuffs, clothing, pharmaceuticals, cosmetics. Principal market: Germany 30.7% (1996) **Population:** 1,924,000 (1996 est) **Language:** Slovene, resembling Serbo-Croat, written in Roman characters **Religion:** Roman Catholic **Life expectancy:** 69 (men); 78 (women) (1995–2000)

Solomon Islands

Area: 27,600 sq km/10,656 sq mi **Capital:** Honiara (on Guadalcanal) (and chief port) **Major towns/cities:** Gizo, Kieta, Auki **Major ports:** Yandina **Physical features:** comprises all but the northernmost islands (which belong to Papua New Guinea) of a Melanesian archipelago stretching nearly 1,500 km/ 900 mi. The largest is Guadalcanal (area 6,500 sq

km/2,510 sq mi); others are Malaita, San Cristobal, New Georgia, Santa Isabel, Choiseul; mainly mountainous and forested **Head of state:** Queen Elizabeth II, represented by governor general Moses Pitakaka from 1994 **Head of government:** Bartholomew Ulufa'alu from 1997 **Political system:** constitutional monarchy **Political parties:** Group for National Unity and Reconciliation (GNUR), centrist coalition; National Coalition Partners (NCP), broad-based coalition; People's Progressive Party (PPP); People's Alliance Party (PAP) **Currency:** Solomon Island dollar **Real GDP per capita (PPP):** ($ US) 2,310 (1994 est) **Exports:** timber, fish products, oil palm products, copra, cocoa, coconut oil. Principal market: Japan 41.1% (1994) **Population:** 391,000 (1996 est) **Language:** English (official); there are some 120 Melanesian dialects spoken by 85% of the population, and Papuan and Polynesian Languages **Religion:** Anglican, Roman Catholic, South Sea Evangelical, other Protestant **Life expectancy:** 70

Somalia

Somali Democratic Republic

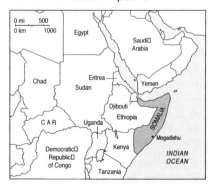

National name: *Jamhuriyadda Dimugradiga ee Soomaliya* **Area:** 637,700 sq km/246,215 sq mi **Capital:** Mogadishu (and port) **Major towns/cities:** Hargeysa, Berbera, Kismayo, Marka **Major ports:** Berbera, Marka, Kismayo **Physical features:** mainly flat, with hills in north **Head of state and government: (interim):** Hussein Aidid from 1996 **Political system:** transitional **Political parties:** parties are mainly clan-based and include the United Somali Congress (USC), Hawiye clan; Somali Patriotic Movement (SPM), Darod clan; Somali Southern Democratic Front (SSDF), Majertein clan; Somali Democratic Alliance (SDA), Gadabursi clan; United Somali Front (USF), Issa clan; Somali National Movement (SNM) based in self-proclaimed Somaliland Republic **Currency:** Somali shilling **Real GDP per capita (PPP):** ($ US) 650 (1995 est) **Exports:** livestock, skins and hides, bananas, fish and fish products, myrrh. Principal market: Saudi Arabia 47.6% (1992) **Population:** 9,822,000 (1996 est) **Language:** Somali, Arabic (both official), Italian, English **Religion:** Sunni Muslim **Life expectancy:** 47 (men); 51 (women) (1995–2000)

South Africa

Republic of

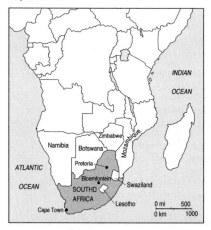

National name: *Republiek van Suid-Afrika* **Area:** 1,222,081 sq km/471,845 sq mi **Capital:** Cape Town (legislative) (and port), Pretoria (administrative), Bloemfontein (judicial) **Major towns/cities:** Johannesburg, Durban, Port Elizabeth, Vereeniging, East London, Pietermaritzburg, Kimberley **Major ports:** Durban, Port Elizabeth, East London **Physical features:** southern end of large plateau, fringed by mountains and lowland coastal margin; Drakensberg Mountains, Table Mountain; Limpopo and Orange rivers **Territories:** Marion Island and Prince Edward Island in the Antarctic **Head of state and government:** Nelson Mandela from 1994 **Political system:** liberal democracy **Political parties:** African National Congress (ANC), left of centre; National Party (NP), right of centre; Inkatha Freedom Party (IFP), centrist, multiracial (formerly Zulu nationalist); Freedom Front (FF), right wing; Democratic Party (DP), moderate, centre left, multiracial; Pan-Africanist Congress (PAC), black, left wing; African Christian Democratic Party (ACDP), Christian, right of centre **Currency:** rand **Real GDP per capita** ($ US) 4,291 (1994) **Exports:** metals and metal products, gold, precious and semiprecious stones, mineral products and chemicals, natural cultured

pearls, machinery and mechanical appliances, wool, maize, fruit, sugar. Principal market: Italy 7.8% (1995) **Population:** 38,000,000 (1996 est) **Language:** English and Afrikaans (both official); main African Languages: Xhosa, Zulu, and Sesotho (all official) **Religion:** Dutch Reformed Church and other Christian denominations, Hindu, Muslim **Life expectancy:** 62 (men); 68 (women) (1995–2000)

Spain

Kingdom of

National name: *Reino de España* **Area:** 504,750 sq km/194,883 sq mi **Capital:** Madrid **Major towns/cities:** Barcelona, Valencia, Zaragoza, Seville, Málaga, Bilbao, Las Palmas de Gran Canarias, Murcia, Córdoba, Palma de Mallorca, Granada **Major ports:** Barcelona, Valencia, Cartagena, Málaga, Cádiz, Vigo, Santander, Bilbao **Physical features:** central plateau with mountain ranges, lowlands in south; rivers Ebro, Douro, Tagus, Guadiana, Guadalquivir; Iberian Plateau (Meseta); Pyrenees, Cantabrian Mountains, Andalusian Mountains, Sierra Nevada **Territories:** Balearic and Canary Islands; in North Africa: Ceuta, Melilla, Alhucemas, Chafarinas Islands, Peñón de Vélez **Head of state:** King Juan Carlos I from 1975 **Head of government:** José Maria Aznar from 1996 **Political system:** constitutional monarchy **Political parties:** Socialist Workers' Party (PSOE), democratic socialist; Popular Party (PP), centre right **Currency:** peseta **Real GDP per capita (PPP):** ($ US) 14,794 (1996) **Exports:** motor vehicles, machinery and electrical equipment, vegetable products, metals and their manufactures, foodstuffs. Principal market: France 20.5% (1995) **Population:** 39,674,000 (1996 est) **Language:** Spanish (Castilian, official), Basque, Catalan, Galician **Religion:** Roman Catholic **Life expectancy:** 75 (men); 81 (women) (1995–2000)

Sri Lanka

Democratic Socialist Republic of (formerly to 1972 **Ceylon)**

National name: *Sri Lanka Prajathanthrika Samajawadi Janarajaya* **Area:** 65,610 sq km/25,332

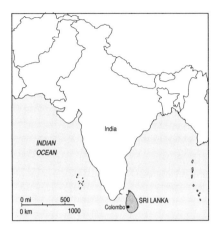

sq mi **Capital:** Colombo (and chief port) **Major towns/cities:** Kandy, Dehiwala-Mount Lavinia, Moratuwa, Jaffna, Kotte, Kandy **Major ports:** Jaffna, Galle, Negombo, Trincomalee **Physical features:** flat in north and around coast; hills and mountains in south and central interior **Head of state:** Chandrika Bandaranaike Kumaratunga from 1994 **Head of government:** Sirimavo Bandaranaike from 1994 **Political system:** liberal democracy **Political parties:** United National Party (UNP), right of centre; Sri Lanka Freedom Party (SLFP), left of centre; Democratic United National Front (DUNF), centre left; Tamil United Liberation Front (TULF), Tamil autonomy (banned from 1983); Eelam People's Revolutionary Liberation Front (EPRLF), Indian-backed Tamil-secessionist 'Tamil Tigers'; People's Liberation Front (JVP), Sinhalese-chauvinist, left wing (banned 1971–77 and 1983–88) **Currency:** Sri Lankan rupee **Real GDP per capita (PPP):** ($ US) 3,277 (1994) **Exports:** clothing and textiles, tea (world's largest exporter and third-largest producer), precious and semi-precious stones, coconuts and coconut products, rubber. Principal market: USA 34% (1996) **Population:** 18,100,000 (1996 est) **Language:** Sinhala, Tamil, English **Religion:** Buddhist 69%, Hindu 15%, Muslim 8%, Christian 7% **Life expectancy:** 71 (men); 75 (women) (1995–2000)

Sudan

Democratic Republic of

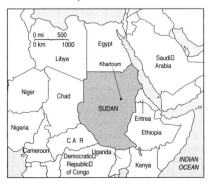

National name: *Jamhuryat es-Sudan* **Area:** 2,505,800 sq km/967,489 sq mi **Capital:** Khartoum **Major towns/cities:** Omdurman, Port Sudan, Juba, Wadi Medani, al-Obeid, Kassala, Atbara, al-Qadarif, Kosti **Major ports:** Port Sudan **Physical features:** fertile Nile valley separates Libyan Desert in west from high rocky Nubian Desert in east **Head of state and government:** Gen Omar Hassan Ahmed al-Bashir from 1989 **Political system:** military republic **Political parties:** officially banned from 1989, but an influential grouping is the fundamentalist National Islamic Front **Currency:** Sudanese dinar **Real GDP per capita (PPP):** ($ US) 1,084 (1994) **Exports:** cotton, sesame seed, gum arabic, sorghum, livestock, hides and skins. Principal market: Saudi Arabia 16.6% (1995) **Population:** 27,291,000 (1996 est) **Language:** Arabic 51% (official), local Languages **Religion:** Sunni Muslim; also animist and Christian **Life expectancy:** 54 (men); 56 (women) (1995–2000)

Suriname

Republic of (formerly **Dutch Guiana)**

National name: *Republiek Suriname* **Area:** 163,820 sq km/63,250 sq mi **Capital:** Paramaribo **Major towns/cities:** Nieuw Nickerie, Moengo, Pontoetoe, Brokopondo, Nieuw Amsterdam **Physical features:** hilly and forested, with flat and narrow coastal plain; Suriname River **Head of state:** Jules Wijdenbosch from 1996 **Head of government:** to be announced **Political system:** emergent democracy **Political parties:** New Front (NF), alliance of four left-of-centre parties: Party for National Unity and Solidarity (KTPI), Suriname National Party (NPS), Progressive Reform Party (VHP), Suriname Labour Party (SPA); National Democratic Party (NDP), left of centre; Democratic Alternative 1991 (DA '91), alliance of three left-of-centre parties **Currency:** Suriname guilder **Real GDP per capita (PPP):** ($ US) 2,950 (1995 est) **Exports:** alumina, aluminium, shrimps, bananas, plantains, rice, wood and wood products. Principal market: Norway 26% (1996) **Population:** 432,900 (1996 est) **Language:** Dutch (official), Sranan (creole), English, Hindi, Javanese, Chinese. Spanish is the main working Language **Religion:** Christian, Hindu, Muslim **Life expectancy:** 69 (men); 74 (women) (1995–2000)

Swaziland

Kingdom of

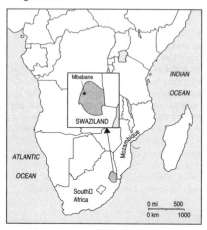

National name: *Umbuso we Swatini* **Area:** 17,400 sq km/6,718 sq mi **Capital:** Mbabane **Major towns/cities:** Manzini, Big Bend, Mhlume, Havelock Mine, Nhlangano **Physical features:** central valley; mountains in west (Highveld); plateau in east (Lowveld and Lubombo plateau) **Head of state:** King Mswati III from 1986 **Head of government:** Barnabas Sibusiso Dlamini from 1997 **Political system:** transitional absolute monarchy **Political parties:** Imbokodvo National Movement (INM), nationalist monarchist; Swaziland United Front (SUF), left of centre; Swaziland Progressive Party (SPP), left of centre; People's United Democratic Movement, left of centre **Currency:** lilangeni **Real GDP per capita (PPP):** ($ US) 2,841 (1994 est) **Exports:** sugar, wood pulp, cotton yarn, canned fruits, asbestos, coal, diamonds, gold. Principal market: South Africa 32% (1994) **Population:** 881,000 (1996 est) **Language:** Swazi, English (both official) **Religion:** Christian, animist **Life expectancy:** 58 (men); 62 (women) (1995–2000)

Sweden

Kingdom of

National name: *Konungariket Sverige* **Area:** 450,000 sq km/173,745 sq mi **Capital:** Stockholm (and chief port) **Major towns/cities:** Göteborg, Malmö, Uppsala, Norrköping, Västerås, Linköping, Orebro, Jönköping, Helsingborg, Borås **Major ports:** Helsingborg, Malmö, Göteborg **Physical features:** mountains in west; plains in south; thickly forested; more than 20,000 islands off the Stockholm coast; lakes, including Vänern, Vättern, Mälaren, and Hjälmaren **Head of state:** King Carl XVI Gustaf from 1973 **Head of government:** Goran Persson from 1996 **Political system:** constitutional monarchy **Political parties:** Christian Democratic Community Party (KdS), Christian, centrist; Left Party (Vp), European, Marxist; Social Democratic Labour Party (SAP), moderate, left of centre; Moderate Party (M), right of centre; Liberal Party (Fp), centre left; Centre Party (C), centrist; Ecology Party (MpG), ecological; New Democracy (NG), right wing, populist **Currency:** Swedish krona **Real GDP per capita (PPP):** ($ US) 19,117 (1996) **Exports:** forestry products (wood, pulp, and paper), machinery, motor vehicles, power-generating non-electrical machinery, chemicals, iron and steel. Principal market: Germany 11.7% (1996) **Population:** 8,819,000 (1996 est) **Language:** Swedish; there are Finnish- and Saami-speaking minorities **Religion:** Evangelical Lutheran (established national church) **Life expectancy:** 76 (men); 82 (women) (1995–2000)

Switzerland

Swiss Confederation

National name: German *Schweiz*. French *Suisse*. Romansch *Svizra* **Area:** 41,300 sq km/15,945 sq mi **Capital:** Bern (Berne) **Major towns/cities:** Zürich, Geneva, Basel, Lausanne, Luzern, St Gallen, Winterthur **Major ports:** river port Basel (on the Rhine) **Physical features:** most mountainous country in Europe (Alps and Jura mountains); highest peak Dufourspitze 4,634 m/15,203 ft in Apennines **Head of state and government:** Arnold Koller from 1997 **Government** federal democracy **Political parties:**

Radical Democratic Party (FDP/PRD), radical, centre left; Social Democratic Party (SP/PS), moderate, left of centre; Christian Democratic People's Party (CVP/PDC), Christian, moderate, centrist; Swiss People's Party (SVP/UDC), centre left; Liberal Party (LPS/PLS), federalist, right of centre; Green Party (GPS/PES), ecological **Currency:** Swiss franc **Real GDP per capita (PPP):** ($ US) 25,141 (1996) **Exports:** machinery and equipment, pharmaceutical and chemical products, foodstuffs, precision instruments, clocks and watches, metal products. Principal market: Germany 23.3% (1996) **Population:** 7,224,000 (1996 est) **Language:** German 64%, French 19%, Italian 8%, Romansch 0.6% (all official) **Religion:** Roman Catholic 50%, Protestant 48% **Life expectancy:** 75 (men); 82 (women) (1995–2000)

Syria

Syrian Arab Republic

National name: *al-Jamhuriya al-Arabya as-Suriya* **Area:** 185,200 sq km/71,505 sq mi **Capital:** Damascus **Major towns/cities:** Aleppo, Homs, Latakia, Hama **Major ports:** Latakia **Physical features:** mountains alternate with fertile plains and desert areas; Euphrates River **Head of state and government:** Hafez al-Assad from 1971 **Political system:** socialist republic **Political parties:** National Progressive Front (NPF), pro-Arab, socialist coalition, including the Communist Party of Syria, the Arab Socialist Party, the Arab Socialist Unionist Party, the Syrian Arab Socialist Union Party, the Ba'ath Arab Socialist Party **Currency:** Syrian pound **Real GDP per capita (PPP):** ($ US) 5,397 (1994) **Exports:** crude petroleum, textiles, vegetables, fruit, raw cotton, natural phosphate. Principal market: Germany 16.7% (1995) **Population:** 14,574,000 (1996 est) **Language:** Arabic 89% (official); Kurdish 6%, Armenian 3% **Religion:** Sunni Muslim 90%; other Islamic sects, Christian **Life expectancy:** 67 (men); 71 (women) (1995–2000)

Taiwan

Republic of China

National name: *Chung Hua Min Kuo* **Area:** 36,179

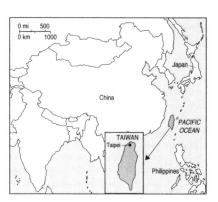

sq km/13,968 sq mi **Capital:** Taipei **Major towns/cities:** Kaohsiung, Taichung, Tainan, Panchiao, Yunlin **Major ports:** Kaohsiung, Keelung **Physical features:** island (formerly Formosa) off People's Republic of China; mountainous, with lowlands in west; Penghu (Pescadores), Jinmen (Quemoy), Mazu (Matsu) islands **Head of state:** Lee Teng-hui from 1988 **Head of government:** Vincent Siew from 1997 **Political system:** emergent democracy **Political parties:** Nationalist Party of China (Kuomintang: KMT; known as Guomindang outside Taiwan), anticommunist, Chinese nationalist; Democratic Progressive Party (DPP), centrist-pluralist, proself-determination grouping; Workers' Party (Kuntang), left of centre **Currency:** New Taiwan dollar **Real GDP per capita (PPP):** ($ US) 11,900 (1994) **Exports:** electronic products, base metals and metal articles, textiles and clothing, machinery, information and communication products, plastic and rubber products, vehicles and transport equipment, footwear, headwear, umbrellas, toys, games, sports equipment. Principal market: USA 23.3% (1996) **Population:** 21,465,900 (1996 est) **Language:** Mandarin Chinese (official); Taiwan, Hakka dialects **Religion:** officially atheist; Taoist, Confucian, Buddhist, Christian **Life expectancy:** 72 (men); 78 (women) (1995)

Tajikistan

Republic of

National name: *Respublika i Tojikiston* **Area:** 143,100 sq km/55,250 sq mi **Capital:** Dushanbe **Major towns/cities:** Khodzhent (formerly Leninabad), Kurgan-Tyube, Kulyab **Physical features:** mountainous, more than half of its territory lying above 3,000 m/10,000 ft; huge mountain glaciers, which are the source of many rapid rivers **Head of state:** Imamali Rakhmanov from 1994 **Head of government:** Yahya Azimov from 1996 **Political system:** authoritarian nationalist **Political parties:** Communist Party of Tajikistan (CPT), pro-Rakhmanov; Democratic Party of Tajikistan (DP), anticommunist (banned from 1993); Party of Popular Unity and Justice, anticommunist **Currencies** Tajik and Russian rouble **Real GDP per capita (PPP):** ($ US) 1,117 (1994) **Exports:** aluminium, cotton lint.

Principal market: the Netherlands 34.1% (1995) **Population:** 5,935,000 (1996 est) **Language:** Tajik (official), similar to Farsi (Persian) **Religion:** Sunni Muslim **Life expectancy:** 69 (men); 74 (women) (1995–2000)

Tanzania

United Republic of

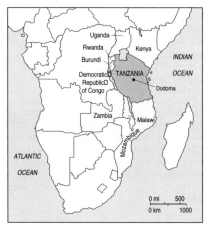

National name: *Jamhuri ya Muungano wa Tanzania* **Area:** 945,000 sq km/364,864 sq mi **Capital:** Dodoma (since 1983) **Major towns/cities:** Zanzibar Town, Mwanza, Tabora, Mbeya, Tanga **Major ports:** (former capital) Dar es Salaam **Physical features:** central plateau; lakes in north and west; coastal plains; lakes Victoria, Tanganyika, and Nyasa; half the country is forested; comprises islands of Zanzibar and Pemba; Mount Kilimanjaro, 5,895 m/19,340 ft, the highest peak in Africa; Olduvai Gorge; Ngorongoro Crater, 14.5 km/9 mi across, 762 m/2,500 ft deep **Head of state:** Benjamin Mkapa from 1995 **Head of government:** Cleoopa Msuya from 1994 **Political system:** emergent democracy **Political parties:** Revolutionary Party of Tanzania (CCM), African, socialist; Civic Party (Chama Cha Wananchi),

left of centre; Tanzania People's Party (TPP), left of centre; Democratic Party (DP), left of centre; Zanzibar United Front (Kamahuru), Zanzibar-based, centrist **Currency:** Tanzanian shilling **Real GDP per capita (PPP):** ($ US) 656 (1994) **Exports:** coffee beans, raw cotton, tobacco, tea, cloves, cashew nuts, minerals, petroleum products. Principal market: Germany 9.2% (1995) **Population:** 30,799,000 (1996 est) **Language:** Kiswahili, English (both official) **Religion:** Muslim, Christian, traditional religions **Life expectancy:** 50 (men); 53 (women) (1995–2000)

Thailand

Kingdom of

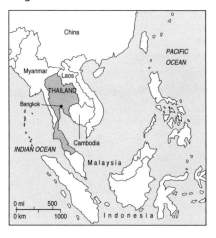

National name: *Prathet Thai* or *Muang Thai* **Area:** 513,115 sq km/198,113 sq mi **Capital:** Bangkok (and chief port) **Major towns/cities:** Chiangmai, Hat Yai, Khon Kaen, Songkhla, Chon Buri, Nakhon Si Thammarat, Lampang, Phitsannlok, Ratchasima **Major ports:** Nakhon Sawan **Physical features:** mountainous, semi-arid plateau in northeast, fertile central region, tropical isthmus in south; rivers Chao Phraya, Mekong, and Salween **Head of state:** King Bhumibol Adulyadej from 1946 **Head of government:** Chavalit Yongchaiyudh from 1996 **Political system:** military-controlled emergent democracy **Political parties:** Democrat Party (DP), centre left; Thai Nation (Chart Thai), right wing, pro-private enterprise; New Aspiration Party (NAP), centrist; Palang Dharma Party (PDP), anti-corruption, Buddhist; Social Action Party (SAP), moderate, conservative; Chart Pattana (National Development), conservative **Currency:** baht **Real GDP per capita (PPP):** ($ US) 7,104 (1994) **Exports:** textiles and clothing, electronic goods, rice, rubber, gemstones, sugar, cassava (tapioca), fish (especially prawns), machinery and manufactures, chemicals. Principal market: USA 17.8% (1995) **Population:** 58,703,000 (1996 est) **Language:** Thai and Chinese (both official); Lao, Chinese, Malay, Khmer **Religion:** Buddhist **Life expectancy:** 65 (men); 72 (women) (1995–2000)

Togo

Republic of (formerly **Togoland**)

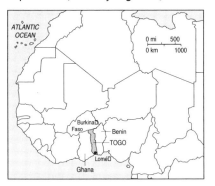

National name: *République Togolaise* **Area:** 56,800 sq km/21,930 sq mi **Capital:** Lomé **Major towns/cities:** Sokodé, Kpalimé, Kara, Atakpamé, Bassar, Tsévié **Physical features:** two savanna plains, divided by range of hills northeast–southwest; coastal lagoons and marsh; Mono Tableland, Oti Plateau, Oti River **Head of state:** Etienne Gnassingbé Eyadéma from 1967 **Head of government:** Kwasi Klutse from 1996 **Political system:** emergent democracy **Political parties:** Rally of the Togolese People (RPT), nationalist, centrist; Action Committee for Renewal (CAR), left of centre; Togolese Union for Democracy (UTD), left of centre **Currency:** franc CFA **Real GDP per capita (PPP):** ($ US) 1,109 (1994) **Exports:** phosphates (mainly calcium phosphates), ginned cotton, green coffee, cocoa beans. Principal market: Canada 9.2% (1995) **Population:** 4,201,000 (1996 est) **Language:** French (official), Ewe, Kabre, Gurma **Religion:** animist, Catholic, Muslim, Protestant **Life expectancy:** 55 (men); 59 (women) (1995–2000)

Tonga

Kingdom of (or **Friendly Islands**)

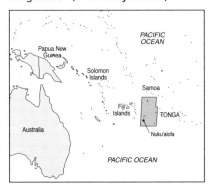

National name: *Pule'anga Fakatu'i 'o Tonga* **Area:** 750 sq km/290 sq mi **Capital:** Nuku'alofa (on Tongatapu Island) **Major towns/cities:** Pangai, Neiafu **Physical features:** three groups of islands in southwest Pacific, mostly coral formations, but actively volcanic in west; of the 170 islands in the Tonga group, 36 are inhabited **Head of state:** King Taufa'ahau Tupou IV from 1965 **Head of government:** Baron Vaea from 1991 **Political system:** constitutional monarchy **Political parties:** legally none, but one prodemocracy grouping, the People's Party **Currency:** Tongan dollar or pa'anga **Real GDP per capita (PPP):** ($ US) 2,160 (1995 est) **Exports:** vanilla beans, pumpkins, coconut oil and other coconut products, watermelons, knitted clothes, cassava, yams, sweet potatoes, footwear. Principal market: Japan 48% (1995) **Population:** 98,000 (1996 est) **Language:** Tongan (official); English **Religion:** Free Wesleyan Church **Life expectancy:** 67 (men); 71 (women) (1996 est)

Trinidad and Tobago

Republic of

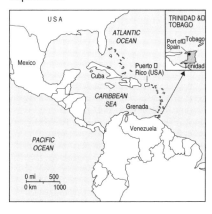

Area: 5,130 sq km/1,980 sq mi including smaller islands (Trinidad 4,828 sq km/1,864 sq mi and Tobago 300 sq km/115 sq mi) **Capital:** Port-of-Spain (and port) **Major towns/cities:** San Fernando, Arima, Point Fortin **Major ports:** Scarborough, Point Lisas **Physical features:** comprises two main islands and some smaller ones in Caribbean Sea; coastal swamps and hills east–west **Head of state:** Noor Hassanali from 1987 **Head of government:** Basdeo Panday from 1995 **Political system:** democracy **Political parties:** National Alliance for Reconstruction (NAR), nationalist, left of centre; People's National Movement (PNM), nationalist, moderate, centrist; United National Congress (UNC), left of centre; Movement for Social Transformation (Motion), left of centre **Currency:** Trinidad and Tobago dollar **Real GDP per capita (PPP):** ($ US) 9,124 (1994) **Exports:** mineral fuels and lubricants, chemicals, basic manufactures, food. Principal market: USA 42.9% (1995) **Population:** 1,297,000 (1996 est) **Language:** English (official); Hindi, French, Spanish **Religion:** Roman Catholic, Anglican, Hindu, Muslim **Life expectancy:** 71 (men); 75 (women) (1995–2000)

Tunisia

Tunisian Republic

National name: *al-Jumhuriya at-Tunisiya* **Area:**
164,150 sq km/63,378 sq mi **Capital:** Tunis (and chief
port) **Major towns/cities:** Sfax, Ariana, Bizerte,
Djerba, Gabès, Sousse, Kairouan, Bardo, La Goulette
Major ports: Sfax, Sousse, Bizerte **Physical features:**
arable and forested land in north graduates towards
desert in south; fertile island of Jerba, linked to
mainland by causeway (identified with island of
lotus-eaters); Shott el Jerid salt lakes **Head of state:**
Zine el-Abidine Ben Ali from 1987 **Head of
government:** Hamed Karoui from 1989 **Political
system:** emergent democracy **Political parties:**
Constitutional Democratic Rally (RCD), nationalist,
moderate, socialist; Popular Unity Movement (MUP),
radical, left of centre; Democratic Socialists
Movement (MDS), left of centre; Renovation
Movement (MR), reformed communists **Currency:**
Tunisian dinar **Real GDP per capita (PPP):**
($ US) 5,319 (1994) **Exports:** textiles and clothing,
crude petroleum, phosphates and fertilizers, olive
oil, fruit, leather and shoes, fishery products,
machinery and electrical appliances. Principal
market: France 28% (1995) **Population:** 9,156,000
(1996 est) **Language:** Arabic (official); French
Religion: Sunni Muslim; Jewish, Christian **Life
expectancy:** 68 (men); 71 (women) (1995–2000)

Turkey

Republic of

National name: *Türkiye Cumhuriyeti* **Area:** 779,500
sq km/300,964 sq mi **Capital:** Ankara **Major
towns/cities:** Istanbul, Izmir, Adana, Bursa, Antakya,
Gaziantep, Konya, Mersin, Kayseri, Edirne, Antalya
Major ports: Istanbul and Izmir **Physical features:**
central plateau surrounded by mountains, partly in
Europe (Thrace) and partly in Asia (Anatolia);
Bosporus and Dardanelles; Mount Ararat (highest
peak Great Ararat, 5,137 m/16,854 ft); Taurus
Mountains in southwest (highest peak Kaldi Dag,
3,734 m/12,255 ft); sources of rivers Euphrates and
Tigris in east **Head of state:** Suleiman Demirel from

1993 **Head of government:** Mesut Yilmaz from 1997
Political system: democracy **Political parties:**
Motherland Party (ANAP), Islamic, nationalist, right
of centre; Republican People's Party (CHP), centre
left; True Path Party (DYP), centre right, pro-
Western; Welfare Party (Refah), Islamic
fundamentalist **Currency:** Turkish lira **Real GDP per
capita (PPP):** ($ US) 6,103 (1996) **Exports:** textiles and
clothing, agricultural products and foodstuffs
(including figs, nuts, and dried fruit), tobacco,
leather, glass, refined petroleum and petroleum
products. Principal market: Germany 23.3% (1995)
Population: 61,797,000 (1996 est) **Language:** Turkish
(official); Kurdish, Arabic **Religion:** Sunni Muslim;
Orthodox, Armenian churches **Life expectancy:** 67
(men); 71 (women) (1995–2000)

Turkmenistan

Republic of

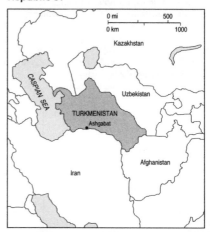

Area: 488,100 sq km/188,455 sq mi **Capital:** Ashgabat
Major towns/cities: Chardzhov, Mary (Merv), Nebit-
Dag, Krasnovodsk **Major ports:** Turkmenbashi
Physical: about 90% of land is desert including the
Kara Kum 'Black Sands' desert (area 310,800 sq km/
120,000 sq mi) **Head of state and government:**

Saparmurad Niyazov from 1991 **Political system:** authoritarian nationalist **Political parties:** Democratic Party of Turkmenistan, ex-communist, pro-Niyazov; Turkmen Popular Front (Agzybirlik), nationalist **Currency:** manat **Real GDP per capita (PPP):** ($ US) 3,469 (1994) **Exports:** natural gas, cotton yarn, electric energy, petroleum and petroleum products. Principal market: Germany 11.4% (1995) **Population:** 4,155,000 (1996 est) **Language:** West Turkic, closely related to Turkish **Religion:** Sunni Muslim **Life expectancy:** 64 (men); 70 (women) (1995–2000)

Tuvalu

South West Pacific State of (formerly **Ellice Islands**)

Area: 25 sq km/9.6 sq mi **Capital:** Fongafale (on Funafuti atoll) **Major towns/cities:** Vaitupu, Niutao, Nanumea **Physical features:** nine low coral atolls forming a chain of 579 km/650 mi in the Southwest Pacific **Head of state:** Queen Elizabeth II from 1978, represented by governor general Tulaga Manuella from 1994 **Head of government:** Bikenibeu Paeniu from 1996 **Political system:** liberal democracy **Political parties:** none; members are elected to parliament as independents **Currency:** Australian dollar **Real GDP per capita (PPP):** ($ US) 800 (1995 est) **Exports:** copra. Principal market: Australia **Population:** 10,000 (1996 est) **Language:** Tuvaluan, English **Religion:** Christian (mainly Protestant) **Life expectancy:** 63 (men); 65 (women) (1995)

Uganda

Republic of

Area: 236,600 sq km/91,351 sq mi **Capital:** Kampala **Major towns/cities:** Jinja, Mbale, Entebbe, Masaka, Bugembe **Physical features:** plateau with mountains in west (Ruwenzori Range, with Mount Margherita, 5,110 m/16,765 ft); forest and grassland; 18% is lakes, rivers, and wetlands (Owen Falls on White Nile where it leaves Lake Victoria; Lake Albert in west); arid in northwest **Head of state:** Yoweri Museveni from 1986 **Head of government:** Kinti Musoke from 1994 **Political system:** emergent democracy **Political**

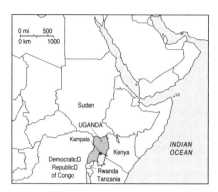

parties: National Resistance Movement (NRM), left of centre; Democratic Party (DP), centre left; Conservative Party (CP), centre right; Uganda People's Congress (UPC), left of centre; Uganda Freedom Movement (UFM), left of centre. From 1986, Political parties: were forced to suspend activities **Currency:** Uganda new shilling **Real GDP per capita (PPP):** ($ US) 1,370 (1994) **Exports:** coffee, cotton, tea, tobacco, oil seeds and oleaginous fruit; hides and skins, textiles. Principal market: Spain 22.8% (1995) **Population:** 20,256,000 (1996 est) **Language:** English (official), Kiswahili, Bantu and Nilotic Languages **Religion:** Christian 50%, animist 40%, Muslim 10% **Life expectancy:** 42 (men); 44 (women) (1995–2000)

Ukraine

Area: 603,700 sq km/233,088 sq mi **Capital:** Kiev **Major towns/cities:** Kharkov, Donetsk, Dnepropetrovsk, Lugansk (Voroshilovgrad), Lviv (Lvov), Mariupol (Zhdanov), Krivoy Rog, Zaporozhye, Odessa **Physical features:** Russian plain; Carpathian and Crimean Mountains; rivers: Dnieper (with the Dnieper dam 1932), Donetz, Bug **Head of state:** Leonid Kuchma from 1994 **Head of government:** Valery Pustovoitenko from 1997 **Political system:** emergent democracy **Political parties:** Ukrainian Communist Party (UCP), left wing, anti-nationalist (banned 1991–93); Peasants' Party of the Ukraine (PPU), conservative agrarian; Ukrainian Socialist Party (SPU), left wing, anti-nationalist; Ukrainian

People's Movement (Rukh), Ukrainian Republican Party (URP), Congress of Ukrainian Nationalists (CUN), and Democratic Party of Ukraine (DPU) – all moderate nationalist; Social Democratic Party of Ukraine (SDPU), federalist **Currency:** hryvna **Real GDP per capita (PPP):** ($ US) 2,718 (1994) **Exports:** grain, coal, oil, various minerals. Principal market: Russia 38.7% (1996) **Population:** 51,608,000 (1996 est) **Language:** Ukrainian (a Slavonic Language) **Religion:** traditionally Ukrainian Orthodox; also Ukrainian Catholic **Life expectancy:** 64 (men); 74 (women) (1995–2000)

United Arab Emirates

(UAE) federation of the emirates of Abu Dhabi, Ajman, Dubai, Fujairah, Ras al Khaimah, Sharjah, Umm al Qaiwain

National name: *Ittihad al-Imarat al-Arabiyah* **Area:** 83,657 sq km/32,299 sq mi **Capital:** Abu Dhabi **Major towns/cities:** Dubai, Sharjah, Ras al-Khaimah, Ajman, Fujairah **Major ports:** Dubai **Physical features:** desert and flat coastal plain; mountains in east **Head of state and government:** Sheik Zayed bin Sultan al-Nahayan of Abu Dhabi from 1971 **Political system:** absolutism **Political parties:** none **Currency:** UAE dirham **Real GDP per capita (PPP):** ($ US) 16,000 (1994) **Exports:** crude petroleum, natural gas, re-exports (mainly machinery and transport equipment). Principal market: Japan 38% (1995) **Population:** 2,260,000 (1996 est) **Language:** Arabic (official), Farsi, Hindi, Urdu, English **Religion:** Muslim 96%; Christian, Hindu **Life expectancy:** 74 (men); 77 (women) (1995–2000)

United Kingdom

of Great Britain and Northern Ireland (UK)

Area: 244,100 sq km/94,247 sq mi **Capital:** London **Major towns/cities:** Birmingham, Glasgow, Leeds, Sheffield, Liverpool, Manchester, Edinburgh, Bradford, Bristol, Coventry, Belfast, Newcastle upon Tyne, Cardiff **Major ports:** London, Grimsby, Southampton, Liverpool **Physical features:** became separated from European continent in about 6000

BC ; rolling landscape, increasingly mountainous towards the north, with Grampian Mountains in Scotland, Pennines in northern England, Cambrian Mountains in Wales; rivers include Thames, Severn, and Spey **Territories:** Anguilla, Bermuda, British Antarctic Territory, British Indian Ocean Territory, British Virgin Islands, Cayman Islands, Falkland Islands, Gibraltar, Montserrat, Pitcairn Islands, St Helena and Dependencies (Ascension, Tristan da Cunha), Turks and Caicos Islands; the Channel Islands and the Isle of Man are not part of the UK but are direct dependencies of the crown **Head of state:** Queen Elizabeth II from 1952 **Head of government:** Tony Blair from 1997 **Political system:** liberal democracy **Political parties:** Conservative and Unionist Party, right of centre; Labour Party, moderate left of centre; Social and Liberal Democrats, centre left; Scottish National Party (SNP), Scottish nationalist; Plaid Cymru (Welsh Nationalist Party), Welsh nationalist; Official Ulster Unionist Party (OUP), Democratic Unionist Party (DUP), Ulster People's Unionist Party (UPUP), all Northern Ireland right of centre, in favour of remaining part of United Kingdom; Social Democratic Labour Party (SDLP), Northern Ireland, moderate left of centre; Green Party, ecological **Currency:** pound sterling (£) **Real GDP per capita (PPP):** ($ US) 18,616 (1996) **Exports:** industrial and electrical machinery, automatic data-processing equipment, motor vehicles, petroleum, chemicals, finished and semi-finished manufactured products, agricultural products and foodstuffs. Principal market: Germany 12% (1996) **Population:** 58,144,000 (1996 est) **Language:** English, Welsh, Gaelic **Religion:** Church of England (established Church); other Protestant denominations, Roman Catholic, Muslim, Jewish, Hindu, Sikh **Life expectancy:** 75 (men); 79 (women) (1995–2000)

United States of America

Area: 9,372,615 sq km/3,618,766 sq mi **Capital:** Washington DC **Major towns/cities:** New York, Los Angeles, Chicago, Philadelphia, Detroit, San Francisco, Washington, Dallas, San Diego, San

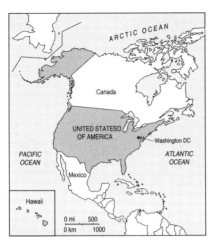

Antonio, Houston, Boston, Baltimore, Phoenix, Indianapolis, Memphis, Honolulu, San José **Physical features:** topography and vegetation from tropical (Hawaii) to arctic (Alaska); mountain ranges parallel with east and west coasts; the Rocky Mountains separate rivers emptying into the Pacific from those flowing into the Gulf of Mexico; Great Lakes in north; rivers include Hudson, Mississippi, Missouri, Colorado, Columbia, Snake, Rio Grande, Ohio **Territories:** the commonwealths of Puerto Rico and Northern Marianas; Guam, the US Virgin Islands, American Samoa, Wake Island, Midway Islands, and Johnston and Sand Islands **Head of state and government:** Bill Clinton from 1993 **Political system:** liberal democracy **Political parties:** Democratic Party, liberal centre; Republican Party, centre right **Currency:** US dollar **Real GDP per capita (PPP):** ($ US) 27,655 (1996) **Exports:** machinery, motor vehicles, agricultural products and foodstuffs, aircraft, weapons, chemicals, electronics. Principal market: Canada 22% (1996) **Population:** 269,444,000 (1996 est) **Language:** English, Spanish **Religion:** Christian 86.5% (Roman Catholic 26%, Baptist 19%, Methodist 8%, Lutheran 5%); Jewish 1.8%; Muslim 0.5%; Buddhist and Hindu less than 0.5% **Life expectancy:** 73 (men); 80 (women) (1995–2000)

Uruguay

Oriental Republic of

National name: *República Oriental del Uruguay* **Area:** 176,200 sq km/68,030 sq mi **Capital:** Montevideo **Major towns/cities:** Salto, Paysandú, Las Piedras **Physical features:** grassy plains (pampas) and low hills; rivers Negro, Uruguay, Río de la Plata **Head of state and government:** Julio Maria Sanguinetti from 1994 **Political system:** democracy **Political parties:** Colorado Party (PC), progressive, centre left; National (Blanco) Party (PN), traditionalist, right of centre; New Space (NE), moderate, left wing; Progressive Encounter (EP), left wing **Currency:** Uruguayan peso **Real GDP per capita (PPP):** ($ US) 6,752 (1994) **Exports:** textiles, meat (chiefly

beef), live animals and by-products (mainly hides and leather products), cereals, footwear. Principal market: Brazil 34.6% (1996) **Population:** 3,204,000 (1996 est) **Language:** Spanish (official) **Religion:** mainly Roman Catholic **Life expectancy:** 70 (men); 76 (women) (1995–2000)

Uzbekistan

Republic of

National name: *Ozbekistan Respublikasy* **Area:** 447,400 sq km/172,741 sq mi **Capital:** Tashkent **Major towns/cities:** Samarkand, Bukhara, Namangan, Andizhan **Physical features:** oases in deserts; rivers: Amu Darya, Syr Darya; Ferghana Valley; rich in mineral deposits **Head of state:** Islam Karimov from 1990 **Head of government:** Otkir Sultonov from 1995 **Political system:** authoritarian nationalist **Political parties:** People's Democratic Party of Uzbekistan (PDP), reform socialist (ex-communist); Fatherland Progress Party (FP; Vatan Taraqioti), pro-private enterprise; Erk (Freedom Democratic Party), mixed economy; Social Democratic Party of Uzbekistan, pro-Islamic; National Revival Democratic Party, centrist, intelligentsia-led **Currency:** som **Real GDP per capita (PPP):** ($ US) 2,438 (1994) **Exports:** cotton fibre, textiles, machinery, food and energy products, gold. Principal market: Russia 22.3% (1996) **Population:** 23,209,000 (1996 est) **Language:** Uzbek, a Turkic Language **Religion:** Sunni Muslim **Life expectancy:** 68 (men); 73 (women) (1995–2000)

Vanuatu

Republic of

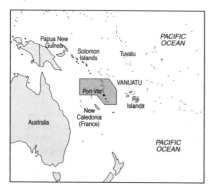

National name: *Ripablik blong Vanuatu* **Area:** 14,800 sq km/5,714 sq mi **Capital:** (and chief port) Port-Vila (on Efate) **Major towns/cities:** Luganville (on Espíritu Santo) **Major ports:** Santo **Physical features:** comprises around 70 inhabited islands, including Espíritu Santo, Malekula, and Efate; densely forested, mountainous; three active volcanoes; cyclones on average twice a year **Head of state:** Jean Marie Leye from 1994 **Head of government:** Donald Kalpokas from 1998 **Political system:** democracy **Political parties:** Union of Moderate Parties (UMP), Francophone centrist; National United Party (NUP), formed by Walter Lini; Vanua'aku Pati (VP), Anglophone centrist; Melanesian Progressive Party (MPP), Melanesian centrist; Fren Melanesian Party **Currency:** vatu **Real GDP per capita (PPP):** ($ US) 2,276 (1994) **Exports:** copra, beef, timber, cocoa, shells. Principal market: Japan 24.1% (1995) **Population:** 174,000 (1996 est) **Language:** Bislama 82%, English, French (all official) **Religion:** Christian 80%, animist **Life expectancy:** 66 (men); 70 (women) (1995–2000)

Vatican City State

National name: *Stato della Città del Vaticano* **Area:** 0.4 sq km/0.2 sq mi **Physical features:** forms an enclave in the heart of Rome, Italy **Head of state:** John Paul II from 1978 **Head of government:** Cardinal Sebastiano Baggio **Political system:** absolute Catholicism **Currency:** Vatican City lira; Italian lira **Real GDP per capita (PPP):** see Italy **Population:** 1,000 (1996 est) **Language:** Latin (official), Italian **Religion:** Roman Catholic **Life expectancy:** see Italy

Venezuela

Republic of

National name: *República de Venezuela* **Area:** 912,100 sq km/352,161 sq mi **Capital:** Caracas **Major towns/cities:** Maracaibo, Maracay, Barquisimeto, Valencia, Ciudad Guayana, San Cristobál **Major ports:** Maracaibo **Physical features:** Andes Mountains and Lake Maracaibo in northwest; central plains (llanos); delta of River Orinoco in east; Guiana Highlands in southeast **Head of state and government:** Rafael Caldera Rodriguez from 1993 **Political system:** federal democracy **Political parties:** Democratic Action Party (AD), moderate left of centre; Christian Social Party (COPEI), Christian, centre right; National Convergence (CN), broad coalition grouping; Movement towards Socialism (MAS), left of centre; Radical Cause (LCR), left wing **Currency:** bolívar **Real GDP per capita (PPP):** ($ US) 8,120 (1994) **Exports:** petroleum and petroleum products, metals (mainly aluminium and iron ore), natural gas, chemicals, basic manufactures, motor vehicles and parts. Principal market: USA 49.2% (1995) **Population:** 22,311,000 (1996 est) **Language:** Spanish (official), Indian Languages 2% **Religion:** Roman Catholic **Life expectancy:** 70 (men); 76 (women) (1995–2000)

Vietnam

Socialist Republic of

National name: *Công Hòa Xã Hôi Chu Nghia Viêt Nam* **Area:** 329,600 sq km/127,258 sq mi **Capital:** Hanoi **Major towns/cities:** Ho Chi Minh City (formerly Saigon), Haiphong, Da Nang, Can Tho, Nha Trang, Nam Dinh **Major ports:** Ho Chi Minh City (formerly Saigon), Da Nang, Haiphong **Physical features:** Red River and Mekong deltas, centre of cultivation and population; tropical rainforest; mountainous in north and northwest **Head of state:** Tran Duc Luong from 1997 **Head of government:** Phan Van Khai from 1997 **Political system:** communism **Political party:** Communist Party **Currency:** dong **Real GDP per capita (PPP):** ($ US) 1,208 (1994) **Exports:** rice (leading exporter), crude petroleum, coal, coffee, marine products, handicrafts, light industrial goods, rubber, nuts, tea, garments, tin. Principal market: Japan 28.5% (1995) **Population:** 75,181,000 (1996 est) **Language:** Vietnamese (official); French, English, Khmer, Chinese, local Languages **Religion:** Taoist, Buddhist, Roman Catholic **Life expectancy:** 65 (men); 70 (women) (1995–2000)

Yemen

Republic of

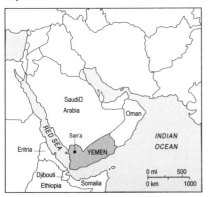

National name: *Jamhuriya al Yamaniya* **Area:** 531,900 sq km/205,366 sq mi **Capital:** San'a **Major towns/cities:** Aden, Ta'izz, Al Mukalla, Hodeida, Ibb, Dhamar **Major ports:** Aden **Physical features:** hot, moist coastal plain, rising to plateau and desert **Head of state:** Ali Abdullah Saleh from 1990 **Head of government:** Abdul Ali al-Rahman al-Iryani from 1998 **Political system:** emergent democracy **Political parties:** General People's Congress (GPC), left of centre; Yemen Socialist Party (YSP), left wing; Yemen Reform Group (al-Islah), Islamic, right of centre; National Opposition Front, left of centre **Currency:** riyal (North); dinar (South), both legal currency throughout the country **Real GDP per capita (PPP):** ($ US) 805 (1994) **Exports:** petroleum and petroleum products, cotton, basic manufactures, clothing, live animals, hides and skins, fish, rice, coffee. Principal market: China 23.4% (1995) **Population:** 15,678,000 (1996 est) **Language:** Arabic **Religion:** Sunni Muslim 63%, Shi'ite Muslim 37% **Life expectancy:** 52 (men); 52 (women) (1995–2000)

Yugoslavia

Federal Republic of

National name: *Federativna Republika Jugoslavija* **Area:** 58,300 sq km/22,509 sq mi **Capital:** Belgrade **Major towns/cities:** Priština, Novi Sad, Niš, Rijeka, Kragujevac, Podgorica (formerly Titograd), Subotica **Physical features:** federation of republics of Serbia and Montenegro and two former autonomous provinces, Kosovo and Vojvodina **Head of state:** Slobodan Milošević from 1997 **Head of government:** Momir Bulatović from 1998 **Political system:** socialist pluralist republic **Political parties:** Socialist Party of Serbia (SPS), Serb nationalist, reform socialist (ex-communist); Montenegrin Social Democratic Party (SDPCG), federalist, reform socialist (ex-communist); Serbian Radical Party (SRS), Serb nationalist, extreme right wing; People's Assembly Party, Christian democrat, centrist; Democratic Party (DS), moderate nationalist; Democratic Party of Serbia (DSS), moderate nationalist; Democratic Community of Vojvodina Hungarians (DZVM), ethnic Hungarian;

Democratic Party of Albanians/Party of Democratic Action (DPA/PDA), ethnic Albanian; New Socialist Party of Montenegro (NSPM), left of centre **Currency:** new Yugoslav dinar **Real GDP per capita (PPP):** ($ US) 4,400 (1995 est) **Exports:** basic manufactures, machinery and transport equipment, clothing, miscellaneous manufactured articles, food and live animals. Principal market: developed countries 40.2% (1996) **Population:** 10,294,000 (1996 est) **Language:** Serbo-Croatian; Albanian (in Kosovo) **Religion:** Serbian and Montenegrin Orthodox; Muslim in southern Serbia **Life expectancy:** 70 (men); 75 (women) (1995–2000)

Zambia

Republic of (formerly **Northern Rhodesia**)

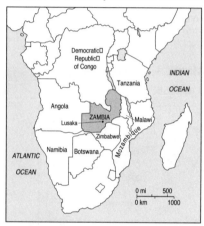

Area: 752,600 sq km/290,578 sq mi **Capital:** Lusaka **Major towns/cities:** Kitwe, Ndola, Kabwe, Mufulira, Chingola, Luanshya, Livingstone **Physical features:** forested plateau cut through by rivers; Zambezi River, Victoria Falls, Kariba Dam **Head of state and government:** Frederick Chiluba from 1991 **Political system:** emergent democracy **Political parties:** United National Independence Party (UNIP), African socialist; Movement for Multiparty Democracy (MMD), moderate, left of centre; Multiracial Party (MRP), moderate, left of centre, multiracial; National Democratic Alliance (NADA), left of centre; Democratic Party (DP), left of centre **Currency:**

Zambian kwacha **Real GDP per capita (PPP):** ($ US) 962 (1994) **Exports:** copper, zinc, lead, cobalt, tobacco. Principal market: Japan 16% (1995) **Population:** 8,275,000 (1996 est) **Language:** English (official); Bantu Languages **Religion:** Christian, animist, Hindu, Muslim **Life expectancy:** 45 (men); 47 (women) (1995–2000)

Zimbabwe

Republic of (formerly **Southern Rhodesia**)

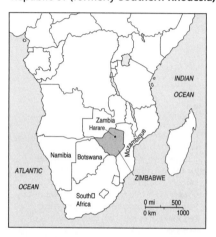

Area: 390,300 sq km/150,694 sq mi **Capital:** Harare **Major towns/cities:** Bulawayo, Gweru, Kwekwe, Mutare, Hwange, Chitungwiza **Physical features:** high plateau with central high veld and mountains in east; rivers Zambezi, Limpopo; Victoria Falls **Head of state and government:** Robert Mugabe from 1987 **Political system:** effectively one-party socialist republic **Political parties:** Zimbabwe African National Union–Patriotic Front (ZANU–PF), African socialist; opposition parties exist but none have mounted serious challenge to ruling party **Currency:** Zimbabwe dollar **Real GDP per capita (PPP):** ($ US) 2,196 (1994) **Exports:** tobacco, metals and metal alloys, textiles and clothing, cotton lint. Principal market: South Africa 13.5% (1995) **Population:** 11,439,000 (1996 est) **Language:** English (official), Shona, Sindebele **Religion:** Christian, Muslim, Hindu, animist **Life expectancy:** 50 (men); 52 (women) (1995–2000)

CALENDAR AND MEASUREMENT

*

The word calendar comes from the Latin *Kalendae*, the first day of each month on which, in ancient Rome, solemn proclamation was made of the appearance of the new moon. All early calendars except the ancient Egyptian were lunar.

The **Western** or **Gregorian calendar** derives from the Julian calendar instituted by Julius Caesar 46 BC. It was adjusted by Pope Gregory XIII 1582, who eliminated the accumulated error caused by a faulty calculation of the length of a year and avoided its recurrence by restricting century leap years to those divisible by 400. Other states only gradually changed from Old Style to New Style; Britain and its colonies adopted the Gregorian calendar 1752, when the error amounted to 11 days, and 3 September 1752 became 14 September(at the same time the beginning of the year was put back from 25 March to 1 January).

The **Jewish calendar** is a complex combination of lunar and solar cycles, varied by considerations of religious observance. A year may have 12 or 13 months, each of which normally alternates between 29 and 30 days; the New Year (Rosh Hashanah) falls between 5 September and 5 October. The calendar dates from the hypothetical creation of the world (taken as 7 October 3761 BC).

The **Chinese calendar** is lunar, with a cycle of 60 years. Both the traditional and, from1911, the Western calendar are in use in China.

The **Muslim calendar**, also lunar, has 12 months of alternately 30 and 29 days, and a year of 354 days. This results in the calendar rotating around the seasons in a 3-year cycle. The era is counted as beginning on the day Muhammad fled from Mecca AD 622.

CALENDAR

Birth Flowers

Month	Flower
January	carnation, snowdrop
February	primrose, violet
March	jonquil, violet
April	daisy, sweet pea
May	hawthorn, lily of the valley
June	honeysuckle, rose
July	larkspur, water lily
August	gladiolus, poppy
September	aster, morning glory
October	calendula, cosmos
November	chrysanthemum
December	holly, narcissus, poinsettia

Birthstones

Month	Stone	Quality
January	garnet	constancy
February	amethyst	sincerity
March	aquamarine, bloodstone	courage
April	diamond	innocence
May	emerald	love
June	alexandrite, pearl	health and purity
July	ruby	contentment
August	peridot, sardonyx	married happiness
September	sapphire	clear thinking
October	opal, tourmaline	hope
November	topaz	fidelity
December	turquoise, zircon	wealth

Chinese Year

The Chinese year is traditionally divided into 12 lunar months, beginning at the second new moon after the winter solstice. As there is a shortfall of approximately 11 days between the lunar and the solar year, an intercalary month is added every $2\frac{1}{2}$ years. The year is also divided into 24 periods of 15–16 days, according to the movement of the Sun.

Both the traditional and, from 1911, the Western calendars are in use in China.

Chinese period	English translation	Chinese period	English translation
Li Chun	Spring Begins	Li Qiu	Autumn Begins
Yu Shui	Rain Water	Chu Shu	Heat Ends
Jing Zhe	Insects Waken	Bai Lu	White Dew
Chun Fen	Vernal Equinox	Qui Fen	Autumn Equinox
Qing Ming	Clear and Bright	Han Lu	Cold Dew
Gu Yu	Grain Rains	Shuang Jiang	Frost Descends
Li Xia	Summer Begins	Li Dong	Winter Begins
Xiao Man	Grain Fills	Xiao Xue	Little Snow
Mang Zhong	Grain in Ear	Da Xue	Heavy Snow
Xia Zhi	Summer Solstice	Dong Zhi	Winter Solstice
Xiao Shu	Slight Heat	Xiao Han	Little Cold
Da Shu	Great Heat	Da Han	Severe Cold

Chinese Zodiac

In the Chinese zodiac, each successive year is named after one of 12 animals. These 12-year cycles are continuously repeated and combined with a sequence of the five elements (water, wood, fire, metal, earth) in a 60-year major cycle.

Dates	Animal	Chinese name	Dates	Animal	Chinese name
1910–20			*1960–70*		
10 February 1910–29 January 1911	Dog	Kou	28 January 1960–14 February 1961	Rat	Niu
30 January 1911–17 February 1912	Pig	Chu	15 February 1961–4 February 1962	Ox	Hu
18 February 1912–5 February 1913	Rat	Shu	5 February 1962–24 January 1963	Tiger	T'u
6 February 1913–15 January 1914	Ox	Niu	25 January 1963–12 February 1964	Hare	Lung
26 January 1914–13 February 1915	Tiger	Hu	13 February 1964–1 February 1965	Dragon	She
14 February 1915–2 February 1916	Hare	T'u	2 February 1965–20 January 1966	Snake	Ma
3 February 1916–22 January 1917	Dragon	Lung	21 January 1966–8 February 1967	Horse	Yang
23 January 1917–10 February 1918	Snake	She	9 February 1967–29 January 1968	Goat	Hou
11 February 1918–31 January 1919	Horse	Ma	30 January 1968–16 February 1969	Monkey	Chi
1 February 1919–19 February 1920	Goat	Yang	17 February 1969–5 February 1970	Cockerel	Kou
1920–30			*1970–80*		
20 February 1920–7 February 1921	Monkey	Hou	6 February 1970–26 January 1971	Dog	Chu
8 February 1921–27 January 1922	Cockerel	Chi	27 January 1971–15 January 1972	Pig	Shu
28 January 1922–15 February 1923	Dog	Kou	16 January 1972–2 February 1973	Rat	Niu
16 February 1923–4 February 1924	Pig	Chu	3 February 1973–22 January 1974	Ox	Hu
5 February 1924–24 January 1925	Rat	Shu	23 January 1974–10 February 1975	Tiger	T'u
25 January 1925–12 February 1926	Ox	Niu	11 February 1975–30 January 1976	Hare	Lung
13 February 1926–1 February 1927	Tiger	Hu	31 January1976–17 February 1977	Dragon	She
2 February 1927–22 January 1928	Hare	T'u	18 February 1977–6 February 1978	Snake	Ma
23 January 1928–9 February 1929	Dragon	Lung	7 February 1978–27 January 1979	Horse	Yang
10 February 1929–29 January 1930	Snake	She	28 January 1979–15 February 1980	Goat	Hou
1930–40			*1980–90*		
30 January 1930–16 February 1931	Horse	Ma	16 February 1980–4 February 1981	Monkey	Chi
17 February 1931–5 February 1932	Goat	Yang	5 February 1981–24 January 1982	Cockerel	Kou
6 February 1932–25 January 1933	Monkey	Hou	25 January 1982–12 February 1983	Dog	Chu
26 January 1933–13 February 1934	Cockerel	Chi	13 February 1983–1 February 1984	Pig	Shu
14 February 1934–3 February 1935	Dog	Kou	2 February 1984–19 February 1985	Rat	Niu
4 February 1935–23 January 1936	Pig	Chu	20 February 1985–8 February 1986	Ox	Hu
24 January 1936–10 February 1937	Rat	Shu	9 February 1986–28 January 1987	Tiger	T'u
11 February 1937–30 January 1938	Ox	Niu	29 January 1987–16 February 1988	Hare	Lung
31 January 1938–18 February 1939	Tiger	Hu	17 February 1988–5 February 1989	Dragon	She
19 February 1939–7 February 1940	Hare	T'u	6 February 1989–26 January 1990	Snake	Ma
1940–50			*1990–2000*		
8 February 1940–26 January 1941	Dragon	Lung	27 January 1990–14 February 1991	Horse	Yang
27 January 1941–14 February 1942	Snake	She	15 February 1991–3 February 1992	Goat	Hou
15 February 1942–4 February 1943	Horse	Ma	4 February 1992–22 January 1993	Monkey	Chi
5 February 1943–24 January 1944	Goat	Yang	23 January 1993–9 February 1994	Cockerel	Kou
25 January 1944–12 February 1945	Monkey	Hou	10 February 1994–30 January 1995	Dog	Chu
13 February 1945–1 February 1946	Cockerel	Chi	31 January 1995–18 February 1996	Pig	Shu
2 February 1946–21 January 1947	Dog	Kou	19 February 1996–7 February 1997	Rat	Niu
22 January 1947–9 February 1948	Pig	Shu	8 February 1997–27 January 1998	Ox	Hu
10 February 1948–28 January 1949	Rat	Niu	28 January 1998–15 February 1999	Tigers	T'u
29 January 1949–16 February 1950	Ox	Hu	16 February 1999–4 February 2000	Hare	Lung
1950–60			*2000–07*		
17 February 1950–5 February 1951	Tiger	T'u	5 February 2000–23 January 2001	Dragon	She
6 February 1951–26 January 1952	Hare	Lung	24 January 2001–11 February 2002	Snake	Ma
27 January 1952–13 February 1953	Dragon	She	12 February 2002–31 January 2003	Horse	Yang
14 February 1953–2 February 1954	Snake	Ma	1 February 2003–21 January 2004	Goat	Hou
3 February 1954–23 January 1955	Horse	Yang	22 January 2004–8 February 2005	Monkey	Chi
24 January 1955–11 February 1956	Goat	Hou	9 February 2005–28 January 2006	Cockerel	Kou
12 February 1956–30 January 1957	Monkey	Chi	29 January 2006–17 February 2007	Dog	Chu
31 January 1957–17 February 1958	Cockerel	Kou	18 February 2007–	Pig	Chu
18 February 1958–7 February 1959	Dog	Chu			
8 February 1959–27 January 1960	Pig	Shu			

Zodiac: Signs

Element	Sign	Symbol	Dates	Element	Sign	Symbol	Dates
Fire	Aries	the ram	21 March–20 April	Water	Scorpio	the scorpion	23 October–22 November
Earth	Taurus	the bull	20 April–21 May	Fire	Sagittarius	the archer	22 November–22 December
Air	Gemini	the twins	21 May–21 June				
Water	Cancer	the crab	21 June–23 July	Earth	Capricorn	the goat	22 December–20 January
Fire	Leo	the lion	23 July–23 August				
Earth	Virgo	the virgin	23 August–23 September	Air	Aquarius	the water bearer	20 January–19 February
Air	Libra	the balance	23 September–23 October	Water	Pisces	the fishes	19 February–21 March

Wedding Anniversaries

In many Western countries, wedding anniversaries have become associated with gifts of different materials. There is variation between countries.

Anniversary	Material	Anniversary	Material	Anniversary	Material
1st	cotton	9th	copper, pottery	25th	silver
2nd	paper	10th	tin	30th	pearl
3rd	leather	11th	steel	35th	coral
4th	fruit, flowers	12th	silk, fine linen	40th	ruby
5th	wood	13th	lace	45th	sapphire
6th	sugar, iron	14th	ivory	50th	gold
7th	wool	15th	crystal	55th	emerald
8th	bronze, electrical appliances	20th	china	60th	diamond
				70th	platinum

Days of the Week

The names of the days are based on the seven heavenly bodies used in traditional astrology (the Sun, the Moon, Mars, Mercury, Jupiter, Venus, and Saturn). These bodies were believed at the time (between 1100–1500) to revolve around the Earth and influence its events. The seven-day week became part of the Roman calendar in AD 321.

English	Latin	Saxon	German	French	Italian	Spanish
Sunday	Dies Solis	Sunnandaeg – Sun's Day	Sonntag	dimanche	domenica	domingo
Monday	Dies Lunae	Mōnandaeg – Moon's Day	Montag	lundi	lunedì	lunes
Tuesday	Dies Martis	Tīwesdaeg – Tiw's Day[1]	Dienstag	mardi	martedì	martes
Wednesday	Dies Mercurii	Wōdnesdaeg – Woden's[2] Day	Mittwoch	mercredi	mercoledì	miércoles
Thursday	Dies Jovis	Thunresdaeg – Thor's Day[3]	Donnerstag	jeudi	giovedì	jueves
Friday	Dies Veneris	Frigedaeg – Frigg's Day[4]	Freitag	vendredi	venerdì	viernes
Saturday	Dies Saturni	Saetern-daeg – Saturn's Day	Samstag	samedi	sabato	sábado

[1] Tiw: Anglo-Saxon name for Nordic Tyr, son of Odin and god of war, closest to Mars (Greek Ares), son of Roman god Jupiter (Greek Zeus).

[2] Woden: Anglo-Saxon name for Odin, Nordic dispenser of victory, closest to Mercury (Greek Hermes), Roman messenger of victory.

[3] Thor: Nordic god of thunder, eldest son of Odin, closest to Roman Jupiter (Greek Zeus).

[4] Frigg (or Freyja): wife of Odin, the Nordic goddess of love, equivalent to Venus (Greek Aphrodite).

Month Equivalents for Gregorian, Jewish, Islamic, and Hindu Calendars

Gregorian equivalents to other calendars are given in parentheses; the figures refer to the number of solar days in each month. (– = not applicable.)

Gregorian (Basis: sun)	Jewish (Basis: combination of solar and lunar cycles)	Islamic[1] (Basis: visibility of the new moon)	Hindu (Basis: moon)
January (31)	Tishri (September–October) (30)	Muharram (30)	Caitra (March–April) (29 or 30)
February (28 or 29)	Heshvan (October–November) (29 or 30)	Safar (29)	Vaisakha (April–May) (29 or 30)
March (31)	Kislev (November–December) (29 or 30)	Rabi I (30)	Jaistha (May–June) (29 or 30)
April (30)	Tebet (December–January) (29)	Rabi II (29)	Asadha (June–July) (29 or 30)
May (31)	Shebat (January–February) (30)	Jumada I (30)	Dvitiya Asadha (certain leap years)
June (30)	Adar (February–March) (29 or 30)	Jumada II (29)	Sravana (July–August) (29 or 30)
July (31)	Adar Sheni (leap years only)	Rajab (30)	Dvitiya Sravana (certain leap years)
August (31)	Nisan (March–April) (29)	Shaban (29)	Bhadrapada (August–September) (29 or 30)
September (30)	Iyar (April–May) (30)	Ramadan (30)	Aswin (September–October) (29 or 30)
October (31)	Sivan (May–June) (30)	Shawwal (29)	Kartik (October–November) (29 or 30)
November (30)	Tammuz (June–July) (29)	Dhu al-Qadah (30)	Agra Hayana (November–December) (29 or 30)
December (31)	Av (July–August) (30)	Dhu al-Hijjah (29 or 30)	Paus (December–January) (29 or 30)
–	Elul (August–September) (29)	–	Magh (January–February) (29 or 30)
–	–	–	Phalgun (February–March) (29 or 30)

[1] These are the months of the Islamic calendar. Their equivalents with the Gregorian calendar vary each year.

Months of the Year

Month	Derivation of name	No. of days	Month	Derivation of name	No. of days
January	Janus, Roman god of doorways and beginnings	31	September	Latin *septem*, 'seven'; September was the seventh month of the earliest Roman calendar	30
February	Februa, Roman festival of purification	28 (29 in a leap year)	October	Latin *octo*, 'eight'; October was the eighth month of the earliest Roman calendar	31
March	Mars, Roman god of war	31			
April	Latin *aperire*, 'to open'	30	November	Latin *novem*, 'nine'; November was the ninth month of the earliest Roman calendar	30
May	Maia, Roman goddess of spring	31			
June	Juno, Roman goddess of marriage	30	December	Latin *decem*, 'ten'; December was the tenth month of the earliest Roman calendar	31
July	Julius Caesar, Roman general and dictator	31			
August	Augustus, Roman emperor	31			

Year Equivalents for Gregorian, Jewish, Islamic, and Hindu Calendars

Gregorian equivalents are given and are AD (Anno Domini).

Jewish (AM)[1]	Gregorian	Islamic (AH)[2]	Gregorian	Hindu (SE)[3]	Gregorian
5753	28 September 1992– 15 September 1993	1413	2 July 1992– 20 June 1993	1914	21 March 1992– 21 March 1993
5754	16 September 1993– 5 September 1994	1414	21 June 1993– 9 June 1994	1915	22 March 1993– 21 March 1994
5755	6 September 1994– 24 September 1995	1415	10 June 1994– 30 May 1995	1916	22 March 1994– 21 March 1995
5756	25 September 1995– 13 September 1996	1416	31 May 1995– 18 May 1996	1917	22 March 1995– 20 March 1996
5757	14 September 1996– 1 October 1997	1417	19 May 1996– 8 May 1997	1918	21 March 1996– 21 March 1997
5758	2 October 1997– 20 September 1998	1418	8 May 1997– 27 April 1998	1919	22 March 1997– 21 March 1998
5759	21 September 1998– 10 September 1999	1419	27 April 1998– 16 April 1999	1920	22 March 1998– 21 March 1999
5760	11 September 1999– 29 September 2000	1420	17 April 1999– 5 April 2000	1921	22 March 1999– 21 March 2000
5761	30 September 2000– 17 September 2001	1421	6 April 2000– 25 March 2001	1922	22 March 2000– 21 March 2001
5762	18 September 2001– 6 September 2002	1422	26 March 2001– 14 March 2002	1923	22 March 2001– 21 March 2002

[1] Calculated from 3761 BC, said to be the year after the creation of the world. AM = Anno Mundi. Some say that the Jewish calendar as used today was formulated in AD 358 by Rabbi Hillel II; others that this formulation occurred later. A Jewish year may have 12 or 13 months, each of which normally alternates between 29 and 30 days, and may be one of the following six types: Minimal Common 353 days; Regular Common 354 days; Full Common 355 days; Minimal Leap 383 days; Regular Leap 384 days; Full Leap 385 days.

[2] Calculated from AD 622, the year in which the prophet Mohammed went from Mecca to Medina. AH = Anno Hegirae. The years are purely lunar, and consist of 12 months with alternately 29 or 30 days, plus one extra day at the end of the 12th month in each leap year, of which there are 11 in each cycle of 30 years. The Islamic calendar being lunar, each month begins on the day immediately following the first observation of the new moon in the night sky. Owing to the Earth's axial rotation, the time of this observation varies from place to place. New Year's Day, and the first days of all the months, are therefore also subject to variation.

[3] Calculated from AD 78, the beginning of the Saka Era (SE), used alongside Gregorian dates in Government of India publications since 22 March 1957. Other important Hindu eras include: Vikrama Era (58 BC); Kalacuri Era (AD 248); Gupta Era (AD 320); and Harsa Era (AD 606).

MISCELLANEOUS MEASUREMENTS

Area: Common Areas

figure	rule for calculating area
rectangle	length × breadth
triangle	half base length × vertical height
parallelogram	base length × vertical height
trapezium	average length of parallel sides × perpendicular distance between them
circle	πr^2, where r is the radius
sector	$\frac{\pi r^2}{360}$ where x is the angle of the sector

Book Publishing: Metric Paper Sizes

Name	Trimmed page	Untrimmed page	Quad sheet	Pages to view	Pages from sheet
metric crown 8vo	186 × 123 mm	192 × 126 mm	768 × 1,008 mm	32	64
metric crown 4to	246 × 189 mm	252 × 192 mm	768 × 1,008 mm	16	32
metric large crown 8vo	198 × 129 mm	204 × 132 mm	816 × 1,056 mm	32	64
metric large crown 4to	258 × 201 mm	264 × 204 mm	816 × 1,056 mm	16	32
metric demy 8vo	216 × 138 mm	222 × 141 mm	888 × 1,128 mm	32	64
metric demy 4to	276 × 219 mm	282 × 222 mm	888 × 1,128 mm	16	32
metric royal 8vo	234 × 156 mm	240 × 159 mm	960 × 1,272 mm	32	64
metric royal 4to	312 × 237 mm	318 × 240 mm	960 × 1,272 mm	16	32

Imperial and Metric Conversion Factors

To convert from imperial to metric	Multiply by	To convert from metric to imperial	Multiply by
Length			
inches	25.4	millimetres	0.0393701
feet	0.3048	metres	3.28084
yards	0.9144	metres	1.09361
furlongs	0.201168	kilometres	4.97097
miles	1.609344	kilometres	0.621371
Area			
square inches	6.4516	square centimetres	0.1550
square feet	0.092903	square metres	10.7639
square yards	0.836127	square metres	1.19599
square miles	2.589988	square kilometres	0.386102
acres	4046.856422	square metres	0.000247
acres	0.404866	hectares	2.469955
Volume/capacity			
cubic inches	16.387064	cubic centimetres	0.061024
cubic feet	0.028317	cubic metres	35.3147
cubic yards	0.764555	cubic metres	1.30795

Imperial and Metric Conversion Factors (continued)

To convert from imperial to metric	Multiply by	To convert from metric to imperial	Multiply by
cubic miles	4.1682	cubic kilometres	0.239912
fluid ounces (imperial)	28.413063	millilitres	0.035195
fluid ounces (US)	29.5735	millilitres	0.033814
pints (imperial)	0.568261	litres	1.759754
pints (US)	0.473176	litres	2.113377
quarts (imperial)	1.136523	litres	0.879877
quarts (US)	0.946353	litres	1.056688
gallons (imperial)	4.54609	litres	0.219969
gallons (US)	3.785412	litres	0.364172
Mass/weight			
ounces	28.349523	grams	0.035274
pounds	0.453592	kilograms	2.20462
stone (14 lb)	6.350293	kilograms	0.157473
tons (imperial)	1016.046909	kilograms	0.000984
tons (US)	907.18474	kilograms	0.001102
tons (imperial)	1.016047	metric tonnes	0.984207
tons (US)	0.907185	metric tonnes	1.10231
Speed			
miles per hour	1.609344	kilometres per hour	0.621371
feet per second	0.3048	metres per second	3.28084
Force			
pound-force	4.44822	newton	0.224809
kilogram-force	9.80665	newton	0.101972
Pressure			
pound-force per square inch	6.89476	kilopascals	0.145038
tons-force per square inch (imperial)	15.4443	megapascals	0.064779
atmospheres	10.1325	newtons per square centimetre	0.098692
atmospheres	14.695942	pound-force per square inch	0.068948
Energy			
calorie	4.1868	joule	0.238846
watt hour	3,600	joule	0.000278
Power			
horsepower	0.7457	kilowatts	1.34102
Fuel consumption			
miles per gallon (imperial)	0.3540	kilometres per litre	2.824859
miles per gallon (US)	0.4251	kilometres per litre	2.3521
gallons per mile (imperial)	2.824859	litres per kilometre	0.3540
gallons per mile (US)	2.3521	litres per kilometre	0.4251

Playing Cards and Dice Chances

Poker

Hand	Number possible	Odds against
royal flush	4	649,739 to 1
straight flush	36	72,192 to 1
four of a kind	624	4,164 to 1
full house	3,744	693 to 1
flush	5,108	508 to 1
straight	10,200	254 to 1
three of a kind	54,912	46 to 1
two pairs	123,552	20 to 1
one pair	1,098,240	1.37 to 1
high card	1,302,540	1 to 1
total number of hands possible	2,598,960	

Bridge

Suit distribution in a hand	Odds against
4–4–3–2	4 to 1
5–4–2–2	8 to 1

Suit distribution in a hand	Odds against
6–4–2–1	20 to 1
7–4–1–1	254 to 1
8–4–1–0	2,211 to 1
13–0–0–0	158,753,389,899 to 1

Dice
(Chances with two dice and a single throw)

Total count	Odds against
2	35 to 1
3	17 to 1
4	11 to 1
5	8 to 1
6	31 to 5
7	5 to 1
8	31 to 5
9	8 to 1
10	11 to 1
11	17 to 1
12	35 to 1

Roman Numerals

Roman	Arabic	Roman	Arabic	Roman	Arabic	Roman	Arabic
I	1	IX	9	LX	60	V̄	5,000
II	2	X	10	XC	90	X̄	10,000
III	3	XI	11	C	100	L̄	50,000
IV	4	XIX	19	CC	200	C̄	100,000
V	5	XX	20	CD	400	D̄	500,000
VI	6	XXX	30	D	500	M̄	1,000,000
VII	7	XL	40	CM	900		
VIII	8	L	50	M	1,000		

SI Prefixes

Multiple	Prefix	Symbol	Example
1,000,000,000,000,000,000 (10^{18})	exa-	E	Eg (exagram)
1,000,000,000,000,000 (10^{15})	peta-	P	PJ (petajoule)
1,000,000,000,000 (10^{12})	tera-	T	TV (teravolt)
1,000,000,000 (10^9)	giga-	G	GW (gigawatt)
1,000,000 (10^6)	mega-	M	MHz (megahertz)
1,000 (10^3)	kilo-	k	kg (kilogram)
100 (10^2)	hecto-	h	hm (hectometre)
10 (10^1)	deca-	da	daN (decanewton)
1/10 (10^{-1})	deci-	d	dC (decicoulomb)
1/100 (10^{-2})	centi-	c	cm (centimetre)
1/1,000 (10^{-3})	milli-	m	mm (millimetre)
1/1,000,000 (10^{-6})	micro-	µ	µF (microfarad)
1/1,000,000,000 (10^{-9})	nano-	n	nm (nanometre)
1/1,000,000,000,000 (10^{-12})	pico-	p	ps (picosecond)
1/1,000,000,000,000,000 (10^{-15})	femto-	f	frad (femtoradian)
1/1,000,000,000,000,000,000 (10^{-18})	atto-	a	aT (attotesla)

SI Units

(French *Système International d'Unités)* A standard system of scientific units used by scientists worldwide. Originally proposed in 1960, it replaces the mks (metre, kilogram, second), cgs (centimetre, gram, second), and fps (foot, pound, second) systems. It is based on seven basic units: the metre (m) for length, kilogram (kg) for mass, second (s) for time, ampere (A) for electrical current, kelvin (K) for temperature, mole (mol) for amount of substance, and candela (cd) for luminosity.

Quantity	SI unit	Symbol	Quantity	SI unit	Symbol
absorbed radiation dose	gray	Gy	mass	kilogram[1]	kg
amount of substance	mole[1]	mol	plane angle	radian	rad
electric capacitance	farad	F	potential difference	volt	V
electric charge	coulomb	C	power	watt	W
electric conductance	siemens	S	pressure	pascal	Pa
electric current	ampere[1]	A	radiation dose equivalent	sievert	Sv
energy or work	joule	J	radiation exposure	roentgen	R
force	newton	N	radioactivity	becquerel	Bq
frequency	hertz	Hz	resistance	ohm	Ω
illuminance	lux	lx	solid angle	steradian	sr
inductance	henry	H	sound intensity	decibel	dB
length	metre[1]	m	temperature	°Celsius	°C
luminous flux	lumen	lm	temperature, thermodynamic	kelvin[1]	K
luminous intensity	candela[1]	cd	time	second[1]	s
magnetic flux	weber	Wb			
magnetic flux density	tesla	T			

[1] SI base unit.

Squares, Cubes, and Roots

Number	Square	Cube	Square root	Cube root	Number	Square	Cube	Square root	Cube root
1	1	1	1.000	1.000	13	169	2197	3.606	2.351
2	4	8	1.414	1.260	14	196	2744	3.742	2.410
3	9	27	1.732	1.442	15	225	3375	3.873	2.466
4	16	64	2.000	1.587	16	256	4096	4.000	2.520
5	25	125	2.236	1.710	17	289	4913	4.123	2.571
6	36	216	2.449	1.817	18	324	5832	4.243	2.621
7	49	343	2.646	1.913	19	361	6859	4.359	2.668
8	64	512	2.828	2.000	20	400	8000	4.472	2.714
9	81	729	3.000	2.080	25	625	15625	5.000	2.924
10	100	1000	3.162	2.154	30	900	27000	5.477	3.107
11	121	1331	3.317	2.224	40	1600	64000	6.325	3.420
12	144	1728	3.464	2.289	50	2500	125000	7.071	3.684

Units: Miscellaneous

Unit	Definition
acoustic ohm	cgs unit of acoustic impedance (the ratio of sound pressure on a surface to sound flux through the surface)
acre	traditional English land measure; 1 acre = 4,480 sq yd (4,047 sq m or 0.4047 ha)
acre-foot	unit sometimes used to measure large volumes of water such as reservoirs; 1 acre-foot = 1,233.5 cu m/ 43,560 cu ft
astronomical unit	unit (symbol AU) equal to the mean distance of the Earth from the Sun: 149,597,870 km/92,955,808 mi
atmosphere	unit of pressure (abbreviation atm); 1 standard atmosphere = 101,325 Pa
barn	unit of area, especially the cross-sectional area of an atomic nucleus; 1 barn = 10^{-28} sq m

Units: Miscellaneous (continued)

Unit	Definition
barrel	unit of liquid capacity; the volume of a barrel depends on the liquid being measured and the country and state laws. In the USA, 1 barrel of oil = 42 gal (159 l/34.97 imperial gal), but for federal taxing of fermented liquor (such as beer), 1 barrel = 31 gal (117.35 l/25.81 imperial gal). Many states fix a 36-gallon barrel for cistern measurement and federal law uses a 40-gallon barrel to measure 'proof spirits'. 1 barrel of beer in the UK = 163.66 l (43.23 US gal/36 imperial gal)
base box	imperial unit of area used in metal plating; 1 base box = 20.232 sq m/31,360 sq in
baud	unit of electrical signalling speed equal to 1 pulse per second
brewster	unit (symbol B) for measuring reaction of optical materials to stress
British thermal unit	imperial unit of heat (symbol Btu); 1 Btu = approximately 1,055 J
bushel	measure of dry and (in the UK) liquid volume. 1 bushel (struck measure) = 8 dry US gallons (64 dry US pt/35.239 l/2,150.42 cu in). 1 heaped US bushel = 1,278 bushels, struck measure (81.78 dry pt/45.027 l/2,747.715 cu in), often referred to a $1\frac{1}{4}$ bushels, struck measure. In the UK, 1 bushel = 8 imperial gallons (64 imperial pt); 1 UK bushel = 1.03 US bushels
cable	unit of length used on ships, taken as $\frac{1}{10}$ of a nautical mile (185.2 m/607.6 ft)
calorie	cgs unit of heat, now replaced by the joule; 1 calorie = 4.1868 J
carat	unit for measuring mass of precious stones; 1 carat = 0.2 g/0.00705 oz
carat	unit of purity in gold; pure gold is 24-carat
carcel	obsolete unit of luminous intensity
cental	name for the short hundredweight; 1 cental = 45.36 kg/100 lb
chaldron	obsolete unit measuring capacity; 1 chaldron = 1.309 cu m/46.237 cu ft
clausius	in engineering, a unit of entropy; defined as the ratio of energy to temperature above absolute zero
cleanliness unit	unit for measuring air pollution; equal to the number of particles greater than 0.5 μm in diameter per cu ft of air
clo	unit of thermal insulation of clothing; standard clothes have insulation of about 1 clo, the warmest have about 4 clo per 2.5 cm/1 in of thickness
clusec	unit for measuring the power of a vacuum pump
condensation number	in physics, the ratio of the number of molecules condensing on a surface to the number of molecules touching that surface
cord	unit for measuring the volume of wood cut for fuel; 1 cord = 3.62 cu m/128 cu ft, or a stack 2.4 m/8 ft long, 1.2 m/4 ft wide and 1.2 m/4 ft high
crith	unit of mass for weighing gases; 1 crith = the mass of 1 litre of hydrogen gas at standard temperature and pressure
cubit	earliest known unit of length; 1 cubit = approximately 45.7 cm/18 in, the length of the human forearm from the tip of the middle finger to the elbow
curie	former unit of radioactivity (symbol Ci); 1 curie = 3.7×10^{10} becquerels
dalton	international atomic mass unit, equivalent to $\frac{1}{12}$ of the mass of a neutral carbon-12 atom
darcy	cgs unit (symbol D) of permeability, used mainly in geology to describe the permeability of rock
darwin	unit of measurement of evolutionary rate of change
decontamination factor	unit measuring the effectiveness of radiological decontamination; the ratio of original contamination to the radiation remaining
demal	unit measuring concentration; 1 demal = 1 gram-equivalent of solute in 1 cu dm of solvent
denier	unit used to measure the fineness of yarns; 9,000 m of 15 denier nylon weighs 15 g/0.5 oz
dioptre	optical unit measuring the power of a lens; the reciprocal of the focal length in metres
dram	unit of apothecaries' measure; 1 dram = 60 grains/3.888 g
dyne	cgs unit of force; 10^5 dynes = 1 N
einstein unit	unit for measuring photoenergy in atomic physics
eotvos unit	unit (symbol E) for measuring small changes in the intensity of the Earth's gravity with horizontal distance
erg	cgs unit of work; equal to the work done by a force of 1 dyne moving through 1 cm
erlang	unit for measuring telephone traffic intensity; for example, 90 minutes of carried traffic measured over 60 minutes = 1.5 erlangs ('carried traffic' refers to the total duration of completed calls made within a specified period)
fathom	unit of depth measurement in mining and seafaring; 1 fathom = 1.83 m/6 ft
finsen unit	unit (symbol FU) for measuring intensity of ultraviolet light

(continued)

Units: Miscellaneous (continued)

Unit	Definition
fluid ounce	measure of capacity; equivalent in the USA to $\frac{1}{16}$ of a pint ($\frac{1}{20}$ of a pint in the UK and Canada)
foot	imperial unit of length (symbol ft), equivalent to 0.3048 m
foot-candle	unit of illuminance, replaced by the lux; 1 foot-candle = 10.76391 lux
foot-pound	imperial unit of energy (symbol ft-lb); 1 ft-lb = 1.356 joule
frigorie	unit (symbol fg) used in refrigeration engineering to measure heat energy, equal to a rate of heat extraction of 1 kilocalorie per hour
furlong	unit of measurement, originating in Anglo-Saxon England, equivalent to 201.168 m/220 yd
galileo	unit (symbol Gal) of acceleration; 1 galileo = 10^{-2} m s^{-2}
gallon	imperial liquid or dry measure subdivided into 4 quarts or 8 pints; 1 US gal = 3.785 l; 1 imperial gal = 4.546 l
gauss	cgs unit (symbol) of magnetic flux density, replaced by the tesla; 1 gauss = 1 × 10^{-4} tesla
gill	imperial unit of volume for liquid measure; equal to $\frac{1}{4}$ of a pint (in the USA, 4 fl oz/0.118 l; in the UK, 5 fl oz/0.142 l)
grain	smallest unit of mass in the three English systems of measurement (avoirdupois, troy, apothecaries' weights) used in the UK and USA; 1 grain = 0.0648 g
hand	unit used in measuring the height of a horse from front hoof to shoulder (withers); 1 hand = 10.2 cm/4 in
hardness number	unit measuring hardness of materials. There are many different hardness scales: Brinell, Rockwell, and Vickers scales measure the degree of indentation or impression of materials; Mohs' scale measures resistance to scratching against a standard set of minerals
hartree	atomic unit of energy, equivalent to atomic unit of charge divided by atomic unit of length; 1 hartree = 4.850 × 10^{-18} J
haze factor	unit of visibility in mist or fog; the ratio of brightness of mist compared with that of the object
Hehner number	unit measuring concentration of fatty acids in oils; a Hehner number of 1 = 1 kg of fatty acid in 100 kg of oil or fat
hide	unit of measurement used in the 12th century to measure land; 1 hide = 60–120 acres/25–50 ha
horsepower	imperial unit (abbreviation hp) of power; 1 horsepower = 746 W
hundredweight	imperial unit (abbreviation cwt) of mass; 1 cwt = 45.36 kg/100 lb in the USA and 50.80 kg/112 lb in the UK
inch	imperial unit (abbreviation in) of linear measure, $\frac{1}{12}$ of a ft; 1 in = 2.54 cm
inferno	unit used in astrophysics for describing the temperature inside a star; 1 inferno = 1 billion K (degrees Kelvin)
iodine number	unit measuring the percentage of iodine absorbed in a substance, expressed as grams of iodine absorbed by 100 grams of material
jansky	unit used in radio astronomy to measure radio emissions or flux densities from space; 1 jansky = 10^{-26} W m^{-2} Hz^{-1}. Flux density is the energy in a beam of radiation which passes through an area normal to the beam in a single unit of time. A jansky is a measurement of the energy received from a cosmic radio source per unit area of detector in a single time unit
kayser	unit used in spectroscopy to measure wave number (number of waves in a unit length); a wavelength of 1 cm has a wave number of 1 kayser
knot	unit used in navigation to measure a ship's speed; 1 knot = 1 nautical mile per hour, or about 1.15 miles per hour
league	obsolete imperial unit of length; 1 league = 3 nautical mi/5.56 km or 3 statute mi/4.83 km
light year	unit used in astronomy to measure distance; the distance travelled by light in one year, approximately 9.46 × 10^{12} km/5.88 × 10^{12} mi
mache	obsolete unit of radioactive concentration; 1 mache = 3.7 × 10^{-7} curies of radioactive material per cu m of a medium
maxwell	cgs unit (symbol Mx) of magnetic flux, the strength of a magnetic field in an area multiplied by the area; 1 maxwell = 10^{-8} weber
megaton	measurement of the explosive power of a nuclear weapon; 1 megaton = 1 million tons of trinitrotoluene (TNT)
mil	(a) one-thousandth of a litre; contraction of the word millilitre; (b) imperial measure of length, equal to one-thousandth of an inch; also known as the thou
mile	imperial unit of linear measure; 1 statute mile = 1.60934 km/5,280 ft; 1 international nautical mile = 1.852 km/6,076 ft
millimetre of mercury	unit of pressure (symbol mmHg) used in medicine for measuring blood pressure

Units: Miscellaneous (continued)

Unit	Definition
morgan	arbitrary unit used in genetics; 1 morgan is the distance along the chromosome in a gene that gives a recombination frequency of 1%
nautical mile	unit of distance used in navigation, equal to the average length of 1 minute of arc on a great circle of the Earth; 1 international nautical mile = 1.852 km/6,076 ft
neper	unit used in telecommunications; gives the attenuation of amplitudes of currents or powers as the natural logarithm of the ratio of the voltage between two points or the current between two points
oersted	cgs unit (symbol Oe) of magnetic field strength, now replaced by amperes per metre (1 Oe = 79.58 amp per m)
ounce	unit of mass, $\frac{1}{16}$ of a pound avoirdupois, equal to 437.5 grains/28.35 g; or 14.6 pound troy, equal to 480 grains/31.10 g
parsec	unit (symbol pc) used in astronomy for distances to stars and galaxies; 1 pc = 3.262 light years, 2.063×10^5 astronomical units, or 3.086×10^{13} km
peck	obsolete unit of dry measure, equal to 8 imperial quarts or 1 quarter bushel (8.1 l in the USA or 9.1 l in the UK)
pennyweight	imperial unit of mass; 1 pennyweight = 24 grains = 1.555×10^{-3} kg
perch	obsolete imperial unit of length; 1 perch = $5\frac{1}{2}$ yards = 5.029 m, also called the rod or pole
pint	imperial unit of liquid or dry measure; in the USA, 1 liquid pint = 16 fl oz/0.473 l, while 1 dry pint = 0.551 l; in the UK, 1 pt = 20 fl oz, $\frac{1}{2}$ quart, $\frac{1}{8}$ gal, or 0.568 l
point	metric unit of mass used in relation to gemstones; 1 point = 0.01 metric carat = 2×10^{-3} g
poise	cgs unit of dynamic viscosity; 1 poise = 1 dyne-second per sq cm
pound	imperial unit (abbreviation lb) of mass; the avoirdupois pound or imperial standard pound = 0.45 kg/7,000 grains, while the pound troy (used for weighing precious metals) = 0.37 kg/5,760 grains
poundal	imperial unit (abbreviation pdl) of force; 1 poundal = 0.1383 newton
quart	imperial liquid or dry measure; in the USA, 1 liquid quart = 0.946 l, while 1 dry quart = 1.101 l; in the UK, 1 quart = 2 pt/1.137 l
rad	unit of absorbed radiation dose, replaced in the SI system by the gray; 1 rad = 0.01 joule of radiation absorbed by 1 kg of matter
relative biological effectiveness	relative damage caused to living tissue by different types of radiation
rood	imperial unit of area; 1 rood = $\frac{1}{4}$ acre = 1,011.7 sq m
roentgen	unit (symbol R) of radiation exposure, used for X- and gamma rays
rydberg	atomic unit of energy; 1 rydberg = 2.425×10^{-18} J
sabin	unit of sound absorption, used in acoustical engineering; 1 sabin = absorption of 1 sq ft (0.093 sq m) of a perfectly absorbing surface
scruple	imperial unit of apothecaries' measure; 1 scruple = 20 grains = 1.3×10^{-3} kg
shackle	unit of length used at sea for measuring cable or chain; 1 shackle = 15 fathoms (90 ft/27 m)
slug	obsolete imperial unit of mass; 1 slug = 14.59 kg/32.17 lb
snellen	unit expressing the visual power of the eye
sone	unit of subjective loudness
standard volume	in physics, the volume occupied by 1 kilogram molecule (molecular mass in kilograms) of any gas at standard temperature and pressure; approximately 22.414 cu m
stokes	cgs unit (symbol St) of kinematic viscosity; 1 stokes = 10^{-4} m^2 s^{-1}
stone	imperial unit (abbreviation st) of mass; 1 stone = 6.35 kg/14 lb
strontium unit	measures concentration of strontium-90 in an organic medium relative to the concentration of calcium
tex	metric unit of line density; 1 tex is the line density of a thread with a mass of 1 gram and a length of 1 kilometre
tog	measure of thermal insulation of a fabric, garment, or quilt; the tog value is equivalent to 10 times the temperature difference (in °C) between the two faces of the article, when the flow of heat across it is equal to 1 W per sq m
tonne	1 unit of mass; the long ton (UK) = 1,016 kg/2,240 lb; 1 short ton (USA) = 907 kg/2,000 lb; 1 metric tonne = 1000 kg/2205 lb
yard	imperial unit (symbol yd) of length, equivalent to 0.9144 m/3 ft

Wind Chill Index

Source: US National Weather Service

To determine wind chill, find the outside air temperature on the top line, then read down the column to the measured wind speed in miles per hour. The point at which the two axes intersect provides the wind chill. For example, if the outside temperature is 0°F and the wind speed is 20 mph, the rate of heat loss is equivalent to −39°F. If the temperature is 0°F and there is no wind, the wind chill is between 0 and 4 mph.

Wind Chill Index A wind chill value of −20°F presents little danger. A wind chill value between −21 and −74°F may cause flesh to freeze within a minute. A wind chill value of −75°F and below may cause flesh to freeze within 30 seconds.

Wind Chill Chart **Wind Speed (mph)** **Temperature (°F)**

	45	40	35	30	25	20	15	10	5	0	−5	−10	−15	−20	−25	−30	−35	−40	−45
0	45	40	35	30	25	20	15	10	5	0	−5	−10	−15	−20	−25	−30	−35	−40	−45
5	43	37	32	27	22	16	11	6	1	−5	−10	−16	−21	−26	−31	−37	−42	−47	−53
10	34	28	22	16	10	4	−3	−9	−15	−22	−28	−34	−40	−46	−52	−59	−65	−71	−77
15	29	22	16	9	2	−5	−12	−19	−25	−32	−39	−45	−52	−59	−66	−72	−79	−86	−93
20	25	18	11	4	−3	−11	−18	−25	−32	−39	−47	−54	−61	−68	−75	−82	−89	−96	−104
25	23	15	8	1	−7	−15	−22	−30	−37	−45	−52	−60	−67	−74	−82	−89	−97	−104	−112
30	21	13	6	−3	−11	−18	−26	−33	−41	−49	−56	−64	−72	−79	−87	−95	−102	−110	−117
35	19	11	4	−5	−13	−20	−28	−36	−44	−52	−59	−67	−75	−83	−91	−98	−106	−114	−122
40	18	10	3	−6	−14	−22	−30	−38	−46	−54	−61	−69	−77	−85	−93	−101	−109	−117	−124
45	17	9	2	−7	−15	−23	−31	−39	−47	−55	−63	−71	−79	−87	−95	−103	−111	−119	−127

INDEX